W9-CTW-104

DATE DUE

| | | | |
|---|---|---|---|
| | | | |
| | | | |
| | | | |
| | | | |
| | | | |
| | | | |
| | | | |
| | | | |
| | | | |

PRINTED IN U.S.A.

FOR REFERENCE

Do Not Take From This Room

# Literature Criticism from 1400 to 1800

# Guide to Gale Literary Criticism Series

| For criticism on | Consult these Gale series |
|---|---|
| Authors now living or who died after December 31, 1959 | ***CONTEMPORARY LITERARY CRITICISM (CLC)*** |
| Authors who died between 1900 and 1959 | ***TWENTIETH-CENTURY LITERARY CRITICISM (TCLC)*** |
| Authors who died between 1800 and 1899 | ***NINETEENTH-CENTURY LITERATURE CRITICISM (NCLC)*** |
| Authors who died between 1400 and 1799 | ***LITERATURE CRITICISM FROM 1400 TO 1800 (LC)***<br>***SHAKESPEAREAN CRITICISM (SC)*** |
| Authors who died before 1400 | ***CLASSICAL AND MEDIEVAL LITERATURE CRITICISM (CMLC)*** |
| Black writers of the past two hundred years | ***BLACK LITERATURE CRITICISM (BLC)*** |
| Authors of books for children and young adults | ***CHILDREN'S LITERATURE REVIEW (CLR)*** |
| Dramatists | ***DRAMA CRITICISM (DC)*** |
| Hispanic writers of the late nineteenth and twentieth centuries | ***HISPANIC LITERATURE CRITICISM (HLC)*** |
| Native North American writers and orators of the eighteenth, nineteenth, and twentieth centuries | ***NATIVE NORTH AMERICAN LITERATURE (NNAL)*** |
| Poets | ***POETRY CRITICISM (PC)*** |
| Short story writers | ***SHORT STORY CRITICISM (SSC)*** |
| Major authors from the Renaissance to the present | ***WORLD LITERATURE CRITICISM, 1500 TO THE PRESENT (WLC)*** |

ISSN 0740-2880

ℓ

Volume 37

# Literature Criticism from 1400 to 1800

Critical Discussion of the Works of Fifteenth-, Sixteenth-, Seventeenth-, and Eighteenth-Century Novelists, Poets, Playwrights, Philosophers, and Other Creative Writers

**Jelena O. Krstović**, Editor

GALE

DETROIT • NEW YORK • TORONTO • LONDON

Riverside Community College
'97 Library
AUG 4800 Magnolia Avenue
Riverside, California 92506

REF
PN86 .L56
Literature criticism from
1400 to 1800 : excerpts fro
criticism of the works of
fifteenth, sixteenth,
seventeenth, and eigh

## STAFF

Jelena O. Krstović, *Editor*

Gerald R. Barterian, Michelle Lee, *Associate Editors*
Dana Barnes, *Contributing Editor*

Aarti Stephens, *Managing Editor*

Susan M. Trosky, *Permissions Manager*
Kimberly F. Smilay, *Permissions Specialist*
Sarah Chesney, *Permissions Associate*
Steve Cusack, Kelly A. Quinn, *Permissions Assistants*

Victoria B. Cariappa, *Research Manager*
Laura Bissey, Julia C. Daniel, Tamara Nott, Michele La Meau, Tracie A. Richardson, Cheryl Warnock, *Research Associates*
Alfred Gardner, *Research Assistant*

Mary Beth Trimper, *Production Director*
Deborah Milliken, *Production Assistant*

Pamela A. Hayes, *Photography Coordinator*
Randy Bassett, *Image Database Supervisor*
Mikal Ansari, Robert Duncan, *Scanner Operators*

Since this page cannot legibly accommodate all copyright notices, the acknowledgments constitute an extension of the copyright notice.

While every effort has been made to secure permission to reprint material and to ensure the reliability of the information presented in this publication, Gale Research neither guarantees the accuracy of the data contained herein nor assumes any responsibility for errors, omissions or discrepancies. Gale accepts no payment for listing; and inclusion in the publication of any organization, agency, institution, publication, service, or individual does not imply endorsement of the editors or publisher. Errors brought to the attention of the publisher and verified to the satisfaction of the publisher will be corrected in future editions.

This publication is a creative work fully protected by all applicable copyright laws, as well as by misappropriation, trade secret, unfair competition, and other applicable laws. The authors and editors of this work have added value to the underlying factual material herein through one or more of the following: unique and original selection, coordination, expression, arrangement, and classification of the information.

All rights to this publication will be vigorously defended.

Copyright © 1997
Gale Research
835 Penobscot Building
Detroit, MI 48226-4094

All rights reserved including the right of reproduction in whole or in part in any form.

This book is printed on acid-free paper that meets the minimum requirements of American National Standard for Information Sciences—Permanence Paper for Printed Library Materials, ANSI Z39.48-1984.

Library of Congress Catalog Card Number 94-29718
ISBN 0-7876-1131-X
ISSN 0740-2880
Printed in the United States of America

10 9 8 7 6 5 4 3 2 1

# Contents

# Preface

*Literature Criticism from 1400 to 1800 (LC)* presents critical discussion of world authors of the fifteenth through eighteenth centuries. The literature of this period reflects a turbulent time of radical change that saw the rise of modern European drama, the birth of the novel and personal essay forms, the emergence of newspapers and periodicals, and major achievements in poetry and philosophy. Many of these historical forces continue to influence modern art and society. *LC,* therefore, provides valuable insight into the art, life, thought, and cultural transformations that took place during these centuries.

## Scope of the Series

*LC* provides an introduction to the great poets, dramatists, novelists, essayists, and philosophers of the fifteenth through eighteenth centuries, and to the most significant interpretations of these authors' works. Because criticism of this literature spans nearly six hundred years, an overwhelming amount of scholarship confronts the student. *LC* organizes this material into volumes addressing specific historical and cultural topics, for example, "Literature of the Spanish Golden Age," or "Literature and the New World." Every attempt is made to reprint the most noteworthy, relevant, and educationally valuable essays available.

Readers should note that there is a separate Gale reference series devoted exclusively to Shakespearean studies. Although belonging properly to the period covered in *LC,* William Shakespeare has inspired such a tremendous and ever-growing corpus of secondary material that the editors have deemed it best to give his works extensive coverage in a separate series, *Shakespearean Criticism.*

Each author entry in *LC* presents a survey of critical response to a topic or an author's oeuvre. Early criticism is offered to indicate initial responses, later selections document any rise or decline in literary reputations, and retrospective analyses provide students with modern views. The size of each author entry is a relative reflection of the scope of criticism available in English. Every attempt has been made to identify and include the seminal essays on each author's work and to include recent commentary providing modern perspectives.

The need for *LC* among students and teachers of literature and history was suggested by the proven usefulness of Gale's *Contemporary Literary Criticism (CLC), Twentieth-Century Literary Criticism (TCLC),* and *Nineteenth-Century Literature Criticism (NCLC),* which excerpt criticism of works by nineteenth- and twentieth-century authors. There is no duplication of critical material in any of these literary criticism series. Major authors may appear more than once in one or more of the series because of the great quantity of critical material available and because of their relevance to a variety of thematic topics.

## Thematic Approach

Beginning with Volume 12, the authors in each volume of *LC* are organized around such themes as specific literary or philosophical movements, writings surrounding important political and historical events, the philosophy and art associated with eras of cultural transformation, and the literature of specific social or ethnic groups. Each volume contains a topic entry providing a historical and literary overview, and several author entries which examine major representatives of the featured period.

## Organization of the Book

Each entry consists of the following elements: author or thematic heading, introduction, list of principal works, annotated works of criticism (each preceded by a bibliographical citation), and a bibliography of further reading. Also, most author entries contain author portraits and other illustrations.

- The **Author Heading** consists of the author's name (the most commonly used form), followed by birth and death dates. (If an author wrote consistently under a pseudonym, the pseudonym is used in the author heading, with the real name given in parentheses on the first line of the biographical and critical introduction.) Also located here are any name variations under which an author wrote, including transliterated forms for authors whose native languages use nonroman alphabets. Uncertain birth or death dates are indicated by question marks. Topic entries are preceded by a **Thematic Heading,** which simply states the subject of the entry.

- The **Biographical and Critical Introduction** contains background information that concisely introduces the reader to the author or topic.

- Most *LC* author entries include **Portraits** of the author. Many entries also contain illustrations of materials pertinent to an author's career, including author holographs, title pages, letters, or representations of important people, places, and events in an author's life.

- The **List of Principal Works** is ordered chronologically, by date of first book publication, identifying the genre of each work. In the case of foreign authors whose works have been translated into English, the title and date (if available) of the first English-language edition are given in brackets following the foreign-language listing. Unless otherwise indicated, dramas are dated by first performance, not first publication.

- **Criticism** is arranged chronologically in each author entry to provide a useful perspective on changes in critical evaluation over time. For the purpose of easy identification, the critic's name and the date of first composition or publication of the critical work are given at the beginning of each piece of criticism. Unsigned criticism is preceded by the title of the source in which it appeared. All titles by the author featured in the critical entry are printed in boldface type. Publication information (such as publisher names and book prices) and some parenthetical numerical references (such as footnotes or page and line references to specific editions of works) have been occasionally deleted to provide smoother reading of the text. Footnotes that appear with previously published pieces of criticism are reprinted at the end of each essay or excerpt. In the case of excerpted criticism, only those footnotes that pertain to the excerpted text are included.

- Critical essays are prefaced by **Annotations** as an additional aid to students using *LC*. These explanatory notes provide information such as the importance of a work of criticism, the commentator's individual approach to literary criticism, and a brief summary of the reprinted essay. In some cases, these notes cross-reference the work of critics within the entry who agree or disagree with each other.

- A complete **Bibliographical Citation** of the original essay or book precedes each piece of criticism.

- An annotated bibliography of **Further Reading** appears at the end of each entry and suggests resources for additional study. In some cases, significant essays for which the editors could not obtain reprint rights are included here.

## Cumulative Indexes

Each volume of *LC* includes a cumulative **Author Index** listing all the authors that have appeared in the following sources published by Gale: *Contemporary Literary Criticism, Twentieth-Century Literary Criticism, Nineteenth-Century Literature Criticism, Literature Criticism from 1400 to 1800, and Classical and Medieval Literature Criticism,* along with cross-references to the Gale series *Short Story Criticism, Poetry Criticism, Children's Literature Review, Authors in the News, Contemporary Authors, Contemporary Authors Autobiography Series, Contemporary Authors Bibliographical Series, Dictionary of Literary Biography, Concise Dictionary of Literary Biography, Something about the Author, Something about the Author Autobiography Series, and Yesterday's Authors of Books for Children.* Readers will welcome this cumulative author index as a useful tool for locating an author within the various series. The index, which includes authors' birth and death dates, is particularly valuable for those authors who are identified with a certain period but whose death dates cause them to be placed in another, or for those authors whose careers span two periods. For example, F. Scott Fitzgerald is found in *TCLC,* yet a writer often associated with him, Ernest Hemingway, is found in *CLC.*

Beginning with Volume 12, *LC* includes a cumulative **Topic Index** that lists all literary themes and topics treated in *LC, NCLC, TCLC,* and the *CLC* Yearbook. Each volume of *LC* also includes a cumulative **Nationality Index** in which authors' names are arranged alphabetically under their respective nationalities and followed by the numbers of the volumes in which they appear.

Each volume of *LC* also includes a cumulative **Title Index,** an alphabetical listing of all literary works discussed in the series. Each title listing includes the corresponding volume and page numbers where criticism may be located. Foreign-language titles that have been translated followed by the tiles of the translation—for example, *El ingenioso hidalgo Don Quixote de la Mancha (Don Quixote).* Page numbers following these translated titles refer to all pages on which any form of the titles, either foreign-language or translated, appear. Titles of novels, dramas, nonfiction books, and poetry, short story, or essays collections are printed in italics, while individual poems, short stories, and essays are printed in roman type within quotation marks.

## A Note to the Reader

When writing papers, students who quote directly from any volume in the Literary Criticism Series may use the following general format to footnote reprinted criticism. The first example pertains to material drawn from periodicals, the second to material reprinted from books.

T. S. Eliot, "John Donne," *The Nation and the Athenaeum,* 33 (9 June 1923), 321-32; excerpted and reprinted in *Literature Criticism from 1400 to 1800,* Vol. 10, ed. James E. Person, Jr. (Detroit: Gale Research, 1989), pp. 28-9.

Clara G. Stillman, *Samuel Butler: A Mid-Victorian Modern* (Viking Press, 1932); excerpted and reprinted in *Twentieth-Century Literary Criticism,* Vol. 33, ed. Paula Kepos (Detroit: Gale Research, 1989), pp. 43-5.

## Suggestions Are Welcome

Since the series began, features have been added to *LC* in response to various suggestions, including a nationality index, a Literary Criticism Series topic index, and thematic organization of entries.

Readers who wish to suggest new features, themes or authors to appear in future volumes, or who have other suggestions or comments are cordially invited to write to the editor (fax: 313 961-6599).

## Acknowledgments

The editors wish to thank the copyright holders of the excerpted criticism included in this volume and the permissions managers of many book and magazine publishing companies for assisting us in securing reproduction rights. We are also grateful to the staffs of the Detroit Public Library, the Library of Congress, the University of Detroit Mercy Library, Wayne State University Purdy/Kresge Library Complex, and the University of Michigan Libraries for making their resources available to us. Following is a list of the copyright holders who have granted us permission to reproduce material in this volume of ***LC.*** Every effort has been made to trace copyright, but if omissions have been made, please let us know.

**COPYRIGHTED EXCERPTS IN *LC,* VOLUME 37, WERE REPRODUCED FROM THE FOLLOWING PERIODICALS:**

***Archive for Reformation History,*** v. 73, 1982 for "From Polemic to Propaganda: The Development of Mass Persuasion in the Late Sixteenth Century," by Miriam Usher Chrisman. Reproduced by permission of the author.—***History Today,*** v. VIII, August, 1958. Copyright © History Today Limited 1958. Reproduced by permission.—***Journal of Ecclesiastical History,*** v. 42, October, 1991 for the "The Two John Knoxes: England, Scotland and the 1558 Tracts" by Jane E.A. Dawson. Copyright © Cambridge University Press 1991. Reproduced by permission of the publisher and author.—***The Journal of Medieval and Renaissance Studies,*** v. 18, Spring, 1988. Copyright © 1988 by Duke University Press. Reproduced by permission.—***The Sixteenth Century Journal,*** v. IV, April, 1973. Copyright © 1973 by The Sixteenth Century Journal Publishers, Inc., Kirksville, Missouri. All rights reserved. Reproduced by permission.

**COPYRIGHTED EXCERPTS IN *LC,* VOLUME 37, WERE REPRODUCED FROM THE FOLLOWING BOOKS:**

Althaus, Paul. From ***The Theology of Martin Luther.*** Copyright © 1966 by Fortress Press. Used by permission of Augsburg Fortress.—Barth, Karl. From ***The Theology of John Calvin.*** Translated by Geoffrey W. Bromiley. English translation copyright © 1995 Wm. B. Eerdmans Publishing Co. All rights reserved. Reproduced by permission.—DeVries, Dawn. From ***Jesus Christ in the Preaching of Calvin and Schleiermacher.*** Westminster John Knox Press, 1996. Copyright © 1996 Dawn DeVries. All rights reserved. Reproduced and used by permission of Westminster/John Knox Press.—Ebeling, Gerhard. From "Luther and the Beginning of the Modern Age," translated by Herbert J. A. Bouman, in ***Studies in the History of Christian Thought, Vol. VIII.*** Edited by Heiko A. Oberman. Brill, 1974. Copyright © 1974 by E. J. Brill, Leiden, Netherlands. All rights reserved. Reproduced by permission.—Ebeling, Gerhard. From ***Luther: An Introduction to His Thought.*** Translated by R. A. Wilson. Copyright © 1970 William Collins Sons & Fortress Press. Used by permission of Augsburg Fortress.—Erikson, Erik H. From ***Young Man Luther: A Study in Psychoanalysis and History.*** Norton, 1958. Copyright © 1958, 1962 and renewed 1986, by Erik H. Erikson. Reproduced by permission of W. W. Norton & Company, Inc.—Garside, Charles, Jr. From ***Zwingli and the Arts.*** Yale University Press, 1966. Copyright © 1966 by Yale University. All rights reserved. Reproduced by permission.—Gerrish, B. A. From ***The Old Protestantism and the New Essays on the Reformation of Heritage.*** T & T Clark LTD. Copyright © 1982 by The University of Chicago. Reproduced by permission.—Greaves, Richard L. From ***Theology and Revolution in the Scottish Reformation: Studies in the Thought of John Knox.*** Christian University Press, 1980. Copyright © 1980 by Chriatian College Consortium. All rights reserved. Reproduced by permission.—Hesselink, John. From "Law and Gospel or Gospel and Law? Calvin's Understanding of the Relationship," in ***Calviniana: Ideas and Influence of Jean Calvin.*** Edited by Robert V. Schnucker. Sixteenth Century Journal Publishers, 1988. Copyright © 1988 by Sixteenth Century Journal Publishers, Inc., Kirksville, Missouri. All rights reserved. Reproduced by permission.—Kingdon, Robert M. From "Calvinism and Resistance Theory, 1550-1580," in ***The Cambridge History of Political Thought: 1450-1700.*** Edited by J. H. Burns with Mark Goldie. Cambridge University Press, 1991. Copyright © Cambridge University Press 1991.

Reproduced with the permission of the publisher.—Lindberg, Carter. From ***The European Reformations.*** Blackwell Publishers, 1996. Copyright © Carter Lindberg 1996. All rights reserved. Reproduced by permission.—Mason, Roger A. From an introduction to ***On Rebellion by John Knox.*** Edited by Roger A. Mason. Cambridge University Press, 1994. Copyright © in the introductory and editorial matter Cambridge University Press 1994. Reproduced with the permission of the publisher.—McEwen, James S. From ***The Faith of John Knox: The Croall Lectures for 1960.*** John Knox Press, 1961. Copyright © 1961 James S. McEwen. Reproduced and used by permission of Westminster/John Knox Press.—Oberman, Heiko A. From " 'Initia Calvini': The Matrix of Calvin's Reformation," in ***Calvinus Sacrae Scripturae Professor: Calvin as Confessor of Holy Scripture.*** Edited by Wilhelm H. Neuser. Eerdmans, 1990. Copyright © 1994 by Wm. B. Eerdmans Publishing Co. All rights reserved. Reproduced by permission.—Oberman, Heiko A. From ***The Impact of the Reformation.*** Eerdmans, 1994. Copyright © 1994 by Wm. B. Eerdmans Publishing Co. All rights reserved. Reproduced by permission.—Oberman, Heiko A. From ***The Reformation: Roots and Ramifications.*** Translated Andrew Colin Gow. Clark, 1994. English translation copyright © T & T Clark Ltd. Published in North America by Wm. B. Eerdmans Publishing Co. All rights reserved. Reproduced by permission.—Oberman, Heiko Augustinus. From ***The Dawn of the Reformation: Essays in Late Medieval and Early Reformation Thought.*** Clark, 1986. Copyright © T. & T. Clark Ltd., 1986. Reproduced by permission.—Oberman, Heiko Augustinus. From ***The Dawn of the Reformation: Essays in Late Medieval and Early Reformation Thought.*** Clark, 1986. Copyright © T. & T. Clark Ltd., 1986. All rights reserved. Reproduced by permission.—Puckett, David L. From ***John Calvin's Exegesis of the Old Testament.*** Westminster John Knox Press, 1995. Copyright © 1995 David L. Puckett. All rights reserved. Reproduced and used by permission of Westminster/John Knox Press.—Rainbow, Jonathan H. From ***The Will of God and the Cross: An Historical and Theological Study of John Calvin's Doctrine of Limited Redemption.*** Pickwick Publications, 1990. Copyright © 1990 by Jonathan H. Rainbow. All rights reserved. Reproduced by permission.—Schaeffer, Francis A. From ***How Should We Then Live? The Rise and Decline of Western Thought and Culture.*** Crossway Books, 1976. Copyright © by Francis A. Schaeffer. All rights reserved. Reproduced by permission.—Skinner, Quentin. From ***The Foundations of Modern Political Thought, Vol. 2.*** Cambridge University Press, 1978. Copyright © Cambridge University Press 1978. Reproduced with the permission of the publisher.—Spitz, Lewis W. From "Humanism and the Reformation," in ***Transition and Revolution: Problems and Issues of European Renaissance and Reformation History.*** Edited by Robert M. Kingdon. Burgess, 1974. Copyright © 1974 by Burgess Publishing Company. All rights reserved. Reproduced by permission.—Stephens, W. P. From ***Zwingli: An Introduction to His Thought.*** Oxford at the Clarendon Press, 1992. Copyright © W. P. Stephens 1992. All rights reserved. Reproduced by permission of Oxford University Press.—Walton, Robert C. From ***Zwingli's Theocracy.*** University of Toronto Press, 1967. Copyright © University of Toronto Press 1967. Reproduced by permission of University Press Incorporated.—Zagorin, Perez. From ***Rebels and Rulers, 1500-1660, Vol. I.*** Cambridge University Press, 1982. Copyright © Cambridge University Press 1982. Reproduced with the permission of the publisher.

**PHOTOGRAPHS AND ILLUSTRATIONS APPEARING IN *LC*, VOLUME 37, WERE RECEIVED FROM THE FOLLOWING SOURCES:**

Calvin, John, photograph of a painting. The Library of Congress.—Knox, John, photograph of an illustration. The Library of Congress.—Luther, Martin, photograph of an engraving.—Luther, Martin, photograph of an illustration.—Zwingli, Huldreich, photograph.

# The Literature of the Protestant Reformation

## INTRODUCTION

Besides its sweeping theological changes, the Protestant Reformation had repercussions on the course of Western cultural history not only in its reaction to Catholic patronage of the arts, but also in its endorsing of universal education. The Reformation questioned the role of the Church as mediator between individual and God and instead emphasized the individual's direct relationship with the Divine through an introspective and active faith. Martin Luther's translation of the Bible into German and the mass distribution of theological writings in the form of instructional pamphlets required widespread literacy and so transformed the audience, medium, and subject matter of literature in early modern Europe.

The alliance between scholasticism (the sanctioned teaching of theology in accordance with contemporary church doctrine) and the Roman Catholic Church faced the challenge of a new humanism in the Renaissance, with its celebration of individualism and fine arts. The church had appropriated many diverse functions during the period and, as a result, had became materialistic and worldly. At the beginning of the sixteenth century the church was more than a religious institution; it had political and economic ties to governments throughout Europe, exerted complete control over the universities, and commissioned most of the continent's artistic production. Frustrated by what they viewed as corruption of spirituality by these materialistic entanglements, the leaders of the Protestant Reformation attempted to return religion to its intellectual and spiritual beginnings. The abuses of power committed by the church during the Renaissance were to be countered by a "universal priesthood" in which each believer has an unmediated relationship with God. Luther demanded a moral recovery based on the active faith of the individual, thereby circumventing the authority of the church and replacing it with a more personal spirituality.

The popular appeal of these ideas initiated various movements throughout Europe, including peasant rebellions in Germany and the establishing of a multitude of Protestant denominations which overturned the power and unity of Christendom. The Reformation also met with the fear of anarchy in the wake of the fragmentation of religious and political institutions. The Protestant emphasis on the individual as the bearer of spirituality liberated theological discussions from the ritualism, traditionalism, and hierarchy of the Catholic Church. The writings of Luther, John Wycliffe, and John Calvin were intended to instigate the general populace to question the basis and practice of faith, and to bring religion out of the institutional setting.

The rigorous spiritual purity of Luther and his followers transformed the cultural humanism of the Renaissance into a focus on religious education through didactic treatises and morality plays. Noting such trends, critics have traditionally claimed that the Protestant Reformation suppressed the cultural flourishing of the Renaissance by harkening back to medieval spirituality. However, the heightened attention given to each individual—of every social class—as the protector of faith required that both the will and the intellect be educated; religious texts and services were translated into the vernacular, printing presses flourished, and Luther advocated the establishment of universal public education. Many twentieth-century critics focus on these humanistic ideals and contend that the Reformation's pluralism and emphasis on education actually stimulated interest in art, music, and literature—as expressions of faith.

---

## OVERVIEWS

### Karl Barth (essay date 1922)

SOURCE: "Reformation and Middle Ages," in *The Theology of John Calvin*, translated by Geoffrey W. Bromiley, William B. Eerdmans Publishing Company, 1995, pp. 13-68.

[*In the following excerpt from a work originally published in German in 1922, Barth surveys the intellectual history of the Protestant Reformation, particularly in relation to the historical period which preceded it.*]

Loofs, *Leitfaden,* 4th ed., 601-62; Tschackert, *Entstehung der lutherischen und der reformierten Kirchenlehre,* 6-33; Seeberg, *Dogmengeschichte,* 2nd ed., IV, 1-55; Troeltsch, "Protestantisches Christentum und Kirche in der Neuzeit," in *Kultur der Gegenwart,* I/4, section 1; and on this Loofs, *Luthers Stellung zum Mittelalter und zur Neuzeit* (Halle, 1907); Troeltsch, *Soziallehren der christlichen Kirchen und Gruppen,* 427-512; Hermelink (in Krüger's *Handbuch der Kirchengeschichte*), 1-58.[1] No matter what our evaluation of them, it will be seen that the works of Troeltsch had the greatest influence on early 20th-century discussion.

In the first instance Calvin's theology naturally interests us in its historical context as an outstanding record of Reformation theology that historically and at times even legally has served as a basis of proclamation in modern Protestant churches. If it is of concern to us as Protestant theologians to be clear where we come from and where we are going as such, then we have every reason to turn again and again to the question how far what we are and think and say does truly, and not merely according to the claim made or displayed on Reformation Days or similar occasions, correspond to what the founders of Protestant theology were and to what they thought and said about God and the world and humanity. And if beyond that perhaps it is also necessary that we should consider the justification of ourselves from a deeper angle, namely, as a question of truth, then we really have cause to be concerned why it was that Protestant theology came into existence as a newborn child, and how in that early period it put to itself and answered the question of truth.

Before we turn to Calvin in particular, we would do well to take our bearings in a brief survey of the relation of the complex of events that we usually call the Reformation to the age which preceded it and also more generally of what this complex meant, as a symptom, for the human situation as a whole. Naturally in this compass I cannot unfold the problem of the Middle Ages and the Reformation in all its breadth. Use the literature on the subject, but with caution. For nowhere is it so obvious how much the historical position of the historian affects the picture given, as we see in the controversies regarding this problem over the last fifteen years.[2] Finally, even though our knowledge of the sources be modest, it is better to try to see with our own eyes than to follow one of the grandiose hypotheses now current, stimulating though these might be in detail. Since Calvin's theology is our theme, I will limit myself to showing how to get a basic grasp of the relation between Reformation theology and that of the Middle Ages which preceded it. When I compare the thinking of the reformers to that of medieval theologians so far as I know them both, the following picture emerges.

I CONNECTION

The first and most direct impression that the comparison gives us is of something strikingly new and different, especially in Luther. We find this man and his thinking moving in the reflection of a great and strange light that falls lightly upon him. We see him faced with an incomparable, unheard-of question and then at once, in and with the question, in possession of an equally incomparable, unheard-of answer. The thoughts in which he tried to give an account of what he saw both to himself and to others are disturbingly and wildly contradictory. Only with difficulty could he put them together, and even then they largely exclude one another. No specific, or, at any rate, no systematic or planned deeper meaning rules in these thoughts; he would clearly have liked to say everything much more simply, but with great embarrassment he constantly ventured paradoxes that in their significance may be placed alongside the boldest insights of philosophical thinking and that in their immediate force put far in the shade the formulations of most philosophers. Even where he does not speak in paradoxes a light like that of the morning sun shines constantly over his trains of thought. They breathe like fresh air after a storm. Was he offering edification? Was he preaching? Was he thinking academically? Who would be so pedantic as to make a distinction? What do categories[3] mean here? In these thoughts something takes place, a decision, a breakthrough, an event. We have the feeling regarding them that the words are not just words. We witness a process of knowledge that we cannot distinguish from an act. And this act, the longer and more radically we let it speak to us in its own true sense, does it not significantly, but also with a claim, and erasing all the borders between here and there, thrust itself into our own existence? Can we escape this word, this act, or do we not feel, like those who heard Zwingli, that we are taken by the hair[4] when we really hear this voice? That is Reformation theology, not just in Luther but also in Zwingli and Calvin and the lesser lights around them, for what counts here is not the genius or originality of the individual thinker but the quality of what all of them were thinking with more or less force and depth.

But precisely when we take seriously our direct impression of this theology, precisely when we believe we have to do here with something new and wholly different, precisely when we are inclined to ascribe to the event that unfolds before our eyes a dignity and significance that a word like "experience"[5] does not really cover even though we do experience something also, precisely then we must be careful in describing this as a new theology compared to the old. If we take the word "different" seriously, what does it mean to confront something totally different?[6] If we are not finally to be guilty of mere bombast, can the *totally* different be one thing in contrast to this or that other different thing? What do "new" and "old" mean when it is a matter of *this* new thing, when it is a matter of the knowledge of *God* in this theology? Who gives us the courage at once to divest the terms of their meaning again by excluding the poor Middle Ages, the old, from this new thing? Precisely when we sense somewhat the superiority of this theology, we must maintain its newness and difference on the plane of historical things only with reservation, only in a relative sense. On the plane of time one thing always and everywhere stands alongside another, certainly with significant differences, but in such a way that great differences often mean very little and little differences mean a great deal.

In assessing what we can see here, those who can only reckon, count, and measure run the risk of hardly being able to avoid serious confusion and mistakes. For the absolute is not directly visible on this world's stage. The great light in the reflection of which we see the reformers and their thoughts move is not itself a phenomenon; it does not become one thing among others. And what we see in the reformers, the reflection in which they stand, is only relatively and not absolutely different from what we see around them, in their predecessors and successors. It is a new and different thing, but not *the* new thing, *the* different thing. It is at every point in continuity with what came before and what came after. *The* new thing is not something that we can establish in the reformers, and *the* old thing is not something that we can postulate of the scholastics and mystics preceding them. On both sides the old and the new confront one another on two fronts, first invisibly, never a perceptible phenomenon, as the distance and fellowship between God and us, eternity and time, infinity and finitude that is the point of the term "sacred history" which we discussed briefly at the outset—and then visibly, in a historically perceptible way, as the historical dialectic of different human possibilities, higher and lower, better and worse, here stronger and there weaker, that point to the original hidden antithesis of old and new, yet never in such a way that a human possibility coincides directly with that which all human possibilities can only indicate, and never in such a way that a human possibility is totally meaningless relative to that hidden antithesis—and we have in mind here the whole range of what is usually called secular history. Always and everywhere that which we see as historical occurrence on the second front stands only in relation to its origin in the primal antithesis, but always and everywhere historical events do to some extent stand in relation to this their origin. Historical events that do so to a higher degree than others can do no more than make us aware that fundamentally even events that do so to a lesser degree do stand in the same relation.

The new thing that in Reformation theology makes on us the impression of something new and totally different is obviously *the* hidden new thing of the first front. We need not be surprised, then, that as we seriously follow up that direct impression, as we translate it from more or less contingent experience to knowledge, we come to see the relative degree of the distinction between the Reformation and the Middle Ages on the historical plane. Those who let themselves be taught by a study of the reformers what is in truth old and what is in truth new can hardly set up a fixed and more mythological antithesis between two ages and historical groups. They will appreciate the distinction, but they will really appreciate it, that is, value it, see its worth. That is, they will see its worth and meaning and point, and also its context, the deeper problematic of which all historical problematic is only a likeness. It will be impossible for them to point to this or that saying in Luther or Calvin, to this or that day in their lives, and to say that here the new and totally different thing was present or was spoken, as though those men could, for example, experience and express the new and totally different thing as others can experience and express what is beautiful. No, even what was there experienced and said is as such relative. It stands in continuity with the old that is so sharply different from it. Calvin and Sadolet were pieces on the same chessboard. Only when we see what they experienced and said in this relation of earthly continuity can it take on significance for us in its difference within the relation. And it is then impossible for us to focus too tenaciously on this or that dubious feature of medieval theology and church life, as though that were really *the* old thing in contrast to the reformers and their position. No, no pope or scholastic was so diabolical as to be able to do or say *the* old thing absolutely, just as no reformer was so heavenly as to be able even for a moment to embody *the* new. Let us leave it to the Roman Catholic philosophy of history to place Protestantism under the category of apostasy, which is so freighted with meaning and for that reason, in the judgment of history, so empty of meaning. Let us not in any circumstances play the same game. What was experienced, thought, and said in the Catholic Middle Ages was also relative, relative, we may say, to the origin that things on the historical plane, be they ever so different, have in common. It stands with the Reformation counterposition in the one basic nexus of the first front where the antithesis is not that of Protestant and Roman Catholic but of God and humanity. Apart from that antithesis, which also means unity, the confessional antithesis was a tragedy in the 16th century and has now become a comedy.[7] If we are aware of the seriousness of the profound problematic of that antithesis, then we have to see the nonseriousness of the confessional antithesis on the second front between Protestantism and Roman Catholicism as historical forces. But one could also put it differently, namely, that the confessional antithesis on the second front can be really serious, important, and full of promise only when we are aware how nonserious it is in the last analysis.

You can check the truth of what I have just said if you reflect again on the direct impression of something new that we get from Luther's commentary on the Psalms or Zwingli's theses[8] so long as we have eyes in our heads. Must we not honestly admit that in these cases *the* new and wholly different thing that speaks forcefully to us confronts not only medieval and modern Catholicism but no less diametrically what we ourselves think and feel? Can we fail to hear, then, the strong accusation that the writings of Luther and Calvin constantly bring against our so-called Lutheran and Reformed Christianity, church life, and theology, not simply because there has been declension from the Reformation, true though that is, but because the new and wholly different thing in the writings of Luther and Zwingli accusingly confronts all Christianity, church, life, and theology even when at their conceivable best? If we accept this judgment, if we recognize the antithesis that runs through the whole four hundred years of Protestant history, how then can the new and wholly other thing four hundred years ago simply be one thing among other historical entities, and how can it have been passed on to Protestant theologians to do with it as they like and with the possibility of handing it down to their successors? Is it not obvious that this new thing critically confronts the theology of the reformers themselves, being absolutely other than the old thing that in its relativity here also is part of the historical plane? And if that is so, must we not conclude that the antithesis between the true new and the true old runs also backward to the time before the Reformation, that what is old in time (i.e., medieval thinking) has its own share, as I see it, in what is eternally old, which is the situation and problem of all history, but that it also has, of course, its share in what is eternally new, the solution to the problem?[9]

So far as I can see, the reformers themselves had a much more restrained view of the epoch-making nature of their work than one might expect and than is often stated in later accounts in church history. It is clear that they had a strong sense of the unique importance of the historical moment in which they stood. Luther spoke again and again about the fact that, in contrast to the past, they were now once more in an age when God was sending forth his Word among us as the most precious of all his gifts. He liked to portray the Reformation under the image of a light that was now kindled and shining for a while.[10] He knew well—perhaps too well—his own personal significance for the process. Calvin, too, in his work against Pighius on the *Liberum Arbitrium* (6, 237) called the Reformation a miracle of supreme divine power, and in sermon 162 on Deuteronomy (28, 466) he could even call it a resurrection from the dead.[11] In his work *On the Need to Reform the Church* he expressly ascribed the same sending to the reformers as to the OT prophets who had to stir people out of the blindness of idolatry (6, 477).[12] In keeping was the eclecticism and the freedom that the reformers allowed themselves vis-à-vis the great theological authority of the early church. "Oh, the fathers were men as we are; we should consider this well and lay what they say on the scales, watching what they say," said Luther in his *Table Talk* ([M. Luther, *Samtliche Werke* (Erlangen, 1826-57); hereafter EA] 62, 109) of the fathers, and of the scholastics he said that they had good heads but did not live in a time like ours (EA 62, 114).[13] As we know, apart from the Bible, the only strong authority for the whole Reformation was Augustine, but if I am right it was Augustine almost exclusively as the opponent of Pelagius and in such a way that Luther at least in his later years moved increasingly apart from this decisive teacher of his theological youth. It is also striking to me that Calvin in his relation to Scholasticism made no use of Anselm's doctrine of the atonement or proof of God as he might well have done in his own system, and that he had no links to Thomas Aquinas, so that there is no connection between the greatest Catholic and the greatest Protestant systematician, and how sparse in him are the references to the late Scholasticism of Duns Scotus, with whom we have the impression today that there would have been many positive points of contact.[14]

From all this we learn that the reformers were aware of standing at a decisive turning point in theological thinking when much that was old was perishing even if much was also at least quietly remaining. At all events, however, the reformers did not share the philosophy of history that we find in a saying of Schwenckfeld that Seeberg quotes and that he calls "monumental": "A new world is coming and the old dies away" (*Lehrbuch,* IV. 2). The Radicals and Humanists talked that way, that is, those specifically who had little awareness of the deeper antithesis that was being played out before them; but for all the zeal with which they, too, took part in the movement in their own way, they were interested for the most part only in what was taking place on the surface. Those who took part genuinely and radically, who saw what it was all about, felt differently, although they too, as we have seen, experienced powerfully enough the historical antithesis between the old and the new.

At least in Luther, however, a more powerful feeling than that of experiencing the dawn of a new age and being its strongest agents and heralds was that of the continuity of the divine work, his reverence for all that had come into being and was now there—a reverence that rested, of course, not merely on insight but also on nature and setting. It was as a monk and in the context of medieval theology that Luther came to his reforming thoughts that snatched him finally out of that context. We know how unwillingly, in obedience to the need,[15] he resolved to build a new church. As long as he lived, his heart still clung to the concept of the one holy catholic church in a way that for reasons deeply rooted in his specific situation was not the case with Calvin.

The fervor of the new age and world, of the new spirit and work, was something that we know again to some extent in our own postwar present. We perhaps find it best among the reformers in Zwingli, it being typically alien to Calvin, although, as I have said, with less sentimental emphasis than Luther, Calvin agreed with the latter that the concept of antiquity was most important for Protestant theology. In the epistle in which he dedicated the *Institutes* to Francis I he could not protest too strongly that what he and those like-minded with him in France were advocating was not something new.[16] He adduced a long list of witnesses from the church's past in which he thought he saw what he called the gospel, and in the *Institutes* itself he was at great pains to prove his agreement with the authorities of the early church. We have said already how eclectic his procedure was, but that does not alter the intention. For him as for Luther, if with an essential difference of mood, the break with the Christianity of the past was not felt to be one of principle. In Luther an example of this is the relatively friendly way in which Bonaventura is treated among the medieval fathers, and in Calvin we note the warmth even with which he speaks of Bernard of Clairvaux.[17] Both were in their different ways typical representatives of what the reformers zealously combated as papism.

An even more striking example is the way in which both Luther and Calvin avoided the man in whom they must have recognized, even if he was not then the most widely read author, and whom they ought to have fought as their most dangerous opponent, the true genius of the Catholic Middle Ages. I refer to Thomas Aquinas. We have in his case a demonstration how often even the greatest among us, precisely in fulfilling their deepest intentions, often do not know what they are doing. The reformers engaged in close combat with late scholastics of the age of decline, about whom we say nothing today, when all the time behind these, and biding his time, stood their main adversary Thomas, in whom all modern Roman Catholicism has come to see more and more definitely its true classic; and apart from a few inconsequential complaints by Luther,[18] they left him in peace, apparently not realizing that their real attack was not on those straw figures but on the spirit of the *Summa,* on the Gothic cathedral and the world of Dante. How could it be possible that in the first half of the 17th century a Lutheran theologian from Strassburg could write a book entitled *Thomas Aquinas, veritatis evangelicae confessor!* (Loofs, 690).[19] All this shows strikingly, however, that the reformers did not see their work in the context of a great philosophy of history but in a fairly relative pragmatic context. Perhaps it is precisely the manner of truly creative people to take this view.

If we ask positively in what they saw the importance of their work, Luther's reply, so far as I can see, would be a sober reference to the fact that the Word of God was again being preached loudly and purely. Thus in a Coburg letter to the elector on May 20, 1530, he described the grace that God gives each of us as follows: "For, of course, your Grace's lands have the most and the very best of good pastors and preachers, more than any other land in all the world, and they teach so faithfully and purely, and help to keep the peace so well. There are thus growing up among us tender young people, boys and girls, who are taught the catechism and scripture so well that it does my heart good as I see how young boys and girls can pray and believe and talk about God and Christ more than all the foundations and monasteries and schools could do or still can" (EA 54, 148).[20] In face of these happy descriptions, no matter what we think of the catechetical success, we cannot possibly say that Luther made great claims for the breadth of his reformation.

There is a similar passage in Calvin. In his work on the need for church reform he described as follows what the reformers had done and achieved: "They aroused the world out of the profound darkness of ignorance to a reading of scripture; they worked hard at a purer understanding and were able successfully to expound certain important concepts of Christian doctrine, whereas formerly foolish fables and no less unnecessary definitions were heard in sermons, the universities echoed with the strife of words, scripture was hardly mentioned, and the clergy had an eye only to money" (6, 473).[21] Calvin did add, of course, that these were improvements that their foes ought to have acknowledged as made, but it is typical that he was content with this rather dry academic description of the significance of the new epoch.

We may note in addition that Luther used the expression "Word of God" both in the absolute and eternal sense that was naturally primary for him and in a relative sense as the Word that takes its course, that comes and goes, that falls like a shower, now here and now there, that can also be chased away and extinguished.[22] It is plain that the latter is the Word of God whose blessings he can extol so eloquently to the elector. For him it is to this category that his own reforming work belongs. It is part of the new thing in the second and relative sense. It is not for him *the* new thing. It is not even as new as appears in most of our historical accounts today, the theological at least. Nevertheless, it is something new, something very new, of course, even if he has to recognize its limits and end: "I am concerned that the light will not last and shine very long, for God's Word has always had its specific course" (57, 19).[23] This looking ahead to the end of the new time, often stated in a bitter and threatening way, is not uncommon in Luther.

Luther could also say once (57, 17) that God's Word comes down always on the same time. I would comment that in its sober but very profound sense this statement is much more monumental than the dictum of Schwenckfeld that a new world was dawning. The context is as follows: "The world now faces God's Word exactly as it did two thousand years ago. God's Word comes down always on the same time. The world is still the world, the devil's bride."[24] The meaning, then, is primarily negative and pessimistic, as was befitting the mood of the older Luther. But be that as it may, the saying embodies the thesis that there are no different times in relation to God, or, as I would put it, that there is no progress in world history. The Word of God, when it makes itself heard, confronts the same world reality in the same tension even when the situation in world reality is supremely critical and significant and God's Word makes itself heard with great power. Indeed, Luther could go so far as to say that at all times from the beginning of the world, when God's Word is purely taught and preached, people are most offended and sins are at their worst and most horrible (57, 22).[25]

Finally, this highly relevant situation had for Luther a positive reverse side. If the world is always the world and even God's Word in history is transitory in its presence and limited in its effects, it is also true that God is always God even when his Word would seem to be lost in history. "God has preserved his Word," Luther can say most unexpectedly, and it is plain that he is not now speaking of a relative and transitory Word: "God has preserved his Word and Christ's kingdom has remained in the world under the papacy" (57, 53). Naturally the fact that this is so, he adds, "is the greatest miracle of our Lord God," but he does count on this miracle.[26] That was the radicalism of Luther's philosophy of history, and it was much greater than that of people of the stamp of Schwenckfeld with their jubilant shouting about the dawn of a new era. The threads of the kingdom of Christ and of God on the one side snap no more than do those of the world on the other, no matter what may be the specific course of God's Word. If it is true that in the so-called new age the old is truly present for the first time, it is also true, and even more true, that the new was also present in the so-called old age. If any had the right to see the old and the new not merely in the light of the kingdom of God but also historically in harsh antithesis, it was the reformers themselves who were engaged in a violent battle in which everything was at stake, life or death. Yet they did not see it that way. They paradoxically left it to those who were further from the fray to view absolutely and mythologically the historical processes of which they were the heroes.

They themselves confirmed the insight that we gained last time by more basic discussion, namely, that nothing really new came into history with the Reformation, that its significance is to be sought instead in a survey of the connection. We must now pursue this insight both negatively and positively.

## 2 CONTRAST

Let us look first at the relation between the Reformation and the Middle Ages as that of opposites, realizing that while the antithesis is great, important, and significant, it cannot in any case be clear-cut or absolute. The spirit of the Middle Ages is hard to grasp and especially to judge. Incredibly often and easily on the Protestant side (even the learned Protestant side; cf. Loofs, 498-99!),[1] efforts are made to characterize the essence of Scholasticism. Terms, highly critical terms, such as "formalism," "pedantry," "credulity," "artificial reconciliation of reason and revelation," and the like,[2] come almost automatically into our minds and on our lips when we hear the word "scholastic." Though there is naturally some truth in them, they are polemically crude, reminding us with some aptness of the foxes who could not get at the grapes.[3] We can hardly complain of formalism if we ourselves have no form at all, nor of pedantry if we want to establish our supposedly better truth no less perspicaciously or simply than the scholastics could do, nor of credulous submission to authority if we are not to ignore the serious problem of authority but be willing to think it out to the end, nor of the way of combining reason and revelation unless we have better counsel to offer on the relation. We have here presuppositions that in general are missing among modern Protestants. Semler was right when he once observed that the poor scholastics have laid themselves open to too much derision, often on the part of those who cannot use them (Hagenbach, 297).[4] Those older theologians had the ability to think and they took pleasure in thinking. They had dialectical courage and consistency. Their academic tradition has had four hundred years of vitality. Once the reformers were no longer present, Protestant theology could do no better than adopt that tradition, and yet comparatively quickly it came to grief, while the older branch from Trent to our own time entered upon a second period of remarkable fruitfulness. All these are things that ought above all to give us respect for medieval theology if we do not already have it. The situation is the same with Scholasticism as with the Roman Catholic church in general. Those who do not admire them, those who are not in danger of becoming scholastics themselves, simply have no inner right to pass judgment on them. We cannot dismiss historical entities of this power by simply tossing around catchwords.

If we are to catch the essence of Scholasticism I would like to propose that we first pursue the direct impression one gets of it when speaking about it unconfused by modern preconceptions. If you ask me how and where to get this direct impression, I would suggest the following indirect way. Go to Cologne cathedral and study it well. Then from a good compendium of the history of philosophy acquaint yourselves with what Aristotle had in mind. Then by means of Dante's *Divine Comedy* learn to know poetically the path of the medievals, as taught by Thomas Aquinas, from hell through purgatory to paradise. You may then take up a dogmatic presentation such as that of Seeberg or Loofs, though I would advise you that in so doing you should check the sources of all the quotations—a history of dogma that consists almost entirely of quotations is that of Hagenbach, 1888.[5] Then perhaps you may try to read a work from the great age of Scholasticism like Bonaventura's *Breviloquium* (ed. Hefele, 1845), supplementing this on the right hand with an ascetic work like the *Analecta* on the history of Francis of Assisi (ed. Boehmer, 1904), and on the left hand with a mystical work like the sermons of Meister Eckhardt (Diederichs, 1911).[6]

The impression that I have gained of medieval theology may be summed up in a phrase coined, I believe, by Luther at the 1518 Heidelberg Disputation: it is a theology of glory.[7] It attempts and achieves a knowledge of God in his glory, purity, and majesty. In the word of the Bible and the theology of the church it does not simply find denoted and described the mystery as such but signposts marking a dialectical path to the heart of the mystery, so that for those who take this path there is no longer any mystery. It recognizes no barrier, no command that it should stop at the object intended in the word of the Bible or in dogma. In the difficulty and obscurity that first conceal the object it simply hears a challenge in some way, notwithstanding the problems, to lay hold of the object. It is venturesome in the way in which it sets its goals and tries to reach them. It is youthfully fresh and healthy and robust and sparkling in all that it does. As readers we feel that we are in the hands of guides who with absolute certainty and confidence know what they want.

Some kind of unequivocal and direct communication of the depths of deity, and perhaps a well-arranged system of such depths, is in any case the goal of our journey if we entrust ourselves to them. In these theologians there is no place for banalities, generalities, or obscurities. Nor is there any place for the basic uncertainty, which oppresses many other theologies, whether theology itself is necessary or useful, nor for the related teeth-chattering question whether and how far theology is a science. Thomas teaches us that *esse* is *intellegere* (to be is to know), that God's essence is his knowledge, that the universal and absolute epitome of all that is known, of all being, is actuality, the first cause in all things.[8] To a lesser degree angels, and to an even lesser degree humans, have a share in this eternal knowledge of God.[9] That is theology. How can it not be a science when it is participation in the knowledge of God,[10] in the a priori of all science? And how can it not be necessary? It is the one thing necessary; it is our blessedness.[11] We have to read the descriptions of heaven that this theology gives[12] if we are to understand what it meant for the people of the Middle Ages.

At this point the academic theology of all the schools is at one with both orthodox mystics and heretical, pantheistic sects. "To have life is to see life," said Peter Lombard.[13] Two hundred years later Tauler, whom Luther greatly honored, said the same thing even more clearly: "Those who see the glory of God, that is paradise" (Hagenbach, 445).[14] According to the *Elucidarium,* an eschatological work of the 12th century, there is a triple heaven: the visible, which is the firmament; the spiritual, where saints and angels dwell; and the intellectual, where the blessed enjoy the vision of the triune God, drink from the fount of God's wisdom, and have knowledge of all things, simply all things and all relations (Hagenbach, 444, 447).[15] Listen to the way Heinrich Seuse, a contemporary of Tauler, puts it: "Look up to the ninth heaven, which is much more than a hundred thousand times bigger than the whole earth, and there is another heaven above, the *Coelum empyreum,* the fiery heaven, not called this because of fire, but because of the immeasurably sparkling clarity that it has by nature, unmovable and unchangeable, the glorious court where the heavenly Lord dwells and the stars praise God together and all God's children rejoice. See around you the countless throng, how they drink from the living, murmuring fountain to their hearts' desire; see how they fix their gaze on the pure and clear reflection of naked deity, on the mirror in which all things are open and manifest" (Hagenbach, 447ff.).[16] Or read the classic description in the final song of Dante's *Paradise:*

> Such keenness from the luring ray I met
> That if mine eyes had turned away, methinks,
> I had been lost, and so emboldened, on
> I passed, as I remember, till my view
> Hover'd the brink of dread infinitude.
> O grace, unenvying of thy boon! that gavest
> Boldness to fix so earnestly my ken
> On the everlasting splendour, that I look'd
> While sight was unconsumed, and in that
>   depth
>
> Saw in one volume clasp'd of love, whate'er
> The universe unfolds, all properties
> Of substance and of accident, and beheld
> Confounded, yet one individual light
> The whole.
>   It may not be
> That one who looks upon that light
> Can turn to other object, willingly, his view
> For all the good, that will may covet, there
> Is summ'd, and all, elsewhere defective, found
> Complete.[17]

That is what Thomas calls the fruition of God and Eckhardt the supraforming of the soul with God, or even the birth of God in the soul.[18] That is the theology of glory, the fiery living heart, the essence of medieval theology. On this vision of God from face to face [1 Cor. 13:12]—and think of the ecstatic portrayal of the faces of the blessed as you surely know it from pre-Renaissance art—that theology counted as on an unheard-of possibility to which it had access by a steep but direct path. Here is the essence of celestial bliss, and for that reason all the medievals, or at least all the more free and profound among them, never spoke of it except with a certain awe and restraint. But it was also part of our human essence, the supreme possibility of the human soul, which in exact parallel to the idea of a triple heaven is depicted in three divisions, as sensuality with the capacity for cogitation, as reason with a capacity for meditation, and finally and supremely as simple intelligence with the capacity for contemplation. This is how Gerson saw it at the beginning of the 15th century and Hugh of St. Victor three hundred years before him.[19]

This basic view of the fundamental accessibility of the mystery and glory (*doxa*) of God is what stamps medieval theology. It changes, of course, in keeping with the teaching of the later schools of Duns Scotus and William of Occam, and especially that of Eckhardt and his followers. Access became extraordinarily difficult,[20] but all the difficulties with which it was seen to be surrounded simply made it higher and more precious and caused it to be lauded more fervently. In a disturbing parallel the cathedral pillars became improbably more lofty and the naked eye had reason to fear they might not ever meet. Yet with unerring certainty they converge in the Gothic arch, even if only in the semi-darkness of the vault. The basic concept of the theology remains intact. It is the serious and final thing in all medieval thoughts about God and the world. It does not rule out sharp antitheses. On the contrary, it evokes them. Triunity as the solution of all puzzles, how can that not be the source of all theses and antitheses? But it also embraces the antitheses. It is always also a synthesis. It stands on both this side and the far side of the tensions of intuitive and dialectical thinking, of world denial and world affirmation, of Aristotelianism and Augustinian Neoplatonism, of devotion and skepticism. It contains all these within itself, ejects them all, and takes back again that which is developed into a unity. For Thomas evil was a lack of good, a corruption of the good, which in the long run could only increase perfection.[21]

The theology includes various individual thinkers and groups of thinkers, an Anselm and an Abelard, and later the Dominican and Franciscan schools, and later still the *via antiqua* and *via moderna,* but all in an invisible discipline and fellowship that only seldom needed the corrective hand of church authority and in relation to which one had to be an outsider like Amalrich of Bena (d. 1205)[22] to be really a heretic, that is, not to be able finally to think the most extreme thoughts under the protection of the same vault along with less radical investigators. Most of the 15th- and 16th-century Humanists saw no good reason to leave that shelter. What nonsense to assume that only the outward, rigid concept of the authority of church dogma had the power to set in motion this host of youthfully fresh seekers and thinkers in its defense, and for half a millennium to keep it in step. It was the basic thought of open and direct access to the final mystery, the conviction as to the necessity and possibility of immediate knowledge of God, that made that possible, and the concept of church authority was simply an outgrowth of the basic perception, and for that reason was not felt to be an alien body that fettered thought.

That this theology was a theology of glory, a bold and confident theology sensing victory, is what we have to remember when we look at the decisions it reached on the individual problems that gave it its characteristic features and over against which the basic contradiction of the Reformation revolted (but only revolted!). If we adopt the same approach as that with which the scholastics tackled these problems, seeing and feeling them in all their unequivocal seriousness and beauty, then we cannot really be surprised that their decisions were so Catholic, but we can also see that the transition from the Middle Ages to the Reformation was not in truth as simple and self-evident as it might often seem if we look only at the polemical positions and counterpositions of individual thinkers and their adversaries.

In the light of that basic concept it was natural that the relation of God, the world, and humanity should be seen at every point as a graded structure of possibilities that are clearly different yet no less clearly in continuity, all leading up to the final possibility of a pure vision of God, and all experiencing their relative consecration and dignity from that supreme pinnacle and in virtue of their continuous connection with it. It was thus that the relation between reason and revelation was fundamentally regulated. They could not really contradict one another. They flowed from the same source, namely, the wisdom of God. So said John Scotus Erigena in the 9th century.[23] On the eve of the Reformation age, as though time had stood still, the Humanist Pico della Mirandola could say similarly: "Philosophy seeks the truth, theology finds it."[24] Between them, of course, lay a whole ocean of possibilities stretching the bow to the very limit. In any case one has to see two sides, not just one, even though one might be called William of Occam, who went as far as is humanly possible in exploring the problems of theology.[25] There was no serious or sharp opposing of reason to revelation or revelation to reason. All along the line the result was a kind of pyramid, the possibility, no matter how paradoxical, of striding across from the one to the other, the supplementing of reason by revelation, the understanding of revelation by means of reason.

Nor could there be any real antithesis between the authority of the Bible and that of the church, problematic though their unity might often appear to be. The authority of the church embodied the idea of the theology of glory, the unbroken possibility of a path to God. No medieval teacher contested the truth that the church's authority rests on that of the biblical revelation, but in the scales against this they all set the dictum of Augustine: "I would not believe the gospel if the authority of the church did not move me to do so,"[26] a saying that caused endless difficulties for his faithful followers, the reformers. Unlike the reformers, the medievals really saw no antithesis between a greater and lesser or a more distant and more immediate authority. Reconciliation was always possible.

In the knowledge of God, too, we have the bold ascent from the demonstrable existence of God to his essence, which is accessible to us humans only by revelation, though in the very same movement from us to God. In mystical terms we have here the movement from the finite to rest in the infinitude of the ground of the soul that is one and the same as God. Either way the step that can be taught and taken is bold but also one that can be envisioned methodically. Thus in the doctrine of God and the world we find the brave thesis that God as first cause is present in second causes, a thesis that leaves the possibility of miracle open but also makes it basically superfluous.

Similarly we have the ingenious and meaningful doctrinal structure of the first estate, the fall, original sin, freedom, grace, and justification, a structure which I cannot in this context depict in detail but relative to which, before we dismiss it with the catchword semi-Pelagianism,[27] we need to consider its basic and helpful and consistently observed practical aim of showing there really is a path from earth to heaven, of giving visibility to eternal paradoxical truth, expounded in time and basically divested of its paradoxical character. Those who want this—and where are the Protestant theologians who are sure they can really do without it?—must at least examine closely the minute scholastic distinctions to see whether they contain just what they seek, or whether, if they despise them, they can truly do without a new and probably much worse semi-Pelagianism. For the Catholic doctrine of the appropriation of grace is truly remarkable in the way it considers all the elements, neglecting none and exaggerating none: nature and grace, humanity and God, freedom and dependence, a justifiable sense of self and humility before God, doing and receiving, meriting and being given, time and eternity. The later Reformation doctrine of salvation hardly contains anything that does not somewhere find a place in scholastic teaching in a heavily emphasized and underlined way.

At the same time there is nowhere any one-sidedness, any ultimate either/or. We always find the way, the possibility, the method, the theology of glory, which knows no final difficulty and is never at a loss vis-à-vis the object before which it stands. Human innocence before the fall consists of a sure combination, free of all friction, between sensuality, understanding, and reason with its vision. Original sin is the absence of righteousness; we have been dealt a wound that is in need of healing. But we can become healthy—that is the famous freedom of the will (*liberum arbitrium*); we can be redeemed if we are diligently concerned, and when love from above, *gratia gratis data,* as Goethe said wholly in the spirit of the Middle Ages, plays its part in us.[28] For grace can make what we do meritorious, or, according to Duns Scotus, God in his grace can accept what we humans do as meritorious.[29] If this happens, then the prior grace that aids and disposes us becomes *gratia gratum faciens* or *infusa,* which is wholly God's work in us but is even so a wholly real and objective event, for grace does not abolish nature but perfects it (Scotus).[30] By it human nature becomes capable of faith, which is *infusa* in terms of its origin and *implicita* in terms of its scope: it orients itself wittingly or unwittingly to what the authority of the church commands us to believe, being formed by love (*caritate formata*) in order that there should be no question as to its efficacy or merit. For the justification of sinners is real *factio iustitiae* (Thomas).[31] It coincides with the infusion of grace.[32] From the work of Christ on the cross that procures forgiveness of sins an unbroken chain of equations leads to the love that is the work of the Spirit of grace. Or, as Eckhardt put it, the conceiving of God in the soul, that triumph of the theology of glory, is the blossom that contains within itself, and will never fail to do so, the action of Martha, the desire and love of virtue, producing them out of itself.[33] I ask again where in Protestant theology we find all this described in a way that is better or more illuminating or credible?

For this reason, too, the church in the Middle Ages was a real saving institution in which something was set up and achieved. As we have seen, the knowledge of God that marked the community of the elect was as such a possessing of God. This community not only had something to show but something to give. In virtue of the infinite merit of Christ's sacrificial death which was its basis, it was the place where grace is present and is dispensed, and outside it was no salvation.[34] We cannot contest this concept by urging against it the usual slogans. It was a bold and titanic concept, significant in its titanism. To overcome it we have to understand it. It explains the dominant position of the sacraments in that church. The sacraments were the visible form of invisible grace,[35] but as Scholasticism laid down with increasing decisiveness and consistency, they were not just signs. As signs they were the thing signified. They were not just signs of power but direct, real, sanctifying power. That is the difference between OT circumcision and NT baptism, taught Peter Lombard and Thomas Aquinas. The one merely signifies and takes its course with faith on the part of the recipient. The other, in the new covenant, has sacramental force (*virtus sacramenti*) by which the recipients are irresistibly given (*ex opere operato*) a sacramental character.[36]

We can see precisely from a study of the doctrine of the Lord's Supper how the principle of a theology of glory gradually established itself in this field that is so important in practice, first in the ideas of Gregory the Great, then in the debates focused on Radbert in the 9th century and Berengar in the 11th, then in the as yet uncertain definitions of Anselm, Hugh of St. Victor, and Peter Lombard, and finally in the full and unequivocal doctrine of transubstantiation proclaimed by Lateran IV in 1215. Later thinkers like Durandus of St. Pourçain, William of Occam, or Peter d'Ailly might express the victorious principle, in this case the equation of bread and wine with Christ's body and blood, in new forms, but in no instance did they question the principle itself.[37] The principle is that of our immediacy to God. That is what triumphed no less in the scholastic doctrine of the Lord's Supper than in Dominican mysticism, and any who are concerned about this principle should ask whether it does not really find justice done to it in the best and most appropriate way in the Roman Catholic church.

In the history of the sacrament of penance again the valleys were filled in and the hills laid low [cf. Isa. 40:4] as obligatory confession developed out of a pious monastic practice, as priestly absolution, which was originally intended to recognize and crown preceding works of satisfaction, became a means of liberation from guilt and of reconciliation to God, to be followed by imposed duties that would make satisfaction and free from sin's penalties, whether in this life or under purgatorial stress in the next life. Irritation at the well-known indulgence system that was meant to soften and regulate the later penitential exercises should not blind us to the intention underlying the whole doctrine. Here again we have something that is often regarded as specifically evangelical, namely, the making of a simple and direct way to God, the principle of immediacy. What Scotus would finally proclaim as the essence of this sacrament was precisely the exclusion of preceding works of merit, even a meritorious heart's attrition, and the immediate relation of the soul to God by grace, the only point being that we have to be *aliqualiter attriti,* that we must not put anything in the way of grace, that we have to receive it. For that reason it could be said of this sacrament—the most personal and incisive, we have to say—that no other way is as simple or as sure.[38] It would not be too hard to express this concept of penance in the language of a modern philosophy of immediacy, the only point being that the scholastics had at the outset the foresight to link the counterweight of works to be done after penance to the boldness of laying hold of what is immediate with such assurance of salvation.

If we try to listen to the whole of medieval theology from which I have selected a few typical details, we are surprised again and again by the great harmony, the mixture of boldness and sagacity, of profundity and common sense, that we find there. It is the harmony of the monastery garden with its rows of cherry trees and its splashing fountains and its surrounding walls that remind us of the world with its joy and grief[39] but also shut it out. Or again, this is the harmony of the Gothic cathedral with its high altar, its soaring pillars, its roomy transepts, its hidden penitential stools, its eternal light, the dark glow of the windows of the choir—the cathedral where sinners and saints, worldlings and penitents, may all join together in common reconciling worship, where the last and deepest things may take place, where the donkey of Palm Sunday and the laughter of Easter are not out of place, where earth and heaven do indeed seem to touch. A "complex of opposites" is what Harnack called this church,[40] and that is also true of its theology.

Let us come back with a few general characteristics to the direct impression that it makes. We are astonished at the certainty about life that the authors display and spread abroad in spite of opposing symptoms. They stand with both feet on the earth precisely because they stride on up to the world above, for that world is also for them a wonderful but attainable possibility. It is only a step between the kingdom of the world and the kingdom of God, between the trivial and the ecstatic, and good care is taken to see that balance is constantly achieved between the two extremes. Even the most broken of these people seem to be able to take the step from below to above and to put the two worlds together. We are astonished at the completeness and subtlety with which this theology handles all its problems no less carefully than radically. What a waltz it dances in its investigations out from the center to every side! Everything is important, everything has to be elucidated and discussed, everything has to be at least prepared for further treatment by means of meaningful divisions and subdivisions in which the numbers three, four, and seven are particular favorites. The question of the hierarchical ranking of angels and the question what happens to Christ's body if the host is accidentally eaten by a mouse come under discussion with equal seriousness.[41]

We come away with the happy impression that we have really heard everything that we might want. We are also astonished at the definite way in which we are told about things regarding which we might at first ask with surprise how the authors can possibly know about them, but then have to admit shamefacedly that they have simply expounded to us in a meaningful and often very poetic way a dialectical possibility that is by no means obvious. Thomas, for example, assures us that the blessed ones in heaven are adorned with a golden crown (*corona aurea*), which, being both golden and circular, signifies the perfection of the *fruitio Dei* in the contemplation and love of which they share. Superadded for martyrs and saints, however, and especially for monks and nuns, is an *aureola* (diminutive of *aurea*) because that essential thing cannot be transcended by anything greater but only by something less.[42] Or listen to what Heinrich Seuse has the damned in hell say about their punishment being eternal: "Woe on us, we did not want anything but this: if a millstone were so broad that it covered the whole earth, and if in the beginning it were so big that it even touched heaven, and if a little bird came every 100,000 years and bit out of it as much as the tenth part of a little millet seed, we wretches would wish nothing more than that when the stone was gone our eternal torment would have an end, and that cannot be."[43]

We are surely barren thinkers if we cannot see what insight is everywhere concealed in the imagery, yet we are no less astounded by the confidence with which these authors translate their insights into imagery that may often be striking. We must also be astounded at the remarkable peace that breathes over their discussions. It is true that here and there, for example, in Abelard or in scholastics of the age of the gathering 14th- and 15th-century storm, we detect highly existential inner conflicts and a hard struggle for composure before things can be as certain and unequivocal on paper as they now are. No doubt Scholasticism is renowned for its controversies and even conflicts. But what distinguishes it is the obvious rule that people spoke only when they were clear about things, only when what they had to say was ripe, so that there was no need to air abroad inner problems or unsolved questions or doubts, only at most to give an account of conflicts that had been ended. Hence, bitter though the quarrels between school and school might be, they took place within the same fellowship and on the same basic premises. The anger and tone of voice that we find in Reformation battles were alien to the Middle Ages. As we have to admit, Reformation contests were like peasant brawls compared to the elegant fencing of the scholastics.... One could then make very radical assertions unhindered without going over the line or really getting out of step. When getting out of step finally began to happen, when a Bradwardine or Wycliffe or Huss began to say really bad things to others, the Middle Ages were at an end. In the best classical age, that was not done, and the stake did not come into action as a theological argument.

But we must stop and ask what all this meant compared to Reformation theology. In relation to Scholasticism, as we have generally described it, that theology was obviously something "wholly other," if we may again put it thus, though we are agreed that there was no real breach of historical continuity. Within the continuity, however, we find first the emergence of a totally new style, the outbreak of a total restlessness, we must say, for along with the intellectual habitus that medieval theology had developed, and in contrast with it, the theological attitude of the Reformation, so long as it was in flux as a true countermovement, was so as a deliberate and angry rejection of that habitus, as a wild and elemental event at the heart of a cultivated land. The harmony of the monastery garden was broken and instead we seem to be in the virgin wilderness of mountain forests, if not in the terrors of the Wolfsschlucht.[44] The harmony of the Gothic cathedral was at an end. The parallel lines to which we referred yesterday no longer intersected in the finite sphere no matter how high they might reach. No, they now relentlessly strove upward to a point of unity and rest in the infinite, the result being that the vault was broken open and heaven's daylight shone in from above. All was sober, nondevout, secular. The glory of God itself brought disaster to the theology of glory.

In saying this we have already disclosed the secret of the new theology. It made the discovery that theology has to do with *God*. It made the great and shattering discovery of the real theme of all theology. The secret was simply this, that it took this theme seriously in all its distinctiveness, that it names God God, that it lets God be God, the one object that by no bold human grasping or inquiry or approach can be simply one object among many others. God *is*. *He* lives. *He* judges and blesses. *He* slays and makes alive [cf. 1 Sam. 2:6]. *He* is the Creator and Redeemer and Lord. The Reformation did not really engender any new thoughts about God. It did the simple thing of underlining the *He*. And that put an end to the Middle Ages. For all the building stone by stone, all the mounting up step by step, all the moving from conclusion to conclusion, all this action in which the Middle Ages found its answers, had to become a question when it was underlined and understood that *He,* God, is the point of the whole enterprise. The basic Reformation view is God *himself* and God *alone, He* the way, *He* the possibility; and therefore all our action, even though oriented to God, is vain even in the very best life;[45] all humanity, the whole world, even in its supreme possibilities, is guilty, lost, but still justified, yet saved only by sheer mercy. The Reformation, too, knew of the glory of God and could speak about it. But it said: To God alone be the glory! That put an end to the theology of glory.

Let us find out first, however, what the emergence of this insight had to involve externally relative to our final survey of the Middle Ages. What are we to say in this regard precisely when we have taken pains to do justice impartially to Scholasticism, precisely when we have learned to like the medieval thinkers, precisely when we have perhaps recognized in them our own deepest longings and desires? May it not be that much of what we have thus far regarded as our supremely modern striving, our whole modern style of religion even with its Christian coloring, is at its deepest level medieval? Who is Goethe closer to, Dante or Luther? That is a question we may at least raise. Where do we belong with our Romanticism, with our drive for immediacy, with our urgent concern to be shown a path that we can tread? Can we stay on those heights on which the reformers ventured, no, on which they were set against their own wishes or expectations, and where an immovable barrier arrests all striving for immediacy, where steps are possible but no path opens up before us, where we can live but only as the dying [cf. 2 Cor. 6:9]? Would we not do better to turn back? Instead of Calvin might we not take Thomas as the one we can really understand better.[46]

If we want the security that we find in the scholastics, then it might be as well for us not to turn to the reformers. Certainty about God, indeed, we may expect that here, but a certainty that entails a supreme lack of security, that makes of life a problem, a question, a task, a need, that makes of the Christian life an unceasing battle: a battle for existence itself in which we constantly confront the impossible and the intolerable that Scholasticism, at least in its teaching, could always adroitly sidestep; a battle in which in truth God wills to be and can be the only helper.

We may well ask whether we are wise to leave the solid Catholic ground of balance and to launch out on the wild sea of Reformation thinking. Even the symmetrical completeness of subtle responses to all that we might want to know is something we cannot seek in Reformation theology. That theology is an emergency structure, not a well-appointed house. It offers no answers at all, or only incidental answers, to many interesting questions. The symmetry of the numbers three, four, and seven, the ladder to heaven that gives us confidence, the theological interplay, the highly intellectual feast—we find none of these things. The only concern in thinking here is to be serious and to keep the real theme in view. What a pile of ruins we have in Melanchthon's *Loci,* what a dark and threatening forest in Calvin's *Institutes!* Not everyone surely can have to tread these desolate places.

Nor may we seek in the reformers what is at least in part such reassuring and profound information about invisible things of which I gave you a couple of examples. The reformers were astonishingly eloquent on those relations between God and us about which one can speak, but astonishingly silent when it came to matters about which one can only be imaginative. They did not deny the possibility of speaking about such things but used the possibility sparingly.

And as for the peacefulness and decorum and good manners that might allow for disagreement but not quarreling, I have told you already that we cannot see these in the reformers. In them we do find quarreling. All the evil spirits of discord seem to have come to life. All the possibilities of quiet academic discussion between one view and another seem to have been excluded. Everything is so much a matter of principle, everything is in such deadly earnest, everything is so angry. Last things are always at issue. Innermost feelings are always exposed. Attacks on opponents are always pressed to the uttermost. For this reason the more delicate like Erasmus who found this hard stayed clear of the tumult so far as possible. Even Calvin would rather have passed his days as a private scholar than as a reformer, and he knew why. As a reformer, he found his life filled with conflicts on every hand concerning which we today can only with difficulty, if at all, convince ourselves that they had to be fought, or had to be fought in the way they were. Lovers of peace cannot possibly approve of this kind of life and this kind of theology in which there was constant hewing and stabbing on all sides. Is that really what the Reformation age involves? we might ask. But we do better to ask why it was that it had to be so and could not be otherwise in this new age.

The slogan that Luther used in the theses of the Heidelberg Disputation to distinguish his own theology from that of the scholastics was "theology of the cross." In what he said then, and in a similar situation and on the same front in his Disputation against Scholastic Theology a year earlier [M. Luther, *Sämtliche Werke,* Opera Latina (Erlangen, 1826 ff.); hereafter EOL] V, Arg. 1, 315ff., 387ff.),[47] we can see how it was that the reformers did not just cause an incidental disturbance but attacked the basic view of the Middle Ages. In essence we find two trains of thought in the records of Luther's initial attack on medieval theology, the first more apparent in the earlier Wittenberg Disputation (1517), the latter more so in the later Heidelberg Disputation (1518), but both deeply involved in one another and both pointing to one another.

The first is a negation, a protest, a sharp offensive. It contains what seemed to those outside the surprising and scandalous theses of the nexus of thought with which the reformers broke out of the circle of medieval possibilities. At Wittenberg we are told that once a person becomes a bad tree then that person can will and do only what is bad (4); or that by nature we cannot will that God be God but will always will that we be God and God not God (17); or that on our part there is no preceding disposition for grace but only the opposite, or even rebellion against grace (30); or that nature knows no righteous command or goodwill (34); or that by nature we cannot overcome our ignorance of God, of ourselves, or of the doing of the good (36); or that we cannot become theologians unless we do so without Aristotle (44); or that the law and the will are two foes that cannot be reconciled apart from grace (72); or that every work done according to the law is outwardly good but inwardly sin (77); or that love for God cannot coexist with love, even the highest love, for the creature (94).[48] Then from the Heidelberg Disputation of 1518 we read that human works, no matter what worth they have or how good they seem, are to be judged as mortal sins (3), or that arrogance is unavoidable, and true hope impossible, if in every human work the sentence of condemnation (God's) is not feared (11).[49] For, as Luther said in explanation, it is not possible to hope in God if one does not despair of all creatures.[50] We read again that those who do what they can to attain to grace heap up sin upon sin and become doubly guilty.[51]

So much from the first and negative train of thought. What is typically and decisively nonmedieval here is not the content in detail but the harsh one-sidedness with which Luther pursued the thought that in all circumstances we stand under judgment. He left no place for an "also" or a "but" or a "nevertheless." He did not look ahead to any higher stage of the way or any further possibility. The last and supreme possibility is that we are sinners. This was not an expression of humility before the eternal God. The Middle Ages knew that, too. By rudely stopping at such humility, Luther's thinking was an assault upon Scholasticism, upon its very heart. What was questioned was not just an aberration or subsidiary teaching of a Thomas, a Dante, or an Eckhardt, but what was best and highest and most inward and vital in them, if Luther's protest was right.

The second train of thought in the Luther of that period was positive, a proclamation or affirmation about God. And what a one it was, of course! Its content is that we live by the grace of God. In itself this is not surprising. It is no more new than the negation. Scholasticism was in truth aware of it, too. But it was suspect and dangerous and even more non-Catholic than the first line of thinking because of its association with the negation, namely, because here the grace of God is taken seriously, with bitter yet saving seriousness, only in connection with that radical protest against us humans as sinners. Set in that context, the proclamation of the mercy of God became the heart of the new Reformation theology.

Listen to Luther himself. At Wittenberg in 1517 he said that the best and infallible preparation for grace, the only disposition for it, is God's eternal election and predestination (29), that the presence of grace is enough to make works meritorious, yet grace is not idly present but present as a living, moving active spirit (54f.), that blessed are those who do the works of grace (81), that the good and life-giving law is the love of God shed abroad in our hearts by the Holy Spirit (85), and that to love God is to hate self and to know nothing outside him (95).[52]

Then at Heidelberg in 1518 he said that the works of God, no matter how hidden they are or how evil they might seem to be, are in truth immortal benefits ("merits").[53] In explanation Luther gave the following important exposition. The Lord humbles and terrifies us by the law and the sight of our sins, so that to others and to ourselves we seem to be empty, foolish, and evil, and truly are so. When we see and confess this, we have no form nor comeliness but live in the hidden God, in the concealment of God, that is, in naked trust in his mercy; and in and of ourselves we can appeal to nothing but sin, folly, death, and hell according to the apostolic saying in 2 Cor. 6 [vv. 9-10]: As sorrowful, but always rejoicing, as dying, and behold we live. That is what Isa. 28 [v. 21] calls God's *opus alienum,* his strange work, for his work has to take place (in us), that is, he humbles us in ourselves by reducing us to despair in order to exalt us in virtue of his mercy, and by bringing us hope, as Hab. 3 [v. 2] says: When you chide, you remember your mercy. When this happens to us, we have no pleasure in ourselves and see no beauty in us but only deformity. Indeed, we do outwardly what must seem foolish and perverted to others.[54] Human existence of this kind under humility and the fear of God is what Luther calls the work of God that is eternally beneficial ("meritorious") in spite of appearances. (It need hardly be said that Luther's use of the category of merit here casts a special light.) We then read that this kind of talk is no reason for despair but is a reason for humility and a spur to the seeking of the grace of Christ (17).[55] For, says Luther in explanation, it is hope and not despair that is preached when the preaching is that we are sinners.[56] Nevertheless, we have to despair of ourselves if we are to be able to receive the grace of Christ (18).[57] For, the explanation adds, if we do not, we still rely on doing what we can, and we remain presumptuous.[58] The good theologian is the one who sees in the cross and passion the visible side of God that is turned to us and does not look directly at the invisible things of God, his majesty and glory, by way of profound spiritual vision.[59]

To support this thesis Luther argues that it helps no one to see God in his glory and majesty if he is not seen in the lowliness and shame of the cross.[60] Along the lines of a theology of glory Philip in John 14 [v.8] says: "Lord, show us the Father," and he receives the answer: "Philip, whoever sees me sees also my Father." True theology and the true knowledge of God lie, then, in the crucified Christ.[61] A theologian of glory calls evil good and good evil, but the theologian of the cross calls things by their right names (21).[62] For, Luther explains, the theologian of glory does not see God hidden in the passion and thus prefers works to suffering, glory to the cross, power to weakness, wisdom to folly; in sum, evil to good. Such are enemies of Christ's cross.[63] Friends of the cross, however, call the cross good and works evil. For the cross demolishes works, and Adam, who is built up by works, is crucified.[64] The wisdom that would know the invisible glory of God by the way of human works puffs up, blinds, and hardens (22).[65] In itself, of course, it is not bad, but without the theology of the cross we make the best worst by ascribing wisdom and works to ourselves (24).[66] We are not righteous by doing much, but by believing much in Christ without works (25).[67] The law says, "Do this," and nothing happens. Grace says, "Believe in him," and all is done already (26).[68] The love of God does not find its object present but creates it (28).[69] For the love of God that is alive in us loves sinners, the wicked, the foolish, the weak, to make them righteous, good, wise, and strong. It overflows and lavishes good on them. Sinners are good, then, because they are loved; they are not loved because they are good.[70]

What we have in these theses of Luther is truly and literally a theology of the cross. Luther, too, sees a horizontal line before him,[71] our human striving, knowing, willing, and doing. The theology of glory thinks that somewhere on an extension of this line it will reach the goal of infinity, the invisible things of God. Its slogan is that grace does not destroy nature but perfects it.[72] Luther does not deny that there is this wisdom, this beatific vision, much, much further along that line. His objection is that one thing is overlooked, namely, that at the center, where each of us stands, we willing and knowing humans with our works, there is a break that throws everything into question.[73] To say human is to say sin, rebellion against grace, invincible ignorance of God, irreconcilable hostility to his law. What is radically set in question by this break in the middle of the line is not simply our banal everyday willing and doing, but just as much what we regard as our love of God, not simply our "sensuality" and reason but just as much our "simple intelligence," as Gerson would put it, at the heart of which, sunk in contemplation, we see God face-to-face.[74]

The theology of glory boldly pushes on beyond the gap that makes all this problematical. It storms ahead without a halt on the horizontal line toward the invisible things of God, not considering how seriously it is threatened in the rear and how much it increases the damage with its striving. In contrast Luther tries to draw attention to the vacuum, to the fact that passion (suffering) stands at the heart of life and speaks of sin and folly, death and hell. These fearful visible things of God, his strange work, the crucified Christ—these are the theme of true theology. A preaching of despair? No, of hope! For what does that break in the center mean? Who is the God hidden in the passion with his strange work, and what does he desire? Explaining Heidelberg Thesis 16, Luther pointed out that the strange work leads on to the proper work, that God makes us sinners in order to make us righteous.[75] The gap in the horizontal line, the disaster of our own striving, is the point at which God's vertical line intersects our lives,[76] where God wills to be gracious. Here where our finitude is recognized is true contact with infinity. He who judges us is he who shows mercy to us, he who slays us is he who makes us live, he who leads us into hell is he who leads us into heaven. Only sinners are righteous, only the sad are blessed, only the dying live. But sinners *are* righteous, the sad *are* blessed, the dying *do* live. The God hidden in the passion is the living God who loves us, sinful, wicked, foolish, and weak as we are, in order to make us righteous, good, wise, and strong. It is because the strange work leads to the proper work that there can be no theology of glory, that we must halt at the sharply severed edges of the broken horizontal line where what we find is despair, humility, the fear of God. For despair is hope, humility is exaltation, fear of God is love of God, and nothing else. The center of this theology, then, is the demand for faith as naked trust that casts itself into the arms of God's mercy; faith that is the last word that can be humanly said about the possibility of justification before God; a faith that is sure of its object—God—because here there is resolute renunciation of the given character of scholastic faith (infused, implicit, and formed) as an element of uncertainty; faith viewed not as itself a human work but as an integral part of God's strange work, sharing in the whole paradox of it.

We see now why this theology was so basically polemical and militant. Without a constant critical debate with the infinitely attractive tendency, represented with such virtuosity by the scholastics, to press on to the goal, with the help of grace, by works, by "high-flying thoughts" (57, 208),[77] the demand for faith cannot possibly be made. Hence a second focal point of this theology was a constantly repeated reference to Christ as God's visible word and work in contrast to the lofty invisible things of the theology of glory. Luther admonished and warned us all to leave off speculating and not to float too high but to stay here below by the cradle and diaper in which Christ lies, in whom dwells all the fullness of the deity bodily (57, 211).[78] This reference to Christ is truly necessary here, grounded in the matter itself, for here Christ does not simply bring grace as a second thing, so that we can then go on without him, as mysticism in particular has blabbed, but he is himself grace, the proper work of God, the promise of the mercy of God that is grasped in faith, the one God who makes us righteous, even as he is the Crucified, the scandal, the strange work of God, which threatens our works at their very root, the same God who makes us sinners in order to make us righteous.

It was this theology of the cross as a theology of the justification of sinners that Luther rediscovered in Romans and the Psalms, and Augustine as the word which finally routs completely even the true longings of mysticism and Nominalist Scholasticism. That this word should be loudly proclaimed and thoroughly heard was for him the Reformation once he became aware that with this concept a reformation of Christendom, the church, and theology had in fact begun. Initially Luther had no other concern than to refer to the forgotten cross at the beginning of our human way, or rather, this one concern basically included all others, though pursuing them could not be for him a matter of incisive or decisive importance. We are forced to say that this one concern in all its one-sidedness is indeed the true essence of the Reformation. Where people have this concern, there is Protestantism; where they do not, or have moved on past it, there is a prolongation of the Middle Ages!

From all this we derive two insights. First, we see why there had to be the sharp clash between the Reformation and the Middle Ages that I have just intentionally depicted for you with almost futuristic vividness. Schwenckfeld was right when he said that two worlds dash against one another here.[79] We cannot both believe with Luther and also engage in mysticism with its devotional excesses, even though it be the finest and most insightful mysticism of an Eckhardt and his school. Medieval mysticism seeks with all its powers to move away from what Luther called God, though it could certainly speak a great deal about the cross and darkness and Christ. Luther turned his back with increasing resoluteness on what mysticism called God, although at first he thought he found his own outlook in the glorious little book of the *German Theology* and in Tauler.[80] We will come back to the connection, which was undoubtedly there. But at the very point where it is there we see clearly that a choice has to be made: Luther or Eckhardt. Once we realize that the Middle Ages also knew the vertical line but lived wholly and utterly on the horizontal, whereas Luther also knew the horizontal but lived wholly and utterly on the vertical, or, more accurately, at the point of the intersecting of the vertical by the horizontal, we need no longer be surprised by the harsh either-or that had to arise there, nor by the shattering of security that the Reformation entailed, nor by the incomplete and fissured nature of its theological presentations, nor by the paucity of its metaphysics, nor by the atmosphere of anger that lay over the whole of the first half of the 16th century and that began to dissipate only when the spirit of the Reformation also fled, nor by the much-noted coarseness of Luther, nor by the cold virulence of Calvin, nor indeed by Ignatius Loyola and the pyres of the Counter-Reformation. When the theology of the cross really becomes part of the theological problem, when theologians begin really to note what is the true theme of their generally peaceful vocation, it is inevitable that something primal, wild, undomesticated, and demonic in religion will be aroused as between friend and foe. It had to be so then, and it might be that if the Creator Spirit brings on the stage another theology of the cross it will have to be so again. Insight into the ineluctability of these consequences will keep us straight when we assess certain secondary phenomena of Reformation history with which we might have little sympathy. It will also keep us from looking for the essence of the Reformation in these secondary phenomena when we might well be in sympathy with them, as can happen.

The second insight clearly arises out of our account of Luther's starting point, where we have to look for what is problematic in the Reformation itself. We obviously turn to the horizontal line of human thought and action in time that is so sharply broken by the vertical line of the knowledge of God in Christ. The problem of human life and striving as the Middle Ages unbrokenly pursued it cannot be simply cut off by being put under the shadow of its finitude, that is, in the light of its origin. What does the attack of the vertical mean for what takes place horizontally? What becomes of all that we will and work here below on the line of death that is suddenly made visible,[81] that we have to will and work because as people in time we are always here below on that line of death? What becomes of all this when we confront the absolute beyond that meets the present world in a way that crushes it but is also full of promise, when we arrive at the sharp edges of despair, humility, and fear of God which... still have their positive side, when we face God the Judge who all the same is none other than the merciful God? The Middle Ages died with Luther's discovery, but their problem, the problem of the active life, of ethics in the broadest sense, did not die with them. Nor can it be put to death. From the very first Luther was aware of this problem in his theology of the cross. Remember Thesis 55 at Wittenberg in 1517: Grace is not idle but a living, moving, active spirit.[82] On innumerable occasions he tried with great seriousness to solve the problem. Simply to make Luther a Quietist is an illegitimate simplifying of the situation. We may at least say that this question was not primarily *his* question. Luther's great concern was for the pure content and free course of the Word, no matter what might become of works. Here, however, in the matter of establishing the positive relation between the vertical and horizontal lines—the cross has to be left open in Luther[83]—we find the point at which the second turn in the Reformation, the Reformed theology of Zwingli and Calvin, had to enter and did in fact do so.

### 3 COMMON FEATURES

What I have said raises the question of features common to the Middle Ages and the Reformation despite the sharpness of their differences. At the beginning of the section I argued that the new thing in the Reformation in the serious sense is something eternally new, and closer investigation confirmed the insight that the new thing then discovered was something so great that it is a priori impossible to assume that it was simply not present at all previously; conversely, the old thing that the reformers vanquished was so all-encompassing and universally human that it could not possibly disappear completely.

The Reformation was the expression of a crisis that secretly ran through all the Middle Ages. I have referred already to the tensions and contradictions that the medieval church was able to reconcile, but in truth the tensions were serious. The Middle Ages were in self-contradiction long before Luther came along and made the contradiction irreconcilable. But the Middle Ages could always find a way victoriously through the tensions to the triumph of the theology of glory. They did not finally accept their own self-contradiction. In spite of every shock, they could always restore equilibrium. We see the existence of that crisis of the medieval spirit at the most varied points.

In this regard we recall especially the problem of monasticism that was always present in the church from Benedict of Nursia by way of the Cluny[1] reform to Francis of Assisi. Originally we had here a real protest of the first order against the theology of glory even though later precisely the Franciscans and Dominicans became that theology's most brilliant champions. Initially monasticism questioned and even attacked a self-assured and worldly Christianity. It was an uplifted finger to remind people that we cannot have the kingdom of God so cheaply. The world took notice and caused the finger to drop. It made a place for asceticism. It offered this hard and dangerous function to the brave who were ready for it. It celebrated a new triumph by putting this possibility too, this highest level of human action, on the church's horizontal line. Thus the ascetics, though often with great pain, as in the case of a Francis, became protagonists of the triumphing world church instead of protesting against it. That does not alter the fact, however, that the Reformation was at least also an extension of the monastic line. The question of true penitence that brought the theology of the cross to the fore was a variation on a typically monastic question. Monasticism now mounted its most powerful offensive. With full seriousness and with no holding back it now broke out of the cloister and became a universal matter. It would now question the world, not as before from outside, but from inside, not in the form of the ascetic lifestyle of the few, but in that of a cross lifted up in the life of all. It achieved perhaps its greatest victory in the man in whom it finally went bankrupt.

To do justice to the new thing that was already concealed in the old we must also look at the innumerable traces that Augustine left in the Western church, and along with Augustine examine Paul's epistles and the philosophy of Plato.[2] Wherever Augustine made an impact, no matter how faintly, there still glowed under the ashes some recollection of the vertical line. In almost every century during the Middle Ages Augustine won over some resolute disciples for himself, and if they were strong enough, also for his own teachers, Paul and Plato. As regards the transcendental knowledge of God, John Scotus Erigena followed in his steps in the 9th century, Anselm in the 11th, Bonaventura in the 13th, and Eckhardt in the 14th. As regards predestination, we find an echo of his teaching in Isidore of Seville in the 7th century, an extreme and defiant proponent in Gottschalk in the 9th, a renaissance in the 14th century in Bradwardine (the profound doctor, who wanted to defend it as "the cause of God" against a Christian world that had fallen into Pelagianism, Elijah against the 450 priests of Baal), and also in Gregory of Rimini, in whose formulas some have sought a source of the theology of Luther.[3] Again, at least as a restraining force, Augustine played a decisive part in the development of the scholastic doctrine of the appropriation of salvation. If at this point the doctrines of free will, of the possibility of earning merit, of infused grace and making righteous were hemmed about by so many distinctions that even in typical representatives of Scholasticism one might at a pinch expound them in better part along Reformation lines, or at least find in them a starting point for Luther's revolution, then unmistakably this was due, if not to the spirit, at least to the shadow, of Augustine. Augustine's spiritual emphasis played a similar role in eucharistic teaching, though here the last powerful opposition to the theology of glory, that of Berengar of Tours, was broken already in the 11th century.[4] Finally medieval theology took over from Augustine something that it found congenial, his mystical devotion and his attachment to the church, while quietly ignoring his less congenial Platonism and Paulinism. Nevertheless, it could no more prevent the latter elements than the former from retaining their vitality. Those latter elements had only to be reasserted, which is precisely what happened with great force.

Along with monasticism and Augustinianism, a third Reformation element in the Middle Ages was undoubtedly the anti-Thomistic theology of Duns Scotus (d. 1308) and the so-called modern way of William of Occam (d. 1349), which had a similar orientation but went even further. With special reference to Calvin we must devote a few moments to these two British thinkers. A first distinctive feature in both was the questioning of the unity of the path of knowledge, of the stairway from reason to revelation. Not metaphysically but methodologically the statements of reason and revelation were for them irreconcilable. We are unable to mount up from reason to revelation. Theology is a practical, not a speculative, discipline, said Duns,[5] and Occam agreed that we cannot know God's existence, essence, or reality intuitively from ourselves or from the things of nature. God cannot be an object for us.[6] Occam went further, however, when he showed that our reason not only cannot prove dogma but might make it appear absurd.[7] Reality consists only of individual things, said Duns, and again Occam went further with his even sharper thesis that this is the reality originating in the idea of God, whereas the terms or names or concepts out of which reason constructs science exist only in the soul of the knowing subjects, so that logic is the only real science.[8] This thesis explains the historical use of the term Nominalism for the Occamist school, though the name by no means exhausts the significance of the school.

Something like the gap in the middle to which we referred in connection with Luther was undoubtedly the result of this agnosticism, and it seems to me totally out of the question that Luther, who could call himself an Occamist,[9] was not methodologically influenced at this point. But the difference comes to light at once when we note to what end the Nominalists made the rent. Unfortunately, at least so far as we can detect their theological purpose, they did not seek like Luther to humble us humans and to make way for the unique self-glory of God. Instead, as apologetics likes to do in every age when it is very refined, they were aiming to bring about a total subjection to all church doctrines, even though these might be as contrary to reason as they are! Occam expressly advocated implicit faith,[10] and their purpose was to make this seem to be the only possible means of rescue from the sea of doubt. If, as they believed, there was no direct path to the theology of glory by way of reason, they would attain to it by the sacrifice of reason.

This maneuver is certainly not the same as Luther's theology of the cross, which simply bids us halt before God himself and appeal to his mercy. We should not fail to see, of course, how insightful and significant it still was from a formal standpoint. We need only look at a saying like that of Occam to the effect that faith is a free gift by which the mind believes on account of God and against itself (Tschackert, 36).[11] Were it not for the fatal knowledge that this believing against the intellect does not lead to pure negation and hence to a true transcendental grounding of natural knowledge, but to the paradoxical superstructure of an additional supranatural knowledge that is not in pure antithesis to the natural; were it not for the knowledge that this believing is simply a secret understanding of a higher type, its object not being the origin of all that may be known, not the crucified Christ, but the hinterland of church dogma that is accepted for all the skepticism, one might say that here an insight into the relation to infinity that takes place precisely in an awareness of human finitude as such (the mind against itself), an insight into the freedom of this relation from any discursive basis ("on account of God"), an insight into its origin by creation ("free gift"), had been wonderfully achieved.

That fundamentally nonmedieval insight did hover before those thinkers even though they did not develop it but were encysted and incapable of the grim seriousness with which Luther proceeded at this point. To see how it hovered before them we need look only at their distinctive doctrine of God.[12] Over against the whole system of causal necessity that we call the world God stands contingently as himself an indeterminate first cause, as free will in the absolute, as will that has its norm only in itself. In virtue of the absolute power of this will the whole world might have been different. In fact, of course, God simply acts in accordance with his plan that aims at the saving of the elect, in accordance with his ordained power. He thus wills everything as it actually is. Nevertheless, and this is the decisive point, the possibility remains, and has to be considered, that God might have willed and acted differently. God is not a prisoner of his own plan that we see worked out in the church, or of the logical and moral orders in which he executes the plan. It might happen, said Duns, that people attain to glory that do not receive the grace, the knowledge of God, that Scotists and Occamists, like other scholastics, think of as infused faith (Seeberg, III, 578). It might be, Occam ventured to say, that God could have made the morally good other than it is in fact, that hatred of God, theft, and adultery could be meritorious, had not God's command ordained the opposite (Loofs, 612).[13] In both the religious and the moral sphere we thus have to consider that things are pleasing to God only because of his acceptance of them on the basis of his free will (Tschackert, 36), and that when we speak of God in the forms of the age, when we speak of what he did, does, or will do, the now of eternity that we mean is the truth of what we say.[14] Only God's own essence is the proper object of his will. To all else he stands in a basically contingent relation; he is free relative to it (Loofs, 593-94).[15] Even Christ's passion is meritorious only by God's "acceptation." An angel or another human might have made reconciliation for the world just as well (Hagenbach, 387).[16] On this path that leads to Luther Occam put out such powerful ideas as that forgiveness of sins is not a making righteous but nonimputation.[17]

Most church historians and histories of doctrine tell us that the God of Duns and Occam was a capricious God,[18] but I believe with Seeberg that this view is wrong. As these theologians studied and deepened the concept of power, their unsettling reminder of God's absolute power was meant to anchor the more firmly the authority of the truth that holds good by God's ordained power.[19] They knew very well that one cannot establish a thing better or more effectively than by taking it back to its premise by the sharpest criticism of the way it is. The premise of all that God has ordained, however, is deity, God's freedom and majesty. What good is all our zeal toward God, or with God, or even for God, if we do not consider at all who and what God is, if there is no basic interruption of our zeal by the recollection that God's thoughts are not our thoughts nor his ways ours [cf. Isa. 55:8]?

To give a sure place to that recollection Duns and Occam introduced into theology a final uncertainty as to God's will and work. They did so for the very same reason—and this is why I deal with the point so fully—as that which would later lead Calvin to think he had found in the doctrine of double predestination the core and lodestar of the doctrine of God. Against the concept of God in Duns and Occam we are not to bring the charge of arbitrariness that has equally wrongly been made against Calvin, but rather—and this is what produced the misunderstanding—that of a charming and playful intellectualism, the lack of seriousness with which, unlike Calvin, they handled these necessary but dangerous ideas. They had no intention at all of using the critical principle of absolute power that they had discovered to call into question the given factor of the church that rests on the ordained power, to subject the church to this critical insight, and in this way actually to destroy the whole theology of glory. Instead they used the insight as a paradoxical means to make a free path for scholastic dogmatics, ethics, and mysticism, for the whole titanic striving of the Middle Ages of immediacy. With this great caveat of the divine freedom they established the validity of such distinctive medieval ideas as infused and implicit faith, free will, merit, grace as habitus, justification as infusion, *opus operatum* in sacramental administration, eucharistic transubstantiation, and penance as a sure and easy path. They could advocate all these things precisely in a more vital way, and by reason of the piquant critical background in a more ingenious way, than the earlier and in the last resort naiver scholastics. Occam was the most important medieval advocate of the inspiration of the Bible and Duns Scotus was the hero of his Franciscan order as the highly regarded pioneering defender of the immaculate conception of Mary.[20]

That matters could take this course naturally forces the word "treason" upon our lips. We recall with shame and anger how 19th-century theologians sat at the feet of Kant in order that with the help of his critique of reason they might justify instead of challenge modern Christianity. Theologians have always been adept at ingeniously toying with the most radical and dangerous thoughts and feelings and then devaluing them in an attempt to justify and confirm contemporary religious thoughts and feelings. But who are we to complain in this regard? It makes no sense to doubt the personal sincerity of those who acted thus in the 14th and 19th centuries. Who among us do not have to complain of ourselves in this regard? Nominalism was a great theological possibility. If for a moment we look beyond the confusing interrelation of excellent intention and lamentable execution, in spite of everything we cannot fail to see how hopeful this theology was. It rendered its historical reforming service and is definitely part of the new thing in the old to the extent that it had a destructive effect on the proud structure of Scholasticism and at least greatly undermined the towers that it was neither able nor willing to overthrow. It is not in vain that we think the thought of God's freedom and majesty, the great and solemn thought of the critical negation of everything given, even though we take the thought no more seriously than did Duns and Occam. If the thought cannot work as a remedy, then it works as a poison. If it does not lay a foundation, then it creates uncertainty. If it does not equip theology for rethinking and renewal, then it results in culpable obduracy. If the Reformation found theology in a state of disarray and uncertainty, of poisoning and hardening; if it found its way easier as a result; if it could succeed in doing what an Anselm or Bonaventura or Thomas perhaps could not do, then that is the tragic merit of Duns, to whom contemporaries gave the honorary title of the subtle doctor, while the frank but crude Gottfried Arnold (*Kirchengeschichte,* I, 421) called him the foremost eccentric,[21] and perhaps he was both. This was also the tragic merit of Occam, whose contemporary honorary title of venerable inceptor was no less ambivalent. Luther called himself an adherent of this school.[22] Calvin, and perhaps also Zwingli,[23] studied in Paris, its main center, and must have been greatly stimulated by it. Yet as an Occamist neither could have become a reformer.

As a fourth line leading to the Reformation we may cite mysticism. You will have noted in the last hours that I regard mysticism only as one factor among others on the soil of the basic common view of the relation of God to us in the Middle Ages, and that I thus see it along with Scholasticism as the latter's finest flower, so that of almost no medieval theologian can we say where the scholastic leaves off and the mystic begins. All of them were to some extent both. We may rightly count many of them as mystics in the narrower sense and then trace a line from Hugh of St. Victor and Bernard of Clairvaux in the 12th century to Bonaventura in the 13th, Meister Eckhardt and his school, Tauler, Seuse, and the author of the *German Theology* in the 14th, and if one will Thomas à Kempis in the 15th.

Yet we should not lose sight of the scholastic element in these mystics, or of the mystical element in the other scholastics, or of the medieval problem common to both. The common factor in medieval mysticism, the human striving for immediacy, Luther was already calling the theology of glory in his 1516 lectures on Romans at the very time when he was also speaking in friendly terms about mysticism and had come into contact especially with German mysticism. He both knew it and rejected it as the theology of glory. He said in the lectures that mystics wish "to hear and contemplate only the uncreated Word Himself, not having first been justified and purged in the eyes of the heart by the incarnate Word" (Tschackert, 41).[24] ... By the "uncreated Word" understand the invisible things of God that the enemies of the cross, as Luther calls them, contemplate, by justification of "the eyes of the heart" understand the strange work of God in which is hidden the proper work of his mercy, and by the "incarnate Word" understand the crucified Christ. Then this critical saying will make sense to you.

Our present task, however, is to trace the positive relations of mysticism to the Reformation. We face the fact that in spite of that and similar sayings Luther did speak in very favorable tones about mysticism, in tones that he never used for Nominalists, and elsewhere only for Augustine and the Bible. He drew from the same source as Bonaventura and Eckhardt, namely, Augustine, and historically the element in Augustine that had the most influence in the Middle Ages was his Neoplatonic mysticism. In later life Luther once expressly confessed that for a long time, and to his hurt, he had been occupied with the mystical theology of Dionysius the Areopagite (Loofs, 724).[26] In the middle of 1516, as we see from the Romans lectures, he was acquainted with Tauler and the *German Theology,* and he was deeply influenced by them, so that a modern scholar could speak of an "acute mystification" of Luther's theology at this time.[27] But what kind of union could there be between the Reformation and mysticism when it obviously could not include what is most striking in mysticism, its striving for immediacy, which Luther here at once perceived and attacked as an enemy? I think I see the unity of the two at three points.

1. It is understandable that Luther should at first unconcernedly greet mysticism as a precious treasure of knowledge even though he was unsympathetic from the outset with its striving for immediacy, its desire to hear and contemplate the uncreated Word. For this desire, this fundamental desire of the Middle Ages, contained within itself a problem that could not be dismissed out of hand even though the desire might be viewed critically. Certainly Bernard of Clairvaux and innumerable followers of his depicted the union of the soul with God in the far too vivid similitude of the union of the bridegroom and the bride in the Song of Songs, and Eckhardt spoke of the ground of the soul in us where we are one with God, or of the birth of God in the soul, just as he also plainly translated the Trinity into the various aspects of the religious process in the soul, or made it our goal to become by grace what God is by nature.[28] What we find in these statements as they stand is the spirit of a religious shamelessness that takes what does not belong to it. We have to see, however, that the more perspicacious of the mystics recognized the danger and warned against the misunderstanding to which the statements can so easily give rise.

Seuse once spoke sharply about the mystic who in his flourishing rationality wanted to see in himself and in all things a part of the eternal, uncreated rationality: "He hurriedly addresses the matter in an unseasonable way, he blossoms out in his mind like fermenting fruit that even so is not yet ripe."[29] We are not to take literally the exaggerated way in which the mystics speak. It is evident that they speak in this way, using extreme and audacious similes and comparisons, because they face the difficulty of wanting to say things that cannot be said even in the strongest terms, and yet are calling out to be said: the actualizing, the taking place, the coming into being, and the actual being of the relation between us and God. The problem that oppresses the mystics is that of dealing seriously with the known truth of God, of the actuality of the revelation of God to us. For all their sharper insight into the difficulty of this problem, the British Nominalists did not feel it or live it out as existentially as the German mystics. If the former were the head of the later Middle Ages, the latter were the heart.

Luther was closer to the heart than to the head. He saw that the problem of the Middle Ages could not be solved with German exaggeration, Roman rationalism, or British skepticism and ingenuity. But he derived from the first of these the great sense of urgency, the profound and heartfelt seriousness, that underlay the whole medieval concern. The word that defied speech had to be spoken. The impossible possibility had to become an event. The very thing that had never been present,[30] that as a human thought or action could be described only as mad folly, that very thing had to come into our lives as the thought and action of God. The Reformation did not ignore the underlying difficulty and hope but for the first time gave it the sharpest expression. It totally rejected and reversed the concern in its existing from, but in reality it still took it quite seriously, Yes, was Luther's reply to the medieval question embedded in mysticism, yes indeed, immediacy, but God's immediacy to us and not vice versa. Yes, life in God, but in the power of his creative Word, not of what is creative in us. Yes, God and the soul, the soul and its God,[31] but *God,* or else it is all error and idolatry. Luther heard what the school of Eckhardt was saying. He understood it. It was alive in him. But because he heard and understood it, he turned aside from the path of Eckhardt as such. There can be no success along that path in terms of the theology of glory, but there is success a hundredfold in terms of the theology of the cross for those who have ears to hear what medieval mystics must surely grasp when they let themselves be taught.

2. Mysticism differs from Scholasticism by stressing the historical person of Jesus. There is, of course, a strange paradox here. None made it more clear than the mystics that the Middle Ages at root did not know what to do with Christ. From the days of Bernard of Clairvaux they anticipated the modern Protestant cult of the gentle, humble, mild, and merciful man Jesus of Nazareth, adorned with all the virtues that they themselves highly rated, and Bernard has often been praised precisely on this account because something particularly evangelical has been seen in it.[32] Neither Bernard,

Tauler, nor Thomas à Kempis could really get beyond the picture of Jesus as the model of our seeking of God and as the invisible head of all those like-minded with him. It is obvious that at this point, as the Reformation saw it, a misunderstanding had to be set aside. The ideal of medieval piety that mysticism equated with Christ, and that it enthusiastically used schematically in its spiritual direction, could not coexist with the theology of the cross, which summoned precisely this ideal of piety to judgment and sought to bring freedom from preoccupation with the self.

But a problem still remained at this point, in short, the problem of the historical element in Christianity, of revelation. The one and only historical Jesus had become important for medieval believers precisely because they came up against historicity, individuality, and uniqueness in their striving for immediacy. They suspected that this was the category under which alone they could grasp the revelation they sought. They ran up hard against the limits of their own individuality within which they finally could not find revelation. They sensed that they could find it precisely where they could not reach, namely, in the historicity, individuality, and uniqueness of the other. The other is the one in whom is revelation, and only as the other speaks directly to me and ceases to be the other, only as[33] he becomes an I, can I have a part in revelation. This other is Jesus Christ as the quintessence of the historical, the individual, and the unique, and therefore as the bearer of revelation. The Bible responds to the search for immediacy, when this seeks clarity about itself, with the wonderful message: The Word became flesh [John 1:14]. Revelation *took place* in the other, in Jesus Christ. The intersecting of the human horizontal line by the divine vertical line *is* a fact. Time *is* related to eternity, this world to the next, I to Thou.

The Middle Ages, too, heard this message. At first, of course, they misheard it—when and by whom is it not misheard? What they heard was that the Word became a pious man, and this went well with their basic view. But the Word that was truly sought and meant was not that. How can a pious man be revelation to me, set me before God, speak directly to me, cease to be another to me? He is and remains a he, the more so the more pious he is. He can demand that I imitate him, but if I try to do that I admit that my supposed finding has again become a seeking. He can be to me only a companion in my striving for immediacy. But he cannot bring this to completion by himself achieving immediacy.

In contrast to the medieval picture of Jesus, the Christ of Luther is not the pious man but the man who is set in the ranks of sinners under judgment, in the shadow of hell and death, the crucified Christ. Not the crucified Christ of edification, who kindles our admiration as a martyr and hero, whom we are to imitate in his submission to the will of God, whom we can depict and tolerate in his tragic beauty, but the nonedifying crucified Christ of Grünewald, who, when painted, proclaims the strange work of God; who has no form nor comeliness [cf. Isa. 53:2]; in face of whom love, the affection lavished so remarkably freely on this Savior in his piety, becomes an offering that we no longer resolve so easily to make; in whose lostness and mortal plight we are forced to see a pointer to God himself and his demand for saving despair, humility, and fear of God. This incarnate Word, the Crucified, can speak directly to me. In him the barrier that makes him another is torn down. In him, if I bow under his judgment, I can see myself, be set before God, be cast into the arms of sheer mercy. Here it is not at all a matter of imitation but of faith, not of a further search for immediacy but of revelation. Here it really happens that a hole is made in the Gothic vault, and God's heaven is seen high above. He who sees me sees the Father [John 14:9].

This incarnate Word then, and not, as we are sometimes told, the so-called historical Jesus, is what Luther rediscovered. Rediscovered? Yes, he was always there. He does not have to come and go with the shifts in understanding or nonunderstanding to which he is subject in the course of history. We hear at least, whether we understand or not; the problem of the human situation as such bears witness to him. This Word is known even when not known. Mystics, too, had no other Christ in view even though they almost always spoke about another. Their love of Jesus, which in the last resort was no other than a special form of their pressing on to the event, was something that Luther could let speak to him. It perhaps spoke more strongly in him than in all of them, and if in him, and in the Reformation in general, the rather thin water of the imitation of Christ with its poetry of blood and wounds became the strong wine of the message of judgment and forgiveness, we simply have here further testimony how seriously what was at issue was the new thing that was also already the old.

3. The third point of contact between Reformation thinking and that of medieval mysticism was the methodological principle of mysticism that we might sum up under the term "abnegation." In infinite variations the mystics tried to describe the outworking of this principle. They spoke of the need for separation, resignation, quiet isolation, simplicity of heart, calm, obedience that gives up all that is one's own, or conversely of entry into the inner ground that is the least we have (Eckhardt), of denying oneself, of imitating the passion of Christ with patient suffering and loving humility, of pressing oneself into this (Tauler), of surrender to God as a captive, of making the transition from creatures to God, of seeking God in pious ignorance and mental darkness (Luther),[34] of laying aside all that is created, I-ness, selfhood, every "me," "to

me," or "mine," of not wanting to be something but nothing, and so on.

We can take all that these expressions denote in two ways. First, we might see them as the description of a temporal process that takes place, or ought to take place, in individuals, and that consists of the achieving—no matter how we think of it—of the greatest possible passivity of the conscious soul with the aim of effecting the souls' union with the deity represented as an event in time. Or, second, we might see them as the description of a timeless transcendental relation of the life of the soul, whether conscious or unconscious, active or passive, to its origin in God. In the first case abnegation is a pastoral injunction, a recipe, a method, a proposal how to proceed. In the second case, in the form of a psychological direction, it is a demand for contemplation or recollection of the truth that is the truth quite apart from any possible or impossible processes in the soul. We need hardly say that the first interpretation is more natural and closer to the text, as it were, than the second. If we read the works of Seuse, for example,[35] we see at once that this man fashioned his whole life upon a constant following of the recipe of abnegation, and with more or less strictness and success almost all mystics did in fact view abnegation as a definite and specific practice. Insofar as mystical abnegation is no more than practice of this kind, it has naturally nothing whatever to do with the Reformation. Instead, it is the supreme and most refined form of what the Reformation combated as works righteousness. How can one more distinctively pursue a theology of glory than by going beyond striving for it and making the negation of all striving itself a striving? (Cf. Gogarten, *Offenbarung und Mystik.*)[36]

We might see here a parallel to the way in which Duns Scotus and Occam made the dangerous dynamite of the doctrine of absolute power a smooth stone in the foundation of church dogmatics. At this third point, however, I think we do mysticism an injustice if we do not look beyond the historical kernel and note how once again it points ahead of itself. Here again dynamite is always dynamite. Note how Eckhardt in his sermons unequivocally negates not just position after position but ultimately negation itself, that is, the psychological path to which he himself previously pointed. Note how he finally seeks a resignation that is not psychological resignation or passivity as a way of life any longer, but that is just as well, or even better as he often says, an active manner of life, so that paradoxically Martha, the busy one, is set above Mary, who sat at the Lord's feet.[37] This means, however, that he sees the transcendental character of the principle of mystical abnegation that is truly meant. He does not cease to be a theologian of glory. He uses the thought of death in the sense of Plato's *Phaedon* (chs. 9-13), which says of the philosopher that at root his only aim is to die and be dead, his work being no other than that of detaching and separating the soul from the body.[38] In my view abnegation for Eckhardt was in the last resort simply Platonic purification, the strongest critical means of clarifying the relation between God and us in which the greatest distance is precisely the greatest proximity. We must insist on this if we are to do full justice to mysticism. In this regard we cannot uphold an absolute antithesis between Luther and Eckhardt, between revelation and mysticism. Luther must have found something related, instructive, and illuminating when he recommended Tauler and the *German Theology;* while Calvin, even though in the latter work seeing and repudiating only medieval spiritualizing,[39] could not refrain, under pressure of the logic of the matter, from himself at a decisive point in the *Institutes* (III, 7-8) depicting the Christian life from the mystical standpoint of self-denial and bearing the cross.

As a fifth force preparing the way for the Reformation, along with monasticism, Augustinianism, Nominalism, and mysticism, we must finally refer, of course, to the 15th- and 16th-century Renaissance. Its positive relation to the Reformation is naturally on a different level from that of the other factors. From the latter, as we have seen, a straight if for long stretches broken line leads to Luther's view of the vertical intersecting the horizontal, to the theology of the cross. We certainly cannot say that of the Renaissance, though technically and formally the new interest in antiquity meant among other things that the original text of the Bible and Augustine, and through Augustine Plato, came into focus and played a part in the Reformation. The result of this rediscovery, especially in Luther, was not intended, however, by the Renaissance, not was it integral to its own logic. The theologically most interested champions of the Renaissance, those great lovers, editors, and expositors of the Bible, Erasmus and Lefèvre d'Etaples (Faber Stapulensis), were completely terrified by the spirits they conjured up,[40] by the bondage of the will and the break with church tradition, and they gave approval and support to the Reformation in neither its Lutheran nor its Reformed manifestation. The interest of the Renaissance was wholly in the direction of the horizontal. It continued the basic classical medieval view, or perhaps translated and reformulated it into the basic classical modern view, which for all the differences has more in common with the Middle Ages than with the Reformation. Common to the Middle Ages and the modern period is the idea of aiming at a goal in step-by-step progress. The goal for both is on the horizontal line. It is a goal of human willing and knowing. The concept alone stood in need of translation. The Middle Ages located the goal somewhere in one of the real or imagined upper worlds, in the so-called hereafter. It sought to mount up to paradise. It wanted to look upon pure deity, as Tauler put it.[41] It wanted ecstasy, as we might put it rationalistically today. Our own age thinks it is much cleverer by not shooting the arrow of longing too far. Impartially we might say: It is more weary and resigned. With a skepticism that is partly more questioning and partly more dogmatic it halts at the gates of the upper worlds. For some centuries the spiritual world has been unknown territory on the suspicion of being unreal. The gaze has been all the keener for what can be perceived directly in time and space, for what is called this world. With the same absoluteness and emphasis the goal is set in nature as we know it and history as we know it. The enthusiasm of pressing on to the immediate that once created the Gothic vault has changed into the enthusiasm for the concrete, for what has come into being, for what can be measured and controlled, for the colorful world of visible things that we can happily attain to without scholastic profundity or mystical abnegation. Goethe once gave classical formulation to the distinction and the common factor when he said that if we want to stride on into the infinite we must simply go on in the finite on every hand.[42] But in my view the difference between the two methods is usually overrated. In the modern age we simply have the Middle Ages now become clever and also weary. The sleep has become half sleep, and who knows, perhaps we might put it the other way round. The Middle Ages could throw back at the modern age the charge of excessive enthusiasm, for the modern age with its rationalism is simply enthusiastic to the point of excess on a different level. The modern age can throw back at the Middle Ages the charge of intellectualism, for the Middle Ages were truly intellectualistic, but on a higher level. The two levels are steps on the same ladder. In principle the distinction in both cases is from the Reformation insight, from Plato and Paul, and therefore from the medieval trends that point back to Plato and Paul and forward to the Reformation.[43] The Reformation and all that is part of it in the Middle Ages and the modern period are both antimodern and antimedieval. The Reformation front cuts right across the opposite contrasting fronts of these two opponents.

This is an insight that I do not find clearly in Troeltsch, Loofs, or Seeberg.[44] In the Renaissance, at first in the form of a rebirth of the rationalism of antiquity, the modern spirit of an emphatic this-worldliness was born and took its first steps. There came to life a strong interest in nature, in the social and political order, in history, in the nation as such, and last but by no means least in the individual human personality. Outstanding Renaissance figures along with Erasmus, the first modern theologian, were Paracelsus, the student of medicine, for whom God did miracles but only human miracles through humans; Machiavelli, who has been called the scientist of the state; Giordano Bruno, who by equating God and the form and matter of the world challenged the reality of the upper world of the Middle Ages,[45] and who was one of the first and rare martyrs of the modern spirit. At root the Renaissance did not take part in Luther's Reformation. Its controversy with the Middle Ages completely bypassed that Reformation. To the degree that it hailed it as a comrade, it misunderstood it. Due to the same misunderstanding the spiritualistic Enthusiasts combined the Reformation with Renaissance aspirations. For all the apparently great contradictions, the Roman Catholic Counter-Reformation was better able to adopt, use, and amalgamate the Renaissance with itself than the young Protestantism that opposed it. The positive significance of the Renaissance for the Reformation was that apart from it, and even against it, it put to it the fateful question: What, in spite of everything, did the Lutheran vertical mean for the horizontal, the theology of the cross for unavoidable human striving? The Renaissance with its most emphatic this-worldliness was needed to put this question to the Reformation, and in this way to bring the crisis to a head, to close the circle of the Reformation movement.

From what has been said it is clear, however, that through the voice of the Reformation the Middle Ages were also calling for a new answer to their own distinctive problem, the problem of ethics, of lifestyle, of the way. With the posing of this fateful question the second turn in the Reformation came that eventually, by a higher curve in the path, would lead back to the beginning and tragically enough, though in a way that is historically understandable, would lead it back onto a newly repaired stretch of the old horizontal highway, to the Christian secularity from which it had once broken free. But those who put the question were not spectators like Erasmus, but Zwingli and Calvin, children of the Renaissance, who, whether dependently or independently, shared the insight of Luther, the born scholastic and mystic. This second development and completion of the Reformation movement in its subsequent controversy with the newly arrived spirit of the modern age as we find that controversy in the theology of Calvin, the man who was both totally the reformer and totally the Renaissance man, which we cannot say of either Luther or Zwingli, will be the main theme, quiet but yet explicit, of our present lectures.

As a sixth group of advocates of the new thing in the old we must finally, for the sake of completeness, mention the Catholic reforming theologians of the 14th and 15th centuries, Bradwardine, Wycliffe, Huss, Gerson, J. Goch, J. von Wesel, Wessel Gansfort, and Savonarola being the best known. There is a book by C. Ullmann, *Reformatoren vor der Reformation* (1st ed. 1841, 2nd ed. 1866), whose title aroused lively opposition especially from Ritschl and his disciples.[46] Those who honor such men with the name of prereformers are not uninfluenced—and this is no disgrace—by the heroic, the tragic, and the sympathetic aspects of their stories. These men were fighters for an insight whose time had not yet come. By their work they did in fact stir up the unrest that became a movement at the Reformation. All of them, with more or less energy and insight, stood at one of the points mentioned from which the prospect of the Reformation insight was a possibility, Bradwardine, for example, as a Neo-Augustinian, Gerson as the champion of a noble and modified mysticism, Savonarola as a proponent of ancient monastic ideals, and Wycliffe as the forerunner of an attempted Christian renaissance, and precisely for that reason the most problematical of all these figures. Nevertheless, these pre-reformers have relatively less systematic interest as we try to elucidate the Reformation than do an Occam or an Eckhardt, for, so far as I can judge, none of them can be hailed as a classical advocate of one of the forward-looking possibilities. The medieval period with its possibilities was inwardly exhausted. The Reformation had not yet come. Why did Bradwardine or Gerson not become a Luther, Savonarola a Zwingli, Wycliffe a Calvin? Why did not the whole Reformation come a hundred years earlier? Who can say? The elements of Reformation were present at the time of the pre-reformers. But their presence alone was not enough. Passionate emphasizing of this or that new approach, passionate negation of the old that was perishing, clever and devout conservation and combination of the balance between the two, but without the will or the power to force through a decision, these were the possibilities for which the pre-reformers worked and suffered. Such possibilities were relative, very relative even within the great relativity of history. The pre-reformers were children of an age of transition, as perhaps we ourselves are again today.[47] A feature of such ages, at least in the judgment of history, is that they cannot achieve more than honorary results. The reformers could always speak of the pre-reformers with respect and admiration, but without owing them anything. This fact gives us cause to reflect, perhaps to our own comfort, that in history bridges of this kind, and not only those that carry it forward, may not be famous but are still of value. And value is the only thing we may strive for at the forum of history, the only thing we can be concerned about. The rest is neither a goal nor a task but grace.

*Notes*

*Connection*

[1] F. Loofs, *Leitfaden zum Studium der Dogmengeschichte,* 4th ed. (1906; enlarged 7th ed. by K. Aland; Tübingen, 1968 [page numbers given in parentheses]); P. Tschackert, *Die Entstehung der lutherischen und der reformierten Kirchenlehre* (Göttingen, 1910); R. Seeberg, *Lehrbuch der Dogmengeschichte,* vol. IV (Leipzig, 1917; 4th ed.), 73, Prolegomena; E. Troeltsch, "Protestantisches Christentum und Kirche in der Neuzeit," in *Die Kultur der Gegenwart* (Berlin and Leipzig, 1906), 254-69; F. Loofs, *Luthers Stellung zum Mittelalter und zur Neuzeit* . . . (Halle, 1907); E. Troeltsch, *Die Soziallehren der christlichen Kirchen und Gruppen,* Gesammelte Schriften, vol. I (Tübingen, 1912); H. Hermelink, *Reformation und Gegenreformation,* part 3 of *Handbuch der Kirchengeschichte,* ed. G. Krüger (Tübingen, 1911).

[2] Barth had in view the thesis of Troeltsch that the Reformation belonged to the Middle Ages and the replies of Loofs and Seeberg. . . .

[3] On the relation between edification, preaching, and academic lectures cf. Barth's *Ein Briefwechsel mit Adolf von Harnack* (1923), in *Theologische Fragen und Antworten, Gesammelte Vorträge,* vol. III (Zurich, 1957, 2nd ed. 1986), esp. 19f., and Harnack's reply, 30f.

[4] According to Thomas Platter; see H. Boos, *Thomas und Felix Platter* . . . (Leipzig, 1878), 39. For an edition of Platter's work in modern German cf. *Thomas und Felix Platters und Theodor Agrippa d'Aubigne's Lebensbeschreibung.,* ed. O. Fischer (Munich, 1911), 64.

[5] Experience was a basic theological and religious category early in the 20th century in the theology of Barth's teacher W. Herrmann, which Barth at first rated highly; cf. Herrmann's *Communion of the Christian with God* (1913); cf. also R. Otto, *The Idea of the Holy* (1923; German, 1917); and many other authors. For Barth's criticisms cf. his *Romans* passim and *Briefwechsel mit Adolf von Harnack,* 10.

[6] For the wholly other cf. Otto, *Idea of the Holy.* How far Barth was dependent on Otto for his use of the term in the 2nd ed. of his *Romans* is contested by scholars. For his view of Otto cf. his letter to Thurneysen on 6.3.1919, in which he expressed his enjoyment of Otto's work in spite of its psychological orientation because it clearly points to the nonrational element in the numinous as the wholly other, the divine in God. He saw here the beginning of a fundamental overcoming of Ritschlianism. There is in it at least a pointer even if things did not go far enough because of the restrained role of the theologian as a spectator, which does not accord with the fairly good understanding of the object.

[7] Cf. K. Marx, *Der achtzehnte Brumaire des Louis Bonaparte,* in Marx and Engels, *Werke,* vol. VIII (Berlin, 1960), 115, in which Marx quoted Hegel's remark that all great historical persons and events come on the scene twice as it were, commenting that Hegel forgot to add that they do so the first time as a tragedy and the second as a farce.

[8] For Luther Barth was thinking of the lectures on the Psalms of 1513-1516, [M. Luther, *Werke, Kritische Ausgabe* (Weimar, 1883ff.); hereafter WA] 3, 11-652 and 4, 1-467. From 1922 he had these in the 2-vol. ed. of J. K. Seidemann (Dresden, 1880). For Zwingli cf. H. Zwingli, *Usslegen and und grund der schlussreden* (1523), [Huldreich Zwingli, *Sämtliche Werke* (Berlin and Zurich, 1905 ff.); hereafter Z] 2., 1-457.

[9] Marginal note in pencil: "Chronik v. Bosshart 89." The reference is to *Die Chronik des Laurencius Bosshart von Winterthur 1185-1532,* ed. K. Hauser, *Quellen zur schweizerischen Reformationsgeschichte,* ed. Zwinglivverein in Zurich, vol. III (Basel, 1905), 89, where it is noted that God revealed his Word through the Greek and Hebrew languages when Zwingli preached the gospel in Zurich, and that this was not of man's doing but God's.

[10] Cf. Luther's admonition against revolt (1522), WA 8, 676, in which he says that it is of God's grace that the light of Christian truth has arisen again.

[11] Cf. the defense of the orthodox doctrine of bondage and liberation against the calumnies of Pighius (1543), [Corpus Reformatorum (Halle, Braunschweig, Berlin, Zurich, 1834 ff.); hereafter CR] 6, 257. For sermon 162 see CR 28, 466.

[12] CO 6, 477.

[13] On the fathers see [Luther's *Werke: Tischreden;* hereafter WA TR] 4, 288, 25f. (no. 4387). On the scholastics, WA TR 3, 543, 18 (no. 3698).

[14] So first A. Ritschl, "Geschichtliche Studien zur christlichen Lehre von Gott," in *Gesammelte Aufsätze,* vol. II (Freiburg, 1893), 67-89; and cf. Seeberg, *Lehrbuch,* IV, 575, on Calvin's doctrine of the divine will.

[15] Cf. Schiller's *Braut von Messina,* V, 1: "Der Not gehorchend, nicht dem eignen Trieb."

[16] [*Ioannis Calvini Opera Selecta,* ed. P. Barth et al. (Munich, 1925ff); hereafter OS] 1, 25, also 27.

[17] For Luther on Bonaventura see WA TR 1, 330, 1 (no. 683): "Bonaventura the best of the scholastic doctors." Cf. 1, 435, 25f. (no. 871), and 3, 294, 35f. (no. 3370a); also WA 7, 774, 13ff.; and 8, 127, 19. For Calvin on Bernard of Clairvaux see [*Ioannis Calvini opera quae supersunt omnia,* ed. G. Braum, E. Cunitz, and E. Reuss (Braunschweig, 1963ff.); hereafter CO] 23.63; 31.540; 49.357; also the many quotations from Bernard in the *Institutes,* e.g., II, 3, 5; III, 2, 25; III, 12, 3; III, 15, 2.

[18] Seeberg, *Lehbuch,* 74 and n. 2.

[19] Loofs, *Leitfaden,* 690 n. 3, quotes the title in this short form. The work was by J. G. Dorsche and was published at Frankfurt in 1656.

[20] [Luther's *Werke: Briefwechsel;* hereafter WAB] 5, 325, 37-326, 44.

[21] CO 6, 473.

[22] Cf. Luther's plea for Christian schools (1524), WA 15, 32, 6-8, in which he says that you know God's Word and grace is a passing shower that does not come again where it has once been; cf. also WA 17/II, 179, 28-33.

[23] Ibid., 4, 151, 11f. (no. 4123).

[24] Ibid., 3, 500, 2-5 (no. 3663).

[25] Ibid., 3, 6-8 (no. 2806b).

[26] Ibid., 3, 6-8 (no. 2806b).

*Contrast*

[1] Cf. Loofs, *Leitfaden,* 498f. (7th ed., 402), for the charge of formalism.

[2] For this evaluation cf. G. Ficker and H. Hermelink, *Handbuch der Kirchengeschichte,* vol. II, *Das Mittelalter* (Tübingen, 1911), 186; also p. 185 on Occam.

[3] Cf. Aesop's *Fables* 33.

[4] K. R. Hagenbach, *Lehrbuch der Dogmengeschichte,* rev. K. Benrath (Leipzig, 1888).

[5] See ibid. Barth commended this work in a circular letter dated 3.26.1922 because the author modestly did not intrude himself but gave many well-chosen and instructive quotations from the sources. He found Loofs less rewarding for his purpose.

[6] Barth used Bonaventura's *Brevioloquium* in the edition of C. J. Hefele (Tübingen, 1845). In a circular letter dated 4.2.1922 he said that he was reading this work so as not to know the Middle Ages only from excerpts. A note in P. Tschackert's *Die Entstehung der lutherischen und der reformierten Kirchenlehre* (Göttingen, 1910), 21, to the effect that the *Breviloquium* represented the church teaching of the time perhaps led Barth to engage in an intensive study of the work, though there are no visible fruits of the study in the lectures. On Francis see *Analekten zur Geschichte des Franciscus von Assisi,* ed. H. Boehmer (Tübingen and Leipzig, 1904). On Eckhardt see *Meister Eckeharts Schriften und Predigten,* tr. and ed. H. Büttner, 2 vols. (Jena, 1909f).

[7] WA 1, 362, 15 and 21.

[8] Cf. Loofs, 535 (437). The quotations are from [*Thomas Aquinas, Summa theologica*; hereafter S. Th.] 1, q. 14 a. 8 i.c., a. 4 i.c., a. 13 i.c.; q. 44 a. 3 i.c. They may be found in Hagenbach, 340 and 354, though in part in incorrect form.

[9] For angelic knowledge in Thomas cf. Hagenbach, 258; and for human knowledge, 331; cf. *S. Th.* 1, q. 12 a. 12 i.c.

[10] Cf. *S. Th.* 1, q. 1 a. 2 i.c.

[11] Loofs, 534 (436), points out that since God is our goal and the goal has to be known but perfect knowledge of God consists of eternal beatitude and is beyond the grasp of human reason—there has to be revelation and revealed knowledge; he gives citations from *S. Th.* 1, q. 1 a. 4 i.c. and a. 1 i.c.

[12] Cf. Hagenbach, 444f.: topography (heaven, hell, and intermediate states).

[13] Peter Lombard, *Libri quattuor sententiarum,* lib. IV, dist. 49A, quoted by Hagenbach, 447.

[14] Good Friday Sermon in Tauler, *Predigten,* vol. I (Leipzig, 1826), 291f.

[15] Hagenbach, 436-50. For the second part of Barth's statement cf. *Elucidarium,* ch. 79. in Hagenbach, 447.

[16] Hagenbach quotes from H. Seuse, *Von der unmässigen Freude des Himmelreiches* in his *Leben und Schriften,* ed. M. Diepenbrock (Regensburg, 1840), 205.

[17] Dante Alighieri, *The Divine Comedy,* Harvard Classics, vol. 20, tr. H. F. Cary, "Paradise," cantox XXXI-II.

[18] For Thomas cf. Loofs, 537 (439), and the text of *S. Th. Suppl.,* q. 96 a. 1 i.ci in Hagenbach, 447 (with some deviation). For Eckhardt see the bull *In agro dominico,* 10, quoted in Hagenbach, 398, with reference to Eckehart, *Predigten,* vol. II, ed. F. Pfeiffer (Leipzig, 1857), 103, 11ff., quoted in Loofs, 628 (521).

[19] Hagenbach, 361, refers to Gerson's (*Considerationes de theologia mystics,* X-XXV) concept of the two basic powers of the soul, the cognitive and affective, and his arrangement of the former as simple intelligence, reason, and sensuality corresponding to contemplation, meditation, and cogitation. For Hugh of St. Victor see Hagenbach, 361 (no examples).

[20] Hagenbach, 330f.

[21] *S. Th.* 1, q. 14 a. 10 i.c.

[22] Hagenbach quotes two passages from Amalrich of Bena, who was condemned posthumously in 1210, to the effect that we are members of Christ by bearing his sufferings on the cross (388) and that having the knowledge of God we have paradise in ourselves, but that if we commit mortal sin we have hell in ourselves like a rotten tooth in the mouth (446f.).

[23] John Scotus Erigena. *De divisione naturae,* I, ch. 68, p. 38, in Hagenbach, 320.

[24] Pico della Mirandola, *Epistola ad Aldum Manutium,* Opera, Basel ed., p. 243, quoted in Hagenbach, 319.

[25] Cf. R. Seeberg. *Lehrbuch der Dogmengeschichte,* vol. III (Leipzig, 1913; 2nd and 3rd ed.), 604-21.

[26] Augustine, *Contra epistolam quam vocant fundamenti,* 5, 6 (CSEL 25/I, 197, 22f).

[27] Loofs, 539 (443), where he points out that to accuse even later Scholasticism of Pelagianism or semi-Pelagianism needs elucidation, though he himself on pp. 613f. (507ff.) describes Nominalism as "the crassest semi-Pelagianism."

[28] J. W. von Goethe, *Faust,* II, lines 11934-11941. On the phrase *gratia gratis data* cf. Hagenbach, 395f. This grace effects our first estate of original righteousness, while *gratia gratum faciens* has an effect oriented directly to justification.

[29] Loofs, 596 (490): For Duns merit is only by divine acceptation. Cf. Seeberg, III. 587.

[30] Hagenbach, 396, states that for Duns there was more human cooperation than for Thomas; cf. *Sent.,* lib. III, dist. 34, 5. We have not to think of grace being infused into us as fire is into a piece of wood, i.e., as if grace were destroying nature.

[31] *S. Th.* Ia, IIae, q. 100 a. 12, in Hagenbach, 395.

[32] Hagenbach, 395, says that by justification Thomas understood not only remission of guilt but at the same time the infusion of grace by which God gives us a share in his own life.

[33] See n. 18 above; also Eckhardt's sermon on Mary and Martha at Luke 10:38 in *Scbriften und Predigten,* ed. H. Büttner (Jena, 1909) vol. II, 119f., where it is shown that the double mention of Martha's name indicates first her perfection in temporal works and then what is needed for eternal salvation, that she might not lack this also.

[34] Cf. Cyprian, *Epistolae,* 73, 21 (CSEL 2/II, 795, 3f.) and Augustine, *De baptismo contra donatistas,* 4, 17, 24 (CSEL 51, 250, 25).

[35] Augustine, *Epistolae,* 105, 3, 12 (CSEL 34/II, 604, 12f.).

[36] Lombard, *Sententiarum,* IV, 1E, in Hagenbach, 408: The OT sacraments promise grace, the NT sacraments give it; cf. also Thomas, *S. Th.* III, q. 62 a. 6 i.c., in Hagenbach, 408. Hagenbach, 409, found the

phrase *ex opere operato* in Gabriel Biel, *Collectorium circa quattuor libros Sententiarum,* IV, dist. 1, q. 3.

[37] On the medieval dogma of the Lord's Supper cf. Hagenbach, 413-23; for Occam and Durandus of St. Pourçain 196, 425-27, divergent views being noted on 426. For Pierre d'Ailly cf. Loofs, 618 (511), directly after Occam.

[38] Duns Scotus, *Opus Oxoniense,* 4, 17, q. un. no. 13f., XVIII, 510f. in Loofs, 600 (493).

[39] Cf. the beginning of the third strophe of J. E. von Eichendorff's *Morgengebet: "Die Welt mit ihrem Gram und Glücke. . . .* "

[40] Cf. A. von Harnack's *What Is Christianity?* (New York, 1912), 264.

[41] Cf. Hagenbach, 257, 357f., on the hierarchy of angels. Cf. also Seeberg, III, 201 n. 1, on the problem whether a mouse eating the host receives Christ's body (with many examples). Cf. also the reference to *S. Th.* III, q. 80, a. 3 ad 3 on p. 468 of Seeberg.

[42] Hagenbach, 446f., on the *corona aurea* and the *aureola* for martyrs and saints, monks and nuns, a superadded prize in *S. Th. Suppl.,* q. 96, a. 1 i.c., according to Hagenbach, 447.

[43] H. Seuse, *Büchlein von der Weisheit,* ch. XI, on the never-ending pains of hell; Hagenbach, 450.

[44] An allusion to act 2 of Weber's opera *Der Freischütz* (1821).

[45] From strophe 2 of Luther's *Aus tiefer Not* (1524).

[46] Cf. Goethe's *Faust,* I, lines 512f.

[47] WA 1, 224ff., 353ff.

[48] Respectively, ibid., 224, 13f.; 225f.; 225, 29f.; 225, 37; 226f.; 226, 16; 227, 26; 227, 35f.; 228, 28.

[49] Ibid., 353, 19f.; 354, 1f.

[50] Ibid., 359, 20f.

[51] Ibid., 354, 11f.

[52] Respectively, ibid., 225, 27f.; 226, 32-227, 2; 228, 4; 228, 11f.; 228, 29.

[53] Ibid., 353, 21f.

[54] Ibid., 356, 37-357, 17.

[55] Ibid., 354, 13f.

[56] Ibid., 361, 12f.

[57] Ibid., 354, 15f.

[58] Ibid., 361, 28-30.

[59] Ibid., 354, 17-20.

[60] Ibid., 362, 11f.

[61] Ibid., 362, 15-19.

[62] Ibid., 354, 21f.

[63] Ibid., 362, 23-26.

[64] Ibid., 362, 29f.

[65] Ibid., 354, 23f.

[66] Ibid., 354, 27f.

[67] Ibid., 354, 29f.

[68] Ibid., 354, 31f.

[69] Ibid., 354, 35f.

[70] Ibid., 365, 8-12.

[71] Barth has a graph in the margin here.

[72] Thomas, *S. Th.* I, q. 1 a. 8 ad 2; cf. n. 30 above.

[73] Barth has a graph in the margin here.

[74] I. Gerson, *Considerationes de theologia mystica,* X, quoted in Hagenbach, 324.

[75] WA 1, 361, 4f.

[76] Barth has a graph in the margin here.

[77] WA TR 6, 38 (no. 6558) refers to high-flying thoughts in the attempt to get to heaven without the ladder of Christ's humanity.

[78] WA TR 1, 108 (no. 257).

[79] See above, 20f.

[80] Cf. Loofs, 701, 709 (524).

[81] The expression "line of death" was an important one for Barth at this period; cf. *Romans.*

[82] See above, n. 52.

[83] Barth has a graph in the margin here.

*Common Features*

[1] The MS by mistake had Clugny.

[2] For Barth's evaluating of Plato along with Paul cf. Barth's *Epistle to the Romans* (Oxford, 1933), p. 111; also his essay "The Christian's Place in Society," in *The Word of God and the Word of Man* (reprinted New York, 1957), 272-327; and *Romans.*

[3] On Bradwardine cf. Hagenbach, 393f.; and Bradwardine, *De causa dei contra Pelagium,* Praefatio, according to Tschackert, 27 n. 1. On the influence of Gregory of Rimini on Luther's view of concupiscence and original sin cf., e.g., Tschackert, 38f.

[4] Cf. Hagenbach, 416f.; Loofs, *Leitfaden,* 500-503 (7th ed. 403ff.).

[5] For Duns see Loofs, 591 (486).

[6] William of Occam, *Super IV libros Sententiarum,* sent. 1, dist. 3, qu. 2, in Hagenbach, 332.

[7] Cf. Seeberg, III, 609-21.

[8] Ibid., 569, in which it is pointed out that for Duns *individualitas* is a reality, the individual entity that constitutes the individual, *haecceitas* as the later expression has it (*Duns metaph.* VII, q. 13, 9). See Ficker and Hermelink, *Das Mittelalter,* 187f., with reference to Occam's agnosticism and Nominalism, or, better, Terminism (the individual thing originating in the idea of God produces a *terminus* in the soul of those who know it, and this is then universalized).

[9] Luther, WA 6, 600, 11f., in his 1520 work against the papal bull.

[10] Seeberg, III, 614, a reference to Occam's *De sacr. alt.* 1.16; quodl. IV, g 35; and cf. 616f.; also Ficker and Hermelink, *Das Mittelalter,* 188.

[11] Tschackert, 36, ascribes this statement to the Occamist Pierre d'Ailly; cf. *Gersonii opera,* I, 68 A.

[12] For what follows cf. Seeberg, III, 577ff.

[13] Occam, *Super IV Libros Sententiarum,* 2, q., 9 litt. O, quoted in Loofs, 612 n. 2 (507).

[14] Duns Scotus, *Opus Oxoniense,* I, dist. 9, q. unica no. 6, quoted in Loofs, 594 (488).

[15] Ibid., I, dist. 39, q. unica no. 22; Loofs, 594 n. 2 (489).

[16] Ibid., III, dist. 19, quoted in Hagenbach, 387, with the comment that Duns undercuts Anselm, for if Christ suffered only according to his human nature, an angel or another man might have suffered just as well.

[17] Occam, *Super quattuor libros sententiarum,* IV, q. 8, according to Loofs, 620 (513).

[18] Cf. the judgment of Loofs, 594 n. 2 (with a reference to F. C. Baur, *Lehre von der Dreieinigkeit,* II, 654f.); also 689 (409, 504); and Ficker and Hermelink, 187f.; Tschackert, 35.

[19] Seeberg, III, 578f., in express opposition (in a note) to Baur, *Lehre,* II, 654ff.

[20] Loofs, 596f. (490f.)

[21] G. Arnold, *Unpartheyische Kirchen- und Ketzer-historie . . . ,* Parts 1 and 2 (Frankfort, 1729), 421.

[22] See n. 9 above.

[23] The reference to Zwingli studying in Paris is based on a note of his friend Gregorus Mangold. It was possible in the years 1499-1500, but a saying of Zwingli's quoted by H. Bullinger refutes the idea. Cf. on the whole question G. W. Locher, *Die Zwinglische Reformation im Rahmen der europäischen Kirchengeschichte* (Göttingen, 1979), 61f.

[24] WA 56, 300, 1ff....

[26] *Disputatio prima contra Antinomos (1537),* WA 39 I, 390, 3-390, quoted in Loofs, 714 n. 2.

[27] Cf. Tschackert, 39f. For a first reference to Tauler cf. the 1516 Romans lectures, WA 56, 378, 13f,; [Luther's Works; hereafter LW] 25, 368. Cf. A. W. Hunzinger, "Luther und die deutsche Mystik," *Neue kirchliche Zeitschrift* 19 (1908), 972-88, quoted in Tschackert, 40.

[28] On the former see Loofs, 522 (425). On the latter see ibid., 628-30 (521f.)

[29] Hagenbach, 334.

[30] Cf. the last lines of F. von Schiller's *An die Freunde* (1802).

[31] Cf. A von Harnack, *What Is Christianity?* (New York, 1902), 61, where it is argued that if religious individualism. "God and the soul, the soul and its God," and subjectivism, if all such things are Greek, then Jesus was in the context of Greek development.

[32] Loofs, 528 (427).

[33] The MS had *dass* here, changed by the editor to *indem.*

[34] On Eckhardt see F. Pfeiffer, *Meister Eckhardt, Deutsche Mystiker des 14. Jahrhunderts,* vol. II (Leipzig, 1857), 155, 21f., quoted in Loofs, 629 (522). See Tauler's sermon on Luke 10:23, quoted in Hagenbach, 388. See Luther's Romans lectures, WA 56, 413, 18f.; LW 25, 404; Barth was using Tschackert, 41.

[35] Barth had Seuse's *Deutsche Schriften,* ed. W. Lehmann, 2 vols. (Jena, 1911).

[36] Cf. Gogarten's essay in *Die religiöse Entscheidung* (Jena, 1921), 65ff.

[37] See n. 33 on 34.

[38] See esp. *Phaedon* 67de.

[39] On Tauler see n. 27; and on the *German Theology* see Luther's prefaces to his 1516 and 1518 editions, WA 1, 153, 378f. Cf. Calvin's letter to the French refugee congregation in Frankfort, 2.23.1559, CO 17, 441f. in which he notes in the *German Theology,* if no major errors, at any rate an obscuring of the simplicity of the gospel. . . .

[40] Cf. Goethe's *Der Zauberlehrling* (1797), V, 91f.

[41] Barth recalls here the quotation from Seuse in Hagenbach, 448, which he used earlier. . . .

[42] Cf. Goethe's *Gott, Gemüt und Welt* (1815), V, vv. 29f....

[45] Seeberg, IV, 12, who quotes Paracelsus but does not give the source. On Machiavelli see Seeberg ad loc. On Bruno cf. K. Vorländer, *Geschichte der Philosophie,* vol. 1, PhB 105 (Leipzig, 2nd ed. 1908), 301.

[46] Ullmann's work was printed in two volumes (Hamburg, 1841 and 1842; 2nd ed. Gotha, 1866). See A. Ritschl, *Die christliche Lehre von der Rechtfertigung und Versöhnung,* vol. I, 4th ed. (Bonn, 1909), 129, 132. Cf. Loofs, 634 (527f.); and Seeberg, III, 640f.

[47] Cf. Barth's letter to Thurneysen and other friends dated 1.22.1922 ([K. Barth and E. Thurneysen, Briefwechsel, ed. Thurneysen, *Karl Barth Gesamtausgabe,* V: *Gespräche,* vol. I: 1914-21 (Zurich, 1973); vol. II: 1921-30 (Zurich, 1974)], II, 30), in which he spoke of being in the corner between Nominalism, Augustinianism, mysticism, Wycliffe, etc., which was not itself the Reformation but from which the Reformation sprang, and then asked whether this was not their own place, in the shadow cast ahead by the Reformation, where there is still no assurance of salvation, no evangelical freedom, etc.

**Will Durant on the lessons of the Reformation:**

. . . [Our sympathy can go to all the combatants of the Reformation.] We can understand the anger of Luther at Roman corruption and dominance, the reluctance of German princes to see German collections fatten Italy, the resolve of Calvin and Knox to build model moral communities, the desire of Henry VIII for an heir, and for authority in his own realm. But we can understand, too, the hopes of Erasmus for a reform that would not poison Christendom with hatred; and we can feel the dismay of devout Roman prelates like Contarini at the prospective dismemberment of a Church that for centuries had been the nurse and custodian of Western civilization, and was still the strongest bulwark against immorality, chaos, and despair.

Nothing of all these efforts was lost. The individual succumbs, but he does not die if he has left something to mankind. Protestantism, in time, helped to regenerate the moral life of Europe, and the Church purified herself into an organization politically weaker but morally stronger than before. One lesson emerges above the smoke of the battle: a religion is at its best when it must live with competition; it tends to intolerance when and where it is unchallenged and supreme. The greatest gift of the Reformation was to provide Europe and America with that competition of faiths which puts each on its mettle, cautions it to tolerance, and gives to our frail minds the zest and test of freedom.

*Will Durant, in* The Story of Civilization, Part IV. The Reformation: A History of European Civilization from Wyclif to Calvin, 1300-1564, *Simon and Schuster, 1957.*

### Heiko A. Oberman (essay date 1994)

SOURCE: "Problems and Perspectives," in *The Impact of the Reformation*, William B. Eerdmans Publishing Company, 1994, pp. 173-200.

[*In the following excerpt, Oberman examines the influence of the Protestant Reformation upon education and literary publications of the sixteenth century.*]

[Battle] is exactly the theme and center of a revealing treatise by Sylvester Mazzolini, named after his birthplace Prierias. On closer scrutiny, the treatise proves to be a pseudepigraphic satire in two distinct parts.[1] The first is dated Rome 1553 and assigned to Prierias, professor of Thomistic philosophy in Rome from 1514 until his death in 1523; from December 1515, Prierias was *Magister sacri Palatii,* chief inquisitor, and responsible for preparing the Roman process against Reuchlin and Luther.

The satirical tone itself must make the reader dubious about one further point of information on the title page, namely that the 1553 edition is a revision of an earlier instruction which Prierias had sent out to all inquisitors in 1519, a manual to detect and convict Lutherans: *in Martini Luteri perditionem et eius sequacium.* But indeed, the satire was published in 1519, in Augsburg, Basel, Cologne, and perhaps in Wittenberg itself.[2] Whereas the Augsburg version is dedicated to Sylvester Prierias by an imaginary younger Dominican under the name of Logumenus (= *loquax* or verbose?), a later edition, printed by Eduard Böcking in the first supplementary volume of his Hutten edition,[3] is assigned not to Prierias but to an unnamed canonist, and directed not against Lutherans but against heresy in general—this time dedicated to both Prierias and the German chief inquisitor Hochstraten. Böcking believes the satire to have been written by Rubianus Crotus (1545), in view of its obvious proximity to the style and tone of the *Letters of Obscure Men.*[4]

The second treatise—added, as its author says, merely in order not to leave precious pages blank (folios 26-40!)—is dedicated to Esprit Rotier (Spiritus Roterus), the French Dominican who functioned from 1523 until 1547 as the vicar-general of his congregation in France, and from 1547 until his death in 1564 (or 1569) as chief inquisitor in Toulouse. This treatise is to be found on the index of Benedict XIV (1758) and assigned to Pietro Paolo Vergerio. Meeting Luther as papal nuncio on 7 November 1535 in Wittenberg, Vergerio had regarded the reformer as the devil incarnate. But afterward increasingly open to the Reformation and despairing of the sincerity of papal reform efforts he converted, ending his life as a Protestant professor at Tübingen in 1565.[5]

What we have here before us in the edition of 1553 is a double plot to ridicule the Inquisition, of which the earlier 1519 treatise presents a more light-footed sample, completely in keeping with the *Letters of Obscure Men.*[6] The second treatise is a much more embittered defense against Rotier's attack on the Genevan Reformation, which Rotier four years earlier in a book published in Toulouse in 1549 had identified as "the new Babylon." The first satire—divided into twelve so-called "rules," perhaps a takeoff on the four *Fundamenta* which Prierias had attached to his 1518 *Conclusiones* against Luther[7]—shows such precise information about theological terminology of the day that one may be inclined to assign it to one of Luther's students or younger colleagues, such as Johann Lang (1487-1548). The Inquisition is ridiculed by having Prierias send out from the Vatican an urgent warning "to all Dominicans and inquisitors in Italy, France, Spain, and elsewhere":

> They should stop interrogating these heretics in public, because of their infectious good faith and convincing knowledge of the Scriptures. They should be killed before it comes to a hearing—on the basis of the "old saw" that the one who sets the fire is always wiser than the one who is burned [*quia semper combustores sum doctiores combustis*]. If only the princes had allowed Reuchlin to receive his due, this thesis could have been wonderfully documented: the German heretic would have been burned; and to be wiser than Reuchlin really means something [*duodecima Regula*] . . . a beautiful feather in the cap of the Inquisition.
>
> The final question raised is why the Holy Church did not burn any heretics in the first 1300 years, until the Council of Constance (1414-1418), yet cannot rule today without burning heretics galore? Answer: I wonder that people can be so stupid that they ask such a question! It is obvious that they have not yet studied their Thomas. I say, therefore, that the solution is short, and, well, thus: at that time, there were not yet inquisitors. If they had been around in the early church, surely the heretics would have been exterminated by fire. Just as the truth grows over the course of time, so does also the purgation of the church increase. In the early church, there were not yet so many gifted students of Scripture as there are today thanks to the tutelage of Aristotle. I sincerely believe that if St. Jerome and St. Augustine were alive today—or even the apostle Paul himself—they would not so easily escape the fires of the Inquisition, because the inquisitors have become real experts today: *bene tibi, Paule, quod vixisti illo tempore, quando non erant subtilia ista ingenia.*

The second satire, edited and added in 1553, follows another procedure: a young respectful trainee of the great French inquisitor Rotier reports a long series of formidable problems he has encountered in defending the opinions of his master. Finding himself gutted time and again by the sharpness of the arguments of the opposition, he is unable—indeed, helpless—to defend Rotier without immediate advice and support. This time, it is not the infallibility of the pope which is carried *ad absurdum,* but Rotier's insistence on the Vulgate and directives against Bible translations. The inquisitor had published a book in Toulouse in 1548[8] to prove that Holy Scripture should not be translated into the vernacular, with the argument that then "the living spirit is converted into the killing letter":

> How then to deal with the feast of Pentecost when the gospel was proclaimed in all languages? Do not think, great master, that in the debate about your thesis I succumbed. Thereby you would underestimate my long breath. However many convincing passages they showed me, they never silenced me. If you think that, you have forgotten my brashness. But it was difficult to argue against their solid proofs of structural weakness in your books, both in grammar and dialectics—especially the difficulty you have in grasping an argument of the opposition and reporting it fairly: how fortunate it is that you have a terrifying, powerful

> institution behind you which scares readers of heretical books from touching them and from comparing them with yours. When they turned to such basic issues as sin and forgiveness, I found it hard to discover a passage in Thomas which could help me. But I hit on the right kind of solution to escape the force of their arguments: I could slither away under the pretext that one is not allowed to debate matters that have already been decided.

At this point, I break off my report on the second treatise. It is just as much a satire as the first one, though different in strategy. Here the young inquisitor reports his embarrassment and thus reveals the weakness of the arguments of his master, instead of the master himself prescribing antidotes for an "obviously" formidable challenge. The power of the Inquisition is ridiculed as a mirror of the disintegration of that Roman Church which sets itself up as infallible and hence as unassailable, and yet can only defend itself with external force.

Amid all similarities, a crucial new element should not be overlooked in the second treatise. The Inquisition is not merely a ridiculous Roman affair—that faraway, unpredictable court before which the great Reuchlin trembled, and where even Paul and Jesus would have had no chance: the Inquisition is now the direct and very present threat to the Genevan Reformation. Thirty-five years later, the struggle dramatically escalates: whereas Geneva is accursed as the New Babylon, the inquisitors are now unmasked as the soldiers of the antichrist. There is not just a difference in time—some thirty-five years—and a difference in locality—from German Lutherans to French Calvinists—but also a difference in a heightened sense of the diabolic power of the opponent: battle has grown out of banter. Behind the shift from irony to sarcasm we discern the growing awareness of the formidable obstacles on the path to reformation: its very impact is threatened.

From haughty banter to harsh battle—this escalation reflected indeed the course of events. From its staging area in Geneva, the third Reformation had sought to close ranks with endemic evangelism and to infiltrate the main bastions of Roman Catholicism in Italy and France. But just as it seemed that the evangelical dreams of such disciples of Valdés (1541) as Bernardino Ochino and Peter Martyr Vermigli under the patronage of Reginald Pole—in touch with Giberti, Contarini, and Cortese—could be translated into structural reform, and just at the time when Viterbo, Modena, and Lucca had become centers of what the Council of Trent would later define and condemn as heresy, the Roman Inquisition was established in July 1542.

Cardinal Caraffa—the later Counter-Reformation Pope Paul IV (1555-1559)—gained control of what he fashioned into a powerful and feared institution.[9] Shortly afterward, in August 1542, Ochino and Vermigli, symbolically just at the time when Contarini was lying on his deathbed, decided to burn their Roman bridges behind them. They were the first in a long line of refugees going the arduous road of emigration over the Alps to Switzerland, and in the case of Vergerio, ultimately all the way to Swabia.

Were these refugees fainthearted or clear-sighted? Less than a decade later, by papal order of 12 August 1553, the Talmud and other rabbinical books were condemned to burning; in the next few months across Italy possibly hundreds of thousands of Hebrew books went up in flames.[10] The *spirituali,* in full accord with the rising tide of antisemitism, did not read the signs of the times, ignoring the medieval sequence "first the Jew, then the heretic".[11]

The index of forbidden books of 1549 was enhanced in 1554 to include works by Dante, Valla, Boccaccio, Machiavelli, and Erasmus.[12] Three years later, Caraffa—now Pope Paul IV—started to round up the *spirituali* in high places. Sanfelice and Soranzo were arrested, Morone sent to the dungeons of St. Angelo, and Pole was recalled from his mission as Papal Legate in England in order to allow the Curia to start proceedings against him. Erwin Iserloh called this crucial period from 1551 to 1559 the "Durchbruch der katholischen Reform."[13] Actually, it was a time of failure for *Catholic* reform and the beginning of the *Roman* Catholic Counter-Reformation.

The refugees could not but feel confirmed in their decision. Those who had stayed behind and clung to the hope for reform from within—peculiarly dubbed, for lack of a proper designation, the *spirituali*—drew the wrath of the refugees, who regarded them as "timorous Nicodemists,"[14] as Vergerio designated Cardinal Reginald Pole.

But if Pole had acceded to the papal throne when, on St. Martin's Eve, the Holy See fell vacant through the death of Pope Paul III (10 November 1549)—on that fateful morning of 5 December Pole needed only one more vote in the conclave!—the *spirituali* would have been in charge of reform from above, and allowed to act so publicly that the charge of Nicodemism would never have arisen. Vergerio's charge is nothing but a red herring: understandable though his "name-calling" may be, it is deceptive, and has indeed deceived scholarship in its search for the roots of Nicodemism. The learned Tübingen professor, by applying a current pejorative term to Italian evangelism, suggests a connection between Nicodemism, cowardice, and spiritualism which most certainly does not apply to Nicodemism as it had emerged ten years earlier in France.

The enigma of Nicodemism is not due to the dissimulation of its adherents, but to the confusing reaction it has evoked among its interpreters, all the way from John Calvin to Carlo Ginzburg.[15] It has been generally recognized that a crucial, but unknown, phase in the history of Nicodemism precedes the intervention of John Calvin.[16] What has not yet been highlighted is the positive connotations associated with Nicodemus, as propagated in late medieval theology,[17] piety,[18] and art.[19] The positive connotation of the term clearly puzzled Calvin: after all, according to the Fourth Gospel, Nicodemus proved to be at the end one of the very few dedicated and steadfast disciples (cf. John 3 and John 19:39). Originally, "Nicodemite" may well have been an apologetic in group designation to express the claim that though one cannot openly profess the gospel, one comes like Nicodemus to the Lord, albeit by night. In this charitable sense, it is used by the reformer of Schwäbisch-Hall Johannes Brenz in a letter of 1 June 1529 to the lord chancellor of Brandenburg-Ansbach. Georg Volger. Brenz expects the secret confession to become a public one.[20] But when Calvin, twice within one year (1543 and 1544), and in no uncertain terms, attacks the French Nicodemites as traitors and apostates, the leader of the third Reformation discredits a movement which would thus be encouraged to subvert, rival, and in certain respects eclipse his own impact on later history.

Thanks to a precious find by that eminent Strasbourg scholar, Jean Rott, we have recovered a missing link in the correspondence of Antoine Fumée (1511-1568?), one of the leaders of French Protestantism in Paris. Long hidden in the library of Corpus Christi College, Cambridge, this letter sheds light on both the creed and the situation of the so-called Nicodemites in France. Writing to Martin Bucer and his colleagues in Strasbourg, Fumée reminds them of the fact that he is not in a position to teach the gospel publicly: "Scitote, fratres, non tam clare et diserte nobis licere, aut per infirmitatem, quam magnam in nobis agnoscimus, aut per assiduas improborum calumnias, docere justificationem hominis solius Dei gratiae esse, non operum."[21] Fumée proceeds to describe his theology in detail. Except for the invocation of the saints—legitimate, he argues, provided it is done in the name of God, and though not attested to in Scripture, not counter to it—it is completely "orthodox." This new letter should be read in conjunction with Fumée's earlier correspondence with Calvin.

Two points should be underscored. In the first place, "Nicodemians" have been erroneously confused with libertinists and epicureans.[22] Yet it was Antoine Fumée himself who alerted Calvin to these very dangers. Even more importantly, Fumée alerts us to the fact that the refugee is not the only true Christian, or the only Protestant prepared to suffer for his faith (after all, Calvin decided to flee); he takes no risks in criticizing those who dared to stick to their social and political responsibility: "hec te illic facile et predicare et monere posse, qui si hic sis aliter forte sentires."[23] Almost exactly a year before, toward the end of 1542, under an alias ("Capnius") Fumée had reported to Calvin the tremendous pressure under which the young French evangelical movement suffered through confusion in its own ranks and police pressure from outside. This had taken on such extreme forms that he expected shortly its *ruina,* and did not doubt "nos diu hoc statu non consistere posse."[24] And indeed, as the records show, the persecutions had intensified since the late summer of 1542, with public burnings in Bordeaux, Toulouse, Rouen, and of course in Paris itself.[25]

It is at this point that the newly found letter of Antoine Fumée is of such importance. A friend of Calvin's since the common study years in Orléans and Paris, he was born into the ruling elite. His grandfather, Paul Fumée, had been the personal physician of Charles VII and Louis XI, ambassador to Rome, and governor of Nantes; his father, Adam Fumée, served as member of Parliament, as did Antoine himself from 1536, at twenty-five years of age.[26] In complete agreement with Calvin as far as the rejection of libertinism is concerned, he takes grave exception to Calvin's attack on those in France who have to assume the posture of Nicodemites, and who do not give in to the temptation to flee—as Calvin had done!—and therefore to make room for people who will subvert the course of the gospel in France.

At this early stage, it is certainly wrong to identify, as Carlo Ginzburg has done, Nicodemism with spiritualism: spiritualism emphasizes an interior religion which is indifferent to externals. Fumée, however, makes it quite clear that he is critical of the spiritualizing interpretation of the eucharist, as it has been reported to him about Strasbourg. The confusion of the two movements, which finds support in George Williams's characterisation of Nicodemism as "prudential spiritualism,"[27] is understandable insofar as Calvin attacks often in one breath a whole series of opponents, from libertines to spiritualists and Nicodemites lurking about in all parts of Europe. In his report of 21 January 1545 to Martin Luther, Calvin makes quite clear that the Nicodemites who "continue to defile themselves with the sacrilegious worship of the papists" are his own fellow countrymen in France. But these compatriots continue not only "to defile themselves" but also to hold out and persevere—they have to give account of their faith under extreme duress.

Nicodemism is not some kind of abstract ideology which *a posteriori* applies what it first, *a priori,* culled out of the pages of a book, as Carlo Ginzburg has argued, when finding the bible of Nicodemism in Otto Brunfels's *Pandectae* (1527)[28] and constructing a school of Brunfels through Wolfgang Capito, Sebastian Franck, Johannes Brenz, Camillo Renato, and Lefevre d'Ètaples. Carlos Eire has convincingly pointed to Ginzburg's overinterpretation of the *Pandectae;* Pierre Fraenkel established that one of Ginzburg's so-called Nicodemite documents actually is a letter of Bucer,[29] and Olivier Millet recently uncovered that the Margarita, whom Ginzburg identified with Margaret de Navarre, is Margreth von Lodieuse, a French refugee in Strasbourg since December 1534. Strasbourg, with its influential preachers around Brunfels, particularly Bucer and Capito, is not a staging area for the export of Nicodemism to France, but rather its court of appeal. The Paris Evangelicals, under the high pressure of royal persecution, *and* simultaneously harshly assailed by Calvin, appeal to Strasbourg to intercede with Calvin and, if need be, to get in touch with Luther and Melanchthon to silence Geneva.

Calvin's sharp reaction is quite understandable in light of the fact that the sensitive point of his absence from the front line as a refugee is called into question. Yet at the same time, as commander-in-chief behind the front, he must keep the troops on the offensive. The impression he creates that the Nicodemists are uninterested in so-called "organized" religion is sheer propaganda. Later, but only after Fumée's forecast had become all too true, and the evangelical movement had met *ruina* under the pressures of the rising tide of the Counter-Reformation, the shift toward spiritualism occurs which Williams and Ginzburg see as its roots. When Calvin, some twenty years later, writes his *Response à un certain holandois* (1546)—successfully identified by George Williams as that enthusiastic follower of Sebastian Frank, Dick Volckertszoon Coornhert—Nicodemism has become that kind of ecumenism which pleads for a "Christianity above confessional diversity" and which relativizes or even dispenses with the visible church, its orders and sacraments.[30] In his creed, Fumée was explicitly a Protestant, and in his sense of priority of charity before faith he stands with Bucer and his colleagues. Yet in his rejection of vituperative and inflammatory attacks in confessional debate and in his insistence on the global Church of Love—which underlies his defense of the invocation of the saints—there are clear lines pointing to that development within the third Reformation which we may best designate as "irenicism."[31] As anti-institutional ecumenism, this is still a force today.

Turning back once more to the situation in the 1540s, Calvin had to respond sharply for personal and programmatic reasons. Eire misinterprets Calvin's silence on the exact identity of his Nicodemite adversaries. Refuting Ginzburg, he holds that Calvin is so given to attacking persons by name that, if there had been an "organized group" with a definite theology, Calvin would have made that explicit.[32] Whereas Eire justly criticizes Ginzburg for assuming a theory which precedes practice, here he himself has lost sight of the historical realities. The Fumée case shows why Calvin could not possibly attack such a person by name. Under daily threat of exposure, Fumée had to write under the pseudonym of Capnius. The one occasion on which Calvin broke the seal of silence was in the horrible case of Michael Servetus; but then, Calvin no longer counted him as a member of the true church. In short, the demarcation line does not run, as Calvin had put it, between the courageous confessor and the dissimulating coward; rather, the alternatives were the *courage to flee,* and become a refugee for the cause of faith, or the *courage to be,* to stay and endure the daily threat of prison and fire.[33]

Fumée's solution, as he so clearly saw, could only remain viable for a limited period of time—an interim, provided relief came soon. The success of the Counter-Reformation in France forced the steadfast soldiers of faith who, like the Nicodemus of the gospel, fought night battles under the cloak of darkness, to embrace a creed of humanity and its divine rights independent of structures, whether of a church state or a state church.

In this new form, the third Reformation was to have a profound impact, even though it would deviate from the vision of its main architect, John Calvin.

Luther is not the father, but neither is he the son, of a single movement. He can—and should—be described as Augustinian, nominalist, humanist and biblical scholar. But all of this would be to no avail if the core of his being is overlooked: he is Luther the Apocalyptic. From the year 1519 onward, he unquestionably understands himself as the forerunner of the coming great Reformation of God. As a Doctor of Holy Scripture, he must instruct the faithful by reopening the treasures of the gospel; as a pastor, he is responsible for gathering the congregation of the faithful "in these last days."[34]

Though widely accepted, this recovery of the "eschatological reformer" has evoked two substantial critical reactions which seem to neutralize each other. The first argues that this apocalyptic reinterpretation of Luther is too comprehensive; the second, that this interpretation is too limited and should be extended beyond Luther to the early leaders of the City Reformation generally. The first critique has been raised by the Hamburg Luther scholar Bernhard Lohse; the second by the Göttingen church historian, Bernd Moeller. Lohse takes issue with the apocalyptic interpretation of the young Luther, for which he finds no evidence; where there is unmistakable evidence, he regards its interpretation as overstretched. Lohse is prepared to admit that Luther regards the Reformation "ultimately" as the work of God, but as he sees it this is from beginning to end for Luther *an historical, not an eschatological event.*[35]

This is not the place to debate the interpretation of single texts. As I see it, Lohse misunderstands the significance of crucial terms, such as the "interim" before the "Day of the Lord"; he renders Christ's *Zukunft* as "future" instead of *Ankunft,* which means the "advent" of Christ.[36] The basic issue is that Lohse feels that he has to opt for an historical *or* for an eschatological interpretation of Luther's understanding of Reformation. It is precisely Luther's point, however, that these last days have already started, and that therefore the "last things" have commenced *in* our historical time, so that the eschatological clock has started to tick: "demoliri coepimus Antichristi regnum."[37] Among a number of other things, this means that Luther, in contrast with the Nicodemite Fumée, does not regard the persecutions as a horrid sign of impending *ruina,* but as the hopeful sign of the recovery of the gospel, since the devil is bound to assail the true gospel and in these last days cannot but persecute its adherents: "Sentit enim Satan potentiam et fructus. . . . "[38] Luther's sense of time is in keeping with Revelation 20:3, and with St. Augustine's interpretation of the last phase of the Thousand Years of history, when—before the coming of the great Reformation—the devil will be loosed for a short time. When the first two martyrs of the Reformation are burned in Brussels in 1523, Luther is not surprised; instead, he is saddened that it is not granted him to sacrifice his own life in order to meet the onslaught of Satan.

From the opposite perspective, Bernd Moeller's criticism appears in an interesting article on the content of preaching in the cities in the early Reformation. He draws on some thirty-two so-called *Predigtsummarien* between 1522 and 1529 to show that in the towns throughout Germany a unified interpretation of the gospel was proclaimed. Moeller documents his findings with references but without quotations, and protects himself with the cautious provisos that these *Predigtsummarien* "leave the impression" that across Germany "more or less the same was preached." One foremost characteristic, Moeller notes, is eschatological urgency: the Kingdom of God has drawn near, and the present is threatened by the antichrist. There is no doubt that Luther's eschatological message was "received" in a wide variety of ways, and well beyond the year 1525.[39] Though I do not dare to go as far as Moeller by claiming that Luther—on the basis of *this* evidence—can be claimed to be a "figure of world history," whatever that may mean, the implications of his apocalyptic view are far-reaching.[40]

Once it is clear, however, that Luther is to be regarded as the apocalyptic prophet, a number of conclusions can be drawn: in the first place, the understandable scepticism of the social historian that under the prophet's cloak the politician is hidden, and that by means of the gospel social control is exercised, is groundless. Luther does not exploit sensitivities concerning usury, tithes, clerical immunities, and clerical indiscipline: all these are rather signs of the end of time and the gruesome extent of the power of the antichrist. Furthermore, far from being one of the calculating *politiques,* the apocalyptic prophet is so much convinced that only the elect will hear his voice that he can concentrate on the content of his gospel, without ulterior motives. The battle cry of *sola Scriptura,* which in the City Reformation came to mean the replacement of Canon Law by Biblical Law, meant for Luther the preaching of the gospel irrespective of political opportunism. As he put it, "This is the time when we have to be prepared to live dangerously."[41] The true Christian should not only be willing to endure persecution, but regard it as the sign of the extent to which we irritate Satan. For this reason, Luther criticized Melanchthon when the latter, during the Augsburg Diet in 1530, was prepared to enter into negotiations to gain political concessions in exchange for a less offensive formulation of the Protestant creed.

It is again the apocalyptic dimension which allows Luther to interpret the doctrine of justification by faith alone in a highly risky fashion, sacrificing the important impetus of reward for moral rearmament. And finally, once this apocalyptic stance is clearly seen, we can measure the distance which separates Martin Luther from a Nicodemite like Antoine Fumée. Though Luther's answer to Calvin has not been preserved, it is quite clear what he could and must have responded to Calvin's earnest question. After all, Fumée the Nicodemite[42] had become the most authentic *politique* of the century in protesting against all forms of sharp controversy, in the hope to avoid *ruina,* by courageously persevering with reform from within.

In trying to fathom the complex question of the impact of the Reformation, we must distinguish between the first, the second, and the third "Reformation," to ensure that our conclusions have the necessary precision.

First, as the history of Christianity shows, apocalyptic moods are not continuous but come in waves—at the time of St. Paul, St. John on Patmos, the churches under Roman persecution, or during the crisis of the Western schism. Thus also the apocalyptic climate which allowed Luther to speak and be heard passed away, re-emerging during the Thirty Years' War and reappearing during successive crises ever since. In such times, the word of Luther is and will be heard afresh, and in this sense we can speak of the lasting impact of Luther. But also, Luther's single-minded, noncalculating investigation of the Scriptures would allow his voice to break through the cultural accretions to the gospel, even when modern findings differ from his.

Insofar as Luther was an active agent in the introduction of visitations, we can indeed speak of "failure," albeit not on the basis of the moral deficiencies reported by the visitation records—proof of moral amelioration is not to be expected there, since the sources are intent on looking for deviation and depravity. But we may speak of failure in so far as Luther expected from the visitations *Besserung,* a limitation of the greed of the ruling elite, which reached out to seize church goods. For Luther, the purpose of the visitations was not only to secure the teaching of Christian basics, but also to make sure that the secularization of the church possessions would furnish ministers' salaries and the founding of good schools.

Luther had counted on another failure: namely, that the gospel would not be victorious in Germany and hence would move elsewhere, like a *Platzregen*—a rainstorm. And finally, regarding the *Fürstenreformation,* whatever our critique may be concerning the development of the *Landesfürst* into the *Notbischof,* and of the prince into the leader of the territorial church in his own territory, the Inquisition and the Index were unable to silence the voice of the apocalyptic prophet. Marjorie Reeves once observed that "men's dreams are as much a part of history as their deeds."[43] With Luther, the prophetic dreams themselves made history.

Second, as far as the significance of the second Reformation—the City Reformation—is concerned, we can be brief. It is a crucial *intermezzo*—an *intermezzo* insofar as it is limited to some twenty-five years until the free cities, which had already lost their economic power on the eve of the Reformation, lost also the last chance for spiritual revitalization, when imperial troops marched in and enforced the Interim, in 1548 and 1549.

At the same time, it is *crucial,* for the *intermezzo* provided the Reformation with more than printing presses and Latin schools, the pulpits, and the learning to understand, interpret, and multiply Luther's voice; it also allowed the political space to experiment with what Bullinger called *enderung,* which encompasses the horizontal dimensions of the Reformation message. Within the city walls, the "semi-monastic" tenets in late medieval lay piety could be translated into laws and a lifestyle which would be its—ambiguous—legacy to the third Reformation.

Third, the impact of the third Reformation—the Reformation of the Refugees—is to be traced along two lines of development. The first is the victorious path of the Revolution of the Saints, who erected and extended the Kingdom of Christ wherever they could seize power and, where such seizure proved impossible, at least survived independently of town council and *Landesfürst,* as congregations under the cross. This Reformation failed to flower in the key territories of France and Italy, but was able to establish itself in many other areas north of the Alps, in Great Britain, and beyond.

The second line of impact has its inauspicious beginnings with the Nicodemites of the 1540s in Paris. Wherever the victory of the Revolution of the Saints collapsed, whether in the Netherlands, Scotland, England, or the New World, the former Nicodemites could provide a new platform of unchurched ethics and voluntary societies—perhaps the stepchild of the Puritan ethic, but pervasive and adaptable to a new civic religion, which would make it a natural ally for socialism and ecumenism. . . .

*Notes*

[1] *Modus solennis et autenticus ad inquirendum et inveniendum et convincendum Luteranos t'alde necessarius, ad salutem sanctae Apostolicae sedis et omnium Ecclestasticorum anno 1519 compositus in Martini Luteri perditionem et eius sequacium per venerabilem Monachum magistrum Sylvestrum Prieratem* [sic] *ex sacrosancto ordine Praedicatorum, Magistrum sacri Palatii et generalem haereticae pravitatis inquisitorem. Anno 1553 revisus et satis bene emendatus ab erroribus per Reverendissimos Cardinales ad officium sanctissimae inquisitionis depuratos* [sic] *per S. D. N. Papam lulium III.* Romae, Per Iordanum typographum Pontificium [sic]. Anno 1553 (40 folios). Cf. [*D. Martin Luthers Werke: Kritische Gesamtausgabe Schriften;* hereafter *WA*] 1.605. I owe the exceptional gift of this rare copy to my colleague James Tanis, the librarian of Bryn Mawr College.

[2] I am indebted to Professor C. Augustijn and to the librarian of the Free University, Amsterdam, B. Lau, for access to the version most probably published in Augsburg in 1519.

[3] E. Böcking (ed.). *Epistolae obscurum virorum (Ulrichi Hutteni . . . opera . . . omnia,* supplementary vol. 1) (Leipzig, 1864; repr. Osnabruck, 1966), pp. 489-99. This version probably printed in Cologne in 1519.

[4] Cf. Otto Clemen in [*D. Martin Luthers Werke: Kritische Gesamtausgabe, Briefwechsel;* hereafter *WA Br*] 1, nr. 236, pp. 604-6. I doubt whether Clemen saw the 1553 treatise himself. Note his incorrect rendering of the title.

[5] The author of the excellent monograph on Vergerio, Anne Jacobson Schutte, informed me in a letter of 17 February 1981 that she doubts Vergerio's authorship:

> Vergerio referred to the work only six years after its publication in Basel. In *Agli inquisitori che sono per l'Italia: Del catalogo di libri eretici stampato in Roma nell'anno presente 1559* (Tubingen [?], 1559), folio 42v, he said that he thought he owned a copy of this rare work and planned to have it reprinted. Since his references to books written and published by others and to books he himself issued are generally very accurate, my tentative conclusion would be that he was *not* responsible for the 1553 edition.

[6] After a deficient bibliographical description, Friedrich Lauchert associates both parts with the *Epistolae obscurum virorum.* In the first treatise Lauchert finds "mehr Gehässigkeit als Witz," citing particularly the irreverent treatment of papal infallibility: satire "durch törichte Verdrehung." Lauchert, *Die italienischen literarischen Gegner Luthers* (Freiburg im Breisgau, 1912), pp. 29-30; 30, n. 1.

[7] Heiko A. Oberman, "Wittenberg's War on Two Fronts: What Happened in 1518 and Why," *The Reformation: Roots and Ramifications* (Edinburgh, 1994), 117-48.

[8] The following treatises of Rotier are alluded to:

*De non vertenda Scriptura Sacra in Fulgarem linguam, deque occidente littera et vivicante spiritu dissertatio* (Toulouse, 1548); *Parergi sive tabellae tres similitudimon, quibus suis coloribus haeretici, vera Ecclesia vulgaresque S. Scripturae traductiones describuntur* (Toulouse, 1548 quarto: 1549 octavo); *Responsio ad epistolam civium novae Babylonis Gebennae a Mornero insigni apostata editam* (Toulouse, 1549).

[9] Dermot Fenlon, *Heresy and Obedience in Tridentine Italy: Cardinal Pole and the Counter-Reformation* (Cambridge, 1972), p. 51.

[10] Paul F. Grendler, *The Roman Inquisition and the Venetian Press, 1540-1605* (Princeton, N.J., 1977), p. 92. The Index of Paul IV is reprinted by F. H. Reusch, *Die Indices Librorum Prohibitorum des 16. Jabrbunderts* (Tübingen, 1886), pp. 176-288.

[11] Cf. Heiko A. Oberman, *Roots of Anti-Semitism in the Age of Renaissance and Reformation* (Philadelphia, Pa., 1984).

[12] Grendler, *Roman Inquisition,* pp. 95-96.

[13] Iserloh, *Handbuch der Kirchengeschichte,* vol. 4, pp. 501-10. Cf., however, Hubert Jedin, "Die Regierung des Caraffa-Papstes war für alle Anhänger der Reform eine graesame Enttauschung," *Geschichte des Konzils von Trient,* vol. 4 (Freiburg im Breisgau, 1975), 15. Jedin placed the breakthrough after 1559: "Der Pontifikat Pius IV. brachte den endgültigen Sieg der katholischen Reform und den Abschluß des Konzils von Trient." *Geschichte des Konzils von Trient,* vol. 4, p. 18. Cf. Donald Nugent's evaluation: "Paul's pontificate was a reign of terror rather than a reformation. . . . Given all this, one can hardly insist that Paul IV launched the Counter-Reformation without allowing at the same time that he was destroying the Catholic Church." *Ecumenism in the Age of the Reformation. The Colloquy of Poissy* (Cambridge, 1974), p. 29.

[14] Anne Jacobson Schutte, *Pier Paolo Vergerio: The Making of an Italian Reformer,* Travaux d'Humanisme et Renaissance 160 (Geneva, 1977), p. 267.

[15] A significant advance is made by C. M. N. Eire. "Calvin and Nicodemism: A Reappraisal," *Sixteenth Century Journal* 10 (1979): 45-69.

[16] Albert Autin, *La Crise du Nicodémisme,* 1535-1545 (Toulon, 1917); cf. Francis Higman (ed.), *John Calvin: Three French Treatises* (London, 1970).

[17] Cf. Gabriel Biel, *Canonis Misse Expositio,* Lectio 18G; 1.157.4; Lectio 34 L; 2.10.22.

[18] Jacobus de Voragine, O.P. (1298), elaborates on the significance of Nicodemus in his influential *Legenda Aurea* (1293). On the wide dissemination of the *Legenda,* see Sherry L. Reames, *The Legenda Aurea: A Reexamination of Its Paradoxical History* (Madison, Wisc., 1985), pp. 197-209.

[19] The account of the deposition in the *Gospel of Nicodemus* and in (Pseudo) Bonaventura's *Meditationes*—visibly represented and propagated in sculptures and paintings throughout Europe—usually presents both Joseph of Arimathea and Nicodemus as the *faithful* disciples who remove the nails from the crucified Christ. Cf. Wolfgang Stechow, "Joseph of Arimathea or Nicodemus?", in W. Lotz and L. L. Möller (eds.), *Studien zur Toskanischen Kunst* (Munich, 1964), pp. 289-302; 290, 292-96.

I am indebted to Dr. Jane Kristof for calling my attention to Stechow's article. In a paper not yet published Dr. Kristof makes a good case for interpreting Michelangelo's Pietà in Florence Cathedral as representing himself as a Nicodemite. Via Vittoria Colonna Michelangelo belonged to the Viterbo circle of the *spirituali.* The Pietà, begun about 1547, was mutilated and abandoned by him before December 1555; by that time the *positive* self-identification with Nicodemus might well have become self-incriminatory.

[20] T. H. Pressel (ed.), *Anecdota Brentiana: Ungedruckte Briefe und Bedenken* (Tübingen, 1868), pp. 31-33; 32. Cf. Martin Brecht, *Die frühe Theologie des Johannes Brenz* (Tübingen, 1966), p. 55, n. 1.

[21] Jean Rott and Olivier Millet, "Miettes Historiques Strasbourgeoises," in P. Barthel, R. Scheurer, and R. Stauffer (eds.), *Actes du Collôque Guillaume Farel (Neuchatel, 29 septembre-1er octobre 1980),* 1, Cahiers de la Revue de Théologie et de Philosophie 9/1 (Geneva/Lausanne/Neuchâtel, 1983), 261-62, 264.

[22] See Marc Lienhard (ed.), *Croyants et sceptiques au XVle siècle. Le dossier, des "Epicuriens,"* Publications de la Société Savante d'Alsace et des Régions de l'Est,

Collection "Recherches et Documents" 30 (Strasbourg, 1981).

[23] A. L. Herminjard (ed.), *Correspondance des Reformateurs,* 9 (Nieuwkoop, 1966), 126.

[24] Herminjard, *Correspondance,* 8 (Nieuwkoop, 1966), 231-32.

[25] Herminjard, *Correspondance,* 8, pp. 107, n. 18; 108, n. 20.

[26] Herminjard, *Correspondance,* 8, p. 228, n. 1.

[27] G. H. Williams. *The Radical Reformation* (Philadelphia, Pa., 1962), p. 598.

[28] Carlo Ginzburg, *Il Nicodemismo: Simulazione e dissimulazione religiosa nell'Europa del 500* (Turin, 1970), pp. xiv, xvi, 154. Cf. Welti, *Kleine Geschichte,* pp. 50, 98.

[29] Pierre Fraenkel, "Bucer's Memorandum of 1541 and a 'Lettra nicodemitica' of Capito's," *Bibliothèque d'Humanisme et Renaissance* 36 (1974): 575-87; Rott/Millet, "Miettes Historiques Strasbourgeoises," p. 271.

[30] Williams, *Radical Reformation,* p. 775.

[31] See G. H. M. Posthumus Meyjes, "Jean Hotman's *Syllabus* of Eirenical Literature," in Derek Baker (ed.), *Reform and Reformation: England and the Continent, c. 1500-c. 1700* (Oxford, 1979), pp. 175-93; 179-80.

[32] Eire, "Calvin and Nicodemism," p. 67.

[33] As an eminent example of the power of narrative history in the service of historical analysis, Geoffrey Elton wrote one of his finest vignettes "Persecution and Toleration in the English Reformation," *Studies in Church History* 21 (1984): 163-87. Though the issue of Nicodemism as such is not treated, the case of John Fox against Thomas More serves to gainsay the assumption that toleration is the child of tired scepticism when, all passions spent, the sober shores of the eighteenth century have been reached. Elton disproves the contention that "only the gradual evaporation of such passions produced a weariness with religious strife which made the return of mutual sufferance to early humanism à la More possible." "Persecution and Toleration," p. 163.

This thesis is not only unfounded because of More's explicit approval of and active support for persecution; more importantly, it is not "weariness" and tired scepticism which lead to the ideal of toleration. Himself a victim of persecution, John Fox is shown to be an advocate of toleration on the basis of his personal experience. "In a very real sense, he knew what he was talking about. Thus one result of the history of religious strife was that people came to experience persecution in reality: it jumped off the page into their lives." "Persecution and Toleration," p. 179. Exactly the same transition from the experience of persecution to the defense of toleration marks the history of the "forgotten" Calvinists.

[34] Heiko A. Oberman, "Martin Luther—Forerunner of the Reformation," in *The Reformation: Roots and Ramifications* (Edinburgh, 1994), pp. 21-52. The extent to which this shaped Luther's development and thoughts from begining to end is spelled out in H. A. Oberman, *Luther: Mensch zwischen Gott und Teufel* (Berlin, 1982; 1985$^3$); Engl. *Luther: Man Between God and the Devil* (New Haven, 1989).

[35] "Vielmehr muß u.E dabei bleiben, daß Luther zwar die Reformation stets letztlich als Gottes Werk ansieht, daß sie für ihn jedoch auch in der Frühzeit ein innergeschichtlicher, nicht ein endzeitlicher Vorgang ist." Bernhard Lohse, "Luthers Selbsteinschätzung," in Peter Manns (ed.), *Martin Luther: Reformator und Vater im Glauben: Referate aus der Vortragsreihe des Instituts für Europäische Geschichte Mainz* (Stuttgart, 1985), pp. 118-33; 122; with pp. 131-32, esp. p. 132, n. 22.

[36] Lohse, "Luthers Selbsteinschätzung," p. 130, nn. 6, 13, 16. The parallel between the use of "interim" at pp. 130, n. 13 and 131, n. 22 is overlooked. To translate "interim" by "vorläufig" in the sentence "una interim Consolation tua erit futuri dies" ("Betont wird viel mehr der zunächst vorläufige Trost," "Luthers Selbststeinschäzung," p. 133, n. 3) is to negate Luther's confident faith and *only* hope during the interim before the imminent end; as Luther's Reformation, the interim itself is *"vor-läufig"!* See further *WA* 40 1.367.13-15; 372.18-32; 581.23-25.

[37] *WA* 40 1.583.29. Commentary on Gal. 4:6; 1531/35.

[38] Commentary on Gal. 3:13; 1531/35; *WA* 40 1.444.28-29.

[39] Bernd Moeller, "Was wurde in der Frühzeit der Reformation in den deutschen Städten gepredigt?" *Archiv für Reformationsgeschichte* 75 (1984): 176-93; 184, 193. Before we lose ourselves in "apocalyptic" vagaries, however, the different types of eschatological expectation in early modern times should first be established. One of the best-known forms was the widespread expectation of cosmic upheaval. From the Tubingen astronomer Johannes Stöffler to the Nuremberg painter Albrecht Dürer the end of the world was calculated to occur sometime between 1524 and 1526. Present research indicates that this upheaval was frequently associated with the intervention of the antichrist. Gustav Hellmann, *Aus der Blütezeit der Astrometeorologie: Johannes Stöfflers Prognose für das*

*Jahr 1524* (Berlin, 1914), pp. 5-67; Lynn Thorndike, *A History of Magic and Experimental Science,* 5 (New York, 1941), 178-233; Dietrich Kurze, *Johannes Lichtenberger: Eine Studie zur Geschichte der Prophetie und Astrologie* (Lübeck, 1960); Paola Zambelli, "Fine del Mondo o inizio della Propaganda?" in *Scienze Credenze occulte Livelli di Cultura* (Florence, 1980), pp. 291-368; 300. This "astrological" eschatology can be used just as well as a weapon *against* the Reformation, and is structurally independent of Reformation theology. Cf. Max Steinmetz, "Johann Virdung von Haßfurt: Sein Leben und seine astrologischen Flugschriften," in H.-J. Koehler (ed.), *Flugschriften als Massenmedium der Reformationszeit,* Spätmittelalter und Frühe Neuzeit: Tübinger Beiträge zur Geschichtsforschung 13 (Stuttgart, 1981), pp. 353-72. Equally, it has been used *against* Luther to "unmask" him as the expected antichrist. Though not convinced that the "forecasts" can properly be divided into "consolation literature" and "apocalyptic warnings" since I regard their ultimate purpose precisely as consolation by placing the evils of the time on the divine timetable, Paola Zambelli has noted the need to develop typologies in order to distinguish varieties of apocalyptic expectation:

> È grosso modo possibile indicare una prevalenza di pronostici consolatori fra gli scrittori che restano fedeli al papato, e al contrario una inclinazione apocalittica fra quelli filo-luterani. "Fine del Mondo," p. 300.

[40] Moeller finds in the *Summarien* such a far-reaching consensus with Luther that he speaks of a "lutherische Engführung" which in turn made "den Theologen Martin Luther zu einer Figur der Weltgeschichte." "Was wurde . . . gepredigt?", p. 193.

[41] Oberman, "Forerunner of the Reformation," pp. 48-51. At this point Moeller inserts a surprising aside: "Heiko Obermans These, die eschatologische Orientierung unterscheide Luther von der übrigen Reformation, läât sich anhand unserer Texte und also für die Frühzeit nicht verifizieren." This statement is all the more surprising when we learn that Moeller wishes to see his interpretation of the "unified Reformation message" confined to the period up to 1525; in his documentation no reason for reducing the span from 1522-1529 to 1522-1525 is adduced. I have been concerned to show that Luther, in the name of a whole series of city preachers, insisted on the introduction of visitations, in complete agreement with Melanchthon. But whereas the latter expected the visitations to establish peace and good order, and ultimately to lead to reconciliation with the papacy, Luther never left any doubt that the Reformation could not be introduced by visitations but only through an act of God announcing the end of the throes of this world. Melanchthon was supported in his view by such leaders of the urban Reformation as Bucer, Zwingli, and to a certain extent also Calvin. By his valuable discovery of the genre of *Predigtsummarien,* Moeller has been able to convey the impact of Luther's eschatological theology, which was not to become characteristic of the urban Reformation; the apocalyptic vision should be seen as one of the hallmarks of the first Reformation.

[42] *Corpus Reformatorum* 12 (Halle a.d. Saale, 1844), 7.

[43] Marjorie Reeves, *The Influence of Prophecy in the Later Middle Ages: A Study in Joachimism* (Oxford, 1969), p. 504.

**Carter Lindberg (essay date 1996)**

SOURCE: "Legacies of the Reformations," in *The European Reformations*, Blackwell Publishers, 1996, pp. 357-81.

[*In the essay that follows, Lindberg argues that the ideals of the Protestant Reformation introduced a cultural and religious pluralism that had a major impact on the social and political history of Europe.*]

> *Listening from the distance of centuries across the death chasms and howling kingdoms of decay, it is not easy to catch everything.*
>
> Thomas Carlyle (1795-1881)

One of the consequences of the Reformations in general and the council of Trent in particular was the splintering of western Christendom. Some of the legacies of this fragmentation of the medieval *corpus Christianum* were almost immediately apparent with, for example, the rise of confessionalization. while the catalytic action of others, such as theological pluralism, were long-term influences. In one way or another, however, the legacies of the Reformations have affected every aspect of modern life and thought. Description and analysis of these legacies already fills more library shelves than most of us can manage. Therefore . . . I shall only suggest some of the Reformations' legacies in the areas of confessionalization, politics and the right of resistance, culture in general, women, the "other," and ecumenism.

### Confessionalization

One of the most obvious consequences of the Reformations was the division of the medieval Catholic church into a number of churches. The process by which these various communities established their own identities is known as confessionalization. In recent German scholarship the term "confessionalization" has become a paradigm of societal history. Confessionalization "designates the fragmentation of the unitary

Christendom (*Christianitas latina*) of the Middle Ages into at least three confessional churches—Lutheran, Calvinistic or 'Reformed,' and post-tridentine Roman Catholic. Each formed a highly organized system, which tended to monopolize the world view with respect to the individual, the state, and society, and which laid down strictly formulated norms in politics and morals" (Schilling 1986: 22; 1992: ch. 5). The Protestant communities began to develop their own cultural and social identities informed by both their specific theologies and their hostilities to each other as well as to the old faith. Catholicism, now properly delimited by the adjective "Roman," did likewise. The late medieval intramural attempts to reform the church became extramural exercises in self-definition. In this process the fluidity of Reformation beginnings rigidified as the edifice complexes of each community structured an identity over against the others.

The decisions of the council of Trent on justification, Scripture, and the sacraments made so definitive the divisions that had arisen in the Reformation that hopes for a reunited Christian church would not begin flickering again until the ecumenical movement of the twentieth century. By the conclusion of the council of Trent, there was a second generation of reformers whose memories of the "one, holy, catholic, and apostolic church" had receded behind the vivid present impressions of the martyrs and confessors of their own particular communities. Loyalty to the "fathers" of the church now came increasingly to mean loyalty to the confessions of faith of the previous generation. Conversations between and even among the churches consisted largely of mutual condemnations and anathemas. The intensity and rancor of these theological and ecclesiastical conflicts is reflected in Philip Melanchthon's sigh on his deathbed that finally he was being delivered from the *rabies theologorum*—the "madness of the theologians." This "madness" contributed to the atrocities of the Thirty Years War (1618-48).

The competitiveness of the churches led to a kind of siege mentality. Protestant theologians became so involved in involved in constructing theological systems to protect their churches and to wall off alternatives that the late sixteenth and early seventeenth centuries came to be known as the period of Protestant orthodoxy or Protestant scholasticism. Both Lutherans and Calvinists developed theories of verbal and plenary inspiration to safeguard the sole authority of Scripture against the Roman Catholic use of tradition on the one hand and the dissidents' use of experience and "inner light" on the other hand. The Reformers' original understanding of faith as trust and confidence in God's promise shifted in the heat of battle to understanding faith in terms of intellectual assent to correct doctrine. The resulting highly rationalized schemata of salvation are exemplified by the chart of election and reprobation drawn up by the Elizabethan Puritan, William Perkins (1558-1602) (Hinson 1976: ch. 7; Muller 1978), and the strict Calvinism formulated at the synod of Dort (1618-19) in the Netherlands. The latter is sometimes referred to as the "Tulip synod" because its decrees may be arranged to spell the flower for which Holland is famed: *T*otal depravity, *U*nconditional election, *L*imited atonement, *I*rresistible grace, *P*erseverance of the saints.

A rationalistic and creed-bound Protestantism and Catholicism contributed politically to the developments of the consolidation of the early modern state and its concomitant imposition of social discipline, and intellectually to the rationalism, Deism, and Pietism that fed the Enlightenment of the eighteenth and nineteenth centuries. The medieval aspiration for a Christian society, the *corpus Christianum,* fragmented into the aspirations of the different confessional groups. Without a unitary sacred ideal for the integration of society and without the means and will to enforce a particular confessional ideal for all Europe, toleration became a path to social peace and the eventual secularization of society. The displacement of a unified sacred society by confessional communities also had psychological and ethical consequences.

> Translated in psychological terms, it meant the internalization of discipline, based on decorum and piety, and the suppression, or at least, the redirection of violence and anger. . . . Described variously as "the civilizing process," or "social disciplining," the transformation of social norms expressed itself also in the spread of bourgeois values, epitomized by the emphasis on learning and self-quest, and by the simultaneous praise of family life and more rigid definition of its sexual boundaries. (Hsia 1989: 184)

## Politics

The Reformations introduced into western culture the problem of pluralism—religious, social, and cultural. Since the modern world is still struggling with this legacy in its classrooms and courtrooms, and on its streets and battlefields, it should not be surprising that the people of the sixteenth century found it exceedingly difficult to live with alternative and competing commitments. This was compounded by a universal fear of anarchy and social disorder (Ozment 1985: 22-7). The first response by all parties was to compel conformity. But religious commitments are not easily swayed by laws and force. In some cases Protestant triumphalism contributed to the development of a "chosen nation" syndrome. England's overcoming of the threats of the Spanish Armada (1588) and the failure of the recusant (English Catholic rejection of the Anglican church) conspiracy to blow up the Houses of Parliament and the king (the Gunpowder Plot, 1605) were interpreted in terms of God's election and blessing of the nation. This messianic sense of being a chosen nation was carried into the new world and contributed to the nascent identity of the United States as a "city set on a hill" with a "manifest destiny," characteristics which continue to exert political influence.

Another response to political pluralism was to assert the rights of the individual conscience. In various ways, Luther's statement to the emperor at the diet of Worms in 1521 has had political echoes ever since: "My conscience is captive to the Word of God. I cannot and will not retract anything, for it is neither safe nor right to go against conscience. I cannot do otherwise, here I stand, may God help me. Amen" ([*Luther's Works,* ed. Jaroslav Pelikan and Helmut T. Lehmann, 55 vols. St. Louis: Concordia/Philadelphia, Fortress, 1955-86; hereafter *LW*] 32: 112-13). Later Luther was equally adamant in defending the freedom of faith against both the theological right (the pope) and left (Karlstadt and Müntzer): "I will constrain no man by force, for faith must come freely without compulsion" (*LW* 51: 77; see *LW* 45: 108). Passive resistance was not confined to Protestants but was common to all those who differed on religion with their rulers, such as Catholics in Elizabethan England.

If a ruling authority is in the wrong, Luther supported conscientious objection. "What if a prince is in the wrong? Are his people to follow him then too? Answer: No, for it is no one's duty to do wrong; we must obey God (who desires the right) rather than men [Acts 5: 29]" (*LW* 45: 125). Soon Lutheran jurists and theologians were developing constitutional and theological arguments for the resistance of lesser magistrates to the emperor's coercion of the faith of his subjects. Protestant political resistance was first defended in the Lutheran Magdeburg confession (1550-1) which in turn directly influenced French Calvinist political thought. Huguenot arguments for a constitutionalism that limited royal power and defended individual conscience were advanced by François Hotman's *Franco-Gallia* (1573), Theodore Beza's *Right of Magistrates* (1574), and Philippe du Plessis-Mornay's more radical *Vindication Against Tyrants* (1579) which authorized individual rebellion on the explicitly religious grounds that God may "raise up new liberators" outside the constitutional framework. In England, John Poynet's *A Short Treatise of Politic Power* (1556), the first break with the English conception of passive obedience, was also influenced by Luther and the Magdeburg confession (Schulze 1985: 209; Hildebrandt 1980; Höss 1963; Skinner 1980). The authority of kings became relative before God, the King of kings. Protestant arguments for resistance to tyranny continued to ferment political change in the eighteenth-century American and French revolutions. These arguments "provided significant ingredients of the constitutionalism that was such an important part of those ideologies. Traces of these sixteenth-century ideas even survive into the twentieth century. They were used in the midcentury struggle against modern totalitarianisms. They are with us still" (Kingdon 1988: 219). That Luther's theological exposition of the duty of political resistance to unjust government is not merely of historical interest is seen in its use in the Norwegian and German resistance to Nazism. In the lapidary phrase of Luther and later of Dietrich Bonhoeffer: "If the coachdriver is drunk, we have to put a spoke in the wheel" (see Duchrow 1987; 34, ch. 3; De Grouchy 1988: 124-30; Berggrav 1951: 300-19; Siemon-Netto 1995).

But the Reformation legacy to politics was not merely rooted in the defense of conscience against compulsion. Many of the doctrinal positions of the Reformation contributed to the rise of a democratic ethos. This point should not be taken anachronistically, for the Renaissance had reinforced centuries of political thought which viewed "democracy" as undisciplined and unprincipled mob rule subject to self-serving demagogues (Kingdon 1973: 187). Nevertheless, Luther's translation of the Bible and his emphasis upon universal education to facilitate reading it, a path followed by other Reformers as well, was a step toward depriving the elite of exclusive control over words as well as the Word. The doctrine of the priesthood of all the baptized proclaimed that the ordained priest or minister is distinguished from all other Christians only by office. For Luther the church is no longer a hierarchical institution but a community of believers in which "no one is for himself, but extends himself among others in love." Thus he translated *ecclesia* not as "church" (*Kirche*) but as "community" (*Gemeinde*), "congregation" (*Gemeine*), and "assembly" (*Versammlung*). And his 1523 pamphlet, *The Right and Power of a Christian Congregation or Community to Judge All Teaching and to Call, Appoint, and Dismiss Teachers, Established and Proved from Scripture,* has been viewed as "a 'whopping endorsement' of *communal* equality and autonomy" (Ozment 1985: 9). The Calvinist idea of the church as a covenanted community contributed to the idea of social contract. These antihierarchical, leveling processes were corrosive of political as well as ecclesiastical structures. In the words of William Tyndale: "As good is the prayer of a cobbler as of a cardinal, and of a butcher as of a bishop; and the blessing of a baker that knoweth the truth is as good as the blessing of our most holy father the pope" (Richardson 1994: 29). Religious egalitarianism could lead to social and political egalitarianism. Politically, the Reformers' goal was the social experience of communion. As John Knox declared: "Take from us the freedom of assemblies and [you] take from us the evangel" (Spitz 1971: 552).

As suggestive as many of these theological motifs are in relation to modern political developments, it is important to remember both that the confessional period coincided with absolutism and that particular confessions cannot be simply equated with political developments. "There is no simple correlation between a particular confession and a political form. Recent research has shown that we need to rethink traditional associations of the Counter-Reformation with the absolutist state, Lutheranism with political conformity, and Calvinism with democratic republicanism" (Hsia 1989: 53; Schilling 1986: 21).

### Culture

The Reformation touched every aspect of culture: work, economics, art, literature, and music. The doctrine of justification by grace alone through faith alone released energy for this world that had hitherto been devoted to achieving the next world. With their new ethos of vocation or calling, the Reformers undercut the medieval dualism of sacred and secular work. In the medieval world only the religious (priests, monks, nuns) had a sacred vocation or calling from God. Those who worked in the secular world were understood by all to be on a lower and less God-pleasing plane. In contrast, the Reformers emphasized that whatever a person did in the world that served the neighbor and helped build up the human community was pleasing to God. All mundane tasks from changing diapers to changing laws were imbued with religious significance, not because human works are salvatory but because God intends neighbors to be served. As Luther once explained his own ministry: "A cow does not get to heaven by giving milk, but that is what she is made for" (Bainton 1957: 299).

### The Reformations and Women

Nowhere was this understanding of vocation applied more explosively to medieval life than in the area of sex and marriage. According to Ozment (1980: 381): "No institutional change brought about by the Reformation was more visible, responsive to late medieval pleas for reform, and conducive to new social attitudes than the marriage of Protestant clergy. Nor was there another point in the Protestant program where theology and practice corresponded more successfully." The Reformers vigorously criticized the Roman church's imposition of celibacy upon priests, monks, and nuns, not only because it was viewed as a good work contributing to salvation but because men and women were thereby removed from service to the neighbor, the divine order of marriage and family was contravened, and the created goodness of sexuality was denied. To Luther and Calvin, marriage was not just the legitimation of sexual fulfillment through procreation but above all the context for creating a new awareness of human community with all its pains and joys. So Luther declared: "Marriage does not only consist of sleeping with a woman—anybody can do that—but of keeping house and bringing up children" (*LW* 54: 441). Those who followed Luther saw in marriage not only a new, joyous appreciation for sexual relations, but also a new respect for women as companions. Luther could not imagine life without women: "The home, cities, economic life, and government would virtually disappear. Men can't do without women. Even if it were possible for men to beget and bear children, they still couldn't do without women" (*LW* 54: 161). For Luther this included the intelligence, piety, and ethics of women.

On the other hand, it would take a very narrow focus indeed to overlook the medieval patriarchalism and sexism, and even misogynism, which continued to find expression in the Reformations. On this subject as well as others which jar contemporary consciousness, it is important that we are not anachronistic. "All of Europe, probably including most women, consistently esteemed women less than men, and the Reformation articulated but did not bring about a marked change in this attitude" (Karant-Nunn 1989: 40). Thus the Spanish humanist, Juan Luis Vives, was in favor of educating women so long as they remained silent. "Considering that women are, 'by nature, sick animals.' Vives concluded that 'much more important than having learned and well-spoken women is having good and honest ones.'" And, in his late sixteenth-century portrayal of the perfect wife, *La perfecta casada*, Fray Luis de León posited that "women are created as an afterthought of God, as only a helper and comfort to men, and are loaded with the constant need to atone since 'from women came the beginning of sin, and by her we all die'" (Costa 1989: 90).

Such misogynist views were not limited to Catholics. Among the Calvinists, John Knox is notorious for his "blast" against women rulers, even though his mother-in-law was instrumental in his theological development (Healey 1994; Frankfurter 1987). Calvin himself believed the government of women "utterly at variance with the legitimate order of nature, . . . to be counted among the judgments with which God visits us" (Duke et al. 1992: 40). Yet this same Calvin carried on extensive correspondence with noblewomen concerned for reform, and was open theologically if not practically to the ordination of women as pastors in the church (Douglass 1985; Thompson 1992). The most extreme misogynist treatment of women must be that of the enforced polygamy at Münster. Yet it has been suggested that along with the desire for male control, this practice was a kind of asceticism that viewed sex solely for increasing the tribe of the elect (Marr 1987: 353). The Anabaptists thus in general shared traditional Catholicism's negative valuation of human sexuality and rejected the magisterial Reformers' positive appreciation of sexual relations as the gift of God's creation. Furthermore, the Anabaptist emphasis on the purity of the church obligated wives and husbands to shun apostate spouses. "In practical terms, Anabaptist women were equal only in martyrdom" (Wiesner 1988: 153).

A frequently asked question is whether the Reformation made any difference for women. Was the Reformation a help or a hindrance to women? The answers usually revolve around the elements sketched above as well as the loss of female saints, especially those associated with childbirth, and the closing of the monastic option for women, thus narrowing their life-choices to spouse and mother. The more recent introduction of gender studies allows another approach to the issue. "Gender" broadens the subject beyond the Reformation's effects on men and women *per se* to its effect on societal determinations of what it means to be male or female. "Unlike biological sex, gender is socially constructed and varies from society to society and over time" (Wiesner 1992: 159).

One example is Luther's effort to redefine what his society thought appropriate for male and female behavior. Medieval society and theology provided considerable sanction to prostitution and civic brothels. Aquinas justified the need for prostitutes by analogy to a cesspit for a palace. They functioned to purify a town which without them would soon become corrupt. The church tolerated prostitution because its gender values denigrated sex and also assumed that male lust was an anarchic, uncontrollable force which if not provided an outlet would pollute the town's respectable women. Since the marital age rose to about twenty-two to twenty-five, so that a youth could master a trade and become able to earn a living before marriage, public brothels for the unmarried were thought to prevent the greater evils of adultery and rape.

The response of Luther and his colleagues was not moralistic but rather an attack on their culture's gender presupposition concerning males. Their point was that the cure (the brothel) is worse than the disease (male sexual desire). In his 1520 *Address to the Christian Nobility,* Luther laments the toleration of brothels. He is aware of their rationale, but "should not the government which is temporal and also Christian, realize that such evil cannot be prevented by that kind of heathenish practice?" (*LW* 44: 214-15). Luther's consistent effort to redefine the gender issue is evident in his lectures on Genesis toward the end of his life: "The example concerning the houses of ill fame which are tolerated in the large cities does not deserve to be discussed; for it is clearly in conflict with the Law of God, . . . It is silly for them to suppose that outcroppings of debauchery and adultery are reduced by this means. . . . Lust is increased rather than cured by this means, . . ." (*LW* 3: 259; Ozment 1983: 56). That these perspectives were not without some impact is indicated by events in Zwickau. Syphilis was present in the town already in 1497, but the brothel was not shut down until 1526. "Venereal disease itself did not drive them to close the brothel. The Reformation did" (Karant-Nunn 1982: 24). Luther and those who followed him attempted to redefine their culture's understanding of male gender from uncontrollable impulse to social responsibility.

## Toleration and the "Other"

Toleration was not the long suit of the Reformations. "Among the convictions of the age and of its law the belief that death by execution in its more horrible forms was a proper reward for those who denied the ultimate and basic loyalties stood firmly entrenched. . . . Of course, one may hold various views of the truth of Christ's Church on earth, and people did. But one needs to recognize that all the representatives of those various views agreed upon the need for an ultimate sanction" (Elton 1977: 206-7). There were, to be sure, the exceptions who proved the rule, such as Castellio and a few French advocates for religious freedom, as well as those Spiritualists who based ecumenism on religious experience. Sebastian Franck exemplifies the latter when he says: "I have my brothers among the Turks, Papists, Jews and all peoples. Not that they are Turks, Jews, Papists and Sectaries or will remain so; in the evening they will be called into the vineyard and given the same wage as we" (Edwards 1988: v).

Similarly, the medieval legend of the three rings related in Bocaccio's *Decameron* advocated tolerance. The legend relates how a great lord declared his heir would be known by possession of his precious ring. Before his death he had exact copies made of his ring which he gave to his three sons, each of whom believed himself the heir. In 1599, Menocchio related this story to his inquisitor with the moral that God had given his law to Christians, Turks, and Jews. Each believes it is *the* heir, but we cannot tell which one is the right one. Menocchio therefore advocated tolerance be extended also to heretics. The consequence was his execution by order of the Holy Office (Ginzburg 1982: 49-51).

Apart from exceptions such as Franck, the Turks were widely feared not only as the "other" but as the forces of Antichrist whose advance into southern and central Europe was a spiritual as well as a military threat. The irony, of course, is that the Turkish military threat to the Empire preoccupied so much of Charles V's time and resources that he was unable to proceed vigorously against the Reformation. Thus from a purely political perspective, Luther might have seen the Turks as an ally against the papacy. But Luther's primary concern was theology not politics, and therefore he saw the Turks in particular as the rod of God's wrath against a sinful Empire, and Islam in general as the enemy of God since Mohammed denies Christ is the Son of God and Savior of the world. It is of interest that Luther rejected the calls for a crusade against the Turks on the same basis that he rejected the religious sanctions for violence advocated by Müntzer: the gospel may not be advanced nor protected by force. Armed conflict against the Turk can only be waged by Christians who repent of their sin and are led by the constituted authority of the emperor (*LW* 46: 155-205). But, for Luther, the Turkish threat was primarily the religious issue of Islam's challenge to the Christian faith. Luther therefore used his influence to make possible Theodore Bibliander's 1542 translation of the Koran on the grounds that it could be refuted only if one knew it. Unlike the medieval interpreters of Islam, Raymond Lull and Nicholas of Cusa, Luther did not view Islam as a kind of "anonymous Christianity" or a Christian sect. For Luther there could be no interreligious dialogue with an "other" who did not acknowledge Jesus Christ as the Redeemer of humankind (Kandler 1993: 8). "As with the Jews, he [Luther] was concerned not about converting the Turks, whom he believed obdurate, but about informing Christians" (Brecht 1993: 354). The Reformations' view of Christian-Islamic conflict as an eschatological confrontation between God and Satan continues to have detrimental influence among some modern Protestant groups.

The most neuralgic subject of the relation of the Reformations to the "other" is the treatment of the Jews. Christian hostility to Jews was not, of course, *sui generis* in the Reformation but has a long, sordid history that extends back to the New Testament and the early church. By the eve of the Reformations the Jews were not only seen as rejected by God for denying Jesus and crucifying him, but were also blamed for the plague, accused of ritual murder of Christian youths and profanation of the eucharistic host, suspected of plots to destroy Christendom, and widely resented for economic reasons (Robinson 1992: 9-22). These myths, legends, and resentments found iconographic expression that reflected and concretized prejudice. The fourth Lateran council (1215) required Jews to wear yellow badges (tragically revived in the Nazi era) for easy identification and thereby social separation. Already in the eleventh century sculptural personifications of synagogue and church, still present in the gothic cathedrals of Europe, contrasted a divinely rejected Judaism as a blindfolded, downcast woman dropping the biblical tablets of the Law with the victorious church as a clearsighted, crowned woman, banner flying from one hand and a chalice in the other (Edwards 1988: 22; Mellinkoff 1993: 1: 48-9). The most demeaning iconography depicted the long-popular association of Jews with excrement. Thus the thirteenth-century *Judensau* image depicting Jews sucking at the teats of a sow included by the fifteenth century the additional depiction of Jews at the animal's rear eating and drinking excrement (Mellinkoff 1993: I, 108; II, pl. IV. 24).

The power of such visual images affected conduct. Jews were slaughtered thousands at a time in pogroms, and were expelled wholesale from England (1290), France (1306), Spain (1492), and Portugal (1497). "In 1555, Paul IV created the Roman ghetto and began to enforce some of the most stringent restrictions on the Jews' freedom in all of Italy and to countenance judicial atrocities against them in the papal state" (O'Malley 1993: 188). However, the antecedent for modern racial antisemitism may well be the pure blood laws instituted by the Spanish Inquisition which "maintained that degenerate Jewish blood was impervious to baptism and grace. . . . Jewishness, then, was not a statement of faith or even a series of ethnic practices but a biological consideration" (Friedman 1987: 16).

What is surprising in light of this tradition is Luther's initial departure from the medieval anti-Jewish legacy. In his 1523 tract *That Jesus Christ Was Born a Jew,* he emphasized that God has honored the Jews above all peoples and that therefore Christians should treat Jews in a brotherly manner (*LW* 45: 200-1). Furthermore, in contrast to the medieval canonical prohibition of Christian-Jewish marriage, Luther wrote:

> Just as I may eat, drink, sleep, walk, ride with, buy from, speak to, and deal with a heathen, Jew, Turk, or heretic, so I may also marry and continue in wedlock with him. Pay no attention to the precepts of those fools who forbid it. You will find plenty of Christians—and indeed the greater part of them—who are worse in their secret belief than any Jew, heathen, Turk, or heretic. A heathen is just as much a man or a woman—God's good creation—as St Paul, St Peter, and St Lucy, not to speak of a slack and spurious Christian. (*LW* 45: 25)

Thus Luther's follower, Urbanus Rhegius (1489-1541), advocated an enlightened toleration of Jews as fellow citizens (Hendrix 1990).

Tragically and shamefully, Luther by the end of his life raged against the Jews and advised destruction of their homes, synagogues, and books as well as prohibition of Jewish civil rights. In light of Nazi use of these later anti-Jewish writings it is important to emphasize that Luther as well as other evangelical and Roman Catholic writers must be seen in their historical context (Oberman 1984; Lindberg 1994; Rowan 1985: Nijenhuis 1972: 38-72), and, more importantly, that Luther's animus toward the Jews was theological not racist. "Luther identified a Jew by his religious beliefs, not by his race. (Identification of a Jew by his race is, in any case, a concept foreign to the sixteenth century). If a Jew converted to Christianity, he became a fellow brother or sister in Christ. For racial anti-Semitism religious belief is largely irrelevant" (Edwards 1983: 139). Nevertheless, "hostile statements by Renaissance and Reformation figures are very likely to seem even more terrible today, against the backcloth of Auschwitz than when they were originally delivered" (Edwards 1988: 51-2).

The Reformations encountered the "other" not only at home but also abroad. Jesuit missionaries were active in China and Japan, and initiated the first steps toward what is now called "inculturation" (Moran 1993; Witek 1988). They wore local dress and followed local customs. Francis Xavier (1506-52), an original member of the Jesuits, through his travels to India, Japan, and China became sensitized to the issues involved in introducing the Christian faith to non-western cultures. His work was advanced in the next generation by Matteo Ricci (1552-1610; Spence 1984). "In Brazil Jesuits took courageous stands against the abuses of slave raids and evoked great wonderment from the natives as word sped through the jungles that among the Portuguese there were some who defended them" (O'Malley 1993: 78). The most renowned opponent to Spanish exploitation of Native Americans is Bartolomé de Las Casas (1474-1566). This Spanish Dominican opposed and exposed both in America and in the Spanish court the atrocities of the Spanish settlers. He advanced his cause through his books *The Brief Account of the Destruction of the Indies* (1552) and *In Defense of the Indians* (ca. 1550). Sadly, Las Casas stood nearly alone in his arguments for a non-Eurocentric vision of the world and equity for all (Friede and Keen 1971; Hanke 1974).

In contrast to the sixteenth-century missionary activity of Roman Catholics, Protestant missions are usually dated from the seventeenth-century evangelization of Native Americans by the Puritans. There was, however, a short-lived Genevan mission to Brazil in the mid-sixteenth century that apparently had Calvin's support. And the Swedish Lutheran pastor Johan Campanius ministered to the Delaware Indians from 1643 to 1648. His translation of Luther's Small Catechism into Lenni-Lenape "is the first attempt by a European to reduce a North American Indian language to writing" (Skarsten 1988: 59).

### Economics, Education, and Science

Perhaps the point where the Reformer's proclamation of vocation has received the most attention in the modern world is where religion and economics intersect. Since the publication of Max Weber's *The Protestant Ethic and the Spirit of Capitalism* it has been popular to associate capitalism with Calvinism. The so-called "Weber thesis" is that Calvinist theology so stressed predestination that anxious believers began to seek signs of their divine election in worldly success such as business. In response to this popular conception of Weber's contribution to theories of modernization (see Schilling 1992: 240, 305, 356-7; Green 1959; Eisenstadt 1968), it should be noted that the profit economy or early forms of capitalism clearly antedated the Reformation, and that Calvin did not associate material success with the individual's standing before God. Calvin's understanding of predestination and providence was not individualistic but communal and world-historical. The doctrine of predestination is an affirmation that despite evil and suffering the ultimate destiny of the world and history rests in the good and infallible hands of God.

Because Calvin's theology was communal not individualistic, he could perceive riches as a divine blessing not in terms of endorsement of the individual's standing before God but rather as God's blessing to be shared with the whole community. Conversely, poverty is an expression of the wrath of God not toward the individual but toward the whole community for sin and thus to be borne by the whole community in support of the poor. The "blame the victim/praise the achiever" ideology of modern times is a secularized and individualized kind of covenant theology which associates worldly failure or success with moral virtue. The biblical answer to this form of "Deuteronomic history" which attributes failure and poverty to intrinsic character flaws and success to moral achievement is the Book of Job. Job is the idealized picture of the person who fulfills the covenant with God, yet nevertheless suffers terribly. His friends, convinced that goodness brings rewards and sin incurs punishments, can only tell him he must have sinned. With friends like that, who needs enemies! The Reformation answer of Luther and Calvin is to recall that God himself suffered, and hence Christians also should not expect that faith promises a rose garden. Already in 1518 at the Heidelberg disputation Luther had asserted that faith and worldly success were not equivalent, and attacked all claims to the contrary as "theologies of glory."

In the realm of economics Luther and Calvin vigorously attacked capitalism as unrestrained greed and called for government control of capitalism. On the other hand, Luther, Zwingli, and Calvin all contributed to the development of modern social welfare. Urban and state welfare programs were instituted sensitive to structural causes of un- and underemployment, and to the necessity for job training and civic responsibility for preventing as well as alleviating poverty.

The Reformation doctrines of justification and vocation also had an impact upon the development of education and the sciences. Building upon the contributions of the humanists, the Reformers stressed education as the resource for preparing persons for service to the whole community. As mentioned earlier, the Reformers liberated the Word and therefore also words from captivity to the elite. If there is to be a priesthood of all believers, then all—including women—should be able to read. It may be that literacy enhanced the self-esteem of women, but that consequence was also perceived as dangerous to the male status quo. Thus Henry VIII attempted—unsuccessfully—to prohibit the Bible to women. It was not accidental that universal literacy was first achieved in Scotland and the Protestant areas of Germany. As Melanchthon declared, "the ultimate end which confronts us is not private virtue alone but the interest of the public weal." And by 1560

Knox and his colleagues had drawn up a vision for a national system of education in Scotland.

But it may be argued that Luther's greatest contribution was not just his tracts on such practical subjects as that towns should establish schools and public libraries and that parents should make sure that their children go to school, but rather his initiation of a new way of thinking. In our time it has become fashionable to call a major change in thinking a "paradigm shift." Luther's thorough rejection of Aristotle and classical "authorities" is no less than a paradigm shift from medieval epistemology based on deduction from textual authorities to an epistemology of induction and experience. Physics was liberated from metaphysics. In his theological context, Luther stated: "It is not by understanding, reading, or speculation that one becomes a theologian, but through living, dying, and being damned" ([*D. Martin Luthers Werke: Kritische Gesamtausgabe,* ed. J. K. F. Knaake, G. Kawerau, et al., 58 vols. Weimar: Böhlau, 1883—; hereafter *WA*] 5: 163). Less dramatically, he also said: "None of the arts can be learned without practice. What kind of physician would that be who stayed in school all the time? When he finally puts his medicine to use and deals more and more with nature, he will come to see that he hasn't as yet mastered the art" (*LW* 54: 50-1). This shift from deduction to induction was recognized by contemporaries who called the maverick physician Paracelsus (1493-1541) "the Luther of the physicians." The point was that Paracelsus shared Luther's view of authority. Similarly, the English thinker Francis Bacon (1561-1626) compared Aristotle to Antichrist and indicted Greek philosophers for conjuring scientific knowledge out of their heads instead of seeking it in nature. The suspicion of metaphysics led to the foundation of modern rationalism in the work of René Descartes (1596-1650) with evidence and mathematics as the keys to interpreting the world in terms of mechanical regularity.

Institutionally Luther and Melanchthon were instrumental in the development of the medical faculty at the University of Wittenberg. On the personal side, Luther's son, Paul, became a respected physician. And Melanchthon's son-in-law Casper Peucer (1525-1602) was a physician as well as a theologian. By the seventeenth century, the University of Wittenberg had a renowned medical faculty. The turn away from the old authorities was evident in the important contributions of Salomon Alberti (1540-1600) in anatomical studies and the contributions of other colleagues to botany.

Ironically, the theological controversies after the death of Luther also contributed to the development of science. For example, Johann Kepler (1571-1630) was not accepted for ordained ministry because his theology of the Lord's Supper was not regarded as orthodox. He then became an assistant to the Danish Lutheran astronomer Tycho Brahe (1546-1601). In spite of his disappointment over rejection for the ministry, Kepler wrote in his first publication, "I wanted to become a theologian. For a long time I was restless. Now, however, observe how through my efforts, God is being celebrated in astronomy." Kepler went on to influence Newton and contribute to the triumph of the Copernican over the Ptolemaic theory of planetary motion.

Similarly, the Royal Society of London focused on scientific studies because they were free from both dogmatism and skepticism. Yet Kepler spoke for many of his scientific colleagues when he described scientists as "thinking God's thoughts after him." By and large these were religious men zealous to discover and admire the works of God in nature.

### Literature and the Arts

From the beginning of the Reformation, historiography played an important role. Luther used history to argue that the papacy of his day was an aberration from the early church, martyrologists such as John Foxe used history selectively to present their case for the truth and witness of Protestantism, and the dissidents argued that the entire church had fallen when it became the establishment under Constantine in the fourth century. The first comprehensive history of the church arose in this context. In 13 volumes the "Magdeburg Centuries" under the general editorship of the Lutheran theologian Matthew Flacius (1520-75) covered the first 13 centuries of the church from the viewpoint that the pope was the Antichrist whose empire of the Roman Church had constantly opposed the work of God. The Catholic response was the equally biased *Ecclesiastial Annals* by Caesar Baronius (1538-1607), which appeared in numerous volumes between 1588 and 1607. Although these histories were designed to make history serve their respective theologies, they did stimulate the development of historical criticism.

National literatures were influenced by their respective great Reformers. There are too many major contributions to even list them here, other than to mention the Elizabethan dramatist William Shakespeare (1564-1616), whose literary brilliance and insight into human life remains unequaled. Behind much of the literary outpouring stimulated by the Reformations was the vernacular Bible. It "worked as a midwife to bring forth a whole great literature. It enabled a tinker of Bedford to write *The Pilgrim's Progress.* In an age when Milton could believe that God had chosen his Englishmen to perform his special tasks, it was the Bible which nerved the arm of Oliver Cromwell and fortified the spirit of the pioneers in New England" (Dickens 1991: 157). Vernacular Bibles were also significant in the norming of languages. The Luther Bible continues to be published in Germany, and the King James Bible (1611) commissioned by James I at the Hampton Court conference in 1604 has influenced English language and expressions up to today.

In art and music the sacramentally oriented Reformations stimulated compositions that continue to enrich modern life. All the Protestant Reformers worked to make the liturgy accessible to the people, but not all complemented the liturgy with art and music as glorious gifts of God. Luther's anti-iconoclastic theology is evident in his appreciation of art and its contribution to faith and politics (Hofmann 1983; Zapalac 1990). Luther also put music in service of the gospel through an extensive hymnody which intended involvement of the whole congregation. He frequently affirmed that "next to the Word of God, music deserves the highest praise" (*LW* 53: 323). By the end of the century some 4,000 Protestant hymns had been written. Many of Luther's hymns continue to be well known and sung today, especially "A Mighty Fortress Is Our God," and the chorales which informed later works by Bach. Indeed, by the time of Buxtehude and Bach the Lutheran tradition of musical worship "had blossomed into a rich musical, liturgical, and spiritual experience, with a wide range of congregational, choral, vocal, organ, and instrumental music" (Leaver 1990: 157; [*Theologische Realenzyklopädie,* ed. G. Krause and G. Muller, Berlin/New York: de Gruyter, 1976-; hereafter *TRE*] 18: 602-29). That Bach's own musical work was rooted in Luther's theology and the Lutheran liturgy is evident not only from his annotations in his two sets of Luther's collected works but also in his use of Lutheran motifs. The well-known Reformation themes of justification by faith alone, law and gospel, and the theology of the cross echo through Bach's works in both music and words (Chafe 1985, Lee 1985).

This was not the case in the Zwinglian and Calvinist Reformations. In Zurich Zwingli, assuming that music distracted from worship and that worship should be a purified service of the Word alone, banned all forms of chant, and in 1524 closed all the organs (Garside 1966: 44). Bern followed suit. We have already seen the contributions of Clement Marot and Calvin himself to the development of psalmody and the Huguenot Psalter. But organ and instrumental music was also prohibited in the Genevan churches. In this the Swiss Reformed were consistent with their iconoclastic orientation toward art in general. In contrast to the Lutheran and Catholic sacramental conviction that the finite is capable of the infinite, the Reformed effort to eliminate all forms of idolatry was informed by a sacramental theology that denied the "real presence," and therefore strictly limited art to the secular realm (Irwin 1993: 28). As Karlstadt had argued for the abolition of images, so Calvin too asserted the validity of the Old Testament prohibition of images. The use of images always leads to idolatry. "Therefore it remains that only those things are to be sculptured or painted which the eyes are capable of seeing: let not God's majesty, which is far above the perception of the eyes, be debased through unseemly representations" (McNeill and Battles 1960: I, 112). The Genevan churches were to be completely free of images. Iconoclasm reflected both the earlier humanist critique of the externalization of religion and a religion and a rejection of the medieval desire for visualization, "the gaze that saves," which had led to adoration of relies and the host rather than participation in the Lord's Supper. There was also the ethical motive that it is better to support the poor than to decorate the church. Erasmus wrote: "How many dedicate candles to the Virgin and Mother of God, even in mid-day when it serves no purpose? How few dedicate themselves equally to a life of chastity, modesty, and love to spiritual things?" (Hofmann 1983: 8; Wandel 1995). The Calvinist emphasis that true decoration of the church consists in the moderation, piety, and virtues of reformed lives rather than costly materials had the effect of "moralizing beauty" (*TRE* 20: 282). It is claimed that the Reformation "decisively advanced the secularization of Western art: theoretically by its desacralization, and practically by reduction of its churchly function" (*TRE* 20: 284).

The council of Trent also expressed concern about idolatrous misuse of art, and sought to reduce "lasciviousness" in art. The most notorious case of this concern for decorum was the painting over of nudity in Michelangelo's great "Judgment of the World." Nevertheless, Roman Catholicism retained the conviction that images may move the heart to recall the preached Word of God.

### Back to the Future: The Reformations and Modernity

The relationship of the Reformations to modernity has been a controversial subject for some time, and raises numerous questions concerning interpretations of both periods. Historians critical of the past hegemony of intellectual and theological interpretations reject simple claims of Reformation patrimony of the modern age. The Reformation is to be understood for its own sake and not (mis-)used for contemporary historical and religious speculation. This is an important warning against "Whiggish" interpretations of the Reformation which view it as the initiation of inevitable progress toward the triumph of truth. "The Reformation remains, in the first instance, the Reformation, and its relationship to modern times is misleading. Historians have a need for modesty" (Nipperdey 1987: 539).

Yet it needs to be said that if historical study includes the purpose of freeing us "from the dead hand of history," then our study of the past entails more than antiquarianism. "When we have finished bewailing the greed, folly and fanaticism of the sixteenth century, the Reformation still stands in mountainous bulk across the landscapes of western Christianity. It concerned significant issues which still live to perplex and divide us" (Dickens 1991: 394-5). There is among historians an increasing willingness to affirm that the Reformation was a turning point with great significance for universal history beyond its religious concerns. This significance has been described in terms of desacralization and deritualization which in the critique of institutions and hierarchies provided space for individual self-determination, the internalization of discipline, and "the civilizing process" (Hsia 1989: 183; Rublack 1993; Blaschke 1993: 511). The prophetic critique of all efforts to ascribe ultimacy to the penultimate was not a force for the past but rather set free intellectual, social, and political impulses toward modernization (Schilling 1992: ch. 7) which brought forth new forms of thought and political-social life. To borrow a concept from modern medicine, the religious, political, and social forces interplayed together like a syndrome to create the specific effects of their interrelationship (Schilling 1988: 86).

Luther certainly did not set out to modernize society, to initiate the modern period, nor even to set off a social revolution. The modern period was already underway when Luther was engaged with his religious struggle to find a merciful God. But it was Luther's religious discovery that righteousness before God is received not achieved which cleared away the obstacles which had till then still prevented the complete breakthrough of the modern world (Blaschke 1993: 520).

This suggests, if I may be allowed some antics with semantics, the relevance of irrelevance. Unlike his contemporaries concerned with fine-tuning the engines of their society so that it would run better, Luther and his fellow-Reformers came to the conclusion that the issue was not running better but running in the right direction. This conclusion was derived from their study of the sources of their society rather than its goals and achievements. We are obviously far removed from the sixteenth century, but also remarkably close to some of the same issues. We too live in a culture rooted in a piety of achievement no less debilitating for all that it is secular instead of religious. The modern concern for the salvation of the economy is no less consuming than the medieval concern for the economy of salvation: and contemporary cathedrals of capitalism and other ideologies require no fewer "good works" than those of the Middle Ages. Study of the distant world of the Reformations thus provides that horizon which offers a perspective on the present. "It questions the self-assurance of our modern existence. For just because it is remote does not mean that it is necessarily totally outdated" (Nipperdey 1987: 535).

Of course the Reformation era was not a golden age; those who hanker for the good old days often are not fully aware of what life then entailed. Yet forgetfulness of the past contributes to incomprehension of the present. Two brief examples may suffice here. Modern Westerners cannot seem to grasp that anything beyond economics and politics could motivate contemporary acts of terrorism or the internal and international policies of other cultures. We have forgotten that our own forefathers quite willingly killed and accepted death on the basis of religious commitments. We ignore religious dynamics at our own peril. Within our own culture we have elevated individual rights to the point of privatism and the erosion of the common good of the whole community. Thus we think of discipline such as that exercised by the Geneva Consistory as punitive social control. At the same time we wonder about the alienation and the breakdown of social relations in our large cities which stems from anomie. We have forgotten that communities where an eye was kept on everyone else's business had the constructive goal of serving and caring for the whole community (see Kingdon 1993b: 679; 1994: 34).

Awareness of the Reformations' contributions to the development of our world both helps us understand how we got this way and provides a critical horizon for evaluation of the results.

*Works Cited*

. . .Bainton 1957: Roland Bainton, *Here I Stand: A Life of Martin Luther.* New York: Mentor. . . .

Berggrav 1951: Eivand Berggrav, *Man and State.* Philadelphia: Muhlenberg. . . .

Blaschke 1993: Karlheinz Blaschke, "Reformation und Modernisierung," in Hans R. Guggisberg and Gottfried Krodel, eds, *Die Reformation in Deutschland and Europa: Interpretationen and Debatten,* 511-20. Gütersloh: Gütersloher Verlagshaus. . . .

Brecht 1993: Martin Brecht, *Martin Luther,* III: *The Preservation of the Church 1532-1546.* Minneapolis: Fortress. . . .

Chafe 1985: Eric T. Chafe, "Luther's Analogy of Faith in Bach's Church Music," *Dialogue* 24, 96-101. . . .

Costa 1989: Milagros Ortega Costa, "Spanish Women in the Reformation," in Marshall 1989, 89-119. . . .

De Grouchy 1988: John De Grouchy, ed., *Dietrich Bonhoeffer: Witness to Jesus Christ.* San Francisco: Collins. . . .

Dickens 1991: A. G. Dickens, *The English Reformation,* 2nd edn. University Park: University of Pennsylvania Press. . . .

Douglass 1985: Jane Dempsey Douglas, *Women, Freedom, and Calvin.* Philadelphia: Westminster. . . .

Duchrow 1987: Ulrich Duchrow, *Global Economy: A Confessional Issue for the Churches?* Geneva: World Council of Churches. . . .

Duke et al. 1992: Alastair Duke, G. Lewis, and A. Pettegree, eds and trs, *Calvinism in Europe 1540-1610: A Collection of Documents.* Manchester: Manchester University Press. . . .

Edwards 1988: John Edwards, *The Jews in Christian Europe 1400-1700.* London: Routledge. . . .

Edwards 1983: Mark U. Edwards, Jr, *Luther's Last Battles: Politics and Polemics 1531-46.* Ithaca: Cornell University Press. . . .

Eisenstadt 1968: S. N. Eisenstadt, ed., *The Protestant Ethic and Modernization: A Comparative View.* New York: Basic. . . .

Elton 1977: Geoffrey R. Elton, "Thomas Cromwell Redivivus," *ARG* 68, 192-208. . . .

Frankfurter 1987: A Daniel Frankfurter, "Elizabeth Bowes and John Knox: A Woman and Reformation Theology," [*Church History* (hereafter *CH*)] 56, 333-47.

Friede and Keen 1971: Juan Friede and Benjamin Keen, eds, *Bartolemé de Las Casas in History: Towards an Understanding of the Man and His Work.* Dekalb: Northern Illinois University Press.

Friedman 1987: Jerome Friedman. "Jewish Conversion, the Spanish Pure Blood Laws and Reformation: A Revisionist View of Racial and Religious Antisemitism," [*Sixteenth Century Journal* (hereafter *SCJ*)] 18, 3-30. . . .

Garside 1966: Charles Garside, *Zwingli and the Arts.* New Haven: Yale University Press. . . .

Ginzburg 1982: Carlo Ginzburg, *The Cheese and the Worms: The Cosmos of a Sixteenth-Century Miller.* New York: Penguin. . . .

Green 1959: Robert W. Green, ed., *Protestantism and Capitalism: The Weber Thesis and its Critics.* Lexington: D. C. Heath. . . .

Guggisberg and Krodel 1993: Hans R. Guggisberg and Gottfried Krodel, eds, *The Reformation in Germany and Europe: Interpretations and Issues.* ([Archive for Reformation History / *Archiv für Reformationsgeschichte* (hereafter *ARG*)] special volume). Gütersloh: Gütersloher Verlagshaus. . . .

Hanke 1974: Lewis Hanke, *All Mankind is One: A Study of the Disputation between Bartolemé de Las Casas and Juan Ginés de Sepúlveda in 1550 on the Intellectual and Religious Capacity of the American Indians.* Dekalb: Northern Illinois University Press. . . .

Healey 1994: Robert M. Healey, "Waiting for Deborah: John Knox and Four Ruling Queens," *SCJ* 25, 371-86. . . .

Hendrix 1990: Scott Hendrix, "Toleration of the Jews in the German Reformation: Urbanus Rhegius and Braunschweig (1535-1540)," *ARG* 81, 189-215. . . .

Hildebrandt 1980: Esther Hildebrandt, "The Magdeburg Bekenntnis on a Possible Link between German and English Resistance Theory in the Sixteenth Century," *ARG* 71, 227-53. . . .

Hinson 1976: Edward Hinson, ed., *Introduction to Puritan Theology: A Reader.* Grand Rapids: Baker Book House.

Hofmann 1983: Werner Hofmann, ed., *Luther and die Folgen für die Kunst.* Munich: Prestel-Verlag. . . .

Höss 1963: Irmagard Höss, "Zur Genesis der Widerstandslehre Bezas," *ARG* 54, 198-214. . . .

Hsia 1988: R. Po Chia Hsia, ed., *The German People and the Reformation.* Ithaca: Cornell University Press.

Hsia 1989: R. Po-Chia Hsia. *Social Discipline in the Reformation: Central Europe 1550 1750.* London: Routledge. . . .

Irwin 1993: Joyee L. Irwin, *Neither Voice nor Heart Alone: German Lutheran Theology of Music in the Age of the Baroque.* New York: Peter Lang. . . .

Kandler 1993: Karl-Hermann Kandler. "Luther and der Koran," *Luther* 64, 3-9.

Karant-Nunn 1982: Susan Karant-Nunn, "Continuity and Change: Some Aspects of the Reformation on the Women of Zwickau," *SCJ* 13, 17-42.

Karant-Nunn 1989: Susan Karant-Nunn, "The Women of the Saxon Silver Mines," in Marshall 1989, 29-46. . . .

Kingdon 1973: Robert M. Kingdon, "Calvinism and Democracy," in John H. Bratt, ed., *The Heritage of John Calvin,* 172-92. Grand Rapids: Eerdmans. . . .

Kingdon 1988: Robert M. Kingdon, *Myths about the St Bartholomew's Day Massacres, 1572-1576.* Cambridge, MA: Harvard University Press. . . .

Kingdon 1993b: Robert M. Kingdon, "Calvinist Discipline in the Old World and the New," in Guggisberg and Krodel, 1993, 665-79.

Kouri and Scott 1987: E. I. Kouri and Tom Scott, eds, *Politics and Society in Reformation Europe: Essays for Sir Geoffrey Elton on his Sixty-Fifty Birthday.* New York: St Martin's. . . .

Leaver 1990: Robin Leaver, "Lutheran Vespers as a Context for Music," in Paul Walker, ed., *Church, Stage, and Studio: Music and Its Contexts in Seventeenth-Century Germany,* 143-61. Ann Arbor: UMI Research Press.

Lee 1985: Robert E. A. Lee, "Bach's Living Music of Death," *Dialogue* 24, 102-6. . . .

Lindberg 1994: Carter Lindberg, "Tainted Greatness: Luther's Attitudes toward Judaism and their Historical Reception," in Nancy Harrowitz, ed., *Tainted Greatness: Antisemitism and Cultural Heroes,* 15-35. Philadelphia: Temple University Press. . . .

McNeil and Battles 1960: John T. McNeill, ed., and Ford Lewis Battles, tr., *Calvin: Institutes of the Christian Religion,* Library of Christian Classics, XX-XXI. Philadelphia: Westminster. . . .

Marr 1987: M. Lucille Marr, "Anabaptist Women of the North: Peers in Faith, Subordinates in Marriage," [*Mennonite Quarterly Review* (hereafter *MQR*)] 61, 347-62.

Marshall 1989: Sherrin Marshall, ed., *Women in Reformation and Counter-Reformation Europe: Public and Private Worlds.* Bloomington: Indiana University Press. . . .

Mellinkoff 1993: Ruth Mellinkoff, *Sings of Otherness in Northern European Art,* 2 vols. Berkeley: University of California Press.

Moran 1993: J. E. Moran, *The Japanese and the Jesuits: Alesandro Valignano in Sixteenth-Century Japan.* London: Routledge.

Muller 1978: Richard A. Muller, "Perkins' *A Gelden Chaine:* Predestinarian System or Schematized Ordo Salutis?," *SCJ* 9, 69-81. . . .

Nijenhuis 1972: W. Nijenhuis, *Ecclesia Reformata: Studies on the Reformation.* Leiden: E. J. Brill.

Nipperdey 1987: Thomas Nipperdey, "The Reformation and the Modern World." in Kouri and Scott 1987, 535-52. . . .

Oberman 1984: Heiko A. Oberman, *The Roots of Anti-Semitism in the Age of the Renaissance and Reformation.* Philadelphia: Fortress.

O'Malley 1988: John W. O'Malley, SJ, ed., *Catholicism in Early Modern History: A Guide to Research.* St Louis: Center for Reformation Research. . . .

O'Malley 1993: John W. O'Malley SJ, *The First Jesuits.* Cambridge, MA: Harvard University Press. . . .

Ozment 1980: Steven Ozment, *The Age of Reform 1250-1550.* New Haven: Yale University Press. . . .

Ozment 1983: Steven Ozment, *When Fathers Ruled: Family Life in Reformation Europe* Cambridge, MA: Harvard University Press.

Ozment 1985: Steven Ozment, "Luther's Political Legacy," in James F. Harris, ed., *German-American Interrelations: Heritage and Challenge,* 7-40. Tübingen: Tübingen University Press. . . .

Richardson 1994: Anne Richardson, "William Tyndale and the Bill of Rights," in John A. R. Dick and Anne Richardson, eds, *William Tyndale and the Law,* 11-29. Kirksville: Sixteenth Century Journal Publishers. . . .

Robinson 1992: John Hughes Robinson, *John Calvin and the Jews.* New York: Peter Lang. . . .

Rowan 1985: Steven Rowan, "Luther, Bucer and Eck on the Jews," *SCJ* 16, 75-90. . . .

Rublack 1993: Hans-Christoph Rublack, "Reformation and Moderne: Soziologische, theologische and historische Ansiehten," in Guggisberg and Krodel 1993, 17-38. . . .

Schilling 1986: Heinz Schilling, "The Reformation and the Rise of the Early Modern State," in Tracy 1986, 21-30.

Schilling 1988: Heinz Schilling, *Aufbruch and Krise: Deutschland 1517-1648.* Berlin: Siedler. . . .

Schilling 1992: Heinz Schilling, *Religion, Political Culture and the Emergence of Early Modern Society: Essays in German and Dutch History.* Leiden: E. J. Brill. . . .

Schultze 1985: Winfried Schultze, "Zwingli, Lutherisches Widerstandsdenken, monomachischer Widerstand," in Peter Blickle, Andreas Lindt and Alfred Schindler, eds, *Zwingli und Europe,* 199-216. Zurich: Vandenhoeck & Ruprecht. . . .

Siemon-Netto 1995: Uwe Siemon-Netto, *The Fabricated Luther: The Rise and Fall of the Shirer Myth.* St Louis: Concordia.

Skarsten 1988: Trygve Skarsten, "John Campanius, Pastor in New Sweden," [*Lutheran Quarterly* (hereafter *LQ*)] 2, 47-87.

Skinner 1980: Quentin Skinner, "The Origins of the Calvinist Theory of Revolution," in Barbara C. Malament, ed., *After the Reformation: Essays in Honor of J. H. Hexter,* 309-30. University Park: University of Pennsylvania Press. . . .

Spitz 1971: Lewis W. Spitz, *The Renaissance and Reformation Movements.* Chicago: Rand McNally. . .

Thompson 1992: John Lee Thompson, *John Calvin and the Daughters of Sarah: Women in Regular and Exceptional Roles in the Exegesis of Calvin, His Predecessors, and His Contemporaries.* Geneva: Droz.

Tracy 1986: James D. Tracy, ed., *Luther and the Modern State in Germany.* Kirksville: Sixteenth Century Journal Publishers. . . .

Wandel 1995: Lee Palmer Wandel, *Voracious Idols and Violent Hands: Iconoclasm in Reformation Zurich, Strasbourg, and Basel.* Cambridge: Cambridge University Press. . . .

Wiesner 1988: Merry Wiesner, "Women's Response to the Reformation," in Hsia 1988, 148-171. . . .

Witek 1988: John W. Witek, SJ, "From India to Japan: European Missionary Expansion, 1500-1650," in O'Malley 1988, 193-210. . . .
Zapalac 1990: Kristin E. S. Zapalac, *"In His Image and Likeness": Political Iconography and Religious Change in Regensburg, 1500-1600.* Ithaca: Cornell University Press. . . .

---

## HUMANISM AND SCHOLASTICISM

### Lewis W. Spitz (essay date 1974)

SOURCE: "Humanism and the Reformation," in *Transition and Revolution: Problems and Issues of European Renaissance and Reformation History,* edited by Robert M. Kingdon, Burgess Publishing Company, 1974, pp. 153-67.

[*In the following essay, Spitz examines the historical link between humanism, a cultural movement that flourished in the Renaissance, and the Protestant Reformation.*]

The intense scholarly debate over historical periodization and the concept of the Renaissance, the "most intractable child of historiography," has resulted in a better understanding of the true nature of the Renaissance and of its relation to the Middle Ages which preceded it. The relation of the Renaissance to the age of the Reformation which followed it, however, has received less careful scrutiny and is less well understood than the importance of the question warrants.

The discussion of this problem has progressed very little beyond the level of the classic exchange between the great German scholars Wilhelm Dilthey and Ernst Troeltsch in the early decades of the twentieth century. Dilthey, the intellectual historian, held the Renaissance and the Reformation to be cultural and religious expressions respectively of a generally progressive and forward looking development in western civilization. They were the twin sources and common cradle of modernity. Troeltsch, the sociologist of religion, on the other hand, held that while the Renaissance was generically related to the Enlightenment and modern tendencies, the Reformation constituted a revival of otherworldly religiosity and was bound by interior lines to the medieval world view, a throwback in that respect to the earlier centuries. The Reformation proved to be the stronger movement, for it was rooted in deep veins of popular religious belief and was institutionally formative and sociologically more productive than was the aristocratic and elitist Renaissance. The Renaissance, according to Troeltsch, went underground and emerged again in the eighteenth century Enlightenment. Troeltsch, however, at least conceded that the Reformation, in both its Protestant and Catholic expressions, was not entirely negative in its effect upon Renaissance culture or destructive of humanist values. For humanist culture was absorbed by the upper classes and was gradually diffused throughout society during the course of the sixteenth century. The nature of this humanist culture requires closer examination if we are to achieve clarity as to the relation of humanism and the Reformation.

The term "humanism" has been used by the historians to describe various intellectual phenomena in modern times. A German pedagogue, F. J. Niethammer, first used the word in 1808 for a philosophy of education which emphasized the importance of the Greek and Roman classics in the school curriculum. The term was also used in the early nineteenth century for the program of Wilhelm von Humboldt and other idealists, who made reason and experience the sole criteria of truth. This variety of humanism was loosely associated with the humanitarian and rationalistic values of the Enlightenment. In the twentieth century humanism has often been militantly anthropocentric or man-centered, and sometimes anti-religious or even atheistic, assuming many different forms such as existential humanism, communist "progressive" humanism, or merely gentle humanitarianism. The historian must clear his mind of these modern connotations in order to grasp the phenomenon in its Renaissance and Reformation context.

It is impossible for the historian to reduce to a simple definition or formula such a protean phenomenon as

Renaissance humanism, for it included a great diversity of emphases and underwent constant change throughout a span of more than three centuries. The noted scholar Paul Joachimsen proposed a simple and fairly concrete definition of humanism as "an intellectual movement, primarily literary and philological, which was rooted in the love and desire for the rebirth of classical antiquity." Humanism was not mere antiquarianism, an interest in classical culture for its own sake. Rather, it was a special way of looking at antiquity and of relating it to the present. Classical culture not only provided the humanists with certain forms for artistic and literary expression, but also with new norms for judging and directing thought and action. The humanist believed that the liberal arts, the *humaniora,* were the studies best designed to perfect and to ornament man. They embraced especially grammar, rhetoric, poetry, history, and moral philosophy. They all held rhetoric in high regard and frequently cited Cicero's definition from his *On Oratory:* "For eloquence is nothing else than wisdom speaking copiously." Wisdom must be applied to life in the most direct and effective way. Wisdom must be so brought home to the hearer that he is both intellectually convinced and emotionally moved to action. The humanists thought of the power of speech as a singular characteristic of man and had great faith in the power of the spoken and written word. Professionally the humanists were teachers of the *ars dictaminis,* the epistolary techniques and skills useful for a city secretary, a chancellor, or church official, and as such they stood in the medieval tradition of the *dictatores.* But they stressed rhetoric and classicism more intensely and the pursuit of eloquence was engaged in by many humanists of other stations in life who were neither teachers nor city secretaries.

In a way there could be a genuine rebirth or Renaissance in all aspects of culture including art only in the Italian homeland. Italy gave birth to the foremost humanists of the Renaissance, to the literary humanists Petrarch, Boccaccio, Poggio, and Filelfo, the civic humanists Salutati and Bruni, the great educators Vergerio, Vittorino da Feltre, Guarino da Verona, philosophers such as Pico, Ficino, and Pomponazzi, and one of the keenest critical minds of all times, Lorenzo Valla. In northern and western Europe, which had once been outlying provinces of the Roman empire or had even lain beyond its frontiers, there developed not so much a genuine rebirth of classical culture during the fourteenth and fifteenth centuries as a gradual development of a humanist literary culture and some artistic adaptation to Italian Renaissance style. One can more appropriately speak of northern humanism than of a northern Renaissance.

During the fifteenth and the sixteenth centuries there was an accelerated two-way traffic of men and ideas between Italy and the North. Italian humanists travelled beyond the Alps as ecclesiastical legates, diplomatic emissaries, or business representatives and served northern bishops, princes, and cities as secretaries. Northerners, in turn, increasingly sojourned in Italy as students of law, medicine, and the liberal arts. As urban culture developed in the wooded North, the atmosphere became less feudal and Gothic, more congenial for the development of a humanist culture. Princes and courts, prince-bishops, and city councils began to emulate Italian practices. The orators and philosopher-poets *(vates)* promoted the liberal arts *(studia humanitatis)* in the universities, competing with the scholastic dialecticians for endowed chairs. As humanist culture began to take hold, enthusiasm for classical culture mounted until humanism developed as a major cultural force in the northern lands.

In each of the major countries in the North one can distinguish three generations of humanists, showing how this intellectual movement began, developed, and finally encountered the Reformation. A pioneering generation expended much of its energy in acquiring the classical languages and wrestling with the normative religious and cultural issues raised by the new learning. A second generation achieved a high degree of mastery of the classics and produced original creations of their own. A third and younger generation set out to put their new learning and ideals into action in order to reform the ills in the church and society which their predecessors had merely criticized. In England such pioneers in classical studies as Grocyn and Linacre were overshadowed by the great humanists Thomas More, John Colet, and Erasmus. They were in turn superseded by such young activists as Thomas Starkey and Richard Morison, expeditors of Tudor statecraft, the latter strongly influenced theologically by Luther, or John Tyndale, Richard Mulcaster, Roger Ascham and others, who led the way in theological and educational reform. In France such early leaders as Fichet, Standonck, and Gaguin were dwarfed by intellectual giants such as Guillaume Budé and Lefèvre d'Etaples. Then young humanists such as Nicholas Cop, Olivetan, and John Calvin were caught up in the evangelical cause and played a key role in the Reformation.

Humanism came earlier to the Germanies because of their geographical proximity to Italy and the many ecclesiastical, political, and educational contacts with Italy, also thanks to an extended period of peace during the many decades while France and England were embroiled in the Hundred Years War. By the mid-fifteenth century some half-scholastic humanists and "migratory poets" had appeared on the scene as harbingers of a new spring. The real "father of German humanism," however, Rudolph Agricola, flourished in the second half of the century as the "Petrarch of the North." He was followed during the last decade of that century and the first two decades of the sixteenth century by such prominent humanists as Celtis, the arch-humanist, Pirckheimer, Wimpheling, Peutinger,

Reuchlin, Mutian, and the ubiquitous Erasmus. The younger or third generation of humanists, Ulrich von Hutten, Eobanus Hessus, Philip Melanchthon, impatient for changes, with Luther made the Reformation. Without the humanists there would have been no Reformation, at least not the kind of Reformation that actually occurred.

Most of the prominent leaders in the Reformation movement passed through a humanist phase into the evangelical reform. Melanchthon, Oecolampadius, Bucer, and Vadian were such humanist-reformers. A larger number of the left-wing or radical reformers, too, had a more respectable humanist education than was formerly fully appreciated, for example, Balthasar Hubmaier, the anabaptist, Sebastian Franck, the spiritualist, Servetus, or Castellio, the evangelical rationalists. A whole army of less well-known younger men were Christian humanists in their formative years and became local leaders in the Reformation movement. Hubmaier once observed that nearly all the learned were Lutherans.

During the course of the decade following the year 1510 a subtle change took place in the world of humanism. The younger humanists were seeking ways of applying their philosophy to life and of effecting the changes necessary for realizing their ethical ideals. In the key cities of the Empire humanist sodalities reinforced their common interest in change. When in 1517 Luther electrified the German nation with his Ninety-Five Theses, the humanist sodalities became the chief agents for their publication and distribution within a fortnight throughout the land. By 1520 Luther was the most widely read author in Germany, rating in popularity even ahead of the militant young humanist Ulrich von Hutten. Without the comprehensive and nearly universal support of the humanists, Luther's reform may well not have succeeded at all. At the outset most of the older humanists, including Erasmus, wished him well. They believed that Luther (or Eleutherius, the free man or liberator, as he styled himself) was one of theirs who would battle for culture and purified religion against the superstitious monks, the barbarous scholastics, and the tyrannous Roman popes. The young humanists greeted Luther with wild enthusiasm as the man who would destroy Aristotle, vindicate Reuchlin, and renovate theology. They appreciated especially Luther's rejection of life-denying scholasticism and his rediscovery and glorification of the Holy Scriptures as the fountain of wisdom. They did not fully appreciate the fact that Luther did not oppose the scholastics as a rhetorician because of their barbarous dialectical style but because of their theology of self-glory. Nor did they adequately grasp the truth that Luther exalted the Holy Scriptures as the sole authority not because it was an ancient source, but because it was the sole carrier of the Word of God, the message of God's full, free, and final forgiveness of the believer's sin thanks to the vicarious suffering and death of Christ, the Son of God.

The year 1520 saw a dividing of the spirits, for Luther's publication of his treatise *On the Babylonian Captivity of the Church,* in which he criticized the sacramental-sacerdotal system and reduced the number of sacraments from seven to a dominical three, opened the eyes of the older humanists to the radical nature of his theology and many of them turned away. They found that in their innermost convictions they were Catholic and wished to remain loyal to the unity and catholicity of the old Church. Mutian, the canon at Gotha, who had taught and inspired so many of the young humanists at the University of Erfurt while Luther was a student there, was shocked at the iconoclasm and violence of some of the protesters, the rockthrowers who even broke some of his windows. But that very treatise of Luther's served as a great stimulus to many of the younger humanists who became fervent evangelicals. Almost all of Luther's followers were young, although not all of the young became his followers. After Luther's stand at Worms in 1521 he became a hero for the younger generation. When Luther nailed his theses to the church door in Wittenberg he was thirty-four years old. Nearly all of his early followers were only thirty years old or younger, many of them humanists turned evangelicals. Nearly all of Luther's major opponents were older, scholastics or humanists, and many of them fifty years old or older, a good number over seventy. There was an obvious generation gap between Luther's most ardent followers and his most distinguished opponents. This, then, is how the humanists related to the Reformation. Equally important for our problem is how the reformers related to humanism.

One of the intriguing and surprising facts about the Reformation is that despite the reformers' subjective principle of authority, Protestantism did not atomize into thousands or countless separate groups of Christians, each asserting its own right to private or individual interpretation of the Scriptures and insisting literally upon the priesthood of every believer. In reality the radicals comprised fewer than one percent of all Protestants and the overwhelming majority of the people remained within the Lutheran, Calvinist, Swiss Reformed, or Anglican communions. The position taken by the magisterial reformers was therefore of crucial importance for the survival and the vitality of humanism.

Luther's attitude was one neither of an unreserved affirmation of secular culture nor of an absolute rejection. Luther gave enthusiastic support to humanist culture in its sphere, and through the years developed an ever-increasing interest in humanist learning, but he sharply rebuffed the encroachments of humanist philosophy into the domain of theology where God's Word and not human letters reigns supreme. Luther owed much to the humanists, to their criticisms of abuses in the church as well as to their cultural reform program. At the University of Erfurt he had enjoyed some contacts with such humanists as Crotus Rubeanus. When he entered the monastery he took along a copy of Virgil and of Plautus. He was a gifted linguist and learned Greek and Hebrew in addition to his Latin. He used the best critical texts available, turning to Erasmus's Greek New Testament (1516) midway through his own commentary on *Romans*. He expressed regret in later years that he had in school and the university been forced to concentrate on dialectics for so many years without an opportunity to study history, poetry, and other humanist disciplines. Through the years, especially during the last decade and a half of his life when the pressure of events had eased up somewhat, under the influence and guidance of Melanchthon, he cultivated his interest in history and other humanist disciplines. He praised the renaissance of the humane letters as a John the Baptist heralding the advent of the evangelical renewal. "Learning, wisdom, and writers should rule the world," he exclaimed, "and should God ever in his wrath take away all learned men from the world, what else would the people who are left be except beasts!"

Even though Luther offered a historical justification and a theological rationale for the aesthetic-literary secular culture of humanism, his own preoccupation was so exclusively theological that he cannot properly be considered a humanist. He was a professor of theology, not of rhetoric. Nor was he a Christian humanist like Erasmus, for his evangelical message with its stress upon sin and grace drew upon greater depths of the Christian faith than did the program of the humanists for religious enlightenment. Luther did not merely advocate the imitation of Christ as the archetype of humanity at its best. Rather, his message was one of the boundless love and mercy of God, the forgiveness of sin which he offers to all men no matter how abject their condition, and the reconciliation of all men to himself through Christ. Theology is not a synthesis of learning and revelation, justification is not a supplementing of nature with grace, nor is salvation a reward for good works together with faith and love. For Luther all worldly culture was a great but conditional good, for its benefits extended to this life only. The gospel, however, was an unqualified good, for it brought benefits not only in this life but also in the eternal life to come.

The second man of the Reformation, the Frenchman John Calvin, was in every way a worthy successor to Luther. On the question of humanism and theology his resolution was virtually the same as Luther's, even though in his personal background he was more thoroughly educated in the humanist disciplines and untrained in scholastic theology compared with the older man. Calvin learned his grammar as a boy living with a noble family. When only fourteen he went to Paris where he studied at the Collège de la Marche with Mathurin Cordier, one of the best Latin teachers of the time. Calvin transferred to the Collège de Montaigu, which was more scholastic and ecclesiastical in nature, and there took the elementary arts course. Calvin seemed destined to take orders in the church, but at that point his father had a falling out with the canons of Noyons and came to favor a law career for John. Even while he was studying law at Orléans, however, Calvin was caught up with the humanistic study of the classics. He studied Roman law with Alciati and learned to read the New Testament in Greek and began the study of Hebrew. In 1532 he published his first book, a Latin commentary on Seneca's *De clementia*. As a self-conscious young humanist, Calvin presented a copy to Erasmus, the prince of the humanists. Less than two years later Calvin fled Paris as a convinced evangelical. He never lost his affection for Cicero, Quintilian, and Plato, but from then on he was dedicated almost exclusively to preaching Christ from the very fountains themselves, the Scriptures.

The third man of the Reformation, the Swiss Ulrich Zwingli, likewise evolved from a learned humanist into an ecclesiastical reformer of major importance. He learned his first letters in Wesen, then at ten moved to Basel, where he studied Latin, dialectics, and music for three years. He continued his studies for two years in Bern under Heinrich Wölflin, a great enthusiast for humanist educational ideals, who instilled in him a keen love of music and the classics. He next attended the University of Vienna, where the liveliest spirit was Conrad Celtis, the German arch-humanist, who taught the classics, directed humanist plays, and served as head of the college of poets and mathematicians. As a loyal Swiss Zwingli returned to Basel where he came under the influence of Thomas Wyttenbach, a reform-minded Erasmian who was opposed to scholasticism and monasticism and urged the study of the New Testament and the patristic writings. As a priest at Glarus Zwingli studied Greek and Hebrew, collected a library of 350 volumes on a wide range of subjects, especially the classics, and came to be known to his friends as "the Cicero of our age." He corresponded with Erasmus and made a pilgrimage to see him in Basel. Zwingli's initial reform experience was more as an Erasmian in criticizing abuses, driving back to the sources, and stressing spirit over letter. Even his teaching of the extreme form of double predestination seems to have originated more from his reading of St. Paul's epistle than from any existential experience of his own. But his close brush with death in the bubonic plague which struck Zurich in 1519, during his first year as preacher in the great minster, and his fervent study of the Scriptures developed in him a very serious mood and inspired him with greater evangelical fervor. It has been contended that he carried over into his theology more evidence of his humanist conceptions than did the other two leading reformers.

Many of the other leading reformers moved from humanism into the evangelical cause, such as Vadian at St. Gallen, Bucer at Strassburg, and Oecolampadius at Basel. In England, too, many reformers and makers of Tudor policy had enjoyed a humanist education designed to prepare them for service to the church and to the commonwealth.

The crucial question was whether the reformers with their powerful theological emphasis and single-minded devotion to the evangelical cause would find a proper and an important place for humanist disciplines in their total program of action. A positive response and happy outcome, which in retrospect may seem to have been predictable, could by no means be taken for granted. Had the revolutionary Muentzer instead of Luther, the less cultured Amsdorf instead of Melanchthon, the fiery Farel instead of Calvin taken over the leadership of the Reformation movement, it might well have spiralled off into an anti-intellectual or anti-humanist direction. There were, after all, anti-intellectual sects and individual cultural atavists who were ready to jettison secular culture along with the world itself. A successful peasant or proletarian revolt might have brutalized culture and destroyed the hard-won and painfully acquired refinements of centuries. Religious wars might have developed much earlier, before the consolidation of the movement or the cultural transition from the Renaissance to the Reformation had been effected. Moreover, the magisterial reformers themselves could have become so preoccupied with purely religious matters that they might well have felt little concern and devoted less energy to the humane studies or liberal arts. That the magisterial reformers assumed a positive stance toward humanist culture as of great value in this life was a factor of tremendous importance for all subsequent western history. The cultivation of humanist learning was for them, like other mundane vocations a *negotium cum deo,* an activity carried on as a co-worker with God. Humanist learning and higher culture remained for these university men a "sphere of faith's works."

It proved to be an equally momentous development that the next generation of young reformers took up the torch of humanist learning, preserved, cultivated, and transmitted it to the centuries which followed. Though some spontaneity and verve was gradually lost and creativity came to be partially smothered by pedantry, the cultural inheritance of the Renaissance was preserved for men in modern times. The attitudes of these younger reformers toward the humanities constitute our special problem. The most satisfactory resolution of this problem is to follow the advice of the English historian James Froude, "To look wherever we can through the eyes of contemporaries, from whom the future was concealed."

The pivotal figure for humanism in the Lutheran Reformation was Philipp Melanchthon, Luther's lieutenant, who came to be known as the *Praeceptor Germaniae*. When he arrived at the University of Wittenberg in 1518 as a brilliant young humanist of twenty-one, he delivered an inaugural lecture "On Improving the Studies of Youth" which was a clarion call to a humanist program. He berated the scholastics, depicted the centuries preceding as the dark ages, called for a revival of the "letters of culture reborn," and spoke out for the entire humanist curriculum, rhetoric first of all, Greek and Hebrew, history, philosophy and science. Luther himself took the initiative, working closely with Melanchthon, in achieving the humanistic reform of the university curriculum at Wittenberg. He hoped that students would enter upon their studies with the theological faculty with a different set of mental habits than had been the case when the arts curriculum was so heavily loaded with dialectics. Melanchthon's many orations, treatises, prefaces, and editions during the following decades promoted the *studia humanitatis* and validated humanist learning for the Protestant world.

Melanchthon became the commanding figure in an aggressive army of penmen who promoted the cause of humanist learning in the age of the Reformation. At the University of Leipzig Peter Mosellanus, who had been Melanchthon's rival for the appointment at Wittenberg, delivered a forceful *Oration Concerning the Knowledge of Various Languages Which Must Be Esteemed*. He inspired Andreas Althamer, who became, in turn, a leading reformer in Brandenburg-Anspach. At the Leipzig debate between Dr. Eck and Luther and Carlstadt in 1519, Mosellanus delivered the preliminary oration on *The Right Method of Disputing*. Leipzig subsequently turned Lutheran and a school of evangelical humanists who had studied with Mosellanus developed, men such as J. Lonicerus and Arnold Burenius. Another "Melanchthonian" humanist, Joachim Camerarius (1500-1574), became one of the leading classical scholars of the century. He studied at Leipzig, Erfurt, and Wittenberg, and then taught history and Greek at the Nuremberg gymnasium for several years. He helped Melanchthon to formulate the Augsburg Confession of 1530, reorganized the University of Tübingen in 1535 and the University of Leipzig, where he devoted the remainder of his life to classical scholarship, in 1541. He wrote more than one hundred and fifty works, and translated many major Greek authors like Homer, Theocritus, Sophocles, Lucian, Demosthenes, into Latin. In a score of orations he praised classical learning, which, when combined with evangelical faith, he believed made possible the fullest development of man's humanity.

A very similar cultural development took place in reformed Switzerland where Zwingli had set the tone. In Geneva Calvin founded the Academy which later became the University of Geneva. On the festive occasion Theodore Beza, the professor of Greek, delivered an *Address at the Solemn Opening of the Academy in Geneva,* in which he praised the good arts and learned disciplines. John Calvin himself made the closing remarks at the ceremony. Calvin's own Latin teacher, Mathurin Cordier, who had followed him into exile from France, lived out his days in Geneva as a model of the evangelical humanist educator. Representative of those Calvinist educators who carried the Geneva ideal to France, Scotland, England, and other areas of Calvinist penetration was Claude Baduel, who taught for many years as a humanist professor at Nîmes. He had been a student of Melanchthon at Wittenberg and a friend of the great Strassburg educator Johannes Sturm. His two great passions were beautiful language and evangelical theology in harmony with the new learning.

The reformers followed the lead of the humanists in emphasizing the great value of education, the classics, rhetoric, poetry, history, and religion. With the possible exception of our own day, never in history was so much published on educational theory and practice as in the Renaissance and Reformation era. The reformers moved beyond the elitism of the Renaissance in pressing for universal compulsory education in order to achieve literacy for boys and girls alike. The idea of the universal priesthood of all believers implied that all who had the wit should at least be sufficiently educated to read the Scriptures. The reformers developed a system of secondary school education in the classical gymnasium or lycée which would prepare students for more advanced work in the university. Formerly boys were often merely twelve, thirteen, or fourteen years old when they were trundled off to the universities. Moreover, the reformers stressed the lofty role of teaching as a divine vocation, second only to the office of preaching. Luther's educational treatises are widely known, such as his *Sermon on the Duty of Sending Children to School* and his *Letter to the Mayors and Aldermen of the Cities of Germany in Behalf of Christian Schools.* We have noted the critical importance of Melanchthon for Protestant education. A typical statement was his *Oration in Praise of a New School,* which he delivered at the opening of the gymnasium or classical secondary school at Nuremberg in 1526, a school which survived the bombing of the second World War and is still in operation today. Johannes Sturm wrote a sizable shelf of books on the nobility of classical letters and his program for Christian humanist education. David Chytraeus published in Wittenberg (1564) an ambitious work on the art of teaching and the right ordering of studies in the individual arts. In England Richard Mulcaster's *Positions* presented the enlightened views of a seasoned sixteenth-century schoolmaster. The prominent English educator and tutor of Queen Elizabeth, Roger Ascham, preached what he practiced as an educator.

The Protestant educators stressed the great value of grammar and rhetoric. The many volumes published on the structure of classical and vernacular vocabulary, figures of speech, rules of syntax, and the art of languages provide ample evidence of the importance which they attached to grammar for exegetical study, homiletical or expository communication. A working knowledge of Greek and Hebrew which was a rarity in the *Quattrocento* became almost a commonplace during the course of the sixteenth and seventeenth centuries. Moreover, the Protestant stress upon preaching and the spoken word of the Gospel coincided harmoniously with the humanist appreciation of rhetoric. They, too, saw man as a "living creature" having the power of speech. They also could appreciate the special power of rhetoric in moving men to action, not merely in convincing them intellectually by syllogisms or other devices of dialectics. Once again, Melanchthon's *Encomium on Eloquence* was one of the finest among many Protestant treatises in praise of rhetoric. Melanchthon wrote a volume on rhetoric himself and his *Loci Communes,* or commonplaces, applied the topical approach of rhetoric to theology. Cicero served as the model of the orator for the reformers as he had been for the humanists. Similarly many of the Lutheran, Calvinist, and Anglican *literati* such as Eobanus Hessus, Jacobus Micyllus, Clement Marot, Georg Major, Michael Neander, or Johannes Secundus Everardus in the Netherlands contributed to poetic culture and hymnody.

The reformers took history very seriously. In part they were thereby following in the footsteps of the humanists who saw a pragmatic purpose in history as moral philosophy teaching by example. If their history was less overtly patriotic than that of many Italians with their fierce city-state loyalties or of the northern humanists with their cultural nationalism, they added a serious religious dimension to the study of history. History was important polemically as a weapon in ecclesiastical controversy. Beyond that, history, like nature, provided evidence of God's having acted. The history of salvation ran like a golden thread through the intricate universal history. Luther not only wrote prefaces to the histories and editions of Galeatius Capella, Lazarus Spengler, Georg Spalatin, Robert Barnes and the like, but he compiled for his own use a chronological outline of world history. Melanchthon composed his famous *Preface to Cuspinian's Chronicle* (1541) which gave expression to the ideas most characteristic of the Reformation view of history. He himself wrote the largest part of *Carion's Chronicle.* Johann Sleidan was the author of the very excellent *Commentaries on the Condition of Religion and the Republic Under Charles V* (1555). Flacius Illyricus set the pattern for a more polemical tradition of historiography with his massive *Catalogue of the Witnesses of Truth* (1556) and the *Magdeburg Centuries* (13 vols., 1559-1574), in which he rewrote ecclesiastical history from a Protestant point of view. The reformers also developed patristic studies further than the humanists, even Erasmus, had brought them. Although the Scriptures remained for them the source and norm (*norma normans*) of doctrine, the fathers were key witnesses to the original and true (*primum et verum*) understanding of doctrine.

The Reformation was at its very heart so much a religious movement and Luther's interests were so predominantly theological as to raise the key question whether secular culture could be related to religious faith in such a way as to maintain an authenticity of its own without capitulating entirely to other-worldly interests. The Reformation determined the destiny of humanism, but humanism helped to define the nature and direction of the Reformation. The reformers basically accepted the stoic-Ciceronian anthropology common to many humanists, which predicated a dualistic compound of body and soul, reason and will, higher and lower impulses. Their disagreement was not with the humanist anthropology as such. They had a high regard for "natural man," whose reason is the loftiest creation of God. Luther expressed a preference for Plato over Aristotle in philosophy, whereas Melanchthon inclined more toward Aristotle, and in due course helped to enthrone the Stagirite in the universities once again. The reformers were inclined to be more realistic about man's finitude, moral flaws, wilfulness, and general limitations than were the humanists, at least in those exalted orations on the dignity of man. "Sweaty realists," Aldous Huxley has called them. But the real test for man, the reformers held, is how he measures up when standing *coram deo,* in the immediate presence of the holy God. Before God man is nothing in terms of his own righteousness, for he is in every way a debtor to God, totally dependent upon God's grace and mercy. All worldly culture, therefore, is merely a relative good, lofty and glorious though its achievements may be. The reformers struggled to relate religion and culture, theology and philosophy in a satisfactory way. Melanchthon himself made a forceful statement on the place of philosophy in religion and learning. A variety of syntheses evolved during subsequent decades, among them a return of Aristotle to theology, despite Luther's efforts to differentiate the respective realms of faith and culture.

The Renaissance and Reformation, then, did not constitute the clear and evident division of European culture into its classic and Christian components. Renaissance humanist learning was not only widespread during the Reformation horizontally on a European scale, but it lived on vertically through the centuries into modern times. This reading of a major problem in European intellectual history depends upon the study of a vast number of addresses, letters, treatises and books by those reformers who carried on in the evangelical movement a sound tradition of Christian humanism. A small sample of these historical documents follows, with Philipp Melanchthon serving as the star witness.

**Francis A. Schaeffer (essay date 1976)**

SOURCE: "The Reformation," in *How Should We Then Live? The Rise and Decline of Western Thought and Culture*, Crossway Books, 1976, pp. 79-104.

[*In the following essay, Schaeffer contends that the Reformation was both a rejection of the increasing humanism of the Roman Catholic Church and a stimulus to new developments in the arts.*]

While the men of the Renaissance wrestled with the problem of what could give unity to life and specifically what universal could give meaning to life and to morals, another great movement, the Reformation, was emerging in the north of Europe. This was the reaction...against the distortions which had gradually appeared in both a religious and a secular form. The High Renaissance in the south and the Reformation in the north must always be considered side by side. They dealt with the same basic problems, but they gave completely opposite answers and brought forth completely opposite results.

As we have seen, there had been forerunners of the Reformation. John Wycliffe (c. 1320-1384), whose life overlapped Giotto's. Dante's, Petrarch's and Boccaccio's, emphasized the Bible as the supreme authority, and he and his followers produced an English translation which had wide importance throughout Europe. John Huss of Bohemia (the heartland of modern Czechoslovakia) was a professor at the University of Prague (the Charles University). He lived between about 1369 and 1415. Thus his life overlapped Brunelleschi's, Masaccio's and van Eyck's. In contrast to the humanistic elements which had come into the church—and which led to the authority of the church being accepted as equal to, or greater than, the authority of the Bible and which emphasized human work as a basis for meriting the merit of Christ—Huss returned to the teachings of the Bible and of the early church and stressed that the Bible is the only source of final authority and that salvation comes only through Christ and his work. He further developed Wycliffe's views on the priesthood of all believers. Promised safe-conduct to speak at the Council of Constance, he was betrayed and burned at the stake there on July 6, 1415. Wycliffe's and Huss's views were the basic views of the Reformation which came later, and these views continued to exist in parts of the north of Europe even while the Renaissance was giving its humanist answers in the south. The Bohemian Brethren, the antecedents of the Moravian Church, were founded in 1457 by Huss's followers, and, like Luther's doctrines later, their ideas were spread not only by their teaching but by their emphasis on music and use of hymns. Huss himself wrote hymns which are still sung today. Another voice was the Dominican monk, Girolamo Savonarola, who drew large audiences in Florence between 1494 and 1498. He was not as clear as Wycliffe and Huss, but he did see some of the growing problems and spoke out against them until he was hanged and then his body burned in the square before the town hall in Florence.

Martin Luther (1483-1546) nailed his Ninety-five Theses to the church door in Wittenberg on October 31, 1517. To put this into historical perspective, we should remember that Leonardo da Vinci lived from 1452 to 1519. Thus, Luther's Theses were set forth just two years before Leonardo's death. Calvin was born in 1509, ten years before Leonardo's death, and the year Leonardo died Luther had his disputation in Leipzig with Dr. Eck. Francis I, who in 1516 took Leonardo to France (where Leonardo died), is the same Francis I to whom Calvin (1509-1564) addressed his *Institutes of the Christian Religion* in 1536.

One must understand that these two things were happening almost simultaneously: First, in the south, much of the High Renaissance was based on a humanistic ideal of man's being the center of all things, of man's being autonomous; second, in the north of Europe, the Reformation was giving an opposite answer. In other words, the Reformation was exploding with Luther just as the High Renaissance was coming to its close. As we have said, Luther nailed his Theses to the door in Wittenberg in 1517. Zwingli led Zürich to its break with Rome in 1523. Henry VIII of England broke with Rome in 1534. (This was at first political rather than religious, but it did lead later to a Protestant England.) Then, as we have mentioned, Calvin's *Institutes* were written in 1536.

But while the Reformation and the Renaissance overlapped historically and while they dealt with the same basic questions, they gave completely different answers. You will remember that to Thomas Aquinas the *will* was fallen after man had revolted against God, but the *mind* was not. This eventually resulted in people believing they could think out the answers to all the great questions, beginning only from themselves. The Reformation, in contrast to Aquinas, had a more biblical concept of the Fall. For the people of the Reformation, people could *not* begin only from themselves, and on the basis of human reason alone think out the answers to the great questions which confront mankind.

The men of the Reformation did learn from the new knowledge and attitudes brought forth by the Renaissance. A critical outlook, for example, toward what had previously been accepted without question was helpful. And while the Reformers rejected the scepticism of Lorenzo Valla (c. 1409-1457), they gladly learned from his study of language. But from the critical attitude toward the traditions which had been accepted without question, the Reformers turned not to man as beginning only from himself, but to the original Christianity of the Bible and the early church. Gradually they came to see that the church founded by Christ had since been marred by distortions. However, in contrast to the Renaissance humanists, they refused to accept the autonomy of human reason, which acts as though the human mind is infinite, with all knowledge within its realm. Rather, they took seriously the Bible's own claim for itself—that it is the only final authority. And they took seriously that man needs the answers given by God in the Bible to have adequate answers not only for how to be in an open relationship with God, but also for how to know the present meaning of life and how to have final answers in distinguishing between right and wrong. That is, man needs not only a God who exists, but a God who has spoken in a way that can be understood.

The Reformers accepted the Bible as the Word of God in all that it teaches. Luther translated the Bible into German, and translations of the Bible began to be available for the people in the languages they could understand. To the Reformation thinkers, authority was not divided between the Bible and the church. The church was *under* the teaching of the Bible—not above it and not equal to it. It was *Sola Scriptura,* the Scriptures only. This stood in contrast to the humanism that had infiltrated the church after the first centuries of Christianity. *At its core, therefore, the Reformation was the removing of the humanistic distortions which had entered the church.*

It is worth reiterating the ways in which the infiltration by humanistic thought—growing over the years but fully developed by 1500—showed itself. First, the authority of the church was made equal to the authority of the Bible. Second, a strong element of human work was added to the work of Christ for salvation. Third, after Thomas Aquinas there had come an increasing synthesis between biblical teaching and pagan thought. This synthesis was not just a borrowing of words but actually of content. It is apparent in many places and could be illustrated in many ways. For example, Raphael in one of his rooms in the Vatican balanced *The School of Athens* (which represents Greek non-Christian philosophic thought) with his pictorial representation of the church, putting them on opposite walls. This representation of the church is called the *Disputà* for it deals with the nature of the mass. Raphael was par excellence the artist of the synthesis. But

Michelangelo, on the ceiling of the Sistine Chapel in the Vatican, also combined biblical teaching and non-Christian pagan thought; he made the pagan prophetesses equal to the Old Testament prophets. Dante's writings show the same mixture.

When in Basel, Guillaume Farel (1489-1565), the Reformer in French-speaking Switzerland before Calvin, showed plainly that there was a second kind of humanism that he stood against, as well as that which had come into the church. This kind of humanism was exemplified most clearly by Erasmus of Rotterdam (1466?-1536). Erasmus helped the Reformers by editing the New Testament in the original Greek (1516) and by urging in the preface that the New Testament be translated into all the vernacular languages. Some have called the view of Erasmus and those with him *Christian humanism,* but it was less than consistent Christianity. Erasmus and his followers wanted only a limited reform of the church, in contrast to the Reformers who wanted to go back to the church as it originally was, with the authority being the Bible only. Thus Farel thoroughly cut himself off from Erasmus to make plain that he stood on principle against either form of humanism. The various branches of the Reformation had differences among themselves, but together they constituted one system—a unity—in contrast to the humanism which had come into the church on one side and to the Erasmian humanism on the outside.

The Reformation was certainly not a golden age. It was far from perfect, and in many ways it did not act consistently with the Bible's teaching, although the Reformers were trying to make the Bible their standard not only in religion but in all of life. No, it was not a golden age. For example, such overwhelming mistakes were made as Luther's unbalanced position in regard to the peasant wars, and the Reformers showed little zeal for reaching people in other parts of the world with the Christian message. Yet though they indeed had many and serious weaknesses, in regard to religious and secular humanism, they did return to the Bible's instruction and the example of the early church.

Because the Reformers did not mix humanism with their position, but took instead a serious view of the Bible, they had no problem of meaning for the individual things, the particulars; they had no nature-versus-grace problem. One could say that the Renaissance centered in autonomous man, while the Reformation centered in the infinite-personal God who had spoken in the Bible. In the answer the Reformation gave, the problem of meaning for individual things, including man, was so completely answered that the problem—as a problem—did not exist. The reason for this is that the Bible gives a unity to the universal and the particulars.

First, the Bible tells men and women true things about God. Therefore, they can know true things about God. One can know true things about God because God has revealed himself. The word *God* was not contentless to Reformation man. God was not an unknown "philosophic other" because God had told man about himself. As the Westminster Confession (1645-1647) says, when God revealed his attributes to people, the attributes are not only true to people but true to God. That is, when God tells people what he is like, what he says is not just relatively true but absolutely true. As finite beings, people do not have exhaustive truth about God, but they can have truth about God; and they can know, therefore, truth about that which is the ultimate universal. And the Bible speaks to men and women concerning meaning, morals, and values.

Second, the Bible tells us true things about people and about nature. It does not give men and women *exhaustive* truth about the world and the cosmos, but it does give truth about them. So one can know many true things about nature, especially *why* things exist and why they have the form they have. Yet, because the Bible does not give exhaustive truth about history and the cosmos, historians and scientists have a job to do, and their work is not meaningless. To be sure, there is a total break between God and his creation, that is, between God and created things; God is infinite—and created things are finite. But man can know both truth about God and truth about the things of creation because in the Bible God has revealed himself and has given man the key to understanding God's world.

So, as the Reformation returned to biblical teaching, it gained two riches at once: It had no particulars-versus-universals (or meaning) problem, and yet at the same time science and art were set free to operate upon the basis of that which God had set forth in Scripture. The Christianity of the Reformation, therefore, stood in rich contrast to the basic weakness and final poverty of the humanism which existed in that day and the humanism which has existed since.

It is important that the Bible sets forth true knowledge about mankind. The biblical teaching gives meaning to all particulars, but this is especially so in regard to that particular which is the most important to man, namely, the individual himself or herself. It gives a reason for the individual being great. The ironic fact here is that humanism, which began with Man's being central, eventually had no real meaning for people. On the other hand, if one begins with the Bible's position that a person is created by God and created in the image of God, there is a basis for that person's dignity. People, the Bible teaches, are made in the image of God—they are nonprogrammed. Each is thus Man with dignity.

That Man is made in the image of God gives many important answers intellectually, but it also has had vast practical results, both in the Reformation days and in our own age. For example, in the time of the

Reformation it meant that all the vocations of life came to have dignity. The vocation of honest merchant or housewife had as much dignity as king. This was strengthened further by the emphasis on the biblical teaching of the priesthood of all believers—that is, that all Christians are priests. Thus, in a very real sense, all people are equal as persons. Moreover, the government of the church by lay elders created the potential for democratic emphasis.

The Bible, however, also says that man is fallen; he has revolted against God. At the historic space-time Fall, man refused to stand in the proper relationship with this infinite reference point which is the personal God. Therefore, people are now abnormal. The Reformation saw all people as equal in this way, too—all are guilty before God. This is as true of the king and queen as the peasant. So, in contrast to the humanism of the Renaissance, which never gave an answer to explain that which is observable in people, the Bible enabled people to solve the dilemma facing them as they look at themselves: They could understand both their greatness and their cruelty.

The Bible gives a different way to come to God from that teaching which had grown up in the church through the previous centuries. The Reformers went back to the teaching of the Bible and the early church and removed the humanistic elements which had been added. The individual person, they taught, could come to God directly *by faith* through the finished work of Christ. That is, Christ's sacrifice on the cross was of infinite value, and people cannot do and need not do anything to earn or add to Christ's work. But this can be accepted as an unearned gift. It was *Sola Gratia,* grace only.

Previously, those who came into the churches were separated from what to them was the center of worship—the alter in the chancel—by a high grill of iron or wood. This was the *rood screen,* so called from the rood, or crucifix, which it often supported or which was hung above it. But with the Reformation, when the Bible was accepted in all its unique authority, these screens were often removed. In some churches the Bible was placed exactly where the screen had been, to show that the teaching of the Bible opened the way for all the people to come directly to God. One such church is in Ollon, Switzerland. You can still see where the rood screen had fit into the wall but was removed; the pulpit was then placed so that the Bible is where the rood screen had previously been.

Guillaume Farel, the early French-Swiss Reformer preached in this church, and from there and nearby Aigle the Reformation began in French-speaking Switzerland. Later, after ministries in Geneva and Lausanne, Farel preached for many years in the cathedral in Neuchâtel. The statue outside that cathedral could well be taken as the mark of the Reformation and of Christianity. This statue has Farel holding the Bible aloft. Thus it is *Sola Scriptura,* the Bible and the Bible only. This is what made all the difference to the Reformers, both in understanding the approach to God and in having the intellectual and practical answers needed in this present life.

Because of their tendency toward purifying religion from an overemphasis on visual symbols, the Reformers are often accused of being antagonistic to the arts. But the Reformation was not against art as art. To some of us the statues and paintings of the Madonna, saints, and so on may be art objects, and perhaps we wish that the people of the Reformation had taken these works and put them in a warehouse for a hundred years or so. Then they could have been brought out and put in a museum. But at that moment of history this would have been too much to ask! To the men and women of that time, these were images to worship. The men of the Reformation saw that the Bible stressed that there is only one mediator between God and man, Christ Jesus. Thus, in the pressure of that historic moment, they sometimes destroyed the images—not as works of art but as religious images which were contrary to the Bible's emphasis on Jesus as the only mediator.

We should note, however, that the Reformers usually distinguished between *cult images* and other works of art, the former alone falling under condemnation. But not even all of the cult images were destroyed. All over Europe in cathedrals and churches we can see thousands of statues which were not destroyed. The reason why some statues were destroyed is pointed out by Bernd Moeller (1931-) in *Imperial Cities and the Reformation* (1962. English translation, 1972). He shows that in certain cases the actual donors of the images smashed them because they represented religiously that which they now rejected as unbiblical. He writes, "Those who donated an image did not merely venerate that image; those who broke an image did not merely hate it. Both the donor and the breaker of images were concerned with eternal salvation." Image breaking parallels in the area of ecology the early Christians' cutting down the sacred groves of trees which were related to the worship of pagan gods. These believers did not cut down the trees because they minimized trees or despised nature; they cut down these specific trees because of their anti-Christian religious significance. Equally, the people of the Reformation did not destroy art objects as art objects. Unlike modern man, the men of that day did not live in a splintered world. Art was an intimate part of life. What is represented had more than an aesthetic value divorced from considerations of truth and religious significance.

The proof that the Reformation was not against art *as* art is seen in the effects of the Reformation on culture. We should not forget that Lucas Cranach (1472-

1553), the German painter and engraver, was a friend of Luther and painted Luther and his wife many times. Cranach also painted Luther's father. The vocal parts of the 1524 hymnbook were probably engraved by Cranach. Luther and Cranach were even the godfathers of each other's children. There is no indication at all that Luther disapproved of Cranach's painting in all the varied forms that it took.

Then, too, we can think of the music which the Reformation brought forth. There was the lively Geneva Psalter, the 1562 hymnbook made up of the Psalms. The tunes were so vivacious that some people in derision called them "Geneva Jigs." The great Theodore Beza (1519-1605), who followed Calvin as leader of the Reformation in Geneva, translated the Psalms' texts, and these were set to melodies selected or composed by Louis Bourgeois (1510-1570). Later this Psalter was used in England, Germany, the Netherlands, and Scotland, as well as in Switzerland. But it was in Luther's Germany where the effects of the Reformation on music are best seen.

Luther himself was a fine musician. He was a singer with a good tenor voice as well as an instrumentalist with skill and verve. In 1524 his choirmaster, Johann Walther (1496-1570), put out a hymnbook (*Wittenberg Gesangbuch*) which was a tremendous innovation. Walther and his friend Conrad Rupff worked on these hymns in Luther's home. Luther himself played out the tunes on his fife. The collection contained Luther's own great hymn "A Mighty Fortress Is Our God," to which he wrote both words and music. As the rood screen was removed in the churches—because with an open Bible the people had direct access to God—so also in a direct approach to God the congregations were allowed to sing again for the first time in many centuries.

We are swept back in this, as in other things, to the practice as well as the teaching of the early church. We are carried back to Ambrose (339-397), bishop of Milan and his antiphonal psalmody, as he, like Luther, wrote hymn texts and taught his congregations to sing them. Luther said in the preface to the *Wittenberg Gesangbuch,* "I wish that the young men might have something to rid them of their love ditties and wanton songs and might instead of these learn wholesome things and thus yield willingly to the good; also, because I am not of the opinion that all the arts shall be crushed to earth and perish through the Gospel, as some bigoted persons pretend, but would willingly see them all, and especially music, servants of Him who gave and created them."

Hymnwriters who later brought forth more complicated forms were Hans Leo Hassler (1564-1612) and Michael Praetorius (1571-1621). Heinrich Schütz (1585-1672) and Dietrich Buxtehude (1637-1707) should also be noted. Schütz was influenced by the baroque music of Giovanni Gabrieli (c. 1557-1612) from Venice, but in the Reformation this style took on its own character and direction. Buxtehude, the organist at Lübeck, had a profound influence on Bach. It is interesting to note that, two years before Bach came to hear Buxtehude at Lübeck, Handel (1685-1759) came there, not only intending to hear Buxtehude, but hoping to inherit Buxtehude's post. In the contract was a clause saying that the new organist was to marry Buxtehude's daughter. Handel did not take the position! The so-called *Abendmusiken* (late Sunday afternoon sacred concerts) were begun by Buxtehude, and both Handel and Bach went to hear them. The Reformation's influence on culture was not just for a favored elite but for all the people. There were also less-remembered men of the period who did remarkable work. We could think of Bach's predecessor as organist at Leipzig, Johann Kuhnau (1660-1722), who wrote biblical sonatas for the harpsichord in 1700.

Johann Sebastian Bach (1685-1750) was certainly the zenith of the composers coming out of the Reformation. His music was a direct result of the Reformation culture and the biblical Christianity of the time, which was so much a part of Bach himself. There would have been no Bach had there been no Luther. Bach wrote on his score initials representing such phrases as: "With the help of Jesus"—"To God alone be the glory"—"In the name of Jesus." It was appropriate that the last thing Bach the Christian wrote was "Before Thy Throne I Now Appear." Bach consciously related both the form and the words of his music to biblical truth. Out of the biblical context came a rich combination of music and words and a diversity with unity. This rested on the fact that the Bible gives unity to the universal and the particulars, and therefore the particulars have meaning. Expressed musically, there can be endless variety and diversity without chaos. There is variety yet resolution.

We must, of course, remember Handel who also stood in the same tradition. One naturally thinks of Handel's *Messiah* (1741), which was in the tradition of the restored Christianity in both its music and its message. Handel's religious music included not only the *Messiah* but *Saul* (c. 1738), *Israel in Egypt* (c. 1738) and *Samson* (1743). The *Messiah* could only have come forth in a setting where the Bible stood at the center. Even the order of the selections follows with extreme accuracy the Bible's teaching about the Christ as the Messiah. For example, Handel did not put the "Hallelujah Chorus" at the end, but in its proper place in the flow of the past and future history of Christ. Many modern performances often place it at the end as a musical climax, but Handel followed the Bible's teaching exactly and placed it at that future historic moment when the Bible says Christ will come back to rule upon the earth—at that point where the Bible prophetically (in the Book of Revelation) puts the cry of "King of kings and Lord of lords!" Handel probably knew Charles Wesley (1707-1788) and wrote the music for a hymn to original words by Wesley, "Rejoice, the Lord is King."

In passing, we should note that English church music followed the same emphasis found in the early music of Reformation Germany. A demand arose for a simplified style which would permit the words to be understood. We could mention here Thomas Tallis (c. 1505-1585) and Orlando Gibbons (1583-1625). In England as in Germany the stress was on content. Music was not incidental to the Reformation's return to biblical teaching; it was a natural outcome, a unity with what the Bible taught. What the Reformation produced musically gives us a clear affirmation that the Reformation was indeed interested in culture. As this was true in music, it was also true in visual art. We have already mentioned Cranach. We must also notice Dürer (1471-1528), Altdorfer (1480-1538), Hans Baldung-Grien (c. 1484-1545), and the Beham brothers: Hans (1500-1550) and Barthel (1502-1540).

Some of the work of Albrecht Dürer was done before the Reformation, yet he must be considered a Reformation artist. In 1521 he was in the Netherlands. (You will remember that Luther nailed his Ninety-five Theses to the door at Wittenberg on October 31, 1517.) There Dürer heard tidings that Luther had been taken captive. The rumor was false. Luther's friends had hidden him to protect his life, but most people thought he was a prisoner. Dürer was keeping a diary which he did not mean to have published. This diary is worth quoting at length (as translated by Udo Middelmann):

> On Friday before Pentecost (17th of May) in the year 1521 the news reached Antwerpen, that Martin Luther had been so treacherously taken prisoner. For when the herald of the emperor Charles had been ordered to accompany him with the emperial guard, he trusted this. But when the herald had brought him near Eisenach to an inhospitable place, he told him that he had no further need of him and rode off. Pretty soon ten riders on horseback appeared; they treacherously led away this deceived, pious man, who was illumined by the Holy Spirit and professed the true Christian faith. And is he still alive?
>
> Or have they murdered him?—which I do not know—in that case he has suffered it for the sake of the Christian truth in that he chastized the unchristian papacy, which resists the liberation by Christ with its heavy burdens of human laws; and also for, this reason has he suffered it, that we should even longer as until now be deprived and completely disrobed of all that is the fruit of our blood and sweat, and that this fruit should shamefully and blasphemously be consumed by idle folk while the thirsty, parched people die because of it.
>
> And especially, the hardest factor for me is that God might possibly want to keep us under their false and blind teaching, which has only been composed and compiled by people whom they call fathers. Because of this, the delicious Word of God is wrongly exegeted or not at all taught in many places.
>
> Oh God in heaven, have mercy on us. Oh Lord Jesus Christ, pray for your people, deliver us at the right time, preserve in us the right, true Christian faith, gather your widely scattered sheep by your voice, which is called the Word of God in Scripture. Help us that we might recognize this your voice and would not follow another tempting call, that would only be human imagination, so that we might never leave you, Lord Jesus Christ! . . . Oh God! You have never burdened a people so horribly with human laws as we are under the Roman chair, who desire daily to be free Christians, redeemed by your blood. Oh highest, heavenly Father! Pour into our hearts by your son Jesus Christ such light, that we might recognize which messenger we are constrained to obey, so that we might reject the burden of the others in good conscience and be able to serve you, eternal heavenly Father, with a glad and cheerful heart.
>
> And should we have lost this man, who has written more clearly than any other that has lived in the last 140 years and to whom you have given such an evangelical spirit, we pray you, Oh heavenly Father, that you would give your Holy Spirit again to someone who would gather your holy Christian Church so that we might live together again in a Christian manner and that because of our good works all unbelievers, as there are Turks, heathen, and Kalicutes, would desire after us of themselves and would accept the Christian faith. . . . Oh Lord! Present us afterwards with the new, decorated Jerusalem that descends from heaven, of which it is written in the Apocalypse, the holy pure gospel, which has not been darkened by human doctrine.
>
> Anyone, after all, who reads Martin Luther's books, can see how his teaching is so clear and transparent when he sets forth the holy gospel. Therefore these are to be honored and ought not to be burned; unless one would throw his opponents, who combat the truth at all times, into the same fire together with their opinions, which want to make Gods out of men; and one should then proceed in this way that new printings of Luther's books would again be available. Oh God, if Luther is dead, who will henceforth proclaim the holy gospel with such clarity? Oh God! What would he not have still been able to write for us in ten or twenty more years?

In a letter to George Spalatin in 1520 Dürer wrote:

> In all subservience may I ask your grace to recommend to you the praiseworthy Dr. Luther, for the sake of the Christian truth, for which we care more than all riches or power of this world, for all this passes with time, only the truth remains eternally. And help me God, that I might get to Dr. Martinus Luther, so that I might diligently picture him and etch him in copper for a lasting memorial of this Christian man who has helped me out of great anxieties. And I ask you, your honor, that if Dr. Martinus produces something new in German, you would send it to me against my money.

There are a number of things to notice in these quotations. Dürer says Luther has written more clearly than anyone for 140 years. John Wycliffe had lived from 1320 to 1384, John Huss from 1369 to 1415. Dürer's diary was written in 1521. When we subtract 140 years from this date, we arrive at 1381, which falls in the lifetime of both Wycliffe and Huss. Dürer may have had both men in mind, but probably he was thinking of Huss, for Huss's influence had remained strong in southern Germany. One thing is clear: Dürer was in the line of these men before the Reformation who had set forth many of the Reformation's basic ideas, especially the Bible as the only final authority. Notice how this fits in with what Dürer wrote about Martin Luther. A second prominent idea of Huss—that salvation did not come through the addition of man's works but through Christ and his work only—is also found echoed in the diary.

Thus Dürer was indeed a man in the stream of the Reformation when he did his great woodcuts illustrating the *Apocalypse* (1498) and his copperplate engravings of *The Knight, Death, and the Devil* (1513) and *St. Jerome in His Cell* (1514), even if he did them before Luther nailed his Theses to the door. Further, notice how he twice quotes from the Apocalypse (the last book in the Bible). This clearly ties in with his previous woodcuts and shows that even when he did them these thoughts were involved. His art is as much a cultural result of the Reformation as is Bach's music. Dürer lived at the same time as Raphael, Michelangelo and Leonardo. When he was thirteen years old, he already took nature seriously. His beautiful watercolors of flowers, rabbits, and so on were a clear exhibition that God's world has value, a real value.

I am not at all saying that the art which the Reformation produced was in every case greater as art than the art of the south. *The point is that to say that the Reformation depreciated art and culture or that it did not produce art and culture is either nonsense or dishonest.*

It is not only Christians who can paint with beauty, nor for that matter only Christians who can love or who have creative stirrings. Even though the image is now contorted, people are made in the image of God. This is who people are, whether or not they know or acknowledge it. God is the great Creator, and part of the unique mannishness of man, as made in God's image, is creativity. Thus, man as man paints, shows creativity in science and engineering and so on. Such activity does not require a special impulse from God, and it does not mean that people are not alienated from God and do not need the work of Christ to return to God. It does mean that man as man, in contrast to non-man, is creative. A person's world view almost always shows through in his creative output, however, and thus the marks on the things he creates will be different. This is so in all fields—for example, in the art of the Renaissance compared to that of the Reformation, or in the direction man's creative stirrings in science will assume, and whether and how the stirring will continue. In the case of the Reformation the art showed the good marks of its biblical base.

It was not only in Germany that the Reformation affirmed painting. The clearest example of the effects of the Reformation culture on painting is Rembrandt (1606-1669). Rembrandt had flaws in his life (as all people do), but he was a true Christian; he believed in the death of Christ for him personally. In 1633 he painted the *Raising of the Cross* for Prince Frederick Henry of Orange. It now hangs in the museum *Alte Pinakothek* in Münich. A man in a blue painter's beret raises Christ upon the cross. That man is Rembrandt himself—a self-portrait. He thus stated for all the world to see that his sins had sent Christ to the cross.

Rembrandt shows in all his work that he was a man of the Reformation; he neither idealized nature nor demeaned it. Moreover, Rembrandt's biblical base enabled him to excel in painting people with psychological depth. Man was great, but man was also cruel and broken, for he had revolted against God. Rembrandt's painting was thus lofty, yet down to earth. There was no need for him to slip into the world of illusion, as did much of the baroque painting which sprang out of the Catholic Counter-Reformation. Nature to this Dutch Reformation artist was a thing to be enjoyed as a creation of God. We can think of Rembrandt's painting *Danae* (1636) in the museum in Leningrad. This is a picture of Rembrandt's nude wife waiting in bed for him. Rembrandt himself is not in the picture. And yet as she waits for him to come from the left side, though still hidden, he is the center of the picture. There is love and gentleness here. Rembrandt understood that Christ is the Lord of all of life. As a Christian, he lived in the midst of God's world and did not need to make himself God. Rather, he could use God's world and its form in his painting.

Many other Dutch artists stood firmly in the stream of Reformation culture. There were portrait painters, landscape painters, and still-life artists; for all of them everyday reality was seen as God's creation and thus as important. This was the right direction, a proper view of nature. Up to a certain point the development of the Renaissance in the south could have gone in a good direction or a poor one. But humanism took over—all was made autonomous and meaning was lost. In the Reformation, the right direction was regained, and nature and the whole of life were things of dignity and beauty.

In 1860 Jacob Burckhardt (1818-1897) in *The Civilization of the Renaissance in Italy* pointed out a crucial difference between the Renaissance and the Reformation. While no one now would follow Burckhardt exactly, his discussion of the contrast between the Renaissance and the Reformation is still the most remarkable one we have and seems to me to be still valid. He indicated that freedom was introduced both in the north by the Reformation and in the south by the Renaissance. But in the south it went to license; in the north it did not. The reason was that in Renaissance humanism man had no way to bring forth a meaning to the particulars of life and no place from which to get absolutes in morals. But in the north, the people of the Reformation, standing under the teaching of Scripture, had freedom and yet at the same time compelling absolute values.

**Charles G. Nauert, Jr. (essay date 1973)**

SOURCE: "The Clash of Humanists and Scholastics: An Approach to Pre-Reformation Controversies," in *The Sixteenth Century Journal*, Vol. IV, No. 1, April, 1973, pp. 1-18.

[*In the essay that follows, Nauert claims that the crisis of the Protestant Reformation was grounded upon earlier, minor controversies within the Catholic Church that provide further insight into the conflict between humanism and scholasticism.*]

History's well-filled dustbin contains many events and persons that once attracted great attention but have since been eclipsed by greater events and greater individuals, and that languish in an historical limbo, disturbed only by an occasional doctoral candidate trying to exhume events and personages that (so far as our general comprehension of the past is concerned) might almost never have existed at all. Yet sometimes these historical non-events can cast light on the greater events which have eclipsed them.

A good case in point is the numerous controversies over religious questions which occurred in Northern Europe during the last decade or two preceding the Reformation. In a general way, most (but not all) of these appear to be confrontations between the educational and church-reform proposals of the humanists, on the one hand and, on the other hand, the established academic and ecclesiastical authorities, especially the scholastic theologians and the religious orders. Historians have traditionally so depicted these controversies, if indeed they have recognized their occurrence at all. With the single exception of the famous conflict between the humanist John Reuchlin and the theological faculty of Cologne, a conflict which produced the scandalous *Letters of Obscure Men,* these controversies have been consigned to oblivion.

The cause is not far to seek. Just think for a moment of the issues which they concerned: whether it was a mortal sin to leave the corpses of executed criminals exposed on the gallows; whether the St. Mary Magdalen of the liturgical tradition was really one person who appeared in the New Testament on three different occasions, or three distinct individuals, only one of whom is correctly identified as Mary Magdalen; whether St. Anne, mother of the Virgin Mary, was married one time or three. Even on their own merits, these subjects seem minor; and when contrasted with the great issues which Martin Luther raised (justification of man, freedom of the will, the nature and authority of the Church, for example), many of these issues which aroused Northern Europe's intellectuals on the eve of the Reformation seem totally inconsequential. If they deserve any mention at all, why not simply list them as minor examples of the irrepressible conflict between humanists and scholastics?

The problem with such a summary dismissal of these and other pre-Reformation controversies is that it neglects two points which (unlike the controversies themselves) are *not* inconsequential. First and most obviously, the system long used to classify them is not itself proven. The relations between humanists and scholastics in pre-Reformation Europe need to be the subject of far more studies than are now available, but already we know enough to say that the idea of an irrepressible conflict needs to be demonstrated, not taken for granted. Humanism was a new and challenging force in the intellectual and ecclesiastical life of the early sixteenth century, but it did not destroy scholasticism or traditional religion, nor even try to do so. In each local situation, and even in each individual, practical accommodations and compromises were not only possible but inevitable. Even the most established members of the scholastic Establishment sometimes admitted that the fruits of humanistic study (for example, reform of grammar, or textual work on ancient authors) ought to be incorporated into the university curriculum, while at the same time humanists not only sought but often achieved a place within the universities for themselves and their studies, and also shared many of the traditional intellectual concerns of the scholastics.[1] Even at Cologne, which probably deserved its reputation for academic conservatism, the humanists had their place; and the dean of Cologne cathedral, the aristocratic Hermann von Neuenar, was in fact the editor of two of the publications that defended John

Reuchlin against the conservative Cologne theologians.[2] In short, humanism and scholasticism were not two irreconcilable philosophies struggling to monopolize the minds and souls of men and the curricula of schools and universities—a point which the work of Professor P. O. Kristeller should already have established long ago.[3] Rather, in the academic and intellectual world of the early sixteenth century, they were two distinct clusters of academic subjects, each with its own distinctive methodology, but neither claiming to represent the totality of culture.

The second reason for not being content to dismiss the minor pre-Reformation controversies without further study is that they provided the immediate context into which the new and more significant debate opened by Martin Luther was injected; and inevitably they conditioned the earliest reactions to Luther's ideas. In the beginning, few people had even the remotest suspicion that the cause of Luther was something other than the cause of the humanist controversialists of the preceding decades. For a brief moment, nearly all the Northern humanists understood Luther as an eloquent new recruit to their own program of church reform; and hence nearly all of them, at least for the crucial two or three years when the Lutheran movement was winning support of its own, sympathized with Luther and urged that no summary and extreme measures be taken against him. Thus these pre-Reformation controversies, because they sheltered the nascent Reformation by obscuring the novelty and profundity of the issues raised by Luther, significantly affected the course of history. This point is in fact well known. Although Luther and the established humanist leaders soon parted ways, humanism provided the mechanisms through which Luther's ideas were first diffused among the intellectuals of Northern Europe.[4]

No doubt because of this obvious connection with the successes of the early Reformation, and also because of our growing awareness of the complexity of relations between humanists and scholastics in the Northern universities, several recent works have attempted to re-evaluate one or another of the controversies. Professor James Overfield has published a thoughtful re-evaluation of the Reuchlin case, seriously questioning whether that bitter conflict was in fact a confrontation between humanists and scholastics, as has been generally believed.[5] Two scholars, Professors Richard Cameron and Anselm Hufstader, have even dared to study topics more obscure than the *Letters of Obscure Men,* namely the attacks by scholastic conservatives on the efforts of the French humanist Jacques Lefèvre d'Ètaples to question the accuracy of the Vulgate Bible and the validity of traditions concerning St. Mary Magdalen and St. Anne.[6] On a slightly earlier period and on a subject perhaps even more obscure, I have myself studied the controversy between the Italian jurist Peter of Ravenna and the Cologne theological faculty.[7] What emerges from these studies is not, I think, mere antiquarian rediscovery of long-dead controversies that might well have been left untouched. Professor Overfield's thesis is essentially that anti-Semitism, not hostility to humanism, was the driving force behind the activities of Reuchlin's foes; and that at least down to the end of 1514, the desire of humanists to study the Greek and Hebrew sources of Christianity was never an issue. He also shows that few of the Northern humanists shared Reuchlin's concern for Hebrew studies or feared that the efforts of the Cologne theologians to destroy Hebrew literature posed a threat to the progress of humanistic scholarship. Overfield also notes the deafening silence of many of the leading German humanists throughout the controversy, and observes that even some who did publicly support Reuchlin, such as Mutianus Rufus,[8] were privately critical. Erasmus, as was his wont, carefully distinguished between the cause of Reuchlin and his own program of studies and reforms, and limited his rare public statements in behalf of Reuchlin to general character-references.[9] Even those humanists who did speak out for Reuchlin were motivated chiefly by resentment at seeing a pious and learned man whom they respected maligned by Dominican friars whom they despised.[10] In their statements they attacked only those individuals who had slandered Reuchlin, not scholasticism as such. Overfield may in fact be underestimating the distaste of the German humanists for scholasticism and exaggerating the uniqueness of Crotus Rubianus and Ulrich von Hutten, chief authors of the *Letters of Obscure Men,* in treating scholastic philosophy and theology as the enemy. Yet he is no doubt correct in his contention that those two extremists in their famous satire went far beyond either the public or the private statements of most humanists. Indeed, Crotus and Hutten were the real creators of the traditional interpretation which teaches that the Reuchlin case was a life-and-death struggle between humanists and scholastics. Thus Overfield's work provides a significant reassessment not only of the Reuchlin case but also of the relations between humanists and scholastics on the eve of the Reformation.

Although they deal with far less publicized conflicts, the works of Professors Cameron and Hufstader on Lefèvre d'Ètaples also demonstrate that even the most obscure controversies involved issues of real significance. The question of authority in religious matters, which was perhaps the fundamental dividing-line between Protestants and Catholics, was clearly raised by Lefèvre and his opponents. Also at issue were such matters as the proper method of Scriptural exegesis, the validity of popular tradition and patristic authority, the criterion by which one distinguishes between truth and falsity, and even the right of (limited) free inquiry by the individual. My own study of Peter of Ravenna at Cologne points to a factor less theoretical than these but perhaps more intensely human: the conflict between the individual's commitment to truth and his need to reach an accommodation with the social group—in this case, the university community—within which he conducted his search for truth; in other words, the constant tension between the need for a sense of community and the need for intellectual consistency and personal integrity. The case of the supposedly renegade humanist Ortwin Gratius, first the friend and later the critic of Peter of Ravenna, and finally the chief butt of the *Letters of Obscure Men,* is a particularly instructive example of this tension.[11]

The whole area of pre-Reformation controversies provides opportunities for further studies which will give historians a clearer and more accurate picture of the intellectual and spiritual situation on the eve of Martin Luther's emergence as the leader of a powerful new movement. Much though Erasmus has been studied already, his conflicts with individuals like Jacobus Latomus, Martin Dorp, Edward Lee, and Jacobus Stunica, and even his later controversies with Noël B da and Alberto Pio,[12] might cast light on the relation between humanism and the defenders of established traditions of learning and religion. Much the same could be said for other leading humanists, notably Lefèvre d'Étaples. Furthermore, much depth might be added to our understanding of the early Reformation if we knew more about some controversies which had little or nothing to do with humanism, such as the struggle over the doctrine of the Immaculate Conception, which reflected the rivalries between the two chief mendicant orders, the Dominicans and the Franciscans. After all, even the humanist Ulrich von Hutten, later one of Luther's most vociferous champions, initially shrugged off the indulgence controversy as a mere quarrel among monks; and there can be no doubt that the rivalries between orders contributed both to the Augustinians' slowness to act against Luther and to the Dominicans' eagerness to prosecute him.

In addition to these and other special studies of individual conflicts of the period, historical scholarship could learn much from a comparative assessment of these and many other controversies, with special attention to the issues of authority, respect for tradition, and freedom for scholarly innovation, and also with attention to party alignments, methods used to conduct the controversies, and tendencies (if any) of one controversy to influence the course of others.

Some of the effects of pre-Reformation controversies are already widely recognized. The rise of a whole literature of controversy, typically expressed in brief, inexpensive, and widely circulated pamphlets, marks the rising power of the press as a means of forming and mobilizing public opinion. This development implied a breakdown of the techniques which the religious orders, the hierarchy, and the universities had heretofore used to maintain their control of public opinion. Not until after the damage was largely done did the established authorities devise effective ways to control the press and prevent its use by critics of the authorities themselves. This use of the press is most strikingly illustrated by the propaganda success of the *Letters of Obscure Men,* which may well have offended even most of the humanists, but which certainly did hold up the monastic and scholastic conservatives to ridicule. Yet it can be seen in earlier controversies also. Peter of Ravenna, in consciously appealing over the heads of the Cologne university authorities to general educated opinion through his published tracts, not only pointed the way to the *Letters of Obscure Men* (whose authors had known his case at first hand) but even prefigured the general picture of the Cologne theologians as a conspiratorial band of ignorant knaves.[13] None of the humanists, of course, not even Crotus and Hutten, could compare with Martin Luther as a controversial pamphleteer; but the pattern of using the printed word as a means of appealing to the people over the heads of the constituted authorities had already been set.

A second obvious effect of the pre-Reformation controversies was that they tended to make the humanists a self-conscious group with a heightened sense of common interests and solidarity and hence made the sympathy of a few key figures such as Erasmus and Pirckheimer sufficient to give Luther the initial wave of support that made German humanism the matrix out of which the new Reformation leadership emerged.[14] Professor Overfield would perhaps qualify this contention by reminding us of the aloofness of many humanists during the Reuchlin case and of the dismay expressed by still more humanists over the coarseness and radicalism of the *Letters of Obscure Men.* Nevertheless, the northern humanists of the early sixteenth century did express distaste for scholasticism frequently enough that it must count as one of their chief characteristics.[15] On balance, the controversies probably tended to draw them closer together.

Thirdly—a point which is little documented but seems obvious enough—the constant dissemination of vague, loose charges of scandalous irreverence, undue levity, and even heresy must have done something to depreciate the seriousness of any accusation of heresy. By the years 1517-1521, when Luther was winning his original base of support in Germany, so many pious and virtuous men (Reuchlin, Erasmus, Lefèvre, for example) had been maliciously accused of heresy, and on such dubious or inconsequential questions, that the charges made against one Augustinian friar by a rival group of Dominican friars were not very likely to convince people that this time the Church did in fact have a real heretic to contend with. Thus at least down to 1520, when his three famous treatises of that year finally alerted some of the more conservative spirits, German humanists tended to shrug off the attacks of Luther's critics as just another example of malevolent and obscurantist hostility to good learning.

These three major effects of the controversies are obvious enough, though each point merits careful further investigation. But the recent studies also suggest some other generalizations which are not so obvious but which may well help us to understand the age if they are borne out by further research.

Of one point my own research on the Peter of Ravenna controversy at Cologne has left me firmly convinced: the emergence of humanism as a new intellectual method and of the printing press as a new way of arousing public opinion posed a serious challenge to the corporate solidarity of the medieval university. Masters and students alike were sworn to observe the statutes of the university, which was a highly privileged corporation with a high degree of self-consciousness and solidarity, and with well established rules of procedure and propriety. Such an institution made allowance for internal disagreements which might arise, but its members bitterly resented any attempt to expose these disagreements to the external world through unauthorized appeals to the press—a trait which they share with more than one university in twentieth-century America. When Peter of Ravenna was first challenged on his teachings concerning the burial of executed criminals in 1507, he was offered the opportunity to defend himself, but only on condition that he did so "in a scholastic manner" and that he not publish any writings on the controversy without the consent of the rector. As a university professor he was under discipline; and what ultimately made his supporters at Cologne abandon him and so left him no choice but to depart was not his original teaching on a disputed point of law, but the offense of publishing works in which he reasserted his opinion and defended himself against his critics. Still worse, his works were emotional and polemical rather than sober and scholarly. He had appealed over the heads of his faculty peers to the general educated (Latin-reading) public, and had even threatened to expose the malevolence and ignorance of Jacob van Hochstraten and his other critics to the whole European world of learning. Such a man had violated the integrity of the university community, and not only had to be forced out of Cologne but also had to be troubled by renewed accusations when he began teaching law at Mainz.[16] The clash between traditional corporate solidarity and individual freedom to challenge corporate opinion, which was one of the central issues of the Reformation, can already be seen in this early and minor conflict; and obviously it was also one issue in the attempts of conservative schoolmen to silence the innovative criticisms which Erasmus and Lefèvre d'Ètaples levelled at various traditions coming out of the medieval period.

The studies of Professors Cameron and Hufstader also suggest that while humanism was certainly not identical with Protestantism, it did in fact contain latent revolutionary tendencies that inevitably made it challenge both the intellectual traditions of medieval scholasticism and the religious traditions of the medieval Church. I find the same point at least implied by the views of Professors Spitz and Moeller about the importance of the "third generation" of German humanists—the ones who were young in 1517—to the success of the Protestant Reformation.[17] In a very real sense, and despite the peaceful coexistence and substantial accommodation which they could at times achieve, humanism and scholasticism really were fundamentally opposed.

After all the sober wisdom which Professor Kristeller has preached about the folly of regarding humanism and scholasticism as two opposed and rival philosophies struggling for the control of intellectual life, one hesitates to speak thus of an inevitable conflict.[18] Yet though there is much truth in Kristeller's suggestion that the conflicts between the two groups sometimes appear analogous to interdepartmental rivalries in a modern university and often involved little more than rivalry for academic positions and prestige,[19] there is nevertheless another respect in which the split between the two traditions was very fundamental indeed. Kristeller defines Renaissance humanism in a very strict and narrow sense, as a movement which emphasized the educational and intellectual importance of a limited number of subjects which ever since ancient times had been regarded as "the humanities" (*litterae humaniores:* grammer, rhetoric, poetry, history, and moral philosophy), all of them studied, of course, through the medium of classical literature.[20] These fields of study in no sense claimed to represent the totality of human learning.

In the opinion of the humanists who taught them, however, they were the most truly practical and valuable fields of learning because they focused on problems of immediate concern in daily life rather than on speculative issues; the "humanities" were indeed "human" because their central focus was the problems of human behavior (i.e., morality, both private and public), and also the techniques useful for controlling human behavior (i.e., the study of rhetoric, the art of persuasive speech and writing). Thus they were more truly central to the problems of real life than were the traditional scholastic fields of study. Hence even though humanism was not in itself a new philosophical system, it did contain philosophical implications about the nature of reality and the ability of human reason to comprehend that reality. These humanistic views are conventially but poorly summarized in the trite and imprecise notion that humanism exalted the dignity of man's life in this world. Their real significance was that they questioned whether it was either part of man's business or part of man's capacity to comprehend eternally valid truths through reason. Perhaps the universe and the powers of man were such that only the practical problems of social relations and behavior (the matters with which humanistic studies chiefly dealt) were of real concern to man, and hence that the scholastic concern with logical and metaphysical questions was useless if not indeed actually harmful.[21] Thus on basic philosophical issues such as the nature of reality and the capacity of man's reason, humanism may have implied new and challenging philosophical views, and in that sense may have been a real philosophical threat to scholasticism.

Of more immediate practical effect, however, was the obvious tendency of humanistic thought, at least from the later fifteenth century, to pass beyond its originally restricted area of competence and to intrude into the subject matter of other, nonhumanistic fields such as law, medicine, theology, and logic. Even Professor Kristeller has noted this tendency and has observed that these humanistic intrusions were the occasion for many of the conflicts between humanists and scholastics in the late fifteenth and early sixteenth centuries. [22] But one wonders whether this tendency to intrude into other fields of study, and the resultant controversies, could have been merely accidental. Although humanism, strictly defined, dealt with only a limited group of subjects, it was something more than the totality of those subjects, for it was also a method of intellectual inquiry. So conceived, its methodological principles were potentially applicable not just to grammar, rhetoric, poetry, and moral philosophy but also to every field of study which rested on the precise interpretation of certain texts universally admitted to be authoritative, as in fact all fields of learning then did. If the critical humanist through his mastery of the arts of grammar and rhetoric were allowed to control the primary interpretation of these texts—such as Aristotle in philosophy, the Bible and the Fathers in theology, the *Corpus Juris Civilis* in law, or Galen in medicine—then in a very real sense he would control the fields of philosophy, theology, law, and medicine. A canon lawyer who was suddenly informed by Valla or Hutten that the Donation of Constantine was a forgery, a civil lawyer who was told that the medieval Italian legal commentators had misunderstood and distorted the law, or a theologian who was told that St. Gregory the Great lived too late to be a valid authority on the identity of Mary Magdalen, or that the Latin Vulgate text at various points misinterpreted the true meaning of the Greek New Testament, was keenly aware that humanism had in fact (if not in theory) intruded into his area of professional competence.

The point is that humanistic *method,* when applied to the texts of received authorities, and especially when accompanied by the typical humanistic animus against all things medieval, did pose a fundamental challenge to the scholastic tradition in all fields of learning. Professor Guido Kisch has ably traced the conflict at the University of Basel which resulted from the attempt of humanist-oriented jurists like Johannes Sichardus to make the new humanistic *mos gallicus* prevail in legal education and to reduce or even destroy the authority of *mos italicus,* the established legal science of the great Italian glossators and commentators of the Middle Ages.[23] The sharpest conflict, however, occurred in the field of theology, for the theologians at Paris, Cologne, Louvain, and elsewhere rather quickly saw that the work of Biblical humanists like John Colet, John Reuchlin, Lefevre d'Étaples, and Erasmus not only involved an arrogant repudiation of centuries of theological learning and ecclesiastical tradition but also in effect amounted to a declaration that the only true way to valid theological learning was through the textual analysis which only humanists trained in the three languages (classical Latin, Greek, and Hebrew) and in philology were qualified to conduct. In other words, they rightly saw in humanism an implication that their own scholastic theological science had no validity at all, and that a lifetime devoted to study of scholastic theology was no real qualification for the theologian's prime business of defining and explaining the content of the Christian faith.[24] Thus even though the established scholastic learning and the new humanist movement coexisted relatively harmoniously at many times and in many places, the conflicts that did break out were not coincidental but did spring from profound differences, arising ultimately from the difference in intellectual method.

The pre-Reformation controversies also illustrate a weakness in late medieval Catholicism which was to have disastrous consequences for the Church during the religious crisis. This weakness was the widespread confusion about the locus of authority within the Church.[25] The Spanish theologian Jacobus Stunica charged that the views of Erasmus and Lefèvre on the Vulgate and on many religious traditions amounted to a dangerously un-Catholic disrespect for authoritative tradition. In defense of their views on St. Mary Magdalen, Lefèvre and his friend Josse Clichtove both maintained that on questions where the Church had not made a dogmatic definition, qualified scholars had a perfect right to challenge traditional opinions, arguing on the basis of scriptural and patristic evidence, and applying the linguistic and historical criteria which humanists had long used in the evaluation of classical literary texts. In assigning relative weight to human testimonies on the Magdalen issue, Lefèvre and Clichtove applied the historical principle that the source chronologically nearest to the events related possesses the greatest authority. They also regarded Biblical evidence as far superior to any tradition, even patristic, and concluded that lack of Biblical testimony for a tradition was a strong argument for rejecting that tradition even in the face of plentiful evidence of other sorts.[26]

This attitude is the result of the characteristic humanistic desire for a return *ad fontes*—to the Bible, basically—in religious belief and practice. This principle did not drive all humanists to reject the authority of the Church or to rebel against all its practices and doctrines, but it may explain the tendency of those humanists who later were converted to Protestantism to take a far more negative attitude toward traditional Catholic beliefs and practices than did the non-humanist Luther. Such a tendency was already apparent in the attitude of Melanchthon and Justus Jonas toward radical reformers at Wittenberg in 1521-1522 and is even more clearly illustrated in the reform career of the ex-humanist Zwingli at Zurich—to say nothing of the humanistic antecedents of many of the early Swiss Anabaptists and of antitrinitarian radicals like Servetus.[27]

All of these tendencies still lay in the future until at least 1520, but some of the conservative critics of Lefèvre's views on Mary Magdalen and of Erasmus' Paraphrase of the New Testament warned of the dangerous implications of the humanists' disregard for non-Scriptural tradition. John Fisher, Bishop of Rochester, a man not unfriendly to humanism, attacked Lefèvre's opinions on the Magdalen and enunciated a theory of authority quite contrary to the humanistic tendency toward *sola Scriptura*. He argued that the centuries-long acquiescence of the faithful in the sermons, liturgical passages, and hymns that contained the Magdalen tradition was normative in establishing the validity of that tradition in such a way that the humanistic criticisms were not permissible. In other words (at least on a question where Rome had not spoken) the community of the faithful through the centuries was the authority in matters of faith and practice. Furthermore, he argued, the sudden casting-aside of such long established traditions by humanist critics would unsettle the minds of the faithful and so should also be rejected on purely pastoral grounds. Bishop Fisher's position was clear even if rather subtle, but his clarity on this point of authority was about as rare as his later willingness to face martyrdom in the cause of a united Christendom.[28]

The other critics of Lefèvre and Clichtove were less perceptive; and while figures like Marc de Grandval, Noël Béda, and Petrus Sutor also warned of the dangers of failing to respect tradition, they did not manage to convince the leaders of educated opinion that reliance on the literal interpretation of Scripture alone, without respect for long-standing traditions or for the exegetical conclusions of the scholastic doctors of the preceding centuries, was dangerous procedure for men who still claimed to be loyal sons of the Roman Church.

Finally, the pre-Reformation controversies already studied suggest one habit of controversial procedure which had grave consequences when applied to the case of Martin Luther. This was the tendency of many conservative schoolmen, even when discussing matters which had not become matters of official dogma and perhaps never would, to regard their own views as unquestionably the opinion of "the Church" and hence to utter loosely phrased charges of heresy against individuals who at worst were taking questionable positions on debatable issues. Thus they often transferred the argument from the issue of concern for discovery of the truth to the issue of loyalty to "the Church"—that is, to the views of the Church as defined not by a council or by Rome but by some pressure group within the Church. Such attempts to overwhelm the opposition sometimes worked. Ortwin Gratius abandoned his defense of Peter of Ravenna at Cologne and bowed to the will of the theological faculty. Josse Clichtove in 1521 retracted his earlier support of Lefèvre's views on the Magdalen and even drew up the text of the *Determinatio* in which the Sorbonne the next year formally condemned Lefèvre's views on Mary Magdalen, though without condemning the humanist by name.[29]

Where a critical humanist was less pliable, he might be subjected to attacks, not only within academic channels but also by public denunciations through the mendicant orders' control of the pulpit. Lefèvre's young admirer at Metz, Agrippa von Nettesheim, found that as a result of his endorsement of Lefèvre's views during private discussions, several friars publicly denounced him from the pulpit as an enemy of the faith.[30] In the same way, somewhat earlier, the Reuchlin controversy really began when the fomentor of all the trouble, Johannes Pfefferkorn, on learning that Reuchlin had privately advised the Emperor Maximilian against the plan to confiscate and burn all Jewish books, published a slanderous vernacular pamphlet accusing Reuchlin of taking bribes from the Jews. Thus not all those who recklessly incited public opinion during the pre-Reformation period where humanists.

But this traditional method of arbitrarily determining a debatable issue by the fiat of some group that presumed to speak in the name of the Church, and then compelling the opponent to recant or face denunciation as a heretic, was not only inherently vicious but also on the point of breakdown. We have seen how in the Peter of Ravenna case, and even more in the Reuchlin case, the accused or his self-appointed defenders used the developing power of the press to appeal to public opinion over the heads of the academic officials, and to balance the power of artfully written appeals to educated opinion over against the friars' traditional use of sermons that appealed to popular hatred of heresy. Furthermore, the humanists were particularly hard for the friars and theologians to silence in this traditional way because the fashion for humanistic culture had spread at the royal courts and among the ruling classes of the towns by the early sixteenth century. This fashion assured the humanists of ready access to the rulers of nations and cities and hence won for them effective protection from the governing authority. Erasmus, for example, corresponded with popes, cardinals, bishops, emperors, kings, nobles, and town councillors. Both by letter and by personal contact he promoted his ideals of scholarship and church reform. The Pope, the Emperor, the Kings of France and England contended for the honor of becoming his patron and protector. Similarly, Lefèvre d'Étaples by the early 1520's was under the special protection of the French royal family. Though on one occasion he found it necessary to flee the kingdom for a time, the influence of his friends at court persistently thwarted the efforts of his opponents to have him condemned as a heretic. Such great humanists could still be opposed, criticized, and even accused of impiety and heresy; but they could not be isolated and silenced.

Thus the system of using broad accusations of impiety and heresy, and of forcing an isolated individual to submit, broke down as the humanists became more numerous, more politically influential, and more skilled at using the printed word in their own defense. Any attempt to compel an earnest critic of scholastic theology and current religious practice to submit, merely by demanding blind obedience to what was in fact a highly uncertain authority, now could lead to successful defiance and even to religious revolution, if that critic possessed the loyal protection of a powerful secular prince, a genius for preaching and for the writing of popular pamphlets, the sympathetic respect of the particular social organism of which he was a member, and the ability to win endorsement from the interlocking directorate of humanistic sodalities which influenced the intellectual and even the political life of the imperial court, the princely states, and the free German cities. Martin Luther was that critic. His greatness as a religious thinker and as a leader of men may transcend the power of historical explanation; but his ability to survive long enough to create a great religious upheaval depended on a specific set of historical circumstances; and some of these circumstances may well have been created by the inherently minor but historically significant controversies of the last pre-Reformation generation.

*Notes*

[1] Lewis W. Spitz. *The Religious Renaissance of the German Humanists* (Cambridge, Mass.: Harvard University Press, 1963), pp. 134-35; Hajo Holborn, *Ulrich von Hutten and the German Reformation,* trans. Roland H. Bainton (New Haven: Yale University Press, 1937), p. 31; and, for the concept of "scholastic" humanism, Paul Joachimsen, *Geschichtsauffassung und Geschichtschreibung in Deutschland unter dem Einfluss des Humanismus* (Aalen: Scientia Verlag, 1968; reprint of ed. Leipzig, 1910), pp. 77-78.

[2] Hermann, Graf von Neuenar, *Epistolae trium illustrium uriorun, ad Hermannum comitcm Nuenarium. Eiusdemy responsoria una ad lo. Reucblinum, et altera ad lectorem* . . . . [Cologne: Eucharius Ceruicornus, 1518]. He also edited Giorgio Benigni, *Defensio praestantissimi viri Joannis Reuchlin.* . . . [N.p., 1517].

[3] Paul Oskar Kristeller, *Renaissance Thought: The Classic, Scholastic, and Humanist Strains,* Harper Torchbooks (New York: Harper & Brothers, 1961), pp. 10, 19-20, and especially 99-102, 108-17.

[4] Lewis W. Spitz, "The Third Generation of German Renaissance Humanists," in *Aspects of the Renaissance: A Symposium,* ed. Archibald R. Lewis (Austin: The University of Texas Press, 1967), pp. 106-08; and Bernd Moeller, "The German Humanists and the Beginnings of the Reformation," in his *Imperial Cities and the Reformation: Three Essays,* trans. H. C. Erik Midelfort and Mark U. Edwards, Jr. (Philadelphia: Fortress Press, 1972), pp. 24-26.

[5] James H. Overfield, "A New Look at the Reuchlin Affair." *Studies in Medieval and Renaissance History,* ed. Howard L. Adelson (Lincoln: University of Nebraska Press, 1971), VIII, 165-207.

[6] Richard Cameron, "The Attack on the Biblical Work of Lefèvre d'Ètaples, 1514-1521," *Church History,* XXXVIII (1969), 9-24; Anselm Hufstader, "Lefèvre d'Ètaples and the Magdalen," *Studies in the Renaissance,* XVI (1969), 31-60.

[7] Charles G. Nauert, Jr., "Peter of Ravenna and the 'Obscure Men' of Cologne: A Case of Pre-Reformation Controversy," *Renaissance: Studies in Honor of Hans Baron,* ed. Anthony Molho and John A. Tedeschi (Florence: G. C. Sansoni: DeKalb, Ill.: Northern Illinois University Press, 1971), pp. 609-40.

[8] Overfield, pp. 194-95.

[9] *Ibid.,* pp. 195-201.

[10] *Ibid.,* p. 201.

[11] Nauert, p. 639.

[12] See, for example, Myron P. Gilmore, "Erasmus and Alberto Pio, Prince of Carpi," in *Action and Conviction in Early Modern Europe: Essays in Memory of E. H. Harbison,* ed. Theodore K. Rabb and Jerrold E. Seigel (Princeton: Princeton University Press, 1969), pp. 299-318.

[13] Heinrich Heidenheimer, "Petrus Ravennas in Mainz und sein Kampf mit den Kölner Dunkelmännern,"

*Westdeutsche Zeitschrift für Geschichte und Kunst,* XVI (1897), 234-40.

Although in a vague sort of way, historians have long recognized the importance of the printing press in the success of Luther's movement, the subject has seldom been investigated in detail. In particular, the emergence of the press as a power during the pre-Reformation controversies has rarely been admitted, except in the spectacular Reuchlin case. There is some acknowledgment of this point in the article of Louise W. Holborn, "Printing and the Growth of a Protestant Movement in Germany from 1517 to 1524," *Church History,* XI (1942), 123-37, especially pp. 125-26, where the role of the "humanist" controversies is understated. See also Lucien Febvre and Henri-Jean Martin, *L'Apparition du Livre* (Paris: Editions Albin Michel, 1958), especially Chapter VIII. For the broadest and most challenging interpretation of the impact of the printed book on the period, see the articles by Elizabeth L. Eisenstein, "Some Conjectures About the Impact of Printing on Western Society and Thought: A Preliminary Report," *The Journal of Modern History,* XL (1968), 1-56; "The Advent of Printing and the Problem of the Renaissance," *Past and Present,* No. 45 (November, 1969), 19-89; and especially "L'avènement de l'imprimerie et la Réforme: Une nouvelle approche au problème du démembrement de la chrétienté occidentale," *Annales: Économies, sociétés civilisations,* XXVI (November-December, 1971), 1355-1382. Professor Eisenstein's interest in the effects of printing passes far beyond its role in the diffusion of protestantism or even the antecedents of that diffusion, but she does give attention to this narrower problem also, especially in the last-cited article.

[14] Moeller, pp. 24-30, 35-36; Spitz, "Third Generation," pp. 106-08, for more detailed evidence.

[15] Spitz, *Religious Renaissance,* pp. 7-8, 275-76, and *passim* (in his discussions of Celtis, Hutten, Pirckheimer, and Erasmus).

[16] Nauert, pp. 637-40.

[17] Spitz, "Third Generation," pp. 106-19; Moeller, pp. 30-35.

[18] Kristeller, p. 113.

[19] *Ibid.*

[20] *Ibid.,* pp. 10, 100-01, 108-11, 122.

[21] For two suggestive recent discussions of the humanists' attitude toward truth and man's ability to discover truth, starting from very different presuppositions but both suggesting that humanism did imply certain characteristic philosophical attitudes, at least in its Italian expressions, see Jerrold E. Seigel, *Rhetoric and Philosophy in Renaissance Humanism: The Union of Eloquence and Wisdom, Petrarch to Valla* (Princeton: Princeton University Press, 1968), and William J. Bouwsma, *Venice and the Defense of Republican Liberty: Renaissance Values in the Age of the Counter Reformation* (Berkeley: University of California Press, 1968), especially Chapter 1.

[22] Kristeller, pp. 19, 100-01, 110, 123-24.

[23] Guido Kisch, *Humanismus und Jurisprudenz: Der Kampf zwischen mos italicus und mos gallicus an der Universität Basel,* Basler Studien zur Rechtswissenschaft, Heft 42 (Basel: Helbing & Lichtenhahn, 1955).

[24] This awareness is expressed in the scholastic attacks on Lefèvre d'Étaples discussed by Cameron and Hufstader. On Erasmus and his critics, Roland II. Bainton, *Erasmus of Christendom* (New York: Charles Scribner's Sons, 1969), pp. 134-40.

[25] Cameron, p. 13.

[26] *Ibid.,* pp. 16-18.

[27] Moeller, p. 34; Spitz, "Third Generation," p. 107.

[28] Cameron, pp. 18-20; Hufstader, pp. 43-53.

[29] Cameron, p. 23.

[30] Charles G. Nauert, Jr., *Agrippa and the Crisis of Renaissance Thought,* Illinois Studies in the Social Sciences, vol. 55 (Urbana: University of Illinois Press, 1965), pp. 61-62.

---

## THE REFORMATION AND LITERATURE

### Perez Zagorin (essay date 1982)

SOURCE: "Agrarian Rebellion," in *Rebels and Rulers, 1500-1660,* Vol. I, Cambridge University Press, 1982, pp. 175-227.

[*In the following excerpt, Zagorin argues for the importance of religious pamphlets, such as the Twelve Articles, in inciting the German peasant revolts of the sixteenth century which contributed to the social rebellion of the Protestant Reformation.*]

The hundreds of articles of grievances put forward in the course of the revolt [German peasant insurrections of the sixteenth century] along with the numerous proposals that emerged looking to freedom. reform, and reconstruction, faithfully reflected the extraordinary political ferment the peasant war aroused. Brief as it was, it stimulated an outburst of ideas and aspirations, a variety of programs, and a hope in new possibilities that were unparalleled in other agrarian rebellions. In its effect on the popular mind it can only be compared with some of the revolutionary civil wars of the early modern age. If unwillingness to be ruled in the old way is one of the hallmarks of a great revolution, as Lenin held, then the peasant war gave ample evidence of this characteristic.

Prominent amid the welter of demands were personal freedom for the serf and autonomy for village and urban communities. The insistence on autonomy, it has been rightly said, runs like a red thread through all the grievances and programs.[1] Peasants desired both emancipation from serfdom and social respect and a recognition of worth from their superiors as the necessary basis for any future cooperation. The will to direct participation in political life through corporative and estate organization was another basic theme in peasant programs. Common, too, in many rebellions was communities' insistence on popular election of their parish clergy. In some ecclesiastical principalities, demands were made for the secularization of the state with the transformation of the bishop into secular ruler. Episcopal cities witnessed a call for the overthrow of the bishop's and chapter's power, the elimination of clerical privileges, and the reduction of both clergy and noble inhabitants to the same level as other citizens. Among the revolts that remained territorially confined, the chief aim was the limitation of the prince's power by the rights and autonomy of the territorial community as expressed through the diet or assembly of estates. In the supraterritorial movements, a frequent goal was the elimination of petty rulers and the absorption of their domains into some larger political structure by a still-to-be-determined reform. Along the same lines, the peasants' articles in some areas expressed the wish to be freed of subjection to their ruler and become immediate subjects of the emperor. Schemes also appeared to strengthen the empire and its institutions in order to make them more representative and curb obstructive particularism.[2]

Because of its wide dissemination and effect, the most important manifesto of the peasant war was the Twelve Articles of the upper Swabian peasantry, produced in March 1525 at Memmingen in the course of the formation of the Christian Union by the upper Swabian *Haufen*. Its draftsmen were two Memmingen Protestants, Christoph Schappeler, a clergyman, and Sebastian Lotzer, a fur dealer, who reduced more than three hundred grievance articles of peasant villages to a concise and representative statement. The Twelve Articles combined a list of practical demands with an ideological justification of the peasant struggle. Replete with Biblical references, they gave eloquent formulation to the conviction of godly justice, which had fused with the revolution and on which the peasants based their case. Despite the fact that the document was composed by religious intellectuals rather than peasants, it was nonetheless an authentic expression of peasant desires and aspirations.[3]

Addressed to the "Christian reader," the Twelve Articles began with a preamble denying that violence was the fruit of the gospel and that the peasants were rebels or against authority. Rather, they wished to live in obedience to Christ and God's word, whereas those who opposed their requests were antichrists and enemies of the gospel. The articles that followed strongly condemned the oppressions of lords, for which redress was sought. They demanded the election of parish clergy, the reduction of tithes, and their administration by the community. The detestable custom of serfdom was to be abolished because Christ's sacrifice has redeemed all men, and "therefore it is proven from Scripture that we are and wish to be free." Other articles required the restoration to the community of wrongfully appropriated common lands and rights to hunt, fish, and cut wood; the reduction of the grievous burden of labor services; the equitable regulation of rents and dues; the removal of arbitrary criminal jurisdiction and evil new laws contrary to custom; and the abolition of the heriot as an intolerable robbery of windows and orphans. In the conclusion, the peasants submitted their claims to the test of God's word; whatever could be shown not in accord with it they promised to make null and void.

The Twelve Articles dealt with fundamental questions of peasant economy, legal and social condition, and independence. Although they did not envisage the overturn of landlordship or rulership, they did project a significant strengthening of the peasant order by ending serfdom and restricting the powers of landlords and seigneurial and ruler jurisdiction. If the Bible and divine justice was their immanent principle, their keynote was the self-assertion of the organized peasant community, the *Gemeinde,* as the voice and vehicle of peasant interests. They captured and condensed to a high degree the essential character of the agrarian rebellion as a *Gemeinde* movement.

For these reasons, the Twelve Articles achieved exceptional influence. Printed first in March 1525, they were reprinted over twenty times in two months and became known throughout the empire and the entire area of the peasant war. They were imitated or adopted by other revolts and served as a model for additional demands. There is evidence, too, that they were read aloud and discussed in large crowds. Not only did they help to spread the rebellion, they gave currency to the revolutionary doctrine of a justice rooted in God's word.[4]

Throughout the peasant war, ideas of common good and common use recurred in demands and grievances. Even though most programs did not conceive of leveling social differences or abolishing landlordship and property, they looked to more fraternal relations, the curbing of privileges, and equitable government. The article-letter of the Black Forest peasants sketched the vague outline of a reformed society, a Christian brotherhood, to relieve the common man in town and country of his oppression. In the name of godly justice, it called upon noblemen, priests, and monks to enter into the brotherhood and live like other folk on penalty of the worldly ban—that is, complete exclusion from all social and economic intercourse.[5] The articles of the Franconian peasantry, imbued with the populist spirit, decreed that all privileged men, spiritual and temporal, shall henceforth possess no greater rights than the ordinary burgher or peasant.[6] The articles of the city of Frankfurt, which were also taken over by other towns, voiced the commonalty's demand for election of pastors, democratization of city government, and economic reforms for the welfare of the lower orders.[7]

Reliance on the estates as the organ of the community was a basic presupposition in the programs of intraterritorial revolts. It probably received its strongest expression in Tyrol in the comprehensive reform plan drawn up at a revolutionary meeting of peasant and town representatives at Meran in May 1525. The Meran articles involked love of Christ, love of one's neighbor, and the common good as justification to create a "new *Landesordnung,*" or territorial constitution. Here peasants and burghers drew on their previous experience of representation in the Tyrolean diet to redefine the territorial community as consisting of their own two orders in a new relation of power to the prince. Although assuming the continuance of Archduke Ferdinand's rule as count of Tyrol, the Meran articles laid down conditions for securing the freedom and autonomy of the common man and territorial community. They took away noble privileges and jurisdiction, abolished the church hierarchy and ecclesiastical property and immunities, provided for the election and dismissal of clergy by towns and villages, and ordained a broad range of political, judicial, and economic reforms as the foundation of a new order.[8]

### *Notes*

[1] . . . Buszello, "Gemeinde, Territorium, und Reich in den politischen Programmen des deutschen Bauernkrieges 1525/26," in Wehler, *Der deutsche Bauernkrieg,* 106.

[2] See the excellent survey of aims and programs in Buszello, *Der deutsche Bauernkrieg.*

[3] The text of the Twelve Articles with their full title is printed in Franz, *Quellen,* 174-9. Schappeler apparently wrote the preface while Lotzer compiled the list of demands. Every English translation I have seen omits the Biblical references. For detailed treatment of their background, content, and significance, see G. Franz, "Die Entstehung der Zwölf Artikel," *Archiv für Reformationsgeschichte* 36, 3 (1939); E. Walder, "Die politische Gehalt der Zwölf Artikel," *Schweizer Beiträge zur allgemeinen Geschichte* 12 (1954); M. Brecht, "Der Theologische Hintergrund der Zwölf Artikel," *Zeitschrift für Kirchengeschichte* 85, 2, (1974); Blickle, *Die Revolution von 1525,* esp. pt. 1, sec. 2, and "The economic, social, and political background of the Twelve Articles," *Journal of Peasant Studies* 3, 1 (1975). Blickle's useful account includes a quantitative analysis of local grievance articles showing the considerable extent to which the Twelve Articles incorporated demands that the peasants regarded as of the greatest importance.

[4] For the range and effect of the Twelve Articles, see Blickle's discussion in *Die Revolution von 1525* and "The economic, social, and political background of the *Twelve Articles,*" and G. Vogler, "Der revolutionäre Gehalt und die räumliche Verbreitung der oberschwabischen Zwölf Artikel," in *Historische Zeitschrift,* Beiheft 4.

[5] Printed in Franz, *Quellen,* 235-6. In all probability, the author was the evangelical preacher Balthasar Hubmayer.

[6] *Ibid.,* 368-9.

[7] *Ibid.,* 455-61.

[8] *Ibid.,* 272-85.

## Miriam Usher Chrisman (essay date 1982)

SOURCE: "From Polemic to Propaganda: The Development of Mass Persuasion in the Late Sixteenth Century," in *Archive for Reformation History,* Vol. 73, 1982, pp. 175-95.

[*In the essay that follows, Chrisman argues that the pamphlets distributed by both Protestants and Catholics during the Reformation were an early form of political propaganda.*]

Polemic can be defined as a controversial argument, a discussion in which opposite views are presented and maintained by opponents. It connotes a two-way process, a dialogue, although it may be a dialogue between the deaf. Propaganda lacks that quality of interchange. It is one-sided, a systematic attempt to propagate a particular opinion or doctrine. Its purpose is to influence men's opinions and attitudes and thus their actions and behaviour.[1] In the sixteenth century ideological formulations experienced the shift from polemic argument to propaganda. Printing presses made it possible to develop new forms of mass persuasion which were directed to the creation and perpetuation of schism, suspicion and hatred between the Christian churches.

When the Reformation began the reformers believed it was a mere matter of time before the Roman church would be won over to see the errors of the past and thus proceed to the purification of doctrine and practise. Luther addressed his *Freedom of a Christian Man* to Pope Leo X in an attempt to maintain some degree of dialogue. As late as 1536 Calvin still hoped that Francis I would accept or at least listen to the new doctrines and dedicated *The Institutes of the Christian Religion* to him. An overwhelming number of polemic pamphlets flowed from the presses between 1520 and 1525, in the city of Strasbourg alone 296 editions were printed.

*Table 1*

Publication of Polemic Pamphlets, Strasbourg, 1520-1529

| | *Protestant* | *Catholic* |
|---|---|---|
| 1520 | 50 | 4 |
| 1521 | 36 | 4 |
| 1522 | 41 | 7 |
| 1523 | 79 | 13 |
| 1524 | 54 | 17 |
| 1525 | 26 | 4 |
| 1526 | 9 | 0 |
| 1527 | 2 | 3 |
| 1528 | 0 | 1 |
| 1529 | 8 | 2 |

Even more flowed from Wittenberg and Nuremberg.[2] The pamphlets were controversial and disputations. They set forth the arguments in favor of the new doctrines and customs. They criticized the errors of the Roman church. But they assumed a rational, if contentious, discourse.

By the middle of the century both sides had changed their tone and their purposes. The schism within the church was accepted as permanent. Faced with the necessity of maintaining the cohesion of its band of faithful in the face of its enemies, each group developed new techniques of indoctrination. As Leonard Doob has observed for the twentieth century, propaganda reflects conflict within a society. Competing groups use methods of persuasion to attract adherents from the ranks of the enemy, from among the neutrals and to strengthen themselves.[3] After 1560, it was no longer a matter of rational argument. The object was to control group attitudes and behaviour. Instead of polemic pamphlets, popular broadsheets, newsheets, songs and woodcuts rolled off the printing presses.[4] Viewed in the light of modern propaganda, the techniques of mass persuasion were already well advanced.

Printing was the instrument of new forms. It had always been possible to influence men's thoughts and actions through the spoken word, through sermons and harangues. Printing gave these words a greater permanence and a greater effect. By the end of the sixteenth century both sides, Catholic and Protestant, began to use the printed word in multiple ways to support their own version of the truth and, above all, to arouse fear of their anatogonists. The core of modern propaganda is stereotyping. Walter Lippmann pointed out that in a complex world men cannot have an accurate picture of reality. Thus they construct their own view of reality to achieve a sense of security.[5] In the sixteenth century this meant the creation of a false image of the opposing religious group. The perceived differences were imbued with emotional and psychological elements as well as religious aspects. The opponent was so separated that his continued existence was viewed as a menace to a stable social order.

The intriguing element for the historian is how the change came about. The polemic tracts of the early years of the Reformation fit clearly into the context of medieval religious, political and scholarly life. Popes, emperors and other princes, for centuries, had used skilled writers like Marsilio of Padua and John of Salisbury to set forth their particular version of a political or religious controversy. Lorenzo Valla, Poggio Bracciolini, Flavio Biondo earned their keep as papal writers, turning out the desired opinion in elegant style. Francesco Filelfo wrote for the Sforzas as well as for the pope. The German humanists were engaged in the bitter Reuchlin controversy just before the Reformation, indeed Ulrich von Hutten moved easily from writing polemic against the Dominicans to writing tracts in support of Luther. What is important to observe is that in the case of Germany until 1525 these battles were open, fought among opponents who knew each other, who openly signed their name to their pamphlets and tracts and who were, by and large, educated men—clerics or scholars. Of the 296 editions of religious polemic published in Strasbourg between 1520 and 1525, only twenty-seven or less than one percent, were published anonymously. All of the polemic on the Catholic side was signed. The overwhelming majority of the Protestant pamphlets were written by clergy who had converted to the new movement and were eager to propagate the religious doctrines of the reformed party.

Then, after the Peasant's War, production of this polemic dropped dramatically (Table 1). Mark Edward's analysis of Lutheran publication in all the major centers of printing. Nuremburg, Augsburg, Wittenberg and Strasbourg shows the same pattern of production in every city—an outpouring from 1520-1525, a sharp decline thereafter.[6] It is impossible not to conclude that the majority of Protestant clergy were afraid that their call for religious reform had been misinterpreted. The Peasant's War was an abyss, a yawning chasm, which opened at their feet. Terrified by the specter of anarchy, they quickly drew back. After 1525 the clergy adopted a far more sober tone, indeed few of them continued to write pamphlets addressed to the populace. It was men like Otto Brunfels, Matthias Flaccius Illyricus or the Anabaptists, none of them accepted by the established reformers, who continued to write for the larger public. The established reformed clergy continued their disputes over doctrine but they addressed each other. They wrote in Latin instead of in German. A few polemic treatises continued to appear. In Strasbourg the Council of Trent created a flurry of activity in the 1540s, then the polemic tracts were reduced to no more than one or two a year. The outpouring of 1520-25 was never repeated.

*Table 2*

Publication of Poletnic Pamphlets in Strasbourg, 1530-1599

| | *Protestant* | *Catholic* |
|---|---|---|
| 1530-39 | 17 | 5 |
| 1540-49 | 26 | 3 |
| 1550-59 | 4 | 1 |
| 1560-69 | 7 | 1 |
| 1570-79 | 1 | 1 |
| 1580-89 | 2 | 0 |
| 1590-99 | 2 | 0 |

Instead, after 1570, new forms began to appear. While they did not reach the totals of the early polemic they outweighed the publication of Protestant doctrine, Biblical commentary or humanist works in these years.

*Table 3*

Publication of Broadsheets, *Zeitung* and Popular Propaganda Songs and Protestant Doctrine, Strasbourg, 1550-1599

| | *Propaganda Materials* | *Protestant Doctrine (including Catechisms)* |
|---|---|---|
| 1550-59 | 6 | 9 |
| 1560-69 | 11 | 17 |
| 1570-79 | 62 | 7 |
| 1580-89 | 24 | 3 |
| 1590-99 | 33 | 2 |

The major propaganda form was the illustrated broadsheet, a large, single sheet with a woodcut that might occupy the entire upper half. The text appeared below. The illustrations were usually in color, color which did much to enhance the dramatic and emotional message. A woodcut of the burning of two Anabaptist women is filled with red: the stockings of the executioner are red; the martyr's dress is red; the jerkin of the attending magistrate is red; the fire is red and yellow. A great cloud, like a wave, engulfs the martyr.[7] The illustration might provide the entire sequence of an event: the assassination of the Prince of Orange in his Palace; the pursuit of the assassin; the latter's conviction and execution.[8] Other broadsheets were in black and white but these were consciously manipulated to create dramatic contrasts. In addition to the illustrated broadsheets there were *zeitung,* usually composed of four leaves, perhaps eight. These were journalistic accounts of a major event, a battle, a political assassination, the St. Batholomew's massacre, important contemporary occurrences. These varied from quite factual accounts written by an eyewitness—the young Francesco Guevara, for example, provided an account of the siege of Malta, written ostensibly as a letter to his family[9]—to strongly biased versions of the close fought battles between the Dutch and the Duke of Alva in favor of the beleaguered Dutch.[10] Poems, published in the form of large or small broadsheets, celebrated the constancy of martyrs to the faith, the bravery of leaders and troops fighting the Catholic or Protestant cause, the treachery of the opponent. Songs were equally, perhaps more important. Songs celebrated the virtues of Protestant heroes. Songs extolled Protestant victories. Songs deplored Catholic cruelty.[11]

A significant element in the German propaganda is its anonymity. The polemic of the 1520s, as we have seen, was far from anonymous. Men and women, seemingly proudly, signed their tracts, bearing personal witness to their own conversion. The propaganda is largely nameless, all the more to be noted because other forms of broadsheets, reports of comets, reports of wonderful events, were usually signed and might even list other witnesses to the event. Thus, a report on the birth of quintuplets in 1566 gives the name of the midwife and those of three other women who attended the birth.[12] a report of a remarkable stalk of wheat which bore 72 kernels on one stem notes that the honorable magistrates of Strasbourg observed this themselves.[13] A description of the capture of a crocodile by one Hieronymus Mantaner stated that the writer, Salvatore Flaminio, had been in captivity with Mantaner and had personally observed the event.[14]

Anonymity was not, then, an integral element of popular publication. Indeed for the wonder publications the opposite seems to have been the case. There was a conscious effort to establish witness and thus credibility. The propaganda broadsheets were an exception to the general rule. The anonymity cannot be causally related to fear of censorship. Most German cities had ordinances invoking censorship and forbidding the publication of *schmähschriften* but it was the printer who was held responsible. Many of the propaganda broadsheets bear the name of the printer or the city.[15] Who wrote these broadsheets? We do not know. It is my own intuition that in the case of the German broadsheets the authors were not clerics. Political accounts may have been the work of writers on the staff of a prince, city secretaries, upper members of the proliferating bureaucracy. It seems likely that the writers were working with certain printers. The writer may have conceivably been the printer himself. In Strasbourg Johann Fischart can be identified as a major propagandist. Although most of his propaganda works were unsigned they have long since been clearly attributed, partially because of his unique use of words. His brother-in-law. Bernhard Jobin, operated one of the largest printing shops in the city at the end of the century. Fischart translated and edited a barrage of propaganda—broadsheets, *zeitung,* poems—defending the Protestant cause in the French wars of religion. Jacob Cammerlander, another Strasbourg printer who made an important contribution to popular scientific and technological publication, printed violent anti-Catholic literature. Anton Bertram, whose major income as a printer came from turning out theses, disputations and other official publications for the Strasbourg Academy, devoted substantial press space to propaganda broadsheets for the Protestant cause.

Broad comparative study of printers in several cities may make it possible to establish some connection between the printing shops and the development of propaganda. It is certainly an area that calls for further study. The printers had discovered the size and the appetite of the popular market during the brief five years of the pamphlet revolution. When the clergy stopped writing these tracts the bottom dropped out for the printers, reflected in the production figures given in the tables. Until 1520 the Catholic church provided the major market for books. The Protestant church, without the monasteries, the chapter libraries, the large bureaucracy with its canon lawyers, never guaranteed the same stable and secure market.

Clearly it was essential for the printers to develop new groups of readers. In Strasbourg the immediate response to the cut-off of religious publication was a burst of popular and scientific treatises. People were health conscious in the sixteenth century and popular medical manuals always sold. By the end of the 1530s new popular writers began to publish novels, short stories and plays for the vernacular market. The journalism after 1560 would seem to be a continuation of this development of materials which would sell to a large audience.[16]

*Table 4*

Catholic and Protestant Publication in Strasbourg, 1480-1599

(includes Doctrine, Sermons, Liturgies, Curates Manuals, and Polemic)

*Catholic Works*

| | |
|---|---|
| 1480-89 | 160 |
| 1490-99 | 134 |
| 1500-09 | 159 |
| 1510-19 | 163 |
| 1520-29 | 99 |
| Total: | 716 |

*Protestant Works*

| | |
|---|---|
| 1520-29 | 504 |
| 1530-39 | 130 |
| 1540-49 | 93 |
| 1550-59 | 55 |
| 1560-69 | 75 |
| 1570-79 | 55 |
| 1580-89 | 47 |
| 1590-99 | 35 |
| Total: | 994 |

The mass market was central to the propagandists. Religious polemic had attempted to change people's religious beliefs but it proceeded in traditional fashion, under the direction of men trained to persuade and to lead. Their writing led to the conversion of ordinary men and women to the new faith, but they did not create a new view of the world. Indeed the moment that the writers felt this had occurred, they stopped writing.

The propaganda created a new view of society, albeit one that had been politically recognized in 155. The world was divided into hostile camps. It was essential for each group to stake out its own claim to the truth and to maintain its separation from the unbelievers. The anonymous propagandists helped to make the separation clear, and laid the foundations of hostility which would end in the prolonged religious struggles of the seventeenth century. Viewed in the light of modern propaganda analysis these writers, whether consciously or unconsciously, adopted the major techniques of mass persuasion and opinion control. One of the primary objectives of the Protestant propagandists was to create a strong sense of identity within the fold by asserting the evils of Catholicism. G. Wylie Sypher has shown that the propaganda written by protagonists of the Catholic League in France had exactly the same aim.[17] In both cases the message was destructive. Its purpose was to create suspicion and distrust of the enemy, to reinforce anxiety and play on the consequences of defeat, principles clearly outlined by Josef Goebbels at a later date.[18]

Portrait broadsheets were important to this type of propaganda. They were an integral element in the process of iconclasm which Louis-Jean Calvet has described as part of revolutionary propaganda. The new consciousness leads to the rejection of old symbols and customs, but the destruction of the old must then be accompanied by the creation of new symbols.[19] Sixteenth century propagandists used religious and political leaders as their symbols. Portrait broadsheets depicted the leaders as heros and heroines, stressing their faithfulness, their constancy, their willingness to endure martyrdom for the cause. They were models of the new way of life, inspiring others to dedicate themselves in the same way.

Jan Hus, for example, exemplified the Protestant cause. A 1550 broadsheet showed him in academic regalia with an open book, symbolic of his preaching of the Holy Word of God. Hus, said the text, had preached the truth of Jesus Christ against the Roman papacy and had revealed the abominable errors of the Roman church. He had then been summoned to the Council of Constance where he went willingly on the strength of the imperial safe-conduct. On arrival, however, he and Jerome of Prague were charged with being stiff-necked and disobedient to the Church of Rome and condemned to be burned. The humiliation of Hus at the hands of his judge was described, but his death was triumphant. As the fire burned fiercely, he sang a hymn of praise in a joyful voice. On the day of his death, Hus said to his captors: "'Today you roast a goose, but after one hundred years a swan will come whom you cannot roast.' With these words he prophesied the coming of Luther. God grant us also such a firm faith that we will all stand by Jesus Christ eternally."[20]

Another broadsheet presented a handsome woodcut of Heinrich Bullinger. The text, written in verse by Johann Fischart, proclaimed that although great age and grey hair were worthy of respect in themselves, they were even more worthy when earned in the service of God, in dedication to the needs of the fatherland and the piety of the common people. Bullinger's name had climbed over the Swiss alps, his virtue was known to foreign people as well as to his countrymen. In every Christian place where God's word was heard, men know of his books which clarified the word and refuted errors. All men schould thank God for such teachers and abide by their doctrines.[21]

A broadsheet by Fischart written after the St. Bartholomew's day massacre extolled, in Latin verse, the virtues of the Admiral de Coligny. His bravery, his skill as leader of the Protestants, had been exemplary. Fischart then shifted into German for a final exhortation: "O Germany, how long will you be blind? How long will your native intelligence atrophy? Greed for gold overcomes all virtue. All fear of God is wiped from your mind and France. Spain and other foreign lands laugh at your dallying . . . O you pious lords and princes take counsel, take counsel. Be unified—behold the Fatherland, the miserable, unprotected people."[22]

In 1587 a Catholic propagandist wrote an anguished account of the martyrdom of Mary Queen of Scots. Imprisoned twenty years before by her rebellious, heretical subjects because of her Catholic faith, Queen Mary had trusted in the Queen of England's promise to replace her on the Scottish throne. Instead she was taken prisoner by Queen Elizabeth and eventually killed by her and her advisors, suffering with great courage and in the full faith of the Holy Roman Catholic religion.[23] Throughout the account these last words reappear almost like a Greek chorus. They were the repeated phrase which would evoke a desired response, another basic technique of modern propaganda.[24]

In the account Mary was portrayed as calm, utterly in control, refusing to see the Queen's deputy until he had presented himself formally at her door to say that he had an official commission for her. She then commanded Melvin, her servant, to convey to her dear son the true account of her death in the Holy Catholic Roman Religion and admonish James to bear no mistrust against the Queen of England. Furthermore, Melvin was to bear witness that Mary had died a Catholic, loyal to Scotland and France. She also asked all her servants to inform the King of France of her Catholic death. Having been denied a priest, she was led to the scaffold which had been prepared. She carried a wooden crucifix in her hand and a book. A gold crucifix hung from her neck and a Pater Noster from her belt. A minister approached her and asked whether she wished to die in sin. She silenced him. Again he approached her and she cried out, "Be quiet, Mr. Doppen, I will not listen to you. I will have nothing to do with you. You are very annoying to me."[25] One of the English nobles, noticing the crucifix, said that it sorrowed him to see her caught in such superstition. The Queen answered that it was a portrait of the Lord Jesus Christ, to remind her of his bitter suffering and death. The Calvinist Doctor then fell on his knees and made a comforting prayer. When he finished, the Queen began to recite a prayer in Latin, holding the crucifix in her hand. She prayed that the Queen of England might rule her kingdom long in peace. She prayed that her son, the King of Scotland, might be converted to the Catholic Roman Religion. Thus, concluded the broadsheet, "did the noble Queen of Scotland have to end her life in the Holy Catholic Religion for the heretical, seduced English who, together with their Queen, fear that the Catholics would come out of Scotland and their Calvinist sect would be endangered. This they prevented by her innocent death."[26]

In the account the old symbols were stressed: the crucifixes, the rosary, the Latin prayers. Mary emerged as pure and constant to Catholicism, merciful towards her persecutor, resisting up to the end the ministrations of the Protestants, turned into Calvinists by the Catholic writer. In contrast, the tyranny, the cruelty, the treachery of Elizabeth were exposed. A Protestant broadsheet gave a similar account of a young woman who was put to death by order of the Cardinal of Trent. While the event lacked the political significance of the death of Mary Queen of Scots, the poem which recounted the martyrdom emphasized similar qualities: mercifulness; constancy; the nobility of her death; unswerving faith.

> There was a godfearing and Christian young woman
> who had ably learned God's word and catechism.
> When she was young she eagerly attending the preaching.
> She was sympathetic to the poor and served them diligently.
> (But) the enemy wished to convert the young maiden to blasphemy.
> With sweet words and harsh words, they talked to her.
> But she stood fast as a wall, as gold in the fire.
> No pains of martyrdom turned her away from Christ.
> Having merited death she held herself nobly
> Crying earnestly to God . . . Lord Christ into thine hands I commit my soul.[27]

Broadsheets were not limited to martyrs. Political, religious and military leadership was also honored. A fine woodcut of Henry of Valois eulogized his accomplishments as King of Poland.[28] Another recounted the contributions to the Protestant cause made by Johann Casimir, Count Palatine. A brave and elegant knight, he had eagerly accepted the teachings of the Reformation. In 1567 he had gone to the aid of the French Hugenots, giving them support when they were in great need. He continued to campaign in France during 1573-76 and then went to the aid of the Dutch against the Spanish. At the death of his brother Ludwig he had succeeded in bringing the Palatinate back into the Reformation.[29] Other broadsheets were devoted to religious leaders: Rudolf Gwalther of Zurich; Matthias Flaccius Illyricus; Martin Bucer.[30] All these portrait broadsheets helped to identify the leadership of the two sides, to publicize their exploits and actions and thus help to develop a sense of identity within the group. Men and women could have confidence in the integrity, wisdom and piety of their leaders. Corruption, dishonesty, deceit, impiety were present only among the opposition.

Attacks on the corruption of the opposition were another major weapon of the propagandists. The licentiousness of the adversary was described in meticulous detail, creating a sterotype of unbridled sexuality. The sexual weapon was particularly important to the development of propaganda techniques. Sexual attitudes and customs are central psychological elements in the development of personality, regulating one of the most fundamental aspects of human behaviour.[31] Accusations of sexual misbehaviour, laxity or perversion helped to undermine the integrity of the opposing side, to heighten distrust and fear.

Much of the Catholic case against the Protestants was based on the latter's sexual behaviour. The polemicists of the Catholic League again and again depicted their antagonists as morally corrupt, indulging in sexual orgies, sodomy and incest.[32] Indeed, they wrote, the Protestants had perverted the concept of Christian love to mean that no woman could refuse to give herself to a man.[33] The Catholic writers conceded that much of this was the fault of the Catholics. The misbehaviour of the Catholic clergy in the past laid a foundation of sexual indiscipline which the Protestants now carried to the extreme. They impregnated nuns and violated young girls. Worse, they maintained that all women should be held in common.[34]

The Protestant propagandists continued to push the old image of the lecherous priest or monk. Young women in the 1570s and 1580s, according to them, were just as liable to sexual molestation at the hands of a priest as their grandmothers and great grandmothers had been in 1500. If anything, their position was more dangerous because of the Jesuits. Protestant broadsheets provided detailed accounts of sexual attacks by priests or monks, each separate step of the incident depicted so that the reader could be conscious of the full hideousness of the event. One such attack resulted in murder rather than rape. A pious young woman, in an advanced stage of pregnancy, had gone into town with her father to make her confession before confinement. The priest who heard the confession noticed her fat purse, waylaid her as she returned home and killed her, plunging his sword into her swollen belly. The black and white woodcut depicted all these events as well as the punishment suffered by the priest. He was boiled in oil.[35]

Another broadsheet recounted the rape of an eight year old girl, the daughter of a poor widow, by a monk. The latter was roused to excitement by his evil spirit. At first the monk tried to resist. He appealed to Mary to save him from his desires, but in vain. " . . . The whoremongering monk carried the young girl by force of violence to the cellar, ripping, tearing, dragging, shoving. He threw her under a barrel and held himself against the innocent child, against her shamefaced eyes, her chaste ears and the tender heart of this small youngling, and did such unnatural and unmanly things so shamefully that it is not to be described."[36] The illustration showed the return of the mother. In dismay and anguish she ran from the house to report to the authorities who quickly proceeded to imprison the culprit. He was later beheaded. All this in the one picture.

Another Protestant broadsheet reported the fate of a poor but honest girl. Twenty years old, pretty and pleasant, she could not find a husband, because her father had no property. The priest from a nearby town asked her to become his mistress. She would eat and drink only the best, never water, only wine. The girl replied that she would never do anything so immoral for she would have to go to hell and suffer eternal pain. Not at all, said the priest. He could fix it all, for he had the power from Rome to overcome the devil and he could forgive sins. Thus he could absolve her and lead her to Heaven. The young woman was persuaded and they lived together for seven years. Then the devil came unannounced, broke open the priest's house and took the maiden by the hand to lead her to hell. At that moment she discovered the priest's powerlessness. Evil, concluded the text, always becomes manifest and priests remain priests.[37]

The Jesuits, in the eyes of the Protestants, represented a particular danger to young women. Johann Fischart carried on a relentless attack against them. Their four cornered hats, he held, were designed precisely for the purpose of covering their devil's horns. They were a constant menace to society, feeding on the innocence and sincerity of young women.[38] A broadsheet with a strong resemblance to the story of Little Red Riding Hood, provided a specific example of the perfidy of the Jesuits. A faithful Protestant young woman had resisted all efforts of a Jesuit to convert her to Catholicism. The Jesuit, undaunted, waited until she had retired to bed and entered her room, disguised as the devil. He was stopped in the nick of time by the arrival of a valiant young man who ran the cleric through with his sword, thus preserving both the virginity and the faith of the young woman.[39]

After forty years the reformed churches were still obsessed by the image of the lecherous priest. Fischart described the high spiritual leaders of the Roman church as stinking rams, caught in their fleshly desires, raging and raving in the herd like proud bucks in heat.[40] The issue of sexual discipline hit close to the core of social stability and the sanctity of the family. In a period when family life was receiving increasing attention, to prove that the enemy was dissolute sexually was to strengthen internal cohesion against him. The moral rectitude, the virtue of each side was reinforced by the depravity of the opposition.

These sexual incidents, based on anecdotal evidence were important elements in building up fear and anxiety. While such incidents did undoubtedly occur, neither Catholic Europe nor Protestant Europe was faced with moral decline in the 1560s or 1570s. The curtailment of personal liberties, the invasion of individual rights was, however, very real. The establishment of the Inquisition, the English Act of Supremacy and the Acts of Uniformity. French legislation against the Protestants, all led to fundamental curtailment of human liberties. The menace of these acts was another major subject for the propagandists, usually in the form of longer polemic *zeitung* or newsheets. The *zeitung* were less blatant than the broadsheets. Since they were not illustrated they lacked the visual impact conveyed by the picture. The text was longer and contained at some point a relatively factual account of the particular event. At the same time their purpose was still to indoctrinate. The strength of the opponent was used to create fear and to demonstrate the absolute necessity of his defeat. Victory by the Catholics would bring disaster and death for the Protestants. Protestant victory, on the other hand, would lead to the destruction of Catholicism.[41]

An early *zeitung* (1546) on the Revolt of the Netherlands gave a six page account of the introduction of the Inquisition. "There is great persecution and pursuit of poor Christians in the Netherlands," the text began, "and a particular misfortune has been created in the new Inquisition." Established by the pope, with the consent of the emperor, it was cruel and terrible because everyone could be examined, high or low, merely on the basis of suspicion. If a person were found guilty both his life and property were taken.[42] The manual of the Inquisition, the *zeitung* continued, contained many unchristian and dangerous articles. For example, men could go into all the houses in the town ask how many people lived there, list their names and leave slips of paper for each person, which had to be signed. Each person was then required to go to confession, to take the Sacrament and present his slip of paper. Those who did not attend would be known because there would be no slips for them. Then, they would be seized, burned, and their property confiscated.[43] Moreover, people were asked not only about their beliefs but about their neighbors—

did the latter attend church and go to confession? Who were their neighbor's friends? The account demonstrated the degree to which men's privacy was violated, the sanctity of the home undermined.[44]

In 1568 another *zeitung* described in even more detail the procedure followed by the Inquisition. The first section described sixteen steps followed in the questioning, beginning with orders to the *familiares* to watch a particular person. Then came the questioning: "They ask them to think whether they have done anything to come before the holy seat of justice. Do you want to make a declaration? Because we would like you to unburden yourself and free your conscience . . . Then, when the individual says some word against himself or others, the inquisitors are pleased, they look at each other and nod to show they like his words."[45] The steps of the inquisitional procedure were described meticulously, the use of witnesses against the accused, the taking of depositions from the accused to inculcate fear.[46] The last section described what happened to those accused. As soon as anyone was imprisoned he was forced to give up his keys to everything, including his chests. His goods were inventoried by a notary, then the neighbors were called in to check the inventory. The monks and priests taught that anyone who had turned away from the teaching of Rome possessed his goods falsely and the king was the legitimate owner. In prison the accused was again asked whether he had anything in his possession like a knife or a ring. If he had, he was forced to give it up. He was then left in prison awaiting further decision on his case. Men had suffered this cruel tyranny now for fifty-seven years, may almighty God soon make an end to it.[47]

A Catholic description of conditions under Queen Elizabeth I of England revealed a similar loss of personal liberties, dwelling on the expanding power of a tyrannical government. Beginning with an inflammatory title, "The Calvinist cruelty . . . in England . . . under the abominable and frightening Calvinist Law."[48] the propagandist described the division and schism within the realm created by Protestantism. The kingdom was now split between Catholics. Protestants and Puritans leading to political as well as religious division.[49] The result had been to stir up obsessional fears on the part of the English. If they saw a ship upon the sea, they were convinced it was coming to invade the realm. If there was political unrest in France, the Netherlands or Spain, they were sure it would spread to England. The whole country was possessed by fear and suspicion with the result that it had been turned into a prison. No one, not even a child or a young person, could leave the country without written permission from the Queen. Everyone entering or leaving was subject to search and examination in all ports. Letters were taken from travellers. Every incoming package was examined in the belief that it might contain an instrument to assassinate the Queen.[50] Worst of all, even the highest and most powerful noble who might try to escape from this tyranny would be stopped in midflight and imprisoned. There was no means of deliverance. The only solution, according to the propagandist, was in the hands of the Catholic monarchs. The king of Spain should serve as a model for all others. He had never permitted heretics in any part of his realm but had rooted them out, hunted them down and dispersed them in order to protect and preserve the true Christian church. He had brought freedom of religion to the Netherlands.[51] Catholics would be safe only when the kings, with the help of the pope, assumed the responsibility of chasing the Protestant wolves away from the flocks.[52]

The extent of the religious polarization emerges clearly. Each side was deeply aware of the loss of personal liberty. English Catholics were restricted within the country, they could neither come nor go freely. Dutch Protestants could neither speak nor write freely and lived precariously under the watchful eyes of their neighbors who might denounce them to the authorities of the Inquisition. While each side recognized the danger of the loss of personal liberty to their own side, neither Catholic nor Protestant was willing to recognize the rights of their opponent. The solution, if one was offered, was to get rid of the enemy. Only then would it be possible to return to peace and tranquility. As long as there were heretics about, according to the Catholics, they would conspire against public order and undermine the monarchy. As long as Catholics were in the community, according to the Protestants, there would be tyranny, and violence would continue against men of firm faith and conscience.

The religious wars were a natural subject for the journalists. There were numerous accounts of the war in the Netherlands, the French wars of religion and local conflicts like the Bishop's war in Strasbourg. For example, there were two accounts of the siege of the city of Middleburg in Zeeland in 1573 and the relief of the siege in 1574 by William, Prince of Orange, with details on the tyranny of the Duke of Alva against the cities of Haarlem, Zutfen and Naarden. There was an illustrated broadsheet showing the pontoon bridge built by the Duke of Parma at the seige of Antwerp and another description of the siege of Ruhrort by Spanish troops in 1587.[53] These accounts, which were based on a factual description of the event, were also used to drive home the strength, the inhumanity, the brutality of the opponent and sometimes reflected similar qualities on their own side. An account of several Protestant victories in the Netherlands told how the Protestant soldiers had taken much booty. They had seized 200 wagons, nine pieces of field artillery and had clothed themselves in the gilded armor of the Spaniards. The captured German mercenaries had beseeched their countrymen to take them as prisoners but the Protestants, said the journalist, had been forced to execute them because the Spaniards never spared their prisoners but hanged them, everyone. The Spanish soldiers for their part, had tried to escape by entering a cloister, even climbing the trees in order to hide. They were shaken from their perches and all were put to death. "It was," concluded the writer, "a praiseworthy and glorious victory."[54]

This account continued with the prayers of the Protestants on the battlefield to stir up the zeal of faithful. Count Louis of Nassau, wrote the reporter, had remained on the battlefield, convinced that Catholic reinforcements might arrive. His Grace held the field with God's help, praying that God the Almighty would grant His mercy, help and victory to these men and all others who fought for His Word so that the abominable Antichrist and his supporters could not say "Where is the stronger God?"[55] In the same way, every stouthearted Christian should not neglect to appeal and pray to the heavenly Father, not only that He will never cease to support the poor, attacked Christians but that he will carry them forward to victory.[56]

Johann Fischart wrote a long account in verse of the defeat of the Spanish Armada, tying this Protestant victory to a Protestant defeat just before. The description of the defeat of the Armada was followed by a long section on the prayer invoked by soldiers of the Protestant Swiss Alliance before an invasion into France in 1587. The question was whether, as one Catholic critic had charged, the prayer had included unchristian petitions.[57] In answer, Fischart reproduced the prayer in full. A summary provides the intent and the tone: "Almighty God . . . (you) know the evil counsel and deceitful practices of thine and our enemy, namely the Antichristian hoards and how they have made an alliance against they son. Jesus Christ, his Holy Word and Gospel . . . and (how) they have poured out the blood of countless Christians . . . There is no surcease in their violence against us . . . so that we are now pressed to take up the offensive in our hands, to come to the help of your hard-pressed Christians in France . . . Now we . . . fully recognize, true God and Father, that we are far too weak and small to stand up against the great power of our enemy and . . . we have earned through our sins that you might reasonably withdraw your hand and help from us . . . Therefore, gracious God and Father, we all come before you and petition you from our hearts that you will pardon our committed sins for the sake of your dear son Jesus Christ . . . but will shower down your violent anger against those who do not acknowledge you nor appeal to you by name . . . And that you will protect us from all evil. You will be the lord of our troops, marching with our commanders. You will be the highest general . . . giving courage to the leaders and strength to our soldiers. You will strike down our enemy with your strong arm . . . and redeem the blood of your servants."[58]

The problem was that these same Swiss troops, having committed themselves to God's cause, had been cut down by the French with terrible losses.[59] Was this because they had prayed erroneously as a Catholic critic had been quick to point out? Was it because they had implored God's help against fellow Christians? No. The defeat of the Armada was witness to their virtue and the righteousness of their request. God had heard the prayer of the Swiss. But because of the sins of the Protestants he had let men feel his heavy hand. Then he had quickly followed the initial defeat with victory—and a far more important victory.[60] For the Armada had involved a far greater effort on the part of the Catholics. It had cost millions in gold since it costs much more to outfit one ship than to lead 1000 horses into the field, and ships had come from all over, from Biscay, Andalusia, Sicily and Ragusa. So much gold and treasure had been spent that a kingdom could have been bought with it.[61] Yet despite all these efforts, despite the fact that the great chaplain in Rome himself had given the benediction, the flags had been consecrated and the sails blessed, God decided to deliver justice and the fleet was drowned in the cold northern sea. The two incidents together bore witness that God would take up the Protestant cause and deliver the Protestants at the right time. He alone, however, knew the time, the place and the people through whom he would carry out justice.[62] In both these accounts, God was clearly proved to support the Protestant cause. He had abandoned the Catholics.

The propaganda which came off the presses in the last decades of the sixteenth century was clearly aimed at certain human reactions and emotions. Basic to propaganda technique, certain words, certain phrases reappear over and over again on both sides: the word *Warnung;* the image of the wolf and the sheep; the words abominable and abomination; the threat of Antichrist; the image of tyrannical rule. The most basic appeal in the newsheets, poems and songs was to fear. If all loyal Protestants, or all loyal Catholics, did not band together in unity these were the terrible consequences which they might expect. Suspicion and doubt were inculcated. The other side was not to be trusted. It was capable of conspiracy of all sorts and at all levels: attempts to convert the faithful; attempts to corrupt morality; attempts to subvert public order and set loose the forces of anarchy and unrest. Horror was another element. Horror at acts of terror and violence such as the assassination of King Henry III, the martyrdom of the Protestant clergy under Mary of England, the martyrdom of Mary Queen of Scots, the St. Bartholomew's day massacre—all these showed the inhumanity and brutality of the opponent. The propaganda created alarm and apprehension in a world already shattered by dissension.

Because the techniques of propaganda were new, the effect may have been particularly deeply felt. Political propaganda mounted by the fascists in the nineteen-thrities did not survive the second World War. The religious propaganda of the sixteenth century was more longlasting. Based on the principle of religious separation. it created fundamental psychological and social distances which would become deeply rooted in Western European culture. The propaganda created a sterotype of The Other, each religious group accepted that stereotype of its antagonist. The Protestant would perceive the Catholic as priest-ridden, harrassed by an ignorant clergy given over to sexual excess and perversion, dominated by a tyrannical pope. The Catholic would see the Protestant as undisciplined spiritually and morally, contentious, willing to undermine the political order for his own ends. These false images made it impossible after 1600 to reestablish a unified society. In the end each group would develop its own life style, its own social mores, its own culture. The seamless garment of Christ was ripped by the religious leaders. It was torn assunder by the propagandists.

*Notes*

[1] Leonard Doob: *Propaganda, its Psychology and Technique* (New York, 1935). 75 76. See also Louis-Jean Calvet: *La production révolutionnaire: slogans; affiches; chansons* (Paris, 1976). 14.

[2] These figures and those which follow are based on my computer study of all surviving books published in the city of Strasbourg from 1480 - 1599. The book analyzes publication by subject matter. See *Books, Lay Culture, Learned Culture, 1480 - 1599.* 2 vols. (New Haven, forthcoming 1982). The statement with regard to Wittenberg and Nuremberg is based on a forthcoming computer study of Luther's publication by Mark U. Edwards, "The Printing and Reprinting of Luther's Works."

[3] Doob, *Propaganda,* 77.

[4] For this paper I have drawn on the printed broadsheets and *Zeitung* in the Wick Collection at the Zentralbibliothek, Zurich (ZB, Z). The illustrated broadsheets are kept in the Graphische Sammlung (G.S.). The numbers given in the footnotes refer to the catalogue of the collection recently completed by the curator, Bruno Weber. The *Zeitung* are kept in the Archives (A) at the Zentralbibliothek. I have also consulted *Zeitung* in the collection of Bibliothèque Municipale at Strasbourg, particularly a small collection made by Rodolphe Reuss.

[5] Cited in Doob, *Propaganda,* 36.

[6] Mark U. Edwards, "Printing and Reprinting of Luther's Works."

[7] ZBZ (GS). PAS II 1/2. *Ein schöner spruch von zweyen Junckfrawen vom Adel zu Delden drey meyl von Deventer verbrantt* (Strasbourg. J. Frölich, 1546).

[8] ZBS (GS), PAS II 21/11. *Demnach ein Spaniardt in Brabant . . .* (no place, no date).

[9] ZBS (A). Wick Ms. F 1713. *Neüwe Zeitung unnd Abschrifft eines Brieffs so letslich von Malta kommen ist* (Strasbourg, T. Berger. 1565).

[10] ZBS (A). *Newezum theil glückliche und sigliche zeittung aus den Niderlander. Wie der Wolgeboren Her Herr Ludwig Grave zu Nassaw und des Printzen von Oranigen . . . mit den Spaniern in Friesland . . . Schlacht begangen unnd verbracht hat* (no place, 1568).

[11] The titles of the following poems and songs provide an idea of the subject matter: *Ein . . . newes Klaglied von einer Jungfrawen mit namen Dorothea wie sie umb der Augsburger Confession . . . jamerlich unnd erbermlich mit dem Schwerdt hingericht ist worden* (Cologne, 1573, another edition Basel, 1573). *Ein neüw Lied von der schlacht so zwischen Hertzog Moritzen von Sachsen . . . und Margraff Albrechten von Brandenburg, anno 1553 gehalten worden* (Strasbourg. T. Berger, 1553). *Ein neuw Lied, von der schlacht in Frankreich, zwischen den Hertzog von Condé und dem Herzog von Guiss . . . anno 1562* (Strasbourg, T. Berger, 1563). *Ein schon und lustig new Lied. von der Edlen Statt Strassburg, und Bistumb da selbs in jetzigen Kriegswesen gantz kurzweilig zu singen* (Strasbourg, B. Jobin, 1592). *Ein Kläglich New Lied . . . von der Lothringischen Bezalung, damit er die Teutsch Knecht unnd Bawren zu Dachstein . . . bezalt, verehrt und begabt hat. Aller Teucher zu trewer Warnung* (Strasbourg, 1592). *Ein Schön Neu Lied von der Wunderkuh so die Jesuiter zu Moltzheim Weyssagen gelehrt* (Strasbourg, 1592). *. . . Klaglied von den absterben . . . Joh. Brentzen 11 September 1570* (Strasbourg, T. Berger, c. 1570). *Ein Lustig Glossierendt Liedt. Uff das Babstlich gedicht, von der Statt Strassburg. . . . Allen Romische Cortisanen und Poetischen Bapstfreuden zugefallen gsungen* (Strasbourg, 1592).

[12] ZBZ (GS). PAS II, 6/6. *In einen Dorff zwischen Augsburg und Dillingen . . . eines armen Baurers weib mit namen Anna Risin . . . fünff lebendiger Kindlein . . . geboren unnd auff Erden gebracht* (Augsburg, M. Francken, 1566).

[13] ZBZ (GS), PAS II, 5/3. *Wunder Weitzenstock* (Strasbourg, T. Berger, 1563).

[14] ZBZ (GS), PAS II, 6/4. *Warhafftige Beschreibung aines grausammen erschroklichen grossen Wurms . . . auff Teutsch Lindwurm genent* (1558).

[15] In a random sample of 40 Broadsheets, 28 (70%) bear the printer's name or give the name of the city where it was printed.

[16] Graphs showing the production curves for the major types of publication in Strasbourg: Catholic, Humanist,

Scientific, Popular Literature can be consulted in my article "L'imprimerie à Strasbourg, de 1480 à 1599" in *Strasbourg au coeur religieux du XVIe siècle,* Actes du Colloque international à Strasbourg, 25 29 mai, 1975 (Strasbourg, 1977), unpaginated, preceding p. 539. A fuller set of graphs and charts accompanies Volume 1 of *Lay Culture, Learned Culture* (New Haven, forthcoming, 1982).

[17] G. Wylie Sypher: "'Faisant ce qu'il leur vient à plaisir:' The Image of Protestantism in French Catholic Polemic on the Eve of the Religious Wars." *Sixteenth Century Journal* XI (1980), 59 84.

[18] Leonard W. Doob: "Goebbels' Principles of Propaganda" in *Public Opinion and Propaganda*, eds. Katz, Cartwright, Eldersvell and Lee (New York, 1954), 520.

[19] Louis-Jean Calvet. *Production révolutionnaire,* 20-25.

[20] ZBZ (GS), PAS II, 13/20. *Johannes Hus* (Augsburg, c. 1550 1560).

[21] ZBZ (GS), PAS II, 12/11. (Johann Fischart) *Heinrich Bullinger Diener der Kirchen zu Zurch* (Strasbourg: B. Jobin, 1571).

[22] ZBZ (GS), PAS II, 10/17. (Johann Fischart) *Epicedion in Mortum Casparis de Coligne, Domini de Castilione . . . una cum suis misere truncatus est; 24 August; 1572* (Strasbourg: B. Jobin, 1573).

[23] ZBZ (GS), PAS II, 24/3-4. *Warhaffter und grundlich bericht welcher Massen die Edel und frumb Konigin auss Schotland Fraw Maria Stuarda von Leben zum Todt in Engeiland hingericht worden ist in disem 1587 jar* (Munich: Adam Berg, 1587).

[24] Leonard W. Doob, "Goebbel's Principles," 518.

[25] *Bericht . . . Fraw Maria Stuarda von Leben zum Todt.*

[26] *Ibid.*

[27] ZBZ (GS), PAS II, 10/27. *Ein warhafftiges newes Klaglied von ein Jungfrawen mit namen Dorothea, wie sie umb der Augspurger Confession . . . mit dem Schwerdt hingericht ist worden . . . durch den Cardinal zu Triendt . . . in disem 1573 Jar* (Coln: Withelm Berek, 1574).

[28] ZBZ (GS), PAS II, 11/1. *Effigies quam accuratissima. Invictissimi. Potentissimique Principis ac Domini D. Henrici Valesii, Henrici Galliarum quondam Regis Filii, modi in regem Poloniae, Lithuaniaque Ducem* (Strasbourg: B. Jobin, 1574).

[29] ZBZ (GS), PAS II, 16/3. *Contrafait des Durchleuchtigen Fürsten unnd Herrn, Herrn Johan Casimirs Pfaltzgrave bei Rhein* (Strasbourg: B. Jobin, 1578).

[30] These portrait broadsheets are described in Bruno Weber: "Die Welt begeret allezeit Wunder", Versuch einer Bibliographie der Einblattdrucke von Bernhard Jobin in Strassburg, *Gutenberg-Jahrbuch* (1976), 270-290. The portraits referred to are, respectively, nos. 13; 15 and 65.

[31] Leonard W. Doob, *Propaganda,* 43.

[32] Wylie Sypher, "Faisant," p. 60.

[33] *Ibid,*. p. 69.

[34] Gentian Hervet: *Epistre aux ministres predicans et supposts de la congregation & nouvelle eglise* (Paris: Nicolas Chesnau, 1561), fol. 200-21R, quoted in G. Wylie Sypher, "Faisant," p. 75.

[35] ZBZ (GS), PAS II, 12/50. *Ein grausamlich mord so geschehen ist in dem Minsterthal . . . da ein pfaff ein schwangere frawen gemordt . . .* (Strasbourg: 1556).

[36] ZBZ (GS), PAS II, 21/9. *Eine schr greuliche . . . History wie ein heilosig Munch zu Dantzk in Preussen ein kleinis junges Megdelein . . . geschendet hat.* (n.p., 1556).

[37] ZBZ (GS), PAS II, 1/1. *Ein wunderbarliche, warhafftige seltzame geschicht von einmen Pfaffin und seines Kellerin . . .* (Strasbourg: A. Fries, 1550).

[38] Bibl. Mun., Strasbourg. Johann Fischart, *Die Wunderlichst, Unerhortest Legend und Beschreigung. Des Abgefuhrten Quartierten . . . und Viereckechten Vierhornigen Hutleins . . .* (Strasbourg: B. Jobin, 1580), passim.

[39] ZBZ (GS), PAS II, 12/74. *Newe zeytung unnd warhaffter Bericht eines Jesuiters welcher inn Teuffels gestalt sich angethan . . .* (Augsburg, 1569).

[40] Johann Fischart: *Im Munster zu Strasbourg, Gegen der Predigstul . . .* (Strasbourg: B. Jobin, 1576).

[41] Leonard W. Doob, "Goebbels' Principles," 520. Goebbels stressed the fact in his journal that propaganda should play on the consequences of defeat. The German people had to remain convinced that the war struck at the basic elements of their lives.
[42] Bibl. Mun., Strasbourg, Coll. Reuss. *Eine Zeytung auss dem Niderland welche anzaygen die Grausame . . . Tyranny wider die armen Christin . . .* (n.p., 1546), folio aii.

[43] *Ibid.*, folio aii$^{v}$.

[44] *Ibid.,* folio aiii.

[45] ZBZ (A), Wick Collection Ms. F. 1823. *Newe wunderseltzame und unchristliche Spannische Zeitung nemlich Wie und mit was sich der Konig von Hispanien durch sein unzifer und weritzeüg der inquisitoren in Hispanisen und Niderlanden . . . viel gute leüt . . . vor ihren Richterstul zu erscheinen . . .* (Strasbourg: T. Berger, 1568), folio ai$^{v}$-aii. There was another edition of this published by Peter Hug in Strasbourg.

[46] *Ibid.,* folio aiii.

[47] *Ibid.,* folio aii$^{v}$.

[48] Bibl. Mun., Strasbourg, Coll. Reuss. *Der Calvinisten Grausambkeit In zweynen Exempeln so in Engellandt newlich fur gelauffen, beschrieben und begriffen. Das Erst, begreifft das grewlich und scheusslich Edict der Calvinisten gegen und wider die Catholische newlich aussganen . . .* (n.p., 1586), title page.

[49] *Ibid.,* folio a2$^{v}$.

[50] *Ibid.,* folio a3.

[51] *Ibid.,* folio B.

[52] *Ibid.,* folio B$^{v}$.

[53] ZBZ (GS), PAS II, 11/2; PAS II, 11/3; PAS II, 22/4; PAS II, 22/5-6; PAS II, 25/5.

[54] Bibl. Mun., Strasbourg. *Newe zum theil gluckliche und sigliche zeittung aus dem Niderland* (n.p., 1568), folio aii.

[55] *Ibid.,* folio aii$^{v}$.

[56] *Ibid.*

[57] Bibl. Mun., Strasbourg, Coll. Reuss. (Johann Fischart). *Uncalvinische Gegen Badstublein. . . .* (Strasbourg; B. Jobin, 1589), unpaginated folio.

[58] *Ibid.,* unpaginated folio.

[59] I am grateful to Professor Hans R. Guggisberg who helped me to identify this incident as the *Tampiskrieg,* an unofficial recruiting activity by Henry of Navarre in Protestant cantons which was tolerated by these governments. A mercenary army of 15-16,000 men from Bern, Zurich, Schaffhausen, St. Gallen, Glarus and other towns marched into France in 1587, getting as far as Estampes near Chartres where they were engaged with heavy losses and disorder. See: *Handbuch der Schweizer Geschichte,* I (Zurich: 1972), pp. 603-605.

[60] Fischart, *Uncalvinisch Gegen Badstublein,* folio B.

[61] *Ibid.,* folio aiii.

[62] *Ibid.,* unpaginated folio.

---

## FURTHER READING

Bainton, Roland H. *Studies on the Reformation.* Boston: Beacon Press, 1963, 289 p.

Centers on Martin Luther and on "the radicals of the reformation."

Buck, Lawrence P., and Jonathan W. Zophy, eds. *The Social History of the Reformation.* Columbus: Ohio State University Press, 1972, 397 p.

Addresses numerous aspects of the Reformation's social history, with essays on the control of morals in Calvin's Geneva, the dynamics of printing in the sixteenth century, "John Foxe and the Ladies," and other themes.

Durant, Will. *The Reformation: A History of European Civilization from Wyclif to Calvin: 1300-1564.* New York: Simon and Schuster, 1957, 1025 p.

Examines the historical background and intellectual development of the Protestant Reformation.

Fernández-Armesto, Felipe, and Derek Wilson. *Reformation.* New York: Bantam, 1997, 324 p.

Overview of the historical and cultural context of the Reformation and the later artistic and religious movements it made possible.

Friesen, Abraham. *Reformation and Utopia: The Marxist Interpretation of the Reformation and Its Antecedents.* Wiesbaden: Franz Steiner Verlag, 1974, 271 p.

Surveys the development of the Marxist interpretation of the Protestant Reformation.

Grimm, Harold. "The Legacy of the Reformation," in *The Reformation Era: 1500-1650,* pp. 569-616. 1954. Reprint, Macmillan, 1965.

Presents a brief overview of the major literary works of the Protestant Reformation.

Hillerbrand, Hans J. *The World of the Reformation.* New York: Charles Scribner's Sons, 1973, 229 p.

Explores the impact of the Protestant Reformation on the politics of European nations.

Holl, Karl. *The Cultural Significance of the Reformation,* Translated by Karl Hertz, Barbara Hertz, and John H. Lichtblau. New York: Meridian Books, 1959, 191 p.

Argues that the Reformation encouraged the development of modern culture, particularly in its emphasis on education and individualism.

Hooykaas, R. "Science and Reformation." In *The Protestant Ethic and Modernization: A Comparative View,* edited by S. N. Eisenstadt, pp. 211-39. New York: Basic Books, 1968.

Argues that Calvinism and Puritanism, outgrowths of the Protestant Reformation, had a "stimulating influence" on scientific progress.

Kingdon, Robert M., ed. *Transition and Revolution: Problems and Issues of European Renaissance and Reformation History.* Minneapolis: Burgess Publishing Company, 1974, 274 p.

Surveys the intellectual and political history of the Renaissance and Protestant Reformation.

Kirk, James. *Patterns of Reform: Continuity and Change in the Reformation Kirk.* Edinburgh: T & T Clark, 1989, 516 p.

Investigates the implications of Protestant ideas such as the doctrine of the "universal priesthood" in Scottish intellectual history and politics.

Kirk, Russell. *The Roots of American Order.* Malibu, California: Pepperdine University Press, 1978, 534 p.

Traces the influence of the Protestant Reformation on American society, philosophy and government.

Littell, Franklin H., ed. *Reformation Studies: Essays in Honor of Roland H. Bainton.* Richmond, Va.: John Knox Press, 1962, 285 p.

Collection of essays that "is so planned as to give attention both to the classical Reformation and to the often-neglected 'Left Wing' of the movement." Contains essays by such scholars as Waldo Beach and John H. Leith.

Lortz, Joseph. *The Reformation in Germany.* Volume 1. Translated by Ronald Walls. New York: Herder and Herder, 1968, 488 p.

Argues that the Protestant Reformation resulted from a complex interaction of spiritual, political, and intellectual conditions.

McGrath, Alister E. *Reformation Thought: An Introduction.* New York: Basil Blackwell, 1988, 212 p.

Examines the history of ideas that brought about and characterized the Reformation.

Overfield, James H. *Humanism and Scholasticism in Late Medieval Germany.* Princeton: Princeton University Press, 1984, 344 p.

Explores the intellectual struggle between scholasticism and humanism from the mid-fifteenth to the early sixteenth century.

Spitz, Leo W., ed. *The Reformation: Material or Spiritual?* Boston: D. C. Heath Co., 1962, 104 p.

Collection of essays by eminent critics of the Reformation, including Roland H. Bainton, Wilhelm Dilthey, and Erik H. Erikson.

Todd, John M. *Reformation.* London: Darton, Longman & Todd, 1971, 377 p.

Provides a general historical introduction to the causes and development of the Protestant Reformation.

# John Calvin

## 1509-1564

French theologian and religious reformer.

### INTRODUCTION

Theologian, bible scholar, and reformer, Calvin towers as a central figure of the Protestant Reformation. Critics agree that this Frenchman, who has been described as a frail man of disciplined and aristocratic demeanor, permanently shaped the emerging Protestant worldview and culture. His method of biblical interpretation was "Sola Scriptura," the Bible alone, but filtered through a scholastic and humanist tradition. Calvin's chief work, *Christianae Religiouis Institutio* (*Institutes of the Christian Religion,* 1536-59), which went through several editions, offered a systematic summary of the free grace doctrines of the Protestant reformers. Following St. Augustine's lead, Calvin emphasized human helplessness and depravity before a righteous God. Building on Martin Luther's justification by faith rather than deeds, he summarized the "doctrines of grace" and revived the controverted Pauline doctrine of Divine Sovereignty, the election and predestination of a chosen people. One of Calvin's most notorious tenets is the assertion that certain people, worthy or not, have been predestined for salvation; others, regardless of merit, will not be saved. Best known for the theological system which later came to bear his name, Calvin's theology can still be felt in our society (sometimes only in critical responses to Calvinism) in the areas of business, law, culture, the arts, and government. The churches associated worldwide with Calvin's theology are called Reformed and Presbyterian.

### Biographical Information

Calvin (in French: Jean Cauvin, in Latin: Johannes Calvinus) was born in Noyon, France, on July 10, 1509, to Gerard and Marie LeFranc Cauvin. His father, a cathedral attorney and secretary to the bishop, first directed his son, at the age of twelve, to Paris to study theology, and later, to Orleans and Bourges to study law, where Calvin earned a degree in 1531. Advancing in his studies of Greek and Hebrew, Calvin moved among the learned circles of Paris, where he became imbued with Renaissance ideas and Reformation principles. In 1532 Calvin published *De Clementia* (*On Clemency*), a commentary on Seneca which displayed his skill with classical texts. In November, 1533, his friend Nicholas Cop delivered an address—possibly ghost-written by Calvin—outlining Protestant and Lutheran ideas. Catholic reaction was highly critical and Calvin and Cop fled Paris. Calvin's conversion to the Protestant cause was followed some years later by the first edition and immediate success of his magnum opus, the ***Institutes***. Later that year, while travelling through Geneva on his way to Basel, Switzerland, he was convinced by Guillaume Farel to settle immediately in Geneva and begin the reformation of that city's church and society. For four years Calvin and Cop struggled against an inconsistently reformed city council, and in 1539 they left Geneva and sought refuge with fellow reformer Martin Bucer in Strasbourg, Germany, where Calvin continued to study, write, and preach. In 1540, he married Idelette de Bure, a widow; their one child died in infancy; his wife died in 1549. In 1541, Calvin was asked to return to Geneva, where the Church was granted more independence from council control. He devoted the remainder of his life in Geneva to pastoral work, systematic preaching, and the writing of his biblical commentaries. Geneva became a reformed publishing center and a haven for the advancement of international Protestantism. One dark cloud in Calvin's life was the episode of Michael Servetus, an anti-Trinitarian, arrested, tried, and executed for the civil crime of blasphemy by the Genevan authorities; Calvin was instrumental in his prosecution. Calvin was a private, hard-working man, and we know little of his inner life except through his published writings and a subjective biography by his successor at Geneva, Theodore Beza. He died on May 27, 1564, and his grave remained, on Calvin's request, unmarked.

## Major Works

The great Calvin scholar Emile Doumergue said, "To know Calvin truly and completely, his thought, character and personality, one must consult not one source but three: his *Institutes,* his sermons, and his letters." An exhaustive division would also include his exegetical commentaries as well as his tracts and treatises. The *Institutes* stand alone as the first and greatest summary of systematic Reformation theology. Published when Calvin was just twenty-six years old, the *Institutes* went through various Latin editions (1539, 1543, 1550, 1559); French texts were published in 1541 and 1560. The organization of the 1541 French edition followed a traditional theological structure: 1) The Ten Commandments, 2) Faith (as expressed in the Apostles' Creed), 3)Prayer, and 4) Sacraments. Sections added from the original version of 1536 included: 5) False Sacraments (an attack on Roman sacramentalism) and 6) Christian Liberty. Though the text of the *Institutes* went through expansion and re-organization, the basic theological framework remained the same. Calvin preached sermons twice each Sunday and three times more each week, not including catechism classes and theology lectures. Much of his sermon material was transcribed by others. Calvin's letters contain a wealth of historical material and include letters to Farel, Bullinger, Cramner, Bucer, John Knox, Melancthon, as well as the royalty of many lands. The greater part of Calvin's commentaries was produced in the latter portion of Calvin's career. His first biblical exposition, *The Commentary on the Book of Romans* (1539), was written while he was in Strasbourg. It treats the major doctrines of the Christian faith: sin, justification, sanctification, and predestination. Calvin also wrote commentaries on Genesis, the Pentateuch, Joshua, Psalms, Isaiah, Jeremiah, Lamentations, Ezekial, Daniel, and the minor prophets. His New Testament commentaries cover all but Revelation. His tracts included argumentative pieces like *The Reply to Sadeleto* (1539), Calvin's Protestant polemical response to Bishop Jacopo Sadeleto's appeal for Geneva to return to the Roman fold. *The Antidote to the Council of Trent* (1547) also contains inflamatory opposition to the papal claims. *A Short Treastise on the Lord's Supper* (1540) is believed by critics to provide a fine example of his sustained theological reasoning.

## Critical Reception

Though of good classical scholarship, Calvin's competant commentary on Seneca brought him little critical success. His fateful link to the Protestant cause and to the reforming society of Geneva propelled him to the forefront of a growing Protestant religious movement. The first edition of the *Institutes* was a startling success in Reformation-oriented intellectual circles. Addressed to the King of France, the *Institutes* were generally not received well by the conservative aristocracy. Yet, among the business and trading classes, the well-thought-out Reformed Christianity, built on the Bible alone, devoid of superstitions, streamlined from ecclesiastical abuses, found growing reception. As C. S. Lewis has pointed out, we mistake the influence of Calvinism if we see it in the light of our dour caricature of Calvin, for his was the progressive philosophy of his day. Calvin's writing had multinational appeal: versions of the *Institutes* appeared in Spanish (1540), Italian (1557), Dutch (1560), and English (1561). Just as Luther's Bible set the tone for standard German, Calvin's writing helped to fix with clarity the French literary style. His critical reception has generally tended to follow on religious and ideological lines: many of his followers have lauded him, some of his religious opponents—Catholics, Anabaptists, Arminians—have attacked him. Calvin's Reformed thought has acted as a recurring motif and counter-motif to Western intellectual history. In the sixteenth-century the Protestant Reformation sparked a Catholic Counter-Reformation. In the seventeenth-century, Calvinism's apparent fatalism galvanized the free-will reaction of Arminianism and, in turn, re-crystallized Reformed thinking at the Synod of Dort. Calvinistic Puritanism was the focal point for England's Cromwellian Protectorate and the anti-Puritan Restoration, and the Calvinist Pilgrims struggled to escape episcopacy by colonizing the New World. In the eighteenth-century, a Calvinistic worldview undergirded George Whitefield's preaching and Jonathan Edwards' philosophy. In the nineteenth-century there was somewhat of a revival of Calvin studies by traditional Calvinists with the printing of Calvin's collected works in English and Latin. It was not until the twentieth-century that objective scholarly commentary, devoid of either reverence or virulent Anti-Calvinism, has engaged critics' attention. Calvin and his works have continued to spark debate among contemporary scholars, but all agree that he is one of the most important theologians in the western European tradition.

---

## PRINCIPAL WORKS

*De Clementia* [*On Clemency*] (essay) 1532
*De Psychopannychia* [*Sleep of the Soul*] (essay) 1534

*The Catechism of the Church of Geneva* (catechism) 1536
*Christianae Religionis Institutio* [*Institutes of the Christian Religion*] (essay) 1536
*The Sinfulness of Outward Conformity to Romish Rites* (treatise) 1537
*Commentary on Romans* (commentary) 1539
*Reply to Sadoleto* (letter) 1539
*A Short Treatise on the Lord's Supper* (treatise) 1540
*Articles concernant l'organisation de l'Eglise* [*Ecclesiastical Ordinances*] (essay) 1541
*A Defense of sound and orthodox doctrine* (treatise) 1543
*Humble Exhortation to Charles V* (letter) 1543
*A short treatise showing what faithful men should do* (treatise) 1543
*The Apology of John Calvin to the Nicodemite Gentlemen* (essay) 1544
*The Necessity of Reforming the Church* (treatise) 1544
*Remarks on the Letter of Pope Paul III* (essay) 1544
*Catechism of the church of Geneva* (catechism) 1545
*Antidote to the Council of Trent* (essay) 1547
*True Method of Reforming the Church and Healing her divisions* (treatise) 1547
*Commentary on all the Epistles of Paul* (commentary) 1548
*De vita hominis Christiani* [*On the Life of the Christian man*] (essay) 1550
*On Scandals* (essay) 1550
*Commentary on the Epistles of Hebrews, and the Epistles of Peter, John, Jude, and James* (commentary) 1551
*Commentary on Isaiah* (commentary) 1551
*Commentary on the Acts of the Apostles* (commentary) 1552
*Commentary on John* (commentary) 1553
*Commentary on Genesis* (commentary) 1554
*Harmony of the Gospels* (essay) 1555
*The Second Defense against Joachim Westphal* (treatise) 1556
*Commentary on Hosea* (commentary) 1557
*Commentary on the Psalms* (commentary) 1557
*Christianae Religionis Institutio* (commentary) 1559
*Commentary on the Twelve Minor Prophets* (commentary) 1559
*Commentary on Daniel* (commentary) 1561
*Comentary on Ezekial* (commentary) 1563
*Commentary on Jeremiah* (commentary) 1563
*Commentary on Lamentations* (commentary) 1563
*Harmony of Exodus, Leviticus, Numbers, and Deuteronomy* (essay) 1563
*Harmony of three Gospels and Commentary on St John* (essay) 1563
*Calvin's Selected Works.* 7 vols. (treatises, commentaries, essays) 1844
*Calvin's Commentaries.* 22 vols. (commentaries) 1847
*Letters of John Calvin.* 4 vols. (correspondence) 1855
*Ioannis Calvini Opera quae supersunt omnia.* 59 vols. (commentaries, treatises, essays) 1863-1900
*Johannis Calvini Opera Selecta.* 5 vols. (commentaries, treatises, essays) 1926-52
*New Testament Commentaries* (commentaries) 1960-
*Supplementa Calviniana: Sermons inedits* (sermons) 1961-

## CRITICISM

### B. A. Gerrish (essay date 1982)

SOURCE: "The Pathfinder: Calvin's Image on Martin Luther," in *The Old Protestantism and the New: Essays on the Reformation of Heritage*, The University of Chicago Press, 1982, pp. 27-48.

[*Below, Gerrish compares the two great Reformers, Luther and Calvin, asserting that, though Calvin never met Luther, Calvin's image of Luther can be fairly well ascertained through the Genevan's correspondence.*]

Martin Luther and John Calvin were, by common consent, the two most eminent figures of the Protestant Reformation. There were other distinguished leaders in both Germany and Switzerland—Melanchthon and Zwingli, for instance—to say nothing of national heroes in other lands. But they do not quite measure up to the stature of the two giants, who can justly be compared only with each other. One naturally expects, then, that the question will have been asked frequently, almost too frequently: What is the relationship between these two? How, in particular, did they think of each other? In actual fact, scholars in the English-speaking world seem to have been strangely uninterested in setting the two Continental Reformers side by side, even when confessional allegiance might have compensated for patriotic indifference. The theme "Luther and Calvin," with variations in approach and content, has been handled rather more regularly in German,[1] occasionally also in French and Dutch.[2] And, of course, the more general studies, such as the biographies of Calvin, always have something more or less weighty to say on the theme, even if only incidentally.[3] But the literature in English is thin.[4]

One reason for the delinquency of British and American scholarship in this respect is perhaps the tendency to concentrate mainly on the ***Institutes*** and (rather less) on Calvin's commentaries. The casual reader of the ***Institutes,*** who is not skilled in identifying unacknowledged debts or anonymous opponents, could be pardoned for concluding that the author had never heard of Luther. Although the pages of Calvin's systematic work bristle with citations from biblical, patristic, scholastic, and classical authors, no explicit reference is made to the great German Reformer. In the commentaries, to be sure, the veil of anonymity is lifted from time to time, and Luther is openly mentioned, often, though by no means always, to illustrate a piece of faulty exegesis.[5] But the most important sources for my theme are among the least read: namely, Calvin's correspondence[6] and the so-called "minor theological treatises."[7] For this reason, and also because some of the pertinent materials are not even available in English translations,[8] I devote a good deal of space, in what follows, to direct quotation of Calvin's most important judgments on Martin Luther.

I

A glance at the dates of some of the articles devoted immediately to my theme (1883, 1896, 1959, 1964) reveals that the sacred festivals of Protestantism—the birthdays or deathdays of the Reformers and the appearance of the definitive edition of the ***Institutes***—have been the chief stimulus to publication. Approaches to the theme have been various. The personalities of Luther and Calvin have been contrasted, with inevitable assistance from ethnology and sociology: the impetuous Teuton is set beside the precise Frenchman, the peasant's son beside the boy who grew up among the gentry.[9] Likewise, the respective theologies of the two Reformers have been compared, and an attempt made to locate the points of difference.[10] Finally, their actual personal relationships and opinions of each other have been reviewed and evaluated.[11] I think it can be said, however, that a special underlying concern often binds essays together which seem, on the surface, quite different in approach. Indeed, *all* the essays which originate from the continent of Europe show traces, some more and some less, of this concern: to see what light the relationships between Luther and Calvin can shed on the division between the two communions that are descended from them. And here, perhaps, a word of caution may be called for.

We cannot help looking back on the Reformation in the light of four centuries of confessional mistrust. This is made particularly plain in the essay by the Dutch scholar A. Eekhof, written during the First World War. He concludes his theme "How did Calvin think about Luther?" with an extraordinary remark from Harnack, who professed to see in the war confirmation of the fact that Calvinism really does have another spirit than Lutheranism. Harnack had written:

> The war shows us that the Reformed territories of Western Europe and America stand over against us with a lack of understanding which makes them susceptible to every defamation. We German Protestants are still just as isolated as three hundred years ago.[12]

Eekhof was able to point to another, possibly wiser statement of Harnack's, published the very same year (1917), in which the German historian reaffirmed his belief in the power of Christianity to induce a sense of unity among the nations. But if, comments Eekhof, it is in fact true that the confessions stand against each other, then another German scholar, August Lang, has shown the way to future reconciliation: we are to learn from the example of Luther and Calvin that the Evangelical church, despite all its divisions, is called to brotherly unity. With this one would not wish to quarrel. But it does already remind us, at least implicitly, that Calvin's situation was not ours, since we are being invited to go back beyond the experience of confessional animosity.

It cannot be too strongly emphasized at the outset that Calvin did not think of himself as "Reformed" in the sense of inner-Protestant polemics. Calvin was not a Calvinist but an Evangelical, and what he thought about Luther can only be understood from this viewpoint. He identified himself wholly with the common Protestant cause and never faced the Wittenbergers as the sponsor of a rival movement. This was at no time made more plain than when Calvin learned of the struggle between the Saxon Lutherans and Heinz von Wolfenbüttel (1545). He immediately obtained permission from the Genevan authorities to hold a special service of intercession, and from his pulpit he exhorted the people of Geneva: "I am not speaking of Geneva alone, but of all towns and territories where the gospel is proclaimed. . . . May we set ourselves apart? May we say, 'They are far away from us'? No, they belong to the church, and we are their members."[13] Moreover, as is well known, Calvin testified to his solidarity with the Lutherans by accepting the Augsburg Confession.[14] Of course, the eucharistic debates repeatedly menaced the relations between Calvin and the Lutherans. But it is common knowledge that on the points at issue between Luther and Zwingli he recognized the validity of Luther's case.[15] And he did not permit even the bitterness of his debate with Joachim Westphal to shake his confidence in the German Reformer, whose memory he continued to cherish.

II

We may say, then, that Calvin's churchmanship and evangelicalism prevented him from being narrowly confessional. Nevertheless, the plain fact is that his affection for Luther was occasioned by the generosity of Luther himself. Calvin's earliest remarks on the Saxon Reformer were inclined to be censorious. But he was utterly disarmed by the news that he himself was more kindly judged in Wittenberg. Not that he ever recanted his early estimate of Luther's character and opinions. Rather, he was enabled to set the negative judgments within the context of a warm admiration for the person and insight of the older man. Further, he learned to view the beginnings of the Reformation from a historical perspective which did not demand of him a plain yes or a plain no to Martin

Luther, but rather led him to adopt the stance of a critical disciple. And, as often happens with strong-willed disciples, he would leap vigorously to his master's defense, and yet claim for himself the right to criticize him freely.

Luther and Calvin never met, and it may be that Calvin's understanding of Luther was hampered by his ignorance of German. This, at any rate, was the accusation brought against him by the Reformers in German Switzerland, as we shall see. Similarly, when the Lutheran Heshusius began his polemics against Calvin, the Swiss Reformer was embarrassed by the fact that his opponent attacked him in German. A third party, Wolph, thoughtfully sent Calvin some selected passages translated into Latin, and explained: "You, most learned Calvin, who are a Frenchman by race and do not understand German, no more understand the insults he spews out against you than I would if insulted in Arabic.[16] We may take it, then, as an established fact that Calvin knew Luther directly only through such of his writings as had been written in Latin or else translated from German.

Further, if Luther and Calvin never encountered each other face to face, neither can one speak of a correspondence between them. We have but one letter from Calvin to Luther, and none from Luther to Calvin. It is true that when the editors of Calvin's works were assembling his correspondence, a certain Count Henri de Sarrau informed them that he had in his possession a latter addressed by the German Reformer to his Swiss counterpart.[17] It bore the improbable inscription *amico et patrono;* and though *patronus* could conceivably mean "advocate" rather than "patron," the letter remained suspect. From an exact copy it was then discovered (by Herminjard)[18] that the count's treasured letter was in fact not from Luther, but from Simon Sultzer, pastor and professor of theology at Berne.

Calvin's earliest sentiments about Luther were expressed in a letter he wrote to Martin Bucer (12 January 1538) during the negotiations which followed the adoption of the Wittenberg Concord (1536). The Concord had achieved reconciliation between the Wittenbergers and the South Germans. The next step was to attempt the inclusion of the Swiss. Calvin was less than enthusiastic. He shared the suspicion of the Swiss theologians that, under the veil of an ambiguous formula, Luther might dream about a transference of Christ's flesh into ours (or of our flesh into Christ's), or might attribute an infinite body to Christ, or, finally, might insist upon a local presence. A "concord" was to be desired such as all good men could accept in sincerity. Calvin then continues with some remarks on Martin Luther:

> If he is able to embrace us with our confession [Calvin means the First Helvetic Confession of 1536] there is nothing that I would more gladly desire. However, he is not the only one in the church of God whom we have to consider. We are thrice unfeeling and barbarous if we take no account of the thousands who are being fiercely reviled under the pretext of the Concord. I do not know what to think of Luther, although I am fully persuaded of his godliness [*pietate*]. I sincerely hope that what many are proclaiming, who otherwise have no desire to be unjust to him, is not true: that there is a bit of obstinacy mixed in with his firmness.[19]

Calvin suspects Luther of being too fond of winning theological victories, and this, he believes, will threaten the Concord. Moreover, he is severely critical of Luther's theological position. Luther is guilty, not just of contemptuousness and abuse, but also of ignorance and gross delusion *(crassissima halucinatione).* This is pretty strong language and does not promise well, one would think, for future relations between the two Reformation giants.

On the other hand, a glance at the first edition of Calvin's ***Institutes,*** already published in 1536, is sufficient to prove that he was deeply indebted to Luther, and this, no doubt, promised better things. Quite apart from the fact, often pointed out, that Calvin modeled the structure of his first edition on Luther's catechisms, he borrowed freely from the fund of Lutheran ideas, not least on the Lord's Supper. His basic understanding of what a sacrament is unmistakably echoed the classic treatment in Luther's *Babylonian Captivity.* In short, unlike Zwingli, who proclaimed his theological independence, Calvin was a conscious debtor, who deliberately appropriated Lutheran insights. It is true that, on this point, Émile Doumergue challenged August Lang, who had argued for Calvin's dependence on Luther in the first edition of the ***Institutes***. Doumergue maintained that, in actual fact, Calvin there rejected the three fundamental ideas of Luther's eucharistic teaching in the *Babylonian Captivity:* consubstantiation, the glorified body of Christ, and the identification of the bread and the body.[20] But, in my judgment, Lang quite rightly refused to recant,[21] since the differences pointed out by Doumergue are not incompatible with agreement on the nature of a sacrament. Calvin criticized Luther's teaching on the mode of Christ's presence in the Eucharist, but he accepted the idea of a sacrament as a sign that confirms the divine promise.[22] Hence we must conclude that, despite the wholly negative appearance of Calvin's remarks to Bucer, he was already under Luther's theological influence.

Then, in 1539, news came from Wittenberg that Dr. Martin held Calvin in high esteem. With almost childlike joy the young Reformer reported the good news to his friend Guillaume Farel, and the entire tone of his judgments upon Luther henceforth changed, even if they remained much the same in content. In a letter to Martin Bucer at Strasbourg, where Calvin was then residing, Luther had ended with these words: "Farewell. And will you pay my respects [*salutabis . . . reverenter*] to John Sturm and John Calvin. I have read their little books with singular enjoyment."[23] Calvin quoted this commendation of his writing when he addressed a letter to Farel (20 November 1539),[24] and he added: "Just think what I say there about the Eucharist! Consider Luther's generosity [*ingenuitatem*]! It will be easy to decide what reason they have who so obstinately disagree with him." Calvin was also able to add two further testimonies of Luther's goodwill. The first was a statement in a letter from Melanchthon (now lost), according to which "Calvin has found great favor." The second was an incident Melanchthon had instructed the messenger to deliver orally. Here is how Calvin repeats the communication to Farel:

> Certain persons, to irritate Martin, pointed out to him the aversion with which he and his followers were alluded to by me. So he examined the passage in question and felt that he was there, beyond doubt, under attack. After a while, he said: "I certainly hope that he will one day think better of us. Still, it is right for us to be a little tolerant toward such a gifted man."[25] We are surely made of stone [Calvin continues] if we are not overcome by such moderation! I, certainly, am overcome, and I have written an apology [*satisfactionem*] for insertion into my preface to the Epistle to the Romans.

Generosity had evoked an answering generosity. Indeed, Calvin's eager testimony to Luther's magnanimous spirit was found embarrassing by later Calvinists. Theodore Beza, who edited Calvin's writings, went through the letter with a censor's quill and crossed out the most compromising phrases.[26] As for Calvin's "apology," Melanchthon persuaded him to leave it out of the preface to his ***Commentary on Romans***.[27] But he did write it, and sent a copy to Farel for his approval.[28] The content of the apology has been thought to shed some light on an interesting question posed by Luther's letter to Bucer: Which book (or books)[29] of Calvin had he "read with singular enjoyment"? Since Luther immediately goes on to make a thrust at Cardinal Sadoleto—"As for Sadoleto, I wish he would believe that God is the creator of men even outside of Italy"—it is natural to suppose that he must have been thinking about Calvin's ***Reply to Sadoleto,*** published earlier that same year (1539). In his apology, however, Calvin refers to the new edition of the ***Institutes,*** which also appeared in 1539, and denies that he there intended to attack the Germans.[30] This does not, I think (pace Doumergue),[31] enable us to identify the ***Institutes*** of 1539 as the "little book" which Luther "read with singular enjoyment." It seems to me more likely that, in his letter to Bucer, Luther really did have the ***Reply to Sadoleto*** in mind. But when confronted with the section on the Eucharist in the new edition of the ***Institutes,*** he refused to retract his favorable opinion of the author. And Calvin, on his side, was wholly captivated by Luther's magnanimity. He hastened to explain that he had not really meant to attack the Lutherans at all.

III

*In the years immediately following the Wittenberg Concord, Luther maintained a friendliness toward the Swiss that contrasts strikingly with the bitterness of the Marburg Colloquy (1529).[32] Indeed, even the common image of Luther as the intransigent antagonist of Zwingli in the castle of Philip of Hesse has been much overdone. At that time he was rather more conciliatory than Philip Melanchthon, even though the conference did begin badly when Luther took his piece of chalk and wrote his text on the table. Despite his tempestuous tirades, Luther was on the verge of giving the Swiss the right hand of fellowship, but Melanchthon dissuaded him.[33] In the 1540s, however, the eucharistic debate flared up once more. Luther's wrath against the Swiss waxed steadily hotter, until even his friend Melanchthon no longer felt safe in Wittenberg. In August 1543, Luther dashed off an angry letter to the Swiss publisher Froschauer, warning him never again to send him anything written by the Swiss, against whom he intended to pray and teach until the end of his days.[34] In 1544 he published his Short Confession on the Holy Sacrament, in which his powers of invective carried him to new heights, as in the the famous description of his adversaries as possessing an eingeteuffelt, durch teuffelt, uberteuffelt, lesterlich hertz und Luegenmaul.[35] In January 1546, shortly before his death, Luther summed up his sentiments in a parody of the first Psalm: "Blessed is the man who walks not in the counsel of the sacramentarians, nor stands in the way of Zwinglians, nor sits in the seat of the Zurichers."[36]*

How, we must now ask, did Calvin's affection for the German Reformer stand up in the face of these vigorous blasts from Wittenberg? The answer is that it remained steadfast as ever. More surprising, Luther, for his part, seems to have been at least half-willing to exempt Calvin from his tirades against the Swiss.

Luther's letter to Froschauer prompted Calvin to write to Melanchthon (21 April 1544), asking him to lay a restraining hand on his colleague and friend:

> Bullinger has recently complained to me that all the Zurichers have been savagely mangled [*atrociter laceratos*] by Dr. Luther. And he sent a copy of a letter in which I, too, feel a lack of humanity. I beseech you, do all you can to restrain, or rather prevent, Dr. Martin from giving way to his violence against that church. Maybe he has reason to flare up against them, but it is proper to deal more gently with godly and learned men.[37]

Indeed, had not Luther himself, in 1539, said the same? Later, when Luther's *Short Confession* had appeared,

Calvin wrote to Bullinger (25 November 1544):

> I hear that Luther has at last broken out with savage invective, not so much against you as against us all. . . . Now I hardly dare ask you to remain silent. For it is certainly not just that the innocent should be molested and denied the chance to clear themselves; and it is hard to decide whether it is even good policy. But I desire you to bear in mind, first, Luther's greatness as a man and his outstanding gifts: the stoutheartedness and steadfastness, the skillfulness, and the effectiveness of teaching with which he has labored to destroy the kingdom of antichrist and spread abroad the doctrine of salvation. I often say that even if he should call me a devil, I should still pay him the honor of acknowledging him as an illustrious servant of God, who yet, as he is rich in virtues, so also labors under serious faults. . . . It is our task so to reprehend whatever is bad in him that we make some allowance for those splendid gifts.[38]

At the very moment when tempers were hottest over the renewed eucharistic debate, Calvin wrote a letter to Luther himself—the only letter ever addressed by one of the two Reformers to the other. The occasion for writing, however, was not furnished by the controversy over the Eucharist, but by persecution of the Protestants in France.[39] Fearing for their lives, some of them had outwardly conformed by attendance at the Roman mass, but remained, as they said, inwardly devoted to the true religion. They were named "Nicodemites," because, like Nicodemus, they came secretly to the Savior. Calvin challenged the weakness of his countrymen with characteristic vigor in his ***Short Treatise Showing What a Faithful Man Should Do, Knowing the Truth of the Gospel, When He Is among the Papists*** (1543).[40] The French Protestants found his imperatives too uncompromising, and even hinted that Geneva was scarcely the most convincing place from which to commend the cross of martyrdom. Calvin wrote a reply, ***The Apology of John Calvin to the Nicodemite Gentlemen Concerning the Complaint They Have Made that He Is Too Rigorous*** (1544).[41] But his countrymen were not convinced, and they felt that a milder verdict could be expected from the Reformers of Wittenberg. They requested Calvin to consult with the Germans by sending a messenger or, if possible, by traveling to Wittenberg himself.

Not surprisingly, Calvin felt unable to make the journey in person. To Wittenberg and back by horse was a two-month ride, and he had neither the leisure nor the constitution for such a rugged journey. Besides, he was handicapped by his ignorance of German and, he admitted, was also too deeply in financial debt to go traveling. Finally, the time for conferring with Luther was still remote, since the passion of controversy had not yet subsided.[42] Instead of a personal visit, then, Calvin translated his two treatises into Latin and sent them by messenger to Wittenberg, together with letters (dated 21 January 1545) to both Luther and Melanchthon.[43] He asked, not for agreement, but for a frank appraisal of what he had written.[44]

In his letter to Luther, Calvin makes profuse apologies for claiming the time of an already overburdened man, and requests Luther to read the two treatises, or have them read, and to give his verdict. Luther is addressed as "most respected father," and Calvin is highly deferential throughout, making plain that he shares with the French Protestants a high regard for Luther's authority.

> Both because I thought it of the most importance for them to be helped by your authority, so that they should not be forever wavering, and also because this was something to be desired by myself as well, I was unwilling to refuse them their request. . . . How I wish I could fly to you there, so that I might enjoy your company for but a few hours! For I should prefer, and it would be much better, to discuss with you in person, not this question only, but others too. But since it is not granted us here on earth, it will shortly be ours, as I hope, in the Kingdom of God.[45]

What, then, it will be asked, did Luther make of Calvin's letter? The answer is that he never received it, and probably never knew that it had been written. Melanchthon wrote back on 17 April that the struggle he had previously avoided was growing worse, and he expected banishment. "I have not shown your letter to Pericles [i.e., Luther]. For he is inclined to be suspicious, and does not want his replies on such questions as you raise to be passed around."[46]

It would be quite unfair to conclude that Calvin had made a gesture of conciliation to Luther, only to be frustrated by the high-handedness of his supposed friend, Melanchthon. Calvin trusted Melanchthon completely. Knowing the situation at Wittenberg, he had sent both letters to Melanchthon, leaving him to determine, at his own discretion, what to do with the letter addressed to his colleague.[47] It has indeed been suggested that Calvin, in a letter to Pierre Viret, "seems to play down the importance of the affair,"[48] as though he wrote to Luther somewhat reluctantly, and solely to pacify his obstinate countrymen. This may well be true.[49] But it is plain that Calvin had hoped to seize the opportunity to assure Luther directly of his deep respect, and one cannot help wondering how Luther might have responded to the younger man's homage. Perhaps Melanchthon knew best, after all. Certainly, Luther's growing intransigence terrified Melanchthon and severely strained Calvin's admiration.

Later in the year (28 June 1545), Calvin urged Melanchthon to greater openness about his eucharistic convictions and, while commending his prudence and moderation, warned him against the policy of appeasement—this time the appeasement, not of Rome, but of Luther. Not that Calvin intended to side with the men of Zurich. He told Melanchthon that he found their answer to Luther (the ***Orthodox Confession*** of 1545) feeble and childish, distinguished more by stubborness than by learning; they excused Zwingli and reproached Luther with equal injustice, and should either have written differently or else have kept quiet. But he could not overlook that they had been deeply provoked by the thundering Pericles of Wittenberg.

> I indeed, who revere him from my heart, am violently ashamed of him. . . . I admit we all owe him much. And I am not reluctant to let him be preeminent with the highest authority, provided he knows how to govern his own self. But in the church we must see that we do not go too far in our deference to men. It would be all over if any one man counted for more than all the rest.[50]

Throughout the renewed crisis, then, Calvin managed to maintain a balance and restraint that prevented him from simply taking the side of the Swiss against Luther. His attitude rested partly on the conviction that neither side had a monopoly on the truth, partly on his refusal to forget the debt that Protestantism owed to the "illustrious servant of God." Indeed, he suspected that Luther was permitting himself to be led by lesser men, especially Amsdorf.[51] And in this he was more than half right.[52] Further, there is evidence that Luther, for his part, did not permit the new phase of the eucharistic controversy to alter his estimate of Calvin. This, however, is another question, and it cannot be allowed to divert us from our theme.[53]

IV

Other features of Calvin's attitude toward Luther could be documented from his correspondence. He had, for instance, some interesting and discerning comments on Luther as an exegete, suggesting that he was a little too quick in drawing the "fruitful" conclusions from the Scripture text.[54] But we must now turn from the correspondence to certain of Calvin's theological treatises in which his picture of Luther takes on sharper contours and is set within the frame of something like a historical interpretation of the Reformation. Three treatises written during Luther's lifetime will be considered first: the ***Short Treatise on the Lord's Supper*** (1541), the treatise against Pighius (1543), and the ***Humble Exhortation*** to Charles V (1543).

The ***Short Treatise on the Lord's Supper*** contains an interesting survey of the eucharistic controversy among the Protestants.[55] There is good reason to believe that Luther himself examined this section of the treatise and gave it his approval.[56] It is characteristic of Calvin to insist at the outset on two points. First, one could hardly expect that a proper understanding of this intricate question would have been attained all at once. "We shall not be at all surprised that they [the disputants] did not grasp everything at the outset." But, second, beneath the outward scandal of disagreement he detects a genuine movement toward unity. With a glad expectancy, later to be disappointed, Calvin anticipates a final settlement of the debate. All are now agreed that "we are truly made partakers of the proper substance of the body and blood of Jesus Christ." It is just that some are better than others at explaining how this happens. Within this movement toward unity both parties erred and refused to hear each other. The case against Luther is that he employed ill-advised similitudes, appeared to teach a local presence, and spoke with too sharp a tongue. But Calvin does not doubt that Luther was right to resist the opposing tendency to reduce the sacrament to a matter of "bare signs." The view of the Zwinglians was entirely too negative and destructive. "For although they did not deny the truth, all the same they did not teach it as clearly as they ought." In any case, Calvin says, our part is not to censure either side, but to recall in thankfulness what we have received from both.

The subject of Calvin's controversy with Pighius is indicated in the full title of his treatise: ***A Defense of the Sound and Orthodox Doctrine of the Bondage and Deliverance of the Human Will against the False Accusations of Albert Pighius***. The first part of the treatise contained a remarkable defense of Luther against many of the charges that are still brought against him in our own day. Whether or not one judges it a merit, Calvin must be acknowledged as a vigorous and skillful polemicist, with a flair for the telling phrase. More important, no doubt, he displays a sensitive appreciation of Luther's thought and personality. He has grasped the meaning of the famous *Anfechtungen* (or "spiritual assaults"), and he recognizes in the admitted extravagance of Luther's style precisely the kind of hero for whom the times cried out.

Calvin refuses to be diverted into a detailed analysis of Luther's moral character.

> As for the denunciations with which he [Pighius] slashes Luther's character and morals, it is no part of my present design to rebut them. They do not contribute much of importance to the subject under debate, neither does Luther need any defense of mine. Pighius behaves just like some hungry, ravenous dog, which, finding nothing to get its teeth into, vents its spite by yapping.[57]

In any case, the worst that Pighius could find to say against Luther's character was that he must have been a very monster from hell, since he was often tormented with oppressive struggles of conscience that were like the anguish of the damned. Calvin retorts that if only the windbag Pighius had the least inkling of what those struggles meant, he would either have held his peace or become Luther's admirer. It is the common lot of the godly to undergo "fearful tortures of conscience," by which they are made familiar with true humility. A man may even say, in times of unusual testing, that he is not only surrounded and beset by the agonies of death, but swallowed up by hell itself. For among the saints there are certain exceptional men whom God has chosen to be the special objects of his strange judgments. The echoes of characteristically Lutheran language in this passage are unmistakable, and they testify to Calvin's insight into the religious struggles of the German Reformer. He would not, I think, have wished to include himself among the *ex sanctis praestantissimi,* the exceptional religious personalities in whom the marvelous judgments of God are displayed. But "spiritual assaults" were not foreign to him, and he knew how Luther understood them theologically.

On the problem of the enslaved will Calvin steps forward as Luther's champion, except that he thinks it necessary to tone down some unguarded and exaggerated language. And he insists that, understood within their historical context, even Luther's extravagant expressions were justified. Pighius deplored, for instance, the fact that Luther was obliged, as a corollary of his views on the bondage of the will, to regard all human works as sins, and that he pressed this theme with gross exaggeration. Calvin replies:

> I grant it, but still say that there was good reason that drove him to such exaggeration. He saw the world stupefied by a false and pernicious confidence in works, as if by a fatal lethargy. What was needed to awaken it was not voice and words, but the trumpet blast, thunder, and lightning.[58]

On the matter of "necessity" in providence and predestination Calvin refuses to be embarrassed by the accusation that there were inconsistencies in Protestant theology, not only between one theologian and another, but even within the writings of a single theologian. There is no reason why all should be expected to use precisely the same mode of expression, nor any reason why an author should be forbidden to improve what he has once written. The expression of the truth is always perfectible. Melanchthon, for example, has adapted to a more popular style much that Luther wrote in the scholastic mode *(scholastico dicendi genere).* And for himself, Calvin's claim is this:

> That which is most important in this question, and for the sake of which everything else is said, we defend today just as it was declared by Luther and others at the beginning; and even in what I have declared less necessary to faith my own concern has been to avoid offense by softening the mode of expression.[59]

In his treatise against Pighius Calvin sums up his understanding of Luther in a single sentence: "We regard him as a remarkable apostle of Christ, through whose work and ministry, most of all, the purity of the Gospel has been restored in our time."[60] The same picture of Luther reappears in the appeal to Charles V, written in the same year and laid before the Diet of Speier in 1544. The appeal was published "in the name of all who desire Christ to reign," under the long-winded title, ***A Humble Exhortation to the Invincible Emperor, Charles V, and the Most Illustrious Princes and Other Orders Now Assembled at the Diet of Speier that They Should Choose Seriously to Undertake the Task of Restoring the Church.*** (From the object of the appeal the treatise is commonly and more manageably titled ***The Necessity for Reforming the Church.***) Here Calvin speaks of Luther as the man whom God raised up at the beginning, along with others, to hold a torch over the path to salvation.[61] Before Luther became known, all the world was bewitched by irreligious opinions about the merit of works.[62] But when the truth of God had been choked by thick clouds of darkness, and when religion had been corrupted by godless superstitions, Luther appeared and others after him, who took counsel together to purge religion from a host of defilements. "In this course," Calvin adds, "we still continue today."[63] He is particularly anxious to present his man as the reluctant reformer driven, against his intention, from protest to revolt. Luther pleaded with the pope to heal the maladies of the church. The plea fell on deaf ears.[64]

> When Luther first appeared, he pointed gently to but a few abuses that were too gross to be endured any longer. So unassuming was he that he did not venture to correct them himself, but rather made it known that he longed to see them corrected. It was the opposing party that promptly sounded the call to arms. As the contention flared up, our enemies judged it the best and shortest way to suppress the truth with force and brutality. . . . And now we have to listen to the same reproach that the godless Ahab once brought against Elijah, that he was a troubler of Israel (1 Kings 18:17). But the holy prophet absolved us with his reply: "It is not I," he says, "but you and your father's house [that trouble Israel], for you have forsaken the Lord and gone after Baalim."[65]

We have it on reliable authority that Luther read the ***Humble Exhortation*** and gave it his glowing recommendation.[66] And well he might! Seldom has a more sympathetic and loyal picture of the Reformer been given outside the limits of his own communion. But one thing stands out clearly in the three treatises of the years 1541 and 1543: for all his devotion to Luther, Calvin never appeals to his ideas as though they were final or definitive. Luther, for him, was not an oracle but a pathfinder—a pioneer, in whose footsteps we follow and whose trail has to be pushed on further. We hurry on, still today, in the path he opened up.[67] The Reformation (if we may so express Calvin's meaning) is open-ended: it had its beginning in the person of that "remarkable apostle of Christ," but it did not end with him. It is this conviction of Calvin's that was sharpened after Luther's death, when a further round of eucharistic debates was opened.

V

The eucharistic controversies of the 1550s were evoked, in part, by the adoption of the Zurich Consensus (1549) as the bond of union between the French- and German-speaking Protestants of Switzerland.[68] In the eyes of the strict Lutherans the consensus showed Calvin in his true colors: all along, he had been one of the "sacramentarians." During the bitter quarrels that followed, Calvin made no attempt to revise his estimate of Luther, but he had to defend it openly on two fronts: against the Swiss, who detested the memory of Luther, and against the ultra-Lutherans, who (in Calvin's opinion) idolized him. And it must be admitted that he did not have much success with either. For the one group, the name of Luther could only evoke bitter recollections of the past, while in the eyes of the other group a nimbus had settled over the deceased Reformer's shoulders.

Calvin's battle may be read in his correspondence during the period. Against Luther's detractors he insisted that Luther could not but give his blessing to the new agreement among the Swiss on the doctrine of the Lord's Supper. He honestly believed that he had discovered the fundamental point of Luther's contention for the real presence, that between the two of them there had never been any disagreement on this point, and that since the point was now unambiguously affirmed by the Swiss theologians Luther, were he alive, could not withold his approval.

> If Luther, that distinguished servant of God and faithful doctor of the church, were alive today, he would not be so harsh and unyielding as not willingly to allow this confession: that what the sacraments figure is truly offered to us [*vere praestari*], and that therefore in the sacred Supper we become participants in the body and blood of Christ. For how often did he declare that he was contending for no other cause than to establish that the Lord does not mock us with empty signs but accomplishes inwardly what he sets before our eyes, and that the effect is therefore conjoined with the signs?[69]

Many of the Swiss theologians were not impressed with Calvin's thoughts on what Luther would doubtless do, were he alive. They found it astonishing that he should persist in making himself Luther's champion.[70] With all the tact they could muster, the pastors of Zurich put it down to Calvin's ignorance of German.

> Possibly you do not know, dear brother, how crassly and barbarously Doctor Luther thought and wrote concerning this spiritual feast. You have not been able to read or understand his books, since he wrote the greater part of this sort in German. . . . So that you may not be ignorant, therefore, of what it had been especially useful to know in this affair, we will rehearse a few particular passages of his. We give the substance faithfully but specify the page, so that, if you like, you can invite an interpreter skilled in the German language to translate for you word for word. And if you do not possess the books, we have them and shall be happy to lend them to you.[71]

As for Calvin's view that Luther would gladly give his hand to those who conceded the union of the sacramental sign with the thing signified, the men of Zurich retort: "Dear Calvin, he would *not* offer us his hand—that right hand which, when living, he did not wish to offer to Zwingli and Oecolampadius, when they were living, though they made all these same concessions and professions."[72]

As far as the other party was concerned—those who refused to move beyond the details of Luther's own eucharistic teaching—Calvin consistently asserted, and not very politely, that there is a difference between a disciple and an ape.[73] This, admittedly, was not a choice of language that was apt to commend his point. Still, the point was worth making, and he could, on occasion, deliver it more courteously, though no less forcefully. Hence to one correspondent he wrote, in reply to the charge that he did not always subscribe to the interpretations of Luther:

> But if now it will not be permitted to each exegete to make public what he thinks about a particular passage of Scripture, to what kind of servitude are we reduced? Indeed, if I was not permitted at any point to depart from the opinion of Luther, it was utterly ridiculous of me to undertake the work of exegesis [*munus interpretandi*].[74]

What Calvin feared was that some of Luther's adherents would make their master's opinions the touchstone of dogmatic truth, thereby repudiating, in effect, Luther's own fundamental principle that the Word of God stands always above the doctrines of men.[75]

Once again, the evidence of the correspondence may be filled out by examining certain of Calvin's theological treatises: in particular, the treatise ***On Scandals*** (1550), the ***Second Defense against Westphal*** (1556), and the ironical work against Gabriel (1561).

Calvin has occasion more than once to speak of Luther in his work ***On the Scandals by Which Many***

***Today Are Deterred, and Some Even Alienated, from the Pure Doctrine of the Gospel.*** For, as he himself remarks, "How many fables have Luther's enemies repeated about him, both in addresses and in published books, for a full five and twenty years!"[76] Among other things, the adversaries of the Protestants alleged that the Reformation was a kind of Trojan war—fought, that is, for the sake of women. Luther, they explained, was spurred on by the lust of the flesh and procured for himself the liberty to marry. It must be admitted that Calvin replies very much in kind. "What could be more ridiculous," he inquires, "than for those who cannot maintain chastity of life to flee from the papacy?"[77] But this, of course, is merely skirmishing beyond the real battle lines.

Of chief interest in the work ***On Scandals*** is what Calvin has to say on the scandal of a divided church.[78] For even "the most prominent teachers of the reborn gospel [*primarios renascentis evangelii doctores*]" are divided on matters of doctrine. Especially unhappy is the contention over the sacraments. Calvin finds it odd that the Protestant differences should somehow appear more scandalous than the fierce theological quarrels among the Roman schools. Further, he reminds the scandalized that among the faithful servants of God there have always been sharp disagreements, such as set Paul against Barnabas and Peter against Paul. But the controversy of Luther and his Protestant opponents, so he argues, moved within the lines of fundamental agreement on the nature of the gospel. "There was a remarkable consensus among them on all that is essential to godliness [*in tota pietatis summa*]." They agreed, for instance, that the whole of salvation resides in the grace of Christ, and they overthrew all confidence in works. "They extolled magnificently the excellence of Christ [*Christi virtutem*], which had lain prostrate or hidden from sight." Only on the sacraments was there dissension. And even on this question Calvin's considered opinion is that only polemical passion and mistrust delayed reconciliation. The miracle is that Luther and others who labored in his day for the restoration of sound doctrine were able slowly to emerge from the darkness of ignorance and error. True, there are those who profess themselves offended because Luther and his contemporaries did not see everything in a flash, and they refuse to continue in the course already begun. But Calvin says of them:

> They are behaving just like the man who blames us because at the first break of dawn [*primo aurorae exortu*] we do not yet discern the midday sun. . . . Surely, those who talk like this are unwilling to allow progress to the servants of God or are distressed that the Kingdom of Christ should move on to something better.[79]

If one may so put it, Calvin here represents Luther, not John Wycliffe, as the "Morning Star of the Reformation." And it is plainly a continuing reformation that he has in mind—reformation as defined by "progress" (*profectus*) and "movement" (*promoveri*). Yet it is still movement from a fixed point, at which stands the extraordinary figure of Martin Luther, God's chosen pioneer.

Luther's name was invoked frequently in the debate between Calvin and Westphal, especially in Calvin's ***Second Defense of the Godly and Orthodox Faith Concerning the Sacraments against the False Accusations of Joachim Westphal.*** That Westphal, the ultra-Lutheran, appealed to Luther's memory, was natural enough.[80] But it is precisely Westphal's right to claim Luther as spiritual father that Calvin contests, recalling the warmth of his own friendship with the first generation of Lutheran Reformers. From the very beginning, when he was just emerging from the darkness of the papacy, he had been turned from Zwingli and Oecolampadius by his reading of Luther. Later, he was kindly received by all Luther's keenest advocates. And Luther's own judgment of him, after examining his writings, can easily be shown through reliable witnesses, including Melanchthon.[81] Calvin's respect for Luther remains unchanged. It is true that the German Reformer was sometimes carried away by his violent disposition, but the flame was sparked by mischief-makers.[82] And it is surely pathetic that some of Luther's followers should choose to mimic only his personal shortcomings. "Ah, Luther! How few imitators of your excellence have you left behind you—and how many apes of your holy belligerence!"[83] As for himself, Calvin rejects the charge that his ***Commentary on Genesis*** was crammed with harsh judgements on Luther, though he leaves us in no doubt that he found more to disapprove in Luther's own commentary than he chose to mention. "More than a hundred times I refrain, out of respect, from mentioning his name." But wherever he does name Luther, the "illustrious servant of Christ" is treated with all due honor.[84]

The point is, then, that although Calvin both regretted Luther's disposition and frankly dissented from some of his expressions,[85] he considered this the legitimate right of an avowed disciple; for the disciple, unlike the epigone, is one who *continues* in the course begun by his master. Calvin insists, as usual, that the *terminus a quo* for a genuine "Lutheran," as far as the Eucharist is concerned, is the efficacious character of sacramental signs. It is here that we have to begin, and not with those unfortunate exaggerations by which Luther himself advanced beyond the essential matter (*ultra . . . progressum esse*).[86] Dogmatic development, so it appears, is not always for the better (*in melius,* as Calvin wrote in the work ***On Scandals***). Indeed, Calvin elsewhere speaks of certain of Luther's opinions as reactionary—a failure to free himself from medievalism, or perhaps a temporary accommodation to the times.[87] Therefore, not progress, but regress! The disciple's duty is to move on. Westphal, however, is like "the man who enters upon the right path, but, as soon as the one who showed him the path turns back, obstinately digs his heels into the one spot and refuses to move on further [*ultra progredi*]."[88]

The last of our sources for Calvin's views on Luther is his ***Congratulation to the Venerable Presbyter Gabriel of Saconay, Precentor of the Church of Lyons, on the Beautiful and Elegant Preface Which He Wrote to the Book by the English King***. Gabriel had reissued Henry VIII's famous polemic against Luther and had furnished it with a preface. For relaxation, Calvin wrote his ironical response and published it anonymously, referring to himself throughout in the third person. Here we find once more judments that are already familiar from the earlier sources. First, Luther was lacking in moderation. It is no wonder that he was shocked by Carlstadt's foolish invention, but he should have listened calmly to men like Oecolampadius. In fact, he overstepped the limits and spoke in anger.[89] Second, it is preposterous to identify as "the last Elijah" either Luther or anyone else. (Gabriel had hinted that Calvin begrudged Luther the title only because he fancied it for himself.)[90] Third, Calvin again presents the idea of a reformation-in-progress. Only now the main thought is, not that the appearance of Luther was one event among others in a continuing movement, but that Luther's own thought was only gradually unfolded. Indeed, we can assume that, were he alive today, he would continue to make progress in the truth.

A key factor in the shaping of Luther's mind was the negative role played by his critics—a thought Calvin had already expressed in his work against Pighius.[91] The positions occupied by his critics forced Luther to more radical offenses against Rome. If, then, Luther once said that the kernel of Christianity is in the papacy, Calvin assures Gabriel that, were the Reformer still alive, he would take that saying back. For what would prevent him from making good progress (*in melius proficere*) in the space of thirty-three years?[92] It is quite true that Luther shifted his position on such matters as the papacy, purgatory, invocation of the saints, the sacrifice of the mass, celibacy, and confession.

> But what, I beg you, was Luther to do at a time when but a faint spark of light had shone upon him? He disclosed, with sincerity, what he knew—that is, little more than nothing. . . . The wonder is that you do not charge him with failure to speak even before he emerged from his mother's womb.[93]

The import of these three treatises from the years 1550, 1556, and 1561 is transparently clear: Calvin wishes to claim for his reformation a continuity with the reformation of Martin Luther. But the claim of continuity is a claim of legitimate development, not of formal identity. In his own estimate, he does not merely transmit the heritage of Luther, but neither does he set his own reformation in opposition to Luther's.[94] In this sense Calvin, in the words of Peter Meinhold, was "the greatest and indeed the only 'disciple' that Luther had."[95] For only he had both the depth of understanding and the creative talents to fashion out of Luther's heritage something that bore the imprint of his own genius. This, at least, was how Calvin himself thought of his relationship to Luther. But it seems less lacking in modesty to have it said by someone other than Calvin.

VI

That Calvin's attitude toward Luther, as I have now described it, raises a whole host of historical and theological problems, hardly needs to be asserted. I have sought only to carry out the first-stage historical task of marshaling such evidence as seems most relevant to my limited theme: What did Calvin actually say about Martin Luther? But the further question suggests itself: Was Calvin right? Was he right in the way he understood his relationship to Luther? Of course, this question, too, is in part historical. But only in part. It also touches on points where theological commitments are at stake.

Even the historical aspects of the question are too complex to be readily solved. What Calvin said about Luther, including what he said about Luther's theology, is a manageable historical problem, which has been adequately handled more than once. But the existing literature is far less satisfactory, in my judgment, where it seeks to compare Luther and Calvin from a neutral standpoint beyond their judgments upon each other. It does not seem to me that historical scholarship has yet sorted out the elements of continuity and discontinuity between the two major Reformers. The attempt to enumerate their theological differences, even though it has often been carried out with sensitivity and insight,[96] leaves much to be desired. Contrasts are too quickly drawn and made to rest upon an insufficiently comprehensive examination of the sources, which are admittedly formidable in bulk for either Reformer alone. Divergent lines of thought are taken to represent a difference between Luther and Calvin, when a more thorough investigation would show that the divergence lies on both sides—that it exemplifies, in fact, the complexity of a theological outlook which the two Reformers had in common. For example, both speak of faith as at once knowledge and trust, and both regard Scripture as at once inspired words and witness to the living Word, Jesus Christ. And yet, by means of "diagonal" comparisons which link the Reformers' unlike utterances instead of pairing the resemblances, it can be alleged that Calvin's idea of faith was more intellectual than Luther's and his understanding of Scripture more inclined toward literalism. By an equally judicious selection of sources the exact opposite could be "proved."[97]

Much more historical research is needed to determine whether seeming differences are really matters of emphasis or even wholly illusory. Only then can we decide how far Calvin was in fact what he claimed to be, a genuine disciple of Luther. However, setting aside this problem for the moment, I content myself with stressing two conclusions of my present theme, which has been concerned only with Calvin's explicit judgments on Martin Luther. In each of these conclusions my interest is in the shape or form of Calvin's thinking rather than in its specific content. I do not ask whether his reading of Luther and the Reformation was correct in detail, but what kind of a reading it was.

In the first place, whether materially justified or not, Calvin's estimate of Luther was historical, not dogmatic, in form. He viewed Luther and the Reformation from a progressive, not an absolutist, perspective, reading Luther's story as a gradual unfolding of the gospel in its various historical relationships—a process in which Luther's opponents played a key role. Calvin rejected not only every effort to elevate Luther's teaching to the status of finished dogma but also any temptation to remove the person of Luther beyond the categories of history—to make him, so to say, an apocalyptic rather than a prophetic figure. Though divinely called, the Reformer was not himself a supernatural person. Calvin did not even object to Luther's being called by the name of Elijah. What he repudiated was the eschatological language which identified him as "the Last Elijah."[98]

It is hardly too much to claim, with Ernst Walter Zeeden,[99] that Calvin anticipated the pietistic-Enlightenment idea of the historical character (the *Geschichtlichkeit*) of Luther and of the Reformation. This is, I think, particularly clear in the treatise against Pighius, where we have found Calvin arguing that theological truth is not formulated once and for all. The *actus tradendi* is also *actus formandi*: "If Pighius does not know it," he wrote, "I want to make this plain to him: our constant effort, day and night, is also to *fashion,* in the manner we think will be best, whatever is faithfully *handed on* by us."[100] This, of course, was not intended by Calvin to allow for changing the content of the Faith. He meant precisely that in the theological task *formare* is always *fideliter tradere,* even though the handing on cannot leave the mode of expression unchanged. Hence he went on to state in these words Melanchthon's intention in preparing the Augsburg Confession: "He had no other wish than to abide by that doctrine which alone is proper to the Church and necessary for saving knowledge."[101]

No doubt, such an interpretation of the theological task is extremely hard to implement, precisely because it poses so acutely the problem of continuity. It does not really furnish exact norms but is rather an announcement of good intentions. Calvin was obliged to argue, for instance, that one could disentangle Luther's essential concern in the eucharistic debates from certain accidental crudities of expression. He never denied that Luther and he disagreed on the idea of an oral manducation (*de substantiali manducatione*). Yet he believed that he had recognized—and, indeed, presented in Luther's own words—the reason why the German Reformer pressed his eucharistic doctrine with such passion:[102] he had kept inviolate Luther's sacramental principle, which stood above their theological differences and was therefore capable of furnishing the basis of unity-in-diversity. But how do we judge what is essential and what is accidental? This is the difficulty in all attempts to "continue the Reformation."

The modern liberal Protestant may turn on Luther and Calvin alike with the judgment that they both stood aside from the real line of progress, which was opened up by Servetus and Socinus. "In the name of progress in Biblical theology," it has been said, "modern Protestantism will proceed to a critical revision of dogma, which the Reformers did not undertake."[103] Here Calvin's own principle of development is, in effect, directed against Calvin himself. But in a sense this serves only to validate his own fundamental point that an earlier theological achievement, however magnificent, cannot relieve the church of the duties of exegesis and dogmatics. Moreover, one can also recognize from his arguments against Westphal that he would by no means concede the subjectivity of his quest for Luther's essential concern. For if he was wrong about Luther, and if, as Westphal argued, Luther condemned indifferently all who denied his understanding of the real presence, how could the unquestionable sympathy between the two Reformers be explained? This is the question that Calvin threw back at Westphal.[104]

In the second place, Calvin's estimate of Luther points to a pluralistic reading of Reformation history, according to which no one party or individual had full possession of the truth. This has to be added to the former conclusion for an obvious reason. It would be easy to assume that Calvin's sole purpose in viewing Luther's work as imperfect was to represent his own work as perfect—or, at least, as very much better. There is, I think, something in this. He does seem, on occasion, to fall into the common illusion of the "progressivist," who may picture the movement of history coming to a halt in his own system. And it cannot be denied that his self-estimate frequently stood in need of the same wisdom he displayed in his sentiments about Luther. Calvin, as we all know, could be dogmatic, overbearing, annoyingly self-confident, and acrimonious in criticism. He possessed a keen theological intellect and was ruthless in exposing the confusions of less gifted rivals. Moreover, he was stubbornly certain that he spoke as God's mouthpiece, although, as he engagingly assures us, he did not make up his mind on a certain matter until he had considered it more than three times.[105] From all of which it certainly seems as though Calvin did not really believe in an *ecclesia reformans,* but merely dated the finished reformation to coincide with his own life and work; so that a fixed norm appears, after all, to be the supposed outcome of the sixteenth-century struggle within the Western church. It must be replied, however, that this appearance is not the whole picture.

If Calvin thought of himself as God's mouthpiece, he thought of Luther in the same way, and this did not prevent him from regarding Luther as fallible.[106] Further, it could be demonstrated from a host of citations that he really did believe in that *gemeinsames Hören,* that hearing the Word along with others, which has been missed in the writings of Luther.[107] In the ***Short Treatise on the Lord's Supper*** his claim is that the truth lay in the dialogue, not on either side of it, and his conclusion is notably undogmatic.[108] In the negotiations that led to the Zurich Consensus he engaged in a remarkably frank correspondence with Heinrich Bullinger, in which each really listened to the criticisms of the other.[109] Further, it could be pointed out that Calvin disapproved on principle of the drafting of confessions of faith by a single hand, citing the legendary origin of the Apostles' Creed in his support.[110] Finally, he longed to see the assembling of an international congress of theologians which might produce a unified Evangelical witness.[111]

In all these ways, Calvin revealed his consciousness of standing under the Word of God along with others. But perhaps the most striking token of his "pluralistic" attitude toward the Reformation and its theology is the interesting phenomenon of the Genevan "congregations," at which the Reformed pastors from the surrounding territory, together with a handful of devout lay people, gathered together to discuss some prearranged passage of Scripture. Calvin believed firmly that this was the proper manner to carry out the interpretation of Scripture. "For as long as there is no mutual exchange, each can teach what he likes. Solitude provides too much liberty."[112] In the last year of his life, when he was too ill to teach or preach, Calvin still—against the counsel of his anxious friends—made his painful way to the Friday morning congregation, whenever he could, and there "added that which God had given him to say upon the text."[113] Practice here coincides perfectly with the principles which he prefaced to his ***Commentary on Romans*** and which have sometimes been identified with the "apology" he promised to the Lutherans in 1539:

> God has never seen fit to bestow such favor on his servants that each individually should be endowed with full and perfect knowledge on every point. No doubt, his design was to keep us both humble and eager for brotherly communication. In this life, then, we should not hope for what otherwise would be most desirable, that there should be continual agreement among us in understanding passages of Scripture. We must therefore take care that, if we depart from the opinions of those who went before us, we do not do so because excited by the itch after novelty, nor driven by fondness for deriding others, nor goaded by animosity, nor tickled by ambition, but only because compelled by pure necessity and with no other aim than to be of service.[114]

In so writing Calvin was loyal to the intention of Luther himself, for whom the Word of God is not given up to the control of any man or any institution, but continually creates for itself a fellowship of hearers and doers.

*Notes*

[1] A. Zahn, "Calvins Urtheile über Luther: Ein Beitrag zur Lutherfeier aus der reformirten Kirche Deutschlands," *Theologische Studien aus Württemberg,* vol. 4, ed. Theodor Hermann and Paul Zeller (Ludwigsburg: Ad. Neubert'sche Buchhandlung, 1883), pp. 183-211; August Lang, "Luther und Calvin," *Deutschevangelische Blätter* 21 (1896): 319-32; Karl Holl, *Luther und Calvin,* Staat, Recht und Volk: Wissenschaftliche Reden und Aufsätze, no. 2 (Berlin: Weidmannsche Buchhandlung, 1919); Hans Grass, *Die Abendmahlslehre bei Luther und Calvin: Eine kritische Untersuchung,* Beiträge zur Förderung christlicher Theologie, 2d ser., vol. 47, 2d ed. (Gütersloh: C. Bertelsmann, 1954); Ernst Walter Zeeden, "Das Bild Martin Luthers in den Briefen Calvins," *Archiv für Reformationsgeschichte* 49 (1958): 177-95; Erwin Mülhaupt, "Luther und Calvin: Eine Jubiläumsbetrachtung," *Luther: Mitteilungen der Luthergesellschaft* 30 (1959): 97-113; Peter Meinhold, "Calvin und Luther," *Lutherische Monatshefte* 3 (1964): 264-69. Cf. also Bernhard Lohse, "Calvin als Reformator," *Luther: Zeitschrift der Luthergesellschaft* 35 (1964): 102-17. I have not been able to see the dissertation of Andrea Wiedeburg, "Calvins Verhältnis zu Luther, Melanchthon, und dem Luthertum" (Tübingen, 1961).

[2] See, in particular: Auguste Lemaître, *Calvin et Luther,* Cahiers de 'foi et vérité', no. 38 [ser. 10, no. 2] (Geneva: Editions Labor et fides, 1959), pp. 3-24; A. Eekhof, "Hoe heeft Calvijn over Luther gedacht?" Nederlandsch Archief voor Kerkgeschiedenis, n.s., 14 (1918): 273-96; A. D. R. Polman, "Calvijn en Luther," in *Vier Redevoeringen over Calvijn,* by D. Nauta et al. (Kampen: J. H. Kok, 1959), pp. 41-53; Charles Boyer, *Calvin et Luther: Accords et différences* (Rome: Gregorian University, 1973).

[3] Of particular note is the full discussion in the magisterial work of Émile Doumergue, *Jean Calvin: Les*

*hommes et les choses de son temps,* 7 vols. (Lausanne: Georges Bridel, 1899-1928), 2:562-87.

[4] David S. Schaff, "Martin Luther and John Calvin: Church Reformers," *Princeton Theological Review* 15 (1917): 530-52, compares the careers, accomplishments, and characters of the two Reformers, but does not consider their actual relationships or opinions of each other. Allan L. Farris, "Calvin's Letter to Luther," *Canadian Journal of Theology* 10 (1964): 124-31, reproduces an old translation of Calvin's letter and adds some historical notes; he does not attempt a general discussion of Calvin's estimate of Luther. Alexander Barclay, in *The Protestant Doctrine of the Lord's Supper: A Study in the Eucharistic Teaching of Luther, Zwingli and Calvin* (Glasgow: Jackson, Wylie, 1927), compares the Reformers on this limited theme only. There are two comparative studies in English of the political opinions of Luther and Calvin: William A. Mueller, *Church and State in Luther and Calvin: A Comparative Study* (Nashville: Broadman Press, 1954), and Duncan B. Forrester, "Martin Luther and John Calvin," in *History of Political Philosophy,* ed. Leo Strauss and Joseph Cropsey (Chicago: Rand McNally, 1963), pp. 277-313. At the time when my own essay first appeared, I had not been able to find any previous study in English devoted directly to Calvin's opinions of Martin Luther; afterwards, I came across an article—by a Dutch scholar, but published in English—that does shed light on my theme: D. Nauta, "Calvin and Luther," *Free University Quarterly* 2 (1952-53): 1-17.

[5] The index to C.O. 23-55 (in C.O. 58) lists ten references to Luther in Calvin's exegetical works, four of which occur in the *Commentary on Genesis.*

[6] C.O. $10^2$-20. Reference will also be made to A.-L. [Aimé-Louis] Herminjard, ed., *Correspondance des réformateurs dans les pays de langue francaise,* 9 vols., vols. 1-4 in 2d ed. (Geneva: H. Georg, 1878-97), whose editorial notes are invaluable.

[7] C.O. 5-9. Some of the treatises will be found also in O.S. 1-2, but I give references only to C.O.

[8] A number of Calvin's letters have been translated in *Letters of John Calvin Compiled and Edited by Jules Bonnet,* trans. David Constable and Marcus Robert Gilchrist, 4 vols. (Philadelphia: Presbyterian Board of Publication, n.d. [ca. 1858]). But this collection is by no means complete and does not contain all the letters that will be discussed in the present essay. A collection of the theological treatises in English has been reprinted: *Calvin's Tracts and Treatises,* trans. Henry Beveridge, 3 vols. (1844-51; reprint ed., Grand Rapids, Mich.: William B. Eerdmans, 1958). It includes only three of the six treatises that are important for our theme: *Short Treatise on the Supper of Our Lord, Necessity of Reforming the Church,* and *Second Defense against Westphal.* Mention may also be made of J. K. S. Reid, ed., *Calvin: Theological Treatises,* Library of Christian Classics, vol. 22 (Philadelphia: Westminster Press, 1954), which also contains in English translation the *Short Treatise on the Lord's Supper* and *Necessity of Reforming the Church.* There is now, in addition, a translation of Calvin's *Concerning Scandals* by John W. Fraser (Grand Rapids, Mich.: William B. Eerdmans, 1978). For simplicity of reference, I cite throughout only C.O., and even where older translations are in existence I have preferred to make my own.

[9] Cf. Lemaître, *Calvin et Luther,* pp. 3-4; Mülhaupt, "Luther und Calvin," pp. 97-99. Mülhaupt also contrasts Luther the scholastic with Calvin the humanist and even describes Calvin as an industrious *Amateurtheologe.*

[10] See the studies by Boyer, Lamaître, Lohse, and Meinhold, referred to above. On particular doctrines there are Barclay, Forrester, Grass, and Mueller. The interesting pamphlet by Karl Holl argues for the complementarity of the thought and activity of the two reformers. He concludes: "Wir sind im Weltkrieg mit calvinischen Mächten zusammengestossen und dabei unterlegen; wäre es nicht vielleicht richtiger, wenn wir einen Tropfen calvinisches Blut in uns aufnehmen?" (p. 19). Contrast Harnack's remark (see n. 12 below)!

[11] So Eekhof, Lang, Nauta, Zahn, and Zeeden. Of course, some of the articles mentioned (e.g., the one by Mülhaupt) display an interest in all three divisions of the theme.

[12] Quoted (in the German) by Eekhof, "Calvijn over Luther," pp. 295-96, from *Theologische Studien und Kritiken* 90 (1917): 225.

[13] Serm. Ps. 115:1-3, C.O. 32:460-61.

[14] C.O. 9:19, 91; 15:336; 16:263, 430; 17:139. But he considered it inferior to the French *Confession de foi,* as his correspondence with the Reformed participants in the Colloquy of Poissey (1561) demonstrates: C.O. 18:683-84 (to Beza), 733 (to Coligny). See chapter 15 below.

[15] C.O. 5:458-60; 9:51; $10^2$:346; 11:24, 438.

[16] John Wolph (Wolf) to Calvin, 1 May 1560, C.O. 18:73 (no. 3189). Cf. Calvin to James André, C.O. 16:553 (no. 2674), where Calvin reports that he had passed on to a friend a book lent by André *quia linguae germanicae sum ignarus.*

[17] C.O. $10^2$:xliv.

[18] Herminjard, *Correspondance,* 7:284-86 (no. 1051).

[19] Calvin to Bucer, 12 January 1538, C.O. $10^2$:138-39 (no. 87). Cf. Herminjard, *Correspondance,* 4:342, n. 11. See also Calvin to Farel, 24 October 1538, C.O. $10^2$:277 (no. 149); Calvin to Farel, April 1539, C.O. $10^2$: 340-41 (no. 169).

[20] Doumergue, *Jean Calvin,* 2:569-70.

[21] Lang's article, "Luther und Calvin," was reprinted in his *Reformation und Gegenwart: Gesammelte Aufsätze* (Detmold: Meyersche Hofbuchhandlung, 1918), pp. 72-87, after publication of Doumergue's second volume, to which a brief allusion is made.

[22] "Principio animadvertere convenit, quid sit sacramentum. Est autem signum externum . . . ut promissionem ipsam firmet atque obsignet . . ." (*Christianae religionis institutio* [1536], C.O. 1:102).

[23] The relevant part of his letter, dated 14 October 1539, is given in C.O. $10^2$:402 (no. 190). Cf. W.A.Br. 8.569.29 (no. 3349); L.W. 50:190-91.

[24] C.O. $10^2$:432 (no. 197).

[25] "Sed aequum est a bono ingenio nos aliquid ferre." Perhaps Luther meant "a man of good character," but in other judgments it was usually Calvin's intellectual ability that seems to have impressed him. The English translation of Calvin's letter by Constable gives a quite different rendering: "It is well that he should even now have a proof of our good feeling towards him" (*Letters* 1:143). This translation appears, without any explanation, in a footnote in C.O. $10^2$:432, n. 18.

[26] Specifically the words translated "Just think . . . disagree with him" and "We are surely . . . to the Romans." See Herminjard, *Correspondance,* 6:131, nn. 49 and 53.

[27] Calvin wrote to Farel on 10 january 1540: "Luther has very kindly inquired after me from Bucer. Philip judged that I should dispense with my apology [*excusatione illa mea . . . supersedendum*]." Herminjard, *Correspondance,* 6:165 (no. 845). But why dispense with it? Because it was thought unnecessary, or because it might have the opposite effect to that intended?

[28] Herminjard reproduces the text (*Correspondance,* 6:132-37). See also his important notes (pp. 131-32), which correct the editors of C.O. at certain points. Misled by an annotation of Farel's on the back of his copy of the *excusatio,* the editors supposed that there were two apologies, one intended for the *Commentary on Romans,* the other for the *Institutes.* The epistle dedicatory does in fact contain an interesting statement on the diversity of theological opinion (see n. 114 below), but this cannot be identified with the apology. A few fragments of the apology were incorporated into the *Institutio* of 1543.

[29] Luther's wording (*quorum libellos*) leaves it open whether he read more than one book by Calvin. He *must* have read at least one each by Calvin and Sturm. He *may* have read more.

[30] Herminjard, *Correspondance,* 6:132-37.

[31] *Jean Calvin,* 2:571-72, n. 6. It should be added here that we have two further testimonies to Luther's approval of the *Reply to Sadoleto:* a letter from Marcus Crodel, a schoolmaster from Torgau, addressed to Calvin on 6 March 1545, C.O. 12:40 (no. 619); and an incident reported by Christoph Pezel in his *Ausführliche, wahrhafte und beständige Erzählung* and cited by Doumergue (*Jean Calvin,* 2:572). According to Pezel, Luther was rereading the *Reply* as he traveled to visit the sick Melanchthon at Weimar (1540). To his travel-companion, Cruciger, he expressed his admiration for the work and predicted that Calvin would complete what he himself had begun against the antichrist. In his *Reply to Sadoleto* Calvin expressly rejects (1) a local presence of Christ's body in the eucharistic bread and (2) the ubiquity of Christ's human nature (*Responsio ad Sadoleti epistolam,* C.O. 5:399-400). Translations of the *Reply* will be found in both *Tracts and Treatises,* vol. 1, and Reid (see n. 8 above).

[32] See, for instance, Luther to the Swiss Reformed Cities, 1 December 1537, W.A.Br. 8.149-53 (no. 3191) and 241-42 (no. 3240).

[33] For Luther's conduct at Marburg, see Bucer to Ambrose Blarer, 18 October 1529, quoted by Walther Köhler, *Das Marburger Religionsgespräch 1529: Versuch einer Rekonstruktion,* Schriften des Vereins für Reformations-geschichte, no. 148 (Leipzing: M. Heinsius [Eger and Sievers], 1929), pp. 139-40.

[34] Luther to Christoph Froschauer, 31 August 1543, W.A.Br. 10.387 (no. 3908).

[35] *Kurzes Bekenntnis vom heiligen Sakrament,* W.A. 54.147.33; L.W. 38:296.

[36] Luther to Jacob Probst, 17 January 1546, W.A.Br. 11.264.14 (no. 4188).

[37] C.O. 11:698 (no. 544).

[38] C.O. 11:774-75 (no. 586).

[39] Cf. the brief account in Beza's life of Calvin (*Vita Calvini,* C.O. 21:138). The circumstances are more fully described in Calvin to Melanchthon, 21 January 1545, C.O. 12:9-12 (no. 606).

[40] *Petit traicté monstrant que c'est que doit faire un homme fidele, cognoissant la verité de l'Evangile, quand il est entre les papistes,* C.O. 6:537-88.

[41] *Excuse de Iehan Calvin a Messieurs les Nicodemites, sur la complaincte qu'ilz font de sa trop grand'rigueur,* C.O. 6:589-614.

[42] Calvin's excuses will be found in a letter, written in January 1545, to an unnamed friend, possibly one of his countrymen (C.O. 12:25-26 [no. 610]).

[43] The two together, in their Latin version, were subsequently published together under the title *De vitandis superstitionibus,* with added comments from Calvin and other leading Reformers (see C.O. 6:617-44).

[44] Calvin to Melanchthon, 21 January 1545, C.O. 12:10 (no. 606).

[45] Calvin to Luther, 21. January 1545, C.O. 12:8 (no. 605).

[46] C.O. 12:61 (no. 632). Luther was being nicknamed "Pericles" at this time because the ancient Athenian had been likened to Zeus the thrower of thunderbolts.

[47] C.O. 12:10 (no. 606).

[48] See Farris, "Calvin's Letter to Luther," p. 128, n. 23.

[49] See Calvin to Viret, 2 February 1545, C.O. 12:26-27 (no. 611).

[50] C.O. 12:99 (no. 657).

[51] See, e.g., Calvin to Bullinger, 25 November 1544, C.O. 11:774 (no. 586).

[52] Cf. Melanchthon to Bucer, 28 August 1544, Herminjard, *Correspondance,* 9:373, n. 16.

[53] "Tu unus semper probatus fueris Luthero," Farel wrote to Calvin on 17 October 1555 (C.O. 15:823). The most interesting testimony to Luther's continuing goodwill is an anecdote related by both Christoph Pezel and Rudolph Hospinian. Moritz Goltsch, a Wittenberg bookseller, brought back the Latin translation of Calvin's *Short Treatise on the Lord's Supper* from the Frankfurt Fair (1545) and presented a copy to Luther, who read the closing section with particular care and announced that, had Zwingli and Oecolampadius spoken like Calvin, there would have been no need for a long dispute. I do not currently have access to either of the two sources, but Pezel's account (the longer of the two) is given in full by Doumergue in French translation (*Jean Calvin,* 2:572-73). Mülhaupt ("Luther und Calvin," p. 103) suspects this story of being a mere embellishment of the incident Calvin reported to Farel in his letter of 20 November 1539, where, as we have seen, the writing in question is not identified. But this is mere guess-work, and the story may well be authentic; Pezel relates it with attention to details and also names the witness (one of Luther's table companions) from whom the incident is derived. On the other hand, it is quite plain from two passages in the *Table Talk* that Luther's attitude toward Calvin in the closing years of his life was a mixture of respect and suspicion: W.A.Tr. 5.51.19 (no. 5303) and 461.18 (no. 6050).

[54] Calvin to Viret, 19 May 1540, C.O. 11:36 (no. 217).

[55] *Petit traicté de la saincte cene de nostre Seigneur Iesus Christ,* C.O. 5:457-60.

[56] See n. 53 above.

[57] *Defensio sanae et orthodoxae doctrinae de servitute et liberatione humani arbitrii adversus calumnias Alberti Pighii Campensis,* C.O. 6:245.

[58] Ibid., 249.

[59] Ibid., 251. Taken in isolation, this passage might seem to imply that differences of expression affect only nonessentials, but I think that subsequent quotations will show that Calvin intended more: he meant that the apprehension of all truth is progressive.

[60] Ibid., 250.

[61] *Supplex exhortatio ad invictissimum Caesarem Carolum Quintum et illustrissimos Principes aliosque ordines Spirae nunc imperii conventum agentes, ut restituendae ecclesiae curam serio velint suscipere,* C.O. 6:459.

[62] Ibid., 466.

[63] Ibid., 472-73.

[64] Ibid., 524-25.

[65] Ibid., 499-500.

[66] " . . . vehementer esse collaudatum." So the Spanish Protestant Dryander (Francisco d'Enzinas) wrote to Calvin (3 August 1545, C.O. 12:127 [no. 673]). Dryander lived at Wittenberg, 1544-46.

[67] "In hoc cursu adhuc hodie pergimus" (C.O. 6:473).

[68] *Consensio mutua in re sacramentaria ministrorum Tigurinae ecclesiae et D. Ioannis Calvini ministri Genevensis ecclesiae,* C.O. 7:689-748.

[69] Calvin to John Marbach, 24 August 1554, C.O. 15:212-13 (no. 1998). For want of a better term to

contrast with "*naked* signs," one could perhaps speak of the bond that Calvin discovers between Luther and himself as the notion of "*efficacious* signs"; and this may be suggested by the last sentence in my quotation from the letter to Marbach. But, for reasons that will become clear in chapters 6 and 7 below, it was in some ways more natural for Calvin to speak of a "sacramental union" between sign and reality. Cf. *Defensio sanae et orthodoxae doctrinae de sacramentis, eorumaque natura, vi, fine, usu, et fructu,* etc. (1555), where Calvin outlined what he believed was at stake for Luther in the eucharistic controversy (C.O. 9:18). But this did not mean, as we shall see, that Calvin revised his earlier judgment of Luther's opinions as in other respects idolatrous. "Ego tamen sepulta esse haec omnia cuperem," he wrote to Bucer in October 1549 (C.O. 13:439 [no. 1297]).

[70] Cf. John Haller's remark to Bullinger, in a letter of 28 December 1554, that Calvin always seemed to defend Luther and Bucer too much (C.O. 15:362 [no. 2072]).

[71] The pastors of Zurich to Calvin, 24 October 1554, C.O. 15:274 (no. 2034). The communication contains *iudicia* on the Zurich Consensus; the original is in Bullinger's hand.

[72] Ibid., col. 276 (my emphasis).

[73] See, e.g., Calvin to Martin Seidemann, 14 March 1555, C.O. 15:501-2 (no. 2148).

[74] Calvin to Francis Burkhart, 27 February 1555, C.O. 15:454 (no. 2123).

[75] "Nam quum Lutherus principium hoc semper tenuerit, nec sibi, nec cuiquam mortalium fas est, nisi ex verbo Dei sapere, mirandum ac dolendum est, tam imperiose eius placitis ecclesiam Dei astringi." *Ultima admonitio Ioannis Calvini ad Ioachimum Westphalum* (1557), C.O. 9:238; *Tracts and Treatises,* 2:477.

[76] *De scandalis quibus hodie plerique absterrenture, nonnulli etiam alienantur a pura evangelii doctrina,* C.O. 8:64.

[77] Ibid., 73.

[78] Ibid., 56-59.

[79] Ibid., 59.

[80] See, for example, *Secunda defensio piae et orthodoxae de sacramentis fidei contra Ioachimi Westphali calumnias,* C.O. 9:61, 69, 80, 109, and 111.

[81] Ibid., 51-52.

[82] Ibid., 52. If Luther failed to make the needed distinctions among the opinions of those who dissented from him, this was because he was provoked by misinformation (col. 69). On Luther's vehemence, cf. cols. 56 and 109.

[83] Ibid., 105. Cf. *Ultima admonitio ad Westphalum:* the faults should be buried, not embraced as virtues (C.O. 9:238). See also Calvin's letter to the pastors of Mömpelgard, 8 May 1544, C.O. 11:704-8 (no. 547). Even at that time Calvin was confident that Luther himself disapproved the *simiae* and *Thrasones*. From Wittenberg, as from Jerusalem, had sprung both the Gospel and also mischief-makers.

[84] *Secunda defensio contra Westphalum,* C.O. 9:54. Here it is relevant to note that on 17 March 1546 Calvin urged Vitus Theodorus to complete the publication of Luther's *Commentary on Genesis* (C.O. 12:317 [no. 781]).

[85] *Secunda defensio contra Westphalum,* C.O. 9:70.

[86] Ibid., 91.

[87] Ibid., 100.

[88] Ibid., 104. Other references to Luther in the *Secunda defensio,* not discussed here, are C.O. 9:93, 94, 101, and 107.

[89] *Gratulatio ad venerabilem presbyterum Dominum Gabrielem de Saconay, praecentorem ecclesiae Lugdunesis, de pulchra et eleganti praefatione quam libro Regis Angliae inscripsit* (1561), C.O. 9:438. Carlstadt's *commentum* no doubt refers to his odd theory that when Jesus uttered the words "This is my body," he pointed not to the bread but to himself. On Luther's *inconsideratus fervor,* see also col. 442.

[90] Ibid., 438.

[91] *Defensio contra Pighium,* C.O. 6:241. To Pighius (loc. cit.), as to Gabriel (C.O. 9:454), Calvin quotes Luther's famous utterance: "Whether I like it or not, my adversaries oblige me to become wiser every day." He does not give Luther's words exactly. See *De captivitate Babylonica ecclesiae praeludium* (1520), W.A. 6.497.7; cf. L.W. 36:11.

[92] *Gratulatio ad Gabrielem,* C.O. 9:442.

[93] Ibid., 453. For other references to Luther in the work against Gabriel, see cols. 428, 435, 437, 441, 443f., 448 (an important reminder that certain of Luther's works were translated and published at Geneva), and 454 (Gabriel hounded Luther even to the grave by claiming that he drank himself to death).

[94] Cf. Eekhof: "Calvijn ziet dus zijne reformatie niet als aan die van Luther tegenovergesteldt, doch als voortzetting en in denzelfden lijn gelegen" ("Calvijn over Luther," p. 283).

[95] "Calvin ist der grösste und wohl auch einzige "Schüler', den Luther wirklich gehabt hat, d.h. der ihn zutiefst verstanden und, von ihm ausgehend, das Werk der Reformation mit einer eigenen Durchdringung der Botschaft des Evangeliums fortgesetzt und zu einer eigenen kirchlichen Gestalt gebracht hat" (Meinhold, "Calvin und Luther," p. 264).

[96] See n. 10 above.

[97] For instance, Luther says that faith is *notitia,* that it is *in intellectu,* that its object is *veritas* (W.A. $40^2$ .25.27ff.; L.W. 27:20-25); Calvin, that even assent is more a matter of the heart than of the mind (*Inst.,* 3.2.8, 33). Again, it was Luther who took his stand upon the letter of Scripture in the eucharistic debate; Calvin, on the other hand, states expressly that the sole function of Scripture is to draw us to Jesus Christ (C.O. 9:815).

[98] *Ultima admonitio ad Westphalum,* C.O. 9:238. Cf. the "Lutherolatry" that angered Bartholomaeus Bertlinus: to Bullinger, 18 July 1554, C.O. 15:191 (no. 1987).

[99] ". . . ich denke an den Gedanken der Geschichtlichkeit des Reformators; an die Idee der Weiterentwicklung der Reformation und an die beherzte Kritik an Luther vom Evangelium her." Hence Calvin could think of certain elements in Luther's teaching as vestigial blemishes. Zeeden, "Das Bild Luthers in den Briefen Calvins," p. 191.

[100] "Nos huc dies noctesque incumbere, ut quae fideliter a nobis *tradita* sunt, in modum etiam, quem putamus optimum fore, *formemus*" (*Defensio contra Pighium,* C.O. 6:250; my emphasis).

[101] Ibid., 251.

[102] *Secunda defensio contra Westphalum,* C.O. 9:91. See also n. 69 above.

[103] Lemaître, *Calvin et Luther,* p. 12.

[104] *Secunda defensio contra Westphalum,* C.O. 9:69, 92.

[105] *Excuse a Messieurs les Nicodemites,* C.O. 6:602.

[106] Cf. *Defensio contra Pighium,* C.O. 6:239-40.

[107] See Karl Gerhard Steck, *Lehre und Kirche bei Luther,* Forschungen zur Geschichte und Lehre des Protestantismus, ser. 10, vol. 27 (Munich: Chr. Kaiser Verlag, 1963), pp. 206-7.

[108] C.O. 5:457-60.

[109] See, for example, Alexander Barclay, *Protestant Doctrine of the Lord's Supper,* chap. 12.

[110] See Jacques Pannier, *Les Origines de la confession de foi et la discipline des églises réformées de France: Étude historique* (Paris: Librairie Felix Alcan, 1936), pp. 90ff.

[111] Calvin to Archbishop Thomas Cranmer, April (or early May) 1552, C.O. 14:312-14 (no. 1619).

[112] Hence the custom of holding congregations is not merely useful but virtually necessary. See Calvin to Wolfgang Musculus, 22 October 1549, C.O. 13:433 (no. 1294).

[113] From Nicolas Colladon, *Vie de Calvin* (1565), C.O. 21:96. I owe this and the preceding reference to the admirable discussion in Rodolphe Peter, ed., *Jean Calvin: Deux congrégations et exposition du catéchisme,* Cahiers de la Revue d'Histoire et de Philosophie Religieuses, no. 38 (Paris: Presses Universitaires de France, 1964), pp. xiii-xiv.

[114] C.O. $10^2$:405 (no. 191). The remarks were made in a dedicatory epistle to Simon Grynaeus, dated 18 October 1539.

**Heiko Augustinius Oberman (lecture date 1986)**

SOURCE: "Calvin's Critique of Calvinism," in *The Dawn of the Reformation: Essays in Late Medieval and Early Reformation Thought*, T. & T. Clark, Ltd, 1986, pp. 259-68.

[*In the following excerpt, originally delivered as a lecture, Oberman treats Calvinism as a movement made up of various traditions and schools of thought that are not necessarily in agreement with their namesake. Oberman believes that a study of the Reformer—especially in the areas of his humanism, issues of renewal and unity, the eucharist, science, piety, and state theory—leads to "Calvin critiquing Calvinism."*]

The theme of our conference as it was originally announced reads: "Reformed Higher Educational Institutions as a Bulwark for the Kingdom of God—Present and Future". And here I am, representing a professedly neutral institution, intended as a bulwark for progress, not for the Kingdom of God, a univeritsy soon to celebrate its 500th birthday, and an Institute which does not deal with the present or future, but with the Middle Ages and the Reformation.

1. SCHOOLS OF CALVIN INTERPRETATION

In approaching our theme it is important to realize in advance that we hail from different worlds, not merely from different continents. Our common bond, however, is that all of us regard this theme as rich—and perhaps even loaded. Let us tax and test this bond to the utmost in challenging each others' presuppositions with the same fearless openness for truth which characterized the Genevan Reformer. The shortest procedure for flushing out these presuppositions may well be a sketch of the history of Calvin research which can then be used as a compass to reveal where each of us stands. Such a sketch is of necessity tendentious; it must ignore the more subtle variations and nuances. Furthermore, this task is a baffling one because of the large number of publications to be taken into account. Dr Kempff's impressive *Bibliography of Calviniania: 1959-1974,* which has recently been published simultaneously in Potchefstroom and Leiden, gives eloquent testimony to the present state of affairs. Since Professor Nauta of the Free University prepared a more comprehensive discussion of recent Calvin research, for the last Calvin Research Congress in Amsterdam, I can limit myself here to what interests us most, the prevailing schools of Calvin interpretation. Enumerated as concisely as possible, I discern six basic types of schools.[1] In the second part of this paper I shall indicate six issues in recent scholarship which I regard as relevant to our theme of Calvin's challenge today.

1. *The classical interpretation.* Even today we can admire the excellent and comprehensive grasp of Calvin's dogmatic treatises and of the ***Institutes*** which was demonstrated by this school. Yet, not unlike the German phenomenon in the field of theology when a reference to Scripture is replaced by a quotation from Martin Luther, the classical school interprets Calvin with the pretence of presenting the Word of God itself. Valid theology is the reiteration of the positions described—and hence prescribed!—by Calvin.

2. *The confessional interpretation.* Calvin is here viewed through the eyes of the Westminster Confession and the Heidelberg Catechism: Scripture and predestination are seen to be the foci of his thought.

3. *The neo-orthodox school:* God's revelation is only grasped in Christ, *through* Scripture, *reflected* in predestination as the covenant of grace ("Gnadenwahl").

4. *The Dutch school* (Abraham Kuyper and Herman Bavinck) stresses the sovereignty of God over all cultural manifestations of life; hence it includes a theology of society, of the state, of politics, yet not in the strict sense of the word 'theocratic'. In his assessment of "Kuypers idee eener christelijke cultuur" Arnold A. van Ruler—a true theocrat, the first to design a theology of hope—concludes that "de gemeene gratie uitsluitend de functie van een leer van het aanknopingspunt in het groot heeft".[2] For Kuyper common grace has the sole purpose of keeping the machine of creation running and of preparing for the conversion and rebirth of individuals, and not, as Van Ruler sees it, of sanctifying creation as the one and single eschatological (= now) purpose of God. We shall return to this point in our discussion of decisive points in contemporary Calvin research.

5. *The anti-orthodox interpretation.* Not characteristic of any particular group, this view builds upon some mythical and some historical elements. Calvin is described as the enemy of culture and of research; as the murderer of Servetus, and the manager of police-controlled Geneva.

6. *The historical school.* Originally in reaction against all forms of 'theological' interpretation, this school has made giant strides by trying to abstain from taking sides in the debate around the right 'use' of Calvin. It thus has little patience with any form of confessional interpretation, be it orthodox or neo-orthodox; yet, *de facto,* it has done the most to answer the theses implied in the anti-orthodox view. The humanist Calvin, the editor of Seneca's *De Clementia,* is shown not to be a passing stage but to determine: 1. his interests in education; 2. his concern with affairs of state—and both with a wide ecumenical horizon.

Although all six 'types' or 'schools' are represented in this country, I expect that most will recognize themselves as belonging to the position I have described as II, III or IV. Yet the most substantial and lasting contribution in the last type described has been made by a South African, André Malan Hugo (1975) who not only provided us with a fine study entitled *Calvijn en Seneca*[3] (Groningen, Djakarta, 1957), but also—together with the English translator of the ***Institutes,*** Ford Lewis Battles—an exemplary critical edition of ***De Clementia*** (Leiden 1969).

We mention André Hugo at the end of our presentation of the six types partly so that we may honour a scholar who died too young, leaving a sizable gap which will not be readily filled in the ranks of international scholarship; and partly because his work shows in a nutshell the extent to which the historical method can help us to demythologize long-venerated Calvin images and allow us ultimately to bridge the divide between the dogmatic and the anti-dogmatic types, orthodox veneration and anti-orthodox iconoclasm.

2. EMBATTLED FRONTS

In the second part of this presentation I intend to touch upon some six key issues which deserve our renewed attention in view of new developments in the field.

Their common scope can perhaps best be designated as "Calvin's critique of Calvinism". As a minority group in a divided world Calvinism is understandably inclined to assume an apologetic attitude, to defend the status quo and to point proudly to the achievements of Calvinistic principles and institutions. An assessment of these from the perspective of Calvin may well provide us with a platform for reorientation, renewal and reform. At the same time, recent research may show us the limits of Calvin himself, the respects in which he was a product of circumstances that do not apply to us to the same extent.

1. *Calvin the Humanist.* Calvin as the twenty-three year old commentator on Seneca is not yet the reformer; as a matter of fact he does not yet see how reform can be possible without detriment to the Church Catholic. Indeed, as Hugo has pointed out, the writing of this commentary may well have "served him as a temporary means of escape from the inner conflict occasioned by that problem".[4] But in 1532, in this year before his conversion—and that means before his discovery that the Church Catholic is a community of believers obedient to the Word of God rather than to the Church of Rome— Calvin placed himself within the ranks of those who were called the *humanistae theologizantes*. In a decree of 22 August 1523 the Sorbonne had decided "that all new translations of the Bible made from Hebrew or Greek into Latin are of no value to the Church, but are pernicious", a decree confirmed by the Council of Trent in 1546. In 1532 Calvin opted for the 'resourcement', the renewal, of the human spirit through a return to the classical sources; in 1533 he found that 'resourcement' in the Scriptures as providing access to the life of the Spirit. For us it is important to realize that it would be a mistake to play off Calvin the Christian against Calvin the humanist scholar. From the very beginning stages of Calvinism these two, the campaign against obscurantism and the struggle for reform of the Church, belong together. Where they are separated an orthodoxy is bound to emerge which is blind to the needs of the mind and the body alike, and which isolates the Church from society.

2. *Renewal and the unity of the Church.* Calvin could very well have become a 'Nicodemian' or an Erasmian Christian, avoiding confrontation (*tumultus!*) and trusting that the new culture of the mind would suffice for the reform of the Church. But Calvin, the student of law—even in that last year of 1532-1533 in Orleans—carried his legal interests over into his study of theology and continued to be concerned with structures, organizations, and politics as the ***Ordonnances Ecclésiastiques,*** as well as Book IV of the ***Institutes,*** document.

In a very bold and—to use an epithet seldom applied in a scholarly presentation—a wise chapter in the volume honouring Paul Oskar Kristeller on his 70th birthday, William Bouwsma discusses the tension between two thrusts in humanism, between two spirits in one breast, the 'Stoic' and the 'Augustinian' elements: on the one hand, Stoic consolation and on the other, the Augustinian call for social engagement and political action.[5] Writing on "The Two faces of Humanism," he observes: "Humanists of more Stoic tendencies, like Erasmus, seem to have been less likely to become Protestants than those of the more Augustinian kind. But the more Augustinian humanist might end up in either the Protestant or Catholic camp".[6]

Why then did the 'Augustinian' Calvin end up becoming a Protestant? As the letter to Cardinal Sadoleto (1539) indicates, it was the doctrine of the Church which proved to be the decisive locus in Calvin's conversion. Augustinianism, Biblical studies and the freedom-hungry protest against tyranny as voiced in his commentary on Seneca were all factors in this event. Yet most importantly in this combination the possibility of opting out of reality and submating the longing for the renewal of the Church through the escape hatch of the invisible Church was excluded. For the whole Reformed tradition it was to be of lasting importance that for Calvin it is impossible to participate in the Church Catholic of the Creed without also participating in the local, visible church. At times in Calvinism this had led to an overemphasis on the completeness of the *ecclesia loci*. But Calvin's vision blocks that kind of cheap ecumenism which transcends and escapes the hardships of urgent Church reform by reference to the invisible Church universal. Within this context, Calvinism has striven from its very beginning for Church unity in faith and order. But it should be added that at the same time Calvinism has suffered most from splinter groups which absolutized their own local traditions. Here I discern the greatest threat resulting from the presently disrupted relations between the churches in this country and the World Council of Churches. Withdrawal can be the necessary attitude over against a political organization, but in the Church of Christ the truly Calvinist course of action is to hang on, to seek communion and to provide for communication—till the partner—churches proceed with *de facto* excommunication . . . much to their own detriment.

3. *Conversion and the Eucharist.* A point of seemingly less immediate interest concerns the two short Latin words "subita conversio". Calvin himself uses these words in his Psalms Commentary of 1559 to describe his conversion.[7] Taken literally, the phrase means "sudden conversion" and it has been understood in this sense by those inside and outside of the Reformed family who have seen in Calvin the divinely ordained prototype of conversion. True conversion has to be sudden, datable; yes, indeed, 'clockable', and those who could not pass this test could not be part of the fold.

Much research has been directed toward understanding this reference to conversion. As a matter of fact, the right understanding of the even smaller word 'subita' could have helped decisively in this effort. Throughout the Middle Ages "subita" marks the work of God in contrast to the time-consuming achievements of man. "Subita" does not refer to a time-unit but to the divine agent, to the vertical in contrast to the horizontal dimension.

Conversion is, as Calvin likes to emphasize, penance, which in turn is the work of the Holy Spirit and which lasts as long as life itself. Conversion cannot be made into an emotional proof of one's belonging to the elect.

The gravest danger, however, proved utlimately not to lurk in a Calvinistic pietism—which I am prepared to defend as the precious core of the Reformed tradition—but in an elitest doctrine of the Eucharist. The "Half-Way Covenant" of the New England Puritans documents[8] how this central sacrament and focal point of Calvin's theology is debased into a sign of progress by the Saints, instead of being regarded as the necessary food for faith—essential for survival on the trek towards the Kingdom.

4. *Scripture and Science.* In 1973 when the 500th anniversary of the birth of Nicolaus Copernicus was celebrated, numerous articles utilized the occasion in order to associate Calvin—as well as the other reformers with obscurantism. The words of Thomas S. Kuhn were readily quoted: "Protestant leaders like Luther, Calvin and Melanchthon led in citing Scripture against Copernicus and in urging the repression of Copernicans".[9]

R. Hooykaas has eloquently opposed the myth that Calvin mentioned and rejected Copernicus in his works: "There is no lie so good as the precise and well-detailed one and this one has been repeated again and again, quotation marks included, by writers on the history of science, who evidently did not make the effort to verify the statement. For fifteen years, I have pointed out in several periodicals concerned with the history of science that the 'quotation' from Calvin is imaginary and that Calvin never mentioned Copernicus; but the legend dies hard".[10]

The reason why the voices of historians were not heeded is no mystery: it was not Calvin, but some of his followers who construed a division between faith and science which tragically forced many a Christian to choose between the two. Hence Calvinists themselves gave credence to this distortion of Calvin.

As far as Calvin himself is concerned, in his commentary on Genesis he points out that the story of creation does not compete with "the great art of astronomy", but that it accommodates and speaks in terms of the unlettered *idiota,* the man in the street.[11]

In the name of Calvin much damage has been done in later times and stores of faith and piety have been sacrificed on the altar of rigid inspiration theories. Calvin's exegetical methods were far ahead of his own time; it is our task not to fall behind him today.

5. *Piety between Theology and Moralism.* My fifth point concerns that elusive entity best called the spirituality of Calvin. It has often been argued that the influence of the *Devotio moderna* (Collège de Montaigu and its principal since 1483, John Standonck!) extends through Calvin far into the Reformation period. And indeed, it is remarkable that a strong Calvinism flourished most easily in those areas which had been centers of the *Devotio moderna:* the Low Countries and the Rhine valley.

However, the more we are able to grasp what it is that characterizes this late medieval reform movement, the better we are able to see some of the unique characteristics in Calvin's spirituality. While *devotio* stood for the fundamental disposition toward God as well as for an attitude of contempt towards the world, *pietas,* Calvin's key word, represents the life of sanctification through intensive involvement in this world. It is another sign of ecumenical openness in Reformation studies[12] that it was a Jesuit, Father Lucien Richard, who made a major advance at this point.[13] He argued that Calvin's *pietas* stands for a new spirituality which is grounded in his understanding of the knowledge of God. Piety is derived simultaneously from the Word of God and the internal testimony of the Spirit. "Simultaneously" is to be underlined since the Spirit provides that inwardness and personalism which are also to be found in the *Devotio moderna.* But at the same time this form of spiritual communication is set in the objective context of theological knowledge of the Word of God. Thus, Calvin's spirituality differs radically from that of the *Devotio moderna* on three essential points. First, it is a spirituality of service to the world; second, it is based on a new Word-directed religious epistemology; and third, it stresses the inner unity of Christian life and theology.[14] In those instances where Calvin's spirituality has given way to Calvinist morality, it has relapsed into the ethics of the *Devotio moderna.* We have a clear task of reform ahead of us here.

*6. Calvinism and the democratic ideal.* Our last point concerns the most highly sensitive issue of the relation of Calvin to democracy.[15] I begin here with some quotations which document the radically opposing interpretations which have been applied to Calvin: "Calvin was as much in favor of the democratic form as he was opposed to the monarchical one".

"Calvin was a great propagator of democracy, but he energetically tried to ward off its abuses and excesses".—Emile Doumergue.

"From considering only his political ideas, one would certainly be entitled to conclude that Calvin was not a precursor of modern democracy".—Charles Mercier.

"If Calvin mixes democratic elements with aristocratic constitutions, he nevertheless remains completely foreign to the dogmas of modern democracy . . . he does not believe either in popular sovereignty or in individual rights".—Marc-Edouard Chenevière.

"'Democracy' is not a term in favor with Calvin. He does not advocate democracy in and of itself: he fears its deterioration into anarchy. Nevertheless, his notion of 'aristocracy tempered by democracy' approaches our conception of representative democracy. It becomes unmistakably clear in his later writings that the ideal basis of government is election by the citizens".—John T. McNeill.

The key to this apparent mystery of these many interpretations is held once again by the historian who is prepared to place Calvin in the context of his time. In this respect I find most validity in the conclusion of Hans Baron: "Calvinist political thought helped more than any other tendency of the time to prevent a full victory of absolutism, and to prepare the way for constitutional and even republican ideas".[16] Michael Walzer has demonstrated the transition from the sixteenth to the seventeenth and following centuries: "What Calvinists said of the saint, other men would later say of the citizen: the same sense of civic virtue, of discipline and duty lies behind the two names".[17]

Yet, in working through the sources I have come to the conclusion that Calvin's own ideal of state government is best described in terms of a form of aristocracy. This is marginally tempered by group interests to which we may validly assign the name 'democratic expressions'. To put it crudely, either reiterating Calvin or using his political views as a blueprint for contemporary society would spell sheer tyranny,[18] the very state of affairs he had challenged as a young humanist. As was the case in each of the previous five aspects I have discussed, this shows us once again that to reiterate is the surest path to distortion.

Allow me to conclude with a quotation from Calvin himself, a statement which bears reiteration because it reveals the living centre of his piety and faith. In his sermon on II Sam. v. 4—'David reigned forty years'—Calvin notes that this was by no means an unchallenged or uninterrupted reign: 'cen'a pas esté du premier coup en perfection'. Then he proceeds ('c'es pour nous, que cecy est ecrit') to apply this text to the contemporary rule of God, giving here his religious testament, which is characteristically at the same time a political eschatology.[19]

> . . . though we know that God rules, yet insofar as our Lord Jesus Christ is hidden in him and his very reign is hidden in this world, it has no splendour but it is little esteemed, indeed rejected by the majority. Therefore, we should find it not at all strange that our Lord Jesus Christ, though he has been established as King by God his Father, does not at all have the authority among men which He is entitled to. Furthermore, today there is no certain time limit ('terme' = kairos) indicated to us. When we see the rule of our Lord Jesus Christ is limited, since there is only a handful of people who have accepted him, and since for every one city which has received the Gospel there are large countries where idolatry rules,—when we thus see that the rule of Jesus Christ is so small and despised according to the world, let us cast our eyes upon this figure which is given us here (in the rule of David), and let us await the end (terme), which God knows, for it is hidden to us. I say, let us await in patience, till his Kingdom is established in perfection and God gathers those who are dispersed, restores what is dissipated and sets in order what is confused.

> . . . let us not desist, as far as it is in us, from praying to God that he advances and enlarges (his Kingdom) and that each man apply to this with all his power; and let us allow ourselves to be governed by him in such a way that he is always glorified in us, both in life and in death.

This text stems from Calvin's last sermons which were not published till recently and hence virtually 'lost'. Yet with this testament of faith and piety in hand, we are in a position to answer the question raised in the theme of this conference quoted at the beginning of this paper.

Whenever and wherever Calvinism did not 'await in patience' but rather sought to establish its own 'kingdom' by force, repression and domination, it did not serve the kingdom of God but its own cultural and political achievements. Calvin's vision of perseverance 'amidst idolatry' is at once critique of and encouragement for the reformed community around the world: ecclesia reformanda quia reformata.

*Notes*

[1] For a more elaborate discussion of the first three schools I refer to Henry Van der Goot: "A typology of 'Schools' of Calvin interpretation in 19th and 20th century theology", prepared for the University of Toronto.

[2] Nijkerk, s.a. (1943), p. 147.

[3] *Calvijn en Seneca. Een inleidende studie van Calvijn's Commentaar op Seneca, De Clementia, De clementia, anno* 1532 (Groningen-Djakarta, 1957).

[4] Ed. cit., p. 16*

[5] *Itinerarium Italicum. The Profile of the Italian Renaissance in the Mirror of its European Transformations. Dedicated to Paul Oskar Kristeller,* H.A. Oberman with Th. A. Brady, Jr., eds. (Leiden, 1975), pp. 3-60; 56.

[6] *Ibid.*, p. 57.

[7] ". . . subita conversione ad docilitatem subiget". *Opera Calvini* 31, 22f. most recently A. Ganoczy: *Le jeune Calvin, Genése et Evolution de sa vocation réformatrice* (Wiesbaden, 1966), pp. 272-304; 298.

[8] Cf. E. Brooks Holifield: *The Covenant sealed: The Development of Puritan Sacramental Theology in Old and New England, 1570-1720* (New Haven, 1974).

[9] *The Copernican Revolution* (Cambridge, Mass., 1957), p. 196.

[10] *Religion and the Rise of Modern Science* (Edinburgh-London, 1972), p. 121.

[11] *Calvini Opera* 23, 20-22.

[12] Cf. R. Bäumer: "sDas katholische Calvinbild" in H. Jedin, R. Bäumer: *Die Erforschung der kirchlichen Reformationsgeschichte seit 1876 und 1931* (Darmstadt, 1975), pp. 99-102. This survey omits the significant contribution by L.G.M. Alting van Geusau: *Die Lehre von der Kindertaufe bei Calvin* (Bilthoven-Mainz, 1962).

[13] *The Spirituality of John Calvin.* (Atlanta, 1974).

[14] Cf. the appreciative review by Joseph N. Tylenda, S.J. in *Theological Studies* 36 (1975), pp. 356-358.

[15] For literature see the excellent workbook by Robert M. Kingdom and Robert D. Linder: *Calvin and Calvinism. Sources of Democracy?* (Lexington, 1970). The following quotations here on p. XIII f.

[16] "Calvinist republicanism and its historical roots", *Church History* 8 (1939), pp. 30-41; 41.

[17] *The Revolution of the Saints* (Cambridge, Mass., 1965), p. 2.

[18] *Basil Hall's words of caution-à propos W. Fred Graham: The Constructive Revolutionary: John Calvin and his Socio-Economic Impact* (Richmond, Va., 1971)—are to the point: ". . . he (Calvin) was a party to reducing the small amount of democratic procedure allowed". "A sixteenth-century miscellany", *The Journal of Ecclesiastical History* 26 (1975), pp. 309-321; 318.

[19] *Supplementa Calvinia* I, 105, 34-36. Cf. my "The 'Extra' Dimension in the Theology of Calvin", *The Journal of Ecclesiastical History* 21 (1970), pp. 43-64; 46. Cf above Chapter 10.

**Calvin on the pastorate:**

Today hardly one in a hundred considers how difficult and arduous it is faithfully to discharge the office of pastor. Hence many are led into it as something trivial and not serious; and afterwards experience teaches them, too late, how foolishly they aspired to the unknown. Others think themselves endowed with great skill and diligence and promise themselves great things from their talent, learning, and judgment; but afterwards they experience too late how limited their equipment is, for their powers fail them at the outset. Others, while knowing there will be many serious battles, have no fear, as though they were born for contention, and put on an iron front. Still others who want to be ministers are mercenaries. We know indeed that all God's servants are wretched in the eyes of the world and common sense, for they must make war on the passions of all and thus displease men in order to please God.

*John Calvin, quoted in* John Calvin: A Sixteenth-Century Portrait, *Oxford University Press, 1988.*

## David C. Steinmetz (essay 1988)

SOURCE: "Calvin and the Absolute Power of God," in *The Journal of Medieval and Renaissance Studies*, Vol. 18, No. 1, Spring, 1988, pp. 65-79.

*[Below, Steinmetz explores Calvin's ideas regarding God's absolute power to act versus His potential to act, noting that Calvin attacked the entire discussion as "speculative doctrine." Disagreeing with the Scholastics on this matter, Calvin decided to accept the mysteries of Divine Sovereignty on a Biblical basis.]*

I

The medieval distinction between the absolute and the ordained power of God is a distinction in Christian theology between what God can do in view of his sheer and unlimited ability to act and what he has chosen to do in the light of his wise and sometimes inscrutable purposes. God cannot, of course, will his own non-existence or suspend the principle of non-contradiction. Omnipotence does not extend to the production of nonsense. But apart from these limitations, the sovereignty of God is absolute. Whatever God chooses to do (excluding, of course, what is inherently self-contradictory), God can do.

That God can do a thing, however, does not mean that he will do it. One may, in this respect draw an analogy, however imperfect, between divine and human activity. Just as human beings choose to do only some of the things which they could in fact do, so, too, God restricts his choices to a limited number of the almost limitless possibilities which lie open to his will. To talk about what is possible for God to do is to talk about the absolute power of God (*potentia dei absoluta*). To focus on the choices and decisions which God has made, is making, or will make (the distinction is in the human mind and not in the utterly simple being of God) is to introduce the subject of the ordained power of God (*potentia dei ordinata*).

In the third book of the ***Institutes*** (III.xxiii.2) Calvin attacked the distinction between the absolute and ordained power of God as a speculative doctrine which separates the omnipotence of God from his justice and which transforms the compassionate Father of the biblical narratives into an arbitrary tyrant. Anyone who has ever tried to trace Calvin's relationship to his sources knows how difficult it is and how few clues Calvin himself provides. What clues are in the text, however, suggest that Calvin is drawn to the position of Duns Scotus—and, to a lesser extent, William Ockham—on several controverted issues. Like Scotus, Calvin stresses the priority of predestination to glory over predestination to grace (III.xxii.9) and argues that whatever God wills, "by the very fact that He wills it, must be considered righteous" (III.xxiii.2). Like Scotus and Ockham, Calvin wishes to preserve the transcendent freedom of God and to stress the radical contingency of the world and of all created being. It therefore comes as a shock that Calvin refuses to accept the very distinction they used to safeguard God's transcendent freedom and to underscore the world's radical contingency.

Later reformed theology did not agree with Calvin's harsh judgment. By the end of the century theologians like Amandus Polanus[1] in Basel and William Ames[2] in Franeker were routinely drawing a distinction between absolute and ordained power in their discussions of divine omnipotence. Even Francis Turrettini[3] in Geneva felt obligated to explain away Calvin's objection to the distinction as an objection to the abuse of this distinction by certain unnamed late medieval scholastics.

Although the distinction between the absolute and ordained power of God is not a subject on which Calvin wrote extensively, he did return to it several times during the period 1551 to 1563. The distinction is mentioned in his commentaries on Genesis 18:13, Genesis 25:29, Romans 9:19, Isaiah 23:9, Jeremiah 12:1, his sermons on Job, as well as in four of his polemical tracts and treatises. Since Calvin is not inclined to use the technical theological language of the medieval Church, his repeated comments on this technical language indicate that the distinction touches on a subject of some importance to him. Calvin seems to object to the distinction as such and not to abuses in the application of the distinction. Yet he is eager to preserve in his own theology many of the points which the medieval distinction intended to protect.

Did Calvin understand this distinction correctly? Did he criticize it fairly? Is Turrettini right when he claims that Calvin's rejection of the distinction between the ordained and absolute power of God is a rejection of its abuse? Or are there internal tensions in Calvin's theology which make him suspicious of this distinction quite apart from the history of its use? In order to answer these and similar questions we need to examine what Calvin says about the absolute power of God both in the context of the antecedent history of this concept and in the context of his own theological commitments.

II

The distinction between the absolute and ordained power of God was first suggested by medieval theologians in the late eleventh century. By the twelfth century it was a distinction common to all the theological schools.[4] In the thirteenth century Thomas Aquinas discussed the distinction in his disputation *de potentia Dei* q.1 a.5 as well in the *Summa theologiae* I.q.25 a.5 and in II *Summa contra gentiles* c.23-30. Thomas used the distinction to make the point that God's actions are free and not subject to necessity. While the created order expresses God's wisdom, justice, and goodness, it does not exhaust them. God could have created *de potentia absoluta* a quite different order of the world and yet one in which his wisdom, justice, and goodness would still have found adequate expression. Thomas made this point in order to reject all necessitarian doctrines of God, whether pagan, Islamic, or Christian in origin, and to emphasize the contingency of the created order.

This distinction, while important, remained marginal to theological debate until the time of Duns Scotus, when it was given broader application.[5] Theologians found increasingly fewer propositions which were, on the face of it, self-contradictory, and increasingly more theological problems which were illuminated by considering the Church's teaching against the background of the hypothetical possibilities inherent in the absolute power of God. Theologians asked whether God could *de potentia absoluta* cause the intuitive cognition of a nonexistent,[6] grant pardon to a *viator* who lacked the habit of grace,[7] or institute a new morality.[8] Some even speculated whether God could have become incarnate in an irrational animal.[9] By invoking divine omnipotence, theologians thought they were better able, in the words of Paul Vignaux, to separate "the accidental from the essential in the object of an investigation."[10]

In addition to the role played by the distinction of the absolute and ordained power of God in late medieval theology, the distinction was of major importance within the enterprise of natural philosophy in this period as well.[11] God's absolute power was appealed to repeatedly (most often without reference to his ordained power) in the critical examination of the tenets or Aristotelian natural philosophy and, especially, in extending the investigation of problems within that natural philosophy from the realm of what was physically possible from the perspective of an Aristotelian system to what was logically possible, an extension that was directly accommodated by the invocation of a divine power limited only by the logically contradictory. Aristotle had asked, for example, whether an actual infinite was physically possible;[12] his fourteenth-century commentators asked in addition whether such actual infinities were logically possible.[13] It is noteworthy that such appeals in natural philosophy to God's absolute power often did not mention this power as such, but tacitly introduced it into the course of an argument by a simple "God could (*Deus posset*)" or by using some hypothetical operation of God that was relevant to the point at issue (for example, God seeing or perceiving the total infinity of points in a line[14] or God annihilating everything save a single physical body).[15]

The theological use of this distinction by Scotus and his disciples—and later by William Ockham and his school—has been the subject of considerable scholarly debate in the twentieth century. Occamism or nominalism (debate has centered for the most part on the use of the *potentia absoluta* by this school) has received a generally negative assessment among such important historians as Gilson,[16] Feckes,[17] Knowles,[18] Lortz,[19] Iserloh[20] and Leff.[21] According to the critics of nominalism, its philosophy and theology are atomistic, sceptical, and fideistic. This understanding of Ockham in particular and of nominalist theology in general has been challenged by many scholars, chiefly E. A. Moody,[22] Paul Vignaux,[23] Gerhard Ritter,[24] Philotheus Boehner,[25] Erich Hochstetter,[26] Léon Baudry,[27] Heiko A. Oberman,[28] Leif Grane,[29] William J. Courtenay,[30] and Albert Lang.[31] While these historians have differed among themselves, they have contributed to a revisionist assessment of nominalism which is increasingly influential.

The revisionists admit that it is true that nominalists celebrate the absolute freedom and transcendence of God. God is *exlex,* free from all claims and demands external to his own will. Prior to his self-revelation God is unpredictable and unknowable. One cannot argue from human conceptions of justice to the justice according to which God guides his actions in history. God is a free and sovereign Lord who acts in a manner which cannot be anticipated and which appears at first glance scandalous and an affront to reason. The absolute power of God means not only that God is utterly free but that the created order is radically contingent.

But while God is radically free from external limitations, he is not free from limitations which he has imposed upon himself. According to nominalist theology God enters into covenants which restrict his freedom and which he regards as permanently binding. God could, if he chooses to do so, justify a sinner who lacks an infused habit of grace or refuse to accept a *viator* who has one. The point is that he does not choose to do so *de potentia ordinata.* Having limited himself by his covenant to justify sinners who are infused by a habit of grace, he remains faithful to his decision. The fidelity of God to his covenants *de potentia ordinata* is a central theme of late medieval nominalism.

When the Scotists and Occamists celebrated the freedom and transcendence of a God who, while under no natural obligation to his creation nevertheless bound himself to fulfill the terms of certain freely assumed covenantal obligations, they were returning to a theme which had a long and venerable tradition in Western thought, beginning with St. Augustine and continuing through such early Franciscan theologians as Odo Rigaldi.[32] Ideas concerning covenant and promise which seem radical in the fifteenth century were already taught by Cardinal Laborans and his contemporaries in the twelfth century.[33] Indeed, the notion that human merit should be established primarily on the basis of the covenant and promise of God[34] rather than on ontological grounds is a dominant motif if one takes the whole Middle Ages and not merely the thirteenth century into account.

The absolute power of God, therefore, must always be kept in tension with his ordained power. The fidelity of God to his covenants is just as important to late medieval theologians as the fact of his utter transcendence and radical freedom. Second causes are not suspended, though God by his absolute power could dispense with them. The point which Scotus and Ockham make is that the present order is radically contingent, not that it is thoroughly unreliable.

The world is governed by divine justice. God is not erratic or arbitrary, even granting that the justice of his will cannot be discovered in advance by human reason. The fact that God is not constrained by external and previously established norms does not mean that he acts unwisely. God is guided by his own inner sense of justice, which, even if it cannot be predicted, commends itself to human reason as self-consistent and reasonable, once it is revealed. God is his own justice. He therefore acts in limited, defined ways. He is committed to upholding the natural order and the process of salvation in spite of their undeniably contingent character.

It is precisely at this point that a disagreement has arisen over the status of miracles. Does a miracle belong to the absolute or the ordained power of God? William J. Courtenay has argued that late medieval theologians use the term "the absolute power of God" to refer to the "total possibilities initially open to God, some of which were realized by creating the established order."[35] The unrealized possibilities remain only hypothetically possible. The ordained power of God, on the other hand, refers to "the complete plan of God for his creation," including both miracle and historical novelty.[36] That God does some things on what appears to be a random or haphazard basis, while he does other things with unvarying regularity, does not mean that the random and occasional acts are any less an expression of the ordained power of God. What God has done, is doing, or will do belongs to the realm of his ordained power, even if that act is the crossing of the Red Sea or the resurrection of Jesus Christ from the dead. Miracle is as much an expression of the ordained power of God as the sunrise or the movement of the tides.

Other historians, among them Francis Oakley[37] and Steven Ozment,[38] have cited authors who use the distinction between the absolute and ordained will of God as a distinction between the way God normally acts and the way he acts on occasion. There is evidence, as Courtenay admits, that Pierre d'Ailly (IV *Sent.* q.1.a.2) and Gregory of Rimini (I *Sent.* d.42-44 q.1 a.2) understood the distinction between the absolute and the ordained power of God in the sense in which Oakley and Ozment have defined them. Even Gabriel Biel (IV *Sent.* d.1 q.1 a.3 dub.2 M; I *Sent.* d.17 q.1 a.3 II) suggested that the rite of circumcision, once established as a requirement for the believing community in the Old Testament by the ordained power of God, has been superseded by baptism and so has fallen back into the realm of the absolute power of God, where it remains a hypothetical but not a real requirement for the Christian Church. John Eck, who lectured on the *Sentences* of Peter Lombard for the last time in 1542, appears to agree with this looser usage and to ascribe miracle both to the absolute power of God and to what he called "special ordained power."[39] It may be that Courtenay's description of the absolute power of God as the realm of the merely hypothetical represents the majority opinion in the thirteenth and fourteenth centuries, but theologians in the fifteenth and sixteenth centuries seem to be more causal in their use of terms.

What remains constant in the history of the use of this distinction is the continuing attempt by medieval theologians to protect the freedom and transcendence of God and to stress, for whatever reasons, the contingency of the created order. Thomas and Ockham did not altogether agree about what threatens the doctrine of that freedom and they certainly differed with each other about what God had bound himself to do. The distinction remained serviceable to Christian theologians who disagreed about many other matters because they shared a common conviction that creation did not exhaust the possibilities open to God and that divine omnipotence stretches beyond the furthest bounds the human imagination can reach.

III

Calvin's rejection of the distinction between the absolute and ordained power of God occurs in three contexts in his biblical commentaries.

1. *Miracles*

The first context is the question of the adequacy of the power of God to perform miracles. According to Genesis 18, when Sarah hears about the promise to Abraham of a son (or, more accurately, over hears the promise, since she is eavesdropping at the time), she "laughs within herself." It is not the laughter of joy, but of unbelief. Sarah is convinced that the natural obstacles—the advanced age of her husband and her own advanced age, compounded by her chronic infertility—are stronger than the Word of God. The angel, who has an unsettling ability to see around corners and to hear inaudible thoughts, rebukes Sarah for her silent laughter with the words, "Is anything too hard for the Lord?" Sarah's sin, as Calvin sees it, is that "she did wrong to God, by not acknowledging the greatness of his power."[40]

Sarah's laughter leads Calvin to make two points to his readers. The first is to warn them not to limit the power of God to the "scanty measure" of their own reason. They doubt God's promises because like Sarah they "sinfully detract from his power." But the second touches on the distinction of the absolute ordained power of God. God's power should only be considered in the context of God's Word, what God can do in the framework of his declared will:

> In this way the Papists plunge themselves into a profound labyrinth, when they dispute concerning the absolute power of God. Therefore, unless we are willing to be involved in absurd dotings, it is necessary that the word should precede us like a lamp; so that his power and will may be conjoined by an inseparable bond.[41]

2. *Providence*

The second context in which Calvin rejects the distinction of the absolute and ordained power of God is the question of the goodness of providence, especially in the face of the continued prosperity of the wicked. Here the prophets Isaiah and Jeremiah stimulate Calvin to reflect on God's power. Jeremiah 12 deals with the "confusion" the faithful experience when they observe that the wicked not only prosper but plead their prosperity as a sign of God's favor. In such circumstances the faithful are tempted to conclude either that the world is governed by chance and therefore not by God or that the God who governs the world is, after all, unjust.[42]

The pagan notion that there are no gods and that the world is at the mercy of irrational fortune is not an idea that Jeremiah seriously entertains. He knows that there is a God and that this God governs the world by his providence. Jeremiah's task is therefore to show that this God is just and that "the disorder in the world"[43] does not reflect any disorder in God. The wicked have mistaken God's forbearance for God's favor. Indeed, the wicked are accumulating a "heavier vengeance" for themselves on the day of judgment by their continued abuse of God's patience.[44] What Jeremiah does not do is "set up the judgments of men against the absolute power of God, as the sophists under the Papacy do, who ascribe such absolute power to God as perverts all judgment and all order; this is nothing less than sacrilege."[45] What he does do is suggest to God (and to the wicked who are listening to this conversation) that it may be time on the basis of God's declared will in the Torah to bring this period of patience and forbearance to an end. God's justice may be slow but it has not arbitrarily been set aside.

Isaiah 23 deals with the judgment of God on the princes of Tyre. Judgments on princes and nations are examples of God's providential ruling of the world. What Isaiah wants to avoid is the notion that the punishment of the princes of Tyre was unmerited or that God is guided in his judgments by anything less than his own sense of justice and equity. It is, of course, true that the justice by which he guides his judgments is not always clear to us. But that is all the more reason never to separate God's "wisdom and justice from his power."[46] The princes of Tyre were brought low, not because they occupied high station, but because they were proud:

> That invention which the Schoolmen have introduced, about the absolute power of God, is shocking blasphemy. It is all one as if they said that God is a tyrant who resolves to do what he pleases, not by justice, but through caprice. Their schools are full of such blasphemies, and are not unlike the heathens, who said that God sports with human affairs.[47]

### 3. *Predestination*

The third context in which Calvin considers the absolute power of God is provided by the doctrine of predestination. Calvin illustrates this problem with the story of Jacob and Esau as told in Genesis 25 and retold in Romans 9. In the commentary on Genesis, Calvin attacks the idea that Jacob's election was based on foreseen merit or Esau's rejection on foreseen demerit. Calvin repeats the Augustinian argument that since all are unworthy to be saved, election is wholly gratuitous. There is no cause outside the will of God for the election of Jacob and that will, which can never be called to account, is itself "the cause of causes."[48]

> And yet Paul does not, by thus reasoning, impute tyranny to God, as the sophists triflingly allege in speaking of his absolute power. But whereas he dwells in inaccessible light, and his judgments are deeper than the lowest abyss, Paul prudently enjoins acquiescence in God's sole purpose; lest, if men seek to be too inquisitive, this immense chaos should absorb all their senses.[49]

In his commentary on Romans 9, Calvin returns to the same set of issues. God is just, even though his justice may be hidden from us, and there is "no higher cause than the will of God."[50] The ungodly, however, wish to blame their predicament on God. They attempt to excuse themselves by accusing God of being a tyrant. As the ungodly see it, God made human beings as they are and, by condemning them, only condemns his own workmanship. God is powerful, but it is a power without justice. "So also the sophists in their schools talk non-sense about what they call his absolute justice, as if God would forget his own righteousness and test his authority by throwing everything into confusion."[51]

When Calvin takes up the problem of the absolute power of God in the ***Institutes*** (III.xxiii.2), he does it in the context of predestination, specifically in response to the objection leveled against it in his commentary on Romans; namely, whether the doctrine of election makes God a tyrant. In responding to this question, Calvin takes a very Scotistic line: "God's will is so much the highest rule of righteousness that whatever he wills, by the very fact that he wills it, must be considered righteous." He combines this answer with the anti-speculative position characteristic of the early Reformation: "it is very wicked merely to investigate the causes of God's will." In short, "when . . . one asks why God has so done, we must reply: because he has willed it." But when Calvin is asked to name this exalted will of God, this "cause of causes," this "law of all laws," he shrinks back from calling it God's absolute will: "we do not advocate the fiction of 'absolute might'; because this is profane, it ought rightly to be hateful to us. We fancy no lawless god who is a law unto himself."[52]

## IV

When we consider Calvin's rejection of the distinction between the absolute and ordained power of God in the context of the history of that doctrine, three things, I think, become clear.

1. *Anti-speculative*

Calvin rejects the distinction in part because he fears that it encourages the natural human tendency to speculate about the being and nature of God apart from revelation. God can only be known where he has made himself known. While Calvin is only too eager to recommend the boundless power of God as a comfort for believers, he does not want the godly to contemplate that power except through the spectacles of Scripture. To investigate the will of God apart from the revealed will of God in the Bible is to lose oneself in a labyrinth of vain speculations.

2. *Power and justice*

Calvin's principal objection to the distinction is that, in his judgment, it separates the power of God from his justice. We have seen already from our survey of the history of the distinction how unfair that judgment is and how close to Scotus Calvin veers in his own conception of the omnipotent will of God. Nevertheless, it is true that scholastic theologians were willing to consider *de potentia absoluta* such hypothetical possibilities as the incarnation of Christ in an irrational animal or the justification of sinners without a created habit of grace. Such arguments served to underscore the wisdom and justice of God's decisions *de potentia ordinata*.

Calvin is unwilling to entertain even a hypothetical separation of God's power from his justice. Of course, Scotus and Ockham do not seriously intend to separate God's power from God's justice, except as an experiment in thought. But Calvin refuses to do even that. God's power and justice are so tightly bound together that they cannot be separated. What the scholastics regard as a useful experiment in thought, Calvin regards as shocking blasphemy.

3. *Potentia inordinata*

Because the distinction, even rightly understood, invites speculative reflection on God outside revelation and allows a hypothetical, if not an actual, separation of God's power from his justice. Calvin's rejection of this distinction must, I think, be understood as a rejection of the distinction as such and not as a protest against its abuse. At no time does Calvin suggest that there is a licit use for this distinction or that it can be salvaged for Christian theology. Calvin reads the distinction between the *potentia absoluta* and the *potentia ordinata,* not as a distinction between the absolute and ordained power of God, but as a distinction between *potentia ordinata and inordinata,* between "ordered" and "disordered" power. What the scholastics call the absolute power of God is a disordered power because it disjoins God's power from his justice. In that sense all power of God, realized and unrealized, actual and potential, is *potentia ordinata,* power ordered by God's justice.

Calvin, who hates and fears disorder in a fallen world, refuses to accept the idea that the disorder and confusion in the world are in any sense a reflection of disorder in the will of God. Whatever God has done, is doing, or plans to do is an expression of his *potentia ordinata,* even if the justice that guides his will is secret and hidden from us. That ordered power is displayed in miracle, in providence, and in predestination. Indeed, even the impenetrable darkness outside revelation cannot rob the godly of their confidence that the hidden power of God is not the power of an arbitrary tyrant, but the infinite power of a just Father. As Calvin writes in his commentary on Isaiah 23:9:

> we ought to contemplate the providence of God in such a manner as to ascribe to his almighty power the praise which it deserves for righteous government. Although the rectitude by which God regulates his judgments is not always apparent or made visible to us, still it is never lawful to separate his wisdom and his justice from his power. . . . in the school of Christ we are taught that the justice of God shines brightly in his works, of whatever kind they are, "that every mouth may be stopped" (Rom. 3:19), and that glory may be ascribed to him alone.[53]

Calvin, in short, is not opposed to the points made by Scotus and Ockham about the freedom and transcendence of God and at times sounds more Scotistic than Scotus himself. But he finds it impossible to make those points by appealing to the theological distinction between the absolute and ordained power of God. Absolute power is for him disordered power, omnipotence divorced from justice. The will of God may be hidden and mysterious; it may even contradict human conceptions of justice, but it is not disordered. Calvin is therefore not only opposed to the abuse of this doctrine, as Turrettini speculated; he is opposed to the distinction as such.

*Notes*

[1] Amandus Polanus von Polansdorf, *Syntagma theologiae christianae* II c.29 (Geneva, 1617).

[2] William Ames, *Medulla theologiae* I.vi.16-20.

[3] Francis Turrettini. *Institutio theologiae elencticae* loc.III q.21 a.3-5 (Edinburgh, 1847).

[4] Cf., for example, Hugh of St. Victor, *De sacramentis* II c.22, *PL* 176.214.

[5] See, for example, Albert the Great, *De caelo et mundo* I tract.III c.6; Alexander of Hales, I *sent.* q.21 m.3 a.1; Bonaventure, I *Sent.* d.44 a.1 q.1.

[6] Philotheus Boehner, "The Notitia Intuitiva of Non-existents according to William Ockham," in *Collected Articles on Ockham* (St. Bonaventure, N.Y., 1958), 268-300.

[7] Cf., for example, Gabriel Biel's discussion of the necessity of a habit of grace considered *de potentia absoluta* in I *Sent.* d.17 with the same habit considered *de potentia ordinata* in II *Sent.* d.27.

[8] William Ockham, II *Sent.* q.19 a.1 ad 30, *Quodlibet* III q.13.

[9] Duns Scotus, *Ox.* III d.2 q.1 a.1; William Ockham, III *Sent.* d.1 q.1 U; Gabriel Biel, III *Sent.* d.1 q.1. a.1. cor.2 E, III *Sent.* d.1. q.1. a.1. concl. resp.

[10] Paul Vignaux, *Philosophy in the Middle Ages* (New York, 1959), 173.

[11] Cf. the role it plays as a fundamental postulate relative to the natural philosophy in the pseudo-Ockham *Tractatus de principiis theologiae,* ed. L. Baudry (Paris, 1936), 45.

[12] Aristotle, *Physics* III, chs. 4-8.

[13] Blasius of Parma, *Quaestiones in Phys.* III q.4; MS VA 2159, fol. 107v-111bv.

[14] Henry of Harclay in MS Tortosa Cated. 88, fol. 88r.

[15] Jean Buridan, *Quaestiones Phys.* (Paris, 1509), fol. 50v.

[16] Etienne Gilson, *History of Christian Philosophy in the Middle Ages* (New York, 1955).

[17] Carl Feckes, *Die Rechtfertigungslehre des Gabriel Biel und ihre Stellung innerhalb der nominalistischen Schule* (Münster i.W., 1925).

[18] Dom David Knowles, *The Evolution of Medieval Thought* (New York, 1962).

[19] J. Lortz, *Die Reformation in Deutschland,* 2 vols. (Freiburg i.Br., 1941).

[20] Erwin Iserloh, *Gnade und Eucharistie in der philosophischen Theologie des Wilhelm von Ockham* (Wiesbaden, 1956).

[21] Gordon Leff, *Bradwardine and the Pelagians* (Cambridge, 1957); idem, *Gregory of Rimini: Tradition and Innovation in Fourteenth Century Thought* (Manchester, 1961); idem, *William of Ockham: The Metamorphosis of Scholastic Discourse* (Manchester, 1975).

[22] E. A. Moody, *The Logic of William of Ockham* (London, 1935).

[23] Paul Vignaux, *Justification et prédestination au XIV$^{e}$ siècle: Duns Scot, Pierre d'Auriole, Guillaume d'Occam, Grégoire de Rimini* (Paris, 1934); idem, *Luther commentateur des Sentences* (Paris, 1935); idem, *Nominalisme au XIV$^{e}$ siècle* (Montreal, 1948).

[24] Gerhard Ritter, *Studien zur Spätscholastik,* 3 vols. (Heidelberg, 1921-22, 1926-27).

[25] Philotheus Boehner, *Collected Articles on Ockham* (St. Bonaventure, N.Y., 1958).

[26] Erich Hochstetter, *Studien zur Metaphysik und Erkenntnislehre Wilhelms von Ockham* (Berlin-Leipzig, 1927).

[27] Léon Baudry, *Lexique philosophique de Guillaume d'Ockham* (Paris, 1949).

[28] Heiko A. Oberman, *The Harvest of Medieval Theology: Gabriel Biel and Late Medieval Nominalism* (Cambridge, Mass., 1963); idem, *Werden und Wertung der Reformation* (Tübingen, 1977); idem, *Die Reformation von Wittenberg nach Genf* (Göttingen, 1986); idem, *The Dawn of the Reformation* (Edinburgh, 1986).

[29] Leif Grane, "Gabriel Biels Lehre von der Allmacht Gottes," *Zeitschrift für Theologie und Kirche* 53 (1956): 53-75; idem, *Contra Gabrielem, Luthers Auseinandersetzung mit Gabriel Biel in der Disputatio contra scholasticam theologiam* (Gyldendal, 1962); idem, *Modus loquendi theologicus: Luthers Kamf um die Erneuerung der Theologie 1515-1518* (Leiden, 1975).

[30] William J. Courtenay, "Covenant and Causality in Pierre d'Ailly," *Speculum* 46 (1971): 94-119; idem, "Nominalism and Late Medieval Religion," in *The Pursuit of Holiness in Late Medieval and Renaissance Religion,* ed. Charles Trinkaus with Heiko A. Oberman (Leiden, 1974), 26-59; idem, "Nominalism and Late Medieval Thought: A Bibliographical Essay," *Theological Studies* 33 (1972): 716-34; idem, "The King and the Leaden Coin: The Economic Background of *Sine Qua Non* Causality," *Traditio* 28 (1972): 185-209.

[31] Albert Lang, *Henry Totting von Oyta* (Münster, 1937).

[32] Odo Rigaldi, *Quaestiones de gratia,* Toulouse, Bibliothéque de la ville, Cod. 737. fol. 208a-220d; II *Sent.*

d.26-29, ed. J. Bouvy, idem, "Les questions sur la grâce dans le Commentaire des Sentences d'Odon Rigaud," *Recherches de Théologie ancienne et médiévale* 27 (1960): 305-43 (d.26 and 27); idem, "La nécessité de la grâce dans le Commentaire des Sentences d'Odon Rigaud," *Recherches de Théologie ancienne et médiévale* 28 (1961): 69-96 (d.28 and 29).

[33] Cardinal Laborans, "De iustitia et iusto," ed. A. M. Landgraf, *FlorPatr* 32 (Bonn, 1932): 6-42.

[34] Odo Rigaldi calls such merit *meritum ex pacto. Quaestiones de gratia* q.35 ad I, fol. 220d.

[35] W. J. Courtenay, "Nominalism and Late Medieval Religion," 39.

[36] Ibid., 39.

[37] Francis Oakley, "Medieval Theories of Natural Law: William of Ockham and the Significance of the Voluntarist Tradition," *Natural Law Forum* 6 (1961): 65-83; idem, "Pierre d'Ailly and the Absolute Power of God: Another Note on the Theology of Nominalism," *Harvard Theological Review* 56 (1963): 59-73; idem, *The Political Thought of Pierre d'Ailly* (New Haven, 1964); idem, *The Western Church in the Later Middle Ages* (Ithaca-London, 1979).

[38] Steven E. Ozment, *Mysticism and Dissent: Religious Ideology and Social Protest in the Sixteenth Century* (New Haven-London, 1973).

[39] John Eck, *In primum librum Sententiarum annotatiunculae* d.42 a.5, ed. Walter L. Moore, Jr. (Leiden, 1976).

[40] John Calvin, *Commentaries on the First Book of Moses called Genesis,* Vol. I, trans. John King (Grand Rapids, Mich., 1984), 475. For the Latin text see John Calvin, *Commentarius in Genesis,* Opera quae supersunt omnia 23, ed. W. Baum, E. Cunitz, and E. Reuss (Braunschweig, 1882), 255. The Latin text will be abbreviated below as *C.O.* For a brief introduction to the problem of the *potentia absoluta* in Calvin's thought see Francois Wendel, *Calvin, Origins and Development of His Religious Thought* (New York, 1963; reprinted Durham, N.C., 1987), 126-29. For a useful examination of many relevant texts, see Armand Aime LaVallee, "Calvin's Criticism of Scholastic Theology" (diss., Harvard Univ., 1967), 60-65, 291.

[41] John Calvin, *Genesis,* 436. *C.O.* 23, 255.

[42] John Calvin, *Commentaries on the Book of Jeremiah and Lamentations,* Vol. II, trans. John Owen (Grand Rapids, Mich., 1984), 122. Idem, *Praelectiones in Ieremiam Prophetam, C.O.* 38 (Braunschweig, 1888), 130. Susan E. Schreiner has written a stimulating and nuanced discussion of "The Concept of Double Justice in Calvin's Sermons on Job" (unpublished essay scheduled to appear in *Church History*). Schreiner shows Calvin's uneasiness with the concept of a justice higher than the justice of the law, by which God could even find fault with the unfallen angels, a concept which comes perilously close to the doctrine of the absolute power of God. Nevertheless, while Calvin rejects the doctrine of the absolute power of God, he retains the doctrine of double justice both in the sermons on Job and in the *Institutes* I.xvii.2, III.xii.I. The passages which Schreiner cites from the sermons show Calvin arguing against the absolute power of God in much the same way as he argues in his biblical commentaries. See, for example, *C.O.* 34, 336: "Job, then supposes that God uses an absolute power (*puissance absolue*) as it is called, that is, 'I am God and I will do whatever seems good to me although it has no form of justice. I will act with an excessive domination.' But here Job blasphemes God. Although the power of God is infinite, to make it 'absolute' is to imagine a tyranny in God which is completely contrary to his majesty. Our Lord cannot be more powerful than he is just; his justice and power are inseparable."

[43] John Calvin, *Jeremiah,* 119. *C.O.* 38, 128.

[44] John Calvin, *Jeremiah,* 121. *C.O.* 38, 129.

[45] Ibid.

[46] John Calvin, *Commentary on the Book of the Prophet Isaiah,* Vol. II, trans. William Pringle (Grand Rapids, Mich., 1984), 152. *Commentarii in Isaiam Prophetam, C.O.* 36 (Braunschweig, 1888), 391.

[47] John Calvin, *Isaiah,* 152. *C.O.* 36, 391.

[48] John Calvin, *Genesis,* II, 51. *C.O.* 23, 354.

[49] Ibid.

[50] John Calvin, *The Epistles of Paul the Apostle to the Romans and to the Thessalonians,* trans. Ross Mackenzie (Grand Rapids, Mich., 1960), 208. *Iohannis Calvini Commentarius in Epistolam Pauli ad Romanos,* ed. T. H. L. Parker (Leiden, 1981), 211.

[51] John Calvin, *Romans,* 208. *Ad Romanos,* 210.

[52] John Calvin, *Institutes* III.xxiii.2. Quotations in English are from the McNeill and Battles edition (Philadelphia, 1960).

[53] John Calvin, *Isaiah,* 152. *C.O.* 36, 391.

**John Hesselink (essay date 1988)**

SOURCE: "Law and Gospel or Gospel and Law? Calvin's Understanding of the Relationship," in *Calviniana: Ideas and Influence of Jean Calvin*, edited by Robert V. Schnucker, Sixteenth Century Journal Publishers, Inc., 1988, pp. 13-32.

[*In the following essay, Hesselink proposes that though Calvin sees an antithesis between Law and Gospel, their relationship is complementary in that humanity is "driven by the law to seek God's grace."*]

The Subject Of Law And Gospel has been a special Lutheran interest. Check any book on Luther or a Lutheran dogmatics and there will usually be a section or chapter on law and gospel.[1] This is not true of studies of Calvin or dogmatics (theologies) written in other traditions. There will be references to, and occasionally treatments of, the law—but rarely will there be a special section entitled "law and gospel" as such.[2] Thus, for centuries this theme has been largely a Lutheran domain.

It has been generally recognized that Calvin also had a special interest in the law but primarily in the third use of the law (the law as a guide for believers) which for him was "the principal use."[3] Although Calvin was in full accord with Luther on the first and second uses of the law (*usus civilis* and *usus elenchticus*), Lutheran scholars tend to denigrate the seriousness with which Calvin takes the accusing function of the law (second use for Calvin, the first for Luther).[4] When Calvin does take up the theme of law and gospel in the larger context of the witness to Christ under the old and new covenants in the ***Institutes,*** in Book II,[5] the Lutheran Old Testament scholar Emil Kraeling tartly comments that here "Calvin really abandons Paul's (and Luther's) antitheses of law and gospel."[6]

For inexplicable reasons Calvin scholars and Reformed theologians generally have not been very interested in defending Calvin on this issue, so the issue has not really been joined in regard to the law-gospel question except briefly by Wilhelm Niesel in his symbolics, *The Gospel and the Churches*[7]. His treatment is brief and is influenced by Barth as can be seen in the title of the chapter dealing with this theme: "Gospel and Law."

This issue might have remained dormant had it not been for Barth's controversial monograph *Evangelium und Gesetz* which first appeared in 1935.[8] Its impact in German-Scandinavian Lutheran theological circles was almost as great as his earlier Romans commentary which was compared to a bomb dropping on a children's playground. By reversing the traditional order, law-gospel, to gospel-law, Barth had attacked a sacrosanct pillar of faith in Lutheranism. The editors of the symposium *Gesetz und Evangelium* explain in their preface that, as a result of Luther research in the nineteenth century, the theme of law and gospel became a "fundamental" theological issue and "was elevated to a central, even distinctive doctrine within Protestantism (*innerevangelischen Unterscheidiungslehre*)."[9]

In the Luther renaissance after World War I, the political notion of a people's law (*Volks-Gesetz*) became an issue which prompted a renewed interest in the broader issue of law on the part of Protestant theologians in Germany. It was in this context that Barth's monograph appeared and "opened . . . a new period of systematic theological discussion and consideration of this original and genuine reformation theme which has lasted until today."[10] The symposium *Gesetz und Evangelium* reflects that discussion and contains seventeen essays which are largely a response to Barth's *Evangelium und Gesetz* (also included). Not surprisingly, almost all of the contributors are German and Scandinavian Lutheran historians and theologians. There are two exceptions, the Dutch Reformed theolgian Hendrikus Berkhof and the Roman Catholic theologian Gottlieb Søhngen.

In 1969, a year after the appearance of *Gesetz und Evangelium,* Gerhard O. Forde's revised Harvard dissertation was published: *The Law-Gospel Debate*. It covers much the same ground, although the scope is much larger. However, as was true in the German symposium, the genesis of the contemporary debate is Barth's reversal of the law-gospel scheme. For, as Forde points out, "Karl Barth startled theologians, especially Lutherans, by suggesting a basic reorientation of the law-gospel dialectic. His essay was the first major attempt at a redefinition of the problem."[11]

Calvin is mentioned only once in passing in Forde's work, and rarely in the German symposium, but Werner Elert is not alone in thinking that Barth's position is basically a Calvinian-Reformed one. He declares that Barth's much-cited assertion in *Evangelium und Gesetz*—that the law is only the form of the gospel—"coincides exactly with the view of Calvin."[12] That this is not true will become apparent in the substance of this essay. Calvin, no less than Luther, recognizes an accusing function of the law and even an *antithesis* between the law and the gospel. There are similarities between Calvin and Barth but there are also fundamental differences. Consequently, a treatment of Calvin's position in regard to this debate is long overdue. The primary purpose of this essay is to attempt to clear up a common misunderstanding regarding Calvin's view of the relation of law and gospel. Indirectly, this brief analysis should also help to clarify the relation between the views of Calvin and Barth which have often been confused.

What is often overlooked by Lutheran scholars who write on this subject and who compare Luther and

Calvin is that they are not always talking about the same thing when they use the expression "law and gospel." Neither of them uses the expression in a fixed way, so that depending on the situation or context, law and gospel can mean any one of a number of things. When the reformers confine themselves to exegesis of given passages, the results are surprisingly similar. As I have demonstrated elsewhere, when they exegete key passages relating to the law and the gospel in their respective Galatians commentaries, Calvin is no less "Pauline" than Luther.[13] The similarities are also striking in their expositions of the ten commandments in their catechisms where Luther's praise of the law is even more exuberant than Calvin's.

*The Different Meanings of Law for Luther and Calvin*

When Luther uses the expression "law and gospel" he is most often thinking in terms of the question of justification and works righteousness. The law accordingly stands either for righteousness by works in opposition to the righteousness of faith or is likened to the "hammer" of God's demands which crushes self-righteous sinners and drives them to the gospel where they experience the free grace of God. The law in this context stands for God's demand, the gospel for God's gift. Therefore the gospel cannot be preached without first preaching the law.[14]

Calvin, on the other hand, often uses the words promise and curse rather than law and gospel when dealing with this issue.[15] He uses the expression "law and gospel" more often to describe the relation between the two covenants. Hence the misunderstanding of Emil Kraeling noted earlier, in reference to the title of Chapter 9 of Book II of the ***Institutes***,: "Christ, Although He Was Known to the Jews Under the Law, Was At Length Clearly Revealed Only in the Gospel." That "law" and "gospel" here refer to the two covenants or dispensations comes out clearly in the next chapter, "The Similarity of the Old and New Testaments."

Calvin's emphasis on the basic unity of the two Testaments is well known. A common charge is that he so stressed their unity that the differences between the two are severely underestimated. Reinhold Seeberg, for example, in his *Dogmengeschichte* declares that "a consequence of Calvin's legalism is that he tends to blur the boundaries between the Old and New Testaments."[16]

What such interpreters fail to recognize is that here Calvin is using the word "law" in a comprehensive sense, in which case the substance of the two covenants is the same: Christ. Only the form of administration differs. For "the covenant made with all the fathers is so much like ours in substance and reality that the two are actually one and the same. Yet they differ in the mode of administration."[17]

It is this sort of statement that has led many scholars to conclude that Calvin does not appreciate or accept what would appear to be the Pauline antithesis between law and gospel. What is not recognized in such cases is precisely in what the difference consists and, most importantly, that for Calvin there is not only a *difference* between the law and the gospel, but also an *antithesis* insofar as the law is opposed to the gospel. (With Calvin the phrase "insofar as" [*quatenus*] is crucial in understanding the nuances of his position.)

Thus, for example, when the Apostle Paul in Gal. 3:19 opposes the law given to Moses to the promise given to Abraham, Calvin observes that the law here is separated from the promises of grace and is being considered only in view of its "peculiar office, power, and end."[18] This law, the law which is the antithesis of the gospel, is the narrow, peculiar sense of the law, the "bare law" (*nuda lex*).[19] The law, so conceived, is separated from its original context, the covenant; it is a bare letter without the Spirit of Christ. It has nothing but rigorous demands which place all humanity under the curse and wrath of God.[20] Concerning the law, so understood, Calvin is no less compromising than Luther in opposing the law to the gospel. Everything depends on what is meant by "law."

The relation between law and gospel, therefore, is not simply a twofold distinction between form and substance, but a threefold distinction:

1. A *unity* of the substance of the doctrine.

2. A *distinction* in the form or mode of instruction (*forma docendi*).[21]

3. An *antithesis* of letter and Spirit.[22]

In the remainder of this essay I shall develop more fully the nature of these distinctions.

*Unity of Substance*

It is impossible to discuss the unity of substance without discussing to some extent the difference in the form of law and gospel. For Calvin invariably makes such distinctions in the context of the same passage. Also, when Calvin discusses the common substance of the law and gospel, another topic frequently enters the picture: the experience of the fathers (i.e., the Old Testament believers) with Christ and the gospel.

It was noted above that the covenant made with the Old Testament "fathers" or patriarchs has the same substance and reality as that made with believers in the New Testament era. This key statement in the ***Institutes,*** (II.10.2) distinguishes Calvin from opponents on two sides: the Roman theologians on the one hand, and the Anabaptists on the other. Calvin, however, was no innovator in this respect, for Zwingli, Bucer, Melanchthon, and Bullinger had made similar distinctions prior to this time.[23]

For Calvin the issue at stake is not only the unity of revelation but the unity of God himself. In those places where the law is opposed to the gospel, Calvin readily recognizes the antithesis, but at the same time he is quick to warn his readers that it would be erroneous to conclude that God is "unlike" or "inconsistent"[24] with himself.[25]

> When we learn that the doctrine of the gospel 'came forth out of Zion' (Isa. 2:3), we conclude from this that it is not new, or a recent innovation, but that it is the eternal truth of God of which a testimony had been given in all ages before it was brought to light. We also gather that it was necessary that all of the ancient ceremonies should be abolished and that a new form of instruction (*nova docendi forma*) should be introduced, although the substance of the doctrine (*doctrinae substantia*) continued to be the same. For the law formerly proceeded out of Mount Sinai (Ex. 19:1), but it now proceeded 'out of Zion,' and therefore it took on a new form.
>
> Two things, therefore, must be observed: First, that the doctrine of God is the same and always agrees with itself (*et sui perpetuo similem*); that no one may accuse God of changeableness (*variationis*) as if he were inconsistent. Although the law of the Lord is the same as always, yet it came out of Zion with new garments (*veste*). Second, when the ceremonies and shadows had been abolished, Christ was revealed in whom their reality was perceived.[26]

In this one quotation it becomes apparent what Calvin means by both the unity and diversity of the covenants. For him there is essentially only one covenant, the covenant of grace, which unites both Testaments. Here Calvin stands on firm ground, for the one covenant promise—"I will be your God and you shall be my people"—is repeated throughout Scripture.[27]

However, Jeremiah and Ezekiel speak of a "new covenant," and in Heb. 8:6-13 we read that this new covenant, which is ratified by the blood of Christ, makes the "old covenant" obsolete. Calvin still insists that the so-called "new covenant" is not contrary to the first covenant. To draw such a conclusion would imply that God is not true to himself and is somehow inconsistent. "For he who once made a covenant with his chosen people has not changed his purpose as though he had forgotten his faithfulness."[28]

What is "new" about the new covenant only refers to its form. The covenants made with Abraham, Moses, and David, and the new covenant promised by Jeremiah and Ezekiel, are all united by the one promise which finds its culmination and fulfillment in Christ. He is the *fundamentum, anima, spiritus, perfectio, scopus,* and *finis* of the law.[29]

Since Christ is the substance of the law, and thereby also of the two Testaments, they are inseparable and interdependent. The gospel does not supplant or supesede the law but rather confirms it and gives substance to the shadows. Consequently, "where the whole law is concerned, the gospel differs from it only in clarity of manifestation."[30]

*Distinction in Form*

The distinction between law and gospel—between the old and new covenants, as we saw earlier—consists principally in the mode of dispensation or manner of instruction. Calvin treats this subject in Book II, chapter 11 of the ***Institutes,*** although he had already dealt with this matter provisionally in chapter 9. The title of this chapter indicates what the principal distinction is: "Christ, although he was known to the Jews under the law, was at length clearly revealed only in the gospel."

The *tota lex* is still the object of inquiry. In this context, the difference between the covenants is only relative, a matter of more or less; the substance is the same. Only the form or manner of God's self-revelation and our understanding and experience of it varies.

In view of all this, it might seem that Calvin has so moderated or smoothed out the differences between the Testaments, or the law broadly conceived, and the gospel, that the distinctions are not really significant. Before dealing directly with that objection, we should examine the five differences or distinctions which Calvin lists in chapter eleven.

1. The Jews were given the hope of immortality under the figure of earthly blessings, but now this inferior method has been suspended.

2. Truth was exhibited by types in the Old Testament, but is now openly revealed in the New, as we see in the Epistle to the Hebrews. This was due to the fact that the Jews were in a state of tutelage, except for the patriarchs who were in advance of their time.

3. The old covenant has the character of the letter, the new, of the Spirit; the old lacks the Spirit whereas the new is engraven on the heart (Jer. 31:31 ff.). The old is deadly because it includes the curse, the new is an instrument of life. The old is a shadow which must pass away; the new will stand forever.

4. The old covenant produces fear and trembling, except for the promises in it which properly belong to the new (so Augustine), whereas the new produces freedom and joy.

5. The revelation of the Old Testament was confirmed to the Jewish nation. In the New Testament the Gentiles are also invited to share in its blessings.[31]

A careful reading of these five differences shows that the third and fourth differences are not of the same character as one, two, and five. These three are of a less radical, more "evolutionary" type of difference whereas three and four come close to representing an antithesis between law and gospel. That is, the difference between the letter and the spirit, works and faith, bondage and freedom, are far greater than the movement from a more limited and obscure revelation to that which is clearer, fuller, and more universal. As Calvin himself points out, "Where the whole law (*tota lex*) is concerned, the gospel differs from it only in clarity of manifestation."[32]

When one speaks of an "antithesis," as in the next section, a much sharper contrast or break is implied. However, even in this case the break or antithesis is never absolute because even the law (although not the *nuda lex*) is *adventitiously* invested with certain qualities of the gospel. This qualification is crucial for understanding Calvin's view of law and gospel and will be illustrated later.

First, however, it is necessary to explore further the nature of the differences between law and gospel. In the following quotation we have a succinct, yet comprehensive, description of that difference in terms of the "more" of the gospel over against the "less" of the law.

> Both [law and gospel] attest that God's fatherly kindness and the graces of the Holy Spirit are offered us in Christ, but ours is clearer and brighter. In both Christ is shown forth, but in ours more richly and fully, that is, in accordance with that difference between the Old and New Testament which we have discussed above. And this is what Augustine means . . . in teaching that when Christ was revealed, sacraments were instituted, fewer in number but more majestic in signification (*significatione*), more excellent in power (*virtute*).[33]

Hence the Old Testament "fathers" also enjoyed God's grace, but they were granted only a small portion, its perfection being deferred until the time of Christ.[34] Calvin uses many similes and metaphors to describe this relative difference. One he employs frequently is that of the shadow (*umbra*) which he contrasts with truth or reality (*veritas*) and body (*corpus*) or substance (*substantia*). Christ is the reality of the shadows and ceremonies of the law which are abolished when he appears.[35] "For the shadows immediately vanish when the body appears.[36] Commenting on John 4:23—". . . will worship the Father in Spirit and truth"—Calvin observes:

> Although the worship of God under the law was spiritual, it was wrapped up in so many outward ceremonies that it had the flavor of carnality and earthliness. . . . Hence we may well say that the worship (*cultus*) of the law was spiritual in its substance, but with respect to its form was somewhat carnal and earthly. For that whole economy (*ratio*) whose reality is now openly manifested to us was shadowy.[37]

The difference between the two ages or dispensations is also described commonly in terms of distance. The simile of a shadow is sometimes used here, too; but in this case the idea is not so much that of insubstantiality as obscurity. That which was distant and obscure is now near at hand. That which was concealed under the law is visible under the gospel.[38]

Col. 2:17 is particularly relevant in this connection: "These are only a shadow of what is to come; but the substance belongs to Christ." According to Calvin, the apostle here

> contrasts shadows with revelation and absence with manifestation. Those, therefore, who adhere to those 'shadows' act like someone who judges a man's appearance by his shadow when in the meantime the man himself is personally present before his eyes. For the substance of those things which the ceremonies anciently prefigured is now presented before our eyes in Christ.[39]

Another way in which Calvin likes to describe the difference between the fathers' experience of God's grace and ours is in terms of eating a meal. The Old Testament believers drew from the same fullness of Christ that we do, but "they had a more scanty taste of the benefits of God." However, when Christ appeared in the flesh, "the blessings were poured out, as it were, with a full hand."[40] They had but a "slight taste" of the grace to which they bore witness. But now that this grace "is placed before our eyes" we "can more richly enjoy it."[41]

Nevertheless, although the fathers had only a taste of that grace which has been so generously poured out on us, even though they saw Christ only through types and figures, and therefore obscurely and at a distance, "yet they were satisfied. . . ."[42] At the same time they desired to see the things which we see, and hear the things which we hear (Lk. 10:24; Mt. 13:17; 1 Pet. 1:10-12). For although they "were content with their lot and enjoyed a blessed peace in their own minds, this did not prevent their desires from extending further (cf. Jn. 8:56; Lk. 2:29). . . . Due to the burden of that curse by which the human race is crushed, it was impossible that they should be anything but inflamed with the desire of a promised deliverance.[43]

This brings us to the most significant difference between the status of believers under the old covenant and the new, one that was alluded to earlier when it was said that the fullness of God's grace was "deferred until the time of Christ."[44] For all the grace which the Old Testament believers enjoyed was in a sense "suspended" (*suspensa*) grace.[45]

It is not simply a matter of more or less, although their knowledge was far more obscure, their experience of God's grace far more scanty. What they knew and experienced was real, not illusory. They had more than bare promises. The promises themselves, being the living Word of God, contained life and provided a genuine hope. But whatever they had, whatever they received and experienced, was all contingent upon the manifestation of the Son of God in the flesh. "Whatever God at that time conferred [on the fathers], it was so to say adventitious (*quasi adventitium*), for all those benefits were dependent on Christ and the promulgation of the gospel."[46]

Those who lived under the law were partakers of the promise; "there was a participation (*societas*) in the same grace" which we enjoy. But "their faith stood, as it were in suspension (*in suspensa*) until Christ appeared in whom all the promises of God are yea and amen."[47] Calvin takes this "suspension" so seriously that he even says that "in a certan sense (*quodammodo*) grace was suspended until the advent of Christ."[48] For "under the law there was no true and real expiation of sins."[49]

"Suspension," therefore, means that "the ceremonies [i.e., of the old covenant] sketch (*adumbrarent*) Christ as though he were absent whereas to us he is represented as actually present."[50] One should not conclude, however, that the Old Testament faithful didn't have some share in the grace of Christ. Calvin, as we have seen, affirms that in various ways. They "possessed him [Christ] but as one hidden and absent . . . because he was not yet manifest in the flesh."[51]

The differences thus are real and significant. All the criticisms about Calvin levelling the differences between the two testaments and failing to recognize the newness of the gospel are seen to be groundless in view of this notion of "suspended grace" which has been overlooked even by sympathetic Calvin scholars like Wilhelm Niesel and François Wendel.

Calvin often warns about confusing different ages (*confusio temporum*),[52] i.e., the two dispensations. However, as to the antithesis of law and gospel, more narrowly conceived, we should keep in mind a characteristic concern and motif of Calvin: the "constancy of God" in all his dealings with humanity.[53]

*Antithesis Between Letter and Spirit*

Now we come to that aspect of the law which most Protestants take for the whole. This law, the law opposed to the gospel, is the law separated from Christ and the Holy Spirit. This is the bare law (*nuda lex*), the accusing law that troubles the conscience, the law in itself (*per se*) and as such which is isolated from the covenant and the promises. This law requires perfection, and where that is lacking, it curses, condemns, and kills. Over against the gospel, when each is taken in its narrower and peculiar sense, this law demands what only the gospel can give.

Does Calvin recognize such a law? Or is this only a minor motif in Calvin's theology, grudgingly conceded because of the strong Pauline evidence in favor of such a view? Is J. S. Whale correct when he affirms that "the gospel as it appears in Paul and John" is found "in clearer and brighter form in Luther than in Calvin"?[54]

The best way to answer such questions is to examine Calvin's exegesis of a few key Johannine and Pauline texts. The first is John 1:17: "The law was given through Moses; grace and truth came through Jesus Christ." On the one hand, Calvin notes that "Moses' contribution was extremely scanty compared to the grace of Christ." This sounds like the comparisons we saw in the last section; it is simply a matter of more and less. But Calvin does not stop here. He proceeds to point out,

> But we must notice the antithesis in his contrasting of the law to grace and truth; for he means that the law lacked both of these. . . . Here we are dealing with . . . the validity of the law in itself (*per se*) and apart from Christ. The evangelist denies that anything substantial is to be found in it until we come to Christ. Moreover, the truth consists in our obtaining through Christ the grace which the law could not give.[55]

A key Pauline text in this regard is Rom. 4:15: "For the law brings wrath, but where there is no law there is no transgression." This is a very negative text, one where Calvin might be tempted to soften its sharpness. But he states unequivocally that

> since the law generates nothing but vengeance, it cannot bring grace. The law would, it is true, point out the way of life to men of virtue and integrity, but since it orders the sinful and corrupt to do their duty without supplying them with the power to do it, it brings them in their guilt to the judgment seat of God.[56]

In any discussion of Paul's view of the law two other texts of a similar nature are always brought forward:

Rom. 5:20 and Gal. 3:19. The former reads, "The law came in to increase the trespass. . . ." Calvin begins his comments by making a characteristic distinction: Paul here, he maintains, "is not describing the whole office and use of the law, but is dealing only with the one part which served his present purpose."[57]

This qualification is crucial to an understanding of Calvin's view of the law: that when Paul speaks in this way of the law, he is not referring to the original meaning of *Torah,* the revelation of God's will for his people. Rather, he is limiting himself to only one aspect and function of the law. Another example of this qualification is seen in his commentary on Rom. 7:2-3. Here, too, Calvin cautions, the apostle "refers only to that part of the law which is peculiar to the ministry of Moses."[58]

The other text which seems to indicate an exclusively negative and secondary role for the law is Gal. 3:19: "Why then the law? It was added because of transgressions." Calvin again begins with characteristic cautions and qualifications.

> The law has many uses, but Paul confines himself to one which serves his present purpose. He did not intend to inquire how many ways the law is of advantage to men. It is necessary to put readers on their guard on this point; for I have found that many make the mistake of acknowledging no other use of the law than what is expressed here. Paul himself elsewhere speaks of the precepts of the law as profitable for doctrine and exhortation (2 Tim. 3:16). Therefore *this defnition of the use of the law is not complete and those who acknowledge nothing else in the law are wrong.*[59] [Italics mine]

The closing warning might be viewed as a criticism of Luther or some of his followers. However, a careful comparison of Luther's and Calvin's exegesis of key law-gospel passages in Galatians shows that the two reformers are in fundamental agreement on this issue.[60] In regard to this text (Gal. 3:19), for example, he continues with this commentarie.:

> However much the law may point out true righteousness, yet, due to the corruption of our nature, its teaching merely increases transgressions until the Spirit of regeneration comes and writes it on the heart; and the Spirit is not given by the law but by faith. The reader should keep in mind that this saying (*dictum*) is not philosophical or political but expresses a purpose of the law which the world has never known.[61]

In Calvin's commentary on Gal. 2:19 one would think that this was Luther, not the Genevan reformer. The text goes: "For I through the law died to the law, that I might live to the law."

> We must not ascribe to Christ what is properly the task of the law. It was not necessary that Christ should annihilate the righteousness of the law, for the law slays its own disciples. . . . It is the law which forces us to die to itself; for by threatening our destruction it leaves us nothing but despair and thus drives us away from trusting in it.

> This passage will be better understood by comparing it with Romans 7. There Paul describes superbly how that no one lives to the law but he to whom the law is dead, i.e., is idle (*otiosa*) and without effect. For as soon as the law begins to live in us it inflicts a fatal would by which we die, and at the same time it breathes life into the person who is already dead to sin. Those who live to the law, therefore, have never felt the power of the law, or even tasted what it is all about; for the law, when truly understood, makes us to die to itself. It is from this source, not from Christ, that sin proceeds.[62]

It is necessary to examine Calvin's exegesis of one more passage, for here, more than anywhere else, the distinctive nuances of Calvin's understanding of the law are clearly delineated. The passage is 2 Cor. 3:6-7: "For the letter [written code," RSV] kills, but the Spirit gives life." Calvin concludes that "letter" or "written code" (*gramma*) here refers to the Old Testament and "Spirit" refers to the gospel. "By the word 'letter' Paul means preaching which is external and does not reach the heart; by 'Spirit' he means teaching which is alive, which works mightily in the souls of men by the grace of the Spirit."[63]

It seems out of character for Calvin to identify the external letter with the Old Testament, but he is convinced that Paul here has Jer. 3:31 in mind and accordingly likens the old covenant to something external whereas in the new covenant the law is written on the heart through the Spirit.

But this raises the question of the faith of the Old Testament believers. Did God only speak to them externally without touching their hearts by his Spirit? Given all that Calvin has affirmed earlier about this subject, this would appear to contradict those affirmations. The first answer to this question is that Paul has in mind here "a special characteristic (*proprium*) of the law."

> Although God was at that time working by his Spirit, he did so not through the ministry of Moses but through the grace of Christ. As we learn from John 1:17, 'The law was given by Moses, but grace and truth by Jesus Christ.' Of course, all that time the grace of God was not inactive; but it is also clear enough that it was not the peculiar blessing of the law. Moses fulfilled his office when he gave the way of life, with its threats and promises. Paul calls the law 'letter' because in

itself it is dead preaching; and he calls the gospel 'Spirit' because its ministry is alive and makes alive.

Secondly, I answer that Paul is not speaking of the law and the gospel absolutely (*non simpliciter*), but only *insofar as* they are opposed to one another for even the gospel itself is not always Spirit. Still, when it comes to a comparison between the two, one must say truly and properly that the nature of the law is such that it teaches literally without penetrating beyond the ear; on the other hand, it is the nature of the gospel to teach spiritually (*spiritualiter*) because it is the instrument of the grace of Christ.[64]

Calvin sharpens the antithesis as he takes up the description of the law as a "ministry (or dispensation) of death" in verse 7. After analyzing various aspects of the comparison, he draws up a summary.

Let us now examine briefly the characteristics of the law and the gospel. But let us remember that the point at issue is neither the whole of the teaching we find in the law and the prophets, nor the experience of the fathers under the Old Testament but rather the peculiar function of the ministry of Moses. The law was engraved on stones and thus it was literal teaching. This defect of the law had to be corrected by the gospel, since the law could not but be breakable, having been consigned to tablets of stone. The gospel, therefore, is a holy and inviolable covenant because under God it was promulgated by the Spirit. It follows that the law as a ministration of condemnation and death, for when men are taught of their duty and are told anyone who does not satisfy God's justice is cursed, they are guilty and found guilty of sin and death. Therefore, they receive nothing from the law but condemnation, for in the law God demands his due (*exigit quod sibi debetur*), but does not confer the power to perform it. The gospel, on the other hand, by which we are regenerated and reconciled to God through the free forgiveness of sins, is the ministration of righteousness and consequently of life itself.[65]

The real problem, however, is not that of demonstrating that Calvin takes the accusing, condemning function of the law seriously. Far more difficult is the matter of showing how he integrates this concept of the law with his understanding of the law as a whole. He frequently reconciles the apparent contradiction between the views of David (as in Psalm 119) and Paul concerning the law by suggesting that David is speaking of the whole law whereas Paul is speaking of the law in a limited sense.

Thus, when David praises the law, he is thinking not only of precepts and commandments but also of the promises of salvation as well. He rejoices in the law of the covenant, God's gift to Israel. Paul, however, is dealing with people who perverted and abused the law. They saw it as a means toward achieving righteousness rather than as a gift to a people already redeemed. They separated it from the grace and Spirit of Christ and hence experienced the law as sheer demand and therefore as deadly.[66]

However, with this explanation we still have not come to the crux of the matter. It is not just a question of the misunderstanding and perversion of the law by the Judaizers (so Barth). Nor is it only a question of the narrower and broader concepts of the law. There is something intrinsic in the law which distinguishes it from the gospel. The antithesis lies in the peculiar office, function, and ministry of the law. When the law is separated from the promises and the gospel, when it is viewed according to its peculiar properties in contrast to those of the gospel, the antithesis is radical and profound.

The explanation lies in the two "offices" (*munera*) of Moses, as Calvin understands them. One was general (*in universum*), "to teach the people the true role of piety." In this sense he was a minister of the whole law and preached repentance and faith. In fact, he proclaimed the promises of free grace and was thus a preacher of the gospel (*evangelii praeconem*)![67]

However, Moses also had another "office," which unlike his general office, he did not have in common with Christ.

This office was particularly imposed upon him, to demand perfect righteousness of the people and to promise them a reward, as if by compact, upon no other condition than that they should fulfill whatever was enjoined upon them, but also to threaten and declare judgment against them if they ever fell from the way. . . . Therefore, it is important to distinguish between the general doctrine (*generalem doctrinam*) which was delivered by Moses and the special commission (*mandatum*) which he received.[68]

When this distinction is understood, it is possible to see how Paul can speak on the one hand of the law as holy and good and on the other as the law of sin and death. The apostle, because of the situation in which he found himself, often pointed to that which was peculiar to Moses and distinct from Christ, even though they are in agreement as far as the substance of their doctrine is concerned.[69] However, when Paul thus refers to that office of the law which was peculiar (*propria*) to the ministry of Moses, he is not referring to the ten commandments, "For the will of God must stand the same forever."[70]

This closing comment may sound like a softening of the antithesis, but Calvin makes two other distinctions which show that the antithesis is real and radical. One concerns the matter of justification. Here Calvin is as uncompromising as Luther. There are two kinds of promises and two kinds of righteousness: legal promises and evangelical promises, the righteousness of works and the righteousness of faith.[71] These are two opposing systems which are totally irreconcilable. For the law requires works; directs us to Christ. This is why Paul often opposes the law to faith when it comes to justification.[72] The law is not contrary to faith. Were that the case, God would be unlike himself! But as far as the cause and method of justification are concerned, the law is completely at variance with faith.[73]

The other difference between the law and gospel relates to sin. Whereas both the law and the gospel can be empty and useless apart from the Spirit of regeneration, there is an inherent quality in the law which makes it particularly deadening. For the law is a less appropriate vessel for the Holy Spirit than the gospel. Therefore, Calvin approves of Augustine's statement, "If the Spirit of grace is absent, the law is present only to accuse and kill us."[74] The same could not be said of the gospel, for

> it is the nature of the gospel to teach spiritually, because it is the instrument of the grace of Christ. That depends on God's appointment (*hoc ex Dei ordinatione pendet*) for it has pleased him to reveal the power of the Spirit more through the gospel than through the law; for it is the Spirit alone who can teach the hearts of men effectively.[75]

The haunting question that has lurked in the background must now be faced. If the original purpose of the law was to condemn and kill—even though its eventual result was salutary—it would reflect both on the law and on God for having willed something which could only hurt and bring a curse. Calvin's answer-and this brings us to the final reason for the antithesis—is that this negative aspect of the law is "accidental" (*accidentale*) and therefore must be attributed to ourselves.[76]

> When Paul calls the law the ministration of death (2 Cor. 3:6), it is accidental on account of the corrupt nature of man. For the law itself does not create sin; it finds it in us. It offers life to us, but because of our corruption we derive nothing but death from it. It is therefore deadly (*mortifera*) only in relation to man.[77]

Consequently, it is not the law as such that is defective, but the weakness of our flesh.[78] The fact that we are not justified by works is not due to the imperfection of the law. The promise is made of no effect by our sin and corruption. It is possible to speak of the "defect" of the law but that defect arises from human infirmity.[79] It was for this reason that the first covenant was made void[80] and only resulted in condemnation.[81]

*If* we had not sinned, *if* our nature had remained pure, then "the law would not have brought death on us."[82] But this is all hypothetical, reminiscent of that crucial phrase which provides the clue to the interpretataion of the first five chapters of the ***Institutes***,: "If Adam had remained upright" (*si integer stetisset Adam*).[83]

Sin may be an intrusion, contrary to the purpose of the Creator, but it is an established reality. Hence the curse and deadly wound of the law is "not only accidental but perpetual and inseparable (*perpetuum et inseparabile*) from its nature. The blessing which it offers to us is excluded by our depravity, so that only the curse remains."[84] "Since our carnal and corrupted nature contends violently against God's spiritual law and is in no way corrected by its discipline, it follows that the law which had been given for salvation, provided it met with suitable (*idoneos*) hearers, turns into the occasion for sin and death."[85]

The gospel is good news, however, because this "defection" of ours is "accidental" and "therefore cannot abolish the glory of God's goodness" in his generous promises. Our failure cannot nullify the steadfast love of the God who condescended to covenant with his people. "God exhibited a remarkable proof of his goodness in promising life to all who kept his law-and this will always remain inviolate (*integrum*).[86] However, since in fact no one has kept the law, the "wickedness and condemnation of us all are sealed by the testimony of the law. Yet this is not done to cause us to fall down in despair, or completely discouraged, to rush headlong over the brink—provided we duly profit by the testimony of the law."[87]

Thus, driven by the law to seek God's grace, we have an even greater evidence of God's goodness and faithfulness—despite our sin and faithlessness. "Thereby the grace of God, which nourishes us without the support of the law, becomes sweeter, and his mercy, which bestows that grace upon us, becomes more lovely."[88]

*Conclusion*

This investigation has shown at least three things:

1. One cannot make any judgments at all about Calvin's understanding of law and gospel without recognizing the various meanings each of those terms connotes and the various qualifications made within those meanings.

2. Calvin does indeed recognize an antithesis or oppostion between law and gospel, as those terms are generally conceived.

3. Accordingly, Calvin is far closer to Luther than to Karl Barth in regard to the whole law-gospel, gospel-law debate. Any schematization fails to do justice to the nuances of Calvin's position, but it might be depicted as law-gospel-law. In any case, at one level, as we have seen, there is an antithesis between law and

gospel, something Barth would not acknowledge. For Barth, the antithesis is only apparent, in that Paul's negative strictures relate only to a *misuse* and *distortion* of the law.[89] For Calvin, as for Luther, there is something intrinsically different between the law and the gospel, and hence neither would probably agree with Barth's famous dictum that "the law is nothing else than the necessary *form* of the gospel, whose content is grace"[90]

*Notes*

[1] See, for example, Philip Watson, *Let God be God. An Interpretation of the Theology of Martin Luther* (London: Epworth, 1947), 152 ff.; Paul Althaus, *The Theology of Martin Luther* (Philadelphia: Fortress, 1966), Chap. 19; Eric W. Gritsch and Robert W. Janson, *Lutheranism: The Theological Movement and Its Confessional Writings* (Philadelphia: Fortress, 1976), 42 ff.; Helmut Thielicke, *The Evangelical Faith* (Grand Rapids: Eerdmans, 1982), vol 3, chap. 11.

[2] In *Calvin: Institutes of the Christian Religion,* ed. John T. McNeill, trans. Ford Lewis Battles, Vols. 20 & 21, Library of Christian Classics, (Philadelphia: Westminster, 1960), 1677, there is a very detailed listing of topics related to the simple heading "Law," one of which is "and gospel." Unless indicated otherwise, quotations from *Institutes,* will be from the McNeil & Battles translation of 1960.

[3] *Institutes* II.7.12.

[4] See Werner Elert, *Law and Gospel* (Philadelphia: Fortress Facet Books, 1967), 7 ff. Some Lutheran theologians view Melanchthon as the villain for introducing a third use of the law into Lutheran theology. Gerhard Ebeling, for example, maintains that Melanchthon first followed Luther's approach, which was a *duplex usus legis* but then in order "to suit the intentions of his own doctrine of the law . . . remodeled it into the scholastic schema of the *triplex usus*."s (*Word and Faith,* [Philadelphia: Fortress, 1963], 74).

However, the Danish ethicist, N. H. Søe, maintains that neither of the reformers is correct in positing a second (first for Calvin) use of the law. Søe, following Barth and Bonhoeffer, maintains that it is not the law but the gospel—and the Spirit—which brings about a sense of sin and unworthiness.

[5] The title of this chapter is "Christ, Although He Was Known to the Jews Under the Law, Was at Length Clearly Revealed Only in the Gospel."

[6] Emil Kraeling, *The Old Testament Since the Reformation* (London: Lutterworth, 1955), 31.

[7] (Philadelphia: Westminster, 1962).

[8] The English translation, "Gospel and Law," appears in *Community, State and Church,* ed. Will Herberg (Garden City: Doubleday, Anchor Books, 1960), 71-100.

[9] Ernest Kinder and Klaus Haendler, Hg. *Gesetz und Evangelium. Beitrage zur gegenwartigen theologischen Diskussion* (Darmstadt: Wissenschaftliche Buchgesellschaft, 1968), xx. Translation mine.

[10] Ibid., xxi.

[11] Gerhard O. Forde, *The Law-Gospel Debate* (Minneapolis: Augsburg, 1969), 137.

[12] Elert, *Law and Gospel,* 8.

[13] John Hesselink, "Luther and Calvin on Law and Gospel in Their Galatians Comm.aries," *Reformed Review* 37/2 (Winter 1984).

[14] Watson, *Let God be God,* chap. 5; Gerhard Heintze, *Luthers Predigt von Gesetz und Evangelium* (Munchen: Chr. Kaiser Verlag, 1958), chap. 9.

[15] See *Institutes,* II.8.4

[16] Reinhold Seeberg, *Lehrbuch der Dogmengeschichte* IV, 2, 5. Auflage (Basel: Benno Schwabe, 1960), 566. Subsequently, Edmund Schlink, confusing Calvin and Barth, asserted that both of them "water down" the 'heilsgeschichtliche' distinction between the two covenants and law and gospel ("Gesetz und Paraklese," in *Antwort,* Festschrift zum 70. Geburtstag von Karl Barth [Zollikon-Zurich: Evangelischer Verlag, 1956], 332).

[17] *Institutes* II.10.2.

[18] Comm. Ex. 19:1, *Harmony of the Last Four Books of Moses,* I: 314. Generally I am using the old Edinburgh edition of Calvin's Old Testament Commentaries (Eerdmans reprint, 1948-50) and the recent Torrance edition of the New Testament commentaries (Grand Rapids: Eerdmans, 1959-72), but occasionally I have altered the translations for the sake of consistency and greater precision.

[19] *Institutes* II.7.2. The contrast here is with the law "clothed (*vestita* translated by Battles as "graced") with the covenant of free adoption" Cf. Comm. Gal. 4:24.

[20] See Comm. Deut. 30:11; Ps. 19:7-8; Rom. 10:5; and 2 Cor. 3:6.

[21] Comm. Isa. 2:3 and Mk. 1:1.

[22] I have adopted this division from Werner Krusche, *Das Wirken des Heiligen Geistes Nach Calvin* (Gottin-

gen: Vandenhoeck & Ruprecht, 1957), 184-202; but I have given these terms a somewhat different content. For Krusche limits the antithesis almost exclusively to a discussion of 2 Corinthians 3, an unwarranted limitation of the scope of this contrast. Andrew J. Bandstra has used the same divisions, based on my Basel University dissertation, "Calvin's Concept and Use of the Law" (1961). Bandstra, professor of New Testament at Calvin Theological Seminary, investigates whether Calvin is a faithful Paulinist in his discussion of law and gospel and concludes affirmatively. See his essay, "Law and Gospel in Calvin and Paul," *Exploring the Heritage of John Calvin: Essays in Honor of John Bratt,* ed. David E. Holwerda (Grand Rapids: Baker, 1976).

[23] See Gottlob Schrenk, *Gottesreich und Bund im alteren Protestantismus* (Darmstadt: Wissenschaftliche Buchgesellschaft, 1967 [reprint of 1923 ed.]).

[24] Comm. Gal. 3:12; Sermons on Gal. 2:15-16; and Gal. 3:11-14.

[25] Comm. Hab. 2:4; Heb. 1:1-2.

[26] Comm. Isa. 2:3. Cf. Comm. Isa. 42:4; Comm. Micah 4:7.

[27] See Lev. 26:12; Jer. 31:31; Ezek. 37:27; 2 Cor. 6:16; Heb. 8:10.

[28] Comm. Jer. 31:31; Cf. Comm. Ezek. 16:61.

[29] Comm. 2 Cor. 3:6-7; Comm. Jer. 31:31-32; Comm. on Matt. 17:3; Comm. Rom. 10:4-5. Cf. *Institutes* II.7.1.]

[30] *Institutes* II.9.4.

[31] This paragraph contains the main points and arguments of *Institutes* II. 11.

[32] *Institutes* II.9.4.

[33] *Institutes* IV.14.26.

[34] Comm. Heb. 11:39.

[35] Comm. Isa. 2:3; cf. Comm. Heb. 4:8.

[36] Comm. Heb. 4:10.

[37] Comm. Jn. 4:23.

[38] Comm. Zech. 13:1; Comm. 1 Pet. 1:10.

[39] Comm. Jn. 4:23.

[40] Comm. Jn. 1:16.

[41] *Institutes* II.9.1; cf. Comm. Acts 13:32; Comm. Isa. 1:19.

[42] Comm. Heb. 11:13.

[43] Comm. Lk. 10:24.

[44] Comm. Heb. 11:39.

[45] I have developed this theme of "suspended grace" in Calvin's thought more fully in an essay, "Calvin and Heilsgeschichte," contributed to a festschrift for Oscar Cullmann's sixty-fifth birthday, ed. Felix Christ, *Oikonomia Heilsgeschichte als Thema der Theologie* (Hamburg: Herbert Reich, 1967).

[46] Comm. Jer. 3:34.

[47] Comm. Acts 13:32.

[48] Comm. Col. 2:14.

[49] Comm. Ex. 24:4; Cf. Comm. Ex. 25:8; Comm. on Dan. 9:25.

[50] Comm. Gal. 3:23.

[51] Comm. I Pet. 1:12.

[52] Comm. Jn. 4:20; Cf. Genesis *Argumentum* (i.e., the preface to his Genesis Commentary).

[53] *Institutes,* II.11.13.

[54] J. S. Whale, *The Protestant Tradition* (Cambridge: Cambridge University Press), 1955, 164.

[55] Comm. Jn. 1:17. Cf. *Institutes* II.7.16.

[56] Comm. Rom. 4:15.

[57] Comm. Rom. 5:20.

[58] Comm. Rom. 7:2-3.

[59] Comm. Gal. 3:19.

[60] See Hesselink, "Luther and Calvin on Law and Gospel in Comm. on Galatians," cited in n 13.

[61] Comm. Gal. 3:19.

[62] Ibid. These and similar commentary should suffice to show that Helmut Thielicke errs when he says, "The Law-Gospel antithesis [in Calvin] is thus to be understood as being quite relative, not unconditional," *Theological Ethics,* Vol. 1 (Philadelphia: Fortress, 1966), 122.

[63] Comm. 2 Cor. 3:6.

[64] Ibid.

[65] Comm. 2 Cor. 3:7.

[66] Cf. Comm. Ps. 19:7-8; Comm. Acts 7:38; Comm. 2 Cor. 3:14-17.

[67] Comm. Rom. 10:5.

[68] Comm. Ex. 19:1.

[69] "The End and Use of the Law," in *Comm.ary on the Last Four Books of Moses,* 3: 1978. cf. Comm. 2 Cor. 3:6-10.

[70] Comm. Rom. 7:2.

[71] *Institutes* III. 11.17; III.17.6.

[72] Comm. Lev. 10:5; Comm. Acts 15:11; *Institutes* II.9.4.

[73] Comm. Gal. 3:12.

[74] Quoted in *Institutes,* II.7.7.

[75] Comm. 2 Cor. 3:6.

[76] "The End and Use of the Law," p. 198; cf. Comm. Deut. 30:19.

[77] Comm. Acts 7:38.

[78] *Institutes* III.17.7.

[79] Comm. Lev. 26:9. Cf. Comm. Rom. 8:3.

[80] Comm. Lev. 26:9.

[81] Comm. Deut. 7:12.

[82] Comm. Rom. 7:19. Cf. *Institutes*. II.7.7.

[83] *Institutes* I.2.1.

[84] Comm. Gal. 3:10. Cf. Comm. Rom. 7:10; Comm. 2 Cor. 3:7f. It is failure to take this reality into account that results in Daniel Fuller's thesis that law and gospel represent a continuum rather than an antithesis. See his *Gospel and Law: Contrast or Continuum?* (Grand Rapids: Eerdmans, 1980), x-xi. In particular, the passages I have just cited show how wrong Fuller is when he concludes: "Calvin never sensed, as biblical theology has begun to perceive, that Paul used the same term 'law' in two ways that are very opposite to each other because of the complicating factor of the power of sin," 204.

[85] *Institutes* II.7.7.

[86] Comm. Ezek. 20:11.

[87] *Institutes* II.7.8.

[88] *Institutes* II.7.7.

[89] *Community, State and Church,* 89-91.

[90] Ibid., 80.

## Heiko A. Oberman (lecture date 1990)

SOURCE: " 'Initia Calvini': The Matrix of Calvin's Reformation," in *Calvinus Sacrae Scripturae Professor: Calvin as Confessor of Holy Scripture*, edited by Wilhelm H. Neuser, William B. Eerdmans Publishing Company, 1994, pp. 113-54.

[*Approaching Calvin from a psychological and literary direction, Oberman looks at the strange reticience of Calvin to open himself up in his theological writings. This lack of self-disclosure sets him apart from the sometimes obtrusive ego of Luther, but may have aided in making Calvin "the compelling spokesman for all* [*Reformed*] *Christians in the European diaspora." This essay was first delivered as a lecture in 1990.*]

> Quand je n'aurais pour moi père ni mère,
> Quand je n'aurais aucun secours humain,
> Le Tout-Puissant, en qui mon âme espère,
> Pour me sauver me prendrait par la main.
>
> Conduis-moi donc, ô Dieu, qui m'as aimé!
> Délivre-moi de mes persécuteurs;
> Ferme la bouche à mes accusateurs,
> Ne permets pas que je sois opprimé.
>
> Clément Marot, Psaume XXVII[1]

### I. "De Me Non Libenter Loquor"

Everyone who sets out to trace Calvin's "Road to Reformation" encounters not only formidable obstacles in the cultural debris separating us from the sixteenth century, but also and especially in the person of Calvin himself. The five short Latin words "De me non libenter loquor"[2] raise a screen of reticence penetrable only at our own risk. Calvin's silence is especially striking when compared with the directness of Martin Luther, the reformer whom he admired as the Inceptor until his death. Whereas Luther's persona looms large on every page of his work, Calvin inclined to be so "private" that it is difficult to discern the person behind the pen and to discover the emotional heartbeat behind his intellectual drive to grasp the mysteries of God and the world. While Luther continued to be a preacher even in the most academic of disputations or exegetical lectures, Calvin remained true to his first office in Geneva as lector, so that even in his sermons he was the teacher charged with enlightening the darkness of human confusion.

Amply displayed in the biblical commentaries of Erasmus, Zwingli, Bucer, or Melanchthon, a general characteristic of this period's biblical humanism was an objective-expository thrust that anticipated the nineteenth-century ideal of descriptive scholarship. Calvin's "ego" surfaced often and explicitly, but served as a scholarly adjudicator rather than as a carrier of personal sentiments. This instructional ideal of communication colored Calvin's sermons and letters—typically the most personal literary genres—and was strengthened by his deep sense of divine immediacy, transforming the prophets and doctors from Moses and Isaiah through Paul and Augustine into instruments of the Word and notaries of the gospel.

Calvin's dislike of self-disclosure is but one of the obstacles on our path to clarify his origins and early development. The Luther scholar has many more hard data to work with thanks to three fortunate constellations, none of which apply in the case of Calvin. As the "Initiator" of the Reformation both in his own eyes and in those of Calvin—the Wittenberger continually had to confront the deeply disturbing question "are you alone wise?", "how dare you contradict the wisdom of so many centuries?" Luther responded to the challenge by relating himself to Occam, Gerson, and Staupitz in a variety of revealing ways. From the very beginning Calvin was never "alone." He provided a rare autobiographical passage in his answer to Cardinal Sadolet (1539), wherein he described his path to the "sudden conversion"[3] and articulated his initial aversion to an ultimate approval of the spokesmen for biblical reform.[4] Confronted by two mutually exclusive claims to truth, Calvin had come to see the weight of the evangelical party's arguments. But he mentioned no specific individuals. Apart from the uncontested impact of Luther, this leaves a wide array of potential candidates as shapers of his earliest thought.

Second, for Luther we can draw on precious and extensive documentation from the periods before and after his Reformation discovery. Though we continue to debate the exact timing of Luther's Reformation breakthrough, we can document stages in his development and reconstruct a remarkably accurate list of books in his library and on his desk while he prepared his first Psalms commentary (1513-15). We possess his marginalia to the works of Augustine, Anselm, and Lombard and know that he studied the sentences commentaries of Occam, d'Ailly, and Biel. Moreover, the most recent discovery documents his early interest in Gregory of Rimini some ten years before the Leipzig disputation (1519).[5] For the preconversion Calvin we have only the Seneca commentary. Although this is indeed a rich source for our knowledge of the young Calvin, its subject matter is not yet biblical theology; hence comparisons with his later works are hazardous.

Finally, for an investigation of Calvin we have to do without what proves so illuminating for Luther research, namely structural interpretive guides that help to describe Luther's place and function as acting vicar within his order or as a professor of biblical theology within his university. Calvin's social and intellectual milieu proves more evasive precisely because the newly emerging phalanx of French biblical humanists did not easily fit into well-established medieval organizations, whether monastic orders or academic institutions. In this light it is understandable that the little we know about the young Calvin during his "student years," from 1523 to 1528 at the Collège de la Marche and the Collège Montaigu in Paris, has had to be squeezed for more information than it could yield. This has led to a history of speculation no less fascinating than fallacious. In the next section we must therefore turn to the task of distinguishing between fact and fancy in the delicate enterprise of retracing and reconstructing the early stages in the development of John Calvin.

## II. The Pitfalls of Pedigree Pursuit

Under the impact of German idealism there has been a phase in the history of ideas in which scholars looked for "systems," for so-called "unfolding principles," and in German research preferably for the right "Ansatz." In this tradition a thinker was declared to be a Platonist, an Aristotelian, or a Kantian; and those elements which did not "fit" this systematic model were declared to be inconsistencies revealing a lack of intellectual vigor. Usually the author of such a study could show himself superior to his subject by pointing to neo-Platonic deviations, to subversive pseudo-Augustinian elements, or, in rare and extremely thrilling cases, to a sniff of Averroism.

Until the middle of this century one liked to write books to show that Calvin was a thoroughgoing Augustinian, Platonist, or Scotist. A new phase in the investigation of the beginnings of Calvin can be discerned in the middle of this century when the awareness emerged that an incontestably original thinker and text-oriented exegete like Calvin is most unlikely to have been systematically derivative or, in any sense of the word, to have been a schoolman. It is to be noted that even though the tendencies of the past proved to be too stubborn to be completely exorcised, and, perhaps because the majority of interpreters were theologians, Calvin continued to be seen as a "thinker" rather than as a real historical person of flesh and blood, who in the decisive stages of his development responded not only to currents of thought, but also and especially to religious needs and political challenges, to personal encounters and social experiences.

In 1950 François Wendel made a new beginning with his study of Calvin's *Origins and Development,* published in English in 1963 and in a revised and enlarged French edition in 1983.[6] For an intellectual biography four decades is a remarkably extensive career; and its end is not yet in sight since it is still the best one-volume introduction to Calvin's theological thought. Perhaps because Wendel could draw even-handedly on French and German scholarship, he does not look for the "master plan" but subtly points to "the echo of Scotus" or to remarkable "traces of nominalism."[7] Admittedly, while looking for the scholastic roots of Calvin's thought, Wendel fails to distinguish between Scotism and nominalism, and (as I will argue) overstates Erasmian influences at the expense of the significance of Lefèvre d'Étaples and the circle of Meaux.[8] Nevertheless, he has set a standard by which succeeding scholarship is to be measured.

Wendel's work whetted the appetite and his allusions unleashed the urge for further clarification. This has been pursued in a series of studies that have in common a search for Calvin's roots, best characterized as the pursuit of the pedigree. In 1963 Karl Reuter published *Das Grundverständnis der Theologie Calvins,*[9] in which he argued for a pervasive "scotisch-scotistische Personalismus" of Calvin after placing him at the feet of John Major (Mair, 1550) until the spring of 1528—even though Major taught from 1518 through 1526 in Glasgow and Saint Andrews and lectured upon his return to Paris at Sainte Barbe. Calvin is said to have learned from Major "eine neue Konzeption antipelagianischer und scotistischer Theologie" as well as a "erneuerten Augustinismus."[10] Behind Calvin's doctrine of sin Reuter discerns the authority of Thomas Bradwardine (1349), who found in Calvin "a true disciple"[11]—"bien étonné de se trouver ensemble!"—even though Calvin never "found" Bradwardine. In 1966 Hiltrud Stadtland-Neumann turned to an analysis of Calvin's understanding of the Sermon on the Mount.[12] The pursuit of the pedigree now leads to the conclusion that Thomas Aquinas, though never mentioned, "exerted no small influence on the thought of Calvin."[13] In the case of the permissibility of an oath, Calvin's direct dependence on Thomas is argued—without consulting the sentences of Peter Lombard, commentaries on canon law, or Duns Scotus's treatment of this burning issue.[14]

In comparison with these speculative constructions of Calvin's dependence on Thomas, Scotus, Bradwardine, or Major, Alexandre Ganoczy's *Le Jeune Calvin,* published in 1966, marked a considerable advance.[15] Ganoczy points to the fact that the young Calvin in and before the first edition of the ***Institutio*** (1536) does not display any knowledge of the leading scholastic theologians, whether they hail from the Thomistic, Scotistic, or Occamistic tradition.[16] Anyone who wants to argue that Calvin had been initiated in scholastic theology in Montaigu, Ganoczy points out, must prove that "Calvin between fourteen and seventeen years of age dared to go against the strict school curriculum and took instead of lectures in grammar, philosophy and science, courses in theology which were the privilege of the much senior students."[17]

Ganoczy does suggest, however, that Calvin in following lectures in scholastic philosophy was introduced to the kind of Aristotelian ethics that were "without doubt rife with scholastic casuistry," and imbibed not only dialectical reasoning but also a "metaphysics which in the nominalist fashion opposed systematically the divine and the human."[18] While this last conclusion, particularly with its loaded word "opposed!" is still the unfortunate remnant of an outdated, Thomist view of nominalism, Ganoczy achieved for Calvin studies what R. R. Post did for the interpretation of the Modern Devotion,[19] facilitating the return ad fontes by cutting through a thick layer of secondary literature.

Whereas it was the strength of Ganoczy that he had limited himself to the works of the young Calvin, in 1982 he revived the pedigree search in his edition—together with Stefan Scheld—of Calvin's annotations to Seneca and Lucanus, dating quite likely from the years 1545-46.[20] On this late basis Ganoczy argues for the formative influence of Stoicism on Calvin in two directions. Always suggestive rather than assertive, and with all of the usual reservations, Ganoczy relates Calvin's so-called "Weltverachtung" to the Stoics, at least as concerns its nonbiblical root, and points to "eine stoische Färbung" in Calvin's emphasis on human beings as clay in the hands of God. He further discerns "die Tendenz einer stoisch beeinflussten Schriftauslegung" in Calvin's biblical doctrine of election and reprobation.[21] Accordingly Ganoczy bases Calvin's sense of vocation not only on Christian faith but also on a Stoic view of the immutable God.[22]

For our purposes it suffices to point out that the young Calvin, writing his ***Institutio*** in 1535—and therefore well before any later elaborations—interprets the immutability of God as the reliability of his Word. As a matter of fact, for Calvin it is the cornerstone of Christian faith that God cannot undo his promise: so certain is God's truth "ut non possit non praestare, quod se facturum sancto suo verbo recepit"; God cannot but deliver what he has laid down in his Holy Word (Rom. 10,11).[23] We discern here not the Stoic but the longstanding medieval vocabulary of commitment that we encounter with Scotus and the nominalist theologians as the *pactum Dei* to which God is bound *de potentia ordinata*.[24] The Stoic notions of tranquility and moderation, which Calvin was willing to accept as biblically sound, he did find with Cicero.[25] As far as Seneca is concerned, he is for Calvin in no sense of the word a Christian. As in earlier research, Ganoczy has overlooked Calvin's uncompromising statement: "For his involvement with Christianity there is nowhere at any time even the slightest indication."[26]

The most recent publication to be considered in this context is an article by Alister E. McGrath, John Calvin and Late Medieval Thought. A Study in Late Medieval Influences upon Calvin's Theological Development.[27] Sufficiently warned by Ganoczy's *Le Jeune Calvin,* McGrath no longer looks for proof but rather for "circumstantial evidence" to establish Calvin's dependence on late medieval theology. Defending and indeed reviving Reuter, McGrath is by no means convinced that Major could not have had a significant influence on Calvin.[28] McGrath finds the circumstantial evidence he is looking for in drawing on the early and late Calvin throughout the period 1536-60. By positing that not only in the fourteenth century, but also in the fifteenth and early sixteenth century, the theology of Gregory of Rimini (1358) was "on the ascendency," he assumes that Gregory—and the "schola augustiniana moderna" associated with him—was so prominent in Paris that Calvin could not possibly have avoided taking note of him.

Beyond a close relationship between Calvin and Gregory of Rimini, McGrath stipulates "the essential continuity between Calvin's thought and that of the later medieval period in general and that of the via moderna in particular."[29] Throughout the footnotes he documents his conclusions with reference to secondary literature, and nowhere is the test-question raised whether or to what extent Calvin's avid reading of St. Paul and St. Augustine can sufficiently—and hence convincingly—explain convictions reemerging (in a markedly different form and context) in the *via Gregorii.* Gregory is never mentioned by Calvin and the *via Gregorii* is not incorporated into the statutes of any of the forty or so Parisian colleges. Furthermore, one of the chief characteristics of the so-called "schola augustiniana moderna" is its programmatic effort to recall the scholastic doctors to read and study the authentic writings of St. Augustine in context and not in excerpts (florilegia). Through the celebrated Basel editions of Amerbach (1503-06) and Erasmus (1520-29; Paris 1531-32), Calvin could bypass the circuitous road of scholastic reception.[30] It is uncontested that already the young Calvin of 1532-35 had an impressively broad and independent access to the *Opera Augustini*.[31]

The preceding survey, which could have been easily extended, is instructive both in alerting us to pitfalls to be avoided and in pointing to promising avenues of approach in four respects:

1. In studying the *initia Calvini* we should apply Occam's razor and control the "plurality" of sources by limiting ourselves to the writings of Calvin prior to 1536, including therefore the first version of his ***Institutio*** written in 1535 in Basel. In this first edition, Calvin—according to an exceptional consensus among all Calvin scholars—speaks to us as a man who has already found both his voice and his message, and addresses the reader as a seasoned spokesman for the embattled evangelical cause. In the later editions from 1539 through 1559 (1560), this first manifest is periodically enlarged and changed; in the course of twenty years of intensive study, taking note of ever new and complex objections, the Genevan reformer had to study a large array of authorities. These additions should not be taken into consideration as the textual basis for studying the origins of the reformer.

2. A promising and already most rewarding avenue of investigation has been opened up by Francis M. Higman in studying Calvin's use of the French language. Higman set out on this path in his important *The Style of John Calvin in his French Polemical Treatises*.[32] Drawing on Higman's study of Calvin's French polemical writings from the forties and applying this to the period before 1536, we can discern the importance of Calvin's first French publication and are indeed struck by the fresh and compact power of Calvin's preface to Olivétan's French Bible. In 1535 Calvin had not only found his theological, but also his "French voice." More generally, Calvin's French writings deserve equal time, and more. My extensive list of Calvin's French expressions and proverbs not only highlights his creative use of a language *in statu nascendi,* but also the extent to which his native tongue was his primary mode of molding experience and shaping reflection.

3. Though it may sound self-evident and therefore redundant, it must be insisted upon that the terminus post quem is as important as the terminus ad quem: in our case this means that the *initia* do not start only in 1532 with his first breaking into print or in 1533 with the computed date of his conversion. We should study Calvin's "beginnings" from 1509 to 1536 and thereby take into consideration that there is far more to influence a person than the books read—including the Scriptures!—namely, political and social as well as psychological and religious experiences. Hence we should apply to the study of Calvin a rule he used with reference to understanding the mysteries of God: " . . . plus in hac inquisitione valere vivendi quam loquendi modum."[33]

4. There cannot be any doubt that it is essential to be committed to the close scrutiny of Calvin's late medieval *resources.* But without clear evidence these resources cannot be transformed into *sources.* They are listening devices or hermeneutical tools to uncover

Calvin's own profile by highlighting—always "zur Stelle" and ad hoc—both continuity and discontinuity. In the case of his final (1562) clarification of the intimate relation between the sacramental sign (*sacramentum tantum, signum*) and the thing signified (*res sacramenti*), we can notice Calvin's application of Scotist terminology to define his position between Zurich and Wittenberg with greater precision.[34] In every such case the interest should be not to construct a pedigree, but rather to show why and how the medieval backdrop is a pertinent and necessary tool for clarifying a particular passage or complex issue.[35] The traditional type of intellectual history is as treacherously reductionist as its twin brother "Ahnenforschung" is racist. For this reason, intellectual history is badly in need of deconstruction, this time not to eliminate but to recover the authorial intention.

Once this is clearly in place, it can be safely said that there is a whole range of themes clustered around Calvin's presentation of the *ordo salutis,*[36] which a hundred years before would have earned him the school ranking "Scotist." Each taken separately, the following seven tenets can be traced back to other traditions, but as a cluster they must have suggested a close proximity to Scotus. We in turn can most readily decode their originality with a Scotistic dictionary in hand:

> 1. The beginning and end of the *ordo salutis* hinge on the sovereign acts of God in predestination and acceptation;
>
> 2. there is a twofold acceptation of the Pilgrim (*Viator*) and of his works;
>
> 3. fundamental and eternal (not cancelled by "disobedience"!) is the covenant of God (*foedus, pactum*) with Israel and the church;
>
> 4. the final acceptation is unmerited "ex mera misericordia" on the basis of God's covenant commitment;[37]
>
> 5. throughout we note the retention of such terms as "ex puris naturalibus"[38] and "facere quod in se est," or (more often) "quantum in se est";[39]
>
> 6. indicative of progressive revelation and the approximation of the end (finis!) is the *felix culpa* doctrine;[40]
>
> 7. of central importance is the "formal" distinction,[41] which also underlies the favorite expression "docendi causa," once succinctly defined by Calvin as "disiungi res inter se coniunctas."[42] It allows for the distinction between the being of God (*essentia*) and his revealed power (*virtus*) which forbids on the one hand "curiosity" about the aseity of God (that is, the "being" behind the "person") and rejects on the other the late medieval expression "de potentia absoluta" as the suggestion of God's use of sheer power (tyranny for Calvin)[43] that improperly separates power and justice.[44]

More important even than such single issues is to grasp the overarching view, which teologians call "eschatological" and philosophers prefer to designate as "teleological": it is characteristic of Calvin's mode of thinking that throughout the Latin "finis" or French "but" *(terme)* is given priority above the second causes or "steps" toward this goal. Hence, metaphysically, "final" causality is given precedence over "first" causality and, psychologically regarded, the human agent is not "pushed" but "reoriented," and "drawn." This perspective is operative in each of Calvin's privileged levels of discourse, which arranged here in temporal sequence has to be read backward "sub specie aeternitatis." It should be kept in mind, moreover, that in the five following paradigms we separate what Calvin would merely distinguish "docendi causa"; actually the five are closely related roles of God:

> 1. "Father"—family (adoption)—protection and discipline—final mercy;
>
> 2. "King"—reign (providence)—obedience—final glory;
>
> 3. "Teacher"—school—exercise—final wisdom;
>
> 4. "Lord of Hosts"—army—oath—final victory;
>
> 5. "Judge"—courtroom—scrutiny—final adjudication s(acceptation/reprobation).

Two examples may serve to illustrate that what could seem an abstract analysis has far-reaching consequences for the interpretation of single aspects. (1) The German rendering of "finis legis" as "Gesetzesende" is misleading: Calvin does not—and indeed, never—mean "the end" of the Law, but its goal or "scopus." (2) "Meditatio futurae vitae" is not only a spiritual exercise, but designates the appropriate mental attitude or frame of mind with which the Christian "sees" and interprets *all* events in the world and in his own life, namely in terms of the eschaton, "the end." "Promissio" and "spes" are as future-orientated as the cosmic order itself. Yet, since faith "knows" and "grasps" the End, the present is already transformed or—more precisely—transfinalized.

Theology and metaphysics can only be distinguished "docendi causa" and only be understood in retrospect. In Calvin's case "sub specie aeternitatis" can only be rendered as "in the light of eternity," if it is understood as "in the light of the End." For Calvin's view of nature and history, the term "second causes" can only be used metaphorically: de facto they are "agents" of God-in-action; human beings come alive when they respond to the call of trekking toward the End.

In this thoroughgoing and radical finalism Calvin is "plus Scotiste que Duns Scot"—so much so that he transcends the boundaries within which such school ties make sense. Indeed, Calvin found this vision already enunciated by the prophet Isaiah: "recte docet Isaias . . . finem spectandum, eoque referenda esse omnia."[45] This is the extent to which the scotistic dictionary can assist us. From hereon in we have to start reading the book of his life itself.

## III. The Historical Calvin: The Growth of a Vision

Confronted with the various claims for Calvin the Platonist,[46] the Stoic, the Thomist, the Scotist, or the nominalist—not to mention the frequent references to "humanism" and the Modern Devotion—it is not too much to conclude that Calvin is caught in a true *captivitas systematica*. What makes Wiliam J. Bouwsma's *John Calvin, A Sixteenth-Century Portrait*[47] the most significant interpretation since François Wendel is his quest for the historical Calvin, not a man of one system but a real human being exposed to a complex bundle of contradictory impulses.

Gingerly Bouwsma wades through the ocean of systematic claims, providing suggestive hints relating the reformer to Budé and Erasmus, Rabelais and Montaigne, rather than to the great medieval schoolmen. Without writing a psycho-history, Bouwsma is acutely aware of the pervasive power of Angst and hope, of terror and trust. One avenue of approach proved here to be particularly rewarding, namely Bouwsma's intent in reading Calvin's major achievement, the biblical commentaries, with a sharp eye for interpretations not required or not immediately following out of the scriptural text.

In consequence there emerge not one but two Calvins, characterized by two favorite expressions: the "labyrinth" and the "abyss." The first Calvin, "the forward-looking humanist and adventuresome discoverer," has escaped from the confusing maze of the labyrinth of medieval scholasticism. The other Calvin is the philosopher, "a rationalist and a schoolman in the high scholastic tradition represented by Thomas Aquinas, a man of fixed principles, and a conservative. . . . This Calvin was chiefly driven by terror that took shape for him in the metaphor of the abyss."[48] While some of Bouwsma's insights will continue to be basic ingredients of every convincing reinterpretation, it is a mark of the significance of this book that it may take scholarship quite some time to refashion these two Calvins into the one historical person.[49]

Inclined to blend out the major theological themes in Calvin's thought, Bouwsma is both a reaction to and a correction of traditional theological Calvin research. At first sight these two approaches seem to be irreconcilable and mutually exclusive.[50] Traditional Calvin interpreters have to be convinced that Calvin's writings contain far more than this doctrina. Bouwsma on the other side has to be convinced that one cannot draw "a sixteenth-century portrait" without retracing the physiognomy of established religious language in order to capture the unique features of the Genevan reformer. And part of these features reflects his lifelong passion: the renewal of theology as the clarification of the gospel.

A case in point is Bouwsma's important discovery of Calvin's predilection for the word and concept of "labyrinth," formerly generally overlooked. Its significance can only be properly assessed, however, against the background of the fact that Erasmus had carved the expression in stone by including it among his *Adagia* (2.10, 15), of which there were twenty-eight editions between 1500 and 1536. But even before Erasmus's *Adagia* had captured the book markets in Paris and Basel, the expression "labyrinth" had already become part and parcel of the humanist arsenal against the "obscurities" of scholasticism. The correspondence in the circle around Jacques Lefèvre d'Étaples amply documents this. Charles de Bovelles—like Lefèvre Calvin a Picardian—employs the term in defense of geometry in 1501, though not yet against a clear target.[51] Hieronymus Gebwiler (1540), writing from Strasbourg to Sebastian Brant in March 1511, seizes upon the image of the "labyrinth"—this time with a specific attack on scholastic logic.[52] And a year later Robert Fortune (1528), teacher of grammar, rhetoric, and philosophy at the Collège du Plessis, contrasts in the preface to his Paris edition of Cyprian (1 Nov. 1512) the clarity and revitalizing power of these writings with the confusing works of the unmentioned scholastics.[53]

Such negative use of the "labyrinth" to decry scholasticism as the prison of the mind had not always been a foregone conclusion. Hardly twenty years before, Wessel Gansfort (1489) invoked the myth of Thesus in a strikingly positive fashion by emphasizing the "thread through the labyrinth" as the classical image for disciplined prayer and well-structured speech.[54] For Gansfort the "labyrinth" is associated with challenge rather than with doom, with the need for direction rather than with loss of orientation. For Calvin the "labyrinth" stands for confusion, and is already part of an established vocabulary that was available to express impatient disdain for scholasticism.[55] It suggests—often as synonymous with "laqueus" or the classical "nassa"—the state of perplexed moral bewilderment, typical of the troubled conscience, overtaxed in the confessional. In its most general application the "labyrinth" characterizes the human condition in terms of a natural knowledge of God that is too dim to find "the right path" but in its frustration creates "fantasies." The *docilitas* that Calvin experienced as the first gift of "conversion" is the only way out of the "labyrinth."[56]

Twice as frequent and far more revealing is Calvin's extensive use of the word "abyssus," to which again Bouwsma was the first to point. In the 1986 Kuyper lectures on "The Heritage of John Calvin" at the Free University of Amsterdam, I had already chosen the same hermeneutical path by identifying a series of favored expressions of Calvin as keys unlocking the existential strata of his thought and pointed to four such catchwords: "nonchalant," "secret" with its Latin equivalent "arcanum," and the expressions "Dei nutu" as well as "meditatio vitae futurae."[57] As fruitful as these four windows proved to be, I must frankly admit that Bouwsma's discovery of "abyssus" opens up even larger horizons—larger, I submit, than even his cultural interpretation admits.

With its biblical roots, "abyssus" is understandably much more prominent[58] than "labyrinth' as the classical shorthand for the intractable maze.[59] One New Testament text in particular makes Calvin reach for the term "abyssus" to describe confusion, the hell of despair, and the threat of ultimate annihilation. A second one, which in the Vulgate version reads "bestia quae ascendit de abysso (Rev. 11:7)," can be mentioned only in passing since Calvin nowhere explicitly invokes or interprets this passage. Yet, in a later version of the ***Institutio*** (1543), pondering why the Scriptures sometimes refer to "the devil" in the singular and sometimes to "devils" in the plural, he explains the singular as indicative of the ongoing war between the kingdom of righteousness under the one-headed leadership of Christ and the kingdom of impiety under the one devil. This adversary will finally be thrown "into the enternal fire, prepared for the devil and his angels (Matt. 25:41)"—and hence ultimately be forced to return to the abyss out of which he emerged.[60] And when Calvin argues that the sinner cannot possibly enumerate all his sins in the confessional, he invokes common sense, that is, the awareness of everybody "quanta esset peccatorum nostrorum abyssus . . . quot capita ferret et quam longam caudam thraheret haec hydra."[61] This abyssmal hydra suggests the biblical "Beast" of the Book of Revelation, which threatens to emerge from the Abyss.

The key biblical text, however, and the ever present context is the story in Luke 8 about the exorcism of the legion of demons who at their own request are sent running into the abyss: "in abyssum irent" (Luke 8:32). It is this powerful image of the crazy[62] yet "voluntary" submersion and death-by-drowning that also stands behind the commentary on Jeremiah 33:44, where Calvin analyzes the unwillingness of the Jews to accept God's offer of grace and forgiveness: "they rather wanted to throw themselves in the abyss of desperation."[63] Without this sense of "existence on the brink" we would not grasp the urgency of Calvin's appeal to his old friend François Daniel, writing on 15 July 1559, "[you are] loath to climb out of the abyss of the papal church in which you have plunged. . . ."[64]

The full import of the term "abyss," with both its emotional and doctrinal freight, is already accessible to us in Calvin's earliest work, the ***Psychopannychia*** (1534), holding treasures that still await mining. In the central and oldest part of this twice rewritten treatise, Calvin first points out that true theology cannot go beyond the boundaries of what the Holy Spirit teaches: to penetrate further and beyond these boundaries is to drown oneself in the abyss, the "abyssum mysteriorum Dei. . . ."[65] He concludes this passage with the warning that those who reach beyond their ken will invariably come to naught: ". . . eos qui supra se nituntur, semper corruere."[66] The classical myth of Icarus had already been transformed into moral advice by Erasmus in the *Adagia:* "quae supra nos nihil ad nos" (1.6.69); and used by Luther in *De Servo Arbitrio* to warn against the penetration of the hidden counsels of God.[67] For Calvin the yonder is "down under."

While Calvin's warning against reaching out for the Deus absconditus has—with the water simile of "drowning"—a flavor all its own, the report on his experience of the wrath of God permits us an unparalleled glimpse into his own psyche.[68] The wider context of this revealing passage is his argument against those who teach that the soul dies at the end of the human life. No, Calvin responds, in reality the soul dies when hit by the judgment of God, when the sinner hears the chilling challenge "Adam, where are you?" This is easier to think than to say, to ponder than to express in words; yet so terrible is the majesty of God that even thinking about it is impossible without having had the experience yourself. Those on whom his wrath falls discover the full terror before the omnipotent God; however they try to escape, they will not succeed, even though "in mille abyssos se demergere parati sunt."[69] Who does not have to admit that this is true death! But to spell this out in words is not necessary for those who have experienced this sharp compunction of the conscience.[70] No doubt Calvin knows what he is talking about.

In the third and final passage we draw on, the experience of conversion has solidified into a doctrine that would become typical for the teachings of Calvin and Calvinism. Often, Calvin points out, the Scriptures mean by "death" not the end of present life nor by "hell" the grave. "To die" and "to descend into hell" frequently mean "alienation" from God and "depression" caused by the judgment of God: it characterizes those who are made attrite [!] by his Hand. In this case hell does not mean physical but spiritual death: "abyssum et confusionem significet."[71]

When in the New Testament the Gospel writers refer to "Hades" they do not mean a place or location but the *condition* of utter misery, exposed to the wrath of God and assigned to exile. This is the meaning of the words in the Creed that Christ has "descended into hell." When the Bible says that "God redeems my soul from the grasp of hell," it means "He has accepted me." The *impius,* who stubbornly *(proterve)* rejects God and instead puts his hope in his own achievements, will die, descend into hell, and disappear in the abyss. But he who trusts in the Lord will be liberated from the power of hell[72] and escape the clutches of the abyss.

Let us venture now to address the implications of our findings. We started out by pointing to Calvin's extreme self-reticence. Then, following the sign-posts of catchwords and favorite expressions, we reached a layer of revealing primordial reactions and gut decisions that can best be described with the German word *Vorverständnis.* Three preliminary conclusions are in order.

1. By concentrating on the earliest layer in Calvin's work, we have found that a firm grasp of late medieval theology is required in order to understand a whole series of terms and assumptions, reaching from God's self-binding covenant (*pactum*)[73] to the inscrutable God (*Deus absconditus*) and the naked state of incapacitating fear (*attritio*). All of these late medieval themes had already been integrated and transformed into a biblical theology that Calvin could have encountered in the French translations and Latin writings of Luther, including *De Servo Arbitrio* of 1525. On a much broader textbase than can be displayed here, an extensive study of Erasmus's *Adagia* must be assumed. Yet the young Calvin is theologically not an Erasmian, but—in view of his different understanding of the *iustitia Dei*[74]—to a remarkable extent in experience and at times even in expression a disciple of Luther.

2. The special characteristic of Calvin's teaching, which can therefore be designated as an extra-Calvinisticum, is to be found in his reinterpretation of hell as a condition,[75] and the descent of Christ into hell as the extreme experience and exposure of the Son of Man to the wrath of God. This extra-Calvinisticum is already part of the earliest stage of Calvin's thought, and with its deep sense of alienation in keeping with his own conversion experience as deliverance "from the pits" ("bourbier si profound").[76] Indeed, the interpreter—and the translator!—of Calvin needs to be as familiar with late medieval terminology as with the Latin and French of that day; yet, I repeat, this is no warrant to construe a medieval pedigree that can be as easily advanced as gainsaid. Calvin did not learn this striking psychological interpretation of the abysmal Descent into Hell in a medieval school but in the school of life.

3. Whereas William Bouwsma marked a significant advance in discovering the centrality of the terms "labyrinth" and "abyss," our analysis places us in a favorable position to start to reunite the two Calvins that Bouwsma sees in tension and even in a crippling conflict with one another. To begin with, the two metaphors are not mutually exclusive; confusion is typical of both. As we noticed, Calvin warns not to penetrate the mysteries of God; such speculation plunges us in the abyss. But this abyss is indistinguishable from the labyrinth when Calvin warns against following Augustine—as Bouwsma himself noted[77]—in speculating how the sin of Adam was transmitted: such puzzling drives you into the labyrinth.

Furthermore, Bouwsma properly points out that it is the "humanistic Calvin who chiefly dreaded . . . entrapment in a labyrinth."[78] This same concern, however, Calvin shared with the humanists of his age, particularly with the circle around Lefèvre d'Étaples in Paris. The alleged "dread" is a stereotypical humanist concern not to slide back into the labyrinth of the man-made "solutions," of scholasticism and canon law.

Finally, Bouwsma is again right in discerning that "Calvin was chiefly driven by a terror that took shape for him in the metaphor of the abyss."[79] Whereas the references to the labyrinth are standing expressions of less than central importance, with the abyss we reach the heart of the matter, and indeed into the heart of the one Calvin. Initiating his conversion is an experience of drowning and annihilation that Calvin regards as generic and applies to all true Christians at all times. It is the experience of hearing God's piercing call, "Adam, where are you?" Scared to death by the majesty of God and caught in the labyrinth of a life without exit, the sinner frenetically flees and, blinded by fear, seeks "refuge" in the abyss of hell and damnation. If saved from drowning by God's outstretched hand,[80] this soul-rending experience gives way to the resuscitating power of God as pledged in his Word. This encounter with naked terror is not left behind, however, but ever present and methodically kept to mind by continuous mediation.[81]

The medieval call "de profundis"—the traditional conclusion of the funeral mass[82]—is rephrased in the language of experience: "obrutus sum, sepultus sum, suffocatus sum"—in the abyss I am drowning, buried, choking.[83] Bouwsma is right: the *timor Dei* as awe for God has marked Calvin for life. But at the same time, knowing about the terrifying abyss neutralizes all other human fears. Such fears Calvin knew very well. He describes his own all-encompassing fear of persecution in a 1562 sermon on II Samuel. Looking back at the time before his refuge, "when tyranny reigned in

France," he remembered that he was scared to death, "j'ay esté en ces destresses là, que i'eusse désiré voulu estre quasi mort pour oster ces angoisses . . .":[84] the same urge to escape the anxiety that drove the "swines of the Gerasenes" into the abyss (Luke 8:26, RSV).

Looking at all the evidence, we reach five conclusions:

1. "Labyrinth" and "abyssus" do indeed provide appropriate lenses—together with "theather" the favorite image drawn from the vital but vitiated world of vision—but the right focus (*scopus*) still has to be established. To present Calvin in his campaign against the "labyrinth" as "the forward-looking humanist and adventuresome discoverer," as does Bouwsma, is to assume a Burckhardtian view of humanism that Calvin shared as little as we do today. With all respect for the *studia humanitatis* as welcome tools and new resources, Calvin does not tire of discrediting all the classical authorities for the moral philosophy of his day: he assails the vagaries of the Platonic dialogues, as well as the implicit or explicit "atheism" of the very best in Virgil, Horace, and Seneca.[85] Except for glimmers ("scintillae") and disparate tidbits of truth ("poetis extortae sunt"!) nothing these unbelievers or *profani homines* can offer alleviates the basic human disorientation, exacerbated by the confusion of scholastic doctors and canon lawyers.

2. There is no "adventurous" way out except by *docilitas and fraenum,* by redirection and by the bridle, so that the "wild horse" can be put back on the right track: *conversio ad docilitatem.*[86]

3. Calvin's undeniable fear for the "abyss" does not reveal him to be the "rationalist" or the "philosopher," let alone the "Thomist." The "abyss" stands for the psychological experience of hell, alienation, and ultimately annihilation when confronted before the *tribunal Dei* with the holy majesty of God the Judge. The "abyssus" is the *finis* of all mankind, except for the elect who experience exactly the same "condition" but then are moved to invoke the mercy of God and thus seize his "extended hand." To use another favorite expression, it can be said *docendi causa* that whereas faith (*revelatio*) is the map leading out of the "labyrinth," hope (*invocatio*) is the escape and life jacket for the drowning creature who has lost his footing in the "abyss." Both metaphors, "labyrinth" and "abyss." relate to confusion: yet the "abyss" does not call for enlightenment but for redemption and has the teleological connotation of the ultimate "discrimination" between life and death. In the "experienced"—and preached!—gospel, Calvin's doctrine of reprobation is sublapsarian: the reprobate are drowning in their own guilt. While the elect throw themselves at the mercy of God the Judge, the reprobate reject his "extended hand."

4. Calvin knows that on the basis of fixed credal points (*fixa stat sententia!*), theology provides a discourse of metaphors. The frequent expression "docendi causa" in the ***Institutio*** alerts the reader to the fact that what follows is a clarification by abstraction, transcending the cohesion of lived experience. Hitherto unnoticed, it is an important warning signal that should be especially heeded by those interpreters who make this teaching manual the mainstay of their interpretation.

In the Commentaries the same function is laid on the slight shoulders of the short word "quasi," which has not drawn the attention it deserves, though it appears some hundred times more frequently than "abyssus." Under this fascinating "quasi"-blanket of expressions, allusions, and approximations lies for Calvin the hard core of psycho-spiritual experiences and traumatic developments such as the growth and shriveling of joy and despair. The Holy Spirit, long recognized as a major and characteristic theme in Calvin's doctrine, is de facto the Divine Analyst *and* Psychotherapist. The Book of Psalms provides the manual for analysis since it offers—to use the phrase that Calvin is proud to have coined—"the anatomy of all parts of the soul."[87] In charge of God's Secret Service (*operatio arcana*), the Spirit penetrates not only the thoughts, words, and deeds, as the tradition had it, but also the *affectus,* transforms external doctrine into persuasion,[88] and above all leads from inner confusion to sanity.[89]

As we shall see, this insight is already the center and heartbeat of the ***Psychopannychia***. At this point it serves to underscore an aspect of Calvin's character to which Bouwsma pointed, but which he saw nipped in the bud: Calvin was indeed an "adventurer," namely an adventurer-into-the interior. He offered both a new diagnosis and a novel therapy for that part of Europe which had broken out of the protection of the confessional and, while risking to live without the benefit of absolution and without the prospect of the "last rites," henceforth found itself directly confronting the tribunal of God with a conscience still trained and sensitized by the medieval interpretation of the Seven Deadly Sins and the Ten Commandments.

The "labyrinth" marks the point of departure, namely the perplexities of the confessional, too heteronomous to assuage and redirect the conscience. The "abyssus," on the other hand, expresses the new priestless life *coram Deo,* where sins can no longer be left behind through the exercise of contrition and the sacrament of absolution. It marks at once the fierce storms outside the confessional and the fiery breath of direct, unmediated exposure to the justice of God.

5. The intensity of the quest for "sincerity" and a "good conscience," as well as the crucible of the *examen pietatis,* reveals the dimensions of the traumatic experience that those generations had to "absorb" (a verb used in connection with "abyss" almost

as frequently as "drown"), who had consciously embraced the Reformation or found themselves in Reformed territories. This "exodus from the confessional" is an important dimension of the social and political exile that marked the audience of Calvin. With this exodus in mind Calvin explored the Scriptures. His Commentaries reveal best the extent to which he himself is not merely an observer but a participant who carried the full brunt of its trauma.

Calvin was at once driven by the ever present awareness (*meditatio!*) of the threat of *drowning* in the abyss of death, devil, and hell, and *drawn* by a deep-seated trust in the promise of God's saving intervention. To him applies not the expression "come hell *or* high water";[90] the diabolical abyss is hell *and* high water. Yet the mercy of God subdues and swallows the power of the Beast, so forcefully formulated in his outcry: "Abyssus tuae misericordiae hanc peccati mei abyssum absorbeat"—May the abyss of my sin be drowned into the abyss of Your mercy.[91]

IV. The Decisive Decade: 1525-35

In six steps we now endeavor to place the young Calvin in his historical context, the increasing threat of persecution.

1. The chaotic structure of the ***Psychopannychia***—notwithstanding or perhaps even due to the double revision in 1536 and 1542—does not facilitate easy access. Even so, it is an amazingly rich treatise[92] for all who try to find the original thread in the labyrinth of Calvin's later thought. The unwieldy structure goes quite a way in explaining why this earliest theological work of the reformer has been given such cursory treatment during the last fifty years. When it was read at all, as in the case of George Hunston Williams, it suffered from a false contrast with Luther, who was claimed to teach the mortality of the soul.[93] This is a misreading not only of Luther,[94] but of Calvin too.

Calvin's point of departure is the immortality of the souls, which he believes to be a truth he can share with all reasonable humans. And indeed he himself refers to the ***Psychopannychia*** (which literally means "The Waking of the Soul") as his libellus "de animarum immortalitate."[95] His point is, however, that just as death strikes when the gospel is rejected, the soul receives life eternal when through justification it is resuscitated and placed on the path of the Kingdom. Calvin explicitly denies that the soul is immortal in and of itself, as if she could subsist without God's care: "sed dicimus, eius manu ac benedictione sustineri"[96]—we learn from experience that it is the might of God and not our human nature that allows us to last in eternity.[97] Not only in this central passage but throughout the ***Psychopannychia,*** we see how the Platonic presuppositions that swayed the minds of the leading humanists in Florence and Paris, around Ficino and Lefèvre d'Étaples, provide Calvin with a point of departure and with a vocabulary that is consciously tested and critically transformed according to the standards of biblical speech.

2. If the major thrust of the ***Psychopannychia*** can be so readily misunderstood, it should not surprise us that a seemingly minor aside in the preface of 1534 has not drawn the attention it deserves. Calvin argues here that "recently" a number of anabapist authors[98] have revived the old heresy of the mortality of the soul, which according to Eusebius was taught by Arabs and sometime later upheld by the "Bishop of Rome,"[99] Pope John XXII (4 Dec. 1334), "whom the University of Paris forced to recant."[100] In one respect the questions raised by this passage have indeed been investigated. It is now well established that Calvin's characterization is mistaken. Pope John, though deviating from the received opinion of the immediate and full vision of the departed souls, never taught the morality of the soul. Rather, he argued for an intermediate state in which the souls of the departed receive the beginning of their reward in seeing the humanity—though not yet the divinity—of Christ, and do therefore not yet enjoy the beatific vision.[101]

The positions of Pope John and John Calvin seem quite similar when compared with the extreme alternatives of mortality and immediate full beatific vision.[102] Joseph Tylenda even concludes, "Calvin's opinion is, in fact, hardly distinguishable from that of John XXII."[103] There is one crucial difference, however, in that Pope John articulates the "not yet" dimension of the intermediate stage in relation to the resurrection, whereas Calvin places an equal emphasis on the "already." Calvin's theme is the progress of the Christian in three stages, from conversion (awakening), resting after death yet fully awake in the joyous expectation of the full beatitude, which will finally be received on the day of the resurrection. The progress of the pilgrim "in dies magis magisque" is already the mark of the earliest thought of Calvin.[104] Contrary to the impression left by Calvin scholarship, the alertness of the soul after death is not a youthful "folly": in none of the later biblical commentaries will Calvin miss an opportunity to illustrate and develop the importance of this theme.[105]

3. For our purposes even more relevant is the question what we can learn about Calvin's *initia* from his reference to the condemnation of Pope John XXII by the University of Paris. The fact itself, that is, the critical Gutachten of twenty-nine Parisian doctors concerning the eschatology of John XXII, dated 2 January 1334, is well documented.[106] The point is, however, that Calvin invokes here with great specificity, as he does again in the ***Institutio***[107] and in his ***Briève Instruction*** of 1544,[108] the authority of Jean Gerson (1429). Calvin does not refer to him in general terms but points ac-

curately to the "first" Easter sermon of the famous chancellor of the University of Paris. This is Gerson's sermon "Pax vobis," preached on Palm Sunday 1394 (April 19) and originally delivered in French. The Latin version was not published until Jacob Wimpfeling (1450-1528) had it translated by a gifted German student in Paris and incorporated it in his *Supplementum* to the 1502 Strasbourg edition, which contains, as he says explicitly, "prius non impressa." This edition, republished in Strasburg (1514), Basel (1518), and Paris (1521), contains two further Easter Sermons and hence explains Calvin's identification of "Pax vobis" as the *first* Easter Sermon.[109] Two centuries later "Pax vobis" was incorporated by L. Ellies Du Pin in his fine edition of Gerson's *Opera Omnia;*[110] the original French version was published for the first time by Palemon Glorieux in 1968.[111]

Since the first preface to the ***Psychopannychia*** is written in Orléans (1534), shortly after Calvin had to flee from Paris and before settling in Basel (1535-36), he may have relied on his memory for the reference to Gerson. It certainly means, however, that if he did not work himself extensively with Gerson manuscripts, he must have used the Wimpfeling edition, that is, the *Supplementum*. In either case it shows that Calvin was early acquainted with the most eminent of late medieval French authors,[112] whose authority was preeminent in Gallican circles that liked to invoke Gerson's authority for that reformation of France for which the chancellor had once delivered such an eloquent blueprint.[113]

Concluding this section on the ***Psychopannychia,*** it may be said that just as the text itself deserves renewed attention as documenting the method, scope, and findings of the young Calvin, the preface points to an even earlier phase when he apparently had access to the works of the great French conciliarist, or moved in circles where Gerson's memory was kept alive.[114]

4. In his plea for the reform of France, Gerson invoked the authority of Seneca. Though admitting that nothing is so poisonous as tyranny, he made quite clear that "sedicion" is rampant rebellion without rhyme or reason: "she is often worse than tyranny." But even so, also to tyranny the rule applies: "Riens violent aussi ne peust durer"—violence has no future. Hence Gerson suggests that the king submit to "reasonable" reform, since to submit to reason does not mean to bow to one's subjects. As Seneca so convincingly put it: "si vis omnia subicere tibi, subice te rationi"[115]—thus Gerson presented his king, Charles VI (1420), with the Stoic yardstick "between severity and clemency" for that enlightened absolutism which a century later would be personified by Francis I (1547).[116]

Calvin's Seneca commentary,[117] understandably often studied for possible hints about his conversion or nascent theological convictions, should rather be road in the context of the politically turbulent situation in France after the Concordat of 1516 and its confirmation in 1519. Initially Parliament resisted, and when it had been placated the University stepped in, blocking the printing of the text of the Concordat.[118] The new alliance between king and pope, which steadied the royal hold on the French Church, presented a challenge to which the older Gallican coalition had to provide new answers. Future interpretations of Calvin's Seneca commentary will want to draw on this challenge to politicians and legal experts as the immediate context of Calvin's earliest publication.

With the commentary on Seneca's *De Clementia* we have access to the earliest phase of Calvin's academic career.[119] At the feet of Pierre Taisan de l'Etoile (Petrus Stella) in Orleans and of Andrea Alciato in Bourges, he was so fortunate as to be introduced to the cutting edge of the political science of his day. Different from the traditional "Fürstenspiegel" in addressing all matters of public administration, and different from a "Utopian" concern by regulating existing legal practice, this new legal prudence found its guiding principles not in canon law but in Roman law. Although Josef Bohatec has convincingly documented the overwhelming extent to which Calvin drew on Guillaume Budé in his later legal thought,[120] for the young Calvin Pierre de l'Etoile was the "prince of the jurists."[121] From Alciato (1550; 1529-33 at the University of Bourges), Calvin occasionally distanced himself as he did in his preface to the "Antapologia" of his friend Duchemin.[122] Yet he may have encountered in Alciato the more significant and innovative legal mind, who, to quote Myron Gilmore, "became the founder of a new school of jurisprudence, based on the principle of humanist exegesis with an appreciation of the importance of the interpretation of the Roman law as a living common law. . . ."[123] This application of Roman law is what Budé tried to achieve in France and what Calvin set out to implement in Geneva. Whereas legal scholars had already been eminent carriers of Renaissance humanism in fifteenth-century Italy, in the sixteenth-century this trend reached France and Germany.[124] In this campaign for the emancipation of civil law from canon law, Alciato was an important transalpine link.

Calvin was fortunate not only in his teachers, but also in the Seneca theme, which he dared to tackle notwithstanding two earlier editions of ***De Clementia*** by Erasmus (1515; 1529). Since 14 February 1531 documented as "Maistre Jean Cauvin, licentié es loix," he published a year later a commentary on the civic virtue of clemency that, as the personalized dimension of the issue of "peace and concord," had been the central theme in political science and reform tracts north and south of the Alps. In measuring the relationship of power and justice, and in reaching for a balance between tyranny and mob rule, "clemency" was sought after as the golden mean.[125] Whereas Calvin's Seneca commentary is too often dismissed as a youthful display of humanistic tools, or praised as the beginnings of "Calvin the exegete," and once even as his "'pagan apprenticeship' to the christian life,"[126] the point of departure for future scholarship will be Calvin as the student of statecraft in the politically volatile situation of an emerging absolutist monarchy.

Drawing on his studies in Orleans (1528-29), Bourges (1529-31), and under the Royal Readers (1531-33), Calvin comes well prepared to design his appeal to Francis I as the preface to his ***Institutio***[127] and to sketch the "humanitatis et civilitatis officia"[128] in its concluding section about power and justice in a Christian society.[129] Without the hermeneutical tool of the Seneca commentary, Calvin's early political theology could be misunderstood as a rhetorical device to win the clemency of Francis I rather than as a programmatic effort to acknowledge *and* regulate royal absolutism between the boundaries of human "aequitas" and the sovereignty of God as "rex regum."[130] Calvin defended by defining both limits and goals: "sunt certique fines!" This is not fear for the abyss, but the common sense of legal circumscription: no humanity without order,[131] no order without checks and balances, no balance without law—which itself is for Calvin the charta of all "true humanism."

Yet even more important than the use Calvin made of his legal training in defending the cause of the French loyal opposition is his vision and ability to create new institutions in the form of the Compagnie des Pasteurs and the Consistory, the General Synod and the Genevan Academy. There is a wise French saying: "Les hommes passent, les institutions subsistent." Calvin did not fade away because he incarnated his vision by designing durable legal structures. His ever growing ***Institutio*** would have been long dated and shelved if he had not initiated viable institutions as the underpinnings of his "textual community," No biography of Calvin can be complete without due attention to the institutional dimensions of his legacy.

5. Calvin did not publish his ***Psychopannychia*** in 1534 because Wolfgang Capito—among the city reformers the most sensitive to winning the radical reformers—strongly advised him against it. This is the first time we learn that the young Calvin had contacts with Strassburg and had apparently already developed such a relationship of respect and trust with Capito that he submitted his theological maidenwork[132] to the scrutiny of this Strassburg reformer.[133] The Strassburg connection cannot surprise us since, after September 1524 when the Reformation had triumphed in this imperial city, it became, to use the expression of Jean Rott, "un centre de propaganda vers les pays de l'Ouest."[134] When on 3 October 1525 the Parliament of Paris decided to take action against the Circle of Meaux, Lefèvre d'Étaples and his chief officers such as Guillaume Farel, Michel d'Arande, and (for a shorter stay) Gerard Roussel sought refuge in Strassburg and were received under the roof of Capito.

From a network of secretive messages[135] we know that a stream of French refugees went to Basel and Zurich, but all of them circulated through Strassburg as the extraterritorial safeplace for the French evangelicals. For a correct understanding of the *initia Calvini,* it is important that instead of the usual opening chapter on "l'Affaire des Placards" in October 1534, the story begins to unfold on 3 October 1525, when Parliament exploited the absence of King Francis I, imprisoned in Spain after the lost battle at Pavia (24 Feb. 1525). At this point in time, Parliament decided to act on the pressure of the Sorbonne to suppress what it called "lutheranism."[136]

Apart from the horror of imprisonment, torture, and death at the stake, the ensuing wave of persecution had a clarifying and accelerating effect. The broad coalition of reform-minded Gallican Episcopalianism, which had taken institutional form in the diocese of Meaux in the years 1521-25, was now broken into three discernible parties, personified by (1) Guillaume Briçonnet, the bishop of Meaux; (2) by his learned vicar Lefèvre d'Étaples, the mastermind of the reform in the diocese; and (3) by Guillaume Farel, the radical student of Lefèvre, who would have such a decisive influence on the course of Calvin's life.

The impact of the persecutions, designed and executed through the cooperation of Parliament and University, forced each party to clarify its understanding of reform. Bishop Briçonnet, in his concern for peace and order the most Erasmian among the "reformists," purged the ranks of his clergy and reinforced traditional devotions to the Holy Sacrament and the Virgin Mary.[137]

Lefèvre d'Étaples, perhaps the most mysterious of the three and certainly the most difficult to place,[138] takes the road to Strassburg and, after his return to France, continues to be in touch with his more radical disciples such as Farel, and may well have met with Calvin two years before his death in 1536. Later Calvin would have counted him among the Nicodemites, but his best modern interpreter can answer this charge in one loaded sentence: "Lefèvre ne se cache pas, il se tait."[139]

Whereas Lefèvre responded to the use of force with the power of silence, Guillaume Farel responded by rejection: he concluded that the Antichrist raged in the Church of Rome and was stretching his greedy fingers to the kingdom of France, forcing the truly faithful to take the counteroffensive.

Reading, side by side, Lefèvre (c. 1440-1536) and Farel (c. 1489-1565)—almost half a century younger—one cannot help but notice the striking new tone of urgency expressed in the intensive and extensive use of Antichrist terminology.[140] Probably early in 1525, the handbook for the reform of instruction and preaching in the diocese of Meaux was published, which Michael Screech has properly called "un ouvrage révolutionnaire."[141] Though it was published anonymously, there can be no doubt as to the authorship of Lefèvre d'Étaples. The *Épistres et Évangiles* follow the text of his translation of the New Testament,[142] and his Paulinism, biblicism, the emphasis on the *gloria Dei,* as well as the revealing silence about the invocation of the saints, inform the preaching examples.[143] Probably inspired by Luther's "Adventspostille" of 1522, it dares to develop a biblical theology that makes it quite understandable that the Sorbonne censured (on 6 Nov. 1525) forty-eight propositions drawn from this text as "diabolical figments" and characterized them as Manichean, Waldensian, Wyclyffite, and Lutheran.[144]

For our intent to measure the difference and, in this case, even the distance between Lefèvre and his disciples, it is important that in the later edition printed by Étienne Dolet (Lyon, 1542),[145] six new "exhortations" were added and quite a number of interpolations were made by changing words, phrases, and sometimes an entire paragraph. The changes reveal a heightened tone of critique and impatience, and are properly characterized by Screech as "plus scripturaires, plus militantes, que celles de Lefèvre lui-même."[146]

### V. Conclusion: "Nous N'Avons Autre Refuge Qu'a Sa Providence" [147]

It is the extended line from Briçonnet via Lefèvre to Farel and his other radical disciples that brings us into the heartland of the *initia Calvini.* In this climate of persecution—and this applies to the whole decade that saw Calvin grow from puberty to adulthood, from 16 to 26 years of age—the themes developed that were to become cornerstones in Calvin's biblical theology: the glory of God,[148] the secret operation of the Holy Spirit, the growth of the Kingdom, the danger of idolatry, and the strategy of Satan.

In Calvin's eloquent preface to the 1535 Bible of Pierre Robert Olivétan (†1538), all of these themes are integrated within the one history of the covenanting God.[149] In this brief summa of the whole history of salvation, one element is novel and deserves our special attention. After relating the liberation from Egypt and before turning to the arrival in the Promised Land, Calvin inserts the revealing sentence: "Il les a accompagnés nuit et jour en leur fuite, étant comme fugitif au milieu d'eux"—he accompanied the Children of Israel night and day on their flight, "present among them as a fugitive himself."[150]

The ten years of ever increasing persecution (1525-35) almost resulted in the annihilation of the Reformed party, but then led increasingly to the radicalization of the "rest" along stages on the line marked by the distance between Briçonnet, Lefèvre, and Farel. The political reality of persecution cried out for a religious interpretation that led to the discovery of the work of the Antichrist, a key phrase in the vocabulary of extra- and anti-hierarchical reform. The yield of this history of persecution, the refuge, made Calvin read the Scriptures anew and allowed him to discover God as the first refugee, trekking with the people of Israel through the desert.[151]

In unfolding his biblical theology and in building his institutions, Calvin used a whole range of authors from Augustine to Luther, from d'Étaples to Budé, from Erasmus to Bullinger; and he reflected currents ranging all the way from Platonism to late medieval Scotism. But at the center of the *initia* stand the never forgotten experience of the abyss as the deadly flight *from* God and the growing insight in the life-giving refuge *with* God.

At times Calvin broke the silence of his reticence. In Genevan exile he confessed, "It is very hard to have to live far from one's fatherland."[152] This experience enabled him to understand and unfold the biblical theme: "I have been a stranger in a strange land" (Exod. 2:22). The threat of the abyss is ever present—but the fugitive God is trekking along, "manum porrexit"—his "hand is stretched out." Both this conviction and this language made Calvin the compelling spokesman for all Christians in the European diaspora. Thus Calvin initiated—after the reformation of Luther and of the cities—the resilient Reformation of the Refugees.

> Ie t'anymeray en toute obeissance,
> Tant que viuray, o mon Dieu, ma puissance:
> Dieu, c'est mon roc, mon rempar haut et seur,
> C'est ma rencon, c'est mon fort defenseur.
>
> En luy seul gist ma fiance perfaite,
> C'est mon pauoys, mes armes, ma retraitte;
> Quand ie l'exalte et prie en ferme roy,
> Soudain recoux des ennemis me voy.
>
> Clément Marot, Psaume XVIII[153]

### Notes

[1] *Clément Marot et le Psautier Huguenot, étude historique, littéraire, musicale et bibliographique,* ed. O. Douen (Paris, 1879; repr. Nieuwkoop: B. de Graaf, 1967), 2.430. In 1541 Calvin incorporated in the new Genevan liturgy psalms that Marot (1544) had begun to "translate" from 1533 onward in what became known as the "style Marotique." Marot provided the dispersed "Churches under the Cross" both with tender hymns commensurate with their refugee experi-

ence and with battle songs preparing for mob action and survival. I open and close this essay with Marot because he has lent Calvin's piety poetic power and is to be regarded as a major cohesive factor offsetting the centrifugal forces operative in this long-dispersed underground movement.

[2] *Responsio at Sadoleti Epistolam* (1539); *Opera Selecta,* 1.460.42. The *Opera Selecta* (henceforth OS), vols. 1-4, ed. P. Barth and G. Niesel (München: Chr. Kaiser Verlag, 1926, 1936), are quoted with page and line references, also where this edition omitted line numbering.

[3] This is Calvin's later—and indeed late: 1557—designation in his Commentary on the Psalms: "subita conversione ad docilitatem subegit . . ." CO 31.21 C. Since the *Calvini Opera* (henceforth CO) do not provide line numbers, I divide the columns into A, B, and C to help the reader locate the quotations in context.

This much-discussed statement deserves a fresh analysis, since it cannot be rendered with the usual—classical or patristic—dictionaries in hand. The most convincing evidence must come from Calvin's Psalms commentary itself. Fortunately, this provides an eloquent answer, and if we include the French rendering of the Preface (if not written by Calvin himself, then certainly by someone thoroughly familiar with his thought and vocabulary), even bilingual evidence. I include supportive references to the French Sermon Series of 1553, in which all the main themes of the Psalms commentary are already available, and which provides the rich extra dimension of French expressions.

Here four points suffice: (1) As in the answer to Sadolet, the wider context of the conversion passage is the argument that Calvin had not sought office on his own account—Sadolet had suggested "ambitio" and "avaritia": lust for power or riches. No, Calvin had been called directly by God—as he shows in other commentaries, David to his throne, Isaiah to his prophecy, and Paul to his apostolate. Hence, even in these two "classical" autobiographical passages, Calvin presents "official" business, speaking "ex officio" about the unexpected intersection of his own designs with God's providence.

(2) In the phrase "subita conversio," conversion means "mutatio" (this can also happen to "impii": CO 31.475 C); the suddenness of "subita," "subito" (adverb), or "repente" refers to an event "praeter spem," beyond all expectation (CO 31.78 B; 459 C; 311 B; cf. CO 48.141 C), at times also applicable to the "secure" enemy (349 B): God intervenes "in a flash." Even in the most hopeless situation, he can "restore" us (as already in the sermon of the 2nd of April, 1553, on Ps. 119) "en une minute de temps" (CO 32.614 C).

(3) Most baffling for interpreters proves to be the clause "ad docilitatem subegit." The French parallel version is more explicit: ". . . par une conversion subite il domta et rangea à docilité mon coeur . . ." (CO 31.22 C). In line with Calvin's favorite image, "dom(p)ter" and "ranger" refer to the taming of wild animals, particularly of wild horses to be placed on track by receiving a "fraenum" ("fraenare": 213 B) or bridle (CO 31.322 C; 32.639 A). Without redirection (*rectitudo legis*), the "wild horses" get lost "in flexuosas vias" (CO 32.200 C) and do not know in or out: they are caught (perplexed) in the "labyrinth" (CO 31.368 C; 32.642 A; cf. 52.447 B), tire out and finally lose their way completely, to be drowned in the "abyss" (CO 31.368 B).

(4) Calvin describes his preconversion situation as the need to be drawn "e profundo luto," "de ce bourdier si profond" (CO 31.21 C; cf. 22 C): He is "stuck in the pits." Though "labyrinth" and "abyss" overlap in the meaning of "confusion" and "disorientation," I am inclined to believe that the labyrinth of ethical directives is intended, when he still was "under the papacy" (CO 31.204 B). In the earlier commentary on Cor. I, Calvin stated explicitly that the "beginning of salvation" is "quod ex peccati et mortis labyrintho extrahimur" (CO 49.331 C). Characteristic of the "abyssus" is the most acute stage of despair which engenders such thoroughgoing "Anfechtungen" that it leaves the believer only one refuge, namely, to call on the mercy of God and his "extended hand." Though the "abyssus" is also the place where, ultimately, the hard of heart, the "protervi" or the "méchants" *(impii)* are "exterminated," the primary function of the "abyssus" is to characterize the human condition *coram Deo:* God is committed *(foedus)* to salvage from death and the sepulchre. The *Psychopannychia* (1534) documents both how early and how seriously Calvin takes this metaphor. See further the concise definition of "docilitas" in CO 7.594 B / C (1549) and the interpretation of the confessional as a threat to the certitude of salvation *(pax conscientiae),* with "the abyssus" as the final consequence: "Haec demum pax est conscientiae, sine qua null est salus, quum indubia est absolutionis fides . . . nihilo minus conficient, quam si aperte iugularetur . . . et tandem abyssus trahet . . . quisquis hunc laqueum sponte induet, sciens ac volens salutem suam proiicit." CO 7.604 A/B.

The Commentary on the Psalms was completed in 1552 and published in 1557. For a clarification of the three types "hidden" in what is usually referred to as "Commentaries"—commentaries proper (the books of Moses, the Psalms, and Joshua), lectures, and sermons—see the fundamental work by T. H. L. Parker, *Calvin's Old Testament Commentaries* (Edinburgh: T. & T. Clark, 1986), 9-41. See here also the helpful list of the known dates of completion and of publication; *ibid.,* 29.

[4] "Ego vero novitate offensus, difficulter aures praebui: ac initio, fateor, strenue animoseque resistebam. Siquidem (quae hominibus ingenita est in retinendo quod semel susceperunt instituto, vel constantia, vel contumacia), aegerrime adducebar, ut me in ignoratione et errore tota vita versatum esse confiterer. Una praesertim res animum ab illis meum avertebat, ecclesiae reverentia. Verum ubi aliquando aures aperui, meque doceri passus sum, supervacuum fuisse timorem illum intellexi, ne quid ecclesiae maiestati decederet. Multum enim interesse admonebant, secessionem quis ab ecclesia faciat, an vitia corrigere studeat, quibus ecclesia ipsa contaminata est. De ecclesia praeclare loquebantur, summum unitatis colendae studium prae se ferebant." OS 1.485.17-30.

[5] Jun Matsuura is presently pursuing the identification of volumes in the Erfurt library of the Augustinians, some containing Luther's marginal notes. See his report, "Restbestände aus der Bibliothek des Erfurter Augustinerklosters zu Luthers Zeit und bisher unbekannte eigenhändige Notizen Luthers. Ein Bericht," in *Lutheriana* ed. G. Hammer and K.-H. zur Mühlen, Archiv zur Weimarer Ausgabe, 2 (Köln: Böhlau, 1984), 315-32.

[6] *Calvin, sources et évolution de sa pensée religieuse* (Paris, 1950; revue et complétée, Geneva, 1985); Eng. trans. *Calvin. Origins and Development of His Religious Thought* (New York: Harper & Row, 1963).

[7] *Calvin. Origins and Development,* 128f.

[8] *Ibid.,* 130.

[9] *Das Grundverständnis der Theologie Calvins unter Einbeziehung ihrer geschichtlichen Abhän gigkeiten.* Beiträge zur Geschichte und Lehre der Reformierten Kirche, Band 15 (Neukirchener-Vluyn: Neukirchener-Verlag des Erziehungsvereins, 1963).

[10] *Ibid.,* 20f. Major, some forty years older than Calvin, was absent from Paris—in Scotland—between 1518 and 1526, and then taught in Sainte Barbe. See James K. Farge, *Bibliographical Register* (Toronto, 1980), 304-11; with full biography and bibliography. Cf. *Orthodoxy and Reform in Early Modern France. The Faculty of Theology at Paris, 1500-1543,* Studies in Medieval and Reformation Thought, vol. 32 (Leiden: Brill, 1985), 100-104. Major went back to Paris in 1521, just long enough to oversee the printing of his vast *History of Greater Britain,* for which he wrote a dedication at the College of Montaigu, where he had taught logic and philosophy since 1499. See Alexander Brodie, *George Lokert: Late Scholastic Logician* (Edinburgh: Edinburgh University Press, 1983), 11. Here, also, the most extensive sketch of the life and works of Major: 4-31. One could only wish for an equally substantial study of Major, for over forty years the friend of Lokert (1548).

[11] *Ibid.,* 162.

[12] *Evangelische Radikalismen in der Sicht Calvins. Sein Verständnis der Bergpredigt und der Aussendungsrede (Matth. 10).* Beiträge zur Geschichte und Lehre der Reformierten Kirche, Band 24 (Neukirchener-Vluyn: Neukirchener Verlag des Erziehungsvereins, 1966).

[13] *Ibid.,* 64, 68f.

[14] For Petrus Lombardus see *Magistri Petri Lombardi Parisiensis Episcopi Sententiae in IV Libris distinctae,* Tomus II, Liber III et IV (Grottaferrata, 1981), III d 39, 4 (153); 218-27. As Calvin's immediate background—and as explanation of any such "Thomistic" traces—Martin Bucer's 1529 Psalms commentary is most pertinent. Attached to his primarily philological interpretation of Psalm 24 is a separate "Disputatio, an Christiano liceat iurare." Thanks to the collegial help of Wim van 't Spijker (Apeldoorn), I could use the Geneva 1554 edition of Robert Stephanus, *Psalmorum libri quinque ad Hebraicam veritatem traducti et summa fide parique diligentia a Martino Bucero enarrati;* here, fol. 155f. In a number of the eighteen inserted "Disputationes" Thomas Aquinas is explicitly quoted. We know that Calvin read this Commentary at an early stage. Though he is critical of Bucer's evasiveness—he felt the first edition was inappropriately "hidden" under a pseudonym: Aretius Felinus—Calvin had high praise for this "opere alioqui praeclarissimo, si quod aliud exstat." A. L. Herminhard, *Correspondance des Réformateurs,* 4 (1536-38) (Genève-Paris, 1872), 347 (henceforth quoted as Herminjard); Letter from Geneva, 12 January 1538.

[15] *Le Jeune Calvin, Genèse et évolution de sa vocation réformatrice.* Veröffentlichungen des Instituts für Europäische Geschichte, Abteilung Religionsgeschichte, Mainz, Band 40 (Wiesbaden: Franz Steiner Verlag, 1966).

[16] *Ibid.,* 191.

[17] *Ibid.,* 192.

[18] *Ibid.,* 192.

[19] See R. R. Post, *The Modern Devotion, Confrontation with Reformation and Humanism.* Studies in Medieval and Reformation Thought, vol. 3 (Leiden, 1968).

[20] *Herrschaft—Tugend—Vorsehung, Hermeneutische Deutung und Veröffentlichung handschriftlicher Annotationen Calvins zu sieben Seneceatragödien und den Pharsalia Lucans.* Veröffentlichungen des Instituts für Europäische Geschichte, Abteilung Religion-

sgeschichte, Mainz, Band 105 (Wiesbaden: Franz Steiner Verlag, 1982), 6f. On the popularity of Lucian, who "had a new vogue in the Renaissance," see Erica Rummel in the introduction to Erasmus's "Tyrannicida," Collected Works of Erasmus, 29 (Toronto, 1989), 72. I do not pursue here the edition of Calvin's annotations to Chrysostom, both because there is no proof that they date from the period before 1536 (Calvin used the Paris edition of 1536 but quoted this Church Father already at the Disputation of Lausanne, Oct. 5, 1536), and whereas the editors emphasize the formative influence on Calvin's hermeneutics, I find Calvin drawing on Chrysostom for support as often as criticizing him for misunderstanding the text. See *Calvins Handschriftliche Annotationen zu Chrysostomus. Ein Beitrag zur Hermeneutik Calvins,* ed. A. Ganoczy und K. Müller (Wiesbaden: Franz Steiner Verlag, 1981). Lucian is quoted in the commentary *In Isaiam,* but merely to show the agreement between biblical and Roman law concerning the legal status of the married woman. CO 36.95 A/B; Com. Is. 4:1.

[21] *Ibid.,* 46, 49.

[22] I quote the relevant passage in toto to illustrate the subtle, cautious, and suggestive formulation of Ganoczy, which in a summary is easily distorted: "Calvins Berufung und Selbstvertrauen wurzeln sicher wesentlich im biblisch-christlichen Glauben. Doch diesem Glauben treten stoische Vorstellungen von einer ewigen und unwandelbaren Bestimmung und Lenkung aller Dinge hilfreich zur Seite und gewinnen nicht zuletzt dort wesentlich an Gewicht, wo der Reformator, über ein christliches Verständnis der Erwählung aller Menschen hinausgehend, eine die Berufung zum Heil kontrastierende Vorherbestimmung zum Bösen und zum ewigen Tod lehrte." *Ibid.,* 52. Apart from the fact that it is improper to leave the impression that Calvin taught a "predestination to evil," there is little in Seneca—or the later Stoic tradition in general—to suggest the providential concern of the deity with the course of individual human lives. See Marcia L. Colish, *The Stoic Tradition from Antiquity to the Early Middle Ages. II: Stoicism in Christian Latin Thought through the Sixth Century*. Studies in the History of Christian Thought, vol. 35 (Leiden, 1985).

[23] *Institutio* (1536), ch. 2; OS 1.69.31. See, however, the version in the *Institutes of the Christian Religion 1536 Edition,* translated and annotated by Ford L. Battles, revised ed. (Grand Rapids: Wm. B. Eerdmans and H. H. Meeter Center for Calvin Studies, 1986 [1975]), 43. Whereas Battles's annotations are generally helpful, the translation is unclear, imprecise, occasionally incomplete, and it times so misleading that a mere revision will not suffice. One of the reasons for these insufficiencies is a lack of familiarity with the medieval matrix of Calvin's thought.

[24] In Calvin's first theological treatise, the *Psychopannychia* (first printed in Strasbourg 1542, but designed probably in Orleans 1534) we find the formulation that will continue to be the shorthand for this "selfbinding of God": "Promisit hoc [i.e., life eternal] nobis qui fallere non potest," CO 5.194.23f. Cf. ed. Zimmerli (see below, n. 56), 50.15f. For the history of this covenant tradition, see Berndt Hamm, *Promissio, Pactum, Ordinatio, Freiheit und Selbstbestimmung Gottes in der scholastischen Gnadenlehre,* Beiträge zur historischen Theologie, 54 (Tübingen, 1977), esp. 345ff.

[25] Quite explicit, for instance, in his Com. on Phil. 4:5; CO 52.60 B. Amid the vast international literature on "Stoic" concepts of mental health and mental growth, I have found most helpful for the interpretation of Calvin Ilsetraut Hadot, *Seneca und die Griechisch-Römische Tradition der Seelenleitung* (Berlin: de Gruyter, 1969), esp. the sections on "securitas" and "tranquillitas animi"; 126-41.

[26] ". . . neque ullo unquam vel minimo indicio se Christianum esse probavit." CO 52.66 C; Com. Phil. 4:22.

[27] *Archiv für Reformationsgeschichte,* 77 (1986), 58-78.

[28] *Ibid.,* 67, 71.

[29] *Ibid.,* 77f.

[30] Luchesius Smits makes a strong case for Calvin's use of the Basel edition of Erasmus, *Saint Augustin dans l'oeuvre de Jean Calvin,* 1 (Assen: van Gorcum, 1957), 201-5.

[31] See J. M. J. Lange van Ravenswaay, *Augustinus totus noster. Das Augustinverständnis bei Johannes Calvin* (Göttingen: Vandenhoeck & Ruprecht, 1990). Two aspects of this work deserve our particular attention: (1) the extent to which Calvin personally identified with the Bishop of Hippo; (2) the extent to which Augustine became such a "key" for doctrinal discernment that it can be argued that (after 1543) Calvin founded his own "schola augustiniana" (*ibid.,* 151f., 180). It should be noted, however, that the claim made in Calvin's "totus noster" is not to be understood as total approval. Augustine is not only incidentally "wrong" in his exegesis (CO 31.310 B; Ps. 31:19; cf. CO 48.137 B; Acts 7:14) but also belongs to those sancti (Cyprian, Ambrose, and more recently Gregory the Great and Bernard) who had the right intention, but ". . . saepe aberrarunt" (CO 49.357 A; I Cor. 3:15).

[32] Oxford, 1967. See also *Jean Calvin, Three French Treatises,* ed. Francis M. Higman (London, 1970). As concerns the period before 1536, see idem, "Dates-clé

de la réforme française: le *sommaire* de Guillaume Farel et *la somme de l'escripture saincte*," Bibliothèque d'Humanisme et Renaissance, 38 (1976), 237-47; idem, "Farel, Calvin et Olivétan, sources de la spiritualité gallicane," *Actes du Colloque Guillaume, Farel . . . 1980* (Genève, 1983), 45-61; idem, "Luther et la pieté de l'église gallicane: le *Livre de vraye et parfaicte oraison*," *Revue d'historie et de philosophie religieuses*, 63 (1983), 91-111.

[33] CO 53.333 A; I Tim. 6:16.

[34] "The 'Extra' Dimension in the Theology of Calvin," in *Dawn of the Reformation: Essays in Late Medieval and Early Reformation Thought* (Edinburgh: T. & T. Clark, 1986), 241ff.; German version, *Die Reformation von Wittenberg nach Genf* (Göttingen, 1986), 266ff. See also the cautious procedure of Jean-Claude Margolin in "Duns Scot et Erasme," *Regnum Hominis et Regnum Dei,* ed. C. Berube (Rome, 1978), 89-112. Commenting on I Tim. 4:6, Calvin points out that "fidelis Christi minister" is an infinitely higher title than to be called a thousand times over "seraphici subtilesque"—the traditional designation of Bonaventure and Scouts! (CO 52.298). The selection of these two names as the standard of comparison strongly suggests that Calvin associates scholasticism with the Franciscan tradition rather than with Thomas and the Dominican tradition.

[35] A fine example of using "background" information to better grasp Calvin's intentions is E. David Willis, *Calvin's Catholic Christology. The Function of the so-called Extra-Calvinisticum in Calvin's Theology,* Studies in the History of Christian Thought 2 (Leiden: E. J. Brill, 1966).

[36] In Part I of his *The Hermeneutics of John Calvin* (Edinburgh: Scottish Academic Press, 1988), Thomas F. Torrance has presented an analysis of Calvin's "Parisian background"—Scotus, Occam, Major—that takes its point of departure in epistemology. Though rich in helpful and at times precious observations in the realm of metaphysics, this abstract "grit" proves to lack the specificity that one likes to find in historical evidence. I am particularly uneasy about "developments flowing from the teaching of Duns Scotus" that are claimed to have a direct bearing on the *Devotio Moderna* (p. 12), which in turn is said to have provided "a spring-board for a leap into the Reformation" (p. 97). In the presentation of Calvin's hermeneutics, however, Torrance's study is exemplary.

[37] CO 52.334 B/C; I Tim. 6:18. Here and in the following notes I indicate only representative passages.

[38] CO 49.343 C; I Cor. 2:14.

[39] CO 31.520 B; cf. 504 C; 523 B; Ps. 51:15; cf. Ps. 50:16; Ps. 51:20.

[40] "In summa, hoc vult Paulus, conditionem, quam per Christum consequimur, longe potiorem esse, quam fuerit sors primi hominis; quia Adae collata fuerit suo et posterorum nomine anuma vivens, Christus autem nobis attulerit spiritum qui vita est." CO 49.558 C; I Cor. 15:45.

[41] The "distinctio formalis" is a distinction "ex natura rei"—in this case "ex natura Dei"—but not "inter rem et rem" (*distinctio realis*). See the glossary in my *Harvest of Medieval Theology* (Cambridge, MA, 1963), 466. Cf. O. Muck in *Historisches Wörterbuch der Philosophie,* hrg. v. J. Ritter, 2 (Basel, Stuttgart: Schwabe Verlag, 1972), 270.

[42] CO 49.522 A; I Cor. 14:14. How far this expression "docendi causa" can take over the function of "de potentia absoluta" appears from the continuation of the definition: ". . . non quia id vel possit vel soleat contingere"!

[43] CO 31.387 C; 402 B; Ps. 38:4; Ps. 39:10.

[44] See David C. Steinmetz, "Calvin and the Absolute Power of God," *Journal of Medieval and Renaissance Studies,* 18 (1988), 65-79. It is to be noted, however, that Calvin can use himself the expression "potentia absoluta." What he opposes is the "nuda potentia absoluta" (CO 31.402 B; cf. 387 C), that is, tyranny. It is Job who—mistakenly—regards God's punishment as "puissance excessive," which threatened to submerge him in the abyss: ". . . comme s'il me vouloit abysmer." Sermon 88 on Job; CO 34.338 A/B; cf. 336 A/B.

[45] CO 36.194 C; Isa. 9:6.

[46] See Charles Partee, *Calvin and Classical Philosophy,* Studies in the History of Christian Thought, vol. 14 (Leiden: Brill, 1977). Though referring to Calvin only once, James Hankins's rich reconstruction of the Platonic discourse in the (later) Renaissance documents how unsuitable Plato is as key to Calvin: *Plato in the Renaissance,* 2 vols. (Leiden: Brill, 1990).

[47] New York: Oxford University Press, 1988.

[48] Bouwsma, *John Calvin,* 230; cf. 233.

[49] See my review "Reforming out of Chaos," *Times Literary Supplement,* 455.4 (Aug. 19-25, 1988), col. 913f.

[50] The divide is not bridged but widened by the view expressed in the extensive review of Bouwsma's *John Calvin* by William Neuser in *Historische Zeitschrift,* 250 (1990), 152-57, which I read with growing concern. Apart from the fact that it is difficult to agree with most of the propositions of Mr. Neuser—even

including his rare points of praise for Bouwsma's achievement—the (for Neuser atypical) condescending tone of the magister correcting a novice in the field does not bode well for the chances of the doctrinal school to catch up *and* thus provide a hearing for its precious tradition. For such a "hearing" see the exemplary review by Edward A. Dowey in the *Journal of the American Academy of Religion,* 57 (1989), 845-48.

[51] "Daedalus inextricabilem labyrinthum fabricavit, quo cuique sine glomere lini improperanti interclusus exitus negabatur." *The Prefatory Epistles of Jacques Lefèvre d'Étaples and Related Texts,* ed. Eugene F. Rice, Jr. (New York: Columbia University Press, 1972), 93.

[52] ". . . praedecessorum nostrorum modorum significandi . . . inextricabiles labyrinthi, quibus totum aevum absumpsere." Rice, 244.

[53] ". . . opus inquam inclitum multis ante saeculis absconditum, cuius lectio dormientes excitet, calcar addat, ad Deum convertat, ad beatorum theologiam invitet et modo quodam ineffabili disponat, nec denique per scabrosa sive ambages et inextricabiles quosdam labyrinthos Gordiive nodo legentium mentes." Rice, 292-93f. For Erasmus see Jean-Claude Margolin, "Duns Scot et Erasme" (as in n. 34 above), 91; Erasmus, *Laws Stuititiae,* Leuvensche bijdragen 4.465C-466A.

[54] "Scalae meditationis," in *Opera* (Groningen, 1614), fol. 269.

[55] For the most immediate foil for Calvin's use of the term "labyrinth," see the concluding passage of the *Praefatio* of Bucer in his Psalms commentary (1529): "Finally, I must say something about the meaning of the word 'Selah,' which is so variously discussed in prefaces of this kind; I follow the opinion of Rabbi Kimhi in order to escape these labyrinths": ". . . ut his me tandem labyrinthis expediam . . ." *Praefatio,* fol. iiiiv. For Calvin's early use and respect for this commentary, see above, n. 14. For Bucer's commentary, see W. van 't Spijker, "Bucers commentaar op de psalmen: Hebraica veritas cum Christi philosophia coniungenda," *Theologia Reformata,* 30 (1987), 264-80.

[56] For this "docilitas" see above, n. 3.

[57] *De Erfenis van Calvijn: Grootheid en Grenzen* (Kampen: J.H. Kok, 1988), 18-22. Since that time I have been pursuing other recurrent terms and phrases, such as Calvin's striking predilection for the word "porro"—his NB or the raised finger of the schoolmaster—his use of "absurd" and "absurdity" at the point were his argument slides from persuasive to coercive discourse, and the unusual frequency of "quasi" in the Commentaries and of "docendi causa" in the *Institutio*.

[58] To give an impression of the relative frequency of occurrence, I Corinthians may serve as a test case for a biblical book in which the terms do not occur and for which we have both a Latin Commentary and French Sermons (CO 49). This yields the following count: In the Commentary (in toto 277 cols.) "labyrinth" 2x, "abyssus" none. In the French Sermons (in toto 249 cols.) "labyrinth" 4x, "abyssus" 5x, but "abysmer" 14x as a verb. A second test case is provided by the first part of the Book of Psalms (Ps. 1-50; CO 31), in which the word "abyssus" does occur in the biblical text (Ps. 36:7; 42:8). Here we find on 470 cols. "labyrinth" 5x, "abyssus" 12x. Throughout the Commentaries the ratio is about 1:2, climbing close to 3 when the French verb "abysmer" is added to "abyssus."

[59] The one dimension of Calvin's abyssus" that overlaps with "labyrinth"—confusion—is articulated in two sources we have reason to believe Calvin to have known. The one is Tractatus XI of Gerson's *Super Magnificat,* where the risk of penetration of the transcendent judgement of God is articulated. See *Oeuvres complètes* 8, no. 418, ed. Mgr. Glorieux (Paris: Desclee, 1968), 485f. Gerson unfolds the "abyssus" in a twofold way, namely as the immeasurable depth of the mercy *and* the immeasurable depth of the severity of God. The other foil is again Bucer's Psalms commentary (see n. 14 above), which either descriptively relates "abyssus" to water (fol. 446, Ps. 136:7; fol. 469, Ps. 148:7) or associates it—as Gerson—with the "iudicia Dei," which should not be penetrated or—according to Bucer—cannot always be grasped: "Neque enim potest animus iusti moerore oppressus, abyssum iudiciorum Dei . . . cognitive consequi" (fol. 73, Ps. 10:1). More in line with Calvin's intensification of the meaning of "abyssus" is the exegesis of Ps. 71:11, where the word indicates to Bucer that no human being can ascend from the abyss on his own power (fol. 299).

[60] *Institutio* 1.14.14; OS 3.165.23-28. This basic discussion of the function of the devil introduces the characterization of his range of operation, which is described as the realm circumscribed "sub Dei potestate," "ipsius nutu"; OS 3.167.21f. Cf. CO 31.445 A: ". . . usque in abyssum fuisse contritos. Nam per 'locum dacronum' non intellego deserta et solitudines, sed profundissimos gurgites maris . . [C] Meminerimus ergo, hoc verum esse pietatis examen, ubi in abyssos deiecti oculus, spes, et vota dirigimus in solum Deum." Ps. 44:20. In keeping with the psychological interpretation of "space" as Christ's descent into hell, the "abode" of the Dragon is utter despair. This characteristic from of demythologization is an aspect of another encompassing shift: in the later Middle Ages—as with Luther—Satan is the anti-type of Christ. With Calvin he is the counterforce to the Holy Spirit, assailing individual sanity and communal stability of the body of Christ, the church.

[61] *Institutio* (1536), cap. V; OS 1.182.10-13.

[62] See the (later) observation on the "typically biblical way" of understanding insanity: "Insanos vocat David in Ps. 5,6 more scripturae, qui caeca cupiditate ad peccandum runt. Nihil enim magis furiosum impiis qui abiecto Dei timore, nocendi libidine ferunter: imo nulla est amentia deterior, quam Dei contemptus, quo fit ut fas omne pervertant homines." CO 31.68 C.

[63] ". . . Quum ergo porrigeret illis Deus manum, malebant sese in abysso desperationis ita demergere, ut nihil levaret eorum animos. Hanc ingratitudinem merito castigat propheta, quod adiudicent terram suam aeterno exitio cuius tamen restitutio promissa fuerat. Perinde igitur est ac si diceret, Superabit Dei misericordia et fides vestram malitiam: quantum in vobis est exstinguitis eius promissiones, aboletis eius gratiam, neque datis locum promissionibus: ipse nihilominus complebit quod pollicitus est," CO 39.48-49 (1551).

[64] "[You are] tardif à sortir de l'abysme, où vous estes plongé . . ." CO 17.585 (nr. 3089). Cited by A.M. Hugo, *Calvijn en Seneca. Een inleidende studie van Calvijns Commentaar op Seneca, De Clementia, anno 1532* (Groningen, 1957), 11. It is highly desirable that this Dutch disseration of Hugo be translated into English and/or German. Only parts of Hugo's insights could be incorporated into the critical edition, but his premature death on 24 January 1975 in Capetown prevented him from fully unfolding his life's theme. See the critical edition, *Calvin's Commentary on Seneca's De Clementia,' with introduction, translation, and notes by F.L. Battles and A. M. Hugo* (Leiden, 1969), 3-71. See also the use of "abimer" ("abysmer") for the final drowning—four times!—in the revealing "Sermon de dernier Advenement," perhaps so consistently overlooked while it is printed between the Latin Commentaries on II Thessalonians and I Timothy: CO 52.232f. The survivor should be grateful to God "q'il nous a retirez de tels abysmes . . ." *ibid.*, 229 A.

[65] CO 5.201.13f. This same concerted effort is assailed by Calvin in the traditional way as "curiosity." See the meticulous study by E.P. Meijering, *Calvin wider die Neugierde*. Bibliotheca humanistica et reformatorica 29 (Nieuwkoop: De Graaf, 1980).

[66] CO 5.201.23f.; cf. the edition of the *Psychopannychia* by Walter Zimmerli, *Quellenschriften zur Geschichte des Protestantismus* (Leipzig, 1932), 60f.

[67] Cf. *Weimarer Ausgabe* 18.685.6f. For the exact parallel with Calvin, see *Institutes* 1.17.2 (ed. 1559).

[68] Whereas Zimmerli already noticed this existential dimension (see his edition, p. 65, n. 1), he failed to see the function of Luke 8:31 in Calvin's formulation of his experience.

[69] CO 5.204.40f.; ed. Zimmerli, 67.12f.

[70] See the rhetorically powerful and personally authentic description of this heart-rending experience of the wrath of God, addressed to those who do not know this from their own experience: "Atque ut quod dictum est in universum, partibus ostendatur: si extra Deum lux non est, quae nocti nostrae luceat, ubi lux illa se subduxerit, anima certe in tenebris suis sepulta, *caeca* est. Tunc *muta* est, quae confiteri non potest ad salutem, quod crediderit ad iustitiam. *Surda* est, quae vivam illam vocem non audit. *Clauda* est, imo se sustinere non potest, ubi non habet cui dicat: Tenuisti manum dexteram meam, et in voluntate tua deduxisti me. Nullo denique vitae officio fungitur"; CO 5.204.52-205.7; ed. Zimmerli, 68.7-15. My use of italics serves to accentuate the realism and completeness of dying in the absence of God: the unforgiven sinner is all but clinically dead—all vital functions have stopped. Two conclusions are called for: (1) this is exactly what it means to be in the "abyss"; (2) once a person is awakened by saving grace, all functions of the soul are so thoroughly revitalized that clinical death can no longer induce "sleep": Conversion is the decisive "Great Awakening": ". . . mors animae alienatio est a Deo. Ergo, qui in Christum credunt, quum prius mortui essent, incipiunt vivere, quia fides spiritualis est animae resurrectio, et animam ipsam quodammodo animat ut vivat Deo . . ." CO 47.262 C; Com. John 11:25.

The briefest formulation of the "Great Awakening" is to be found in the Commentary on Isa. 19:22: "Hinc collige, conversionem esse quasi resurrectionem ab aeterna morte," CO 36.347 B.

[71] "Infernus ipse non sepulcrum sed abyssum et confusionem significet." CO 5.223.43f.; ed. Zimmerli, 97.20-22. N.B.: the "confusion," characteristic of being in the "labyrinth," is here identified with the "abyss." The "labyrinth," however, has the connotation of the self-made (CO 32.551 B) contraption (and trap) of "fantasies" or "inventions"; "abyssus" designates the human condition *coram Deo,* that is, "drowning, naked, without refuge"—were it not for the extended hand of God.

It should be noted that the content of "attritus" is anything but Scotistic. As its usage in many parallel contexts shows, it means far more than "regret," namely something in the range between "beggarized" and annihilated, broken-down (in German: *zerrieben*): CO 36.202 A; 265 C; Isa. 9:10; 13:12.

[72] CO 5.224. 13-46; ed. Zimmerli, 98.5-99.2. Zimmerli establishes that the reference to Hades is an addition of 1545.

[73] For its far-reaching consequences in Reformed orthodoxy, see the clear analysis of Richard A. Muller,

*Christ and the Decree: Christology and Predestination in Reformed Theology from Calvin to Perkins.* Studies in Historical Theology, vol. 2 (Durham, NC: Labyrinth Press, 1986).

[74] This contrast calls for further investigation. Here are some preliminary observations: Luther's description of his exegetical breakthrough by interpreting the righteousness of God as "iustitia passiva" (grasped in faith), articulated in the *Praefatio* to the first edition of his Latin works (Wittenberg, 1545), may very well have been read by Calvin. More importantly, he contradicts the validity of this interpretation. Careful to interpret the expression "iustitia Dei" always in terms of the changing biblical context, Calvin in interpreting the Psalms does relate "iustitia" to "fides," yet not to the faith of the believer but to the "active" faithfulness of God as the stable foundation of salvation. See his exegesis of Ps. 7:18 (CO 31.87 B); Ps. 22:31 (*ibid.,* 237 B). When *iustitia Dei* is interpreted as the goodness of God ("pro bonitate accipitur"), it means an attribute of God: Ps. 51:16; CO 31.520 C. Though in all these contexts, *iustitia Dei* does not refer to the punishing justice of God—which Luther rejected—it does not mean the righteousness received by faith as in the case of Luther's *iustitia passiva.* See my article in the *Festschrift* for G. W. Locher (in press).

[75] I owe a special debt of gratitude to my colleague Alan E. Bernstein, who, in the process of completing an extensive history of the concept of hell ranging from early mythology through the works of Dante, helped me in tracing the importance of Calvin's formulation. See his "Esoteric Theology: William of Auvergne on the Fires of Hell and Purgatory," *Speculum,* 57 (1982), 509-31; and "The Invocation of Hell in Thirteenth-Century Paris," *Supplementum Festivum, Studies in Honor of Paul Oskar Kristeller,* ed. J. Hankins, J. Monfasani, and F. Purnell, Jr., Medieval and Renaissance Texts and Studies, 49 (Binghamton, New York, 1987), 13-54.

[76] CO 31.21 C.

[77] Com. Ps. 51:7; as quoted by Bouwsma on 271, n. 101.

[78] Bouwsma, 231.

[79] Bouwsma, 230.

[80] The "extended hand" of God stands for his "potentia ac virtus." CO 48.260 B.

[81] The young Calvin reflects on this transition and is conscious of going his own way—"meo quidem iudicio"—in defining the biblical meaning of "poenitentia." *Inst.,* cap. V; OS 1.170.1-172.38; 171.20; cf. 172.37f. In the following section, he criticizes and rejects scholastic solutions from Lombard onward (OS 1.172.39-202.30), proving to be well informed and showing his legal training by pointing to the "pugna inter canonistas et theologos scholasticos," a rift overlooked by earlier reformers (OS 1.175.22f.). His own view of "penance," however; is worked out by correcting the respected pre-Scholastic tradition ("docti quidam viri, longe etiam ante haec tempora"; OS 1.170.1f.)—which I take to reach from Augustine and Ambrose to Hugo and Richard of St. Victor—recently edited in Paris. See the ten books of Richard's *Liber Exceptionum* (c. 1160), published in Paris 1526—under the name of Hugo—for Jean Bordier. A second part had already been published in Paris 1517 by Henri Etienne, and seen through the press by Josse Clichtove—at that time still in close touch with Lefèvre d'Étaples. See Jean-Pierre Massaut, *Critique et tradition à la veille de la Réforme en France* (Paris, 1974), 81-99. Reading Calvin's Old Testament Commentaries side by side with the *Liber Exceptionum,* one is struck by such parallels (per se inconclusive) as the frequent use of "manifestare" for the "Son of God." Cf. Calvin's favored formulation "Deus manifestatus in carne." See *Liber Exceptionum* IV, cap. 1; ed. Jean Chatillan (Paris, 1958), 267f.

The second respected tradition, which Calvin reports before choosing his own course (OS 1.171.8-10), draws on Luther and Melanchthon. The point that Calvin finds missing in the fine insights of the Fathers and the reformers is the *lasting* function of the fear of God ("verus ac sincerus timor Dei"; 171.22), first in compunction and conversion, but then in the *mortificatio.* This is not a passing stage in life—left behind in the "great awakening"—but a lasting characteristic of the Christian life: "ut morti Christi insertus poenitentiam meditetur" (172.36f.). This highly unusual formulation and spiritual directive Calvin regards as "sententia . . . simplicissima omnium"; OS 1.172.37.

[82] Jean Delumeau has articulated the related question, what it meant for the first generation(s) of Reformed Christians to live without the assurance of pardon, which medieval Europe had received in the confessional; they are now directly confronted with the wrath of God. Whereas Luther reformed this key sacrament by relating it to baptism, the young Calvin placed it in the category of "false [= misleading, diabolical] sacraments"; OS 1.162.22f. For Delumeau look beyond the too impressionistic "dossier" in *L'aveu et le pardon. Les difficultés de la confession XIII-XVIII siècle* (Paris: Fayard, 1990) to the more intriguing volume *La Peur en Occident (XIV-XVIII siècle)* (Paris, 1978), and—again less cohesive and convincing—*Le Péché et la peur, La culpabilisation en Occident XIII-XVIII siècle* (Paris, 1983).

[83] The images of "abyss" and "drowning" can indeed be related to the sacrament of penance as the second plank after baptism. Yet, Calvin's cry "de profundis" is so suggestive of the experience of death that in his case we must pay at least equal attention to the impact of dying without extreme unction. The central theme of the *Psychopannychia*—the "Great Awakening" is not interrupted by physical death—can be read as the elimination of the need of the "last rites."

The "pain" experience in the absence of absolution and extreme unction is the missing link in a volume full of insight: *Conscience and Casuistry in Early Modern Europe,* ed. Edmund Leites (Cambridge: Cambridge University Press, 1988).

[84] Sermon of 1 July 1562 on 2 Samuel 5:12-17, *Predigten über das 2. Buch Samuelis,* Supplementa Calviniana, Sermons inedits, ed. Hanns Rückert (Neukirchen: Moers, 1936-61), 122.27f.; identified by Paul Sprenger, *Das Rätsel um die Bekehrung Calvins,* Beiträge zur Geschichte und Lehre der Reformierten Kirche, Band 11 (Neukirchen: Moers, 1960), 29, n. 5.

[85] For the "blasphemy" of Virgil, CO 39.517 C; Lam. Jer. 1:8. For Horace as the "impurus Dei contemptor," CO 31.287 C; Ps. 29:4. For Seneca see CO 52.66 C; Phil. 4:19. The rich and creative French translations of the Latin poets, which I take to be Calvin's own work, deserve to be overlooked no longer: "by heart" he knew the giants he was dwarfing!

[86] See above, n. 3.

[87] For this view Calvin does not refer to tradition, but to his own way of speaking: "Librum hunc non abs re vocare soleo 'anatomen' omnium animae partium. Immo omnes . . . spiritus sanctus ad vivum repraesentavit"; CO 31.15 C.

[88] See CO 39.587 C; 586 B.

[89] See CO 39.576 B; 586 C.

[90] "Water" as a threat was available to Calvin in the exegetical tradition (Richard and Hugh of St. Victor!) and a commonplace in the Scriptures, as Bucer observed (Ps. 42:8; fol. 229). It is not surprising to find it to be prominent with the Dutchman Wessel Gansfort (1489); see my contribution to the forthcoming proceedings of the 1989 Gansfort fifth centennial, edited by A. J. Vanderjagt, Yet in some respects closer to home for Calvin is the revealing "naked" poem (1547) written by Marguerite de Navarre (1575), to whom since 1524 all "Lutherans" in France had looked for help. See the opening two lines: "Navire loing du vray port assablée, / Feuille agitée de l'impétueux vent . . ."; edited by Robert Marichal, *La navire ou consolation du Roi Francois Ier à sa soeur Marguerite* (Paris: Librairie Champion, 1956), 237. Cf. the observation of the editor in the Introduction: ". . . on ne peut relire l'Institution [of Calvin] sans se rappeler en maint endroit la *Navire*"; *ibid.,* 17. For differences see p. 21.

[91] *Institutio* (1536), cap. V; OS 1.183.23. This is Calvin's rendering of the public confession: "Domine, propitius esto mihi peccatori" (Luc. 18:13). For the uninitiated a bombastic statement of baroque proportions, for Calvin this sentence expresses at once the pain of the price of emancipation and the bold hymn of praise for the God who liberates from the "pit of despair." The other side is expressed in the 4th sermon on I Cor. 10:8f.: The "vileins," the enemies of the church, "sont dignes d'estre abysmez au profound des abysmes." CO 49.625 B.

[92] Under the unassuming title "Quelques indications bibliographiques," B. Roussel provides essential information in "Francois Lambert, Pierre Caroli, Guillaume Farel . . . et Jean Calvin (1530-1536)," in *Calvinus Servus Christi,* ed. W. H. Neuser (Frankfurt a.M., 1984), 35-52; 43f. Throughout alert to the dangers of "reconstruction," Calvin is placed in the wider context of the opponents of the Sorbonne, "ces autres acteurs de l'agitation religieuse." *Ibid.,* 48.

[93] *The Radical Reformation* (Philadelphia: Westminster Press, 1962), 104f. Even more explicitly Williams writes eighteen years later: ". . . at the University of Wittenberg Luther sustained a still more radical view, namely, that the soul dies with the body and that only at a Second Advent of Christ and as a consequence of the Last Judgement of the quick and of the dead, resurrected for that end, would salvation be experienced by the righteous." "Commentary to Lionel Rothkrug," in Lionel Rothkrug, "Religious Practices and Collective Perceptions: Hidden Homologies in the Renaissance and Reformation," *Historical Reflections,* 7 (1980), 259-64;259.

[94] From his first statement in 1522 onward, the sleeping of the souls (*dormire*) has for Luther the connotation of "quies," the "rest" so important to Calvin; *WA Br,* 2.422.4-423.44; Jan. 1, 1522 to Augsburg: To sleep, Luther writes, is *not* to be dead, but to be certain of the resurrection; WA 46.470.17f. (1538).

[95] See his letter of 11 September 1535 (from Basel to C. Fabri, i.e., Libertet), which does not prove a publication in print, but rather refers to the manuscript of which we still possess the preface, signed "Orleans, 1534," and first printed in 1542 under the title *Psychopannychia.* See Herminjard, *Correspondance des Reformateurs,* 3.349. Cf. CO 10.38f. Though we still have the letter in which Capito dissuades Calvin from publishing (CO 10.45f.; nr. 35; 1535), in 1538 Calvin points to Bucer as "qui editionem antea dissuaserat, nunc est mihi hortator"; CO 10.260 B.

[96] CO 5.222.18-20.

[97] "Nam quum dicimus spiritum hominis esse immortalem, non affirmamus contra manum Dei stare posse, aut sine eius virtue subsistere. Absint a nobis hae blasphemiae. Sed dicimus, eius manu ac benedictione sustineri . . . experimentoque discamus, quoniam ex illius magnitudine, et non ex nostra natura habemus in aeternum perseverantiam"; CO 5.222.18-22; ed. Zimmerli, 95.7-16.

[98] On closer scrutiny the tracts of Karlstadt and Westerburg invoked by George Williams do not teach "mortality" in any form or fashion. See Karlstadt's *Ein Sermon vom stand der Christglaubigen Seelen von Abrahams schoß und fegfeür / der abgeschydnen Seelen* (Wittenburg, 1522). As the preface by Wolfgang Kuch forcefully highlights, this pamphlet is directed against "das arme elende unselge fress und geytzvolck / Münch und Pfaffen" (fol. a i v); cf. fol. a iiii r. Karlstadt: What Devil permitted you to declare the departed souls to be "unselig"?: "Sy haben ain ewig leben und sein nicht todt vor gott . . ." (fol. b ii v / b ii r). The same point is made by "Gerhart Westerburch" in his pamphlet *Vom fegefeuer und standt der verscheyden selen: eyn Christliche meynung* (Cologne, 1523). Before the resurrection the departed souls are "in der Schoss Abrahe zuruwen, genomen. Dan got ist nit eyn got der verstorben [the dead], sunder der lebendigenn . . ." (fol. a iiii v). Like Luther, Westerburg can use the image of "sleep" (*eyn süsser schlaf*), not, however, as a form of death but of life "dieweyl yr leben trefflich und köstlich worden ist durch abkleydung yrer beschwerlicher leychnamen" (fol. b ii r). Since the young Calvin could have met Karlstadt in Basel, where this early ally of Luther spent the last phase of his life (1534-41) as a professor (particularly of Old Testament), it is important to note that Karlstadt also in his last publications (1535, 1538, 1540) discusses the resurrection from the perspective of the renewal (the awakening by grace) in this life. Just as Calvin did in 1534! See M. A. Schmidt, "Karlstadt als Theologe und Prediger in Basel," *Theologische Zeitschrift,* 35 (1979), 155-68; esp. 160f.

Though the Italian debate around Pomponazzi establishes indeed how "current" the problems of immortality were, they cannot explain Calvin's reference to "anabaptist authors." Since Calvin explicitly says that he had not seen these anabaptist tracts himself, he may well have relied on the information found in Zwingli's *Elenchus* of 1527. Bernard Roussel has pointed to evidence in the Orleans Preface for Calvin's use of Alphonsus de Castro, *Adversus omnes haereses,* s.v. "Anima" and "Resurrectio," published at the beginning of October 1534. Whereas this would require an exceptionally rapid transmission from Cologne to Orleans to reach Calvin, and to allow him time for reaction at the latest in December 1534, it is more likely that Alphonsus and Calvin reacted to the same common source. Most convincing, I find Roussel's suggestion that Calvin, in his attack on these as yet unknown anabaptist authors, lines up with the "politique religieuse 'allemande' du Roi" in disassociating political and heretical revolt (in Germany!) from the genuine reform intended by those falsely called "Lutherans" at the Sorbonne. See "Histoire et théologies de la Réforme," *Annuaire, École pratique des Hautes Études,* Section des sciences religieuses, 95 (1986-87), 389-97; 393.22.

[99] Ganoczy properly observes that the *Psychopannychia* is still void of anti-Roman sentiment; *Le Jeune Calvin,* 77. All the more striking, however, is the designation of Pope John as "Bishop of Rome," which I am inclined to interpret as a "Gallican" statement.

[100] CO 5.170-71.32-35; here I follow Walter Zimmerli's edition (see n. 66 above), 16-17: "Neque tamen nunc primum nascitur. Siquidem legimus arabicos fuisse quosdam huius dogmatis auctores, qui iactarent animam cum corpore una emori, in die iudicii utrumque resurgere. (Eus. eccl. histor. 1.6. c. 37—Augustinus lib. de haeresibus c. 83). Et aliquanto post tempore Joannem episcopum Romanum, quem schola Parisiensis ad palinodiam adegerit (Joan. 22. de quo Gers. in serm. pasch. priore)."

[101] See Marc Dykmans, ed., *Les Sermons de Jean XXII sur la Vision Béatifique, Texte précédé d'une introduction et suivi d'une Chronologie de la Controverse avec la liste des Écrits pour et contre le Pape,* Miscellanea Historiae Pontificiae, vol. 34 (Rome, 1973); Marc Dykmans, ed., *Pour et Contre Jean XXII en 1333. Deux Traités Avignonnais sur la Vision Béatifique* (Citta del Vaticano, 1975); cf. *La Vision Bienheureuse. Traité envoyé au pape Jean XXII,* Edite avec une introduction et des notes par Marc Dykmans, Miscellanea Historiae Pontificiae, vol. XXX (Rome, 1970).

[102] The best analysis to date is provided by Joseph N. Tylenda, "Calvin and the Avignon Sermons of John XXII," *Irish Theological Quarterly,* 41 (1974), 37-52. To his extensive references should be added the reliable summary in G. C. Berkouwer, *De Wederkomst van Christus,* 1 (Kok: Kampen, 1961), 55-60; 57.

[103] "Calvin and the Avignon Sermons of John XXIII," 47.

[104] Cf. *Institutio* (1536), cap. I; OS 1.6.3. After death the believer is no longer a pilgrim in the sense that he is no longer "in via": the *mortificatio* begun at baptism is then perfected when ". . . ex hoc vita migrabimus ad Dominum." *Institutio* (1536), cap. IV; OS 1.132.8-10.

[105] See CO 31.491 C; Ps. 49:16. CO 7.28 C / 29 A; Articuli . . . cum antidoto (1544), art. 17 cum antidoto. CO 48.319 A; Acts 9:41.

[106] "Litterae viginti novem magistrorum Parisiensium in theologia ad Philippum VI, regem Francorum, de statu animarum corpore exatarum," *Chartularium Universitatis Parisiensis,* ed. H. Denifle (Paris, 1841), 2.429-32; 429; quoted by Tylenda, 49, n. 48 (see n. 102 above).

[107] OS 5.130.23-33; *Institutio* (1543).

[108] "Brieve instruction pour armer tous bons fideles contra les erreurs de la secte commune des Anabaptistes," CO 7, col. 43-142; 127. The most extensive and reliable treatment of Calvin's lifelong debate with the "Anabaptists" is presented by W. Balke, *Calvijn en de doperse radikalen* (Amsterdam: Bolland, 1977 [1973]). Here the title page of the *Instruction* and a regest of the *Psychopannychia,* 318-23.

[109] I am grateful to the rare book department of the Universitätsbibliothek, Tübingen, which allowed me to make this comparison by providing me with the collection of early prints of Gerson's works. For the early printing history see the article on Gerson by Chr. Burger in *Theologische Realenzyklopädie,* 12.535f. In the "Prologus" to his *Supplementum* Wimpfeling acknowledges royal support for his work, which the Court must have regarded as the presentation of high French political and religious culture to the European learned world: "Novissime vero his diebus . . . alia quaedam in intimis Parrhysiensis gymnasii penetralibus ac diversis Galliae locis quaesita et nutu summae maiestatis inventa sunt, quorum nonnulla cum Gerson gallica lingua scripsisset, aut in concionibus popularibus disseminasset operae pretium fuit ilia in latinam utcunque interpretari atque transferre." Fol. I$^{v}$. The ambivalent compliment for the German student-translator expresses respect for the French original: "Si non eleganter, tamen fideliter traducta sunt." In Wimpfeling's copy—preserved in the Haguenau Stadtbibliothek (Inc. 539)—this student is identified as Johannes Brisgoicus; see Herbert Kraume, *Die Gerson-Übersetzungen Geilers von Kaysersberg, Studien zur deutschsprachigen Gerson-Rezeption* (München: Artemis Verlag, 1980), 81.

[110] L. E. Du Pin (Antwerp, 1706), 3.1204-14.

[111] ". . . pour quoy en seurplus appert la fausseté de la doctrine au pape Jehan le XXIIe qui fut condempnée aux boix de Vincennes devant le roy Philippe vostre aieul, par les théologiens de Paris, de visione beata. Et en cru plus les théologiens de Paris que la court," Jean Gerson, *Oeuvres complètes* VII*, ed. Mgr. Glorieux (Paris: Desclee, 1968), 779-93; 780. I am indebted to my Leiden colleague, G. H. M. Posthumus Meyjes, who alerted me to the complex publication history of this sermon, incompletely presented by Glorieux. For the preceding assembly at Vincennes, see his volume *Jean Gerson et l'Assemblée de Vincennes (1329). Ses conceptions de la jurisdiction temporelle de l'Église, Accompagné d'une édition critique du 'De Jurisdictione Spirituali et Temporali,'* Studies in Medieval and Reformation Thought, vol. 26 (Leiden: E. J. Brill, 1978).

[112] See Christoph Burger, *Edificatio, Fructus, Utilitas. Johannes Gerson als Professor der Theologie und Kanzler der Universität Paris,* Beiträge zur historischen Theologie 70 (Tübingen, 1986). All three terms prove to be central to Calvin's program, in his French works gathered in the one concept "profit"—the (tenuous) basis for the later Weber thesis.

[113] See Gerson's Gutachten for the King on the Reformation of the Kingdom, dated 7 November 1407; ed. Glorieux VII*, 1137-85; esp. 1183f.

[114] Herbert Kraume has particularly pursued the German reception of Gerson, and in this context dedicates a special section to the circle around Wimpfeling in Strassburg. Kraume assumes that partly due to Wimpfeling's edition, Gerson was better known at the end of the fifteenth century in Germany than in France. See his *Die Gerson Übersetzungen Geilers von Kaysersberg* (as in n. 108 above), esp. 79-90; 82. But Wimpfeling apparently also found a new readership for Gerson in France.

[115] *Oevres complètes,* ed. Glorieux, VII*, 1159f; 1160.7. Seneca, *Epistula* 37.

[116] R. J. Knecht, *Francis I* (Cambridge, 1984 [1982]), 62f.

[117] In *De Clementia,* cap. V, Seneca formulated the revealing parallel "clementia rationi accedit" amid the Stoic thesis of *misericordia* as "sickness of the soul." Understandably, this context draws Calvin's full attention—and critique!—so that we do not have his explicit response to the main clause (ed. Battles and Hugo, 360-68). His later works amply make up for this early lacuna!

[118] What is best designated as Calvin's "Parisian view" of royalism and of Gallican reform in the kingdom has recently been sharply criticized as "traditionalism," and once even explained as "manichaeism." So W. Fred Graham, who invokes Bouwsma's reconstruction of Calvin's fear of the "abyss." See "Calvin and the Political Order. An Analysis of the Three Explanatory Studies," in *Calviniana. Ideas and Influence of Jean Calvin,* ed. R. V. Schnucker, Sixteenth Century Essays and Studies," vol. 10 (1988), 51-61; 57ff. A further study of the Gallican-royalist tradition of jurisprudence seems to promise a stricter control of the evidence.

[119] In a precious, recently discovered ear-and-eye-witness report of February 2, 1534, we have the first evidence of the academic impact of the young Calvin. The Erasmian "regens" at the Collège de Beauvais in Paris, Claude Despence, attended in the Collège de Fortet some lectures by "a certain Calvin" on Seneca, and now reports that the audience—with the exception of one small-minded colleague—was impressed: "Calvinum istum nescioquem aliquoties audivi ennarantem Senecam suis commentariis illustratum in aula Forteretica, cuius eruditionem tantum non admirabitur Simon Bouterius [unknown to the editor] vix anxie eruditus . . ." J. Dupebe, "Un document sur les persécutions de l'hiver 1533-1534 à Paris," Bibliothèque d'humanisme et renaissance 48 (1986), 405-17; 406. Since the letter reports on recent events, I am disinclined to follow the editor in dating these lectures of Calvin as early as 1531 or 1532. Since Calvin could not have publicly lectured after the address by Cop (November 1, 1533), I am rather inclined to date Calvin's Seneca course in the late summer or early fall of 1533. The rest of the letter vividly documents—with rich footnotes provided by the editor—how small and vulnerable the "network" is of the Protestant underground ("évangélisme lutheranisant"). A central pawn proved to be the poet Nicolas Bourbon (*Nugae,* 1533; perhaps also the unknown author of the Placards), who was indirectly in touch with Nicolas Cop—and hence brings us as close to Calvin as hitherto possible. This may well be the time and the situation Calvin refers to in his late Samuel sermon, in which he recounts "the time of terror" in which one blow "could have silenced us" (see n. 84 above). The editor properly calls attention to the growing distance between the "Erasmian" Despence and the "Lutheran" group (also called "Gerardini" after Gerard Roussel, like Farel a radical disciple of Lefèvre d'Étaples). The academic address of Cop—with its use of both Erasmus and Luther—may have to be seen inter alia as an effort to bridge this divide and thus to forge a coalition, which in Germany had already broken down. For the development of Calvin, the probable author, this appeal to the Rotterdammer should not be taken as proof of the direction of his own loyalties. Francis Higman kindly called my attention to the fact that Claude d'Espence dedicated in May 1547 to Marguerite de France, daughter of Francois I, a "Consolaytion en adversite" to console her on the death of her father—six years later condemned by the Sorbonne: it is a straight translation of Luther's "Tesseradecas Consolatoria" (1519). See *Index des Livres Interdits, I, Index de l'Université de Paris 1544, 1545, 1547, 1551, 1556,* ed. J. M. Bujanda, F. M. Higman, and J. K. Farge (Sherbrooke: Droz, 1985), nr. 528; on the remarkable career of d'Espence "between the fronts" see nr. 527, p. 433.

[120] Josef Bohatec, *Budé und Calvin, Studien zur Gedankenwelt des französischen Frühhumanismus* (Graz, 1950), 440.

[121] CO 9.875 B. In 1530 de l'Etoile was sufficiently prominent to be drawn into the efforts of Henry VIII to find legal support on the Continent for his divorce case. See the rich dossier gathered by Guy Bedouelle and Patrick le Gal, *Le 'Divorce' de Henry VIII. Études et documents.* Travaux d'Humanisme et Renaissance, 221 (Geneva, 1987), 399.

[122] "Nicolai Chemyni Aureliani antapologia adversus Aurelii Albucii defensionem pro Andrea Alciato contra D. Petrum Stellam nuper editam Paris 1531"; cf. Bohatec, *Budé und Calvin,* 439, n. 5 and n. 6. For the legal principles of the later Calvin—with only two references to Seneca—see Bohatec, *Calvin und das Recht* (Graz, 1934). Among the works of Guido Kisch, see esp. *Erasmus und die Jurisprudenz seiner Zeit. Studien zum humanistischen Rechtsdenken* (Basel, 1960), note here the important appendix with relevant legal texts and extensive bibliography, 473-538.

[123] Myron P. Gilmore, *Humanists and Jurists: Six Studies in the Renaissance* (Cambridge, MA: Harvard University Press, 1963), 79.

[124] After a brief stay in Orleans, some thirty years before Calvin's arrival, Erasmus started to get "Heimweh" and long for the North, since—in his opinion—"Accursus, Bartolin and Baldus," that is, the faculty of law, created a climate unfavorable for the "Musae," the true spirit of humanism. Letter from Orleans, dated 20 Nov. 1500; *Opus Epistolarum Des. Erasmi,* ed. P. S. Allen, nr. 134, I (1484-1514) (Oxonii, 1906), 312.25-27. For the resonance of Budé's critique in Germany, see Gerald Strauss, *Law, Resistance and the State. The Opposition to Roman Law in Reformation Germany* (Princeton, 1986), 42f.

[125] See A. M. Hugo, *Calvijn en Seneca. Een inleidende studie van Calvijns Commentaar op Seneca, De Clementia, anno 1532,* 14 (as in n. 64 above).

[126] Ford Lewis Battles, "The Sources of Calvin's Seneca Commentary," *Studies in John Calvin* (Courtenay Studies in Reformation Theology), 1 (1965), 38-60; 56f.

[127] OS 1.21-36. Cf. as a parallel the dedication to Francis I by Zwingli, ten years earlier, of *De vera et falsa religione commentarius* (1525), *ZW* 3 (Corpus reformatorum 90), 626-37.

[128] *Institutio* (1536), cap. VI; OS 1.232.34. Robert Kingdon has repeatedly called attention to Calvin's activity as an expert lawyer in Geneva. See "Calvin and the Government in Geneva," in *Calvinus ecclesiae Genevensis Custos,* ed. W. H. Neuser (Frankfurt a.M., 1984), 49-67; esp. 59f. Cf. the seminar report "Calvinus Regislator [sic!]: The 1543 'Constitution' of the City-State of Geneva," in *Calvinus Servus Christi,* ed. W. H. Neuser (Budapest, 1958), 225-32; esp. 226.

[129] OS 1.270.17-280.15. Cf. Harro Höpfl, *The Christian Polity of John Calvin* (Cambridge: Cambridge University Press, 1982), 43ff.

[130] OS 1.36.18 and 279.40.

[131] See the conclusion of Jane Dempsey Douglass: "For Calvin a reformation requires more than preaching; it needs order." *Women, Freedom, Calvin,* The 1983 Annie Kinkead Warfield Lectures (Philadelphia: Westminster Press, 1985), 21.

[132] I find the arguments advanced by Jean Rott for Calvin's authorship of "Cop's academic address"—held on 1 November 1533 in Paris—convincing. However, since we cannot exclude the possibility of at least partial authorship by Nicolas Cop and—more generally—since we cannot determine the precise interaction between ghost-writer and public speaker, I find it advisable not to draw on this document—so important for the history of the decisive "events"—for the analysis of the *initia Calvini.* See Jean Rott, "Documents strasbourgeois concernant Calvin," *Regards Contemporains sur Jean Calvin. Actes du Colloque Calvin, Strasbourg 1964* (Paris: Presses Universitaires de France, 1965), 28-73; 42. Together with a number of other precious documents, the critical edition can be found on pp. 43-49.

[133] A year later Calvin and Capito cooperated again. Whereas Calvin wrote the Preface on the history of salvation (see below, n. 148), Capito contributed "le discours aux lecteurs juifs de la Bible," signed "V.F.C. . . . ," behind which we will have to discern "Wolfgang Fabritius Capito." As in the case of Bucer's Psalms commentary of 1529, the intended readership in France could not be reached if the police authorities could make out the name of one of the Strassburg preachers. For Bucer's role in the publication of the *Psychopannychia,* see also n. 95.

[134] "L'Eglise des refugiés de langue francaise à Strasbourg au XVI siècle," *Bulletin de la sociéte d'histoire du protestantisme français,* 122 (1976), 525.

[135] The dangers for the "reformistes," even before Oct. 3, 1525, are vividly described by Gerard Roussel in a letter dated 25.IX.1525 from Meaux to Farel: " . . . hactenus prohibuit Christi clementia." *Correspondance des Reformateurs,* ed. A.-L. Herminjard, 1 (Geneva, 1866), nr. 162, p. 391. See esp. p. 390, n. 4.

[136] See James K. Farge, *Orthodoxy and Reform in Early Reformation France,* esp. 255-68. Cf. Augustin Renaudet, *Humanisme et Renaissance* (Geneva, 1958), 214ff.

[137] See the well-documented and nuanced analysis of Michel Veissiere, *L'Évêque Guillaume Briçonnet (1470-1534). Contribution à la connaissance de la Réforme catholique à la veille du Concile de Trente* (Provins, 1986), esp. 386f.

[138] See Guy Bedouelle, *Lefèvre D'Étaples et l'intelligence des écritures* (Geneva: Droz, 1976).

[139] *Ibid.,* 131. See the conclusion, "Sans se situer nécessairement au-dessus de la melée, alors qu'il était proche des intuitions théologiques des Réformateurs et de leur interpretation de l'écriture, Lefèvre a préféré le silence qui-dit-plus que les disputes"; *ibid.,* 235. Of course Faber had been "speaking" and still "spoke" loud and clear through his *Opera* in the Dedication of his Psalms Commentary (to the eldest son of Francis I). Martin Bucer acknowledges his indebtedness and calls Faber "pietissimus ille et erudissimus senex." Psalms Com., *op. cit.* (above, n. 14), fol. iii$^r$.

[140] *Guillaume Farel 1489-1565.* Biographie Nouvelle écrite d'après les Documents Originaux par un groupe d'Historiens, Professeurs et Pasteurs de Suisse, de France et d'Italie (Neuchâtel and Paris: Editions Delachaux & Niestle, 1930); Christoph Burger, "Farels Frömmigkeit," in *Actes du Colloque Guillaume Farel,* Cahiers de la Revue de Théologie et de Philosophie, 1, 2 (Geneva, 1983), 149-50. Not only by "swearing" Calvin into service in Geneva was Farel "direct" in his vocabulary. See Michel Peronnet, "Images de Guillaume Farel pendant la Dispute de Lausanne 1536," in *La Dispute de Lausanne 1536. La théologie réformée après Zwingli et avant Calvin* (Lausanne, 1988), 133-41; 140f. We are in the fortunate position that such reading impressions can be objectified. Henry Heller's *The Conquest of Poverty. The Calvinist Revolt in Sixteenth Century France,* Studies in Medieval and Renaissance Thought, vol. 35 (Leiden, 1986), contains an important chapter, "Popular Roots of the Reformation: The Lutherans of Meaux" (1525-46) in which the social unrest and the vulnerability of the cloth industry in Meaux are spelled out. Cf. pp. 27-69. I call particular attention to Heller's discovery of the fuller Nicolas Boivin, who was interrogated after he fled the persecutions of 1525 in Meaux; Heller, 58-60. Heller's characterization of Boivin fits exactly the case of Farel: biblicism, justification by faith, the priesthood of all believers, and religious certitude: "They supply him with the means not merely of rejecting the old faith but also give him the self-confidence of a new one." *Ibid.,* 60.

[141] See his introduction to the facsimile reproduction of the edition of Simon Du Bois, *Jacques Lefèvre d'Étaples et ses disciples. Épistres & Évangiles pour les Cinquante & deux Sepmaines de l'An* (Geneva: Droz, 1964), 9-28; 13. In the following I draw on this substantial introduction with texts.

[142] Cf. the edition with introduction by M. A. Screech of *Jacques Lefèvre d'Étaples: le Nouveau Testament.* Facsimilé de la première édition Simon de Colines, 1523, 2 vols. (Paris, 1970).

[143] "Lefèvre 'Étaples est donc l'auteur de notre texte, dans le sens où c'est lui qui a fourni la traduction des péricopes et où c'est lui le maître qui, en toute humilité, a donné au travail de quatre de ses disciples l'empreinte de sa personnalité, de son style et de sa doctrine." Screech, introduction to *Épistres & Évangiles,* 12.

[144] See the text in Appendix B of Screech's introduction; *ibid.,* 41-51; 51.

[145] On the complex task of placing Dolet (1546) amid the reform currents in France, see B. Longeon, "Étienne Dolet: Années d'enfance et de jeunesse," in *Réforme et Humanisme. Actes du IVe Colloque* (Montpellier, 1975), 37-61. Of the same age as Calvin—born 1509 in Orléans—after studies in Padua, he describes in his *Commentarii Linguae Latinae* (Lyon, 1536), dedicated to Guillaume Budé, the wide variety of positions on the "(im)mortality of the soul": "Has de animae mortalitate, vel immortalitate sententias, simul varia de religione iudicia, sectasque hominum in deo colendo diversas discutimus iis libris, qui de opinione posteritati à nobis relinquentur, ut nos planè viros vixisse intelligat, non ineptiis cruciatos elanguisse"; quoted by Longeon, p. 55, n. 3. Cf. Judith R. Henderson, "Dolet," in *Contemporaries of Erasmus,* 1 (Toronto, 1985), 394-96.

[146] See the documentation for the adaptation made in the Dolet edition in Appendix A, Screech, *ibid.,* 28-40; 28.

[147] CO 53.273.

[148] Suzanne Schreiner graciously allowed me to read the galleys of her illuminating *The Theatre of His Glory* (Durham, NC: The Labyrinth Press, 1990). The function of the "theater" with Calvin deserves a separate treatment under the heading of the "rhetoric of the eyes." Since Bouwsma presented "Rhetoric" and "Theater" in two separate chapters (7 and 11), Neuser could wonder what "drama" has "letzlich" to do with Calvin's understanding of the Christian life (*art. cit.*—as in n. 50 above, p. 156). In my view the answer can be brief: "letzlich" everything! But to document this view would require a separate treatment.

[149] For Olivétan and his bible, see *Olivétan: traducteur de la bible,* ed. A. Casalis and B. Roussel (Paris, 1987). For an excellent introduction and the text, see Irena Backus et Claire Chimelli, "L'Épitre à tous amateurs," *"La Vraie Piété," Divers traités de Jean Calvin et Confession de foi de Guillaume Farel,* Histoire et Société, nr. 12 (Geneva, 1986), 17-38.

[150] Ed. Backus, 27.6f. Some ten years later (1546), after one of his frequent sharp asides against the philological deficiencies of Erasmus ("Erasmi cavillum") Calvin insists that Christ already in the desert was the *mediator and dux ecclesiae:* ". . . qui in itinere semper adfuit populo." CO 49.459 B; I Cor. 10:9.

[151] This reevaluation highlights the contrast between Calvin and the so-called city reformers. With reference to Theodore Beza, Donald Kelley has pointed to the far-reaching consequences of exile in terms of the "substitution of confessional roles for familial ones": fellow exiles became brothers and sisters. *The Beginning of Ideology. Consciousness and Society in the French Reformation* (Cambridge: Cambridge University Press, 1981), 57: Beza, not only the successor of Calvin in Geneva but also following on a similar path (Bourges, Orleans, Paris, Lausanne, Geneva), found his refugee experience reflected in Abraham's sacrifice—rather than in the trek through the desert—and could perhaps therefore describe it as free choice: I went to Geneva "in exilum voluntarium." Letter to Melchior Volmar, Geneva 12, III, 1560, no. 156, in *Correspondance de Théodore de Bèze,* ed. Henri Meylan et Alain Dufour, Tome III (1559-61), (Geneva, 1963), 47, 25.

[152] ". . . et scimus hoc esse durius, ubi quis longe abstrahitur a patria." CO 38.399 B; Comm. on Jer. 22:28. Cf. "Scimus enim durum esse exilium." CO 39.511 A; Lam. of Jer. 1:3 (1563).

[153] O. Douen, *Clément Marot . . . ,* 1.504; as above, p. 113, n. 1. The translation of Psalm 18 catches the threatened existence of the transients-in-exile in a form commensurate with what the editor calls a "véritable chef-d'oeuvre de poésie orientale." *Ibid.,* 503. See further C. A. Mayer, *La religion de Marot,* Travaux d'Humanisme et Renaissance, vol. 39 (Geneva: Droz, 1960).

**Jonathan H. Rainbow (essay 1990)**

SOURCE: "Christ and Election in Calvin's Theology," in *The Will of God and the Cross: An Historical and Theological Study of John Calvin's Doctrine of Limited Redemption,* Pickwick Publications, 1990, pp. 64-88.

[*In the following excerpt, Rainbow treats Calvin's views on Predestination in contradistinction to Arminian theologians like the seventeenth-century Frenchman Moyse Amyraut. Rainbow shows that the doctrines of Divine Election, Limited Atonement, and*

*Assurance of Salvation, are intricately knotted together in Reformed theology.*]

There is no single place where Calvin addressed the extent of Christ's redemption in a systematic fashion. The absence of such a *locus* in the ***Institutes*** has led some scholars to think that it was not important for him, but this was not the case. Calvin, unlike Bucer, was never much involved in controversies about the extent of redemption; like Augustine, his most significant statements are to be found in biblical exposition and preaching. This means for us that the evidence is strewn about, in the ***Institutes*** but also in the commentaries, the sermons, and the tracts, and I have attempted to gather together in a reasonably complete way Calvin's teaching that bears on our question. That is, above all, what needs to be done.[1]

But how to arrange the large body of evidence that emerges from Calvin's writings? Here the existence of the Amyraut thesis has tended to influence my approach. On the one hand, there is a body of evidence from the side of the Amyraut thesis, consisting of Calvin's statements about Christ's death for "all" and the "world," which needs to be evaluated. Advocates of the Amyraut thesis, as a matter of fact, have only scratched the surface here, especially in regard to Calvin's statements to the effect that souls perish for whom Christ died. To reach a valid conclusion about Calvin, it is essential to face this theological theme head-on, not simply to explain it away, but to account for its strong presence in Calvin's thought.

On the other hand, there is decisive evidence that Calvin was a limited redemptionist. Holding center stage in this group of evidence are Calvin's exegeses of the famous universalistic texts of the New Testament, John 12:32, I Timothy 2:4-6, I John 2:2, and the like. We have seen already how limited redemptionists from Augustine on handled these texts, and their importance in deciding the question was recognized by Kendall when he said that Calvin "generally leaves verses like these alone, but never does he explain, for example, that 'all' does not mean *all* or 'world' does not mean the *world,* as those after him tended to do."[2] This assertion of Kendall's was a huge mistake, and catastrophic for his whole case. As we shall see, in almost every case Calvin follows the Augustinian interpretation of the text.

The claims of the Amyraut thesis will also lead us beyond those Calvin passages that deal in some explicit way with the extento of redemption. It is claimed, for example, that Calvin maintained a universal saving will of God; that he did not link Christ's death to the decree of election, nor to Christ's work of intercession; that his doctrine of assurance was grounded in his doctrine of universal redemption. These claims take us beyond the proof-texts for or against limited redemption and demand a close look at some of Calvin's larger soteriological themes. It is with these that we begin.

Along the way we will hold Calvin's theology up against Amyraut's version of his theology (as expressed both by Amyraut and by his modern supporters), and find that the Saumur professor extensively distorted the reformer's thought.

## The centrality of the death of Christ

As I worked through the Calvin *corpus,* I was, naturally, looking for Calvin's view of the extent of redemption. Other things came into focus too, things not so much looked for as felt by sheer repetition and accumulation. One of these things was that the center of Calvin's theology was Christ.

The "quest" for the center of Calvin's theology has yielded other answers. Alexander Schweizer argued in the mid-nineteenth century that predestination was Calvin's *Centraldogma.*[3] This viewpoint has been repeated innumerable times since and has even passed into the popular consciousness. Certainly predestination was Calvin's dominant *polemical* topic.[4] Others have maintained that the doctrine of justification by faith alone formed the heart of Calvin's outlook.[5] There are good arguments for this contention as well, not least Calvin's own statement—certainly an echo of Luther's famous comment on justification as the article of the standing or falling church—that justification by faith alone is the "main hinge on which religion turns."[6]

But prominence must not be mistaken for centrality. Predestination and justification were extraordinarily important doctrines without which Calvin's theology would not be the same. Their prominence and frequency in his writings, however, was the special product of historical struggle. The deeper principle underlying both predestination and justification was for Calvin, as for the other magisterial reformers, that of *sola gratia.* Here was the chief treasure, the soul of the Reformation, and the heart of the gospel itself: salvation by God's grace alone, the radical reduction of man in his potentialities and abilities and the equally radical elevation of God in the sovereignty of his saving grace. Calvin perceived this principle to be under mortal assault, both from the side of Tridentine Catholicism with its affirmation of meritorious good works, to which Calvin counterposed justification *sola fide,* and from the side of the Anabaptists with their championing of free will, to which he counterposed predestination. The assaults on justification by faith alone and on predestination were for Calvin assaults on something that lay behind them in the theological holy of holies: the principle of grace. Salvation by grace was the treasure in the heart of the fortress, justification and predestination the outer bastions where most of the blood was spilled. Salvation by grace was the king on the chessboard, justification and predestination its queen and rooks.

But this still does not go deep enough. What does the abstract slogan *sola gratia* really embody? Calvin's answer to this, if I have absorbed anything at all from his writing and preaching, would be *Christ*. Simply Christ, incarnate, obedient, crucified, and risen. For what John Calvin really delighted to expound, lecture, and preach, when he was unencumbered with the burden of doing polemical battle with some enemy, was Christ. Christ, and the grace of Christ, is everywhere—in the commentaries, in the sermons, in the ***Institutes*** preeminently, in the Old Testament as well as the New, at the center of ethical instruction as well as soteriology, as much in the midst of the prayers of the Psalms as in the gospel narratives.[7]

Calvin was well aware of this Christological orientation of his thought, and often called attention to it explicitly. Especially did he focus in on the death and resurrection of Christ as the irreducible core of the gospel:

> For there is no part of our salvation which may not be found in Christ. By the sacrifice of his death he has purged our sins . . . by his resurrection he has purchased righteousness for us.[8]

> The principal thing he did for our salvation was his death and resurrection.[9]

Or even, at times, simply the death of Christ alone. In one place, after an eloquent recitation of the benefits which the Messiah would bestow—satisfaction for sin, reconciliation, righteousness, regeneration—Calvin stated "that all those things were fulfilled in the person of Jesus Christ crucified."[10] "We have in his death the complete fulfillment of our salvation."[11] "The whole accomplishment of our salvation, and all the parts of it, are contained in his death."[12] "His sacrifice was the most important part of his redemption."[13] The Christ of Calvin's gospel is the Christ who is "never to be separated from his death."[14] The death of Christ is his "principal office," and from "this source flow all the streams of blessing."[15] If the death of Christ is seen this way, it necessarily becomes the focal point of the believer's own apprehension of salvation: "The whole assurance of life and salvation rests upon the Lord's death."[16] Calvin could express this all with a terse and paradoxical equation: "The death of Christ is our life."[17]

It has not often been appreciated to what extent Calvin's theology was a *theologia crucis,* not only as a soteriology but as theology of the Christian life. There was in Calvin's thought, in a way that must remind us strangely of the Anabaptists themselves, the vision of the life of the church and the life of the individual Christian lived under the humility of the cross.

Theological systems rooted in moralism or metaphysics could conceivably bypass the question, for whom did Christ die? But Calvin's theology was a *theologia crucis,* with a *crux* on which the Redeemer saved men by suffering vicariously in their place. The death of Christ was, to be only a little hyperbolic, everything. So, to conclude, as a few historians have, that for Calvin the extent of redemption was a non-issue, is not only to be unaware of the history of the doctrine which we have traced (of which Calvin could not have been ignorant), but to say that Calvin did not think through his own most central tenet. Calvin had a position, which can be felt even as he speaks of the relationship of the Father and the Son in the work of salvation.

### The work of the Father and the Son

If Calvin's theology was Christocentric, it was also Trinitarian. For Calvin, the eternal ontological unity of the Godhead was the premise of the work of salvation, so that the work of each person of the Godhead—whether Father, Son, or Spirit—is also the work of the whole Godhead; the classic orthodox doctrine of the Trinity is therefore closely reflected in the divine accomplishment of salvation.

> For this reason we obtain, and, so to speak, clearly discern in the Father the cause (*causa*), in the Son the substance (*materia*), and in the Spirit the effect (*effectus*) of our purgation and regeneration.[18]

Calvin in this remark borrowed the philosophical terminology of multiple causation to describe the unity-in-diversity of the work of the Trinity. This concept posits the most intimate kind of unity between the saving purpose of the Father and the saving work of the Son and Spirit. The particular interest of this study is with the relationship of the Father and the Son, and specifically with the question: in Calvin's thought, did the saving work of the Son correspond in scope and intention to the electing work of the Father?

To appreciate the importance of this topic it is necessary to return briefly to the theology of Moyse Amyraut, who believed that the will of the Father in regard to man's salvation was twofold. There was, first, a particular, predestinating, saving will of God directed toward the elect alone and effectuated through calling and the work of the Spirit. There was also a general saving will of God directed toward every human being and effectuated through the death of Christ and the general preaching of the gospel. Amyraut called these wills "covenants," respectively, the *foedus absolutum* and the *foedus hypotheticum.* The activity of God was a two-pronged thing with a clear division of labor between the Son, as the executor of one purpose, and the Spirit, as the executor of the other. Thus, in Amyraut's theology it was possible to say both, "God desires only the elect to be saved," and, "God desires every human being to be saved." Although Amyraut formally conceded that there must be some ultimate unity between these wills, he resisted the urge to reconcile them, preferring instead to emphasize the distinction and to leave them side by side. He summed it up well in these words:

> No, my brethren, when on the one hand the word of God will teach me that he has reprobated some and consigned them to eternal punishment, and that on the other hand this same word invites them to repent, that he extends his arms to them . . . although my reason found there some things which seemed to be in conflict, although whatever effort I exert I am not able to harmonize and reconcile them, still I will not fail to hold these two doctrines as true.[19]

The pivotal point in all this is that Amyraut linked the death of Christ to the general saving will of God and not to the electing will of God. The death of Christ was thus the effectuation of the *foedus hypotheticum;* it got its intention, its *telos,* from God's will to save every human being.[20] Then, that only the elect are actually saved was the result of the outworking of the *foedus absolutum,* effectuated by the Spirit. "The Spirit makes effective to the particular believer what Christ had accomplished for the world."[21]

Amyraut claimed Calvin in support of this conception, appealing to passages in which Calvin distinguished a "secret" and a "revealed" will of God,[22] and, of course, to passages in which Calvin taught that Christ died for "all" and for the "world." Amyraut was correct that there was in Calvin the identification of a revealed will of God by which God calls every man to salvation through the preached word. This doctrine of Calvin concerning the universal offer of the gospel will be examined more closely in another connection. The substructure of this teaching, however, for all its resemblance to that of Amyraut, was not the same. For Calvin was not content to be left with a double will of God. In the ***Institutes*** (1.18.3) he energetically argued that God's will is "one and simple," and explained its apparent duality not (as Amyraut) by appeal to two covenants in the eternal counsel of God, but to the imperfection of human perception.[23] While there may appear to humans to be two wills of God, in reality there are not. The duality of the divine will was for Calvin an epistemological thing; for Amyraut it assumed an ontological existence, to the extent that it could become for him a tool for the ordering of systematic theology.

The crucial question here is whether in Calvin's theology the saving work of Christ was linked to the particular saving purpose of God the Father. Amyraut said no; others, Kendall for instance, said no. But was Amyraut actually following Calvin? To come back to our earlier question, did the scope of the redemptive work of the Son correspond for Calvin to that of the electing work of the Father?

The answer must be yes. So identical in intention are the works of the Father and the Son that the term "Savior" is interchangeable between them:

> The Father is called our Savior, because he redeemed us by the death of his Son . . . and the Son, because he shed his blood as the pledge and the price of our salvation. Thus the Son has brought salvation to us from the Father, and the Father has bestowed it through the Son.[24]

Both the Father and the Son are "Savior"; it may also be properly said that each "gave himself" for us, though in different ways, the Father by decreeing redemption from eternity and the Son by carrying it out in history.[25]

This harmonious and connected work of the Father and the Son had to do, in Calvin's theology, not with a general intention to save every human being, but with the salvation of the elect. God's saving will is at this point "one and simple"; it is directed toward the elect, and is entrusted for its accomplishment (its *materia,* to use the causal term) to Christ. At precisely this juncture in Calvin's thought, the statement of Jesus, "All that the Father gives me will come to me" (John 6:37), always an important text in the discussions of predestination, became a central theme. Calvin commented on the passage:

> Faith is not a thing which depends on the will of men, so that this man and that man indiscriminately and at random believe, but . . . God elects those whom he hands over, as it were, to his Son.[26]

This giving of souls by the Father to the Son is the language of John's gospel for what Paul would call election, as Calvin recognized. Whereas "election" and "predestination" denote mental acts, "giving people to the Son" denotes a relational act; it draws the Son into the act of election. Largely as a consequence of the Johannine language, Christ became in Calvin's view the executive, the trustee, of the election decree.

> Christ brings none to the Father but those given to him by the Father; and this donation, we know, depends on eternal election; for those whom the Father has destined to life, he delivers to the keeping of his Son, that he might defend them.[27]

The donation of the elect by the Father to the Son is thus a transaction rooted in predestination, and one that also faces the future; that Christ has been made the sole Protector of God's chosen people guarantees their final perseverance. We would surely perish

> were we not safe under the protection of Christ, whom the Father has given to be our guardian, so that none of those whom he has received under his care and shelter should perish.[28]

The Father gives the elect to the Son; the Son brings the elect to the Father; the Father wills their salvation and perseverance; the Son carries it out. All this was implied in Calvin's understanding of John 6:37, and because of the richness of the image and its appropriateness for the doctrine Calvin wanted to express, the picture of the Father entrusting the elect to Christ was an image that permeated his writing and preaching.

But where did the death of Christ, specifically, fit into this picture for Calvin? Did Christ, having received the elect as his peculiar donation from the Father, to bring them to the Father, to keep them and defend them, then proceed to give his life on the cross for every human being indiscriminately? It sounds strangely out of joint; but this is exactly what the Amyraut thesis asks that we believe about Calvin. The truth is otherwise.

"Let us therefore learn that every part of our salvation depends on [election]."[29] In Calvin's theology the free election of God was the source to which all other blessings of redemption must be traced. The dual involvement of Father and Son in election, implied in Calvin's teaching on John 6:37, suggests that Christ himself is an integral part of Calvin's doctrine of election. We turn now to an examination of Calvin's concept of the relationship of Christ to election. Here we will identify four themes: that Christ is the elector; that election is in Christ; that Christ is the executor of election; and that the assurance of election is to be found in Christ.

### Christ the elector

Calvin never lost sight of the fact that Christ, who for the salvation of men took to himself a human nature and became thereby the Mediator between God and men, nevertheless preexisted as the fully divine and sovereign second person of the Trinity. "Unchangeable, the Word [i.e. the Son] abides everlastingly one and the same with God, and is God himself."[30] Here again was Calvin's premise that the persons of the Trinity operate in unity; as eternal God, the Son necessarily participated in the decree of election.

> Meanwhile, although Christ interposes himself as Mediator, he claims for himself, in common with the Father, the right to choose . . . From this we may infer that none excel by their own effort or diligence, seeing that Christ makes himself the author of election (*electionis authorem*).[31]

The right of Christ to designate himself as the *author electionis* rests, not only upon his own personal authority as Deity, but upon the intimate sharing of function which exists between the Father and the Son, a kind of *communicatio officiarum*:

> That Christ declares himself to be the author of both [election and ordination] is not to be wondered at, since it is only by him that the Father acts, and he acts with the Father. So then, both election and ordination belong equally to both.[32]

So while it was Calvin's usual pattern of thought to ascribe election to God the Father, he could also on occasion speak of Christ as the one who "has chosen and set apart the church as his bride,"[33] and of the church as elected by Christ.[34] These references to Christ as *author electionis,* while not numerous, were direct and clear. While Calvin normally saw Christ in his servant-mediator role, he never forgot that Christ did not cease to be God, even in his incarnation.

### Election in Christ

The complexity of Calvin's thought concerning the relationship of Christ to election begins to appear even more clearly in his concept of Christ as the *locus* of election, or the one in whom election takes place. In this role Christ stands, not as the one facing man and acting sovereignly upon him, but as the Mediator standing alongside his people as they are considered by God as objects of his election.

The passage Ephesians 1:4 ("[God] chose us in him before the foundation of the world.") exercised an enormous influence on Calvin, as it had on predestinarians before him; it furnished him not only with a prooftext for the doctrine of election, but also with a Christological connection: "in him." Calvin derived from these words the principle that the union of the redeemed with Christ began "before the foundation of the world." He used this idea to push Christology back into election: Christ did not begin to function as mediator only at his incarnation, but was present and involved when the elective decree of God was made.

This doctrine suffused Calvin's writing and preaching. In the short space of one paragraph of a sermon on Esau and Jacob, he said: "God chose us before the creation of the world in Jesus Christ . . . St. Paul says that he chose us in Jesus Christ . . . Our election is founded in Jesus Christ."[35]

What did Calvin mean by this? He meant that in the act of election God regarded those whom he chose, not as they were in themselves (that is, as they would be when they were created), but as they were (or would be!) in union with Jesus Christ. It was, one might say, a matter of how God graciously chose to perceive his elect. Given this, certain things followed for Calvin.

First, election in Christ meant for Calvin that human merit was excluded, not only in the course of the individual's historical life, not only at conception and birth, but at the absolute fountainhead of salvation in the decree of God. This was Calvin's comment on Eph. 1:4:

> "In Christ." This is the second proof that the election was free; for if we were chosen in Christ, it is not of ourselves. It is not from a perception of anything that we deserve, but because our heavenly Father has introduced us, through the privilege of adoption, into the body of Christ. In short, the name of Christ excludes all merit, and everything which men have of their own; for when he says that we are chosen in Christ, it follows that in ourselves we are unworthy.[36]

This is one of the arguments with which Calvin countered the notion, urged by his antipredestinarian opponents, that election was based upon God's foreknowledge of something the individual would do as the condition for the bestowal of grace. Calvin argued that if this were the case, there would be no need for God to elect us *in Christ*. The intervention of Christ even at the point of divine election therefore excludes merit.

> Those whom God has adopted as his sons are said to have been chosen not in themselves but in his Christ; for unless he could love them in him, he could not honor them with the inheritance of his kingdom.[37]

> Now if they are elect in Christ, it follows that . . . each man is elected without respect to his own person.[38]

The doctrine of election in Christ also functioned in Calvin's theology to buttress the doctrine of perseverance, the endurance of the elect to the end in faith. Much more than a stark divine decree, election defined in this Christocentric way is the creation of an indissoluble personal bond, very much like a marriage, between Christ and the elect. To describe this elective union Calvin resorted habitually to the Pauline image of Christ as the "head" of his "members":

> We must, in order that election may be effectual and truly enduring, ascend to the head, in whom the heavenly Father has gathered his elect together and has joined them to himself by an indissoluble bond.[39]

This redemptive organism of head and members, once created, can never be torn asunder; therefore the effectuation of election is certain. The "members of Christ," once "ingrafted to their head," are "never cut off from salvation."[40]

As a result of this, the doctrine of election in Christ meant for Calvin that the whole weight of the believer's assurance of his own election must rest on Christ. If the effectuation of election flows from head to members, then the members must always look to the head. This leads us logically to the topic of assurance, which, as we will shortly see, was for Calvin Christocentric.

Calvin's doctrine of election in Christ, and particularly his insistence that God's consideration of the elect in Christ excludes merit, brings up a form of the cart-and-the-horse question: if God saw the elect in Christ as he elected them, then how did they come to be in Christ in the first place? Was election the act of God's *placing* humans in Christ, or was it—as the recently quoted statements would suggest—the act of God's *seeing* the elect already in Christ and setting their destiny? Calvin was not unaware of this question, and addressed it directly:

> Although we are elected in Christ, still in terms of order God's considering us as among his own people is first, and his making us members of Christ is second.[41]

God's determination to save came first in terms of logical order, and his determination to save through union with Christ came second. Yet both, taken together as a unity, constituted election for Calvin. Election was, to revert to the language of John 6:37, the act by which God the Father handed over a people to the Son.[42]

### Christ the executor of election

Was the Christ who was himself the elector, and in whom election took place, also for Calvin the one who carried out the decree of election by his own redemptive work? This is the most important question we have posed so far. For the Amyraut thesis *must* say no to this. If Christ is the executor of election, then his death, as the centerpiece of his work, must be for the elect.

F. Wendel affirmed that Calvin saw Christ as the executor of election.[43] R. T. Kendall, however, denied this: "The decree of election, however, is not [for Calvin] rendered effectual by the death of Christ."[44] Kendall was at this point fighting for the life of his thesis about Calvin; he realized that if Christ was the executor of election through his death, limited redemption follows as a consequence. But the texts support Wendel.

> A third time he repeats that the decree was eternal and unchangeable, but that it must be ratified by Christ, because in him it was made.[45]

The mediatorial work of Christ is that means by which God's decree was ratified (*sanciri*). And Calvin rooted this arrangement in the fact that the decree of election took place "in him." An election which took place *in* Christ is most fittingly carried out *by* Christ. Again, the same doctrine:

> [Christ] has been manifested to the world in order to ratify (*ratum faciat*) by his own work (*ipso effectu*) what the Father has decreed concerning our salvation.[46]

> For, by the coming of Christ, God executed what he had decreed.[47]

Because it was through the Mediator that God "ratifies" and "executes" his eternal decree,[48] Christ was the "channel" (*canalis*) through whom our salvation, eternally hidden in the predestination of God, flows to us.[49] And the nexus between election and the mediatorial work of Christ can be described as that between a plan and its fulfillment.[50]

Election, important as it was for Calvin, was in itself an empty act, ineffectual for the salvation of men, if not ratified and executed. Christ is the one who did this by his redemptive work. The eternal covenant of adoption, made with the elect, must be made firm "through the hand of Christ (*per manum Christi*)."[51]

Calvin made a parallel point when he spoke of Christ as the one through whom the secret purpose of God was revealed. The emphasis here was not effectuation but manifestation. God's hidden purpose was made "clear and manifest" by the appearance of Christ.[52] "The predestination of God is in itself hidden, but it is manifested to us in Christ alone."[53] The same nexus between the work of Christ and election underlies this theme. And because the manifestation of Christ in human history was the revelation of election, Christ becomes, again from this new angle, the focal point of assurance.

Yet another path into Calvin's thought on the relationship of election to Christ is his doctrine of the love of God. There was for Calvin a sense in which God "loves" all his creatures, including even the reprobate, but this love amounts in the final analysis to God's present patience with them and his bestowal upon them of many temporal blessings before the final judgment day. This concept was not akin to Wyclif's idea of "secondary benefits" of redemption; Calvin never connected the idea to the sacrifice of Christ. In this connection we might also mention that there was no trace in Calvin's theology of the idea, often ascribed to him, that worldly prosperity is a visible sign of election. God causes the rain to fall on the unjust as well as the just (Matt. 5:45). This universal "love" of God is then a kind of universal benevolence.[54] But it is not the soteriological love of the gospel which issues in the redemption and renewal of sinners. Calvin reserved the love of God in this sense for the elect alone. His salvific love is directed to "his elect"[55] and to "the whole church."[56] And the following statement is blunt: "God embraces in fatherly love none but his children."[57]

God's love in this sense was for Calvin synonymous with election. Here again the Ephesians 1 passage had a formative role in Calvin's thought since it designates the divine love as the motive for God's predestination of the elect (1:5). So Calvin often intertwined the themes of election before the beginning of time and God's love. The Father's favor is "the love with which God embraced us before the foundation of the world,"[58] and the elect are "those whom he loved before the creation of the world."[59] Furthermore, God's love, like his election (or, perhaps more accurately, because love and election are simply two aspects of the same divine act), is *in Christ.* Christ is the person in whom the elect are loved;[60] since sinners are inherently odious to God, it is necessary that God love them in the acceptability and merit of Christ, the Beloved Son.

Finally—and in this sense too Calvin's doctrine of God's love resembled his doctrine of election—God's love was expressed and effectuated through the redemptive work of Christ. He is, said Calvin, the "mirror" of God's love.[61] The love of the Father for his children cannot remain a mere sentiment; it must take expression in redeeming action.

> For how comes it that we are saved? It is because the Father loved us in such a manner that he determined to redeem and save us through the Son.[62]

The redemption which the Father effected through the Son was, then, the outworking of his special love for the elect. Calvin captured something of the New Testament linkage of the divine love with the divine gift which appears in passages like John 3:16 ("God so loved the world that he gave . . ."), Galatians 2:20 ("the Son of God, who loved me and gave himself for me"), and Ephesians 5:25 ("Christ loved the church and gave himself for her"). God loved and so he gave, and the giving of which these passages speak is specifically the giving of Christ in his sacrificial death; following this pattern, Calvin coupled God's love with the death of Christ:

> How did God begin to embrace with his favor those whom he had loved before the creation of the world? Only in that he revealed his love when he was reconciled to us by Christ's blood.[63]

> The love with which God embraced us before the creation of the world was established and grounded in Christ. These things are plain and in agreement with scripture, and beautifully harmonize those passages in which it is said that

> God declared his love toward us in giving his only begotten Son to die (John 3,16).[64]

The sense of these passages is that Christ's death is the revelation and effectuation of God's love for the elect.

According to Calvin, Christ was the executor of election. He was also, and specifically in his death, the manifestation and effectuation of the love of God for the elect. Surely, as even Kendall recognized, the logical outcome of such a Christology is the doctrine of limited redemption.[65]

Christ and the assurance of election

The role of Christ in the believer's assurance was a dominant theme for Calvin R. T. Kendall claimed that Calvin's Christocentric doctrine of assurance, based on universal redemption, was replaced in the "experimental predestinarian" theology of the English Calvinists by an introspective mode of assurance; he claimed that this change was the result of the introduction of the idea of limited redemption through Beza. "Beza's doctrine inhibits the believer from looking directly to Christ's death for assurance," he stated.[66] "Had Christ died for all, we could freely know that we are elected," he asserted; however, because of limited redemption, assurance "must be sought elsewhere than in Christ."[67] This contention needs to be tested against Calvin's own exposition of Christ's role in assurance.

Calvin's doctrine of assurance was bordered by two premises which, like the banks of a river, determined its direction and shape. On the one side lay the fact that election is secret. Calvin often reminded his hearers and readers that God's predestination, considered in itself, is inscrutable and inaccessible to human knowledge. He described election characteristically as "secret" or "hidden." As he began his treatment of election in the ***Institutes,*** he warned that those who presumptuously rush into this doctrine in order to satisfy their own curiosity will find themselves in a labyrinth.[68] Philosophical and speculative inquiries into election are ruled out. There is absolutely nothing man can do to discover his election.

On the other side lay the necessity to know one's own election. Such knowledge Calvin considered essential for spiritual health. He took a staunch stand, as a Reformation theologian, against the medieval doctrine of uncertainty which was formulated emphatically at Trent. He said, "Satan has no more grievous or dangerous temptation to dishearten believers than when he unsettles them with doubt about their election."[69] He considered it no part of piety or humility to be in doubt about one's own election. Rather, piety was, for Calvin, to be certain of it and therefore to be able to ascribe the praise for such grace to God with a confident heart. True piety flows from certainty.

So the question arises: how does the believer know something which must be known but which cannot be known through direct knowledge? Calvin asked this question himself: "What revelation do you have of your election?"[70] The word "revelation" is crucial here; it signals one of Calvin's important assumptions. If there is to be any knowledge of election, it will have to be because God reveals it, not because man has found it out in an empirical manner. But Calvin had good news: God does in fact reveal to the believer the knowledge of his election.

How? Calvin's answer to his own question was multilayered. The believer's calling—the awakening of faith which is the work of the Holy Spirit through the gospel—is incontestable evidence of election,[71] since "those whom he predestined, he also called" (Rom. 8:29). Knowledge of election is also to be sought and found only in the word.[72] But in the end it is Christ himself on whom Calvin focused his doctrine of the assurance of election. For it is Christ whom the word reveals, and it is Christ to whom the elect person is drawn through calling. To push through the implications of Calvin's theology is to find oneself again and again, and from every possible angle, face to face with Christ.

> We must always come to our Lord Jesus Christ when it is a question of our election.[73]

> How do we know that God has elected us before the foundation of the world? By believing in Jesus Christ.[74]

> Do you want then to know that you are elect? Consider yourself in Jesus Christ.[75]

Only by founding the assurance of election on Christ can the believer avoid despair on the one hand and the quagmire of speculative investigation of God's unsearchable mind on the other. Certainty of election is through Christ alone, and all who inquire into it by any other means are "insane to their own destruction."[76]

Building on this Christocentric foundation, Calvin employed a rich variety of verbal images to express the place of Christ in the assurance of election. To apprehend God's election, faith directs itself to Christ, who is the "pledge of election" (*electionis arram*).[77] Christ, that is, can be likened to the down payment or earnest money which proves the good faith of the giver and is in fact a portion of that which has been promised. The gospel, when received by believers, is an "authentic letter"—a faithful and trustworthy copy of the original document—of their election, because it is "signed" by the blood of Christ.[78] Calvin also refers to Christ's blood as a "sacred seal" (*sacrosanctum sigillum*) which erases the doubt that so often assails the believer.[79]

So Christ was for Calvin the pledge, the notarized copy, and the sacred seal of election. But the most important and common of Calvin's analogies was that of Christ as the "mirror" (*speculum*) of election. This image, as the following passage from the ***Institutes*** shows, was grounded in the concept of election in Christ. If election was in Christ, reasoned Calvin, then it is only in Christ that assurance may be found.

> But if we have been chosen in him, we shall not find assurance of our election in ourselves; and not even in God the Father, if we conceive him as severed from his Son. Christ, then, is the mirror wherein we must, and without self-deception may, contemplate our own election.[80]

The same analogy occurred frequently in the sermons,[81] once with a striking double vantage point: not only is Christ the mirror in which we behold our election, but also the mirror in which God beholds us to find us acceptable.[82] There was for Calvin, it would seem, no direct relationship between the Father and his elect. Christ stands always between.

But what did it mean that Christ is *speculum electionis*? To answer this it is possible to draw on a wealth of references to *speculum* and *miroir* in Calvin's writings to form a definition. Indeed, to read the Calvin *corpus* at any length is to be struck by how often the term comes up. In a few cases, Calvin used "mirror" in a way that was roughly equivalent to "example": the history of the church in Acts is a mirror of perseverance in tribulation,[83] and the godly family described by Paul in Titus is a mirror of chaste behavior.[84] But this was not the typical meaning. Almost always it had a deeper sense. The "mirror" in Calvin's mind was a symbolic or even a typological thing, a bearer of meaning beyond itself in which a more profound or general truth may be glimpsed. The Old Testament types, Calvin said, were mirrors of heavenly reality;[85] man is a mirror of God's glory;[86] the word is a mirror of God himself;[87] David is a mirror of Christ,[88] Jacob of the whole church of the elect,[89] nature of the glory of God,[90] and the Lord's Supper of Christ's death.[91] The physical creation, redemptive history, and the Scripture itself formed for Calvin a complex revelatory structure through which God, who is always fundamentally *deus absconditus,* wills to reveal himself. The mirrors are the vehicles of this revelation. Through them man learns about the true God in indirect ways. The knowledge of God for Calvin was always this kind of mirror-knowledge, true but indirect.

Christ himself was the mirror *par excellence*. In the person of Christ the necessity of prying into the secrets of heaven is obviated, for in his face the God who would otherwise be hidden and distant appears.[92] Christ is the mirror of God's grace,[93] of God's love,[94] of all ethical perfection,[95] and therefore of Christian conduct.[96] He stands at the very center of the revelatory structure of God. To see and to understand the Mediator is for Calvin to see and understand God, indirectly but truly.

This is the larger context of Calvin's references to Christ as the *speculum electionis*. The image is not poetic or allusive, but precise and theological. It meant in Calvin's usage that Christ is the point at which God's election pierces, as it were, through the cloud of secrecy in which God's decree is normally veiled. To behold Christ in faith is to behold one's own election. Beyond Christ it is not only unnecessary but unlawful to pry to find certainty of election. And the Chris who, seen with faith, is the mirror of election was undoubtedly for Calvin Christ crucified: "Therefore, whenever our hearts waver, let us remember that we should always go to the death of Christ for confirmation."[97] Because the election of God is revealed in the death of Christ, believers may find assurance at the cross.

The figure of Christ the Mediator loomed over the landscape of Calvin's doctrine of election like a mountain. There was literally no doctrine of election without him. He was there, at the making of the decree of election, as its co-author. He was there also as the one in whom election took place, covering the elect already, in the divine counsel, with his merit. He undertook, in history, as the incarnate God, to execute and reveal the decree of election by his life, death, and resurrection. He presents himself, through the word, as the anchor of assurance.

This all points logically to the doctrine of limited redemption. If Christ elected his people, it would seem to follow that it was for them he died. If Christ was the executor of election, it would seem to follow that his task was to redeem the elect. There was no trace in Calvin's theology of the doctrine attributed to him by Amyraut, that Christ came to carry out something other than the predestinating decree of God for the salvation of the elect. Everywhere Calvin's doctrine was that Christ's redemptive work was linked to, flowed from, and carried out the election of God.

What about Kendall's claim that Puritanism lost Calvin's doctrine of assurance because of limited redemption? On a theological level the sense of this is not clear. How can a Christ who died for everyone, even the nonelect who will perish, be a source of the assurance of election? Kendall misread both the mind and the heart of the predestinarians who advocated limited redemption. If anything is clear in theologians like Beza, Perkins, and Whitaker—whom Kendall treated—it is that limited redemption was for them *precisely a doctrine of assurance*.[98] Kendall was convinced that only a universal redemption can bring assurance to be focused on Christ. But the limited redemptionists were convinced that only a limited redemption can accomplish this. For, as they argued, if Christ died for everyone but only the elect will be saved, then there are humans for whom Christ died but who will perish anyway. So it does the troubled soul no good to know that Christ died for him; he may be "redeemed" but still on his way to hell. He still does not know if he is elect. The Puritans argued that only when the scope and intention of Christ's work corresponds to that of the Father's election does Christ function meaningfully in assurance. If I know that Christ died for me (which knowledge is, in Calvinism, imparted by the testimony of the Spirit), then I know, without further probing or speculation, that I am elect. And this is exactly what Calvin himself meant by calling Christ the "mirror of election."

*Notes*

[1] Treatments of Calvin's doctrine of election in its relationship to Christology can be found in Wilhelm Niesel, *The Theology of Calvin* (Philadelphia: Westminster Press, 1956); Paul Jacobs, *Prädestination und Verantwortlichkeit bei Calvin* (Clark, 1956); Wendel, *John Calvin;* and Muller, *Christ and the Decree.*

[2] Kendall, p. 13, footnote 2.

[3] Alexander Schweizer, *Die Protestantischen Centraldogmen in ihrer Entwicklung innerhalb der Reformierten Kirche,* 2 vols. (Zurich, 1854-56). This interpretation has been upheld more recently in David Wiley, *Calvin's Doctrine of Predestination: His Principal Soteriological and Polemical Doctrine* (Ph.D. dissertation, Duke University, 1971).

[4] For example, *Defensio sanae et orthodoxae doctrinae . . .* (1543), *CO* 6:225-404; *De aeterna Dei praedestinatione* (1552), *CO* 8:249-366; *Sur L'Election Eternelle* (1551), *CO* 8:85-118; *Brevis responsio Io. Calvini . . .* (1557), *CO* 9:253-66; *De occulta dei providentia* (1558), *CO* 9:285-318.

[5] E.g. E. Doumergue, 4:267-71.

[6] Inst. 3.11.1.

[7] Richard Muller (*Christ and the Decrees*) proposed an alternative approach to the whole question of a "Centraldogma" in Calvin's theology. He refuted the notion that either Calvin or Reformed orthodoxy had a starting doctrine from which everything else was logically deduced, and argued that the central feature of Calvin's theology was actually the tandem (or the "multiple foci") of predestination and Christology. "The predestinarian structure (the decree and its execution) and the christological structure (the Son and his manifestation in the flesh) together provide a basis for the parallel development and mutual interpenetration of the doctrines of predestination and person of Christ." (p. 38)

[8] Comm. on Acts 20:21, *CO* 48:463.

[9] Sermon on Acts 1:1-4, *CO* 48:586.

[10] Comm. on Acts 28:23, *CO* 48:569.

[11] *Inst.* 2.16.13.

[12] Comm. on John 19:30, *CO* 47:419.

[13] Comm. on Luke 24:26, *CO* 45:806.

[14] Comm. on Hebrews 9:22, *CO* 55:116.

[15] Comm. on John 1:29, *CO* 47:25.

[16] *Inst.* 4.17.37.

[17] *Inst.* 4.17.37.

[18] *Inst.* 4.15.6.

[19] Moyse Amyraut, *Sermons sur divers textes de la sainte ecriture.* 2nd ed. (Saumur: Desbordes, 1653). Armstrong's translation, p. 184.

[20] "La grace de la redemption qu'il leur a offerte et procurée deu estre egale et universelle." Amyraut, *Brief Traitté de la predestination et de ses principales dependances* (Saumur: J. Lesnier, 1634), p. 77.

[21] Armstrong, p. 177.

[22] *CO* 8:301; Comm. on II Peter 3:9, *CO* 55:476.

[23] *Inst.* 1.18.3.

[24] Comm. on Titus 1:3, *CO* 52:407.

[25] Comm. on Galatians 1:4, *CO* 50:170.

[26] Comm. on John 6:37, *CO* 47:146.

[27] Comm. on Hebrews 2:13, *CO* 55:31.

[28] Comm. on Jude 1, *CO* 55:488. Cf. also *CO* 58:66.

[29] Comm. on John 13:18, *CO* 47:311. Election is understood here by the context.

[30] *Inst.* 1.13.7.

[31] *Inst.* 3.22.7. Cf. also *CO* 47:311.

[32] Comm. on John 15:16, *CO* 47:347.

[33] Inst. 4.1.10

[34] Comm. on Luke 8:2, CO 45:356.

[35] Sermon on Genesis 25:19-22, *CO* 58:49. Calvin's Christological concept of election was in line with Bucer's. In his comments on Ephesians, Bucer stressed

that election is "through Christ," and "in Christ," and is enacted only "by the merit of Christ's blood." Cf. Stephens, p. 25.

[36] Comm. on Eph. 1:4, *CO* 51:147. Cf. also *CO* 51:269, where Calvin called Christ *le vray registre* of election.

[37] *Inst.* 3.24.5.

[38] *Inst.* 3.22.2.

[39] *Inst.* 3.21.7.

[40] *Inst.* 3.21.7.

[41] *CO* 9:714.

[42] Perhaps it is here, in connection with the topic of election in Christ, that we should mention Calvin's reference to Christ as the *object* of election. This comment (*Inst.* 2.17.1) was wholly dependent on Augustine (*De praedestinatione sanctorum liber, MPL* 44:981). Since Calvin used the idea only here, and that for a special polemical purpose, it should not be considered a major element of his view of election and Christ.

[43] F. Wendel, *Calvin,* pp. 231-2.

[44] Kendall, p. 15.

[45] Comm. on Eph. 3:11, *CO* 51:183.

[46] Comm. on John 6:38, *CO* 47:146.

[47] Comm. on I Peter 1:20, *CO* 55:226.

[48] Comm. on John 6:40, *CO* 47:147.

[49] Comm. on Matt. 11:27, *CO* 45:319.

[50] Sermon on II Timothy 1:9-10, *CO* 54:54.

[51] *Inst.* 2.6.4.

[52] Sermon on II Tim. 1:9-10, *CO* 54:59.

[53] Comm. on John 17:6, *CO* 47:379.

[54] Comm. on Mark 10:21, *CO* 45:541.

[55] Comm. on John 17:24, *CO* 47:390.

[56] Comm. on Matt. 12:18, *CO* 45:331.

[57] Comm. on Mark 10:21, *CO* 45:540.

[58] *Inst.* 2.16.4.

[59] *Inst.* 2.17.2.

[60] Cf. *CO* 45:540-41, 47:390.

[61] *Inst.* 2.12.4.

[62] Comm. on I Tim. 1:1, *CO* 52:249.

[63] Cf. *Inst.* 2.16.4.

[64] *Inst.* 2.16.4.

[65] Kendall, p. 15.

[66] Kendall, p. 29.

[67] Kendall, p. 32.

[68] *Inst.* 3.21.1.

[69] *Inst.* 3.24.4.

[70] *Inst.* 3.24.4.

[71] *Inst.* 3.24.4.

[72] *Inst.* 3.21.2.

[73] Sermon on II Tim. 1:9-10, *CO* 54:58.

[74] Sermon on Eph. 1:4-6, *CO* 51:281.

[75] *Sur L'Election Eternelle, CO* 8:114.

[76] Comm. on I John 4:10, *CO* 55:353-54.

[77] Comm. on Acts 13:48, *CO* 48:314. The Latin *arrha* and its closely related synonym *arrhabo* appear to be borrowed from the Greek *arrabon,* which Paul uses in II Cor. 1:22, 5:5, and Eph. 1:4 to characterize the work of the Spirit. The application of the term to Christ is Calvin's own idea.

[78] Sermon on II Tim. 1:9-10, *CO* 54:57.

[79] Comm. on I Tim. 6:13, *CO* 52:330.

[80] *Inst.* 3.24.5.

[81] Sermon on II Tim. 1:9-10, *CO* 54:54.

[82] Sermon on Eph. 1:4-6, *CO* 51:281-82. Cf. also *CO* 51:269.

[83] Comm. on Acts 16:11, *CO* 48:375.

[84] Comm. on Titus 1:16, *CO* 52:410.

[85] *Inst.* 2.11.1.

86 *Inst.* 2.12.6.

87 *Inst.* 3.2.6.

88 Sermon on Matt. 26:40-50, *CO* 46:854.

89 Sermon on Gen. 27:11-19, *CO* 58:174.

90 Sermon on II Thess. 1:6-10, *CO* 52:230.

91 Comm. on Matt. 26:29, *CO* 45:709.

92 Comm. on John 5:22, *CO* 47:114.

93 Comm. on Eph. 1:20, *CO* 51:158.

94 Comm. on John 15:9, *CO* 47:342.

95 Sermon on Matt. 27:11-26, *CO* 46:900.

96 Comm. on Philippians 2:9, *CO* 52:28.

97 Comm. on I Tim. 6:13, *CO* 52:330.

98 Dewey Wallace noted the proper emphasis of the doctrine of limited redemption in Puritan theology in *Puritans and Predestination* (Chapel Hill: University of North Carolina Press, 1982), p. 48.

**David L. Puckett (essay 1995)**

SOURCE: "Calvin's Exegetical Via Media," in *John Calvin's Exegesis of the Old Testament*, Westminster John Knox Press, 1995, pp. 105-38.

[*Puckett examines Calvin's judicious use of typology in interpreting the Old Testament through the eyes of the New, noting that Calvin is the first great developer of the Protestant Biblical hermeneutic of grammatical historical exegesis.*]

Christian interpreters before Calvin generally believed that the New Testament served as a reliable exegetical guide to the Old Testament. But in answering the question "What kind of guidance does it provide?" they were far from being of one mind. Origen believed that the usage of the Old Testament by New Testament writers established precedent for nonhistorical exegesis. Paul's use of [*allegoroumena*] in Galatians 4:22-24 justified (or even demanded) the use of allegorical exegesis throughout the Old Testament. The apostle Paul intended his words to be a reproach to those who did not understand the spiritual meaning of the law. "They who do not believe that there are allegories in the writings do not understand the law."[1] Theodore of Mopsuestia, on the other hand, argued that allegorists could draw no support for doing away with the historical meaning of the Old Testament from the apostle's use of [*allegoroumena*].

> There are people who take great pains to twist the senses of the divine Scriptures and make everything written therein serve their own ends. They dream up some silly fables in their own heads and give their folly the name of allegory. They (mis)use the apostle's term as a blank authorization to abolish all meanings of divine Scripture. They make it a point to use the same expression as the apostle, "by way of allegory," but fail to understand the great difference between that which they say and what the apostle says here. For the apostle neither does away with history nor elaborates on events that happened long ago.[2]

Calvin agreed with Theodore. In so doing, he placed himself in opposition to much of the Christian exegetical tradition. To Hunnius it seemed that Calvin was siding with Jews against Christians. In this chapter I will explore Calvin's exegetical reasoning in several areas in which Christian and Jewish traditions often opposed one another. He was unable to agree fully with either tradition concerning how best to handle allegory and allegorical interpretation, typology, and the interpretation of Old Testament prophecies.

ALLEGORY

Calvin believed that allegorical interpretation of scripture was superficially appealing. As it was practiced in the church, it appeared to offer a plausible explanation of scripture but could not stand up under scrutiny.

> I am aware of the plausible nature of allegories [*Scio allegorias esse plausibiles*], but when we reverently weigh the teachings of the Holy Spirit, those speculations which at first sight pleased us exceedingly vanish from our view. I am not captivated by these enticements myself, and I wish all my hearers to be persuaded of this—nothing can be better than a sober treatment of Scripture.[3]

The term *allegorical* has in modern times been commonly employed to designate an approach to interpreting the Bible that ignores the historical meaning of a text in favor of a higher or spiritual meaning. Some early Christian practitioners of allegorical interpretation do appear to have treated the literal meaning as little more than a husk that hides a spiritual kernel of truth. The task of exegesis necessitated going beyond the historical sense of the text. The basic characteristic of such allegorization, according to Greer, is that it was essentially nonhistorical. "When Gregory of Nyssa allegorizes the life of Moses into a sketch of the Christian's spiritual life, there is really nothing left of the historical events of Moses' life, even though the events are still a part of Gregory's exegesis."[4] Modern Old Testament scholars often rule out allegorical exegesis because it finds the historical meaning of the text "indifferent or even offensive" and pushes it aside to make room for the spiritual sense.[5]

Calvin appears to endorse such a negative evaluation of allegorical exegesis. He calls interpretations "allegorical" if they disregard the historical context or if they interpret the details of a biblical text apart from a consideration of the immediate literary context. Allegorical exegesis is the antithesis of historical exegesis. His severest criticism—apart from his criticism of Jewish interpreters—is reserved for those who allegorize scripture excessively. He contrasts his own method (which is concerned only with what is useful) with the allegorical approach of other interpreters (which serves simply as a display for their cleverness).[6] "Let those who choose to hunt for subtle allegories receive the praise they covet; my object is only to profit my readers."[7]

Calvin has little appreciation for the quality of Origen's exegesis, but he is fully aware that many others in the church have found Origen's approach to their liking, Origen, "by hunting everywhere for allegories, corrupts the whole of Scripture." Others have followed his example and "extracted smoke out of light." In all of this, "not only has the simplicity of Scripture [*scripturae simplicitas*] been vitiated, but the faith has been almost subverted, and the door opened to many foolish dotings."[8] In his comments on one of the most frequently used proof texts for allegorical interpretation, 2 Corinthians 3:6 ("The letter kills, but the spirit gives life"), Calvin lays the blame for the evils of allegorical interpretation at Origen's door.

> This passage has been distorted and wrongly interpreted first by Origen and then by others, and they have given rise to the most disastrous error that Scripture is not only useless but actually harmful unless it is allegorized. This error has been the source of many evils. Not only did it open the way for the adulteration of the natural meaning of Scripture [*germanum scripturae sensum adulterandi*] but also set up boldness in allegorizing as the chief exegetical virtue. Thus many of the ancients without any restraint played all sorts of games with the sacred Word of God, as if they were tossing a ball to and fro. It also gave heretics a chance to throw the Church into turmoil, for when it was an accepted practice for anybody to interpret any passage in any way he desired, any mad idea, however absurd or monstrous, could be introduced under the pretext of an allegory. Even good men were carried away by their mistaken fondness for allegories into formulating a great number of perverse opinions.[9]

Calvin does not regard allegorization as simply a foolish indulgence. It is literally diabolic. Allegorical interpretation originates with the devil (as does its polar opposite, Jewish interpretation). Allegorization is a means by which Satan attempts to undermine the certainty of biblical teaching. "We must, however, entirely reject the allegories [*allegoriae*] of Origen, and of others like him, which Satan, with the deepest subtlety, has endeavored to introduce into the Church, for the purpose of rendering the doctrine of Scripture ambiguous and destitute of all certainty and firmness."[10] The plan of Satan had been most successful.

> For many centuries no man was thought clever who lacked the cunning and daring to transfigure with subtlety the sacred Word of God. This was undoubtedly a trick of Satan to impair the authority of Scripture and remove any true advantage out of the reading of it.[11]

Calvin usually simply states that allegorical interpretations are neither solid, nor simple, nor genuine and offers no further refutation.[12] He rejects the "allegorical" application of Augustine, who made Noah's ark a figure of the body of Christ because he finds there "scarcely anything solid [*solidi*]."[13] He points out that Genesis 15:4 is often interpreted allegorically by others, "but we maintain what is more solid [*magis solidum*]."[14] In his exegesis of Daniel 7:9 he recognizes that "subtle allegories [*subtiles allegoriae*] are pleasing to many," yet he argues that one should be satisfied only with what is solid (*solidum*).[15] In his interpretation of Deuteronomy 12:4 he contrasts allegory with the solid scholarship that is needed in the interpretation of scripture.

> But my readers must now be requested not only to pardon me for abstaining from subtle speculations [*argutis speculationibus*], but also themselves willingly to keep within the bounds of simplicity [*simplicitatis*]. Many have itching ears, and in our natural vanity, most men are more delighted by foolish allegories [*inanes allegoriae*] than by solid erudition [*solida eruditio*]. But let those who shall desire to profit in God's school learn to restrain this perverse desire of knowing more than is good for them, although it may tickle their minds.[16]

Elsewhere he comments, "It seems to me far too frivolous [*nimis frivolum*] to search for allegories. We should be content with true simplicity [*simplicitate*]."[17] A simple exposition of the true sense of scripture (*simplex veri sensus expositio*) will dispose of all the subtle triflings (*futiles omnes argutias*) of those who delight in allegory.[18] He contrasts the genuine meaning (*genuino sensu*) with that of the allegorical interpreters whose chatter is entirely contrary to the prophet's meaning.[19] He declares that an allegorical interpretation is forced (*nimis coactum*) and offers in its place the genuine intention of the prophet (*genuinam prophetae mentem*) that is supported by the context.[20] Instead of embracing allegory, we "ought reverently and soberly to interpret the prophetic writings and not to fly in the clouds but ever to fix our foot on solid ground."[21]

Calvin's commentary on Galatians 4 is a pertinent text for his view of allegorical interpretation. He admits that Paul appears to interpret the story of Isaac and Ishmael allegorically, but he does not believe the passage provides any justification for Origen's method of allegorization.

> Origen, and many others along with him, have seized this occasion of twisting Scripture this way and that away from the genuine sense [*genuino sensu*]. For they inferred that the literal sense is too meagre and poor and that beneath the bark of the letter there lie deeper mysteries which cannot be extracted but by hammering out allegories. And this they did without difficulty, for the world always has and always will prefer speculations which seem ingenious, to solid doctrine. With such approbation the licence increased more and more, so that he who played this game of allegorizing Scripture not only was suffered to pass unpunished but even obtained the highest applause.[22]

When he indicates that the Old Testament story was an allegory, Paul is not suggesting that Moses intended to write it as such. He simply means that the story may be understood figuratively with no departure from the literal meaning.

> An anagoge [*anagoge*] of this sort is not foreign to the genuine and literal meaning [*genuino literae sensu*], when a comparison was drawn between the Church and the family of Abraham. For as the house of Abraham was then the true Church, so it is beyond doubt that the principal and most memorable events that happened in it are types [*typi*] for us. Therefore, as in circumcision, in sacrifices, in the whole Levitical priesthood there was an allegory [*allegoria*], as there is today in our sacraments, so was there likewise in the house of Abraham. But this did not involve a departure from the literal meaning [*a literali sensu*]. In a word, it is as if Paul says that there is depicted in the two wives of Abraham a figure of the two covenants, and in the two sons a figure of the two peoples.[23]

Paul uses the term [*allegoroumena*] imprecisely in Galatians 4. He interprets the Old Testament narrative typologically;[24] he does nothing that would undermine contextual exegesis.

Calvin observes that allegorists have tried to use other New Testament passages to support their rejection of historical exegesis. He opposes their view that Paul establishes precedent for allegorical exegesis in Romans 10:18 by interpreting Psalm 19:4 allegorically ("Their voice goes out through all the earth, and their words to the end of the world. In them he has made a tent for the sun"). "Those who have imagined that Paul departed from the literal sense [*a literali sensu*] of David's words are grossly mistaken."[25] "Those who were more reverent and proceeded more modestly in their interpretation of Scripture are of the opinion that Paul has transferred to the apostles what the psalmist had properly said of the architecture of heaven."[26] He rejects the opinion of allegorists that the writer of Hebrews allegorized Psalm 104:4 ("who makes the winds thy messengers, fire and flame thy ministers").[27] He denies their contention that Matthew 2:18 ("Then was fulfilled what was spoken by the prophet Jeremiah. "A voice was heard in Ramah, wailing and loud lamentation, Rachel weeping for her children; she refused to be consoled, because they were no more'") interprets Jeremiah 31:15 allegorically in applying it to Herod's slaughter of the male children in Bethlehem.

> This passage is quoted by Matthew, where he gives an account of the infants under two years old who had been slain by the command of Herod: then he says that this prophecy was fulfilled, even that Rachel again wept for her children. But the explanation of this is attended with no difficulty; for Matthew meant no other thing than that the same thing happened at the coming of Christ as had taken place before, when the whole country was reduced to desolation. . . . To no purpose then do interpreters torture themselves by explaining this passage allegorically; for Matthew did not intend to lessen the authority of ancient history, for he knew in what sense this had been formerly said, but his only object was to remind the Jews that there was no cause for them to be greatly astonished at that slaughter, for that region had formerly been laid waste and bereaved of all its inhabitants, as though a mother, having had a large family, were to lose all her children.[28]

In light of his often harsh critique of allegorical interpretation, it may come as a surprise that Calvin sometimes approves of what he clearly regards as an allegorical understanding of the text. One such instance is found in his commentary on Daniel 4:10-16.

> There is no doubt at all of the whole discourse being metaphorical—nay, properly speaking, it is an allegory, since an allegory is only a continued metaphor [*continua metaphora*]. If Daniel had only represented the king under the figure of a tree, it would have been a metaphor, but when he pursues his own train of thought in a continuous tenor, his discourse becomes allegorical.[29]

Metaphor and allegory belong in the same class of figures; the writers of scripture use both.

Calvin believes that many of the Old Testament promises of a future kingdom were meant to be taken allegorically. He finds an allegory in Isaiah 30:25 ("And upon every lofty mountain and every high hill there will be brooks running with water, in the day of the great slaughter, when the towers fall").

> When the prophets describe the kingdom of Christ, they commonly draw similitudes [*similitudines*] from the ordinary life of men; for the true happiness of the children of God cannot be described in any other way than by holding out an image of those things which fall under our bodily senses, and from which men form their ideas of a happy and prosperous condition. . . . But those expressions are allegorical and are accommodated by the prophet to our ignorance, that we may know, by means of those things which are perceived by our senses, those blessings which have so great and surpassing excellence that our minds cannot comprehend them.[30]

Old Testament texts that, if taken literally, promise a time of great earthly blessing for God's people, are usually given a spiritual (or allegorical) interpretation by Calvin. He usually demonstrates the validity of his spiritual exegesis by pointing out that the prophecy in question has not had a literal fulfillment. He takes the magnificent restoration of Jerusalem promised in Jeremiah 31 as a promise of the spiritual kingdom of Christ.

> Though Jerusalem before Christ's coming was eminent and surrounded by a triple wall, and though it was celebrated through all the East, as even heathen writers say that it excelled every other city, yet it was never accomplished that the city flourished as under David and Solomon. We must necessarily come to the spiritual state of the city, and explain the promise as the grace that came through Christ.[31]

He insists that, in adopting this type of spiritual interpretation, he is not guilty of twisting scripture—something he charges that the allegorists do. He is forced to the interpretation because there has been no literal historical fulfillment. He observes that anyone who looks for a literal fulfillment of the prophecy recorded in Amos 9:15 ("And I will plant them on their land and they shall no more be pulled up out of their land which I have given them") will be disappointed. The prophecy, therefore, must be fulfilled in Christ.[32]

It is axiomatic for Calvin that "whatever is foretold of Christ's kingdom must correspond to its nature and character." And what is the nature of Christ's kingdom? It is spiritual. "When Scripture, as we have seen, promises a large produce of corn and wine, an abundance of all good things, tranquillity and peace, and bright days, it intends by all these things to set forth the character of Christ's kingdom."[33] When the prophet warns of the judgment of God in Joel 2 ("I will give portents in the heavens and on the earth, blood and fire and columns of smoke. The sun shall be turned to darkness, and the moon to blood, before the great and terrible day of the LORD comes"), he intends to warn God's people not to find their happiness in this world. "The prophet here checks vain imaginations, lest the faithful should think that Christ's kingdom would be earthly, and fix their minds on corn and wine, on pleasures and quietness, on the conveniences of the present life."[34] It was never God's intention that the coming kingdom of Christ be understood as earthly.

> We must again call to remembrance what is the nature of Christ's kingdom. As he does not wear a golden crown or employ earthly armor, so he does not rule over the world by the power of arms, or gain authority by gaudy and ostentatious display, or constrain his people by terror and dread; but the doctrine of the gospel is his royal banner, which assembles believers under his dominion. Wherever, therefore, the doctrine of the Gospel is preached in purity, there we are certain that Christ reigns, and where it is rejected, his government is also set aside.[35]

The language of Isaiah 11:6 ("The wolf shall dwell with the lamb, and the leopard shall lie down with the kid, and the calf and the lion and the fatling together, and a little child shall lead them") is to be understood spiritually. "By these modes of expression he means nothing else than that those who formerly were like savage beasts will be mild and gentle, for he compares violent and ravenous men to wolves and bears which live on prey and plunder, and declares that they will be tame and gentle, so that they will be satisfied with ordinary food, and will abstain from doing any injury or harm." In defense of his spiritual interpretation, Calvin appeals to the apostle Paul, who in Ephesians 1 and Colossians 1 teaches that "Christ came to gather together out of a state of disorder those things which are in heaven and on earth."[36] The text refers to the time when men are cleansed of their depraved natures by the Spirit of regeneration.[37]

In his interpretation of Amos 9:15 he again argues that "what is said here of the abundance of corn and wine must be explained with reference to the nature of Christ's kingdom." Since this kingdom is spiritual, the blessings must also be.

> If anyone objects and says that the prophet does not speak here allegorically, the answer is ready at hand, even this—that it is a manner of speaking everywhere found in Scripture, that a happy state is painted as it were before our eyes by setting before us the conveniences of the present life and earthly blessings: this may especially be observed in the prophets, for they accommodated [*accommodabant*] their style, as we have already stated, to the capacities of a rude and weak people.[38]

Why did God communicate in allegories? Partly to prevent the ungodly from understanding the message. "We know that God sometimes spoke enigmatically [*aenigmatice*] when unwilling to be understood by the impious and disbelieving."[39] But more importantly, the enigmatic nature of the allegory was intended to induce the people of Old Testament times to listen more carefully to the prophet's message. When the prophets used ordinary language, the people often ignored their message.[40] "If the prophet had spoken simply and in his accustomed language, they would not have been so attentive."[41] God's use of allegories is a gracious condescension to the ignorance of his people. The prophets "borrow their similitudes [*similitudines*] from an earthly kingdom, because our ignorance would make it almost impossible for us to comprehend, in any other way, the unspeakable treasure of blessings."[42] "Whenever the prophets speak of Christ's kingdom, they set before us an earthly form, because spiritual truth, without any figure [*figura*], could not have been sufficiently understood by a rude people in their childhood."[43] The prophets "accommodated [*accommodabant*] their style to the capacities of a rude and weak people."[44] When God offers us the conveniences of earthly life "it is not because he wishes that our attention should be confined to our present happiness, which alone hypocrites value, and which entirely occupies their minds, but in order that, by contemplation of it, we may rise to the heavenly life, and that, by tasting so much goodness, he may prepare us for the enjoyment of eternal happiness."[45]

> Christ's kingdom and his dignity cannot be perceived by carnal eyes, nor even comprehended by the human intellect. . . . Our minds cannot naturally comprehend these things. No wonder, then, if mortals judge erroneously of Christ's kingdom, and are blind in the midst of light. Still there is no defect in the prophet's expressions, for they depict for us the visible image of Christ's kingdom, and accommodate [*accommodant*] themselves to our dullness. They enable us to perceive the analogy between things earthly and visible, and that spiritual blessedness which Christ has afforded to us, and which we now possess through hope in him.[46]

Calvin indicates that the difference between his approach and that of the allegorists is one of degree—he is moderate; they are excessive. In his commentary on Isaiah 55:13 ("Instead of the thorn shall come up the cypress; instead of the brier shall come up the myrtle; and it shall be to the LORD for a memorial, for an everlasting sign which shall not be cut off"), he distinguishes his spiritual exegesis from the allegorical approach, which he opposes. The passage is rightly interpreted as a promise of the spiritual kingdom of Christ. "When they say that these things relate to the kingdom of Christ and on that account ought to be understood spiritually [*spiritualiter*], I agree with them." But when the allegorists begin to draw meanings out of each of the particulars of the text, they have gone too far. "In expositions of that kind ingenuity is carried to excess."[47]

Calvin's principle for determining which Old Testament passages are allegories is this: if there has been no historical fulfillment of the promise, one should look for a fulfillment that is not literal. Since New Testament reality was often presented in an earthly, shadowy form in the Old Testament, it is reasonable to look for a spiritual interpretation of prophecies that were not literally fulfilled. Calvin's approach does not reflect a lack of concern for historical exegesis. On the contrary, it could be argued that his view is necessitated by that concern—specifically, by his failure to find an earthly historical fulfillment of Old Testament promises.

TYPOLOGY

Calvin's reservations about allegorical interpretation do not carry over to typological interpretation. In an exposition of Isaiah 33:17, where he argues that Hezekiah was a type of Christ, he expresses concern that someone might confuse his approach with allegorization. "Let no man imagine that I am here pursuing allegories, to which I am averse." Hezekiah, he believes, functioned as a type to lead the Jewish people to a knowledge of Christ. But this does not allow the interpreter to simply leap over Hezekiah to get to Christ.[48] In his explanation of the Old Testament sacrificial system, Calvin again distinguishes his typology from allegory. Typological interpretation of Old Testament cultic practices acknowledges that something more than purely historical interpretation is called for, yet differs from allegorical interpretation in not seeking meanings in all of the details of the ceremonies.

> All the ancient figures were sure testimonies of God's grace and of eternal salvation, and thus Christ was represented in them, since all the promises are in Him. . . . Yet it by no means follows from hence that there were mysteries hidden in all their details, since some, with mistaken acuteness, pass over no point, however trifling, without an allegorical exposition.[49]

Throughout the history of the church even opponents of allegorical interpretation have often found typology to be useful.[50] It has been adopted as a tool of twentieth-century biblical theology, and has thus escaped some of the criticism leveled at allegorical interpretation. It is considered by some to be acceptable because it is grounded in the historical meaning of the text.[51] Eichrodt argues that typology may have a legitimate role in modern exegesis.[52] Lampe agrees that legitimate historical typology is useful in understanding scripture because, while not denying the role of historical exegesis, it provides a way of emphasizing the unity of scripture.

> If we admit the unity of Scripture in the sense that it is the literature of people whose thought was controlled by a single series of images, and that it is a body of writings whose explicit or implicit theme is the people and the Covenant, and if, further, we hold that Christ is the unifying centre-point of Biblical history, deliberately fulfilling the various images presented by that literature and bringing together different threads within it to form a consistent pattern, then we have no objection to a typology which seeks to discover and make explicit the real correspondences in historical events which have been brought about by the recurring rhythm of the divine activity.[53]

Frei agrees that the unity of scripture is the underlying presupposition of typological interpretation. Typology is actually literal interpretation "at the level of the whole biblical story," and thus may be regarded as "a natural extension of literal interpretation."[54]

That Calvin made extensive use of typological interpretation has been noted by many scholars. One writer states that without typology "Calvin would not be Calvin."[55] He has been faulted for having a "weakness for typology."[56] It has been charged that he "is often in danger of letting in allegory by the back-door of typology,"[57] and that he avoids allegory only by "falling into typology."[58] It should not be surprising that one who stresses the unity of scripture as strongly Calvin does would use typology extensively.

Typology for Calvin is true prophecy, albeit shadowy and somewhat obscure.[59] God chose to accommodate his revelation to the weakness and ignorance of his people in Old Testament times by presenting spiritual truth under earthly symbols. The symbols did not set forth the full truth, but directed the people toward the truth. The symbols varied, but in almost every instance they were intended as pictures of the redeemer who was to come.[60] Calvin believes an understanding of the symbolic nature of persons and institutions is absolutely indispensable if one is to profit fully from the study of the Old Testament.[61]

In conformity with much of the Christian exegetical tradition, Calvin views the ceremonial laws of the Old Testament as shadows of the coming Messiah. "The whole cultus of the law, taken literally and not as shadows and figures [*umbras et figuras*] corresponding to the truth, will be utterly ridiculous."[62] He finds typological significance in almost every ceremony. He learns from the New Testament that the Sabbath was typical. "We learn especially from Paul that the Sabbath day was enjoined in order that the people might look to Christ; for well known is the passage in Colossians 2:16 where he says that the Sabbath as well as other rites were shadows [*umbras*] of Christ to come, and that he was the substance of them."[63] Similarly, the passover is to be understood as a type of Christ:

> It is not to be wondered, therefore, that God should now require the Passover to be one year old, and without blemish, that the Israelites might know that in order to propitiate God, a more excellent price was required than could be discovered in the whole human race; and since such excellency could much less exist in a beast, the celestial perfection and purity of Christ was shown forth by this visible perfection of the lamb, or kid. It was with reference to this also that they were commanded to keep it up separate from the rest of the flock, from the tenth until the fourteenth day of the month. As to God's will, that the side-posts and lintel should be sprinkled with blood, by this sign He plainly taught them, that the sacrifice would profit none but those who were stained and marked with Christ's blood; for this sprinkling was equivalent to their bearing each one the mark of His blood upon their forehead.[64]

He adds of the paschal lamb that "there is no doubt that by this visible symbol, he raised up their minds to that true and heavenly exemplar, whom it would be absurd and profane to separate from the ceremonies of the law."[65]

The mediatorial function of the Levitical priesthood appears to Calvin to be an obvious picture of the priestly role of Jesus Christ. "It is unquestionable that the Levitical priests were the representatives of Christ, since, with respect to their office, they were even better than the very angels; which would be by no means reasonable, unless they had been the image [*imago*] of Him, who is Himself the head of the angels."[66] He finds a foreshadowing of the work of Jesus Christ in the detailed description of the Levitical garments.

> This robe was above the oblong coat between that and the ephod, and from its lower edge hung the bells and pomegranates alternately. Although there was no smell in the pomegranates, yet the figure [*figura*] suggested this to the eyes, as if God required in that garment a sweet smell as well as a sound; and surely we who stink through the foulness of our sins are only a sweet smell unto God as being covered with the garment of Christ. But God would have the bells give a sound, because the garment of Christ does not procure favor for us except by the sound of the Gospel, which diffuses the sweet savor of the Head among all the members.

Calvin acknowledges that he has crossed the line in this interpretation from typology into allegory, so he hastens to insist that there is nothing speculative about his reasoning. "In this allegory there is nothing too subtle or far-fetched [*In hac allegoria nihil est nimis argutum, vel procul quaesitum*], for the similitude of the smell and the sound naturally leads us to the honoring of grace and to the preaching of the gospel."[67]

Although Calvin does in the case of the Levitical vestments elaborate on the particulars, as a general rule he suggests that one not seek a deeper meaning for every detail of the ceremonial law.

> Nothing is better than to contain ourselves within the limits of edification, and it would be puerile to make a collection of the *minutiae* wherewith some philosophize, since it was by no means the intention of God to include mysteries in every hook and loop; and even although no part were without a mystical meaning, which no one in his senses will admit, it is better to confess our ignorance than to indulge ourselves in frivolous conjectures. Of this sobriety, too, the author of the Epistle to the Hebrews is a fit master for us, who, although he professedly shows the analogy between the shadows of the Law and the truth manifested in Christ, yet only sparingly touches upon some main points, and by this moderation restrains us from too curious disquisitions and deep speculations.[68]

As the Levitical priesthood typifies Christ as priest, so David and his descendants typify him in his kingly role. Calvin makes both points in his commentary on Jeremiah 33:17.

> Now we know that in David was promised a spiritual kingdom, for what was David but a type of Christ [*Christi typus*]? As God then gave in David a living image of his only-begotten Son, we ought ever to pass from the temporal kingdom to the eternal, from the visible to the spiritual, from the earthly to the celestial. The same ought to be said of the priesthood; for no mortal can reconcile God to men, and make an atonement for sins; and further, the blood of bulls and goats could not pacify the wrath of God, nor incense, nor the sprinkling of water, nor any of the things which belonged to the ceremonial laws; they could not give the hope of salvation, so as to quiet trembling consciences. It then follows that the priesthood was shadowy [*umbratile*], and that the Levites represented Christ until he came.[69]

Not only David but also his royal successors typically represented Christ. Hezekiah was a type of Christ "as David and the rest of his successors also were."[70] And it was not just the pious kings of Old Testament times who served as types. All the posterity of David (and even his predecessor, Saul) represented Christ (*Christi imaginem*). In his exposition of Lamentations 4:20 Calvin explains, "Zedekiah is here rightly called the Christ of Jehovah, by which term Scripture designates all kings, and even Saul; and though his kingdom was temporary, and soon decayed, yet he is called 'the Anointed of Jehovah.' '[71] Joseph was a type of Christ.[72] Aaron was a type of Christ; the supreme power of Christ was represented in him.[73] Samson, who was set apart from his mother's womb and separated from the rest of the people by his Nazirite vow, was a type of Christ.[74] Joshua, the high priest, was a type of Christ, together with his successors.[75] Zerubbabel was a type of Christ, as one who was despised by the world, yet esteemed by God.[76] Even Cyrus was a type of Christ. In him things were foreshadowed that were ultimately fulfilled in the reign of Christ.[77]

In Jesus Christ the priestly and kingly are roles combined. The cult and government were given to ancient Israel by God so that they might not be ignorant of the basis of their salvation.

> All our salvation depends upon these two points; first, that Christ has been given to us to be our priest, and, secondly, that he has been established king to govern us. This God showed to his ancient people under figures [*sub figuris*]. The sanctuary erected on mount Zion was intended to keep their faith fixed upon the spiritual priesthood of Christ; and in like manner, by the kingdom of David, there was presented to their view an image [*imago*] of the kingdom of Christ.[78]

Calvin recognizes that he is walking a very narrow path in his use of typology. He cannot follow the Jewish approach, which denies that the ceremonies and events of the Old Testament find their ultimate fulfillment in Jesus Christ. Nor can he follow Christian exegetes who disregard the significance of Old Testament history in their eagerness to find Christ in every passage. Jewish exegetes are guilty of maliciously misconstruing the words of the Bible in order to obscure the references to Jesus Christ in the Old Testament. Christians, unfortunately, give the Jews reason to object when they sophistically apply to Christ things that do not directly refer to him.[79]

In order to stifle any Jewish protest against his typological interpretations, Calvin attempts to substantiate the validity of his approach.[80] He depends on two basic arguments: first, the New Testament writers treat Old Testament texts as prophecies that are fulfilled in Jesus Christ; second, the language does not suit the reign of David or any other Old Testament figure, yet it perfectly suits the reign of Christ.[81] These two arguments are his standard defense of typology throughout his Old Testament commentaries.

Calvin's primary argument is his appeal to the use of the Old Testament by Jesus[82] and the New Testament writers (most often the apostle Paul[83] and the writer of Hebrews),[84] yet he insists that he is able to make the case on Old Testament evidence alone. Arguments from the Old Testament itself are strong enough, he believes, to refute even those who reject the authority of the apostles. However, he doesn't think it is very productive to limit one's arguments to the Old Testament. He has little hope of convincing a skeptical Jew, but he does believe that his reasoning may strengthen the faith of the Christian who is perplexed by Jewish arguments. He suggests that when the language of the Old Testament writer does not seem appropriate for the Old Testament setting, it is normally a clue that the writer is presenting a type. The language of joyful submission to the king in Psalm 47 ("Clap your hands, all ye peoples; shout unto God with the voice of triumph") fits neither David nor Solomon. "Many nations were tributary to David, and to his son Solomon, but while they were so, they ceased not, at the same time, to murmur, and bore impatiently the yoke which was imposed upon them."[85] Isaiah 16:5 ("Then a throne will be established in steadfast love and on it will sit in faithfulness in the tent of David one who judges and seeks justice and is swift to do righteousness") was taken by the Jews as a prophecy of restoration under Hezekiah, but "the Psalmist is clearly speaking of a more important restoration of the Church than that which occurred in Hezekiah's reign."[86] In his exposition of Isaiah 33:6, Calvin writes that the kingdom of Hezekiah was "but a slender straw of the kingdom of Christ."[87] "In Christ alone is found the stability of that frail kingdom."[88]

Apart from the question of the size and strength of the kingdom, there are other descriptions that make little sense if applied to an Old Testament person or office but seem to fit Christ perfectly. The description of the Levitical priesthood as even better than angels certainly must be viewed typologically.[89] The qualities attributed to David in Jeremiah 33:17 could not fit any earthly king or priest: one who can reconcile God to men; one who can make atonement for sins; one who can quiet troubled consciences by giving them the hope of salvation.[90]

Finally, some Old Testament practices are simply absurd unless they are conceived as types—the Old Testament sacrificial system, for instance. In his exposition of Exodus 12:21, Calvin asks "what could be more childish than to offer the blood of an animal as a protection against the hand of God, or to seek from thence a ground of safety?"[91] In the same commentary he writes, "Surely if Christ be put out of sight, all the sacrifices that may be offered differ in no respect from mere profane butchery."[92] Only a typological fulfillment could explain why God says in Psalm 40:6 that sacrifices are of no value. Apart from leading people higher to the knowledge of the spiritual fulfillment in Christ, they were of no use.[93]

Although Calvin rarely appeals to the immediate literary context to justify his typological interpretations, he does do so on at least one occasion. Psalm 45 cannot refer primarily to Solomon because the context will not allow it. "As the Jews and other ungodly men refuse to submit cordially to the force of truth, it is important to show briefly from the context itself [*ex contextu*], the principal reasons from which it appears that some of the things here spoken are not applicable fully and perfectly to Solomon."[94]

Most of Calvin's arguments justifying typological exegesis are intended to support the faith of Christians in the face of Jewish objections to a christological reading of the Old Testament. But many Christians have no difficulty accepting the reality of Old Testament prophecies of Christ. More often their problem is that they see little else. He sometimes has to justify a typological interpretation to those who want to interpret a text as an explicit prophecy of Christ with no contextual referent. He is embarrassed by his fellow Christians' views concerning the referent of Psalm 72.

> Those who would interpret it simply as a prophecy of the kingdom of Christ, seem to put a construction upon the words which does violence to them; and then we must always beware of giving the Jews occasion of making an outcry, as if it were our purpose, sophistically, to apply to Christ those things which do not directly refer to him. . . . What is here spoken of everlasting dominion cannot be limited to one man, or to a few, nor even to twenty ages; but there is pointed out the succession which had its end and complete accomplishment in Christ.[95]

In his interpretation of Isaiah 61:1 ("The Spirit of the LORD God is upon me, because the LORD has anointed me to bring good tidings to the afflicted; he has sent me to bind up the brokenhearted, to proclaim liberty to the captives, and the opening of the prison to those who are bound") he again displays his sensitivity to criticism by the Jews.

> As Christ explains this passage with reference to himself (Luke 4:18), so commentators limit it to him without hesitation, and lay down this principle, that Christ is introduced as speaking, as if the whole passage related to him alone. The Jews laugh at this, as an ill-advised application to Christ of that which is equally applicable to other prophets.[96]

He counsels his fellow Christians that prophecy need not deny a historical referent in Old Testament times.[97] That is just the point with typology. It has an Old Testament referent, yet its perfect fulfillment comes later in the person of Christ. This approach allows Calvin to guard the unity of scripture without requiring him to discard historical exegesis.[98]

Calvin justifies his typological approach against both Jewish and Christian misinterpretations. The Jewish approach robs Jesus Christ of his honor; the Christian approach robs the Old Testament of significance for its original audience. A mediating position is necessary. His interpretations of Psalm 2, Psalm 22, Psalm 89, and Psalm 110 provide excellent examples of his method of exegetical reasoning as he tries to avoid the pitfalls often encountered by Jewish and Christian interpreters.

Calvin sees David in Psalm 2 boasting that his kingdom, though assailed by powerful enemies, will reach to the ends of the earth and last forever. All this he insists "is typical and contains a prophecy concerning the future kingdom of Christ [*Caeterum hic typus vaticinium continet de futuro Christi regno*]."

> As David's temporal kingdom was a kind of earnest to God's ancient people of the eternal kingdom, which at length was truly established in the person of Christ, those things which David declares concerning himself are not violently or even allegorically [*violenter vel allegorice*] applied to Christ but were truly predicted concerning him. If we attentively consider the nature of the kingdom, we will perceive that it would be absurd to overlook the end or scope [*fine vel scopo*], and to rest in the mere shadow [*umbra*].[99]

Calvin's proof of the correctness of a typological interpretation of the psalm begins with an appeal to the New Testament. "That the kingdom of Christ is here described by the spirit of prophecy is sufficiently attested to us by the apostles, who seeing the ungodly conspiring against Christ, arm themselves in prayer with this doctrine."

Calvin believes that the New Testament writer's use of Psalm 2 is an adequate demonstration that the psalm should be understood typologically. But apart from this explicit citation, it is still possible to prove that the psalm refers to Christ. "To place our faith beyond the reach of all cavils, it is plainly made manifest from all the prophets that those things which David testified concerning his own kingdom are properly applicable to Christ."[100] The language of verse 6 ("I have anointed my king upon my holy hill of Zion") has reference to David, yet more appropriately to Christ.

> Although David in these words had a regard to the promise of God, and recalled the attention of himself and others to it, yet, at the same time, he meant to signify that his own reign is holy and inseparably connected with the temple of God. But this applies more appropriately to the kingdom of Christ, which we know to be both spiritual and joined to the priesthood.[101]

Verse 7 ("I will tell of the decree of the LORD: He said to me, 'You are my son, today I have begotten you'") again fits Christ much better than David. David "protests that he did not come to the throne without a sure and clear proof of his calling. . . . But this was more truly fulfilled in Christ, and doubtless, David, under the influence of the spirit of prophecy, had special reference to him." David "could with some propriety be called the son of God on account of his royal dignity."

> But here God, by the singularly high title with which he honours David, exalts him not only above all mortal men, but even above the angels. . . . David, individually considered, was inferior to the angels, but in so far as he represented the person of Christ, he is with good reason preferred far above them. By the Son of God in this place we are therefore not to understand one son among many, but his only begotten Son.[102]

The language of verse 8 ("Ask of me, and I will give thee the heathen for thine inheritance, and the uttermost parts of the earth for thy possession") cannot possibly be understood as fulfilled in the person of David. He had many great victories and conquered other nations, yet David's empire was not large compared with other monarchies. "Unless, therefore, we suppose this prophecy concerning the vast extent of the kingdom to have been uttered in vain and falsely, we must apply it to Christ, who alone has subdued the whole world to himself, and embraced all lands and nations under his dominion."[103] The language of verse 9 ("Thou shalt break them with a rod of iron, and dash them in pieces like a potter's vessel") also demands fulfillment in someone other than David. While it is true that David vanquished many enemies through military force, yet "the prediction is more fully verified in Christ, who, neither by sword nor spear, but by the breath of his mouth, smites the ungodly even to their utter destruction."[104]

For Calvin, Psalm 22 was unquestionably a prophecy of Christ.[105] The psalm opens with the words "My God! my God! why have you forsaken me?"—words which, according to Matthew 27:46, were uttered by the Savior while he was suffering on the cross. Calvin complains that older interpreters in their overenthusiasm for showing how the psalm teaches about Christ, could not even wait until they got beyond the psalm's heading before flying off into allegorical excesses. "They thought that Christ would not be sufficiently dignified and honored unless, putting a mystical or allegorical sense upon the word 'hind,' they viewed it as pointing out the various things which are included in a sacrifice." Calvin finds nothing solid (*nihil solidi*) in these subtleties. He opts for a more simple (*simplicius*) and genuine (*genuinum*) interpretation. The word *hind,* he suggests, is the beginning of some common psalm, and has no relation whatever to the subject matter.[106]

According to Calvin, David in Psalm 22 "sets before us, in his own person, a type of Christ." David understood "by the Spirit of Prophecy" that the things of which he wrote were true of the humiliation of Christ that took place prior to his exaltation.[107] Calvin insists he can prove that in this psalm "under the type [*typo*] of David, Christ has been shadowed forth [*adumbra-*

*tum*]."[108] He explains that he is not trying to convince the Jews that David is a type of Christ. (They are too obstinate and opinionated to be reasonable.) He does, however, hope to demonstrate the truth of his interpretation to Christians who are in danger of being confused by the Jewish exegesis of the psalm. He is especially concerned with the Jewish charge that Christians have deliberately overthrown the literal sense of the psalm in their translation of verse 16 ("they have pierced"). He argues that if one accepts the Jewish reading of the text, the passage will be wrapped in obscurity.[109] He challenges the motives of the Jews, who he believes are guilty of tampering with the Old Testament text in order to rid it of whatever evidence there is that Christ is the redeemer. He is aware that, even if he wins the textual argument, he must still answer the Jewish argument that since David was never nailed to the cross, the language cannot refer to crucifixion. The answer to this is easy; the language must be metaphorical. David in the psalm declared "that he was not less afflicted by his enemies than the man who is suspended on a cross, having his hands and feet pierced through with nails."[110] Metaphorical language is also used in verse 17 ("They parted my garments among themselves, and cast lots for my cloak"). "It is as if he had said that all his goods have become a prey to his enemies, even as conquerors are accustomed to plunder the vanquished." In Matthew 8:16-17, the evangelist uses this verse of the psalm without the figure in reference to Christ—a perfectly legitimate practice if David is regarded as a type. "The heavenly Father intended that in the person of his Son those things should be visibly accomplished which were shadowed [*adumbrata*] forth in David."[111] If any question should remain about the propriety of viewing David as a type of Christ, all doubt is removed by verse 27 ("All the ends of the earth shall remember"). This language could never be applied to David's reign. First, David's kingdom was great, but not so great that it reached to the ends of the earth. Second, the nations David subdued were not converted to the true worship of God. The type reached fulfillment in Christ. With amazing speed his reign was extended to the Gentiles throughout the world. They were truly converted to his rule.

Calvin adopts the same line of argument in defending his typological interpretation of Psalm 89:26 ("He shall cry to me, Thou art my Father"). The language of the psalm best fits Christ—in fact, it can fit no one else. The psalmist presents God speaking of the king. This has to be a reference to Christ, because it was the privilege of "only one king in this world to be called the Son of God." If the description can fit anyone other than Christ, then the writer of Hebrews is reasoning inconclusively—even absurdly—when he uses this text to prove that Christ is superior to the angels. Calvin observes that in verse 27 David is given a dignity above men and angels when he is called the firstborn and one who is elevated above all the kings of the earth. Anticipating an objection to this comparison, he reasons: "If he is considered in himself, he cannot justly be elevated to the same rank with them, but with the highest propriety he may, in so far as for a time he represented the person of Christ."[112] The next two verses of the psalm picture David's descendants sitting upon the throne forever, a final proof that "this prophecy cannot have its full accomplishment in any till we come to Christ, in whom alone, in the strict and proper sense, this everlasting duration is to be found."[113] For Calvin a typological interpretation of this psalm is no uncertain matter. It is unquestionably correct for the same two reasons he highlights in his exposition of Psalm 22: first, the New Testament writer supports it; second, the language fits no one else.

> To limit what is here said to the ancient people of Israel is an exposition not only absurd, but altogether impious. In the first place, I take it as a settled point, which we have already had occasion often to consider, that this kingdom was erected to be a shadow [*umbratile*] in which God might represent the Mediator to his Church: and this can be proved, not only from the testimony of Christ and the apostles, but it may also be clearly and indubitably deduced from the thing considered in itself. If we set Christ aside, where will we find that everlasting duration of the royal throne of which mention is here made? . . . The obvious conclusion then is that perpetuity, as applied to this kingdom, can be verified in Christ alone.[114]

Calvin admits that the New Testament plays a major role in guiding him to a typological interpretation of this psalm. He does not concede, however, that he has no other reasons. Apart from the testimony of the writer of Hebrews, it is obvious that a typological interpretation is the only one that can do justice to the language of the text. Throughout the psalm he uses his normal justifications, especially arguing from context.[115] He apparently sees no tension between his typological approach and his usual method of determining the intention of the human writer through an understanding of language and a careful consideration of context.

Calvin launches his most sustained defense of typological interpretation in his exposition of Psalm 110.

> Having the testimony of Christ that this psalm was penned in reference to himself, we need not apply to any other quarter for the corroboration of this statement; and, even supposing we neither had his authority, nor the testimony of the apostle, the psalm itself would admit of no other interpretation; for although we should have a dispute with the Jews, the most obstinate people in the world, about the right application of it, we are able, by solid arguments [*firmis rationibus*], to compel them to admit that the truths here stated relate neither to David nor to any other person than the Mediator alone.

Here again are Calvin's two recurring arguments for typological interpretation: the New Testament relates the psalm to Christ, and the language fits no one but Christ. Since Christ himself tells us the psalmist refers to him, no further substantiation should be required. Even the Jews, who refuse to accept the testimony of Christ or his apostles, have to admit that this can only be fulfilled in the mediator. "It cannot be asserted of him [David], or of any of his successors, that he should be a king whose dominion should be widely extended, and who, at the same time, was a priest, not according to the law, but according to the order of Melchizedek, and that for ever."[116] Though David did bring a few of the neighboring nations into subjection, "his kingdom, when contrasted with other monarchies, was always confined within narrow limits."[117] The problem of the priestly office fitting anyone in Old Testament times is twofold. First, another priestly office could not be established without depriving the Levites of their place of honor. Second, the longevity of the priesthood described here could not fit any one man—except Jesus Christ.[118]

It is thus clear from Calvin's defense of typology in his commentary on Psalms 2, 22, 89, and 110 that he believes typological interpretation as he practices it rests on a solid defensible base. He argues that the Jews are able to cite no adequate referent for the texts in Old Testament times, and thus a christological interpretation is necessary. Against fellow Christian exegetes he argues that one cannot tear a text out of its historical context in order to apply it to Christ.

SPROPHECY

Jewish and Christian writers agreed that the Old Testament contained numerous explicit promises, predictions, or prophecies. Among these were assurances of deliverance from hardship and the restoration of God's blessing. Jewish exegetes believed these to be fulfilled either in some event before the Christian era (e.g., deliverance from the Babylonian captivity) or in the Messiah for whom they were still waiting. In no case could the predictions be correctly related to Jesus Christ. Christians reasoned differently. Since Jesus Christ is the Messiah, promises of future deliverance may be taken as clear, direct prophecies of his life and work.

The dominant approach to interpreting Old Testament prophecy in the early church disregarded the setting in which the prophet lived and the circumstances in which he made his predictions. According to Greer:

> The exegesis by means of fulfillment of prophecy . . . tends so to see all events in terms of their fulfillment, that the events themselves become unimportant and meaningless. Prophecy then becomes not a speaking to the contemporary scene, but purely prediction of events to come in the distant future.[119]

Things had changed little by the Middle Ages. Preus indicates that a characteristic of much medieval Old Testament exegesis was that "the interpreter does not place himself with the Old Testament writer in time."[120] Calvin was uncomfortable with traditional Christian exegesis of Old Testament promises because he believed interpreters were wrong to ignore the historical circumstances in which the promises were originally given.

He finds something of value in both Jewish and Christian approaches. In his commentary on Isaiah 59:19 ("So they shall fear the name of the LORD from the west, and his glory from the rising of the sun; for he will come like a rushing stream which the wind of the LORD drives") he notes that the Jews refer the prophecy "exclusively to the deliverance from Babylon while the Christians refer it to Christ alone." His solution is to embrace elements of both views. "I join with both, so as to include the whole period after the return of the people along with that which followed down to the coming of Christ."[121] In his commentary on Isaiah 43:19 he argues that Christian commentators are undoubtedly mistaken in "referring absolutely to the coming of Christ." Jewish interpretations are no more correct in limiting the fulfillment to the return from the Babylonian captivity. "As I have frequently remarked, we ought here to include the whole period which followed the redemption from Babylon, down to the coming of Christ."[122]

It is the exclusivity of the positions that Calvin rejects. He opposes the "either/or" mentality that characterizes Jewish and Christian approaches to Old Testament promises. His approach recognizes the significance of the historical fulfillment in Old Testament times (return from Babylon) without divorcing it from the complete fulfillment that only comes in Christ.[123]

His comments on Isaiah 52:10 ("The LORD has bared his holy arm before the eyes of all the nations; and all the ends of the earth shall see the salvation of our God") show the middle way he found between Jewish and Christian views:

> This prophecy is maliciously restricted by the Jews to the deliverance from Babylon, and is improperly restricted by Christians to the spiritual redemption which we obtain through Christ; for we must begin with the deliverance which was wrought under Cyrus (2 Chronicles 36:22, 23), and bring it down to our own time. Thus the Lord began to display his power among the Medes and Persians, but afterwards he made it visible to all the nations.[124]

Calvin finds the "either/or" approach of both Jewish and Christian interpreters to be defective in the interpretation of Joel 3:1-2 ("In those days and in that time, when I shall bring again the captivity of Judah and Jerusalem, I will also gather all nations").

> This time the Jews limit to their return: they therefore think that when liberty to return was granted them by Cyrus and Darius, what the prophet declared here was fulfilled. Christian doctors apply this prediction to the coming of Christ, but both interpret the words of the prophet otherwise than the circumstances of the passage [*circumstantia loci*] require. The prophet, no doubt, speaks here of the deliverance we have just noticed, and at the same time includes the kingdom of Christ, and this, as we have seen in other parts, is very commonly done. While then the prophets testify that God would be the redeemer of his people, and promise deliverance from Babylonian exile, they lead the faithful, as it were, by a continuous train or course, to the kingdom of Christ. For what else was the Jewish restoration, but a prelude of that true and real redemption, afterwards effected by Christ? The prophet then does not speak only of the coming of Christ, or of the return of the Jews, but includes the whole of redemption, which was only begun when the Lord restored his people from the Babylonian exile; it will then go on from the first coming of Christ to the last day.[125]

Calvin also offers an "extended" interpretation in his comments on Jeremiah 32:37 ("Behold, I will gather them from all the countries to which I drove them in my anger and my wrath and in great indignation; I will bring them back to this place, and I will make them dwell in safety").

> Whenever the prophets prophesied of the return of the people, they extended [*extendunt*] what they taught to the whole kingdom of Christ. For liberation from exile was no more than the beginning of God's favor: God began the work of true and real redemption when he restored his people to their own country, but he gave them but a slight taste of his mercy. This prophecy, then, with those which are like it, ought to be extended [*extendi*] to the kingdom of Christ."[126]

Another text misinterpreted by Jews and Christians alike was Jeremiah 32:41, in which God promised to "plant" his people in the land. Calvin sees a problem with the Christian approach in its failure to recognize a historical fulfillment in Old Testament times. The Jews, however, correctly saw the earthly fulfillment, but failed to see anything else. "The Jews, who reject Christ, stop in that earthly deliverance." Calvin prefers an extended fulfillment that begins with the return of the people from exile and continues through the time of Christ. The prophets "set Christ also in the middle, that the faithful might know that the return was but a slight taste of the full grace, which was to be expected from Christ alone; for it was then, indeed, that God really planted his people." The fulfillment of this prophecy must be found in God's redemption of his people in Christ. Nothing that Psalm 80 used similar language to describe the conquest of the land under Joshua, Calvin reasons that God initially planted his people in the land under Joshua's leadership. "God had brought his vine out of Egypt and planted it in the promised inheritance." But this was not the true planting, because the people did not put down firm roots. Jeremiah 32 promises something new and unusual—a perpetual planting that was based upon a covenant relationship. The planting after the exile was only a first step in the fulfillment of the promise. The complete fulfillment comes in Christ. The prophecy must be extended beyond what Jews and Christians traditionally say. "The Church was fixed in Judea until the coming of Christ, who brought in the real accomplishment of this plantation."[127]

Calvin believes that the fulfillment of Old Testament promises relating to the establishment of the kingdom sometimes extends as far as the final advent of Christ. Concerning Isaiah 26:19 ("The dead shall live, their bodies shall rise. O dwellers in the dust, awake and sing for joy! For thy dew is a dew of light, and on the land of the shades thou wilt let it fall") he writes: "Isaiah includes the whole reign of Christ; for, although we begin to receive the fruit of this consolation when we are admitted into the Church, yet we shall not enjoy it fully until that last day of the resurrection is come, when all things shall be most completely restored."[128] Concerning the promise of the restoration of God's people in Isaiah 60 he explains:

> The Prophet does not speak of a few years or a short period, but embraces the whole course of redemption, from the end of the captivity to the preaching of the gospel, and finally down to the end of the reign of Christ. . . . We know that this prediction was never accomplished in that external restoration of the people, or during the commencement of it, and even that the temple which was afterwards erected was far inferior to the former. It follows, therefore, that the Prophet, to whom a full redemption was exhibited in spirit, not only relates what shall happen immediately after the return of the people, but discourses concerning the excellence of the spiritual temple; that is, of the Church of Christ. We must, therefore, come down in uninterrupted succession to Christ, if we wish to understand this prophecy.[129]

In his commentary on Isaiah 66:10ff. ("Rejoice with Jerusalem, and be glad for her, all you who love her; . . . I will extend prosperity to her like a river, and the wealth of the nations like an overflowing stream") he explains his principle for treating prophecies of restoration: "We ought to abide by the general rule, of which we have often spoken already, namely, that those promises must be extended [*extendendas esse*] from the return of the people down to the reign of Christ, and to the full perfection of that reign."[130] He understands Ezekiel 17:22 ("I myself will take a sprig from the lofty top of the cedar, and will set it out; I will break off from the topmost of its young twigs a tender one, and I myself will plant it upon a high and lofty mountain") to be a prophecy of the reign of Christ. He explains: "When, therefore, the reign of Christ is treated, we must date its commencement from the period of the building of the temple after the people's return from their seventy years' captivity: and then we shall take its boundary, not at the Ascension of Christ, not yet in the first or second centuries, but through the whole progress of his kingdom, until he shall appear at the last day."[131] In his comments on Zephaniah 3:16-17 ("On that day it shall be said to Jerusalem: 'Do not fear, O Zion; let not your hands grow weak. The LORD, your God, is in your midst, a warrior who gives victory; he will rejoice over you with gladness, he will renew you in his love; he will exult over you with loud singing'") he writes: "We must ever bear in mind what I have already stated—that it is not one year, or a few years, which are intended, when the prophets speak of future redemption; for the time which is now mentioned began when the people were restored from the Babylonian captivity, and continues its course to the final advent of Christ."[132]

Calvin's clearest explanation of why God might have his prophets speak in such a manner is found in his commentary on Isaiah 54:1 ("Sing, O barren one, who did not bear; break forth into singing and cry aloud, you who have not been in travail! For the children of the desolate one will be more than the children of her that is married, says the LORD"). Some Christian interpreters, he notes, believe the passage speaks of the church. Such interpreters are mistaken and "only succeed in increasing the obstinacy of the Jews, who perceive that the Prophet's meaning is twisted." In articulating his own position Calvin explains that the Old Testament period was the youth of the church and the period since Christ's advent is the adulthood. Only when this analogy is recognized is it possible to fully understand the prophets.

> This prophecy began to be fulfilled under Cyrus, who gave the people liberty to return, and afterwards extended to Christ in whom it has its full accomplishment. The church therefore conceived, when the people returned to their native country; for the body of the people was gathered together from which Christ should proceed, in order that the pure worship of God and true religion might again be revived. Hitherto, indeed, this fertility was not visible, for the conception was concealed, as it were, in the mother's womb, and no outward appearance of it could be seen; but afterwards the people were increased, and after the birth the church grew from infancy to manhood, till the gospel was preached. This was the actual youth of the church; and next follows the age of manhood, down to Christ's last coming, when all things shall be fully accomplished.
>
> All these things must be taken together if we wish to learn the prophet's genuine meaning [*genuinum prophetae sensum*].[133]

Calvin believes his views can be justified against the traditional interpretations of Jews and Christians. The rationale he offers for rejecting traditional Christian exegesis is grounded in his historical sensitivity. He rejects Christian interpretations that ignore the historical meaning of the text. In his commentary on Jeremiah 32:41 ("I will plant them in this land in faithfulness") he explains that prophecies belong first to the time in which they were given. "When Christians explain this passage and the like, they leave out the liberation of the people from Babylonian exile, as though these prophecies did not belong at all to that time; in this they are mistaken."[134] In his interpretation of Jeremiah 50:5 ("They shall ask the way to Zion, with faces turned toward it, saying, 'Come, let us join ourselves to the LORD in an everlasting covenant which will never be forgotten'") Calvin does not follow Christian exegetes because the words need to be taken literally—"that God would never forget his covenant, so as to retain the Jews in the possession of the land." He contrasts his own view with the "allegorical" view, which does not allow for any fulfillment in Old Testament times. Yet he insists that the language must also be understood spiritually. The Jews had never received the favor of God to the degree described in this passage. Whenever the prophets spoke of the return of the people they referred not just to the return from Babylon; they also spoke of "the chief deliverance." While it is true that the passage does indicate that God will favor the Jews by putting them back in their land, "this would have been a very small thing had not Christ come to bring real happiness."[135] The fact that the Jews were suffering in the land suggests that the promise was not fulfilled then, yet their return to the land should be understood as the beginning of the fulfillment.

Calvin finds Christian interpreters of Micah 4 ("Arise and thresh, O daughter of Zion, for I will make your horn iron and your hoofs bronze; you shall beat in pieces many peoples, and shall devote their gain to the LORD, their wealth to the Lord of the whole earth") to be guilty of engaging in unnecessary allegorization—they again fail to see that the fulfillment of prophecies of the kingdom of Christ begins with the return of the Jews from foreign exile.[136] In his comments on Micah 7 ("The nations shall see and be ashamed of all their might; they shall lay their hands on their mouths; their ears shall be deaf; they shall lick the dust like a serpent, like the crawling things of the earth; they shall come trembling out of their strongholds, they shall turn in dread to the LORD our God, and they shall fear because of thee") he allows an interpretation that sees fulfillment taking place in the preaching of the gospel, but cautions that "deliverance must always be made to begin with the ancient people. For if anyone would have this to be understood exclusively of Christ, such a strained and remote exposition [*tam coacta et remota expositio*] would not be suitable."[137] Calvin rejects "exclusively" christological interpretations because they fail to grasp the historical meaning of the Old Testament text. The Old Testament must be interpreted historically because the prophets had their eyes on the Jews of that day so that they might give them hope in their difficult circumstances. The texts must be understood as partly fulfilled in Old Testament times when God freed the Jews from the domination of foreign despots, giving them a foretaste of the blessing that was to come in Jesus Christ.[138]

Calvin sharply rebukes some Christian interpreters in his interpretation of Jeremiah 31 ("Thus says the LORD of hosts, the God of Israel: 'Once more they shall use these words in the land of Judah and in its cities, when I restore their fortunes: 'The LORD bless you, O habitation of righteousness, O holy hill!' And Judah and all its cities shall dwell there together, and the farmers and those who wander with their flocks"). These interpreters fly into allegories without understanding what the prophecies would have meant to the people to whom they were originally delivered:

> Now, were anyone to ask, when was this fulfilled? We must bear in mind what has been said elsewhere—that the prophets, when speaking of the restoration of the Church, included the whole kingdom of Christ from the beginning to the end. And in this our divines go astray, so that by confining these promises to some particular time, they are compelled to fly to allegories, and thus they twist [*torquere*] and even pervert all the prophecies. But the prophets, as it has been said, include the whole progress of Christ's kingdom when they speak of the future redemption of the people. The people began to do well when they returned to their own country, but soon after distresses came as Daniel had predicted. It was, therefore, necessary for them to look for the coming of Christ. We now taste of these benefits of God as long as we are in the world. We hence see that these prophecies are not accomplished in one day, or in one year, no, not even in one age, but ought to be understood as referring to the beginning and the end of Christ's kingdom.[139]

Usually Calvin's defense of his exegesis of prophecy is aimed at refuting Jewish interpretations. In his commentary on Jeremiah 49:2 ("Therefore, behold, the days are coming, says the LORD, when I will cause the battle cry to be heard against Rabbah of the Ammonites; it shall become a desolate mound, and its villages shall be burned with fire; then Israel shall dispossess those who dispossessed him, says the LORD") he justifies his "both/and" approach by arguing that the language of the prophecy cannot conceivably be regarded as having been fulfilled under the Old Testament kings.

> It may be asked, when was this prophecy fulfilled? God, indeed, under David, gave some indication of their future subjection, but Israel never possessed that land. Indeed, from that time Ammon had not been brought low until after the overthrow of Israel. It then follows that what Jeremiah predicted here was not fully accomplished except under the kingdom of Christ. David humbled that nation because he had received a great indignity from the king of Ammon, and he took also Rabbah, as it is evident from sacred history. He was yet satisfied with making the people tributary. From that time they not only shook off the yoke, but exercised authority within the borders of Israel; and that the Israelites had recovered what they had lost, we nowhere read. Then Israel began to possess power over the Ammonites when the kingdom of Christ was established; by which all heathen nations were not only brought into subjection and under the yoke, but all unworthy of mercy were also reduced to nothing.[140]

Concerning verse 6 of the same chapter ("But afterward I will restore the fortunes of the Ammonites, says the LORD") Calvin argues that the prophecy must refer to Christ because the calling of the Gentiles did not occur until Christ came.[141]

In his interpretation of Isaiah 60:21 ("Your people shall all be righteous; they shall possess the land forever") he again argues against the Jews that the language of the text was not fulfilled in Old Testament times—at least not perfectly. A later fulfillment is demanded. "This was not in every respect fulfilled in the Jews, but a beginning was made in them, when they were res'ored to their native country, that, by their agency, the possession of the whole earth might afterwards be given to them, that is, to the children of God."[142] Calvin finds the Jewish interpretation of Jeremiah 50:5 ("They shall ask the way to Zion, with faces turned toward it, saying, 'Come, let us join ourselves to the LORD in an everlasting covenant which will never be forgotten'") to be inadequate because "this would have been a very small thing, had not Christ come forth, in whom is found the real perpetuity of the covenant, because God's covenant cannot be separated from a state of happiness; for blessed are the people, as the Psalmist says, to whom God shows himself to be their God." Since the Jews were miserable rather than happy, it is evident that the fulfillment was not conspicuously present. "We must therefore come necessarily to Christ."[143]

So it is clear that in his treatment of allegory, typology, and prophecy in the Old Testament, Calvin adopts a moderate position in which he believes he has avoided the temptations that too often befell Jewish and Christian exegesis. He has not uprooted the Old Testament from its historical soil nor has he been content to look at the roots once the full flowering has taken place in Jesus Christ. He uses the New Testament interpretation of the Old to establish the meaning of the Old Testament text. Yet even if he could not find confirmation in the New Testament, he believes he can demonstrate through clear philological and historical reasoning that his interpretation is correct—and even necessary.

*Notes*

[1] Origen, *On First Principles,* trans. G. W. Butterworth (Gloucester, Mass.: Peter Smith, 1973), IV.2, 280.

[2] Theodore of Mopsuestia, "Commentary on Galatians 4:22-31," in *Biblical Interpretation in the Early Church,* trans. and ed. Karlfried Froehlich, Sources of Early Christian Thought (Philadelphia: Fortress Press, 1984), 96. Frances Young has argued that a key to understanding the differences between Antiochene and Alexandrian exegesis is the training in rhetoric received by the Antiochenes ("The Rhetorical Schools and Their Influence on Patristic Exegesis," in *The Making of Orthodoxy,* ed. Rowan Williams [Cambridge: Cambridge University Press, 1989], 196).

[3] Comm. Dan. 10:6 (C.O. 41.199).

[4] Rowan A. Greer, *Theodore of Mopsuestia: Exegete and Theologian* (London: Faith Press, 1961), 94-95. Christian use of allegorical interpretation has in the past sometimes been viewed as finding its intellectual roots in Philo of Alexandria and later Clement and Origen, but in fact, it was already in use in the interpretation of pagan literature. Discussions of the early history of allegorical interpretation may be found in R. M. Grant, *The Letter and the Spirit* (London: SPCK, 1957); R.P.C. Hanson, *Allegory and Event: A Study of the Sources and Significance of Origen's Interpretation of Scripture* (Richmond: John Knox Press, 1959); M. J. Pépin, *Mythe et allégorie: Les origines grecques et les contestations judéo-chrétiennes,* rev. ed. (Paris, 1976).

[5] Walther Eichrodt, "Is Typological Exegesis an Appropriate Method?" in *Essays in Old Testament Hermeneutics,* ed. Claus Westermann (Richmond: John Knox Press, 1963), 227. Barr has challenged the use of history as a criterion to make a clear and absolute distinction between typology and allegory: "The idea that allegory is definitely and ineluctably antihistorical does not seem to me to be true. It depends on the choice of examples." See James Barr, *Old and New in Interpretation: A Study of the Two Testaments* (London: SCM Press, 1982), 104, 105. Paul K. Jewett has also questioned the sharp distinction often drawn between allegory and typology ("Concerning the Allegorical Interpretation of Scripture," *Westminster Theological Journal* 17 [1954-55]: 1-20).

[6] Torjesen effectively demonstrates that the allegorical approach of Origen was deeply rooted in his practical piety, and thus cannot be rejected on the basis that it is primarily a speculative exercise. Karen Jo Torjesen, "Hermeneutical Procedure and Theological Structure in Origen's Exegesis" (Ph.D. diss., Claremont School of Theology, 1982); see also her essay "'Body,' 'Soul,' and 'Spirit' in Origen's Theory of Exegesis," *Anglican Theological Review* 67 (January 1985): 17-31; Allan E. Johnson, "The Methods and Presuppositions of Patristic Exegesis in the Formation of Christian Personality," *Dialog* 16 (1977): 186-90.

[7] Comm. Lev. 1:1 (C.O. 24.506).

[8] Comm. Gen. 21:12 (C.O. 23.302).

[9] Comm. 2 Cor. 3:6 (C.O. 49.40-41).

[10] Comm. Gen. 2:8 (C.O. 23.37).

[11] Comm. Gal. 4:22 (C.O. 50.236).

[12] Comm. Gen. 1:6 (C.O. 23.18); 3:1 (C.O. 23.54); 3:14 (C.O. 23.68); 3:23 (C.O. 23.80); 49:1 (C.O. 23.590); 49:11 (C.O. 23.603); Comm. Ex. 17:10 (C.O. 24.180); 20:24 (C.O. 24.397); 31:18 (C.O. 25.80); Comm. Lev. 3:16 (C.O. 24.514); 11:9 (C.O. 24.349); Comm. Num. 17:8 (C.O. 25.231); Comm. Ps. 12:8 (C.O. 31.131); 22:1 (C.O. 31.219); 27:10 (C.O. 31.277); 36:6 (C.O. 31.362); 38:8 (C.O. 31.389-90); 74:11 (C.O. 31.696); 132:6 (C.O. 32.344); Comm. Isa. 13:12 (C.O. 36.264); 29:18 (C.O. 36.498); 42:16 (C.O. 37.70); 55:13 (C.O. 37.292-93); 66:20 (C.O. 37.452); Comm. Jer. 16:16 (C.O. 38.251); Comm. Ezek. 5:9-10 (C.O. 40.126); Comm. Hos. 1:8-9 (C.O. 42.215); 3:2-5 (C.O. 42.259); 4:12 (C.O. 42.282); Comm. Joel 3:7 (C.O. 42.588); Comm. Zech. 9:16 (C.O. 44.283); 10:2 (C.O. 44.287); 14:4 (C.O. 44.365); Comm. Mal. 2:12 (C.O. 44.449).

[13] Comm. Gen. 6:14 (C.O. 23.123). What Calvin calls allegorical interpretation may be better categorized as typology.

[14] Comm. Gen. 15:4 (C.O. 23.210).

[15] Comm. Dan. 7:9 (C.O. 41.121).

[16] Comm. Deut. 12:4 (C.O. 24.391).

[17] Comm. Dan. 8:24-25 (C.O. 41.121).

[18] Comm. Ex. 3:4 (C.O. 24.37).

[19] Comm. Ezek. 16:10-13 (C.O. 40.343).

[20] Comm. Hab. 3:10 (C.O. 43.577-78). He notes that the context is against the allegorical interpretation. Elsewhere he notes that allegorists seek to find meaning in small units and fail to interpret them in light of the larger context. They attempt to give "an ingenious exposition of every clause." Comm. Isa. 5:2 (C.O. 36.104). Barr argues that "de-contextualization" is one of the defining characteristics of the allegorical approach of the early church. "Ancient and mediaeval allegory is, in very large measure, de-contextualizing, and in two ways: firstly, in that it works from very small pieces of the text (as when each of Jacob's wives has an allegorical sense, but there isn't an allegorical sense for the passage as a whole) and interprets them in ways that are irreconcilable with the context within the books; secondly, that it uproots them from the culture in which they have meaning." Such an approach, he argues, has no validity. "All valid understanding of a passage as having allegorical features must depend on contextual considerations within the linguistic semantics, the literary context, the cultural background and the historical setting." James Barr, "The Literal, the Allegorical, and Modern Biblical Scholarship," *Journal for the Study of the Old Testament* 44 (1989): 14.

[21] Comm. Zech. 6:1-3 (C.O. 44.202). Parker appears to be correct in observing that Calvin's "attacks on 'allegory' are directed against an over-elaborated use of allegory in its general sense of extended metaphor as well as against an allegorical interpretation imposed arbitrarily on a passage." T.H.L. Parker, *Calvin's Old Testament Commentaries* (Edinburgh: T. & T. Clark, 1986), 70.

[22] Comm. Gal. 4:22 (C.O. 50.236).

[23] Ibid.

[24] See discussion in Alexandre Ganoczy and Stefan Scheld, *Die Hermeneutik Calvins: Geistesgeschichtliche Voraussetzungen und Grundzüge,* Veröffentlichungen des Instituts für Europäische Geschichte Mainz, Abteilung für Abendländische Religionsgeschichte, no. 114 (Wiesbaden: Franz Steiner Verlag, 1983), 157-59.

[25] Comm. Ps. 19:4 (C.O. 31.198).

[26] Comm. Rom. 10:18 (C.O. 48.207).

[27] Comm. Ps. 104:4 (C.O. 32.86).

[28] Comm. Jer. 31:15, 16 (C.O. 38.665).

[29] Comm. Dan. 4:10-16 (C.O. 40.657). For Calvin's recognition of allegory as extended metaphor in the Old Testament, see also Comm. Isa. 9:15 (C.O. 36.204); 16:8 (C.O. 36.308); 22:22 (C.O. 36.382); 27:1 (C.O. 36.448); 44:27 (C.O. 37.125); 65:25 (C.O. 37.434); Comm. Ezek. 17:4 (C.O. 40.404); Comm. Dan. 7:7 (C.O. 41.47); Comm. Hos. 4:13-14 (C.O. 42.286).

[30] Comm. Isa. 30:25 (C.O. 36.525).

[31] Comm. Jer. 31:38-40 (C.O. 38.704).

[32] Comm. Amos 9:15 (C.O. 43.176).

[33] Comm. Zech. 14:8 (C.O. 44.375).

[34] Comm. Joel 2:30-31 (C.O. 42.571).

[35] Comm. Isa. 11:4 (C.O. 36.240).

[36] Comm. Isa. 11:6 (C.O. 36.242).

[37] Comm. Isa. 11:8 (C.O. 36.243).

[38] Comm. Amos 9:15 (C.O. 43.176).

[39] Comm. Ezek. 17:1-2 (C.O. 40.403).

[40] Comm. Ezek. 17:11-16 (C.O. 40.408).

[41] Comm. Ezek. 17:1-2 (C.O. 40.403).

[42] Comm. Isa. 32:19 (C.O. 36.554).

[43] Comm. Jer. 33:15 (C.O. 39.67).

[44] Comm. Amos 9:15 (C.O. 43.176).

[45] Comm. Isa. 1:19 (C.O. 36.47-48).

[46] Comm. Dan. 7:27 (C.O. 41.82).

[47] Comm. Isa. 55:13 (C.O. 37.292).

[48] Comm. Isa. 33:17 (C.O. 36.572).

[49] Comm. Ex. 20:8. See also Comm. Jer. 11:19 (C.O. 38.124).

[50] Richard M. Davidson provides a concise, well documented survey of the history of typological interpretation in *Typology in Scripture: A Study of Hermeneutical* [TYPOS] *Structures,* Andrews University Seminary Doctoral Dissertation Series, no. 2 (Berrien Springs, Mich.: Andrews University Press, 1981), 15-45. For the use of typology in the early church, see Jean Daniélou, *From Shadows to Reality: Studies in the Biblical Typology of the Fathers,* trans. Wulstan Hibberd (Westminster, Md.: Newman Press, 1960).

[51] Francis Foulkes, *The Acts of God: A Study of the Basis of Typology in the Old Testament,* Tyndale Old Testament Lecture for 1955 (London: Tyndale Press, n.d.), 35-40.

[52] Eichrodt, "Is Typological Exegesis an Appropriate Method?" 245.

[53] G.W.H. Lampe, "The Reasonableness of Typology," in *Essays on Typology,* ed. G.W.H. Lampe and K.J. Woollcombe (Naperville, III.: Alec R. Allenson, 1957), 29.

[54] Hans Frei, *The Eclipse of Biblical Narrative: A Study of Eighteenth and Nineteenth Century Hermeneutics* (New Haven, Conn.: Yale University Press, 1974), 2.

[55] Thomas M. Davis, "The Traditions of Puritan Typology," in *Typology and Early American Literature,* ed. Sacvan Berkovich (Amherst, Mass.: University of Massachusetts Press, 1972), 38.

[56] Jackson Forstman, *Word and Spirit: Calvin's Doctrine of Biblical Authority* (Stanford, Calif.: Stanford University Press, 1962), 106.

[57] Kemper Fullerton, *Prophecy and Authority: A Study in the History of the Doctrine and Interpretation of Scripture* (New York: Macmillan, 1919), 135.

[58] Basil Hall, "Biblical Scholarship: Editions and Commentaries," in *The Cambridge History of the Bible,* vol. 3: *The West from the Reformation to the Present Day,* ed. S. L. Greenslade (Cambridge: Cambridge University Press, 1963), 88. Hall defends Calvin against this charge, arguing that his use of typology was sparing compared to that of others in his day—including Hunnius.

[59] Davidson cautions that contemporary biblical typology should not be confused with the typology of earlier generations. While typological exegesis has experienced a revival in the Biblical Theology movement in the twentieth century, the modern understanding, which "describes typology in terms of historical *correspondences* retrospectively recognized within the consistent redemptive activity of God," is actually different than the typological interpretation of earlier writers, which "views typology in terms of divinely preordained and predictive *prefigurations.*" According to the older view, "God not only acts consistently but also has ordained and superintended specific persons / events / institutions to mutely predict the coming of Christ." The typical element is "already to be found within the context of the historical root event." According to the contemporary view, persons / events / institutions are only seen to be typical "in retrospect after the appearance of the antitype." Davidson, *Typology in Scripture,* 94-97. Calvin, not surprisingly, held the view of typology as predictive prophecy. In his exposition of Psalm 2 he insists that David prophesied concerning Christ-he knew his kingdom was merely a shadow of the future kingdom. If we carefully consider the nature of the kingdom we will see that it would be absurd to overlook the end and rest on the shadow only. Comm. Ps. 2: 1-3 (C.O. 31.42-43). See also Comm. Ps. 21:3 (C.O. 31.213); 22:1 (C.O. 31.219); 84:9 (C.O. 31.783); 89:18 (C.O. 31.817).

[60] This view of the predictive nature of Old Testament ceremonies was opposed by Michael Servetus. See Jerome Friedman, "Servetus and the Psalms: The Exegesis of Heresy," in *Histoire de l' exégèse au XVIe siècle,* ed. Olivier Fatio and Pierre Fraenkel, Etudes de Philogie et d' Histoire, no. 34 (Geneva: Librairie Droz, 1978), 170.

[61] Comm. Ps. 18:50 (C.O. 31.194).

[62] *Inst.* II.vii.1 (O.S. 3.326-27).

[63] Comm. Jer. 17:22 (C.O. 38.287).

[64] Comm. Ex. 12:5 (C.O. 24.288).

[65] Comm. Ex. 12:21 (C.O. 24.136).

[66] Comm. Ex. 28:1ff. (C.O. 24.426).

[67] Comm. Ex. 28:31 (C.O. 24.431-32).

[68] Comm. Ex. 26:1 (C.O. 24.415).

[69] Comm. Jer. 33:17 (C.O. 38.70).

[70] Comm. Isa. 16:5 (C.O. 36.304).

[71] Comm. Lam. 4:20 (C.O. 39.624).

[72] Comm. Gen. 37:2 (C.O. 23.482). Calvin believes that careful attention to the context will prove his typological approach to be correct.

[73] Comm. Num. 3:5 (C.O. 24.444).

[74] Comm. Num. 6:2 (C.O. 24.304).

[75] Comm. Zech. 3:6-7 (C.O. 44.174).

[76] Comm. Hag. 2:20-23 (C.O. 44.122).

[77] Comm. Isa. 60:10 (C.O. 37.361).

[78] Comm. Ps. 122:4 (C.O. 32.305).

[79] Comm. Ps. 72, pref. (C.O. 31.664).

[80] Russell argues that a great deal of subjectivity is present in Calvin's approach to the Psalms. In his

defense of typological exegesis Calvin succumbs to one of the chief pitfalls of typological exegesis: the temptation to account for discrepancies in description of type and antitype through the necessity of maintaining the difference between promise and fulfillment. This forces him to defend his typological exegesis through two contrary arguments: (a) the similarity of language and function between two realities shows they are related; (b) dissimilarity in language and function between two realities shows that one is superior in comparison to the other. S. H. Russell, "Calvin and the Messianic Interpretation of the Psalms," *Scottish Journal of Theology* 21 (1968): 42-43.

[81] Bucer seems to have relied on the same arguments. See R. Gerald Hobbs, "How Firm a Foundation: Martin Bucer's Historical Exegesis of the Psalms," *Church History* 53 (December 1984): 489.

[82] Comm. Ps. 110:1 (C.O. 32.160).

[83] Comm. Ex. 20:8 (C.O. 24.577); Comm. Ps. 68:19 (C.O. 31.628); Comm. Jer. 17:22 (C.O. 38.287).

[84] Comm. Ex. 20:8 (C.O. 24.577); 26:1 (C.O. 24.415).

[85] Comm. Ps. 47:1 (C.O. 31.466).

[86] Comm. Isa. 16:5 (C.O. 36.304).

[87] Comm. Isa. 33:6 (C.O. 37.563).

[88] Comm. Isa. 33:17 (C.O. 37.572).

[89] Comm. Ex. 28:1-43 (C.O. 24.426).

[90] Comm. Jer. 33:17, 18 (C.O. 38.70).

[91] Comm. Ex. 12:21 (C.O. 24.136).

[92] Comm. Ex. 29:38-46 (C.O. 24.489).

[93] Comm. Ps. 40:7 (C.O. 31.410-11).

[94] Comm. Ps. 45:1 (C.O. 31.449).

[95] Comm. Ps. 72:1 (C.O. 31.664).

[96] Comm. Isa. 61:1 (C.O. 37.371).

[97] Comm. Ps. 109:6 (C.O. 32.148); Comm. Isa. 50:4 (C.O. 37.218).

[98] Frei argues that "the reason for Calvin's confidence in the harmony of grammatical and pervasive Christological interpretation is his unquestioned assumption of a natural coherence between literal and figural reading, and the need of each for supplementation by the other." Calvin's "application of figural interpretation never lost its connection with literal reading of individual texts." Frei, *Eclipse of Biblical Narrative,* 27-31.

[99] Comm. Ps. 2, pref. (C.O. 31.41).

[100] Comm. Ps. 2:1-3 (C.O. 31.43).

[101] Comm. Ps. 2:6 (C.O. 31.45).

[102] Comm. Ps. 2:7 (C.O. 31.46). Ps. 2:7 had been used as a proof of the eternal generation of the Son since the time of Origen. Calvin rejects this interpretation, arguing that Paul, "a more faithful and a better qualified interpreter of this prophecy," in Acts 13:33 relates this text to the time of the mainfestation of the glory of Christ to men. In adopting this view Calvin maintains that these words have reference to David as well. Here Calvin uses the New Testament writer as an authoritative interpreter of the Old Testament, not against Jews, but against other Christian interpreters.

[103] Comm. Ps. 2:8 (C.O. 31.47).

[104] Comm. Ps. 2:9 (C.O. 31.48).

[105] The typology of David and Christ is examined by Gilbert Vincent in "Calvin, commentateur du Psaume XXII," *Bulletin du Centre Protestant d'Etudes et de Documentation* 293 (July-August 1984): 32-52.

[106] Comm. Ps. 22, pref. (C.O. 31.219).

[107] Ibid.

[108] Comm. Ps. 22:22 (C.O. 31.231).

[109] See the discussion of what Calvin believes is a textual problem of this text, in "Criticism of Jewish Exegesis" in chapter 4.

[110] Comm. Ps. 22:22 (C.O. 31.231).

[111] Comm. Ps. 22:17 (C.O. 31.229).

[112] Comm. Ps. 89:27-28 (C.O. 31.820-21).

[113] Comm. Ps. 89:29-30 (C.O. 31.821).

[114] Comm. Ps. 89:31 (C.O. 31.822).

[115] Comm. Ps. 89, pref. (C.O. 31.811); 89:6 (C.O. 31.814); 89:7 (C.O. 31.814).

[116] Comm. Ps. 110, pref. (C.O. 32.159-60).

[117] Comm. Ps. 110:2 (C.O. 32.162).

[118] Comm. Ps. 110, pref. (C.O. 32.159).

[119] Rowan A. Greer, *Theodore of Mopsuestia: Exegete and Thelogian* (London: Faith Press, 1961), 95.

[120] James Samuel Preus, *From Shadow to Promise: Old Testament Interpretation from Augustine to the Young Luther* (Cambridge, Mass.: Belknap Press, 1969), 164.

[121] Comm. Isa. 59:19 (C.O. 37.350).

[122] Comm. Isa. 43:19 (C.O. 37.94).

[123] Calvin finds an extended fulfillment including an incomplete historical fulfillment near the time of the prophet and a later complete fulfillment in Jesus Christ in the following texts: Comm. Ex. 23:31 (C.O. 24.254-55); Comm. Num. 24:20 (C.O. 25.294); 61:6 (C.O. 31.583); 72:8 (C.O. 31.668); 102:22 (C.O. 32.71); Comm. Isa. 9:6 (C.O. 36.195); 11:13-14 (C.O. 36.248); 14:1 (C.O. 36.273); 14:25 (C.O. 36.288); 40:1 (C.O. 37.4); 41:19 (C.O. 37.48); 43:8 (C.O. 37.85-86); 46:1 (C.O. 37.153); 49:9-12 (C.O. 37.201-3); 49:19 (C.O. 37.207); 58:12 (C.O. 37.333); 60:10 (C.O. 37.361); 60:17 (C.O. 37.366); 60:21 (C.O. 37.368); 61:9 (C.O. 37.379); 62:11 (C.O. 37.390); 66:10 (C.O. 37.445); Comm. Jer. 3:17-18 (C.O. 37.566); 50:20 (C.O. 39.413); 50:39 (C.O. 39.429); Comm. Dan. 7:27 (C.O. 41.82-83); Comm. Micah 5:5 (C.O. 43.373); 7:12 (C.O. 43.421); Comm. Zeph. 3:10 (C.O. 44.62); 3:16-17 (C.O. 44.73); Comm. Zech. 3:10 (C.O. 44.180), 10:4 (C.O. 44.290-91); 14:13 (C.O. 44.380).

[124] Comm. Isa. 52:10 (C.O. 37.249-50).

[125] Comm. Joel 3:1-3 (C.O. 42.581).

[126] Comm. Jer. 32:36, 37 (C.O. 39.37).

[127] Comm. Jer. 32:41 (C.O. 39.45-46).

[128] Comm. Isa. 26:19 (C.O. 36.442).

[129] Comm. Isa. 60:15, 17 (C.O. 37.365).

[130] Comm. Isa. 66:10 (C.O. 37.445).

[131] Comm. Ezek. 17:22 (C.O. 40.417).

[132] Comm. Zeph. 3:16-17 (C.O. 44.73).

[133] Comm. Isa. 54:2 (C.O. 37.270).

[134] Comm. Jer. 32:41 (C.O. 39.45-46).

[135] Comm. Jer. 50:5 (C.O. 39.397).

[136] Comm. Micah 4:11-13 (C.O. 43.362).

[137] Comm. Micah 7:16-17 (C.O. 43.426).

[138] Comm. Isa. 35:1 (C.O. 36.590).

[139] Comm. Jer. 31:24 (C.O. 38.682).

[140] Comm. Jer. 49:2 (C.O. 39.349).

[141] Comm. Jer. 49:6 (C.O. 39.352).

[142] Comm. Isa. 60:21 (C.O. 37.369).

[143] Comm. Jer. 50:5 (C.O. 39.397). Calvin indicates in the following commentaries that the language of the prophets was not fulfilled in Old Testament times: Comm. Ps. 68:31 (C.O. 31.635); Comm. Isa. 11:11 (C.O. 36.246); 61:9 (C.O. 37.379); Comm. Jer. 32:36-37 (C.O. 39.36-37); 49:2-6 (C.O. 39.348-52); 50:3-5 (C.O. 39.392-97); Comm. Hos. 3:2-5 (C.O. 42.263); Comm. Amos 9:11 (C.O. 43.171); Comm. Obad. 19-20 (C.O. 43.198-200); Comm. Micah 5:9 (C.O. 43.398).

**Dawn DeVries (essay date 1996)**

SOURCE: "Calvin on the Word as Sacrament," in *Jesus Christ in the Preaching of Calvin and Schleiermacher*, Westminster John Knox Press, 1996, pp. 14-25.

[*In the following excerpt, De Vries analyzes the importance of Calvin's notion of the Word of God as a "means of grace" and as a paradigm shift.*]

Calvin, like Luther before him, borrowed from Augustine the notion that sacraments were "visible words."[1] While this meant that the Reformers tended to verbalize the sacraments, it also led them to "sacramentalize" the Word.[2] In order to understand the significance of Calvin's doctrine of the Word, however, we must first explore how preaching was understood by Calvin's predecessors.

THE DOCTRINE OF THE WORD AND THE TASK OF PREACHING BEFORE CALVIN

While it cannot be asserted that the Reformers of the sixteenth century invented the notion of the Word as a means of grace, it is commonly said that they raised the discussion to a wholly new level.[3] Already in Origen one can discover an appreciation for the importance of the preaching of the Word in the life of the faithful.[4] But in Augustine's writings against the Donatists, the parallelism of Word and sacrament first receives explicit statement.[5] Both Word and sacraments are instruments for communicating the grace by which God justifies and sanctifies the elect: the Word is the seed of regeneration.

At the same time, however, Augustine also understood the Word as a means of instruction for the faithful. And it is the didactic understanding of the Word that came to prevail in the Middle Ages, when, increasingly, the infusion of grace was taken to be the special office of the sacraments of Baptism and Eucharist. The preached Word was a means of teaching, communicating the truth, and preparing people to receive the sacraments. But it was only the *preparation for,* and not the instrument of communicating, the grace of salvation.[6]

This preparation should consist in two things: catechetical instruction and moral urging. The average churchgoer in the Middle Ages was not well instructed in the rudiments of the faith. If he or she knew how to say the Lord's Prayer, or the Ave Maria, for example, he or she was considered remarkably educated. Much medieval preaching, then, simply tried to convey the words of prayers and creeds, and their meaning, to the hearers of sermons.[7] At the same time, however, medieval preachers tried to stimulate in their hearers the desire to receive the church's sacraments by stressing the demands of the moral law, the fleetingness of life, and the terrors of hell.[8] The preached Word itself, so far from conveying the healing medicine of divine grace, was rather a prescription for the medicine that was available only in the sacraments.

By the end of the Middle Ages, this conception of preaching was beginning to come undone. Even before Luther and the first generation of Protestant reformers, the Augustinian notion of the Word as a means of grace was being recovered.[9] But Luther went farther: he took Romans 10:17 as a radical principle for reform. Faith comes from hearing; thus, the grace of God is infused primarily through the preaching of the Word, and only secondarily through the sacraments.[10] Even the life of Jesus is interpreted through the lens of the sacramental Word. Luther states:

> If I had to do without one or the other,—either the works or preaching of Christ,—I would rather do without His works than His preaching; for the works do not help me, but His words give life, as He Himself says. Now John writes very little about the works of Christ, but very much about His preaching, while the other Evangelists write much of His works and little of His preaching; therefore John's Gospel is the one, tender, true chief Gospel, far, far to be preferred to the other three and placed high above them. So, too, the Epistles of St. Paul and St. Peter far surpass the other three Gospels,—Matthew, Mark and Luke.[11]

Calvin, then, was following an old and established tradition—freshly appropriated in the sixteenth century—in understanding the Word as the primary means of grace to which the sacraments are but "appendages."[12] But now we must ask what precisely Calvin meant by "the Word."

THE WORD OF GOD: SCRIPTURE PREACHING, AND THE INCARNATION

Calvin's use of the term "Word of God" is ambiguous at best. It is often unclear to what exactly the "Word" refers.[13] Certainly Calvin wishes to maintain that the Word of God is found reliably in scripture. But Calvin does not simply equate the words of scripture with the Word of God.[14] For, as he puts it in his commentary on 2 Timothy 3:15, "False prophets also make use of it [scripture] as a pretext; and so, in order that it may be useful to us for salvation, we have to know how to use it rightly."[15] The correct use of scripture involves seeking in it what we need to know for our salvation—or, more correctly, *whom* we need to know, namely, Jesus Christ. Thus, the center of scripture, its unifying purpose, is to present Christ and his saving work to those who are to be saved.[16]

One of Calvin's favorite shorthand terms for the center of scripture is "gospel." The gospel is "an embassy [*legatio*], by which the reconciliation of the world with God, once for all accomplished in the death of Christ, is daily conveyed to men."[17] The gospel, in other words, is not only the announcement, but the actual gift imparting God's promised grace. It communicates or presents Christ to its hearers, and unites them to God through Christ. In fact, Calvin goes so far as to say that the gospel itself *brings* salvation.[18] In presenting Christ, the gospel reveals the fatherly goodwill of God, and so enables the hearers of the Word, if God wills, to receive the gifts of justification and sanctification.[19]

Calvin is very clear, however, that the gospel comes to us, or communicates Christ to us, only in the proclaimed Word of preaching and sacraments.[20] Private reading of and meditation on scripture is not sufficient. In a fascinating passage in his ***Commentary on John*** (Jesus' reference to the story of Moses' lifting the brazen serpent over the people in 3:14), Calvin argues explicitly that the preaching of the gospel is to be understood sacramentally.

> To be lifted up means to be set in a lofty and eminent place, so as to be exhibited to the view of all. This was done by the preaching of the gospel; for the explanation of it which some give, as referring to the cross, neither agrees with the context nor is applicable to the present subject. The simple meaning of the words, therefore, is that by the preaching of the gospel, Christ would be raised on high. . . . Christ introduces [the illustration of the brazen serpent] in this passage, in order to show that he must be placed before the eyes of all by the teaching of the gospel, that all who look at him by faith may receive salvation. And so we ought to infer that Christ is clearly shown to us in the gospel . . . and that faith has its own faculty of vision, by which to perceive

> him as if present; as Paul tells us that a lively portrait of Christ with his cross is portrayed, when he is truly preached (Gal. 3:1). . . . A question now arises: Does Christ compare himself to the *serpent,* because there is some resemblance; or, does he pronounce it to have been a sacrament, as the Manna was? For though the Manna was bodily food, intended for present use, yet Paul testifies that it was a spiritual mystery (1 Cor. 10:3). I am led to think this was also the case with the brazen serpent.[21]

This passage is remarkable for several reasons. First, Calvin speaks of the preaching of the gospel as a kind of manifestation of Christ's presence. "Faith has its own faculty of vision [*fidei adspectum*] by which to perceive Christ as if present." Thus, the gospel not only conveys information about, but also renders the veritable presence of, Jesus Christ. It is interesting that Calvin goes out of his way to deny the obvious interpretation of the text: that Jesus was alluding to his death on the cross. Even more remarkable, however, is the suggestion with which he concludes his comments on this verse: namely, that Jesus refers to the serpent because it was a sacrament. Calvin's understanding of the unity of the Old and New Testaments in one covenant of grace required that he discover in the Old Testament "types" of significant aspects of New Testament faith. Thus, with regard to the sacraments, circumcision is the Old Testament type of baptism.[22] It seems that in the passage above, Calvin is arguing that the brazen serpent was the Old Testament type of the New Testament sacrament of the Word—the preaching of the gospel. But Calvin is more certain that the Word is sacramental than he is that he has given the only possible interpretation of this passage in John: he concludes that "if anyone comes to a different opinion about this, I do not debate the point with him."[23]

The Word of God, then, refers first and foremost to Jesus Christ, the incarnate *Logos,* who secured the reconciliation of elect humanity with God. For present-day believers, an encounter with Christ the Word is possible when the words of scripture are truly preached and heard. Preaching under the power of the Holy Spirit focuses, as it were, the vision of believers on the center of scripture—Christ—and in that moment of insight, faith perceives the immediate presence of the Redeemer.[24] Thus preaching itself becomes the Word of God, in the sense that it discloses the person of Christ and Christ's witness to his Father.[25]

### THE FUNCTION OF THE SACRAMENTAL WORD

Calvin frequently states that the Word and the sacraments have the same purpose or office: to offer and present Christ.[26] Thus it should not surprise us that Calvin describes the function of the preached Word as analogous to the function of sacraments—both are instruments of divine grace.[27] He often speaks of preaching as a mirror in which we can behold the face of Christ and of God.[28] The Word in this sense reveals the gracious character of God and the love of the Savior. Yet Calvin is not satisfied with an understanding of the Word that could be merely educational and would appeal only to the cognitive faculties of human beings. Like the sacraments, preaching works, according to Calvin, in appealing to the entire person (not just the intellect) through an attractive picture. Preachers present Christ so forcefully that their hearers can "see" and "hear" Christ themselves as if he were confronting them directly.[29]

The verb Calvin frequently uses to describe the function of the sacramental Word is *exhibere:* to present or represent.[30] The Word and the sacraments are exhibitive signs—they present or offer what they represent. Calvin explicitly rejects a merely memorialistic understanding of representation, that is, that the sacraments are like pictures that remind the partakers of things they represent.[31] On the contrary, the sacraments themselves confer grace. Calvin explains that by "exhibit" he means nothing less than to *give.*[32]

As in his discussion of sacraments, Calvin explicitly denies that the Word is a *bare* sign—that is, a sign devoid of the reality it represents. The Word itself is efficacious—it brings what it portrays.[33] The gift of the Word is the presence of Christ with all the benefits that he has secured for the elect—specifically, the twofold grace of justification and sanctification.[34] In addition, the preaching of the Word is itself the true exercise of the keys of the kingdom: it has the power both to save and to damn.[35] Calvin even speaks of preaching as "ratifying" the salvation secured in Christ's death.[36]

God uses the instrument of the Word, however, in such a way that its power and efficacy remain God's own. Calvin is careful to avoid what he takes to be the mechanistic implications of the Roman Catholic view that sacraments function *ex opere operato.*[37] Only when the Word is effectively sealed by the Holy Spirit can it be said to offer and present Christ to us. And if Calvin reserves the possibility that God can work faith in the hearts of the elect quite apart from any outward signs, he also insists that God is not bound to communicate grace only through the Word.[38] Nonetheless, Calvin is quick to insist that preaching, like the sacraments, is the regular and ordinary means by which God chooses to communicate the benefit of Christ's work.[39]

Both Word and sacraments are "accommodations" to human weakness. God "provides for our weakness in that he prefers to address us in human fashion through interpreters in order to draw us to himself, rather than to thunder at us and drive us away."[40] Likewise, since we are "creatures who always creep on the ground . . .

he condescends to lead us to himself even by these earthly elements, and to set before us in the flesh a mirror of spiritual blessings."[41] Some people, Calvin says, have difficulty accepting such accommodations. They believe God's Word is "dragged down by the baseness of the men called to teach it" and that they could benefit just as much from private meditation on the scripture.[42] They believe it improbable that a "drop of water" suffices to assure us of remission of sins, or that "a piece of bread and a drop of wine suffice to assure us that God accepts us as his children" and that in them we receive Jesus Christ and all his benefits.[43] Such doubts are understandable in respect to the true lowliness of the instruments consecrated to God's use, but they do not excuse believers from the necessity of acknowledging God's presence in the events of preaching and sacraments.

Calvin offers several explanations for why God chooses to work through all too fallible human instruments. First, the human mediation of the Word is an exercise in humility. If God were to speak to us directly from heaven, everyone would hear and believe, because everyone would be terrified at the majesty of God's glory. "But when a puny man risen up from the dust speaks in God's name, at this point we best evidence our piety and obedience toward God if we show ourselves teachable toward his minister, although he excels us in nothing."[44] Second, the ministry provides "the chief sinew by which believers are held together in one body."[45] If individuals were allowed to interpret scripture for themselves in isolation, each would despise the other, and there would be as many churches as there are individuals.

Ultimately, however, the use of human mediation for the Word is, like the incarnation itself, part of the mystery of divine grace in salvation. For the incarnation itself was also an accommodation to human weakness. Christ, the Mediator, was known to the patriarchs under the law. And the work of the Mediator was the same in the Old Covenant as it is in the New: to reveal the parental goodwill of God toward the elect.[46] But in emptying himself and taking on human flesh, the Mediator assures us, in the weakness of our conscience, that he is approachable—that we need not be afraid to come to him for help. Indeed, it is Christ who has come to *us* and extends his hand to us. As Calvin says in his commentary on Hebrews:

> It was not, indeed, the Apostle's object to weary us with . . . subtleties . . . but only to teach us that we have not to go far to seek a Mediator, since Christ of his own accord extends his hand to us, that we have no reason to dread the majesty of Christ since he is our brother, and that there is no cause to fear, lest he, as one unacquainted with evils, should not be touched by any feeling of humanity, so as to bring us help, since he took upon him our infirmities in order that he might be more inclined to succor us. . . . And the chief benefit of . . . [this] is a sure confidence in calling on God, as, on the other hand, the whole of religion falls to the ground, and is lost, when this certainty is taken away from consciences.[47]

This work of restoring human confidence in the goodness of God is carried on through the proclamation of the gospel. For Christ's own office of proclaiming the name of God and of filling all things is fulfilled in the ministry.[48] Thus the preached Word not only conveys Christ, but also continues Christ's living presence in the world. The sacramental Word is a re-presentation of the person and work of Christ. In this sense, the Word itself gives life and salvation, for it enables the hearers to receive the benefit of Christ's reconciling work.[49]

### THE SACRAMENTAL WORD AND THE TASK OF MINISTRY

If the preaching of the gospel is the very continuation of the presence of Christ in the world, it should not surprise us that for Calvin, and the Reformed tradition after him, the sermon takes on a liturgical significance not unlike that of the Eucharist itself. Calvin insisted that Word and sacrament must never be separated. He could not imagine a Eucharist without the proclamation of the gospel in preaching. But neither did he believe that preaching alone, without a celebration of the Eucharist, was sufficient for regular worship. He argued for years with the magistrates of the city of Geneva, trying to convince them of the importance of weekly Communion. But finally he compromised and agreed to a quarterly celebration of Communion (even though he was preaching almost daily). From that time on, churches in the Reformed tradition tended to elevate preaching to a position of relatively greater importance than that of the sacraments.[50]

There is a certain ambivalence to this emphasis on the Word. On the one hand, Reformed worship can be aridly intellectual and devoid of the mystical element that always remained a part of Calvin's piety.[51] And Reformed ministers—perhaps even Calvin himself—sometimes appear to arrogate to themselves inordinate authority because of their office of proclaiming God's Word to the church. On the other hand, however, the Reformed theology of the Word captures the scandal of particularity that is the scandal of incarnation itself: the Word of God comes in the form of human flesh.

It can hardly be overemphasized what a paradigm shift this understanding of the Word represented in sixteenth-century theology. Grace was no longer an incrementally infused quality but renewed personal relationship, made possible by God's initiative in addressing sinners.[52] The Roman Church, in the Council of Trent, decisively rejected this concept of grace. While they recognized the necessity of preaching and reading the Bible, the Tridentine fathers never attributed to preaching the function of conveying grace. The reference to Romans 10:17 in the "Decree Concerning Justification" falls in a chapter on *preparation* for receiving grace.[53] Like their medieval predecessors, the theologians at Trent could not see preaching as anything more than a preparation for receiving the sacraments "through which all true justice either begins, or being begun is increased, or being lost is restored."[54]

For Calvin, on the contrary, the one thing necessary is the Word that offers and presents Christ; without this Word, the sacraments are nothing more than vain superstitions.[55] But how can the preacher do this? How must sermons be constructed in order to be effective means of grace? Calvin never wrote a technical treatise on homilestics, and so we must look at his own preaching practice for answers to these questions. . . .

*Notes*

[1] *Inst.,* 4.14.6 (ET, 2:1281). Augustine, *In Joannis Evangelium Tractatus,* lxxx.3 (J. P. Migne, ed., *Patrologiae cursus completus, series Latina,* 221 vols. [Paris, 1844-1900], 35.1840).

[2] T.H.L. Parker describes this feature of Calvin's doctrine of preaching in his *The Oracles of God: An Introduction to the Preaching of John Calvin* (London: Lutterworth, 1947), 53-56. Ernst Bizer notes the same characteristic in Luther's theology in his important study *Fides ex auditu: Eine Unterschung über die Entdeckung der Gerechtigkeit Gottes durch Martin Luther* (Neukirchen: Verlag der Bucchandlung des Erziehungsvereins, 1958), 160. Others have referred to the sacramental Word in Calvin's theology. See B. A. Gerrish, "The Reformers' Theology of Worship," *McCormick Quarterly* 14 (1961): 29; Richard Stauffer, "Le Discours à la première personne dans les sermons de Calvin," in *Regards contemporains sur Jean Calvin* (Paris, 1965); Georges Bavaud, "Les Rapports entre la prédication et les sacrements dans le contexte du dialogue oecuménique," in *Communion et communication: Structures d'unité et modèles de communication de l'évangile. Troisième Cycle romand en thélogie practique (1976-77)* (Geneva: Labor et Fides, 1978), 69-73; B. A. Gerrish, *The Old Protestantism and the New: Essays on the Reformation Heritage* (Chicago: University of Chicago Press, 1982), 106-17; John H. Leith, "Calvin's Doctrine of the Proclamation of the Word and Its Significance for Today," in *John Calvin and the Church: A Prism of Reform,* ed. Timothy George (Louisville, Ky.: Westminster/John Knox Press, 1990), 211-12, 219; B. A. Gerrish, *Grace and Gratitude: The Eucharistic Theology of John Calvin* (Minneapolis: Augsburg Fortress Press, 1992), 82-86.

[3] See the articles, "Predigt," and "Wort Gottes," in *Die Religion in Geschichte und Gegenwart,* 3d ed., ed. Hans von Campenhausen et al., 6 vols. (Tübingen: J.C.B. Mohr [Paul Siebeck], 1957-62), 5:516-39, 6:1809-21. Cf. the article "Preaching," in *The New Schaff-Herzog Encyclopedia of Religious Knowledge,* ed. Samuel Macauley Jackson et al., 12 vols. (New York and London: Funk & Wagnalls, 1908-14), 9:158-89.

[4] Jean Daniélou, *Origen,* trans. W. Mitchell (New York: Sheed & Ward, 1955), 65.

[5] As Harnack notes, "To begin with it was an immense advance, only possible to so spiritual a man as Augustine, to rank the Word along with the Sacraments. It is to him we owe the phrase 'the Word and the Sacraments.' If he did not duly appreciate and carry out the import of the 'Word,' yet he perceived that as gospel it lay at the root of every saving rite of the church" (Adolf von Harnack, *History of Dogma,* trans. from the 3d German ed. by Neil Buchanan, 7 vols. [London, 1900; reprint, Gloucester, Mass.: Peter Smith, 1976], 5:155). Cf. Reinhold Seeberg, *Textbook of the History of Doctrines,* trans. Charles E. Hay, 2 vols. (Grand Rapids: Baker Book House, 1952), 2:282. See also Richard H. Grützmacher, *Wort und Geist: Eine historische und dogmatische Untersuchung zum Gnadenmittel des Wortes* (Leipzig: A. Deichert'sche Verlagsbuchhandlung [Georg Böhme], 1902), 1-7.

[6] Grützmacher attributes the increasing emphasis on the didactic character of the Word to the intensification of Augustine's predestinarianism in his later years and the corresponding need he felt to distinguish sharply between the inner work of the Spirit and the outer Word of preaching (*Wort und Geist,* 1-7). But in addition it should be noted that the Augustinian doctrine of sin and redemption created the need for a system of penance and satisfaction that rendered the Word as such less important for growth in grace.

[7] See T.H.L. Parker, *The Oracles of God,* 13-21; cf. Elmer Carl Kiessling, *The Early Sermons of Luther and Their Relation to the Pre-Reformation Sermon* (Grand Rapids: Zondervan Publishing House, 1935), 9-41; cf. also the articles on "Preaching," in *New Catholic Encyclopedia,* vol. 11 (New York: McGraw-Hill Book Co., 1967), 684-702. Of course the preaching theory and practice of the Middle Ages is a complex subject in its own right, and the paragraphs above are not intended to serve as anything more than a simple background to the discussion of Calvin's understanding of preaching that follows.

[8] See Michel Zink, *La Prédication en Langue Romane avant 1300* (Paris: Editions Honoré Champion, 1976), 431-75.

[9] For example, the Strassburg preacher John Geiler of Keisersberg (1445-1510) seems to have understood

preaching as a means of grace (E. Jane Dempsey Douglass, *Justification in Late Medieval Preaching: A Study of John Geiler of Keisersberg,* 2d ed. [Leiden: E. J. Brill, 1989], 82-91).

[10] See Ernst Bizer, *Fides ex auditu.* Harnack states: "Luther reduced the sacraments . . . to one only, namely, the Word of God. . . . For Luther . . . the sacraments are really only the 'visible word' . . . but the Word which is strong and mighty, because in it God himself works upon us and transacts with us. In the last analysis, it is a contrariety in the view of grace that comes out with special directness here. According to the Catholic view, grace is the power that is applied and infused through the sacraments, which, on condition of the cooperation of free will, enables man to fulfill the law of God and to acquire the merits that are requisite for salvation. But according to Luther grace is the Fatherly disposition of God, calling guilty man for Christ's sake to himself and receiving him by winning his trust through the presentation of the picture of Christ" (Harnack, *History of Dogma,* 7:216-17); cf. Seeberg, "Medieval theology constructed the doctrine of the sacraments. Luther was the first to frame a doctrine of the Word of God" (Seeberg, *Textbook of the History of Doctrines,* 2:282).

[11] Martin Luther, *Preface to the New Testament* (1545 [1522]), in *Luther's Works,* ed. Jaroslav Pelikan and Helmut T. Lehmann, 55 vols. (St. Louis: Concordia Publishing House; Philadelphia: Fortress Press, 1955-76), 6:443-44. This statement could have been made *verbatim* by F.D.E. Schleiermacher some three hundred years later. See chapter 4 below. One can find many more references to the Word as sacrament in Luther's works. See, for example, his sermon for Christmas Day 1519: "All the words and all the narratives of the Gospel are a kind of sacraments: that is, sacred signs by which God effects in believers what the narratives signify" (*D. Martin Luthers Werke: Kritische Gesamtausgabe* [Weimar, 1883-], 9.440.3; hereafter cited as *WA*). In his 1519 *Commentary on Galatians* Luther states, "The Word, I say, and the Word alone is the vehicle of divine grace" (*WA* 2.509.13).

[12] *Inst.,* 4.14.3, 14 (ET, 2:1278, 1289-90). It must be noted, however, that Luther and Calvin do not understand the sacramental Word in precisely the same way. In fact, their respective views on preaching mirror their different understandings of the sacraments. See T.H.L. Parker, *The Oracles of God,* 45ff.

[13] For an excellent discussion of this problem, see John T. McNeil, "The Significance of the Word of God for Calvin," *Church History* 28 (1959): 131-46, esp. 139.

[14] *Inst.,* 1.7-9 (ET, 1:74-96). See also B. A. Gerrish, *The Old Protestantism and the New,* 58-64, 296-300; Alexandre Ganoczy and Stefan Scheld, *Die Hermeneutik Calvins: Geistesgeschichtliche Voraussetzungen und Grundzüge,* Veröffentlichungen des Instituts für Europäische Geschichte Mainz, vol. 114 (Wiesbaden: Franz Steiner Verlag, 1983), 90-92; H. Jackson Fortsman, *Word and Spirit: Calvin's Doctrine of Biblical Authority* (Stanford, Calif.: Stanford University Press, 1962).

[15] *Comm. 2 Tim.* 3:15 (*CO* 52:382).

[16] See, for example, his preface to Olivetán's New Testament (*CO* 9:815) and *Comm. John* 5:39 (*CO* 47:125). For more discussion of the limits of Calvin's biblicism, see B. A. Gerrish, *The Old Protestantism and the New,* 61-62, and H. Jackson Forstman, *Word and Spirit,* 39-41.

[17] *Comm. Harm. of the Gospel* (*CO* 45:1).

[18] *Comm. Gal.* 1:7 (*CO* 50:173); *Comm. 1 Peter* 1:13 (*CO* 55:221); *Comm. Titus* 1:3 (*CO* 52:407); *Comm. 1 John* 1:3 (*CO* 55:302), *Comm. Acts* 5:20 (*CO* 48:106-7); *Comm. Eph.* 3:7 (*CO* 51:180).

[19] *Comm. Eph.* 2:17 (*CO* 51:173).

[20] See, for example, *Comm. Rom.* 1:16; 16:21 (*CO* 49:19, 290); and *Comm. Titus* 1:3 (*CO* 52:407). It is quite appropriate to take preaching as the primary sense in which Calvin used the term "Word of God," since he almost always translated *verbum Dei* as "la Parole de Dieu," a term that is used only for the spoken, not the written, word. In this matter, however, Calvin was not original. Erasmus before him, in his Latin translation of the New Testament, had rendered John 1:1 as "In the beginning was the speech [*sermo*]" (*Un inédit d'Erasme: La première version du Nouveau Testament: copiée par Pierre Meghen, 1506-1509,* ed. Henri Gibaud [Angers: H. Gibaud, 1982], 188).

[21] *Comm. John* 3:14 (*CO* 47:62-63). It is interesting that Calvin gives essentially the same explanation of this event and Jesus' reference to it when he comments on the Old Testament passage that originally recounts it (*Comm. Num.* 21:8-9 [*CO* 25:249-50]). Schleiermacher argues in a similar fashion that, "if one understands the 'lifting up' to refer to the crucifixion of Christ, that is a totally capricious interpretation; nothing more is meant by 'lifting up' than to become generally visible" (*Das Leben Jesu* [SW I/6:345]). Calvin speaks of Christ "as if" present, in this passage, not to deny the real presence of Christ, but to distinguish his spiritual presence from a crassly physical or local presence. This is exactly the same move Calvin makes when speaking of the presence of Christ in the Lord's

Supper. See B. A. Gerish, *Grace and Gratitude,* 145n, 180-81n.

[22] *Inst.,* 2.9-11, 4.14.18-26 (ET, 1:423-64, 2:1294-1303).
[23] *Comm. John* 3:14 (*CO* 47:63).

[24] *Comm. John* 7:33 (*CO* 47:178).

[25] This understanding of the preaching event was taken up into the Reformed tradition and preserved in the *Second Helvetic Confession* (1566), written by the Zurich reformer Heinrich Bullinger (1504-66). It states: "Proinde cum hodie hoc Dei verbum per praedicatores legitime vocatos annunciatur in Ecclesia, credimus ipsum Dei verbum annunciari et a fidelibus recipi, neque aliud Dei verbum vel fingendum, vel coelitus esse exspectandum" (*The Creeds of Christendom,* ed. Philip Schaff [New York: Harper, 1877; 4th ed., 1919], vol. 3, 237).

[26] The second passage I used for an epigraph to this chapter states this clearly (*Petit traicté de la Saincte Cene de nostre Seigneur Iesus Christ* [*CO* 5:435]).

[27] *Inst.,* 2.5.5, 4.14.12 (ET, 1:321-23, 2:1287); *Comm. Acts* 16:14 (*CO* 48:378); *Comm. Eph.* 5:26 (*CO* 51:223-24).

[28] See sermon 31 on the harmony of the Gospels (*CO* 46:378); see also *Comm. Matt.* 4:1 (*CO* 45:128); *Comm. Luke* 2:30 (*CO* 45:90); *Comm. John* 3:14 (*CO* 47:62-63); *Comm. John* 8:19 (*CO* 47:195); *Comm. 1 Peter* 1:13 (*CO* 55:221).

[29] *Comm. Isa.* 11:4 (*CO* 36:240); *Comm. Gal.* 3:1 (*CO* 50:202-3).

[30] For example in *Inst.,* 1.9.3 (ET, 1:95-96); cf. the argument to the sermons on the Harmony of the Gospels (*CO* 46:v).

[31] This was Zwingli's understanding of the sacraments. For Calvin's criticism of it, see his letter to Heinrich Bullinger, February 25, 1547 (*CO* 12:480-89).

[32] *CO* 12:483-88.

[33] *Inst.,* 4.17.5, 10 (ET, 2:1364-65, 1370-71); *Comm. John* 1:12 (*CO* 47:12); *Comm. John* 6:51 (*CO* 47:153); *Comm. Heb.* 4:2, 12 (*CO* 55:45-46, 49-52); *Comm. 1 Peter* 1:23, 25 (*CO* 55:228-31); *Comm. 1 John* 1:1-2 (*CO* 55:301-2).

[34] *Petit traicté de la Saincte Cene* (*CO* 5:435); *Comm. John* 15:3, 17:17 (*CO* 47:340, 385); *Comm. Acts* 5:20, 10:36 (*CO* 48:106-7, 244).

[35] *Inst.,* 4.1.22 (ET, 2:1035-36); cf. *Comm. Matt.* 3:12 (*CO* 45:123); *Comm. 1 Tim.* 4:16 (*CO* 52:303-4).

[36] *Comm. Acts* 26:18 (*CO* 48:542); cf. *Comm. John* 20:23 (*CO* 47:441).
[37] *Inst.,* 4.14.14 (ET, 2:1289-90); cf. *Comm. Acts* 7:35 (*CO* 48:149).

[38] *Inst.,* 1.7, 1.8.3, 4.14.14, 17 (ET, 1:74-81, 83-84, 2:1289-90, 1292-94); *Comm. Acts* 16:14 (*CO* 48:378); *Comm. Eph.* 5:26 (*CO* 51:223-24).

[39] *Comm. Rom.* 10:14, 11:14 (*CO* 49:205, 219).

[40] *Inst.,* 4.1.5 (ET, 2:1016-20).

[41] *Inst.,* 4.14.3 (ET, 2:1278).

[42] *Inst.,* 4.1.5 (ET, 2:1016-20).

[43] *Serm. Luke 2:1-14* (*CO* 46:960).

[44] *Inst.,* 4.3.1 (ET, 2:1054).

[45] *Inst.,* 4.3.2 (ET, 2:1055).

[46] *Inst.,* 2.6.2-4 (ET, 1:342-48).

[47] *Comm. Heb.* 4:15-16 (*CO* 55:54-56).

[48] *Inst.,* 4.3.2 (ET, 2:1054-55); *Comm. Heb.* 2:11 (*CO* 55:29).

[49] The first epigraph I chose for this chapter conveys just this point (*Inst.,* 2.10.7 [ET, 1:434]).

[50] William D. Maxwell, *An Outline of Christian Worship: Its Development and Forms* (London: Oxford University Press, 1936), 112-19.

[51] In trying to explain the nature of Christ's presence in the sacrament of the Lord's Supper, Calvin states that "I experience rather than understand it" (*Inst.,* 4.17.32 [ET, 2:1403]).

[52] See Melanchthon's discussion of grace in his *Loci Communes Theologici,* in *Melanchthon and Bucer,* Library of Christian Classics, vol. 19, ed. Wilhelm Pauck (Philadelphia: Westminster Press, 1969), 86-88.

[53] *Canons and Decrees of the Council of Trent: Original Text with an English Translation,* trans. H. J. Schroeder, O.P. (St. Louis: B. Herder Books, 1941), 26, 32, 305, 311.

[54] *Canons and Decrees of the Council of Trént,* 51, 329.

[55] *Inst.,* 4.14.3-4 (ET, 2:1278-80).

## FURTHER READING

### Bibliography


Bihary, Michael. *Bibliographia Calviniana.* N. J.: Princeton University Press, 1992, 194 p.

Comprehensive bibliographic resource.

Gamble, Richard C. "Current Trends in Calvin Research." In *Calvinus Sacrae Scripturae Professor*, pp. 91-112. Grand Rapids, Mi.: Eerdmans, 1990.

A bibliographic essay surveying historical, linguistic, and theological scholarship on Calvin.


### Biography


Bouwsma, William J. *John Calvin: A Sixteenth-Century Portrait.* New York: Oxford University Press, 1988, 310 p.

Biography that "tries to interpret Calvin as a figure of his time: As a representative Freud intellectual, an evangelical humanist and therefore a rhetorician, and an exile."

McGrath, Alister E. *A Life of John Calvin.* Oxford: Blackwell, 1990, 332 p.

General biographical survey.


### Criticism


Barth, Karl. *The Theology of John Calvin.* Grand Rapids, Mi.: Eerdmans, 1995, 424 p.

The preeminent Swiss neo-orthodox theologian thoroughly treats his Reformation predecessor.

Battenhouse, Roy W. "The Doctrine of Man in Calvin and in Renaissance Platonism." *Journal of the History of Ideas* 9, No. 4 (October 1948): 447-71.

Revisionist argument by a noted literary scholar who sees humanistic Platonism and even Pelagian roots in Calvin's thought.

Battles, F. L., et al. *John Calvin.* Grand Rapids, Mi: Eerdmans, 1966, 228p.

Anthology containing essays, among others, on Calvin's letter writing and sermons.

Belloc, Hilaire. *How the Reformation Happened.* London: Jonathan Cape, 1928, 293 p.

Anti-Calvinist polemic by a pre-Vatican II triumphalist Catholic.

Butin, Philip Walker. *Revelation, Redemption, and Response: Calvin's Trinitarian Understanding of the Divine-Human Relationship.* New York: Oxford University Press, 1995, 232 p.

Assesses the significance of Calvin's understanding of the divine-human relationship and its importance to the historical development of Christian doctrine.

Davies, Rupert E. *The Problem of Authority in the Continental Reformers: A Study in Luther, Zwingli, and Calvin.* Westport, Conn.: Greenwood Press, 1978, 158 p.

Davies examines the central epistemological problem of Protestantism, and indeed of all theology, "Is there any accessible source of religious truth which is wholly authorative?"

Dickens, Arthur Geoffrey. *Reformation and Society in Sixteenth-Century Europe.* London: Thames and Hudson, 1966, 216 p.

Illustrated introduction to the Reformation milieau.

Doumergue, Emile. *Jean Calvin, les hommes et les choses de son temps.* 7 vols. Lausanne: 1899-1927.

Monumental scholarly source on Calvin, available only in French.

Eire, Carlos M. N. *War against the Idols.* Cambridge: Cambridge University Press, 1986, 325 p.

Addresses Protestantism's attack at the use of images in Catholic worship.

Elton, Geoffrey R. *Reformation Europe 1517-1559.* London: Collins, 1963, 349 p.

Overview of the European situation and key personalities at the time of the Reformation.

Foxgrover, David. "Calvin as a Reformer: Christ's Standard Bearer." In *Leaders of the Reformation,* pp. 178-210. London and Toronto: Associated University Presses, 1984.

Analysis of Calvin's self-assessment as one called to restore a church in ruins.

Gerrish, Brian A. *The Old Protestantism and the New: Essays on the Reformation Heritage.* Chicago: University of Chicago, 1982, 422 p.

Essays on various Reformation issues relating to the clarification of Reformation principles.

_____. *Grace and Gratitude: The Eucharistic Theology of John Calvin.* Minneapolis: Fortress, 1993, 210 p.

A study of the Lord's supper in Calvin.

Graham, W. Fred. *The Constructive Revolutionary.* Richmond: John Knox Press, 1971, 271 p.

Thorough survey of the effect of Calvin and Calvinism on socio-economic life.

Hall, Charles. *With the Spirit's Sword.* Zurich: Evz-Verlag, 1968, 227 p.

Traces the Pauline theme of spiritual warfare in the theology of Calvin.

Hancock, Ralph C. *Calvin and the Foundations of Modern Politics.* Ithaca and London: Cornell University Press, 1989, 221 p.

Calvin is shown to encourage and critique democratic theory.

Hesselink, I. John. *Calvin's Concept of Law.* Allison Park, Penn.: Pickwick Publications, 1992, 311 p.

The law of God is treated as a positive aspect of Calvin's theology expressing God's rule.

Hoitenga Jr., Dewey J. *Faith and Reason from Plato to Plantinga.* Albany: State University of New York, 1991, 263 p.

An introduction to Reformed epistemology.

Kendall, R. T. *Calvin and English Calvinism to 1649.* Oxford: Oxford University Press, 1979, 238 p.

Historical and theological dissertation regarding Calvin's thought as found in the works of Theodore Beza, and further transposed into the English setting of William Perkins and the Westminster Assembly.

Leith, John H. *John Calvin's Doctrine of the Christian Life.* Louisville: Wesminster/John Knox, 1989, 230 p.

Discussion of piety in relation to Calvin's theology.

Littell, Franklin H., ed. *Reformation Studies: Essays in Honor of Roland H. Bainton.* Richmond: John Knox Press, 1962, 285 p.

Collection two essays on Calvin regarding his theological method and his view of the relation of God's Grace to His Glory.

McNeill, John T. "The Democratic Element in Calvin's Thought." *Church History* 18, No. 3 (September 1949): 153-71.

A study of Calvin's political theory—defending liberty, fraternity through God's Fatherhood, but having doubts about the possibility or benefit of equality.

_____. *The History and Character of Calvinism.* New York, 1954, 466 p.

Very thorough study of Calvinism in western culture.

_____. "The Significance of the Word of God for Calvin." *Church History* 28, No. 2 (June 1959): 131-46.

Summary of Calvin's views on the supremacy of scripture in faith and practice.

Parker, T.H.L. "The Self-Revelation of the Creator." In *The Doctrine of the Knowledge of God: A Study in the Theology of John Calvin*, pp. 7-24. London: Oliver and Boyd, 1952.

Contends that for Calvin, mankind's knowledge of God, though innate through the created order, is most fully comprehended in the Special Revelation of Scripture.

_____. "Christianae Religionis Institutio." In *John Calvin: A Biography*, pp. 34-50. Philadelphia: The Westminster Press, 1975.

Analyzes the *Institutes*, giving a picture of its character, purpose, treatment of the Law, faith, prayer, sacraments, and Christian Liberty. He further notes that its summary of standard catechismal topics according to the "Bible Alone" hermeneutic helped define the emerging Reformed Faith.

_____. *Calvin's Preaching.* Louisville, Kent.: Westminster/John Knox Press, 1992, 202 p.

An updated, and rearranged version of Parker's 1947 *The Oracles of God: An Introduction to the Preaching of John Calvin,* which, like its predecessor, attempts to show "a Calvin very different from the unattractive effigy" that has characterized our English speaking image of the Reformer."

Partee, Charles. "Calvin's Central Dogma Again." *The Seventeenth Century Journal* 18, No. 2 (Summer 1987): 191-99.

Suggests that we move from the central doctrine God's Sovereignty to "Union with Christ" in studying Calvin.

Richard, Lucien Joseph. *The Spirituality of John Calvin.* Atlanta, Ga.: John Knox Press, 1974, 207 p.

Examines the roots and fruition of Calvin's spirituality relating to devotion, piety, and wisdom.

Selinger, Suzanne. *Calvin Against Himself.* Hamden, Conn.: Archon Books, 1984, 238 p.

Psycho-history that sees Calvin as a product of his times and culture.

Steinmetz, David C. *Calvin in Context.* New York: Oxford University Press, 1995, 235 p.

General introduction to Calvin's thought, with context provided by the writings of Calvin's own contemporaries and their sources.

Warfield, B. B. *Calvin and Augustine.* Philadelphia: Presbyterian and Reformed Publishing, 1980, 507 p.

Appreciative essays of Augustine and his chief disciple by the Princeton's turn of the century Biblical inerrantist.

Wendel, Francois. *Calvin.* New York: Harper and Row, 1950, 383 p.

An exposition of the theology of Calvin stressing the origins and development of his religious thought.

Zachman, Randall C. *The Assurance of Faith.* Minneapolis: Fortress Press, 1993, 258 p.

Calvin and Luther are both shown to agree that assurance of salvation "lies in the grace and mercy of God towoard us in Jesus Christ crucified, revealed to us in the gospel."

# John Knox

## 1514?-1572

Scottish religious reformer, theologian, and historian.

### INTRODUCTION

Credited by Thomas Carlyle as the man who caused the people of Scotland to *live,* Knox was a key figure in the Scottish Reformation and the founder of Scottish Presbyterianism. Considered by many to be responsible for Scotland's religious and political freedom, Knox was the author of many letters and pamphlets which attacked the Catholic Church, which he termed the "Antichrist," and its priests, "vermin of shavelings utterly corrupted." It was Knox's fervent belief that all worshipping and service invented by man without God's expressed commandment was idolatry; the Roman Catholic mass fit this criterion and so constituted idolatry. In addition to trying to rid religion of the influence of the hated Pope, Knox also vocally attacked women as rulers. *The First Blast of the Trumpet against the Monstrous Regiment of Women* (1558) was aimed at Mary Tudor, Queen of England, but was interpreted generally, with international application. Knox's preaching inspired and incited Scotland to fight the Catholic Church; eventually the Pope's authority was abolished, as were the jurisdictions of the prelates, and celebration of the mass was made a crime. His *Scots Confession* (1560), co-written with five other ministers at the end of the Scottish Civil War, became the Scottish church's official theological text.

### Biographical Information

The exact date of Knox's birth is unknown. Although 1505 was generally believed to be the year of his birth, this date was challenged, and now 1514 is widely accepted as the correct date. Knox was born near the burgh of Haddington in East Lothian. Little is known of his parents or of Knox's early life. It is presumed that Knox attended the University of St. Andrews to train for the priesthood and that he took his priestly orders around the age of twenty-five. He also held a minor governmental post and worked as a tutor. Knox met George Wishart in the winter of 1545-46, just weeks before the reformer was burned at the stake by Cardinal Beaton. Knox was inspired by Wishart and soon became a zealous Protestant. From this point on most of Knox's life would be spent in violent opposition to the ruling powers about him. When Beaton was assassinated, Knox was accused of plotting the murder and fled to a castle garrison at St. Andrews. In June of 1547 Knox was the preacher at the castle when it fell to the French, and he soon found himself a galley slave. His first work, directed to his congregation of St. Andrews, now prisoners of France, was written during his nineteen-month imprisonment. Upon his release Knox traveled to England and preached there for five years. After Mary Tudor became Queen, Knox fled to the continent. In Geneva he met and studied with John Calvin; although heavily influenced by him, Knox did not hesitate to differ with Calvin in print. It is thought that *The First Blast of the Trumpet against the Monstrous Regiment of Women* was published anonymously so as not to openly disagree with the powerful Calvin, but it was widely known that Knox was the author of the pamphlet. The first half of 1558 also saw the publication of two other of his most important writings: the *Appellation from the Sentence Pronounced by the Bishops and Clergy: Addressed to the Nobility and Estates of Scotland,* and the *Letter Addressed to the Commonalty of Scotland.* Knox attempted to bring Mary, Queen of Scots, to Jesus; she in turn offered bribes of political power to Knox to bring him back to Catholicism. Neither was swayed, though Mary is said to have feared the sight of Knox on his knees in prayer more than all the assembled armies of Europe. Although Knox was successful at removing the Catholic Church from Scotland, starting a new church proved much more difficult, as he was hampered at every turn, and his final ten years were full of disillusionment. Knox died in Edinburgh on November 24, 1572.

### Major Works

*The First Blast of the Trumpet against the Monstrous Regiment of Women,* invoking the words of the Old Testament against female rule, is an attack on the Catholic Mary Tudor, referred to as Jezebel. Its publication unfortunately coincided with the accession of the Protestant Elizabeth I, and Knox spent much effort on assuaging the feelings of the new Queen. Two planned sequels were never realized, although Knox published an outline of the proposed second work. *The Appellation from the Sentence Pronounced by the Bishops and Clergy* is a response to having been tried in absentia by the prelates, condemned, and burned in effigy. Knox calls on the nobles to exercise their duty to defend the innocent and punish the evil. He calls for the establishment and defense of Protestant worship and resistance to "idolatrous" tyrants. In *Letter Addressed to the Commonalty of Scotland* Knox again urges everyone to heed the word of God, insisting that it is one's duty to oppose false religion and one's right to defend one's conscience against persecution. *The History of the Reformation of Religion within the Realm of Scotland* was not published during Knox's lifetime, possibly because the political situation described therein was rapidly changing. When it was published in London in 1587, Queen Elizabeth immediately suppressed it.

### Critical Reception

Critics have pointed out that Knox was not a systematic thinker or writer. His individual writings were intended for particular purposes and addressed to particular audiences, so there is no one work that encompasses Knox's views in a fully developed fashion. This has led many critics to charge Knox with being disorganized, contradictory, and inconsistent. *The First Blast of the Trumpet against the Monstrous Regiment of Women* received quick critical response, from both Catholics full of opposition and Protestants wishing to distance themselves from what they felt were Knox's overly strong views against women. One writer called the author an "impudent, vile and shameless villain traitor." Even in the century after his death Knox was considered a threat to established order in England and his writings were banned and burned at Oxford University. Knox did not appear to have literary ambitions; he wrote to incite his readers to follow God's word, and there is general agreement among scholars that he was a forceful motivational speaker. B. K. Kuiper has likened Knox's preaching to a spark in a keg of gunpowder. But other critics have also focused on aspects of Knox's writing style. William Croft Dickinson has commented that Knox's English is "robust in style and rich in vocabulary" and that "in language and style the *History* is a masterpiece written by a man who could marshal words to meet his mood." Kevin Reed has described Knox the author as riveting, possessed of extraordinary zeal and knowledge. Emphasizing his influence on Scottish history, P. Hume Brown has written that Knox "revealed the heart and mind of the nation to itself." Many Scots still revere Knox and consider him the greatest man their nation has produced.

## PRINCIPAL WORKS

*A Vindication of the Doctrine that the Sacrifice of the Mass Is Idolatry* (essay) 1550
*A Faithful Admonition to the Professors of God's Truth in England* (essay) 1554
*Two Comfortable Epistles to His Afflicted Brethren in England* (letters) 1554
*The Copy of a Letter Delivered to the Lady Marie, Regent of Scotland* (letter) 1556; augmented 1558
*The Appellation from the Sentence Pronounced by the Bishops and Clergy: Addressed to the Nobility and Estates of Scotland* (letter) 1558
*The First Blast of the Trumpet against the Monstrous Regiment of Women* (essay) 1558
*Letter Addressed to the Commonalty of Scotland* (letter) 1558
*The Scots Confession* [co-author] (manifesto) 1560
*The History of the Reformation of Religion within the Realm of Scotland* (history) 1587

## CRITICISM

### Robert Louis Stevenson (essay date 1882)

SOURCE: "John Knox and Women," in *Familiar Studies of Men & Books*, Chatto and Windus, 1882, pp. 295-356.

[*In the following excerpt, the famous English novelist discusses the political expediency of Knox and the compromises Knox made concerning the controversial issue of female rule.*]

When first the idea became widely spread among men that the Word of God, instead of being truly the foundation of all existing institutions, was rather a stone which the builders had rejected, it was but natural that the consequent havoc among received opinions should be accompanied by the generation of many new and lively hopes for the future. Somewhat as in the early days of the French Revolution, men must have looked for an immediate and universal improvement in their condition. Christianity, up to that time, had been somewhat of a failure politically. The reason was now obvious, the capital flaw was detected, the sickness of the body politic traced at last to its efficient cause. It was only necessary to put the Bible thoroughly into practice, to set themselves strenuously to realise in life the Holy Commonwealth, and all abuses and iniquities would surely pass away. Thus, in a pageant played at Geneva in the year 1523, the world was represented as a sick man at the end of his wits for help, to whom his doctor recommends Lutheran specifics.[1]

The Reformers themselves had set their affections in a different world, and professed to look for the finished result of their endeavours on the other side of death. They took no interest in politics as such; they even condemned political action as Antichristian: notably, Luther in the case of the Peasants' War. And yet, as the purely religious question was inseparably complicated with political difficulties, and they had to make opposition, from day to day, against principalities and powers, they were led, one after another, and again and again, to leave the sphere which was more strictly their own, and meddle, for good and evil, with the affairs of State. Not much was to be expected from interference in such a spirit. Whenever a minister found himself galled or hindered, he would be inclined to suppose some contravention of the Bible. Whenever Christian liberty was restrained (and Christian liberty for each individual would be about coextensive with what he wished to do), it was obvious that the State was Antichristian. The great thing, and the one thing, was to push the Gospel and the Reformer's own interpretation of it. Whatever helped was good; whatever hindered was evil; and if this simple classification proved inapplicable over the whole field, it was no business of his to stop and reconcile incongruities. He had more pressing concerns on hand; he had to save souls; he had to be about his Father's business. This short-sighted view resulted in a doctrine that was actually Jesuitical in application. They had no serious ideas upon politics, and they were ready, nay, they seemed almost bound, to adopt and support whichever ensured for the moment the greatest benefit to the souls of their fellow-men. They were dishonest in all sincerity. Thus Labitte, in the introduction to a book[2] in which he exposes the hypocritical democracy of the Catholics under the League, steps aside for a moment to stigmatise the hypocritical democracy of the Protestants. And nowhere was this expediency in political questions more apparent than about the question of female sovereignty. So much was this the case that one James Thomasius, of Leipsic, wrote a little paper[3] about the religious partialities of those who took part in the controversy, in which some of these learned disputants cut a very sorry figure.

Now Knox has been from the first a man well hated; and it is somewhat characteristic of his luck that he figures here in the very forefront of the list of partial scribes who trimmed their doctrine with the wind in all good conscience, and were political weathercocks out of conviction. Not only has Thomasius mentioned him, but Bayle has taken the hint from Thomasius, and dedicated a long note to the matter at the end of his article on the Scottish Reformer. This is a little less than fair. If anyone among the evangelists of that period showed more serious political sense than another, it was assuredly Knox; and even in this very matter of female rule, although I do not suppose anyone nowadays will feel inclined to endorse his sentiments, I confess I can make great allowance for his conduct. The controversy, besides, has an interest of its own, in view of later controversies.

John Knox, from 1556 to 1559, was resident in Geneva, as minister, jointly with Goodman, of a little church of English refugees. He and his congregation were banished from England by one woman, Mary Tudor, and proscribed in Scotland by another, the Regent Mary of Guise. The coincidence was tempting: here were many abuses centring about one abuse; here was Christ's Gospel persecuted in the two kingdoms by one anomalous power. He had not far to go to find the idea that female government was anomalous. It was an age, indeed, in which women, capable and incapable, played a conspicuous part upon the stage of European history; and yet their rule, whatever may have been the opinion of here and there a wise man or enthusiast, was regarded as an anomaly by the great bulk of their contemporaries. It was defended as an anomaly. It, and all that accompanied and sanctioned it, was set aside as a single exception; and no one thought of reasoning down from queens and extending their privileges to ordinary women. Great ladies, as we know, had the privilege of entering into monasteries and cloisters, otherwise forbidden to their sex. As with one thing, so with another. Thus, Margaret of Navarre wrote books with great acclamation, and no one, seemingly, saw fit to call her conduct in question; but Mademoiselle de Gournay, Montaigne's adopted daughter, was in a controversy with the world as to whether a woman might be an author without incongruity. Thus, too, we have Théodore Agrippa d'Aubigné writing to his daughters about the learned women of his century, and cautioning them, in conclusion, that the study of letters was unsuited to ladies of a middling station, and should be reserved for princesses.[4] And once more, if we desire to see the same principle carried to ludicrous extreme, we shall find that Reverend Father in God the Abbot of Brantôme claiming, on the authority of some lord of his acquaintance, a privilege, or rather a duty, of free love for great princesses, and carefully excluding other ladies from the same gallant dispensation.[5] One sees the spirit in which these immunities were granted; and how they were but the natural consequence of that awe for courts and kings that made the last writer tell us, with simple wonder, how Catherine de Medici would "laugh her fill just like another" over the humours of pantaloons and zanies. And such servility was, of all things, what would touch most nearly the republican spirit of Knox. It was not difficult for him to set aside this weak scruple of loyalty. The lantern of his analysis did not always shine with a very serviceable light; but he had the virtue, at least, to carry it into many places of fictitious holiness, and was not abashed by the tinsel divinity that hedged kings and queens from his contemporaries. And so he could put the proposition in the form already mentioned: there was Christ's Gospel persecuted in the two kingdoms by one anomalous power; plainly, then, the "regiment of women" was Antichristian. Early in 1558 he communicated this discovery to the world, by publishing at Geneva his notorious book—***The First Blast of the Trumpet against the Monstrous Regiment of Women***.[6]

As a whole, it is a dull performance; but the preface, as is usual with Knox, is both interesting and morally fine. Knox was not one of those who are humble in the hour of triumph; he was aggressive even when things were at their worst. He had a grim reliance in himself, or rather in his mission; if he were not sure that he was a great man, he was at least sure that he was one set apart to do great things. And he judged simply that whatever passed in his mind, whatever moved him to flee from persecution instead of constantly facing it out, or, as here, to publish and withhold his name from the title-page of a critical work, would not fail to be of interest, perhaps of benefit, to the world. There may be something more finely sensitive in the modern humour, that tends more and more to withdraw a man's personality from the lessons he inculcates or the cause that he has espoused; but there is a loss herewith of wholesome responsibility; and when we find in the works of Knox, as in the Epistles of Paul, the man himself standing nakedly forward, courting and anticipating criticism, putting his character, as it were, in pledge for the sincerity of his doctrine, we had best waive the question of delicacy, and make our acknowledgments for a lesson of courage, not unnecessary in these days of anonymous criticism, and much light, otherwise unattainable, on the spirit in which great movements were initiated and carried forward. Knox's personal revelations are always interesting; and, in the case of the ***First Blast,*** as I have said, there is no exception to the rule. He begins by stating the solemn responsibility of all who are watchmen over God's flock; and all are watchmen (he goes on to explain, with that fine breadth of spirit that characterises him even when, as here, he shows himself most narrow), all are watchmen "whose eyes God doth open, and whose conscience he pricketh to admonish the ungodly." And with the full consciousness of this great duty before him, he sets himself to answer the scruples of timorous or worldly-minded people. How can a man repent, he asks, unless the nature of his transgression is made plain to him? "And therefore I say," he continues, "that of necessity it is that this monstriferous empire of women (which among all enormities that this day do abound upon the face of the whole earth, is most detestable and damnable) be openly and plainly declared to the world, to the end that some may repent and be saved." To those who think the doctrine useless, because it cannot be expected to amend those princes whom it would dispossess if once accepted, he makes answer in a strain that shows him at his greatest. After having instanced how the rumour of Christ's censures found its way to Herod in his own court, "even so," he continues, "may the sound of our weak trumpet, by the support of some wind (blow it from the south, or blow it from the north, it is of no matter), come to the ears of the chief offenders. *But whether it do or not, yet dare we not cease to blow as God will give strength. For we are debtors to more than to princes, to wit, to the great multitude of our brethren,* of whom, no doubt, a great number have heretofore offended by error and ignorance."

It is for the multitude, then, he writes; he does not greatly hope that his trumpet will be audible in palaces, or that crowned women will submissively discrown themselves at his appeal; what he does hope, in plain English, is to encourage and justify rebellion; and we shall see, before we have done, that he can put his purpose into words as roundly as I can put it for him. This he sees to be a matter of much hazard; he is not "altogether so brutish and insensible, but that he has laid his account what the finishing of the work may cost." He knows that he will find many adversaries, since "to the most part of men, lawful and godly appeareth whatsoever antiquity hath received." He looks for opposition, "not only of the ignorant multitude, but of the wise, politie, and quiet spirits of the earth." He will be called foolish, curious, despiteful, and a sower of sedition; and one day, perhaps, for all he is now nameless, he may be attainted of treason. Yet he has "determined to obey God, notwithstanding that the world shall rage thereat." Finally, he makes some excuse for the anonymous appearance of this first instalment: it is his purpose thrice to blow the trumpet in this matter, if God so permit; twice he intends to do it without name; but at the last blast to take the odium upon himself, that all others may be purged.

Thus he ends the preface, and enters upon his argument with a secondary title: ***The First Blast to awake Women degenerate***. We are in the land of assertion without delay. That a woman should bear rule, superiority, dominion or empire over any realm, nation, or city, he tells us, is repugnant to nature, contumely to God, and a subversion of good order. Women are weak, frail, impatient, feeble, and foolish. God has denied to woman wisdom to consider, or providence to foresee, what is profitable to a commonwealth. Women have been ever lightly esteemed; they have been denied the tutory of their own sons, and subjected to the unquestionable sway of their husbands; and surely it is irrational to give the greater where the less has been withheld, and suffer a woman to reign supreme over a great kingdom who would be allowed no authority by her own fireside. He appeals to the Bible; but though he makes much of the first transgression and certain strong texts in Genesis and Paul's Epistles, he does not appeal with entire success. The cases of Deborah and Huldah can be brought into no sort of harmony with his thesis. Indeed, I may say that, logically, he left his bones there; and that it is but the phantom of an argument that he parades thenceforward to the end. Well was it for Knox that he succeeded no better; it is under this very ambiguity about Deborah that we shall find him fain to creep for shelter before he is done with the regiment of women. After having thus exhausted Scripture, and formulated its teaching in the somewhat blasphemous maxim that the man is placed above the woman, even as God above the angels, he goes on triumphantly to adduce the testimonies of Tertullian, Augustine, Ambrose, Basil, Chrysostom, and the Pandects; and having gathered this little cloud of witnesses about him, like pursuivants about a herald, he solemnly proclaims all reigning women to be traitoresses and rebels against God; discharges all men thenceforward from holding any office under such monstrous regiment, and calls upon all the lieges with one consent to *"study to repress the inordinate pride and tyranny" of queens*. If this is not treasonable teaching, one would be glad to know what is; and yet, as if he feared had not made the case plain enough against himself, he goes on to deduce the startling corollary that all oaths of allegiance must be incontinently broken. If it was sin thus to have sworn even in ignorance, it were obstinate sin to continue to respect them after fuller knowledge. Then comes the peroration, in which he cries aloud against the cruelties of that cursed Jezebel of England—that horrible monster Jezebel of England; and after having predicted sudden destruction to her rule and to the rule of all crowned women, and warned all men that if they presume to defend the same when any "noble heart" shall be raised up to vindicate the liberty of his country, they shall not fail to perish themselves in the ruin, he concludes with a last rhetorical flourish: "And therefore let all men be advertised, for THE TRUMPET HATH ONCE BLOWN."

The capitals are his own. In writing, he probably felt the want of some such reverberation of the pulpit under strong hands as he was wont to emphasise his spoken utterances withal; there would seem to him a want of passion in the orderly lines of type; and I suppose we may take the capitals as a mere substitute for the great voice with which he would have given it forth, had we heard it from his own lips. Indeed, as it is, in this little strain of rhetoric about the trumpet, this current allusion to the fall of Jericho, that alone distinguishes his bitter and hasty production, he was probably right, according to all artistic canon, thus to support and accentuate in conclusion the sustained metaphor of a hostile proclamation. It is curious, by the way, to note how favourite an image the trumpet was with the Reformer. He returns to it again and again; it is the Alpha and Omega of his rhetoric; it is to him what a ship is to the stage sailor; and one would almost fancy he had begun the world as a trumpeter's apprentice. The partiality is surely characteristic. All his life long he was blowing summonses before various Jerichos, some of which fell duly, but not all. Wherever he appears in history his speech is loud, angry, and hostile; there is no peace in his life, and little tenderness; he is always sounding hopefully to the front for some rough enterprise. And as his voice had something of the trumpet's hardness, it had something also of the trumpet's warlike inspiration. So Randolph, possibly fresh from the sound of the Reformer's preaching, writes of him to Cecil:—"Where your honour exhorteth us to stoutness, I assure you the voice of one man is able, in an hour, to put more life in us than six hundred trumpets continually blustering in our ears."[7]

Thus was the proclamation made. Nor was it long in wakening all the echoes of Europe. What success might have attended it, had the question decided been a purely abstract question, it is difficult to say. As it was, it was to stand or fall, not by logic, but by political needs and sympathies. Thus, in France, his doctrine was to have some future, because Protestants suffered there under the feeble and treacherous regency of Catherine de Medici; and thus it was to have no future anywhere else, because the Protestant interest was bound up with the prosperity of Queen Elizabeth. This stumbling-block lay at the very threshold of the matter; and Knox, in the text of the ***First Blast,*** had set everybody the wrong example and gone to the ground himself. He finds occasion to regret "the blood of innocent Lady Jane Dudley." But Lady Jane Dudley, or Lady Jane Grey, as we call her, was a would-be traitoress and rebel against God, to use his own expressions. If, therefore, political and religious sympathy led Knox himself into so grave a partiality, what was he to expect from his disciples? If the trumpet gave so ambiguous a sound, who could heartily prepare himself for the battle? The question whether Lady Jane Dudley was an innocent martyr, or a traitoress against God, whose inordinate pride and tyranny had been effectually repressed, was thus left altogether in the wind; and it was not, perhaps, wonderful if many of Knox's readers concluded that all right and wrong in the matter turned upon the degree of the sovereign's orthodoxy and possible helpfulness to the Reformation. He should have been the more careful of such an ambiguity of meaning, as he must have known well the lukewarm indifference and dishonesty of his fellow-reformers in political matters. He had already, in 1556 or 1557, talked the matter over with his great master, Calvin, in "a private conversation"; and the interview[8] must have been truly distasteful to both parties. Calvin, indeed, went a far way with him in theory, and owned that the "government of women was a deviation from the original and proper order of nature, to be ranked, no less than slavery, among the punishments consequent upon the fall of man." But, in practice, their two roads separated. For the Man of Geneva saw difficulties in the way of the Scripture proof in the cases of Deborah and Huldah, and in the prophecy of Isaiah that queens should be the nursing mothers of the Church. And as the Bible was not decisive, he thought the subject should be let alone, because, "by custom and public consent and long practice, it has been established that realms and principalities may descend to females by hereditary right, and it would not be lawful to unsettle governments which are ordained by the peculiar providence of God." I imagine Knox's ears must have burned during this interview. Think of him listening dutifully to all this—how it would not do to meddle with anointed kings—how there was a peculiar providence in these great affairs; and then think of his own peroration, and the "noble heart" whom he looks for "to vindicate the liberty of his country"; or his answer to Queen Mary, when she asked him who he was, to interfere in the affairs of Scotland:—"Madam, a subject born within the same!" Indeed, the two doctors who differed at this private conversation represented, at the moment, two principles of enormous import in the subsequent history of Europe. In Calvin we have represented that passive obedience, that toleration of injustice and absurdity, that holding back of the hand from political affairs as from something unclean, which lost France, if we are to believe M. Michelet, for the Reformation; a spirit necessarily fatal in the long run to the existence of any seet that may profess it; a suicidal doctrine that survives among us to this day in narrow views of personal duty, and the low political morality of many virtuous men. In Knox, on the other hand, we see foreshadowed the whole Puritan Revolution and the scaffold of Charles I.

There is little doubt in my mind that this interview was what caused Knox to print his book without a name.[9] It was a dangerous thing to contradiet the Man of Geneva, and doubly so, surely, when one had had the advantage of correction from him in a private conversation; and Knox had his little flock of English refugees to consider. If they had fallen into bad odour at Geneva, where else was there left to flee to? It was printed, as I said, in 1558; and, by a singular *mal-à-propos,* in that same year Mary died, and Elizabeth succeeded to the throne of England. And just as the accession of Catholic Queen Mary had condemned female rule in the eyes of Knox, the accession of Protestant Queen Elizabeth justified it in the eyes of his colleagues. Female rule ceases to be an anomaly, not because Elizabeth can "reply to eight ambassadors in one day in their different languages," but because she represents for the moment the political future of the Reformation. The exiles troop back to England with songs of praise in their mouths. The bright occidental star, of which we have all read in the Preface to the Bible, has risen over the darkness of Europe. There is a thrill of hope through the persecuted Churches of the Continent. Calvin writes to Cecil, washing his hands of Knox and his political heresies. The sale of the ***First Blast,*** is prohibited in Geneva; and along with it the bold book of Knox's colleague, Goodman—a book dear to Milton—where female rule was briefly characterised as a "monster in nature and disorder among men."[10] Any who may ever have doubted, or been for a moment led away by Knox or Goodman, or their own wicked imaginations, are now more than convinced. They have seen the occidental star. Aylmer, with his eye set greedily on a possible bishopric, and "the better to obtain the favour of the new Queen,"[11] sharpens his pen to confound Knox by logic. What need? He has been confounded by facts. "Thus what had been to the refugees of Geneva as the very word of God, no sooner were they back in England than, behold! it was the word of the devil."[12]

Now, what of the real sentiments of these loyal subjects of Elizabeth? They professed a holy horror for Knox's position: let us see if their own would please a modern audience any better, or was, in substance, greatly different.

John Aylmer, afterwards Bishop of London, published an answer to Knox, under the title of *An Harbour for Faithful and True Subjects against the late Blown Blast, concerning the government of Women.*[13] And certainly he was a thought more acute, a thought less precipitate and simple, than his adversary. He is not to be led away by such captions terms as *natural* and *unnatural.* It is obvious to him that a woman's disability to rule is not natural in the same sense in which it is natural for a stone to fall or fire to burn. He is doubtful, on the whole, whether this disability be natural at all; nay, when he is laying it down that a woman should not be a priest, he shows some elementary conception of what many of us now hold to be the truth of the matter. "The bringing-up of women," he says, "is commonly such" that they cannot have the necessary qualifications, "for they are not brought up in learning in schools, nor trained in disputation." And even so, he can ask, "Are there not in England women, think you, that for learning and wisdom could tell their household and neighbours as good a tale as any Sir John there?" For all that, his advocacy is weak. If women's rule is not unnatural in a sense preclusive of its very existence, it is neither so convenient nor so profitable as the government of men. He holds England to be specially suitable for the government of women, because there the governor is more limited and restrained by the other members of the constitution than in other places; and this argument has kept his book from being altogether forgotten. It is only in hereditary monarchies that he will offer any defence of the anomaly. "If rulers were to be chosen by lot or suffrage, he would not that any women should stand in the election, but men only." The law of succession of crowns was a law to him, in the same sense as the law of evolution is a law to Mr. Herbert Spencer; and the one and the other counsels his readers, in a spirit suggestively alike, not to kick against the pricks or seek to be more wise than He who made them.[14] If God has put a female child into the direct line of inheritance, it is God's affair. His strength will be perfected in her weakness. He makes the Creator address the objectors in this not very flattering vein:—"I, that could make Daniel, a sucking babe, to judge better than the wisest lawyers; a brute beast to reprehend the folly of a prophet; and poor fishers to confound the great clerks of the world—cannot I make a woman to be a good ruler over you?" This is the last word of his reasoning. Although he was not altogether without Puritanic leaven, shown particularly in what he says of the incomes of Bishops, yet it was rather loyalty to the old order of things than any generous belief in the capacity of women, that raised up for them this clerical champion. His courtly spirit contrasts singularly with the rude, bracing republicanism of Knox. "Thy knee shall bow," he says, "thy cap shall off, thy tongue shall speak reverently of thy sovereign." For himself, his tongue is even more than reverent. Nothing can stay the issue of his eloquent adulation. Again and again, "the remembrance of Elizabeth's virtues" carries him away; and he has to hark back again to find the scent of his argument. He is repressing his vehement adoration throughout, until, when the end comes, and he feels his business at an end, he can indulge himself to his heart's content in indiscriminate laudation of his royal mistress. It is humorous to think that this illustrious lady, whom he here praises, among many other excellences, for the simplicity of her attire and the "marvellous meekness of her stomach," threatened him, years after, in no very meek terms, for a sermon against female vanity in dress, which she held as a reflection on herself.[15]

Whatever was wanting here in respect for women generally, there was no want of respect for the Queen: and one cannot very greatly wonder if these devoted servants looked askance, not upon Knox only, but on his little flock, as they came back to England tainted with disloyal doctrine. For them, as for him, the occidental star rose somewhat red and angry. As for poor Knox, his position was the saddest of all. For the juncture seemed to him of the highest importance; it was the nick of time, the floodwater of opportunity. Not only was there an opening for him in Scotland, a smouldering brand of civil liberty and religious enthusiasm which it should be for him to kindle into flame with his powerful breath; but he had his eye seemingly on an object of even higher worth. For now, when religious sympathy ran so high that it could be set against national aversion, he wished to begin the fusion together of England and Scotland, and to begin it at the sore place. If once the open wound were closed at the Border, the work would be half done. Ministers placed at Berwick and such places might seek their converts equally on either side of the march; old enemies would sit together to hear the gospel of peace, and forget the inherited jealousies of many generations in the enthusiasm of a common faith; or—let us say better—a common heresy. For people are not most conscious of brotherhood when they continue languidly together in one creed, but when, with some doubt, with some danger perhaps, and certainly not without some reluctance, they violently break with the tradition of the past, and go forth from the sanctuary of their fathers to worship under the bare heaven. A new creed, like a new country, is an unhomely place of sojourn; but it makes men lean on one another and join hands. It was on this that Knox relied to begin the union of the English and the Scotch. And he had, perhaps, better means of judging than any even of his contemporaries. He knew the temper of both nations; and already during his two years' chaplaincy at Berwick, he had seen his scheme put to the proof. But whether practicable or not, the proposal does him much honour. That he should thus have sought to make a love-match of it between the two peoples, and tried to win their inclination towards a union instead of simply transferring them, like so many sheep, by a marriage, or testament, or private treaty, is thoroughly characteristic of what is best in the man. Nor was this all. He had, besides, to assure himself of English support, secret or avowed, for the reformation party in Scotland; a delicate affair, trenching upon treason. And so he had plenty to say to Cecil, plenty that he did not care to "commit to paper neither yet to the knowledge of many." But his miserable publication had shut the doors of England in his face. Summoned to Edinburgh by the confederate lords, he waited at Dieppe, anxiously praying for leave to journey through England. The most dispiriting tidings reach him. His messengers, coming from so obnoxious a quarter, narrowly escape imprisonment. His old congregation are coldly received, and even begin to look back again to their place of exile with regret. "My First Blast," he writes ruefully, "has blown from me all my friends of England." And then he adds, with a snarl, "The Second Blast, I fear, shall sound somewhat more sharp, except men be more moderate than I hear they are."[16] But the threat is empty; there will never be a second blast—he has had enough of that trumpet. Nay, he begins to feel uneasily that, unless he is to be rendered useless for the rest of his life, unless he is to lose his right arm and go about his great work maimed and impotent, he must find some way of making his peace with England and the indignant Queen. The letter just quoted was written on the 6th of April 1559;

and on the 10th, after he had cooled his heels for four days more about the streets of Dieppe, he gave in altogether, and writes a letter of capitulation to Cecil. In this letter,[17] which he kept back until the 22nd, still hoping that things would come right of themselves, he censures the great secretary for having "followed the world in the way of perdition," characterises him as "worthy of hell," and threatens him, if he be not found simple, sincere, and fervent in the cause of Christ's gospel, that he shall "taste of the same cup that politic heads have drunken in before him." This is all, I take it, out of respect for the Reformer's own position; if he is going to be humiliated, let others be humiliated first; like a child who will not take his medicine until he has made his nurse and his mother drink of it before him. "But I have, say you, written a treasonable book against the regiment and empire of women. . . . The writing of that book I will not deny; but to prove it treasonable I think it shall be hard. . . . It is hinted that my book shall be written against. If so be, sir, I greatly doubt they shall rather hurt nor (than) mend the matter." And here come the terms of capitulation; for he does not surrender unconditionally, even in this sore strait: "And yet if any," he goes on, "think me enemy to the person, or yet to the regiment, of her whom God hath now promoted, they are utterly deceived in me, *for the miraculous work of God, comforting His afflicted by means of an infirm vessel, I do acknowledge, and the power of His most potent hand I will obey. More plainly to speak, if Queen Elizabeth shall confess, that the extraordinary dispensation of God's great mercy maketh that lawful unto her which both nature and God's law do deny to all women,* then shall none in England be more willing to maintain her lawful authority than I shall be. But if (God's wondrous work set aside) she ground (as God forbid) the justness of her title upon consuetude, laws, or ordinances of men, then"—Then Knox will denounce her? Not so; he is more polite nowadays—then, "greatly fears" that her ingratitude to God willl not go long without punishment.

His letter to Elizabeth, written some few months later, was a mere amplification of the sentences quoted above. She must base her title entirely upon the extraordinary providence of God; but if she does this, "if thus, in God's presence, she humbles herself, so will he tongue and pen justify her authority, as the Holy Ghost hath justified the same in Deborah, that blessed mother in Israel."[18] And so, you see, his consistency is preserved; he is merely applying the doctrine of the ***First Blast***. The argument goes thus: The regiment of women is, as before noted in our work, repugnant to nature, contumely to God, and a subversion of good order. It has nevertheless pleased God to raise up, as exceptions to this law, first Deborah, and afterward Elizabeth Tudor—whose regiment we shall proceed to celebrate.

There is no evidence as to how the Reformer's explanations were received, and indeed it is most probable that the letter was never shown to Elizabeth at all. For it was sent under cover of another to Cecil, and as it was not of a very courtly conception throughout, and was, of all things, what would excite the Queen's uneasy jealousy about her title, it is like enough that the secretary exercised his discretion (he had Knox's leave in this case, and did not always wait for that, it is reputed) to put the letter harmlessley away beside other valueless or unpresentable State Papers. I wonder very much if he did the same with another,[19] written two years later, after Mary had come into Scotland, in which Knox almost seeks to make Elizabeth an accomplice with him in the matter of the ***First Blast***. The Queen of Scotland is going to have that work refuted, he tells her; and "though it were but foolishness in him to prescribe unto her Majesty what is to be done," he would yet remind her that Mary is neither so much alarmed about her own security, nor so generously interested in Elizabeth's, "that she would take such pains, *unless her crafty counsel in so doing shot at a further mark*." There is something really ingenious in this letter; it showed Knox in the double capacity of the author of the ***First Blast***, and the faithful friend of Elizabeth; and he combines them there so naturally, that one would scarcely imagine the two to be incongruous.

Twenty days later he was defending his intemperate publication to another queen—his own queen, Mary Stuart. This was on the first of those three interviews which he has preserved for us with so much dramatic vigour in the picturesque pages of his history. After he had avowed the authorship in his usual haughty style, Mary asked: "You think, then, that I have no just authority?" The question was evaded. "Please your Majesty," he answered, "that learned men in all ages have had their judgments free, and most commonly disagreeing from the common judgment of the world; such also have they published by pen and tongue; and yet notwithstanding they themselves have lived in the common society with others, and have borne patiently with the errors and imperfections which they could not amend." Thus did "Plato the philosopher": thus will do John Knox. "I have communicated my judgment to the world: if the realm finds no inconvenience from the regiment of a woman, that which they approve, shall I not further disallow than within my own breast; but shall be as well content to live under your Grace, as Paul was to live under Nero. And my hope is, that so long as ye defile not your hands with the blood of the saints of God, neither I nor my book shall hurt either you or your authority." All this is admirable in wisdom and moderation, and, except that he might have hit upon a comparison less offensive than that with Paul and Nero, hardly to be bettered. Having said thus much, he feels he needs say no more; and so, when he is further pressed, he closes that part of the discussion with an astonishing sally. If he has been content to let this matter sleep, he would recommend her Grace to follow his example with thankfulness of heart; it is grimly to be understood which of them has most to fear if the question should be reawakened. So the talk wandered to other subjects. Only, when the Queen was summoned at last to dinner ("for it was afternoon") Knox made his salutation in this form of words: "I pray God, Madam, that you may be as much blessed within the Commonwealth of Scotland, if it be the pleasure of God, as ever Deborah was in the Commonwealth of Israel."[20] Deborah again.

But he was not yet done with the echoes of his own ***First Blast***. In 1571, when he was already near his end, the old controversy was taken up in one of a series of anonymous libels against the Reformer affixed, Sunday after Sunday, to the church door. The dilemma was fairly enough stated. Either his doctrine is false, in which case he is a "false doctor" and seditions; or, if it be true, why does he "avow and approve the contrare, I mean that regiment in the Queen of England's person; which he avoweth and approveth, not only praying for the maintenance of her estate, but also procuring her aid and support against his own native country?" Knox answered the libel, as his wont was, next Sunday, from the pulpit. He justified the ***First Blast*** with all the old arrogance; there is no drawing back there. The regiment of women is repugnant to nature, contumely to God, and a subversion of good order, as before. When he prays for the maintenance of Elizabeth's estate, he is only following the example of those prophets of God who warned and comforted the wicked kings of Israel; or of Jeremiah, who bade the Jews pray for the prosperity of Nebuchadnezzar. As for the Queen's aid, there is no harm in that: *quia* (these are his own words) *quia omnia munda mundis:* because to the pure all things are pure. One thing, in conclusion, he "may not pretermit"; to give the lie in the throat to his accuser, where he charges him with seeking support against his native country. "What I have been to my country," said the old Reformer, "what I have been to my country, albeit this unthankful age will not know, yet the ages to come will be compelled to bear witness to the truth. And thus I cease, requiring of all men that have anything to oppone against me, that he may (they may) do it so plainly, as that I may make myself and all my doings manifest to the world. For to me it seemeth a thing unreasonable, that, in this my decrepit age, I shall be compelled to fight against shadows, and howlets that dare not abide the light."[21]

Now, in this, which may be called his *Last Blast,* there is as sharp speaking as any in the ***First Blast*** itself. He is of the same opinion to the end, you see, although he has been obliged to cloak and garble that opinion for political ends. He has been tacking indeed, and he has indeed been seeking the favour of a queen; but what man ever sought a queen's favour with a more virtuous purpose, or with as little courtly policy? The question of consistency is delicate, and must be made plain. Knox never changed his opinion about female rule, but lived to regret that he had published that opinion. Doubtless he had many thoughts so far out of the range of public sympathy, that he could only keep them to himself, and, in his own words, bear patiently with the errors and imperfections that he could not amend. For example. I make no doubt myself that, in his own heart, he did hold the shocking dogma attributed to him by more than one calumniator; and that, had the time been ripe, had there been aught to gain by it, instead of all to lose, he would have been the first to assert that Scotland was elective instead of hereditary—"elective as in the days of paganism," as one Thevet says in holy horror.[22] And yet, because the time was not ripe, I find no hint of such an idea in his collected works. Now, the regiment of women was another matter that he should have kept to himself; right or wrong, his opinion did not fit the moment; right or wrong, as Aylmer puts it, "the ***Blast*** was blown out of season." And this it was that he began to perceive after the accession of Elizabeth; not that he had been wrong, and that female rule was a good thing, for he had said from the first that "the felicity of some women in their empires" could not change the law of God and the nature of created things; not this, but that the regiment of women was one of those imperfections of society which must be borne with because yet they cannot be remedied. The thing had seemed so obvious to him, in his sense of unspeakable masculine superiority, and his fine contempt for what is only sanctioned by antiquity and common consent, he had imagined that, at the first hint, men would arise and shake off the debasing tyranny. He found himself wrong, and he showed that he could be moderate in his own fashion, and understood the spirit of true compromise. He came round to Calvin's position, in fact, but by a different way. And it derogates nothing from the merit of this wise attitude that it was the consequence of a change of interest. We are all taught by interest; and if the interest be not merely selfish, there is no wiser preceptor under heaven, and perhaps no sterner.

Such is the history of John Knox's connection with the controversy about female rule. In itself, this is obviously an incomplete study; not fully to be understood, without a knowledge of his private relations with the other sex, and what he thought of their position in domestic life....

*Notes*

[1] Gaberel's *Eglise de Genève,* i. 88.

[2] *La Démocratie chez les Prédicateurs de la Ligue.*

[3] *Historia affectuum se immiscentium controversiae de gynoecocratia*. It is in his collected prefaces, Leipsic, 1683.

[4] *Œuvres de d'Aubigné,* i. 449.

[5] *Dames Illustres,* pp. 358-360.

[6] Works of John Knox, iv. 349.

[7] M'Crie's *Life of Knox,* ii. 41.

[8] Described by Calvin in a letter to Cecil, Knox's Works, vol. iv.

[9] It was anonymously published, but no one seems to have been in doubt about its authorship; he might as well have set his name to it, for all the good he got holding it back.

[10] Knox's Works, iv. 358.

[11] Strype's *Aylmer,* p. 16.

[12] It may interest the reader to know that these (so says Thomasus) are the *ipsissima verba Schlusselburgii.*

[13] I am indebted for a sight of this book to the kindness of Mr. David Laing, the editor of Knox's Works.

[14] *Social Staties,* p. 64, etc.

[15] Hallam's *Const. Hist. of England,* i. 225, note[m].

[16] Knox to Mrs. Locke, 6th April 1559. Works, vi. 14.

[17] Knox to Sir William Cecil, 10th April 1559. Works, ii. 16, or vi. 15.

[18] Knox to Queen Elizabeth, 20[th] July 1559. Works, vi. 47, or ii. 26.

[19] Knox to Queen Elizabeth, 6[th] August 1561. Works, vi. 126.

[20] Knox's Works, ii. 278-280.

[21] Calderwood's *History of the Kirk of Scotland,* edition of the Wodrow Society, iii. 51-54.

[22] Bayle's *Historical Dictionary,* art. Knox, remark G.

**Edwin Muir (essay date 1929)**

SOURCE: "The End," in *John Knox: Portrait of a Calvinist,* The Viking Press, 1929, pp. 291-302.

[*In the following excerpt, Muir considers Knox's personal strengths and weaknesses.*]

. . . [Knox was] a man who, for almost a generation, had amazed everybody, princes, statesmen, divines, burghers, students and common people alike, by three magnificent qualities: his vehemence, his persistence, and his incorruptibility. The first of these was his distinguishing quality; the others only served to emphasise it. Other great men of action have been vehement and placable, capable of both devouring ardour and repose; what distinguished Knox was the uniformity of his vehemence, his perpetual possession of an extreme ardour. To him the excessive was the normal. He was not, even to his contemporaries, so much a great natural force, like Luther, as a terrible and inexplicable natural portent. It was this that gave his denunciations, drawn appropriately from the terrible arsenal of the Hebrew prophets, their overwhelming force. It was this that made even the hardened Scottish nobles look upon him as an almost supernatural figure. Yet he had not been designed by nature, it seemed, to make peoples tremble. He was of insignificant stature; his health was delicate; his temper at the beginning timid and apprehensive. One-half of his equipment was in keeping with this: his extraordinary adroitness in changing his opinions when it suited him, his almost feminine skill in personal debate, his employment of threatenings, his instinct for and delight in damaging gossip about his enemies, his indefatigable capacity for twisting and turning. The man who in England proclaimed that subjects were bound to obey their prince; who in Dieppe incited subjects to murder their prince; who in Geneva exhorted the faithful in Scotland to depose their prince; who in Dieppe once more declared that the Anabaptists certainly, but the faithful never, would harm their prince; who in Scotland helped to drive one prince after another from the throne while loudly proclaiming his loyalty; who maintained that two brutal murders were admirable in the sight of God, and that a third, less brutal, must be wiped out by the execution of an unfortunate woman who had no direct part in it, and whose guilt could not be proved; who pursued that woman to disgrace and destruction, and yet called another man a murderer because he did not love his enemy: this man was clearly not that model of consistency and strength which history and his biographers have set before us. He was rather a man who, when his object required it, was always ready to contradict himself, and used any means which suited him.

This was one element in Knox, the substratum of weakness from which developed all the qualities which made him unassailable. What was it that transformed a man so timid and apprehensive into a heroic figure? So far as one can tell it was a theory now completely outworn; a belief that before the beginning of the world God had ordained that mankind should be separated into two hosts, the reprobate and the elect; that the elect should prevail, and that after death they should enjoy everlasting bliss; and finally, that it was alike fated that they should fight and that they should win. To embrace this creed was to enrol in an invincible army; to remain outside was destruction. At a crisis in his life Knox found himself a soldier in it. From that time forward his fear and his thirst for power alike made him work to make that army supreme. As its power increased, however, so did his, and it was the Church Triumphant in Geneva that finally turned him into the marvellous instrument which changed the fate of Scotland.

It is easy to point out Knox's faults, and it is impossible to deny their seriousness. He had no sense of justice; what he praised in his friends he condemned in his enemies. He was not sagacious; his wild epistles to England, and his treatment of the young Scottish Queen intensified the calamities which they were intended to avert. He was disingenuous, as all his writings prove. He was vindictive in his unrelenting pursuit of Mary Stuart, he was ruthless towards the Catholics, repeatedly clamouring for their extermination. Normally he was altogether without self-control; he could, however, assume it in an emergency. He was incapable of living in peace; he quarrelled in succession with almost all his friends, with Cranmer, the English at Frankfort, Calvin, Moray, Kirkcaldy, Lethington; he fought in his maturity with queens, and in his dotage with the nonentities of St. Andrews.

His greatness lay in two qualities: the inexhaustible vehemence of his powers, and the constancy of his aim. The effect he had on men less unrelenting was like that of a wind, which blows with a steadfast violence, and by its persistence bends everything and keeps it bent. His will, like the *mistral,* had something in it unnatural and mechanical. It never relaxed, because it could not. It went on, as if independent of him, when his body was powerless, and he was lying on his deathbed; it lived in his last gesture, the hand stubbornly upraised as he gave up his spirit. It had goaded the Scottish nobles to revolt and Mary to shame and destruction: it had not given its possessor a respite for thirteen years. It was cruel and terrible, but it is perhaps the most heroic and astonishing spectacle in all Scottish history.

### J. H. Burns (essay date 1958)

SOURCE: "John Knox and Revolution, 1558," in *History Today*, Vol. VIII, No. 8, August, 1958, pp. 565-73.

[*In the following essay, which emphasizes Knox's writings of 1558, Burns explores the motivating factors that led Knox to become openly political.*]

Early in 1558 John Knox returned to Geneva from Dieppe. He had gone there in the previous autumn, having been invited by four Protestant leaders to come back to Scotland and resume the successful preaching of the winter of 1555-56. But "contrary letters"—and, as he later acknowledged, certain hesitations of his own—interrupted his journey at the Channel. His final return to Scotland was delayed until May 1559. Before that he published three important pamphlets, all written in the first half of 1558: the notorious ***First Blast of the Trumpet against the Monstrous Regiment of Women,*** the ***Appellation of John Knox,*** and the ***Letter to the Commonalty***. In so far as Knox made history by writing rather than by speech and action, these, together perhaps with the ***First Book of Discipline,*** are his most important works.

The impatient rebel who appears in their pages was no youthful firebrand. Knox's date of birth is disputed; but he was by now at least in his middle forties and may have been ten years older. He was thrice an exile: from his native Scotland, when the Protestant defeat of July 1547 brought him to the galleys; second, from England, which was his home from the spring of 1549 till the early months of 1554; and last, from Scotland again, after his period of preaching between the autumn of 1555 and the spring of 1556. Religion was the key to these repeated exiles, and to Knox's whole life. That religion was entangled in politics goes without saying. The two could not in that age be separated, even by those who most desired their separation—and Knox was to have good cause to fear and hate political contamination. A politician willy-nilly, Knox can none the less hardly be understood without due recognition of the overmastering importance for him of his own intensely held conception of "Christ's truth." On his deathbed on November 24th, 1572, he asked his wife to read from the 17th chapter of St. John's Gospel, "in which he had first cast anchor." That great prayer of love and reconciliation may seem remote from the harsh polemic, the rigid dogmatism with which Knox's name is usually associated. But this is an essential clue; and one need not share Knox's version of Christian belief to understand that his faith was passionately sincere.

Ordained priest sometime in the 1530's and subsequently a notary apostolic, by the mid-1540's Knox was acting as tutor to the children of East Lothian lairds who patronized the leading Protestant preacher of the day in Scotland, George Wishart. The first crisis of Knox's life was his meeting with Wishart at mid-winter 1545-46, six weeks before the preacher died a heretic's death at St. Andrews. Thenceforward Knox was, in some sense, committed to the Protestant cause. This commitment had political implications. The lairds who had been Wishart's patrons, and were Knox's employers, were deeply involved in the English interest. For the moment, power lay with the rival party, headed by Cardinal Beaton, Chancellor of Scotland since 1543. They had successfully resisted the proposal of an English marriage for the infant Mary Queen of Scots, and had inaugurated an intensified campaign against the Protestants, culminating in the burning of Wishart. When Beaton was killed, three months after Wishart's death, it was in part for political reasons, not simply because he was "an obstinate enemy against Christ Jesus and his holy evangel." Knox was soon taught what was to be a familiar lesson: that the tangled motives in such affairs make impossible the emergence of any such simple issue as the triumph of "good" over "evil." He himself, after seven months' precarious wandering, had to take refuge with the Protestant murderers and their allies—the "Castilians" of St. Andrews. In that extraordinary society, compact of debauchery and piety, Knox's oratorical and controversial gifts brought inevitably a "call" to undertake public preaching. After much heart-searching, he accepted. "Master George Wishart spoke never so plainly," men said of his first sermon, "and yet he was burnt: even so will he be." It was true that Knox had decisively accepted his vocation and its perils. From death itself, however, he was saved by the terms of the "Appointment" made when the Castle was surrendered after French forces had joined in the siege. By this agreement all the "Castilians" were handed over to France. The "principal gentlemen" were committed to various French prisons, the smaller fry, including Knox, went to the galleys. There, despite "the grudging and murmuring complaints of the flesh" of which he himself afterwards wrote, for nineteen months his faith held firm. The essentials of his religious belief were fixed when release from the galleys came in the spring of 1549.

Scotland was barred to the liberated prisoner; but in England he soon found a place as a licensed preacher paid by the Privy Council of Edward VI. As usual, he made his mark on the society he lived in. Minister first at Berwick, then at Newcastle, he became a royal chaplain and was offered the Bishopric of Rochester (which he declined). He could not altogether avoid turbulence; and, especially in his relations with John Dudley, Duke of Northumberland, he evinced what later became a characteristic attitude—disgusted impatience with the rulers of this world. Relatively, however, this was a peaceful and happy time for Knox, when he was forming personal ties of a strong and lasting kind—especially with Mrs. Bowes, sister-in-law to the Warden of the East Marches, and her daughter Marjory, later Knox's first wife. The accession of Mary Tudor was for Knox a personal catastrophe as well as a public calamity. Her reversal of religious policy soon drove him into exile; and by February 1554 the most settled period of an unsettled life was at an end.

For a considerable part of his life in exile, Knox's attitude was that of an Englishman by adoption. The prospect of any change for the better in the Scottish situation must have seemed bleaker than ever in the spring of 1554. The Regency passed from James Hamilton, Earl of Arran, who, whatever his backslidings, had once at least favoured the reformed religion, to the Queen Mother, Mary of Lorraine, a daughter of the House of Guise from whom Knox had little to hope. In England, on the other hand, the foundations of reform had been firmly laid, and Mary Tudor's new regime might not last. Here, again, politics and religion met and mingled. Any sorrow Knox felt at the failure of Northumberland's attempt to prevent Mary's accession must have been far from unalloyed, in view of his hostility to its leader. But he could hardly help seeing that political factors, such as dislike of the proposed Spanish marriage, might serve his cause. Perhaps he now understood for the first time that politics of some kind must enter into the triumph of "true religion."

Hitherto Knox's political views, to judge from the rather scanty evidence, had been the orthodox views of early Protestantism, with the emphasis heavily upon the Christian duty of submission to temporal rulers. The roots of this attitude, in conviction and convenience alike, were too deep for Protestant thinkers lightly to abandon it. Certainly Knox did not do so. Writing to his English congregations from Dieppe at the end of February 1554, he urged them "to avoid all fellowship with idolatry": if this meant disobeying the civil power, they must disobey. But active resistance is not for them. To slay idolaters "were the office . . . of every civil Magistrate within his realm." Knox had not yet solved the problem that arose when the magistrate himself was committed to "idolatry." This was one of the problems he took to Calvin at Geneva. Geneva was to become for Knox the "perfect school of Christ," with a clarity in doctrine and discipline that his own unsystematic mind would never have attained. But, on this first brief visit, it was with means rather than ends that he was concerned. We do not know, in detail, how Calvin answered Knox; but we know that his answers were not materially different from those given by Bullinger in Zurich, where Knox proceeded direct from Geneva. The answers were dusty enough. Bullinger would not argue against female sovereignty; he would not countenance organized resistance to an idolatrous authority nor advise the faithful to support those who did resist. Such actions *might* be justified. But the question must be decided circumspectly by those in full possession of the facts, bearing in mind the ease with which motives in such cases become contaminated. The moment for that great turningpoint in Protestant political thinking, which has been called "the break from Calvin," had not yet come.[1]

Thus advised, Knox wrote two further letters in May to his English brethren from Dieppe. Then, in July 1554, he published his ***Faithful Admonition unto the Professors of God's truth in England***. The notorious invective of this pamphlet has perhaps tended to obscure the absence from it of any new *political* doctrine. True, Knox resorts for the first time to a purely political argument. Mary is "an open traitoress to the Imperial Crown of England," since her marriage will "bring in a stranger, and make a proud Spaniard king," whereas "the ancient laws and acts of Parliament pronounceth it treason to transfer the Crown of England into the hands of a foreign nation." But Knox, paralysed by the doctrine of Christian obedience reinforced by the advice of Calvin and Bullinger, draws no operative conclusion from this, any more than from his denunciation of idolatry. Four years later he could say:

> I fear not to affirm that it had been the duty of the Nobility, Judges, Rulers and People of England, not only to have resisted and againstanded Mary, that Jezebel, whom they call their Queen, but also to have punished her to the death, together with all such as should have assisted her.

But he affirmed no such thing in 1554. The ***Faithful Admonition,*** like the May letters, urges that purity of faith be preserved by passive disobedience, and, for the rest, recommends patient trust in God, who will

> for his great mercy's sake, stir up some Phineas, Elias, or Jehu, that the blood of abominable idolaters may pacify God's wrath, that it consume not the whole multitude.

To hope and pray for an inspired tyrannicide is not to recommend organized and, as it were, "constitutional" rebellion.

The ***Faithful Admonition,*** nevertheless, proved a useful weapon in the hands of Knox's enemies. It was effectively employed against him in the controversy in which he became embroiled in the winter of 1554-55, within the English congregation at Frankfurt, whose minister he had become. It is too easy, in retrospect, to see Knox's defeat in this conflict as the decisive severing of his English connection. What it did mean was that his future in England now depended on the fortunes of the ecclesiastical party later known as Puritan. But it was far from certain, when Knox left Frankfurt at the end of March 1555, that he had no English future at all. It was as minister to another English congregation that he settled at Geneva; and his return to Scotland in the autumn of 1555 was in a sense accidental. He had gone to the north of England, evidently without enthusiasm, on family business. The summons had come from his mother-in-law, Mrs. Bowes, hard-pressed in her struggle to maintain the faith Knox had taught her, amid a predominantly Catholic family, in a country where Catholic authority had been restored. The death of her brother-in-law, Sir Robert, never a friend to Knox, seemed to offer some hope of a more permanent settlement. It was to explore the possibility of a life with his family in Scotland that Knox crossed the Border. Preaching was not his mission; and his unconcealed surprise at the fruitful soil for missionary work he found there shows how little he had expected from his native country. For months he travelled about, forming wherever he went congregations with "the right use of the Lord's Table." This was the end of the beginning of the Scottish religious revolution; and it brought Knox into Scottish politics for the first time in nearly a decade.

The omens were not unfavourable. The policy of Mary of Lorraine was not that of Mary Tudor. When Knox himself was at last summoned by the Church authorities to answer for his preaching, "that diet held not"—thanks, it would appear, to the Queen Regent's intervention. Hope based on her virtual neutrality, if not on her conversion, may have been considered not unreasonable by those nobles who had now openly gone over to the new religion. Some of these leading men seem to have influenced Knox at this time; and their influence was all in favour of caution. Hence the letter that Knox addressed to the Regent in the summer of 1556 is, for him, all deference and respect. Nor need we doubt his sincerity when he says that the honour due, by God's command, to lawful magistrates "containeth in itself, in lawful things obedience, and in all things love and reverence." He insists, indeed, that the ruler's duties include those of upholding "true religion" and correcting "the negligence of Bishops," and that failure in these respects must mean "dejection to torment and pain everlasting." But there is no hint of any temporal or political sanction. In this posture of affairs, Knox's departure for Geneva may seem puzzling. It can be ascribed to cowardice on Knox's part—on other occasions Knox freely acknowledges such motives as "the love of this life, or the fear of corporal death"—or to deliberate policy on the part of his patrons. But less speculative motives suffice to explain his departure: his obligations towards his wife and mother-in-law, and his duty to his Geneva congregation, who had formally elected him, together with Christopher Goodman, as their minister in November 1555 and now "commanded" his return. Here, again, full allowance must be made for the strength of Knox's English connections and loyalties, and care must be taken to avoid reading back into his situation in 1556 a sense of destiny as the maker of the Scottish Reformation.

Knox, then, went back to the "perfect school of Christ." But Scotland would not leave him alone. In May 1557, he received a letter from the Protestant leaders, which took him, again without enthusiasm, on the journey towards Scotland that was interrupted at Dieppe in the autumn. In the letters and other writings of the closing months of that year, there is a picture of Knox's mind as it was just before the vigorous pamphleteering of 1558. It was a mind divided and uncertain. On the one hand, Knox was developing a new notion of the duties of the nobles whose vacillation had helped to break his journey: "for," he told them in October, "only for that cause are ye called Princes of the people . . . by reason of your office and duty, which is to vindicate and deliver your subjects and brethren from all violence and oppression, to the uttermost of your power." And this holds good "be it against Kings of Emperors." On the other hand, Knox evidently could not readily accept all the possible implications of this view. When he next wrote to the Protestant lords in mid-December, he had heard rumours of "contradiction and rebellion . . . made to the Authority by some in that realm." Of this he declared:

> my conscience will not suffer me to keep back from you my counsel, yea, my judgement and commandment which I communicate with you in God's fear, and by the assurance of his truth; which is, that none of you that seek to promote the glory of Christ do suddenly disobey or displease the Authority in things lawful; neither yet, that ye assist or fortify such as for their own particular cause and worldly promotion would trouble the same.

This caution had a complex political background. An alliance might naturally have been expected between the Protestant party and the movement of opposition to the Queen Regent, especially to her foreign policy, which seemed to make Scotland a mere make-weight for France. But the alliance was obstructed by the political role of the house of Hamilton, with its dynastic ambitions. Arran, the head of the house, was, till the birth of James VI and I in 1566, next heir to the Crown after Mary with no inconsiderable hope of succeeding her.[2] A movement led by Arran, the ex-Regent and renegade Protestant, now Duke of Châtelherault, and by his brother the Archbishop of St. Andrews, was no place for the "professors of Christ's truth." So Knox thought, as is plain from scathing references to Châtelherault in the letter just quoted. At the same time, the Regent's position was such that she could ill afford to alienate unnecessarily any influential section of the nobility. And the "Lords of the Congregation," as they became known after the signing of their "Common Band" at the beginning of December 1557, were men of influence and power. Some of their leaders were members of the commission sent to France early in 1558 to negotiate the marriage between the fifteen-year-old Queen of Scots and the Dauphin that was now the keystone of the Regent's policy. A moderate course might still succeed from the Protestant point of view. But it was not political expediency alone that induced Knox's hesitancy. The same ambivalence appears in a context quite divorced from Scottish politics—the Additions he wrote, about this time, to his translation of the ***Apology*** of the French Protestants then imprisoned in Paris. There he labours to show how politically reliable the new religion is; but, contemplating the "heap of inquity" to which "the regiment of Princes is this day come," he feels that either the Princes must be "reformed" or else "all good men depart from their service and company." Even here, it is noteworthy, a "nonviolent" alternative to rebellion is suggested. As 1557 closed, Knox was on the verge of a momentous change in his political thinking. He had not yet made that change.

Others, meanwhile, were not so hesitant. Already in 1556, John Ponet, sometime Bishop of Rochester and of Winchester, had published in exile his *Short Treatise of politic power*. In this, which has some claim to be reckoned the most notable piece of Protestant political writing before George Buchanan and the Huguenot controversialists of the 1570's, Ponet develops a systematic argument to show that royal power is necessarily limited and that infringement of its limits may be punished by deposition, imprisonment, and even death. More recently, the thoughts of Knox's colleague in the Geneva ministry, Christopher Goodman, had been moving in a similar direction. During Knox's absence (it seems likely) Goodman preached a sermon on the theme of obedience to God rather than man, out of which grew the pamphlet he published at the beginning of 1558, entitled *How Superior Powers ought to be obeyed of their subjects*. The spirit and language of the pamphlet are such as have come to be thought typical of Knox. It has even been suggested that Goodman was merely Knox's "mouthpiece." But the evidence is against this. Goodman's pamphlet is dated January 1st, 1558; so that it must have been written at a time when Knox, as we have seen, was still far from sure of his political position. In Goodman, there is no such hesitation. Behind his rhetoric there is a clarity and decision that Knox was hardly ever to attain and had certainly not attained by this time. Goodman not only firmly maintains the duty of counsellors and nobles to "bridle" their Princes; he insists that the duty of resistance to "wicked commandments" binds "all men . . . of what state and condition so ever they be," and that resistance, at least in such extreme cases as idolatry and oppression, must be pressed to the point of deposing and slaying the offending sovereign. Goodman is not devoid of caution; but, though he claimed that "This is no doctrine of rebellion," it is manifestly something far nearer such a doctrine than Knox had yet gone.

Circumstances, however, soon drove Knox in the same direction. Politically, he was alarmed by the rapid progress of the negotiations for the French marriage of the Queen of Scots. In religion, though the news of revived persecution in Scotland cannot have come soon enough to affect his first publication in 1558, there must have been ample news at Dieppe of the continuing persecution in England. Finally, Knox received news about this time of a personal affront—the sneer with which Mary of Lorraine had received his carefully phrased letter in the summer of 1556—and of a personal attack—his burning in effigy by the clerical authorities after he had left Scotland. Public and private indignation conspired to produce the astonishing polemical outburst of 1558.

***The First Blast of the Trumpet against the Monstrous Regiment of Women*** was published anonymously in Geneva sometime before May 1558.[3] Its central theme, namely, that

> To promote a Woman to bear rule, superiority, dominion, or empire, above any Realm, Nation, or City, is repugnant to Nature; contumely to God, a thing most contrarious to his revealed will and approved ordinance; and finally, it is the subversion of good Order, of all equity and justice,

was in itself less startling than might be thought. As a statement of general principle, certainly many—perhaps most—thinkers of the age would have accepted it. The scandal it occasioned—"my FIRST BLAST," Knox wrote ruefully a year later, "hath blown from me all my friends in England"—was, in part, due to an historical accident. A few months after it was published, Mary Tudor died: Elizabeth's succession meant that the hopes of English Protestantism centred upon a female sovereign. But the scandal was also due to Knox's application of his principle. If the divine and natural order had been subverted, he argued, there was a duty to restore it. This was incumbent on the nobility, the estates, and the people of a realm afflicted with a female ruler; they must "remove from honour and authority that monster in nature," they must "pronounce . . . and . . . execute . . . the sentence of death" against any who "presume to defend that impiety." With queens regnant in both England and Scotland, this was indeed a revolutionary manifesto.

Yet the application of the argument to the case of female "regiment" was less significant than the argument itself. To argue that the existence of something "contrarious" to God's order implied and imposed a duty to set matters right was to open up immense possibilities. One possibility was Knox's main concern—the use of this weapon against "idolatry." Implicitly in the ***First Blast,*** explicitly in the draft of the abortive ***Second,*** he asserts the right and the duty of subjects to "depose and punish" rulers who are "Tyrants against God and against his truth known." The political caution Knox had once shown is cast aside. To the charge of subversion he answers (in the expanded, 1558 version of his letter to the Queen Regent) "with the prophet Isaiah, 'That all is not reputed before God sedition and conjuration, which the foolish multitude so esteemeth'; neither yet is every tumult and breach of public order contrary to God's commandment."

In the ***Appellation,*** Knox insists that "the Reformation of religion in all points" is the duty of "Nobles and Estates," as well as kings; and, if kings fail in their duty, the nobles must remember that God has appointed them "to be as bridles to repress the rage and insolency of your Kings." But, if these duties fall especially upon the "princes of the people," the people themselves have heavy obligations. This argument is developed in the ***Appellation,*** and more especially in the ***Letter to the Commonalty of Scotland,*** published at the same time. Appealing to the doctrine of Christian equality, Knox draws drastic conclusions from it:

> For albeit God hath put and ordained distinction and difference betwixt the King and subjects, betwixt the Rulers and the common people, in the regiment and administration of Civil policies, yet in the hope of the life to come he hath made all equal . . .

> . . . ye, although ye be but subjects, may lawfully require of your superiors . . . that they provide for you true Preachers, and that they expel such as, under the name of Pastors, devour and destroy the flock. . . . And if in this point your superiors be negligent . . . most justly may ye provide true preachers for yourselves . . .

> . . . as your Princes and Rulers are criminal with your Bishops of all idolatry committed, and of all the innocent blood that is shed for the testimony of Christ's truth. . . . So are you criminal and guilty . . . of the same crimes.

And the obligation goes further than giving "plain confession" against idolatry. In the ***Appellation*** Knox affirms that "the punishment of such crimes as are idolatry, blasphemy, and others, that touch the majesty of God, doth not appertain to kings and chief rulers only, but also to the whole body of that people, and to every member of the same." The position taken in his first letters from exile in 1554 has been neatly and completely reversed.

The position of Calvin, too, has been left far behind. Calvin's teaching was, with almost complete consistency, that the Christian must submit to the powers, going no further than passive resistance to commands repugnant to God's law. He was prepared to entertain the hypothesis that, in some cases, the Estates might have powers similar to those of the Spartan ephors or the Roman tribunes. But, confronted by the French Protestants with a concrete case at the time of the conspiracy of Amboise, he carried caution to the point of a virtual prohibition of active resistance. He explicity condemned the views of Knox and Goodman. But the logic of the situation was with them and against Calvin; and the views they, together with Ponet, had advanced became increasingly characteristic of the warring Protestants of the later sixteenth century.

Knox may be said to have provided the "ideology" of the revolution that, between 1558 and 1560, dealt the old order in Scotland blows from which it could never recover. But ideologies do not make revolutions. In Scotland, as elsewhere, other factors had to be at work before the Reformation could triumph over the political and diplomatic obstacles in its path. Those factors were found in the age-old, and seemingly irremediable, weakness of the Scottish Crown; in the incurable turbulence and ambition of the nobility; and perhaps, too, in a new kind of national consciousness among the gentry—the "lesser barons" who resisted the policies of Mary of Lorraine. In the successive pronouncements of the Lords of the Congregation, between 1557 and 1559, can be traced the gradual intermingling of political and religious motives that finally brought about the victory of 1560. Of the dangers inherent in this mingling of motives Knox was well aware. Risk became reality when the revolution passed from destruction to construction. The ideal society of the ***First Book of Discipline***—a people dedicated to the fulfilment of "God's perfect ordinance"—presupposed two conditions, neither of which was realized. The first was a single-minded devotion to the cause on the part of those who had made the revolution. For this, there were too many who proved to be devoted to "their own particular cause and worldly promotion." The second was something too often forgotten in assessing Knox's political beliefs: it was the rule of a sovereign devoted to the service of "Christ's truth"—a "covenanted king," as he would later be called. To such a sovereign the duty of Christian obedience would be simple and absolute. It is a mistake to think of Knox as professing a "philosophy of revolution," or a general theory of limited or constitutional rule. These were not matters in which he had more than a peripheral interest. No doubt, the king must, like every other "estate," be subject to Kirk discipline. But, within his civil sphere, he would reflect, Knox said in 1565, the "power, terror, and majesty" of God Himself; and "who soever should study to deface the order of regiment that God hath established . . . and bring in such a confusion as no difference should be betwixt the upper powers and the subjects, doth nothing but evert and turn upside down the very throne of God."

Knox was neither a clear nor a systematic thinker; and it is evident that the arguments of his 1558 pamphlets must have tended to bring in the "confusion" that he here condemns. But it seems clear that his purpose in 1558 was to bring down the "idolatrous" sovereignties he saw around him, and not to subvert sovereignty itself. He was neither the first nor the last idealist to discover that means and ends are not so easily separable; that the method penetrates and changes the purpose it is intended to serve.

*Notes*

[1] It is true that the refusal of the Protestants of Magdeburg to accept the Interim in 1548 had been defended in a copious pamphlet literature between that date and 1550. But, though this literature was subsequently cited in argument (notably by Knox himself in his debate with Maitland of Lethington at the General Assembly of 1564) it does not seem to have had any immediate effect upon Protestant political thinking as a whole.

[2] Provided the legitimacy of his birth were accepted. Doubts about this were the basis of the dynastic hopes of the house of Lennox, whose head was the father of Lord Darnley, later Mary's second husband.

[3] Knox did not long preserve his anonymity. By publishing with his *Appellation,* under the heading "John Knox to the Reader," an outline of the proposed *Second Blast* (which was never completed), he implicitly acknowledged his authorship of the *First*. This publication probably took place in the late summer of 1558 (after mid-July).

## James S. McEwen (lecture date 1960)

SOURCE: "Predestination," in *The Faith of John Knox: The Croall Lectures for 1960,* John Knox Press, 1961, pp. 61-79.

[*In the following excerpt, originally delivered as a lecture at New College, Edinburgh, McEwen compares and contrasts Knox's sometimes inconsistent views on predestination with the views of Calvin and of Luther, and examines Knox's interpretations of election, assurance, free-will, and reprobation.*]

There are certain historical facts that are known to everybody: as, for example, that the Norman Conquest dated from 1066, and that Calvinism was a predestinarian faith. One might go further and say that everyone is aware that Calvinism was not only predestinarian, but adjectivally predestinarian—sternly, crudely, harshly predestinarian, and so on.

The main use of adjectives of this type is to induce the reader or hearer to pass judgment on purely emotional grounds, without asking to see the facts; thereby saving trouble all round, and producing the desired result more rapidly and certainly than argument and explanation could do it. For, of course, if a thing is stern, crude or harsh, it must be wrong; and we need think no more about it.

A wise man is instantly on the alert when he comes across such damnatory epithets. They may express an honest indignation: more often they indicate a desire to communicate an irrational dislike.

When applied to the Calvinist doctrine of predestination, these unpleasant adjectives are usually appeals to irrational emotion: for the most that the majority of those who use them know about predestination is the rather vague impression that it means that the good will go to Heaven no matter how naughty they are, while the bad will be damned no matter how well they behave. And I do not think that John Knox would recognize this as an adequate statement of his faith, or that anyone who reads what he has written on the subject would think so either.

Adjectives therefore, however colourful, will not excuse us from the task of acquainting ourselves with Knox's views. And that will be no easy task. For although Knox has left us a long treatment of the subject,[1] it is far from being a systematic one. It is a reply to an Anabaptist who had published an attack on Calvin's teaching on predestination; and instead of developing his own argument in an orderly way, Knox assails the Anabaptist's book, chapter by chapter, with all the ammunition he can lay his hands on. The result is much repetition, and repetition that is by no means always consistent with itself; so that it is often difficult to decide what is Knox's true view.

One has to bear in mind also that Knox was passionate and excitable, and that in the heat of debate he could be carried away to extremes to which, in his calmer moments, he was perhaps not prepared to commit himself.

And there is this further possible complication, that Knox's head may have been somewhat at variance with his heart. Intellectually, he was captivated by the theology of Calvin—as well he might be. But when he speaks and writes strictly as a pastor, one hears rather the voice of Martin Luther. I do not think that he was particularly interested in systematic theology, but rather in its pastoral and homiletic applications. For these reasons, I should be a little hesitant about assuming that the reply to the Anabaptist can be taken as representing Knox's own inmost convictions, or as the teaching that he communicated to his congregations. One has to weigh against it, rather carefully, references to predestination in his pastoral letters and elsewhere. Incidentally I must dissent from Percy's judgment that Knox was no pastor, and did not care for pastoral work.[2] His letters seem to me to reveal a man who was a pastor first, last, and all the time.

I am all the more inclined to doubt whether logical consistency is to be looked for in Knox's **"Treatise on Predestination,"** by the fact that in it he was following Calvin; and Calvin laid little store by logical consistency on this, or indeed on any other subject related to faith. We constantly hear references, of course, to Calvin's "ruthless (another damnatory adjective!) French logic", which pushed principles to their ultimate uncomfortable conclusions, without leaving any of these blurred edges or woolly compromises which, to the British mind, are infallible guarantees of balanced commonsense. One suspects that those who thus judge have been misled, by the limpid clarity and meticulous orderliness of Calvin's literary style, into supposing that the thought which it expresses is just as pellucid and neatly logical. This is not so, as anyone who tries to make a *précis* of his theology will quickly discover. His aim was to expound the truths of Biblical faith, as he understood them, without distortion: and he will not distort them, even in the interests of logical consistency. Again and again we are confronted with unresolved antinomy and paradox. Thus, after a lucid exposition of the majesty and sole sovereignty of God, he will proceed to stress the terrible reality and power of evil; not in order to offer any neat logical solution of the antinomy, for he has no such thing to offer—but simply because both sides of the antinomy are facts of Biblical witness, and of Christian faith and experience; and both, therefore, require the clearest statement that can be given them. A logical thinker would blur both sides of the antinomy in an effort to reach some sort of rational reconciliation between them, paring away something of the sovereignty of God, and something of the reality of evil;—until, with a limited God on the one hand, and evil that is not really evil but rather undeveloped good on the other, he could build some kind of logical bridge between the two. Calvin does no such thing. He states both sides of the antinomy with extreme sharpness, because both are, to him, incontrovertible facts which must not be minimized in any way, though they cannot be reconciled by logic. Truth, not logic, is his aim.

His treatment of Predestination is similar. On the one hand, he insists on outright and extreme predestination. On the other hand, no theologian ever put greater stress on human responsibility, and the importance and reality of human choice and decision, than Calvin. He states both sides without compromise or dilution, because he believes that both are *facts* which we dare not minimize or ignore; though how we are to reconcile them is an absolute mystery. We may call Calvin an extreme thinker if we like, provided we remember that his extremes are usually balanced by opposite extremes. He never nibbles the sharp edges off what he takes to be the facts. But the last thing we can accuse him of is "ruthless logic". It is the woolly-minded harmonizer who is really the ruthless logician—ruthless, all too often, with inconvenient facts and truths.

In his **"Treatise on Predestination,"** Knox is following Calvin's arguments pretty closely; and not only his arguments, but his methods also. Knox presents us with the same sharp statement of apparent contradictories. It would be a cheap victory, and a useless one, to rake out the numerous inconsistencies in his treatise. Knox would reply, like Calvin, that his aim was to state facts as he knew them to be, not to explain how they could be what they were. And, if it would be cheap simply to parade Knox's inconsistencies, it would be downright dishonest to label him as an "extremist" for his uncompromising assertion of one side of an antinomy, without pointing out that in the very next chapter he probably is just as extreme in his statement of the opposite truth. Indeed, Knox's views on Predestination are a balance of opposite extremes; a fact which the careless and hurried reader of his work is apt to miss.

There has been so much denunciation of the "ugly predestinarianism" of Calvinism and of John Knox—particularly on the part of some Scottish literary writers whose itch to pontify on theology seems scarcely to be warranted by the apparent sketchiness of their acquaintance with the subject[3]—that it seems to be altogether necessary to point out that neither Calvin nor Knox invented the doctrine, nor is it by any means peculiar to them.

The doctrine is Biblical. And it is Biblical not only in the sense that a Biblical basis can be found for it in certain utterances of St Paul, and of the prophets Isaiah and Jeremiah. The truth is (and it was the merit of Calvin and of Knox after him that they realized this) *that the Bible is a book about predestination*. Predestination is its theme from start to finish. If the attempt is made to purge predestination from the pages of the Bible, what remains falls to pieces and loses significance, just as a beautiful necklace falls to meaningless bits and pieces when the string is withdrawn.

Consider how predestinarian the Bible is. In the Old Testament God is represented as sovereign in nature and in grace. His name is "I am", and He is God, and beside Him there is none other. His sovereign will, and only His will, ordains what is and what shall be. He created the world, down to its last detail; and He maintains it, down to its smallest event. Each morning He appoints to the sun its daily course, and each evening He brings out the stars by their number. The beasts of the forest receive their meat in due season from His hand; and when it is His pleasure to take away their breath, they die and return to the dust from which He created them. All nature, in all its details, is subject to His will; and all events come about as He ordains.[4]

Man, too, lives out his life in the hollow of God's hand, and the issues of that life lie with God's sovereign will. There is no escaping that divine surveillance which is so magnificently described in the 139th Psalm: "Thou knowest my very thoughts from afar . . . and before ever a word comes to my tongue, Thou knowest it altogether. Thou art on every side, behind and before, and layest Thy hand on me. . . . If I take the wings of the morning and dwell in the uttermost parts of the sea, even there would Thy hand reach me, and Thy right hand would grasp me." But the Psalmist is sure not only of God's ordaining of all his life, but of His fore-ordaining of it: "All the days of my life were foreseen by Thee, set down within Thy book; ere ever they took shape, they were assigned me, ere ever one of them was mine."[5]

Here indeed is predestination! In the Old Testament—if we except the cynicism of Ecclesiastes—there is no such thing as chance or fate. All things fall out by the sovereign will and determination of God. And, since He sees the end from the beginning, not just by His determination but by His pre-determination or predestination. Not even evil is excepted from this sovereign determination of God—and this despite the constant stress upon His holiness and goodness: "Shall there be evil in a city, and the Lord hath not done it?[6]" "I make peace, and create evil: I the Lord do all these things."[7]

As in the realm of nature, so also in the realm of grace: God chose Israel when Israel was nothing, and of sheer grace, and of His own good pleasure, elected Israel to be His chosen people and the instruments of His purposes of blessing. The destiny of the nation was determined by God, not for any special qualities which Israel had, for God gave all these qualities subsequently to His choice. The choice of God determined in all details the destiny of the people: it was a pre-destination.[8]

The New Testament, too, is saturated with Predestination. In the fulness of time—at the appointed and determined hour—God sent His Son, and sent Him to do a pre-determined work. The events of His life fell out "that it might be fulfilled which was spoken by the prophets." As He faced death, Our Lord exclaimed "For this cause came I unto this hour." And to the disciples on the Emmaus journey He said "O fools and slow of heart to believe all that the prophets have spoken: ought not Christ to have suffered these things, and afterwards to enter into His glory"—was not this the role appointed and fore-ordained for Him by God?

As the Lord's destiny was fore-ordained, so was the disciples'. "I have manifested Thy Name," says Christ in His High Priestly prayer, "to the men Thou gavest me out of the world. Thine they were, and Thou gavest them to me . . . Thou hast given Thy son power over all flesh, that He should give eternal life to as many as Thou hast given him." They did not choose; they were chosen. These last words come (significantly) from that 17th chapter of St John's Gospel where Knox said that he "cast his first anchor". Who could cast anchor there, and not be a predestinarian out and out?

And finally, the end to which all the processes of nature and grace are moving—the final consummation—is hidden in the determinate foreknowledge of God. "Of that day and hour knoweth no man, no, not the angels of heaven, but my Father only."

Surely enough evidence has now been adduced to show that the doctrine of Predestination does not rest precariously on a few doubtful proof-texts. Predestination is what the Bible is about, and no theology can claim to be Biblical which is not strung on this same predestinarian thread.

It is unnecessary, therefore, to apologize for the predestinarian strain in Knox's theology. It was his business to expound the Biblical faith, and the Biblical faith is predestinarian from end to end. It is those who object to his predestinarian teaching who must show how it can be rejected without rejecting the Bible as well.

What can be questioned, however, is whether certain emphases in Knox's handling of the doctrine give a really balanced presentation of this fundamental element of the Biblical testimony.

One question suggests itself immediately. If all the Reformers were thorough predestinarians (as indeed they were) why does Calvinism have the reputation of being an ultra-predestinarian creed? The main reason is that Calvin's theological interests, and therefore his dogmatic formulations, range over a wider field than Luther's, so that there is more for him to be predestinarian about. Luther was a monk and an anti-humanist with a strong distaste for speculation: his interest was practical, and was focused to one burning point—man's sin and need, and what God has done to meet that need. At that point he is, of course, predestinarian; perhaps even more completely so than Calvin. On the wider fields of theology, however—especially where it borders on speculation and philosophy—Luther has, comparatively speaking, less to say. His predestinarianism is therefore displayed on a fairly narrow front.

Calvin, on the other hand, was a converted humanist—yet a humanist still with wide-ranging interests. He begins his theology, not at the subjective point of sinful man's predicament, but with God in His infinite glory and sovereignty; and from this he passes down through the whole range of the divine creation and scheme of redemption before reaching the application of that redemption to the individual sinner. His method of thought thus compels him to present predestination over a far wider front than Luther did: and it is the wide range of his predestinarianism, corresponding to the wide range of his theology, that is the main cause of the general impression that Calvinism is abnormally predestinarian.

In his **"Treatise on Predestination"** however, Knox follows Luther's method rather than Calvin's: that is to say, he begins from predestination as it bears directly on our own personal salvation. From that central point he makes excursions into the wider field of Christian philosophy, and back towards those eternal decrees of God on which predestination is conceived to be founded. His chief interest is in the relation between God's fore-ordination and our salvation, and the topics that take up his attention are those of election and reprobation, the nature of human responsibility, the problem of assurance and of the perseverance of the saints, and the relationship between election and the mediation of Christ.

Knox begins, as do all the Reformers, with the assertion that salvation is altogether of God's grace, and rests not in the smallest measure on our good works. He grounds this assertion not only on the fact that sinful man cannot produce good works with which to justify himself before God, but must ever be a debtor to God's mercy and grace—Luther's starting-point: much more does Knox found himself on the insight that Assurance is an essential factor in salvation—not just an additional comfort which the saved man may hope to enjoy, but can very well get along without. Assurance of salvation is essential, says Knox, because without assurance we must alternate miserably between hope and fear, never certain that we are acceptable to God.[9] But uncertainty and fear about our acceptability are distrust of God's redeeming mercy and love. And such distrust is the exact antithesis of the trust and self-commitment, of the faith in Himself and in His promises, that God calls for, and which are of the very essence of salvation.

We are saved by trusting God. But we are not trusting Him at all, so long as we doubt His assurance that we are acceptable, and are accepted by Him, for Christ's sake. To be told *that* in our inward hearts by God, is to have salvation offered to us. To believe it, when we are told it, is to be saved. Assurance therefore, assurance that God does accept us and has accepted us, is of the very essence of salvation.

Now, of course, if our acceptability to God depended on anything in ourselves—on the firmness of our faith, or the quality of our deeds—we never could have assurance. For our faith is frail, and our best deeds tainted with evil.

Assurance can only be reached (says Knox) when we realize that our acceptability with God rests on nothing in ourselves, but entirely on the election of God. And this election, since it proceeds from God's free and sovereign grace, and is exercised without respect to anything in us, does not vary with our changing moods, our successes or failures, our faith or our doubt, but abides constant and unchanging through them all.[10]

Election, therefore, is the true ground of assurance. Only conviction of election can produce such perfect trust. And perfect trust is essential; not only for the hour of conversion, but for the whole of the Christian life that follows after. For true service of God cannot spring from doubt and fear, but only from trust and love.[11]

The doctrine of election, then, produces Assurance—that joyful certainty that the love and mercy of God are ours—which was one of the new things that the Reformation brought to men. The mediaeval Church had awakened men to a profound and disquieting sense of sin. This sense of sin is indeed the leading factor in mediaeval religious life. But the mediaeval Church had signally failed to give men the assurance of salvation: it had taught them to seek assurance through austerities and good works, and they had sought diligently and failed to find it. The Reformation, with its teaching that we are not saved by our works but only by God's gracious election of us to salvation, gave men the assurance they craved, and indeed required, for Christian living.

But it is an extraordinary thing that Knox did not clearly realize—none of the Reformers apparently realized—

that by grounding assurance on election, rather than on merit, they were only pushing the problem of assurance back one stage, and pushing it into what appeared to be an even more terrifying form. For if salvation depends on merit, and I doubt of my salvation, I can at least do something about it: I can try harder to be good. But if salvation depends on God's election, and I doubt my election, I land in complete and hopeless paralysis. There is nothing I can do about that. If God has not elected me, what hope or help have I? Apparently none.

The first generation of Reformers, and Knox among them, had few doubts on this score. They had been led out of the "errors of Romanism" into the gracious light of the evangelical truth. They had known, in their own hearts, the reality of God's forgiving love. How could they doubt, in face of these facts, that they were elect to salvation?

It was only after the fire of this new experience was spent that gloomy doubts began to rise in some Calvinist circles. How could a man be sure that he was one of the elect? So long as a man could point to the fact that he had been led out of the "synagogue of Satan", and had braved persecution for the true faith, he could be persuaded that he was elect to salvation. But when Protestantism was established, and Tom, Dick and Harry were all Protestants, the question arose how Tom, Dick and Harry could all be sure that they were elect?

Knox was first seriously confronted with this problem in the person of his neurasthenic mother-in-law Mrs Bowes, and sorely he was perplexed both by her and by it. He treated her neuralgic conscience with extraordinary patience and gentleness; but I gravely doubt the wisdom of some of his pastoral counselling to her, and of the solutions he despairingly suggests for her recurrent doubts.[12]

He advocates the perilous method of self-inspection. Election should produce certain fruits, and if the fruits are there, we can be reasonably certain of our election. We must remember that even the elect may sin, and even sin grievously. Mrs Bowes is not, therefore, to despair of her election because of isolated lapses into sin. But if we find in ourselves a steady delight in some evil course, persistent wrong-doing, an ingrained aversion to godliness, then we do well to doubt our election and to be seriously alarmed.[13]

But to what end should Mrs Bowes, or anyone else, be seriously alarmed, if everything depends on election, and election depends only on God's will, and on nothing in us? With sublime but perhaps saving inconsistency, Knox introduces at this point an exhortation to Mrs Bowes to "make her calling and election sure". It is not clear to me what he means by this. Clearly he does mean that greater efforts after righteousness are urgently called for in such a case. But is this because God's election of us is not final and decisive, but awaits confirmation in the light of our subsequent behaviour—so that it is never too late to mend?

This is to skate on very thin ice over the doctrine of merits, if not to crash through right up to the neck. To say this would indeed be a violent departure from his principles; though I should not put it past Knox to make it. The pastor in him was always mercifully strong enough to overcome the theologian in a really tight corner.

More probably, he means no more than that the spectacle of our progress in godly living will increase our own assurance of our election—assuming that we are elect. And in the case of Mrs Bowes he did assume that as beyond question; she could not have thought so highly of his sermons if she had not been elect. Yet, even to the elect, this is risky pastoral counselling: and it does nothing to meet the problem of those who have a basic and miserable doubt of their election.[14]

Surely the true answer to all such gloomy questionings is to get the victim to look outwards, not inwards. Assurance can never be internally grounded at all, but must rest altogether on the promise of God. The assurance is correlative to the promise, and cannot be introspected in abstraction from the promise. If God gives a promise, and I trust that promise—then I trust it, and that is the end of the matter. It is perversity thrice perverted to go on to ask whether my trust is a valid trust, whether my faith is a saving faith. It is a saving faith, if it believes a saving promise. It is a valid trust, if the promise itself is valid. Assurance of election can lie in nothing else than in the simple fact that we do believe in the mercy of God in Jesus Christ.

To seek to prop up this assurance by any other means than taking a closer and stronger grip on the Promise, is really to undermine and eventually to destroy it: to lead towards that miserable situation where men look into themselves for the evidences of election, and inevitably fail to find them. It would have been well if Knox had been clearer on this point than he was.

There is a related point on which Knox seems equally to waver, or perhaps rather to assert two sides of an antinomy with equal vehemence—the question of the Perseverance of the Saints: whether a man can fall from election, or whether election is final and irreversible, so that it must issue in full salvation.[15] To understand Knox on this point we must know something of what he means by free-will and obedience to God. He holds—and none has ever held it more strongly—that man's will is free. In a striking passage[16] in his **"Treatise on Predestination,"** he shows how Annas and Caiaphas, the Scribes and the Sanhedrin, Judas and

Pilate, all acted freely in bringing about the crucifixion of Christ. Each man did precisely what he wanted to do, and purposed to do: yet, also, each man did precisely what God had predestinated him to do, in such a way that at the predetermined time, and in the predetermined way, Christ gave His life on the Cross for sinners. From all the ages, the Cross had been ordained, yet those who brought it about acted responsibly and freely in doing it.

The natural man, therefore, is free in all things but one. The one thing he cannot do is to obey God's will. He does God's will, unwittingly, because he is predestinated to do it. But obedience involves voluntary co-operation with the known will of God; and this the natural man cannot render, because he does not know the will of God, and would not do it if he did know it.

With conversion, obedience to the will of God becomes possible for the first time, for that will is now revealed to us in Christ, and is impressed in us by the Holy Spirit. But Knox is quite clear that the meaning of obedience is voluntary self-identification with the will of God. It would not be obedience if it was not voluntary. The whole difference between the elect and the non-elect at this point lies in the fact that the non-elect do God's will involuntarily, while the elect obey it voluntarily.[17] But does this mean that, after conversion, a man may fail in this voluntary self-identification with the will of God—may, by stubborn refusal to will God's will, reject the salvation that was his, and make his election of none effect? God can, and does, ensure that all men do His will, without infringing their freedom. But can even God guarantee a man's *voluntary* obedience and co-operation? Is it not clear that the redeemed man is free to withdraw this obedience, and so lapse from grace?

When Knox contemplates the Sovereign Majesty of God, he cannot believe this. What God has predestinated will come to pass. His election cannot fail. The saints will persevere unto full salvation, though they fall often, and sometimes (for a season) seem to fall away altogether.[18]

But when Knox contemplates the hearts of men, and his own heart, he is not so sure: and the pastor's voice rings out, calling men to watchfulness and care, lest in the end they be not found in the company of the redeemed. Once again, both sides of the antinomy are stated; and the anxious pastor corrects the confident theologian. Knox will have no man use the doctrine of the perseverance of the saints as a feather bed.

It remains to take a brief glance at the seamy side of the doctrine of Predestination: the matter of Reprobation. Knox grounds this partly on experience, partly on his understanding of God's nature, and wholly upon his understanding of the Bible.

Experience seems to show that while some men accept the Gospel, others steadily reject and despise it to their dying day, and delight in iniquity and mock at goodness. Since nothing in this world happens by chance, but all falls out according to the will of God, we must conclude that while God has elected some to salvation, He has reprobated others and predestinated them to damnation.[19]

Knox finds the reason for this double-edged predestination in the nature of God.[20] In Catholic theology, God had been regarded as substance. By the Scotists He was regarded as arbitrary will. The Reformers conceived of God rather as the embodiment of moral law, though the old conception of arbitrary will was not absent from their thoughts. The Calvinist system distinguished between the nature and the will of God; the stern necessity of justice belongs to His nature. By His nature, He is, and must be, just. But in His will God is absolutely free: and this divine freedom is expressed by showing mercy to those who would otherwise be the objects of God's stern justice.

But neither justice nor mercy could reveal themselves fully in a world that was devoid of evil.[21] Both the justice of God's nature, and the mercy of His will, require evil as the foil against which they can be displayed. God could not reveal Himself, in all His fullness, to a sinless humanity. All men must sin, in order that the elect may know His mercy, and all may know His justice. Hence God ordained the fall, creating man good, but giving man free-will, and ordaining that by the exercise of free-will man should fall.

Knox insists vehemently that Predestination must never be thought of as constraining man's free-will in the slightest degree—though by his own free-will man does exactly what God has predestinated him to do.[22] In this way Knox seeks to avoid the odium of making God responsible, for sin. He fore-ordained it, but He did not compel man to it. Man was free, and therefore man was responsible. No doubt man could not have acted otherwise; but he did not desire to act otherwise. He sinned because he wanted to sin, and chose to sin. And (says Knox plaintively) how can people say that our doctrine of Predestination destroys man's free-will, when we keep insisting that man does just as he chooses, and exactly as he desires? Can you conceive of a will more free than that? This is not, of course, an attempted solution of the problem of evil, so much as an outright assertion of both sides of the antinomy: God is absolutely sovereign, and man is absolutely free. Man does just what he chooses, and, in so doing, does just what God chooses.

Confronted now by a fallen humanity, both God's justice and His mercy have free play to manifest themselves. Knox is fully prepared to cry *"O felix culpa!"*—O happy fault, that brought Christ into the world for our redemption! For had we not sinned and fallen, we should never have known all the greatness and wonder of God's mercy.[23]

But God's justice must be displayed as well as His mercy, for God is justice as well as mercy: and He cannot make Himself known without revealing His justice. Therefore, out of the mass of fallen humanity, God elects some to salvation, to manifest His mercy: others He leaves to their merited punishment, in order to manifest His justice. The reprobate are as necessary to God's self-manifestation as the elect. (This is the infra-lapsarian theory—that God's election operates on man as fallen, not on man as innocent. In a few passages Knox appears to incline to the supra-lapsarian doctrine; but on the whole, he is infra-lapsarian. Like Calvin, he had probably never thought the matter out.)

The principle by which God elects certain sinners to salvation, and leaves others to their merited fate, is entirely opaque to us. It is due to no quality in the sinners themselves, for all alike are worthy of damnation. Yet Knox insists that the principle of selection cannot be other than a just principle, since it proceeds from a God whose very nature is justice. This is part of His secret counsel which is too high for mortal mind to comprehend.[24] And, as Knox very pertinently remarks, if we could understand why God elects some and reprobates others, God would not be God. God cannot be questioned on this point—not because His election and reprobation are arbitrary and unjust; but because we could not understand the answer even if we got it. All we can do at this point is to lay our hand upon our mouths, and be dumb. Some might be tempted to feel that Knox might with advantage have laid his hand on his own mouth just a little sooner.

He may even have felt this himself: for it is a remarkable fact that all this religious speculation is rigorously excluded from the ***Scots Confession***. Predestination is not discussed at all, and under the heading of election[25] we are told simply that it was Christ who was predestinated from all eternity to be our Saviour, and that we are elected in Him. This passage in the ***Scots Confession*** rests so directly on Knox's "anchor passage" in John 17—"Thine they were, and Thou gavest them to me"—that I do not doubt that here we have the simplicity of Knox's own faith: not a bowdlerization of his views forced upon him by his more cautious colleagues.

Knox can fly high in controversy, and speculate daringly. And if men must speculate on such subjects (and I suppose that nothing will ever stop them doing so) then I think that Knox's speculative theology is worthy of a good deal of respect. But Percy is probably correct in his judgment that the Treatise on Predestination was something of a *tour de force,* and that Knox's heart was not really in it.[26]

Certainly, when he folds his speculative wings, it is to a simple Christocentric faith that he returns—and to one that points towards that fine flowering of Federal theology which comes in Thomas Boston, a Scottish theologian whose work has too long been neglected.[27] Knox's Christocentric faith (and Boston's after him) is this: that the immediate object of God's election is Christ, not men. It is by Christ's calling of us, and in our union with Him, that we partake in this election of God. It is not ours directly, but only mediately, through Christ.

In this way, election does not by-pass and short-circuit the sacraments, as it does when stated speculatively. If we ourselves are the direct objects of God's election, then Baptism, and the Eucharist itself, must be emptied of much of their significance. For a man will then tend to rest himself on this eternal decree, rather than on any event that takes place in Time. But if it is Christ who is the object of election, and we are elect only in Him, then the sacraments in which we are united to Him grow and increase in significance.

I have already pointed out the stress that Knox lays on the Sacrament of Communion. The statement on election in the ***Scots Confession*** links up directly with this. It is in the Christocentric, Johannine mysticism of the doctrine of election in the ***Scots Confession*** that Knox's true faith is displayed. One wishes that Knox, instead of writing that arid and speculative **"Treatise on Predestination,"**[28] had laboured instead at the rich mine of this, his own distinctive and personal comprehension of what election really means. Yet he points to where the riches lie; and others have gathered, and will gather, wealth from this mine.

*Notes*

[1] This treatise on Predestination occupies the greater part of Vol. V of his *Works.*

[2] *John Knox,* p. 59.

[3] A recent substantial work of literary criticism contains the statement that the cruel doctrine of the damnation of unbaptized infants was brought to Scotland from Geneva by John Knox! Can theological absurdity and misrepresentation go further? Probably it can, and will.

[4] See Psalm 104.

[5] Moffatt's translation.

[6] Amos 3: 6.

[7] Isaiah 45: 7.

[8] Cf. Leviticus 20: 26.

[9] Preface to the treatise, *Works* V, pp. 21-30.

[10] *Op. cit.* pp. 26-27.

[11] *Op. cit.* p. 30.

[12] A series of letters to her will be found in *Works* III, pp. 331-402.

[13] See also the Treatise on Predestination, *Works* V, p. 210.

[14] Mrs Bowes's doubts on this point were pathological and incorrigible. She had an exasperating knack of discovering the weak spot in every argument that Knox designed for her comfort.

[15] *Works,* V, p. 210.

[16] *Works,* V, p. 142f.

[17] *Works,* V, pp. 144, 182.

[18] *Works,* V, p. 210; III, 364.

[19] *Works,* V, p. 124 sq.

[20] *Works,* V, p. 406.

[21] *Works,* V, pp. 91-92.

[22] *Works,* V, pp. 41, 112f, etc.

[23] *Works,* V, p. 92.

[24] *Works,* V, p. 114, etc.

[25] *Confession,* Cap. VIII.

[26] *John Knox,* p. 247.

[27] A new study of Boston and of Federal Theology, by Dr Donald Bruggink, is shortly to be published.

[28] To do Knox justice, it should be noted that the centrality of Christ in Election is by no means ignored in his Treatise on Predestination. Indeed, it is stated with peculiar force and beauty at one point—*Works,* V, pp. 50 to 54.

**Richard L. Greaves (essay date 1980)**

SOURCE: "Calvinism, Democracy, and Knox's Political Thought," in *Theology and Revolution in the Scottish Reformation: Studies in the Thought of John Knox*, Christian University Press, 1980, pp. 169-82.

[*In the following excerpt, Greaves finds certain of Knox's writings to have some, albeit unintended, democratic implications.*]

In the course of the long-standing debate on the possibility of democratic tendencies in the thought and practice of John Calvin and his followers, recent attention has focused on limited case studies. Certain of these studies have a direct relevance to understanding the role of John Knox in the history of Calvinism. It is [my] purpose. . . to reexamine Knox's position, in part by the use of these studies, in order to clarify that position and to add a further dimension to the broader debate. It is not, however, [my] purpose. . . to engage in an exercise of comparative government to determine whether or not Knox's Scotland was more or less democratic than its sister states. Nor will an endeavor be undertaken to shift the focus of this historic and worthwhile debate from its principal question: Are the sources of modern democracy to be found in the thought and practice of Calvin and his disciples? Although the essence of modern democracy is debatable, for the purpose of this essay it is used in the sense of a society governed directly or indirectly by the people, with power originating in a broadly based citizenry whose rights as individuals are guaranteed through constitutional or legal means. Modern democracy obviously did not exist anywhere in sixteenth-century Europe, but there is a clear relevance in understanding how and where it developed.

At the outset it must be remembered that Knox, like Calvin, had a great deal to say about politics, but not about the ideal form of government. According to Knox, government was divinely instituted for man because of his inability to live in peace without it. To the secular authorities God entrusted two basic powers, that is, the punishment of vice and the maintenance of virtue. This authority of the secular rulers was not without limit, but was to be exercised for the profit and comfort of the governed, not the benefit of the governors.[1] The authority of rulers was conceived by Knox to be strictly limited by the precepts of divine law, which meant especially that they "should admitte into their kingdomes no worshipping of God, except that which is commanded in the Scriptures."[2] Knox was totally committed to the divine Law as expressed in the Bible, which led him on occasion to urge violations of temporal law. Overall, however, his actions manifest a deep respect for the rule of law in society, as exemplified, for example, by his adherence in England to the *Book of Common Prayer* (despite his strong criticisms of it), his compliance with the Frankfurt magistrates after he lost his quarrel with the Coxians,[3] and his concern for the work of the Scottish Parliament. Consequently, although Knox did not set forth an exposition of the ideal form of government, it is clear that any form which would be acceptable to him would have to rest on the basic principles of the divine origin of sovereignty, the limited powers of secular authority, and the primacy of law—especially divine Law as revealed in Scripture.

These principles are not incompatible with monarchy, aristocracy, or democracy (i.e., polity). They are principles which Calvin also accepted, although John T. McNeill has argued that the repeated criticism of kings throughout Calvin's writings logically resulted in a depreciation of monarchical government.[4] Certainly in the last chapter of the *Institutes of the Christian Religion* Calvin states a clear preference for a government which is an aristocracy or an aristocracy tempered by a democracy (polity).[5] Yet Calvin's experience of royalty in his formative years was in many respects different from Knox's. Calvin's initial difficulties occurred with Francis I, a strong Renaissance prince often regarded as one of the "new monarchs." The controversy surrounding Nicholas Copp's inaugural address (which Calvin helped compose) at the University of Paris and the persecution which followed the affair of the placards forced Calvin's flight to Basel and ultimately Geneva, where his contacts were with aristocratic governments tempered with democratic elements. Knox, in his formative years, experienced weak sovereigns whose authority was exercised by prominent nobles, namely, the Earl of Arran, the Duke of Somerset, and the Duke of Northumberland. Not until Mary Tudor ascended the throne did Knox encounter a reasonably strong monarch who ruled personally and imposed a policy of persecuting Protestants. The conjunction of Mary's rule in England with the repressive policy in Scotland of the regent Mary of Lorraine drove Knox to his most extreme criticism of monarchs in his 1558 tracts, but the accession of Elizabeth I the same year and subsequent weakening of the French position in Scotland may have been responsible for his not adopting a critical position on monarchical government akin to Calvin's.

No matter how attractive the government of a city-state such as Geneva might have been to Knox—and there is no hard evidence that it was—such a government would clearly have been inapplicable to the much larger and less urbanized Scotland of the sixteenth century. He did not, therefore, criticize monarchy itself, though he had some definite things to say regarding its nature. Sovereigns did not receive their right to govern from lineal descent, popular sovereignty, or military force, but from God.[6] Any attempt by a monarch to impose commands which contravened divine precepts could legitimately be disobeyed. Although Knox believed that sovereigns had perverted the institution of monarchy by failing to fulfill their divinely appointed obligations, at no time does he conclude that monarchy itself must be abolished, or even that another form of government is preferable to monarchy. Nor does he advocate either an elective or a constitutional monarchy, either of which would have had obviously democratic implications.

One of the most potentially democratic principles in Knox's political thought is his developed doctrine of resistance by the people against tyrannical rulers. His earlier writings do not explicitly embrace this position, though they rest on the principle that obedience to rulers is required in all things except those contrary to divine precepts. In his ***Admonition or Warning,*** written in December and January 1553-54, Knox contends that it is the duty of every "Civill Magistrate" to "slay all ydolateris."[7] The Scottish scholar J. H. Burns takes Knox's phrase "Civill Magistrate" to mean only the sovereign, in which case Knox was not thinking of active resistance.[8] Knox, however, may be using the phrase in a broader sense, since the same work refers to the defense of Jeremiah (albeit from "pestilent preistis," not a king) by princes and nobles.[9] In any case, by May 31, 1554 he was willing to encourage his English friends that God would "styr up one Jehu or other to execute hys vengeaunce uppon these bloudde-thyrsty tyrauntes and obstinate idolators."[10] The following July he called to God to provide a Phinehas, Elijah, or Jehu to topple Mary Tudor, and praised Jeremiah's exhortation to cease obedience to one's princes and obey the enemies of one's state.[11] In July 1558, in his ***Appellation*** to the Scottish nobles and estates, Knox set forth the responsibilities of the inferior magistrates to remove a tyrannical sovereign. The same responsibility had been asserted in ***The First Blast of the Trumpet,*** which was published in Geneva in the spring of 1558.

Before 1558 Knox had not explicitly gone beyond what Calvin himself had written in the last chapter of the *Institutes*. ***The First Blast,*** however, made it the duty of the people as well as the magistrates to see that a tyrannical monarch (such as Athaliah) was overthrown and executed.[12] The ***Appellation*** made the punishment of idolaters and blasphemers, regardless of status, the concern of every person in the state in accordance with his Christian vocation and the possibility afforded to him by God to wreak vengeance.[13] Knox's letter to the commonalty of Scotland, which accompanied the ***Appelation,*** asserted that subjects could lawfully require from their temporal rulers the provision of godly ministers and the expulsion of false prophets. If the rulers declined, the commonalty could provide for and defend such clergy against government persecution. Yet Knox also made it clear that the people ought to work with the estates and nobility rather than against them.[14] There is thus no demand for the creation of a democratic state in these works, but a clarion call for religious reform in the context of the existing social and political structures of England and Scotland. Simultaneously, however, the assertion of individual responsibility in the context of limited government has democratic implications, even if Knox did not intend this to be the case.

The question then arises as to whether or not Knox's development of resistance theory is a logical working out of Calvin's political principles. The answer to this question is partially suggested by the research of Helmut Koenigsberger, whose studies of the Huguenots, the Catholic Leagues, and the Dutch Beggars led him to the conclusion that "religion was the binding force that held together the divergent interests of the different classes and provided them with an organization and a propaganda machine capable of creating the first genuinely national and international parties in modern European history. . . . "[15] The crucial point which Koenigsberger so effectively demonstrates is that the French Catholic Leagues manifested many of the organizational and propagandistic characteristics of the Calvinist-inspired Huguenot and Beggar movements. Consequently these organizations are the response of religious minorities, willing to use force as a tactic, to the growing power of the state. The source of rebellion is essentially external, not an ideological outgrowth of Calvin's political principles.

If Koenigsberger's thesis is applied to Scotland, certain difficulties immediately appear. The relative remoteness of the region, the absence of a powerful regent backed by effective military forces, and the largely independent ways of the Scottish nobility cannot be ignored. Nevertheless, the Scottish Protestants, like their counterparts in France and the Netherlands, represented the social spectrum. The role of the Lords of the Congregation is too well known to need recounting, and W. Stanford Reid has recently demonstrated the role of the burgesses in the coming of the Reformation to Edinburgh.[16] It was lords such as the Earl of Glencairn, Lord Lorne, Erskine of Dun, and Mary Stewart's half-brother, Lord James Stewart, who led the reform movement while Knox was in exile in Geneva, though he had been in Scotland in 1555 and communicated with Scottish leaders from Geneva in the next three years. It was the burgesses of Edinburgh who took the lead in July 1559 in denying the authority of the regent, Mary of Lorraine, by calling Knox to become minister of St. Giles' Kirk.[17] As on the Continent, the moving force behind the activities of the lords and burgesses appears in large measure to have been a response to external political conditions, in particular Mary's recent crackdown on Protestantism in the aftermath of the Peace of Cateau-Cambrésis.[18] In both, cases, however, Calvin and Knox respectively contributed advice and encouragement to the rebel forces.

Behind the revolutionary activities, particularly of the nobles, was another factor; that is, Knox's insistent demands that the Scottish Protestants fulfill their covenant responsibilities. It was in the covenant context that Knox developed and urged his doctrine of resistance to tyrants. In ***An Admonition or Warning*** (1554), where Knox called on civil magistrates to slay idolaters, "the league betuixt God and us" is set forth as the basis for this demand. "The league betuixt God and us requyreth avoyding of all ydolatrie," but "the slaying of ydolateris appertenis not to everie particular man."[19] Four years later, however, the "covenante" obligations were delineated in such a manner as specifically to require the commonalty to wield

> the sworde in their own hand to remove such enormities from amongest them. . . . If any go about to erect and set up idolatrie, or to teach defection from God, after the veritie hath bene receaved and approved, that then, not only the Magistrates, to whom the sword is committed, but also the People, are bound, by that othe which they have made to God, to revenge to the uttermost of their power the injurie done against his Majestic.[20]

Because the extension of tyrannicide to the common people has democratic implications,[21] it would bolster the arguments of those who find democratic tendencies in Calvin's thought, if it could be demonstrated that Knox derived his covenant principles from the Geneva reformer. But this is not the case, at least in terms of their theological writings. . . . Calvin's concept of the covenant is essentially promissory in nature, though it is possible to see a more reciprocal covenant notion at work in his efforts to persuade the Genevans to accept *Les Ordonnances Ecclesiastiques.* Theologically Knox treated the covenant as a conditional promise calling for man's reciprocal obedience. Apart from the Old Testament, the possible theological sources for Knox's concept of the covenant include the writings of William Tyndale, Oecolampadius, and Heinrich Bullinger (through John Hooper), all of whom stressed the conditional nature of the covenant. But a more important source was the ancient Scottish custom of banding, which originated in the feudal era in conjunction with the oath of fealty and the clan-family relationship. Scotland had a long tradition of men banding together by sworn pledges of fidelity, despite prohibitory royal legislation.[23] In 1556 the gentlemen of the Mearns entered into such a band for the purpose of maintaining Protestant preaching. At the time Knox was visiting the laird of Dun. The following year Knox urged the reform-minded lords and lairds to get on with the task, with the result that such men as the Earls of Argyll, Glencairn, and Morton, the Lord of Lorne, and John Erskine of Dun signed a Protestant covenant on December 3, 1557.[24] Thus Knox's concept of the covenant, which provided the foundation for his doctrine of resistance, had its origins in the world of Scottish feudal politics, but was thereafter developed in altered political circumstances into the basis for a revolutionary party akin to the kind described by Koenigsberger in France and the Netherlands.

Having been freshly reminded of the Scottish rite of banding by the gentlemen of the Mearns, Knox returned to Geneva in September 1556. Within the next two years he completed the development of his doctrine of resistance, with its democratic implications. One cannot discount the influence on this development of his discussions early in 1554 with Calvin, Bullinger, and Pierre Viret. Hans Baron has demonstrated the importance of the civic experience of Strasbourg in Martin Bucer's exposition of the legitimacy of resistance by *magistratus inferiores,* that is, the Strasbourg magistrates.[25] Calvin, of course, almost certainly was influenced by Bucer in this regard. Bucer's influence on Knox's doctrine of the Lord's Supper (through the medium of the *First Helvetic Confession*) has been demonstrated. It also appears that Bucer may have influenced Knox's development of resistance theory through the agency of Pierre Viret.

The advice Knox received in 1554 from Calvin and Bullinger would not have encouraged him to undertake a more democratic enunciation of resistance doctrine.[27] There is no record of what Viret told Knox, but the recent research of Robert Linder makes possible a reasonable reconstruction. Viret justified armed resistance against tyrants if two preconditions were fulfilled, the first of which was the trying of other means, including prayer and patience. The second condition was that armed resistance must be led by legitimate lesser magistrates whose authority derived from the people. Viret never sanctioned Christians to resist actively as individuals, such as Knox subsequently did, but he linked liberty and religion by asserting that "once the people somehow had gained a measure of political and religious freedom, they possessed the authority to resist any tyrannical encroachments upon it."[28] The advice, therefore, that Knox received from Viret in 1554 may have been an additional factor in motivating Knox to express a more democratic resistance theory.

Attempts have been made to find democratic implications in the theological doctrines of Calvin. Since Knox shared many of these doctrines, one can reasonably expect to find the same democratic implications, if they exist. The evidence, however, distinctly indicates that Knox did not develop any political implications that may be inherent in his (or Calvin's) theology. In his long treatise on predestination,[29] Knox does not take occasion to argue either that the special role of the elect should mean an aristocratic government of the chosen, or that the universal depravity of all men (hence their spiritual equality) should lead to a democratic state. Because Knox is openly critical of the masses in the pages of his ***History of the Reformation in Scotland,*** it seems quite apparent that he was unsympathetic to democracy. This is also clearly reflected in his predestination treatise when he recounts Calvin's attempts to impose discipline in Geneva:

> The Consistoire called for justice to be executed, and for penalties to be appointed, for the inobedient and open contemners. But nothing coulde prevaile; for the multitude of the wicked was so great, that in votes and voices they did prevaile. And so was the iniquitie of the wicked mainteined for a long ceason.[30]

Clearly a democratic government determined by "votes and voices" could be prejudicial to the establishment of a godly commonwealth. Even when considering the democratic implications of Knox's doctrine of resistance, one must remember that it is the godly individuals who share the responsibility of tyrannicide, not the reprobate. When equality is mentioned, it occurs in a spiritual, not a political, context. The ***Book of Discipline,*** of which Knox was a coauthor, stipulates, for example, that there is to be no respect of persons, since all are equal in God's sight. This position is elsewhere stated: "In the hope of the life to come he hath made all equall."[31] The priesthood of all believers and the perspicuity of Scripture, making it available to all (illumined) men, similarly deal with equality in the spiritual realm in Knox's writings, but are not given any political connotations. This does not rule out the possibility that a later disciple of Knox might read democratic political principles into these doctrines, but there is nothing inherent within them that would make such a reading either logical or compelling.

Attempts have also been made to show that Calvin's ecclesiastical polity, with its elements of popular participation, was conducive to the development of political democracy. Robert M. Kingdon has already analyzed the debate between two Calvinists—Jean Morely, who advocated a form of Congregational polity, and Theodore Beza, who defended a Presbyterian position. Morely specifically made an analogy between Congregational polity and political democracy, in which he defended a democracy dominated by law as the best type of civil government. Morely's supporters were largely obliterated in the Huguenot wars, but a similar debate subsequently developed in England between the Presbyterians and the Independents.[32] In Scotland during Knox's lifetime debate over polity ranged between presbyterian and episcopalian poles,[33] bypassing the question of congregational polity. Nevertheless, the type of church government established for the reformed Kirk of Scotland by Knox and his colleagues included a good deal of popular participation—perhaps more than in Calvin's Geneva.

The coauthored ***Book of Discipline*** gave the primary responsibility for the selection of a minister to the local congregation, which had forty days to choose a candidate. If it failed to do so, the superintendent and his council were empowered to intervene. In Geneva, on the other hand, primary responsibility rested with the Venerable Company of Pastors and the Little Council, with the local congregation having essentially the right of ratification. The Scottish candidate did, of course, have to undergo an examination of his doctrine, personal life, and ability by the ministers and elders of the

Kirk as well as the congregation. If his life, doctrine, and abilities were found acceptable by the ministers, elders, and local congregation, the latter was normally obligated to accept him as its minister. In practice the differences between Scotland and Geneva were probably minimal.[34]

There was fairly broad participation in the procedures laid down for the selection of superintendents, though in practice there were only five, and these were appointed by the Council. According to the ***Book of Discipline*** subsequent superintendents were to be selected in a more representative manner. When a vacancy occurred, the ministers, elders, deacons, and magistrates or council of the principal town in the district were to nominate two or three suitable candidates. The latter were to be examined by the ministers of the province and the neighboring superintendents, with the final selection being determined by election.[35] Because these provisions were not carried out, it is difficult to imagine that anyone derived democratic ideas from them.

The laity were given an even more direct role in the governing of the church through the institution of elders and deacons. Elders were to be elected annually by the congregation, with no limit on the successive number of terms as long as the freedom of the annual election was maintained. Elders had the responsibility of assisting the minister in the governance of the church, especially in the supervision of both the ministers and the members. Deacons also were elected annually, though they could not be reelected until a three-year period had elapsed. Their responsibility was to handle the church's financial affairs, including the distribution of alms to the needy.[36] All male members of the congregation could participate in the church's decisions at the local level, and under Melville Scottish Presbyterianism operated democratically through elected representatives. Moreover, the General Assembly of the church which Knox helped establish included clergy and laity, and functioned in a democratic manner. Later in the century it played a major role in battling the absolutist tendencies of James VI.

Certainly the polity established by Knox and his colleagues for the selection of elders and deacons was more democratic than that in Geneva, where these officers were chosen by the Little Council, with the advice of the ministers and subject to the approval of the Council of Two Hundred. Of the twelve elders, two had to be members of the Little Council, four of the Council of Sixty, and six of the Council of Two Hundred. With Calvin himself participating in the work of constitutional revision, these councils had come to be selected in a more aristocratic manner, further underscoring the differences in the mode of selecting elders and deacons in Geneva and Scotland. It must be remembered, of course, that Calvin's concept of aristocracy was one of worth, not heredity.

If there is any merit in considering popular participation in church government as a school for preparing men for civil democracy, then the polity of the Kirk of Scotland was more effective than Calvin's church in Geneva. It is, however, essential to bear in mind that the reformed Kirk had to struggle desperately for survival during its early years. Not only did Mary Stewart and her followers oppose it, but the Protestant lords and lairds themselves refused to enact the ***Book of Discipline*** into law and provide the reformed Kirk with the financial support it required. The Kirk retained marked elements of the earlier revolutionary character, because it faced the hostility of a Catholic sovereign and a nobility determined to retain its hold over ecclesiastical lands. The democratic elements in the polity must be seen as at least in part a reflection of the continuing revolutionary nature of the Reformed churches, and not as a conscious preparation for the creation of democracy in the state.

Knox's position on the relationship of church and state is also relevant to the question of democratic tendencies. His comments sometimes have an Erastian tone, but such comments occur in the context of discussions in which the godly character of the state is asserted or assumed. Given a godly state, Knox's preference was that it support and protect the church, but not directly control it. This is reflected in the ***Scots Confession,*** which asserts that rulers and magistrates are obligated to maintain true religion and suppress idolatry and superstition. By 1567 it had been long apparent to Knox and his colleagues that the state was less than godly. The ***Book of Discipline*** had not received governmental sanction, nor had the queen's mass been abolished. Three years earlier the General Assembly had apointed a committee to look into the matter of ecclesiastical jurisdiction. In 1567 Parliament appointed a committee, which included Knox and his colleague, John Craig, "to searche more speciallie, and consider what other speciall points or causes could apperteane to the jurisdictioun, priviledge, and authoritie of the said kirk. . . . " Parliament already recognized ecclesiastical jurisdiction with respect to preaching, the administration of the sacraments, and the correction of manners. The General Assembly agreed with the purpose of the committee, but appointed its own, again with Knox and Craig among its members. It is obvious that Knox and his friends were interested in establishing a more independent jurisdiction from the state.[37]

Knox favored less involvement of the state in church affairs than did Zwingli, Bullinger, and possibly Calvin. All sought a harmonious relationship between church and state based on the ideal of a godly magistracy. Knox preferred to restrict the state's function in religion to certain specific areas. First, the state was to support the true faith and suppress idolatry and atheism. Secondly, the state was to serve as a higher court of appeal from judgments rendered by a corrupt church, provided always that the members of a godly church had the right to disobey the state if the latter contravened divine precepts. Thirdly, the state was to collect tithes and dispense the appropriate portion to the church. Fourthly, the state was to punish vices repugnant to God as well as traditional crimes. In effect, the state was to create and maintain an environment in which Protestantism could flourish.

The church for its part was to refrain from the participation of its ministers in the government, though all members of the church had a responsibility to scrutinize critically the affairs of the government in the light of biblical principles. Knox made this point manifest in his debate with Sir William Maitland of Lethington at the meeting of the General Assembly in June 1564: "The servants of God mark the vice of kings and queens, even as well as of other offenders, and that because their sins be more noisome to the Commonwealth than are the sins of inferior persons." Knox freely acknowledged that the secular power was divinely ordained, but he distinguished between the power and the ordinance upon which it was based on the one hand, and the recipient of the power on the other. The ordinance was holy and perpetual, but the "men clad with the authority, are commonly profane and unjust; yea, they are mutable and transitory, and subject to corruption. . . ." On this basis Christians could judge the behavior of their ruler and, if it violated biblical precepts, resist his authority without defying that power which was divinely ordained.[38] It was then a possible step—though Knox did not take it—to move from the right of the people to judge the religious policy of the government and intervene in it if necessary to the right of the people to participate in government. This implicit conclusion plus Knox's explicit principle of limited monarchical authority helped lay the foundation for the eventual establishment of a constitutional monarchy.

A final area which is relevant to the question of democratic sources is the educational reform proposed in the ***Book of Discipline,*** of which Knox was a coauthor. Calvin was an active educational reformer whose principal contribution was founding the Geneva Academy, in part to enable citizens to serve the commonwealth. Although the Academy was not established until 1559, Knox was influenced by Calvin's work with the educational system in Geneva. When he returned to Scotland he helped chart a course of reform characterized by a universal education at the basic level, aid for poor students, and a revised curriculum. Certainly such a system is necessary, if there is to be a functioning political democracy; and the advocacy of universal schooling is significant in this regard. Likewise the proposal to provide education based on ability rather than wealth or social status is a democratizing principle. Nevertheless, it is apparent that Knox had no democratic political principles in mind. The educational system was to be infused with religious ideals and governed by the church, which was responsible for schools and schoolmasters. Students who were not certified by the church as godly could not attend the universities, and teachers and administrators had to undergo theological examinations. In the long run this system, which was not enacted for financial reasons, would probably have created intellectual dissent and corroded ecclesiastical authority, but its proposers obviously did not have this in mind.

In conclusion, it is reasonable to accept the fact that there are democratic implications in Knox's thought, though these are definitely not intended to suggest the establishment of a political democracy in the state. Secular authorities have limited power and must govern in accord with divine law. Monarchs who become tyrannical can be actively resisted by individuals, but the individuals must be godly and engage in such action as part of their covenant obligations. These individuals also play important roles in the churches to which they belong, both in the selection of ministers, elders, and deacons, and in their participation in the government of the church through the latter offices. To the extent to which these practices reveal democratic tendencies, the credit must go less to Calvin than to other, primarily external sources. Chief among these is the revolutionary nature of the Reformed party in Scotland, with its strong ties to the feudal custom of banding. Some influence also comes from Knox's associations on the Continent with such men as Viret and Calvin. On the whole this examination of John Knox does not lend much support to those scholars who have argued that Calvinism fostered the growth of democracy, but neither does it repudiate the fundamental thesis that certain seeds are present in the Reformed tradition out of which democracy slowly developed.

*Notes*

[1] Knox, *Works,* 6:235-37.

[2] Ibid., 3:26.

[3] *A Brieff Discours off the Troubles begonne at Frankford in Germany* (1574).

[4] John T. McNeill, "The Democratic Element in Calvin's Thought," *Church History* 18 (September 1949):159-61.

[5] Calvin, *Institutes,* IV, xx, 8.

[6] Knox, *Works,* 6:236.

[7] Ibid., 3:194.

[8] Burns, "The Political Ideas of the Scottish Reformation," p. 254.

[9] Knox, *Works,* 3:188.

[10] Ibid., 3:247.

[11] Ibid., 3:309, 312, 325-26.

[12] Ibid., 4:415-16.

[13] Ibid., 4:500-501.

[14] Ibid., 4:527, 533-35.

[15] Helmut G. Koenigsberger, "The Organization of Revolutionary Parties in France and the Netherlands during the Sixteenth Century," *Journal of Modern History* 27 (December 1955):336; cf. pp. 335-51. Cf. J. H. M. Salmon, "The Paris Sixteen, 1584-1594: The Social Analysis of a Revolutionary Movement," *Journal of Modern History* 44 (December 1972):540-76. For the English situation see Leo F. Solt, "Revolutionary Parties in England under Elizabeth I and Charles I," *Church History* 27 (September 1958):234-39.

[16] W. Stanford Reid, "The Coming of the Reformation to Edinburgh," *Church History* 42 (March 1973):27-44.

[17] Reid, *Trumpeter of God,* pp. 163-64, 176.

[18] Ibid., pp. 166-67.

[19] Knox, *Works,* 3:194.

[20] Ibid., 4:506.

[21] The best case for the democratic tendencies in Calvin's resistance theory is made by Winthrop Hudson. "Democratic Freedom and Religious Faith in the Reformed Tradition," *Church History* 15 (1946):177-94....

[23] Burrell, "The Covenant Idea," pp. 339-41.

[24] *Knox's History,* 1:22, 136-37.

[25] Hans Baron, "Calvinist Republicanism and Its Historical Roots," *Church History* 8 (1939):30-42....

[27] Calvin did not respond in writing to queries posed by Knox, but his political views in these years are well known. Bullinger's written replies to Knox are found in Knox's *Works,* 3:221-26. Cf. Burns, "Knox and Bullinger," pp. 90-91.

[28] Robert D. Linder, *The Political Ideas of Pierre Viret* (Geneva: Droz, 1964). p. 138; see Chapter Seven. Also cf. Linder, "Viret and the English Protestants," pp. 149-71.

[29] Knox, *An Answer to a Great Nomber of Blasphemous Cauillations,* in *Works,* 5:21-468. Toward the end of this treatise Knox recounts the story of the Anabaptist experiment at Münster, using it as an occasion to condemn those who claim "libertie that no man should be troubled for his conscience, cloking under that title all blasphemie and diabolical doctrine" (5:461).

[30] Ibid., 5:213.

[31] *Knox's History,* 2:309; Knox, *Works,* 4:527.

[32] Robert M. Kingdon, "Calvinism and Democracy: Some Political Implications of Debates on French Reformed Church Government, 1562-1572." *American Historical Review* 69 (January 1964):393-401. Calvin opposed Morely, whose congregational proposals were rejected by the national synod at Orleans in 1562. The political implications of polity were recognized in England: cf. the remark of a Royalist pamphleteer: "He that would rightly understand them must read for Presbytery, aristocracy; and democracy, for Independency." Cited in Christopher Hill, *The Century of Revolution,* 1603-1714 (Edinburgh: Thomas Nelson and Sons, 1961), p. 165.

[33] Donaldson, "The Polity of the Scottish Church," pp. 212-26. Donaldson observes that real controversy over episcopacy did not commence until the arrival of Andrew Melville in 1575, three years after Knox's death.

[34] *Knox's History,* 2:283-85. Cf. Calvin, *Institutes,* IV, iii, 15.

[35] *Knox's History,* 2:293-95.

[36] Ibid., 2:309-12.

[37] Ibid., 2:271: *Booke of the Universall Kirk,* p. 50; Calderwood, *History,* 2:390, 396-97. In 1560, however, Knox defended Parliament when it defied the Treaty of Edinburgh by enacting laws to institute religious reform.

[38] *Knox's History,* 2:115, 117....

### Jane E. A. Dawson (essay date 1991)

SOURCE: "The Two John Knoxes: England, Scotland and the 1558 Tracts," in *Journal of Ecclesiastical History*, Vol. 42, No. 4, October, 1991, pp. 555-76.

[*In the following essay, Dawson maintains that Knox's writings were intended for different readers and various purposes, and that attempts to interpret them as a unified whole are misguided.*]

The tracts which John Knox wrote in 1558 are regarded as the core of his political writings and the key to his entire political thought.[1] The most famous—and infamous—of his works, ***The First Blast of the Trumpet Against the Monstrous Regiment of Women,*** was published in the spring and was followed in July by ***The Letter to the Regent (Augmented), The Appellation*** and ***The Letter to the Commonalty of Scotland***.[2] These tracts have suflered from two serious misconceptions. The first is the natural tendency to link all the 1558 material together and in particular to treat the ***First Blast*** and the July tracts as a unified whole. This has distorted the meaning of all the pamphlets and led to vain efforts to mould them into a composite unit which can then be labelled 'Knox's political thought.' In fact, it is extremely important to separate them and to make a sharp distinction between their intended audiences and purposes. Crucially, the ***First Blast*** was written primarily for an English audience and the July tracts intended for a Scottish one.

The second misconception, the result of historical hindsight, has produced an anachronistic approach to Knox's writings and has destroyed the proper historical context of each of his tracts. It is the assumption. frequently made, that Knox must have written with a revolution in mind because a revolution actually occurred in Scotland during 1559-60, when the Lords of the Congregation overthrew the Regency and themselves assumed power. This muddles the eventual outcome of the particular Scottish situation with Knox's ideas at an early stage in its evolution. In 1558 Knox did not know he was about to assume the role of hero of the Scottish Reformation.

The 1558 tracts were all completed and published before any prospect of real change seemed to exist either in the English regime or in the Scottish government. In both countries Catholic power appeared unchallenged, though different policies were pursued towards Protestants: rigorous persecution in England and relative tolerance within Scotland. Knox responded in separate ways to the problems of the two countries and his expectations for each nation were correspondingly different. He wrote his tracts hoping for a revolution in England and planning for gradual change in Scotland. Yet in London change came in the unspectacular guise of a new monarch when Elizabeth I succeeded to the throne on 17 November 1558. In Scotland Knox returned in May 1559 to find himself taking part in a revolution. This was the exact opposite to what he had imagined at the beginning of 1558 and of the analysis which had informed his writings during that year.

When the distorting spectacles of the Scottish Revolution of 1559-60 and the false assumption that the ***First Blast*** was specifically directed towards the changing situation in Scotland are removed, a new, convincing and consistent message emerges. The three July tracts offered advice and encouragement for the Scots in the confusing situation of the spring and summer of 1558. They also advocated a programme of action for all Scottish Protestants. If these writings are placed within their precise historical context a better understanding of their meaning ensues. That Knox was a more consistent thinker than is usually assumed, is also demonstrated.

By 1558 there were two Knoxes: Knox the Scotsman by birth and Knox the Englishman by adoption.[3] As is well known, John Knox spent most of the decade after 1549 in England or in the company of Englishmen and Englishwomen. After his release from the French galleys he became minister at Berwick-upon-Tweed and at Newcastle.[4] He later moved to London preaching at court and throughout the home counties. Knox fitted remarkably easily into the radical wing of the Edwardian Church. He was busy doing what he did best—preaching the Word and ministering to congregations of the faithful. At Mary's accession in 1553 he went into exile on the continent with his fellow Edwardian Protestants. Like many of the other English preachers, he felt considerable guilt about abandoning his English flock and wrote a series of pamphlets to comfort and exhort his congregations and to justify his own withdrawal.[5] He was equally concerned at England's religious plight and questioned his Swiss hosts about possible methods of overturning Queen Mary's Catholic policies. Even as early as 1554 Knox was prepared to consider varieties of resistance as a way to tackle the English situation.[6] He took a leading part in the bitter dispute among the exiles at Frankfurt and as a result was expelled from the city. In November 1554 he went to Geneva, which became his base for the remainder of his exile. Throughout this period Knox moved among the other English exiles, becoming minister to their congregations at Frankfurt and Geneva and immersing himself in the problems of the English exile community.

This phase of Knox's life was interrupted by his celebrated Scottish trip in 1555-6. The return to Scotland was unplanned. He had originally gone to the north of England at the request of his mother-in-law, Mrs Elizabeth Bowes. It was probably at this time that he formally married her daughter Marjorie and then crossed the border in search of a safe place for them to stay. Once in Scotland he was astonished at the progress of Protestantism and the number of underground congregations which welcomed him. His trip turned into a triumphant missionary tour. As he explained to Mrs Bowes:

> Gif I had not sene it with my eyis in my awn contrey, I culd not have beleivit it . . . the fervencie heir doith fer execid all utheris that I have sene . . . for depart I can not, unto sic tyme as God quenche thair thrist a litill. Yea, Mother, thair fervencie doith sa ravische me, that I can not but accuse and condemp my sleuthfull coldness.[7]

Despite the obvious success of this progress and the protection he had received from sympathetic members of the Scottish nobility, Knox decided to return with his wife and mother-in-law to Geneva. His return to exile confirmed, not any lack of courage, but rather that at this point in his life his strongest ties were with the English rather than the Scottish Protestants. His explanation for leaving Scotland was that the English exile congregation in Geneva, 'commanding him in God's name, as he was their chosen pastor, to repair unto them, for their comfort'.[8]

The following year Knox again demonstrated a marked reluctance to assume the mantle of 'The Scottish Reformer'. A group of Scottish noblemen had written to him in March 1557 inviting him to come to Scotland. He received the letter in May but procrastinated until late September, finally having to be told by Calvin and other pastors in Geneva: 'That he could not refuse that vocation, unless he would declare himself rebellious unto his God, and unmerciful to his country.'[9] By the time Knox arrived at Dieppe at the end of October another letter had arrived from the Scottish nobility instructing him to delay his journey. Knox remained for several months at his 'listening-post' in the French seaport receiving the latest news of events in England. Scotland and France. By the winter of 1557-8 he was being pulled in different directions. He remained loyal to his English congregations and his family but was becoming involved in developments in Scotland. Never a man to remain idle, he was also becoming concerned for his hosts and friends in the French Protestant community. Whilst awaiting further instructions Knox wrote to the Scottish Lords and composed most of ***The First Blast of the Trumpet*** as well as editing and arranging for the English translation of *An Apology for the French Protestants.*[10] He then made a wide circuit through Huguenot France, finally reaching Geneva by the summer of 1558.

Thus there were two Knoxes. The first the man who had been absorbed into the struggles of the English Protestant Church under Edward and Mary and had become an Englishman by adoption. The second was Knox the Scotsman by birth who was both confused and pleased by his recent discovery that the Protestant cause was flourishing in his native country and that a number of influential Scots were looking to him for leadership. Although he possessed two distinct voices, Knox had only one aim, that of seeing Protestantism established in both England and Scotland. He was dedicated to achieving this goal and was prepared to employ all manner of arguments and persuasions to convince the English and the Scots. His absolute commitment gave him both the passion to argue his case and the flexibility to adopt those two distinct voices. The two John Knoxes were united in a single religious purpose. In 1558 Knox wrote in both his personae. In the spring the ***First Blast*** was published anonymously, but from the pen of Knox the Englishman. In July Knox the Scotsman wrote, signed and had printed his three Scottish tracts. He addressed each of his countries in separate works, adapting his message to suit their very different circumstances. The tracts for Scotland and the ***First Blast*** are normally treated as a single unit and have suffered from the conflation of the two John Knoxes.

The greatest confusion has arisen over the purpose of Knox's ***First Blast,*** which discussed the question of whether or not women were ever permitted to rule. It has been assumed that the work was addressed to an international audience or at least to both the kingdoms of England and Scotland, which were ruled by women. The subject was of universal interest and when treated as a matter of general principle it was eminently suitable for an international readership. However, this is where the error has crept in. The subject matter and the type of argument employed in the ***First Blast*** have been confused with its proposed audience and the programme of action which Knox wished certain of his readers to adopt. The tract's arguments were plainly universal and international, but the intended audience was very specific. Knox addressed the people of England and urged them to remove their queen, but he employed broad general arguments to convince them.

In order to prove his case Knox chose to argue from a basic principle—that a woman should not rule a kingdom. This proposition had universal application, was supported by a wide variety of examples and fitted into an already well-established debate.[11] Knox's ideas on female rule were bound to be read and noted by an international audience. He probably welcomed such a wide readership, though no attempt was made to translate the work into the international language of Latin, and he initially tried to keep his authorship secret. What mattered far more to Knox than the general circulation of his views was that the purpose of the ***First Blast*** be achieved. His aim in writing the book was to convince the English people by his rational arguments and to incite them to depose their queen. Knox was more concerned about the programme of action he hoped would follow his appeal than his intellectual contribution to the debate upon female rule. The arguments themselves were available for general consumption but their 'application' was directed solely at the English.[12] The negative aspect of Knox's purpose is even more important. Although he employed examples from Scotland and Scottish history Knox did not intend that the ***First Blast*** should be 'applied' immediately in Scotland because he was not directly addressing the Scots. In his writings to the Scottish nobility Knox never assumed that because Scotland also possessed a female ruler she should automatically be deposed. In the July tracts he had a very different message for the Scottish people. Despite its wide-ranging arguments the ***First Blast*** was directed solely towards the English.

The tract was written for a single audience because its specific aim was the removal of Mary Tudor. When explaining himself on 4 September 1561 to another Queen Mary, the Scottish sovereign, Knox excused his work by saying,

> for in very deed, Madam, that book was written most especially against that wicked Jezebel of England . . . If the realm finds no inconvenience from the regiment of a woman, that which they approve shall I not further disallow than within my own breast, but shall be as content to live under your Grace as Paul was to live under Nero; and my hope is, that so long as that ye defile not your hands with the blood of the saints of God, that neither I not that book [*First Blast*] shall either hunt you of your authority.[13]

His defence did not impress Mary, Queen of Scots. She could not accept that his generalised attack upon female rule might be excused on the grounds that it was directed at Mary Tudor. Her fellow monarch, Queen Elizabeth of England, was in complete agreement.[14]

Knox's contemporaries recognised that the ***First Blast*** was aimed primarily at Mary Tudor. Those who sought to refute or explain away his arguments acknowledged that the book would have been acceptable if his propositions had remained as specific as his target. As John Aylmer explained, Knox's mistake was to go beyond the attack upon Queen Mary and to induced all female rulers. Aylmer was even willing to concede that, 'if he had kept him in that particular person [Mary] he could have said nothing to(o) muche, nor in suche wyse, as could have offended any indifferent man'.[15] In the opinion of many contemporaries Knox had committed a cardinal error by failing to restrict his fire to Queen Mary. His indusion of all regnant queens and his general statements on the subject of gynaecocracy produced a wide variety of defences of female rule. None of the subsequent refutations defend Mary Tudor and her regime.

The accession of Elizabeth to the English throne, providing yet another queen regnant, deepened the embarrassment of the Protestant exiles over Knox's generalised attack. Elizabeth was greeted as the new Deborah who would lead the English Church back into the light after the darkness of Catholicism. In their struggle to find favour with the new queen the Protestants who hastily returned from exile sought to distance themselves from Knox's untimely outburst against female rule. Encouraged by the other exiles, Aylmer rushed off his glowing defence of Elizabeth and the English constitution.[16] The Confession of Faith which was presented to the queen in January 1559 roundly declared that the Scripture did permit women to rule. These efforts to cleanse themselves from the taint of Knox, Goodman and even Geneva itself were not entirely successful. Years later Calvin and Beza were still complaining that Queen Elizabeth remained unsympathetic because of their supposed association with Knox and his views.[17]

The unfortunate timing of the ***First Blast*** was not lost on Knox. Even he admitted, in his own letter to Queen Elizabeth, that his target had been her half-sister and tacitly acknowledged that he had employed arguments which he would now be willing to modify: 'My conscience beareth me record, that malicioustie nor of purpose I never offended your Grace nor your realme . . . my booke tuichest not your Grace's person in especiall, neyther yit is it prejudiciall to anie libertie of the realme, if the time and my writing be indifferentlie considered.' He offered the new English queen what he regarded as a reasonable compromise on the subject of female rule—one which Elizabeth did not feel inclined to accept![18]

It was ironic that Knox's attempt to broaden his attack upon Mary into a general principle should subsequently have caused him so much trouble. By the winter of 1557 Knox and most of his friends in the English exile community were convinced that Queen Mary should not be allowed to continue her disastrous reign in England. From 1556 a whole range of works advocating resistance were written.[19] They employed a wide variety of arguments but all advanced the same proposition—that Mary should be removed from her throne. Knox's ***First Blast*** was an important part of a general radical movement within the English exile community. The Marian exiles responded to the immense pressure of their unique situation by producing a series of revolutionary works.[20] In its specific aim his tract was seeking precisely the same result as was sought by his English colleagues. Where he differed from his fellows was not in his aim nor his intended audience but in the arguments he chose to accomplish their common purpose.

In the ***First Blast*** Knox rested his case exclusively upon general propositions concerning female rule. He sought to produce a non-sectarian argument to support Queen Mary's deposition. He was deliberately attempting to extend his audience to include all Englishmen and not confine his appeal to the godly minority. To achieve this aim he widened his particular attack upon Mary into a general condemnation of female rulers. Knowing that her gender was a source of considerable disquiet for Catholic and Protestant alike, he concentrated on the demonstrable fact that she was a female ruler.[21] By fixing upon the broad question of female rule Knox could appeal to men of all religious and political persuasions.[22] He could shift attention away from the bitter divisions concerning the queen's policies and on to the problem of her 'unsuitable' sex. The English queen could not remove the disadvantages which contemporaries believed accompanied all members of the female gender. Such constraints produced peculiar difficulties for a ruler, as the political implications of Mary Tudor's marriage had demonstrated.[23]

Once Knox's premise that only men were capable of ruling a kingdom was accepted, his conclusions were inevitable. Irrespective of her policies Mary could never be a suitable monarch, simply because she was female. That inescapable biological fact ensured that a compromise or settlement with Mary could not be negotiated or even contemplated. The queen must be removed and replaced by a male ruler. Knox's spotlight upon Mary's gender enabled him to present his argument and conclusions in the simple black and white terms which he relished.[24] In his mind the purpose of the ***First Blast*** was to present a case against Mary based on law, logic and reason, in themselves non-controversial and widely acceptable authorities. He also sought to provide an explanation, which did not rest upon purely Protestant assumptions, for the disasters England was experiencing under Mary's rule. The arguments against female rule seemed to fulfil both these criteria extremely well. They gave Knox the opportunity to convince as wide a range of the English 'political nation' as possible by his rational arguments and, by mobilising their support, to remove the English Queen from her throne. The reasons for choosing the general argument instead of a particular and personalised attack upon Mary were tactically sound, though perhaps in the circumstances rather shortsighted! The switch to a non-sectarian approach presented in an ordered and rational way was one which George Buchanan, the Huguenots and the Dutch were to employ to great advantage twenty years later.[25]

Knox's strategy for presenting a calm and rational case for Mary's deposition should have been a great success. However, the main problem for Knox in the ***First Blast,*** as elsewhere, was that this task did not come easily to him. When he strove to be rational Knox reverted to the training of his university days and his grounding in the syllogistic methods of the 'schools'.[26] This had a dampening effect upon his usually ebullient style and made the opening section of the book ponderous and boring. Knox began with a formal proposition:

> To promote a Woman to beare rule, superioritie, dominion, or empire above any Realme, Nation, or Citie, is repugnant to Nature: contumelie to God, a thing most contrarious to his reveled will and approved ordinance; and finallie, it is the subversion of good Order, of all equitie and justice.[27]

He then proceeded to demonstrate the truth of his proposition in the time-honoured manner by adducing a large number of examples and proofs. Knox normally preferred to rely solely upon Scripture to validate his points and would rarely acknowledge any other source for his ideas.[28] Departing from his usual practice in the ***First Blast,*** he was prepared to appeal to any and every argument from authority: the working of nature, divine law, the hierachical ordering of society, and justice and equity. He cited a wide range of sources, including Aristotle, Augustine and the Roman Law.[29] The very fact that he was willing to support his case by referring to texts other than the Word of God demonstrated his desire to reach and persuade as many Englishmen as possible.

Knox was unable to sustain the style of calm exposition, and periodically slipped into passionate exhortation. The first time he caught himself and apologised to his readers: 'Albeit I have thus (talkinge with my God in the anguishe of my harte) some what digressed'.[30] He strove to continue but found the greatest difficulty in restricting himself to measured proofs. The image suggests itself of Knox writing at his desk, his face becoming redder by the minute until he could contain himself no longer and his prose exploded into prophetic fury against Mary Tudor. The arguments of the ***First Blast*** changed from rational assertions supported by legal and historical examples to biblical exposition and exhortation. The style became livelier and the tempo of the book quickened. Knox was a master of righteous denunciation. Because 'the power of rebuking magnificently produces great polemic', this change ensured a dynamic and hard-hitting book.[31] Unfortunately, it also guaranteed that it would fail to achieve its initial purpose of a calm and rational case for the deposition of Mary Tudor.

The manner of Knox's failure makes it easier to explain why the ***First Blast*** provoked such a storm of protest throughout Europe. The basic argument of the book was that women were not fit to rule over kingdoms. This was conventional wisdom and by itself did not justify the opprobrium heaped on Knox. In the sixteenth-century debate he was part of the 'conservative' group which resisted the new and radical idea that women were capable of ruling. The precise nature of his views on women has been analysed extensively elsewhere and in this particular context are less important than his willingness to enter that debate and his whole style of presenting his case.[32]

The intellectual content of Knox's arguments was neither particularly original nor startling, but his method of using and applying those assertions shocked his contemporaries deeply. They were upset by the way in which he transformed his relatively uncontroversial basic premise into an immutable law. The identification of absolute laws was a technique which he had borrowed from his Old Testament exegesis.[33] He used it to establish rigid rules, which must be obeyed because they were endowed with all the authority of a direct divine command. By tying his rules to the absolute authority of God Himself, Knox sought to place them beyond doubt or contradiction. Any variations permitted by local laws, habit or custom could then be ignored. The rules were declared to be absolutely binding and applicable to each and every circumstance, place and person. This elevation of a rule to the status of an immutable law removed the possibility of compromise. Knox could then present the case as a matter of stark alternatives, obedience or disobedience to a great principle of law. In the ***First Blast,*** as in most of his other works, Knox was intent upon establishing a single absolute rule which permitted no exceptions. Having fixed this law, Knox could designate any deviation as 'monstrous' and insist that it be removed.[34] He could then declare that the rule itself was a categorical imperative for action, which was the message he was so concerned to ram home.

Knox used this method to insist that male rule was a universal and inviolable law which could never tolerate an exception. As such, it should always override any contrary national laws and customs, particularly in the highly sensitive area of hereditary succession. This in itself was a profoundly worrying statement, but what upset contemporaries even more was the revolutionary practical conclusions Knox drew from this position. He was convinced that if an immutable law were broken it was necessary to remedy the lapse without delay. Unless immediate action was taken, Knox argued, the whole system of divine and human law would be made ridiculous and placed in jeopardy. According to his premises a female ruler was ineligible for rule and so was by definition a usurper. Having no legitimate title or qualification, a woman who called herself queen should be deposed immediately. These conclusions flowed from Knox's basic premises. He then rigorously applied them to the particular contemporary situation of the English monarchy.

Contemporaries were naturally alarmed by this move from theoretical argument to practical political action. Knox did not hesitate to point out that England's possession of a reigning queen was a direct breach of the general principle forbidding female rule. The contravention of a universal law could not be tolerated and was extremely dangerous to the whole kingdom. The integrity of that law and with it the whole principle of order needed to be re-established. This could only be achieved by the immediate removal of Queen Mary. Knox declared that the English, 'oght, without further delay, to remove from authority all such persons as by usurpation, violence or tyrannie, do possesse the same . . . They oght to remove frome honor and authoritie that monstre in nature . . a woman against nature reigning above man . . . They oght not to feare first to pronounce, and then after to execute against them the sentence of deathe'.[35] As everyone was well aware, Knox was specifically calling upon the English people to depose and execute Mary Tudor forthwith. The same message, though employing a different set of arguments, was being proclaimed by other English exiles such as Ponet, Goodman and Gilby.[36] What horrified Europe was the unequivocal and radical demand for the removal of the present English monarch.

Knox's explicit call for immediate revolutionary action was directed at England and it was not intended to apply to Scotland too. When this is understood, the other 1558 tracts can be recognised as a separate Scottish whole. These works comprise Knox's angry reply to the Scottish Lords in October 1557, his more constructive and conciliatory letters of December and then the three open and published letters penned in July 1558. When they are taken together a distinct and consistent pattern emerges. By removing the distracting voice of Knox the Englishman, his Scottish message can be heard loud and clear.

In this period the Scottish Lords were seeking advice on how to consolidate the surprising gains already made by Protestantism.[37] They looked to Knox for a programme of action for the future, and wanted him to return to Scotland to lead their campaign in person. Between March 1557 when they sent their initial request and the autumn when they asked him to wait, the Lords of the Congregation, as they called themselves after the First Band of December 1557, had changed their minds about Knox's immediate return. This was a tactical decision about timing and not a change of direction. The Lords were reacting to the changes in the political climate, particularly in the attitude of the regent, Mary of Guise.[38] Their request that Knox wait for a better opportunity to return did not merit his angry outburst. There is a suspicion that, having had to be pushed very hard to accept the invitation in the first place and having keyed himself up to face the danger, Knox's anger arose as much from his own ambivalent reaction to the delay as from the political reasons behind it. The Lords and Knox were of one mind about the broader strategy to be followed, although they might disagree as to the appropriate tactics. They all accepted that the main task was to ensure that Protestants could worship openly and safely in Scotland. Once the full recognition and toleration of Protestantism was achieved, it was assumed that the innate superiority of their faith would bring complete victory.

Knox was particularly concerned that the Protestant cause should not be contaminated by political considerations. At this stage all his advice to the Lords emphasised the need for pure religious motives; hence his suspicion over the delayed return. He wished to ensure that the campaign for Protestant worship would not be associated with sedition or treason. Although in later letters his attitude towards the civil authorities became increasingly bitter, Knox was always adamant that there should be no *direct* or offensive attack upon the young Scottish queen or her mother the regent.[39] This was most clearly stated in the letter of 17 December to the Scottish Lords:

> nane of yow that seik to promote the glorie of Chryst do suddanlie disobey or displeas the establissit Autoritie in things lawfull; . . . I exhort yow, that with all simplicitie and lawfull obedience, joynit with boldnes in God, and with open confessioun of your faith ye seik the favours of the Autoritie, that by it (yr possibill be) the cause in whilk ye labour may be promotit, or at the least not persecuted.[40]

Knox's positive proposals also strove to maintain a sharp distinction between the Catholic Church and royal authority. In the long-standing Protestant tradition he asked for a public disputation on points of contention between himself and the Roman Catholics.[41] He also reiterated his hope that the queen regent would see the light and embrace the true religion herself. If not, she would face the eternal consequences of her blindness, a fate he was happy to spell out at some length in the augmented version of his ***Letter to the Queen Regent***. Such things needed to be said despite the fact that Mary of Guise's conversion was extremely unlikely. These dire warnings to the monarch and her regent were essentially personal rather than constitutional. At this stage Knox was more concerned about the soul of the ruler than her qualification to rule. He was threatening Mary of Guise with damnation and not with deposition. Within a Scottish context Knox had not yet moved to the belief that the ruler's Catholicism in itself made her unfit to govern, though he had already adopted that attitude towards the English situation. It took six tumultuous months in the middle of the Wars of the Congregation for Knox's views on the Scottish constitutional position to develop to the point where he felt able, in October 1559, to justify the suspension of Mary of Guise as regent by the Lords of the Congregation.[42]

Having made his obligatory appeal to the regent, Knox, with more practical considerations in mind, turned his attention to the Scottish nobility and the common people. He wanted the nobility to establish Protestant worship, a goal which had been discussed during his visit and had been fiercely debated by the leading Scottish Protestants throughout 1557. The precise programme of action which he envisaged was set out in the letter of 17 December. Following directly on from his advice first to seek the assistance of the civil authorities. Knox explained,

> whilk thing, efter all humill requeist yf ye can not atteane, then, with oppin and solempn protestatioun of your obedience to be gevin to the Autoritie in all thingis not plainlie repugnyng to God, ye lawfullie may attempt the extreamitie, whilk is, to provyd, whidder the Autoritie will consent or no, that Chrystis Evangell may be trewlie preachit, and his halie Sacramentis rychtlie ministerit unto yow, and to your brethren, the subjectis of that Realme.[43]

The 'extremity' to which he referred, establishing Protestant worship without the consent of the civil government, had been the main theme of discussion among the Scottish Protestants, and Knox was advocating the direct and more radical approach. However, it does seem rather pallid when compared with the extreme measures of deposition and regicide which Knox was simultaneously recommending to the English.

In the Scottish context Knox was prepared to go one step further, Having established public Protestant worship, the Lords should then defend its practice against persecution by the Catholic Church and even against the secular authorities. After conceding this point Knox immediately warned against the danger of turning the right to defend true religion into political rebellion:

> And farther, ye lawfullie may, yea, and thairto is bound to defend your Brethrene from persecution and tyranny, be it aganis princes or empirouris, to the uttermost of your power, provyding alwayis, as I haif said, that nether your self deny lawfull obedience, nether yit that ye assist nor promot thois that seik autoritie and preeminence of wardlie glorie.[44]

In the ***Appellation*** Knox expounded at considerable length the whole range of duties of the nobility or inferior magistrates, especially in respect to religion.[45] In practical terms he wanted the nobility to establish Protestant worship and defend it. He also urged them to remove and punish the Catholic clergy so that the people were no longer deceived by false doctrine. In the last resort the nobility must be prepared to defend Protestantism against all threats, even those from the crown. Knox drew a sharp distinction between defending the true religion and a full-scale offensive to establish it throughout the kingdom. He wanted the Protestant nobility to establish true worship within their households and the areas which lay under their direct control. He urged them also to protect the preachers who ministered to them. What Knox was suggesting was the type of spirited support and defence put up by Archibald Campbell, fourth earl of Argyle, on behalf of his minister John Douglas who was accused of heresy by Archbishop Hamilton, the primate of Scotland.[46] Knox was not yet ready within a Scottish situation to employ the idea of the right to defend the true religion as a justification for a revolution to establish Protestantism throughout Scotland.

Following the lead set by the godly nobility, Knox also envisaged a role for the common people of Scotland and he addressed one of his letters specifically to them.[47] He told them to demand the establishment of public worship. In the first instance they should not themselves seek to accomplish that task but should support and urge the nobility to do it for them. Knox explained.

> althoghe ye be but subjects, (you) may lawfully require of your superiours, be it of your king, be it

of your Lordes, rulers, and powers, that they provide for you true Preachers . . . if in this point your superiours be negligent, or yet pretend to maintaine tyrantes in their tyrannie, most justly ye may provide true teachers for yourselves, be it in your cities, townes or villages: them ye may maintaine and defend against all that shall persecute them.[48]

This was a considerably more limited area of action and responsibility than that permitted to the nobility. The common people should support and defend their Protestant minister, but they were not expected to establish public reformed worship by themselves. The first action secured true doctrine and was, therefore, a matter of faith. It could be performed by the common people. The second was a public action affecting the ordering of the commonwealth and so entered into the civil and political sphere. It could only be performed by those who held civil office and so the common people had no authority to undertake a change themselves: that was a task for the nobility.

Knox derived the religious duty of the common people from his belief in the religious equality of all men. There were no social distinctions before God in the matter of salvation; every man, however humble, was entitled to seek out the true faith which would save him. This was a fundamental Christian liberty enjoyed and exercised by all men. Knox rousingly declared, 'Beloved Brethren, ye are Goddes creatures, created and formed in his own image and similitude . . . For albeit God hath put and ordened distinction and difference betwixt the King and subjects . . . yet in the hope of the life to come he hath made all equall.'[49]

In his view true faith was nourished by the proper food of the soul—the Word of God. The preaching of the Word was the main task of the Protestant minister and so access to a 'true Preacher' was essential to the spiritual welfare of every individual. Knox's whole case was based upon the *religious* equality of all men. The fundamental Christian liberty which belonged to each individual to hear the Word of God did not extend to the political arena. He categorised the full establishment of Protestant worship as a matter of public and social organisation and not of religious liberty. Consequently, he was prepared to allow the common people to maintain and defend a minister but not to establish Protestant worship. The religious equality of all Christians was to be exercised within narrowly defined limits.

In addition to maintaining a minister Knox asked the common people to withhold their tithers from the Catholic Church. This would gravely weaken the ecclesiastical institution by starving it of funds. By presenting it as a tax-strike to force the clergy to do their job properly, it could be justified as a means of protecting the faith;

Ye may, moreover, withold the frutes and profetts which fals Byshoppes and Clergie most injustly receyve of you, unto such time as they be compelled faithfully to do theyr charge and dueties, which is to preach unto Christ Jesus truely, ryghtly to minister his Sacramentes according to his own institution, and so to watche for the salvation of your soules.[50]

The violence of the language which Knox employed to describe the Catholic elergy and the people's attitude towards them has obscured the limited nature of the demands he actually made for action by the common people. They did have a part to play in the 'reformation of religion', but it was a strictly subordinate one, and Knox always justified their participation by reference to a universal religious equality. The very restricted possibilities for popular action were a direct consequence of this premise. What is noticeable by its absence is any mention of the special obligations of every member of a convenanted nation which gave each individual the right and the duty to act for himself in both political and religious matters.[51]

At one level, the Scottish programme of action was very radical. Its aim was nothing less than the swift establishment of public worship, and full toleration and recognition of Protestantism. This was to be achieved by increasing pressure upon the regent and, if that failed, by direct action by the nobility and to a lesser extent by the common people. What Knox demanded in his 1558 tracts was that the Scottish Protestants should come further out into the open. To some extent the plan reflected what was already happening in France.[52] In certain areas of strength the Huguenots were worshipping and organising more openly, despite a much harsher royal attitude than prevailed in Scotland. In both countries the main target was the Catholic Church and its elergy. The Protestants asserted that they were loyal subjects of the crown and made no attacks upon the secular government.[53] In all his letters Knox heaped abuse upon the Catholic priesthood and sought their complete destruction, but he carefully avoided any direct threat to the civil authorities.

If Knox's radical programme had been followed in Scotland it would have had very serious and violent consequences leading eventually to armed confrontation. It would have been impossible to maintain the distinction which Knox wished to make between an attack upon the Catholic Church and one upon the civil authorities. However, whatever the practical outcome, on an ideological level the programme fell a long way short of a call for an immediate insurrection. In Scotland Knox advocated a policy of mounting pressure to establish Protestantism. It provided a sharp contrast to his demand that the English overthrow their Catholic regime, depose their monarch and substitute a godly Protestant commonwealth. The two voices of

Knox can be recognised most easily in these two very different programmes for Protestant action in Scotland and England.

There is one point in his ***Appellation*** where it seems as if Knox wanted to go beyond this gradualist approach. This is in his discussion of idolatry, a subject which always aroused his fury, and from there Knox moved directly into the covenant argument.[54] He began by assuming that Scotland could be treated just like Israel in the Old Testament with its full panoply of covenant promises and obligations. Following the great biblical prophets, he could then recall the country to its religious duty and urge a return to its covenant with God. It was a slip of the mind and pen. In the summer of 1558 Scotland was not, in Knox's view, a covenanted nation because it had not yet openly avowed the Gospel and thereby entered into a covenant with God. All his previous uses of the covenant argument had been in relation to England, which had accepted the covenant despite its present backsliding under Mary. In his memorable phrase, 'we haif refusit the fellowship of God, and hes schakin hands with the Devill'.[55]

In writing this section of the ***Appellation*** Knox was clearly thinking about England. He concluded his discussion of the covenant obligation with a radical statement about the *English* and not the Scottish situation:

> I fear not to affirm that the dutie of the Nobilitie. Judges, Rulers and People of England, not only to have resisted and againstanded Marie, that Jesabel, whome they call their Queen, but also to have punished her to the death, with all the sort of her idolatrous Preestes, together with all such as should have assisted her, what tyme that shee and they openly began to suppresse Christes Exangil, to shed the blood of the sainets of God, and to erect that most divellish idolatrie . . . which ones most justly by commone othe was banished from that realme.[56]

If Knox had seriously intended to employ the covenant argument in a Scottish context he would have done so in the ***Letter to the Commonalty***. In this tract he relied entirely upon the premise that men shared a basic religious equality. There was no hint of the obligation upon each individual to maintain and defend the covenant both personally and collectively.[57]

The relatively cautious nature of Knox's programme of action for Scottish Protestants has been obscured by its association with the ***First Blast*** and by the confusing covenant passages in the ***Appellation***. It has also been difficult to see its moderation behind the extremely violent and corrosive language Knox habitually employed in his writings. His main target was the Catholic priesthood, which was unsparingly attacked with rich invective punctuated by remarks about its tyranny.[58] This was a reference to the spiritual tyranny of the clergy and their religious persecution of the Protestants. The closest Knox came to attacking political tyranny was the assertion that the elergy were usurping political power and manipulating rulers to achieve their ends: a charge that was an old favourite of Protestant polemic.

Despite this attack upon the Catholic Church and his harsh words to the queen regent as an individual, Knox remained silent about her constitutional position and that of her daughter, Mary Queen of Scots. The situation was complicated by the minority of the queen and her continued absence from Scotland, leaving the country to be ruled by a regent for the foreseeable future. Knox believed that during such a regency the Scottish nobility were in a special position of authority.[59] He combined these Scottish constitutional traditions with similar views found in the theory of inferior magistracy.[60] This set of ideas had been developed by the Lutherans within the context of the Holy Roman Empire.[61] They proved remarkably adaptable, and were successfully transposed to fit the very different constitutional arrangements which prevailed elsewhere. They were enthusiastically employed by Calvinist and other Protestant groups who found themselves in opposition to the kings and queens of Europe. Knox was acquainted with the Lutheran theories through such works as the *Magdeburg Confession* and through his extensive discussions about the possibility of resistance in an English context during his exile.[62] He seems quite naturally to have linked these ideas to the traditional view of the role of the nobility within the Scottish kingdom. He added and stressed the religious dimension to the general responsibilities of the nobles. Knox explained that in order to fulfil those onerous duties the nobility had been directly endowed by God with political power. In the ***Appellation*** he spelt out the duties of the Scottish nobility:

> That ye whome God hath appointed heades in your commune welth . . . do studie to promote the glorie of God; to provide that your subjects be rightly instructed in his true religion; that they be defended from all oppression and tirannie; that true teachers may be maintained, and such as blynde and deceave the people . . . may be removed and punished as God's Law prescribeth.[63]

It is worth nothing in passing a suprising omission in Knox's ***Appellation.*** Though he had borrowed extensively from the Lutheran theorists, he failed to exploit an obvious opportunity to employ one of their well-known arguments. In their search for a convincing legal basis for resistance Gregory Bruck and the lawyers of Saxony had developed the doctrine of the 'unjust judge'.[64] They had taken the precept from canon law and combined it with the Roman private-law concept of repelling unjust force with force. They produced the argument that in certain circumstances it was legitimate to resist an unjust judge. They then transferred the whole doctrine of resisting an unjust judge into the public and constitutional realm and used it to justify resistance against the Emperor Charles v. Three types of case which permitted resistance to an unjust judge were identified. The first was when an appeal was pending: the second if a judge acted outwith his jurisdiction; and the third if a judge, though competent to try the case, then acted unjustly—and in the latter two instances the resulting injury was 'notorious' and 'irreparable'. These were then applied to the case of the emperor's dealings with the Protestants, particularly after the Diet of Augsburg in 1530 and the Protestant fear of the enforcement of its decrees. According to the theory the emperor had ceased to be a competent judge in the matter, and so it was possible for the Protestants to use the natural right of self-defence against an unwarranted attack. In this instance, because the emperor had ignored the appeal to the General Council of the Church, had acted outwith his jurisdiction, and had committed 'notorious' injustices, he ceased to have the authority to coerce and became a 'private man'. Any attempt by this 'private man' to enforce his will would constitute 'unjust force' and could be legitimately repelled. A legal justification for resistance to the emperor in defence of the Protestant cause had been formulated and was even accepted, with considerable reluctance, by Luther himself as part of the Torgau Declaration.[65]

The main burden of the theory rested upon the recognition of an 'unjust judge' and the matching of one or more of the three typical cases to a new set of circumstances. In the Lutheran situation, once the initial identification had been made, attention moved on to the question of 'notorious' injury and the restriction of a private individual's right to repel unjust force.[66] However, in his own recent experience Knox had all the key ingredients to make a case concerning an unjust judge and so be able to employ the whole theory of resistance which rested upon the identification. As its title indicated,[67] the ***Appellation*** was an appeal against a sentence of heresy. Knox had been tried in his absence and sentence pronounced after he had left Scotland in 1556. His effigy was subsequently burnt at the Cross of Edinburgh.[68] The process had angered Knox and so he had written the tract in his own defence. He first attacked the legal proceedings and then demanded the establishment of Protestantism in Scotland. The link between the two subjects was tenuous, being based upon the assumption that the heresy of which Knox was accused was in fact true doctrine and so should be recognised and established throughout Scotland. Knox used the association of ideas and not any formal connection to join his personal predicament to the general cause of promoting Protestantism. In the first dozen pages of his work Knox put forward his legal appeal before moving on to deal with the duties of the inferior magistrates and the need to establish Protestant worship.[69]

The legal opening fell into two main sections, based upon two very different arguments. The first section appeared to be providing, in a careful and calculating manner, all the necessary ingredients for the identification of an unjust judge both on the grounds of a pending appeal and for injurious and unjust proceedings.[70] Knox demonstrated that to appeal his sentence was an established right, and that his particular appeal was legitimate. He also put forward arguments to suggest that the judges in this case were not impartial and so were not competent to sit in judgement against him. Knox seemed to have brought together from his own personal case all the requirements for the unjust judge theory which would enable him to move from his own specific legal action to a more general theory of resistance.

At this stage he halted and entirely changed his legal defence. He made a completely separate appeal from the ecclesiastical court (whose sentence he now appeared to recognise) to the secular ruler. Knox's new plea was that his case should be freed from the judgement of the visible church and moved to the jurisdiction of the temporal magistrate. He declared, 'it is laufull for the servantes of God to call for the help of the Civile Magistrate against the sentence of death'.[71]

Knox turned to his new theme with enthusiasm. He justified the wide jurisdiction over ecclesiastical matters enjoyed by the temporal ruler through the use of biblical examples. In particular he cited the troubles of Jeremiah and St Paul's appeal to the Roman Emperor. In this section Knox came very close to the full Lutheran position that the secular magistrate had jurisdiction over all aspects of temporal life including ecclesiastical ones.[72]

The most obvious explanation for Knox's hasty retreat from using the doctrine of the 'unjust judge' to advocate resistance was that its implications were too radical for the Scottish situation in 1558. It had been used by Knox's friend Christopher Goodman to justify the call for resistance to a ruler by any individual irrespective of social status.[73] As with the covenant, such ideas were appropriate to the English situation and acceptable to Knox the Englishman, but were not employed by him in a Scottish context. Knox's abandonment of this argument in his ***Appellation*** as inappropriate for Scotland highlights his two voices. It demonstrates how important it is for the understanding of his religious and political thought to distinguish between his intended audiences. The purpose of the ***First Blast*** can only be properly understood when its English audience is recognised. Knox employed the general attack upon female rule as an approach to the problem of Mary Tudor rather than out of wholehearted commitment to the principle. His own subsequent willingness to accept female rulers, the Catholic Mary Queen of Scots as well as the Protestant Elizabeth, was less of a *volte-*

*face* than has been supposed.[74] In its proper context as an 'English' tract the ***First Blast*** forms part of that special category of revolutionary works produced by the English exiles, especially those based at Geneva.

It is the Scottish writings which have suffered most from their association with Knox the Englishman. Freed from their revolutionary appendages they emerge as a coherent whole advocating a practical programme for the establishment of Protestantism by the Scottish Lords and commons. In their new guise they fit neatly into the broader canvas of Knox's personal and intellectual participation in the Scottish Revolution itself. The old tension is removed between Knox's relatively quiescent political statements and behaviour after his return in May 1559 and his writings of the previous year. Shorn of these premature revolutionary elements, Knox's Scottish thought becomes more consistent and his co-operation with the Lords of the Congregation explicable. During those dramatic months of 1559-60 Knox's ideas changed to suit a rapidly developing situation.[75] These modifications are easier to detect now that the basic position has been established. The developments within Knox's political thought can be seen more clearly, and a more subtle and convincing explanation given of the changes which his thinking underwent throughout the whole of the 1550s and early 1560s.

As well as improving his overall consistency, the new perspective on Knox's Scottish thinking partly exonerates him from another charge. His shrewd Catholic adversary, Ninian Winzet, accused Knox of being an alien in his native country and by preference an Englishman, full of 'southron' speech and thinking.[76] As has been shown, Knox was indeed an Englishman by adoption, but he did not make the mistake of confusing his two homelands. At this stage he did not try to export his English ideas to Scotland, and offered a very different type of advice to each national group of Protestants. In his political and religious thought, if not in his English accent, Knox was careful to remain two men: the Scotsman by birth and the Englishman by adoption.

*Notes*

[1] For example, the latest collection of Knox's writings: *The Political Writings of John Knox,* ed. M. A. Breslow, Granbury, NJ 1985.

[2] As Breslow does not print any of the original sidenotes to the text, the best edition remains *The Works of John Knox,* ed. D. Laing, 6 vols. Edinburgh 1816-64 (thereinafter *Works*). Vol. iv contains all the 1558 tracts.

[3] This phrase has been borrowed from J. H. Burns, 'John Knox and Revolution', *History Today* viii (1958), 566. The perceptive points which Professor Burns made in this article and his other writings on Knox (see below nn. 6, 44, 60) have not been properly appreciated.

[4] The standard biographies of Knox cover his movements. though none of them produces a full and accurate itinerary of his exile: E. Percy. *John Knox,* London 1937, sections 3, 4; W. S. Reid, *Trumpeter of God,* New York 1974, chs. vi-viii; J. Ridley, *John Knox,* Oxford 1968, chs. vi-xvi.

[5] These were his *Declaration of the True of Nature of Prayer; Exposition upon the Sixth Psalm; Godly Letter of Warning; Two Comfortable Epistles*; and *A Faithful Admonition,* written between Jan. and Aug. 1554: *Works,* iii.

[6] Knox had addressed a series of questions to Bullinger and Calvin on the matter of resistance: *Works,* iii. 217 26; J. H. Burns. 'Knox and Bullinger', *Scottish Historical Review* xxxiv (1955), 90-1.

[7] Knox to Mrs Bowes, 4 Nov. 1555, *Works,* iv. 217-18

[8] *John Knox's History of the Reformation in Scotland,* ed. W. C. Dickinson, 2 vols, Edinburgh 1949, i. 123.

[9] *Ibid,* i. 131-6. at p. 133.

[10] *Works,* iv. 297-347.

[11] For the debate see C. Jordan, 'Women's rule in sixteenth-century British political thought', *Renaissance Quarterly* xl (1987); J. E. Phillips, 'The background to Spenser's attitude toward women rulers', *Huntington Library Quarterly* v (1941 2), 5 32; P. L. Scalingi, 'The scepter and the distaff: the question of female sovereignty, 1516-1607', *The Historian* xli (1978), 59-75; R. L. Greaves, *Theology and Revolution in the Scottish Reformation,* Washington 1980, ch. viii and Mandy Shephard's forthcoming thesis.

[12] The 'application' of a text to the contemporary political situation was a feature of many Protestant sermons, particularly in King Edward's reign. See J. N. King. *English Reformation Literature,* Princeton 1982.

[13] *John Knox's History,* ii. 15 and see below n. 74. In the 1550s when Knox used the Old Testament example of Jezebel it was always with reference to Mary Tudor.

[14] Knox also wrote directly to Queen Elizabeth, 20 Jul. 1559: *Works,* vi. 47-50. His letter was taken, carefully-annotated and its main points refuted: BL Add. MS 32,091, fos 167-9.

[15] J. Aylmer, *An Harborowe for faithfull and trewe subjects,* Strasbourg 1559. sig. B2. The refutations of

Knox fell into two categories, those written by contemporaries and fellow exiles within a few years of the appearance of the *First Blast* and those written considerably later, usually with the defence of Mary Queen of Scots in mind. Most of the first group defended Knox personally whilst attacking his views on female rule. Aylmer's book was written in the 'more in sorrow than in anger' style and he was at pains not to criticise Knox himself: *Harborowe,* sig. B1. Lawrence Humphrey also strove to exonerate Knox: *De religionis conservatione et reformatione vera,* Basle, 1559, 100, trans. in M. Knappen, *Tudor Puritanism,* Chicago 1970 ed., 176-7. John Foxe's letter to Knox is now lost, but the reply gives some indication of the criticism which he made of the *First Blast: Works,* v. 5-6. John Jewel was rather harsher on Knox when he was defending the Protestant cause from Harding's attack in his *Defence of the Apology* in *The Works of John Jewel,* ed. J. Ayre, 4 vols, Cambridge 1845-50, iv. 664-5. The most interesting refutation was by Richard Bertic, BL Add. MS 48,043, fos 1-9. I am most grateful to Mandy Shephard for discussions with her on the Bertie manuscript and for allowing me to read the relevant portions of her thesis in advance.

[16] Although he valued Elizabeth as a person, Aylmer was not particularly complimentary about the capacity of women to rule. He argued that England was safe in female hands because it enjoyed a mixed monarchy and was governed by the laws and not solely by the monarch; *Harborowe,* sig. H3.

[17] The joint statement of faith presented by the exiles to Elizabeth also declared that the principle of female rule was consonant with Scripture: Knappen, *Tudor Puritanism,* 172. However, despite the mild attacks, Knox wrote to Mrs Anne Locke on 6 Apr. 1559, 'my First Blast hath blowne from me all my friends in England': *Works,* vi. 14. Calvin and Beza both felt that they were unfairly associated with the English exiles' views and that in consequence Queen Elizabeth was suspicious of all their friendly gestures towards her: *Zurich Letters,* ed. H. Robinson, 2 vols, Cambridge 1842-5, ii. 34-6, 131.

[18] *Works,* vi. 48, and n. 14 above.

[19] For a general discussion of these see G. Bowler, 'Marian Protestants and the ideal of violent resistance to tyranny', in P. Lake and M. Dowling (eds), *Protestantism and the National Church,* London 1987, 124-143. For the way in which events in England affected the exiles see B. Peardon, 'The politics of polemic: John Ponet's *Short Treatise of Politic Power* and contemporary circumstance, 1553-6,' *Journal of British Studies* xxii (1982), 35-49.

[20] For a full discussion of this pressure see J. Dawson, 'Revolutionary conclusions: the case of the Marian exiles'. *History of Political Thought* xi (1990), 257-72.

[21] For an example of some of the difficulties which might arise see C. Levin, 'Queens and claimants: political insecurity in sixteenth-century England', in J. Sharistanian (ed.), *Gender, Ideology, and Action,* New York, 1986, 41-66.

[22] Stimulated by his dislike of Mary and her Catholic policies, Knox had been mulling over the question of female rule since 1554. It had been the subject of one of the famous questions which he had asked of Bullinger and Calvin that year. See above n. 6.

[23] For the consequences of Mary's marriage to Philip of Spain see D. M. Loades, *The Reign of Mary Tudor* London, 1979), chs iv, vii.

[24] On 18 May 1559 Knox wrote to Foxe, 'to me it is yneugh to say that black is not whit, and man's tryannye and foolishnes is not Goddes perfite ordinance': *Works,* v. 5. For this general approach see R. Mason, 'Knox, resistance and the moral imperative', *History of Political Thought* i (1980), 411-36.

[25] Q. Skinner, 'The origins of the Calvinist theory of revolution', in B. C. Malament (ed.), *After the Reformation,* Manchester 1980, 309-30.

[26] For Knox's polemical style see D. Murison, 'Knox the write', in D. Shaw (ed.), *John Knox,* Edinburgh 1975, 33-50.

[27] *Works,* iv. 473. There are assorted modern editions of the 'First Blast', none of which is as satisfactory as Laing's edition.

[28] Greaves, *Theology and Revolution,* ch. i; R. Kyle, *The Mind of John Knox,* Lawrence, Kansas 1984, ch. ii.

[29] For example, *Works,* vi. 374-6, 383-4.

[30] Ibid. 396.

[31] The aphorism from C. S. Lewis is cited in E. G. Rupp, 'The Europe of John Knox', in Shaw, *Knox,* 6-7.

[32] Jordan, 'Women's rule', 426; and above n. 15.

[33] R. Kyle, 'John Knox's methods of biblical interpretation: an important source of his intellectual radicalness', *Journal of Religious Studies* xii (1986), 57-79.

[34] Jordan, 'Women's rule', 436.

[35] *Works,* iv. 416.

[36] Christopher Goodman had said, 'it is lawful for the people, yea it is their duty to do it [punishment] them-

selves, as well as upon their own rulers and Magistrate as upon other of their brethren': *How Superior Powers Oght to Be Obeyd,* Geneva 1558, 189-90; J. Dawson, 'Resistance and revolution in sixteenth-century thought: the case of Christopher Goodman', in J. van Berg and P. Hoftijzer (eds.), *Church, Change and Revolution* (Publications of the Sir Thomas Browne Institute New Series, XII), Leiden 1991, 69-79.

[37] For the situation in Scotland see G. Donaldson, *The Scottish Reformation,* Cambridge 1960, ch. ii; I. Cowan, *The Scottish Reformation,* London 1982, chs v-vi; and for the composition of the Lords of the Congregation, G. Donaldson, *All the Queen's Men,* London 1983, chs. ii-iii.

[38] The First Band was signed on 3 Dec. 1557: *John Knox's History,* i. 136-7. On the regent see R. Marshall, *Mary of Guise,* London 1977, chs ix-xi.

[39] The burning of Walter Myln (28 Apr. 1558) provoked Knox to harsh criticism of the regent and the archbishop of St. Andrews: *John Knox's History,* i. 153 and the 'Additions' revealed a much sharper edge to his comments than in his original *Letter to the Regent, Works* iv, 431-60. Myln's execution was part of the hardening of the regent's attitude made possible by the celebration of Mary Queen of Scots' marriage to the French dauphin on 24 Apr. 1558; J. Wormald, *Mary Queen of Scots,* London 1988, 89.

[40] *Works,* iv. 284-5. At the end of 1557 Knox wrote three letters to the Scottish Lords: 27 Oct., *John Knox's History,* i. 133-6; 1 Dec., *Works,* iv. 261-75; 17 Dec., ibid 276-86.

[41] Ibid. 524. In the *Appellation* Knox even set out the rules for the disputation, 518-19.

[42] *John Knox's History,* i. 249-56.

[43] *Works,* iv. 285.

[44] Ibid. See J. H. Burns 'The political ideas of the Scottish Reformation', *Aberdeen University Review* xxvi (1955-6), 256-8.

[45] *Works,* iv. 480f.

[46] *John Knox's History,* i. 138, ii. 246-54.

[47] *Works,* iv. 523-40. Knox addressed 'his beloved brethren the Communaltie of Scotland': p. 523.

[48] Ibid. 534.

[49] Ibid. 526-7.

[50] Ibid. 534.

[51] For a full discussion of the covenant argument see Dawson, 'Resistance and revolution' and idem, 'The Early Career of Christopher Goodman and his place in the development of English Protestant Thought', unpubl. PhD diss., Durham 1978.

[52] R. M. Kingdom, *Geneva and the Coming of the Wars of Religion in France, 1555 63,* Geneva 1956: C. Eire, "'Prelude to sedition:' Calvin's attack on Nicodemism and religious compromise," *Archiv für Reformationsgeschichte* lxxvii (1985), 120-45. The setting up of a national synod in 1558 was an important step, especially as the Huguenots felt able to hold it in Paris where in the previous September there had been the incident at the Rue St Jacques. It had provoked a pamphlet war of which Knox's *Apology* was part: B. Diefendorf, 'Prologue to massacre: popular unrest in Paris, 1557-1572', *American Historical Review* xc (1985), 1067-91; D. Kelley. *The Beginning of Ideology*, Cambridge 1981, ch. iii.

[53] For example in Knox's *An Apology for the Protestants who are holden in Prison at Paris, Works,* iv. 324-5.

[54] R. Mason. 'Covenant and commonweal', in N. Macdougall (ed.), *Church, Politics and Society*. Edinburgh 1983, 97-126. I am grateful to Dr Mason for our discussions on this point. On Knox's obsession with idolatry see R. Kyle. 'John Knox and the purification of religion: the intellectual aspects of his crusade against idolatry', *Archiv für Reformationsgeschichte* lxxvii, (1986), 265-80. The general links between iconoclasm, and resistance theories are discussed in C. M. N. Eire, *War Against the Idols*, Cambridge 1986, ch. vii.

[55] *Works,* iii. 199. This is found in *A Godly Letter of Warning or Admonition to the Faithful in London, Newcastle and Berwick* [1554], *Works,* iii. 157-216, which contains Knox's basic treatment of the covenant in relation to England: see Greaves, *Theology and Revolution*, ch. vi. On Knox's views about Scotland and the covenant in this period see R. Mason, 'Kingship and Commonweal: political thought and ideology in Reformation Scotland', unpubl. PhD diss. Edinburgh 1983, 289.

[56] *Works,* iv. 507.

[57] This argument had been developed by Christopher Goodman, *How Superior Powers.*

[58] *Works.* iv. 515.

[59] I am grateful to Professor J. K. Cameron for this important suggestion. Traditionally the nobility had a major part to play during a regency in Scotland: Wormald, *Mary Queen of Scots*, 44-6.

[60] For the Scottish constitutional tradition see Mason, 'Kingship', pts I and II: J. H. Burns, 'The Theory of Limited Monarchy in Sixteenth-century Scotland', unpubl. PhD diss., Aberdeen 1952, and see above nn. 3, 44; Greaves, *Theology and Revolution,* sect. 3; Kyle, *The Mind of John Knox*. For the most comprehensive treatment of the European theory of inferior magistracy see R. Benert, 'Inferior Magistrates in Sixteenth-Century Political Thought', unpubl. PhD diss., Minnesota 1967, chs. i-iv.

[61] Q. Skinner, *The Foundations of Modern Political Thought,* 2 vols, Cambridge 1978, ii. ch. vii; C. Shoenberger, 'The development of the Lutheran theory of resistance: 1523 30', *Sixteenth-Century Journal* viii (1977), 61-76; idem, 'Luther and the justifiability of resistance to legitimate authority', *Journal of the History of Ideas* xl (1979), 3-20; W. D. J. Cargill-Thompson, *Studies in the Reformation,* London 1980, chs. i-ii, and idem, *The Political Thought of Martin Luther*, Brighton 1984.

[62] E. Hildebrandt, 'The *Magdeburg Bekenntnis* as a possible link between German and English resistance theories in the sixteenth century', *Archiv für Reformationsgeschichte* lxxi (1980), 227-53; R. M. Kingdon, 'The first expression of Theodore Beza's political ideas', in Kingdon (ed.), *Church and Society in Reformation Europe,* London, 1985, ch. x; R. C. Gamble, 'The Christian and the tyrant: Beza and Knox on political resistance theory', *Westminister Theological Journal* xlvi (1984), 125-39.

[63] *Works,* iv. 480, 481-2.

[64] Skinner, *Modern Political Thought,* ii, 198-9.

[65] Cargill-Thompson, *Political Thought,* 104-5.

[66] Skinner, *Modern Political Thought,* ii, 201-38.

[67] The full title ran 'The Appellation of John Knox from the cruell and most iniust sentence pronounced against him by the false bishoppes and clergie of Scotland, with his supplication and exhortation to the nobilitie, estates and communaltie of the same realme': *Works*, iv. 465.

[68] *John Knox's History,* i. 124.

[69] *Works,* iv. 467-79.

[70] Ibid. 469-72.

[71] Ibid. 473.

[72] Ibid. 472-9: Skinner, *Modern Political Thought,* ii. ch. i; Cargill-Thompson, *Political Thought,* ch. vi.

[73] Goodman, *How Superior Powers,* 185.

[74] *John Knox's History*. ii. 15, and above n. 13. As late at 1571 Knox's attempts at compromise encouraged his enemies to charge him with inconsistency in attacking female rule and later supporting and praying for Queen Elizabeth; D. Calderwood, *The History of the Kirk of Scotland,* 8 vols, Edinburgh 1842-9, iii. 51-4.

[75] For the later developments of Knox's thought and their Scottish context see Mason, 'Covenant and Commonweal', and 'Kingship and Commonweal', nn. 54-55 above.

[76] *Certain Tractates by Niman Winzet,* ed. J. Hewison.... *Cf. Works,* iv. 439; J. H. Burns, 'Catholicism in defeat: Ninian Winzet, 1519-92', *History Today* xvi (1966), 788-95.

**Robert M. Kingdon (essay date 1991)**

SOURCE: "Calvinism and Resistance Theory, 1550-1580," in *The Cambridge History of Political Thought: 1450-1700,* edited by J. H. Burns with Mark Goldie, Cambridge University Press, 1991, pp. 194-218.

[*In the following excerpt, Kingdon asserts that Knox and others whose arguments were based on Calvinism had little impact on Political thought in Europe*.]

Well before Calvin's death . . . one group of his followers developed a body of resistance theory. These were the English and Scottish Marian exiles, refugees from the England of Mary Tudor and the Scotland of Mary of Guise, resident in a number of Reformed cities on the continent, including Calvin's own Geneva. Like many ideological refugees before and since, these Marian exiles spent much of their time in conspiring against the government which had driven them out, in looking for ways to create a more congenial government that might make possible their return home. The Marian exile was short, as exiles go, for Mary Tudor sat upon the throne of England for only five years, from 1553 to 1558, and few of the refugees were gone from Britain for that entire period. But her rule was precarious, many of her subjects uncertain and upset, and this could only encourage their compatriots in foreign exile to call most stridently for resistance. A number of these exiles wrote political pamphlets and had them printed in major Protestant publishing centres on the continent, for circulation among fellow exiles to keep strong their commitment to the cause and for smuggling into England to encourage subversion of the government. Among these exiles, three wrote particularly interesting statements of resistance theory. They were John Ponet, the former bishop of Winchester, in exile in Strasburg; Christopher Goodman, a former professor at Oxford, in exile in Geneva; and John Knox, the future leader of the Reformation in

Scotland, with Goodman in Geneva. It can be argued that none of these three was a true Calvinist, that their theologies had been formed under the influence of Swiss and Rhenish theologians well before they came to know Calvin. Still they fell under his spell while on the continent, most obviously Knox, and their followers helped plant Calvin's thought as the reigning form of theology back in Britain after the exile. For these reasons it is fair to call their resistance ideas an early form of Calvinist theory.

The first of these three to publish a political tract was Ponet. His *A Shorte Treatise of Politike Power, and of the true obedience which subjectes owe to kynges and other civile governours . . . ,* was printed anonymously in 1556 in Strasburg.[1] It was not only one of the earliest statements of a Calvinist theory, it was also one of the most radical—for it called for popular revolution and tyrannicide. In form this treatise is divided into eight sections, the first seven in turn exploring separate political questions, the last issuing a general warning to the lords and commons of England. Of these sections, the most important for an understanding of Ponet's resistance theory is number 6, devoted to the question: 'Whether it be lawful to depose an evil governor and kill a tyrant.' Ponet's answer is a resounding yes, documented by many examples of depositions and assassinations drawn from the Old Testament, ecclesiastical history, and English history. They include general uprisings, depositions by legal process, and assassinations by individuals. Ponet gives the impression that anyone who can get away with an act of violent resistance to a tyrant should. He does not limit the duty of resistance to any particular kind of agent. Some of his examples, however, do suggest a limitation of a sort that was to be important in later Calvinist theory. He points out, for example, that the popes who were deposed at the Council of Constance were deposed by the cardinals who created them (pp. 103-5), thus intimating that the grating of power in an election is conditional and can be revoked if that power is misused. And in an earlier section, number 1, on the origins of government, a classic Christian argument that all governing power is derived from God fleshed out with an Aristotelian analysis of the types of government, he points to institutions within many governments designed to hold rulers to their duties, to prevent tyranny. These include the ephors of Sparta, the tribunes of Rome, the members of the imperial 'council or diet' in Germany, the members of the parliaments in England and France, all representatives of the people charged with keeping a check on executive power (pp. 11-12). Ponet does not return to these institutions in his analysis of resistance, however, so they do not play a very important role in his theory.

Ponet's target, furthermore, is not so much the government of England as it is her church. The individuals he singles out for his most violent attacks are her Catholic bishops, most notably Stephen Gardiner—his Catholic rival for Winchester—and Edmund Bonner—who supervised in London the greatest number of burnings of Protestants. He also attacks in vaguer terms the Spanish advisers to the queen, as foreigners seeking to force Englishmen out of their rightful positions. But he never mentions Mary Tudor at all. And he makes it clear that he did not approve of the attempt engineered by John Dudley, duke of Northumberland, to substitute Lady Jane Grey for Mary at the beginning of her reign. The government which Ponet wants to see deposed is an ecclesiastical government; the tyrants he wants to see assassinated are its bishops. His theory, therefore, is still very much a part of the general Protestant struggle against Catholics that marked the early stages of the Reformation. It is religious; it is sectarian; it does not have the more political and secular significance of later theories.

There is an important shift in target in the pamphlets of Goodman and Knox which appeared two years later, in 1558, from the press of Jean Crespin in Geneva. They still lambast the Catholic bishops and Spanish advisers, but their primary target is Mary Tudor, and there is an almost hysterical misogyny to their argument. Goodman is the more comprehensive and the more interesting of the two for students of theory. His *How Superior Powers Oght to be Obeyd of their Subjects* began as a sermon on Acts 4, but was extended into a full treatise on resistance, developing one general lesson: we must obey God rather than man.[2] It has some of the shape of a scholastic treatise, with two chapters, 8 and 9, raising objections to his own argument from first the New Testament and then the Old Testament, followed by formal refutations to each. Goodman was also radical, as radical as Ponet, calling for popular revolution and tyrannicide. The unusual feature of his argument is its misogyny. Applying his general precept, that we must obey God rather than man, he proceeds to argue that we must obey God in the principles by which we choose rulers rather than follow our own fantasies. But those principles preclude the choice of a woman for that 'is against nature and God's ordinance' (p. 52). Just as a woman is incapable of ruling a family or holding an inferior office within a government, so is she totally unfit for supreme rule. Mary is unfit not only because she is a woman, furthermore, but because she is a 'bastard by birth' (p. 97) and thus barred by the laws of inheritance from rule, and is also an 'open idolatress' (p. 99) who deserves death. Furthermore, this sentence can be executed by anyone who can manage it. Goodman explicitly refuses to limit the right of resistance to magistrates and inferior officers, arguing that 'common people also' (p. 142) must make their princes obey God's laws. The vengeance of God upon an idolatrous community will fall upon the entire community, not just its leaders. It is therefore the responsibility of all to avert the calamity which the pollution of idolatry will otherwise bring upon the community. A good example, says Goodman, is Matathias in the books of the Maccabees who 'was no public person' (p. 76) yet led the revolt against Antiochus that ended in the killing of the tyrant. Goodman's treatise, like Ponet's, is religious and sectarian, and indeed has an even nastier polemical edge. But it does have a more openly political content, since its prime target is the head of state, the queen.

There is an even more sharply developed misogyny in Knox, for Knox spent much of his life organising resistance to the rule of women—first Mary Tudor, then Mary of Guise as regent of Scotland, finally her daughter Mary Stuart. Knox was also much more prominent as an actual leader of resistance than either Ponet or Goodman. Ponet, indeed, died before he could return to England. But Knox became the chief ideological leader of the Protestant movement in Scotland, with some influence south of the border into England. Knox's political writings, in consequence, have some of the practical quality of an active leader, closely adapted to the circumstances for which they were written.

The first and best known of these writings is his ***First Blast of the Trumpet Against the Monstrous Regiment of Women*** (Knox 1846-64, IV, pp. 363-420). It is a real classic of misogyny, elegantly organised and developed with a relentless scholastic logic. His purpose, he tells us in the preface, is to demonstrate 'how abominable before God is the Empire or Rule of a wicked woman, yea, of a traiteresse and bastard' (p. 365). He then develops three separate proofs of this proposition: the first is from nature, quoting Aristotle and the Corpus Juris Civilis to the effect that women are inherently unstable and should thus not possess political or judicial authority; the second is from Scripture, quoting Genesis and St Paul to suggest that God himself prefers that women be subject not only to their husbands but to men in general; the third is from order and equity, and advances an organic analogy, comparing society to a body and man to its head, backed by analogies from the animal kingdom. In proper scholastic fashion he then states and refutes objections drawn from the Old Testament, the New Testament, and the history of certain other governments. He concludes that it is a duty of the nobility and estates that had elected women as rulers to correct their mistake by deposing those women. Only at this point does the argument enter the domain of resistance theory, and the conclusion is not elaborated very much. Knox's primary target throughout this treatise is Mary Tudor of England, but he acknowledges in passing that the argument also applies to Scotland, then ruled by Mary of Guise, as regent for Mary Stuart.

Knox then turns to his native Scotland and writes a number of pamphlets attacking its government. They are *The Copy of a Letter Delivered to a Lady Marie, Regent of Scotland* (first printed in 1556), *The appelation...to the nobilitie, estates, and communaltie* (of Scotland), and *A Letter Addressed to the Commonalty of Scotland*, all published in Geneva in 1558 (Knox 1846-64, IV, pp. 429-60, 465-520, 521-40). These three treatises take the form of appeals against a sentence issued by the convocation of the Catholilc church of Scotland back in 1556, convicting Knox of heresy and ordering his execution. In form, therefore, they are primarily diatribes against the Catholic clergy and pleas for intervention by the secular authorities in this as in other matters of church business. The tyrants Knox attacks are Catholic bishops and abbots, the resistance he encourages is by laymen against clerical rule. In this they are reminiscent of Ponet, or for that matter of Protestant polemic in general. The most temperate of the three is the letter to the queen regent, Mary of Guise. It is polite and respectful, almost courtly in tone. There is almost none of the misogyny of the *First Blast*, save for one rather condescending passage in which he expresses regret that the instability that goes with her sex will make it impossible for her rule to last very long (p. 452). Above all it is a plea that she intervene to lift the condemnation of Knox and other Protestants, even though she remains Catholic, and inaugurate a policy of toleration for the two faiths. His emphasis on the power of a ruler to control religious matters led one king, James VI of Scotland and I of England, to claim in this pamphlet support for his own Erastian views on the rights of a monaraach to control a national church, although James exaggerates the point somewhat (Knox 1846-64, IV, pp. 425-8).

Knox's argument is expanded and made somewhat more concrete in the *Appellation*. Here he develops the contention that his condemnation by the Catholic clergy violated due process of law, as codified by the civil lawyers, and that in any event the matter should be settled in a secular court. He goes on to argue that it is the primary purpose of all secular government to see to the 'reformation of religion...and punishment of false teachers' (p. 485), and thus calls upon their assistance in his campaign to rid Scotland of its Catholic clergy. He insists that this is an obligation laid by God not only upon kings but also upon all magistrates and other officers of government, particularly in times when a king fails to undertake this duty. In fact he argues that each and every member of a community is responsible for the suppression of idolatry, his code word for Catholicism, and that God will punish the entire community if this is not done. He follows the scholastic format of the *First Blast* in raising and then refuting a number of objections to this thesis. Most of his examples of proper suppression of idolatry are drawn from the Old Testament, which he insists must continue to serve as a guide to Christians in matters of this sort. In an aside, he says that is 'the duty of the Nobility, Judges, Rulers and People of England' to resist and put to death Mary Tudor, for permitting the return of 'idolatry' to that country (p. 507). This is the only open appeal to resistance in the pamphlet. His target is primarily the Catholic clergy of

Scotland, he rarely mentions its royal government; his goal is to persuade the lay nobility of the realm to join his campaign against Catholicism.

Finally in *Letter to the Commonality* Knox again appeals that his condemnation be lifted so that he might have freedom to preach, and calls upon the general population to join in this campaign. He does not advise them to join in any form of armed resistance, however, contenting himself with asking them to disobey the Catholilc clergy and refuse to pay tithes and other financial dues owed to them.

At the very end of this piece, Knox adds an outline of a proposed *Second Blast of the Trumpet*. In this outline he promises to develop the following propositioins: (1) lawful kings do not receive their power by inheritance but rather by election; (2) it is never legitimate to elect an idolater as king or to any public office; (3) even a promise to an elected idolater is not binding; (4) if an idolater has been mistakenly elected to public office, those who elected him can and should depose him. Here at last is a real resistance theory, insisting upon the conditional nature of all political power, designed to justify Protestant attempts to overthrow Catholic rulers. But it is only an outline, without any development. Knox never did get around to writing this treatise.

Taken together, these pamphlets of Knox's hardly provide a resistance theory of any generalilty. They argue for resistance to women and Catholic clergymen, not to governments in general. They also did not have much influence. The *First Blast*, in particular, proved to be a considerable embarrassment to the general Calvinist community. Its arguments quite obviously applied not only to Mary but also to Queen Elizabeth I. She was fully aware of them and never forgave Knox or his Genevan hosts for issuing this pamphlet. In vain Calvin wrote to Elizabeth's chief minister, William Cecil, to protest that he had not read and certainly had nor approved of the misogynous writings published by the English in his city.[3] In vain Calvin's chief lieutenant, Theodore Beza, added a clause on this matter to the next version of the *Confession* he prepared as an authoritative summary of the Calvinist faith, a summary printed in many editions and translations throughout the rest of the century. That clause supported the occasional rule of women, specifically denying that the biblical texts used by Knox on the subjection of women to men were applicable when it came to deciding who should rule a kingdom.[4]

It is possible that Knox's appeals to the Scots had more effect. Soon after they were issued, Knox returned to Scotland and helped the covenanted Lords of the Congregation overthrow the government of the queen regent and establish a Reformed church of Scotland. In this case, however, action really went beyond theory. In any case Scotland was peripheral to most of Europe and its policies were not followed closely elsewhere.

In general, then, these English Calvinist arguments for resistance, radical though they were in part, had little general impact, even within the Calvinist community. Most Calvinist resistance theory followed a very different line of development and built upon a somewhat different set of sources. An important ingredient in those sources was Lutheran.

*Notes*

[1] Hudson 1942 includes as an appendix a facsimile reprint of the *Shorte Treatise of Politike Power*.

[2] Goodman's *How Superior Powers Oght to be Obeyd* (1558) is available in a facsimile reprint with a brief introduction by C.H. McIlwain.

[3] Calvinus Cicellio, n.d. (probably March 1559), in Calvin 1863-1900, XVII, pp, 490-2.

[4] The relevant passage of Beza's *Confession de la foi chrestienne* (1560) is reprinted as an annexe II to Beza 1971, pp. 70-5.

**Roger A. Mason (essay date 1994)**

SOURCE: An introduction to *On Rebellion*, by John Knox, edited by Robert A. Mason, Cambridge University Press, 1994, pp. viii-xxiv.

[*In the following excerpt, Mason provides an overview of Knox's ideas, the political world around him, and his major writings.*]

I

There was little in John Knox's background to suggest that as a self-styled instrument of God he was destined to wield considerable influence over the course of the Reformation in Britain. Of his early life, in fact, very little is known. Even the date of his birth—c. 1514—is conjectural, though we can say that he was born of humble parentage in the Scottish burgh of Haddington in East Lothian and was probably educated at the local grammar school before attending St Andrews University. There is no record of his graduating from St Andrews, but he did take holy orders in the later 1530s and, unable to obtain a benefice, eked out a living as a notary apostolic (a minor legal official) and a tutor to the children of the gentry. The date of his conversion to Protestantism is similarly obscure, but it must have occurred in the early 1540s as Knox was closely involved with the ministry of George Wishart who returned to Scotland in 1543 after five years of exile in England and on the continent. Wishart's return appears to have been prompted by the Protestant and anglophile policies pursued by the Regent Arran following the death of James V in 1542 and the accession to the Scottish throne of the infant Mary Stewart. If so, it proved a fatal miscalculation. The powerful Catholic and pro-French party, led by the queen mother, Mary of Guise, and ably seconded by the archbishop of St Andrews, Cardinal David Beaton, ensured that Arran's 'godly fit' was short-lived. Wishart was arrested in January 1546 and burned at the stake outside the cardinal's castle at St Andrews two months later.

It was fear of suffering the same fate as his mentor that drove Knox to seek refuge in the castle the following year. There he joined the Protestant lairds who had avenged Wishart's death by murdering the cardinal and who were now under siege vainly awaiting relief from England. It was in these inauspicious circumstances, during a prolonged armistice, that in April 1547 Knox preached his first Protestant sermon. According to his own account, however, he did so only reluctantly, at first refusing 'to run where God had not called him'. It was only when publicly summoned in the face of the congregation and after several days of soul-searching that he became convinced that this was a 'lawful vocation' which he could not deny. It is surely significant that, while he tells us nothing about his conversion in his ***History,*** Knox describes the circumstances of his calling in such detail (Laing, vol. I, pp. 185-93; Dickinson, vol. I, pp. 81-86). If he suffered a conversion experience, it paled into insignificance when set beside the public drama—and personal trauma—of discovering his vocation. Nor is this surprising. For it was precisely the fact of having been singled out by God through the agency of the congregation which justified for Knox the very public role which he thereafter assumed. Throughout his career as a reformed preacher, it was to his vocation that he constantly referred to legitimise his public actions and utterances.

It was a vocation, moreover, which he repeatedly identified with that of the Old Testament prophets. Knox was not alone among Protestant preachers in turning to the prophets for inspiration and example, but his sense of kinship with them was unusually strong. Time and again in his writings he had recourse to the careers of Isaiah, Ezekiel and particularly Jeremiah to justify his conduct. In part, this stemmed from a kind of biblical 'legalism' to which we shall return in a moment. But it was also founded on Knox's deep-rooted conviction that, like his biblical predecessors, he had an 'extraordinary' vocation which bound him to proclaim the divine will and warn the disobedient of the fearful consequences of their iniquity. Not unnaturally, the vehemence of his prophesying varied in proportion to the adversity he faced. Exiled from England during Mary Tudor's reign, he indulged in an orgy of prophetic denunciation quite unrestrained in its violent abuse of Catholicism. Yet while his identification with the Old Testament prophets was only fully realised in exile, it was firmly rooted in the conviction—dating from 1547—that he was indeed a chosen instrument of God.

In 1547, however, Knox's future as a prophet looked decidedly bleak. Within months of his debut in the pulpit, St Andrews castle fell to the French and he was to spend almost two years as a prisoner on a French galley. He was released in March 1549, but rather than return to Scotland, where English military intervention had failed to prevent Mary Stewart being sent to Catholic France and to an eventual French marriage, he settled in Protestant England. There he was licensed to preach by Edward VI's reforming privy council and ministered to congregations at Berwick and Newcastle before his growing reputation as a preacher led to his appointment as a royal chaplain and the offer (which he declined) of the bishopric of Rochester. His years in England were in retrospect probably among the happiest of his career. But at the time Knox was less than satisfied with the slow pace of reform. While the offer of a bishopric is evidence of his growing stature within the English church, his rejection of it testifies to his refusal to conform with a moderate ecclesiastical establishment. His opposition to kneeling at communion, and hence to Cranmer's 1552 Prayer Book, clearly aligned Knox with the radicals in the English Protestant movement. At the same time, it betrayed a reluctance to deviate from biblical precept and precedent which is the most fundamental feature of his thought.

If sixteenth-century Protestantism was pre-eminently the religion of the Word, Knox was one of those who pressed the doctrine of *sola scriptura* to extremes. Certainly, in the ***First Blast,*** he shored up his argument with any authority—legal, classical or patristic—which came to hand. But this is the exception that proves the rule. For Knox took such authorities seriously only when they accorded with the will of God as revealed in the Word. Indeed, it was in the ***First Blast*** that he declared that the fundamental authority was 'the law moral . . . the constant and unchangeable will of God to the which the Gentile is no less bound than was the Jew' (p. 30). The effect of this biblical literalism was to turn the Scriptures—particularly the Old Testament—into a source book of 'legal' precedents which were as binding on the kingdoms of England and Scotland as they had been on Israel and Judah. At its most arid, this could give rise, as in the ***First Blast,*** to an obscure discussion of Jewish inheritance practices as evidenced by the daughters of Zelophehad (pp. 38-9). More generally, however, it meant that when Knox identified himself with Jeremiah, or Mary Tudor with Jezebel, he was doing much more than invoking convenient scriptural parallels or paradigms. He was appealing to biblical 'case law' to establish precedents which were universally binding because they revealed to man the immutable laws of God.

In the England of Edward VI, however, the immediate focus of Knox's biblical literalism was the Roman Catholic mass. Manifestly, he argued, the mass was a human invention and *ipso facto* an idolatrous ceremony repugnant to the divine law he had been called to proclaim. As a preacher and a prophet, Knox was bound in conscience to warn the people of the hideous consequences of participating in what he knew to be the most perverted ceremony of an antichristian church. 'For so odious and abominable I know the mass to be in God's presence', he wrote in 1550, 'that unless ye decline from the same, to life can ye never attain. And therefore, Brethren, flee from that idolatry rather than from the present death' (Laing, vol. III, pp. 69-70). With the accession in July 1553 of a Catholic sovereign to the throne of England, such advice was to strike sharply home among those Protestants who—unlike Knox—were in no position to seek solace and sanctuary in continental exile.

II

For those Protestants who did remain in England, Mary Tudor's accession, and the Catholic reaction she initiated, created an agonising dilemma. It posed in the acutest possible way the problem of whether the allegiance of the faithful was owed to the commands of God or to those of man. Knox himself, of course, had no doubt which was the sovereign authority. After arriving in Dieppe early in 1554, he wrote a series of letters to his former congregations in England whose leading theme was the absolute necessity 'as ye purpose and intend to avoid God's vengeance', of eschewing 'as well in body as in spirit, all fellowship and society with idolaters in their idolatry' (Laing, vol. III, p. 166). While such an uncompromising stance was fairly predictable, the main argument which Knox deployed in its support was not. For it was in this context that he made use for the first time of the idea that to participate in the mass was irrevocably to violate 'the league and covenant of God' which 'requires that we declare ourselves enemies to all sorts of idolatry' (Laing, vol. III, p. 193). Formulated in terms of a renewed Mosaic covenant, the avoidance of idolatry was transformed from a simple scriptural precept into a clause in a formal 'contract' drawn up between God and the elect. Moreover, according to Knox, just as the reward for fulfilling the terms of the covenant was eternal salvation, so the penalty for their infraction was eternal damnation. In effect, in the context of Mary Tudor's reign, this crudely conditional interpretation of the covenant rendered civil disobedience a precondition of salvation.

While Knox had thrust the convenant firmly into the political arena, it is important to emphasis that he did not at this stage view forcible resistance to ungodly rule as one of its terms. Certainly, when formulated in terms of a binding contract, the injunction to obey God rather than man represented a formidable challenge to power structures founded on human rather than biblical precepts. Nevertheless, Knox expressly warned his English brethren 'that ye presume not to be revengers of your own cause, but that ye resign over vengeance unto Him' (Laing, vol. III, p. 244). Such a policy of non-resistance was as distasteful to Knox as it was dangerous for his fellow Protestants in England. But in 1554 it was the only option available to him. For just as his belief that allegiance was owed to God rather than man had an impeccable biblical source (Acts 5.29), so too did the claim that the powers that be were ordained by God and whoever resisted them resisted the ordinance of God and would suffer eternal damnation (Romans 13.1-7). The latter Pauline injunction was the most influential biblical precept of the age and, beyond advocating a policy of passive disobedience in all things repugnant to the law of God, Knox was in no position to deny it.

His stance conformed, moreover, with the views of the leading lights of European Protestantism. Knox's attempt during a tour of the Swiss churches early in 1554 to elicit a more aggressive response from John Calvin and Heinrich Bullinger proved unsuccessful. Bullinger responded cautiously that, while it *might* be possible to justify rebellion in the cause of God and the Word, the great danger was that baser motives would masquerade under the cloak of religious zeal. Of Calvin's response we know only that it differed little from Bullinger's and offered Knox no great encouragement. Given their emphatic belief in the divine nature of political authority and their anxiety to distance themselves from the excesses of the Anabaptist sects, Calvin and his associates were ill-equipped to forge any justification of resistance in the early 1550s. Knox became more sensitive to these constraints as he fell directly under Calvin's influence during his exile. As a result, he continued to urge on the faithful in England the orthodox Calvinist policy of disobedience in all things repugnant to the law of God, but passive acceptance of any persecution that such a stance might bring upon them.

Gradually Knox did learn how to interpret St Paul's injunction to obey in such a way as to admit the possibility of armed resistance to an idolatrous ruler. But he did so only with significant reservations. After all, as Calvin surely made clear to him, to admit the general principle of resistance was to provide also the means of challenging those very powers to whom he looked for the imposition of godly rule. Knox was no more a radical antinomian than he was a popular constitutionalist. His aim was the establishment of a godly commonwealth ruled by a godly prince in strict accordance with the law of God. It was against the background of a Calvinist ideal of a severely disciplined society, a society in which obedience to the temporal power was of paramount importance, that his theory of resistance was evolved. To understand its development, however, we must see it in the context, not just of Knox's relations with Marian England, but also of his complex reaction to events in contemporary Scotland.

III

Knox spent the winter of 1554-5 ministering to the English congregation at Frankfort and locked in a bitter dispute over his radical liturgical views. Forced to leave Frankfort, he spent the summer months in Geneva before returning to Berwick in the autumn of 1555 to marry the Englishwoman, Marjory Bowes, to whom he had been betrothed before his flight to the continent. While there, he ventured into Scotland and was astonished at the warm reception he received. Although Mary of Guise had formally assumed the regency the previous year (buying off the earl of Arran, a former supporter of reform, with the French duchy of Châtelherault), her hostility to her Protestant subjects was tempered by her need to win their acquiescence in the marriage of her daughter to the French dauphin. Unlike their English counterparts, therefore, Scottish Protestants were not being actively persecuted and, during the winter of 1555-6, Knox was able to undertake a hastily improvised mission criss-crossing the country ministering to congregations assembled in the houses of sympathetic brethren. He returned to Geneva in July 1556, but not before the Scottish bishops, increasingly alarmed at his activities, summoned him to Edinburgh to face a charge of heresy. The trial never took place. Unwilling to risk a confrontation with her Protestant subjects, Mary of Guise had the proceedings quashed.

It is indicative of the impact of his mission that, after his departure, the Scottish bishops did condemn Knox as a heretic and publicly burned his effigy. As he preached mostly in private and to audiences already sympathetic to his cause, he can have done little to extend the existing base of Protestant support. But his rapid movement around the country lent the scattered congregations a sense of common purpose which they had never previously experienced. For the first time both Knox and the lay leaders of the localised Protestant cells became aware of the possibility of adding a concerted political dimension to what had hitherto been a haphazard spiritual movement. In this respect, the most crucial aspect of his visit was his success in establishing contact with sympathetic noblemen. For it was these men—the future lords of the Congregation—who were to turn the fledgling movement for reform into a significant political force. In securing the support of such notables as Lord James Stewart and the earls of Glencairn and Argyll, Knox had laid the foundations of the organised Protestant party which within a few years was to embark on revolution. If he still remained reticent as to the legitimacy of resistance, he had gone some way towards consolidating a movement capable of armed rebellion.

But Knox's reticence may only have applied to his public utterances. It is likely that privately he did broach the possibility of some form of organised resistance with the nobility. Certainly, they appeared to be acting with the foreknowledge of his approval when, in March 1557, they wrote to him in Geneva asking that he return once again to Scotland and assuring him that they were now prepared 'to jeopard lives and goods in the forward setting of the glory of God' (pp. 133-4). Knox duly responded to the call, but he had travelled only as far as Dieppe before he received further letters intimating that the nobles had changed their minds. Understandably incensed, on 27 October 1557 he wrote an indignant reply upbraiding them for their irresolution and affirming that, as noblemen, their 'office and duty' bound them 'to vindicate and deliver your subjects from all violence and oppression to the uttermost of your power' (p. 137). It is tempting to read into this letter the full-blown theory of armed rebellion which Knox was to set out in the ***Appellation*** the following year. As we shall see, however, the ***Appellation*** is much less radical in the demands it makes of the Scottish nobility than is commonly supposed. The same applies to Knox's correspondence of 1557. Although an earlier letter in which he explained what he expected of the nobility was 'lost by negligence and troubles' (p. 137), in one of 17 December, he made it plain that, while they were duty bound to defend their brethren from persecution, they were under no circumstances to deny 'lawful obedience' to the regent (pp. 147-8).

Paradoxically, however, it was while advising the Scottish nobility to respect the authority of Mary of Guise, that Knox began to write his classic diatribe against the very principle of female government itself. Although not published until he returned to Geneva in the spring of 1558, Knox began work on the ***First Blast*** in Dieppe in the latter months of 1557. Here there was none of the caution evident in his Scottish correspondence. Writing in the style of the schools, but enlivening his scholastic reasoning with outbursts of prophetic invective, Knox took as his starting-point the wholly unambiguous proposition that nature and the Scriptures, both of which were revelations of the divine will, demanded the total exclusion of women from power. He then proceeded to marshal an array of authorities, ranging from Aristotle to Augustine and from the civil law to secular history, to support his claim. But he was patently more at home when he turned to biblical 'case law' and was able to exercise his exegetical talents on the precedents set by such exemplars of vicious female rule as Athaliah and Jezebel. Well armed with scriptural references, he had no difficulty in proving that 'the regiment of a woman is a thing most odious in the presence of God'. Less predictably, however, he then concluded that those who 'have most heinously offended against God, placing in authority such as God by His Word hath removed from the same . . . ought without further delay to remove from authority all such persons as by usurpation, violence or tyranny do possess the same' (pp. 43-4). This was, without doubt, an unequivocal call to revolution.

Although its conclusion was extreme, in terms of sixteenth-century attitudes to women, the premises on which the ***First Blast*** was based were hardly exceptional. Knox was merely articulating, albeit in his characteristic language of imperatives, a prejudice common among his contemporaries. But it was not a view which was to commend itself to Protestants in Scotland or England over the next few years. With the accession of Elizabeth only months later, the publication of the ***First Blast*** proved a source of acute embarrassment to those—including Knox and the Scottish Congregation—who were to look to the English queen for aid. Subsequently, in an interview with Mary Stewart, Knox refused to retract the principles expounded in the ***First Blast,*** but argued that 'that book was written most especially against that wicked Jezebel of England', Mary Tudor (p. 177). He was substantially correct. For although God's law was universal and immutable, Knox chose in the ***First Blast*** to apply it only to England. He was certainly aware that Scotland too was ruled by a female regent on behalf of a female sovereign, but it was only the English whom he explicitly instructed to fulfil the divine ordinance and destroy the 'monster' who reigned over them (p. 46). That this was not an oversight, but was based on a deliberate distinction between the two countries, is borne out by the ***Appellation,*** but it is also evident in the very different attitude that Knox displayed towards Mary of Guise in the ***Letter to the Regent.***

As published in the summer of 1558, the ***Letter to the Regent*** was a revised version with substantial additions of an appeal which Knox had addressed to Mary of Guise while in Scotland in May 1556. To some extent, this explains the difference in tone between it and the ***First Blast.*** In 1556, Knox thought it possible that the regent might be persuaded to extend her policy of conciliating Protestants to one of formal toleration and perhaps even to embrace the 'true religion' herself. It would have been a dereliction of his duty not to warn her of the terrible fate she was courting by continuing to participate in idolatry. But his central purpose was to instruct her in her duty to reform religion in accordance with the Word of God. If Knox was far from confident of success, in 1556 he at least wrote more in sorrow than in anger. By 1558, however, his attitude had hardened and the additions to the original text betray a less temperate spirit. A discordant note is introduced by citing the untimely death of the regent's husband and two male children as evidence of 'the anger and hot displeasure of God' (p. 66), while more pertinently, in an echo of the ***First Blast,*** she is reminded that 'seldom it is that women do long reign with felicity and joy' (p. 65). Yet this was as close as Knox came in the ***Letter to the Regent*** to pronouncing against Mary of Guise the sentence he had already pronounced against Mary Tudor. That this was not simply a matter of expediency—the faint and fading hope that the regent might yet be persuaded to forsake idolatry—is apparent from the ***Appellation.*** For there it becomes clear that the contrasting agendas which Knox was setting for Scotland and England rested on compelling ideological foundations.

IV

The ***Appellation*** is the most important as well as the most easily misconstrued of Knox's political writings. Taking shape in his mind as he wrote the ***Letter to the Regent,*** it was published in Geneva in July 1558 together in a single volume with its companion piece, the ***Letter to the Commonalty,*** and a summary of the questions which he intended to address in his ***Second Blast of the Trumpet.*** The latter was never written, but the former three were clearly intended by Knox to be read as one. Having defined the duties of a godly prince, it was his purpose now to make clear those of the nobility and estates (in effect, the Scottish landed elite) and finally those of the common people.

As its title suggests, the ***Appellation*** is an appeal to the Scottish nobility and estates against 'the cruel and most injust sentence' which the Scottish clergy had pronounced against Knox in 1556. In this, it has much in common with the ***Letter to the Regent*** where Mary of Guise was similarly implored to protect the preacher from the bishops' wrath and allow him to defend himself against the charge of heresy. Underlying this argument lay the Erastian contention that the authority of the church was subject at all times to that of the crown. As a whole, Knox's writings hardly suggest consistent support for the idea of the royal supremacy. But the belief in the primacy of the civil sword is fundamental to the case he presented in 1558. On the basis of such precedents as the subjection of Aaron to the authority of Moses, he argued in the ***Appellation*** that, just as the civil magistrate was duty bound to reform religion, so he possessed the authority to discipline the clergy. This applied, however, not simply to the supreme magistrate—the crown—but also to the inferior magistrates of the realm—the nobility. It was a crucial extension of the principle. For it was in pursuing this argument that Knox finally established the grounds which, without denying the authority of Romans 13, allowed him nevertheless to elaborate a theory of aristocratic resistance to ungodly rule.

The key element in this theory was the idea that, as St Paul had said that the 'powers' (plural) were ordained by God, there must exist in each kingdom alternative—albeit inferior—magistrates whose office was, like a king's, of divine institution, and whose duty it was, again like a king's, to reform the religion in accordance with the law of God. The inferior magistrates of Scotland were, primarily, the nobility. It was to them, therefore, as 'lawful powers by God appointed' (p. 72), that Knox addressed his ***Appellation***. That his reasoning was squarely based on Romans 13 is revealed by a passage where, after quoting the appropriate verses, he went on to explain to the nobility that 'if you be powers ordained by God (and that I hope all men will grant), then by the plain words of the Apostle is the sword given unto you by God for maintenance of the innocent and for punishment of malefactors' (p. 85). Like a godly prince, the godly nobility were to wield the sword of justice in the cause of Christian discipline. Even when the superior power commanded the contrary, the inferior magistrates were bound to fulfil the function assigned to them by God. That being so, Knox could now insist that a godly Protestant magistrate was duty bound to protect the innocent elect from a godless Catholic prince. Moreover, from this position it was but a short step to the more radical conclusion that those 'whom God hath raised up to be princes and rulers . . . whose hands He hath armed with the sword of His justice' were also 'appointed to be as bridles to repress the rage and insolency of your kings whensoever they pretend manifestly to transgress God's blessed ordinance' (p. 102). Apparently, unlike in 1557, this was a step which Knox was now prepared to take.

Yet it was not a step which he could base solely on the expedient of pluralising the Pauline maxim that the powers are ordained by God. Of itself, the idea of an inferior magistracy did nothing to counter the injunction to obey in Romans 13. On the contrary, it confused the issue by positing a plurality of powers to each and all of whom obedience was theoretically due. It was, of course, palpably absurd to invite a situation in which divinely ordained magistrates were opposed to a divinely ordained prince, both of whom were demanding obedience in accordance with the divine will. But how was such a scenario to be avoided without denying that *all* the powers are ordained by God and must not be resisted? According to Knox, the answer lay in distinguishing between a prince acting according to God's ordinance and a prince acting *ultra vires*. When faced with the contention that the powers are to be obeyed 'be they good or be they bad', Knox retorted that, when kings acted wickedly, God 'hath commanded no obedience, but rather He hath approved, yea, and greatly rewarded, such as have opponed themselves to their ungodly commandments and blind rage' (p. 95). Although not fully articulated here, Knox was working towards the conclusion that there was a great difference between the power ordained by God and the person who wielded that power. As a divine ordinance, the former was perfect and unchallengeable, but the latter was prone to all the imperfections stemming from man's fallen nature. In the General Assembly debate of 1564, Knox made the distinction much more explicitly in defending the proposition 'that the prince may be resisted and yet the ordinance of God not violated' (pp. 191-2). But it is already present in embryo in the ***Appellation***. In addition to having located a magistracy empowered to resist an ungodly prince, Knox had found a way of sanctioning rebellion without negating the divine ordinance of obedience to the royal office.

Knox's use of these ideological devices was crucial to the radicalisation of his political thought. It should be stressed, however, that they were by no means original to him. Knox's theory was a variation on the constitutionalist case for resistance developed by Lutheran theologians in the 1520s and 1530s. Radical French reformers like Pierre Viret and Theodore Beza had already learned to tap this tradition and Knox, together with his fellow Marian exiles, John Ponet and Christopher Goodman, was to do the same. A key document here was the Magdeburg *Confession* of 1550 which, drawn up by the city's Lutheran pastors to vindicate their defiance of the emperor, summed up many of the ideas on resistance promulgated by previous generations of Protestants in their struggles with Charles V. It was to prove a valuable source for militant Calvinists whose own leaders were unable to provide ideological backing for their revolutionary schemes. Although there is no proof that Knox was aware of its existence before 1564 (p. 204), the *Confession* does contain the key elements of the theory set out in the ***Appellation***. As with the ***First Blast,*** however, it is important to distinguish between the general principles espoused by Knox and the particular circumstances in which he thought them applicable. For, whatever the source of his theory, at no point in the ***Appellation*** did he instruct the Scottish nobility to act on it against duly constituted authority. On the contrary, it was only the inferior magistrates of England who received such explicitly radical instructions.

What lay behind this distinction was the belief that, while England was a covenanted nation, Scotland was not. 'I fear not to affirm', Knox wrote in the ***Appellation,*** 'that the Gentiles (I mean every city, realm, province or nation amongst the Gentiles embracing Christ Jesus and His true religion) be bound to the same league and covenant that God made with His people Israel' (p. 103). In the case of England where, under Edward VI, the magistrates and people had 'solemnly avowed and promised to defend' God's truth, Knox insisted that the terms of such a covenant still applied. Consequently, he had no compunction about arguing that there it was 'lawful to punish to the death such as labour to subvert the true religion'—including 'Mary that Jezebel whom they call their queen' (p. 104). Unlike the English, however, the Scots had never officially embraced Protestantism and were not bound under the convenant in the same way. Knox's instructions to the Scottish nobility, therefore, fall far short of demanding the execution of their sovereign,

Mary Stewart, or of her representative, Mary of Guise. In contrast to the remarks which immediately precede it, his advice to the Scottish nobility was aimed at the punishment, not of the crown, but only of the Catholic clergy: 'if ye know that in your hands God hath put the sword . . . then can ye not deny but that the punishment of obstinate and malapert idolaters (such as all your bishops be) doth appertain to your office' (pp. 104-5).

While it is true that there is no explicit mention of the covenant in the ***First Blast,*** the way it is used in the ***Appellation*** does help to resolve the puzzle of the different programmes of action which Knox set out for Scotland and England in the 1558 tracts. But where does it leave the claim that in the ***Letter to the Commonalty*** Knox developed a populist theory of resistance? It is certainly the case that his colleague, Christopher Goodman, propounded such a theory in his *How Superior Powers Ought to be Obeyed,* also published in Geneva in 1558. But there is nothing in the ***Letter to the Commonalty*** to suggest that Knox accepted Goodman's extreme views. Admittedly, there are undeveloped references in the ***Appellation*** to a people's obligation under the covenant to punish idolaters and revenge the injuries committed against God's majesty. But on each occasion Knox introduced a note of ambiguity by adding such qualifying phrases as 'according to the vocation of every man' (pp. 99-102). The implications of this are explained neither in the ***Appellation*** nor in the ***Letter to the Commonalty***. The latter, in fact, goes no further than to advise the people to demand true preachers of their superiors, themselves to establish and defend them if necessary, and 'to withhold the fruits and profits'—the tithes— 'which your false bishops and clergy most injustly receive of you' (pp. 123-4). This hardly amounts to a radically populist theory of resistance. As with the other tracts of 1558, the ***Letter to the Commonalty*** suggests that Knox's Scottish agenda was far less extreme than is often supposed.

V

This interpretation of the 1558 tracts is borne out by the development of Knox's views after he returned to Scotland in May 1559 and threw his weight behind the Congregation's armed defiance of the regent. It was the marriage of Mary Stewart to the French dauphin in April 1558, followed six months later by the accession of Elizabeth to the English throne, which led Mary of Guise to abandon her conciliatory policy towards her Protestant subjects and which made some form of confrontation inevitable. But it was Knox who brought matters to a head when, immediately on his arrival in Scotland, he preached a sermon against idolatry which led to a wave of iconoclastic rioting. The rebellion had effectively begun and Knox had found an arena in which his theory of resistance could be tested in practice.

Although there is no proof that Knox wrote the series of public documents issued by the rebels in the course of 1559, the imprint of his ideas on the Congregation's propaganda is unmistakable. At the outset of the rebellion, a justification of resistance was deployed which, heavily reliant on the distinction between the office and the person of a prince, is strikingly similar to that developed in the ***Appellation*** (pp. 153-4). There was, however, no attempt to use this theory to justify the regent's overthrow. By August, in an attempt to broaden their appeal, the Congregation had abandoned their exclusively religious demands in favour of a wholesale indictment of her administration designed to tap the Scots' fear of French military occupation (pp. 159-65). But at the same time, in response to the regent's assertion that the preachers were encouraging disobedience to the 'higher powers', it was claimed that they had always maintained that 'they ought to be honoured, feared, obeyed, even for conscience sake, provided that they command nor require nothing expressly repugning to God's commandment and plain will, revealed in His Holy Word' (p. 166). Certainly, if wicked rulers commanded wicked things, then those who 'may and do bridle' them 'cannot be accused as resisters of the authority, which is God's good ordinance' (p. 166). But if this passage was written by Knox, it is as close as he came in 1559 to pressing on the Scots the extreme solution to the problem of ungodly rule which he had earlier urged on the English.

There were, of course, sound tactical reasons for sparing Mary of Guise the full rigour of the death sentence which he had pronounced against Mary Tudor. Not only would it have proved too extreme for the Scottish political community to stomach, but it would have done nothing to encourage Elizabeth to lend the Congregation her much-needed support. Consequently, when in October 1559 the Congregation formally 'suspended' Mary of Guise from the regency, they did so on the grounds that she was an enemy of the commonwealth rather than because she was a Catholic idolatress (pp. 171-4). Tactical considerations aside, however, Knox's attitude to Mary of Guise still appears remarkably moderate. In the debate among the Congregation which preceded her suspension, while agreeing with John Willock's views on the legitimacy of resistance, he added significant reservations: firstly, that her suspension, should not detract from the obedience owed to Mary Stewart and her husband; secondly, that it should not be motivated by 'malice and private envy'; and thirdly, that 'upon her known and open repentance, and upon her conversion to the commonwealth and submission to the nobility, place should be granted unto her of regress to the same honours from the which, for just causes, she justly might be deprived' (pp. 170-1). While the second condition is reminiscent of Bullinger's fears regarding rebellion, the others reflect a pragmatism far removed from the imperatives which Knox thought binding on a covenanted nation.

Knox's attitude underwent a marked change, however, once the intervention of Elizabeth had ensured the Congregation's success and the Reformation Parliament of August 1560 had given a Protestant settlement statutory backing. Although never ratified by Mary Stewart, the acts renouncing papal authority, abolishing the mass and adopting a Protestant Confession of Faith were assumed to have the force of law. Scotland had publicly embraced the 'true religion' and, like England under Edward VI, had entered into a covenant with God. It is not surprising, therefore, that Mary Stewart's return to Scotland in August 1561 was met by Knox with a furious tirade against the reintroduction of the mass to the heart of the realm. It threatened apostasy on a scale equal only to that of England under Mary Tudor. It also led to the first of a series of 'reasonings' with the queen during which he refused to retract the arguments against female rule laid down in the ***First Blast***. Although, as we have seen, he maintained that it was directed primarily against Mary Tudor, he otherwise conceded only that, if the realm found 'no inconvenience from the regiment of a woman', he would be 'as well content to live under your Grace as Paul was to live under Nero' (p. 176). Moreover, he added that, irrespective of their gender, when 'princes exceed their bounds . . . and do against that wherefore they should be obeyed, it is no doubt but that they may be resisted, even by power' (p. 178). Knox was thinking here of princes who actively persecuted the faithful. Nevertheless, it was an argument capable of much broader interpretation.

If Knox's interviews with the queen were intended to charm him into silence, they did not succeed. He continued to denounce her mass from his Edinburgh pulpit and to demand that the nobility deprive her of it. Indeed, preaching on Romans 13 during a meeting of the General Assembly in June 1564, he finally applied to Scotland the arguments which in the ***Appellation*** he had reserved only for England. When asked the following day to defend his views in a debate with William Maitland of Lethington, he reaffirmed that the distinction between the office and the person of a prince empowered men to 'oppone themselves to the fury and blind rage of princes; for so they resist not God, but the devil, who abuses the sword and authority of God' (p. 192). Now, however, he did not hesitate, as he had before, to apply this in Scotland to its fullest extent. Asked by Lethington 'whether that we may and ought to suppress the Queen's mass?', Knox replied without equivocation that 'Idolatry ought not [only] to be suppressed, but the idolater ought to die the death' (p. 195). As with 'the carnal seed of Abraham', in the time of their Egyptian bondage the Scots had been obliged only to avoid idolatry, but having taken full possession of the land of Canaan they were now duty bound to suppress it (pp. 196-7). Like the English before them, they had entered into a covenant with God which bound them to fulfil the divine injunction that idolaters—including royal idolaters—must die the death.

VI

It would have marked a fitting climax to Knox's career had Mary Stewart been deposed in 1567 for her manifest idolatry rather than her alleged adultery. As it was, though he advocated her execution from the pulpit, he was already on the political sidelines and was to remain there throughout the ensuing years of civil war, revising and extending his ***History,*** until his death in 1572. To expect consistency in a writer as unsystematic as Knox, whose works were all written in haste and in response to rapidly changing circumstances, would be to expect too much. Nevertheless, it is possible to discern a clear logic in the development of his ideas on rebellion and, just as importantly, in the limits of their application. Throughout his career, these limits were set, as his political vision was defined, by the intense biblicism which is the true hallmark of his thought. It is conceivable that, had he written his ***Second Blast of the Trumpet,*** he might have developed a secular theory of the accountability of kings to their subjects akin to that which he attributes in the General Assembly debate to his colleague John Craig (pp. 206-8). Yet it hardly seems likely. When a fellow member of the General Assembly, George Buchanan, published his theory of contractual monarchy in 1579, his solution to the problem posed by Romans 13 was to dismiss Paul's words as relevant only to the historical context in which they were written. Such a blatant disregard for the immutable will of God was wholly alien to the closed world of biblical precept and precedent inhabited by John Knox.

## FURTHER READING

### Biography

Brown, P. Hume. *John Knox: A Biography*. 2 vols. London: Adam and Charles Black, 1895.

Classic scholarly examination of Knox.

Cowan, Henry. *John Knox: The Hero of the Scottish Reformation*. 1905. Reprint, New York: AMS Press, 1970, 404 p.

Examines Knox's career and works in historical context.

Lang, Andrew. *John Knox and the Reformation*. 1905. Reprint, Port Washington, N.Y.: Kennikat Press, 1967, 281 p.

Sound historical study, but unsympathetic to Knox's religious views.

Percy, Lord Eustace. *John Knox*. 1937. Reprint, Richmond, Va.: John Knox Press, 1965, 343 p.

Very highly praised volume.

Ridley, Jasper. *John Knox*. Oxford: Clarendon Press, 1968, 596 p.

Study of Knox's life; includes substantial bibliography.

## Criticism

Burns, J. H. "The Political Ideas of the Scottish Reformation." *Aberdeen University Review* 36, No. 3 (Spring 1956): 251-68.

Considers the problem of political obligation and obedience in regards to the Scottish Protestants in the years of 1548 through 1570.

Dickinson, William Croft. An introduction to *John Knox's History of the Reformation of Scotland*, Vol. 1. Edited by William Croft Dickinson, pp. xv-lxxxvi. Edinburgh: Thomas Nelson and Sons, 1949.

Examines the development of the exiled Knox's philosophy of rebellion, the political situations of England and Scotland, respectively, and proposals outlined in Knox's *Book on Discipline*.

Kyle, Richard G. *The Mind of John Knox*. Lawrence, Kan.: Coronado Press, 1984, 347 p.

Study of Knox's intellectual life, including Knox's influences, his concepts, and his development of resistance theory.

Murison, David D. "Knox the Writer," in *John Knox: A Quatercentenary Reappraisal*. Edited by Ducan Shaw, pp. 33-50. Edinburgh: The saint Andrews Press, 1975.

Considers different aspects of Knox's work, quoting from his private letters, his theological treatises, his public letters, and his historical work.

Watt, Hugh. *John Knox in Controversy*. New York: Philosophical Library, 1950, 109 p.

Collection of essays that focuses on various aspects of Knox's formative years as well as his more controversial periods.

# Martin Luther

## 1483-1546

German theologian and religious reformer.

The following entry contains critical essays focusing on Luther's role in the Protestant Reformation. For further information on Luther, see *LC*, Vol. 9.

### INTRODUCTION

Luther's challenges to the ecclesiastical authority and doctrines of the Roman Catholic Church precipitated the Protestant Reformation and eclipsed the hegemonic power of the papacy in the West. The splintering of the church and the formation of Protestantism ranks as a seminal historical event with profound social, cultural, and political repercussions. Luther's rebellion against the absolutism of church dogma and his insistence on the primacy of Scripture as the source of religious authority weakened both the power and the religious authority of the church. Initially seeking to reform the church from within, Luther's doctrinal departures elicited papal charges of heresy and resulted in his excommunication by Pope Leo X in 1521. Luther's first public quarrel with Rome was an indictment of the practice of granting indulgences for monetary donations, a fund-raising method that had become very corrupt by Luther's day. Luther's criticisms escalated from a reproach of ecclesiastical practices to a renegade attack upon sacrosanct Catholic dogma. He believed in the justification by faith alone, which meant that redemption was a free gift of God's love, and not contingent upon one's merit or the performing of good works. Luther's reform efforts emboldened other dissidents to challenge the ubiquitous grasp of Rome. The end result of the Reformation was not the successful reform of the church, but the creation of new Protestant denominations throughout Western Europe, culminating in the establishment of the Anglican Church in Britain by the middle of the sixteenth century. The growth of independent churches, often with national ties, occurred with the rise of nation-states in the West. Luther's translation of the Bible into the German vernacular and his composition of hymns and prayers also contributed to the cohesion of German culture and burgeoning nationalist sentiment. While scholars contest the degree to which Luther contributed to the demise of medieval piety and ushered in the modern age, there is unqualified agreement that he ranks as one of the most vital figures in Western history.

### Biographical Information

Luther was born at Eisleben in the province of Saxony. Although descended from peasant stock, Luther's father, Hans, became a prosperous copper miner at Mansfeld and was able to provide a superior education for his son. Luther received both his bachelor's and master's degrees from the well-regarded University of Erfurt before beginning legal studies there in accordance with his father's wishes. He soon abandoned the law, however, and entered the monastery of the Augustinian Hermits at Erfurt upon undergoing a profound religious conversion experience. In 1507 Luther was ordained a priest. At the urging of his mentor, Johann von Staupitz, he pursued theological studies and earned a doctorate from the newly founded University of Wittenberg in 1512; upon graduation Luther accepted the chair in biblical theology at the university. He taught philosophy and Biblical literature while grappling with the question of salvation: how could God love and forgive human beings so flawed that they could never possibly live up to his laws? An exploration of the Book of Romans provided Luther with his answer, and he formulated his doctrine of justification through faith alone. Luther believed that faith, not good works, was the means of redemption, and that the suffering and death of Jesus Christ provided both the basis and the proof of God's unconditional love. The tenet that salvation ultimately depended on the willingness of sinners to embrace God's grace and mercy through acts of faith implicitly attacked the Sacrament of Penance since it meant that only God, not clerics, had the capacity to absolve people of their sins; thus Luther condemned the Church's practice of selling indulgences. He became particularly critical when Dominican Johann Tetzel peddled indulgences in Saxony to raise funds for the building of St. Peter's Basilica in Rome. Luther posted his objections on the door of the church in Wittenberg in the form of a series of theological propositions, *The Ninety-Five Theses* (1517). This document was widely disseminated and discussed throughout Europe and created particular excitement in Germany. *The Ninety-Five Theses* prompted Johann Tetzel to compose his own list of theses as a retort and to hold a public burning of Luther's work. Luther's students retaliated by conducting their own burning of Tetzel's work. The controversy increasingly alarmed church elders in Rome. In 1518 Pope Leo X ordered Luther to appear before Cardinal Cajetan in Augsburg and recant his views within sixty days. He refused and instead demanded that his opponents offer Biblical proof that his beliefs were wrong. Luther spent the next several years defending his beliefs to his fellow monks, and even traveled to Leipzig to publicly debate with theologian Johann Eck, a blatant critic of his theology. In 1520 Leo X issued the papal bull (or official proclamation) *Exsurge domine* which branded Luther as a heretic. Luther responded by publicly burning the bull before the students, theologians, and townsfolk of Wittenberg. The Pope officially excommunicated Luther several months later and ordered him to stand trial before Holy Roman Emperor Charles V at a special council, the Diet of Worms. It is here that Luther is said to have proclaimed, "Here I stand: I can do no other. God help me. Amen." Facing certain imprisonment or death, Luther was taken into hiding at Wartburg castle by friends operating under the protection of Elector Frederick III of Saxony. He spent the next eight months in concealment, devoting his time to translating Scripture into German and writing intensively. When danger had passed, Luther returned to Wittenberg, where he continued to teach throughout most of the remainder of his life. In 1525 he married Katharina von Bora, a former nun, and together they had six children in a happy marriage. Luther continued his prodigious literary output throughout his lifetime. Biographers have claimed that he was highly temperamental and expressive, given to periods of doubt and despair, pain and joy; his energy was boundless and the passion of his convictions sparked a reforming spirit in many of his contemporaries. Luther's last few years were marked by declining health; he died in 1546 and is buried at Wittenberg.

## Major Works

During his life Luther created a body of written work that was extraordinary for both its range and its quantity. He is credited with composing more than 450 essays, 3000 sermons, and 2600 letters. Luther also composed numerous hymns, including the well-known "Ein' feste Burg ist unser Gott" ("A Mighty Fortress Is Our God"). *The Ninety-Five Theses*, in which Luther chastised the practice of granting indulgences, inaugurated his public career as a polemicist. Its appearance elicited disapproval but not wholesale condemnation from ecclesiastical officials; Luther responded to church criticism of his views with a vigorous flurry of new writing that further exacerbated strained relationships. In *Eyn Sermon von Ablasz und Gnade* (1518; *Sermon on Indulgence and Grace*), Luther challenged the scope of papal authority. He furthered his doctrinal attack in a group of seminal essays collectively known as the *Reformationsschriften (Reformation Writings)*, published in 1520. In *An den Christlichen Adel deutscher Nation: Von des Christlichen Standes Besserung (Address to the Nobility of the German Nation)* Luther asserted the need for greater German autonomy from the secular influence of the church, proposing a reduction in the amount of monetary tribute collected from the German people and sent to Rome. Luther also called for an end to celibacy for clergy in the same treatise. He outlined some of his most radical departures from church dogma in *De captivitate Babylonica ecclesiae praeludium (On the Babylonian Captivity of the Church)*. Most of the seven sacramental rites of the church, along with the doctrine of transubstantiation, a cardinal tenet of Roman Catholicism, come under attack in *On the Babylonian Captivity of the Church*. Another important essay, also published in 1520, *Von der Freyheyt eynes Christen Menschen (The Freedom of a Christian Man)*, outlines in halcyon rhetoric the joys and duties of Christian life. Luther laid out his doctrine of faith, not good works, as the basis for Christian salvation in *Von den Guten Wercken, Treatyse of Good Workes* (1520). Collectively these early essays contain the essence of an emerging Lutheran canon. Luther continued to write throughout his life and the remainder of his work includes two important catechisms, hundreds of essays, hymns and prayers, and thousands of letters and sermons. In order to supplement their income, Luther and his wife took in students as borders. Many recorded dinner conversations with their guests are gathered in *Trschreden* (1566; *The Table Talk*).

### Critical Reception

Luther's appearance on the world stage was not a historical anomaly. The Renaissance of the fourteenth and fifteenth centuries had fostered a burgeoning interest in education and created a cultural climate fertile for intellectual growth. The appearance of Johannes Gutenberg's printing press facilitated the dissemination of new ideas and promoted a return to the reading of Scripture and literary texts. The humanists called for a return to the reading of ancient texts and the writings of the early church fathers as an alternative to scholasticism. Scholastics sanctioned teaching theology in accordance with contemporary church doctrine and practices while stressing the role of the individual in his salvation. This view was at odds with the evangelical component of Luther's belief that redemption resulted from acts of faith. The humanists shared common ground with Luther's faith in the ability of the individual to direct the spiritual aspects of one's life without the intercession of clerical mediators. Desiderius Erasmus, a leader in the humanist movement committed to reforming the church from within, was an early champion of Luther but his support waned when he feared that Luther's attacks were destabilizing the church. While Erasmus feared that Luther went too far, many contemporary rebels felt he did not go far enough. The moral authority of the ecclesiastics had come under siege by Luther's time. Many of the Renaissance popes were notorious for living lives that were less than exemplary, given to venality, nepotism, and greed. Luther struck a particularly resonant chord with a laity eager for spiritual renewal. Excoriated by Roman Catholic Church elders, Luther was championed by members of dissident groups throughout Europe. He experienced some disfavor with the populace, however, when he issued a stern pamphlet condemning the rebellious actions of serfs and artisans during the Peasants' War (1524-26). Although Luther did call for a more democratic church in which all believers, not just clerics, shared in the priesthood, he never abandoned his belief in a divinely ordered state. All members of society, according to Luther, were required to submit to secular authority except in the most extreme circumstances. Still, Luther won many converts and remained the catalyst for the growth of Protestant sects throughout Europe. In Switzerland the Reformation began in Zurich under the guidance of Ulrich Zwingli, a priest influenced both by the Christian Humanists and Luther. Another important evangelical, John Calvin, galvanized religious reform in both Switzerland and France. In 1530 Philipp Melanchthon, a prominent Luther disciple, presented the doctrines of Protestantism in *The Augsburg Confession* before a tribune called by Charles V at Augsburg, Germany. Ultimately the church failed to stave the schisms that ended her unqualified supremacy in the West. New European principalities emerged and promoted their own state-sponsored churches. Luther's confrontation with the institutional power of the church helped open the door to the questioning of other entrenched social and political institutions. Thus, Luther's challenge to Rome not only irreparably altered the theological world, but influenced the course of Western political and social history as well. Contemporary scholarship on Luther and the Reformation increasingly focuses on Luther's psychic profile, the influence of medieval piety, the socio-economic conditions of fifteenth-century Europe, and the emergence of modern nation-states.

---

## PRINCIPAL WORKS

**Disputatio pro declaratione virtutia indulgentiarum* [*The Ninety-Five Theses,*published in *The Origins and Results of the Ninety-Five Theses of Dr.M Luther*] (theses) 1517

*Die Sieben busspsalm mit deutscher au-siegung nach dem schrifftlichen synne tzu Christi und gottes gnadden, neben seynes selben, ware erkentniss grundlich gerichtet* [*The Seven Penitential Psalms,*published in Vol.14 of *Luther's Works,*1958] (psalms) 1517

*Eyn Sermon von dem Ablasz und Gnade* [*Sermon on Indulgence and Grace*] (sermon) 1518

***Epistola Lutheriana ad Leonem decimum summum pontificem. Dissertatio de libertate christiana per autorem recognita* [*A Treatise,Touching the Libertie of a Christian*, 1579; also published as *The Freedom of a Christian Man,* 1901] (letter and essay) 1519; also published as *Von der Freyheyt eynes Christen Menschen* [abridged translation]

*In epistolam Pauli ad Galatus* [*A Commentarie of M. Doctor Martin Luther upon the Epistle of S. Paul to the Galatians*, 1535] (lecture) 1519; revised edition, 1535

***An den Christlichen Adel deutscher Nation: Von des Christlichen Standes Besserung* [*Address to the Nobility of the German Nation* published in *First Principles of the Reformation*, 1883] (essay) 1520

***De Captivitate Babylonica ecclesiae praeludium* [*On the Babylonian Captivity of the Church*, published in *First Principles of the Reformation*, 1833] (essay) 1520; also published as *Von der babylonischen Gerfencknues der Kirchen*

***Von den Guten Wercken* [*Here after Ensueth a Propre Treatyse of Good Workes*] (sermon) 1520

*Warumb des Babits und feuner Jungernn bucher von Doct. Martino Luther vorbrant jeunn* [*On the Papacy in Rome Against the Most Celebrated Romanist in Leipzig*, published in Vol. 39 of *Luther's Works*] (essay) 1520

*De votis monasticis Martini Lutheri judicium* [*The Judgment of Martin Luther on Monastic Vows,* published in Vol.44 of *Luther's Works*] (essay) 1521
*Enarrationes epistolarum et evangeliorum quas postillas vocant* (sermons) 1521
*Contra Henricum regem Angliae* [*A Copy of the Letters, wherin...Kyng Henry the Eight...made Answere unto a Certayne Letter of Martyn Luther, Sent unto Him by the Same, and also the Copy of the Foresaid Luthers Letter*] (letter) 1522
*Das newe Testament Deutzsch* [translator] (Bible) 1522
*Eyn Sermon tzu Sant Michael gethan, tzu Erffordt auff den Tag der XI tausent Juchfrawe vom Glauben und Wercken* (sermon) 1522 <l>*De servo arbitrio* [*Martin Luther on the Bondage of the Will*] (essay) 1525; also published as *Das der freie Will nicht sey*
*Praefatio methodica totius scripturae in Epistolam Pauli ad Romanos* [*A Methodociall Preface Prefixed before the Epistle of S. Paul to the Romanes*] (essay) 1524
*Wider die morderischen und reubischen Rotten der Bawern* [*Against the Robbing and Murdering Hordes of Peasants,* published in Vol. 46 of *Luther's Works*] (essay) 1525
*Deudsche Messe und Ordnung Gott is Diensts* (mass) 1526
*Dom abendmal Christi, Bekendis* [*Short Confessions concerning Christ's Supper,* published in Vol. 37 of *Luther's Works*] (essay) 1528
*Deudsch Catechismus* [*Larger Catechism* published in *Luther's Primary Works, Together with His Shorter and Larger Catechisms*] (catechisms) 1529; revised edition, 1533
*Enchiridion. Der kleine Catechisms* [*Luther's Small Catechism*] (catechism) 1529
*Warnung D. Martini Luther an seine lieben Deudschen* [*Dr. Martin Luther's Warning to His Dear German People* published in *Luther: Selected Political Writings*] (essay) 1531
****Biblia; das ist, Die gantze heilige Schrifft Deudsch* [translator, with others] (Bible) 1534; revised editions 1539, 1540, 1541, 1546
***Artickel, so da hetten sollen auffs Concilion zu Mantua, oder wo es wurde sein, uberantwortet werden von unsere Teils wegen* [*The Last Wil and Last Confession of Martyn Luthers Faith concernng thr Principal Articles of Religion Which Are in Controversy, Which He Wil Defend...until His Death, agaynst the Pope and the Gates of Hell...*] (essay) 1538; also published as *Die Heubtartikel des Christlichen Glaubens, wider den Babst, und der Hellen Pforten zu erhalten* [enlarged edition], 1543
*Von den Conciliis und Kirchen* [*Martin Luther's Authority of Councils and Churches*] (essay) 1539
*Geistliche Lieder* [*Hymns of the Reformation*] (hymns) 1543
*Kurtz Bekentnis D. Mart. Luthers, vom heiligen Sakrament* [*Brief Confession concerning the Holy Sacrament,* published in Vol. 38 of *Luther's Works*] (essay) 1554
*Tischreden; oder, Colloquia* [*Dris. Martini Lutheri Colloquia Mensalia; or, Dr. Martin Luther's Divine Discourses at His Table...*; also published as *The Table Talk or Familiar Disocurse of Martin Luther*] (conversations) 1566
*****D. Martin Luthers Werke: Kritische Gesammtausgabe.* 58 vols. (essays, sermons, lectures, hymns, cathecisms, letters, and gramar) 1883
******Luthers Vorlesung uber den Romerbrief* [*Lectures on Romans*] (lectures) 1908
*Luther's Correspondence and Other Contemporary Letters.* 2 vols. (letters) 1913-18
*Luther's Works.* 56 vols.(essays, sermons, lectures, catechisms, theses, conversations, letters, and songs) 1955-

*This work is usually referred to as *95 Thesen.*
**These works are collectively referred to as *Die Reformationsschriften (The Reforming Writings).* The German version of *Dissertatio de libertate christiana per autorem recognita* does not include the letter *Epistola Lutheriana ad Leonem decimum summum pontificem.* The English translations cited contain both works.
***This work contains a revised version of the earlier *Das newe Testament Deutzsch.*
****Known as the Weimer Edition, this definitive collection is considered indispensable for advanced Luther studies.
*****This work comprises lectures delivered between 1515 and 1516 at the University of Wittenburg.

## CRITICISM

### Joseph Priestley (essay date 1803)

SOURCE: "The Progress of the Reformation," in *The Theological and Miscellaneous of the Works Joseph Priestley, Vol. X,* edited by J. T. Rutt, 1803. Reprint by Kraus Reprint Co.,1972, pp. 112-27.

[*In the excerpt below, Priestley traces Luther's increasing conflict with papal authority and the rise of his popularity with the laity.*]

It is something remarkable that Luther began his reformation independently of any thing that had been done before him; so that he was truly a great original in that way. He ever dreaded the reproach of heresy, and it was by slow degrees that he was brought to any connexion with those who had been denominated heretics; but the affinity between his doctrines and those of the Hussites in Bohemia could not but soon be perceived, and all his enemies eagerly propagated reports of his connexion with them. Some colour was given to them by the publication of a sermon this year, in which he expressed a wish that the church, assembled in general council, would restore the cup to the laity. The bishop of Misnia censured this piece,[1] and forbade the reading of it in his diocese; and the duke of Saxony wrote to the elector to complain of it. But he answered with great prudence, that he did not take upon him the defence of any of the writings of Luther, though there were persons of acknowledged piety and good sense who saw nothing reprehensible in them.

Luther easily defended himself from this accusation, in two publications. The first bore the title of ***An Apology,*** in which he shewed that the Bohemians could not be called heretics on account of their receiving the communion in both kinds, because they did it with the consent of the church; nor could he be called a heretic for having expressed a wish that the communion in both kinds might be restored, unless Pius II. was a heretic, for having wished that the priests might be allowed to marry. The second piece contained a refutation of the sentence of the bishop of Misnia, in which he was very severe on two or three ecclesiastics, whom he considered as the authors of it. This publication was disliked by the electoral court, and the impression of it was stopped for fear of provoking the Pope.

This interference of the court displeased Luther; and what he wrote to Spalatin on the occasion, discovers his firmness and the justness of his way of thinking; "You would have me," he says, "continue to teach, but how can this be done without offending the Pope? The Scriptures condemn the abuse of sacred things, and the popes will never bear the condemnation of the abuses of which they are the authors. I have devoted myself to the service of God, and may his will be done. Let us leave this business to him, and make ourselves easy. What can they do? They may take my life, but this I cannot lose more than once. They may defame me as a heretic, but was not Jesus Christ condemned by the wicked? Every time that I meditate on the sufferings of our Saviour, I am concerned to perceive that my trials appear so great to many persons. This comes from our not being used to suffer, that is, to live as the disciples of Christ. Let them do what they please. The more they endeavour to destroy me, the more I deride their efforts. If I did not fear to involve our prince in my destruction, I would write all I think without reserve, in order to provoke them the more."

At this time the new emperor was expected in Germany, and it was thought that he would be favourable to Luther, as it was well known that the Pope had opposed his election. He therefore addressed a respectful letter to the emperor,[2] in which, however, he expressed himself with proper firmness, explaining his sentiments, and expressing the hope he had of his protection; concluding with saying, that if there was any thing that would do honour to his memory in future ages, it would be, his not suffering the wicked to trample upon the righteous. But previous to this he had adopted other conciliatory measures. He had made a public protestation of his resolution to live and die in the communion of the catholic church, that he was ready to renounce all disputation in order to employ himself in more useful works, and to appear before any ecclesiastical or secular judges, provided he could have a safe-conduct; praying the public to excuse his faults, since he aimed at nothing but the edification of the church, and the discovery of truth.

In a short time after,[3] he wrote with the same spirit of moderation to the archbishop of Mentz, and to the bishop of Mersberg. The answer he received from the former was mild, and did the writer much honour. He had the greater expectation from this prelate, in consequence of a letter which Erasmus had written to him the year before,[4] as it was a complete justification of his conduct, and a condemnation of that of his enemies. It shewed at the same time the necessity of a reformation. This letter Erasmus, agreeably to his usual caution, wished to be kept secret; but Ulric of Hutten, who was then at the court of the bishop, made it public, which gave the author much concern. In this letter he made heavy complaint of the mendicant friars, as the great supporters of superstition, and whose practices would exterminate all Christian piety. In mentioning their artifices, he referred to the history of Jetzer, at Bern.[5] Erasmus also wrote to the elector of Saxony to the same purpose, adding, that such was the artifice of the monks, that, as they saw all the learned to be against them, they endeavoured to persuade the people that the study of languages, of eloquence, and of literature in general, was the source of the heresy of Luther, and his great support.

These two letters were of great service to Luther, as the writer was universally esteemed both for his knowledge and moderation; so that the censures of the universities of Cologne and Louvain, which were now published, did Luther less harm than the testimony of Erasmus did him good. Indeed, Luther's own replies to these censures were so bold and just, as to be of great service to his cause. In them he mentioned a number of most respectable persons whom they had censured, especially Erasmus and Reuchlin, saying, it was the opinion of all the learned that they had lost nothing of their just reputation, having been calumniated by men whose pride and passion were equal to their ignorance, and that whatever advantage they had gained over such men, had been by their intrigues, or their authority.

At this time, however, Luther did not wish wholly to abolish the authority of the Pope, thinking it might be of use to preserve the unity of the Western church; but he was desirous of moderating its authority, since it was become tyrannical, and the avarice and ambition of the court of Rome encouraged those abuses which were the source of their wealth. To accomplish this end, he this year published a treatise in the German language, addressed to the emperor and the nobility of the empire, in which he sapped the foundation of the papal tyranny by arguments which went further than his own views. The foundations of this tyranny he said were three: 1. The prerogative which the clergy assumed over the laity; whereas, the Scriptures made no such distinction as then prevailed between them, and laymen might exercise the functions of the Christian ministry in case of necessity. 2. The right which the popes claimed to determine the sense of Scripture, when they were as liable to error as other men. 3. The sole power of calling general councils, which properly belonged to the princes, and had been usurped by the popes.

He then gave a detail of the abuses of the court of Rome, and proposed the means of rectifying them; and this he did in so able a manner as appeared extraordinary in a man who had been educated at a distance from the business of the world. He particularly exposed the pretensions of the popes to the giving of the empire to the Germans, after taking it from the Greeks. On the contrary, he shewed that they had revolted from the emperors, whose subjects they were. He also dwelt upon their artful and unjust methods of exhausting Germany. He acknowledged, however, that the popes had a spiritual authority over the emperors, as they preached the word of God, and administered the sacraments, which Ambrose did to Theodosius. But, said he, "Let the emperor shew at length that he is emperor and their sovereign, and let him not be surprised by the tricks of Rome. Let him not suffer the Pope to seize upon his authority, and take from him the sword which God has put into his hands."

Though these things were well known before, the emperors not having been ignorant of their rights, this work of Luther's made a great noise. The friends of the court of Rome were inexpressibly enraged, and the friends of Luther trembled for him: thinking that, after such an affront, the Pope would never forgive him. This publication was, however, of service to him with the nobility, but hurt him with the ecclesiastics in general, who were not pleased to see themselves reduced to a level with the laity. He was much urged by his friends to suppress this piece, but he said it was impossible, and four thousand copies were soon sold. He added, "We are persuaded, that the Papacy is the seat of Antichrist, and we expose his impostures." He did not, however, mean any thing more at this time than to reduce the power of the Pope within due bounds.

At this time, the elector of Saxony having some business to manage at Rome, in which he did not succeed to his wishes, was told that he could not wonder that it went so ill, while he protected such a man as Luther. But he answered, that he had never arrogated to himself the right of judging Luther, and was far from defending him; and that he had let him alone, on his assurance that he was ready to defend his opinions before a proper tribunal, as soon as he should have a safe-conduct for that purpose; that Luther himself had voluntarily proposed to leave his estates, but that the legate Miltitz had opposed the measure, fearing that he might write with more freedom in some other place. In order to prevent their proceeding to the excommunication of Luther, he observed that Germany was not now what it had been; that it abounded with learned men; that all persons were passionately bent upon reading the Scriptures; and that if the court of Rome was determined to treat Luther with rigour, it might occasion a revolution as fatal to the Pope as to others.

The Pope, somewhat intimidated by this remonstrance, wrote to the elector, praising him for his moderation, but still speaking of Luther as the most wicked and detestable of all heretics, who had no mission but from the devil. He further informed him, that the doctrine of Luther had been condemned in a congregation held for that purpose, and that it he did not retract in the time prescribed, he desired the elector to secure his person.

About this time Luther found other friends and protectors in Germany. Sylvester de Schaumberg, a nobleman of Franconia, and Francis Seckingen, a person of great wealth and influence in the empire, wrote to him, desiring him not to take refuge in Bohemia, as that would make his cause generally odious; but they assured him that there were a hundred gentlemen who were determined to protect him from any injury till his affairs should come to some regular decision. These friends, gained by nothing but the justice and goodness of his cause, greatly encouraged Luther to despise the thunders of the court of Rome, and he signified to the elector, that it might answer a good purpose to intimate this to his friends at Rome; hoping it might stop the excommunication which he knew was preparing against him. He added, "As for myself, my determination is taken. I equally despise the favours and the frowns of Rome. I will have no peace or communion with them. Let them condemn me, and burn my books if they will. I will condemn and burn their decrees, and renounce for ever all submission. I have gone too far in this way to recede. I doubt not God will finish his work either by me, or by some other."

Luther did not, however, always retain this degree of courage. About this very time, or not long after, he wrote to Spalatin to request his mediation in the business; saying, that he would agree to every thing except an absolute retractation, submitting to the brand of heresy, and the deprivation of his liberty to preach the word of God. He had, however, he said, an asylum in the hearts of the Germans. We cannot wonder at this vacillation in a man whose temper was naturally violent, and therefore subject to extremes, in a conjuncture of such great difficulty and importance.

All this time Luther continued to write, and now he published a book which surprised by its title, and not less by its contents. It was entitled, ***De Captivitate***

***Babylonicâ,*** in which he treated of the sacraments; as nothing had contributed more to raise and maintain the authority of the Pope, than their number and supposed efficacy, and his exclusive power of administering them. In this work he reduced the sacraments to three—baptism, the eucharist, and penance; though this last, he said, was not properly a sacrament. He maintained, on clearer ground than he had done before, the right of communion in both kinds; but though he denied the doctrine of transubstantiation, he retained that of the *real presence;* saying, that, as the divine nature of Christ became flesh without the flesh being changed into the divine nature, so the bread became the body of Christ without any change in its substance. This doctrine was called *consubstantiation,* and Luther illustrated it by the comparison of fire being in the substance of hot iron, where both subsisted together. In this work he took great pains to prove that the eucharist was no proper sacrifice, and therefore that no person can offer it for another, that therefore the priest can no more communicate for the people, than he could be baptized for them. Consequently, that all anniversaries, masses for the dead, or for the living who are absent, and the foundations which supported them, ought to be abolished, which would ruin an infinite number of priests and monks, who had no employment besides the celebration of such masses. With respect to sacraments in general, he said that they did not justify, but the faith which men have in the promise of God; as Abraham was not justified by circumcision, because he was justified before he was circumcised.

In the mean time Miltitz, whose interest it was not to offend either the court of Rome or the elector, was indefatigable in his endeavours to bring about a reconciliation; and for this purpose he applied to the archbishop of Treves, to whose judgment Luther had made no objection. But this prelate, perceiving the difficulty of the business, referred him to the approaching diet. He then applied to the chapter of the Augustines, and they appointed Stupitz, who had resigned the office of their vicar-general, and Vinceslas Lincius, who had succeeded him, to confer with Luther for the purpose. Accordingly they both went to Wittemberg, and actually prevailed upon Luther to promise that he would write to the Pope, assuring him of his filial submission; and Miltitz was overjoyed at this success. But in the mean time Eckius arrived from Rome; and having brought the bull of excommunication, Luther changed his opinion, and informed Spalatin, that as he had not actually written the letter which he had promised to write, he would not now do it. This letter to Spalatin is dated October 3, [1520].

This was a great mortification to Miltitz, but he did not yet despair. He applied again to Luther, and promised the electoral court that, if Luther would abide by his promise to the Augustines, he would procure the bull to be revoked or moderated, in one hundred and twenty days. On this, Luther again consented, and promised to write to the Pope within twelve days a letter that should be dated the 6th of September, that it might not appear to be written after the arrival of the bull, or extorted for fear of the excommunication. Miltitz's design was to go himself to Rome before the expiration of the one hundred and twenty days, and negociate the business with the Pope. Luther then actually wrote his letter, and sent it to the Pope, together with a book he had just published on the liberty of a Christian, in which he maintained the seeming paradox, that a Christian is at the same time subject to no one, and yet subject to all the world, taking advantage of the saying of Paul, *though I am free, I am servant of all.* This work gave offence to some, as favouring sedition, and was incautiously written. The court of Rome might, however, have borne with it, if it had been capable of moderation, or had consulted its interest.

But the conduct of Miltitz was by no means approved at Rome. It was thought that he had acted with too much meanness; and Eckius, who was then at Rome, had so boasted of his superiority in the conference at Leipsic, and so exaggerated the heresy of Luther, that he succeeded in procuring a bull against him, which, after much difficulty with respect to particulars, it was agreed should contain a condemnation of Luther's doctrine in forty-one propositions, but should allow him to retract in six days. All the books which he had ever published, or that he should publish, were ordered to be burned, and all Christian princes were exhorted to seize his person and his adherents, after that time should be expired, with a promise of a reward for so great a service, and an interdict was laid upon any place to which he should retire. In this bull,[6] Luther himself is treated as the greatest of heretics. The Pope, however, expresses his extreme concern for the state into which this heresy had brought the German nation. Even the composition of this bull, though exceedingly elaborate, did no credit to the composers of it; the periods being uncommonly long, and perplexed with parentheses, as well as objectionable on many other accounts.

Ulric de Hutten, a nobleman of Franconia, but a man of letters,[7] and deeply impressed with the prevailing abuses of the times, caused this bull to be published, and at the same time exposed its defects, adding, at the close of his remarks, the words of the Psalmist, Psalm ii. *Let us break their bonds asunder, and cast their cords from us.*

Eckius having obtained the character of nuncio, returned to Germany with this bull; but his reception was very different from his expectations; and at Leipsic, where he had disputed with Luther, and where he hoped to have met with the greatest applause, he was worse treated than in any other place. Even the duke of Saxony forbade the publication of the bull, without an express order from the bishop of Mersberg; and when it appeared, the people and the students tore it in pieces, and threw it into the dirt. Eckius himself was so much insulted, that he took refuge in the monastery of the Dominicans. Leaving Leipsic in the night, he presented the bull to the university of Erfort; but there it was not received, on the pretence of the want of some formality. In this place also it was torn, and thrown into the water, and the students kept him besieged in his own house.

The bishop of Bamberg made the same objection to the reception of the bull that had been made at Erfort, and the bishop of Eickstadt, where Eckius was a canon, was the first who at length published it. The bishop of Mersberg deferred the publication, till April in the year following, and the bishop of Misnia, the most violent against Luther, did not do it till the 7th of January. At Vienna, it was not published till Easter, in A. D. 1521, and then the senate ordered all the people to withdraw before the reading of it. The bishop of Brandenberg, though accompanied by the elector, and Albert, duke of Mecklenberg, went to Wittemberg to publish it there; but finding the favourable opinion the people there had of Luther, and both the elector and the duke his brother speaking favourably of him, they left the place without doing any thing in the business.

Thus encouraged, we are not surprised to find that Luther treated this bull with contempt. At first he thought to advise the elector of Saxony, who was then at Aix, attending the coronation of the emperor, to obtain an imperial rescript, forbidding the condemnation of him till he should be convinced of heresy out of the Scriptures. But finding by a letter from Erasmus that the emperor was surrounded with monks, who had prepossessed his mind against him, he did not wish to expose his master to the inconvenience of a refusal, and thought it would be better that he should appear to have no knowledge of the matter. The first step that he took was to attack Eckius, in a work in the German language, in which he exposed his vices and hypocrisy, and for the first time openly vindicated John Huss; having now read his books, and approved of them. He also renewed his appeal to a general council, the Pope having condemned him without giving him a hearing. The Pope himself he treated as a tyrant, an apostate, and Antichrist, and conjured the emperor, and the states of the empire, to respect his appeal, and suspend the execution of the bull till he should be heard and convinced of his errors out of the Scriptures.

Not content with this, he attacked the bull itself in two publications. In the first he gave the lie to the Pope, who had said that he made him an offer of money to defray the expenses of his journey to Rome. On the other hand, he said it was well known that there was a sum of money in the hand of some bankers, to reward the villain who should assassinate him. Keeping, therefore, now no measures with the Pope, he said, "If you do not renounce your blasphemies and impieties, know, that not only I, but all who serve Jesus Christ, regard your church as the damnable seat of Antichrist, which we will not obey, and to which we will not be united. We shall bear with joy all your unjust excommunications, and even voluntarily devote ourselves to death. But if you persevere in the fury with which you are now actuated, we condemn you, and deliver you to Satan, with your bulls and your decretals." In the second publication he defended the propositions which the court of Rome had condemned.

In the mean time the Pope's bull had been received at the universities of Cologne and Louvain,[8] and in consequence of it, the writings of Luther were publicly burned in those cities. This was on the day on which the emperor set out from Spain. The same was attempted at Antwerp, but without success. Those who undertook to do it at Mentz, were in great danger, hardly escaping the rage of the people. In other places the monks purchased of the magistrates the liberty of doing it, and it generally cost them dear. In return, Luther, accompanied by the doctors of the university of Wittemberg, with the students and the people, having lighted a great fire, threw into it the Pope's bull with all the decretals; at the same time pronouncing these words; "Since thou hast troubled the holy one of God, may eternal fire consume thee." This was transacted December 10, A. D. 1520.

Luther followed this bold action with a public justification of it, in which he alleged, that, being a doctor in theology, it was his duty to prevent the increase of impiety, and that all the world ought to be informed, that he, Luther, convinced that the Pope was Antichrist, had thrown off his yoke, and was resolved to sacrifice every thing to the truth which he had taught. In this work, which he entitled ***An Apology,*** he inserted thirty propositions drawn from the decretals, and shewed them to be impious. They were such as these: "The successors of St. Peter are not subject to the command which this apostle gave to all the faithful to obey the temporal powers; that the Pope has all power in heaven and in earth; that he can absolve from all oaths and vows; that he does not depend upon the Scriptures, but that the Scriptures derive their authority from him," &c. &c. &c. He concluded with quoting Rev. xviii. 6: *Do unto Babylon as she has done unto you, render unto her, double.* The next day, in lecturing on the Psalms, he discoursed on the necessity of renouncing obedience to the Pope, telling his pupils that there was no medium, and that they who aspired to the ministry of the gospel, must either expose their lives in resisting the reign of error, or renounce eternal life; and that he had taken his own measures accordingly.

In the mean time the Pope used his utmost endeavours to gain the elector, and for this purpose had appointed two nuncios, whom he sent to Germany to wait upon him. One of them was Aleander, a person of Jewish extraction, bishop of Brindisi.[9] He was a man of whom Luther said that though born of a Jew, he was not of the sect of the Pharisees, living as if he disbelieved the resurrection of the dead, his life was so notoriously profligate. The other was Carraccioli, sent more particularly to congratulate the emperor on his arrival in the Low Countries.[10] Both these nuncios applied to Frederic, and after a long preamble, acquainted him with the request of the Pope, which was, that he would order the books of Luther, and himself also, to be burned, or at least that he would keep him in close custody, if he did not choose to send him in irons to Rome, which would be most agreeable to his holiness.

The elector heard them both with great patience, and replied, that he would consider of the business. And after a few days he commissioned his counsellors to tell them, that he had determined to have nothing to do in the business of Luther; and after repeating what he had said on a former occasion, about his sending Luther to Augsburg and the archbishop of Treves, he said that people judged so differently of his writings, that he thought there had been precipitation in burning them before they had been examined, and he desired the nuncios to suspend the execution of the bull till the Pope had granted that Luther should be judged by German divines of known capacity and probity; and he said that if Luther should be convicted of error from the Scriptures, he would not fail to do honour to the holy see, and every thing that his holiness could require of an obedient son. The nuncios seeing no prospect of gaining their point with the elector, told the counsellors that the Pope did not wish to take the life of Luther.

Erasmus being at Cologne at this time, the elector consulted him about his conduct in this business, and in the grave and serious manner that was natural to him. After pausing some time, Erasmus said that Luther had committed two great crimes, he had touched the crown of the Pope, and the bellies of the monks,[11] which made the elector, who before had been very grave, to laugh outright. He then said more seriously, that Luther was justified in checking the abuses that had been introduced into the church, and that his doctrine was right, but he wished he had used more moderation. Soon after this, Erasmus gave his opinion more at large in writing, concluding with saying, that the state of the empire, and the interest of the emperor, required that the beginning of his reign should not be stained with blood; that it was the interest of the Pope himself to have affairs accommodated; that the adversaries of Luther had advanced things which all divines disapproved; that now all the world sighed for the evangelical doctrine, and that it would be dangerous to oppose their inclination in an odious and violent manner.

There was great boldness in this conduct of Erasmus, considering that he had come to a resolution to be neuter in this controversy. Dreading the consequences of having delivered his sentiments with so much freedom, he wrote to Spalatin, requesting that the letter might be returned to him. This was done, but not till a copy had been taken of it, and this being by some means published, gave great offence both to Erasmus and Luther. In consequence of this, Aleander, though before a friend of Erasmus, did every thing he could to ruin him, especially after having endeavoured in vain to engage him, by the promise of a bishopric, to write against Luther.

The elector, confirmed in his judgment by the opinion of Erasmus, prevailed upon the emperor to allow Luther a hearing before he should be condemned; and the emperor, highly respecting his character, being under great obligations to him, and indeed wanting his assistance, desired him to bring Luther to Worms, where the diet was to be held; but he forbade him in the mean time to write any thing more against the Pope. The elector with his usual prudence declined having any thing to do with the conduct of Luther; who, however, was far from having any objection to appear at Worms, on the summons of the emperor, which he said he should consider as the call of God; and with great piety and magnanimity he expressed his firm resolution to go at all events, though his death should be the consequence of it.

At this time there was a very general wish for a reformation. The emperor himself was not disinclined to it, and this was even the case of some of the ecclesiastical princes. The archbishop of Mentz, though a voluptuous man, was not much averse to it, and the archbishop of Treves, though attached to the Pope, had prevented the burning of Luther's books, in his diocese. George, duke of Saxony, though a rival to the elector, and disliking Luther, was so much persuaded of the necessity of some reformation, that he carried to the diet of Worms a proposal in twelve articles, which concluded with his saying, "We must labour for an universal reformation, and as it cannot be effected more commodiously than in a general council, we all demand the immediate calling of one." Notwithstanding these favourable appearances, the friends of Luther, who knew the situation of the emperor, and especially how desirous he was to gratify the Pope, in order to gain his interest to oppose Francis, king of France, were not a little apprehensive for his safety.

However, the enemies of reformation dreaded the appearance of Luther at Worms, much more than his friends, and nothing that they could do was spared to prevent it; and when the diet was met, Aleander, on the 13th of February, delivered a flaming invective against Luther, in which he said that his books were full of as many heretics, as would justify the burning of a hundred thousand heretics, and declared that they could not avoid ordering them to be burned without offering an affront to the emperor, and especially the elector of Mentz and Cologne. Of himself, he said that he was not of Jewish extraction, but descended from the marquisses of Istria.

But all the influence of the Pope and his partisans could not prevail upon the diet to take any harsh measures with respect to Luther, though they thought the authority of the Pope well-founded, and only wished to correct the abuses of it. The sentiments of Erasmus being desired on this occasion, he wrote his advice at large, blaming the enemies of Luther, who, he said, were the enemies of literature; for their violence, as the cause of his advising moderate measures; asserting the necessity of a reformation, and saying that the old theology was nothing but a heap of useless subtleties; that the people were every where longing for the doctrine of the gospel, and that if the sources of this knowledge were shut to them, they would open them by force. In his opinion, he said, the only method of terminating the differences was, by the emperor, the kings of England and Hungary, who could not be suspected by either party, choosing out of their estates prudent and enlightened persons to take cognizance of the writings of Luther. The Pope he allowed had a right to judge in all matters of faith, but that on this occasion he ought to decline it, and leave the business to others.

In this state of things, Glapius, confessor to the emperor, had many conferences with Pontanus, the chancellor of the elector of Saxony, the object of which was, to prevent the public discussion of Luther's sentiments, to have the business settled in some private manner, or to amuse the people with some slight reformation. But the issue of the whole tended to confirm the elector in his opinion that Luther had much reason on his side, and that he ought to protect him.

The emperor, being thus assailed on all sides, thought of an expedient, which he imagined would satisfy all parties for the present. It was, that the books of Luther should not be burned, nor yet suffered to be circulated, but that the magistrates of each place should take them into their custody. Accordingly, an ordonnance was made to that purpose. But the magistrates said that this measure could not answer any good end, since the doctrine of Luther was not now confined to his books, but was fixed in the minds of the people, from which it was not in their power to force it. They, therefore, thought that the better way would be to require him to retract what he had written, and that if he refused, they would employ all their force to second his majesty's intentions; but they added their entreaty, that he would correct the abuses by which the court of Rome was ruining Germany. This advice was approved, and the emperor gave orders for the citation of Luther, and also that a memorial should be drawn up of the abuses complained of. Notwithstanding this seeming moderation, it sufficiently appeared that the emperor was gained by the enemies of Luther, and he even joined with them in having recourse to expedients unworthy of his dignity, to prevent his appearance; and several things were proposed in the diet, which, if they had been carried, would certainly have prevented his journey. The emperor also endeavoured to draw the elector of Saxony into some difficulty, by advising him to grant the safe-conduct. But Frederic had too much prudence to be thus surprised; and when the summoning of Luther could not be prevented, and a safe-conduct must be given, not only by the emperor, but by all the princes through whose estates he was to pass, he did not give his, till he received an order from the emperor so to do. At length, not only was the safe-conduct given in the fullest manner, but it was accompanied with a respectful letter from the emperor to him, requiring him to attend at Worms within twenty-one days, there to give an account of his doctrine and his writings. No mention was made in it of retractation, or any prohibition to preach, on his journey. Accordingly, he set out respectably attended, and on his way he preached at Gotha, Erfort, and Eisenach.

Still the partisans of the Pope entertained some hope that they should be able to prevent his coming, and with this view they spread a report which was calculated to intimidate him, and it had such an effect upon his friends, that they endeavoured to persuade him to return. But though he was at that time in a bad state of health, he persisted in his purpose, and said he would go to Worms in spite of all the powers of hell. When he was within three leagues of the city, he received a letter from Spalatin, conjuring him once more not to proceed any farther. But he replied that he would go to Worms, though there should be as many devils there as there were tiles upon the houses.[12]

Another attempt was made to divert him from his purpose, by deferring the execuion of the imperial ordonnance to take his books into custody, till the very evening before his arrival. This induced Seckingen to send Bucer to him, to persuade him to retire to some castle in the neighbourhood, where Glapius would be ready to confer with him on the subject of religion. But he replied, that only two days remained of his safe-conduct, and that this was not sufficient for any conferences with the emperor's confessor. He therefore proceeded, and arrived at Worms the same day, April the 16th. His entering resembled a triumph rather than that of a man accused of heresy. A herald walked before him, in his habit of ceremony, a number of courtiers, who had gone to meet him, walked along with him, and the streets were crowded with people eager to see him. He was lodged with the ministers of the elector of Saxony, where he received the visits of many persons of distinction.[13]

*Notes*

[1] "On the 24th of January, 1520." *Life,* p. 25.

[2] "Dated January 15, 1520." *Life,* p. 26.

[3] "On February 4th of the same year." *Ibid.*

[4] See Jortin's *Erasmus,* A.D. 1520, 4to, pp. 233-235.

[5] See *supra,* pp. 62-69.

[6] Dated June 15, 1520.

[7] See *supra,* p. 101, *Note ad fin.*

[8] At this time *Margaret,* the emperor's aunt, was governess of the Netherlands, who, when the *Masters of Louvain* lamentably complained that Luther, with his writings, did subvert all Christendom, asked of them, what manner of man this Luther was. They told her that he was an *unlearned* monk. 'Why then,' replies she, 'see that all you learned men, being a great multitude, write against that one unlearned fellow, and doubtless the world will give more credit to many of you, being learned, than to him, being but one, and unlearned.'" *Hist. of Popery,* II. p. 311.

[9] "Afterwards a cardinal. He was taken prisoner with Francis I. at the battle of Pavia, and died at Rome in 1542. *Nouv. Dict. Hist.* I. p. 83.

[10] Charles was crowned at *Aix-la-Chapelle,* October 21, and appointed a meeting of the Diet to be held at Worms, January 26, 1521.

[11] "Duo magna esse Lutheri peccata, quod ventres monachorum et coronam Papæ attigisset." *Hist. of Popery,* II. p. 309.

[12] *Brandt,* p. 119. His friends had reminded "him of the safe-guard granted to John Huss, which had been violated." *Life,* p. 33.

[13] I am enabled here to add to this edition of the *History,* some curious notices of Luther and his contemporaries, with which I have been favoured by a friend well acquainted with Germany and the German language.

> "In the year 1814, a literary and graphical curiosity made its appearance at Berlin, under the title of *Lucas Cranach's Stammbuch,* or Album. Cranach was one of the most celebrated German painters of the 16th century, the intimate friend of Luther, and a zealous reformer. It has been known for more than a century, that there existed a volume of miniature portraits of the German Reformers, in water colours, on parchment, by Cranach, each portrait being accompanied by the autograph of the subject of the painting. The history of the volume is very obscure, but the painter's well-known monogram, and the date 1543 upon the miniatures, sufficiently confirmed the authenticity of the work. It was purchased at Nuremberg 1797, by Baron Hardenberg, and transmitted to king William the Second of Prussia, in November of that year. The death of that monarch at that time occasioned the loss of the volume, which was found 1812. It has been published in three editions, one of which contains a coloured fac-simile of the paintings. There are ten portraits.
>
> 1. The Saviour.
> 2. Frederick III. surnamed the Wise, Elector of Saxony, Æt. 59.
> 3. The Elector John Frederick, the Generous, Æt. 40.
> 4. Duke Ernest of Saxe-Cobourg, Æt. 32.
> 5. Luther, Æt. 60....

## Thomas M. Lindsay (essay date 1900)

SOURCE: "The Three Great Reformation Treatises," in *Luther and the German Reformation*, T. & T. Clark, 1900, pp. 93-112.

*[Below, Lindsay, outlines several of Luther's early works that challenged the power of Rome, and describes the subsequent reactions by the German people.]*

### THE THREE GREAT REFORMATION TREATISES

#### 1. "CHRISTIAN LIBERTY" AND "THE CAPTIVITY OF THE CHURCH"

In 1520 Luther published the three writings which contain the principles of his reformation. They appeared in the following order: ***To the Christian Nobility of the German Nation, respecting the Reformation of the Christian Estate,*** probably in the beginning of August; ***The Babylonian Captivity of the Church,*** probably before the end of September; and ***Concerning Christian Liberty,*** early in October. These three books are commonly called in Germany the "Three Great Reformation Treatises," and the title befits them well. Luther wrote and published them after three years of controversy, following upon the publication of the theses, had made his position perfectly clear to himself, and at a time when he knew that he had to expect nothing from Rome but a sentence of excommunication. However the details of his teaching may have afterwards changed, it remained in all essential positions unaltered from what we find it in these three books.[1]

The short tractate on "**Christian Liberty**" had a somewhat pathetic history. The good Miltitz still hoped that the final breach between Luther and the papacy might be avoided; and he earnestly counselled Luther to write a friendly letter to the Pope, and send His Holiness a short, simple statement of what his inmost religious beliefs were. Luther did so; and this booklet was the result. It has for its preface the letter to Pope Leo, which concludes thus: "I, in my poverty, have no other present to make you, nor do you need anything else than to be enriched by a spiritual gift. I commend myself to your paternity and blessedness, whom may the Lord Jesus preserve for ever. Amen."

The short treatise is a brief statement, free from all theological subtleties, of the priesthood of all believers, which is the result of justification by faith. Luther begins by an antithesis: "A Christian man is the most free lord of all, and subject to none; a Christian man is the most dutiful servant of all, and subject to everyone"; or, as St. Paul puts it, "Though I be free from all men, yet have I made myself servant of all." He expounds this by showing that no outward things have any influence in producing Christian righteousness or liberty; neither eating, drinking, or anything of the kind, neither hunger nor thirst, have to do with the liberty or the slavery of the soul. It does not profit the soul to wear sacred vestments or to dwell in sacred places, nor does it harm the soul to be clothed in worldly raiment, and to eat and drink in the ordinary fashion. The soul can do without everything except the Word of God, and this Word of God is the gospel of God concerning His son, incarnate, suffering, risen, and glorified, through the Spirit the Sanctifier. "To preach Christ is to feed the soul, to justify it, to set it free, to save it, if it believes the preaching; for faith alone and the efficacious use of the Word of God bring salvation." It is faith that incorporates Christ with the believer, and in this way "the soul, through faith alone, without works, is, from the Word of God, justified, sanctified, endued with truth, peace, liberty, and filled full with every good thing, and is truly made the child of God." For faith brings the soul and the Word together, and the soul is acted upon by the Word, as iron exposed to fire glows like fire, because of its union with the fire. Faith honours and reveres Him in whom it trusts, and cleaves to His promises, never doubting but that He overrules all for the best. Faith unites the soul to Christ, so that "Christ and the soul become one flesh." "Thus the believing soul, by the pledge of its faith in Christ, becomes free from all sin, fearless of death, safe from hell, and endowed with the eternal righteousness, life, and salvation of its husband Christ." This gives the liberty of the Christian man; no dangers can really harm him, no sorrows utterly overwhelm him, for he is always accompanied by the Christ to whom he is united by faith.

"Here you will ask," says Luther, "'If all who are in the Church are priests, by what character are those whom we now call priests to be distinguished from the laity?' I reply, By the use of these words, 'priest,' 'clergy,' 'spiritual person,' 'ecclesiastic,' an injustice has been done, since they have been transferred from the remaining body of Christians to those few who are now, by a hurtful custom, called ecclesiastics. For Holy Scripture makes no distinction between them, except that those who are now boastfully called Popes, bishops, and lords, it calls ministers, servants, and stewards, who are to serve the rest in the ministry of the Word, for teaching the faith of Christ and the liberty of believers. For though it is true that we are all equally priests, yet we cannot, nor ought we, if we could, all to minister and teach publicly."

The first part of the treatise shows that everything which a Christian man has goes back in the end to his faith; if he has this he has all; if he has it not, nothing else suffices him. In the same way the second part shows that everything that a Christian man does must come from his faith. It may be necessary to fast and keep the body under; it will be necessary to make use of all the ceremonies of divine service which have been found effectual for the spiritual education of man. The thing to remember is that these are not good works in themselves or in the sense of making a man good; they are all rather the signs of his faith, and are to be done with joy, because they are done to the God to whom faith unites us.

This brief description of what Luther called a "summary of the Christian life" will give an idea of the little book which perhaps most clearly manifests that combination of revolutionary daring and wise conservatism which was the most outstanding feature in Luther's character. It maintains that ceremonies, or what may be called the whole machinery of the Church, are most valuable, and indeed indispensable, provided they are looked at from the right point of view, and are kept in their proper place; while, on the other hand, they may become harmful to, and indeed almost destructive of, the true religious life, if they are considered in any other sense than as means to an end. It therefore follows that, if through human corruption and neglect of the plain precepts of the Word of God, those ceremonies instead of aiding the true growth of the soul are hindering it, they ought to be changed or done away with; and the fact that the soul of man, in the last resource, needs absolutely nothing but the Word of God dwelling in it, gives men courage and tranquillity in demanding their reformation. It is the assertion of this principle, at once simple and profound, which places Luther in the forefront of all reformers of religion, and which marks him off from all previous witnesses for the truth, however courageously they may have testified against the ecclesiastical abuses of their days. The principle itself is the doctrine of Justification by Faith stripped of theological accessories, and stated in the simple language of everyday life.

The immediate application of this principle which Luther made, to define by it the relative positions of the clergy and the laity, was so important that it may be called a second principle. It is the assertion of the spiritual priesthood of all believers. He declared that men and women living lives in the family, in the workshop, and in the civic world, held their position there, not by a kind of indirect permission wrung from God out of His compassion for human frailties, but by as direct a vocation as that which called men to what by a mistake had been deemed the only religious life. The principle of the spiritual priesthood of all believers was able to deliver the laity from the vague fear of the clergy which enthralled them, and was also a potent spur to incite them to undertake a reformation of the Church which was so sorely needed.

These principles Luther at once applied in his two longer treatises on the Church and on the Christian Estate or Commonwealth.

In the ***Babylonian Captivity of the Church*** Luther declares that everything must be brought to the one test of the authority of the Word of God. This shows us how Luther thought that his principle of Christian liberty is to be applied, and what limitations were to be placed on its exercise. The essence of the liberty of a Christian man is the faith which he possesses, and faith is not mere abstract sentiment, but a personal trust in a personal Saviour who has given promises to be trusted in and messages to be accepted. These promises and messages are given us in the Word of God, which is a tissue of promises and prayers, and thus exhibits the union and communion of the believing man and the Saviour God. The promises may be simple promises, or they may be promises wrapt in a visible sign, or they may be contained in pictures of the life of a believing man or nation in communion with God. However they are given, they are contained in the Word of God, which is therefore the rule—both of the exercise and of the limitations of our Christian freedom. He applies this to a criticism of the elaborate sacramental system of the Roman Church, and the result of the application is to convince him that the Roman Curia has held the Church of God in bondage to human traditions and commandments of men, which run counter to the plain messages and promises of the Word of God. The ideas which guide him throughout the book are brought together at the close; and there we learn that while Luther considers it possible to apply the word "sacrament" to all those things to which a divine promise has been made, such as prayer, the Word, the cross, yet it is best to limit the use of the word to those promises which have visibly and divinely appointed signs attached. The results is that there are only two sacraments,—Baptism and the Lord's Supper, or the Bread as Luther calls it,—and that the other so-called sacraments are but ceremonies of human institution, salutary or otherwise.

It is unnecessary to describe the contents of this book at any length, but it may be interesting to notice briefly what Luther has to say on the one topic of Christian marriage.

Nothing in the whole round of Romish interferences with scriptural commands and messages excited Luther's indignation like the way in which it had degraded the whole conception of Christian marriage. "What shall we say of those impious human laws by which this divinely appointed manner of life has been entangled and tossed up and down? Good God! it is horrible to look upon the temerity of the tyrants of Rome, who thus, according to their caprices, at one time annul marriages and at another time enforce them. Is the human race given over to their caprice for nothing but to be mocked and abused in every way, and that these men may do what they please with it for the sake of their own fatal gains. . . . And what do they sell? The shame of men and women, a merchandise worthy of these traffickers, who surpass all that is most sordid and most disgusting in their avarice and impiety." Luther points out that there is a clear and scriptural law on the degrees within which marriage is unlawful, and that no human regulations ought to forbid marriages outside these degrees or permit it within them. He declares himself in favour of the marriage of priests, and says that there is nothing in Scripture or in the usages of the early Church forbidding it. He says that personally he detests the thought of divorce, "and even prefers bigamy to it"; but that it is clearly permitted by Christ in certain cases, and that the Roman Curia, now forbidding and now permitting, have defied all laws human and divine for the sake of money-making.

The justness of Luther's indignation at the scandals of the Roman Curia in relation to the Church's matrimonial legislation can only be appreciated by those who have studied the havoc it made in the family life of palace, castle, and burgher's home in the fifteenth and sixteenth centuries.

### 2. The Reformation of the Christian Estate

In his address ***To the Nobility of the German Nation, respecting the Reformation of the Christian Estate,*** Luther applied the principles laid down in his treatise on ***Christian Liberty*** to the reformation of the political Commonwealth. No writing coming from Luther's pen produced such an instantaneous, widespread, and powerful effect as this treatise did. It was issued from the printing-press some time in the beginning of August (the exact date is unknown), and before the 18th of the month four thousand copies were in circulation throughout Germany, and the presses could not print fast enough for the demand. Such a circulation was extraordinary for the times, and was quite unprecedented. The treatise was a thoroughgoing antidote to the Bull of excommunication which was soon to be published in Germany. It was the political and social manifesto of the Reformation, and its effects were seen at the two Diets held at Nürnberg in 1522 and 1524, where its indictment of the Roman Curia was practically adopted by the Diet. It owed its power to the spiritual insight, the moral energy, and the tact which, in spite of occasional violence of language, it displayed throughout. The spiritual insight is to be seen in the way in which it lays down the principle of the independence of the human soul of all merely human powers and arrangements, in which it insists on the equal spiritual rights and responsibilities of layman and cleric, and in which it asserts the true sanctity and spirituality of all natural relationships of family, home, trade, and profession, of noble, burgher, artisan, and peasant. The moral energy is displayed in the way in which one abuse after another is brought forward in swift irresistible succession, and the veil of legal chicanery is stripped from one monstrous exaction after another, and in the boldness with which the author points to plague-spots which were due to the vices of the people themselves. Its wonderful tact is disclosed in the modest beginning; "It is not out of mere arrogance and perversity that I, an individual poor man, have taken upon me to address your lordships." It appears in the courteous address to the young Emperor, Charles v., from whom German patriots were expecting so much, and in whom they were soon to be sadly disappointed: "God has given us a young and noble sovereign, and by this has roused great hopes in many hearts; now it is right that we too should do what we can, and make good use of time and grace." It is seen in the deft omission from the title of all reference to the Holy Roman Empire and the delicate suggestion thereby of a "Germany for the Germans"; in the appeal to the nobles who were, with the Emperor, the legal representatives of the German nation, and on whose shoulders the author lays the responsibilities for the good government of the realm; and in the use of the German language, which makes the address an appeal to the whole German people—nobles, burghers, and peasants.

The great source of the clamant evils which oppress the German people is, according to Luther, the Pope and the Roman Curia, and the reason why the nation has been slow to deliver itself from the evils which overwhelm it is because its arch-enemy has entrenched itself behind a triple fortification believed to be impregnable. The first thing to do is to tear down these defences, which are: (1) that the Temporal Power has no jurisdiction over the Spiritual; (2) that they cannot be admonished from Scripture, since no one may interpret Scripture but the Pope; (3) that they cannot be called in question by a Council, because no one can call a Council but the Pope. These are their defences, and Luther proceeds to demolish them.

The Romanists assert that the Pope, bishops, priests, and monks are the *spiritual estate,* while princes, lords, artificers, and peasants are the *temporal estate;* but this is simply an hypocritical device. All Christians are of the spiritual estate, and there is no difference between them save that of office and of work given to do. Every man has work given him to do for the commonwealth, and he may be restrained and punished if he does not do it properly, whether he be Pope, bishop, priest, monk, tailor, mason, or cobbler.

As for the statement that the Pope alone can interpret Scripture—if that were true, what is the need for the Holy Scriptures? "Let us burn them, and content ourselves with the unlearned gentlemen at Rome, in whom the Holy Ghost dwells, who, however, can dwell in pious souls only. If I had not read it, I could never have believed that the devil should have put forth such follies at Rome and find a following."

The third "wall" falls of itself with the other two; for we are plainly taught in Scripture that if our brother offends we are to tell it to the Church, and if the Pope offends, as he often does, we can only obey the Word of God by calling a Council; and this the Emperors used to do.

Then comes the indictment. There is in Rome one who calls himself the Vicar of Christ, and who lives in a singular state of resemblance to our Lord and St. Peter, His apostle; for this man wears a triple crown (a single one does not content him), and keeps up such a state that he requires a larger personal revenue than the Emperor. He has surrounding him a number of men, called cardinals, whose only apparent use is that they serve to draw to themselves the revenues of the richest convents, fiefs, endowments, and benefices, and spend the money thus got in keeping up the state of a wealthy sovereign in Rome. When it is impossible to seize upon the whole revenue of an ecclesiastical benefice, the Curia joins some ten or twenty together, and mulcts each in a good round annual sum for the benefit of a cardinal. Thus the priory of Würzburg gives one thousand gulden yearly, and Bamberg, Mainz, and Trier pay their quotas. The papal court is enormous—three thousand papal secretaries and hangers-on innumerable, and all waiting for German benefices, whose duties they never fulfil, as wolves wait for a flock of sheep. In this way Germany pays to Rome a sum of three hundred thousand gulden annually—more than it pays to its own Emperor. "Do we still wonder why princes, noblemen, cities, foundations, convents, and people grow poor? We should rather wonder that we have anything left to eat." Then look at the way in which Rome robs the German land. Long ago the Emperor permitted a Pope to take the half of the first year's income from every benefice—the *annates*—for the special purpose of providing money for a war against the Turk. This money was never spent for the purpose destined; yet it has actually been regularly paid for a hundred years, and the Pope regards it as a regular and legitimate tax, and employs it to pay posts and offices at Rome. "Whenever there is any pretence of fighting the Turk, they send out commissions for collecting money, and often send out Indulgences under the same pretext . . . They think that we Germans will always remain such great and inveterate fools that we will go on giving money to satisfy their unspeakable greed, though we see plainly that neither *annates,* nor absolution money, nor any other thing—not one farthing—goes against the Turks, but all goes into their bottomless sack . . . and all this is done in the holy name of Christ and St. Peter." He then enumerates the ways, many of them mere legal chicanery, by which the Pope gets the right to appoint to German benefices. He exposes the gross exactions connected with the bestowal of the *pallium* on German prelates; the trafficking in benefices, in all manner of exemptions and permissions to evade ecclesiastical laws and restrictions, the most shameless instances being those connected with marriage; and describes the Curial Court as a place "where vows are annulled; where a monk gets leave to quit his Order; where priests can enter married life for money; where bastards can become legitimate; and dishonour and shame may arrive at high honours; all evil repute and disgrace is knighted and ennobled; where a marriage is suffered that is in a forbidden degree, or has some other defect. . . . There is a buying and a selling, a changing, blustering and bargaining, cheating and lying, robbing and stealing, debauchery and villainy, and all kinds of contempt of God that Antichrist could not reign worse."

Luther, lastly, proceeds to give some suggestion for amending matters—twenty-seven in number. The first eight and the seventeenth are such that if carried into effect they would have the result of creating a German National Church with an ecclesiastical Council, to be the highest court of ecclesiastical appeal, and to represent the German Church as the Diet did the German State. Suggestions nine, ten, eleven, and twenty-six aim at the complete abolition of the supremacy of the Pope over the State. In most of the others he deals with ecclesiastical abuses which do not spring from the supremacy and greed of Rome, but which are productive of much religious and social evil. Luther would check the multitude of pilgrimages, which he thinks do not tend to good morals, and lead men to pursue a life of wandering beggary. For the same reason he would limit or suppress the mendicant orders. "It is of much more importance to consider what is necessary for the salvation of the common people, than what St. Francis, or St. Dominic, or St. Augustine, or any other man, laid down, especially since things have not turned out as they expected." He would bring some daylight into the convents both for men and women, and believes that everyone who wishes to leave the convent ought to be allowed to do so, since God will accept voluntary service only. He thinks that there are too many saints' days and ecclesiastical festivals, which are only seasons of gluttony, drunkenness, and debauchery, and would retain the Sunday only. He also considers that it is time that the German Church came to some terms with the Bohemians, who, whatever their sins, did nothing so bad as deliberately break a solemnly given safe-conduct. In one of his suggestions (fourteenth), he deals with the terribly sad condition of the German country parish priests, and he does this in a tender and sympathetic way. "We see also how the priesthood is fallen, and how many a poor priest is encumbered with a woman and children, and burdened in his conscience, and no one does anything to help him, though he might very well be helped." Luther's sympathy goes out to the man; ours goes forth more to the woman. The priest's concubine, the Pfaff's Frau, is the common butt of the mediæval rustic poetry; and she is accused of all manner of things in the coarse wit of the times. Even Hans Sachs has his gibe at her:

> Nach dem der Messner von Hirschau,
> Der tanzet mit des Pfarrherrn Frau
> Von Budenheim, die hat er lieb,
> Viel Scherzens am Tanz mit ihr trieb.

"I will not conceal," says Luther, "my honest counsel, nor withhold comfort from that unhappy crowd, who now live in trouble with wife and children, and remain in shame, with a heavy conscience, hearing their wife called a priest's harlot, and the children bastards. . . . I say that these two (who are minded in their hearts to live together always in conjugal fidelity) are surely married before God."

His remaining paragraphs treat briefly of social evils which cannot be called ecclesiastical. He refers to the rampant beggary which disgraces Germany and which comes both from the mendicant monks and from the numerous vagrants. He calculates how much a town of ordinary size actually taxes itself when it supports by casual almsgiving the troops of sturdy rogues who wander through it. His remedy for the disease is that each town should support its own poor in a charitable fashion. He has also some solemn words addressed to the luxury and the licensed immorality of the cities; and with these words of warning he closes the address.

This call to the Nobility of the German Nation appealed to all Germans, and produced a great effect on the very class to which it was directly addressed. Apart from its immediate effect on Luther's relation to his contemporaries, it ought to be remembered that it is really the first definite announcement that Germans ought to work all together for a united Germany, and was the first practical step taken in the movement to create a German nationality which has made such an advance in our own generation, and whose end is not yet.

Meanwhile at Rome the Bull condemning Luther had been prepared, and was published there in the middle of the month of June. It seems to have been drafted by Eck, Cajetan, and Prierias, and the workmanship was mainly Eck's. It is a very curious document. It begins pathetically: "Arise, O Lord, plead Thine own cause; remember how the foolish man reproacheth Thee daily; the foxes are wasting Thy vineyard which Thou hast given to Thy Vicar Peter; the boar out of the wood doth waste it, and the wild beast of the field doth devour it." St. Peter is then invoked, and the Pope's distressful state at hearing the news of Luther's misdeeds is described at length. The Bull then cites forty-one propositions, said to be Luther's, and condemns them. It is worthy of notice that there is no condemnation of Luther's evangelical principles, but of the objections to Romish practices which flowed from these principles. All Luther's writings, whenever and wherever found, are ordered to be burnt. The Pope details his many "fatherly dealings" with his rebellious son, and adds that even yet, if he will only recant, he is prepared to welcome him back to the fold; if he remains obstinate there is nothing before him but the fate of a heretic.

This Bull was published, by Eck and by the Roman legate Aleander, in some parts of Germany. When it reached Wittenberg both the Elector and the university took no notice of it, notwithstanding threats that the privileges of the university would be withdrawn. The Elector, some time later, asked Spalatin to find out what effect the Bull was having on the students and citizens, and the chaplain reported that there were nearly six hundred students in Melanchthon's classes and over four hundred in Luther's, while the crowds of people attending Luther's preaching were so great that the churches could scarcely contain them. The Bull had not caused the people of Wittenberg to shun Luther. The legate was determined to make a personal appeal to the Elector; he waylaid him at Cologne as he was returning from the coronation of the young Emperor, and demanded that he should publish the Bull in his dominions, publicly burn Luther's writings, and deliver up Luther himself to the Pope as a heretic. He added the curious threat that if this was not done, the Pope would withdraw the title of Holy Roman Empire from Germany and treat the land as Constantinople and the Eastern Empire had been treated. Upon this Frederic secretly consulted Erasmus. The cautious Dutchman told him "that Luther had sinned in two points; he had touched the crown of the Pope and the bellies of the monks"; while in an interview with Spalatin the great humanist declared that the attacks upon Luther came from ignorance enraged at science and from tyrannical presumption. Thus fortified, the Elector replied to the legate that he had never made common cause with Luther, nor would he protect him if he attacked the Pope, but that as matters stood Luther must have a fair trial. His Elector therefore protected Luther, and the Reformer was able to go on preaching, teaching, and writing in peace.

The Bull was proclaimed in some parts of Germany, and copies of Luther's writings were seized and burnt; but the curious *Documenta Lutherana,* published a few years ago by the Vatican, reveal that this was done with increasing difficulty, and that the excitement caused by burning Luther's books was so great that the legate sometimes trembled for his life.

Meanwhile Luther worked on indefatigably with his pen. Attacks on the Bull and its authors in Latin and in German flowed from the Wittenberg press, and among others an elaborate defence and explanation of the forty-one propositions cited in the Bull. Luther also solemnly renewed his appeal to a General Council, and published it in Latin and in German.

When tidings came to him that his writings had been burnt in several parts of Germany, he resolved on the momentous step of burning the Book of Decretals, that part of the Canon Law in which the papal supremacy is supported by many a fictitious document, and with them the Bull itself. So on the 10th of December 1520 he posted a notice inviting the students of Wittenberg to witness the burning of the "Antichristian Decretals" at nine o'clock in the morning. A great multitude of students, burghers, and professors collected in the open space before the Elster Gate, where a great bonfire had been built. One of the masters kindled the pyre; Luther laid the Books of Decretals on the glowing mass, and they caught the flames; then in solemn silence Luther placed a copy of the Bull in the flames, saying in Latin: "As thou hast wasted with anxiety the Holy One of God, so may the eternal flames waste thee" ("Quia tu conturbasti Sanctum Domini, ideoque te contubernetignis aeternus"). He waited till the flames had consumed the paper and then with his fellow-professors and other friends slowly re-entered the town and went back to the university.

The opportunity was too good a one to be lost by the students. The solemnity of the occasion at first impressed them, and some hundreds standing round the flames sang the "Te Deum." Then the spirit of mischief seized them, and they began to sing funeral dirges in honour of the burnt Decretals. Thereafter they got a large peasant cart, erected a pole in it, and hung on it a banner six feet long emblazoned with a copy of the Bull. They piled the cart with the works of Eck, Emser, and other Romish controversialists, hauled it through the town and through the Elster Gate, and tumbling Bull and books on the still glowing embers of the bonfire, they burnt them together. Then sobered again they sang the "Te Deum" and separated.

It is scarcely possible for us in the nineteenth century to understand the thrill that went through all Germany, and indeed all Europe, when the news sped that a poor monk had burnt the Pope's Bull. It was not the first time that a Bull had been burnt, but the burners had been great monarchs, with trained armies and a devoted people behind them, while in this case it was a monk with nothing but his manhood to back him. It meant that a new world had come into being, and that the individual human soul had found its own worth. It is as impossible to date epochs as it is to trace the real fountainhead of rivers. In the one case a guess is made and some event is fixed on as the beginning of the new period, and in the other some nameless rill is selected as the source. But it is easy to see the river when it begins to roll in volume of water, and to discern the epoch when some utterly unlooked-for event startles mankind. So this burning Pope Leo's Bull showed that modern history had begun.

An oak tree now stands between the Elster Gate and the Elbe River, planted long ago to mark the spot where the Bull was burnt.

*Note*

[1] These three treatises, exhibiting the principles of the Lutheran Reformation, together with the theses against Indulgences and Luther's Short and Greater Catechisms, have been translated and published in English, with two explanatory Essays—one on the "Primary Principles of Luther's Life and Teaching," by Prebendary Wace, and the other on the "Political Course of the Reformation in Germany (1517-1546)," by Professor Bucheim. London: Hodder & Stoughton, 1896. I have taken the translation of the extracts quoted from this volume.

**Thomas Carlyle on Luther's character:**

Luther's character, on the whole, is one of the most characteristic in Germany, of whatsoever is best in German minds. He is the image of a large, substantial, deep man, taht stands upon truth, justice, fairness, that fears nothing, considers the right, and calculates on nothing else; and. . . does not do it spasmodically, but adheres to it deliberately and calmly, through good report and bad. Accordingly, we find him a good-homoured, jovial, witty man, greatly beloved by every one, and though his words were half battles, as Jean Paul says, stronger than artillery, yet among his friends he was one of the kindest of men. The wild kind of force that was in him appears in the physiognamy of the portrait by Luke Chranak, his painter and friend, the rough plebian countenance, with all sorts of noble thoughts shining out through it. That was precisely Luther as he appears through his whole history.

*Thomas Carlyle, in* Lectures on the History of Literature, *Charles Scribner's Sons, 1892.*

**Erik H. Erikson (essay date 1958)**

SOURCE: "Faith and Wrath," in *Young Man Luther: A Study in Psychoanalysis and History*, W. W. Norton & Company, Inc., 1958, pp. 223-50.

[*In the excerpt below, Erikson examines Lather's writings, provides a psychoanalysis of the reformer, and describes the dynamics of his theology.*]

The importance of Luther's early lectures lies in the fact that they bear witness not only to the recovery of his ego, but also to a new theology conceived long before he suddenly became famous as a pamphleteer in the controversy over indulgences. To the Catholic scholar, his theological innovations seem pitiful, mere vulgarized fragments of the order he disavowed; to the Protestant, his theology is powerful and fundamentally new. The historical psychologist, however, can only question how efficacious an ideology is at a given historical moment. Obviously, when this monk spoke up he presented in his words and in his bearing the image of man in whom men of all walks of life were able to recognize in decisive clarity something that seemed right, something they wanted, they needed to be. Whatever theological rationale unified Luther's teachings as an evangelist was transcended by his influence on men in his own and in other reformers' churches, in his and in other countries, and even on the Catholic Church's own Counter Reformation.

There are a number of conflicting historical views about Luther's importance for the great movement called the Reformation. These views, strongly tinged by partisanship, attest to his original leadership or suggest that his was merely an adroitly timed episode on the order of Wycliffe's or Huss's; they affirm a divine providence in his survival and ascendance, or maintain that luck, in the form of his adversaries' fatal hesitation, permitted him to complete his rebellion when according to the criteria of his time he had forfeited his life to the stake many times over. He is revered as a voice of genuine inspiration, or made out to be the tool of a conspiracy of crude economic forces which were in need of a bit of evangelical polish. Be all this as it may, Luther was the herald of the age which was in the making and is—or was—still our age: the age of literacy and enlightenment, of constitutional representation, and of the freely chosen contract; the age of the printed word which at least tried to say what it meant and to mean what it said, and provided identity through its very effort.

It is true, of course, that both Wycliffe in England and Huss in Bohemia had focused with fanatic affront on holy issues which had been widely argued about even by dignitaries and writers within the Church for more than a century before Martin's birth: the entrusting of the sacraments, especially confession, to priests with dirty ears; the administering of the Mass by equally dirty hands; the extortion by the same hands of money, at first as an adjunct to, but then increasingly as a substitute for, that contrition which it was a priest's job to insist upon; and finally, the problem of all problems, the infallibility of the foreign and distant Roman papacy whose sanction lifted these priests and their performances above all earthly criticism. Wycliffe, a hundred years before Luther's birth, had translated the Bible into the English of his contemporaries, so that they could hear the original Word freed from its captivity by the Roman monopolists. Huss, in turn, had objected to the adoration of images and the emphasis on works; with a more decidedly nationalist flair, he had likewise translated the Bible into the Czech vernacular, insisting, as Luther would, that he would have to be *shown* that he was wrong from the *Book*.

Literacy, and a conscience speaking the mother tongue—these pillars of our present-day identity had long been in the building. But Gutenberg had, as it were, waited for Luther; and the new technique of mass communication was thus available to Luther's theological performance, which so attracted the charisma, the personality cult, of a nation. It would be fatal to underestimate the degree to which the future always belongs to those who combine a universal enough new meaning with the mastery of a new technology. The Church, however, whose influence had already been impaired by the development of national monarchies elsewhere, clung to its fateful investment in the German nation which because of its position in the center of Europe held then, as it still holds, the balance between the great isms of the world.

As we discuss a few of the events which brought Luther to prominence, we cannot hope to retell what the history books and the movies have told and retold, or give consistent historical meaning to the dogmatic moralism, the diplomatic corruption, or the popular foolery which this young monk outshouted and outprinted for a few historical moments. Nor can we in any way try to do justice to the relation within Luther between his continued inner conflicts and his public leadership. We can only outline what we are reasonably competent to perceive, namely, the step from Martin's identity crisis to that crisis of middle-age which occurs when an original man first stops to realize what he has begun to originate in others.

Here are a few dates:

EVENTS OF LUTHER'S THIRTIES AND FORTIES

1513-16 Started lecturing at the age of thirty, and delivered the great trilogy on the Psalms, Romans, and Galatians.

1517 Nailed the ninety-five theses against indulgences on the door of the Castle Church in Wittenberg.

1518 Appealed the Pope's Bull threatening excommunication.

1520 Publicly burned the Bull. Wrote his great pamphlets, culminating in ***On the Freedom of a Christian Man***.

1521 Appeared before the Diet at Worms. Imperial ban. Hid on the Wartburg.

1522 New Testament published in German.

1525 Pamphlet against the peasants. Marriage.

1526 Son Hans born.

1527 Sickness and depression. ***A Mighty Fortress***.

1546 Death at the age of sixty-three.

The matter of indulgences set off the time bomb which had been ticking in Luther's heart. The Church had, over the centuries, developed a system of high spiritual finance, made tangible in the imagery of accrued credit in heaven, and a kind of universal community chest. Some saints, it was claimed, had amassed a credit of salvation far above their personal needs; the Church had naturally been entrusted with its distribution among the deserving. There was some abundance available within this Catholic system, but there was no salvation whatsoever outside its monopoly. Gradually the transactions within the system—the dealings of the employees with each other, and their dealings with the masses of customers—became increasingly dominated by ideas of earthly cash. The most pitiful display of this commercialization was the number of small coins dropped in sundry boxes by the masses of the poor, at first as an accessory to ritual observance, then in the assumption that the money itself had a direct magic influence through the Church's vertical line on the accounting above.

The Jubilee of 1500 provided an excuse for a worldwide campaign to increase the number of indulgences. The money so raised was to help complete St. Peter's as an anchor for the vertical, outshining the capitol of any merely horizontal empire. Indulgences were collected by expert friars, who were sometimes accompanied by agents of banking houses to whom some of the pious money was already owed, and for purposes other than those advertised in the campaign. Still, Luther typically did not raise his voice about indulgences until the campaign made itself felt in his home town and electoral province.

His own archbishop, Albrecht von Brandenburg, used the Jubilee collection to pay his personal debts, and this with the Pope's permission. Brandenburg had borrowed the money which he had to pay to the Pope for the insignia of his third archbishopric from the Augsburg house of Fugger. The Pope permitted the Fuggers to repossess this money by taking out of the indulgence boxes half of the still warm coins which the people had dropped in them to save themselves from some temporal penance, and the souls of their loved ones from centuries in purgatory. When one collecting party, headed by an especially unprincipled salesman, Tetzel, approached the borders of Electoral Saxony, both Luther and his Elector pricked up their ears.

The Elector was through with taxation without representation. He had previously kept in his own treasury the sums donated by people in Wittenberg who had viewed the Electoral relic collection expecting to gain spiritually from its radiation. The Elector was damned if he was going to release this money to pay the overhead of the agency in Rome. The money he collected was going to be applied to *his* pride, the University of Wittenberg. There is no evidence that Luther was either a party to this diversion of pious funds into his own institution or that he objected to it. But he was highly incensed at the limitless promises made by Tetzel, a Dominican at that, to Luther's constituents who were flocking over the border to participate in the fun as well as in the gain of the noisy campaign. Tetzel had, in certain cases, dispensed with confession altogether, and was distributing sealed letters of credit for sins as yet contemplated; even worse, he suggested that potential purchasers of indulgences could go to confessors of their own choosing, so that they could avoid those who might maintain a too pronounced austerity in the time of the Jubilee. This was too much; it undercut the psychological conditions for individual piety on the part of Luther's Wittenberg constituents.

Furthermore, Luther also came to realize the incompatibility of principle between his own teachings and preachings and the monetary habits and images of the organization in whose name he spoke. As he always did in decisive moments, he acted without seeking the counsel of those who might have restrained him; his entry into the monastery is an earlier example of this behavior, and his marriage is a later one. His closest friends were unaware of the fact that on the day before All Souls, when masses of people came to see the Elector's relics spread out on the castle square as if at a country fair, he had nailed the ***Ninety-Five Theses*** on the door of the castle church. This was a custom generally used whenever one wished to invite the public disputation of a controversy. It usually neither touched the populace, nor reached the higher-ups. This time, however, Luther had a copy of the Latin text delivered to the archbishop, from whom he intended to get an answer over and above private disputation. But the answer came from elsewhere, from everywhere. The German translation of the theses evoked an immediate, wide, and emphatic echo: from the general public, who were anti-Italian and patriotic; from the dispossessed, who were anticapitalist and equalitarian; from the petty plutocrats, who were antimonopolistic; from the princes, who were particularist and territorial; from the educated, who were anticlerical and secularist; and from the knights, who were Teutonic and anarchistic. From all of these groups came encouragement so personal and folksy that it can be rendered in American only as "Atta boy, Monk!" The response of the educated, including Erasmus and Dürer, was what it has remained over the centuries: "When Luther, in his immense manly way, swept off by a stroke of his hand the very notion of a debit and credit account kept with individuals by the Almighty, he stretched the soul's imagination and saved theology from puerility."[1]

The explosiveness of the popular response immediately warned both Luther and the Church that many kinds of rebellious desires had been ignited by this one issue of alien taxation. There were moments in the following months when Luther seemed ready to recant, and when the Pope made amazing concessions by publicly "clarifying" some of the excessive claims for the papal power of divine intercession which had been made, implied, or not denied by his operatives. But Luther and the Pope acted mostly like animals who withdraw when they hear the echoes of their own growls, then are emboldened by the other's withdrawal, and soon find themselves irrevocably engaged. There is no retreat once blood is drawn. A year after the theses had been published, Luther wrote to the Pope: "Most blessed Father, I offer myself prostrate at the feet of your Holiness, with all that I am and have. Quicken, slay, call, recall, approve, reprove, as may seem good to you. I will acknowledge your voice as the voice of Christ, residing and speaking in you. If I have deserved death I will not refuse to die."[2] Yet, summoned to Rome, he refused to go; as a matter of fact, the Elector refused to let him go, having been told by the Emperor "to take good care of that monk." Soon, however, Luther began to refer to the Pope as "Antichrist"; to the Pope Luther was the "child of Satan."

Luther once again promised submission to the Pope; but then he used a legalistic excuse to break his promise of silence, and entered into public debate with the experienced Eck, who cornered him into statements which amounted to an outspoken heretical doubt in the God-givenness of the Roman Pope's supremacy in Christendom. Although (or perhaps because) he had shown himself inferior to Eck in the disputation itself, Luther began to play to the gallery, and to develop and enjoy a certain showmanship. The point of no return was soon reached; Luther preached open revolt, even suggesting that it would be entirely in order "to wash our hands in the blood" of cardinals and popes.[3] I will not quote from the rhetoric, so boring in its monotonous excess, which this once quiet and tortured monk released against the "sink of the Roman Sodom." It is enough to say that on July 10, 1520, he wrote to Spalatin: "I have cast the die . . . I will not reconcile myself to them in all eternity."[4] A few days later, the Pope published a bull threatening Luther's excommunication. Knowing that there was no way to avoid this ultimatum, Luther openly attacked specific fundamentals previously assailed by Wycliffe and Huss: the sacraments of penance and of baptism, and finally of the Eucharist itself. His views on theological matters were an applied extension of his earlier lectures, but about 1520 he appeared in an entirely new role: as a German prophet and ideological leader. He published a trilogy of pamphlets in German, the titles of which are like fanfares: ***An den christlichen Adel Deutscher Nation (To the Christian Nobility of German Nationality); Ueber die Babylonische Gefangenschaft der Kirche (On the Babylonian Captivity of the Church);*** and ***Von der Freiheit eines Christenmenschen (About the Freedom of a Christian).***

The three prehistoric lectures on the Psalms, Romans, and Galations had developed a new vertical, a new theology of the praying man, rediscovering the passion of Christ in each man's inner struggles. These three pamphlets of 1520 outlined a new horizontal, a civic reformation in which such prayer could exist. We will mention only his claims for the equality of all Christians; for every Christian's priesthood, prepared for by baptism, and confirmed by his receptivity for the Word of the Scriptures; and for the necessity for elected councils as the true representation of all the faithful. It must interest us that he urged the postponement of monastic vows until the age of thirty—the age when sexual drive has passed its peak, when identity is firmly established, and when man's ideological pliability comes to an end. The Pope pronounced his ban in September, 1520. Luther took the Pope's Bull out by one of the Wittenberg gates and burned it, together with other printed works. The students loved it. Rarely have young people been in on such decisive events as the students and faculty of that frontier University of Wittenberg. The next day, Luther announced that nobody could be saved except by following him out of the Church of Rome.

Luther was gladder about this pyrotechnic deed, he told Staupitz, than about anything he had said in his whole life. Even as hearing his own words had previously inspired his convictions, seeing the fire he set seems to have inflamed his rebelliousness. From this time on, the struggle set in between the Word and the Deed, between the method of persuasion and the method of fire. Every one of his words aroused his countrymen to deeds; every one of their deeds made him reaffirm: "By the Word the world has been vanquished, by the Word the Church has been saved, by the Word it will again be put in order, and the Antichrist . . . will fall without violence."[5] His verbosity could inspire chorales apt (as Goethe remarked) to lift heart and roof; but the heartlifting would persistently be matched by the roof-destroying. Almost before he knew it, Luther uttered words of violence which to him no doubt were often nothing more than poems of wrath; but to his followers, his words were tantamount to acts which obliged and justified concrete deeds.

The occasion of his most decisive oratory is the most famous moment of his life. Books and movies which have depicted his appearance before the Diet in Worms have more often than not adjusted the historical setting to fit the eternal quality of his words: a large hall, a dignified audience, and the sonorous resonance of his voice. It is too bad that history has not yet recognized the drama inherent in the rare clear voice which transcends both the anxiety within the speaker and the tense bedlam of the surrounding scene. Gettysburg should remind us how to visualize an unrehearsed historic scene; although in Worms they did crowd in to see and hear the featured speaker.

Luther had been warned not to appear, in spite of his Imperial passport. He was guided into town by a bodyguard of robber barons, and at the first brief session could hardly speak for fright or discomfort. But friends, beer in the evening, and a night's sleep restored him, and in the morning his voice was clear. In his native German he spoke those words of conscience which were a new kind of revelation achieved on the inner battlefield. At Worms Luther faced ostracism and death, not for the sake of an established creed or ties of ancestry and tradition; he did so because of *personal* convictions, derived from inner conflict and still subject to further conflict. The conscience he spoke of was not an inner sediment of a formalized morality; it was the best a *single man* between heaven, hell, and earth could know. If Luther did not really say the words which became most famous: "Here I stand," legend again rose to the occasion; for this new credo was for men whose identity was derived from their determination to stand on their own feet, not only spiritually, but politically, economically, and intellectually. No matter what happened afterward—and some terrible and most terribly petty things did occur because of it—Luther's emphasis on individual conscience prepared the way for the series of concepts of equality, representation, and self-determination which became in successive secular revolutions and wars the foundations not of the dignity of some, but of the liberty of all.

True, Luther did not really contemplate armed rebellion: "Had I desired to foment trouble, I could have brought great bloodshed upon Germany. Yea, I could have started such a little game at Worms that the

Emperor would not have been safe. But what would it have been? A fool's game. I left it to the Word."[6] And he would soon so act as to deserve to be called a great reactionary. Historical dialectics refuses to acknowledge the principle that a great revolutionary's psyche may also harbor a great reactionary; but psychological dialectics must assume it to be possible, and even probable.

The new Emperor, only twenty-one years of age, and obviously stirred by the proceedings, reaffirmed *his* identity: "I am descended from a long line of Christian emperors. . . . a single friar who goes counter to all Christianity for a thousand years must be wrong . . . I will have no more to do with him."[7] He put a ban on the monk. But the Elector arranged for Luther to be kidnapped and taken to a secret hideout on the Wartburg, only a mile from Eisenach and the Cottas.

After his father's house, this castle was Luther's most fateful residence. He was still a monk, committed to obedience, prayer, and celibacy; but at the castle he was without monastery or observances, without brethren or prior. From his window he could see the wide world, now (as messages conveyed) full of his name, and full of sinister threats. That world needed his leadership as much as he, so abruptly awakened to action, was ready to assume leadership. But at the very moment of his readiness, he was forced back into anonymity and inactivity, forced to read his own obituaries written by mourning friends whom he could have joined in reform and revolution.

Deprived of institutional routine, he was prey to the ego's double threat: the id within him, and the mob around him. His letters from the Wartburg frankly reveal how the mature man, grown beyond his tortured attempt at monasticism and abruptly blocked in his development as a leader, was tormented by desire. His enjoyment of food and beer under his immobile circumstances aggravated his tendency to be constipated, which in turn increased his demonological preoccupation with the lower parts of the body. All the *tentationes* from which he had fled as a young man into the monastery obsessed him as a grown man and the potential leader of a nation. His lust for power turned into furious anger with himself, with his circumstances, and with the devil. Much has been said about his hallucinations; but what would he have done without the devil, without being able to lump the grotesque and embarrassing paradoxes of his condition into one personalized creature—not invented by him, but confirmed by tradition (black dog and all) and thus "real" enough to permit a degree of hallucinatory projection, and, above all, now and then a superhuman temper tantrum? Luther on the Wartburg apparently at times suffered from something akin to a prison psychosis, which brought out in somewhat spectacular fashion those elements of unresolved infantile conflict which later, when he could not blame prison walls for his exposure to "the devil," turned into spells of brooding melancholy.

But despite his laments in the form of confessions to his friends (and this orator, as others of his kind, was also a colossal crybaby) he worked and could work. Under these conditions he wrote his pamphlet ***On Monastic Vows,*** the one which he prefaced with a letter to his father. The pamphlet stated as a general principle what the father had predicted for this particular son, namely, that the sexual instinct is essentially insurmountable, and, except in the case of rare and naturally celibate individuals, should not be subjected to attempts at suppression lest they poison the whole person. Marriage, he said, is the answer. Nevertheless, the father had been wrong because God alone could be right; and only Martin could have found this out—by becoming a monk.

He also began translating the New Testament from Erasmus's Greek version into German. It became his and his nation's most complete literary achievement. All the facets of a many-sided personality and all the resources of a rich vernacular were combined to create a language not intended as poetry for the few, but as inspiration in the life of the people. As Nietzsche put it: "The masterpiece of German prose is, appropriately enough, the masterwork of Germany's greatest preacher: the Bible so far has been the best German book. Compared with Luther's Bible, almost everything else is 'literature,' that is, a thing which has not grown in Germany and has not grown, and does not grow, into German hearts as the Bible has done."[8] Jacob Grimm, a scholar considered to be the founder of German linguistics, said that the later flowering of German literature would have been unthinkable without Luther's work. "Because of its almost miraculous purity and because of its deep influence, Luther's German must be considered the core and the fundament of the new German language. Whatever can be said to have nursed this language, whatever rejuvenated it so that a new flowering of poetry could result—this we owe to nobody more than to Luther."[9] Almost literally thunderstruck in the choir, this man translated the Lord's Prayer so that most Germans came to feel that Christ conceived it in German; and beside his diatribes of hate and blasphemous filth, wrote lyrics which have the power and the simplicity of folksong.

*"Ein Woertlein kann ihn faellen":* a tiny word can topple the devil. Luther's muteness was more than cured. The cultivation of national vernaculars was part of the growing nationalism; it was also part of the verbal Renaissance, one of the principles of which was that man, to reaffirm his identity on earth, needed to be able to say what is most worth saying in his native tongue. At any rate, language was the means

by which Luther became a historical force in Ranke's sense; that is, "a moral energy. . . . which dares to penetrate the world in free activity."[10] Or, as Luther put it: "God bestows all good things; but you must take the bull by the horns, you must do the work, and so provide God with an opportunity and a disguise."[11]

Here, in a way, our story ends. We could leave to mass psychology and political philosophy what mankind made of Luther's insights and doctrines; and we could ascribe to endogenous processes or to early aging the residual conflicts which marred the further development of Luther's personality. But a completed identity is only one crisis won.

Luther's letters from the Wartburg indicate the psychological setting for his future actions: having openly challenged Pope and Emperor and the universal world order for which they both stood, and having overcome his own inhibitions in order to express this challenge effectively, he now fully realized not only how ravenous his appetites were, and how rebellious his righteousness, but also how revolutionary were the forces which he had evoked in others. He was again moved to universal action by provincial events; Wittenberg and Erfurt, so he was informed, were falling to pieces. The friars had disbanded and married; even worse, they and the students, supported by a mob and led by Luther's friends, had planlessly changed such procedures as the holy Mass, destroyed sacred images, and banned music from the churches. Here, then, was initiated revolutionary puritanism—that strange mixture of rebellious individualism, aesthetic asceticism, and cruel righteousness which came to characterize much of Protestantism. Luther could hardly recognize what he had generated. Against all command or advice, he hurried to Wittenberg and for a week preached daily, with power, restraint, and humor. If one destroyed everything which one *might* abuse, he said, why, one would have to abolish women and wine too. How he got away with this last remark in the capital of Saxon beer brewing, I do not know; but he did make his point. He also made his first enemies among his own friends, who began to call him a reactionary.

The development of Luther's personal and provincial life, on the one hand, and of the general social dislocation, rebellion, and evolution, on the other, now took on a combination of naive eagerness, unconscious irony, and righteous frightfulness fit for a drama of Shavian dimensions. The Augustinian monastery in Wittenberg, abandoned by the friars, was turned over by the Elector to Luther's personal use. After his marriage it was shared by his wife, a former nun, and their children—certainly an ironic architectural setting for the first Lutheran parsonage. Then, just as he was about to settle down, his revolutionary poetry came home to roost. The peasants rose up all over Germany. He had said about the priests and bishops: "What do they better deserve than a strong uprising which will sweep them from the earth? And we would smile did it happen."[12] He had said: "In Christendom . . . all things are in common and each man's goods are the other's, and nothing is simply a man's own."[13] He had said, "The common man has been brooding over the injury he has suffered in property, in body, and in soul. . . . If I had ten bodies . . . I would most gladly give all to death in behalf of these poor men."[14]

The peasants published a Manifesto of the Twelve Articles, and sent it to him.[15] Peasants had revolted before and had been massacred before; but this time they were speaking as a class with a leader and a book—a new identity. They spoke with simplicity and dignity: "seeing that Christ has redeemed and bought us all with the precious shedding of his blood, the lowly as well as the great," they promised each other to retreat only "if this is explained to us with arguments from the Scripture"—the divine, the only, constitution. Otherwise they demanded that each, for his work, receive "according to the several necessities of all." It is easy to agree today that they were as moderate in their demands as they were immoderate wherever violence sprang up. Luther had previously warned of such violence, and did so again in ***An Earnest Exhortation for all Christians, Warning Them Against Insurrection and Rebellion***. He emphasized, in measured tones, that "no insurrection is ever right no matter what the cause . . . my sympathies are and always will be with those against whom insurrection is made."[16] He objected to the concept of political and economic freedom; spiritual freedom, he said was quite consistent with serfdom, and serfdom with the Scriptures. This, of course, corresponded to his medieval notions of the estate to which the individual is born; he wished to reform man's prayerful relation to God, not change his earthly estate. This dichotomy between man's spiritual freedom and his station in social life, which Luther subsequently tried to formulate convincingly, haunts Protestant philosophy to this day. For among the estates, the offices, and the callings which he defined as equally God-given and God-guided, he forgot to mention his own vocation of reformer and revolutionary. But he had burned the Bull publicly. He had called for rebellion; and his original Word-deed now left him far behind.

The peasants, as it were, quoted Martin back to Luther. He advised compromise, and he, Hans' son, found that he was being disobeyed and ignored. He could forgive neither the peasants for this, nor later the Jews, whom he had hoped to convert with the help of the Scriptures where the Church had failed to do so. In 1525 he wrote his pamphlet ***Against the Robbing and Murdering Hordes of Peasants,*** suggesting both public and secret massacres in words which could adorn the gates of the police headquarters and concentration camps of our time. He promised rewards in heaven to those who risked their lives in subduing insurrection. One sentence indicates the full cycle taken by this once beaten down and then disobedient son: "A rebel is not worth answering with arguments, for he does not accept them. The answer for such mouths is a fist that brings blood from the nose."[17] Do we hear Hans, beating the residue of a stubborn peasant out of his son?

Luther now went too far even for some members of his own family. One of his brothers-in-law asked him whether he wished to be "the prophet of the overlords," and accused him of cowardice—an accusation which was unfair. Luther wrote against the peasants when they were advancing in his direction like a steamroller; and he refused to flatter the princes when he needed them most. It makes him more understandable, even if it does not make his immediate influence more palatable, to realize that his excessive statements were always directed against deliberate disobedience. Otherwise, he could be entirely tolerant and express outright liberal views. He pleaded with the princes to permit free discussion of sectarian views; and he established the principle for a clergyman "never to remain silent and assent to injustice, whatever the cost."[18] If he did become the prophet of the overlords, it was because he would not begin political history anew as the leaderless enthusiasts wanted him to. In the long run, one may fairly say that this reactionary established some of the individualist and equalitarian imagery, and thus the ideological issues for both the rightists and the leftists in the revolutions then to come.

In May, 1525, the peasants were massacred, first by superior artillery, then by ferocious footsoldiers, in the battle of Frankenhausen. All in all, 130,000 peasants were killed in that war. In June, Luther wrote "all is forgotten that God has done for the world through me. . . . Now lords, priests, and peasants are all against me and threaten me with death."[19] But the Reformation was on its way, and Luther was safe in Wittenberg, master of the empty monastery and the recipient of an increased salary as professor and pastor.

In July, he suddenly married and settled down in his parsonage. He married, he said, because his father wanted him to, a statement so incomprehensible to some that they think it must have been a joke; yet his father, when he heard of Luther's hesitation, urged him to continue the family name which was endangered by the death of his brothers. And marriage was part of the belatedly manifest identification with his father which at this time, openly and secretly, began to determine much of Luther's life. No doubt, also, he loved children; he loved a combination of children and homemade music most of all, so that again, one must assume some early happiness in his own childhood. True, once settled in his domesticity and in his fame, he said awful things in the children's presence, and not in Latin, either. But this is just one aspect of his many-cornered mouth. "*Homo verbosatus,*" he called himself, leniently. A superior resiliency is suggested by the fact that despite having been a captive after years of monastic abstinence and a virginal youth, he could at the age of forty-five enter an apparently happy marriage. To be sure, one finds in his remarks references to a kind of eliminative sexuality, a need to get rid of bodily discharge which one could ascribe partially to a persistent preoccupation with the body's waste products. . . . But here as elsewhere, he was, up to a point, merely more frank and less romantic in expressing what dominates the sexual urge of most ordinary men, and what, in refined men, leads to conflicts with their sense of propriety and personal affection. He also said deep, sweet, humorous, and novel things about marriage.

In 1526, his son was born, and christened: Hans.

In this quiet after the storm, Luther again developed severe anxiety, this time protracted and bordering on a deep melancholia. How can this be? asks the psychiatrist; wasn't Luther at the height of his influence, happily married and out of the range of danger? He obviously had no reason to be sad again, sadder than ever; his "psychosis" must have been endogenous, dictated by strictly biological changes within him; so it would be foolish to look for meaningful reasons. Our sociologist, in contrast to the psychiatrist, feels that Luther had reason to be troubled far more than he was: "That he was able to effect such a volte-face without being stricken in his conscience shows that he did not feel that he was betraying a principle which he felt to be fundamental."[20] The fact is that Luther, facing the full consequences of his oratory, stood before a new crisis which—and here his constitution helped to determine his symptoms—brought back his sadness in a new and incongruous context.

Luther, now a father himself, abnegated much of his postadolescent identity. This is (or was) a not uncommon phenomenon in Europe, and especially in Germany.[21] Except for a few more and more hypothetical Christians, Luther increasingly perceived man as a potentially dangerous child, if not a ravenous beast. The only safe men were the *Landeskinder,* the children of the petty principalities, whose head was the *Landesvater* (the father of the country), as all the heads of the tiny states and of their churches came to be called. In 1528, Luther expressed the opinion that Moses' commandment "Honor thy father," applied to these princes, and is, therefore, equivalent to an injunction against political rebellion.[22] Famous and infamous are his words: "The secular sword must be red and bloody, for the world will and must be evil"[23]—a statement plausible enough from the view of common sense, and from that of Luther's political philosophy which assumes that the prince in power is born to a singular function in the commonwealth. Since he is a Christian, he is subject to the same injunctions against a personal abuse of his calling, and to the same obligation to be guided by prayer, as is any other man in any other position; otherwise, as Luther admitted, he might "start a war over an empty nut."[24] But even then he must be obeyed, although under pronounced protest.

The ordinary man thus surrendered to ordinary princes, lost much of what Luther's early lectures had stood for. The same praying man whose soul Luther had emancipated from Roman authoritarianism was now obliged to accept the ruling family, the economic practice, and (so the law of territorial identify soon decreed) the religious creed which were dominant in his prince's domain. In Protestant states, Luther established Consistorial Councils as the governing religious bodies. These councils were headed by the prince in power, and were composed of two theologians and two jurists; they could imprison a man and exclude him from all work, decree his social boycott, and take away his civic rights. The Protestant Revolution thus led to a way of life in which a man's daily works, including his occupation, became the center of his behavioral orientation, and were rigorously regimented by the church-state. Such a condition Luther had once decried as "Mosaic law." Now he rationalized it: since a Christian man has not only a soul, but also a body living among other bodies, he must "resign himself to Moses" (*sich in Mosen schicken*).[25] Even praying man should take council not only with himself, but with the rulers, in order to be sure of perceiving all the signs of God's plan. This new face of a God, recognizable in prayer, in the Scriptures, *and* in the decisions of the *Landesvater,* became the orientation of a new class, and of a religiosity compliant to the needs of progress in the new, the mercantile, line of endeavor. In spite of having reacted more violently than anyone else against indulgences and against usury, Luther helped prepare the metaphysical misalliance between economic self-interest and church affiliation so prominent in the Western world. Martin had become the metaphysical jurist of his father's class.

This is the Luther known to most, and quoted most in sociological treatises of our time by authors from Weber[26] to Fromm.[27] These treatises quickly proceed from cursory biographic sketches of Luther to the Reformation at large, as personified in Calvin and Knox and institutionalized in the various Protestant sects. Tawney sharply contrasts Luther with Calvin, who, impressed in his youth with Luther's writings, was to be the real lawgiver of Protestantism:

> Luther's utterances on social morality are the occasional explosions of a capricious volcano, with only a rare flash of light amid the torrent of smoke and flame, and it is idle to scan them for a coherent and consistent doctrine. . . . His sermons and pamphlets on social questions make an impression of naivete, as of an impetuous but ill-informed genius, dispensing with the cumbrous embarrassments of law and logic, to evolve a system of social ethics from the inspired heat of his own unsophisticated consciousness. It was partly that they were *pièces de circonstance,* thrown off in the storm of a revolution, partly that it was precisely the refinements of law and logic which Luther detested. . . . He is too frightened and angry even to feel curiosity. Attempts to explain the mechanism merely enrage him; he can only repeat that there is a devil in it, and that good Christians will not meddle with the mystery of iniquity. But there is a method in his fury. It sprang, not from ignorance, for he was versed in scholastic philosophy, but from a conception which made the learning of the schools appear trivial or mischievous.[28]

The younger Luther remained the personification of universal rebellion; but the older, the often "frightened and angry" Luther—his reformation remained a provincial one. His theology had announced a Secret Church of all the truly faithful whom only God could know; his reformation led to the all-powerful church-state. His doctrines included Predestination; but his reformation opened the future to petty-bourgeois optimism. His theology was based on the inner experience and the clear expression of meaning it; his influence, in the long run, furthered the humorless and wordy phraseology of "right thinking." His principal recourse was to the Scriptures as perceived in prayer; his own juristic habits made them a legal text rationalizing all kind of practical compromise. Only when other constitutions began to offer healthy competition to the Bible, guaranteeing the individual rights which Luther had helped secularize only against his will and intention, did Protestantism make its contribution to a way of life at times singularly free from terror. But with this contribution went developments for which moral philosophers like Kierkegaard, who saw in Luther the potentially truest religious figure since Christ and Paul, could not forgive him.

Hypersensitive Kierkegaard, another melancholy Dane, had to live in a Protestant monarchy which is one of the smallest and best-fed, best-natured, and most self-satisfied nations in the world, and does not easily betray the chronic melancholy underlying its mandatory happiness. Philosophically, Kierkegaard had to do again all that Luther had done; but he deliberately remained a philosopher without a country and without a family. "For a few years of his life," he wrote about Luther, "he was the salt of the earth; but his later life is not free of the staleness of which his tabletalks are an illustration: a man of God, who sits in small-bourgeois coziness, surrounded by admiring followers who believe that if he lets go of a fart, it must be a revelation, or the result of an inspiration. . . . Luther has lowered the standards of a reformer, and has helped create in later generations that pack, that damned pack of nice, hearty people, who would all like to play at being reformers. . . . Luther's later life has accredited mediocrity."[29] Kierkegaard blames two trends for this calamity, which now we can claim to understand better: first, that Luther spent himself in attacks on one high office and, in an increasingly personal fashion, on the officeholder, the Pope, thus diverting energy from the true object of reformatory fervor—the evil in man's soul; and secondly, that as a reformer, Luther was forever *against* something, and therefore was supported by those who (as Burckhardt also said pointedly) "would rather *not* have to do this or that any more" (*gerne einmal etwas nicht mehr wollen*).[30] "Luther," said Kierkegaard, "in a certain sense, made it too easy for himself. He should have known that the freedom for which he fought (and in this fight itself he was right) is apt to make life, the life of the spirit, immeasurably more strenuous than it had been before. If he had held to this, nobody would have held with him, and he would have been given the taste of the great Double-Danger. Nobody holds with another just to make his own life more strenuous."[31] As Kierkegaard saw it, Luther did not concentrate enough energy on the refinement of those introspective steps which he had outlined in the lectures on the Psalms; and he spent too much venom in a personal animosity and contrariness against his enemies and, above all, against the Pope. Luther, incidentally, was quite aware of his excessive vindictiveness; but he argued that at least he was not needling in a poisonous fashion, that he poked only with pigs' pokes which did not leave any wounds, and that, at any rate he was not as bad as the "*Koenig von Engellandt*"[32] [Henry VIII].

Is it not shocking, however, that even a Danish philosopher can think of no better simile than an anal one to criticize Luther's private verbosity? Luther would probably not have felt criticized; he had said himself, and proudly, that a wind in Wittenberg, if occasioned by him, could be smelled in Rome. . . .

*Notes*

[1] James, *Varieties of Religious Experience,* 348.

[2] Charles Beard, *Martin Luther and the Reformation in Germany* (London, Philip Green, 1896), 231.

[3] *L.W.W.A.*, [Martin Luther, *Werke* (Weimarer Ausgabe, 1883)] VIII, 203.

[4] Enders, II, 432-33.

[5] Enders, III, 73.

[6] *Works of Martin Luther* (Philadelphia, A. J. Holman Co., 1916), II, 400.

[7] Bainton, Ref. 7, Chapter III, 186.

[8] Nietzsche, Ref. 32, Chapter III, VII, 216.

[9] Jacob Grimm, *Vorrede zur Deutschen Grammatik,* 1, 1822, 11 (quoted in Bornkamm, Ref. 31, Chapter II, 176-77).

[10] *Ibid.,* 40.

[11] *L.W.W.A.*, XXX, 1, 436; translated by Gordon Rupp in *The Righteousnes of God* (London, Hodder and Stoughton, 1953), 293.

[12] *L.W.W.A.*, XXVIII, 142.

[13] Will Durant, *The Reformation* (New York, Simon and Schuster, 1957), 378.

[14] Ref. 6, IV, 206-207.

[15] "The Twelve Articles," *ibid.,* IV, 210-16.

[16] *Ibid.,* III, 211-12.

[17] *L.W.W.A.*, XVIII, 386.

[18] *L.W.W.A.*, XXVIII, 286.

[19] Smith, Ref. II, Chapter II, 165.

[20] Pascal, Ref. 27, Chapter II, 178.

[21] See the chapter on Hitler in *Childhood and Society.*

[22] *L.W.W.A.*, III, 1, 70.

[23] Pascal, 187.

[24] *L.W.W.A.*, XXXI, 1, 196.

[25] *L.W.W.A.*, IV, 274.

[26] Max Weber, Ref. 29, Chapter II.

[27] Erich Fromm, *Escape from Freedom* (New York, Rinehart and Co., 1941).

[28] Tawney, Ref. 30, Chapter II, 88-89.

[29] Kierkegaard, Ref. 1, Chapter I, XI, 44, No. 61.

[30] Quoted in Bornkamm, Ref. 31, Chapter II, 57.

[31] Kierkegaard, Ref. 1, Chapter I, X, 401, No. 559.

[32] *L.W.W.A.*, X, 2, 237.

**Gerhard Ebeling (essay date 1964)**

SOURCE: "The Way Luther Speaks of God," in *Luther: An Introduction to His Thought*, translated by R. A. Wilson, Fortress Press, 1970, pp. 242-67.

[*In the following excerpt from a work originally published in 1964, Ebeling describes how Luther's conception of an "omnipresent" God shaped his faith.*]

There is something challenging about the way Luther speaks of God. We cannot turn to his works without our own way of speaking about God faltering or falling silent or being brought into question, or without doubt being cast upon it. This implies that Luther's way of speaking of God expresses more than an ordinary degree of personal involvement, and therefore also involves us. All consideration of historical data in some respects involves the participation of the observer, so that the false ideal of a 'purely historical' consideration is neither possible nor desirable. In the same way, what has been said about God and handed down in tradition is even less capable of being dealt with by a 'purely historical consideration'. For to speak of God implies his essential presence, and this is true even of the statement 'God is dead', as can be seen from the way Nietzsche asserts the presence of the slain God: 'Do we still smell nothing of the divine putrefaction?'[1]

At a time when it has become exceedingly difficult to defend any attempt to speak about God, the decisiveness with which Luther spoke of God acts as a challenge—though he did not speak of him with an ill-considered facility, but with the utmost readiness to defend what he was doing, and with a certainty which seems completely alien to our problem of the vindication of any attempt to speak about God.

One might attempt to explain this on the basis of the change in basic assumptions which has taken place since then. Luther lived at a time—it might be argued—in which the word 'God' was still understandable without further discussion, and the claim it implied, together with the right to speak of God, was taken for granted. In spite of this, of course, or strictly speaking because of this, what was said of God was so much the subject of dispute that virtually all other disputed matters at that period were attracted by and drawn into the dispute about God, which took place in the denominational schisms and conflicts. All shared the assumption that the existence of God could be taken for granted, and besides this, there was a virtually undisputed recognition of the doctrine of the Trinity and of the Incarnation of the Son of God according to the testimony of the holy scripture and the Church. On this basis, in fact, a conflict arose which to this day cannot be regarded by Western Christianity as having been solved. Nevertheless, the situation has fundamentally changed, in that it is evident that the automatic assumption of the validity not only of the Christian idea of God, but of the idea of God as a whole, has finally and irrevocably ceased to be accepted.

It is true that proper distinctions must be made, in order to avoid a rough-and-ready argument on the basis of the automatic assumption of the existence of God at that period and the disappearance of such an assumption at the present day. But this does not alter the basic fact that not merely popular opinion but theology itself proceeded at that period from this automatic assumption, and as it were 'counted on it'. Scholasticism included the acceptance of the existence of God amongst the so-called *praeambula fidei,* that is, as something which was not in the strict sense the object of faith, because it was already evident to the apprehension of natural reason. Luther too was able to ascribe to all men either by nature, or by virtue of a universal tradition difficult to distinguish from nature, a knowledge of God, which was a knowledge of his existence, although not a knowledge of his will (he did not classify this knowledge of God in the dogmatic category of a *praeambulum fidei*). On the other hand, simultaneously with the virtual disappearance of the automatic assumption of the existence of God, modern Protestant theology from Schleiermacher to Karl Barth has made an increasingly radical attempt to eliminate any idea of a natural theology, although it has not adequately taken into account the consequences of so doing.

All the same, it is not possible to equate or even to confuse the automatic assumption of the existence of God, in however restricted a form, with the firm decisiveness of Luther's way of speaking about God. This forms a challenge to modern man, but did so to Erasmus as well, and is remarkable also by contrast with the scholastic tradition. This decisiveness is manifested in discussing matters which are not automatically self-evident, in so far as 'self-evident' is understood in the trivial sense of the knowledge of immediately obvious facts, which it would be superfluous and a mere waste of words to discuss. 'What is not self-evident', of which Luther speaks so decisively in his language about God, does not mean any arbitrary matter, but what can only be said of God, and therefore what can only be said because it comes from God, can only be understandable through him, and is, therefore, in a profound sense 'self'-evident because it provides in itself the only assurance of its truth. But this must be stated, confessed and asserted in *words*. It therefore requires to be spoken, and so appears in two aspects: it must be spoken with decisiveness, because it can only be *spoken;* and it needs to be spoken with *decisiveness*.

That Luther lays such an emphasis on the mode of speech and therefore on the situation that comes about in speech, follows from the substance of what is spoken. This cannot be derived from Luther's temperament or special charisma. We can ignore his person except in so far as it was given to him to realize with great force that one can only speak of God in form of a decisive assertion. Erasmus found Luther's categorical style a source of offence. Luther reproached him: 'It is not the way of a Christian heart to fail to delight in decisive assertions; rather, one must delight in them, or one is not a Christian . . . Sceptics and academics are far from us Christians, but those are welcome to us, who, twice as obstinately as the Stoics themselves, present what they have to say with decisiveness. Tell me, how often did the apostle Paul insist on *plerophoria,* full assurance, that is, assertion with the utmost certainty, as firm as a rock to the conscience? . . . Nothing is better known and more familiar to a Christian than decisive assertion. Do away with decisive assertions, and you have taken away Christianity . . . The Holy Spirit is not a sceptic and has not written doubtful matters and mere opinions in our hearts, but decisive assertions which are more certain and sure than life itself and all experience.'[2]

These utterances concerning the appropriate way to speak of God naturally go much further than the mere assertion of God's existence. On the one hand they extend to the whole of Christian doctrine, and on the other hand they recognize that human existence is drawn into it and is involved in it. But it would not be accurate to say of Luther that he developed the basic assertion of the existence of God in these two directions. What seem to be two different issues which are drawn together are in fact a single point. Nothing would be said of God, if the whole of Christian doctrine and man also were not already involved. But the reason for this is that what is at issue in Christian doctrine and also in human existence is nothing other than the basic assertion of the existence of God.

The way Luther speaks of God—and this explains his decisiveness—has both an all-embracing and inclusive tendency, and also a radical and exclusive tendency. The latter, as is well known, finds its expression in the so-called *particula exclusiva,* the word 'alone', which is found in his formulation of the decisive points of his theology, and always has the same purpose of giving pointed utterance to a true theological understanding: 'God alone', 'Christ alone', 'the scripture alone', 'the word alone', 'faith alone'. Of course when the exclusive particle is used in this way its meaning must be precisely elucidated. An unthinking and emotional profession of faith, or an uncomprehending and reckless assertion would be quite out of place in this mode of theological thought. What must be realized is that in spite of the different ways in which it is applied, the recurrent word 'alone' expresses a fundamental theological understanding: that whenever anything is said about God, it must be made fully evident that it is God who is being discussed. But if God is to be spoken of at all, then it is necessary for God's sake to rely on God alone, on Christ alone, on the scripture alone, on the word alone, and on faith alone; that is, one must exclude everything which prevents God from being God, and which gives an opportunity of speaking of theological matters in an untheological or pseudo-theological way.

But this exclusive tendency, which concentrates everything upon a single issue, is not modified and compensated by an opposed tendency to an all-inclusive comprehensiveness; this would be meaningless. For the point of the exclusive particle itself is to discuss everything in a single light, rather than isolating individual aspects. No less characteristic of Luther's theological thought than the term 'alone' is the apparently contradictory, but, if properly understood, closely associated term 'at the same time', which is likewise used in various ways, and is best known in the formula, 'righteous and a sinner at the same time'. One could term it the *particula inclusiva,* which does not weaken the sense of the *particula exclusiva,* but clarifies it and makes it more precise.

It will scarcely be disputed that the use of the particle 'alone' expresses the distinctive nature and also the decisiveness of Luther's way of speaking about God. Proceeding from this, however, his power of drawing everything together into a single theme is also a characteristic of his way of speaking of God. Luther does not allow the content of Christian doctrine to be fragmented into a profusion which is coherent only in a positivist and historical sense. It is foolish to deny, as is often done, that he possesses the power of systematic thought. But he displays it not in the summarizing and harmonizing architectural structure of a system of doctrine, nor in the speculative derivation of numerous lines of thought from a single principle, but rather by a critical and a liberating demonstration that God is God indeed, in the language of the biblical tradition. It is a complete misunderstanding of the concentration of Luther's theological thought on the doctrine of justification to regard it as the arbitrary choice of a partial aspect of doctrine, to which he wilfully adds a special emphasis of his own. According to Luther it points to the way in which God can be made God indeed in the whole of Christian doctrine. For the whole of Christian doctrine consists not of a profusion which forms a supplement to the doctrine of God itself, but of the doctrine of God and nothing more. Christian doctrine is a guide to the right way to speak of God.

But from this it is obvious that to the extent that it is God who is being spoken of, man is also involved whenever this takes place and does not have to be brought in later. Similarly, what is said of God does not have to be applied later to man. Thus what is said of God is addressed to man. For how could it be possible to speak of God if what was said were not the direct concern of man? But if what is said of God possesses certainty, then it brings certainty with it when it is addressed to someone. This is not a formal aspect which is additional to the concept of what is said of God, nor is it merely one partial aspect, which is present in so far as God has to do with man. For Luther certainty is the essence of God's being with man and therefore of man's being with God. In the presence of God, and there alone, there is no uncertainty. But uncertainty is man's sin, and certainty is salvation.

We began by observing the decisive way in which Luther spoke of God. From this we were able to see the vast extent of what he has to say of God; and at the same time we saw this whole vast extent gathered together into a single point. This justified the hope of seeing the essence of Luther's theology in what he says of God, and moreover, of being able to apprehend what he says of God from a single point of view. Finally, if in this way we have attained to the very heart of all Luther says about God, he can help us, in spite of our different situation, to answer the problem which faces us at present, of how to vindicate any attempt to speak of God. When he was a theological student, only twenty-five years old, Luther expressed the view in a letter that the only theology which was of any value was that which penetrated the kernel of the nut and the germ of the wheat and the marrow of the bones.[3]

By beginning with the decisive way in which Luther speaks of God, we have in fact already arrived at the kernel of the nut. All that is necessary is a more precise and penetrating statement, to give us as it were the basic formula from which it is possible to understand and expound how the attempt to speak of God can be vindicated. This basic formula is as follows: *God and faith belong together*. This follows from the whole structure of Luther's theology, and does not require a detailed demonstration. We shall nevertheless give an example of it from a particular text, which because of its original purpose is of particular importance, and must be regarded as having been formulated with great care. We can use it as the starting-point of our development of this basic formula. For our further inquiry into the way Luther speaks of God will consist of nothing other than the further consideration of this basic formula; and of how far the fact that God and faith belong together enables us to understand what God is.

The text is found in the 'Greater Catechism' at the beginning of the exposition of the first commandment: '"You shall have no other gods." That is, you shall regard me alone as your God. What does this mean, and how is one to understand it? What does it mean to have a god, or what is God? Answer: A god is that on which one should rely for everything good, and with which one can take refuge in every need. Thus to have a god is nothing other than to trust and to believe in him from the heart—or, as I have often said, that only trust and faith in the heart make both God and a false god. If your faith and trust is right, then your God is right as well, and again, where the belief is false and wrong, then the right God is absent too. For the two belong together, faith and God. So that to which you give up and hand over your heart is truly your God.[4]

We will admit at once how dangerous this text is. While our first approach, to the decisive way in which Luther speaks of God, gave us the impression that he is very remote from the spirit of the present day, in this passage he seems strangely close to us. One could almost imagine that one was listening to Ludwig Feuerbach, who taught that God was the projection and product, or even the essence of man; a theology transformed and swallowed up in anthropology! This apparent similarity is confirmed by a demonstrable connection between the two. Feuerbach, who was a theologian himself at first, was thoroughly well-acquainted with Luther's works, and, as a supplement to his work ***The Nature of Christianity*** (***Wesen des Christentums***), published in 1844 a study of 'The Nature of Faith According to Luther'. Not that he simply obliterated the difference: 'No religious doctrine is more consciously and deliberately contrary to human understanding, thought and feeling, than that of Luther. No other seems more firmly to reject the basic idea of ***The Nature of Christianity***, and no other provides such evidence of the origin of what it contains outside and above man; for how could he arrive of himself at a doctrine which degrades and humbles man to the utmost degree, and which in the sight of God at least, that is before the highest and therefore the only decisive court of appeal, denies him all honour, all merit, all virtue, all willpower, all value and trustworthiness, all reason and understanding whatsoever? This is how it seems; but what seems to be is not necessarily the case.'[5] Feuerbach implies that in his very opposition to Luther he can appeal to Luther himself, and to the real consequences of his basic ideas.

Theologians have been horrified at the thesis of Feuerbach, that the mystery of theology is anthropolgy. In the desire to defend theology against the destructive tendencies of modern psychology and historicism, they have turned to their task anew, and this has meant a change from an anthropocentric to a theocentric theology. Karl Barth in particular has led the struggle against even the most disguised tendency on the part of theology to turn to anthropology—quite rightly, in so far as it really represents the abandonment of the true theme of theology in the sense of the exclusive 'alone' of the Reformation. Certainly, under the influence of Feuerbach's interpretation of Luther, Barth became suspicious of Luther[6] and came to believe it necessary to seek the methodological foundation of his dogmatic theology not in Luther but in Anselm of Canterbury, in order to restore an objective basis to theology.

It has been necessary at least to hint at the heated dispute in which we become involved if we attempt to go deeper into the meaning of what Luther says about God, under the guidance of his statement that 'faith and God belong together.' We cannot embark at length upon a dialogue with Feuerbach and Barth. We must restrict ourselves to a mere outline of what is contained in this conjunction of God and faith, and there are three guiding principles which will provide our starting-point. What God is can be made clear by interpreting this basic formula in the light of the phrases 'God alone', 'through faith alone', and 'through the word alone'.

1. The very passage in which Luther gives the most precise definition of what he means by 'God alone', in his exposition of the first commandment, is that which contains his suspicious association between God and faith. At a point where everything should be concentrated upon authority and unconditional obedience, Luther, regardless of the fact that the word 'God' is something which he is supposed to be able to take for granted, stresses the question of *understanding:* 'What does this mean, and how is one to understand it? What does it mean to have a god, or what is God?' It seems immediately suspicious that he should combine the question of the meaning of 'to have a god' and that of the being of God, and should attempt to answer both simultaneously. Surely it is necessary to affirm what God *is* before it is possible to say what it means to *have* him? Surely the being of God must be laid down and clarified before dealing with the question of 'letting God be God'? Surely it is the fundamental definition of the nature of God that nothing precedes him, that nothing imposes any conditions upon him, that he alone is the origin of all things, and that, as is expressed by the technical term 'aseity', he derives his being from himself?

It would be nonsense to try and impute to Luther the denial or watering-down of this idea, and to interpret the phrase 'that only trust and faith in the heart make both God and a false God' in such a sense that man becomes the creator and God the creature. But the idea of the aseity, the underived existence of God is not sufficient in itself to maintain with the utmost rigour that to be God and to be the creator are identical, and to be man and to be a creature are identical. The implications of the idea have not been fully considered as long as one fails to take into account the fact that man himself is involved in thinking and uttering this idea. This does not mean that it is justifiable to jump to the conclusion that this implies the dependence of God upon man, in such a way that the assertion of the aseity of God would be a logical contradiction. For the very aim and purpose of the idea of aseity is to define the position of the creature and of man. Without this specific application there would be nothing left of the idea of aseity. The emphasis on the independence of God from man is addressed to man.

The objection to such metaphysical statements about the nature of God is not so much to what they say, but rather to what they conceal as the result of a deficient doctrine of the understanding, an unsound hermeneutic theory. The objection lies in the significance for *what* is said of the fact that it is *said.* No account is taken of the fact that the metaphysical theorist is not suspended in a no-man's-land between God and the world. He is himself affected by what he thinks, and addresses what he says to his fellow-men, and therefore he ought to give consideration to the significance of the assertion of God's aseity on the concrete process of its utterance. The aseity of God thought out in abstract terms is in fact self-contradictory, because it is dependent on the abstract independence and individuality of man, who carries out the process of abstraction. Ignoring the question of whether metaphysics suffers in any essential respect from this short-sighted theory of the understanding, it ought at least to be clear that the question 'What is God?' is not being conducted along false lines, but in the only adequate way, when God is spoken of and understood as the absolute concern of man and is considered with regard to the way in which he is the absolute concern of man.

Thus we are concerned not with a proof of God's existence, something which at least in the conventional sense is directly contradictory to the divinity of God, but with a demonstration of the reason why man is addressed whenever anything is said about God. The purpose is not to *derive* the being of God from the being of man, but to *direct* man towards the situation in which he can understand what is said of God. This situation is not one which is essentially alien to his nature—in which case it would be a baseless fantasy to speak of God—but is a situation which decisively affects him, and in which he already finds himself.

The word 'faith' refers to this basic human situation. It would be an inadequate if not a misleading explanation of the statement that faith and God belong together, to say that because God is invisible and beyond experience we have to make do with faith, as a substitute as it were. For this would fail to explain what obligation or right there is to do this at all, and in what situation faith, understood as a substitute for knowledge, can be regarded as something necessary.

If one examines this problem, it becomes clear that it is possible to understand how far faith brings knowledge with it, not in the bad sense of uncertain conjecture or a mere probable opinion but as a rock-like certainty, only on the basis of the situation in which man is driven to seek certainty. Luther says simply: 'In every need'. Thus the nature of faith is that of a knowledge which brings help, salvation, courage, hope and relief in need. Accordingly, what is said of God tells man that he is obliged to wait and hope, that he is concerned with what still lies beyond him, outside his control, so that man is always reaching out beyond himself and is drawn outside himself and beyond his own control. He cannot avoid this sallying out beyond himself, this attempt to make uncertainty certain, which Luther calls hanging his heart on something; he must have something to rely on, to trust and to believe. This situation always exists. Consequently, it is the basic human situation, although the degree to which it is palpable and obvious varies greatly. We shall not analyse it in detail, but we must warn against one or two misunderstandings which readily arise.

It can appear as though God is now made a substitute for our power, just as it was suggested before that faith might be seen as a substitute for our knowledge. But it must be noted that the emphasis is not on flight *from* need, but on a refuge *in* need, not upon a change in circumstances, but on a changed attitude to the circumstances, not on the affirmation that the saving action has taken effect, but on certainty with regard to an effect which is still to come and is still awaited. Nevertheless, the suspicion still lingers that this is a theology which only brings in God to satisfy a human need. But one must be cautious in advancing this objection. It would be a dangerous theology which was *not* orientated towards human need and therefore towards the aspect of necessity.

Of course everything here depends upon the proper understanding of what is absolutely necessary and therefore on the apprehension of what true faith and trust is. Only a superficial view can suppose that it is possible to escape the question of truth by approaching the matter from the point of view of human need. Luther gives offence by seeming to stand the relationship between faith and God upon its head: 'If faith and trust are right, then your God is right as well, and again, where the belief is false and wrong, then the right God is absent too.' But it must be pointed out that it is in purity of faith, that is, in the radical degree to which the situation of faith is maintained, that it can be seen whether God is taken seriously as God, or whether he is furtively avoided and replaced by idols of man's own making. In his lectures on the Epistle to the Romans Luther says of the love of God that it is exclusively directed towards the one God alone, and not towards his gifts. Thus its place is where there is nothing visible or accessible to experience, either inwardly or outwardly, in which one can place one's trust, or which one can love or fear; but it is drawn beyond everything else to the invisible and incomprehensible God, beyond experience, and hidden in the innermost darkness.[7] Here, though still with borrowings from the language of mysticism, the meaning of the way in which faith and God belong together is clearly set out. It is no accident that the context of what is said of God is one in which there is only a hair's breadth distinction between it and every from of idolatry. To let God be God, that is to believe rightly, means not to make gods for oneself in any way, but above all to allow oneself to be deprived of deity and brought to nothing, so that one is hurled outside oneself and the whole creation into nothingness, and one is certain of having fallen into the hands of God.[8] That faith and God belong together is the theology of the cross, a theology not based on human wishes, but upon the will of God.

2. We have spent some time in discussing the text from the 'Greater Catechism' with reference to our first guiding principle, 'God alone'. That God and faith belong together is in no sense contrary to the principle of 'God alone', but is what actually makes it possible. For only to faith is God alone of value, and God is God in that he desires nothing but faith. Thus the second guiding principle, 'by faith alone', is already implied in the first. But it must be evaluated on its own if we are to make any progress with the question, 'What is God?' For until we come to this principle, the answer is largely a negative one: God takes away the power of false gods as faith takes away the power of superstition. And just as faith is a trust which reaches out into the darkness, so God is the presence, affirmed in spite of every experience of his absence, of the one being who is worthy of faith, never disappoints, never fails, and deserves total reliance. But what kind of knowledge of God is implied by faith in the strict sense?

In Luther's longer series of lectures on the Epistle to the Galatians we read: 'See what faith is—something incomparable and of immeasurable power, that is, to give honour to God. It does not do something for God; but because it believes, faith accords wisdom, goodness and omnipotence to God, and imputes everything divine to him. Faith is the creator of deity, not in person, but in us. Apart from faith, God loses his righteousness, glory, riches, etc., and there is no majesty or deity where there is no faith. You see what great righteousness faith is . . . God demands only that I make him God. If he possesses his deity pure and unspotted, then he has everything that I can accord him. This is the wisdom beyond all wisdom, religion beyond all religion. This is what makes the highest majesty, which faith bestows upon God. That is why faith justifies; for it pays what it owes, and whoever does this is righteous.'[9] This again is put in a very bold and paradoxical way. Yet is it not in fact paradoxical that man should be called to honour God, and to give him what God alone has of himself, that is, to give God what is divine? But what is called faith creates the divine in man, which man accords to God. The creative power of faith—Luther terms it, with unsurpassed boldness, *creatrix divinitatis*—means nothing other than that faith is not the work of man, but the work of God, or as Luther says in a play on words, not a *facere Deo* (something done for God) but *facere Deum* (making God). But this means nothing less than to let God act, to let God be God, to do justice to God through faith alone. If one takes God seriously, one cannot attain to God by an action, but through faith alone, or shall we say, by delighting in God. The only adequate way to speak of God is in praising him, not in the sense of a particular literary form, but as the basic definition of all proper speech about God.

Then why does Luther adopt such paradoxical turns of phrase? Not because he confuses delight in God with delight in paradox; but because to speak of God is to speak of something that happens, of the way in which God establishes himself as God, and finds faith. One cannot as it were first speak of God in himself, disregarding the actual situation of the way God is dishonoured, even in religion itself, and excluding the question of how God obtains his rights. In this world, in fact, God is humiliated and insulted, seeks his honour only by calling for faith, and desires to be honoured through faith alone. What is at issue is not the description of passive attributes, such as what God is in himself, what man is in himself, and how they are related. What is said of God is concerned with something that happens, of which what is said itself forms part. This is the key to the understanding of Luther's work ***De servo arbitrio*** (***The Bondage of the Will***), which could equally be called *De Deo*. Because God is being spoken of, so must man be spoken of. For self-knowledge and the knowledge of God form a unity, and the reason for this is that they are both concerned with an inseparable association which consists of something that *happens*. To know God means to know what God can and does do, not his power and his potentialities, but his power as it is actually at work in everything that exists, an omnipotence that is active.[10] But if man has to know, for the sake of his salvation and his certainty, what he is capable of with regard to his salvation, then he evidently knows neither what he is capable of, nor what God is, until he knows for certain that he can *do nothing* towards his salvation. And that very inability permits him to be certain of salvation, which is based upon the act of God alone. One can have no inkling of God, if one has not a clear understanding of the problem of the bondage of the will in matters of salvation. To engage in a dialogue with God on the basis of the will is godless. Thus it is necessary for salvation to be able to distinguish between the action of God and the action of man, not in order to weigh one against the other as cooperating forces, but to make a fundamental distinction between them. By contrast with man, God is an unlimited force, whereas by contrast with God, man cannot be considered as one who acts, however much action may be demanded from him in the sight of God towards the world. Man's understanding of himself in relation to God only does justice to God if man regards himself as one who has been made what he is, as one who is subject to God's will, has received all he has as a gift, and is therefore a creature, righteous not by works, but through faith alone.[11] Only when man lays claim to freedom of action before God is man radically enslaved; by understanding himself as the work of God, that is through faith, he becomes free, participating, as one who belongs to God, in the freedom of God.

3. We turn now to the question of what takes place in the conjunction of God and faith, how God can be honoured, and how faith can come about. The answer we receive from Luther is, *through the word alone*. This answer provokes numerous questions. We shall reduce them to three fundamental objections to the way Luther speaks of God, which must now be raised and considered as the conclusion of our study. Is not the word too little? How far does the course of history matter? What is the place of our fellow-men?

The first objection is, *is the word not too little?* 'Through the word alone' forms a strict parallel to 'by faith alone'.[12] In both these principles Luther is radically opposed to scholastic theology and Roman Catholic doctrine, which in fact allege here that 'the word alone' is 'too little', that a mere 'verbal revelation' is replacing a 'revelation of reality', to quote the slogans of modern controversial theology,[13] and that mere faith takes the place of perfection through a real change in man. Thomas Aquinas based the precedence of love amongst the so-called theological virtues, faith, love and hope, on the assertion that, like hope, faith also implied a separation from its object, that is, from God, whereas love united one with the beloved.[14] This shows with great clarity the difference between the denominations. By contrast to an understanding of God, the aim of which is the perfection of nature until it is supernatural, Luther's view is that in fact the overriding action which derives from God can take place in a way appropriate to God and to faith through the word alone. In this way the basis of salvation remains strictly outside man as a promise which is believed. Indeed, man himself is drawn out of himself towards the word of Christ. The word must guarantee that faith is *extra nos;* this is essential if what is said of God is to be certain. Luther says: 'Our theology is certain, for it places us outside ourselves.'[15] The word makes it possible to distinguish between God and man and to maintain this distinction. To desire more than the word alone would result in having less. For what God gives to man for his salvation can be imparted essentially and effectively only through the word. 'One thing and that alone is needful for life, for righteousness and for Christian freedom. That is the holy word of God, the gospel of Christ . . . We should regard it as certain and irreversible: the soul can do without everything except the word of God, without which nothing at all is of any use to us. But who ever possesses the word is rich and needs nothing, for it is the word of life, of truth, of light, of peace, of righteousness, of salvation, of joy, of freedom, of wisdom, of power, of grace, of glory and of everything good, in an inestimable way . . . But since these promises of God are holy, true, righteous, free and peaceable words, and are full of pure goodness, it comes about that the soul which clings to them with firm faith is so united, or even absorbed by them, that it does not merely partake in them, but becomes sated and drunk with all their power . . . As the word is, so it makes the soul.'[16]

The second question is, *how far does the course of history matter*? Luther's way of speaking of God can be suspected of implying a radical retreat into the inner life and spiritualization, which, if it does not abandon the relationship between God and the world, God and history and God and living reality, does not seem to take adequate account of them. One ought not to be too hasty in qualifying this impression, which is caused by the fact that what Luther says of God is concentrated to an extraordinary degree upon the conscience. 'Conscience', of course, does not mean what it means in the usual but questionable interpretation of the conscience as the essence of the normative contents of the consciousness and of the autonomous faculties of judgement, that is, the presence of the decisive norm and appeal within man himself. Rather, what Luther understands by 'conscience' is the reliance of man upon the word, in the sense that he is always, and not merely in some particular respect but in his very person, claimed, commanded, questioned, and subjected to judgement, so that in one way or another he is always a determined, listening and receiving conscience; either confused or arrogant in an imaginary freedom, which means his bondage to the powers of this world; or assured and comforted in obedient attention to God, which is true freedom with regard to the world. This understanding of the conscience is decisive for the understanding of what Luther says of God. For it makes clear that the sole aim of the apparent retreat into the inner life and spiritualization, is to locate what is said of God at the point where a universal event in the strictest sense takes place, and God and the world, and God and Satan, struggle with one another like two riders struggling to possess their mount.[17] Thus the concentration on the conscience is a concentration upon the process in which the most powerful and most strictly opposed powers that exist are at work, a process which, precisely because it is centred upon the hidden heart of man, gives rise to the most powerful consequences in his outward and visible life.

It is therefore essential to Luther's way of speaking of God, concentrating as it does upon faith alone and the word alone, not to understand God as something which exists in a remote place, outside and beyond the world, and which has nothing to do with the everyday experience of the world. On the contrary: if the word is to be believed, and faith is to be brought about by the word, then God and the world must be thought of simultaneously and together in such a way that there can sometimes be a suspicion of pantheist or even atheist language. With an amazing freedom Luther subjected theological argument in naïve theistic terms to a ruthless criticism, condemning it as rationalism disguised as devotion. Thus he says of the conception of heaven: 'The deity does not come down from heaven, like someone from a mountain, but is in heaven and remains in heaven, but at the same time is upon earth and remains upon earth . . . Is there any need to discuss this at length? Surely the kingdom of heaven is upon earth. The angels are both in heaven and upon earth at once. Christians are both in the kingdom of God and upon earth, in the sense in which "on earth" is understood, as they say, *mathematice* or *localiter* . . . Ah, they speak childishly and foolishly about heaven, making a place for Christ up above in heaven, like the stork makes a nest upon a tree, and they do not know themselves what they are saying.'[18] Or again, with regard to the concept of God's omnipresence: ' . . . as though God were a great and vast being who filled the world and extended beyond it, as when a sack is full of straw, and the straw sticks out at the top and the bottom.'[19] Luther portrayed the omnipresence and omnipotence of God with such perception, that in the way he speaks of God it is impossible to ignore the reality of the world. 'Thus he [God] must himself be in every creature at its very heart and in every way, all about, through and through, above and below, before and behind, so that there can be nothing more present or more deep-rooted in all creatures than God himself with his power . . . Indeed, who knows what it is that is called God? He is above the body, above the mind, above everything that one can say, or hear or think: How can such a being at the same time be wholly and entirely present in every body, creature and being everywhere, and again be bound to be and able to be nowhere, outside and above every creature and being; for our faith and the scripture testify both things of God. Here reason must give up at once and say, "Alas, there is certainly no such thing, and there must be no such thing!"'[20] 'God is not an extended, long, broad, thick, high, or deep being . . . but a supernatural and inscrutable being, who at the same time is wholly and entirely in every grain of corn, and yet is in and above and outside every creature. Thus there is no need for any fence to be built round him . . . for a body is far too great for the deity, and many thousands of deities could be contained in it, and yet it is far too small, for not a single deity could find room in it. Nothing is so small that God is not smaller, and nothing is so large that God is not larger, nothing is so short that God is not shorter, nothing is so long that God is not longer, nothing is so wide that God is not wider, nothing is so narrow that God is not narrower, and so on; he is an ineffable being above and beyond everything that one can name or think.'[21]

This presence of God in the world, which goes far beyond the conventional alternative between transcendence and immanence, and which it shows to be a completely mistaken approach to the question, is also true of history. God's omnipotence is the power at work in everything, and without it nothing would exist and nothing would happen. The rigour with which

Luther maintains this idea sometimes suggests the horrible conception that God is the motor in a gigantic machine which it would be impossible to stop, even if the men were cleared away from it and carried out to die, unless one blasphemously desired God to cease to be God.[22] It is not Luther's intention to lose sight of the difficult problems that arise here. For the sake of God and of faith he does not with to conceal them nor to leave it to the blasphemers to stir them up.

For in truth, if God is seen in his naked majesty and encountered in his concealment, which is the same thing, and the attempt is made to understand him as God, God presents the same fearful countenance which reality ultimately displays if one encounters it without God's word and without faith, and tries to think about it. The result is unrelieved despair, idolatry or atheism. But these are not fundamentally different alternatives. Luther can do not more than warn against undertaking speculation about God in his majesty, in his concealment. It is necessary to speak of God from below, beginning in the depths with the fact that the word of God became flesh, became history, and gave the power to carry out the act of preaching; that is, the starting-point must be Jesus, the crucified.[24] Of course to turn away from the hidden God and to turn towards the revealed God does not mean that the concealment of God is no longer the concern of faith. For revelation itself is concealed beneath its contrary, beneath the cross.[25] Faith is only faith because it is exposed to the forces of temptation. Consequently, it is necessary to speak of the *Deus absconditus,* in order that the revealed God may be taken seriously as God in his revelation.[26]

The last question, that of *the place of our fellow-men in what is said of God,* arises from the idea that the thought of Luther is preoccupied with a religious individualism which is concerned only with the blessedness of the individual. It is suggested that it is to this that the doctrine of justification owes its central place in Luther's theology. To answer this objection, it would be necessary to go on to consider Luther's ethics and his doctrine of the Church. We shall limit ourselves, however, to one fundamental point. Luther's ethics and his doctrine of the Church—in so far as one can use these academic classifications at all, since Luther always sees all aspects as they are involved with each other—are not as it were complementary to what he says about God, but can only be understood in their proper sense as ways of speaking about God. But it then becomes obvious, with regard to both points, how a concentration upon the word and faith which is apparently orientated entirely towards the individual also includes our fellow-men in its scope. The word which creates faith, the word of the gospel, deals with the law which accuses and slays, and therefore it deals with man under the pressure of his existence in the world, the decisive and determining aspect of which is his involvement with his fellow-men. The basic experience of man is that a demand is always being made upon him, and that he is constantly aware of having failed, and the claim which the gospel makes upon man is a response to this, a response to the voice of the law. Consequently, the expression 'in every need' in the 'Greater Catechism' is primarily exemplified in man's unfulfilled common humanity, the disappointments he has suffered and caused, and his inability to overcome hatred, to arouse trust, or to love creatively. It is the need brought about by his failure to be what he really ought to be as God's creature: the image of God who has shared our humanity. If the essence of the gospel is that God shares our humanity, then faith can do nothing other than be effective in love. Faith is really no less than the courage to love on the basis of love received in faith, the freedom to love on the basis of the liberating promise of love.

But on no account must the distinction between faith and love laid down here be obscured. Because, as Luther says, faith is the doer and love the deed,[27] everything depends upon the source of the doer's life. Consequently the relationship between faith and love corresponds to the relationship between doctrine and life. Life is usually given precedence over doctrine, but instead Luther gives the pre-eminence to doctrine, precisely for the sake of the life created and desired by God. Doctrine is heaven, life is the earth.[28] For doctrine, the word of God, is, to put it briefly, the bread of life.

Thus with regard to the Church, our humanity is not displayed in the first instance in the manifestations of the common life of the Church, but in the fundamental event which makes the Church into the Church, the word of faith, which takes place between one person and another, and reveals its divinity by making men human. The community of the Church, which is based upon what takes place in the word, is an indication that true community ultimately lives entirely by the word and by faith. For what takes place in the true word is love. Thus the word of God, by making faith possible, also makes love possible; for—this is the source and the conclusion of all that is said about God—God is love, or as Luther, who was horrified at Erasmus's frigid, ice-cold way of speaking about God,[29] said with the full assurance of ultimate certainty: 'A glowing furnace full of love'.[30]

*Works Cited*

References to the Weimar Edition of Luther's works (*Kritische Gesamtausgabe der Werke D. Martin Luthers,* Weimar, 1883 ff.) are given only by volume, page and line number. References to the selected edition published in Bonn, to the Weimar editions of the German Bible, Luther's Table Talk and his correspondence, and to the English translation of a selection of Luther's works by Bertram Lee Woolf are given as below. The year of each quotation is given in parentheses, and in the case of the letters, the exact date.

Bonn Ed. *Luthers Werke in Auswahl,* ed. by O. Clemen.

WA, Br *Kritische Gesamtausgabe,* etc. (*Briefwechsel*), Weimar Ed. (Correspondence).

*Notes*

1 *Fröhliche Wissenschaft,* p. 125.

2 18; 603, 10-12. 22-24. 28 f. 605, 32-34 (1525); Bonn Ed. 3; 97, 31-33. 98, 6-9. 13-15. 100, 31-33.

3 WA, Br 1; 17, No. 5, 43 f. (17.3.1509). Cf. above, pp. 76 f.

4 30, 1; 132, 32-133, 8 (1529); Bonn Ed. 4; 4, 21-32.

5 *Feuerbachs Sämtliche Werke,* ed. by W. Bolin, and Fr. Jodl, VII (1903), 311.

6 K. Barth, 'Ludwig Feuerbach' (1926). In: K. Barth, *Die Theologie und die Kirche,* 1928, 212-239, esp. 230 f.

7 56; 306, 26-307, 15 (1515/16); Bonn Ed. (2nd Ed.) 5; 250, 10-30.

8 5; 167, 38-168, 7 (1519/21).

9 40, 1; 360, 2-361, 1 (1531).

10 18; 718, 28-31 (1525); Bonn Ed. 3; 214, 11-14.

11 18; 614, 1-26 (1525); Bonn Ed. 3; 106, 25-107, 15.

12 E.g. 6; 516, 30-32 (1520); Bonn Ed. 1; 448, 8-11.

13 W. H. van de Pol, *Das reformatorische Christentum im phänomenologischer Betrachtung,* 1956, 259 ff. Cf. my article 'Worthafte und sakramentale Existenz. Ein Beitrag zum Unterschied zwischen den Konfessionen', in *Im Lichte der Reformation. Jahrbuch des Evangelischen Bundes VI,* 1963, 5-29, esp. 13 ff. Reprinted in my book *Wort Gottes und Tradition. Studien zu einer Hermeneutik der Konfessionen,* 1964, 197-216; an English translation appears under the title 'Word and Sacrament' in *The Word of God and Tradition,* Collins, London, and Fortress Press, Philadelphia, 1968, 206-224.

14 S. th. 1, II q. 66 a. 6.

15 40, 1; 589, 8 (1531). Cf. above, p. 174.

16 7; 50, 33-51, 3. 53, 15-18. 26 f. (1520).

17 18; 635, 17-22 (1525); Bonn Ed. 3; 126, 23-28. Cf. above pp. 222 f.

18 26; 421, 16-422, 10 (1528); Bonn Ed. 3; 445, 32-446, 5.

19 26; 339, 27-29 (1528); Bonn Ed. 3; 404, 20-22.

20 23; 135, 3-6, 137, 25-31 (1527).

21 26; 339, 33-340, 2 (1528); Bonn Ed. 3; 404, 26-38.

22 18; 712, 19-24 (1525); Bonn Ed. 3; 207, 26-32....

24 18; 689, 18-25 (1525); Bonn Ed. 3; 182, 8-17.

25 E.g. 18; 633, 7-23 (1525); Bonn Ed. 3; 124, 16-37.

26 18; 685, 3-686, 13 (1525); Bonn Ed. 3; 177, 12-178, 25.

27 17, 2; 98, 25 (1525). Cf. above p. 159.

28 40, 2; 51, 8 f. (1531). Cf. above pp. 172.

29 18; 611, 5 (1525); Bonn Ed. 3; 104, 27 f.

30 36; 425, 13 (1532).

**Paul Althaus (essay date 1966)**

SOURCE: "The True Church and the Empirical Church," in *The Theology of Martin Luther,* translated by Robert C. Schultz, Fortress Press, 1966, pp. 333-44.

[*In the following excerpt, Althaus explains how Luther used scriptural authority to distinguish between the "true" Church and the exercise of ecclesiastical power.*]

THE AUTHORITY OF TRADITION AND ITS LIMITATION

For Luther the Christian church is, without detriment to its spiritual nature, a historical reality, which constantly existed through all the centuries from the time of the apostles till his own time. The Evangelicals are not another and a new church but "the true old church, one body with the entire holy Christian church, and one community of saints."[1] In spite of all his heartfelt criticism of the Roman Church, Luther remained certain that God had, in spite of everything, miraculously preserved the true church even in the midst of its Babylonian captivity.[2] The Evangelicals received the great Christian inheritance from the hands of the pre-Reformation church—for this inheritance was not lost even under the papacy. "We on our part confess that there is much that is Christian and good under the papacy; indeed, everything that is Christian and good is to be found there and has come to us from this source. For instance, we confess that in the Papal Church there are the true Holy Scriptures, true baptism, the true sacrament of the altar, the true keys to the forgiveness of sins, the true office of the ministry, the true catechism in the form of the Lord's Prayer, the Ten Commandments, and the articles of the Creed."[3] The things which Luther lists are, with the exception of the last, "the articles of the Creed," all biblical material. The fact that he names these together with materials taken directly from the Bible leads us to conclude that he, in spite of many concerns about details, received the creeds of the ancient church as essentially corresponding to biblical truth.[4] He found genuine Christian content in the Roman mass together with what was contrary to the gospel. He expressed this position also in his German mass.[5] In the same way, he adopted a by no means small number of collects which had been written in the Middle Ages. (His translation of them into German was admittedly often a creative reconstruction).[6] And since he includes "many good songs and hymns both Latin and German" in the evidence proving that God preserved the substance of Christianity even in the ancient church,[7] he also introduced these into the German service of worship and into the worship of the evangelical communities. He translated a number of the best Latin hymns and other accepted musical texts from the liturgy and composed them in the form of German songs. ("We are determined to preserve the best Latin songs for particular festivals. They certainly have our heartfelt approval.") In addition, he took the most powerful German songs of the Middle Ages, purified them from unevangelical thoughts, and added some verses to them.[8]

Thus Luther thankfully received not only biblical substance in the direct sense of the term from the hands of the ancient and medieval church but also elements of ecclesiastical tradition. Not the least of these was the church's custom of baptizing children. Since, in Luther's judgment, it is not expressly commanded in the Holy Scriptures, his opposition to the Anabaptists' rejection of infant baptism gave him an opportunity to express himself basically about the authority of tradition in the church.[9] Luther asserts: The consensus of the entire church in a doctrine or a custom is binding insofar as it is not contrary to Scripture. He opposes the spiritualistic interpretation of the Lord's Supper by declaring: "The witness of the entire holy Christian church (even if we had nothing else) should be enough for us to maintain this doctrine and neither to listen to nor tolerate any sectarian objections. For it is dangerous and terrible to hear or believe anything contrary to the common witness, faith, and doctrine which the entire holy Christian church has maintained from the beginning until now—for more than 1500 years throughout all the world."[10]

Luther did not, as is obvious, in any sense advocate an absolute biblicism. He did not absolutize the Bible in opposition to tradition. He limits neither Christian dogma nor the ethical implications of the gospel to what is expressly stated in Scripture. He does not demand that the truth of Christianity be reduced to biblical doctrine. The Holy Spirit led not only the apostles but also Christendom since the time of the apostles. Luther, however, strongly emphasized the difference between the two cases. This establishes the right and the validity of the Christian tradition. It is to be tested only as to whether or not it contradicts the truth of the gospel clearly contained in Scripture. Whatever passes this test should be preserved.

In this sense then, Scripture is the standard of what can and cannot claim to be good tradition of the church. Since Luther emphatically asserts the validity of this standard, his basic affirmation of the church's tradition cannot be unconditional. Rather, it contains the possibility of disagreement. This "no" to tradition is not a basic and universal "no," but is always spoken in a specific situation and based on Scripture. We cannot, however, avoid such rejection of tradition whenever it cannot be harmonized with Scripture because it obviously contradicts it.

Luther himself tells us that he found it bitterly difficult to express this "no." For his confidence in the continuity of the church and the uninterrupted leadership of it through the Holy Spirit were an indispensable part of his faith. His opponents argued against him: "The church, the church: Do you suppose that God is so merciless that he would reject his whole church for the sake of a few Lutheran heretics? Do you suppose that he would leave his church in error for so many centuries?"[11] "Do you really imagine that you are the only one who is wise?"[12] Every rejection of an essential part of the tradition placed the entire historical development of the church, even the entire dogma of the church in question. "The church, the church"—the rallying cry of the pope and of his followers caused Luther considerable inward difficulty. "That blow really strikes home," that is, this constant insistence upon the reality of the church and the power of its truth. As late as 1538 he discusses this temptation in a sermon.[13] The Roman Church claims that it is the true church. And Luther himself cannot deny what he constantly recognized: "The papacy has God's word and the office of the apostles, and we have received the Holy Scriptures, baptism, the sacrament, and the office of preaching from them." Does this not mean that whoever opposes the Roman Church also opposes the church of Christ and Christ himself? This is what the opponents ask and Luther feels it is extremely difficult to deprive them of this argument and to talk them out of it. "Yes, we ourselves find it difficult to refute it. . . . Then there come rushing into my heart thoughts like these: Now I see that I am in error. Oh, if only I had never started this and had never preached a word! For who dares oppose the church, of which we confess in the creed: I believe in a holy Christian church. . . . "

Luther overcame this difficult temptation and decisively attacked ecclesiastical tradition. "No one likes to say that the church is in error; if the church teaches anything in addition to or contrary to God's word, we must say that it is in error."[14] At this point a new problem admittedly arises. What is "God's word?" Luther had to experience opposition to his doctrine and his criticism of tradition that itself was based on Scripture passages. A formal legalistic biblicism would not have been enough to get at his opponents. Luther's ultimate authority and standard was not the book of the Bible and the canon as such but that Scripture which interpreted itself and also criticized itself from its own center: from Christ and from the radically understood gospel. For Luther the authority of Scripture is strictly gospel-centered.[15] One may characterize his attitude in this way: The canon itself was, as far as Luther was concerned, a piece of ecclesiastical tradition and therefore subject to criticism on the basis of God's word. Roman Catholic theology has, up until the present day, frequently condemned Luther's method of approaching and validating the authority of Scripture as subjective and arbitrary. But Luther is as far as the heaven is from the earth in determining the center of Scripture by himself and self-confidently presenting his theology as this center. Rörer in his notes on the lectures on Galatians of 1531 has preserved the Reformer's remark that he constantly found within himself contradictions against the gospel as he understood it.[16] But he also knew that he was always overcome and compelled by the witness of the Apostle Paul, and he found Paul's basic melody in the entire Scripture—anything within the canon which did not agree with this was an exception and could make no claim to the authority of God's word.[17]

In all of this Luther maintains a decisive thesis as the material criterion of his theology. This basic principle was the theocentric character of the gospel and the preservation of God's honor as he who creates out of nothing. Luther tells us that Staupitz once comforted him in his doubts by pointing out that Luther's doctrine gave all honor to God and not to men. "One cannot give too much to God." Luther accepted this criterion and used it to overcome the temptation which came to him because he contradicted tradition. "I still know this for certain, that what I teach is not from men but from God (cf. Gal. 1:10). That is, I attribute everything solely to God and nothing at all to men . . . it is far safer to ascribe too much to God than to men."[18] "My teaching . . . lets God be God and it gives God the glory . . . therefore it cannot be wrong."[19] But even this criterion for the truth of his interpretation of the gospel was not something which he arbitrarily established. It was given to him by the Apostle Paul in Romans 4:17, "Abraham believed in the God who calls into existence the things that do not exist."

THE AUTHORITY OF SCRIPTURE AND
THE AUTHORITY OF THE CHURCH

For Luther, there is no unconditional authority in the church parallel to and apart from the word of God. Whenever anyone refers to the "opinion of the church" on matters of Christian faith and life, we must ask what this means. Is it the true opinion of the church which can be recognized by the fact that it stands in and is based on Scripture or is it a self-fabricated opinion "found outside of Scripture" which someone only claims to be the true opinion of the church. Only the former has authority, because it alone is based on Scripture and agrees with Christ's will and command. "The church believes and thinks nothing except what Christ has thought and commanded, much less something contrary to what he thought and commanded." Such an opinion of the church cannot err any more than God's word can.[20] It is only in this sense, then, that we can and may cite the authority of the church. It is relative to and dependent on the Holy Scripture.

The authority of the church as such, of its fathers, of its traditions, of its officials and organs cannot be an unconditional authority. For the church can err, as the Lord himself predicted (Matt. 24:24). For this reason we cannot simply cite the church fathers to establish our position. "We can neither rely nor build very much on the life and works of the fathers but only on God's word."[21] The Old Testament, through the examples of David and Nathan, shows that the church can err. The New Testament presents no less evidence of this, since even the apostles "often sinned and failed," for example, Peter erred, as Paul reports in Galatians 2:11 ff.[22] For this reason, the church, without prejudice to its holiness, must daily pray the fifth petition of the Lord's Prayer which asks for forgiveness. This must be prayed not only by individual members of the church but also by the church as a whole.[23] The church "remains an obedient sinner before God until the last day and is holy only in Christ her Savior through grace and the forgiveness of sins."[24] For this reason a Christian cannot unconditionally obey the church. We owe Christ unconditional obedience, but we pass judgment on the apostles, the church, and even on angels according to the standard of God's word. (For this reason, the apostles must also permit us to measure them by the standard of Christ's word even though they have greater authority than the church does.) "We obey the apostles and the church insofar as they bear the seal of that man [Christ]," that is, if they preach the gospel according to Christ's commission in Matthew 28:19 f. "If they do not bear this seal we do not pay any more attention to them than St. Paul did to Peter in Galatians 2." Paul did not listen to Peter but rebuked him because he had deviated from the gospel. Under such circumstances, an appeal to the authority of the church carries no weight.[25] The authority and thereby also the duty to obey is based on and limited by the gospel, that is, because and insofar as the church bears true witness to the gospel and thus demonstrates that it has been sent by Christ.

The Christian's obedience to the church must therefore take the form of obedience to Christ. But these two can be different. It can happen that, for the sake of obeying Christ, we must refuse to obey the church. And there is also an obedience to human authority that is disobedience against God. In a memorable statement, Luther expressly names the church among such human authorities. "Let all obedience be damned to the depths of hell which obeys the government, father, mother, or even the church in such a way that it disobeys God. At this point I know neither father, mother, friendship, government, or the Christian church."[26] The church thus occupies no special place in relationship to the other earthly authorities which are named. All are embodied in men and "to err is human." Luther emphasizes this particularly with reference to the church.[27] The church is exempt neither from humanity nor sinfulness. Both of these factors forbid any of these authorities from claiming unconditional authority and demanding unconditional obedience. But doesn't the church occupy a special position among all authorities since the Holy Spirit has been promised to it? Luther deals with this question, too—we will come to it in the following.

Luther concretized these thoughts about the limits of the church's authority and its capacity for error by specifically applying them to the councils.[28] A council as such does not possess unconditional spiritual authority any more than the church and its tradition do. The councils have constantly claimed that they assemble in "the name of Christ" and thus that they are not able to err—according to Christ's promise in Matthew 18:20 ("Where two or three are gathered together in my name . . ."). Luther points out that the mere claim to have gathered in the name of Christ does not yet mean that a council really has done so and possesses Christ's authority. "If they have come together in the name of Christ, they will show that by acting according to Christ and not contrary to the gospel." Thus the content of the council's decrees will determine whether a council has actually gathered in the name of Christ. "Even though saints are present at the council, even though there are many saints, and even though angels are there, still we do not trust personalities but only God's word, since even saints can make mistakes. There is no excuse for saying that a man was a saint and is therefore to be believed. Most certainly not; Christ says just the opposite, believe him only if he speaks correctly about me." This is not a majority decision; rather "if I see someone who thinks correctly about Christ I ought to kiss him, throw my arms around his neck, and let all the others who think falsely alone." Thus the pure truth of the gospel gives genuine authority to the men of the church who witness to Christ. Luther asserts the same thing when he says that only those have assembled in the Holy Spirit who bring the "analogy of faith" and not their own thoughts.[29]

When a council does not err but bears witness to the truth, we should not take it for granted. Such a council does not necessarily witness to the truth because it is ecumenical or because of its formal authority; when a council does so, that is an empirical and "accidental" fact (in distinction from that which can be taken for granted. Each such instance is a particular sign of Christ's grace toward his church, whether he uses an individual "saint" in the council or the voice of the entire church. As has been said, this is a particular grace and does not simply follow from the council's authority. Truth is not guaranteed by the authority of the council, but Christ's free gift of truth in a specific instance gives a council its authority.[30] The mere fact that a council "represents" the church also does not mean that it itself is the church, the true church. This is, as has been said, not something to be taken for granted and not simply given with the assembling of the council, but is a purely empirical and "accidental" fact.[31]

Luther recognizes that the Holy Spirit has been promised to the church of Christ. But this is not necessarily promised to the gathering of the bishops or the council. This means that no council can cite the promise of the Holy Spirit to prove its decrees and derive binding authority for its canons from this promise of the Holy Spirit.[32] The ecclesiastical legitimacy of such a gathering does not necessarily include its spiritual legitimacy. This latter depends completely on the apostolicity of its doctrines and resolutions.[33] We hardly need mention that Luther would say the same about the claim of the highest teaching office of the church. The First Vatican Council's dogma that the pope's teaching *ex cathedra* is infallible is subject to the same criticism as the dogma that the council is infallible.

### THE HOLY SPIRIT IN THE HISTORY OF THE CHURCH

Luther's evaluation of the councils clarifies the distinction between the Roman and the evangelical understanding of how the Spirit leads the church. The difference is not that the Roman Catholic Church recognizes the leadership of the Spirit and evangelical thought does not recognize it. Luther is as sure and confident as his opponents are that Christ remains with his church through his Holy Spirit and that he guides and leads it into all truth. He can say, "We, too, confess that the church does everything right."[34] And although he definitely denies that any one individual in the church after the time of the apostles can claim to be infallible in matters of faith, he is equally certain that the universal church can not err.[35] But where is the church of which all this is true and what sort of church is it? At this point, Luther's theology of the cross once again enters the picture. It determines his understanding of the church of Christ. It says that the true church of Christ and historical Christendom are not identical. The true church is hidden[36] and not to be identified with the official church and its history—the official church has not even recognized the true church as church. This true and hidden church is ruled by Christ's Spirit; it cannot err, even in the smallest article of faith; for Christ has promised to remain with it until the end of the world. It is the "pillar and bulwark of the truth" (I Tim. 3:15).[37] His promise is, however, not automatically valid for the entire organization of the church and for the official church. The apostolic succession of its bishops, which the official church. The apostolic succession of its bishops, which the official church claims for itself, does not necessarily imply the succession of truth and of the genuine apostolic gospel as something which can be taken for granted. The former is not inseparably connected with the latter.[38]

A theory of church history formulated in terms of the organic development of the church cannot simply explain the decisions and development of the empirical church by assuming that the Holy Spirit has led the church. Luther can understand the history and the reality of the empirical ecclesiastical organization only by assuming that it also stands under God's wrath.[39] Or to use other words, Luther, in a thesis that is sharply and polemically formulated, declares that we must always ask whether the papal and other official decrees and regulations of Rome came from the Holy Ghost or from Satan.[40] Certainly, Luther's statements about the differences and contradictions between the official and the hidden church are conditioned by his struggle with Rome, and thus, by the concrete polemical situation. We may not, however, ignore the fact that the basis and meaning of these statements extend far beyond this situation. Luther finds that this law which describes the church's nature is also present in the Old Testament, for example, at the time of Elijah and in the entire history of God's people since then. He applies this principle to the entire history of the church. It has always been true "that some were called the people and saints of God who were not, while others, who were among them as a remnant, were the people and saints of God, but were not so called."[41]

The official and the secret church are identical at the point of the gospel, sacraments, office of the keys, etc. Luther finds all these present also in the official church. This assures him that the hidden church is not a Platonic ideal. According to Luther, it has historical reality. The theology of the cross which says God's people, the community of Christ, are not identical with the historic form of the official church but are hidden under it, is complemented by the theology of the resurrection. According to the theology of the resurrection God has always preserved his church, even under a church organization such as the papacy which erred in many ways. He has done this by marvelously preserving the text of the gospel and the sacraments; and through these many have lived and died in true faith. This remains true even though they were only a weak and hidden minority within the official church. Luther repeatedly says this.[42] Thus he sees a line of truth in the actual history of the church along which the promise that the Holy Spirit will lead the church has again and again been fulfilled.

In this sense, the true church is the object not only of "nevertheless" faith but also of historical experience; it is part of an obvious historical continuity which Luther always recognized. But this continuity of leadership through the Spirit and of the preservation of the true church is definitely not identical with and is not guaranteed by the official tradition and supposed apostolic succession of the ecclesiastical structure.[43] In every age, God chooses his witnesses to the truth how and where he wills. Luther, as we have seen, points out, that in a specific situation in the church, one single individual might have the truth; he then must constantly maintain it against the authorities of the official church. This prevents us from understanding the Holy Spirit's leadership in hierarchical or supernatural evolutionistic terms. God allows the official church to err in order to destroy the ever present danger that men trust in the church rather than in God's word alone.[44] Then, however, God again sends the church witnesses to his truth.

*Works Cited*

*BOW*—Martin Luther, *The Bondage of the Will,* translated by J. I. Packer and O. R. Johnston (Westwood, N. J.: Fleming H. Revell, 1957).

*LW*—American Edition of Luther's Works (Philadelphia and St. Louis, 1955- ).

*PE*—*Works of Martin Luther,* 6 vols., (Philadelphia, 1915-1943).

*WA*—*D. Martin Luthers Werke.* Kritische Gesamtausgabe (Weimar, 1883- ).

*Notes*

1 *WA* 51, 487.

2 *WA* 38, 220.

[3] *WA* 26, 148; *LW* 40, 231 f. Cf. *WA* $40^{1}$, 69; *LW* 26, 24. At this place Luther specifically mentions the church in the city of Rome. Cf. *WA* 51, 501. *WA* $39^{11}$, 167.

[4] Cf. p. 7.

[5] *WA* 19, 72; *LW* 53, 61.

[6] Paul Althaus d. Ä. [Sr.], *Forschungen zur evangelischen Gebetsliteratur* (Gütersloh: Bertelsmann, 1927), pp. 195 f. Cf. *LW* 53, 129-146.

[7] *WA* 38, 221.

[8] Paul Althaus d. Ä. [Sr.], *Luther als Vater des evangelischen Kirchenliedes* (Leipzig: Deichert, 1917), pp. 29 ff. Cf. *LW* 53, 191-309.

[9] Cf. pp. 359 ff.

[10] *WA* 30III, 552.

[11] *WA* 40I, 54 f. (Rörer's printed edition and notes); *LW* 26, 15. Cf. *WA* 40I, 130; *LW* 26, 65.

[12] *WA* 46, 22; *LW* 24, 323.

[13] *WA* 46, 5 f. [edited by Cruciger]; *LW* 24, 304.

[14] *WA* $40^{I}$, 132; *LW* 26, 66 f.

[15] Cf. p. 82.

[16] *WA* $40^{I}$, 131; cf. *LW* 26, 65 f. It should be noted that the printed text [on which the English translation is based] tones down Luther's explicit statement, "and I also often think contrary to this teaching [*ego qui saepe sentio contra hanc doctrinam*]."

[17] Cf., e.g., *WA* $40^{I}$, 458; *LW* 26, 295. For Luther's statement on James, see *WA* $39^{II}$, 199.

[18] *WA* $40^{I}$, 131 f.; *LW* 26, 66.

[19] *WA* $17^{I}$, 232; *LW* 12, 187.

[20] *WA* 38, 203, 216 ff. Cf. *WA* 51, 518.

[21] *WA* 38, 206.

[22] *WA* 38, 208. Cf. *WA* 12, 417, 419.

[23] *WA* 38, 208, 216. Cf. *WA* $40^{I}$, 132; *LW* 26, 66. *WA* $39^{I}$, 351. *WA* $40^{III}$, 506; *LW* 13, 89.

[24] *WA* 38, 216. "The appearance of the church is the appearance of a sinner." *WA* $40^{II}$, 560; *LW* 12, 263.

[25] *WA* 38, 208.

[26] *WA* 28, 24.

[27] Luther points out that the fathers of the church have also erred as do all men. *WA* 7, 711. Luther declares that the true interpretation of Paul's doctrine of justification cannot be determined on the basis of what the recognized fathers of the church said. "Were they not equally blind? Did they not ignore Paul's clear and understandable statements?" *WA* 18, 771; *BOW*, 294. *WA* $39^{I}$, 185.

[28] Cf. the *Disputation on the Authority of a Council* (1536), *WA* $39^{1}$, 189 f. Cf. Theses 12 ff., *WA* 391, 185 f. In addition, Luther's criticism of the councils in his *On the Councils and the Churches* (1539), *WA* 50, 509-624; *PE* 5, 157-263.

[29] *WA* 39I, 186.

[30] *WA* 39I, 185.

[31] *WA* 39I, 186 f.

[32] *WA* 39I, 186.

[33] *WA* 39I, 187.

[34] *WA* 7, 713.

[35] "Hence, after the Apostles no one should claim this reputation that he cannot err in the faith, except only the universal church." *WA* $39^{I}$, 48; *LW* 34, 113. Cf. *WA* 6, 561; *LW* 36, 108. *WA* 6, 615.

[36] "The church is hidden away, the saints are out of sight." *W A* 18, 652, *BOW*, 123. This is true in the Old Testament. The true people of God are hidden and not to be identified with the Jewish religious community. On the contrary, in the Old Testament the true church is always opposed by those who pretend to be the church, but who persecute the true church; cf. the references in H. Bornkamm, *Luther und das alte Testament*, pp. 176 ff.

[37] *WA* 18, 649; *BOW*, 120. Cf. *W A* 51, 511.

[38] *WA* 39I, 191. Cf. *W A* $39^{II}$, 176 f.

[39] *WA* 5, 43; *LW* 14, 306.

[40] *WA* 7, 713.

[41] *WA* 18, 650; *BOW*, 121. On the hiddenness of the true church, see also *WA* $40^{III}$, 504f.; *LW* 13, 88 ff.

[42] *WA* 18, 651; *BOW*, 121. *WA* $39^{II}$, 167 f. *WA* $40^{III}$, 505; *LW* 13, 89.

[43] *WA* $39^{II}$, 176.

[44] *WA* 12, 418.

**Gerhard Ebeling (essay date 1972)**

SOURCE: "The Way Luther Speaks of God," in *Luther: An Introduction to His Thought*, translated by R. A. Wilson, Fortress Press, 1970, pp. 242-67.

[*In the excerpt below from a work originally published in 1970, Ebeling discusses the problem of historical periodization, suggesting a way to transcend the attempts of Ernst Troeltsch and Hegel to assign Luther to either the medieval or modern age.*]

I. TOWARDS THE HISTORY OF THE PROBLEM

1. *Interpretation in the Manner of Salvation History*

In his lectures on the philosophy of history Hegel calls the Reformation "the all-illuminating sun, which follows that day-break at the end of the Middle Ages."[1] This metaphor of the dawning day to which the night gives way has a long history as an expression for a decided break in history.[2] Here the picture is recalled only as an allusion and only in so far as it affects an understanding of the Reformation.

In the age of the Reformation and of Orthodoxy an ever recurring theme of the Protestant understanding of the Reformation event is that after a time of Egyptian darkness the light of the gospel arose again through Luther's word and deed.[3] For that matter, this picture can also be applied to the inner illumination which Luther experienced, instead of to the general spread of the gospel.[4] These phrases give expression to an ecclesiastical and salvation-historical interpretation of Luther's appearance.

In Hegel's statement, however, Luther and the Reformation are integrated in the history of thought. To this we must immediately add a twofold explanation. First, for Hegel, history as such is the history of thought. Hence here "history of thought" (*geistesgeschichtlich*[5]) does not have its usual sense, only *one* aspect of history among others. Furthermore, in the process of the spirit that reaches an awareness of itself, Luther and the Reformation are assigned a niche which in a sense also has a salvation-historical, yes, an eschatological dignity. It is a matter of "the new, the last banner . . . , around which the nations gather, the flag of the free spirit."[6] By the use of the same metaphor the word "Enlightenment" likewise connotes such a pathos of salvation. The way in which the Enlightenment appealed to the Reformation and integrated it into its self-understanding[7] indeed seems by comparison to Hegel as superficial. On a higher level of reflection Hegel was intent on maintaining the connection with the innermost theological concerns of the Reformation.[8]

Yet even the sharply negative assessment of the Reformation by such men as Jacob Burckhardt[9] and Friedrich Nietzsche[10] and their followers insists on qualifying soteriologically the beginning of the modern age as a transition from night to day. Of course the role of the Reformation receives a diametrically different evaluation. Nietzsche is of the opinion, "If Luther had been burned like Huss, the dawn of the Enlightenment might perhaps have come a little earlier and more brilliantly than we can now imagine."[11] Alexander Ruestow thinks that the Reformation, together with the Counter Reformation, for which Luther and Calvin also are said to be responsible, ushered in a new period of darkness, a relapse into extreme medievalism, and this after the onset of a new era was already well on the way in the late Middle Ages and in the Renaissance.[12]

The concept of dawning implies not only the sharp contrast between darkness and light but permits also shadings in the transition from one extreme to the other. Dawn proclaims the end of the night, the aurora, the sunrise. This, in turn, is only the beginning of the day in which the all-illuminating sun runs its course and performs its task. As far as I can see, the obvious thought of the ultimately returning sunset does not overshadow the application of that history-interpreting metaphor to the Reformation and the modern age. The light of the gospel may be threatened by ever recurring periods of darkness; nevertheless, it has the character of finality, even as the conviction that a definitive source of light has risen is combined with the light of reason.

It is true, in that original salvation-historical interpretation of the Reformation only very limited use is made of the possibility of differentiation. There is indeed an awareness of certain omens and antecedents of Reformation insights.[13] As far as Luther's Reformation breakthrough is concerned, in his autobiographical remarks he makes much of the fact that he was held captive for a long time in his papistical bias from which he extricated himself only with great difficulty.[14] Farthest from the mind of the reformatory self-understanding and the orthodox understanding of the Reformation, at least within Lutheranism, was the thought of an evolving development. The left wing of the Reformation had indeed raised the complaint early that the Reformation had gone only half-way, yes, had retrogressed in a reactionary way, and was therefore still awaiting its consummation.[15] Very early the need was felt to distinguish between the lights and shadows of Luther's personality.[16] Not until the age of Pietism did the idea arise also in Lutheranism that the Reformation had remained unfinished and needed to be continued.[17] All of these differentiations with reference to the prehistory and progress of the Reformation, as well as with reference to the evaluation of Luther's person, were extraordinarily intensified later, during and since the Enlightenment, because of an increasing awareness of historical conditionalities and changes.[18]

*Martin Luther burns the papal bull.*

2. *Hegel*

Strictly speaking, it was Hegel who first assumed the task of integrating the Reformation into the history of thought. Its precondition is a view of history which does not stop with external symptoms, such as incidental abuses in the Middle Ages, but takes note of the inner movement of the event and for that reason encompasses everything in its dialectical necessity and in its comprehensive context.[19] With Hegel this assumes the character of a universal teleological view of history, that sees the changes as evolving aspects of a single basic theme, progress in the consciousness of freedom.[20] This constitutes the grandeur but also the problematics of his understanding of history. Therefore the predominant impression is that here, because of a dogmatic prejudice, Luther's Reformation is understood as turned toward the modern age without a break, and the integration into the history of thought is not at all regarded as a problem. Nevertheless, Hegel's historical judgment of Luther and the Reformation is more carefully differentiated than seems to be the case. From Luther to the Middle Ages on the one hand and to the modern era on the other, there are intimately intertwined positive and negative relationships. Hegel indeed knows that the principle of subjectivity did not simply arise because of the Reformation.[21] All of the well-known phenomena, which demonstrate that man had recovered confidence in himself and enjoyment of the earth, are part of the daybreak at the close of the Middle Ages that preceded the all-illuminating sun.[22] However, it is only in relationship to God that freedom authenticates itself, loses its particularity, and thus its nearness to the barbaric, and is recognized not only as permitted but simply as necessary.[23] Thus, according to Hegel, the reformatory faith provides the true legitimation, but with that also the critical norm for that movement from the Middle Ages to the modern age, a movement that is in progress *per se* apart from the Reformation but is not on the right track without the Reformation.

True, the main accent is on the antithesis to the Middle Ages. According to Hegel, their corruption arises from the fact that the presence of the Eternal in the world, the linking of the finite with the infinite—the "this," as he expresses it in an enigmatic formula[24]—has been externalized.[25] Superstition, external authority, asceticism, and the materialization of the means of salvation are the symptoms.[26] As the most pregnant phenomena he names the adoration of the host and the yearning for the possession of the Holy Land, especially the Holy Sepulcher, which then, however, as a conquered empty grave elicited an experience of disappointment and therewith brought about the crisis of the Middle Ages.[27] But Hegel would be completely misunderstood, if he is understood as trying to dissolve the connection between the secular and the eternal. On the contrary, he is concerned precisely about the right place and the correct manner of this connection.[28] In this point, as an advocate of the Christian faith in the modern age, Hegel is in agreement with Luther:

> Luther's simple teaching is this, that the "this," the infinite subjectivity, that is, the true spirituality [*Geistigkeit*], Christ, in no respect is present and real in an external manner, but is attained as spiritual at all only in the reconciliation with God, in faith and in partaking [that is, *in usu,* not *extra usum*].[29]

Hence, according to him, the essence of the Lutheran faith consists in

> that man is in a right relationship to God and . . . his piety requires . . . that his heart, his innermost being, is involved. . . . The individual himself must repent, himself be contrite in his heart, and his heart must be filled with the Holy Spirit.[30]

This is what Hegel has in view in reducing the essential content of the Reformation to the formula: "Man is destined through himself to be free."[31]

Nevertheless, the relationship of the Reformation to the modern age is ambivalent. The spirit does not at once appear in the full consummation.[32] Just as the church's doctrine was only gradually developed after the beginnings of Christianity, so correspondingly here. The freedom of the spirit began with Luther, only embryonically, and therefore required subsequent explication.[33] At first it was restricted to the religious sphere.[34] But this principle had then also to be brought into the world and above all to penetrate the political realm.[35] Both aspects must be emphasized: What is already present in the Reformation and what is not yet there; that the modern age rightly goes beyond the Reformation and yet, correctly understood, can be nothing else than an actualization of the legacy of the Reformation.

Here indeed is the cause of conflicts between the modern age and the empirical shape of Protestantism. The religious content was conserved as something historically given and remained something external and foreign to faith, instead of being speculatively tested as to its truth. As a result the germ of an unspiritual mode of comprehension entered the freedom of the spirit.[36] Consequently the subjective religious principle was separated from philosophy. This constitutes a step backward even in relation to medieval scholasticism.[37] Either a bad subjectivity, emptied of the objective, remains, abandoned to the torture of religious self-contemplation,[38] or the biblical texts are surrendered to a purely historico-philological exegesis which strangles the spirit in the test.[39] Both phenomena, pietism and rational biblical scholarship, which are generally regarded as marks of transition from Old Protestantism to Neo-Protestantism, Hegel regards as degeneracy. The reason for this state of affairs is that there has been no self-critical reshaping of the Reformation for modern time.

3. *Troeltsch*

The terms, Old and Neo-Protestantism, are not in Hegel's vocabulary, but were coined by [Ernst] Troeltsch. Therefore they come from that late phase in which the thought-historical treatment of Luther and the Reformation was expanded into the cultural-historical method of study.[40] It was only at this point, though not without preparation by Dilthey[41] and Harnack,[42] that the self-evident manner in which the predominant opinion, that assigned Luther and the Reformation to the modern age, was subjected to so startling a critique that for the first time the historical classification became a controverted problem, and indeed a problem, and of extraordinary range. For the position one takes with regard to this problem manifestly determines the significance that one assigns to Luther for the present and the future.

As Hegel's conception was simplified to mean that Luther was the standard bearer of the modern age, so Troeltsch's thesis caused a stir in its exaggerated form that Luther was a representative of the Middle Ages. However, if the nuances in both are observed, they approach each other more closely. Already with Hegel the outlines of the problem are delineated. They are met with again in Troeltsch, filled with a far richer historical perception and therefore essentially differentiated better, but also accentuated differently. Both thinkers are agreed on a passionate affirmation of the turn from the Middle Ages to the modern age, and both feel themselves obligated to Luther's innermost intention. Both are opposed to a superficial derivation of the modern age from Luther and the Reformation, since before, contemporaneously, and afterwards, radically different forces promoted the modern age. The new religious impulses and their roles in the upheaval of the times must be carefully distinguished from these. Finally, both Hegel and Troeltsch are aware also of the ambivalence of the Reformation and its historical effects, the twilight zone of the already and the not yet, the contradictory trends of further development and retrogressive encasement.

Nevertheless, with Troeltsch[43] there is an unmistakable change in perspective. Although he ultimately agrees with Hegel in the premise of an integration of religion and philosophy;[44] nevertheless, in contrast to him (Hegel), he does not claim to outline the necessary explanation of the idea. Rather, he confines himself in a purely experiential-imminent way to clarifying the extremely complicated relationship of the cultural types that succeed and overlap each other.[45] For that reason his way of reflecting and presenting oscillates sharply and changes the accent and emphasis from one sketch to another.[46] As he himself knows, in this procedure empirical orientation and construction wrestle with each other,[47] knowledge of historical details and an instinct for historical relationships that often are not matched by a corresponding knowledge, a combination which again is not unlike what is found in Hegel, eliciting at once admiration and criticism. But what allows Troeltsch's understanding of history to diverge from Hegel's not only in method but also in content is the fact that Troeltsch, born about a century later, is conditioned by a more advanced experience with the modern age.

For Hegel the antithetical relationship between modern times and the Middle Ages was still a necessary aspect within the realization of the Christian principle which coincides with the goal of the movement of the world spirit itself. For Troeltsch, on the contrary, the essential aspects of the modern age are throughout independent of what is Christian. Therefore he contrasts the modern age with the churchly culture of the Middle Ages in a way that immediately creates the impression of being anti-Christian:[48] over against theology, rationalism; over against authority, autonomy; over against the infallible truth of revelation, relativism; over against an ascetic orientation toward the life to come, this-worldliness; over against the pessimism of sin, the optimism of progress.[49] In short, the individualism of the human person and the imminence of the divine are the two chief principles of the modern age.[50] Not that Troeltsch saw the modern age moving irresistibly toward a complete lack of religion. But he is profoundly obsessed by the thought that the configuration of religious life in the modern world presents an extremely dark problem.[51] Thus in one sense the antithesis between the Middle Ages and modern times became more acute; but in another respect it indeed was relativized, because the direct connection with internal Christian controversies was dissolved. From the viewpoint of the history of culture Catholicism and Protestantism are moving into a continually closer relationship. In spite of the break between the Middle Ages and the modern age, the Middle Ages can nevertheless be valued now as "the mighty maternal lap of all West European life."[52]

Hegel already restricted the positive participation of Luther and the Reformation in the rise of the modern age to the religious aspect. But since it seemed to him that the modern age was inseparably connected with the idea of Christianity, the religious factor in the genesis of the modern age had a different value for him than for Troeltsch. On the one hand, Hegel could unequivocally equate the Protestant principle, as it is relevant for the modern age, with the essence of Luther's reformatory teachings. On the other hand, he expected of this Protestant principle an immediate impact on culture as a whole. For Troeltsch, however, the direct impact of Protestantism in its original form on modern culture did not come into consideration at all.[53] For the Reformation was still embedded in the churchly culture of the Middle Ages as a religious renewal, and historically constituted itself in an analogous form. For that reason Troeltsch can formulate his well-known provocative judgements. Protestantism appears, first of all, "as a completely medievalistic reaction, which swallows up the already achieved beginnings of a free and secular culture."[54] Protestantism "similar to, or even more than the Counter-Reformation, is a second blossoming of the Middle Ages . . . which deprives the already formed sprouts and buds of a secular culture of their sap."[55] The Reformation was "a reformation of the urban class of the Late Middle Ages."[56] Of course, "by shattering the sole authority of the Catholic church Protestantism has broken the power of ecclesiastical culture in general, in spite of its transitory revival"[57] and participated in this way negatively in the rise of the modern era. Troeltsch also concedes that modern individualism and rationalism, autonomy and faith in progress have their deepest roots in the religious personalism which has its origins in the Old Testament prophets and in Christianity.[58] But these are only subconscious and hidden, indirect and secularized influences in which Protestantism also participates to the extent that it has elevated this religious personalism to a principle. However, the area in which Protestantism actually became creative for the modern world is that area in which the modern age itself is deficient, namely the religious life.[59] Under this aspect, Troeltsch gives the question a shift in direction. He moves from that which constitutes the new age, to that which it lacks; from the impact of Protestantism on the modern age, to the impact of the modern age on Protestantism. The first, because according to Troeltsch the modern era cannot be sufficient unto itself, but is in need of a religious-metaphysical tie.[60] The second, because Protestantism of itself cannot provide the modern era with a religion appropriate to it, without itself experiencing a profound transformation under the influence of the modern age.[61] Therefore the service which Protestantism is rendering to the modern era is not really one of shaping the culture—according to Troeltsch Christianity can no longer do this—rather, if I may say so, it is one of providing therapy for the culture.

Therefore, too, according to Troeltsch, the relationship between the Middle Ages and the modern age appears in Protestantism itself as the relationship between Old and Neo-Protestantism. From this process of change, and only from it, the ideas that were already concealed in Luther and the Reformation are disclosed, ideas that point forward to the modern age but remained bound to the Middle Ages in their historical form. For the central teachings of the Reformation are still under the spell of medieval questions, a spell which they do not break even as newly formed answers.[62] Hence a definition of Protestantism is possible after all only as a reflection on its relationship to the Middle Ages and to the modern age.[63] In its historical form it is a phenomenon of transition composed of inner contradictions.[64] Only the dissolution of its classical form permits the comprehension of its true kernel. It is true, in one sense Troeltsch exempts Luther himself from this judgment. Although with him too the new and the medieval are intertwined, he juts out into the arena of the timeless and universal-human.[65] The catchword, "religious individualism," which is intended to fix the congruence between the "exploding new spirit" in Luther and the spirit of the modern era,[66] calls to mind the principle of subjectivity which according to Hegel was brought to its decisive breakthrough by Luther. According to Troeltsch, however, Hegel would say that the emptying of all dogmatic content results in a bad subjectivity, in an individualism which emancipates itself from the power of the universal.[67] In the end Troeltsch seems to draw Luther more forcibly to the side of the modern age than Hegel did.

### *4. The Development of the Question after Troeltsch*

The attempts to integrate Luther and the Reformation into the history of thought are themselves conditioned by the history of thought. On their part they document an increasingly sharpened wrestling with the relationship between theological and thought-historical ways of thinking. Hegel's claim of the philosophical perfection of theology was transformed by Troeltsch into a mere administration of the theological legacy, in so far as this legacy after its historical decline could still be made use of at all in the philosophy of religion. It is understandable that a tendency to mutual repulsion increased. Dialectical theology believed it could derive a theological profit from the thought-historical antithesis between the modern age and the Reformation. But on the other hand the philosophical concern for the "legitimacy of the modern age"[68] went beyond Troeltsch and identified theology thoroughly with the Middle Ages. For the change from one age to the other Luther and the Reformation are now worthy only of marginal comment. Driven to extremes, theological absolutism is said to reveal completely its human unbearableness and involuntarily to legitimize man's self-assertion,[69] this basic trait of the spirit of the new age. Alongside that, the efforts within theology continued to bring the theological and thought-historical view into a relationship fruitful for both. Together with the systematicians Paul Tillich, Emanuel Hirsch, and Friedrich Gogarten, grateful mention should be made of historians and Luther researchers like Heinrich Bornkamm, Walter von Loewenich, Wilhelm Pauck, and Hanns Rückert. This task requires further work.

## II. Fundamental Considerations to Lluther's Thought-historical Significance

If I add some further considerations to these analyses, it will seem doubly presumptuous in view of how much thought has already been given to this matter and how much still needs to be considered to make some essential progress. But we would not be doing justice to our assignment, if we should want to spare ourselves the exertion of further consideration.

The nature of the theme and its destiny require very general reflections to discover where and how the detailed work on the texts—the really rewarding business in dealing with history—must begin anew to expedite the solution of our problem.

I begin with the following observation: The more we move toward the center of Luther's theology, the stronger the impression becomes that his way of thinking is in contrast both to the spirit of the Middle Ages and to the spirit of the modern age, and to both at the same points. Luther's understanding of sin would be an example. Others could be adduced with equal justification. And all of them together probably constitute a single state of affairs.

This surmise draws explicit support from the well-known fact that Luther reduced to a common denominator the dissimilar opponents on his two battle fronts, the so-called papists and the so-called Enthusiasts, the scholastics and the humanistic theologian Erasmus. Thus he had to stress the same points in both directions.[70] Even though one does not unreservedly accept the wide-spread thesis that spiritualists and humanists of all shades were farther removed from the Middle Ages and closer to the modern age than Luther, one must still admit: In the fermenting sixteenth century they represented a stance that evokes the sympathy of modern times, already because of the contrast to Luther and the Catholic tradition. What differentiates Luther's position among his contemporaries, it seems to me, has a much greater significance for his position between the Middle Ages and the modern era.

We do not deny a relative right to the customary thought-historical form of questioning as Troeltsch in general has handled it brilliantly and impressively, though individual details may be challenged. Without doubt it is profitable heuristic procedure which in the historical studies opens one's eyes and sharpens the awareness of the problem, when we assign the historical phenomena as a whole either to the Middle Ages or to the modern era, indeed in most cases more appropriately, in part thus, in part so, in respect to the many factors and the complexity of their interrelationships. For this Luther provides inexhaustible material: from starkly medieval conceptions of the devil to critical expressions regarding the Bible: from the most daring acts of breaking with tradition to a cautious conservation of the status quo, "an infinitely conservative revolutionary," as Troeltsch once put it.[71] Even in such historical confrontations, that more readily lead us to expect a heightening of his characteristic medieval features, certain aspects provoke in us astonishing claims for his modernity. Karl Marx regards him as the oldest German national economist;[72] Erik H. Erikson sees him as the forerunner of Sigmund Freud.[73]

Even when this way of interpretation is employed with a high degree of sensitivity and one perceives the modern already under the medieval and the medieval still under the modern, since both do not stand side by side but interpenetrate each other, this is hardly the way to get at the essential in Luther. What is appropriate is not a coordination with regard to the Middle Ages and the modern era according to the scheme either-or, or both-and, but here evidently neither-nor is valid.

With this consideration we would be on the wrong road if we wanted to withdraw the theological question from contact with the history of thought and pit it dogmatically against the latter. Even the distinction between shell and kernel, form and content must be regarded as unsatisfactory—this peaceful separation which has served since the rise of historical consciousness as a formula for the co-existence of the variable and the constant, the transitory and the permanent. The intention would indeed be understandable, but the difficulty of the problem would not be pondered sufficiently, if the thought-historical consideration were concerned only with elements of form: forms of thought, of style, of society, etc., of which the theologically relevant would be untouched, so that one could be isolated from the other as formal and material aspects. The study of history is necessarily compartmentalized into a large number of aspects and questions. But precisely this makes the sharp twofold division into history of thought and history of theology questionable. One would even have to say that in the final analysis they become one, if history in its theological aspects is interpreted correctly. To obtain clarity on this point both are necessary: To interrogate theology about its relation to history, and the thought-historical interpretation about its ultimate presuppositions.

Self-evidently, problems of this sort are encountered not only in connection with Luther. Yet his stature in its historical context and its future historical effect—one would almost like to say—compels in a unique way and in exemplary acuteness the question about the thought-historical classification and at the same time makes the relationship of thought-historical and theological patterns a problem. That is a symptom of the historical rank of Luther's person and of the objective relevance of his work. And it provides the explanation why a treatment of the theme, "Luther and the Beginning of the Modern Age," cannot withdraw from the onslaught of the general problem of the understanding of history.

2. *The Essence of Historical Relationship*

To a certain degree historical relationship may perhaps be grasped by means of physical causality or biological evolution. But these means for comprehending history miss the essential, the specifically human. All action and suffering, all experience and expression, all contemplation and planning, all destruction and construction, societal processes and individual control of life, insensibility and communication, enmity and friendship, hatred and love, despair and hope, unbelief and faith—all of this is actualized by the medium of language and is condensed therein to thought and conversation, to understanding and analysis. History as the context of language in a sense is actualized on two planes. First, in the immediate controversy of the time event and, correspondingly, the immediate influence on history so that word becomes deed and deed becomes word; but language also becomes institutionalized and institutions become means of regulating language. Secondly, in the transmission of fixed language and in its understanding across long distances of time, so that what was once thought and spoken, experienced, and decided asserts itself anew in a different situation and thus influences history mediately.

Therefore historical interest tends in two directions. On the one hand, it asks about the historical genesis of specific phenomena; on the other, about their present significance. The center of gravity of historical interest lies in the first, to recognize how something came to be. Naturally this includes also the question about its further development as the genesis of its change in form. Aspects of the history of transmission and effect are also included in so far as they likewise contribute to the clarification of its historical genesis. At the same time they form the bridge to the interest in the present. Consciously or unconsciously this interest in the present time is involved in all historical interest. But it gains the upper hand when the transmitted material is studied with a hungry heart because history promises to meet something the present needs. Only then, when the historical distance is taken seriously, can a gift for the present grow out of the dialogue with history.

"Luther and the Beginning of the Modern Age"—according to this theme Luther can be investigated in his historical dimension, the growth and development of his personality, and especially his theology. To what extent do essential features of modern thought assert themselves among all of the influences which impinged on Luther and the way in which he utilized them? The ties with the Middle Ages, which received little attention formerly, are being noted more and more today, but have not yet been interpreted adequately. In contrast, as I see it, the influences on Luther of the dawning modern age, influences which can be grasped only with great difficulty, have been neglected by research, because especially here we cannot be satisfied with mere literary references but very subtle problems will have to be dealt with. Such problems are: What germs of the modern age are contained in Occamism or in late medieval mysticism and were transmitted from them to Luther? Or, to say it somewhat crudely, what is the relationship of the modernity of the *via moderna* and the *devotio moderna* to modern day modernity? Or, how much of the humanistic climate, beyond Luther's known modest relationship to humanism, made an impact on him and at least elicited some reactions? To what extent did the Renaissance-consciousness of life and the times influence him, perhaps in the development of his historical self-consciousness and his picturesque literary style?

But the theme can also be considered in the opposite direction, with regard to the contribution which Luther made to the beginning and the continuation of the modern age; through the acceleration—or retardation—of developments that were already on the way, through new insights that were translated into historical forces pregnant with the future, or through thought forms which did not affect history until much later, perhaps still awaiting adequate consideration. This line of questions therefore necessarily points beyond the genesis of the modern age to its continuity to the present. We simply cannot examine Luther's impact on the beginning of the modern age without being swept out onto the open sea of the modern age. This has implications for our treatment of Luther here. We must transcend the very necessary concentration on the biographical and, the historical in the narrow sense, in his appearance. Therefore, we were forced again and again to mention Luther and the Reformation in one breath, not to make them identical, but to indicate the historical forces which continue in the history of Luther's influence to the present. But now also the previously indicated shift to the dominance of interest in the present arrives on the scene, a shift no longer merely to the question about what Luther contributed to the rise of the modern age once upon a time, but what Luther contributes to the continuation of the modern age to the present.

If in this way our theme comprehensively brings into play all aspects of the interest in history, then critical reflection on the thought-historical method of treatment up to this point suggests the question whether this method was handled openly and broadly enough. I cannot enter further into the most obvious criticism of the concept of the history of thought today. If one has in mind the restriction to an absolutized partial aspect, because of which the reference to other aspects is improperly neglected, then already Troeltsch's expansion into the history of culture and society indicates both that corrections must be made and how they are to be made meaningfully. However, if one is offended by the conception of the spirit as historical *movens,* a conception which, diluted in comparison with Hegel, stands behind the customary usage of the term *Geistesgeschichte,* then the following must be borne in mind: The concept of the history of thought (*Geistesgeschichte*) is inseparably connected with the task of determining far-ranging periods of history according to the norm of their characteristic facial features, hence physiognomically. The spirit of the times, in the sense of what finds expression in the face of a period, may serve as interpretation of the controverted concept of the history of thought (*Geistesgeschichte*) until further notice.

### 3. *Toward Designating Epochs and Periods*

It is incontestably proper to examine history in terms of epochs, outstanding moments of history in which time, as it were, holds its breath and a pause in the movement of time occurs; or, to use Hegel's picture which in an opposite way expresses the same thing, epochs in which the spirit seems to have donned seven-league boots after a long snail's pace.[74] In this sense, beyond doubt the appearance of Luther is eminently epochal. Even if it is remembered that his appearance occurs in the broader phenomenon of the onset of an epoch, its epochal character is hardly diminished, but, if anything, enhanced. Also incontestable is the necessity to proceed from such epochs and delimit periods in both directions, contracted, or stretched out, depending on the dominant point of view, and provided with correspondingly smaller or larger transitional phases. The more universally the many strata of life and strains of events in a given time are embraced, the farther the beginnings of the epochs are separated from each other and the more complex they become.

To take a century as a period is a practical procedure which has the advantage of completely neutral labeling. If it is handled with chronological breadth, it is less mechanical than it seems. But this is not adequate. The continued, very problematical, labeling of the overlapping periods of Western history as Ancient History, the Middle Ages, and the Modern Era, whose original humanistic interpretation has long been rejected, betrays a corresponding need and at the same time an embarrassment. It is obvious that we are dealing with profoundly different ages. But to give them names oriented to their content, names universally acknowledged, appears impossible in view of the complexity of the state of affairs. For that reason those customary formal designations have the advantage of ciphers which permit free play to the constantly new search for historical knowledge. Moreover, the humanistic evaluation of at least the relationship between the Middle Ages and the Modern Era is quite compatible with the predominant modern evaluation of history.

If now the understanding of Luther has been derived from his place between the two periods, the way in which their essence is determined will be decisive. It is evident that the so-called Middle Ages, as a Christianized era, constitute a cohesive period of history, even though the chronological boundaries are disputed, and the way in which Christianity and culture were fused requires critical interpretation. It is much more difficult to define the Modern Era. As an open-ended period its total picture is constantly subject to changes in perspective. This is all the more so, since in contrast to the strong continuity of the Middle Ages, revolution has entered into the essence of the modern age, in one sense, as a principle. Yet even from this perspective the so-called Modern Era is sharply differentiated from the Middle Ages through all of its changes, and is clearly recognizable as an historical period with its own stamp by its progressive emancipation from the sacral structure of order in the medieval world as well as by the rapidly advancing scientific-technical conquest of the world.

By this yardstick Luther undoubtedly occupies a highly complicated intermediate position. Closely bound to the Middle Ages according to his origin, he was, because of his own transformation, more deeply involved in conflict with this age than any one else; and for that very reason, because he was on such intimate terms with the heart of the Middle Ages, he moved into opposition to the Middle Ages just at this point, rather than at merely peripheral issues. As for the dawn of the Modern Era, however, as far as it already appeared, Luther himself was not so much inspired by it, but only illumined by it from the outside. And that all the more, the more visibly he stood at the focus of his time; and yet, the more deeply he touched, also in this direction, the innermost part of what constitutes an age, he was in one sense far ahead of the course of the modern age, precisely because he was in opposition to its principal trend.

That here a both-and is affirmed, and yet is transferred into a neithernor, appears as a contradiction. So as not to fall prey to this impression prematurely, we must go behind the acknowledged periodization of history and ask what, in the last analysis, constitutes a period of history. What is the nature of its unifying force? According to the common understanding a historical period is to some extent a closed monad—to borrow this metaphysical concept from Leibniz in a hackneyed expression[75] and apply it to the problem of history—, a monad which is determined by principle. Even though the idealistic tracing back of complex historical movements to principles which are realized in them has long since yielded to a more modest pragmatic view, yet the converse with historical periods and the attempt to reduce them to formulas betray the over-simplifying tendency to conceive of them as ultimately pure monads. But already the observation that the peculiarity of a period can be determined only by comparison with another and by its delimitation against another opposes such an approach. Yet the following is more important.

What is constitutive for an age is the constellation of a series of longlasting data of the most diverse character, factors having to do with geography, population, tradition, etc. But what is characteristic about it is not simply a status of one kind or another, but the constellation of a task, the creation of elbow room or a restricted arena, within which the problematics of an age come to a final decision. To point it up paradoxically, one could say: What unifies an age is that about which there is conflict. Especially also the matters, which are self-evident for an age and which are so characteristic for its image, contribute to its profile primarily by determining the playing field and the rules of the game, and within these boundaries the great discussions of an age are carried on. For the Middle Ages this can be illustrated by the persistent struggle for Christendom's diversified unity, while for the modern age this can be done by the struggle for world change. The fact that every age is dominated by the discussion about its true image is not the least indication of how much an age's assigned struggle belongs to its essence. Since this constantly also involves ideas of the goal which pertain to humanity and the state of the world, one can say that an age is characterized by its soteriological situation.

Intimately connected with this is the fact that no age is sufficient to itself. Every age transcends its boundaries in a threefold respect. First, into the past: It is dependent on what is transmitted, what it has not produced itself and with which it must come to terms in order to gain spiritual nourishment which is again transformed into new traditions. Hence every age is characterized by where outside itself it has its sources of life and what it does with them. Secondly, into the future: Since it is never at the goal and never completely satisfied with itself, every age is occupied with its change, strives beyond itself for better times, and, not only through revolutionary means but also through conservative endeavors, consciously or unconsciously prepares changes which will finally consolidate into the onset of a new epoch. Finally, every age transcends its own concrete time and becomes a part of history as such. At all times mankind is confronted by the problematics of becoming and passing away, of living and dying, of time lost and fulfilled, hence basic questions of humanness. These questions by no means always remain timelessly the same as to their explication, yet in all ages they are kindled at the same neuralgic points, because they are evoked by the temporality of existence.

These three directions, in which an age has, as it were, open windows, belong together as dimensions of a single state of affairs. The task which arises from the specific constellation of an age—its soteriological situation, as I formulated it—, calls for a sovereign word which is suitable for the time and able to cope with its problems. But this requires that those three directions are given attention in the same measure: the source of the great historical traditions, the goals of historical responsibility, and the basic questions of historical existence. A contemplation of history that is open to the breadth and depth of the dialogue of an age will therefore have to take note of the controversial correlation of situation and word. With this catchword I refer to the distinction which Troeltsch employed for our problem, between medieval questions to which Luther is said to have given unmedieval answers; and furthermore, to Arnold Toynbee's historical categories of challenge and response, as well as to Paul Tillich's theological method of correlation[76] by means of which he relates to each other the questions from the situation and the answers from the message. It must be said by way of criticism that the new answer also changes the way the question is to be put, or already presupposes a change in the questions. For in the understanding of the situation, there is already an intimation of what is needed to master it.

4. *Correction of the Treatment of Luther's Classification in the History of Thought*

The net gain of this far-ranging excursion into basic problems of the understanding of history may be summed up in the following observation: The traditional handling of Luther's integration in the history of thought made a one-sided, and therefore false, use of opposing viewpoints. It affirmed a comprehensively exclusive opposition between the Middle Ages and the Modern Era, so that the question about the classification was simply posed disjunctively. Consequently this approach reduced the belonging to an age to a conformity free of contradiction and reckoned the remaining antitheses to the succeeding ages. For that reason, this historical method was not capable of doing adequate justice to the theological aspects and brought about a sham opposition to the theological concepts. So as not to surrender this criticism to the misunderstanding that the valid aspects in the thought-historical questioning were being denied, the three critical viewpoints shall be elucidated further.

First: The experience of liberation, which is so characteristic of the transition from the Middles Ages to the Modern Era, understandably produced the fascination of a purely antithetical reference of the periods to each other. The implications given by the labels to the periods have confirmed this impression. In spite of everything that is correct here, an age presents a far more complex state of affairs, when one extricates oneself from the notion of a windowless monad. The contrast between the Middle Ages and the Modern Era becomes alive and differentiated only in the context of what they have in common: the abiding factors, the overlapping problems, and a dialogical confrontation of the ages which does not really begin until one age has succeeded another. As much as belonging to the Modern Era demands its affirmation and excludes the medieval world as a possibility, so, on the other hand, this No can be as little a simple disparaging as the Yes can do without criticism.

Secondly: By its position in the transition from Middle Ages to the Modern Era a historical figure seems to be surrendered to the contraries of the old and the new, and so in a special measure to the transitory. Yet the opposite is the case with Luther, because heterogeneous elements were not accidentally mixed in him. Rather, in him a process of upheaval was accomplished, the poles of which simply were not only Late Middle Ages and Early Modern Era, but, on the one hand, the fountain of Christian faith which precedes even the Middle Ages, and, on the other hand, the future of the Modern Era into which the reformatory understanding of the Gospel makes its way without restriction. Thus Luther was occupied with a state of affairs that transcends Middle Ages and Modern Era. Precisely this qualified him to criticize in both directions. He broached anew the essentially Christian and discovered that this had been distorted just in the Christianized age. In this way he assisted in the demise of the Christianized age to a high degree and, at the same time, prevented the beginning of the modern age from continuing and completing itself in the same way in which it had started, namely as an immediate issuing from the Middle Ages. Because a new consideration of what is essentially Christian was injected, the detachment of the Modern Era from the Middle Ages took place under greatly changed conditions. Because of the Reformation, the Christian faith could approach the dialogue with the problems of the Modern Era in a form different from the medieval. Because the Christian faith was not identical with the age that was passing away, it was capable of a confrontation with the new age such as the medieval form of Christianity could not have achieved. To use Hegel's beautiful phrase, it was the "infinite elasticity of Christianity" which created the possibility of going into the new age without falling prey to it. However, the history of Old and Neo-Protestantism shows how much this possibility was endangered and in how many ways it failed to be realized.

Thirdly: If the thought-historical approach is corrected in the sense of that opening and differentiation, which I could only indicate, the foolish rivalry with the theological interest falls away. Room is provided for the appropriate grasp of the theologically relevant aspect in historical research, as far as this research in a self-critical way, resists its contraction. That this really does justice to the theological questioning is clear from the insight that the reference to time is essential for the Christian faith. The Word, to which it must cling and which it must transmit, is not a rigid formula that ostensibly would be removed from time. All the more for that very reason it is subjected to it, but it is a living word event which always demonstrates its superiority to time in a superior manner by entering into time. Hence it becomes concrete only when it confronts the temporal situation and only in that way does it demonstrate its power. For that reason the Christian faith is not definitively bound up with a specific period of culture, even though it can integrate itself so thoroughly with an age that in its expressions of life it seems to be identical with it. Although the Christian faith is not dependent for its existence on a Christianized culture, it constantly knows itself responsible for the total life of an age, as long as it itself is alive. Thus it is to the advantage of the theological questioning if, by an appropriate inclusion of the culture-historical aspects, it is preserved from a pseudo-theological restriction, while by an inappropriate intrusion of these aspects it is indeed perverted into the pseudo-theological. It would be the task of a fundamental theology to explicate this further. . . .

*Works Cited*

*ARG Archiv für Reformationsgeschichte.*

*CR Corpus Reformatorum* (Halle, 1834ff.).

*LW Luther's Works* (American edition; Philadelphia and St. Louis, 1955ff.).

*NZST Neue Zeitschrift für Systematische Theologie und Religionsphilosophie.*

*RGG Religion in Geschichte und Gegenwart* (3rd ed.; Tübingen, 1957).

*WA D. Martin Luthers Werke: Kritische Gesamtausgabe* (Weimar, 1883ff.).

*WA, Br D. Martin Luthers Briefwechsel* (Weimar, 1930ff.).

*WA, Tr D. Martin Luthers Werke: Tischreden* (Weimar, 1912ff.).

*Notes*

[1] I quote Hegel, unless otherwise indicated, according to H. Glockner, ed., *Georg Wilhelm Friedrich Hegel, Sämtliche Werke, Jubiläumsausgabe in zwanzig Bänden* (Stuttgart-Bad Canstatt, 1956-1965); here, XI, 519. Cited as *Werke.*

[2] Compare the eschatological use in Rom. 13:12.

[3] Evident already in Melanchthon's funeral oration on 22 February 1546, CR, XI, 728: "Lutherus veram et necessariam doctrinam patefecit. Fuisse enim tenebras in Doctrina de poenitentia densissimas, manifestum est." Translated into German in E.W. Zeeden, *Martin Luther und die Reformation im Urteil des deutschen Luthertums* (Freiburg, 1952), II, 3.

See also especially Matthias Flacius Illyricus, *Ecclesiastica historia, Cent. II, Praef.*, as given with translation in Zeeden, II, 46: ". . . tempora quidem Germanici prophetae MARTINI LUTHERI, cuius voce ac ministerio lux Evangelii quasi e tenebris Aegyptiacis revocata est, propemodum Apostolorum aetati respondent."

J.F. von der Strass (Sub Presidio J.C. Dannhaueri), *Memoria Thaumasiandri Lutheri* (Strasbourg, 1661), pp. 1-2, as given with translation in Zeeden, II, 125-26: "Lux haec preciosissima, post Christi in coelos ascensionem ( . . . ) ministerio Apostolorum et Apostolicorum virorum ore et calamo per totum mundum clarissime diffusa fuit. Sed dormientibus hominibus sub Antichristi tyrannide (heu quanta miseria) obscurata est ( . . . ) Obducto itaque his rebus pessimis Ecclesiae coelo, tenebrae erant crassae, non quidem penitus lux Evangelii interierat, nec tamen etiam ita fulsit, ut diem quis dicere posset et non nisi raro tenues emisit radios. ( . . . ) Misertus igitur est Deus Ecclesiae suae, Papali tyrannide pressae, et votis et gemitibus piorum exoratus Heroem Christianum ( . . . ) excitavit, qui doctrinam Evangelii a variis corruptelis ita repurgavit, ut piis novam lucem exoriri videretur. Heros ille fuit MARTINUS LUTHERUS, . . . cf. Zeeden, II, 43, 66; also *ibid.*, II, 15, 20, 24.

[4] Johannes Müller, *Lutherus defensus: Das ist Gründliche Widerlegung dessen was die Bäpstler D. Lutheri Person fürwerffen* (Arnstadt, 1645), pp. 250-51, in Zeeden, II, 113-14: "Also sehen wir am Tage / dass es Liecht worden sey [gemeint ist die Luther widerfahrene Erleuchtung] / ob wir gleich die Minut nicht wissen / wann das Liecht vollkommen worden sey. Also thut auch nicht vonnöthen / dass wir genaw müssen wissen / welch Jahr und Tag Lutherus vollkommen sey erleuchtet worden . . ." This was written in 1634.

[5] In contrast to the much discussed concept *Geisteswissenschaften* the history of the word *Geistesgeschichte* with its derivative *geistesgeschichtlich* has not been investigated, so far as I know. Hegel does not use the word, it seems. Evidently we are dealing here with an inner scientific method resulting from a narrowing to

a particular aspect of history. For instance, compare H. Rickert's critical delimitation in opposition to this "that someone orientates himself unilaterally to the so-called *Geistesgeschichte* in contrast to political or economic history." *Die Grenzen der naturwissenschaftlichen Begriffsbildung: Eine logische Einleitung in die historischen Wissenschaften* (5th ed.; Tübingen and Leipzig, 1929), p. 591. Compare also the frequent distinctions between Church History or History of Theology and (general) *Geistesgeschichte.*

[6] *Werke,* XI, 524.

[7] See Zeeden, II, 269-300 (J.S. Semler); *ibid.,* II, 300-25 (G.E. Lessing); *ibid.,* II, 328-40 (Fredrick the Great). G. Hornig, *Die Anfänge der historisch-kritischen Theologie: Johann Salomo Semlers Schriftverständnis und seine Stellung zu Luther* (Göttingen, 1961), especially ch. V, "Semlers Lutherkritik," ch. VI, "Semlers Luthernachfolge." H. Bornkamm, *Luther im Spiegel der deutschen Geistesgeschichte: Mit ausgewählten Texten von Lessing bis zur Gegenwart* (2nd ed.; Heidelberg, 1970), pp. 16-21. There further literature about Lessing's relations to Luther. W. von Loewenich, *Luther und der Neuprotestantismus* (Witten, 1963), pp. 16-22.

[8] E. Hirsch, *Fichtes, Schleiermachers und Hegels Verhältnis zur Reformation* (Göttingen, 1930). H. Bornkamm, pp. 31-36. W. von Loewenich, pp. 28-33. E.-W. Kohls, *Das Bild der Reformation in der Geisteswissenschaft des 19. Jahrhunderts (G. W. F. Hegel, L. von Ranke, J. Burckhardt), NZSTh,* IX (1967), 229-46.

[9] Bornkamm, pp. 91-92, 266-74. W. von Loewenich, *Jacob Burckhardt und die Kirchengeschichte,* in: W. von Loewenich, *Humanitas-Christianitas* (Witten, 1968), pp. 103-29. Kohls, pp. 242-45.

[10] Bornkamm, pp. 92-94 (see for additional bibliography), pp. 305-14.

[11] Fr. Nietzsche, "Menschliches, Allzumenschliches: Ein Buch für freie Geister," 1878, no. 237, in: *Nietzsches Werke* (Leipzig, 1899-1904), I, ii, 224-25. See also Bornkamm, pp. 306-7.

[12] A. Rüstow, *Ortsbestimmung der Gegenwart: Eine universalgeschichtliche Kulturkritik,* vol. II, *Weg der Freiheit* (Erlenbach-Zürich, 1952), 303.

[13] The references to prophesies which are said to have been fulfilled in Luther (cf., e.g., Zeeden, II, 12, 63-66, 98), imply the direct opposite from the historical, genetic questions which were far removed in that time. Luther made some allusions, granted very subjectively colored, in this respect to Tauler, Hus, von Staupitz, and others.

[14] Especially in the preface to vol. I of the *Opera Latina* of the 1545 Wittenberg edition. *WA,* LIV, 179: 22ff., 183: 21 ff.

[15] For example, Thomas Müntzer, "Hochverursachte Schutzrede . . ." (1524), in *Thomas Müntzer: Politische Schriften mit Kommentar,* ed. C. Hinrichs, (Halle [Saale], 1950), p. 101: 545-46. Cf. p. 97: 479-81; Thomas Müntzer, *Schriften und Briefe: Krit. Gesamtausgabe,* ed. G. Franz (Gütersloh, 1968), pp. 342-43:27-28; cf. p. 340:14-16). I am indebted to Reinhard Schwarz for the references.

[16] See Zeeden, II, 4 (Melanchthon); *ibid.,* II, 104 (E. Willich); *ibid.,* II, 129-30 (J. M. A. Musäus); *ibid.,* II, 157-58 (V.L. Frhr. von Seckendorf); *ibid.,* II, 186, 188-89, 191 (Ph. J. Spener); *ibid.,* II, 218-22 (G. Arnold).

[17] Zeeden, II, 198-200 (Ph. J. Spener).

[18] Historical preparation: see Zeeden II, 270 (J.S. Semler); *ibid.,* II, 352-53 (I. Iselin). Continuing Reformation: *ibid.,* II, 278-79 (J.S. Semler). Luther's person: *ibid.,* II, 275, 281 (J.S. Semler); *ibid.,* II, 303-4 (G.E. Lessing).

[19] *Werke,* XI, 519-20.

[20] G.W.F. Hegel, *Die Vernunft in der Geschichte,* ed. G. Lasson, Ph. Bibl. 171a, 40.

[21] *Werke,* XIX, 255; see p. 253: "Die Haupt-Revolution ist in der lutherischen Reformation eingetreten . . ."

[22] *Werke,* XI, 518; *ibid.,* XIX, 266-67.

[23] *Werke,* XIX, 255: "Diess Gelten des Subjektiven hat nun jetzt einer höheren Bewährung und der höchsten Bewährung bedurft, um vollkommen legitimiert zu seyn, und sogar zur absoluten Pflicht zu werden; und um diese Bewährung erhalten zu können, hat es aufgefasst werden müssen in seiner reinsten Gestalt. Die höchste Bewährung des Princips ist nun die religiöse Bewährung: so dass diess Princip der eigenen Geistigkeit, der eigenen Selbständigkeit erkannt wird in der Beziehung auf Gott und zu Gott; dann ist es durch die Religion geheiligt. Die blosse Subjektivität, blosse Freiheit des Menschen, dass er einen Willen hat, und damit diess oder jenes treibt, berechtigt noch nicht; der barbarische Wille, der sich nur mit subjectiven Zwecken erfüllt, die nicht vor der Vernunft Bestand haben, ist nicht berechtigt." *Werke,* XIX, 256: "So ist hier das Princip der Subjecktivität, der reinen Beziehung auf mich, die Freiheit, nicht nur anerkannt: sondern es ist schlechthin gefordert, dass es nur darauf ankomme im Kultus, in der Religion. Diess ist die höchste Bewährung des Princips, dass dasselbe nur vor Gott gelte, nur der Glaube des eigenen Herzens, die Überwindung des eigenen Herzens nöthig sey; damit ist denn diess Prin-

cip der christlichen Freiheit erst aufgestellt, und zum Bewusstseyn, zum wahrhaften Bewusstseyn gebracht worden."

[24] About *dieses* as the concrete content of the direct assurance of the *jetzt* and *hier,* see *Werke,* II, 81-92; in religious respect, *Werke,* II, 494-99, 520-23.

[25] *Werke,* XIX, 265.

[26] *Werke,* XI, 520-21.

[27] *Werke,* XI, 494-99.

[28] *Werke,* XIX, 266: "Das Princip der inneren Versöhung des Geistes war an sich die Idee des Christenthums, aber selbst wieder entfernt, nur äusserlich, als Zerrissenheit, unversöhnt. Wir sehen die Langsamkeit des Weltgeistes, diese Äusserlichkeit zu überwinden. Er höhlt das Innere aus,—der Schein, die äussere Gestalt, bleibt noch; aber zuletzt ist sie eine leere Hülse, die neue Gestalt bright hervor."

[29] *Werke,* XI, 522; *ibid.,* XIX, 257: "Nur im Genuss und Glauben stehe ich in Beziehung zu Gott."

[30] *Werke,* XIX, 256; *ibid.,* XIX, 253: "Aus dem Jenseitigen wurde so der Mensch zur Präsenz des Geistes gerufen; und die Erde und ihre Körper, menschliche Tugenden und Sittlichkeit, das eigene Herz und das eigene Gewissen fingen an, ihm Etwas zu gelten."

*Ibid.,* XI, 523: "[Der Glaube] ist überhaupt nicht Glauben an Abwesendes, Geschehenes und Vergangenes; sondern die subjektive Gewissheit des Ewigen, der an und für sich seyenden Wahrheit, der Wahrheit von Gott. Von dieser Gewissheit sagt die lutherische Kirche, dass sie nur der heilige Geist bewirkt, d.h. eine Gewissheit, die nicht dem Individuum nach seiner particularen Besonderheit, sondern nach seinem Wesen zukommt."

[31] *Werke,* XI, 524.

[32] *Werke,* XI, 532.

[33] *Werke,* XIX, 254-55.

[34] *Werke,* XIX, 258: "Diess Princip nun ist zuerst aufgefasst innerhalb der Religion, dadurch hat es seine absolute Berechtigung erhalten, ist aber zunächst nur in Beziehung auf religiöse Gegenstände gesetzt erschienen; es ist noch nicht ausgedehnt auf die weitere Entwicklung des subjektiven Princips selbst."

*Ibid.,* XI, 532: "Die Versöhnung Gottes mit der Welt war zunächst noch in abstracter Form, noch nicht zu einem Systeme der sittlichen Welt entwickelt."

[35] *Werke,* XI, 524; *ibid.,* XI, 526: "Doch war zu einer politischen Umgestaltung, als Consequenz der kirchlichen Reformation, die Welt damals noch nicht reif."

[36] *Werke,* XIX, 258.

[37] *Werke,* XIX, 259.

[38] *Werke,* XI, 532-33.

[39] *Werke,* XIX, 261: "Ein anderes und unrichtiges Verhalten zu dem Inhalt ist, demselben äusserlich zu nehmen, z. B. nach dem grossen neuen Princip der Exegese, dass die Schriften des neuen Testaments behandelt werden sollen, wie ein griechischer oder lateinischer und anderer Schriftsteller, kritisch, philologisch, historisch. Das wesentliche Verhalten des Geistes ist nur für den Geist. Und es ist ein verkehrtes Beginnen einer störrischen Exegese, auf solche äusserliche philologische Weise die Wahrheit der christlichen Religion zu erweisen, wie diess die Orthodoxie gethan hat; der Inhalt wird so geistlos."

[40] With this designation I indicate how in historical questions, especially by taking up sociological aspects, Troeltsch maintains a (real or supposed) narrow approach to considerations in the history of thought. However, I am conscious that he wants to use the concept *Kulturwissenschaften* as little as *Geisteswissenschaften.* See *Gesammelte Schriften* (Tübingen, 1912ff.), III, 84: "Die Bezeichnung historisch-ethische Wissenschaften für die Zusammenfassung von entwickelnder Geschichtsdarstellung, soziologisch vergleichender Systematik, systematischen Geisteswissenschaften und Ethik ziehe ich den gangbaren Bezeichnungen 'Geisteswissenschaften' (Mill und Dilthey) vor, die bald psychologistisch, bald spiritualistisch verstanden werden und den Anteil der Natur an der Geschichte ausser Augen lassen und 'Kulturwissenschaften' (Hermann Paul und Rickert), die bald soziologistisch, bald werttheoretisch aufgefasst werden. Die Doppelbezeichnung weist zugleich auf den engen Zusammenhang von Sein, Werden und Sollen auf diesem Gebiete hin. Auch der Unterschied gegenüber der gar nicht zu leugnenden, aber andersartigen Naturgeschichte und-entwicklung ist damit ausgesagt."

[41] E.g., in W. Dilthey, "Auffassung und Analyse des Menschen im 15. und 16. Jahrhundert" (1891-92), *Gesammelte Schriften* (5th ed.; Stuttgart, 1957), II, 56-57: ". . . dieser mit der grossen Tradition der Kirche einige Glaubensinhalt gab den Reformatoren die heroische Kraft, Apparat und Disziplin der Kurie abzuschütteln und kirchenbildend zu wirken. Aber zugleich muss es doch dabei bleiben: dieser Zusammenhang religiöser Begriffe ist nicht der Ausgang des Dogma, das 'Ende des alten dogmatischen Christentums' . . . , sondern hat dieses überall zu seiner notwendigen Voraussetzung. Er steht und fällt selbst mit

dem Dogma. Ja sogar das mönchische, franziskanische religiöse Ideal muss als die Voraussetzung für die Lehre von der Sünde und von dem Unvermögen zum Guten angesehen werden. In dem Masse, in welchem die Erbsündenlehre von dieser dualistisch motivierten Unterlage losgelöst wurde, musste sie zu einer ganz unhaltbaren Darstellung der Erfahrungen über die Menschennatur greifen." See H. Bornkamm, pp. 100-3, 314-23; W. von Loewenich, pp. 48-55; E.-W. Kohls, "Das Bild der Reformation bei Wilhelm Dilthey, Adolf von Harnack und Ernst Troeltsch," *NZSTh,* XI (1969), 269-91.

[42] *Lehrbuch der Dogmengeschichte* (5th ed.; Leipzig, 1932), III, 809: "Die Reformation, wie sie sich in dem Christenthum Luther's darstellt, ist . . . in vieler Hinsicht eine altkatholische, resp. auch eine mittelalterliche Erscheinung, dagegen auf ihren religiösen Kern beurtheilt, ist sie es nicht, vielmehr Wiederherstellung des paulinischen Christenthums im Geiste einer neuen Zeit." 810f: "Es ist eine ganz einseitige, ja sträflich abstracte Betrachtung Luther's, die in ihm den Mann der neuen Zeit, den Helden eines heraufsteigenden Zeitalters oder den Schöpfer des modernen Geistes feiert." See H. Bornkamm, pp. 83-84, 290-97; W. von Loewenich, pp. 118-29; W. Pauck, *Harnack and Troeltsch: Two Historical Theologians* (New York, 1968); E.-W. Kohls, pp. 278-85.

[43] From E. Troeltsch's writings I cite the following: "Protestantisches Christentum und Kirche in der Neuzeit," in *Kultur der Gegenwart* (2nd ed.; Berlin and Leipzig, 1909), I, iv, 1 (1906), 431-755; "Luther, der Protestantismus und die moderne Welt," in *Ges. Schr.,* IV, 202-54 (to this two previous essays provided by the compilation of the editor, H. Baron, "Luther und die moderne Welt," 1908, and "Luther und der Protestantismus," 1917—see *ibid.,* IV, xi-xiv); "Die Bedeutung des Protestantismus für die Enstehung der modernen Welt," *Historische Zeitschrift,* XCVII (1906), 1-66, or "Beiheft" 2 of the *Historische Zeitschrift* (cited as "Die Bedeutung"). For Troeltsch's concept of Luther and the Reformation: H. Bornkamm, pp. 107-10, 373-83; H. Fischer, "Luther und seine Reformation in der Sicht E. Troeltschs," *NZSTh,* V (1963), 132-72; W. von Loewenich, 130-40; W. Pauck; E.-W. Kohls, 285-91.

[44] *Ges. Schr.,* IV, 253: "Die religionslose Philosophie und die unphilosophische Religion müssen schwinden, wenn es wieder Gesundung und geistigen Zusammenhang geben soll, und wer die Dinge in diesem Lichte sieht, der beobachtet auch in dem Werden des modernen Geistes überall die Arbeit an jenem Gedanken der coincidentia oppositorum, dem weder Theologie noch Philosophie der alten Zeit gewachsen waren. Hegel hat das Problem des Cusaners wieder aufgenommen, und das moderne Denken sucht im Grunde neue Mittel zur Lösung der Hegelschen Probleme."

[45] "Die Bedeutung," p. 7.

[46] An exact, chronological, comprehensive investigation of the problem how Troeltsch changed his accents and nuances in the historical arrangement of the Reformation and under what influences this happened, in consideration of the revision of individual writings from edition to edition as well as with reference to the interdependent circumstances would be a very difficult, but perhaps a rewarding task.

[47] "Die Bedeutung," pp. 6-7.

[48] *Ibid.,* p. 12: "An diesem Gegensatze erhellt nun das Wesen der modernen Kultur. Sie ist überall die Bekämpfung der kirchlichen Kultur und deren Ersetzung durch autonom erzeugte Kulturideen, deren Geltung aus ihrer überzeugenden Kraft, aus ihrer immanenten und unmittelbar wirkenden Eindrucksfähigkeit folgt. Die wie immer begründete Autonomie im Gegensatz gegen die kirchliche Autorität, gegen rein äussere und unmittelbare göttliche Normen, beherrscht alles. Auch wo man neue Authoritäten prinzipiell aufrichtet oder tatsächlich befolgt, wird doch deren Geltung selbst auf rein autonome und rationelle Überzeugung begründet; und auch, wo die älteren religiösen Überzeugungen bestehen bleiben, wird doch ihre Wahrheit und verpflichtende Kraft, wenigstens bei den Protestanten, in erster Linie auf eine innere persönliche Überzeugung und nicht auf die herrschende Autorität als solche begründet."

[49] *Ibid.,* pp. 8-16. See also the essay, "Das Wesen des modernen Geistes" (1907) in *Ges. Schr.,* IV, 297-338.

[50] *Ges. Schr.,* IV, 230.

[51] "Protestantisches Christentum und Kirche," p. 433.

[52] *Ibid.*

[53] "Die Bedeutung," p. 16.: "Es ist damit nicht gesagt, dass alle israelitisch-christlichen Kräfte des religiösen Lebens wurzellos geworden seien. Aber so, wie sie die Erlösungsanstalt der autoritativen, für das Jenseits erziehenden und disziplinierenden Kirche zu begründen vermochten, sind sie allerdings ausserordentlich matt und schwach geworden. Sie können keine kirchliche Kultur mehr erzeugen und tragen."

*Ibid.,* p. 30: ". . . von einer Wirkung des Protestantismus zur Herbeiführung der modernen Kultur kann nur in bezug auf die verschiedenen Gruppen des Altprotestantismus die Rede sein, während der Neuprotestantismus selbst ein Bestandteil der modernen Kultur und von ihr tiefgreifend beeinflusst ist."

*Ges. Schr.*, IV, 215: "In Wahrheit ist die neue Religion der Gnade, des Glaubens und der Erwählung eine ungeheure Vereinfachung der Religion, eine gründliche Verinnerlichung und Verpersönlichung, eine Wiedereinsaugung des Moralismus in die religiöse Idee; es bedurfte nur der Ablösung von dem scholastischen Weltbild, von den christologisch-trinitarischen Dogmen, von der übernatürlichen Offenbartheit der Schrift und von der anthropomorphen Gottesidee, um daraus die ganze Welt heutiger religiösser Innerlichkeit und persönlicher Glaubensïberzeugung hervorzubringen. In Wahrheit ist Christliches und Weltliches, Staat und Kirche, Kultur und religiöse Innerlichkeit doch scharf getrennt und nur nachträglich und mühsam wieder zu einer Analogie der mittelalterlichen Lebenseinheit zusammengebogen . . ."

[54] "Die Bedeutung," p. 44; *ibid.*, pp. 44-45: ". . . so erlebte Europa trotz gleichzeitiger Verbreitung der Ideen und Lebensformen der Renaissance wieder zwei Jahrhunderte mittelalterlichen Geistes. Wer freilich von der Geschichte des Staatsleben oder der Wirtschaft herkommt, wird diesen Eindruck nicht haben, da hier die Ansätze des Spätmittelalters sich ungebrochen weiterentwickeln, ja den Protestantismus zum guten Teil in ihren Dienst nehmen. Aber wer von der Geschichte der Religion, des Ethos und der Wissenschaft herkommt, wird sich dem Eindruck nicht entziehen können, dass erst der grosse Befreiungskampf des endenden 17. und 18. Jahrhunderts das Mittelalter grundsätzlich beendet."

[55] *Ges. Schr.*, IV, 214.

[56] *Ges. Schr.*, IV, 215: "Wie im Frühmittelalter Ritter und Mönch die Brennpunkte einer Ellipse bildeten, so wird jetzt die Verschmelzung von Bürger und Christ der Mittelpunkt eines geschlossenen Lebenskreises. Ein verinnerlichtes, verpersönlichtes und verbürgerlichtes, in seiner religiösen Tiefe bis zum höchsten Glauben und bis zum Fanatismus neu erregtes Spätmittelalter steht hier vor uns."

[57] "Die Bedeutung," p. 46; *ibid.*, "Dazu kommt weiter, dass die innere kirchliche Struktur der protestantischen Kirche, vor allem des Luthertums, doch bedeutend schwächer ist als die des Katholizismus und daher gegenüber der modernen Ideenwelt weniger dauernde Widerstandskraft besass als der Katholizismus."

[58] *Ibid.*, pp. 22-23: "Indem der Protestantismus gerade an der Herausbildung dieses religiösen Individualismus und an seiner Überleitung in die Breite des allgemeinen Lebens seine Bedeutung hat, ist von vornherein klar, dass er an der Hervorbringung der modernen Welt erheblich mitbeteiligt ist."

See also within the context of the citation in the previous note *ibid.*, p. 47: "Die geringere Widerstandskraft allein hat es nicht getan. Der Protestantismus besass vielmehr allerhand der modernen Welt entgegenkommende Strebungen, die ihn befähigten, im Konflikt nicht bloss zu unterliegen, sondern sich mit dem neuen zu amalgamieren, und zwar viel stärker zu amalgamieren, als das auf seine Weise auch der Katholizismus in der Kultur der Gegenreformation und in seiner modernen Entwicklung gekonnt hat."

[59] *Ibid.*, p. 88: "Die eigentliche und letzte Frage, wenn es sich um die Bedeutung des Protestanismus für die moderne Welt handelt, ist daher die, in welcher Beziehung gerade seine religiöse Kraft und Grundidee zu dem religiösen Wesen des modernen Geistes steht, ob dieses, wie es auch in der Gegenwart seine relative Unabhängigkeit von den einzelnen Kulturgestaltungen besitzt, in ihm wesentlich wurzelt und von ihm bestimmt ist. Die Frage nach seiner Bedeutung für die Entstehung der modernen Welt fällt nicht zusammen mit der nach seiner Bedeutung für die der modernen Kultur. Denn diese ist nicht identisch mit dem in ihr sich aufringenden religiösen Leben. Es bleibt die letzte Frage die nach dem Verhältnis der protestantischen Religiosität zur modernen Religion, zu der mit der modernen Kulturwelt zusammenhängenden, aber in ihr nicht erschöpften Religion."

*Ges. Schr.*, VI, 206-7: "In England haben Locke und der Deismus, in Frankreich Rousseaus Menschenrechte und Gefühlsreligion, in Deutschland die mit Leibniz, Lessing und Kant eröffnete deutsche Religionsphilosophie eine neue Religiosität nicht aus sich begründet, aber von sich aus bedingt und zur Einfügung in ein neues Bild der Dinge und in ein neues Ideal der Gesellschaft und Kultur genötigt. Alles das ist nicht ohne den Protestantismus geschehen, negativ überhaupt durch Zerbrechung des Kirchentums ermöglicht und positiv aus vielen Lebenssäften des Protestantismus genährt, aber nach andern Seiten hin von den Nachwirkungen der Renaissance und des Humanismus und von dem konfessionell gänzlich unberührten Geiste der neuen Philosophie aufgebaut. So gesehen erscheint der Protestantismus als Vorbedingung und Anreger einer neuen, spezifisch modernen, jedenfalls von dem Kirchenwunder und altchristlichen Dogma gelösten Religiosität."

[60] Troeltsch, "Die Bedeutung," p. 92, posits it for a *geschichtlicher Erfahrungssatz*" dass ohne religiöse Grundlage, ohne Metaphysik und Ethik, ein einheitlicher und starker Kulturgeist unmöglich ist." "So wird man auch rein tatsächlich sagen dürfen, dass die Religion der modernen Welt wesentlich vom Protestantismus bestimmt ist und dass hierin seine stärkste historische Bedeutung liegt. Freilich ist es kein einheitlicher Protestantismus. Es ist ein tief und innerlich gewandelter . . ."

Compare also Troeltsch's judgment about the historical dependence of the three new force (the modern natural sciences, the new philosophy which is related to them, and the new political system of national superstates) on the old forces (antiquity, Christianity, and the Roman-Germanic spirit of the Middle Ages) and his judgment of the enduring references to these. *Ges. Schr.*, IV, 203: "Dieses Neue hängt nun aber mit den alten Urgewalten nicht bloss überall näher oder enger entwicklungsgeschichtlich zusammen und trägt sie dadurch sozusagen in seiner Tiefe mit sich, sondern ist überdies so wenig befähight, den ganzen Lebenswillen auszufüllen und zu formen, dass daneben eine selbständige, ununterbrochene Mitwirkung jener drei alten Urgewalten stattfindet, die nun nicht mehr bloss unter sich ihre Gegensätze, Verwandtschaften, Berührungen und Fortentwicklungen auszuwirken fortfahren, sondern auch mit den neuen modernen Elementen die verschiedenartigsten Verbindungen eingehen und Gegensätze hervorrufen."

[61] "Die Bedeutung," p. 30: ". . . von einer Wirkung des Protestantismus zur Herbeiführung der modernen Kultur kann nur in bezug auf die verschiedenen Gruppen des Altprotestantismus die Rede sein, während der Neuprotestantismus selbst ein Bestandteil der modernen Kultur und von ihr tiefgreifend beeinflusst ist."

[62] "Protestantisches Christentum und Kirche," pp. 438-39; "Die Bedeutung," p. 32; *Ges. Schr.*, IV, 212, 214.

[63] Cf. Hanns Rückert, "Die geistesgeschichtliche Einordnung der Reformation," *Zeitschrift für Kirche und Theologie*, LII (1955), 48 where he cites correctly as a masterful formulation Troeltsch's statement from "Protestantisches Christentum und Kirche," p. 436: Der Protestantismus "ist *zunächst* in seinen wesentlichen Grundzügen und Ausprägungen eine Umformung der mittelalterlichen Idee, und das Unmittelalterliche, Moderne, das in ihm unleugbar bedeutsam enthalten ist, kommt als Modernes erst voll, in Betracht, nachdem die erste und klassiche Form des Protestantismus zerbrochen oder zerfallen war."

[64] *Ges. Schr.*, IV, 205: "[Die Reformation und der Protestantismus bilden] eine grossartige und mächtige Übergangserscheinung, nicht in dem Sinne, wie alle geschichtlichen Schöpfungen aufblühen und abwelken und neuen Platz machen, sondern in dem Sinne, dass ihr ganzes inneres Wesen sich aus dieser Zwischenstellung erklärt und das Alte und Neue eigentümlich und unwiederholbar verbunden in sich trägt. Nicht ihre Vergänglichkeit, von der ja bis jetzt gar nicht die Rede sein kann, sondern ihre widerspruchsvolle innere Zusammengesetztheit bedeutet also der Ausdruck 'Übergangserscheinung'." Also *Ges. Schr.*, IV, 231.

[65] *Ges. Schr.*, IV, 231: ". . . diese Charakterisierung als Übergangsgebilde gilt nur vom protestantischen Kirchentum, genauer gesagt vom orthodoxen Altprotestantismus. Sie gilt nicht von dem Manne, der den Ausgangspunkt und Sammelpunkt aller dieser Kräfte bildet, von Luther selbst. Wenigstens kann sie von ihm nur sehr viel eingeschränkter gelten. Er ragt . . . in die Region des Zeitlosen und Allgemein-Menschlichen hinein, . . . durch die Ursprünglichkeit und Kraft seines religiösen Erlebnisses."

[66] "Die Bedeutung," pp. 20ff; *Ges. Schr.*, IV, 220.

[67] "Die Bedeutung," pp. 12-13: "Eine absolut überindividuelle Bindung bringt nur eine so ungeheure Macht wie der Glaube an eine unmittelbare supranaturale göttliche Offenbarung hervor, wie sie der Katholizismus besass . . ." Here one must ask, of course, how Troeltsch relates individualism to "the region of the timeless and common "hamanness." See note 2 above.

[68] H. Blumenberg, *Die Legitimität der Neuzeit* (Frankfurt-M., 1966).

[69] *Ibid.*, pp. 143-44, 59. The interpretation of Luther as the radical epitome of Nominalism is likely the weakest passage in this volume, which in many respects is stimulating.

[70] Cf. e.g., the well-known statement of the Smalcald Articles. *WA*, L, 245: 1-247: 4; *Die Bekenntnisschriften der evangelisch-lutherischen Kirche* (6th ed.; Göttingen, 1967), pp. 453: 16-456: 18.

[71] *Ges. Schr.*, IV, 236.

[72] See H. Bornkamm, p. 75.

[73] E. H. Erikson, *Der junge Mann Luther: Eine psychoanalytische und historische Studie* (Hamburg, 1958), pp. 9, 53, 236, 238, 278-79.

[74] *Werke*, XIX, 266.

[75] See E. Heintel, *Die beiden Labyrinthe der Philosophie: Systemtheoretische Betrachtungen zur Fundamentalphilosophie des abendländischen Denkens* (Munich, 1968), I, 59.

[76] P. Tillich, *Systematische Theologie* (Chicago, 1951ff.), I, 74ff.

[77] *Werke*, XI, 514.

**Quentin Skinner (essay date 1978)**

SOURCE: "The Principles of Lutheranism," in *The Foundations of Modern Political Thought, Vol. 2*, Cambridge University Press, 1978, pp. 3-19.

[*Here, Skinner describes how Luther's theological tenets ultimately required individual obedience to secular authority.*]

**Søren Kierkegaard on Luther's role in history:**

. . . [Christians in the Middle Ages] came up with the idea of meritoriousness, thought that they earned merit before God through their good works. And it became worse: they thought they had merit so such a degree through thier good works that they thought they benefited not only the person himself but one could, like a capitalist and bondsman, let others benefit. And it grew worse; it became an out-and-out business: people who had never once thought of producing some of these so-called good works themselves now had plenty to do with good works, inasmuch as they were put into business as hucksters who sold the good works of others at fixed but cheap prices.

Then Luther appears. This condition, he declares, is spiritlessness; otherwise you who think to earn salvation by good works are bound to perceive that this is the sure road eiher to *presumptuousness*, consequently to the loss of salvation, or to *despair*, consequently to the loss of salvation. To want to build upon good works—the more you practice them, the stricter you are with yourself, the more you merely develop the anxiety in you, and new anxiety. On this road, if a person is not completely devoid of spirit, on this road he comes only to the very opposite of peace and rest for his soul, to discord and unrest. No, a person is justified solely by faith. Therefore, in God's name, to hell with the pope and all his helpers' helpers, and away with the monastery, together with all your fasting, scourging, and all the monkey antics that come into use under the name of imitation. . . .

*Søren Kierkegaard, in* For Self-Examination; Judge for Yourself, *edited and translated by Howard V. Hong and Edna H. Hong, Princeton University Press, 1990.*

To begin the story of the Lutheran Reformation at the traditional starting-point is to begin in the middle. Luther's famous act of nailing up the ***Ninety-Five Theses*** on the door of the Castle Church at Wittenberg on the Eve of All Saints in 1517 (which may not even have happened) [1] merely marks the culmination of a long spiritual journey on which he had been travelling at least since his appointment over six years before to the chair of Theology in the University of Wittenberg. One of the main achievements of Lutheran scholarship in the past generation has been to trace the course of Luther's intellectual development during this formative time. The basis for this reinterpretation has been provided by the rediscovery of the materials he used in giving his lectures on the Psalms in 1513-14, on the Epistle to the Romans in 1515-16, and on the Epistle to the Galatians in 1516-17. The outcome has been the suggestion that it would only be a 'slight exaggeration', as Rupp puts it, to claim that 'the whole of the later Luther' can already be discerned in the pages of these early lecture-notes (Rupp, 1951, p. 39). The implication is that it may be best to begin the story where Luther himself began: with the development of his new theology, which provided him with the framework for his subsequent attack not just on the Papacy's traffic in indulgences, but on the whole set of attitudes, social and political as well as religious, which had come to be associated with the teachings of the Catholic Church.

### THE THEOLOGICAL PREMISES

The basis of Luther's new theology, and of the spiritual crisis which precipitated it, lay in his vision of the nature of man. Luther was obsessed by the idea of man's complete unworthiness. To a modern psychologist this may appear as evidence of a particularly severe crisis of identity, an 'integrity crisis' in which the sufferer comes to have a total mistrust in the value of his own existence (Erikson, 1958, p. 254). Luther's more conventional biographers, however, have been content to see this simply as a case of 'pitting one type of Catholicism against another, Augustinianism against Thomism' (Bainton, 1953a, p. 36). Luther's vision caused him to reject the optimistic view of man's capacity to intuit and follow the laws of God which the Thomists had characteristically emphasised, and led him back to the earlier and more pessimistic Augustinian emphasis on man's fallen nature.

This doctrine not only represented a break with Thomism, but an even sharper rejection of the elevated view of man's virtues and capacities which, as we have seen, the humanists had more recently popularised. Luther was thus prompted to mount a violent attack on the humanist ideal of a *philosophia pia,* and in particular on the 'heathen and publican' Erasmus, the most dangerous exponent of their arrogant creed. The occasion for this definitive breach with the humanists was provided by the publication of Erasmus's discourse *On the Freedom of the Will* in 1524. Erasmus had at first appeared as a cautious ally of the Reformation, applauding the ***Ninety-Five Theses*** and helping to ensure that Luther was not condemned unheard by the Imperial authorities (Rupp, 1953, pp. 264-7). He soon became more evasive, however, especially after Luther had been excommunicated. We find him writing to Wolsey in 1519 to deny that he had read Luther's works, and to Luther himself at the same time to urge him to proceed more cautiously (Allen, 1906-58, III, pp. 589-606). By 1521 he was insisting a trifle mendaciously that he had 'opposed the pamphlets of Luther more than any other man', and two years later he finally yielded to the demand—voiced by the Pope and Henry VIII amongst others—that he should compose an anti-Lutheran tract (Allen, 1906-58, IV, pp. 536-40). Luther's doctrine of man presented the obvious target for his humanist talents, and the outcome was the treatise *On the Freedom of the Will,* in which he not only opposed Luther's views with copious citations from the scriptures and Church Fathers, but also prefaced his discussion with the characteristically dismissive remark that he would 'prefer men to be persuaded not to waste their time and talents in labyrinths of this kind' (p. 41).

Luther clearly felt goaded as well as alarmed by this somewhat unexpected attack from such an influential quarter. He quickly produced an elaborate and exceptionally violent reply, in which he developed a comprehensive statement of his own theological position, and included a definitive presentation of his anti-humanist and ultra-Augustinian doctrine of man. This was published in 1525 as ***The Bondage of the Will***. Gerrish has emphasised that it would be a mistake to characterise this assault on the idea of a *philosophia pia* as a completely 'irrationalist' one (Gerrish, 1962, p. 25). Luther certainly never seeks to deny the value of natural reason, in the sense of man's reasoning powers, nor does he condemn the use of 'regenerate reason' when it is 'serving humbly in the household of faith' (Gerrish, 1962, pp. 25-6). He even makes a residual use of the concept of natural law, although he usually equates this source of moral knowledge simply with the promptings of a man's conscience (McNeill, 1941). He is implacably opposed, however, to Erasmus's central and typically humanist contention that it is open to a man to employ his powers of reasoning in order to understand how God wishes him to act. He repeatedly insists that in this context all man's reasoning powers are simply 'carnal' and 'absurd' (pp. 144, 224). We have all 'fallen from God and been deserted by God', so that we are all completely 'bound, wretched, captive, sick, and dead' (pp. 130, 175). This makes it ridiculous as well as sinful to suppose that we can ever hope 'to measure God by human reason' and in this way to penetrate the mysteries of His will (p. 172). The true situation, as Luther seeks to indicate in the title of his tract, is that our wills remain at all times in total bondage to sin. We are all so 'corrupt and averse from God' that we have no hope of ever being able to will 'things which please God or which God wills' (pp. 175-6). All our actions proceed from our 'averse and evil' natures, which are completely enslaved to Satan, and thus ensure that we can 'do nothing but averse and evil things' (pp. 98, 176). The result is that 'through the one transgression of the one man, Adam, we are all under sin and damnation', and are left with 'no capacity to do anything but sin and be damned' (p. 272).

This vision of man's bondage to sin commits Luther to a despairing analysis of the relationship between man and God. He is forced to acknowledge that since we cannot hope to fathom the nature and will of God, His commands are bound to appear entirely inscrutable. It is at this point that he most clearly reveals his debt to the Ockhamists: he insists that the commands of God must be obeyed not because they seem to us just but simply because they are God's commands (p. 181). This attack on the Thomist and humanist accounts of God as a rational lawgiver is then developed into the distinctively Lutheran doctrine of the twofold nature of God. There is the God who has chosen to reveal Himself in the Word, whose will can in consequence be 'preached, revealed, offered and worshipped' (p. 139). But there is also the hidden God, the *Deus Absconditus*,[2] whose 'immutable, eternal and infallible will' is incapable of being comprehended by men at all (pp. 37, 139). The will of the hidden God is omnipotent, ordaining everything that happens in the world. But it is also beyond our understanding, and can only be 'reverently adored, as by far the most awe-inspiring secret of the divine majesty' (p. 139).

Luther is also forced to accept a second and even more despairing implication of his doctrine of man. Since all our actions inexorably express our fallen natures, there is nothing we can ever hope to do which will justify us in the sight of God and so help us to be saved. This is really the chief point at issue between Erasmus and Luther, and the main theme of ***The Bondage of the Will*** (Boisset, 1962, pp. 38-9). The debate with Erasmus is not about the freedom of the will in the ordinary philosophical sense. Luther is quite prepared to concede that men can freely 'eat, drink, beget, rule', and even that they can freely perform good acts by following 'the righteousness of the civil and moral law' (p. 275). What he is concerned to deny is Erasmus's definition of the freedom of the will in terms of 'a power of the human will by which a man can apply himself to the things which lead to eternal salvation' (p. 103). Luther insists on the contrary that 'since men are flesh and have a taste for nothing but the flesh, it follows that free choice avails for nothing but sinning', and that all men are 'consigned to perdition by ungodly desire' (pp. 214, 226). The despairing conclusion of ***The Bondage of the Will*** is thus that 'free choice is nothing' and virtuous acts are of no value in relation to salvation (p. 241).

These conclusions suggest to Luther a further implication which, as he goes on to tell us, at one time brought him 'to the very depth and abyss of despair' (p. 190). He has conceded that man's impotence is such that he can never hope to be saved by his own efforts. He has argued that God's omnipotence is such that the hidden God who 'works all in all' must already have a complete foreknowledge of all future as well as past events. (Luther even takes sides at this point in the scholastic debate over the nature of God's foreknowledge, affirming (p. 42) that 'God foreknows all things, not contingently, but necessarily and immutably'.)[3] The implication of these claims, as he is forced to admit, is a doctrine of double predestination—the contention that some men must already be predestined to be saved while others are predestined to be damned. And this thunderbolt, as he calls it, seemed to open up an unbridgeable gulf between God and man (p. 37). God appears terrifyingly inexorable: it is entirely for Him to decide, and He must already have decided, which of us is to be spared. And man is left completely helpless: it is possible that we are all damned, and it is certain that no one can ever hope to change his fate.

This conclusion at first induced in Luther a prolonged spiritual crisis. His affliction appears to have begun as early as 1505, when he suddenly abandoned his proposed career in law after a series of traumatic personal incidents and decided instead to enter the Augustinian monastery at Erfurt (Fife, 1957, p. 73). The crisis seems to have deepened in 1510, after he returned from a visit to Rome which seems to have left him, as Fife suggests, 'disillusioned and to some extent disheartened' about the state of the Church (Fife, 1957, p. 176). Luther himself gives an account of his spiritual condition during these years in the autobiography which he published in 1545 as a Preface to the Wittenberg edition of his Latin works (pp. 336-7). He tried the traditional monastic remedies of fasting and prayer, but these failed to bring him any solace. He turned to the study of Augustine, but this merely confirmed his sense of hopelessness. He found himself driven to the frightening blasphemy of cursing and hating God for providing men with a law which they are unable to keep, and then righteously damning them for failing to keep it. He speaks of coming to hate the very word 'righteousness' (*iustitia*), which he understood to refer to the justice of God in punishing sinful men, and he found himself unable even to look at those parts of the New Testament—especially the Epistles of St Paul—in which the concept of God's righteousness is assigned a central place (Boehmer, 1946, p. 110).

Then, after years of deepening anguish, Luther suddenly attained a tremendous new insight which brought him permanent relief. The moment evidently came to him while he was engaged in the mundane academic task of preparing a new lecture-course, working in the tower-room of the monastery at Wittenberg.[4] While reading over and paraphrasing the Psalms, he was struck by a completely new interpretation of the crucial phrase in Psalm 30, 'Deliver me in thy righteousness'—*in iustitia tua libera me* (Boehmer, 1946, p. 109). It suddenly occurred to him that the concept of the righteousness of God referred not to His punitive powers, but rather to His readiness to have mercy on sinful men, and in this way to justify them by delivering them from their unrighteousness. After this, as Luther himself reports in his autobiography, he felt that he had been 'altogether born again and had entered paradise itself through open gates' (p. 337).

Luther himself speaks of his 'tower-experience' (*Turmerlebnis* both in his autobiography and in the ***Table Talk*** recorded by Conrad Cordatus (pp. 193-4). A number of commentators have recently sought to show that the outcome, his ultra-Augustinian doctrine of justification, was in fact the product of a gradual evolution in his thought. But all the scholars who pioneered the study of Luther's intellectual development—in particular Vogelsang, Bornkamm and Boehmer—agreed in seeing this doctrine as the fruit of a sudden epiphany, which they all dated to some time in the year 1513. The dating will doubtless continue to be a subject of learned debate,[5] but the crucial significance of the episode in Luther's development is not in doubt: it suddenly enabled him to bridge the agonising gap between God's omnipotence and man's unrighteousness. It was at this point that he at last felt able, under the promptings of his spiritual adviser, Johann von Staupitz, to turn to the intensive study of St Paul's Epistles, and to compose his commentaries on Romans, Galatians and Hebrews. The outcome was the complete new theology in terms of which he then turned and rent the Papacy and the whole Catholic Church.

The core of Luther's theology is constituted by his doctrine of justification *sola fide,* 'by faith alone'. He continues to stress that no one can ever hope to be justified—that is, granted salvation—by virtue of his own works. But he now argues that it must be open to anyone to perceive God's *gratia*—the 'saving grace' which He must already have granted as a totally unmerited favour to those whom He has predestined to be saved. He is thus able to propose that the sole aim of the sinner must be to achieve *fiducia*—a totally passive faith in the righteousness of God and in the consequent possibility of being redeemed and justified by His merciful grace.

Once Luther attained this fundamental insight, all the other distinctive features of his theology gradually fell into place. He was able first of all to give a complete account of the concept of justification underlying his pivotal doctrine of faith. This was first fully stated in the sermons and disputations of 1518-20, and in particular in the sermon of 1519 entitled ***Two Kinds of Righteousness*** (Saarnivaara, 1951, pp. 9-18, 92-5). Here Luther moved decisively beyond the traditional patristic idea of justification as a gradual process of eradicating the believer's sins. He now sees it as an immediate consequence of *fides apprehensiva*—'a grasping and appropriating faith' which enables the sinner suddenly to seize Christ's righteousness for himself, so that he becomes 'one with Christ, having the same righteousness as he' (p. 298; cf. Althaus, 1966, p. 230). The result is an intensely strong emphasis on the idea that the righteousness of the believer is never *domestica*—never achieved by himself, and still less deserved. It can only be *extranea*—an 'alien righteousness, instilled in us without our works by grace alone' (p. 299). The believer is at all times seen as *simul justus et peccator*—at once a sinner and justified. His sins are never abrogated, but his faith ensures that they cease to count against him.

Luther next proceeded to relate this account of faith and justification to the process by which the life of the sinner comes to be sanctified. This further theme also emerges clearly for the first time in the sermons of 1518-20 (Cranz, 1959, pp. 41-3). The Christian is now pictured as the simultaneous inhabitant of two realms—that of Christ and that of worldly things. The justification of the sinner comes first, and happens 'not piecemeal but all at once' (Cranz, 1959, p. 126). As Luther phrases it in his sermon on ***Two Kinds of Righteousness,*** the redeeming presence of Christ 'swallows up all sins in a moment' (p. 298). The process of sanctification then 'follows gradually' once the sinner has acquired his faith (Cranz, 1959, p. 126). The result is a distinction which is central to Luther's social and political thought, and also underlies Melanchthon's influential doctrine of 'adiaphora': the distinction between a primary and passive concept of justice which Christians are able to attain in the realm of Christ, and an active or civil justice which is not a part of salvation, but remains essential to the proper regulation of worldly affairs.

Luther's pivotal belief in God's redeeming grace next enabled him to resolve the cruel dilemma posed by the Old Testament, with its law which no one can hope to follow and its threat of damnation for those who fail to follow it. His answer, first explicitly stated in ***The Freedom of a Christian*** in 1520, takes the form of marking a sharp antithesis between the message of the Old and the New Testaments, an antithesis between God's impossible commands and his redeeming promises (p. 348). The purpose of the Old Testament is now said to be to 'teach man to know himself', in order that 'he may recognise his inability to do good and may despair of his own inability'—as Luther himself had so profoundly despaired (p. 348). This is 'the strange work of the law'. The contrasting purpose of the New Testament is to reassure us that although we may be unable to attain salvation 'by trying to fulfil all the works of the law', we may be able to attain it 'quickly and easily through faith' (p. 349). This is 'the proper work of the gospel'. The implication of this 'law-gospel dialectic', as McDonough has labelled it, is thus that it corresponds exactly to the individual's 'despair-faith' experience of sin and grace. And with Luther's contrast between these two positions, as McDonough adds, we return to 'the very heart and core of his basic convictions' (McDonough, 1963, pp. 1-3).

The relation between these doctrines serves in turn to illuminate a further characteristic feature of Luther's theology: his account of the significance of Christ. It is Christ who transmits to men their knowledge of God's redeeming grace. It is thus through Christ alone that we become emancipated from the impossible demands of the law and receive 'the good news' that we may be saved. This means that in spite of Luther's emphasis on the powers of the hidden God, there is nothing mystical about his outlook, in the sense of inviting us merely to contemplate God's remoteness and infinity. Luther is always at pains to present his theology as a *theologia crucis,* in which Christ's sacrifice remains the key to our salvation. Christ is 'the only preacher' and 'the only saviour', who not only lifts from us the burden of our moral worthlessness, but also serves as 'the source and the content of the faithful knowledge of God' (Siggins, 1970, pp. 79, 108).

Given this view of Luther's christology, it seems somewhat misleading to suggest—as Troeltsch has done in his classic account of Luther's social thought—that Luther found 'the objective revelation of the moral law' entirely in the Decalogue, and took this law to be 'simply confirmed and interpreted by Jesus and the Apostles' (Troeltsch, 1931, p. 504). This judgment certainly holds good for Calvin, who always laid a strong emphasis on the immediate moral relevance of the Old Testament. When applied to Luther, however, it appears to obscure the transforming role he assigned to Christ's sacrifice. For Luther, far more than for Calvin, Christ is perceived as coming not only to fulfil the law, but also to release the faithful from its demands by His redeeming merit and love. The consequence is that for Luther, though not for Calvin, it is always essential to understand the commands of the law in the light of the gospel, not the gospel in the light of the law (Watson, 1947, p. 153).

Finally, Luther's solfidianism—his doctrine of justification 'by faith alone'—leads him to enunciate the two main features of his heretical concept of the Church. He first of all devalues the significance of the Church as a visible institution. If the attainment of *fiducia* constitutes the sole means by which the Christian can hope to be saved, no place is left for the orthodox idea of the Church as an authority interposed and mediating between the individual believer and God (Pelikan, 1968). The true Church becomes nothing more than an invisible *congregatio fidelium,* a congregation of the faithful gathered together in God's name. This Luther saw as a sublimely simple concept, completely encapsulated in his claim that the Greek word *ecclesia,* which is habitually used in the New Testament to denote the primitive Church, should be translated simply as *Gemeinde* or congregation (Dickens, 1974, p. 67). Despite his assurance, however, that 'a child of seven knows what the Church is', his apparently simple doctrine was widely misunderstood, especially by those who took him to be saying that he wished 'to build a church as Plato a city, which nowhere exists'.[6] In his mature theological writings he sought to counter these misconstructions by adding that while the Church is merely a *communio,* it is also a *republica,* and as such needs to have a visible embodiment in the world (Watson, 1947, pp. 169-70; Cranz, 1959, pp. 126-31). His treatise ***On the Councils and the Church,*** first issued in 1539, even includes an influential enumeration of the 'marks' or signs which are taken to be necessary (though never sufficient) for distinguishing a fellowship which genuinely constitutes 'a Christian holy people' from a mere group of papists or 'Antinomian devils' (Luther was thinking of the Anabaptists) who might claim to have received the divine light (p. 150). While introducing these later concessions, however, Luther continued to insist that the true Church has no real existence except in the hearts of its faithful members. His central conviction was always that the Church can simply be equated with *Gottes Volk,* 'the people of God living from the word of God' (Bornkamm, 1958, p. 148).

The other distinctive feature of Luther's concept of the Church is that, in stressing the idea of the *ecclesia* as nothing more than a *congregatio fidelium,* he also minimises the separate and sacramental character of the priesthood. The outcome is the doctrine of 'the priesthood of all believers' (Rupp, 1953, pp. 315-16). This concept and its social implications are most fully worked out in the famous ***Address*** of 1520 directed 'To the Christian Nobility of the German Nation'. Luther argues that if the Church is only *Gottes Volk,* it must be 'a piece of deceit and hypocrisy' to claim that 'Pope, bishop, priests and monks are called the spiritual estate, while princes, lords, artisans and farmers are called the temporal estate' (p. 127). Luther wishes to abolish all such false dichotomies, and to insist that 'all Christians are truly of the spiritual estate', since they belong to it not in virtue of their role or rank in society, but simply in virtue of their equal capacity for faith, which makes them all equally capable of being 'spiritual and a Christian people' (p. 127). He deploys this argument partly as a way of claiming that all believers, and not just the priestly class, have an equal duty and capacity to help their brethren and assume responsibility for their spiritual welfare. But his main concern is clearly to reiterate his belief in the ability of every faithful individual soul to relate without any intermediary to God. The result is that throughout his his ecclesiology, as in his theology as a whole, we are continually led back to the central figure of the individual Christian and his faith in God's redeeming grace.

### THE POLITICAL IMPLICATIONS

Luther's theology carried with it two political implications of major importance, which together account for most of what is distinctive and influential about his social and political thought. First of all, he is clearly committed to repudiating the idea that the Church possesses jurisdictional powers, and thus has the authority to direct and regulate Christian life. It is of course the abuse of these alleged powers which Luther mainly denounces, and especially the traffic in indulgences, the subject of his original outburst in the ***Ninety-Five Theses***. The sale of indulgences was a longstanding scandal (already satirised in Chaucer) which had been given a theological basis as early as the Bull *Unigenitas* in 1343.[7] This declared that the merit Christ had displayed in sacrificing himself was even greater than the amount needed to redeem the entire human race. It went on to proclaim that the Church has the power to dispense this extra merit by selling indulgences (that is, remissions of penance) to those who confess their sins. The doctrine was dangerously extended by Sixtus IV in 1476 with the claim that souls in purgatory could also be helped by the purchase of an indulgence on their behalf. It was a short step from this doctrine to the popular belief—cited by Luther in the twenty-first of his ***Ninety-Five Theses***—that by offering an immediate cash-payment for an indulgence one might eventually curtail one's sufferings after death (p. 127). It will already be evident why this system was particularly liable to spark off Luther's protests. To Luther, the belief in the efficacy of indulgences was simply the most wicked perversion of a general doctrine which he had come to believe as a theologian to be wholly false: the doctrine that it is possible for the Church to enable a sinner to attain salvation by means of its authority and sacraments. As we have seen, he had reached the conclusion that if a sinner attains *fiducia,* he will be saved without the Church; if he does not, there is nothing the Church can do to help him. The Papacy's claim to remit the wages of sin thus appeared to Luther as nothing more than the most grotesque of all the Church's attempts to devalue these central truths. The point is fiercely made in the attack on the Papacy and its agents which takes up most of the ***Address*** to the Christian nobility. 'For payment of money they make unrighteousness into righteousness, and they dissolve oaths, vows and agreements, thereby destroying and teaching us to destroy the faith and fealty which have been pledged. They assert that the Pope has authority to do this. It is the Devil who tells them to say these things. They sell us doctrine so satanic, and take money for it, that they are teaching us sin and leading us to hell' (p. 193).

The real focus of Luther's attack, however, was not so much on the Church's abuses of its powers, but rather on the Church's right to claim any such powers in Christian society at all. This first of all prompted him to repudiate all the institutions of the Church which were based on the assumption that the clergy constitute a separate class with special jurisdictions and privileges. This attack simply followed from his belief in the spiritual nature of the true Church, and in particular from the doctrine that, as the ***Address*** puts it, 'we are all consecrated priests through baptism' (p. 127). One outcome was a complete rejection of the canon law. Luther insists in the ***Address*** that the only reason why 'the Romanists' wish to maintain this separate legal system, which 'exempts them from the jurisdiction of the temporal Christian authority', is in order that 'they can be free to do evil' and remain unpunished (p. 131). One of his concluding proposals is thus that 'it would be a good thing if canon law were completely blotted out', since 'the greater part smacks of nothing but greed and pride' while the absolute authority of the Pope over the interpretation of its contents makes any serious study of it 'just a waste of time and a farce' (p. 202). Within six months of publishing the ***Address*** Luther had followed his own advice. He presided over a book-burning at Wittenberg in December 1520 at which he not only destroyed the Papal Bull *Exsurge Domine,* in which his excommunication had been pronounced, but also committed the *Decretals* and commentaries of the canonists to the flames at the same time (Fife, 1957, p. 581). This urge to reject the idea of a separate clerical estate also led him to attack the mendicant orders, and to repudiate the whole ideal of the monastic way of life. He broaches this theme in the ***Address,*** which includes the demand 'that the further building of mendicant houses should not be permitted' and that all existing convents and monasteries should be regulated 'in the same way they were regulated in the beginning, in the days of the Apostles' (pp. 172-4). But his main attack occurs in the major treatise of 1521 entitled ***The Judgment of Martin Luther on Monastic Vows***. The monastic life is denounced both for violating 'evangelical freedom' and for assigning a misplaced value to works, and in this way being 'against the Christian faith' (pp. 295-6). The book ends with a defence of the sweeping assertion that 'monasticism is contrary to common sense and reason', in the course of which Luther ridicules the monastic ideal of celibacy and mounts a vigorous defence of clerical marriage (p. 337).

Luther's objections to the status and powers of the Church also led him to repudiate every claim by the ecclesiastical authorities to exercise any jurisdiction over temporal affairs. It is sometimes said that this involved him in defending 'the separate jurisdiction of the State as distinct from the Church' (Waring, 1910, p. 80). His central belief about the Church, however, was rather that, since it is nothing more than a *congregatio fidelium,* it cannot properly be said to possess any separate jurisdiction at all. It is true that his argument is easily misunderstood at this point, since he continues to speak of the Two Kingdoms (*Zwei Reiche*) through which God exercises His complete dominion over the world. The Christian is said to be a subject of both these 'regiments', and Luther even speaks of the government of the spiritual kingdom as 'the government of the right hand of God' (Cargill Thompson, 1969, pp. 169, 177-8). It is generally clear, however, that what he has in mind when discussing the rule of the spiritual kingdom is a purely inward form of government, 'a government of the soul', which has no connection with temporal affairs, and is entirely dedicated to helping the faithful to attain their salvation. This interpretation can readily be corroborated by considering the important tract of 1523, on ***Temporal Authority: to what extent it should be obeyed,*** one of the key documents of Luther's social and political thought. He bases his discussion on the distinction between the immediate justification and the later sanctification of the faithful sinner (p. 89). He agrees that all Christians live simultaneously in two kingdoms, that of Christ and that of the world. He then goes on to equate the first with the Church and the second with the realm of temporal authority. The Church is thus taken to be ruled entirely by Christ, whose powers are entirely spiritual, since there is by definition no need for true Christians to be coerced. The realm of temporal authority is equally claimed to be ordained by God, but is seen as wholly separate, since the sword is granted to secular rulers simply in order to ensure that civil peace is maintained amongst sinful men (p. 91). All coercive powers are thus treated as temporal by definition, while the powers of the Pope and bishops are said to consist of 'nothing more than the inculcating of God's word', and are thus 'not a matter of authority and power' in the worldly sense at all (p. 117). It follows that any claims by the Pope or the Church to exercise any worldly jurisdictions in virtue of their office must represent a usurpation of the rights of the temporal authorities.

Luther's theological premises not only committed him to attacking the jurisdictional powers of the Church, but also to filling the power-vacuum this created by mounting a corresponding defence of the secular authorities. He first of all sanctioned an unparalleled extension of the range of their powers. If the Church is nothing more than a *congregatio fidelium,* it follows that the secular authorities must have the sole right to exercise all coercive powers, including powers over the Church. This does not of course impinge on the true Church, since it consists of a purely spiritual realm, but it definitely places the visible Church under the control of the godly prince. This does not mean that the *rex* becomes a *sacerdos,* nor that he is granted any authority to issue declarations about the content of religion. His duty is simply to foster the preaching of the gospel and to uphold the true faith. But it does mean that Luther is prepared to envisage a system of independent national Churches, in which the prince is given the right to appoint and dismiss the officers, as well as to control and dispose of the Church's property. The point is emphatically made at the start of the ***Address,*** where Luther affirms that 'since the temporal power is ordained of God to punish the wicked and protect the good, it should be left free to perform its office in the whole body of Christendom without restriction and without respect to persons, whether it affects Pope, bishops, priests, nuns or anyone else' (p. 130). For Luther, this means that the tremendous theoretical battle waged throughout the Middle Ages by the protagonists of the *regnum* and the *sacerdotium* is suddenly brought to an end. The idea of the Pope and Emperor as parallel and universal powers disappears, and the independent jurisdictions of the *sacerdotium* are handed over to the secular authorities. As Figgis expresses it, Luther destroyed 'the metaphor of the two swords; henceforth there should be but one, wielded by a rightly advised and godly prince' (Figgis, 1960, p. 84).

Luther committed himself to an even more radical defence of the secular authorities when he turned to consider the basis of the powers they might rightfully claim to exercise. He is emphatic in declaring that all their enactments must be treated as a direct gift and expression of God's providence. This makes it strange to say, as Allen has done, that Luther never concerns himself 'with any question of the nature or derivation of authority' (Allen, 1957, p. 18). Luther could scarcely be more explicit in acknowledging that all political authority is derived from God. The text to which he constantly recurs, and which he regards as the most important passage in the whole Bible on the theme of political obligation, is the injunction of St Paul (at the start of Chapter 13 of the Epistle to the Romans) that we should submit ourselves to the highest powers, and treat the powers that be as ordained of God. Luther's influence helped to make this the most cited of all texts on the foundations of political life throughout the age of the Reformation, and it furnishes the basis for the whole of his own argument in the tract on ***Temporal Authority***. He begins by demanding that 'we must provide a sound basis for the civil law', and his opening argument is that this must above all be sought in St Paul's command: 'Let every soul be subject to the governing authority, for there is no authority except from God' (p. 85).

This commitment in turn leads Luther's discussion of the power of princes in two different directions. He first of all stresses that the prince has a duty to use the powers God has given him in a godly way, and above all to 'command for truth'. The main exposition of this theme occupies the final section of the tract on ***Temporal Authority***. The prince 'must really devote himself' to his subjects. He must not only foster and maintain true religion amongst them, but also 'protect and maintain them in peace and plenty' and 'take unto himself the needs of his subjects, dealing with them as though they were his own needs' (p. 120). He must never exceed his authority, and must in particular avoid any attempt 'to command or compel anyone by force to believe this or that', since the regulation of such a 'secret, spiritual, hidden matter' can never be said to lie within his competence (pp. 107-8). His main duties are simply 'to bring about external peace', to 'prevent evil deeds' and in general to ensure that 'external things' are 'ordered and governed on earth' in a decent and godly way (pp. 92, 110).

Luther does not in fact believe that the princes and nobles of his own day have been educated in such a way as to make them adequately aware of these duties. As he insists at the end of his ***Address*** to the nobility, very few of them have any sense of 'what an awful responsibility it is to sit in high places' (p. 215). In the ***Address*** he denounces the training offered in the universities, where godly students are exposed to the false moral and political principles of 'the blind heathen teacher Aristotle' (p. 200). And in the treatise on ***Temporal Authority*** he pours scorn on the fashionable humanist ideals of noble and princely conduct, ridiculing all 'the princely amusements—dancing, hunting, racing, gaming and similar worldly pleasures' (p. 120). The effect of all these pernicious influences is that 'a wise prince is a mighty rare bird' (p. 113). Luther repeatedly insists that in practice the leaders of political society are usually 'consummate fools' and 'the worst scoundrels on earth' (pp. 106, 113). He even despairingly concludes at one point that 'God almighty has made our rulers mad' (p. 83).

Luther makes it clear, moreover, that no respect or obedience is due to such worthless rulers when they attempt to involve their subjects in their ungodly and scandalous ways. He sets a firm boundary to the authority of princes by insisting, in a favourite phrase, that they are merely the 'masks' or *larvae* of God. If a ruler tears off the mask which identifies him as God's lieutenant, and commands his subjects to act in evil or ungodly ways, he must never be obeyed. The subject must follow his conscience, even if this means disobeying his prince. The point is underlined in the form of a catechism at the end of the tract on ***Temporal Authority***. 'What if a prince is in the wrong? Are his people bound to follow him then too?' The answer is 'No, for it is no one's duty to do wrong' (p. 125). Luther is unwavering in his emphasis on this aspect of his theory of political obligation. He treats all claims to absolute power as a misunderstanding and perversion of the authority God has granted to princes (Carlson, 1946, p. 267). And he repeatedly appeals for the confirmation of this view-point to a passage in the book of Acts which unequivocally demands that 'We must obey God (who desires the right) rather than men'.[8] For Luther, no less than for the later reformers who continually reverted to the same text, this is always taken to establish a decisive limitation on the general duty of political obedience.

Luther is equally pulled in the opposite direction, however, by his over-riding emphasis on the Pauline doctrine that 'the powers that be are ordained of God'. Despite his stress on the idea that an ungodly ruler must never be obeyed, he is no less insistent that such a ruler must never be actively resisted. Since all powers are ordained, this would still be tantamount, even in the case of a tyrant, to resisting the will of God. This harsh contrast between the equal duties of disobedience and of non-resistance to tyranny is clearly brought out in the central section of the tract on ***Temporal Authority***. If the prince commands you to do evil, you must refuse, saying that 'it is not fitting that Lucifer should sit at the side of God'. If the prince should then 'seize your property on account of this and punish such disobedience', you must passively submit and 'thank God that you are worthy to suffer for the sake of the divine word' (p. 112). Luther in no way mitigates his previous emphasis on the claim that such behaviour is tyranny, and that we must never 'sanction it, or lift a little finger to conform, or obey'. But he still insists that there is nothing further to be done, since tyranny 'is not to be resisted but endured' (p. 112).

In the early 1530s, when it seemed likely that the armed forces of the Empire might destroy the Lutheran Church, Luther suddenly and permanently changed his mind over this crucial issue. Throughout the 1520s, however, he had a special motive for wishing to emphasise the doctrine of non-resistance as strongly as possible. He shared the common fear of the reformers that their demands for religious change might become associated with political radicalism and in consequence discredited. This was the reason for the ***Sincere Admonition*** of 1522, which Luther addressed 'to all Christians', warning them 'to guard against insurrection and rebellion'. He optimistically predicted that, in spite of the wickedness of the Catholic Church, there would not in fact be any rebellion against it. But he also took the opportunity to remind his readers in a far more alarmed tone that 'God has forbidden insurrection' and to plead with those 'who read and rightly understand my teaching' to recognise that there is nothing in it which excuses or justifies any attempt to bring about political revolution (pp. 63, 65).

When the Peasants' Revolt broke out in Germany in 1524, Luther's fears that the radicals might distort his political teachings reached a peak of hysteria, and prompted him to react to the revolt with shocking brutality.[9] Before the serious fighting broke out, his initial response was to travel to Thuringia, one of the centres of unrest, and to publish there an eirenic ***Admonition to Peace***. This merely urged the princes to attempt conciliation, and reminded the peasants that 'the fact that the rulers are wicked and unjust does not excuse disorder and rebellion' (p. 25). By May of 1525, however, the peasants had won major victories in Thuringia, and were pillaging throughout the south of Germany. Luther then responded with his famous outburst ***Against the Robbing and Murdering Hordes of Peasants***. This brief but shattering tirade simply takes its stand squarely on St Paul's command that 'every person be subject to the governing authorities'. The peasants have totally ignored this command, and 'are now deliberately and violently breaking this oath of obedience'. This constitutes such a 'terrible and horrible sin' that all of them 'have abundantly merited death'. Since they have all attempted to resist the will and ordinance of God, we may safely conclude that all of them have already 'forfeited body and soul' (pp. 49-50).

It was not merely an immediate terror of rebellion which caused Luther to lay such an absolute emphasis on the duty of non-resistance, and it is impossible to excuse the tone of his tract against the peasants by treating it as a momentary aberration induced by an immediate political crisis. The stance he took up was a direct outcome of his key theological belief that the whole of the existing framework of social and political order is a direct reflection of God's will and providence. This appears most clearly in the major political tract he published in the year following the Peasants' Revolt on the question of ***Whether Soldiers too can be Saved***. This begins by repeating all over again that the people must be prepared to 'suffer everything that can happen' rather than 'fight against your lord and tyrant' (pp. 112-13). Some of the reasons are practical: 'it is easy to change a government, but it is difficult to get one that is better, and the danger is that you will not' (p. 112). But the main reason is essentially theological: since the establishment of political rule lies 'in the will and hand of God', it follows that 'those who resist their rulers resist the ordinance of God, as St Paul teaches' (pp. 112, 126).

It might seem that such a stringent doctrine of non-resistance is bound to lead to one awkward consequence: it appears to make God the author of evil, since it commits us to saying that God ordains the rule of the madman and tyrant no less than that of the godly prince. Luther acknowledges and deals with this difficulty in the tract on whether soldiers can be saved. He propounds an extremely influential answer, derived from St Augustine, which is not merely compatible with his basic doctrine of non-resistance but actually contrives to enhance it. He simply insists that the reason why evil and tyrannical rulers are from time to time ordained by God is, as Job says, 'because of the people's sins'. It is 'blind and perverse' of the people to think that sheer power sustains the wicked ruler, and thus that 'the tyrant rules because he is such a scoundrel'. The truth is 'that he is ruling not because he is a scoundrel but because of the people's sin' (p. 109).

Luther's major political tracts may thus be said to embody two guiding principles, both of which were destined to exercise an immense historical influence. He treats the New Testament, and especially the injunctions of St Paul, as the final authority on all fundamental questions about the proper conduct of social and political life. And he claims that the political stance which is actually prescribed in the New Testament is one of complete Christian submission to the secular authorities, the range of whose powers he crucially extends, grounding them in such a way that their rule can never in any circumstances be legitimately resisted. The articulation of these principles involved no appeal to the scholastic concept of a universe ruled by law, and scarcely any appeal even to the concept of an intuited law of nature: Luther's final word is always based on the Word of God.

*Works Cited*

Allen, J. W. (1957), *A History of Political Thought in the Sixteenth Century* (revised edn, London, 1957).

Allen, P. S. (1906-58), *Opus Epistolarum Des. Erasmi Roterodami,* 12 vols (Oxford, 1906-1958).

Althaus, Paul (1966), *The Theology of Martin Luther* (Philadelphia, 1966).

Bainton, R. H. (1953), *The Reformation of the Sixteenth Century* (London, 1953).

Bendry, L. (1950), *La Querelle des futurs contingents* (Louvain, 1465-75) (Paris, 1950).

Boehmer, Heinrich (1946), *The Road to Reformation,* trans. J. W. Doberstein and T. G. Tappert (Philadelphia, 1946).

Boisset, Jean (1962), *Erasme et Luther: Libre ou serf arbitre?* (Paris, 1962).

Bornkamm, Heinrich (1958), *Luther's World of Thought,* trans. Martin H. Bertram (St Louis, Mo., 1958).

Cargill Thompson, W. D. J. (1969), 'The "Two Kingdoms" and the "Two Regiments": Some Problems of Luther's *Zwei-Reiche-Lehre*', *The Journal of Theological Studies* 20 (1969), pp. 164-85.

Carlson, Edgar (1946), 'Luther's Conception of Government', *Church History* 15 (1946), pp. 257-70.

Cranz, F. Edward (1959), *An Essay on the Development of Luther's Thought on Justice, Law and Society* (Cambridge, Mass., 1959).

Dickens, A. G. (1974), *The German Nation and Martin Luther* (London, 1974).

Erikson, Erik H. (1958), *Young Man Luther: A Study in Psychoanalysis and History* (London, 1958).

Fife, Robert H. (1957), *The Revolt of Martin Luther* (New York, 1957).

(1960), *Political Thought from Gerson to Grotius, 1414-1625,* with an Introduction by Garrett Mattingly (New York, 1960).

Gerrish, B. A. (1962), *Grace and Reason: a Study in the Theology of Luther* (Oxford, 1962).

Green, V. H. H. (1964), *Renaissance and Reformation,* 2nd edn (London, 1964).

Iserloh, Erwin (1968). *The Theses Were not Posted: Luther between Reform and Reformation* (London, 1968).

McDonough, Thomas M. (1963), *The Law and the Gospel in Luther* (Oxford, 1963).

Mackensen, Heinz F. (1964), 'Historical Interpretation and Luther's Role in the Peasant Revolt', *Concordia Theological Monthly* 35 (1964), pp. 197-209.

Mackinnon, James (1925-30), *Luther and the Reformation,* 4 vols (London, 1925-30).

McNeill, John T. (1941), 'Natural Law in the Thought of Luther', *Church History* 10 (1941), pp. 211-27.

Pelikan, Jaroslav (1968), *Spirit versus Structure: Luther and the Institutions of the Church* (London, 1968).

Rupp, E. Gordon (1951), *Luther's Progress to the Diet of Worms, 1521* (London, 1951).

———. (1953), *The Righteousness of God* (London, 1953).

Saarnivaara, Uuras (1951), *Luther Discovers the Gospel* (St Louis, Mo., 1951).

Siggins, Ian D. Kingston (1970), *Martin Luther's Doctrine of Christ* (New Haven, Conn., 1970).

Spitz, Lewis W. (1953), 'Luther's Ecclesiology and his Concept of the Prince as *Notbischof*', *Church History* 22 (1953), pp. 113-41.

Troeltsch, Ernst (1931), *The Social Teaching of the Christian Churches,* trans. Olive Wyon, 2 vols (London, 1931).

Waring, Luther H. (1910), *The Political Theories of Martin Luther* (New York, 1910).

Watson, Philip S. (1947), *Let God be God! An Interpretation of the Theology of Martin Luther* (London, 1947).

*Notes*

[1] For this allegation see Iserloh, 1968, esp. pp. 76-97.

[2] The reference is to Isaiah, Chapter 45, verse 15.

[3] For a discussion of this debate, as conducted at the University of Louvain in the fifteenth century, see Baudry, 1950, esp. pp. 27-46.

[4] But folklore tells a less polite story at this point, as W. H. Auden reminds us in the appropriate section of *About the House* (London, 1965, p. 117):

> Revelation came to
> Luther in a privy.

[5] The evidence in favour of an evolutionary interpretation has been best presented by Saarnivaara, 1951, pp. 59-120. The original interpretation has been powerfully restated, however, in a reply to Saarnivaara by Bornkamm, 1961-2. The debate is well surveyed by Dickens, 1974, pp. 85-8, who inclines cautiously to Saarnivaara's side.

[6] For these references, and for an account of Luther's response to these misunderstandings, see Spitz, 1953, esp. pp. 122ff.

[7] I take the following details about the history of indulgences from Green, 1964, pp. 113-14, 119-20.

[8] See *Temporal Authority*, p. 125. The allusion is to Acts, Chapter 5, v. 29.

[9] For a suvvcy of discussions about Luther's role, see Mackensen, 1964. For a full account of his activities, see Mackinnon, 1925-30, vol. 3, pp. 159-210.

## Heiko Augustinus Oberman (essay date 1986)

SOURCE: "Simul Gemitus et Raptus: Luther and Mysticism," in *The Dawn of the Reformation: Essays in Late Medieval and Early Reformation Thought*, T. & T. Clark Ltd, 1986, pp.126-34.

[*Below, Oberman outlines approaches to studying Luther and mysticism, and discusses Luther's own understanding of the role of mysticism in faith.*]

"We will deal with that material than which none is more sublime, none more divine, and none more difficult to attain . . ." Jean Gerson[1]

"That [mystical] rapture is not the passageway [to God]." Martin Luther[2]

### 1. INTRODUCTION

It cannot be our task to determine whether Luther is to be regarded as a mystic. For an empathic biographer it is interesting that Luther himself testifies to the highest degree of mystical experience when he writes: "once I was carried away (*raptus fui*) to the third heaven."[3] Yet, in complete accordance with a widespread concern and hesitancy almost monotonously expressed in late medieval pastoral literature, he also states in 1516 that this "negotium absconditum" is a rare event.[4] Furthermore there are grave dangers in the pursuit of the *suavitas* which "is rather the fruit and reward of love than love itself."[5] Luther never based his authority on special revelations or high mystical experiences, nor does he write for the "aristocrats of the Spirit" who are granted a special foretaste of the glory to come. Rather it is our task to investigate the relation between Luther and medieval mystical theology and its possible significance for the formation and understanding of Luther's theology.

The fact that *mysticism* is a form or degree of religious experience, and hence to some extent individually determined, makes this topic highly elusive. We have to turn, therefore, to mystical theology, which is the effort of those who may or may not have had these experiences themselves to report, order, or teach the methods and goals of "the mystical way." Even so we shall find that there is a considerable variety of views both as to the method and goal germane to Christian mysticism. Furthermore, in the particular case of Luther, I believe that a consensus can be reached among scholars in the field that it is highly precarious to separate the mystical tissue from the living organism of Luther's spirituality. The tissue of mysticism cannot be treated as one aspect of Luther's theology, such as his relation to certain historical events, men, or movements (e.g. the Black Death, Karlstadt, or the Hussites) but it is part and parcel of his overall understanding of the Gospel itself and therefore pervades his understanding of faith, justification, hermeneutics, ecclesiology, and pneumatology.

### 2. METHODOLOGICAL CONSIDERATIONS

In view of the complexity of the question before us it is not my intention to offer any final solutions, but rather to indicate a series of desiderata for research and suggest the direction in which the problem might be fruitfully pursued in the years ahead.

Centuries of controversy are reflected in the varying views presented on Luther's relation to mysticism: the tension between Philippism and Pietism; the differing views on the relation of the young Luther to the mature or—more descriptively—the old Luther; the evaluation of the thesis of "the Reformers before the Reformation"; the Holl-Ritschl debate on justification as impartation (*sanatio*) versus imputation; the intimate interplay of politico-nationalistic and theological factors in the clash of *Deutsche Christen* and the *Bekennende Kirche* reflected in the confrontation of Luther as the spokesman of an endemic "Deutsche" or "Germanische Mystik" (Eckhart-Luther-Nietzsche!) versus an appeal to Luther as the witness to the God who is *totaliter aliter,* without a natural point of contact (*Seelengrund,* etc.) in man; the unclarity regarding the relation of the *Via moderna* to the *Devotio moderna*—and more generally of nominalism to mysticism. It will prove to be impossible to bypass these battlefields, but we will have to approach them with appropriate caution.

Yet the greatest obstacle methodologically is doubtless the fact that the terms "mysticism" and "mystical theology" themselves shift in meaning from author to author. The preliminary question is therefore: what is mysticism and with what structure of thought do we compare Luther?

On first sight the most obvious procedure for answering this question, which has indeed recently been suggested, is: "What is common to mystics, and where do we find these common elements in Luther?"[6] On two scores we cannot accept this solution. In the first place there is no guarantee that the common denominator gathers in much more than a general structure such as *purgatio, illuminatio, unio,* or the contrast between scholastic theology and mystical theology as *sapientia doctrinalis* versus *sapientia experimentalis.* Perhaps more important, the search for the common mystical denominator presupposes that one knows what authors are to be regarded as mystics and therefore the proper subject of investigation.

The alternative approach is a dogmatic answer. Protestant theologians are not too helpful for our purposes because they have by and large chosen the *via negativa* in their evaluation of mysticism, inclined to regard the *Christus pro nobis* and *extra nos* as alternatives to the *Christus in nobis.*

A clearer answer can be garnered from Roman Catholic manuals and encyclopedias. In Thomistically oriented works one frequently encounters the name of Philipp of the Holy Trinity, well known as interpreter of St. Thomas and famous for his *Summa Theologiae Mysticae,* first published in Lyon in 1656. His influential definition is: "mystical and heavenly theology is a kind of knowledge of God drawn forth or produced by divinely infused light through the union of the will with God."[7] We are fortunate in that there is a recent and learned example of the application of this standard to a topic similar to ours: Augustine's relation to mysticism.[8] Without explicitly mentioning the definition quoted above, the author relies on Philipp for the corresponding description of the stages leading to mysticism in the strict sense of the word. In a few words we report his outline to clarify both his final conclusion and the technical terms we shall use later on. The first stage is ascetics or mysticism in the general sense of the word. It starts with oral prayer and meditation characterized by "discursive, decisional thinking."[9] Not study as such but love is the goal, and the more love is elicited the more an irrational element characteristic of love is introduced so that finally in persistent meditation the intuitive mode replaces the discursive mode of thought. From the resulting affective prayer, "the state of meditation, in which purification and inner unification is achieved, transforms itself, with the aid of God's grace, into an acquired state of contemplation."[10] The ensuing peace of soul and enjoyment of divine truth should not be confused with mysticism proper. What is important is that "the acquired state of contemplation is a habit and a fully controllable act which is accessible to every individual soul, given the assistance of ordinary grace."[11]

It is only from here onward that one embarks upon the *via mystica* proper—to which I shall refer as "high mysticism"—when the soul suffers in sheer receptivity and passivity the divinely infused contemplation, is transformed in spiritual marriage, and finally absorbed into God, gazing upon God Himself or upon the Holy Trinity. Applying this definition to the thought of St. Augustine, Hendrikx argues that Augustine teaches merely the achievement of *sapientia* with the aid of ordinary grace, typical of acquired and not of infused contemplation; therefore "in the closed system of Augustinian convictions there is no place for mystical knowledge of God in the genuine sense of the word."[12]

Since the two stages of acquired and infused contemplation are alien to Luther's thought, acceptance of Hendrikx' definition of mysticism would mark the end of this essay. Furthermore, this scholastic understanding of mysticism—which is anachronistic with regard to Augustine—excludes with St. Augustine a large group of eastern and western theologians from the realm of mystical theology "in the genuine sense of the word," since it presupposes the thirteenth century secularization of Neoplatonic and Augustinian epistemology.

In addition to the phenomenological and dogmatic solutions, there is still a third option, namely, the historical-genetic approach. Again in the year 1936 Erich Vogelsang made a significant contribution by no longer operating with the general and usually vague concept of mysticism. After first enumerating the mystical authors said to be known to Luther—Dionysius Areopagita, Hugh and Richard of St. Victor, Bernard, Bonaventure, Gerson, Brigit of Sweden, Tauler, and "the Frankfurter"—Vogelsang distinguished between

"Dionysian mysticism" (*areopagistische Mystik*), "Latin mysticism" (*romanische Mystik*), and "German mysticism" (*Deutsche Mystik*). With this more differentiated view of mysticism, Vogelsang could give a more refined answer to our question: (1) From 1516 onward Luther renders the clear verdict of "No" to "Dionysian mysticism" as a speculative bypassing of the incarnate and crucified Christ;[13] (2) *re* "Latin mysticism" both a "Yes" to its emphasis on the earthly Christ and on mysticism as experience rather than doctrine, and a "No" to its bypassing spiritual *Anfechtung,* to its erotic marriage mysticism, and to its ultimate goal of ecstatic union with the uncreated word;[14] (3) an enthusiastic "Yes" characterizes Luther's evaluation of the third type of mysticism, "German mysticism," in which Luther found what he hailed in "Latin mysticism," but beyond that a spiritual understanding of purgatory as self-despair characteristic of the Christian life, and the idea of the *resignatio ad infernum,*[15] both presented in his German mother tongue and representative of a nearly forgotten, submerged, genuinely German theological tradition.

Insofar as Erich Vogelsang works here with concepts and categories which have been operative and influential in Luther research until this present day, it is appropriate to raise some fundamental questions which lead us, I believe, *in medias res.*

The medieval use of authorities is seldom characterized by a total endorsement of an earlier theologian as such; rather it is an effort to establish support on a particular point under discussion, while leaving ample room for overt criticism in another context. The relation of Thomas Aquinas to Augustine, of Jean Gerson to Bernard of Clairvaux, and of John Eck to Gregory of Rimini may serve here as three well-known examples drawn from the traditions of the *theologia speculativa* and the *theologia affectiva.* The same "sic et non" procedure can be amply documented with regard to Luther's attitude toward many preceding theologians, including Augustine, Bernard, Thomas, and Scotus.[16]

Hence it is inappropriate to chart on the basis of one or two references, whether positive or negative, reliable lines of relationship and dependence. When Luther refers to or praises a medieval doctor whose thoughts on other accounts prove to be completely alien to his own theology, it is often suggested that Luther "misunderstood" him, or—as it is sometimes put more nicely—that Luther is led into a "productive misunderstanding." If one collects these kinds of statements from a wide range of Luther studies, one cannot but conclude that Luther is uniquely naïve and ignorant!

In the case of Pseudo-Dionysius we have the very positive statement by Luther in 1514 that the *via negativa* is the most perfect. "Hence we find with Dionysius often the word 'hyper,' because one should transcend all thought and enter darkness."[17] Luther seizes here upon an aspect of the theology of Dionysius[18] which in the *Disputation Against Scholastic Theology* in 1517 will be formulated as "the whole of Aristotle relates to theology as shadow to light."[19] I am inclined to classify this theme with the earliest statement on this matter in 1510: "Theology is heaven, yes even the kingdom of heaven; man however is earth and his speculations are smoke. . . ."[20] It is the "hyper" element which Luther approves and by no means the anagogical *facere quod in se est* of man which would bypass God's revelation in Christ.[21]

In 1514 it is already clear that "darkness,"—*tenebrae, umbra,* or *caligo*—shares in the double meaning of *abscondere* and *absconditus:* not only apart from faith is God obscured in our speculations, but even in faith the faithful live "in umbraculo," in God's protective custody,[22] as friends of God on earth. If one turns for comparison to a passage from the hand of such a true disciple of Pseudo-Dionysius as Dionysius the Carthusian (1471), where he discusses the *unio mystica* in terms of the most intimate sons of God (*secretissimi filii Dei*), elevated halfway between the blessed and the average believers and through love and rapture absorbed in the ocean of God's infinity,[23] one sees immediately that it would be misleading to overlook the "sic et non" character of this and other asides Luther makes to Dionysius in the early years.[24] When from 1519-1520 onward Luther attacks "Dionysian speculations" there is no reason to base on this finding a theory of development, let alone of reversal. Rather, he now associates the name of Dionysius with a theological position which had never been his own, a phenomenon perhaps not unrelated to the fact that his earliest opponents had started immediately to make use of Pseudo-Dionysius to defend the validity of the papal hierarchy.[25]

Turning now to the second category of "Latin mysticism," we begin by stating that it makes exceedingly good sense to establish a separate category for medieval authors from Bernard to Gerson who, in contrast to the tradition characterized by the *Doctor Ecstaticus,* Dionysius, do not allow for the absorption of the believer into the abyss of the Godhead. As Etienne Gilson has shown clearly for Bernard, the Christian has to lose his *proprium* in the process of union with God through love, but this *proprium* is not the individuality of the *viator,* but rather the distortion of his image by the impact of sin.[26]

In Bernard's influential *De diligendo Deo* there is an acute awareness of the limits and limitations of man's bond with God on this earth. After distinguishing four degrees of love—of oneself for one's own sake (*se propter se*), of God for one's own sake (*Deum propter se*), of God for God's sake (*Deum propter Deum*), of oneself for God's sake (*se propter Deum*)—of which the first three are familiar to us from late medieval scholastic debates as *amor sui, amor concupiscentiae,* and *amor amicitiae*. Bernard confesses that he is not certain that anyone can attain to the fourth degree in this life: "I for one confess that it seems impossible to me. But without doubt this will come about when the good and faithful servant will have entered into the joy of his master, exhilarated by the abundance of God's house."[27]

It is not without good reason that in so many fifteenth century meditations and sermons Bernard and Gerson constitute the two major authorities, often mentioned in one breath and interchangeably. Without denying Gerson's independent synthesis in his *Theologia mystica speculativa,* it is, e.g., at such a climax in his work as the description of the several interpretations of transformation and union with God that Gerson falls back on *De diligendo Deo*. In a fascinating sermon preached on the Feast of St. Bernard, dated August 20, 1402, he appropriates Bernard's heritage, and extols the *Doctor Mellifluus* by having Bernard speak autobiographically.[28] Here three stages of contrition, meditation, and contemplation are described as the way to peace and union with Christ with the usual reference to Gal. 2:20: "it is no longer I who live, but Christ who lives in me."[29] Gerson selects two points which the young Luther would also associate with Bernard: (1) not to progress is to regress (*non progredi, regredi est*),[30] and (2) the hermeneutical principle that for a proper interpretation one has to clothe oneself in the affective state of the writer (*affectus induere scribentis*).[31] In my opinion the most revealing index of the intimate relation between Gerson and Bernard is the fact that on the one point at which Gerson warns his listeners against Bernard, he refers to a Pseudo-Bernardian work. Not yet five months before the exuberant encomium and completely in accord with the "sic et non" tradition, Gerson expresses his disapproval of a too intimate and proleptic description of the union of love in Bernard's *Epistola ad fratres de Monte Dei,* which actually is from the hand of William of St. Thierry.[32]

I am not convinced that Bonaventure should be mentioned in the same breath with Bernard and Gerson. Though one can interpret Gerson's theological program as an effort to reestablish in the Parisian theological faculty the balance of mind and heart which had characterized Bonaventure's *opus* a century and a half before, and though Gerson regrets that the Franciscan *moderni* abandoned the great tradition of Bonaventure, [33] it is questionable whether Bonaventure would have reciprocated this admiration and whether he would have sided with the Parisian Chancellor in his critique of Ruysbroeck's transformation (eucharistic) mysticism, or would have appreciated Gerson's insistence on the "conformitas voluntatis" as the axis of mystical theology.[34]

Furthermore, when Bonaventure develops his own typology[35] in accordance with the threefold spiritual sense of Scripture, and hence distinguishes between *doctores* (*fides*), *praedicatores* (*mores*), and *contemplativi* (*finis utriusque*), Bernard of Clairvaux is classified as a preacher rather than with Dionysius and Richard of St. Victor as one concerned with the *stadium contemplativorum*. Whereas Hugh of St. Victor[36] forms the apex of Bonaventure's typology, embracing the offices of doctor, preacher, and contemplative, we find in a parallel typology with Luther's later opponent, Kaspar Schatzgeyer, that Bonaventure has replaced Hugh of St. Victor. In his *De perfecta et contemplativa vita,* a hitherto hardly noticed work dating from 1501,[37] Schatzgeyer distinguishes—according to a psychological instead of an exegetical scheme—between doctors who have special gifts "in vi rationali" (Augustine, Ambrose), "in vi irascibili" (Jerome), and "in vi concupiscibili" (Gregory the Great, Bernard). While Jerome does not seem to have any intellectual progency, Thomas, Alexander, Scotus, and the later commentators on Lombard stand in the succession of Augustine and Ambrose. Bonaventure, however, stands out as the appropriate guide for all those in orders, since he combines the characteristic gifts of both Augustine and Bernard.[38]

This classification finds its echo in Luther's evaluation. He can place Bernard before Augustine as the *preacher* of Christ[39] but refers to Bonaventure as "the highest among the scholastic *doctores*."[40] It is exactly where Bonaventure straddles the two schools and combines the *theologia speculativa* with the *theologia affectiva* that Luther deviates from him and testifies: "he almost drove me out of my mind, because I wanted to feel the union of God with my soul, as a union of both the intellect and the will."[41]

From the point of view of Luther, it is not so obvious that Gerson should be classified under the rubric of "Latin mysticism" rather than with Tauler and the Frankfurter as "German mysticism." Conceding that Luther hails in Tauler a concept of spiritual temptation,[42] we note that it is exactly this aspect of Gerson's writing which leads Luther to say: "Gerson is the first who came to grips with the issue which concerns theology; he too experienced many temptations."[43] And: "Gerson is the only one who wrote about spiritual temptation."[44]

In 1516 Luther notes explicitly the anthropological parallel between Gerson and Tauler[45]—characteristically replacing their *apex mentis* and *syntheresis,* regarded as the highest part of the soul, by faith.[46] In view of the dramatic importance sometimes attached to the influence of Tauler upon Luther, it may be noted that this position of Luther can be traced back to a reference to Gerson in the earliest layer of the *Dictata,* more than two years before the discovery of Tauler.[47]

If the different classification of Gerson and Tauler is argued on the basis of Gerson's adherence—with Bernard and Bonaventure—to the mystical ascent by way of (*per christum*) rather than *to* the incarnate Christ (*in christum*), we may recall that Luther noted in 1516 that Tauler preached one sermon on the basis of *theologia mystica,* which for Luther is characterized by its concern with the spiritual birth of the *uncreated* word, in contrast with theology in the normal sense (*theologia propria*), which is concerned with the spiritual birth of the *incarnate* word.[48] Luther insists on the right relation between the two—"Leah [*theologia propria*] ought to precede (*prius . . . ducere oportet*) Rachel [*theologia mystica*]"[49]—but does not now or later deny the possibility or validity of "high mysticism" in the sense indicated above, however qualified it is as *difficile* and *rarum.* When the "old Luther" refers to Gerson in a most revealing comment on Genesis 19, probably sometime in 1538, he notes first that Caspar Schwenckfeld *cum suis* speculates about God as the monks used to when they bypassed Christ. Against this dangerous *commercium* with the *Deus nudus* Luther pits the true specultive life which concerns God's *potentia ordinata,* the incarnate and crucified Son.[50] It is quite clear, however, that Luther does not here condemn Gerson as the spiritual father or ally of Schwenckfeld.

Whereas it is often argued that the young Luther was a mystic until he saw the dangers of mysticism in the encounter with the left wing of the Reformation,[51] we note that Luther's reference to Gerson in 1538 reveals basically the same attitude as in his marginals to Tauler's sermons of 1516. High mysticism is not said to be out of the question or impossible, but "often extremely dangerous and a sheer trick of the Devil. . . . If one wants to be safe, one had best flee these speculations altogether. . . . "[52] Not even in this last stage of his development does Luther put Gerson on the Index. To the contrary, he exhorts his audience to study Gerson (and other authors of his genre), though with a restriction similar to that we noted with Gerson vis à vis Bernard: he should be read "cum iudicio."[53]

One could, of course, argue that beyond the earlier qualifications of the mystical union as "difficult" and "rare", the old Luther adds the warning "dangerous." However, we find this implicitly[54] stated in Luther's comment on Romans 5:2, dating from approximately the same time as his marginals on Tauler. Again, as in the example of Leah and Rachel, Luther insists on the priority of *accessus to raptus,* of justification by faith through the incarnate and crucified word to the *raptus* by the uncreated word. "But," Luther concludes this passage, "who would consider himself so clean, that he would dare to pursue this, unless he is called and, like the Apostle Paul, lifted up by God (II Cor. 12:2). . . . In short, this 'raptus' cannot be called 'accessus.'"[55]

There is here a transition from "rare" to "dare", from *rarum* to *periculose;* yet this transition is not so unexpected and is understandable in the light of the fact that in the prologue of the most important nominalistic *Sentences* commentaries, the Apostle Paul is introduced on the basis of II Cor. 12 as an exception to the rule *de potentia ordinata* according to which the status of the *viator* is contrasted with that of the *beatus* in that he is not yet a *comprehensor,* not yet face to face with God, and hence without immediate knowledge of God.[56] Though Luther employs the concept of the *potentia ordinata* of God, so characteristic for nominalistic theology; in his commentary on Genesis, he gives it a Christological point instead of its primary epistemological meaning: the *potentia ordinata* is here not primarily the order established by the inscrutable free God who could as well have established another order, but it is clearly the order of redemption in Jesus Christ, established out of God's mercy to provide sinful man with a refuge from danger. If we remind ourselves of the striking parallel with the *Dictata* passage (early 1515), which insists, against those who want to be more immediately related to God, on the protection (the *umbraculum*) which is necessary in this life because we are not yet face to face with God,[57] we are forced to conclude that there is a basic continuity throughout this large span of years (1515-1538), not-with-standing Luther's encounter with Tauler and the *Schwärmer.*

The fact remains that Tauler seems exempted from the "sic et non" rule which generally applies to all Luther's authorities. This cannot be due—as in the case of Wessel Gansfort[58] and Pupper of Goch[59] or the author of "Beatus Vir"[60]— to temporary enthusiasm and later disappearance from the sources. Bernd Moeller was able to compose a list of twenty-six references to Tauler over the years 1515-1544 which remain positive to the very end.[61] We believe that Tauler and the *Theologia Deutsch*[62] are and remain of vital importance for Luther, among other things because they showed the growing Reformer how the mystical *affectus* could be retained while breaking with both the synergistic elements in the *contemplatio acquisita* and the speculative elements in the *contemplatio infusa*. Indeed, it is a question whether it was not precisely this mystical *affectus,* with its proximity to *sola* categories, which made it possible for Luther to carry out this double break, or at least to formulate it theologically.

It is important that we do not assume that all the so-called "mystical authors" listed by Vogelsang have been read by Luther as *mystical* authors. In the first place and more generally one can point to the democratization of mysticism[63] in late medieval devotional literature: what is retained of such an author as Bernard of Clairvaux or Hugh of St. Victor is often his piety, not his mysticism.[64] There is still a margin left for the "aristocrats of the Spirit," but the traditional mystical terminology is appropriated for the description of the Christian life of the average believer.[65] The *Via moderna* and the *Devotio moderna* share a common concern for the *theologia affectiva* rather than for the *theologia speculativa,* for ascetics rather than for mysticism, for the *contemplatio acquisita* rather than for the *contemplatio infusa*.[66]

In the second place, and more specifically with regard to Tauler: the very fact that Luther comes to the conclusions that Tauler develops one particular sermon on the basis of mystical theology[67] alerts us to the fact that Luther apparently does not assume this always to be the case. It is a daring step to build around Tauler—and the *Theologia Deutsch*[68] mentioned by Luther in the same breath—a whole category of so-called "German mysticism," especially if this is to include, as it usually does, an author such as Meister Eckhart to whom Luther has not related himself in any sense. Granted the generally acknowledged proximity of Eckhardt and Tauler, there are noticeable differences which, when seen from the vantage point of Luther, are too formidable to overlook.[69] At any rate, the main conclusion drawn by Luther from the *Theologia Deutsch* is certainly not mystical: " . . . man should not confide in anything else but in Jesus Christ alone, not in his prayers, not in his merits or his works. Since it is not due to our efforts that we are to be saved but due to the mercy of God."[70] As appears from the final words of the 1518 preface to "Eyn deutsch Theologia" Luther regards it as a representative of the category "German Theology" rather than that of "German Mysticism": "hence we will find that the German theologians are without doubt the best theologians. Amen!"[71]

### Christ's Embrace: Death and Hell[72]

Although we seemed to remain within the realm of methodological issues when we discussed the problems involved in extracting from Luther a "Yes" or "No" with respect to schools of mystical theology which did not present themselves as such to him, we have already moved beyond the state of formal considerations. The only viable method open to us is to study and define mysticism on the basis of Luther's description and evaluation, hence, at least initially, bypassing the issue of the appropriate definition of mysticism as such and of the classification of its several schools.

On the basis of the foregoing discussion we can come to the following preliminary conclusions:

a) There is as yet no reason to assume that Luther rejected mystical theology as such.[73] Rather he opposes the dangers of what we called "high mysticism."

b) The first characteristic of this form of mysticism is for Luther the union of soul and body ("unio animae et corporis"). So far as I know, this is not a standard expression. Altenstaig brings in his *Vocabularius theologie* a definition of "beatitude" which includes both soul and body.[74] It may be that Luther hints at this form of final beatitude to expose the proleptic nature of this high mysticism as a presumptuous *theologia gloriae*. More specifically, however, the context of his remarks indicates that he has in mind a psychosomatic experience through which the human senses experience the object of speculation,[75] i.e. the union of the soul with Christ.[76]

Luther's stance is not due to the fact that he rejects the idea of union as such or that he holds that spiritual realities cannot be experienced. On the contrary, while they cannot always be formulated, they can be experienced, and on the basis of experience they can be learned. The point is, however, that true negative theology is "theology of the cross" and, as we shall see, its corresponding experience is the crying and groaning of the soul, the "gemitus inenarrabiles" (Rom. 8:26).[77]

c) The second characteristic of the kind of mysticism rejected by Luther is the bypassing of Christ in order to rest *in Deo nudo*. In his comment on Romans 5:2 Luther had insisted on the double requirement "per fidem" and "per Christum."[78] The single requirement "per Christum" could still be—and indeed was generally—understood as the necessary preparation for union and contemplation since it axiomatically presupposed the earlier and now transcended stage of faith. Especially the meditation upon the passion of Christ as the basis of all merits is advocated as the most useful means to generate intense devotion.[79]

A treatise by Schatzgeyer, in time (1501) close to Luther and filled with that monastic spirituality which was to evoke Luther's wrath, has by no means slighted Christ. The "pro nobis"—in this warm treatise put as "pro te"—establishes the intimate bond between Christ and the believer.[80] Furthermore the treatise insists that "there is but one way to heaven, through the cross of Christ." This proves, however, to evoke love and lead to the sweet embrace of Christ.[81] The true Christian turns away from the bitterness of this valley of tears to the beauty and splendor of Christ. Over against this *per Christum (et charitatem)* Luther places *per Christum* in the abiding context of faith (*per fidem*).[82] For Luther the embrace with Christ is not sweet but death and hell:[83] "God wants us to be trained (by the cross), not absorbed."[84] The Christian does not turn away from the bitterness of this world but is in that very valley of tears identified with the cross of Christ.[85]

d) At this point one may wonder whether the question as to Luther's relation to mysticism has not already been answered. If, indeed, the *contemplatio acquisita* is ruled out because it presupposes man's strenuous cooperation with grace,[86] and if *contemplatio infusa* is ruled out as presumptuous *theologia gloriae,*[87] it seems that no latitude is left. Yet the contrast of *accessus* and *raptus* is not the last word. If Luther, on the one hand, rejects the *raptus,* he indicates, on the other hand, that the *accessus* takes on a number of traits which are usually characteristic of the *raptus* itself. Although the embrace and union cannot be experienced through the senses and the *gemitus* continues to characterize the human crying need for the full manifestation of God (Rom. 8:26),[88] still the embrace and union are not ruled out but grasped by faith. As appears from the third Galatians commentary, the confrontation with the left wing of the Reformation does not force Luther to break with his alleged mystical past. The amazing thing is that he does not criticize the *Schwärmer* for being too radical, but for not being radical enough. They separate faith in the heart and Christ in heaven, whereas, for Luther, these are inseparably interwined. As regards this identification of Christ and the Christian Luther says concisely: "Es geht nicht speculative sed realiter zu"—it is not an imagined but a real matter.[89] It is important for us that this "realiter" is interpreted—undoubtedly expressing Luther's intention precisely—as the Christ in us who works "realiter," clarified by the eolquent adverbs "most present" (*praesentissime*) and "most efficaciously" (*efficassime*).

In the concluding section we want to probe Luther's use of typical mystical terminology in a series of thesis-like short paragraphs. To collect Luther's explicit statements *re* mystical theologians and their theology would prove to be an illegitimate short-cut. We have to take here the same seemingly unexciting or at least unspectacular way as in the study of other aspects of Luther's theology: patient comparison with the preceding tradition, with a special emphasis on the devotional tradition immediately before him.

### The Mystical Context: Fundamental Concepts

1. *Exegetical mysticism.* When one consults such a source as Altenstaig's *Vocabularius theologie*—published in the same year that Luther published his 95 theses—for the contemporary understanding of such technical mystical terms as "excessus," "extasis," and "raptus," one notices that the article on "extasis" is drawn up on the basis of two authorities. The first witness is the late medieval Church father, Gerson;[90] but in second place we find the Augustinian bishop and biblical exegete Jacobus Perez de Valencia.[91]

In the Prologue to the Psalms Commentary (1484) of Perez, we read that the *excessus* is the gift of vision to all prophets, a supernatural illumination which transcends the capacity of human knowledge. *Extasis* is a higher stage in which one is alienated from one's inner senses, as if he were outside himself (*quasi extra seipsum*). The third and final *elevatio* is called *raptus,* which is granted to but a few.[92] Perez, just like Luther half a century later, could and probably did find this description dispersed throughout the works of Augustine.[93]

In the exegetical application, however, Perez does not retain the indicated distinctions. In commenting upon Psalm 115:11, Vulgate: "I said in my *excessus:* every man is a liar"—"excessus" is identified with "extasis" and interpreted by the verb "rapi" to describe the transition of David from "fides sola" to "contemplatio." Thus David is able to foresee the mysteries of the New Testament as prefigured in the law of Moses.[94] More important for the hermeneutical implications, exactly the same applies to the Apostles. First they have an implicit faith in Christ; but after Pentecost their minds are brought into ecstasy so that they grasp the mysteries of faith.[95] One may use here the term "exegetical mysticism" since it is the elevated state of mind, *excessus* or *extasis,* which allows the Apostles to understand Scripture.[96] The humiliation of which the preceding verse 10 speaks ("I am completely humiliated") is understood by Perez as the "sacrificium intellectus," the preparatory pre-Pentecostal state of mind. Thus, in a second stage, the "excessus" takes place in which David, the interpreter, comes to understand that only the divine law is reliable in the sense revealed by the Spirit.[97]

When we turn now to Luther's exposition of this text, we find that in his first comment on the *Psalterium* of Faber Stapulensis, the "excessus" is related to self-knowledge: elevated above himself man sees himself as he is, full of clouds and darkness.[98] Luther refers back to his exposition of Ps. 30 (:21) where he had said even more explicitly that *humiliation* is the result of the "excessus" or "extasis."[99] In contrast to Perez, humiliation is not the preparation for but the result of the "extasis."

In the interlinear gloss on the words "in my excessus," Luther notes the two meanings of "excessus" as either "raptus" or fear,[100] as he charts the four possible meanings of *extasis.*[101] Apart from this second connotation of fear, Luther interprets the term "excessus" ("extasis") in its mystical sense first as related to the "raptus" and the clear knowledge of faith; second, it stands for the understanding of faith (*sensus fidei*) which exceeds the literal understanding (*sensus litere*). This first understanding is the *true* literal sense;[102] the "sensus litere" is the interpretation on which the unbelievers stubbornly insist. The understanding of faith is the understanding of Scripture, the Gospel itself, the "face" of God, elsewhere distinguished from the eschatological vision of God's face in heaven.[103]

In his comments Luther makes three successive attempts to interpret this text. He is especially concerned to bring together the "excessus" as (1) the transition of the sinful man (*homo mendax*) to the man who is spiritual through faith (*homo spiritualis per fidem*), and

(2) as the state of man stricken by fear particularly the fear due to persecution,[104] in which the believer experiences his complete dependence upon God.[105] "In my excessus" proves to become a synonym for both "in faith" and "in struggle"; it designates man's place "coram Deo" where the demarcation between "verax" and "mendax" is revealed.[106] This "excessus" does not imply the transcendence of this valley of tears and a rest in the peace of God, but the "demasquer" of the enemies of truth (i.e. the flesh and the world) and marks the beginning rather than the end of the battle.[107] There is definitely an elevation involved in the "excessus," an elevation which gives the believer a true perspective on the "futura bona" and produces the humiliating acknowledgment that he has no claim to these.[108]

Though the exegetical tradition concerning Ps. 115:11 will have to be explored in more detail, we suggest that four conclusions can be drawn from the preceding exposition.

a) The mystical term *excessus* is related by Luther to the idea of battle or struggle typical for the life of the *viator,* the soldier of Christ.[109] As such this is by no means unusual; ever since Augustine it had been noted that *excessus* refers to an extraordinary state of mind either due to fear and suffering or to revelation. It would remain for Luther characteristic that the *excessus* through which the *homo mendax* becomes the *homo spiritualis* continues to be seen in the context of *pugna, tribulatio, Anfechtung*. What must have fascinated Luther most in Tauler is the idea that man *suffers* the birth of God.[110] This is what Luther means when he contrasts "realiter" with "speculative."

b) There is another aspect to this very same contrast. The "realiter" also means that one does not leave Scripture behind as a mere starting motor for the *affectus*.[111] Against the usual monastic order of *lectio (oratio), meditatio, contemplatio,* Luther prescribes a *lectio* initiated by *oratio* and leading toward *relectio*. When compared with the preceding tradition, it is striking that Luther no longer regards *lectio* (letter) and *meditatio* (spirit) as two *successive* stages. In 1539, dealing explicitly with the proper order, it is stated that true *meditatio* is *lectio* and *relectio*.[112] The axis of this Scripture-oriented meditation is not speculation (*prudentia-intellectus*) but the affective state (*affectus*) which prepares man's intellectual powers for the sudden insights and break-throughs which we should not limit to a once and for all *Turmerlebnis*.[113] The scope of the *affectus* is exactly the reality *coram Deo* which, as we saw, is revealed *in excessu mentis,*[114] when the knowledge of *futura bona* and the self-knowledge that *omnis homo mendax coincide*.[115] Luther can refer here to the believers exactly because it is to them, as the *spirituales* or the *mystici,*[116] that the mysteries of redemption and Incarnation are revealed.

c) Just as Luther rejects a false Christological mysticism—which, as we saw, speculates on the uncreated word and is not satisfied with the "homo abscondens divinitatem"—so also he rejects a false exegetical mysticism which forces access to the Father "through the mysteries of Scripture." Either way makes for pride or desperation, *superbi* or *desperati,* a traditional allusion to the two erring groups on the left and the right of the *via media* of the Church militant.[117]

d) The dual aspects of the *excessus mentis* as faith and tribulation may help us to explain why, in the first lectures on the Psalms (1513-1515), Luther repeatedly slights the fourth sense of Scripture, the anagogical interpretation.[118] It is certainly not completely absent; but when it occurs it stands increasingly for the horizontal perseverance of the faithful and not for the vertical ascent of the aristocrats of the Spirit. Accordingly, in one central passage the anagogical work of God is not mystical elevation but the goal of God's work in history, either in heaven or in hell.[119] The deviation from the principles of Bonaventure[120] and from the practice of men like Dionysius the Carthusian and Kaspar Schatzgeyer cannot escape our attention. I am inclined to find here support for the conclusion of Gerhard Ebeling, accepted by the editors of *WA* 55, that the reduction of the fourfold sense is to be related to another hermeneutical schema: head-body-members.[121] Just as its head, Jesus Christ, so does the body, the *ecclesia militans,* march toward history's goal through the same valley of tears as its suffering Lord:[122] "Therefore if you look for a sign of the grace of God or wonder whether Christ himself is in you: no other sign is given to you but the sign of Jona. Therefore if you were to be in hell for three days, *that* is the sign that Christ is with you and you in Christ."[123]

2. *Raptus*. Not only *excessus* but also *raptus* and *rapi* function in Luther's theological vocabulary. The well-known sharp contrast between the *temporalia* and the *aeterna,* etc., referring to the difference between existence *coram hominibus* and *coram Deo*, can be summarized by Luther on the inside of the title-page of his Psalter with the words: "In Holy Scripture the most important thing is to distinguish the Spirit from the letter; this is what truly makes one a theologian."[124] In a significant parallel in early 1514, Luther had noted that a true theologian is born "in rapture and ecstasy; this is what makes a true theologian" (*in raptu et extasi, et hec facit verum theologum*).[125] After we have seen that *excessus* or *extasis* is at once *fides* and *pugna,* we are no longer tempted to oppose without far-reaching qualifications the mystical Luther of 1514 to the mature one of 1520 who states in the *Operationes in Psalmos:* "By living, indeed by dying and being damned, one becomes a theologian, not by thinking and reading and speculating" (*Vivendo, immo moriendo et damnando fit theologus, non intelligendo, legendo aut speculando*).[126]

*Raptus* is the reliance on the righteousness of Christ outside ourselves (*extra nos*) and can be described as a complete transformation into Christ (*in Christum plane transformari*).[127] Again, as we noted with *excessus, raptus* does not mean an ontological transformation but a transformation of *affectus* and *fiducia,* of our love and trust. Hence we do not argue that Luther is a mystical theologian because of his use of these terms. Rather we stress that their new function cannot be understood without a thorough grasp of their original mystical context. If future research confirms my suggestion that Luther's concept "extra nos" is related to *raptus,* one of the major arguments for a forensic interpretation of Luther's doctrine of justification has been preempted.[128] Though we have no claim to the *iustitia Christi* which is not our "property" (*proprietas*), it is granted to us as a present possession (*possessio*).[129] *Extra nos* and *raptus* indicate that the *iustitia Christi*—and not our own powers—is the source and resource for *our* righteousness.[130] Epithets such as "external" and "forensic" righteousness cannot do justice to Luther's doctrine of justification.

Luther can use the *raptus* not only because of its connotation of "extra nos" but also because of its implication of absolute passivity. According to what we called "high mysticism," sheer passivity is typical of the last stage of true mysticism experienced by the elect few. Luther takes this term and applies it to the life of faith as such and hence to *all* true believers. Parallel to his deletion of the wall of separation between the *praecepta* and the *consilia evangelica*—the shaking of the foundations of monasticism—Luther's particular kind of democratization of mysticism robs high mysticism of one of its main characteristics. At the same time, its original context alerts us to the fact that when Luther uses *rapi* in one breath with *duci* and *pati,*[131] the sinner is not a dead instrument of the omnipotent God, and justification by faith is not quietism.

3. *Gemitus.* Both *excessus* and *raptus* imply that faith and justification are not the harmonious realization of man's capacities and desires. In his Romans commentary Luther uses a term which he could have read in Gerson's *De mystica theologia,* the "juxtaposition of opposites" (*antiperistasis*), synonymous with "sub contrario," in the transcript rendered as "in abscondito."[132] Here we are in the immediate proximity of Luther's own use of the word mystical: all wisdom and love are hidden in the suffering and dying Christ—"hidden because visible to mystical and spiritual eyes (*mysticis et spiritualibus oculis visibiles*)."[133]

At this point we should at least mention the term *gemitus,* though its absence in the relevant literature and the limits of this paper do not allow for more than some introductory observations. In the light of the preceding tradition with regard to *gemitus,* two points are particularly noteworthy in Luther's earlier works. In the first place the parallel between *fides* and *gemitus.* Justification, and more precisely the nonimputation of sin, takes place "on account of faith and groaning" (*propter fidem et gemitum*), and culpable sin is not found "in those who believe and cry out [to God]" (*in credentibus et gementibus*).[134] *Gemitus* is not another word for *facere quod in se est* or *humilitas* as some kind of condition for justification; rather it characterizes the life of the *sancti,* whose righteousness is hidden.[135] It describes the state of complete identification with Christ.[136] Whereas in the connection between *gemitus* and true penitence there is a basis for comparison with Abelard,[137] Bernard and Gerson refer to *gemitus* as part of the preparatory stage in the triad "purgation-illumination-contemplation"[138] or as initiation of the birth of God in the soul.[139]

The real significance of the fact that Luther can combine *gemitus* and *fides* appears, however, when we realize that the use made of *gemitus* by both Bernard and Gerson as a stage on the mystical way is by no means a coincidence. According to an influential gloss by Jerome *gemitus* refers to *synderesis,* which means that the gloss attributes to the human spirit what Romans 8:26 describes as the operation of the Holy Spirit: "the Spirit petitions for us with unutterable groanings."[140] This combination of *gemitus* and *synderesis* functions in scholasticism in such a way that we are not allowed to study the one concept without the other. For Bonaventure the *synderesis* is the affective power in man which intercedes with God with "unutterable groanings,"[141] since it makes man desire the good. Since this *synderesis* is an inalienable part of man, Geiler can exhort his readers to self-purgation by going "diligently into the inner ground [of the soul]."[142] It is this same virginal part of man which, according to Dionysius the Carthusian, is kindled by love until the soul is completely absorbed in God.[143] And it is in a call for the full exploitation of these divine resources in man that Schatzgeyer's 1501 treatise on the spiritual life culminates in the Epilogue.[144]

As is well known, there is a marked interest with the young Luther in the *synderesis,*[145] which I am inclined to relate to his early defense of the *facere quod in se est* and the *merita de congruo.*[146] Yet in the most explicit statement in this period it is quite clear that the *synderesis* points man to the proper *goal* but does not show him the *way* to that goal.[147] Even here the *gemitus* is not the emotional expression of the *synderesis* but the mark of its impotence and hence of man's absolute dependence on God. The *synderesis* characterizes man's *esse,* not his *bene esse.*[148] Schatzgeyer had—in accordance with the tradition—based his high expectations of man's innate *synderesis* on Ps. 4:7: "the light of your face is manifest to us, O God." In the ***Dictata*** (1516) and again emphatically in the ***Operationes in Psalmos*** Luther says explicitly that this interpretation is false: "The first principle of all good works is faith."[149] *Gemitus* (just as much as *oratio*) presupposes faith and does not refer to a stage of preparation or to a virginal sinproof part in man, but to the life of faith itself: "Prayer is his desire for Christ; the cry is for Christ to transfigure his wretchedness."[150]

Reviewing our conclusions it can be said that Luther has gathered in terms characteristic of the extremes of the *via mystica* to clarify its center and axis. On the one hand *excessus* and *raptus,* on the other *gemitus* have been put to the service of clarifying the Christian life. It is exactly in the balance of these ideas that I discern the genius of Luther's theology of the Christian life. The *gemitus* aspect neutralizes the dangers of the *theologia gloriae* of the mystical *raptus*. The *excessus* and *raptus* aspect neutralizes the synergistic elements in the traditional scholastic combination of *synderesis* and *gemitus*. The test for this conclusion can be carried out in a separate discussion of Luther's use of bridal imagery and his view of the *unio fidei,* which we cannot execute here. Searching our way among the many pitfalls inherent in the theme "Luther and Mysticism," we hope to have shown that this crucial area cannot be regarded as a side issue in the rich world of thought of the Reformer.

One can designate the theology of Luther with the generally recognized summarizing formula, "simul iustus et peccator"—simultaneously righteous and sinful. The very same reality which is summarized by this formula can be expressed in the language of mystical spirituality, and that means for Luther in the language of the personal experience of faith, by the formula, "simul gemitus et raptus."[151] For both formulas it is characteristic that they do not indicate a *via media,* but a *simul* which reveals a *coincidentia oppositorum.*

*Notes*

[1] *De mystica theologia, Tractatus primus speculativus. Prologus,* ed. André Combes (Lucani, 1958), cons. 2, pp. 27-29.

[2] *WA* 56,300 7f.; Cl. (= *Luthers Werke in Auswahl,* I-*VIII,* hrsg. von Otto Clemen). 5.248.16f (to Rom. 5:2; 1516).

[3] *WA* 11.117. 35f. (1523): cf. 2 Cor. 12:2. Thomas Aquinas relates the "third heaven" to the *contemplatio intellectus,* and he understands the rapture of Paul as a higher level "quod pertinet ad affectum." (S. Th. II/II, q. 175, a. 2, c.a.).

[4] *WA* 9.98.19 (Marginal Notes on Tauler's Sermons, 1516). See Johannes Ficker, "Zu den Bemerkungen Luthers in Taulers Sermones (Augsburg, 1508)." *Theol. St. u. Kritiken* 107 (1936), 46-64

[5] *WA* 9,100. 38f.; Cl. 5,308.11f. (1516).

[6] Artur Rühl, *Der Einfluss der Mystik auf Denken und Entwicklung des jungen Luther* (Theol. Diss. Marburg, 1960), p. 6.

[7] "Theologia mystica coelestis est quaedam Dei notitia per unionem voluntatis Dei adhaerentis elicita vel lumine coelitus immisso producta." So reported by Thomas de Vallgornera O.P., *Mystica theologia divi Thomae* (Barcelona, 1662). Philipp and Thomas were both dependent upon the commentary of John of St. Thomas (†1644) on Thomas of Aquinas, *S. Th.* I/II, q. 67-70, Cf. *Les dons du Saint Esprit,* trans. R. Maritain (Juvisy, 1950²).

[8] Ephraem Hendrikx O.E.S.A., *Augustins Verhältnis zur Mystik* (Theol. Diss. Würzburg, 1936); in abbreviated form in *Zum Augustin-Gespräch der Gegenwart,* ed. Carl Andresen (Darmstadt, 1962). pp. 271-364.

[9] *Ibid.,* p. 272.

[10] *Ibid.,* p. 274. L. G. Mack points out: "Above all the humanity of Christ should be meditated upon, for man is more deeply impressed by visible objects. . . . As to the acquired contemplation, Domenichi seems to admit a contemplation, inferior to the infused, it is true, yet genuine contemplation, which can be reached by a human efforts." *The Liber de contemplatione Dei by Dominicus de Domincis, 1416-1478* (Rome, 1959), pp. 14, 16f. In the Thomistic mystical tradition it is unthinkable that the higher levels of mysticism should be subject to the efforts of man. Marie Louise von Franz suggests that this Commentary could be a transcript of the last words which Thomas Aquinas spoke in his ecstasy on his deathbed. *Aurora consurgens: A document Attributed to Thomas Aquinas on the Problem of Opposites in Alchemy* (New York, 1966), pp. 430f. On the other hand, the identity of the soul with God, which in one place even looks to such union from the side of man (*ibid.,* p. 363), suggests the opposite conclusion.

[11] Hendrikx (note 8), p. 275.

[12] *Ibid.,* p. 346. It may be noted that a generally respected authority on mystical theology, writing in the same year as Hendrikx and working with a different definition of mysticism, came to the opposite conclusion about Augustine. Joseph Maréchal, *Etudes sur la psychologie des mystiques* II (Brussels, 1937), 180ff.; cf. 250, 255. A more balanced judgment is made by Ernst Dassmann in regard to Ambrosius: "Ein wie auch immer akzentuierter *moderner* Begriff von Mystik kann nun aber wiederum nicht als Maszstab an die Aus-

sagen des Ambrosius gelegt werden." *Die Frömmigkeit des Kirchenvaters Ambrosius von Mailand* (Münster, 1965), 181.

[13] "Luther und die Mystik," *Luther-Jb,* 19 (1937), 32-54, esp. 35. Vogelsang was not the first to go beyond an often unrewarding general definition of mysticism. He acknowledges the merits of Hermann Hering, *Die Mystik Luthers* (leipzig, 1879). Cf. also W. Köhler, *Luther und die Kirchengeschichte I* (Erlangen, 1900), 368, where an "areopagitische und germanischbernhardinische Mystik" are described.

[14] Vogelsang (note 13), pp. 40f. In his later essay, "Die unio mystica bei Luther," *ARG* 35 (1938), 63-80. Vogelsang focuses his earlier exposition as he now expressly applies the "yes" and "no" to bridal and union mysticism; see especially the reference (p. 70, n. 4) to Luther's emphasis on faith as "copula." Cf. further Friedrich Th. Ruhland, *Luther und die Brautmystik nach Luthers Schrifttum bis 1521* (Giessen, 1938), pp. 54ff., 142f. Vogelsang could still write in 1937 that Luther preferred Tauler to Bernard because, among other things, the bridal mysticism "bei Tauler ganz zurücktrat" (42). Cf. however Ruhland, pp. 59ff., and Vogelsang, *ARG* 35 (1938), 78ff.

[15] On the spiritual nature of temptation (*Anfechtung*) and the *resignatio ad infernum* in Jean Gerson. cf. Walter Dress, *Die Theologie Gersons. Eine Untersuchung zur Verbindung von Nominalismus und Mystik im Spätmittelalter* (Gütersloh, 1931), pp. 167, 180ff.

[16] For Augustine see *WA* Tr. 1,140.5; Cl. 8,45.36 (Nr. 347); cf. *WA* 54,186.16. For Bernard esp. *WA* Tr. 3,295.6 (Nr. 3370b). For Thomas: *WA* Tr. 1,135.12 (Nr. 329). For Scotus: *WA Tr.* 3,564.3; Cl. 8,150.4 (Nr. 3722).

[17] *Schol* to Ps. 64(65):2 (*WA* 3,372.13-27; early 1514). Martin Elze has warned that one cannot interpret this passage as a positive reference to Dionysius; see his important article, "Züge spätmittelaterlicher Frömmigkeit in Luthers Theologie." *ZThK* 62 (1965), 381-402, 395, n. 51. If one examines this text as a whole, one finds that in the "attamen"-sentence Luther indeed says that the text of Dionysius should not be undertood in an anagogical sense. In the sentence which begins "Nam ut dixi . . ." however, it is necessary to understand the words "unde nimis temerarii sunt nostri theologi" as a reference to the "hyper" of Dionysius. Cf. also the *Schol.* to Ps. 17 (18):12 (*WA* 3,124.29-39; Cl. 5,94.14-25).

[18] Soon thereafter, perhaps in the summer of 1514, Luther emphasizes in the *scholion* to Ps. 79 (80):3 the "supra rationem" of faith. This passage shows that by "contemplativi" Luther can mean not the spiritually privileged among the faithful, but the faithful as such: "Christi fides non potest esse nisi in iis, qui supra rationem contemplativi sint. Apparet enim, quando in eum creditur. Sed credere nequent, nisi filii Rachel, elevate mentis." *WA* 3,607.22-24. On the significance of "in eum credere" in place of "eum credere" or "eo credere" cf. my book *The Harvest of Medieval Theology* (Cambridge, Mass., 1963), pp. 229, 119. I fully agree with the important observation of Bernhard Lohse that "positiv . . . die contemplatio letztlich mit dem Glauben identisch gesetzt (wird)" and that Luther "zumindest der Sache nach die contemplatio mit dem Glauben gleichsetzt oder doch auf die entscheidende Bedeutung des Glaubens hinweist." *Mönchtum und Reformation. Luthers Auseinandersetzung mit dem Mönchsideal des Mittelalters* (Göttingen, 1963), pp. 230f. To be sure, to the extent to which *Contemplatio = elevatio mentis = excessus mentis,* Luther's interpretation is not completely without precedent; cf. infra, n. 93. But in the *Dictata* for the most part "contemplativi" refer to a particular group in the Church and is often connected with the "doctores." For further documentation of this point see Joseph Vercruysse, *Fidelis Populus. Een onderzoek van de ecclesiologie in Martin Luthers Dictata super Psalterium (1513-15)* (Diss. Gregoriana, Rome, 1966), typed ms., pp. 176-182.

[19] *WA* 1,226,26; Cl. 5,324.8.

[20] *WA* 9,65.14-16; Cl. 5,9.29-31 (Marginal Notes to Lombard, *Sent.* I, d. 12, c.2). In regard to Luther's rejection of the "facere quod in se est" between reason and revelation, cf. my essay "Robert Holcot O.P. and the Beginnings of Luther's Theology," *HThR* 55 (1962), 317-342, esp. 330ff. [See Chapter IV above]. On sinful blindness as "caligo" in the later years, cf. the commentary on Gen. 42. *WA* 44.472.38; 473.42 (1535-45)....

[21] See Luther's later statement in the *Operationes in Psalmos,* Ps. 5:12 (*WA* 5,176.29-33).

[22] *Schol.* to Ps. 90(91):1 (perhaps early 1515; *WA* 4.64.24-65.6; cf. 65.28-31). In Ps. 121 (122):3, another aspect of this theme is touched upon. Here Luther warns: be careful with the idea of participating in Christ! In this life, he writes, not even the most perfect of the saints have the whole Christ (". . . nunquam habet aliquis sanctorum totum Christum, sed quilibet partem eius, etiam perfectissimi"). *WA* 4.401.25-30. The significance of this passage has been noted by L. Pinomaa, "Die Heiligen in Luthers Frühtheologie," *St Theol.* 13 (1959), 1-47, 6f., and by B. Lohse (note 18), p. 230. n. 15, who quotes the second half of the citation. It is precisely the first half of the citation, however, that shows that Luther consciously sets forth this theme as a major and not a minor motif. Luther's conclusion, the Bernardian "stare est regredi," harkens back to the "in hac vita": in this life the *activi* and the *contemplativi* remain *viatores.*

[23] Dionysius the Carthusian, *Enarratio in canticum canticorum Salomonis in D. Dionysii Cartusiani Enarrationes piae ac eruditae in quinque libros sapientiales* (Coloniae, 1533), *Opera omnia* VII (Monstrolii, 1898), 386 B-387 B.

[24] Although I do not believe that John Eck was in any way decisively indebted to the Aeropagite, Eck still makes reference in a completely understandable way to the *via negativa* of Dionysius as representative of the tradition of the Church. *Chrysopassus, Centuria* IV, 44 (Augsburg, 1514), Cf. *WA Tr.* I, Nr. 257.

[25] See in regard to Eck, *WA* 2,55.34-56.1 (1519). Ambrosius Catharinus Politus (†1552) writes: "As the great theologian Dionysius says, the ecclesiastical hierarchy is as much like the heavenly hierarchy as possible." *Apologia pro veritate . . . adversus impia ac valde pestifera Martini Lutheri Dogmata* (1520), ed. Josef Schweizer, *Corpus Catholicorum* 27 (1956), 2.7.18f. One finds this concept of the Church also with Sylvester Prierias. *De potestate papae dialogus* (1518) in Valentin Ernst Loescher, *Vollständige Reformations-Acta und Documenta,* II (Leipzig, 1723), 14. For the insistence upon the authenticity of the works of Dionysius as a disciple of Paul by Johannes Cochläus, see Martin Spahn, *Johannes Cochläs. Ein Lebensbild aus der Zeit der Kirchenspaltung* (Berlin, 1898; 2nd ed. Nieuwkoop, 1964), p. 234. For the high rating of Dionysius among northern humanists in the beginning of the sixteenth century we note, besides the well-known analysis by Nicolas Cusanus and the editorial work of Faber Stapulensis (cf. Eugene F. Rice, *Renaissance Studies* XI [1962], 126-160; 142), a letter by Konrad Peutinger (Augsburg, June 13, 1513), where Dionysius heads the list of the Greek and Latin Church fathers. *Briefwechsel des Beatus Rhenanus,* ed. Adalbert Horawitz and Karl Hartfelder (Leipzig, 1886; Hildesheim 1966[2]), pp. 57f. In a letter of Dec. 1, 1508. Beatus Rhenanus ranks him even with Paul and John as an instrument of revelation (*ibid.,* p. 18). Shortly before (Oct. 10, 1508), Rhenanus had already indicated as the most important reading "altissimam Dionysianae theologiae lectionem," "sublimem Cusani de Sacris philosophiam," "Bonaventurae commentarios"—"the other theologians are not worth your time"—and the *Quincuplex Psalterium* of Faber. *Ibid.,* pp. 576f. In the later letters Dionysius is no longer mentioned!

[26] *La théologie mystique de Saint Bernard* (Paris, 1947), pp. 21, 138, 155. The destruction of the false *proprium* means "reformation"; "transformamur cum conformamur." *Cant. Cant.* 62.5. as cited by Friedrich Ohly, *Hohelied-Studien. Grundzüge einer Geschichte der Hoheliedauslegung des Abendlandes bis um 1200* (Wiesbaden, 1958), p. 152.

[27] *De dilig. Deo* 15.39 (*PL* 182, 998 D).

[28] *Jean Gerson, Oeuvres complètes,* v: *L'Ouevre oratoire,* ed. P. Glorieux (Paris, 1963), 326.

[29] *Ibid.,* p. 329

[30] *Ibid.,* p. 335. Cf. Luther, *WA* 9,69.36f.; 107.23. See also the *scholion* to Ps. 4:2 in the Vatican Fragment: *Unbekannte Fragmente aus Luthers zweiter Psalmenvorlesung 1518,* ed. Erich Vogelsang (Berlin, 1940), p. 41. On Bernard, *Ep.* 91.3 (*PL* 182, 224).

[31] Gerson (note 27), p. 334. Cf. *WA* 3,549.27-37.

[32] Sermon "A Deo exivit" (Mar. 23, 1402), 14. Cf. *PL* 184, 337.

[33] *Opera omnia,* ed. L. Du Pin. I (Antwerp, 1706), 91 D.

[34] Cf. my book, *The Harvest of Medieval Theology,* pp. 338f.

[35] *De reductione artium ad theologiam,* cap. 5, ed. Julian Kaup (Munich, 1961), 246.

[36] On the relation between Hugo of St. Victor and the Pseudo-Dionysius, see Roger Baron, *Etudes sur Hugues de Saint-Victor* (Angers, 1963). Baron, who edits Hugo's commentaries, regards them as late works, ca. 1130-40 (*Ibid.,* p. 88).

[37] Otfried Müller cites from this work without calling attention to its early date. *Die Rechtfertigungslehre nominalistischer Reformationsgegner: Bartholomäus Arnoldi von Usingen O.E.S.A. und Kaspar Schatzgeyer O.F.M.* (Breslau, 1939). The same is true for another work on Schatzgeyer by Heinrich Klomps, *Freiheit und Gesetz bei dem Franziskanertheologen Kaspar Schatzgeyer* (Münster, 1959). Together with the equally neglected yet quite significant *Apologia status fratrum ordinis minorum de observantia* (1516). *De Perfecta et contemplatita vita* forms the main source of our knowledge of Schatzgeyer before 1517, and hence it permits us by way of comparison with the *Scrutinium* and other later works to measure the influence of the *causa Lutheri* on the development of Schatzgeyer's thinking. The pre-Reformation writings of Counter-Reformation authors deserve our special attention. Cf. the conclusion of Ernst Walter Zeeden: "Der Protestantismus hatte Augen, Herzen und Sinne auch der Katholiken geöffnet für das Wirken der Gnade." "Aspekte der Katholischen Frömmigkeit in Deutschland in 16. Jahrhundert," in *Reformata Reformanda. Festgabe für Hubert Jedin,* ed. Erwin Iserloh and Konrad Repgen. II (Münster i. W. 1965), 1-18; 12.

[38] Kasper Schatzgeyer, *De perfecta atque contemplativa vita* (Conventus Monarchiensis, 1501) in *Opera omnia* (Ingolstadt, 1534[2]), fol. 318r-333v; directio 20, fol. 325.

[39] *WA Tr.* 1,435.32f (Nr. 872); *WA Tr.* 3,295. 6-8 (Nr. 3370b); *WA* 40/3.354.17.

[40] *WA Tr.* 1,330 I (Nr. 683).

[41] *WA Tr.* 1,302.30-34; Cl. 8.80.17-22 (Nr. 644). Cf. *WA* 40/3,199.32-35 (Ps. 126:6-1532-33, pub. 1540).

[42] In the *Dictata* Luther breaks consciously with medieval tradition in the *scholion* to Ps. 90 (91):6 (*WA* 4.69.6-22—probably early 1515), in that he interprets the text not in the sense of "tentationes corporales," but as "tentationes fidei."

[43] *WA Tr.* 2,114.1-3 (Nr. 1492); cf. *WA Tr.* 5.213.16 (Nr. 5523).

[44] *WA Tr.* 1,496.7 (Nr. 979). Vogelsang notes "Gersons Sonderstellung" and refers to his earlier book, *Der angefochtene Christus bei Luther* (Berlin, 1932), p. 15, n. 56. Nevertheless, he finds with Gerson the same bypassing of the incarnate Christ as with Bernard and Bonaventure, "wenn auch auf dem methodisch gestuften Umweg über den Menschgewordenen, Gekreuzigten." *Luther-Jb.* (1937), p. 41 and n.I.

[45] *WA* 9,44.38-39; Cl. 5,307.22 (Marginal Notes to Tauler's Sermons).

[46] *WA* 9,103.41; Cl. 5.310.27. I do not pursue this further pending the study by S.E. Ozment of the influence of Gerson and Tauler on the anthropology of the young Luther (a Harvard Ph.D. dissertation). [Now in print: *Homo Spiritualis: A Comparative Study of the Anthropology of Johannes Tauler, Jean Gerson and Martin Luther (1509-16)* (Leiden, 1969).] On the solidarity of Thomas and Tauler vis à vis Luther who "misunderstood" Tauler, cf. Heinrich Denifle, *Luther und Luthertum* I/I (Mainz, 1904$^2$), pp. 150ff. Cf. also A.M. Walz, "Denifles Verdienst um die Taulerforschung," in *Johannes Tauler. Ein deutscher Mystiker; Gedenkschrift zum 600. Todestag,* ed. E. Filthaut O.P. (1961), pp. 8-18. For Protestant assessments of the independent nature of Luther's appropriation of mysticism see Reinhold Seeberg, *Die religiösen Grundgedanken des jungen Luther und ihr Verhältnis zu dem Ockhamismus und der deutschen Mystik* (Berlin, 1931), p. 30; Willhelm Thimme, "Die 'Deutsche Theologie' und Luthers 'Freiheit eines Christenmenschen,'" *ZThK* NF 13 (1932), 193-222, esp. 222; and Hering (note 13), p. 27.

[47] *WA* 3,151.5-13 (*schol.* to Ps. 26 [27]:9—ca. Autumn, 1513). Cf. Gerson, *De mystica theologia* (note 1) 28.42-29.47; 34.24-35.31; 97.35f.

[48] *WA* 9,98.20-25; Cl. 5,306.28-307.3.

[49] *WA* 9,98.34: Cl. 5,307.13. For a parallel to this in a sermon from Aug. 15,1517 (according to Vogelsang it is from 1520—see *Z K G* 50 [1931], 132, 143), see *WA* 4,650.5-15; Cl. 5,434.19-30. To my knowledge the earliest treatment of this matter is in Luther's use of "deinde" with reference to the transition from the *vita activa* to the *vita contemplativa* in the *scholion* on Ps. 52 (53):7 (*WA* 3,298.31). Cf. the almost hymnic development in the *scholion* on Ps. 113(114):9 (*WA* 4,94.40-95.11), where an attack on the "prius" is already considered dangerous. Cf. the striking parallel to this "pirus" in John Geiler of Kaysersberg in L. Dacheux, *Die ältesten Schriften Geilers von Kayserberg* (Freiburg I. Br., 1882), pp. 215f. Cf. also the letter written a century earlier by Geert Groote, "Ad curatim Zwollensem" (1382), which warns of the importance of the "prius" by calling on the authority of the Pseudo-Dionysius, *Geraldi Magni Epistolae,* ed. W. Mulder, S.J. (Antwerp, 1933). p. 135. On Groote cf. K. L. C. M. de Beer, *Studie over de Spiritualiteit van Geert Groote* (Brussels, 1938), pp. 84-187. Groote warns of the serious danger of a mystical contemplation which is not preceded by ascetic purification (*ibid.,* pp. 186f.). While he has praise for Heinrich Seuse, Groote is very critical of Meister Eckhart and speaks in a qualified way about Jan van Ruysbroeck. It is noteworthy that Luther warns us not "festinari ad opera . . . antequam credimus." (*WA* 57,143.5f.—Hebr. 3.7, 1517).

[50] Cf. *WA* 43,72.9-14, 22-28 (to Gen. 19:14).

[51] More cautious is Johannes von Walter, *Mystik und Rechtfertigung beim jungen Luther* (Gütersloh, 1937), p. 21. Horst Quiring presents a representative view when he argues that Luther's (negative) relation to mysticism after 1520 is determined by his "Antithese zum Schwärmertum." "Luther und die Mystik," *ZSTh* 13 (1936), 150-174, 179-240, 234. Over against this view cf. Karin Bornkamm's instructive juxtaposition of Luther's exposition of Gal. 2:20 ("Vivo autem non iam ego, sed vivit in me Christus") in 1519 and in 1531. *Luthers Auslegungen des Galaterbriefs von 1519 und 1531. Ein Vergleich* (Berlin, 1963), p. 98. In 1531 the intimacy of the union between Christ and the believer is described in stronger terms " . . . multo arctiore vinculo quam masculus et femina" (*WA* 40/1.286.1). Despite our emphasis on continuity, we do not deny a certain fluctuation and noteworthy parallels in the lectures on Romans and especially in the lectures on Hebrews. Cf. J. P. Boendermaker's study which comes to the conclusion that Luther's lectures on Hebrews are concerned "die neuen Erkenntnisse in alten, grösstenteils von der deutschen Mystik geprägten Begriffen auszudrücken." *Luthers commentaar op de brief aan de Hebreeën 1517-18* (Assen, 1965), p. 119; cf. p. 101. As we are trying to demonstrate, such was Luther's effort to depict the "*vera* vita contemplativa" from the very beginning.

[52] *WA* 43,73.11-13, 21-23.

[53] *WA* 43, 72.31-73.9.

[54] More explicit is the comment on Tauler at *WA* 9,100.28-30. Cf. Luther's Aug. 1517 (?) sermon. *WA* 4,647.19-25, 35-40; 648.13-16.

[55] *WA* 56,299.17-300.8. Cf. *WA* 57,168.18-22; 167.17f.; *WA* 56,298.1f. On the basis of Luther's contrast between *raptus* and *accessus* Otto Scheel concludes: "So verliert die mystische Theologie ihre Bedeutung für die Praxis des religiösen Lebens . . ." "Taulers Mystik und Luthers reformatorische Entdeckung." in *Festgabe für Julius Kaftan* (Tübingen, 1920), pp. 298-318, esp. 318.

[56] Cf. my *Harvest of Medieval Theology,* p. 41. On the debate between Ockham, d'Ailly, and Biel, cf. Altenstaig, under article "Viator," fol. 263[rb]-264[va].

[57] *WA* 4, 64.24-65.6.

[58] Cf. the preface to Gansfort's *Epistolae, WA* 10/2,316f. (1522); 317.3.

[59] Cf. *WA* 10/2 329f. (1522). R. R. Post, the *connoisseur* of the *Devotio moderma,* has recently established that Pupper is a typical late medieval theologian. "Johann Pupper van Goch," *Nederlandsch Archief voor Kerkgeschiedenis* 47 (1965-66), 71-97, esp. 93.

[60] Luther declares that he has nowhere found a better (i.e. nonphilosophical) treatment of original sin than in the "Beatus vir" (i.e. "De Spiritualibus ascensionibus") of Gerhard Groote (i.e. Gerhard Zerbolt von Zütphen). *WA* 56,313.13-16; Cl. 5.252.23-26. Cf. the Cologne ed. (1539), chap. 3. J. van Rooij considers Luther's praise a misunderstanding, since Zerbolt did not represent a "Protestant" doctrine of the total corruption of man. *Gerhard Zerbolt van Zutphen* (Nijmegen, 1936), p. 254.

[61] "Tauler und Luther" in *La mystique Rhénane* (Paris, 1963), pp. 157-168, esp. 158, n. 3.

[62] See the preface to the first, incomplete edition of the *Theologia Deutsch* (1516). *WA* 1,153: ". . . ist die matery fasst nach der art des erleuchten doctors Tauleri, prediger ordens." Henri Strohl points out that Tauler by comparison is more Thomistic (Dominican), whereas the *Theologia Deutsch* is more Scotist. *Luther* (Paris, 1962), p. 191.

[63] Cf. *Harvest of Medieval Theology,* pp. 341ff.

[64] Cf. Elze (note 17), esp. pp. 391ff. Cf. Jean Chatillon, "La devotio dans la langue chrétienne," in *Dic. de Spiritualité,* III (Paris, 1957), 705-716, esp. 714.

[65] François Vandenbroucke characterizes this era as marked by "le divorce entre théologie et mystique," *La Spiritualité du Moyen Age* (Paris, 1961), p. 533. Indeed, a general upsurge of affective theology can be noted, usually critical of the debates "in scholis." If theology is understood in this latter academic sense, Vandenbroucke's conclusion can be amply validated. Late medieval affective theology, however, with its elaborate use of mystical terminology, can perhaps better be assessed as a protection against such a divorce. This upsurge of affective theology and what I have called the democratization of mysticism are two sides of the same coin.

[66] I shall deal elsewhere more extensively with the relation between the Observant movement and the *Devotio moderna.*

[67] *WA* 9,98.20; Cl. 5,306.28.

[68] On Luther's description of the *Theologia Deutsch,* see the title page of the second (and first complete) edition (1518), *WA* 1,376.A. Cf. the exposition of Ps. 51:3 in 1517. *WA* 1,186.25-29. Finally, cf. *Eine Deutsche Theologie,* cap. 42, modernized by Joseph Bernhart (Munich, 1946), p. 229.

[69] On the distinction between Eckhart and Tauler see Käte Grunewald, *Studien zu Johannes Taulers Frömmigkeit* (Berlin, 1930), p. 41: "Statt einer Schaumystik also eine in diesem neuen Sinne wirklich voluntaristische Mystik." We do not, of course, deny that there are parallels between Eckhart and Luther; it is a more complex matter than mere "Verbindunglinien," as Rühl argues (note 6), p. 91. If Rühl is justified in describing as *the* point of distinction between scholasticism and mysticism the "Denkform" of the latter which "von einem Begriff ausgeht, andere anschliesst und wieder zum Ausgangsbegriff zurükkehrt" (38), and hence "die essentielle Einheit von diametral entgegengestzten Konzeptionen enthüllt" (45), then the question must be raised: is not a minimal interpretation of just this "Denkform" encountered in every affective theology and hence no further typical for "high mysticism" in the described sense of the word? To the extent that one seeks an interpretation which would embrace "high mysticism," the "Denkform" rests then upon a "Denkinhalt" which presupposes a thorough-going monism in which opposites are present only in appearance. Further, Rühl's effort to distinguish Luther and mysticism generally on the basis of anthropology is unclear and does not take account of the fact that the anthropologies of Eckhart and Tauler are different. Cf. Grunewald, p. 8. Finally, there is a decisive difference between Luther's and Eckhart's understanding of creation. While for Eckhart creation is alienation (cf. *Harvest of Medieval Theology,* p. 326), it is for Luther "gnad und wohltat." *Tagebuch über Dr. Martin Luther,* ed. H. Wrampelmayer (Halle, 1885), p. 1559.

[70] *WA Br.* 1,160.10-20; Cl. 6,10.15-18.

[71] *WA* 1,379.11f.

[72] *WA* 5,165.23. See note 82.

[73] Cf. the discussion of Luther's use of the concept of bridal mysticism in my article, "'Institutia Dei' and 'Iustitia Christi': Luther and the Scholastic Doctrines of Justification," *HThR* 59 (1966), 1-26, esp. 25f. On the use of the expression, "du bist min, ich bin din," among German mystical authors, see the register assembled by Grete Lüers. *Die Sprache der deutschen Mystik des Mittelalters im Werke der Mechthild von Magdeburg* (Munich, 1926), pp. 309f. On the use of the expression, "minnende Seele," cf. Romuald Banz, *Christus und die minnende Seele. Zwei spätmittelhochdeutsche mystische Gedichte* (Breslau, 1908), p. 119.

[74] "Illa autem unio animae et corporis . . ." (*WA* 43,73.11). Altenstaig writes in the article on "beatitudo," fol. 25[ra]. "Beatitudo est duplex (ut scriptis reliquit Richardus di. XLIX ar. V, q. 2, li. IV), sc. anime et corporis." Under the article on "unio" (fol. 269[va]) he writes: "unio quedam est corporalis, quedam spiritualis," although it is only in regard to the latter that mystical experience is discussed.

[75] Bonaventure writes of such an experience: *Itinerarium mentis in Deum,* ed. Julian Kaup (Munich, 1961), IV,3. 112-114.

[76] Cf. *WA* 40/3, 199.5-10.

[77] *Enarratio* Ps. 90:7 (1534-35. pub. 1541), *WA* 40/3,542.27-31; 543.8-13. A similar point is made in *WA Tr.* 1,108.1-11 (Nr. 257; 1532), where Luther writes against Eck as a disciple of Plato.

[78] See note 54.

[79] See Schatzgeyer (note 37), fol. 329[b], Dir. 32. Cf. John Geiler of Kaysersberg in Dacheux (note 48), p. 247, and Jane Dempsey Douglass. *Justification in Late Medieval Preaching* (Leiden, 1966), pp. 180ff. In this connection we refer the reader to Gerson's "Ars bene vivendi," which appeared in Wittenberg in 1513 "apud Augustinianos" with Luther's publisher Johannes Grunenberg. It is inconceivable that Luther should not have known this edition, and it increases the number of Gerson's works which Luther probably had read.

[80] Schatzgeyer (note 37), fol. 325[b], Dir. 21.

[81] *Ibid.*, fol. 329. Dir, 29.

[82] Compare by way of contrast Dionysius the Carthusian, *Opera* VII, 301 D-302 A.

[83] *Operationes in psalmos,* Ps. 5:2 (1519-20), *WA* 5,165.21ff.: "Sicut et filii patrem carnis dulcius amant post virgam, qua verberati sunt, Ita carni contraria voluptate sponsus sponsam suam afficit Christus, Nempe post amplexus. Amplexus vero ipsi mors et infernus sunt."

[84] Cf. note 75. For both parallel and contrast cf. the emphasis on *exercitium* in Gerhard Zerbolt, note 59.

[85] See the *scholion* to Hebr. 2:14 (1517), *WA* $57^3$, 129.20-25.

[86] *WA Br.* 1.160.

[87] Cf. the exposition of Hebr. 9:5, *WA* $57^3$,201.15-202.6. Cf. the earliest exposition of Ps. 17:11 ("Ascendit et volavit super pennas ventorum") in *WA* 3,114.15; 124.16ff. On the two theologies which Luther contrasts in his exposition of Hebr. 9:5—"sapientia Christi gloriosi" and "sapientia Christi crucifixi"—cf. *WA* $39^1$,389.10ff.

[88] As we hope to show, this "gemitus" is closely related to the "syntheresis." On Luther's assessment and use of the concept "syntheresis," see Emanuel Hirsch, *Lutherstudien* (Gütersloh, 1954), pp. 109-128. Without connecting "gemitus" and "syntheresis" with one another, M. A. H. Stomps collects a series of citations under the viewpoint "expectatio"—a term which is central for Luther's *theological* anthropology. *Die Anthropologie Martin Luthers. Eine philosophische Untersuchung* (Frankfurt a. M., 1935), esp. pp. 14ff.

[89] Commentary on Galatians 3:28 (1531). *WA* $40^1$,546-8, and the printed text of 1535. *WA* $40^1$.546.25-28.

[90] Luther speaks of "Gerson et ceteri patres" (*WA Tr.*2.27.6f. [Nr. 1288]-1531). On the pulpit of the Amanduskirche in Urach, which was constructed in the last third of the 15th century, Gerson is depicted together with the four fathers of the Church. Cf. Georg Dehio, *Handbuch der Deutschen Kunstdenkmäler,* III (Berlin, 1925[3]), 548.

[91] See Altenstaig, *Vocabularius theologie* under article on "extasis" (fol. 83[va]); cf. the article on "raptus" (fol. 213[va-b]). Cf. also the earlier *Vocabularius* (Tübingen, 1508; 2nd ed. Basel, 1514) under article on "ecstasis" (fol. 25[3-4]). As the epigram of Heinrich Bebel put it, this Latin schoolbook was considered an "antidote" to such little-valued books as the "Catholicon." The "Catholicon," a comprehensive book completed in March, 1286, and often published (there is a Cologne, 1497, edition), was a lexicon compiled by Joannes Balbus de Janua (Giovanni Balbi), and it was still used as an authority by Luther in 1509-10. Cf. *WA* 9,68.14. In 1524 Luther considered it (along with the *Florista, Grecista, Labyrinthus,* and *Dormi secure*) typical of the "tollen, unnützen, schedlichen, Müniche bücher," which glutted the libraries. *An die Ratherren aller*

*Städte deutsches Lands, WA* 15.50.9f.; CI. 2,461.10f. Humanists north of the Alps probably followed the variegated judgment of the work by Erasmus; *Opus Epistolarum* I, 115.89 (1489); 133.85 (1494); 172.32 (1497). At the time he wrote his first lectures on the Psalms (1513-15), Luther still considered the "Catholicon" authoritative.

[92] *Prologus in Psalterium, tract.* II, a.2(Venetiis, 1581), 16 F-17 B. For the larger context cf. Wilfrid Werbeck, *Jacobus Perez von Valencia. Untersuchungen zu seinem Psalmenkommentar* (Tübingen, 1959), pp. 81f. Cf. Luther *WA* 3,185.26f.: "in spiritu raptus intellexit in eo facto quid mystice significaret."

[93] Cf. the by no means dated work of A. W. Hunzinger, *Lutherstudien, I, Luthers Neuplatonismus in der Psalmenvorlesung von 1513-1516* (Leipzig, 1906), pp. 105ff., esp. p. 106, n. I, Cf. p. 74, where Hunzinger argues that Luther's Neoplatonism is not that of the Pseudo-Dionysius. For a necessary clarification of the basic differences, cf. the characterization by J. Koch, "Augustinischer und dionysischer Neuplatonismus und das Mittelalter," *KantSt.* 58 (1956-57), 117-133. I owe this reference to F. Edward Cranz, "The Transmutation of Platonism in the Development of Nicolaus Cusanus and of Martin Luther," which appears as part of the reports of the Cusa Congress of 1964.

[94] Perez (note 91), fol. 837 F-838 A.

[95] *Ibid.,* fol. 838 B.

[96] *Ibid.,* fol. 838 D/E.

[97] *Ibid.,* 383 E/F.

[98] *WA* 4,519.26-29. Cf. Augustine, *Enarr.*, in Ps. 115, n. 3; Gl. ord., *PL* 113, 1038A; Peter Lombard, *PL* 191, 1030B.

[99] *WA* 3,171. 19-24.

[100] *WA* 4,265.22 (Spring, 1515). Cf. Altenstaig, *Vocabularius* (1508), fol. 253-254.

[101] *WA* 4,265.30-36. With Cassiodorus the connection between *excessus* and martyrdom is given prominence. See his exposition of Ps. 115:10f., *Corpus Christianorum* 98, col. 1042, lines 9-16.

[102] Cf. *WA* 4,492.5-8 (Ps. 40, Faber). Luther's comments here are an exact mirroring of Faber's prologue to his Psalter. This important text is discussed in my book, *Forerunners of the Reformation* (New York, 1966), pp. 281-296.

[103] *WA* 4,482.25-483.4. On this usage of "face" (*vultus/facies*), cf. John Staupitz, *Tübinger Predigten,* ed. G. Buchwald and E. Wolf (1927), pp. 239.13-15. Cf. also the study by David C. Steinmetz, *Misericordia Dei: The Theology of Johannes von Staupitz in its Late Medieval Setting* (Leiden, 1968).

[104] *WA* 4,267.16-33; Cl. 5,196.16-197.2. Compare Augustine's interpretation. *Enarr.* in Ps. 115, n. 3; *Corpus Christianorum* 40, col. 1654, lines 1-27.

[105] *WA* 4,268.29-35.

[106] *WA* 4,269.3-15.

[107] *WA* 4,269.15-20.

[108] *WA* 4,273.14-22.

[109] Cf. Olavi Tarvainen, "Der Gedanke der Conformitas Christi in Luthers Theologie," *ZSTh* 22 (1953), 26-43, esp. 40. See also the *Operationes in Psalmos.* Ps. 5:12 (*WA* 5, 167.36-168.7). Cf. *WA* 5, 188.30-32.

[110] *Schol.* to Ps. 4:2 (Autumn, 1516), *WA* $55^2$,57.3-58.11. On Tauler's view of passivity as spiritual self-elevation, cf. Bengt Hägglund, "The Background of Luther's Doctrine of Justification in Late Medieval Theology," *Lutheran World* 8 (1961), 24-36, esp. 30f.

[111] *WA* 4,467.24-26.

[112] *WA* 50,659.22-24; cf. the discussion in "'Iustitia Christi' and 'Iustitia Dei'" (cited in note 72), p. 12. See above Chapter V.

[113] For a more exact analysis of the term "affectus" in the young Luther, cf. Göttingen, Metzger, *Gelebter Glaube. Die Formierung reformatorischen Denkens in Luthers erster Psalmenvorlesung* (Göttingen, 1964). Metzger's definition of "extasis" in the excursus on "excessus" (*ibid.,* pp. 111f) requires further work.

[114] Cf. Reinhard Schwarz, *Fides, Spes und Caritas beim jungen Luther* (Berlin, 1962), p. 148, n. 213.

[115] Cf. *WA* 1,342.37-343.8 (*Sermo de Passione,* 1518).

[116] Comments on Rom. 8:6 as an explanation of Ps. 31(32):9; *WA* 3,176.14-24; Cl. 4,107.25-108.1.

[117] *WA* 4,647.24f. (Sermon, Aug., 1517 [?]).

[118] Cf. the discussion of this important discovery by Gerhard Ebeling, "Die Anfänge von Luthers Hermeneutik," *ZThK* 48 (1951), 172-230, esp. 226, and "Luthers Psalterdruck von Jahre 1513," *ZThK* 50 (1953), 43-99, esp. 92ff. Cf. also the suggestion by Werbeck (note 91), p. 104, that in the medieval tradition the anagogical sense "weniger häufig . . . zum Zuge kam." Cf.

Henri de Lubac, *Exégèse médiévale. Les quatre sens de l'Ecriture,* I (Paris, 1959), 139.

[119] *Schol.* to Ps. 76(77):13, *WA* 3,532.7f.; Cl. 5,160.28f.

[120] Cf. above, pp. 226-229.

[121] Ebeling (note 117), pp. 95ff.; cf. *WA* 55/1,9.28ff.

[122] Although the early ecclesiology of Luther is not a topic for detailed discussion here, I believe that the usual criticism by Roman Catholic scholars, which spies in the first lectures on the psalms documentation for an individualistic interpretation of the "congregatio fidelium," must be corrected by Luther's conception of anagogy as the *common* history of the people of God, without foregoing individual exceptions. On the literature, cf. Gerhard Müller, "Ekklesiologie und Kirchenkritik beim jungen Luther," *Neue ZSTh* 7 (1965), 100-128.

[123] *Schol.* to Ps. 68 (69):17, *WA* 3,433.2-4; Cl. 5,147.7-10.

[124] *WA* 55/1,4.25f.

[125] *Schol.* to Ps. 64(65):2, *WA* 3,372.23-25; Cl. 5,130.11f.Cf. *WA* 1,336.10-12 (*Sermo de passione Christi,* 1518).

[126] *WA* 5,163.28f.

[127] *WA* 8,111.29-5 (1521).

[128] Cf. Thomas M. McDonough O.P., *The Law and the Gospel in Luther: A Study of Martin Luther's Confessional Writings* (Oxford, 1963), p. 53: "Indisputably, Luther understands imputative righteousness as an extrinsic or forensic relation. . . ."

[129] *WA* $39^{I}$,109.1-3 (*Disputatio de iustificatione,* 1536). In the Roman legal tradition "possessio" and "ususfructus" from the contrast to "proprietas" or "dominium." Cf. Max Kaser, *Eigentum und Besitz im älteren römischen Recht* (Weimar, 1943), pp. 310ff. and Ernst Levy, *West Roman Vulgar Law: The Law of Property,* (Philadelphia, 1951), pp. 19ff.

[130] One should concede that in one of its very earliest statements the "extra se (nos)" designates simply the contrast between God's aseity and the dependence of man on divine providence. *WA* 4,481.20f. (to Faber, *Quincuplex Psalterium,* Ps. 15(16):2). The "extradimension" is, therefore, not only applicable to fallen man and his justification, but also to man as a created being.

[131] *WA* 5,144.34-36 (1519-21); *ibid.,* 176.12. *WA* $40^{I}$,41.3-5. Cf. Karl Holl, *Ges. Aufs. zur KG,* 1,131.Cf. *WA* 56,386.24f., where it is clear that "rapi" need not necessarily mean an "excessus mentis" to God.

[132] Gerson (note 1), pp. 190, 129f. Luther, *WA* 56, 387.2-4; Cl.5,270.14-16. Cf. the transcript. *WA* 57, 199.6ff.

[133] *WA* 1,340.35-341.3 (*Sermo de passione,* 1518).

[134] *Schol.* to Rom. 4:7; *WA* 56,289.18-21; Cl. 5,245.11-15. *Ibid.,* 276.7ff; 289.29-31.

[135] *WA* 56,290.18-22; Cl. 5,245.30-34.

[136] *WA* 1,558.4f (1518).

[137] Peter Abelard, *Ethica* c. 19 (*MPL* 178, 664, p).

[138] Bernard, *Tractatus de gradibus humilitatis et superbiae,* c. 6, n. 19 (*MPL* 182, 952).

[139] Gerson, *In festo S. Bernardi* (Aug. 20, 1402), Glorieux, v, 336.

[140] Commentary on Ezekiel 1:10 (*MPL* 25, 22); cf. Commentary on Malachi (*MPL* 25, 1563).

[141] II *Sent.,* d. 39, a. 2, q. I, ad 4; *ibid.,* ad I. Cf. *ibid.,* a, 2, q, 3, ad 5. Cf. also Alexander of Hales, *Summa* I/II (*Ad Claras Aquas II,* Nr, 418); Scotus, *Ox.* II, d. 39, q. I (Vives, XIII, 409ff); *Rep., ibid.* (Vives, XXIII, 203). For our purposes it is not important to discuss further the relation of *synderesis* and conscience or to distinguish *synderesis, apex mentis,* and *scintilla animae.* In this regard cf. Hirsch (note 87). pp. 11ff. An interesting variation of this concept appears in Wessel Gansfort. *De Providentia* in *Opera omnia* (Groningen, 1614), p. 722.

[142] Geiler of Kaysersberg, fol. $6^{b}$ (note 48), p. 222.

[143] *Opera,* VII, 313 a/b.

[144] Schatzgeyer (note 37), *Epilogus et conclusio,* $330^{b}$.

[145] *WA* 1,32.1-16 (Sermon, Dec. 26, 1514).

[146] Cf. my "Facientibus quod in se est Deus non denegat gratiam," *HThR* 55 (1962), 317-342, esp. 333ff. See above Chapter IV.

[147] *WA* 1,32.33-40 (Sermon, Dec. 26, 1514), *ibid.,* 33.36f.; 34, 4-7.

[148] *Ibid.,* 36.37-37.1 See the connection between *gemitus* and *homo vetus, Operationes in Psalmos,* Ps. 5:12; *WA* 5.164.22-31. For a more detailed analysis of the texts which deal with the *synderesis* and *fides,* see S.E. Ozment (note 45).

[149] *WA* 5,119.12-18 (1519-21); cf. *WA* $55^2$,80.29-81.2 (1516) and the detailed annotations in *WA* $55^1$ 22.34-25.9. Cf. the thesis of Arnold of Heisterbach in Gerhard Ritter, *Via antiqua und Via Moderna* (Heidelberg, 1922; Darmstadt, 1963), 155.16ff.; cf. 63f.

[150] *WA* 1,196.25f. (*Die sieben Busspsalmen,* 1517).

[151] *Operationes in Psalmos*. Ps. 5:12; *WA* 5,176.11-22.

**Carter Lindberg (essay date 1996)**

SOURCE: "The Dawn of a New Era," in *The European Reformations*, Blackwell Publishers, 1996, pp. 56-90.

[*In the excerpt below, Lindberg gives a brief overview of the medieval worldview and the religious practices of the day, focusing on Luther's opposition to the Church's granting of indulgences for monetary donations.*]

> *It is through living, indeed through dying and being damned that one becomes a theologian, not through understanding, reading, or speculation.*
>
> Martin Luther

Luther came from an upwardly mobile family. His grandfather was a peasant farmer but his ambitious, determined father worked his way up in the mining industry to the position of a small employer. Luther himself was the first of his family to gain a formal education and become an academic. It is striking that other leading Reformers—Melanchthon, Zwingli, Bucer, and Calvin—came from similar backgrounds.

The poor to modest circumstances of Luther's youth were ameliorated as his father's mining ventures prospered. Indeed, as a smelter-master, Hans Luther earned sufficient income to provide Martin with a university education. After the younger Luther's marriage, his prince gave him the Augustinian monastery in Wittenberg for living quarters; he and his family had meat, fish, and fruit to supplement the medieval staple of life, bread, and Luther's wife—by his account—made the best beer available.

The educational system Luther encountered as a youth was certainly effective, although he did not find it at all edifying. Knowledge was literally beaten into the students. Luther probably started school around the age of seven. The techniques by which he was forced to learn Latin as the basis for later studies included coercion and ridicule. Unprepared students were forced to wear an image of a jackass and addressed as an ass. A student speaking German rather than Latin in class was beaten with a rod. Even music, Luther's favorite subject, was presented in a utilitarian fashion in order to train youths for church choirs. In short, the education of children was at best dull and at worst barbaric. Luther later recalled that one morning he was caned fifteen times for not mastering the tables of Latin grammar.

Those who did master Latin could go on to more advanced education. At fourteen Luther went to Magdeburg, where he lived and studied at a school run by a pious lay religious organization, the Brethren of the Common Life. From there he went on to study in Eisenach. All the students literally sang for their suppers: after classes they roamed the streets in children's choirs to beg for food. Toward the end of his studies in the Eisenach school, Luther was fortunate to find some supportive teachers who recognized his abilities. They introduced him to the Latin classics and history, which made a life-long impression on him and gave him great pleasure. In later life, he translated Aesop's fables into German, and insisted that everyone should study the classics and history. It was a university education, however, that opened doors for commoners to careers in medicine, law, and the church. Like Calvin's father a generation later, Luther's father was eager for Martin to improve the family status and wealth by going to university and becoming a lawyer. Thus Luther attended the University of Erfurt, where he received both his Bachelor of Arts and Master's degrees.

The medieval university consisted of an arts faculty and the three professional faculties of medicine, law, and theology. The language of instruction was Latin, and the method of instruction was detailed study and commentary on texts with particular attention to *the* authority, Aristotle, and his writings on logic. Disputations, an adversarial style of presentation central to this process, not only allowed display of intellectual skill but served the search for the truth. Disputants presented the evidence for their position in the form of theses; opponents then presented alternative evidence to support their own position. Every professor was required to hold public disputations to show how this was done, and both faculty and students were required to attend weekly disputations on selected topics. Disputations educated students in logical thinking. The teacher assigned a set of theses to a students who then defended them according to the rules of logic. This was also the form for the final examination for a degree. Today's oral examination of PhD students in our universities during which they defend their dissertation or thesis is but a pale reflection of the rigorous academic exercises common to the medieval university. The disputation is precisely the form in which Luther cast his ***Ninety-Five Theses*** as well as many of his other Reformation writings. In this as well as other ways, the Reformation was a movement from within the universities.

As a movement within the universities, the Reformation benefited greatly from the approach known as humanism, which strove to apply the critical intellectual recovery of ancient sources to education, the church, and society as a whole. The significance of humanism as a reforming party is conveyed by Bernd Moeller's (1982: 36) succinct phrase: "No humanism, no Reformation." The sources and norms for humanism included Scripture and the church fathers, whose writings were newly accessible through the recovery and improvement of scholarship in Greek, Hebrew, and Latin. The widespread approval of Luther as "our Martin" by humanists in the years up to the edict of Worms (1521) reflected their view of him as a prominent representative of the new learning who opposed their common enemies of scholastic and ecclesiastical abuses of religion and power (Grane 1994).

Luther's move from the study of law to monastic life and the study of theology occurred in the context of the piety of his day. Chapter 2 presented the late medieval period as a time of crisis and insecurity prompted not only by the physical difficulties of the time but also by the rapid social changes that called into question the values and traditional truths by which people had lived. The church exacerbated these insecurities by promoting a type of pastoral care designed to make people uncertain about their salvation and thus more dependent upon the intercessions of the church. The Christian pilgrimage toward the heavenly city was a balancing act between fear and hope. Visitors to medieval cathedrals and churches can still see representations of Christ on the throne of judgement with a sword and a lily on opposite sides of his mouth. The lily represented the resurrection to heaven, but the sword of judgment to eternal torment was more vivid in the minds of most people. A sandstone relief of this common depiction of Christ seated on rainbow "graced" the Wittenberg parish churchyard and so terrified Luther that he refused to look at it.

Everywhere in everyday life the medieval person was surrounded by images serving to remind him or her of eternity and how to achieve it. As the early medieval pope, Gregory the Great (d. 604) had said, "images are the books of the laity." Medieval churches presented the Bible and the lives of the saints in stone, stained glass, and wood. The medieval person did not compartmentalize life into sacred and secular spheres. Thus "the books of the laity" were evident at the town fountain and town hall, carved in the doorways and painted on the walls of homes and public buildings. Where people walked, worked, and gathered for news and gossip, there were religious reminders of their origin and their destination in heaven or hell.

Since hell was not the preferred option, the church and its theologians developed a whole set of practices and exercises to assist people to avoid it. The irony was that in attempting to provide security in an insecure world, the church largely mirrored the new urban and economic developments that exacerbated human insecurity. Suspended between hope and fear, the individual had to achieve his or her goal through a whole system of *quid pro quo* services that reflected the new ledger mentality of the urban burgher absorbed in the developing profit economy. Taken as a whole, Christendom at the end of the Middle Ages appeared as performance-oriented as the new business enterprises of the day.

The very effort of late medieval theology and pastoral practice to provide security only led an insecure world to more insecurity and uncertainty about salvation. One of the key scholastic ideas that led to this uncertainty about salvation was expressed in the phrase *facere quod in se est:* do what lies within you; do your very best. That is, striving to love God to the best of one's ability—however weak that may be—will prompt God to reward one's efforts with the grace to do even better. The Christian's life of pilgrimage toward the heavenly city was increasingly perceived, literally and not just theologically, as an economy of salvation. As mentioned earlier, this "mathematics of salvation" concentrated upon achieving as many good works as possible in order to merit God's reward. In religion as in early capitalism, contracted work merited reward. Individuals were responsible for their own life, society, and world on the basis and within the limits stipulated by God. Pastoral care was intended to provide an avenue to security through human participation in the process of salvation. This theology, however, enhanced the crisis because it threw people back upon their own resources. That is, no matter how grace-assisted their good works, the burden of proof for these works fell back upon the performers, the more sensitive of whom began asking how they could know if they had done their best.

Most people, however, were grateful for whatever help they could get in their quest for salvation. Saints' bones and other relics were avidly collected and venerated with the conviction this was efficacious in reducing sentences to purgatory. Thus the Wittenberg Castle church was dedicated to All Saints; and within it Luther's prince, Frederick the Wise, housed one of the largest relic collections of the area—over 19,000 pieces, worth more than 1,900,000 days' indulgence. This pious intoxication with numbers is also evident in the celebration of masses. In 1517 at the Wittenberg Castle church of All Saints more than 9,000 masses were celebrated which consumed 40,932 candles (over 7,000 pounds of wax!) costing 1,112 gulden (Brecht 1985: 118). Frederick's relic collection included a piece of the burning bush, soot from the fiery furnace, milk from Mary, and a piece of Jesus' crib, to name but a few of his treasures acquired at great cost and lavishly displayed in expensive containers (Hillerbrand 1964: 47-9). Luther's contemporary, Cardinal Albrecht, believed his relic collection was worth 39,245,120 days' indulgence.

The extraordinary prosperity of the indulgence trade was fueled as much by the desires of believers as by the financial interests of the church. If this seems surprising, think of the similar appeal and success of modern media evangelists who promise to satisfy modern desires to control God and conquer insecurity. Late medieval Christendom has been characterized as having "an immense appetite for the divine." Scholars have sometimes puzzled over the great surge of popular piety in the late Middle Ages. No other period celebrated so many religious festivals and processions, nor threw itself so wholeheartedly into church construction. Mass pilgrimages, frequently sparked by some perceived miracle usually associated with the Lord's Supper, caught on like wildfire. The dark side of this devotion erupted in mass attacks upon Jews and persons thought to be witches. Miracles seemed to multiply everywhere in the Empire. The veneration of saints reached its peak and changed its form. Saints were depicted life-size, individualized, and garbed in contemporary dress. Saints were now aligned with the arrangement of society and made patrons for every human exigency. The practice of giving children saints' names became so widespread that the old German names all but disappeared. Insecure about salvation, people attempted to guarantee it by capturing mediators between themselves and God.

Why did people throw themselves into such a piety of achievement? Why was the treadmill of religious performance thought to be the path to security and certainty of salvation? Perhaps because in times of crisis people tend to yearn for the "good old days," and try harder to emulate what they think they were. Hidden behind the late medieval surge in piety there "was an oppressive uncertainty about salvation together with the longing for it. By capturing the mediators between them and God, men attempted to force a guarantee of salvation. Death seems never to have been more realistically considered than in this era, and hardly ever so anxiously feared" (Moeller 1971: 55). Even today we are still fascinated by the bizarre paintings of Hieronymous Bosch (ca. 1450-1516) with their weird, rapid-breeding hybrid creatures associated with lust and fertility but which in the end symbolize sterility and death. Artistic realism blossomed in popular manuals on the art of dying, depictions of the dance of death, and deeply moving representations of Christ's passion.

Religious and psychological anxiety appears to have been heightened by the imposition upon people of clerical standards of morality and behavior. The place where every real or imagined failure to meet clerical norms was ferreted out was the confessional. The laity were expected to go to confession frequently. There the priest pried into every aspect of their lives, especially their sexual lives. The lists of sexual sins in the confessional manuals of the day were so complete that even sexual thoughts were categorized according to the particular danger of damnation consequent on them. Whether or not sexual relations within marriage were serious sins was debated, but there was agreement that at least in principle they were sins. One catechism from 1494 listed sex for enjoyment rather than procreation as a sin. The other side of this coin was the elevation of celibacy and the cloister as the supreme form of a God-pleasing life. Marriage and family were demeaned as necessary evils for the propagation of the community. It is no wonder that the Reformers' attack upon mandatory celibacy for the clergy, and their renewed appreciation of the joy of sex in marriage, were so well received by the laity (Ozment 1992: 152-3; 1983: 12; Tentler 1977: 162-232).

Everyday life on the eve of the Reformation included elements regarded today as superstitions: belief in witches, magic, and astrology. But before we look too quickly down our collective modern nose at late medieval superstitions, we might recall that most of our daily newspapers include horoscopes, and that the "health and wealth" gospels utilizing contemporary media appeal to the same fears and desires that motivated the medieval person to seek out supernatural healers and diviners of the future.

Luther's reform movement was not initiated by the righteous and moral indignation of a Savonarola or an Erasmus directed against perceived superstitions or the corruption of the Renaissance papacy. Luther's movement was rooted in his own personal anxiety about salvation; an anxiety that, if the popular response to him is any indication, was widespread throughout Europe. This anxiety was an effect of the crises of the late medieval period already sketched, but its root cause was the uncertainty of salvation in the message of the church.

### Theological and Pastoral Responses to Insecurity

According to Thomas Aquinas, grace does not do away with nature but completes it. So the famous scholastic phrase *facere quod in se est,* "do what lies within you," means that salvation is a process that takes place *within* us as we perfect ourselves. Put another way, we become righteous before God as we do righteous acts, as we do good works. But to an anxious and insecure age, the question became: "How do I know if I have done my best?"

The answers came primarily from the parish priests, most of whom were unversed in the subtleties of academic theology. The most common answer was "try harder!" This is the clue to that great surge in popular piety mentioned earlier. When in doubt about your salvation, examine yourself to determine if you have done your best, and then put more effort into achieving the best you can. In order to encourage more effort, pastoral practice consciously stimulated anxiety and introspection by citing the church's translation of Ecclesiastes 9:1, "No one knows whether he is worthy of God's love or hate." The church's pastoral theology suspended people between hope and fear—a sort of spiritual carrot-and-stick incentive system.

Catechisms provide a clue to the religious sensibilities of the people and the lower clergy. Priests used these simplified expositions of basic theology, usually in question and answer format, in daily pastoral practice. Widely popular, these catechisms were translated from Latin into the vernaculars, and in this process reflected the spiritual needs of the people. Dietrich Kolde's *Mirror of a Christian Man* indicates the deep religious fear and anxiety of the people up to the eve of the Reformation, and thereby provides a clue for understanding Luther's reform movement.

Kolde's *Mirror* was very popular. First printed in 1470, it appeared in 19 editions before the Reformation and continued to be reprinted after it. Translated into various European vernaculars, Kolde's work was probably the most widely used Catholic catechism before and during the early years of the Reformation. The significant point of this catechism for our purposes is the author's expression of the people's widespread lack of certitude about salvation. Kolde summed up this anxiety when he wrote: "There are three things I know to be true that frequently make my heart heavy. The first troubles my spirit, because I will have to die. The second troubles my heart more, because I do not know when. The third troubles me above all. I do not know where I will go" (Janz 1982: 182).

Luther's first steps on his own quest for certainty about his relationship to God paralleled those of many before him and countless others since: he entered a "seminary." In Luther's case it was the Augustinian monastery in Erfurt. Again, not unlike countless other seminarians past and present, Luther's decision greatly upset his father. Hans Luther was by this time making a decent living. He had sent Martin to Erfurt University with the ambition that he would earn a law degree, return home to the town of Mansfeld, and perhaps eventually become mayor. But Luther had barely begun his law studies when his father's dreams were shattered by the same lightning bolt that knocked Martin to the ground as he walked to Erfurt after a visit home. In terror, Martin implored St Anne, the patron saint of miners, for help, shouting, "I will become a monk."

And become a monk he did. In July 1505 he entered the Black Cloister (so-called because the monks wore black) of the Observant Augustinians in Erfurt. The Black Augustinians were known for their rigorous pursuit of spiritual benefits that more than matched in intensity the pursuit of material benefits practiced by Luther's father and other budding entrepreneurs. It was no less the business of monks to earn spiritual currency for themselves and others than it was the business of the early capitalists to earn material currency.

In the monastery, Luther threw himself wholeheartedly into efforts to achieve salvation. Between the six worship services of each day, which began at 2:00 a.m., Luther sandwiched intense prayer, meditation, and spiritual exercises. But this was just the normal routine, which Luther in his zeal to mortify his flesh and make himself acceptable to God soon surpassed. "I tortured myself with prayers, fasting, vigils, and freezing; the frost alone might have killed me" (*LW* [*Luther's works,* ed. Jaroslav Pelikar and Helmut T. Lehmann, 55 vols. St. Louis: Concordia/Philadelphia: Fortress, 1955-86] 24: 24). It has been suggested that his long periods of fasting, self-flagellation, and sleepless nights in a stone cell without a blanket all contributed to the continual illness that plagued him for the rest of his life. Later in life, Luther remarked: "I almost fasted myself to death, for again and again I went for three days without taking a drop of water or a morsel of food. I was very serious about it" (*LW* 54: 339-40).

In fact, Luther was so serious about perfecting himself in order to gain God's acceptance that he soon became a burden to his fellow monks. Monastic practice prized introspection and self-examination that probed the conscience: "Have I really done my best for God?" "Have I fully realized my God-given potential?" No sensitive person under such introspective pressure to achieve righteousness before God can answer these questions affirmatively. Luther was in a continual state of anxiety about his righteousness. He constantly sought out spiritual guidance and confessors. Years later Luther remarked about all this: "Sometimes my confessor said to me when I repeatedly discussed silly sins with him, 'You are a fool . . . God is not angry with you, but you are angry with God.'" (*LW* 54: 15). Ironically, Luther entered the monastery to overcome his uncertainty of salvation, but there was confronted by the very introspection, intensified to a fine art, that had caused his very anxiety before God.

Luther's monastic superior, Johann von Staupitz, directed him to continue his theological studies to a doctoral degree. Luther protested he was too ill, unworthy, and inadequate. Staupitz was unimpressed. In 1512, Luther became a "sworn Doctor of the Holy Scripture" and embarked on his life-long career as professor of biblical studies at Wittenberg. Later, in his controversies with the church, he appealed to his doctoral oath in which he vowed to exposit and to defend the Scriptures. He believed he had a mandate from the church, and that his efforts for reform were not just a personal crusade.

At this point a brief description of Luther's Wittenberg context is in order. This small town of about 2,500 was the capital of Electoral Saxony. The duchy of Saxony had divided in the late thirteenth century, and in 1356 the area including the town of Wittenberg was granted electoral dignity by the Golden Bull, the decree regulating imperial elections. The prince of Electoral Saxony when Luther arrived was Frederick III, known as "the Wise" (1463-1525). Frederick was not only wealthy but also politically powerful and astute. Loyal to the Habsburg line, he nevertheless opposed expansion of imperial power as well as the powers of the neighboring states of Ducal Saxony and Brandenburg. Frederick was also well traveled and personally concerned for the well-being of his people, land, church, and education. By the turn of the century, he was engaged in rebuilding the castle and the church of the All Saints Foundation and establishing the university.

The division of Saxony into Ducal and Electoral territories left Electoral Saxony without a university, since Leipzing University was in Ducal Saxony. By 1503 Frederick obtained papal confirmation for a new university for which the All Saints Foundation would serve as chief financial support. Frederick also poured his own resources into the university and in 1508 published its statutes. The establishment in 1502 of the Augustinian monastery in Wittenberg by Staupitz provided the university with many of its faculty. That is how Luther came to be in Wittenberg. At first about 200 students enrolled annually. After Luther's burst into notoriety in 1517, the enrollment mushroomed. A student saying of the time suggested that if you want an education go to Wittenberg, if you are looking for amusement go elsewhere. The university was Frederick's pride and joy; he would be reluctant to allow one of his prize professors to be burned at the stake! Besides, Frederick had invested a good sum in the promotion of Luther to the doctorate on the promise that Luther would serve in the professorship of Bible for life; it would be a poor investment to allow that life to end unnaturally soon.

Luther began lecturing at the university in the winter semester of 1513-14. The exact time-frame for his lectures is uncertain, but the sequence up to the controversy over indulgences included lectures on the Psalms (1513-15), Romans (1515-16), Galatians (1516-17), and Hebrews (1517). There is nothing quite like having to explain a text to others to intensify one's own study of the material. Luther had at his disposal a good library of biblical commentaries, various biblical translations, and, after 1516, the new edition of the Greek New Testament by Erasmus. But Luther's intellectual focus was further sharpened by his own personal religious quest for certainty of salvation, the resolution of which occurred in this academic context. His conversion experience was, in the words of Gerhard Ebeling (1970), a *Sprachereignis,* a language event.

Luther's intense study of the language and grammar of the Bible, assisted by the linguistic tools provided by the Renaissance humanists, radically changed his understanding of salvation. He learned that the righteousness of God is not a demand to be met by achievement but a gift to be accepted by faith. Luther's conversion experience set medieval piety on its head. He came to see that salvation is no longer the goal of life but rather its foundation. On the basis of this discovery the theology faculty at the University of Wittenberg instituted a curriculum reform that replaced scholastic theology by biblical studies. In the spring of 1517, Luther wrote to a friend in Erfurt: "Our theology and St Augustine are progressing well, and with God's help rule at our University. Aristotle is gradually falling from his throne, and his final doom is only a matter of time. . . . Indeed no one can expect to have any students if he does not want to teach this theology, that is, lecture on the Bible or on St Augustine or another teacher of ecclesiastical eminence" (*LW* 48: 42). The authority of Aristotle was displaced by the authority of the Bible.

What Luther discovered, and what so moved his faculty colleagues and students, was an understanding of God and salvation that overthrew the anxiety-ridden catechetical teachings of priests like Kolde. Luther's biblical study led him to the conviction that the crisis of human life is not overcome by striving to achieve security by what we do, but by the certainty of God's acceptance of us in spite of what we do. The gospel, Luther argued, repudiates "the wicked idea of the entire kingdom of the pope, the teaching that a Christian man must be uncertain about the grace of God toward him. If this opinion stands, then Christ is completely useless. . . . Therefore the papacy is a veritable torture chamber of consciences and the very kingdom of the devil." Luther now never tired of proclaiming that the burden of proof for salvation rests not upon a person's deeds but upon God's action. This conviction delivered Luther from what he called "the monster of uncertainty" that left consciences in doubt of their salvation. For Luther theology is certain when "it snatches us away from ourselves and places us outside ourselves, so that we do not depend on our own strength, conscience, experience, person, or works but depend on that which is outside ourselves, that is, on the promise and truth of God, which cannot deceive" (*LW* 26: 386-7).

Medieval theology and pastoral care had attempted to provide religious security by what we may call a covenantal theology which said that if we do our best then God will not deny us grace. Although theologians employed numerous and subtle qualifications, the gist of the universal theme *facere quod in se est* ("do your best") was that people could at least initiate their salvation. That is, if you strive to love God to the best of your ability, weak as that may be, God will reward you with the grace to do even better. God, the medieval theologians claimed, has made a covenant to be our contractual partner in creation and salvation. In religion, as in the rest of life, work merited reward. Individuals were to be responsible for their own life, society, and world on the basis and within the limits of the covenant God stipulated. The theological and pastoral concern here was to provide an avenue of security through participation in the process of salvation. The consequence of this theology, however, was to enhance insecurity and uncertainty because it threw individuals back on their own resources. . . .

The concept came from Aristotle. If we look briefly at how medieval theologians applied just two of Aristotle's ideas, we can see how influential he was. In logic Aristotle posited that like is known by like. Applied to theology, this meant that fellowship with God can only take place when the sinner is raised to likeness with God. The sinner must become holy because God is holy and does not associate with the unholy. To the question of where fellowship with God may be achieved, the answer could only be: on God's level. The sinner must become "like" God, that is, perfected and raised to where God is. Hence the popularity of ladder imagery in medieval theology.

The widespread imagery of a ladder to heaven graphically depicted the idea that salvation requires ascent to God. Thus the twelfth-century *Hortus deliciarum* ("Garden of Delights") includes the picture of the "ladder of virtues" leading from earth to heaven. The top of the ladder enters a cloud from which the hand of God extends offering the crown of life to the climber who reaches the top. The rungs of the ladder correspond to the virtues the climber must acquire. At the foot and side of the ladder are demons who try to hinder human ascent. Angels with swords fight these demons. The persons on the rungs represent various social and religious roles: a soldier and a laywoman, a cleric, a nun and a mendicant monk, a monk from an enclosed cloister, a hermit, and, at the top, "charity," who alone reaches the goal. All the others fall off the ladder as they reach for their respective temptations below them. The hermit is attracted by his garden, the monk by his bed, the mendicant and nun by money, the cleric by food and friends, the soldier and laywoman by the goods of the world. On the ladder itself is inscribed: "Whoever falls can start climbing again thanks to the remedy of penance."

But how is the sinner to accomplish this feat? Aristotle's other idea comes into play at this point. Aristotle spoke of self-improvement in terms of what he called a *habitus,* a personal modification through habitual activity, through practice. People acquire skills through practice. A person becomes a guitarist by practicing the guitar, a good citizen by practicing civic virtues, ethical by practicing moral virtues, and so on. Through such habits or practices ethics becomes a kind of second nature.

Medieval theologians took this basically commonsense idea and applied it to achieving righteousness before God. They "baptized" Aristotle's philosophy by saying that God through the sacraments infuses a supernatural "habit" in us. On the basis of this habitual grace, we are responsible to actualize it; to do what now lies within us. In so far as we perfect the gifts God has given us, we merit more grace. Thomas Aquinas (1225-74) stated that grace does not do away with nature but perfects it. Thus, the famous scholastic phrase "do what lies within you" means that salvation is a process that occurs *within* us as we perfect ourselves. Put another way, we become righteous before God as we do righteous acts, as we do good works. But again the question becomes: "How do I know if I have done enough good works to merit salvation?"

Luther could not believe that God was placated by his efforts to do his best for his salvation. Toward the end of his life Luther reflected on his struggles with this covenantal theology. He wrote: "Though I lived as a monk without reproach, I felt that I was a sinner before God with an extremely disturbed conscience. . . . I hated the righteous God who punishes sinners . . . Nevertheless, I beat importunately upon Paul at that place, most ardently desiring to know what St Paul wanted" (*LW* 34: 336-7).

"That place" is the passage in Romans 1:17, "For in it [the gospel] the righteousness of God is revealed through faith for faith; as it is written, 'He who through faith is righteous shall live.'" Up to this point Luther, like so many of his contemporaries, had heard the gospel as the threat of God's righteous wrath because medieval theology and pastoral care presented the righteousness of God as the standard that sinners had to meet in order to achieve salvation. Luther now came to realize that we are not to think of the righteousness of God in the active sense (that we must become righteous like God) but rather in the passive sense (that God gives us his righteousness). The good news, Luther discovered, is that justification is not what the sinner achieves but what the sinner receives. That is, it is not the sinner who is changed, but rather the sinner's situation before God. In short, the term "to be justified" means that God considers the sinner righteous (*LW* 34:167). "God does not want to redeem us through our own, but through external, righteousness and wisdom, not through one that comes from us and grows in us, but through one that comes from outside; not through one that originates here on earth, but through one that comes from heaven. Therefore, we must be taught a righteousness that comes from the outside and is foreign" (*LW* 25:136).

So Luther turned the medieval piety of achievement on its head. We do not do good works in order to become acceptable to God; rather, because God accepts us we do good works. Justification by grace alone through faith alone thus is a metatheological proclamation. That is, it changes the language of theology from an "if . . . then" structure to a "because . . . therefore" structure; from a language of conditions to be fulfilled in order to receive whatever is promised, to a language of unconditional promise (Gritsch and Jenson 1976: 42).

This radical shift is clearly expressed by Luther's move from a theology of covenant and contract to a theology of testament, as in a person's last will and testament. If a person is named in a will as an heir then the only condition necessary for inheritance is the death of the one who made the will. In his discussion of Hebrews 9:17, Luther wrote: "You would have to spend a long time polishing your shoes, preening and primping to attain an inheritance, if you had no letter and seal with which you could prove your right to it. But if you have a letter and seal, and believe, desire, and seek it, it must be given to you, even though you were scaly, scabby, and most filthy" (*LW* 35: 88; see Hagen 1974).

The language of testament is unconditional promise. God has named us in his will, and with his death on the cross the will is in effect. The "language event" of Luther's biblical study presented "a totally other face of the Scriptures" to him. "Thereupon I ran through the Scriptures from memory. I also found in other terms an analogy, as, the work of God, that is, what God does in us, the power of God, with which he makes us strong, the wisdom of God, with which he makes us wise, the strength of God, the salvation of God, the glory of God" (*LW* 34: 337).

### Theological Implications

I have belabored Luther's understanding of the sinner's righteousness before God because it is at the heart of everything Luther said and did after his conversion. At this point we need to take a moment to sketch the difference this made in other areas of Luther's theology.

The Reformation is sometimes described in terms of the watchwords "grace alone," "Scripture alone," and "faith alone." We have already seen what Luther meant by grace alone. But what did he mean by the other two *solas*? He did not mean by these battle cries what some modern Protestants mean by them. According to Luther, the Word of God is primarily Christ. Secondarily, the Word of God is the preached or spoken Word. He was fond of emphasizing that faith comes by hearing the promise of God because he was aware that we can look away from written words but have more difficulty closing our ears to spoken words. Only on a third level did Luther relate the Word of God to the written words of the Bible. The Bible is rather "the swaddling clothes and the manager in which Christ lies . . . Simple and lowly are these swaddling clothes, but dear is the treasure, Christ, who lies in them" (*LW* 35: 236).

Faith is trust and confidence in God's promise of acceptance in spite of being unacceptable. Faith is not belief in particular doctrines. Faith is a relationship with God based on trust in God. The tendency among Protestants to speak of "salvation by faith alone" can lead to the misunderstanding that faith itself is an achievement. The confusion of faith with intellectual belief in particular doctrines or in biblical stories may lead to a kind of "can you top this" contest in which the person who believes the most unbelievable things is considered the most Christian. Then faith becomes the intellectual or psychological equivalent of medieval good works. This is far afield from Luther's understanding. "Faith is not a paltry and petty matter . . . ; but it is a heartfelt confidence in God through Christ that Christ's suffering and death pertain to you and should belong to you" (*LW* 22: 369).

Luther's radical understanding of justification brought with it a radical understanding of the person before God. Luther departed from all religious anthropologies that divide the person, whether it be into body and soul; body, soul, and spirit; flesh and spirit; or inner and outer. For Luther, the person is always the whole person. Luther could use traditional terminology, but he redefined it. Thus the distinction between flesh and spirit is no longer dualistic and anthropological but biblical and theological. Flesh and spirit do not designate parts of the person but refer to the whole person's relationship to God. Living according to the flesh means the whole person in rebellion against God. Living according to the spirit means the whole person in confidence in God's grace. "Flesh and spirit you must not understand as though flesh is only that which has to do with unchastity and spirit is only that which has to do with what is inwardly in the heart. . . . Thus you should learn to call him 'fleshly' too who thinks, teaches, and talks a great deal about lofty spiritual matters, yet does so without grace" (*LW* 35: 371-2).

Human beings have no intrinsic capacity that entitles them to a relationship with God. The whole person, not just some "lower" aspect, is a sinner. Luther understood sin theologically rather than ethically. Sin is not doing bad things but rather it is not trusting God. "Unbelief is the root, the sap, and the chief power of all sin" (*LW* 35: 369). In other words, the serpent's question to Eve is whispered in everyone's ears. Sin is the egocentric compulsion to assert self-righteousness against God; it is the refusal to allow God to be God.

Acknowledgement of sin and the acceptance of God's judgment enable the sinner to live as righteous in spite of sin. By "letting God be God," that is by ceasing one's efforts to be like God, the sinner is allowed to be what he or she is intended to be—human. The sinner is not called to deny his or her humanity and to seek "likeness" to God. Rather, the forgiveness of sin occurs in the midst of life. The Christian before God is therefore at one and the same time both sinner and righteous; "a sinner in fact, but a righteous man by the sure imputation and promise of God that He will continue to deliver him from sin until He has completely cured him. And thus he is entirely healthy in hope, but in fact he is still a sinner" (*LW* 25: 260).

The theological motif that relates justification and anthropology is the dialectical distinction of law and gospel. To Luther this is the essential nerve of theological thinking; it is what makes a theologian a theologian. "Nearly the entire Scripture and the knowledge of all theology depends upon the correct understanding of law and gospel" (*WA* [D. Martin Luthers Werke: Kritische Gesamtausgabe ed. J.K.F. Kraake, G. Kawer au, et al., 58 vols. Weimar: Böhlau, 1883-] 7: 502). Throughout his career Luther never tired of emphasizing the distinction between law and gospel as the key to correct theology. He believed that without this distinction the Word of God will be confused with human judgment.

The distinction between law and gospel is the distinction between two fundamental kinds of speech. The law is the communication of demands and conditions; it is the language of covenant. The law imposes an "if . . . then" structure on life. All law-type communication presents a future contingent upon human achievement: "If you hold up your end of the bargain, then I will hold up mine." The gospel however is the communication of promise. It is the language of testament with the pattern of "because . . . therefore." "Because I love you I will commit myself to you." But even in the best of human relationships this analogy breaks down. There are all sorts of contingencies over which we have no control. Death is the clearest example. We may be committed to our children but death may take us away just when they need us the most. But Luther's point is that we are not the gospel. The gospel is the unconditional promise of God. It is unconditional because God has already satisfied all conditions, including death. In this sense, then, justification is not just a particular doctrine among others. Rather, justification is *the* language that is always unconditional promise.

Indulgences: The Purchase of Paradise

At the same time as Luther was reaching a radical theological reversal of his received tradition in the context of his biblical lectures, he was also carrying out pastoral responsibilities in the Wittenberg parishes. It is important to remember that while the form of the ***Ninety-Five Theses*** was that of an academic disputation, the context of this disputation was pastoral. Luther was propelled into the public arena by concern for his parishioners, who believed they could purchase paradise if they bought letters of indulgence. "I am," Luther later wrote, "a sworn doctor of Holy Scripture, and beyond that a preacher each weekday whose duty it is on account of his name, station, oath, and office, to destroy or at least ward off false, corrupt, unchristian doctrine" (*LW* 31: 383).

Indulgences grew from the sacrament of penance. Baptism incorporated a person into the pilgrim community of the church which was always in process of traveling to its true home with God in the heavenly city, and the eucharist nourished the pilgrims during their trip. However, pilgrims continually faced the danger of shipwreck on earthly delights. The church's response to this danger was to offer what the early church called the "second plank after shipwreck," the sacrament of penance.

The sacrament of penance was the subjective side of the objective sacrament of the mass. Through the sacrament of penance, the church provided not only the absolution of guilt but also the means for satisfying the socially disruptive and religiously offensive actions of persons. It has been suggested that the idea of atoning for crimes by rendering commensurate satisfaction has Germanic and feudal roots. Secular penal practice allowed the "redemption" of a punishment for money. Applied to religious practice this meant that a fast could be replaced by the cost of the meal or a pilgrimage by the cost of the journey.

The significance of penance for medieval life and religion cannot be overrated. The term itself derives from the Latin *poena,* which means not only punishment but also compensation, satisfaction, expiation, and penalty. St Augustine had spoken of the necessity of punishment for sin that will be satisfied either here through human acts or hereafter by God. From this perspective there developed the doctrine of purgatory and its purifying fire, the pastoral and disciplinary life of the church, and the indulgence system for commuting penitential impositions too severe for completion outside the monastic regimen. Thus when the austere eleventh-century reformer, Cardinal Peter Damian (1007-72) imposed a 100-year penance on the archbishop of Milan for simony, he also indicated how much money would commute each year of penance. Although the intent of the indulgence system was to adjust satisfaction for sins to changing social conditions (a developing urban environment made certain penances difficult), by the late Middle Ages it was becoming an abused instrument for clerical social control and revenue raising.

By the twelfth century, the norm was a private penance before a priest that consisted of contrition (a heartfelt repentance), confession, and satisfaction. By the eve of the Reformation some wags spoke of contrition, confession, and compensation! A development that eased the sacrament of penance substituted attrition (fear of punishment) for contrition. Theoretical justification for remission of the ecclesiastical satisfaction imposed on the penitent rested on the thirteenth-century theological development of the treasury of grace available to the church. This treasury of the church contained the accumulated merits of Christ and the saints (mainly the works of monastics) which, since they were superfluous for those who originally achieved them, were available for ordinary sinners in the church. Here again, we see a ledger mentality, a calculating frame of mind concerned with "the account books of the beyond." An indulgence, then, drew on the treasure of the church to pay off the debt of the penitent sinner who would otherwise be obliged to pay off the penance by works of satisfaction. The possibility of a capitalist interpretation of this system may be seen in the story of the nobleman who decided to invest in futures. The story goes that after Tetzel made a large sum of money from indulgences in Leipzig, a nobleman approached him and asked if he could buy an indulgence for a future sin. Tetzel agreed upon the basis of an immediate payment. When Tetzel departed from Leipzig, the nobleman attacked and robbed him with the comment that this was the future sin he had in mind (Hillerbrand 1964: 44-5).

The popular mind, abetted by some preachers, twisted the meaning of indulgence from that of the church's remission of a temporal penalty imposed because of sin to that of a ticket to heaven. The hard-sell medieval indulgence sellers such as Tetzel, whom Luther attacked, offered direct access to heaven even for those who were already dead and in purgatory. One of Tetzel's sales jingles was, "As soon as the coin into the box rings, a soul from purgatory to heaven springs." Would you buy a used car from this man? Well, crowds of anxious contemporaries believed they could buy salvation from him. He was good at his job, but then he was also rewarded handsomely.

Tetzel's routine would have been the envy of Madison Avenue, had it existed. His advance men announced his arrival some weeks before he came to town. They also compiled a special directory of the town that listed the financial resources of its citizens so they would know how much they could charge. Tetzel's entrance into the town was accompanied by a fanfare of trumpets and drums and a procession complete with the flags and symbols of the papacy. After a vivid sermon on hell and its terrors in the town square, he proceeded to the largest church and gave an equally vivid sermon on purgatory and the sufferings not only awaiting the audience but presently endured by their dead relatives and loved ones. "Do you not hear the voices of your dead parents and other people, screaming and saying: 'Have pity on me, have pity on me . . . for the hand of God hath touched me' [Job 19: 21]? We are suffering severe punishments and pain, from which you could rescue us with a few alms, if only you would.' Open your ears, because the father is calling to the son and the mother to the daughter" (Oberman 1989b: 188). After the next sermon picturing heaven, his audience was sufficiently prepared and eager to buy indulgences. There was always something for everyone because he had a sliding scale of prices depending upon the person's financial resources.

Tetzel was not allowed in Wittenberg because Frederick the Wise did not want competition for his own relic collection with its associated indulgences. But Luther's parishioners overcame this inconvenience by going out to Tetzel. Luther was appalled when they returned and said they no longer needed confession, penance, and the mass because now they had tickets to heaven. Indeed, it was said that a papal indulgence "could absolve a man even if he had done the impossible and had violated the mother of God" (*LW* 31: 32). As a priest responsible before God for his parishioners, Luther had to warn them against spiritual pitfalls.

This is the immediate context for the ***Ninety-Five Theses*** of 31 October 1517, the traditional date of the beginning of the Reformation. But that was not Luther's first criticism of current indulgence practice. As early as 1514 Luther had denounced the abuse of indulgences and in sermons in 1516 had criticized his own prince's relic collection. Frederick was not amused. Luther was not only questioning his prince's devout piety but also undermining a source of revenue for his own university: indulgences, "the bingo of the sixteenth century" (Bainton 1957: 54), were a source of revenue for construction projects ranging from bridges to cathedrals.

The ***Ninety-Five Theses*** were a typical academic proposition for a university debate. They were written in Latin, and most Wittenbergers could not even read German. Thus the popular image of Luther the angry young man pounding incendiary theses to the church door is far more romantic fiction than reality. In fact there has been intensive historical discussion about whether they were posted or posted, i.e. nailed or mailed (Iserloh 1968; Aland 1965). How, then, did this document for debate cause such an uproar? Luther sent it to Tetzel's superior, Albrecht, the archbishop of Mainz, with the naïve thought that Albrecht did not know that his hireling was abusing the authority of the church. The document was then sent on to Rome. The result was an explosion that startled and frightened Luther as much as anyone else. Luther had unknowingly touched some very sensitive nerves concerning papal authority and far-reaching political and ecclesiastical intrigue.

The Squeaky Mouse

Although Pope Leo X reputedly first dismissed Luther as another drunken monk, envious of the Dominicans, the case was given to the papal theologian Sylvester Mazzolini, known as Prierias after his birthplace, Prierio. Prierias, a Dominican, was the first literary opponent of Luther (Lindberg 1972; Bagchi 1991: 17-44; Hendrix 1981: 46-52). He had already played a role in the infamous trial of Reuchlin, the famous humanist Hebraist charged with heresy by another Dominican, Pfefferkorn. That long trial was the occasion for the humanist satire against the clergy, *Letters of Obscure Men*. The Dominicans, still smarting from the Reuchlin affair, saw the indulgence controversy and the attack on the Dominican Tetzel in the context of university reform, Dominican-Augustinian rivalry, and their own role as champions of the papacy. The curricular reform at the University of Wittenberg had displaced Thomistic and scholastic studies by Augustine and biblical studies. The Dominicans understood themselves to be the appointed guardians of Catholic doctrine and, since the mid-fifteenth century, the champions of papal primacy and authority. Under Leo X the curia included a number of Dominicans. Thus Luther's attack on indulgences appeared as an attack on Thomistic-scholastic theology, papal authority, and Dominican (curial) jurisdiction over heretics. Luther, on the other hand, understood his questioning of indulgences as an academic dispute to which he was entitled under his doctoral oath (*LW* 34: 103). From this understanding of his position as a servant of the church in the office of doctor, Luther insisted on proof of his error by a convincing refutation of his teaching. This was both shocking and infuriating to the Dominicans.

Prierias quickly formulated a response to Luther: *Dialogue Against the Arrogant Theses of Martin Luther Concerning the Power of the Pope*. This "dialogue" accused Luther of heresy by framing the indulgence controversy in terms of papal authority. To be sure, Luther's theses raised a number of questions concerning the pope (Why doesn't he empty purgatory for love rather than money? Why doesn't he build St Peter's with his own money?) and pointed out that the true treasure of the church is the gospel, but Prierias's perspective was basically formed by an anticonciliarist papalism. His four fundamentals of the papacy, already essentially formed before the ***Ninety-Five Theses***, ended dialogue before it could begin. These fundamentals stated that "virtually it is the pope who is head of the church, though in another manner than Christ;" that "the pope cannot err when he in his capacity as pope comes to a decision;" that "he who does not hold to the teaching of the Roman Church and the pope as an infallible rule of faith, from which even Holy Scripture draws its power and authority, is a heretic;" and that "the Roman Church can establish something with regard to faith and ethics not only through word but also through deed. . . . In this same sense custom acquires the power of law, . . . And it follows [that he is] a heretic who wrongly interprets the teaching and actions of the church in so far as they relate to faith and ethics." In case Luther does not get the point, Prierias concludes: "He who says in regard to indulgences that the Roman Church cannot do what she has actually done is a heretic."

Luther's initial reaction to the *Dialogue* was shock and fear. "Then I thought, 'Good God, has it come to this that the matter will go before the pope?' However, our Lord God was gracious to me, and the stupid dolt wrote such wretched stuff that I had to laugh. Since then I've never been frightened" (*LW* 54: 83). Although Luther later said that Prierias as the first to come forth against him "squeaked like a mouse and then perished," this "squeak" was such that, echoing in the successive attacks by Cajetan and Eck, it shaped the future discussion.

It is, I think, no accident that during these days (1518-21) Luther's existential epistemology is so clearly expressed in the words from his second series of lectures on the Psalms: "It is through living, indeed through dying and being damned that one becomes a theologian, not through understanding, reading, or speculation" (*WA* 5: 163, 28-9).

Luther was now forced to recognize that a particular "abuse," indulgences, could not be reformed without addressing the larger context of the church's self-understanding and theology. In this sense, the original issue of the Reformation appears to be papal authority, not justification (Bagchi 1991; Lindberg 1972; Headley 1987). The ensuing conflict clarified and sharpened Luther's thought, driving him to study church history and preparing him for future confrontations with Cajetan and Eck. This conflict is also the context for Luther's 1520 appeal to the German nobility for a council and for his suspicion that the papacy was the Antichrist.

Politics and Piety

Prierias's *Dialogue* formed the basis for the citation summoning Luther to appear in Rome within 60 days of its receipt. Both documents reached Wittenberg on 7 August 1518. But before the grace period had expired Rome decided that Luther was a heretic and should be delivered to the authorities. That Luther did not suffer the fate of Hus owes much to the peculiar mix of local and imperial politics with piety. This larger context had two main foci: political jockeying for the impending imperial election in 1519; and Pope Leo

X's desire to impress his secular rivals by completing the building of St Peter's, begun by Julius II. Luther escaped the normal fate of a heretic through the loopholes left by the interweaving of these concerns.

Religion and politics had been inextricably intertwined since the emperor Constantine had called the council of Nicea in 325. By the Middle Ages the papacy exercised direct temporal power and the imperial ideal included the mandate to protect the church and the true faith. Although there were open as well as latent tensions between the papacy and the German emperors in the late Middle Ages, Habsburgs such as Maximilian and Charles V took their religious duty seriously. Indeed, Charles V's reign was marked by his striving to achieve hegemony in Europe on the one hand and to combat heresy on the other. Charles's profound attachment to the Catholic church supported his perceived duty to preserve it against the Reformation. But this gets ahead of our story.

Since 1257 certain princes had claimed the right of electing the emperor. This group consisted of the duke of Saxony, margrave of Brandenburg, king of Bohemia, count palatinate of the Rhine, and the archbishops of Cologne, Trier, and Mainz. This tradition was codified in the Golden Bull of 1356, the so-called Magna Carta of German particularism, which provided an orderly procedure for an imperial regime on a federative basis, exempted the seven electors from imperial jurisdiction, and excluded papal participation in the election. The Habsburgs had been emperors since 1438 but that did not mean their election would be automatic. The dynastic rivalry of the time was between the Habsburgs and the Hohenzollerns. Since 1517 the Emperor Maximilian had tried to line up the electors in favor of his grandson, Charles of Spain. On the eve of both the Reformation and the election of a new emperor, the elector of Brandenburg, Joachim, was a Hohenzollern. In 1513 three important church positions were vacant: the archbishoprics of Magdeburg, Halberstadt, and Mainz. The last of these, see of the primate of Germany, carried a vote in the electoral college. Elector Joachim saw this situation as an opportunity to strengthen the Hohenzollern house and to influence the imperial election by having two of the seven votes in his pocket. Joachim therefore determined to acquire these positions for his younger brother Albrecht.

The difficulty with Joachim's plan was that Albrecht, under canonical age for an archbishop, was not even a priest, and it was illegal to hold more than one church office. It was, of course, possible to get papal dispensations for these impediments; but dispensations for matters of this importance were very expensive. But, as Reynard the Fox said, money talks. Albrecht negotiated a price with Rome for the archbishopric of 29,000 Rhenish gold gulden. This was clearly more than the credit of both Joachim and Albrecht. Leo, however, was a reasonable man and willing to work out a financial arrangement. The curia proposed that Albrecht take a loan from the Fugger banking house. Leo demanded a down payment of about 25 percent in cash, and granted Albrecht the right to sell indulgences to raise the rest of the money. As the money came in, half of it was to go to the papacy to finance the building of St Peter's, and the rest to repay the enormous Fugger loan and its interest. It is not surprising that Albrecht would hire the best indulgence salesman he could find in order to pay off his debt as quickly as possible.

The imperial election which took place in Frankfurt am Main on 28 June 1519 was one of the most hotly contested and significant political events of sixteenth-century Germany. The traditional three-cornered power struggle between the Empire, France, and the papacy was sharpened as both France and the papacy realized the immense world holdings that would be brought together under the Habsburgs if Charles were elected. Charles was already duke of Burgundy, king of Spain and Naples-Sicily, and, with his brother Ferdinand, heir to the lands of Austria. The search for alternative candidates and funds for propaganda and bribery began before the death of Maximilian. Even Henry VIII of England was briefly considered, although it was clear that Francis I of France had a more credible position. One candidate significant for Luther's personal well-being and for the course of the Reformation was his prince, Frederick the Wise, elector of Saxony. Papal efforts to persuade Frederick to be a candidate in order to counter Habsburg power rendered the papacy rendered the papacy hesitant to proceed with full force against Luther, Frederick's prize professor; and the Habsburg effort to garner Frederick's support to the extent of a marriage alliance between Charles's sister, Catherine, and Frederick's nephew, John Frederick, meant the imperial desire to root out heresy also had to be tempered.

Charles was elected, but the machinations engaged in to achieve this result left political and financial impediments in their wake. Politically, Charles accepted the so-called "capitulation of election" as a precondition of his election. Its intent was to confirm existing constitutional order and maintain the laws and customs of the Empire. Important imperial decisions were not to be made without consultation with the German estates, German and Latin were to be the official languages, foreigners were to be excluded from German imperial offices, foreign troops were not permitted in Germany, and imperial resources were not to be used for dynastic interests. Financially, the Habsburg investment in this election approached a million gulden. The Fugger banking house supplied so much of this capital that later Jacob Fugger could brazenly request repayment with the reminder that "It is known and thus need not be emphasized that your Majesty could not have obtained the Roman crown without my help" (Hillerbrand 1964: 87). Charles V became emperor, but not with a totally free hand. His empire was geographically at least close to the medieval aspiration for a *corpus Christianum,* but he himself was forced to recognize German "liberties;" emperor and empire were no longer a unity but an opposition. His chancellor, Gattinara, argued for an imperial ideology to stabilize the empire. But imperial hegemony was a perpetual problem, now intensified by the rise of nations and the opposing powers of France and the papacy. Charles faced numerous problems with his huge empire. He had inherited everything but conquered nothing. He had to deal everywhere with the complex structures and institutions of the late phase of medieval feudalism with all their complicated privileges, precedents, and exemptions. The person of the monarch held it all together, but in a pre-jet age it took him months to get around. In all this Germany played a secondary role. Charles himself knew little German and resided mainly outside the Empire. The politics of the time were in Luther's favor as he was impelled toward confrontation with pope and emperor at the diet of Worms.

From the Diet of Worms to the Land of the Birds

Events accelerated rapidly after the publication of the ***Ninety-Five Theses*** Luther received significant support from his prince, Frederick the Wise, the founder and proud patron of the University of Wittenberg. Frederick had earlier prohibited indulgence selling in his lands not only because of his own relic collection but as a measure against his rivals, the Hohenzollerns of Brandenburg, especially the archbishop Albrecht. Also, Frederick's university was in the process of a significant curriculum reform, led by Luther and his colleagues, that displaced scholasticism with biblical and patristic studies. Frederick knew that the Dominicans opposed this new theological orientation in Wittenberg and moved to protect his talented professor of Scripture against opponents in the arenas of both politics (archbishop Albrecht) and education (the Dominicans), whom he suspected of fomenting heresy charges in order to discredit Wittenberg and its university. If Frederick had doubts concerning Luther they seem to have been dispelled by Erasmus's clever reply to Frederick's question of what he thought of the Luther affair: "He has committed great sin—he has hit the monks in their belly, and the Pope in his crown!"

As a professor, Luther had the status of a state official of Electoral Saxony. On this basis, Frederick "allowed" Luther to attend his order's chapter meeting in Heidelberg. There, rather than being silenced by his superior, he was encouraged to set forth his theology. The famous Heidelberg disputation took the younger theologians by storm, some of whom, such as Martin Bucer (1491-1551), went on to become major Reformers in their own right. In the meantime, Prierias's report on Luther served as the basis for a formal indictment before an ecclesiastical judge, and Luther was cited to appear in Rome within 60 days to answer the charge of heresy against him.

When Luther received the citation to Rome, he wrote to Frederick, who was at the imperial diet at Augsburg, requesting the prince to intervene on his behalf with the pope. The request was for a hearing in Germany before an impartial judge or group of university theologians. This was not a unique request in this period, when rulers often expressed concern that their subjects in matters of ecclesiastical dispute were too often taken to Rome. Also, coupled with the German national pride in this matter was the ostensible claim that the issue was an academic matter that affected the good name of the University of Wittenberg.

Frederick could count on a sympathetic hearing from Leo X because Leo was at this time urging the members of the diet to mount—at great cost to themselves—a crusade against the Turk. The papal legate, Cardinal Cajetan (a Dominican) had been sent to address the diet, arguing that not only the future of religion but that of humanity itself was threatened if Croatia and Hungary fell to Turkish advances. The German estates were dubious about this enterprise, which would entail a tax of up to 20 percent, and they gave an evasive answer to the pope.

In this context Frederick arranged Luther's meeting in Augsburg with Cajetan. Meanwhile Cajetan received a papal letter instructing the summary trial and imprisonment of Luther unless Luther recanted and requested forgiveness. Another papal letter, sent to Frederick at the same time, voiced a much more subtle request for assistance because the pope did not want to offend such a powerful prince at the very moment he needed his support. The prince, the pope wrote, should think of his good family name, although of course the pope did not believe all the ugly rumors that Frederick was supporting a heretic.

Frederick insisted upon Luther's safety if he were to meet with Cajetan. Furthermore, there was to be full examination and proof of charges; Luther would be given the opportunity to defend himself; and no definitive judgment was to issue from this meeting.

The first interview with Cajetan quickly relieved Luther of any illusion of dialogue. The cardinal told Luther to do three things: repent and revoke his errors; promise not to teach them again; and refrain from future disruptive activity. Three further interviews did nothing but escalate tempers and fray nerves, for Luther insisted on a theological discussion of the issues. Cajetan cut short the last interview, telling Luther not to come back unless he were ready to recant. Days passed in silence and rumors spread that Luther was to be seized and sent to Rome in chains. Luther's friends panicked and hustled him out of town. He later learned he had escaped just in the nick of time.

The furious Cajetan complained to the elector of Luther's insolence. Frederick passed this complaint on to Luther, who responded that Cajetan had broken his promise of discussion and ended by saying he would be willing to leave Electoral Saxony. He then made preparations to leave. At the farewell dinner Luther was giving on 1 December, two letters dramatically arrived. The first expressed Frederick's surprise that Luther was still around; the second said Luther must remain. The latter was probably prompted by the arrival of the papal emissary, Miltitz, on a mission concerning the imminent imperial election. On 18 December, Frederick made up his mind that Luther would not go to Rome or into exile unless he was first duly heard and properly convicted. On 12 January 1519 Emperor Maximilian died, and papal and imperial politics superseded the supposed peril of heresy.

Enter Dr Johann Eck of Ingolstadt. Eck had struck up a friendship with Luther in 1517, so Luther was hurt and angered when Eck now attacked Luther's theses. Eck did not attack Luther directly, instead challenging Luther's faculty colleague, Andreas Bodenstein von Karlstadt (ca. 1480-1541), to a public disputation; but it was clear that he was after Luther. The disputation negotiations dragged on for months, and in the process led to a small pamphlet war. Karlstadt got his artist friend, Lucas Cranach, to draw a cartoon showing two wagons, one bearing the cross on the way to heaven, and the other loaded with scholastic writings on the way to hell. The Leipzig theologians and clerics were furious, and even went to the extent of questioning people in the confessional whether they had laughed at the "wagon cartoon."

Luther now suggested that at the time of Gregory I (d. 604), the Roman church was not above all other churches. Eck chose this for the focal point of his attack (recall that the Catholic controversialists saw the issue to be that of papal authority). In response to Prierias and now Eck, Luther turned to an intensive study of church history and canon law. In his thirteenth thesis against Eck, Luther wrote: "That the Roman Church is superior to all churches is indeed proved by the far # fetched decrees put out by the Roman pontiffs in the last 400 years. But this ecclesiastical dogma is contrary to the approved histories of 1100 years, the plain teaching of Scripture, and the decrees of the Council of Nicea, the most sacred of all councils." Luther frequently scared his friends as much as his enemies, and Karlstadt and Spalatin expressed their concern that he had gone too far. Luther responded that their caution almost made him sick to his stomach.

The Leipzig debate began in early July 1519. The Wittenbergers arrived in wagons flanked by numerous armed students on 24 June. The first wagon contained Karlstadt and all his precious books. The second wagon included Luther, Melanchthon, and the rector of the University of Wittenberg. As the procession reached the city gate of Leipzig, Karlstadt's wagon crashed, flinging Karlstadt into the muck. The Leipzigers were delighted. This was undoubtedly a good omen, for Eck to have the perpetrator of the infamous "wagon cartoon" hurled from his wagon. Karlstadt lost more than his pride in this incident; badly shaken, he was given medical treatment and bled twice. Altogether, the debate was a bad scene for Karlstadt. He had had a tiring trip from Wittenberg, a public humiliation, and two bleedings as prelude to facing a vicious and clever debater already licking his lips in anticipation of an upcoming roasting—literal as well as intellectual—of Karlstadt and Luther. Furthermore, Karlstadt was not good at thinking and speaking on his feet; he needed his reference works, which was why he brought all his books with him.

Duke George placed his castle at the disposal of Leipzig University for the debate. But the duke himself was not about to let a little theological fracas intrude on his vision of reality. He grumbled that they should finish soon because he had a hunting party coming; and he said to Luther: "God's law or man's law, what does it matter? The pope is the pope!" Luther's immediate problem, however, was obtaining permission to join the debate since he was not originally invited; permission was granted only after much ranting and cajoling.

The debate itself had a long wind-up, beginning at 7 a.m. with a mass written for the occasion, followed by a lengthy and tedious harangue in Latin on the procedure of the debate, then more music, and finally lunch. The debate itself began after lunch. Eck and Karlstadt spent the first week on grace and free will. Eck played to the audience and won their approval, while Karlstadt searched for references in his many texts. But since the debate would be judged by faculties from other universities on the basis of the written record, Eck finally persuaded the referee to prohibit Karlstadt from entering data into the transcript from his books.

It soon became apparent to the laity that disputations were not the most fun to watch. Indeed, even the theologians were falling asleep as they sat through the hot afternoons following big lunches. On the other hand, it has been suggested that it was safer to feign sleep because if you were later asked about volatile issues you could always plead ignorance due to a nap. The livelier debates were carried on by students in the taverns.

On 4 July Luther came into the debate. Eck prodded him with charges of being a "Hussite" and a "Bohemian." This was tantamount to being labeled a communist in the 1950s, because this area still recalled the numbers of Germans expelled from Bohemia during the Hussite revolt. Luther protested Eck's charges but finally went to the library and looked up Hus's teachings. When he returned, he stated that many of the condemned Hussite articles were truly Christian and evangelical, and ought not to be condemned by the church. After a moment of shocked silence, there was uproar. Eck pressed on and got Luther to state that both the papacy and councils may err. This was an immediate triumph for Eck. After this, Karlstadt returned to take up the debate again, but Duke George was anxious to bring the whole thing to a close.

Eck spent the following weeks gloating about his success and fantasizing about receiving a cardinal's hat. Luther was now fully face to face with the implications of his ***Ninety-Five Theses***. His opponents had put questions to him that led him farther than he at first thought he would go. Ironically, the debate had not pursued Luther's more radical attack on scholastic authorities. That was now taken up by scholastic theologians who began writing that "having arrogantly abandoned holy teachers and basic philosophy and having decided to interpret Scripture according to their own minority methods, Luther and Carlstadt had not only thrown away any chance they might have had of making their views appear reasonable but had also cut themselves off from the historic faith of the church." The Italian controversialists such as Prierias "identified the source of all Luther's errors as his rejection of Aristotle and thus of Aquinas" (Bagchi 1991: 73, 76). The faculties of Paris and Erfurt had been chosen as judges of the debate, but they stalled on giving their opinion.

The Leipzig debate was of great significance to Luther's development because here he publicly stated his evangelical conception of the church in unmistakable terms, and revealed that in the last analysis his sole authority in matters of faith was Scripture. He stated without reservation that not only the papacy but also church councils could err. This made reconciliation with the Roman church virtually impossible, and led to his excommunication.

After the Leipzig debate, Eck went to Rome to help prepare the condemnation of Luther, the papal bull *Exsurge Domine* (15 June 1520). Eck was further honored with the responsibility of disseminating the bull in Germany. He and the papal nuncio, Aleander, however, soon discovered that while they might be heroes in Rome, they were intensely disliked in Germany as respectively a traitor and a foreigner. The bull, "Arise, O Lord, judge thine own cause," listed and condemned 41 errors in Luther's writings. Luther was enjoined to return to mother church within 60 days of its posting. If Luther failed to recant, then his very memory was to be wiped out. But this was easier said than done, for by now much of Germany was rallying to Luther's side. Not only were many humanists supporting his cause, so were nobles, such as Sylvester von Schaumburg, who offered Luther the protection of 100 Franconian nobles; and Franz von Sickengen and Ulrich Hutten, who later led the Knights' Revolt, hailed Luther as the potential liberator of Germany. When the bull was posted in Germany, it was frequently defaced. When inquisitors went about with orders to burn Luther's writings they often encountered students who gleefully substituted the writings of scholastics for those of Luther. Eck himself added more fuel to the fire by adding names of his personal enemies to the list of those condemned by the bull.

On the 60th day of grace granted Luther, 10 December 1520, Melanchthon led the Wittenberg faculty and students out to the banks of the nearby Elbe river for their own book-burning ritual. There, along with classic scholastic and legal texts, and some of Eck's writings, Luther consigned to the flames both the papal bull, *Exsurge Domine,* and a copy of the *Copus iuris canonica,* the legal foundation for the medieval *corpus Christianum.* This was clearly a revolutionary act, comparable to burning the United States Constitution. Luther was quite aware of the significance of what he had done, and spoke of it in class (*LW* 31: 381-95). After singing the Te Deum and the De Profundis, the faculty returned to the university. The students, however, continued demonstrating against the pope until after two days the town authorities put a stop to it. On 3 January 1521, the final bull of excommunication, *Decet Romanum Pontificem,* appeared.

## The Diet of Worms

Aleander urged the new emperor, Charles V, to issue a mandate against Luther in Germany. But Charles had agreed in his coronation oath that no Germans should be condemned unless his case was heard in Germany by an impartial panel of judges. In this context, Charles V had three basic options. He could yield to Rome and condemn Luther by imperial mandate, since he was already under the papal ban; try private negotiations to attempt to persuade Luther to bow to Rome; or permit Luther to appear before the imminent diet of Worms for an investigation. Charles chose the last course, partially because of the arguments of Frederick the Wise, and partially for political leverage against Rome, promising that Luther would not be condemned unheard, and would be given a safe conduct to Worms.

Luther's popularity is indicated by the fact that when the papal nuncio Aleander arrived in Worms he could not find a comfortable room, even though he had plenty of money; when he walked in the streets people threatened him, and when he looked in bookshops he found them full of Luther's writings. Aleander wrote to the pope: "Nine-tenths of the people are shouting 'Luther,' and the other tenth shouts, 'Down with the Pope!'" When Aleander heard of Luther's rebellious burning of the bull and the canon law, he persuaded Charles to revoke the permission to come to Worms. However, other voices counter-persuaded Charles to compromise and maintain the safe conduct, although limiting Luther's hearing to the question of whether or not he would recant.

Luther's journey to Worms became a spectacle of cheering mobs in town after town. His preaching services were so jammed that in one place the church balcony threatened to collapse. Although Luther's friends warned him of the fate of Hus, who also had had a safe conduct, Luther vowed he would go to Worms even if all the tiles of the roofs became devils. Such bravado escaped him when he was ushered into the hall to face the leadership of the world. Asked whether he would recant the pile of his writings placed before him, he begged leave to consider his response for an extra day. Luther was brought back the next day. There, before the emperor, princes, and lords—a whole world away from his monastic cell and dingy classroom—Luther did not receive the hearing he had hoped for. Rather, he was presented with a pile of his writings and asked to recant their errors. Luther's brief answer included the memorable lines: "Unless I am convinced by the testimony of the Scriptures or by clear reason . . . I am bound by the Scriptures I have quoted and my conscience is captive to the Word of God. I cannot and I will not retract anything, since it is neither safe nor right to go against conscience. I cannot do otherwise, here I stand, may God help me. Amen" (*LW* 32: 112-13).

The German princes were in general impressed by this skinny monk standing up to the powers of the world; such courage they could understand, even if the theological issues might escape them. A lasting impression was made on the young duke of Schleswig-Holstein who when he became King Christian III of Denmark immediately decreed that his subjects (including Norway and Iceland) should become Lutherans. The Spanish soldiers, however, shouted: "Into the fire!" And the emperor declared: "He will not make a heretic out of me!"

After Luther's political supporters left the diet, a rump diet voted to place Luther under the imperial ban. The edict of Worms outlawed Luther and all who gave him support. All subjects were forbidden to assist or even communicate with Luther on pain of arrest and confiscation of their property. All his writings were condemned as heretical and ordered burned. Now outlawed by the state as well as excommunicated by the church, Luther was compelled by his conscience and faith to defy both church and state. Deprived of help by the great medieval authorities, Luther now relied upon his prince and also appealed directly to the people. The latter move had already been noted by the Catholic controversialists as a rebellious stance that could only lead to insurrection. In short, Luther was now the leader of a religious movement that in effect had become a revolution.

*Bibliography*

Aland 1965: Kurt Aland, *Martin Luther's 95 Theses*. St Louis: Concordia.

Bagchi 1991: David V. N. Bagchi, *Luther's Earliest Opponents: Catholic Controversialists 1518-1525*. Minneapolis: Fortress Press.

Bainton 1957: Roland Bainton, *Here I Stand: A Life of Martin Luther*. New York: Mentor.

Brecht 1985: Martin Brecht, *Martin Luther*, I: *His Road to Reformation 1483-1521*. Minneapolis: Fortress.

Ebeling 1970: Gerhard Ebeling, *Luther: An Introduction to his Thought*. Philadelphia: Fortress.

Grane 1994: Leif Grane, *Martinus Noster: Luther in the German Reform Movement 1518-1521*. Mainz: Zabern.

Gritsch and Jenson 1976: Eric W. Gritsch and Robert W. Jenson, *Lutheranism: The Theological Movement and Its Confessional Writings*. Philadelphia: Fortress.

Hagen 1974: Kenneth Hagen, *A Theology of Testament in the Young Luther: The Lectures on Hebrews*. Leiden: E. J. Brill.

Headley 1987: John M. Headley, "The Reformation as Crisis in the Understanding of Tradition," *ARG* 78, 5-23.

Hendrix 1981: Scott Hendrix, *Luther and the Papacy: Stages in a Reformation Conflict*. Philadelphia: Fortress.

Hillerbrand 1964: Hans J. Hillerbrand, ed., *The Reformation: A Narrative History Related by Contemporary Observers and Participants*. New York: Harper & Row.

Iserloh 1968: Erwin Iserloh, *The Theses Were Not Posted: Luther Between Reform and Reformation*, tr. Jared Wicks, SJ. Boston: Beacon.

Janz 1982: Denis Janz, *Three Reformation Catechisms: Catholic, Anabaptist, Lutheran*. New York/Toronto: Edwin Mellon.

Lindberg 1972: Carter Lindberg, "Prierias and his Significance for Luther's Development," *SCJ* 3, 45-64.

Moeller 1971: Bernd Moeller, "Piety in Germany around 1500," in Ozment 1971, 50-75.

Moeller 1982: Bernd Moeller, *Imperial Cities and the Reformation: Three Essays,* ed. and trans. H. C. Erik Midelfort and Mark U. Edwards, Jr. Durham: Labyrinth. (First publ. 1972.)

Oberman 1989b: Heiko A. Oberman, *Luther: Man between God and the Devil.* New Haven: Yale University Press.

Ogment 1971: Steven Ogment, ed., *The Reformation in Medieval Perspective.* Chicago: Quadrangle.

Ozment 1983: Steven Ozment, *When Fathers Ruled: Family Life in Reformation Europe.* Cambridge, MA: Harvard University Press.

Ozment 1992: Steven Ozment, *Protestants: The Birth of a Revolution.* New York: Doubleday.

Tentler 1977: Thomas N. Tentler, *Sin and Confession on the Eve of the Reformation.* Princeton: Princeton University Press.

## FURTHER READING

### Bibliography

Grimm, Harold J. *The Reformation Era: 1500-1600.* New York: Macmillan, 1966, 703 p.

Contains an extensive bibliographic essay and survey of the literature on Luther and Reformation scholarship.

### Biography

Bainton, Ronald H. *Here I Stand: A Life of Martin Luther.* New York: Abingdon-Cokesbury Press, 1950, 422 p.

Important biography spanning Luther's entire life, by a leading Luther scholar.

Brecht, Martin. *Martin Luther: His Road to Reformation 1483-1521*, translated by James L. Schaaf. Philadelphia: Fortress Press, 1985, 557 p.

Biography of young Luther utilizing recent scholarship in specialized fields of historical research.

Brendler, Gerhard. *Martin Luther: Theology and Revolution*, translated by Claude R. Foster, Jr. New York: Oxford University Press, 1991, 383 p.

Biography of Luther that emphasizes his historical context—"the first revolution in German history"—and posits that "he thought like a theologian and acted as an intellectual in a princely dukedom."

Lohse, Bernard. *Martin Luther: An Introduction to His Life and Work,* translated by Robert C. Schultz. Philadelphia: Fortress Press, 1986, 288 p.

Comprehensive introduction to Luther's life and writings that also includes a survey of the interpretation of Luther.

### Criticism

Atkinson, James. *The Great Light: Luther and Reformation.* Great Britain: Paternoster Press, 1968, 287 p.

Discussses the evangelical dimension of Luther's work, focusing on concurrent theological reform initiatives in Britain and Switzerland, and on the theology of John Calvin.

———. *The Trial of Luther.* New York: Stein and Day, 1971, 212 p.

Detailed account of Luther's excommunication by Pope Leo X and his appearance before Charles V at the Diet of Worms.

Bagchi, David V. N. *Luther's Earliest Opponents: Catholic Controversialists, 1518-1525.* Minneapolis: Fortress Press, 1991, 305 p.

Detailed examination of the Catholic response to Luther's ideas, focusing on the view of Luther as a challenger of church authority.

Davies, Rupert E. *The Problem of Authority in the Continental Reformers: A Study in Luther, Zwingli, and Calvin.* Westport: Greenwood Press, 1978, 158 p.

Argues that the question of religious authority is at the heart of the Reformation and that Luther's radical encounter with God made him a rebel rather than a reformer; also discusses why Zwingli and Calvin became rebels.

Edwards, Jr., Mark U. "The Mature Paradigm." In *Luther and the False Brethren*, pp. 112-26. Stanford: Stanford University press, 1975.

Discusses how Luther compared himself to St. Paul as an apostle engaged in a historical struggle between the "true" and "false" church.

Edwards, Mark. and Tavard, George. *Luther: A Reformer for the Churches.* Philadelphia: Fortress Press, 1983, 96 p.

Very brief introduction to Luther and his ideas.

Gerrish, B. A. *The Old Protestantism and the New: Essays on the Reformation Heritage.* Chicago: University of Chicago Press, 1982, 422 p.

Collection of essays that explores myriad facets of Reformation history with an emphasis on the differences between Luther and Calvin.

Grane, Leif. *Martinus Noster: Luther in the German Reform Movement 1518-1521.* Mainz: Verlag Philipp von Zabern, 1994, 326 p.

Examines Luther's role in the reform movement and his relationship to humanist theologians challenging the scholastic tradition and the authority of the Church.

Johnson, Roger A., ed. *Psychohistory and Religion: The Case of Young Man Luther*. Philadelphia: Fortress Press, 1977, 198.

Collection of essays by various authors evaluating the methodology and scholarship of psychohistorical approaches to Luther and his theology, focusing on Erik Erikson's seminal biography, *Young Man Luther*.

McSorley, Harry J., C.S.P. *Luther: Right Or Wrong? An Ecumenical-Theological Study of Luther's Major Work, "The Bondage of the Will."* New York: Newman Press, 1969, 398 p.

Study of Luther's conceptions of free will and justification by faith with an examination of the relevant theology of St. Paul, St. Augustine, Erasmus, and others.

Steinmetz, David C. *Luther in Context*. Bloomington: Indiana University Press, 1986, 146 p.

Collection of essays that contextualizes the contribution of Luther's ideas within sixteenth-century knowledge of theology and awareness of other religious figures in western history.

**Additional coverage of Luther's life and career is contained in the following source published by Gale Research: *Literature Criticism from 1400 to 1800*, Vol. 9.**

# Huldrych Zwingli

## 1484-1531

Swiss religious reformer, theologian, and essayist.

### INTRODUCTION

A contemporary of Martin Luther and a forerunner of John Calvin, Zwingli was a founder of the Reformed Churches and an important figure in the Protestant Reformation in sixteenth-century Europe. Concerned with political and social life as well as theology, Zwingli broke with the Roman Catholic hierarchy and medieval theology and encouraged theocratic social organization. More radical theologically than Luther and more political than Calvin, Zwingli had a profound influence on the debates that framed the development of Protestantism. Despite some pacifist tendencies, he believed in fighting to establish and defend his vision of a Christian society.

### Biographical Information

Zwingli was born in Wildhaus, in the Toggenburg valley, in the rural district of St. Gallen, Switzerland. His family were farmers and magistrates, essentially well-to-do peasants. A good student, Zwingli was educated first in his village, then by his uncle, a pastor in Wesen, until he was ten. Thereafter he was sent to school in Basel and Bern. At fourteen he entered the University of Vienna, where he took a baccalaureate degree in 1504. He returned to Basel, taught classics at a local school, and took his master's degree in 1506. That same year he was ordained by the Bishop of Constance and assigned to the parish of Glarus. He continued studying on his own, learning Greek and reading Erasmus and other humanist thinkers. He remained largely at Glarus for ten years and gradually began his career as a reformer. His first published writings, *The Fable of the Ox* (1510) and *The Labyrinth* (1516), were political allegories critical of the Swiss practice of hiring out mercenaries in European wars, the results of which he had observed first hand, having served as military chaplain in Italy in 1513 and 1515. These views were politically unpopular in Glarus, and Zwingli was forced to leave town, though he did not formally lose his post as pastor. He went temporarily to Einsiedeln, where he stayed for three years and began to actively preach in what became the reform tradition, holding that the Bible was the supreme authority for God's will and criticizing such Roman Catholic practices as the selling of papal indulgences. In 1518 he competed for, and eventually won despite some political difficulty, the post of people's priest at Zurich, where he launched his reform movement in earnest. He took up his position in January, 1519, beginning a series of sermons on the New Testament, critical both of practices of the Catholic Church and the immoral behavior of the citizens. Later that year he fell ill with a plague that struck Zurich and nearly died. His poem *Gebetslied in de Pest* (1519; *Prayersong in the Plague*) described the experience, which generally made him more serious and urgent about his goal of reform. By 1522 his ideas had begun to take hold in Zurich and that spring a number of people chose not to observe the Lenten fast, some quite publicly. Zwingli wrote *Von Erkeisen und Freyheit der Speysen* (1522; *Regarding the Choice and Freedom of Food*) arguing that there was no Biblical injunction against eating meat during Lent. The controversy, and condemnation by the papal authorities, led to the historic First Disputation, a debate convened by the City Council of Zurich. There he presented his *Sixty-Seven Theses* (1523), which became the core of his theology. His arguments won over the council of Zurich and led to an unprecedented break with the bishopric of Constance. Among the ideas presented there was a rejection of the celibacy of priests and in 1524 he married Anna Reinhart, with whom he had been living for two years. The following year he published his major work, *De vera et falsa religione commentarius* (1525; *Commentary about the True and False Religion*), a thorough presentation of his theological ideas. Many of the ideas set forth here, especially those concerning the meaning of the Eucharist, put Zwingli at odds with Luther. The two debated the issues in a number of treatises and met in 1529 at the Marburg Colloquy to try to reach an agreement that could allow for a unified reform movement. Their efforts failed and the nascent Protestant movement broke into two camps. During these years Zwingli's preaching and writing had been having an effect in Zurich; in 1524 the council ordered all images and music removed from the churches, and in 1525 the mass was discontinued, replaced by a simpler ceremony in the vernacular language rather than Latin. But the growing success of Zwingli's ideas in Zurich, Bern, and Basel led to increasing conflicts with more conservative Swiss districts that maintained their papal affiliation. The tensions finally came to a head in 1531, when a civil war broke out between the Evangelical Swiss and the Five Cantons, rural districts which rejected the reform movement. Zwingli was killed carrying the banner in the battle of Kappel, in October 1531.

## Major Works

Zwingli developed his key theological ideas over the course of a decade, beginning with *Archeteles* (1522; *The Beginning and the End*), his first major treatise, which criticized many of the doctrines of the Roman Catholic Church, and ending with his *Christianae Fidei Expositio* (1531; *Exposition of Christian Faith*). In between, he published dozens of essays, sermons and letters expounding and defending his views. In the *Sixty-seven Theses*, Zwingli affirmed the primacy of scriptural authority and rejected papal indulgences, prayers to the saints or any other intermediary between individuals and God, transubstantiation and the mass, the use or display of images and music in churches and worship ceremonies, and the celibacy of priests. He elaborated on these tenets later that year in *Auslegung der Gründ der Schlussreden* (1523; *An Exposition of the Articles*). His most comprehensive theological tract was the *Commentary about the true and false Religion* (1525). Other essays addressed specific and controversial issues, such as: *Vom Touf, vom Wiedertouf, und vom Kindertouf* (1525; *Baptism, Rebaptism, and Infant Baptism*) and *Ein klare Unterrichtung vom Nachtmal Christi* (1526; *A Clear Briefing about the Lord's Supper*). Some of his last works addressed basic Christian beliefs: *De Providentia Dei* (1530; *On Divine Providence*), *Fidei Ratio* (1530; *Confession of Faith*), and the *Christianae Fidei Expositio* (1531; *Explanation of Christian Faith*). In all his writings Zwingli sought to free the church from the perceived idolatry of Roman Catholic practices and to build a theocratic community in which local civil leaders would have the right and the duty to regulate church teaching and social life. In this he was as much a political and social reformer as a religious one, and his thinking shows the influence of the humanist thinkers he read and studied. A contemporary of Luther, he insisted as early as 1519 that he had come to his ideas on his own, through reading and interpreting the Gospel, and rejected the notion that he was in any way a follower of Luther. In fact, the two men were in sharp disagreement about many points, most especially the meaning of the Eucharist. In general, Zwingli made a stronger break with Roman Catholic theology. Nowhere was this more clear than in his insistence that the Eucharist was a remembrance, not a repetition of Christ's sacrifice, and that the communion wafer was purely symbolic.

## Critical Reception

Perhaps because of his sudden and early death, Zwingli is often forgotten as a founder of the Reformation, along with its giants, Luther and Calvin. While his successor Heinrich Bullinger continued to advance his ideas, he also gradually made concessions. The most significant was at the Zurich Consensus of 1549, where Calvin's more moderate ideas about the Eucharist won. Calvinist doctrine was subsequently adopted by the Swiss Reform Church and spread to other parts of Europe and the British Isles. Among the ways Calvinism differs are a position closer to Luther's on the Eucharist, a rejection of theocracy, and a stricter view on predestination. As Calvinist doctrines grew and spread, Zwingli's name and writings were largely forgotten outside of his native Switzerland. Luther and his followers invoked his work to criticize the Calvinist strain of Protestantism; Catholic theologians went even further, condemning him as a heretic and banning his writings. In the twentieth century, scholars of religious history and theologians have returned to Zwingli's work and ideas. While there is some disagreement about whether there is a coherent and distinct body of thought which can be termed "Zwinglianism," there is no doubt that Zwingli was the founder and leader of the Zurich Reformation, a profound influence on Calvin, and a major voice in debates that shaped the course of Protestantism.

---

## PRINCIPAL WORKS

*The Fable of the Ox* (verse) 1510
*The Labyrinth* (verse) 1516
*Gebetslied in de Pest* [Prayersong in the Plague] (poem) 1519
*Archeteles* [*The Beginning and the End*] (essay) 1522
*Von Erkeisen und Fryheit der Speysen* [*Regarding Choice and the Freedom of Food*] (essay) 1522
*Auslegung der Gründ der Schlussreden* [*An Exposition of the Articles*] (essay) 1523
*Lehrbuchlein* [*On the Education of Youth*] (essay) 1523

*A Short Christian Introduction* (essay) 1523
**The Sixty-Seven Theses* (speech) 1523
*Von der göttlichen und menchlichen Gerechtigkeit* [*On Divine and Human Righteousness*] (sermon) 1523
*Der Hirt* [*The Shepherd*] (sermon) 1524
*Ein Antwort, Valentin Compar Gegeben* [*An Answer to Valentin Compar*] (essay) 1525
*De vera et falsa religione commentarius* [*Commentary about the True and False Religion*] (essay) 1525
*Vom Touf, vom Wiedertouf, und vom Kindertouf* [*Baptism, Rebaptism, and Infant Baptism*] (essay) 1525
*Ein klare Unterrichtung vom Nachtmal Christi* [*A Clear Briefing about the Lord's Supper*] (essay) 1526
*Plan for a Campaign* (essay) 1526
[*De Providentia Dei* [*On Divine Providence*] (essay) 1530
*Fidei Ratio* [*Confession of Faith*] (essay) 1530
*Christianae Fidei Expositio* [*Explanation of Christian Faith*] (essay) 1531
*Werke*. 4 vols. (essays, verse, sermons, and letters) 1545
*Huldreich Zwingli's Werke*. 8 vols. (essays, verse, sermons, and letters) 1828-42
*Huldreich Zwinglis Sämtliche Werke* (essays, verse, sermons, and letters) 1905-

*This work was expanded by Zwingli's followers after his death and was republished in 1536 as *The First Helvetic Confession*.

## CRITICISM

### Charles Beard (essay date 1883)

SOURCE: "The Reformation in Switzerland," in *The Reformation of the 16th Century: In Its Relation to Modern Thought and Knowledge,* 1883. Reprint by The University of Michigan Press, 1962, pp. 225-61.

[*In the following excerpt from his important study of the Reformation, Beard analyzes the Reformation in Switzerland, comparing the ideas of Zwingli with those of Calvin.*]

The history of Swiss Protestantism is peculiar in the fact that it follows a double line of development. It boasts two names of the first rank, Zwingli and Calvin: it had two centres, Zürich and Geneva. And it is obvious to remark that one of these is German, the other French; that standing in close relation to the Rhineland, this to France, Italy, Savoy. The movement in Switzerland divides itself into two parts, chronologically as well as geographically. Zwingli was born on the 1st of January, 1484, and was therefore less than two months younger than Luther. He was at work in his own way—a way which I shall try to describe presently—as early as Luther was. The scene of his activity was the northern and German-speaking Cantons of Switzerland, Glarus, Zürich, St. Gall, Schaffhausen, and afterwards Basel and Bern; while many of the free cities on the German side of the frontier, Strasburg, Constanz, Ulm, Augsburg, Reutlingen, adopted with more or less unanimity his opinions on the Eucharist. But when in 1531 he fell in the Battle of Cappel, in which Zürich was defeated by the five Forest Cantons, and his friend and helper Œcolampadius died a few weeks after, it seemed as if the cause of Swiss Protestantism would fall from the comparatively feeble hands of their successors. It was at this moment of crisis that a young refugee from northern France, John Calvin, stepped into the breach and held it victoriously. He was a full generation younger than Zwingli and Luther: born in 1509, the first edition of his "Institution" was published in 1536, five years after Zwingli's death: the period of his theocratic sway at Geneva extended from 1541 to his death in 1564. Henceforth the little free city on Lake Leman is the centre of Swiss, I had almost said of European Protestantism. Here were gradually developed that scheme of theological thought, that method of ecclesiastical organization, those principles of church discipline, which, in more or less modified form, were destined to so wide a prevalence. There is little direct intellectual relation to be traced between Calvin and Zwingli; indeed, the great systematizer was wont to speak in higher terms of the Saxon Reformer than of his own immediate forerunner. But not the less was his work a continuation of Zwingli's. The leading ideas of Calvinism are ideas which Zwingli had already put forward in a less precise and systematic form. There is a well-marked sense in which the Swiss theology as a whole can be compared and contrasted with the German. It would serve no good purpose were I to attempt in this place to define the shades of difference which in the middle years of the sixteenth century separated the Swiss churches from one another, and all from the Saxon Reformers. They led to many controversies; they are embodied in many confessions. But the final result was that the Calvinistic type of doctrine prevailed, especially in the foreign churches. The Confession of La Rochelle, the Decrees of the Synod of Dordt, the Westminster Confession, have nothing in them which can be called distinctively Zwinglian. But it is at least an allowable speculation that the milder, more rational, humaner spirit of the great Reformer of Zürich reappeared in the Arminian theology which in the seventeenth century was so powerful a factor of European thought.

The doctrine of Zwingli was Lutheranism with a difference. Like Luther, he substituted the authority of the Bible for the authority of the Church; like Luther, he preached justification by faith alone; like Luther, he maintained the true priesthood of every Christian man. Under the influence of the same forces, the Reformation, all over Europe, assumed the same forms: Lutheranism, Zwinglianism, Calvinism, even when the most is made of their differences, resemble each other much more than any of them the faith of the Church to which they were all opposed. And we should miss a significant fact if we failed to note that Zwingli was a religious phenomenon parallel with Luther, but not dependent on him. While the Reformer of Zürich speaks in admiring language of the Reformer of Wittenberg, he will not be called a Lutheran: he drew his doctrine, he said, from the Scriptures; he had preached it before ever he heard the name of Luther: why should he not rather be called by the name of Paul or of Christ? At the same time there were differences in the original constitutions of the men, as well as in the training which they had received, which influenced their apprehension and presentation of what was substantially the same group of truths. We can find in Zwingli no trace of the mysticism which Luther had learned from Tauler and the *Theologia Germanica*. There is nothing in his life-history at all answering to the spiritual crisis which drove Luther into the monastery at Erfurt, and there left him to his almost solitary struggle for deliverance and peace. He bears about with him no marks of conflict. He does not, as Luther did, retire into the darkness for a season, coming back trembling and chastened. There is an admirable and cheerful good sense about him, a keen apprehension of the simplicities of piety, a firm grasp of religion on the ethical and practical side. But the sense of mystery does not weigh upon him: the contemplation of divine things neither excites him to paradox nor awakens him to rapture.

The fact is that, much more than Luther, Zwingli was a humanist. First at school, at Basel and at Bern, next for two years at the University of Vienna, then for four years more again at Basel, he gave himself up to the studies of the day. It was at Basel, already a centre of busy literary activity, that he fell under the influence of Thomas Wyttenbach,[1] one of those grave scholars of the Rhineland who found the keenest admiration of ancient literature not inconsistent with an earnest Christian faith, and who directed his pupil to the study of the Scriptures apart from scholastic commentary. At a later period he learned for this purpose first Greek and then Hebrew, copying out with his own hand all the Epistles of Paul, that he might know them through and through. But he was not on this account untrue to his first classical preferences. He learned Valerius Maximus off by heart. Thucydides and Aristotle, Plutarch and Lucian, were familiar to him. He thought Plato had drunk at the fountain of Divine Wisdom; he extolled the piety of Pindar;[2] he gave the great heroes and poets of pagan antiquity a place in the Christian heaven. When Luther, in the first ardour of his Biblical zeal, was forswearing all philosophy, Zwingli was burying himself in the speculations of Pico della Mirandola. In relation to these and similar facts, the word Switzerland is apt to lead us astray. What we have really to do with are not the narrow valleys, the lofty pastures, the sparse population of the Forest Cantons, so much as the wide and fertile Rhineland, a great highway of nations, having on either side a broad belt of cities, free, wealthy, enlightened, the region of central Europe where civilization had reached its highest point, the chosen home of the German revival of letters. Here were the oldest Universities, the most celebrated schools: here had taught the mystics: here the mediæval sects had honeycombed society: here art went hand in hand with letters: here the citizens of many little republics had learned the secret of a life in loosest dependence on the Church. On the other hand, the learning and civilization of Saxony, and of North Germany in general, were of later origin, and had penetrated the popular life less deeply: society was constituted on more aristocratic principles: the prince went for more, the burgher for less. It would be difficult to think of Erasmus at Wittenberg, nor had Luther ever a firm hold on the Rhineland.

In this connection I must point out that the republican constitution of Switzerland gave direction and colour to all Zwingli's activity. He was born only seven years after the Confederates had vindicated their independence in leaving Charles the Bold dead under the walls of Nancy; and the patriotic glow which that marvellous event had kindled in men's hearts must have been fresh as he grew up to manhood. But this victory and those which preceded it taught the Swiss a fatal lesson, in making them acquainted with the strength of their right arms and the force of their disciplined onset: they were brave and they were poor: what more natural than that they should sell their swords? So a system grew up pregnant with national demoralization: now the Pope, now the King of France, recruited in the mountains an army of lanzknechts, whose courage decided many a battle: the spoils of war corrupted the simplicity of republican life: rival potentates bound their friends to their cause by pensions and gratuities: foreign and interested influences turned the currents of Confederate politics. Against this system Zwingli set his face at the very beginning of his career. He had been required as army chaplain to attend more than one expedition into Italy; he had been present at the Battle of Marignano, and as patriot and reformer he deplored the evils which he could not choose but see in their true colours. These things provided him with a policy which the forms of republican life enabled him to carry out. He aimed at concentrating the life of the Confederacy within its own frontiers, at detaching its several members from foreign alliances, at raising the chief citizens of its republics to a sense of national dignity, and its incompatibility with royal pensions and mercenary service. His friend and biographer Myconius describes his object as the restoration of ancient virtue. After the Battle of Pavia in 1525, in which the Swiss soldiers suffered severely, Zwingli, standing in the Minster pulpit of Zürich, drew from the misfortune a trenchant political moral.[3] He told his hearers that when, of old time, their life had been simple and pious, God had given them great victories, and that unless they returned to their former way, there was nothing before them but Divine wrath and utter ruin. All his life long he had a double purpose, the reformation of the Church and the reformation of the State, which were indeed in his view but one. You may say, if you will, that he took religion more on the social, Luther more on the personal side; that while the latter thought of individual salvation and the soul's union with God, the former had before him the ideal of a well-ordered state, a righteous and peaceful community. But this is the answer to the reproach sometimes directed against Zwingli that he was a politician, and as such degraded religion by bringing it down to the level of earthly intrigue and passion. It is not easy to see what else he could be. He was the first citizen of Zürich, as Calvin afterwards of Geneva; and in that capacity endeavoured to guide the policy of the Republic to the advantage of righteousness and the interests of the Protestant Church. Would he not have been justly open to the imputation of cowardice if, sheltering himself behind his clerical character, he had always worked by others' hands and others' voices, and so thrown on his colleagues the responsibility of measures which were really his own? It is impossible now to say that he did not sometimes succumb to the peculiar temptations of politics, and give himself to widely-reaching schemes of European alliance and attack: let the statesman bear the blame of the stateman's errors. Had Zürich conquered on that field of Cappel where Zwingli left his life, had the tide of Swiss Reformation in consequence risen over the whole land, her Reformer might have escaped heavy censure and much invidious comparison with Luther.

These facts stand in close relation, on the one hand, with the popular character of ecclesiastical government in the Reformed Churches; on the other, with the ethical type of Zwinglian religion. Calvin in Geneva worked under substantially the same political conditions as Zwingli in Zürich, and the result is that the organization of the churches which descend from him is neither Episcopal nor Consistorial, but Presbyterian. To take the instance with which we are most familiar, it is easy to trace a likeness between the Presbyteries, Synods and Assembly of the Church of Scotland, and the greater and lesser Councils of Zürich or Bern, deriving their power from the citizens at large. I do not mean that one set of institutions is the direct copy of the other, or that the Presbyterian organization of the Church does not sincerely claim for itself the authority of scriptural precedent and primitive example. But men are unconsciously swayed by the circumstances in which they have been brought up, and easily find in the Bible what they go there to look for. On the other hand, Zwingli's application of religion to the reform and guidance of the State, partly shows how ethical his conception of it was, partly made it more ethical still. One of the distinctions that may be drawn between Lutheran and Zwinglian religion is, that the former is more than anything else a justification of the sinner effected by faith; the latter, a law of God which asks obedience of all believers. And in accordance with this, we find in Zwingli's works many ethical definitions of religion in which an experienced ear will detect the absence of any Lutheran ring.

> "Piety," he says, "is a fact and an experience, not a doctrine or a science."[4] "The Christian life is innocence. . . . But no soil produces innocence more richly than contempt of oneself."[5] "All the writings of the apostles are full of this opinion, namely, that the Christian life is none other than a firm hope in God through Jesus Christ, and an innocent life after Christ's pattern."[6]

There is a little work of Zwingli's, covering only a few pages, ***"Quo pacto adolescentes formandi,"*** addressed to his step-son, Gerald Meyer, in which he depicts a noble ideal of active manliness:

> "For God, as He is an Energy, which, itself unmoved, turns and moves all things, will not suffer to be slothful one whose heart He hath drawn to Himself. And the truth of this is approved, not by reasoning, but by experience, for only the faithful know how Christ allows no ease to his own, and how cheerfully and joyfully they engage in toil."[7]

Again:

> "An ingenuous mind will in the first place think thus with itself, that as Christ offered himself for us and is made ours, so it behoves thee to be offered for all, to think thyself not thine own but another's; for we are not born that we may live to ourselves, but that we may be all things to all men. These things alone, justice, fidelity, constancy, will it meditate from its tender years, in what things it may profit the Christian commonwealth, in what its native country, in what all mankind, one by one. Those are languid minds which look only to the attainment of a quiet life; nor are they so like God as those who study, even at their own risk, to do good to all."[8]

And once more:

> "It is the part of a Christian man not to talk magnificently of doctrines, but always, with God, to do great and hard things."[9]

In Zwingli's view, the church and the state were practically one body under different aspects. How the realization of this idea is facilitated by republican institutions is clear at first sight. In Germany it was a necessity of the case that the subject should follow the religion of his ruler: but for the succession of three devoutly Protestant Electors, the Reformation could not have subsisted in Saxony. When Duke Henry succeeded Duke George, his people abandoned Catholicism at once: with the best will in the world, Protestantism was unable to maintain itself in Austria and Bavaria. But in Zürich, in Basel, in Bern, the church and the state were administered through the same institutions by the same persons. Each step in the process of revolt against Catholicism, of the adoption of Protestantism, was marked by a public debate, and a solemn decision arrived at by the authorities of the city. The change in religion, with all that it involved, was the will of the people, and therefore held to be binding upon the people, in the same way as any regularly enacted law, any legally concluded alliance. It is in this light that we have to look at that persecution of Anabaptists which throws a dark shadow upon this phase of religious administration. They were held to be offenders against the expressed will of the commonwealth, and therefore justly liable to be treated like any other criminals. They were fined, they were banished, they were imprisoned; and it was only upon their repeated and impenitent obstinacy that at least some of their leaders were made to pay the forfeit of their lives. And from the same idea of the identity of church and state follows that conception of ecclesiastical discipline as a thing to be enforced by the secular arm, which was afterwards worked out with such relentless logic by Calvin in Geneva. Here, as in so many instances more, the beginnings of Calvinism are to be traced back to Zwingli. If the citizens of a particular state are also members of the church of Christ, what more natural and expedient than that the laws of the church should be enforced in the same way and by the same means as the laws of the state? Nor if it is true that the prosperity of the state is built upon the righteousness of the people, is the attainment of the political, possible except in the attainment of the moral and religious ideal. In this connection, the Proclamation which was issued on the 26th of March, 1530, by the Burgomaster, in conjunction with the greater and lesser Councils of the city of Zürich, is a curious and significant document.[10] It prescribes that all the people shall go to church, remain there till the sermon is over, and refrain from talking against the preacher. The number of taverns is to be diminished. All kinds of games—not cards and dice only, but others which lead less directly to gambling—are forbidden. Profane swearing is made an offence against the law. All these moral delinquencies are punished by fines of greater or less amount. In some cases the culprits are to be excluded from their guild, or forbidden the exercise of their trade or calling within the city. These things, as we shall presently see, were carried much further in Geneva, but the principle of Calvinistic discipline is already conceded in Zürich.

Zwingli adopted to the full the Reformation principle of the authority of Scripture. In the public disputations or conferences, which were the republican way of settling all controversies approved at Zürich, the Bible was solemnly put forward as the rule of faith and practice. Each of these disputations, as, for instance, that in which Zwingli defended his doctrine against the Pope's Vicar,[11] those against the Anabaptists,[12] that which secured the alliance of Bern,[13] was therefore a public re-assertion of this fundamental principle. But a distinction has been drawn between Luther's attitude to Scripture and Zwingli's, which, if not easy to support by specific quotations from their writings, is, I think, a legitimate deduction from their practice. Luther, it is said, was willing to abide by any existing doctrine or usage which he did not find expressly forbidden in Scripture, while Zwingli demanded distinct warrant of Scripture for whatever he was willing to allow. It is easy to see that the latter rule is of much more sweeping application than the former, and to trace to its operation the more rigid severity of worship in the Reformed than in the Lutheran Church. But if Zwingli was more precise than Luther in bringing all matters of faith and practice to the test of Scripture, he also took a wider view of what Scripture was. He was more Biblical than Pauline. While in the main agreeing with Luther in his conception of spiritual religion, he did not so exclusively take his gospel from the Pauline Epistles and then read it into the whole Bible. He had a scheme of scriptural instruction, which he explains more than once, as if its use were habitual to him.[14] It began with the Gospel of Matthew, which was succeeded first by the Acts of the Apostles and then by the two letters to Timothy. Only when he had laid this foundation of gospel teaching and primitive practice, did he proceed to explain the Epistle to the Galatians, followed by the Epistles of Peter and that to the Hebrews. It is significant that the Epistle to the Romans finds no place in this series. This method, which makes a selection from the New Testament in which most of the varied elements of its teaching are fairly represented, would evidently lead to a different result than that which begins and almost ends with Paul.

The religious faith which Zwingli was engaged in establishing—and it must not be forgotten that we are criticising an incomplete and violently interrupted work—has frequently been charged with containing a rationalizing element. If the word rationalism be used in the definite sense now attached to it, this is no more true of Zwinglianism than of the other great presentations of Reformation theology. Zwingli neither declaims against reason like Luther, nor, like Luther, erects his own theological preferences, his own untaught insight, into a rule of Biblical criticism. What he might have done had he lived longer, we cannot tell; but as a fact he did not call in the aid of human reason, as did Calvin, to pour the fluid and indeterminate elements of his thought into the rigid mould of a system. But at the same time there is a breezy atmosphere of good sense about his religion. It was meant for every-day use among the affairs of men. Its ultimate object was practical: if it aspired to soar on wings of faith into the heavenly abyss of the Divine decrees, it always came back to earth with a message of innocence and purity and justice between man and man. Zwingli's sympathy with Erasmus and the scholars of the Rhineland, which never failed him, both prevented him from becoming narrowly ecclesiastical and helped to keep him human. His conception of baptism, as a pledge of fidelity on the part of the recipient rather than as a mystical channel of grace—that explanation, in the words of institution, of "is" by "signifies," which so vexed the soul of Luther—his designation of original sin as a disease (*morbus*) rather than as an offence (*peccatum*)—his substitution of a mere figure of rhetoric for the mysterious transference of qualities from the divine to the human nature of Christ, which the Lutherans knew as the *communicatio idiomatum*—are all instances of what we may call his religious common sense. To this answered the character of the man, strong, kindly, sincere. He was of untiring energy both in study and in affairs, taking delight in simple pleasures, a musician like Luther, and a performer upon several instruments.[15] His disposition and habits were social: his campaigns, no less than his active participation in politics, had given him a large knowledge of men: he mingled with the citizens in their guilds, with the peasants at their merry-makings, and had an acceptable word for all. What would have been the course of events had he lived—whether he would have been drawn more and more into the whirlpool of Confederate or European politics—whether he would have thrown his thought into a more systematic form, or worked out his principles of faith to further consequences—who can say? When Œcolampadius died, no man of originating power was left to take Zwingli's place: Bullinger, Myconius, Leo Jud, fell naturally into the second rank; and after a few years of wrangling controversy on their part, with Geneva on the one side, with Germany on the other, it was clearly seen that the task of moulding and guiding Swiss Protestantism henceforth belonged to Calvin.[16]

It is, however, impossible to understand Calvin's place and work in the church, until we clearly apprehend that he belongs to a later stage in the development of the Reformation than Luther and Zwingli. The period of his commanding influence in Geneva stretches from 1541 to his death in 1564. The epoch of creative religious thought is now past. But the process of doctrinal development is still going on: systems are being built up and shaped into symmetry: the churches are only just entering upon a period of arid and minute and bitter controversy. The conflict with Rome is without remedy or recall, and the line of battle, from which after ages have found it difficult to depart, is determined. Nor is the Reformation any longer a merely national thing, Saxon or Swiss: in France, in Holland, in England, in Scotland, in the Northern kingdoms, everywhere indeed, the struggle is going on with more or less violence, and the time is rapidly coming at which Europe will find itself divided into two camps, a Protestant and a Catholic, owning the force of neither alliances nor enmities but such as spring from this distinction. Think now of the movements and changes of fortune in the religious world upon which Calvin looked out from his fortress under the shadow of the Alps! The twenty-three years of his rule at Geneva comprehended in Germany the death of Luther, the Schmalkaldic War, the defeat of Mühlberg, the melancholy period of the Interim, the abdication of Charles V., and the settlement of Passau. Just as it closed, Philip II. and the Duchess Margaret were making ready for Alva in the Netherlands; while in Scotland, Mary Stuart was contending with John Knox, and in all the insolence of power and beauty preparing the tragedy of her own downfall. During these years the first generation of Huguenots in France are maintaining an unequal fight with Catharine de Medici and the Guises, and the day of St. Bartholomew is soon to follow. They cover in English history almost exactly the interval between the Six Articles of Henry VIII. and the Thirty-nine of Elizabeth: what a time of hope, and feverish expectation, and wild terror, and good cheer renewed, lies between! The Council of Trent met for the first time in 1545, and was finally dissolved in December, 1563: to it, the Church of Geneva and the "Institution of the Christian Religion" were the most resolute and the most complete answer of the Reformation. When Calvin's theocratic rule began, Paul III., a Farnese, the last of the old line of Popes who founded families and clutched their own advantage in utter disregard of the interests of Christendom, sat in the fisherman's chair: when it ended, Pius IV. had succeeded Paul IV., both, by comparison, grave and austere Pontiffs, the Inquisition had been re-founded, and the Counter Reformation had begun. For already in 1540, Paul III. had sanctioned the incorporation of the Society of Jesus; and in command of these new and splendid soldiers of the faith, the Church of Rome, stunned and perplexed for the moment by the brilliant onset of Luther, had recovered her courage and advanced once more to the attack.

During these years, then, Calvin gradually grew to the height of a commanding figure in Europe. He is the only one of the great Reformers who can justly be called international. Though he never re-entered France after his first flight from it, he is the director of the French Reformation, dictating, as it were, to the Huguenots both their theology and their church government. During the reign of Edward VI. he is the adviser to whom Somerset and Cranmer listen with the deepest respect, while it is from Geneva that John Knox goes out to mould and to teach Scotland. Among the Swiss Reformers he is something more than *primus inter pares:* when Luther is gone, and Melancthon is more and more the mark for the rage of theologians, he represents the Reformation in the eye of Pope and Emperor. And I do not think that we shall do him justice unless we look upon Geneva as a fortified post of the Reform, to be held against all comers, and within whose walls, always open to attack, the sternest discipline is necessary. When Calvin took it and made it his own, it was just struggling into independent political life. Originally a free city, subject to its Bishop, it had fallen under the dominating influence of the House of Savoy, which it shook off only after many struggles. The Reformation introduced a new line of division among its citizens: the partizans of Genevese independence were mostly Protestant; the friends of Savoy clung to the old faith; while there were many who, without any faith at all, disliked the new austerity of manners, the stern restraint of license. Calvin failed in his first attempt to impose his theocracy on the mixed and mobile population of Geneva: I am not sure that if he had had to deal with it alone, he would ever have succeeded. But Geneva soon became a city of refuge. From France especially, and from Italy, men fled for their lives to this secure haven, where they could worship God in their own way (so long as it happened to be Calvin's way too), and bring up their children in the saving knowledge of the gospel. And these men naturally gathered round Calvin, and upheld him in all his measures. His convictions were their convictions, and they found it no hardship to submit to his ecclesiastical rule, however sharp it might seem to be to those who remembered and loved the easy days of old. Between them, they made Geneva at once a city of God after their own pattern, and a frontier fortress of the Reformation. I suppose that, little by little, cruel persecution and stern, steady repression crushed out the rebellious elements of Genevese life: the partizans of the old régime; the sect of the Libertines, in whom wild Pantheistic speculation is said to have undermined all moral conviction; the genuine lovers of freedom, who rebelled against the tyranny of preachers and an inquisition disguised under the name and forms of consistory. But whatever Geneva became, Calvin must have the credit or the shame of it. It is a mistake to suppose, as some seem to do, that he held the reins of power in his own hands and openly wielded the authority of a dictator. It is equally a mistake to attempt to lift from his shoulders the responsibility of what was done at Geneva, by pointing to the civil institutions of the place. His was the kind of influence, the most powerful, the most pervading of all, which bends independent minds to itself, and works by the hands of others. There were councils of various kinds, syndics, a consistory; but from 1541 to 1564, Geneva was John Calvin.

Of Calvin as a systematizing theologian I shall have to speak at another time: we are concerned with him now as the founder and governor of a church. It has been said, with as much truth as such antitheses usually contain, that Catholicism is a religion of priests, Lutheranism of theologians, Calvinism of the believing congregation. And it is obvious at first sight that Calvin availed himself of the republican constitution of Geneva to establish a religious community as distinct in its outline, as definite in its faith, as rigid in its administration, as the Papal system itself had been in its palmiest days. It is not, with Luther, "the freedom of the Christian man" on which he insists; much more he delights to magnify the office and authority of the church. With him, the individual depends on the community; the unit is part of a well-ordered whole. Have not the following words, which stand at the beginning of his exposition of the theory of the church, more of a Catholic than a Protestant sound?[17]

> "But because our rudeness and slothfulness, yea, and vanity of wit, do need outward helps, whereby faith in us may both be engendered and grow and increase in proceeding towards the mark whereunto it tendeth, God hath also added them thereby to provide for our weakness. And that the preaching of the gospel might flourish, He hath left this treasure with the church. He hath appointed pastors and teachers, by whose merits He might teach them that be His: He hath furnished them with authority: finally, He hath left nothing undone that might avail to the holy consent of faith and right order. . . . I will begin at the church, into whose bosom God will have His children to be gathered together, not only that they should by her help and ministry be nourished while they are infants and young children, but also be ruled by her motherly care till they grow to riper age and at length come to the mark of faith. For it is not lawful that those things be served which God hath conjoined; that to whom He is a Father, the church be also their mother; and *that,* not only under the Law, but also since the coming of Christ, as Paul witnesseth, which teacheth that we are the children of the new and heavenly Hierusalem."

This is a very different tone from that of the Saxon Reformers, who were satisfied with an ecclesiastical constitution which had shaped itself according to circumstances, or even of Hooker, who strove to penetrate, and as it were to interpret by his own theory, one which had just weathered the storm of reformation. It is the utterance of the self-confident legislator who rejoices to be able to go back to first principles and to apply them upon new ground. And not only was Calvin's theory of the relation between church and state definite enough, but he was prepared to carry it out by the use of a discipline which did not yield for weight and edge to any weapon that Catholic Bishop or Inquisitor ever wielded.

Discipline is the constant dream of churchmen of every kind. Give them but power enough, they say, and they will cleanse the church of all heresies and unfaithfulnesses, transforming her into the likeness of the pure Bride of Christ, without blemish and without taint. In their rage against error, they forget the wheat and the tares that are to grow together till the final harvest. In their anger against open manifestations of vice, they overlook the subtler sins which no inquisition can detect, which no severity can cast out, but which not the less canker the Christian life at its core. But Europe, in the sixteenth century, had had enough of discipline as administered by clerics; and when the whole system by whose terrors it had been enforced crumbled into ruins, there was no basis on which to erect another. Princes would not, and churchmen could not, take up again the rod that had fallen from Papal hands. Error indeed might be repressed, but vice was perforce left to itself. So deeply, however, is this passion for moral judgment engrained in the hearts of theologians, that I doubt not Luther and Melancthon would gladly have set up, if they could, a discipline analogous to that of Rome, if perchance milder: fortunately for themselves and the church, they were compelled to rely upon moral and religious influence alone. Still the Reformation had everywhere to contend against a relaxation of morals which its enemies put down to its own account, which its friends declared to be a legacy of the past: perhaps in Geneva, with its mixed population, with its southern blood, with the turbulence of its recent history, things were worse than elsewhere. However this may have been, reformation of morals was henceforth a matter of life and death struggle between the Genevese and their new pastor. He had come to Geneva for the first time in 1536, and had been expelled from it, on this very quarrel, in 1538: when in 1541 he was recalled, it was on the understanding that the life of the city was to be controlled and organized as he would have it.

I cannot here enter into the particulars of the ecclesiastical constitution which Calvin established, or define with accuracy the different functions of the Councils and the Consistory. He calmly lays it down in the "Institution" that the church knows of no punishment save exclusion from the Lord's Supper. "For the church hath not the power of the sword to punish or restrain, no empire to command, no prison, no other pains which the magistrate is wont to lay upon men."[18] But what if the state, penetrated through and through with the spirit of the church, acts upon its information, makes crimes of its offences, and is prompt to inflict the severest punishments upon its criminals? Two things are especially to be noticed in the holy reign of terror which Calvin established and left behind him as a legacy to Geneva: first, the vast extension given to the idea of crime, and next, the worse than Draconian severity of the punishments inflicted. Adultery was repeatedly punished with death. A child was beheaded for having struck father and mother. Banishment, imprisonment, in some cases drowning, were penalties inflicted on unchastity. To sing or even to have in one's possession lewd songs was a crime: to laugh at Calvin's sermons, or to have spoken hot words of him in the street, was a crime: to wear clothes of forbidden stuff or make was a crime: to give a feast to too many guests or of too many dishes was a crime: to dance at a wedding was a crime:—to all of which, with many others of like sort, appropriate punishments were meted out. Everybody was obliged to attend public worship: everybody was required to partake of the Lord's Supper: no sick man might lie in bed for three days without sending for the minister of the parish. Do not let it be thought that these penalties were of infrequent enforcement, unwelcome breaks in a smooth current of civic life: in the years 1558 and 1559 alone, there were in the little city four hundred and fourteen of such prosecutions.[19] Now and then, as might be expected, there was a sharp spasm of rebellion against so grinding a tyranny. The Libertines were not wholly suppressed. The old spirit of Genevese freedom was not quite dead. Some man, or as often some woman, was goaded into open revolt, which almost inevitably took such a form as gave a plausible pretext for fresh severity on the part of the guardians of faith and order. Then the prison, the pillory, the scaffold, did their work, and the reign of repressive holiness was resumed.

Did this method of church government succeed or fail? This question will be answered differently according to the side from which it is approached. It must not be forgotten that its story has been chiefly told by Calvin and his friends; and, in particular, that his book against the Libertines is still quoted as the best, and indeed almost the only authority for their false and immoral doctrines. But it is never safe to accept against heretics the testimony of the orthodox doctor who glories in having put them down: heresy, in the common judgment, always involves a taint of immorality, and is only too easily associated with it. The Genevese must have been either more or less than human if the rigid and minute discipline of the Consistory had not now driven sin beneath the surface, and again excited it to bravado: an over-strained severity of criminal jurisprudence is quite as much provocative as remedial. In opposition to the writers who hold up the Geneva of Calvin and Beza as a model community, there are others who, relying on the irrefragable evidence of public records, assert that at no period was its immorality fouler or more deeply seated than when it was covered over with the thickest varnish of religious observance. On the other hand, there can be no doubt that in some respects Calvin largely succeeded in reaching his own ideal. Geneva was to all external appearance sound in the faith. The majority of the inhabitants submitted willingly to the new discipline, while those who hated it maintained, with occasional outbreaks, a sullen silence. Refugees, if only they reached the standard of Genevese orthodoxy, were safe beneath the shelter of the city walls. A flourishing University became the centre from which the Calvinistic theology was diffused. Geneva was, as it were, the High Change of Protestant thought and action: hither came missionaries to be instructed and inspired: hence they issued, to preach all over Europe the gospel of the Divine decrees. But in spite of the admiration which this polity still continues to excite in some minds, we must pronounce the Geneva which Calvin created but a poor and mechanical imitation of the City of God. The true holiness is that which men live and grow into in the strength of high principles and noble affections, not that which is bolstered up by regulations and protected by penalties. I do not even discuss the question whether the ideal of life was in itself a lofty one: the polity by which it was sought to be promoted condemns itself.

Calvin's principles of church government led straight to persecution. In this respect he was neither before nor behind his age: he differed from other Reformers, if at all, in the calm and logical outspokenness with which he defended his position. If sins and crimes are obnoxious to the same kind of judgment—if adultery is punishable with death, reading loose books with imprisonment, neglect of divine ordinances with a fine—why should not heresy, the immoral character of which orthodoxy is always ready to assume, receive the same treatment? Who can be a greater offender in a theocratic state than the heresiarch who is active in the propagation of his soul-destroying errors? Then there is that distinction between heresy and blasphemy of which I have already spoken, and the duty, as to the obligation of which Calvin never entertained a doubt, of being jealous for the honour of God. The chief victims of this theory of upholding religious truth and repressing religious error were Gruet and Servetus. No doubt Gruet was a scoffing unbeliever of a very coarse type; but the evidence on which this fact rests was not discovered till three years after long torture had crushed out of him a confession which led him to the scaffold:[20] while the crime for which he actually suffered was that of having affixed to Calvin's pulpit at St. Peter's a scurrilous and threatening placard. The case of Servetus I shall not re-open. All the world, except the few persons who are determined to clear Calvin's fame by any means, is agreed about it. His only defence lies in the proof afforded by the approval of Melancthon and the Swiss churches, that the act was not out of accord with the spirit of the age. He wanted to give the world at large, and the Papacy in especial, an assurance of the fact that such heresy as that of Servetus was no more tolerable in Geneva than in Rome, and bade men read his witness in the smoke that went up to heaven from the faggots of Champmel. Two damning facts, neither of which can be denied or explained away, blacken the deed with special infamy: first, that terrible phrase in Calvin's letter to Farel of February, 1546, seven years before its threat was fulfilled, *"nam si venerit, modo valeat mea auctoritas, vivum exire nunquam patiar;"* and next, that Servetus was only a stranger in Geneva, taking it as one temporary resting-place on his flight into Italy, over whom therefore neither Consistory nor Council had any pretence of jurisdiction. But the lurid light which surrounds the death of Servetus, and the controversy which it continues to excite, have done much to draw away attention from the fact that it was only part of a system and the logical outcome of a theory. In a long letter to the Protector Somerset, written in the name and with assumption of the authority of Christ, Calvin lays down with great distinctness the duty of repressing heresy by force:[21]

> "From what I understand, my Lord, you have two kinds of rebels who have risen up against the King and the State of the realm. The one are fantastic people, who under colour of the gospel would cast all into confusion; the other, obstinate adherents to the superstitions of the Roman Antichrist. Both alike well deserve to be repressed by the sword which is committed to you, seeing that they attack not the King only, but God who has seated him upon the throne, and has entrusted to you the protection as well of his person as of his majesty."

In the latter part of the same letter, the Protector is exhorted for the honour of God "to punish the crimes which men are not accustomed to hold in much account," adultery, unchastity, blasphemy, drunkenness. The state, however theoretically independent of or even superior to the church, is practically to be its instrument in enforcing a scheme of doctrine, in carrying out a method of polity, which are assumed to be in complete accordance with the mind and purpose of God.

To turn to considerations of a more general kind, the Calvinistic type of theology differs from the Lutheran, not so much in the doctrines which it includes, as in the relative importance which it gives to such as are common to both. Its centre of gravity is not the same. Both are Augustinian in their origin and essence: both assume the absolute foreknowledge and determining power of God, the servitude of the human will, the corruption and incapacity of man's nature. But while Lutheranism crystallizes round the idea of justification by faith, and is, so to speak, anthropological, Calvinism, beginning and ending with the supremacy of God, is theological. Another side of this distinction has been expressed in the statement, that while Lutheranism chiefly opposed itself to the Judaizing element in the Papal system by cutting at the root of ceremonial piety, Calvinism stood in stronger contrast to its Paganism by merging all forms of idolatry in the awe of the Supreme. In the one, the main thing is the sinner's personal relation to Christ, his appropriation of the Saviour's work, his resurrection from sin and death to holiness and life; in the other, the majesty of God, who is over all and in all, and the awful omnipotence of the Divine decree fixing the unalterable succession of events, and rigidly determining the eternal fate of men from a period before time was. And when we come to look a little more closely at the constituents of Calvinistic theology, we see how this master-thought runs through it all. In the process of salvation, it at once shuts out all co-operation of the human will, and assures the final perseverance of the elect: shall not God begin, round off, complete His own work? We have no doctrine here of a *communicatio idiomatum:* the attributes of the deity of Christ cannot be transferred to his manhood. The sacraments may be signs or seals or what you will; a veil of words may be drawn over the too naked simplicity of the Zwinglian conception; but no true Calvinist could admit an actual presence of the Living God under the species of bread and wine. To the same source may be traced the bareness of Calvinistic worship and its unwillingness to charm the soul through the senses: God, the Omnipotent and the Omnipresent, will choose and occupy and mould His own, without the vain help of audible and visible things. The one thought of God dominates, almost engulfs, all others; and it is a God whose will binds the world and men in bonds of adamant.

It would seem at first sight as if such a conception of religion must be fatal to morals. If the essence of Calvinism be, as John Wesley put it, that the elect shall be saved, do what they will, and the reprobate damned, do what they can, what motive is left for self-restraint in the one, for effort in the other? In what does the convinced Calvinist differ from the Moslem fatalist who resigns himself with *Allah Ackbar,* to be a counter in the hands of Omnipotence? Yet so far is Calvinism from producing slackness of will and feebleness of character, that Calvinists have been among the most strenuous of men: Calvin himself, John Knox, William of Nassau, Oliver Cromwell. The secret lies in that communication between earth and heaven for which Mohammedanism makes no provision, except in the case of the world's great prophets. No true Calvinist, save one perhaps here and there, ever believes that he is finally reprobate: as in the case of Cowper, "that way madness lies:" on the contrary, he feels himself to be an instrument of the Omnipotent Will, and bends to whatever toil he undertakes in the unshakable conviction that he is on the side of God. How copious a spring of energy lies in this thought I need not tell you; nor is it without a power of moral consecration too. It is customary to say that Calvinism is a more distinctively ethical form of religion than Lutheranism: that while the latter represents it as a grace that is imparted, the former holds it up as a law to be obeyed. But does not the ethical efficacy of Calvinism take a direction of its own, and act within limits? There are specific moral dangers in the absolute identification of God's will with our own conception of it, from which, it seems to me, neither Calvin nor some of the most eminent of his followers have been able to escape. Nothing is more difficult than to be jealous for the Divine honour and to abate all personal pretension. To hate the enemies of God and to love one's own, are practically incompatible precepts.

The relations of Calvinist and Lutheran theology to the Bible are in theory the same. Luther and Calvin alike appealed from the authority of Pope, Church, Schoolmen, Tradition, to that of the Scriptures themselves. The Genevese Reformer, as I have already pointed out, true to his systematizing instinct, developed the theory of Biblical authority into a somewhat more definite form; but in the general both stand upon the same ground. Yet Calvin, it must be confessed, was the more consistent scripturalist of the two. He was a not less industrious expositor of Scripture than Luther, and probably more acute and systematic; while the literary and theological difficulties which the latter found in the Bible, and cut asunder rather than solved by his trenchant good sense, did not trouble him. He believed that all Scripture was written under the direct dictation of the Holy Spirit, and was to be received by the church as a living voice from heaven. So given to men, it could not possibly contain discrepancy or contradiction: to question its genuineness, was simple rebellion against God. Calvin went to the New Testament for his theory of church government, and claimed a Divine sanction for Presbyterianism; while Luther in setting up his Consistories did not look beyond the practical necessities of the case and the prejudices of his pious Electors. And, like Zwingli, Calvin took the Bible much more as a whole than Luther did. He was full of a Hebrew spirit: he went back willingly to Jewish precedents, and used them to modify the too great humanity of the gospel. The apologists for some of his questionable actions defend him on this line: "Whoso ventures to judge him," says a late biographer, "judges the Hebrew Prophets too." When the Duchess Réné of Ferrara alleges that the example of David in hating his enemies is not applicable to those who live under the milder dispensation of the gospel, he sternly replies[22] that "such a gloss would upset all Scripture," and alleges that the Holy Ghost has in this respect set David before us as a pattern. "And, in fact," so he continues, "it is declared to us that in this ardour he is the type of our Lord Jesus Christ. Now, if we assume to surpass in sweetness and humanity him who is the fountain of piety and compassion, woe be unto us!" What of this kind the English Puritans thought and said is known to all, and how in the seventeenth century the Old Testament, the Mosaic legislation, the Jewish kingdom and church, assumed a place in religious thought and practice to which the earlier history of Christianity offers little that is like. This particular phase of Calvinistic thought has in the main passed away; nor do fanatical politicians or wild social reformers now, as under the Commonwealth, borrow the language of the Old Testament. But Calvin's way of looking at Scripture still survives in much uncritical apprehension of the relation between the Old Testament and the New, and a method of exposition which takes little account of differences of age and authorship.

To conclude: Calvinism is the last word of what may be called the orthodox Protestant Reformation. It stands further from Rome than Lutheranism, and is at the same time a compacter system, a more reasoned protest, a more pronounced antithesis. In its appeal to the authority of Scripture over the whole ground of faith and practice, it breaks more decisively with tradition. Whatever we may think of Calvin's attempt to find a middle place between Luther and Zwingli for his doctrine of sacraments, Calvinistic, in a very different way from Lutheran churches, have always been opposed to Rome in that great and critical controversy. Partly in the line of natural development, partly in that of reaction, the process of doctrinal decay in the Reformed Church has often led to rationalism. Calvinism is an intellectual system, proceeding by logical method from premiss to conclusion, having all its parts duly subordinated to the whole, and held together by the strongest argumentative cement. But when thought is once encouraged to activity, who shall prescribe limits? And, on the other hand, there are demands upon belief of such a kind as to provoke unqualified rejection, if they do not meet with submissive assent. From the beginning, Calvinism has been at the opposite pole from Rome in the application of art to the service of religion: it rejects all symbolism, it sets up no cross, it lights no candles, it has inspired no architecture, it distrusts even music. Lutheran hymnology began with Luther, and from the first put forth a strong and sweet luxuriance; but it was only in the eighteenth century that Calvinism learned how to write hymns, the help of which Scottish piety does not even yet value. But while it is almost Papal in its theory of the church, and would, if it could, exercise as rigid a rule as Rome over men's minds and actions, it stands in long historical opposition to Papal politics. "No Bishop, no King,"[23] said James I. at the Hampton Court Conference; and, on the other hand, your true Calvinist is always on the side of freedom and national independence. He has not been as tender of others' rights as strenuous to maintain his own: the children of the Dutchmen who had withstood Alva, exiled the Remonstrants: the Puritans, who had fled for freedom of worship to New England, banished Baptists and branded Quakers. But in the incidental mention of these names, I have done enough to vindicate for Calvinism an honourable place in history. It was the form of faith in the strength of which the Dutch Republic was sustained and the American Republic was founded: to propagate which, Tyndale gave to the English people the Bible in their own tongue, and with it his life: which formed the royal intellect of Cromwell, and inspired the majestic verse of Milton. Shall I say more, or is not this enough?

## Notes

[1] In connection with the passage above quoted, Zwingli says that it was from Wyttenbach, and not from Luther, that he learned the true character of indulgences: "dann ich vorhin von dem ablass bericht was, wie es ein betrug und farbe wär, us einer disputation die doctor Thomas Wytembach von Biel, min herr und geliebter trüwer leerer, vor etwas zyten ze Basel gehalten hatte, wie wol in minem abwesen." Opp. I. p. 254.

[2] Vid. Zwingli's preface to an edition of Pindar, edited by Cœporinus: Opp. IV. 159.

[3] Bullinger: *Reformationsgeschichte,* I. 259.

[4] *De Vera et falsa religione:* Opp. III. 202.

[5] Ibid. III. 285.

[6] Ibid. III. 201.

[7] *Quo pacto adolescentes formandi:* ibid. IV. 152.

[8] *Quo pacto adolescentes formandi:* Opp. IV. 155.

[9] Ibid. IV. 158.

[10] Bullinger: *Reformationsgeschichte,* II. 277.

[11] January 29, 1523.

[12] January 17, March 20, 1525.

[13] January 6, 1528.

[14] *Apologeticus Archeteles adpellatus:* Opp. III. 48. Conf. I. 151, 485, for slightly differing forms of the same statement.

[15] Bullinger: *Reformationsgeschichte,* I. 31.

[16] I may refer here to an excellent essay in the Theologische Studien und Kritiken for 1862, p. 631, by Hundeshagen, "Zur Charakteristik Ulrich Zwingli's und seines Reformationswerkes unter Vergleichung mit Luther und Calvin." Another essay in the same periodical, to which I am under obligation throughout this Lecture, is one by Ullmann, "Zur Charakteristik der Reformirten Kirche," 1843, p. 749.

[17] *Instit. Christ. Rel.* IV 1. I have adopted Norton's translation.

[18] *Instit. Christ. Rel.* IV. 11, 3.

[19] I lay no stress upon the fact that the registers of the city of Geneva show that within the space of sixty years a hundred and fifty poor wretches were burned for witchcraft; that the application of the torture was an incident of almost all criminal trials; that thirty-one persons were burned at one time for the fantastic offence of spreading the plague. These cruelties, these

popular terrors, were common to all Europe, and cannot be specially laid to the charge of either Calvin or Geneva. Yet they belong to the delineation of this City of God, upon which so much strange admiration has been spent, and must be suffered to remain and to darken the picture.

[20] Gruet was executed in July, 1547: it was not until April, 1550, that a MS. book of his handwriting was discovered under the roof of his house, severely characterized by Calvin in a still extant document, and ordered to be burned by the Syndics. Henry: *Leben Calvin's,* II. 439 et seq.; Beilage 16, p. 120.

[21] The letter is dated October 22, 1548. Henry: *Leben Calvin's,* II.; Beilage 4, p. 26 et seq.

[22] Henry: *Calvin's Leben,* I. 452, 453.

[23] Fuller: *Church History of Britain,* III. 180.

**Frank Hugh Foster (essay date 1903)**

SOURCE: "Zwingli's Theology, Philosophy, and Ethics," in *Huldreich Zwingli: The Reformer of German Switzerland, 1484-1531,* edited by Samuel Macauley Jackson, revised edition, G. P. Putnam's Sons, 1903, pp. 365-401.

[*In this essay, Foster gives an overview and explanation of the main precepts of Zwingli's theology.*]

The Protestant Reformation rendered two separate and great services in the realm of thought to its age and to the world. One of these was in the protest which it delivered against the Roman doctrinal system; and the other was in its positive contribution to the enrichment and development of Christian theology. The Roman idea of human merit and its relation to salvation had led to a conception of grace, of the operation of the sacraments, of the atonement and the divine forgiveness, to a system of morals, and to methods of discipline, which the adherents of the Protestant faith declared must be swept away, with all their practical consequences in the conception and the conduct of life, and in their stead new conceptions must be introduced. But the system of thought was even then defective. It was not up to the level of Christian experience. It had to be enlarged and perfected. A new doctrine, justification by faith, had to be adjusted to the old, and to be supplemented by a group of other new doctrines which should first bring the system into some degree of completeness. This work Protestantism also undertook, and under its able leaders in Wittenberg it gave to the Christian world the first system of Christian dogmatics which could claim to have treated the doctrines of grace with anything like the necessary fulness, and to have welded them into a consistent whole with the heritage which had come down from the ancient and uncorrupted Church.

To obtain a complete view of Zwingli's theology, both of these elements in the general work of Protestantism must be brought into the consideration, for they are both represented in his labours. With the rest of the Reformers he was led to those general positions in respect to the sole mediatorship of Jesus Christ, salvation by faith in Him, the helplessness of man as a sinner, and the authority of the Christian congregation in distinction from the papacy, which constituted the more direct recoil from Rome. In all these doctrines Zwingli showed marked independence of view, vigour, and originality, but in none of them did he render any service that could be called especially his own, or bring out anything which belongs properly to his contributions to the system of developed Protestant doctrine. For our present purpose our theme, therefore, admits of a limitation. We do not need to pass in review every doctrine which Zwingli held, not even every one which he wrought out independently, and which in another environment would have to be reckoned to his most marked service. He was as clear as Luther upon the doctrine of justification by faith, and entirely independent in his method of approach to it and in his manner of holding it. But as historians we must ascribe that doctrine to Luther and not to Zwingli. Luther alone gave it to the world and made it the rallying cry of the mighty movement. But Zwingli had his own peculiar field, and to this we must give more especial attention.

A word needs to be said as to the underlying philosophy of Zwingli before we enter upon the direct consideration of that which is more distinctively theological. He brought with him to the construction of his theology, from the formative and educational period of his life, two great currents of influence, the one having its origin in the enthusiasm for liberal culture nourished by the period of the Renaissance, and the other springing from the fountain of the New Testament Scriptures. The latter made his theology biblical and Protestant; the former gave to it its liberal tone. Many individual ideas may be traced to a classic origin which might be denominated not improperly philosophical. Zwingli was not without something which may be styled a philosophy of a very great type. But it cannot be said that his system was dominated by the philosophy of the ancient or even of the mediæval schools. He followed a distinct trend of thought upon the themes embraced within the scope of philosophy, but it is a trend developed in the Christian Church and distinctly belonging to theology. It has its roots in the Hebrew religion. It was held by those writers in the Old Testament who attributed all agency, even that producing evil, to God. Among Christian theologians, the first to express it with so great emphasis as to associate his own name with it was Augustine. Augustinianism has been a synonym for stress laid upon the sovereignty of

God. It was Augustine's favourite thought that "everything good was either God or from God." The same tendency had its representatives in the Middle Ages, and among them was Thomas Aquinas. It reappeared in the Reformation in Luther's doctrine of predestination and of the bondage of the will, in which, for a purely religious reason, Luther affirms in the strongest way the absolute and sole causality of God. In the year 1520, long before the controversy with Erasmus had given occasion to a flow of feeling which may seem to have been unfavourable to impartial thought, he wrote: "I would that the word 'free-will' had never been invented; neither is it in the Scripture, and might better be called self-will, which is of no use."[1] Later he derives the sole causality of God from His omnipotence, and rejoices in it as in the ground of the Christian's confidence in God, since God thus foreknows everything, and hence proposes and performs everything, He can therefore never be defeated. "By this thunderbolt," he says, "is cast down and ground to powder the freedom of the will."[2] Luther's doctrine was far more the result of his general point of view and of his impressions as to the necessary foundation of the doctrines of grace, than of any philosophical opinions he held. The same is true of Calvin, whose position is too well known to require even a mention here. Zwingli shared the same atmosphere with these other Reformers, was moved by the same great spiritual opposition to Rome, which had practically, if not confessedly, taken the opposing view, and hence it was natural that he should revert to Augustinianism, as they did. And thus we find him, for the most part from purely theological interests, upon the side of that philosophical doctrine which exalts the sovereignty of God.

It would, therefore, be of little value if we sought to trace the system of Zwingli to any distinct philosophical root. What biblical elements there are in it will best appear if we simply follow in the natural line of exposition as his system is presented in his principal dogmatic writings. Of these there is an interesting series brought out by the special exigencies of Zwingli's public life. We need consider only his ***Sixty-Seven Articles,*** with the ***Explanation*** of the same,[3] the ***Christian Introduction***[4] (all of the year 1523), the ***Commentary on True and False Religion***[5] (1525), the confession of faith presented to the Diet of Augsburg (1530) and entitled ***Ratio Fidei,***[6] the treatise upon ***Divine Providence*** (1530),[7] and his last important production, published posthumously, the ***Explanation of the Christian Faith*** (1531). The earlier of these are of great historical interest, and the last is not without dogmatic importance; but the central member of the group, the elaborate and comprehensive ***Commentary,***[8] written after his views had attained maturity and consistency, must ever remain the chief source of information as to his theological system, and will be the best starting-point in our exposition.

This work opens with a definition of religion as the system which comprises the whole of Christian piety, viz., its faith, life, rites, laws, and sacraments. As such, it is fundamentally a relation existing between God and man, and hence, to understand it, the terms between which it exists must be understood first. Hence the treatise begins with the doctrine of God. We thus meet the first and most important peculiarity of the Zwinglian system, the prominence given to the doctrine of God, at the outset of our study. It is now to be noted that it flows naturally out of his conception of religion, and that he could scarcely begin at any other great doctrine, having once defined religion as he does. The Lutheran theology was anthropological in its starting-point, and was determined largely by this element, in spite of the emphasis laid upon the divine causality by Luther, because its absorption in the spiritual experience which gave it its birth kept the eye fixed upon man rather than upon God.

Zwingli opens the discussion of the doctrine of God by considering His knowability. Although it may be above human understanding to know *what* God is, it is not above it to know *that* He is. Hence, the knowledge of God's existence is obtained from the light of nature; and nature is itself defined, in accordance with the tendency to exalt God which we are now noting, as "the continual and perpetual operation of God and His disposition of all things."[9] Thus the heathen have known the existence of God and some even His unity, though these have been few. But believers advance far beyond this. They are such as not only know that there is one only omnipotent and true God, but have more than a mere knowledge, since they trust in Him alone. They thus know in some measure what He is, but not from the unaided operation of their own faculties or from any merely human instruction which they may receive. The Scriptures testify that God is a hidden God, and that only the Spirit of God possesses knowledge of Him so as to become the source of knowledge to human hearts. Hence it is deception and false religion to pretend to derive the knowledge of God from philosophy. It is produced by the power and grace of Him in whom believers trust. The only source of the knowledge of God, in the full and Christian sense of such a word, is, therefore, the "mouth of God," by which term Zwingli designates the Bible, illuminated to the reader by the Spirit in his heart.

Upon such a basis, the discussion of the nature of God must be a purely biblical discussion, and Zwingli begins his treatment of this point with a study of Exodus iii., 14: "I am that I am." This is interpreted to mean that God is "the sole essence of all things" (*solum rerum omnium Esse*).[10] The word "essence" is here to be understood, apparently, as signifying the true being, the fundamental and ultimate reality of all things. Zwingli does not intend to identify God with nature in the pantheistic fashion, or to anticipate later idealism in what men have often attributed to it,—the denial of the existence of matter; but it is his design rather to refer nature entirely to God as its living energy. Thus he declares this to be "first in the knowledge of God, that we should know that He is, who is nature, who is Himself, and receives His existence from no one else."[11]

But now God not only is and is independent of all other existence, but He has a determinate and definite existence. "That being is as really good as He is being."[12] Zwingli thus passes from the nature to the attributes of God, at the summit of which, as the comprehensive expression of them all, he puts goodness. This very comprehensiveness of goodness will, however, be seen somewhat to modify its meaning. The proof of the goodness of God is drawn from the world which He has made. If this be "good," as the Scriptures declare, then the source of the world must Himself be good, and that of Himself, since the source of His goodness, truth, righteousness, justice, and holiness must be the same as the source of his being, viz., His own infinite self.

We are not, however, to think of the goodness of God as of some passive and inactive quality. His very nature, as the philosophers say, involves His constant activity, since He is the perfect, efficacious, and consummating force. Hence, He speaks and creation comes into existence. It is thus the product of His power; but it is also permeated by His other attributes. His wisdom, knowledge, and providence must so pervade all things that there shall be nothing that is hidden from Him or that fails to obey Him. The proof of this statement Zwingli draws from the general idea of His goodness (*bonum*), which is thus shown to embrace more than merely moral goodness. It is, in fact, a synonym in his mind for perfection, embracing all good, natural as well as moral. The argument might be summarised thus: God is the sum of all excellence; therefore He has this excellence, viz., wisdom.

It may serve to bring out more clearly the force of this argumentation, as well as to give a view of Zwingli's theological style, if we pause here in our analysis for a longer quotation. Says Zwingli[13]:

> This Good is, therefore, no idle or inactive thing, to lie supine and unmoved, neither moving itself nor other things, for, a little above, it was evident that it is the essence and conservation of all things, which is nothing else than that all things are moved, contained, and live through it and in it. It itself is called by the philosophers . . . perfect, efficacious, and consummating power, which, since it is perfect, never shall desist, never cease, never waver, but continually preserve all things, turn them, rule them, that in all things and actions no fault may be able to intervene to impede His power or to defeat His counsel. Which, again, is manifest by His own word. For thus you have it in the beginning of the creation, And God said, Let there be light, and there was light. See how the light when summoned does not only immediately present itself, but, that it may obey the command of its creator, is made of nothing. For so great is His power that when He calls things which are not, they appear, exactly as those things which are, even if they must first be born of nothing. . . . Since, therefore, all things which either move or live, so live and move as they are (for, unless they were, they could not move or live; but what they are, they are in God and through God); it may be thence inferred most clearly that God, as He is the being and the preservation of all things is also the life and movement of all things which live and move. . . . Nor, again, is He the life and movement of all things in such a way that either He himself should purposelessly inspire or move them, or that those things which are inspired or moved, should purposelessly seek of Him that they may live and move. How should they seek this of Him, which could not even be, except they were of Him, or how could they seek before they were? It follows that God is not only, like a kind of material, that from which all things are, by which all things are moved and live; but he is, at the same time, such wisdom, knowledge, and providence, that nothing is hidden, unknown, remote, and disobedient to it.

To resume the course of our analysis, Zwingli derives all other excellences in God from His supreme excellence as the highest being. "That only is God which is perfect, that is, absolute[14] and to which nothing is lacking, to which also all things are present which befit the highest good."[15] Among these attributes are God's foreknowledge and His providence, "upon which topic the whole matter of free-will and merit depends."[16]

Zwingli now advances to the proof of the benevolence and mercy of God by the following course of reasoning:

> Now, it were vain, fruitless, and useless to mortals if this highest Good, God, were wise for Himself alone, as is said, if He were goodness, life, motion, knowledge, providence for Himself alone; for thus He would differ in no respect from mortals, who have this by their own nature, that they sing for themselves, care for their own things, prefer themselves to others. It is necessary, therefore, that this highest Good, which is God, should be by its own nature kind and bountiful, not with that bounty with which we wish ourselves to seem to have given, sometimes considering reward, sometimes glory, but with that by which He wishes to benefit those to whom He has given, and considers this solely and alone, that those things which have been done by Himself may be theirs; for He will be freely drawn upon. For, as He is the fountain of all things (for no one merited, before He was, that he should be generated of Him), so He is perennially bountiful towards those whom He begot to this one end, that they should enjoy His bounty. In a word, this is the respect in which that Good differs from all other

> things which are called good: these do not expend themselves . . . gratuitously, since they are squalid and needy; that, on the contrary, neither will nor can be expended except gratuitously. Again, those things which are good in appearance spare themselves, for they can satisfy very few, since they are limited and mean. But that Good so abounds that it surpasses all the desires of all to satiety; for it is infinite and loves to be drawn upon. It cannot itself enjoy other things, for they are inferior to it, and except they enjoy it, from which they are, they cannot exist at all.[17]

This, in outline, is his doctrine of God. Passing now to the doctrine of man,—the other term of the relation which religion was defined to be,—we meet with distinct agreement with Augustine, but still with marked individuality of conception. Man was originally formed in the image of God. He was forbidden to eat of a specified tree. Tempted of the devil through his wife, he consented and ate, and thereby fell, and, in accordance with the threat of the law, he died. So far the narrative is one of plain facts. In what, now, did this "death" consist? It was not a death of the body, for Adam did not die immediately as the law threatened; and yet his ultimate physical death was for no other reason than for his transgression of the law at this time. But he died in some sense as soon as he ate. The death meant by the threatening of the law must therefore have been a death of the soul, not of the body. What death was it? Zwingli collects the answer from Romans v., 12. The death of the soul suffered at this time was sin.

Hence Zwingli comes next to discuss the topic of sin. Men are led into sin by desire. We have therefore to inquire what desire influenced Adam when he fell. It was the desire to be equal with God and to know good and evil by his own power. Evidently this desire had its origin in self-love. This, then, is the root and characteristic of sin. In this sin there is a corrupting power which infects our whole nature, so that there is a viciosity of nature (*vitium naturæ*).[18] Man has become flesh by the fall. Hence he thinks the things of flesh, and this makes him an enemy of God. "Therefore his mind (*mens*) is bad, and his disposition (*animus*) is bad from the beginning of his life."[19] Zwingli uses language even stronger than this, for he says: "They who have been born of one dead are themselves also dead. The dead Adam could not generate one free from death,"[20] that is, sin, for death is here to be understood of the love of self which is the essence of sin. Zwingli is unique among the three great Reformers for the clearness with which he makes the fundamental distinction between the corruption of our nature and what is properly sin, for he says there are two kinds of sin received in evangelical doctrine: first the disease (*morbus*) which we contract from the author of the race by which we are addicted to self-love, and the second that which is done contrary to the law.[21] In the ***Ratio Fidei*** he repeatedly makes this distinction, and says that the sin derived from Adam is only improperly called sin.[22] Adam was brought into the condition of a slave by sin and we are born in that condition. Hence death hangs over our heads. Thus, while essentially Augustinian, Zwingli shows the free spirit of inquiry which will carry him still farther towards new views in later portions of his system.

The topic of sin also raises the question of the agency of God in its appearance in this world, and therefore involves the theologian at once in the discussion of His providence and of His wisdom and goodness. Zwingli has given us a special treatise upon these subjects, to which it will be worth while to turn for a little.[23] Although written considerably later than the ***Commentary***, it proceeds to establish the doctrine of providence upon the basis of those principles as to the essential nature of God which have been already drawn out. The title of the first chapter contains its doctrine, that "Providence is necessary because the highest good necessarily cares for and disposes of all things."[24] The course of the argument has been substantially sketched above. The relation of God's providence and wisdom is this, that the wisdom is the power, and the providence the operation of God. It is His "constant and unchangeable government and administration of all things."[25] The entire harmony between God's providence and wisdom is therefore a postulate of Zwingli's thinking. So absolute, however, is God's government of all things that Zwingli now proceeds to deny second causes entirely. Nothing material can be of itself: it must derive its being from Him who alone is all being. "There is nothing which is not from Him, in Him, and through Him, yea, He Himself."[26] Any single finite force is "called a created power because the universal or general power is exhibited in a new subject and new form."[27] If finite things truly proceeded from other finite things, then these all must also proceed from still other finite things like themselves, and so *ad infinitum.* Since God can derive the being He gives them from none but Himself, He gives them His own being, and hence they are He. They are because they are in Him who always is and who is the only true being. Thus there is one Cause, and all the rest are no more causes than the ambassador of a sovereign is the sovereign himself.

It might be feared lest this entire identification of the creature with the Creator might lead to its degradation in the scale of being, as having no individuality or importance in itself. Such is, however, not Zwingli's tendency. All things become of the divine species,—not merely man, but even all the creation beneath man, although there remains a distinction in their nobility and gifts. In fact, the idea of God as the essence of all things introduces a new view of spheres of life which Christians were apt to relegate to the realm of unmingled evil. Zwingli thus attains a breadth of view which was denied to Luther. The heathen who have written holy and wise things are cited to sustain Zwingli's views upon the Deity, and this procedure he defends as right and proper because, whenever a good or holy thing is found in them, it is to be regarded as an emanation from the divine fountain.[28] The conception of the all-permeating activity of God is thus a liberalising element in Zwingli's conception of the world and its worth.

But does not this view of God's causality rob man of all real being and especially of responsibility? Such had been in Zwingli's day, as it has ever since, a common conclusion, and appeal had been made to him to clear up this point. He therefore now proceeds to consider man and the divine law.[29] Man is the most remarkable and wonderful being, since he is both a heavenly being, as possessing a spirit, and an earthly, as clothed in a visible, earthy body. The body which is given to him that he may be a part of the world over which he rules, is nevertheless a source of corruption to him. He is like a stream of pure water befouled with a mass of clay and thrown into the greatest commotion by this disturbing element. Why has God placed man in so unfortunate a position? And why, when he falls into sin, which arises from his connection with the body, does God punish the spirit, although it is the flesh which is the cause inciting to sin?[30] Thus sharply does Zwingli formulate the ever-recurring question as to man's responsibility. His answer is by no means as keen. The soul is punished because it has offended against the law.[31] But why has God given man the law, against which he was sure to offend, when He might have left him to ignorance and innocence?[32] The answer to this is that the law is the expression of the essence of God. It is light, the expression of the reason and the will of God. It is for us a law; for God it is not law but nature and essence. Thus from the command to love God we learn that *the nature of God is love*.[33] All that He does, therefore, will be according to His nature, though He is above the law under which we are bound. But the flesh does not understand and agree with this law and is led by it necessarily into sin. All this results by the knowledge and will of God, since He is the sole true cause. How, then, can the spirit be punished for what is the operation of God Himself? Zwingli's sole answer to this question is that it has sinned against the law.[34] This suggests the still sharper formulation of the question, Whether God Himself has not sinned in the sin of men, because their sin is His own operation? To this there are substantially two answers in Zwingli: one, the formal one, that God has not sinned against the law, because He is above the law and cannot sin against it; and, second, the more substantial one, that, considered as an act of the creature, a certain thing is sin which, considered as the act of God, since it is done for other and greater reasons, is no sin at all. But what "other and greater reason" can there be for the introduction of sin into the world by the act of God? Zwingli's answer here is that sin is as necessary to holiness as some evil is to all good. Without it holiness cannot be known. Hence, God produced sin in the world by means of the creature, whose sin was wrought by God through the instrumentality of the Tempter, for the good of the creature, that is, "that he might come to a knowledge of righteousness." The goodness of God in it all is the more evident in that He provided redemption.[35] This line of reasoning is more consistent than successful.

Zwingli passes by a natural transition to the discussion of election,[36] which he defines as "the free determination of the divine will concerning those who are to be made blessed." It is an act of the free-will of God in distinction from His mere wisdom. In opposition to Thomas Aquinas, Zwingli makes election to be independent of all foreknowledge of our faith. He had once been inclined to this opinion of Aquinas's, but rejected it because it endangers God's goodness and omnipotence, since He must have foreseen Judas's becoming bad, and must then be conceived as unable to hinder it; and also destroys His sole causality, ascribing some reason for His activity to the creature.[37] Yet the other attributes of God, wisdom, love, etc., are not unconcerned in election, though it is primarily a matter of the will. And faith, which is the condition of justification, is the gift of God and follows upon election;[38] so that election, rather than faith, may be said to be the justifying principle. "Faith follows election as its symbol." With such theories, Zwingli of course denies the freedom of the will, as is evident from innumerable expressions scattered here and there through his works, though there is no special treatise devoted to this theme.

Zwingli's whole discussion of the topic of sin may be sharply criticised as vitiated by arguments which are verbal and not material. To say that what is wrong to man because against law is not to God since He is above law, amounts to but little. But Zwingli did not intend to engage in mere logomachy. Law is viewed, it is true, too mechanically as an outward standard to which man must conform. But he meant, when he said that God must be above law, to ascribe to Him a peculiar and glorious excellence. It is a fine remark when he says, in attempted expression of this thought, that what is law to man is to God His own nature and essence.[39] He illustrates his breadth of view by this distinction. The whole treatment of the subject is an endeavour to state the facts of the case and make them consistent with the theory of God's operation which Zwingli had conceived. The failure lies in the impossibility of making such a theory fit the facts of human action and responsibility. Zwingli was as successful, perhaps, as anyone of his age in solving the difficulties which he had the perfect candour to acknowledge and to present.

Zwingli had defined religion as a relation existing between God and man.[40] Having described the terms between which this relation exists, he now returns to discuss religion itself.[41] Man, having fallen from God, will, if left to himself, never return. God in His great mercy now goes out after man and exhibits him to himself so that he recognises his disobedience, loss, and misery, as Adam did. Thus He produces despair of himself in man's soul. But God also shows him the divine mercy, and this he sees to be so great that he cannot be separated from it. He thus comes to trust God, treats Him as a parent, adheres to Him. Thus is established the relation which is described by the term "religion," which is, therefore, entire dependence upon God. False religion, on the contrary, is trusting in anyone else than God, especially in any creature.

All this is general and true of any religion. The specifically Christian religion gathers about the person of Christ. Hence Zwingli devotes a special paragraph to the definition of Christianity.[42] Christ is the certainty and the pledge of the grace of God. But how is this grace to be bestowed upon men who have wandered from God and will not come to Him, since God is just, and justice demands the punishment of sinners? God needs to exhibit Himself as He is, both just and also merciful and good. To this end His justice must be satisfied. But how is this to be done? Can man do it? He is too sinful to correspond to the spotless law of God. Neither have good works in themselves any merit to satisfy the justice of God. It remains, therefore, that God must provide for such satisfaction, which He has done by sending His Son incarnate to make satisfaction in our behalf. To this end Christ was prophesied; miraculously conceived; and born of the Virgin Mary (to avoid the stain of original sin); suffered all things which were to be inflicted upon us in consequence of sin, such as want, cold, and every other evil; and especially surrendered Himself to death. "For this was justice, that He, through whom we were all created, in whom there was no sin, . . . innocently bore those things which we had merited by sinning, but which He bore in our behalf."[43] Zwingli here places himself distinctly upon the ground common to the Reformers, that the death of Christ was a sacrificial satisfaction of justice in our behalf. The individual words and phrases employed by him are clear in their implications, such as *lito* (to make atonement for), *expiatio* (expiation), *ea ferre quæ nos peccando commeruimus* (to bear those things which we had merited by our sins), *redemptionis pretium* (price of redemption); but there is, further than this, no theoretical development of the doctrine.

In the ***Christianæ Fidei Expositio***[44] there is a fuller treatment of this theme in which, in connection with the general style of thought which had been prevalent since the days of Anselm, Zwingli presents the same conceptions of the work of Christ from a slightly different viewpoint. He derives the work of atonement from the goodness of God which must control in every plan and act. Through goodness God clothed His Son in flesh that He might exhibit to, and provide for, the world redemption and renovation. "Since His goodness, that is, His justice [note this identification], and His mercy are holy, that is, firm and immutable, His justice required expiation, His mercy pardon, His favour new life."[45] Hence this incarnate Son was made a victim that He might placate affronted justice and reconcile it with those who did not dare to approach God's face in their own innocence, since they were conscious of guilt. This was because, though He was merciful, yet virtue could not bear the repudiation of its own work [the law], and justice could not bear impunity. Justice and mercy are, therefore, so mingled that the latter should furnish the victim and the former should accept it for the expiation of all sins.

Such being the central point of the Christian religion distinguished from religion in general, Zwingli is now prepared to define the Gospel, which he does in the words, "that in the name of Christ sins are remitted."[46] The progress of salvation begins in the illumination of God, whereby we come to a knowledge of ourselves. Thereupon we fall into despair. We flee to the mercy of God, but His justice throws us into dismay. Eternal Wisdom finds a way whereby it can itself render satisfaction to its own justice, a thing which is absolutely impossible for us. God sends His Son to make satisfaction for us and become an indubitable security for us. But the fruits of this sacrifice become ours only upon the condition that we become new creatures, put on Christ, and so walk. Consequently the whole life of the Christian is a constant repentance. Here Zwingli pauses to discuss, in sharp distinction from the compulsory and hypocritical penance of the false Church, the marks of true repentance.[47]

Upon this head and several of the following, our present purpose does not call us to linger. Zwingli maintains, with many a minor peculiarity, the great Protestant doctrines upon the law, sin, the keys, and the Church. The law he reduces to the fundamental command of love to neighbour as its substance and root.[48] The keys are keys to open, like those of a castle, and not to shut, and are the knowledge and ability given to the servants of God to lead others unto salvation.[49] The Church he elsewhere defines more fully as the assembly (*concio, cœtus*), by which he means the local assembly of the Christian people in any city or town.[50] This external Church comprises all those who call themselves Christians, even though they are not truly such. This is not, however, the Church of which mention is made in the Apostles' Creed in the phrase, "I believe in the Catholic Church." The true spouse of Christ, "the Catholic Church," is composed of those who believe in Christ: it is the communion of saints, and is known to God alone. In this distinction between the visible and invisible Church Zwingli entirely agrees with the other Protestant Reformers. He differs, however, somewhat in the place he ascribes to the local Church.[51] This possesses all the powers which are conferred upon the Church at large. It may exercise the power of excommunication.[52] It also judges its pastors and the Word preached to it; and yet this is done not by the outward Church as such, but by the true spouse of Christ which is embosomed in it, since the judgment is given according to the Word of God in the minds of the faithful. For legislative purposes, Zwingli conceives the local Church of any city as represented in the government of the city—that is, in its board of magistrates. More distinctly individual is the claim which he asserts for the local Church to the attribute of infallibility. He puts this infallibility in the sharpest opposition to the infallibility of the Roman Church.[53] The Roman Church errs because it rests upon its own word: the true spouse of Christ "cannot err" because it "relies upon the word of God alone."[54] The source of this infallibility is the fact that the Church does not propose to set up anything of its own accord, but simply listens to the word of God and accepts what it finds there. Its infallibility is, therefore, the infallibility of the word of God, and Zwingli's doctrine of the infallibility of the local Church is like that of the other Protestant leaders as to the "perspicuity of the Scriptures." The Scriptures are plain in the great outlines of the way of salvation, so that no one who trusts himself to them will fail of eternal life; and the infallibility of the Church is such that when, in the exercise of her God-given authority, she tries to find out God's will in the great matters of salvation, she will be infallibly led into the knowledge of it.

The discussions of the ***Commentary***, as we have thus followed them, have been of the greatest importance to the establishment of a sound and comprehensive theology, but they have been defective in many respects and have had little in them upon which Zwingli's distinctive fame as a theologian could rest. They were defective, for example, in omitting all formal discussion of the doctrine of the Trinity, though there are many passages in which the substance of the doctrine is well expressed.[55] Doubtless Zwingli did not intend to traverse the ground where he agreed substantially with the ancient, and even with the Roman Church. Luther and his friends misunderstood this reticence and thought Zwingli a denier of the unmentioned doctrines, though Melanchthon's silence in the earlier editons of the *Loci* upon the same points, and his exprĕssion of some degree of contempt for such studies, might have led to worse conclusions as to his orthodoxy. But we now come into the region in which the great contest between Luther and Zwingli was waged, and in which Zwingli made an advance upon all his contemporaries,—to the doctrine of the Sacraments.

In this discussion the ***Commentary*** was the first production of Zwingli's by which he was willing to stand. He expressly says that his previous treatment of the theme in the Sixty-seven Articles was written for the times rather than to declare the whole truth, "that he might not cast pearls before swine."[56] The ***Commentary*** represents his matured views, and although he wrote much afterwards in his controversy with Luther, the history of which has already been elsewhere detailed,[57] he added nothing and modified nothing of any importance to the understanding of his theological system.

He begins by mentioning three views,[58] all of which he rejects, viz.: (1) That the sacrament is something which by its own power liberates the conscience from sin [the magical theory of the sacraments]; (2) that it is a sign upon the performance of which the thing signified is internally performed; (3) that it is a sign given for the purpose of rendering him who receives it certain that that which is signified by the sacrament has already been performed. In opposition to these he defines his own view. It is that the sacrament is a dedication and a consecration (*initio et oppignoratio*) and a public setting of the person apart (*publica consignatio*). "Having been initiated, a man must do that which the function, order, or institute with which he has connected himself demands."[59] It follows at once from this conception that the sacrament has no power to liberate the conscience. God alone can cleanse the soul. The first of the above theories is thus disposed of. As for the second, if the cleansing be performed, the subject is conscious of it, for it is done by the inward act of faith; and faith must be conscious. Zwingli's great purpose in opposing Luther's doctrine as well as that of Rome comes here into view. It was to rescue the true character of faith. In reply to the third he says, that for the same reason one does not need a pledge that the cleansing has already been performed. If it has, he knows it, and that is enough. The great gift of God is thus, in Zwingli's mind, a matter of experience. He sometimes makes it identical with faith, this being, upon one side, a conscious act, and upon the other, the sum and substance of the life into which the Christian is ushered through forgiveness. He lives a life of faith—that is, faith may designate his highest experiences. And this faith, he says over and over again, is a fact, an experience, not a mere matter of intellectual knowledge and imagination, or a mere opinion. It is trust in Christ, a new direction of the purposes and affections of the man, a wholly internal operation of the soul itself; and it is therefore produced not by external means, which can produce only external changes, but by the Holy Spirit. Neither is the Holy Spirit bound to external means or limited by them. The object of faith, likewise, is always Christ or God as revealed in Christ, and it can therefore have no material thing, like the body of Christ, or the nature of the elements in the sacrament of the altar, for its proper object. Whether the elements of the sacrament are bread and wine or the real body and blood of the Lord is a question for the determination of the mind by means of sensation and perception, not for faith, which has nothing to do with such objects. When the theologians of the Roman

Church say, "We *believe* that we *perceive* the real body and blood of the Lord at the alter," they utterly confound faith with what is totally different. Zwingli also objects to Luther's view as obscuring the nature of faith and as confounding its object.[60]

This effort of Zwingli in behalf of a consistent definition of faith may well be counted as among his most important contributions to the cause of evangelical truth. That faith is a spiritual process, produced by spiritual means, is a far-reaching principle of the utmost importance. Much as Protestant theology has insisted upon faith, it has long been obscure in defining it. Could Zwingli's fundamental ideas have been fully received, that faith is an act of self-committal, that it is a spiritual process of the soul, that it is conscious, and that it is the eternal life which Christ promised, already in exercise and possession, then long and gloomy chapters in the history of Reformed Theology, in which the story of spiritual paralysis in consequence of ignorance of the way of salvation and positive misrepresentation of the gift of divine forgiveness, might have been spared the world. Even the theologian, evangelist, and saint, Jonathan Edwards, could say to an inquirer:

> You must not think much of your pains, and of the length of time; you must press towards the kingdom of God, and do your utmost, and hold out to the end; and learn to make no account of it when you have done. You must undertake the business of seeking salvation upon these terms and with no other expectation than this, that *if ever God bestows* mercy, it will be in His own time, and not only so, but also, when you have done all, *God will not hold Himself obliged* to show you mercy at last.[61]

But Zwingli would never have written such a travesty of the Gospel, and Zwingli's clearness and breadth would have spared generations of Calvinists, before Edwards and after him, from the necessity of consequent darkness and pain.

In accordance with this general view of the sacraments Zwingli defines the first sacrament which he discusses, which is baptism,[62] matrimony being excluded from the number of true sacraments. Baptism is not a sacrament which conveys the grace which it signifies. To John the Baptist it was an essential part of his teaching. It said as by a visible word that, as one bathed comes forth from the bath cleansed, so they that are baptised ought to put off the old life of sin and begin a new life. It also pledged them to this. Such baptism is to be distinguished from the baptism of the Holy Spirit, which is of two sorts: an inward baptism, which is equivalent to the creation of true faith, and an outward, such as that through which the Apostles spoke with tongues. In our day, not all receive the latter baptism, but all who are truly religious have become so through the illumination and drawing of the Holy Spirit. There is, however, no distinction between the baptism of John and that of Christ. Christ did not demand a new baptism of His disciples when they had once been baptised by John, nor is the purpose of the two baptisms different. Both preached repentance, and both baptised with the same purpose. Christian baptism is baptism into the name of the Father and the Son and the Holy Spirit, by which they who formerly served the Devil now consecrate themselves to the Father, Son, and Spirit.[63]

In the special treatise upon "Baptism, Re-Baptism, and Infant Baptism"[64] the same general views reappear. Baptism is a sign that obligates the one baptised to the Lord Jesus, but salvation is not dependent upon it. It cannot wash away sins. It is not necessary to rebaptise those who were baptised in the Roman Church, because infant baptism is itself valid and because we may be reasonably certain of our baptism, since there are numerous witnesses of it. And then baptism is essentially a single act, not to be repeated. The validity of infant baptism rests upon the analogy of circumcision, and is equally proper with that as a sign to hold children to their duty to God. Infant baptism probably began in the time of Christ, for there is nothing against it in the New Testament, and much that may be cited for it. Indeed, the children of Christians, as standing under the covenant of God with His people, and as the children of God, ought to be baptised.

In regard to the Lord's Supper, Zwingli defines it, with special reference to the Greek word *eucharist,* as a thanksgiving, a festival of thanksgiving among those who proclaim the death of Christ. It involves also the element of self-consecration, and is an act more for the community of Christians before whom the communicant professes thus his faith in Christ than for the communicant himself. Hence Zwingli came to the view that its nature is that of a symbol, and he adopted the tropical interpretation of the word "is" in the words of institution, "This is my body," paraphrasing it, "This represents my body," thus sweeping away at once the whole theory of what has been called consubstantiation, as well as transubstantiation.[65]

The following year after the appearance of the ***Commentary***, Luther began the series of controversial writings which were interchanged between himself and Zwingli, and from that time until the Marburg Colloquy in 1529 the pen of neither of them had very long repose. Zwingli developed his views with great acuteness and dialectic skill, but he added little to their substance. The Colloquy brought him neither instruction nor change. It was more evident there, however, what was the fundamental question at issue, and this was, in a word, the spirituality of religion. Zwingli, in accordance with the natural consequences of the emphasis which he laid upon the sole causality of God, maintained the freedom of the Spirit of God in his converting operations, and exhibited a surprising breadth of view, embracing within the gracious operations of God even noted cases of moral excellence among the heathen, like Socrates.[66] Luther, influenced excessively by the historical tendencies of the Roman Church, was inclined to emphasise the necessity of the means, and to restrict the operations of the Spirit to those to whom the Word was preached and the sacraments administered. To him the Gospel appeared to be evacuated of its power and rendered superfluous if such men as Socrates, who had never received it, could nevertheless be saved. With all his large-heartedness, Luther was seriously limited in his horizon. In Zwingli there appeared the tendency which has been characteristic of the Reformed Theology ever since—the tendency to ascribe perfect reasonableness to the doctrines of the Gospel and to interpret the Scriptures largely upon the supposition that they must be reasonable, while yet yielding to them the cordial assent of simple faith in regions where evidently they speak above human comprehension.

Discussions upon the sacrament, inasmuch as they had to do with the human Christ, naturally led, both in Luther's and in Zwingli's case, to further consideration of the subject of Christology. With Luther, this developed in the period before Marburg into discussions of the eternal pre-existence of Christ's body, and into the doctrine of the "Communication of Properties" (*communicatio idiomatum*), whereby each nature was supposed to communicate to the other its peculiar properties, while at the same time it did not itself cease to be what it was. Luther subsequently developed this doctrine still farther and involved himself in difficulties both conscious and unconscious. Zwingli remained rather upon the ground of the simple doctrine of Chalcedon: that there are two natures, human and divine, each perfect and entire, that they are not confounded, and that each remains what it is according to its own character. His phraseology shows in many places a tendency to that balancing of the two natures over against one another which is characteristic of the creed of Chalcedon.[67] He sought to explain the phenomena of the Scriptures upon which Luther had based his communication of properties by means of . . . transference. This takes place when "one names one of the two natures and understands the other; or names that which they both are and understands nevertheless only one of the two."[68] This is enough, he thinks, to explain the whole of the matter. With him, as with the ancient theologians, the divine Logos is the personalising principle of the Christ. But into further efforts to clear up the mystery of the nature of Christ, he does not go. His strength in this direction seems to be consumed by the many efforts he makes to exhibit the inconsistencies and absurdities of Luther's ideas and to win him to a simpler theory of the Eucharist.

With this theme is naturally connected the doctrine of the work of Christ, upon which Zwingli often lets fall incidental remarks in passing and which he treats more at length in the ***Fidei Christianæ Expositio***.[69] In these scattering remarks the various points which needed emphasizing against the papal corruptions of the day are brought out fully and cogently. The fact that the death of Christ is the only meritorious cause of our salvation against the doctrine of good works, His sole mediatorship between God and man, His death as the great exhibition of God's love towards men, the redemption of men from death and the devil, the perfect revelation through Him of the will of God, are thus incidentally developed.

Zwingli's theology, as thus sketched by him, is in substantial agreement with that of the other Reformers both Lutheran and Calvinistic. It subsequently admitted without difficulty the practical union of the German with the French Swiss in doctrine and practice. At Marburg he was able without difficulty to subscribe a statement of doctrine drawn up by Luther, with whom his only great difference was that upon the nature of the sacrament of the Lord's Supper. He was, however, decidedly marked by the freer and broader spirit of the humanistic circles. Luther was a man of greater heart, of a profounder emotional nature, and of a more vivid experience of the great life forces of Christianity. He seized upon the truth by intuition and defended it with stormy and violent eagerness. He was but to a small degree capable of putting himself in the place of an antagonist, estimating him correctly, and meeting him successfully. He often refused to read his adversaries' writings. Zwingli was clearer, keener, calmer, informed himself accurately upon the subjects which he would discuss, and debated them with more comprehensiveness. Above all, he was broader in his view of things in general, as he was to a larger degree a man of affairs. He could ascribe merit to those with whom he disagreed, and could embrace even the pagan world in his scheme of the universe. Luther denied the freedom of the will to emphasise the certainty of salvation from God. Zwingli denied it to emphasise God's causality. Luther thus looked upon man as so sinful in his enslaved condition that there was no hope for him aside from the established means of grace. Zwingli saw the operation of God in all the world and hoped for the operation of grace beyond the bounds of the Church. This freer spirit Zwingli handed down to the Reformed theology; and though it was often eclipsed by other elements, it has not been without its continuous influence to the present day.

Zwingli's ethics received no systematic development at his hand with the single exception of the treatise written in 1523 upon the "Education of Noble Youths,"[70] and here only in connection with the general subject of education. The whole theme is discussed from a Christian standpoint, the object of the education which Zwingli describes being to develop the highest type of Christian manhood. Education begins, therefore, in the knowledge of God, whose nature as manifested in creation and providence is to be taught the youth. The effort is here to be made to lead the young man from a knowledge of his sins to the knowledge of the Redeemer and to the living and personal apprehension of the way of salvation. Upon the basis of such a religious change in the soul, the teacher is to seek to form a blameless life. To this end he is to inculcate constant acquaintance with the Word of God. To this, the knowledge of languages is necessary, and here Zwingli warns against temptations to use superior knowledge as a means of gratifying wantonness, ambition, love of power, deceitfulness, vain philosophy, etc. On the contrary, the youth must be instructed in the duty of modesty and reticence in discourse, propriety and conformity to usage in the choice of words, in gesture, and delivery; in temperance and simplicity in the reception of food and drink and in clothing and personal adornment; in chastity and self-control in his relations with the female sex. He is especially to be warned against the desire of money and fame, and is to be taught to imitate Christ in all these things. He may learn fencing, but only so far as is necessary to the defence of the fatherland. Especially is idleness to be avoided, and no one is to be received into the citizenship of the state who has not a trade by which he can earn his own living. The law of love to our neighbour is to be impressed and enforced. It demands a true, inner sympathy and participation in the lot of others, whether joy or sorrow. This leads to a discussion of social relations with our fellow men; and while festivals and parties are not forbidden, they are to be enjoyed with moderation. Obedience to parents is to be insisted upon. Self-control, as of the temper, is to be sought. Games may be played, but not those which furnish no exercise for the mind, like dice and cards. In all things should genuineness and love control the conduct towards one's fellow men. "It is the work of a Christian not to be able to utter great things upon the dogmas, but to render great and weighty services, by the help of God."[71]

In this brief outline we get the general conception of a Christian life which Zwingli had. Without asceticism or undue severity, it was to be a sober, God-fearing, earnest, and useful life.

*Notes*

[1] *Werke,* Erlangen edition, xxiv., 146.

[2] *De Servo Arbitrio,* cap. xvii.

[3] Zwingli, *Werke,* ed. Schuler u. Schulthess, i., 169-424.

[4] *Ibid.,* i., 541-565.

[5] *Ibid.,* iii., 145-325.

[6] *Ibid.,* iv., 1-18.

[7] *Ibid.,* iv., 79-144.

[8] Zwingli, *Werke,* ed. Schuler u. Schulthess, iv., 42-78.

[9] Zwingli, *Werke,* ed. Schuler u. Schulthess, iii., 156.

[10] Zwingli, *Werke,* ed. Schuler u. Schulthess, iii., p. 158.

[11] *Ibid.,* p. 159.

[12] *Ibid.,* p. 159.

[13] Zwingli, *Werke,* ed. Schuler u. Schulthess, iii., pp. 159 *sq.*

[14] *Hoc solum deus est quod perfectum est, id est, absolutum et cui nihil desit, cuique omnia adsint qua summum bonum deceant.* It would be an error to suppose these expressions to have anything in common with modern ideas of the "Absolute" so much favoured in our own country. "Absolute" means to Zwingli, as this context shows, simply "complete," "perfect."

[15] P. 160.

[16] P. 163.

[17] P. 163.

[18] P. 168.

[19] P. 169.

[20] P. 169.

[21] III., p. 203.

[22] IV., p. 6 *ff.*

[23] IV., 79-144.

[24] P. 81.

[25] P. 84.

[26] P. 85.

[27] P. 86.

[28] P. 93.

[29] P. 98.

[30] P. 101.

[31] P. 102.

[32] *Ibid.*

[33] P. 104.

[34] P. 106.

[35] P. 108.

[36] P. 111.

[37] P. 113.

[38] P. 121.

[39] P. 104.

[40] III., p. 155.

[41] P. 173.

[42] P. 179.

[43] P. 189.

[44] IV., 42.

[45] IV., 47.

[46] III., 192.

[47] III., 199.

[48] P. 203.

[49] P. 273 *f.*

[50] P. 226; *cf.* i., 469.

[51] III., 226; *cf.* i., 469.

[52] III., 135.

[53] P. 128; *cf.* i., 468, 470.

[54] P. 128.

[55] *E. g.*, iii., 251.

[56] III., 239 *sq.*

[57] See Chapter XIV and Index.

[58] III., 228.

[59] P. 229.

[60] III., 248.

[61] *Works,* Dwight edition, v., 467.

[62] P. 232.

[63] In his *De Providentia Dei* (iv., 125), Zwingli says: "Since all the elect were elected before the establishment of the world, and the infants of the faithful are of the Church, there is no doubt that when these infants die they are received into the number of the blessed according to election, which the Apostle says remains sure."

[64] German, of the year 1525, *Werke,* ii., 1. 230 *sqq.*

[65] III., 253.

[66] IV., 65.

[67] IV., 181; ii., 2, 67.

[68] II., 68.

[69] IV., 47 *sq.*

[70] IV., 148 *sqq.* See this volume, pp. 211, *sq.*

[71] IV., 158.

## Karl Barth (essay date 1922)

SOURCE: "Calvin, Luther, and Zwingli," in *The Theology of John Calvin,* translated by Geoffrey W. Bromiley, William B. Eerdmans Publishing Company, 1995, pp. 69-128.

[*In this excerpt from his noted study of Calvin, originally published in 1922, Barth discusses Zwingli's thought in relation to that of both Calvin and Luther.*]

In taking Calvin as the specifically and typically Reformed reformer as distinct from Luther, what I have in mind is that because of Zwingli's early death we have only Calvin's and not Zwingli's Reformed theology before us in developed systematic form, and it was Calvin, not Zwingli, who in large part left his imprint on the Reformed world. For a proper understanding of Calvin, however, we must not overlook the fact that the so-to-speak classical representative of the Reformed possibility was Zwingli. In a pure, one-sided, not too cautious, and very exposed form, the Reformed trend is much more prominent in him than in Calvin, who worked out much more sharply the dialectical relation to Lutheranism and thus took some of the edge off the antithesis. In the relation Zwingli was a pure type like the younger Luther. But the pure, or relatively pure, is not always historically the most powerful, and Zwingli's theology could no more establish itself than that of the younger Luther. Since the gods did not love Luther enough to grant him an early death, his early theology was given a historically viable form by the later Luther, then above all by Melanchthon.[1] In Zwingli's case, however, the death of its author, the lack of an executor of Melanchthon's stature, and above all the superior competition of the system of Calvin, which better met the general situation, did not allow his theology, or spared it, that type of conservation. We thus have to compare Luther and Zwingli but then compare both with Calvin as a new and third force if we are to see how the latter, having the experience of both behind him, uniting the possibilities they chose in some sense in himself, and even pressing them to their final logic, proclaimed perhaps a higher synthesis of the two, and perhaps spoke the last and ripest word of the Reformation. We can then see that in Calvin we have the harvest time but certainly also the melancholy late summer of the Reformation. We can then see how he is—as I simply indicated earlier—the truly tragic and the most profoundly problematic figure of the Reformation age.

First, however, we must see what linked Zwingli and Calvin together. I have referred to the resolutely taken step from the knowledge of God into the real world. These two were the prophets of the new Christian ethos. On three sides they spoke words that sounded very much the same.

1. The advocates of a moderate reform of the Catholic church had already throughout the 15th century and even earlier laid down the postulate of a renewal of Christian life according to the laws of God. The early 16th-century religious Humanists, of whom we have already spoken, powerfully took up their message. The new thing in Reformed activism as compared with the good and pious ideals of those sincere friends of progress was its unconditional nature. Earlier the postulate of a "reformation of both head and members"[2] had been a possibility; on the lips of Zwingli and Calvin it was a "Notwithstanding," a moral imperative with an estranging otherworldly emphasis because it was paradoxically related to a break with belief in our natural human goodness such as we never find in Wycliffe or a hundred years later in Erasmus, and because it was grounded in a concept of God such as they had never envisioned. The OT was discovered, and in it the majesty of God, and therewith the shattering seriousness of the problem of a real Christian life in the world. The Reformed started out with the thought of the divine providence that encompasses all things.[3] They viewed the Bible as simply the divine confirmation of the natural law that is written in the conscience.[4] These ideas naturally sounded congenial to Humanist ears. But the resultant ardor for the glory of God, with its bitter Mosaic taste, was accepted by none of those enlightened thinkers, to whom nothing could be more alien than the strange zeal for God that their converted colleagues represented.

2. The Enthusiasts too, whether along the lines of a free, mystically based individualism or along more moral, legal, and ascetic lines, demanded a reconstruction of life by the Holy Spirit, about whom they read in the Bible and on whose presence they thought they might count. There was certainly a link, though not a direct one, between the Reformed glory of God and the radical offensive launched by such circles. Martin Bucer sympathized with them, and Bucer's Christianity seems to have influenced Calvin. But if we look more closely we see that the attacks were different on the two fronts. The Anabaptists were separated from the Reformed by the same thing as the Humanists, namely, by the optimism with which they believed that a little of the Spirit and love would bring about a transformation of life. But then—and this is even more important—they encountered in the Reformed the soberness, or, let us openly say, the rationalism with which the latter asserted the unconditional nature of the divine command in which the Anabaptists also believed. The new knowledge of the grace of God in Christ did not give the Reformed any cause to leave the solid ground of this world's reality and to lose themselves to God's glory in the boundlessness of religious feeling. Instead, it gave them every reason to set themselves for the first time firmly on that solid ground, and there—where else?—to do to God's glory, not the impossible, but all that they could do within the limits of the possible. They grasped the thought and took it to its logical conclusion, that the God of creation is one and the same God as the God of redemption, that his providence rules over the kingdom of nature as well as that of grace, and that even though our knowledge of it has been obscured by the fall, the natural law that underlies the written laws of family, society, and the state is simply confirmed by the law revealed in the Bible. Again it was the OT that rendered the decisive service at this point, by marking out at least the bridge between that natural law and the demands of, for example, the Sermon on the Mount. Living according to the law and living according to the gospel are just as surely one and the same thing as the God of Moses and the Father of Jesus Christ are one and the same.

3. Luther was also on the scene. He, too, had something to say about ethics. He, too, was enthusiastically hailed by friends of light of every type, including Radicals on the extreme left. The new thing in the Reformed as compared to Luther was not something really new, as we have seen already. It was simply that they were in a position to take what Luther said more seriously than he did himself: without his separation of law and gospel, of the kingdom of the world and the kingdom of God, by which he had quickly alienated the hearts of both Humanists and Enthusiasts; without the slight hesitation of the former monk face-to-face with the need truly and unconditionally to accept things as they are in the world with all that that acceptance entails; yet also without the romantic explanations with which, basically alien to the world, he artfully evaded things as they are; in short, without the zigzags that

betray his great uncertainty in this area. The NT with a similar earthly comprehensibility and applicability as the OT; the apostles of Jesus Christ with the same total ruthlessness as Moses or Elijah; a message of divine mercy sounding forth like the blast of a trumpet; a Christianity equipped for action and armed to the teeth, stripped of the most beautiful illusions and prepared for the worst eventualities—there we have the new thing in the Reformed as compared to Luther. Something involving decisive renewal was undoubtedly here, something incomparably more important than the new thing that the Humanists and Anabaptists thought they found in Luther, but also something incomparably more dangerous. For precisely in the hesitant uncertainty of Luther face-to-face with the ethical problem lies the primary meaning and vitality of the Reformation, which at all events cries out for a second turn to complete it, but not for a step that will betray and surrender the new knowledge and return to the harlot reason[5] and the ungodliness of the papacy, as Luther might put it.

Two things could happen when the Reformation took leave of Luther's hesitation and emerged unequivocally as an ethical Reformation. It might, as we have said, lose its primary meaning and basis, spread itself abroad without power or worth, and merge into the cultural and political movements of the age. Or, with all the power and worth of its primary meaning and basis, it might take the form of the most radical and principled movement of all, surpassing and absorbing all the other movements, advancing into every area of human existence in the power of the knowledge of God, in an act of self-reflection and conversion on the part of Western humanity with unimaginable consequences, in short, in an event of almost eschatological breadth—though naturally we say "almost," for *last* things do not take place on earth, and yet why should not *little* things and even *great* things do so? Why should we not be allowed to believe that great things may also take place in history? Zwingli believed this, naively, firmly, confidently, more consistently than Calvin. That was his greatness and his problem. Luther also had this belief that great things are possible in history. Why not? It is almost impossible to think that he, too, did not dream the bold dream of a renewal of human life in the West, at least in the years 1517-1520. He knew, however, why he hesitated to take the great step in this direction, why he was so cautious. He recognized the greatness of the undertaking, of attempting this transformation of a purely religious movement with all the power of its origins. He was aware of the immeasurable danger that threatened, namely, that the transformation might be successful but the incomparable and priceless origins might be lost. Can we ever say how it came about that Luther's holy fear for the cause of God finally overcame his hope? We can only accept the result. Luther decided against that breakthrough into the world for the sake of the purity of what had to break through. He devoted his whole concern to guarding the priceless treasure, the noble Word of God, to keeping the gospel free of any admixture of nature, law, or reason.

It was for this reason that of all his opponents, with an antipathy surprising even in him, Luther called "den Zwingel," as he named him, a non-Christian, who did not teach the Christian faith correctly in any point, and who was seven times worse than if he had been a papist (30, 225).[6] He saw in Zwingli the man who in the most open way conceivable did the opposite of what he himself regarded as right in the interests of the cause of God. His heartfelt difficulty with Zwingli finds especially clear expression in a passage in the *Table Talk* (61, 16) under the heading "Enthusiasts Are Presumptuous and Foolhardy":

> The presumption and foolhardiness of the Enthusiasts is very harmful, for by it they fall and plunge themselves into trouble and distress. Listen to Zwingli's call: "Nothing can stop us, let us break through, in three years you will see that Spain, France, England, and all Germany will come to the gospel and accept it." They are so certain of this, only reluctantly praying our Lord God even once that his name be hallowed, etc., but let us break through, he said. With this fabled triumph and victory, however, he harmed himself, gave the gospel a bad name so that it was blasphemed, and strengthened the papacy. (How sad, all the Swiss have gone over to the papacy and built churches and altars, etc., except Zurich, Bern, and Basel, and unfortunately they will not hold out long.) This is what they have done with their *perrumpamus,* their breaking through; they are proud, presumptuous, and rely on their own good cause. And even if they had a truly good cause (which they have not), they should pray to God for success and blessing. For what is more right than the gospel! Yet we must always pray: Hallowed be thy name! Righteousness and progress and good fortune and good counsel must kiss each other. And the fools, even though in truth they are uncertain of their teaching, still do not pray.[7]

Luther's complaint against Zwingli was that with too great self-confidence, especially without praying the first petition of the Lord's Prayer, he wanted to lead the gospel to triumph in the world under the slogan *perrumpamus* or breakthrough, thus doing the greatest possible harm to it and bringing himself to ruin. How heartfelt was this complaint may be seen from the fact that he not only pursued Zwingli when alive with all conceivable invective, but even after his death spoke of his fate with pitiless and sanctimonious narrow-mindedness: "I could wish from my heart that Zwingli were saved, but I must fear the contrary, for Christ commands us to judge and decide as follows, that God will not know those who deny him and do not know him, or those who deny him and give the lie to him for the people. Those who do not believe are condemned already" (62, 15).[8]

We have to admit that Luther could think of Zwingli in no other way. Zwingli was indeed reckless. He could not understand, let alone even in the slightest share, Luther's concern for the purity of the gospel. He could not take this into account. He knew no restraint. Probably the idea that sheer movement might lead to the loss of the origins and goal never entered his head. He was the overconfident one who seemed to know only one question: How do we do it? That the whole Zwingli is described with that *perrumpamus* and a total forgetting of the first petition of the Lord's Prayer, and that there is no little corner for him in heaven, is a judgment that rests on Luther's nearsighted perspective, but how else could Luther see and depict him? It is not from Luther but from modern Lutherans that we should demand that Zwingli be finally treated with rather more objectivity and respect than is still the case. Eternally repeating Luther's narrow-mindedness does not really give credibility to the ongoing spirit and work of Luther.

At that time there could be no reconciling the antithesis. The two were both peasant sons. They both had sound but incorrigibly stubborn minds. They both had the same urge. They were both deeply claimed by the problems of the great movement of the age of which they were representatives and spearheads. Both were thus born leaders. For the rest, they were totally different. On the one hand was a heavy-blooded and troubled Thuringian, on the other hand an awakened and orderly and not easily overturned East Swiss such as one may still find in St. Gall canton, who would not let recollection of the last things in any way disturb his initiatives for the present, not in the least! Luther the North German was full of respectful regard for the system of divinely willed realities and dependencies, so that he was most incensed that Zwingli had supposedly once said that a window is as easily seen through as a pious prince (59, 248).[9] Zwingli had no fundamental reverence or regard for anything smacking of mediatorship, intermediate rule, or provisional authority—a quality I must beg you to take into account today if you want to understand us Swiss. The one was the child of a politically and culturally rather backward zone, the other was at the heart of what was then the blossoming urban culture of the German South. In the Reformation period there were Zwinglians in East Friesland, and there was a Lutheran party in Switzerland, especially Basel and Bern, from the early 1530s; indeed, Lutheran thinking and sentiments are not uncommon in Switzerland even to our own time, the proof being that today Ritschlian theology, as we may calmly admit, is the dominant theology among us.[10]

The decisive difference between Luther and Zwingli was the difference between the hesitation of the one with its basis in faith and the *perrumpamus* of the other with its basis in ethos. It is easy enough constantly to see Zwingli through Luther's spectacles and then, like Loofs and Tschackert and others before them,[11] to offer the caricature that associates Zwingli with the Anabaptist Enthusiasts as a former Humanist who could not properly differentiate religion and culture, Christianity and politics. It is equally easy, as we see especially in Ragaz in modern Switzerland, to detest Luther, accusing him of being the great Quietist and the father of an exclusive focus on divine grace that results in reaction.[12] In my view both these evaluations are impermissible simplifications of the historical truth, and a judicious Lutheran or Reformed theologian will have to come beseechingly into the midst and ask above all else for a little calm and justice on both sides. We must not tear apart the unity of the problem that links Luther and Zwingli even though we must strongly emphasize the difference between them within this context.

Since ethics, the turning to life with all that it involves, was Luther's problem too, inadequate though his solution might be, we must again underline this fact. Yet we must also say that Zwingli was undoubtedly a *total* Humanist, a *total* man of the Reformation, a *total* politician, a *total* Swiss. He was all these things totally, astonishingly, and often annoyingly, unrestrainedly, unbrokenly, and one-sidedly. But if the monasticism from which Luther came, and which gave him a tendency toward resignation, proves nothing against his ethical seriousness, the Humanism from which Zwingli came, and which gave him a tendency toward activism, proves nothing against the seriousness of his faith. Nor can we say that the antithesis of Saxon or Swiss, of reverence or lack of it, of being a man of spirituality or of reform, of being born with the mind of a subject or with a sense of political democracy in the kingdom of God, played any decisive role. Luther too, in his creatureliness, was what he was *totally* in a way no less annoying and questionable than that of Zwingli. If we do not see this in the haze that surrounds Luther, I can only assure you that it is so when we look at him more clearly from a greater distance. We must demand that on both sides regard should be had not to what is creaturely but to the sign preceding what is creaturely. We miss the main point in characterizing Zwingli if we do not go on to say: Yes indeed, a Humanist, a man of the Reformation, a politician, a Swiss, but also a converted Humanist, man of the Reformation, politician, and Swiss, who in intention at least had his basis in God, in the God of Luther and Paul. Were not all the creaturely elements that we see in him, and also in Luther, possibilities—no more, yet possibilities, equally good and bad in both cases? And who gives whom the right as a historian to call into question the purity of Zwingli's intention to a higher degree than anything that is human?

Certainly there was something secular and worldly and daylight-clear about Zwingli's style. In him we look in vain for the half-light, the obscurity, and the mystical bent of the German mind. In the eucharistic controversy the deep-rooted instinct of Luther that some mediation of salvation is needed collided with the equally deep-rooted instinct of Zwingli that salvation is only from God, from the *one* God. Mediation came for him when the voice of the heavenly Captain was heard and his banner was perceived on earth.[13] There is nothing soulful about that. Yet the first turn in the Reformation did not come in Luther's German mind but in his faith. In comparison with the German mind Zwingli's Swiss and urban activism is not at any rate a nuance in the colorful array of legitimate human possibilities that necessarily means exclusion from the kingdom of heaven. In worth and significance the zeal for monotheism is at least on a par with the zeal for the thought of mediation.

We can indubitably describe as rationalism Zwingli's stubborn fight for the purely intellectual nature of Christianity that historically and in principle was his starting point and at least historically the point at which he parted company with Luther. But no matter how much or how little he had in common with what we call the Humanism of the time, we must ponder the fact that Erasmus at all events rejected Zwingli no less than he did Luther.[14] We then have to realize that this rationalism was paradoxically the same as the exclusive belief in revelation that so sharply opposed any transposition of the this-worldly into the otherworldly because it so emphasized the transposition of the otherworldly into the this-worldly, the glory of God in the world. This rationalism is the essence of what I have called the second turn in the Reformation. Are we to say that rationalism is a possibility for which there is no place in the kingdom of God? Are Plato and Kant divided from Christ because they were decided rationalists? Is the rationalisitic spirit of antiquity and of the modern period less capable of a conversion, of a resurrection from the dead, than the irrationalistic spirit of the Middle Ages? Does not everything depend upon the preceding sign? Those who are justified by faith alone must give glory *alone,* give *glory,* to the Justifier. To this urgent concern everything mystical, sacramental, and cultic, everything that is an image of deity, cannot but appear to be a hindrance and disruption. The *ratio* of the justification that is grasped in faith has to be at once the *ratio* of moral action. What is ruled out is the ambivalence of a religious world that comes between an equally resolutely affirmed otherworldly and this-worldly. For Zwingli religion was the knowledge of God and obedience, not a third thing. Christ does not give his people anything passive (4, 152).[15] That is what seemed to the Lutherans to be so secular in Zwingli, the rationalistic element.

In spite of his Christian rationalism, no, because of it, Zwingli opened up the abyss of the fall, original sin, justification, and faith no less profoundly than Luther. His view, reminiscent of Abelard, that original sin is not guilt but *morbus,* a *Prästen,* was certainly not meant to excuse the *philautia* (self-love) of which the *Prästen* consists, but to show that we have here a plight that is so great that the moral term "guilt" cannot cover it, so great that there is only one answer to it, namely, the grace and election of God.[16] Again, the elect pagans with whom Zwingli peopled heaven, Hercules to Seneca,[17] were not an indication that he took any the less seriously our lost estate. Instead, they indicate that he did not see the division between heaven and hell, between Christ and unredeemed humanity, as directly dependent upon the presence or absence of Christian means of grace in the church, but wanted to anchor the Christianity or otherwise of individuals in the freedom of the redeeming God—a thought that is simply unavoidable if we think through strictly the concept of grace and take seriously the redemption effected in Christ, but that has nothing whatever to do with any glorifying or even saving of what we are by nature.[18] "We as little know what God is as the scarabeus knows what a human being is" (***On True and False Religion,*** 1, 157).[19]

Like Luther, Zwingli called the Spirit of God who brings us self-knowledge, and assures us of forgiveness, an alien power or force (1, 192).[20] He expressly adopted the central thesis of Luther that the whole of the Christian life must be penitence (1, 194).[21] He was indeed an optimist and enthusiast, but we find in him not the slightest trace of optimism regarding our nature and situation apart from the grace of God, nor of any enthusiastic overrating of our human possibilities apart from the divine possibility. He recognized the full paradox of the relation between God and us. Nevertheless, again at one with Luther in principle, beyond that abyss and in light of the divine possibility, he not only saw but thought he could tread with a sure step the ground of our relative possibilities, the ground of ethics and history. The paradoxical confidence with which he not only demanded this step but thought it through and carried it through with all its implications is what distinguished him from Luther. At first he envisioned a carrying through of the Reformation, of the renewal of life, in the very banal and local form of opposition to the abuses in the Switzerland of his day associated with foreign mercenary service.[22] But then he had the vision of a renewal of the whole of Western cultural life in the spirit of the Pauline doctrine of justification. He not only dreamed up this possibility but thought it out clearly and set to work soberly enough to achieve it even to the point of the daring plan of a European alliance against the Hapsburgs as the leading papal power.[23] This was the *perrumpamus* that Luther took so ill.

We must do justice to Luther's objections. As criticisms of Zwingli's attitude they were right. But the attitude of Luther underlying them was also not free from criticism. We might well say to Zwingli: Where is the humility? Where is the waiting? But we can just as well say to Luther: Where is the courage? Where is the hastening?[24] There is no reason to accuse Zwingli one-sidedly if we keep in view the dialectic of the whole Reformation. It will not do simply to depict Zwingli's common sense as a lack of religious depth, his clarity of understanding as intellectualism, his urgent cry from the heart for a brave deed as moralism, his total and boldly direct relating of God to the things of this world as pantheism,[25] his more lofty and more mundane political action as typically religio-social arrogance. We must try to understand, in the first instance without evaluating, the intention and intuition behind all such things, the Reformation offensive that he had in view. Certainly he often gave a bad impression with what he did and said, but in the opposite sense this was no less true of Luther's hesitation. In reality Zwingli, too, kept in mind the infinite gap between Creator and creature, the "finite not capable of the infinite,"[26] and much better indeed than his later critics and teachers.

It was precisely this awareness, however, awareness of the remoteness of God that is also his nearness, which in relative distinction from Luther would not let him hesitate but drove him sharply into action. We may stand before his incomplete life and work as before the fragments of an unfinished house, and shaking our heads ask whether it could ever possibly have been complete, yet not forgetting that beyond our human wisdom the truth still holds that in great things it is enough to have the desire.[27] And what do we really know? Perhaps if Zwingli had lived any longer he might have been like the man who wanted to build a tower without counting the cost [Luke 14:28], and his enterprise would have ended up choked and sterile and brutalized and secularized and divorced from the church because the power and worth of its origins were no longer in it. But was not that the fate of the whole Reformation, even of the Lutheran Reformation with its much more modest spirit of adventure? It might also have been, however, that the great thing that Zwingli expected from God, and that he believed he should fight for, would actually have come to pass. Zwingli's vitality, at least, was not broken even when he fell on the field of Cappel.

No matter how we assess the possibilities, however, one thing is sure: in the work of this remarkably restless and remarkably cold-blooded man from the Toggenburg, who was well adapted for it both by nature and by grace, we see an attempt to do what Luther wanted to do purely but also for profound reasons did not want to do. In other words, we see the Reformed possibility in its most distinctive form. Dilthey said of Zwingli: "No man of the Reformation age understood Christianity in a way that was more manly, healthy, or simple" (1, ch. 525).[28] This secular verdict is unjust to Luther. For in a way no less manly, healthy, and simple, Luther was at the opposite pole of the movement. We must not expound his concern for the purity of the cause as the antithesis of the qualities extolled in Zwingli. There was also a restraint that was manly, healthy, and simple. Nevertheless, we must not take it amiss if a secular philosopher like Dilthey is especially warm to the second meaning of the Reformation, its ethical turn. The children of the world are often wiser than the children of light [cf. Luke 16:8]. And if Dilthey found a type of this in Zwingli, as his words surely indicate, then in this regard he was right.

*Notes*

[1] Cf. Plautus, *Bacchides,* IV, 7, 18, on the basis of a verse from Menander, *Fragments,* 125. Cf. Melanchthon's *Loci Communes* in the 1521, 1535, and 1542 editions.

[2] The demand for reform in head and members was a common one at Constance in 1414-1418, and we find it in the council decrees; cf. H. Jedin, ed., *Handbuch der Kirchengeschichte,* vol. III, 2 (Freiburg, Basel, and Vienna, 1968), 551f.; H. Bettenson, *Documents of the Christian Church* (London, 1975), 135.

[3] First found in the *Sermon on Providence;* cf. Z 6/III, 64ff.

[4] See n. 37 above on 86.

[5] Cf. Luther's *Wider die himmlischen Propheten . . .* (1525), WA 18, 164, 25-27: "die vernunfft des teuffels heurer."

[6] Cf. Luther's *Vom Abendmahl Christi, Bekenntnis* (1528), WA 26, 342, 21ff.

[7] WA TR, 3, 56, 11ff. (no. 2891b).

[8] Ibid., 1, 436, 27ff. (no. 875).

[9] Ibid., 3, 572, 3ff. (no. 3729).

[10] In East Friesland cf. esp. the work of John à Lasco (1499-1560) and his reforms as superintendent in Emden from 1543 to 1549. On the work of Lutheran-minded pastors in Bern and the Lutheran party there and in Basel from 1522 to 1540, cf. C. B. Hundeshagen, *Die Conflikte des Zwinglianismus, Lutherthums, und Calvinismus in der Bernischen Landeskirche von 1532-1558* (Bern, 1842), 59ff. Cf. K. Barth, "Die kirchlichen Zustände in der Schweiz" (1922), in *Vorträge und kleinere Arbeiten 1922-1925,* ed. H. Finze, vol. III of *Gesamtausgabe* (Zurich, 1990), 35.

[11] Loofs, *Leitfaden,* 800f.; and Tschackert, 257, who thinks Zwingli was closer politically to Savonarola than Luther.

[12] Cf. L. Ragaz, "Von den letzten Voraussetzungen der schweizerischen Neutralität," in *Die geistige Unabhängigkeit der Schweiz* (Zurich, 1916), 44, accusing Lutheranism of being Quietist and of accepting even the worst of earthly rulers under God's supreme rule. Cf. also M. Mattmüller, *Leonhard Ragaz und der religiöse Sozialismus; Fine Biographie,* vol. II (Zurich, 1968), 82.

[13] Cf., e.g., Zwingli's *Usslegen und gründ der schlussreden oder artiklen* (1523), thesis 6; Z 2, 52, 2-4; also Z 5, 307, 20ff.; and G. W. Locher, "Christus unser Hauptmann," in *Huldrych Zwingli in neuer Sicht* (Zurich, 1969), 55ff.

[14] Cf. Erasmus on Luther in a letter to Zwingli dated 8.31.1523, Z 8, 118, 2ff. (no. 315). As regards his attitude to Zwingli cf. his letter to him dated 9.8.1522, Z 7, 582, 1ff. (no. 236).

[15] Z 2, 542, 4, from *The Education of Youth;* cf. LCC, XXIV, 107: "Confidence in Christ does not make us idle."

[16] For Abelard's doctrine of original sin cf. Hagenbach, 368, who notes stress on sin as willing act and on motivation. Cf. Zwingli's *Usslegen und gründ . . .* on article 5; also *Züricher Einleitung* (1523), BSRK 8, 5, 21f.; 9, 9, 17; 13, 23; 51, 21, 23f.; also Hagenbach, 514; and Loofs, 805f.

[17] *Exposition of the Faith,* LCC, XXIV, 275. Seneca is not listed here, but there are many references to him; cf. 106.

[18] The view rejected by Barth is taken by Tschackert, 245, who traces the idea of the election of pagans to a weak view of sin.

[19] *Commentary on True and False Religion* (1525), Z 3, 643, 1ff.

[20] Ibid., 3, 692, 16ff. Luther, *Disputatio pro declaratione virtutis indulgentiarum* (1517), WA 1, 233, 10f.

[21] Zwingli, Z 3, 695, 20.

[22] Cf. the sermon to the Swiss Eidgenossen in May 1522, Z 1, 165ff.

[23] Cf. G. W. Locher, *Die Zwinglische Reformation im Rahmen der europäischen Kirchengeschichte* (Göttingen and Zurich, 1979), 514ff.

[24] In the two terms from 2 Pet. 3:12 Barth found the two aspects of Christian life in light of the eschaton as he saw it esp. in C. Blumhardt; cf. Barth, *Römerbrief,* 1st ed., vol. II of *Gesamtausgabe* (Zurich, 1985), 126 n. 20; and idem, *Ethics* (New York, 1981), §15.

[25] Cf. Loofs, 800; Tschackert, 243; W. Dilthey, "Das natürliche System der Geisteswissenschaften im 17. Jahrhundert," 225, who speaks of Zwingli's panentheism.

[26] Z 5, 354, 6ff. The actual formula does not occur in Zwingli or Calvin, but we find it in Lutheran-Reformed controversies in the later 16th century. Cf, A. Adam, *Lehrbuch der Dogmengeschichte,* vol. II (Gütersloh, 1st ed. 1972), 396; Barth, *Die christliche Dogmatik* (1927), vol. II of *Gesamtausgabe* (Zurich, 1928), 251f.

[27] Propertius, *Elegies,* II, 10, 5.

[28] Dilthey, *System,* 226.

**Rillet assesses Zwingli's overall importance to the Reformation:**

If Zwingli is the least known of the reformers, this is doubtless because of his Swiss origins. Not only is the scene on which his activity took place more restricted than the Germany of Luther, or the France of Calvin, but also the language which he used—the crude dialect of his Alpine valley—often remains incomprehensible to the foreign reader. He was born, he preached, he struggled and he died on a territory which hardly exceeded in size the limits of a province. His studies at Berne, Vienna and Basle, the military campaigns in Italy, and the colloquy of Marburg, alone free him at times from his narrow horizon. He possessed neither that passionate violence which made of the Saxon monk the inaugurator of a new era, nor the dialectical power which enabled the reformer of Geneva to publish at the age of twenty-seven his *Institutes of the Christian Religion.* The writings of the reformer of Zürich are difficult to compare with those of his two brilliant protagonists. Yet, the position which he occupies at their side is by no means a contemptible one. The lucidity of his mind and the radicalism of his views suffice to save him from oblivion. . . . .

*Jean Rillet, in* Zwingli: Third Man of the Reformation, *Lutterworth Press, 1964.*

**Charles Garside, Jr. (essay date 1966)**

SOURCE: "The Answer to Valentin Compar," in *Zwingli and the Arts*, Yale University Press, 1966, pp. 161-78.

*[In this excerpt, Garside analyzes Zwingli's rationale for his rejection of ecclesiastical and liturgical images and music.]*

Early on the second day of the Second Disputation Zwingli had remarked in passing that by comparison with the question of the Mass, that of images was a "childish matter" (2, 733, 8-9). Nevertheless, he was unable thereafter to dismiss those images so lightly. Unprepared as he had been to give Myconius genuinely effective advice in December 1522, he had found himself similarly unprepared for the September demonstrations of 1523. Of his extant works, the section on images in ***A Brief Christian Introduction*** marks his first attempt to deal systematically with the visual aspects of the cult of the saints. From November 1523 until July 1524, when the images were finally removed from the city churches, the practical problem of ecclesiastical art had been ever with him. Against the immediate background of their removal, he prepared a defense of his iconoclasm, published August 18, 1524,[1] in reply to the judgment of ***A Brief Christian Introduction*** by the Bishop of Constance. For the remainder of that year he was absorbed in work on his great ***Commentary on True and False Religion***.

He had not yet done with the problem of images. At some time late in 1524 or early 1525[2] Valentin Compar, the land-secretary of Canton Uri, sent to Zwingli a critique of the Reformer's theology centering around four fundamental articles: his doctrine of the Gospel, his understanding of authority, his iconoclasm, and his denial of Purgatory. This document, unhappily lost, must have been restrained in tone as well as judicious in temper, for Zwingli later acknowledged publicly in his ***Answer*** that Compar has "more good grace in his writing than all those who write against one another at this time" (4, 53, 10-11).[3] He determined, therefore, to reply to Compar as soon as the ***Commentary*** was completed.

It is of considerable significance that in the latter work Zwingli had intended originally not to discuss images at all, perhaps because he thought that what he had written on that subject in his reply to the Bishop of Constance was sufficient. Yet the pressure was such that he acquiesced, explaining the brevity of his discussion in the ***Commentary*** by stating that he would thereafter write a book devoted entirely to the subject (3, 900, 2-6).[4] Compar's critique must thus have inspired him to think through again, and formulate on a larger scale, the theological reasons for his rejection of ecclesiastical and liturgical art. Although the separate book was never published, what would have been its contents must have been incorporated into Zwingli's reply to Compar's third article, since of the four parts into which the ***Answer*** is divided, that on images is the longest and most carefully wrought; it is indeed, as Zwingli confessed, his "complete opinion" (84, 15) on the subject. The phrase is important: on this occasion he produced a synthesis of all that he had thought and written on ecclesiastical art since his arrival in Zurich. Moreover, inasmuch as the ***Answer*** opens with a double salutation, one to the Confederacy and one to Compar, Zwingli clearly intended the document to be something more than a local polemic. The ***Answer to Valentin Compar*** must thus be understood as a defense and an explanation to the rest of Switzerland of the whole Reformation as it had thus far affected the visual arts in Zurich.

### THE DEFINITION OF TRUE BELIEF

The massive indictment of images in the ***Answer to Valentin Compar*** rests entirely on Zwingli's radical discrimination between a true Christian belief and a false Christian belief. He begins by putting the question: what is the ultimate object of Christian belief—that is to say, how is the Christian properly to understand the content of the word God? The word is defined here as "that good from which all things arise and come, in which all things exist, and are sustained, to whom all men should go in all their evil and vileness" (86, 22-25). It must follow, then, that true Christian belief can consist only in a reliance on this absolute unconditional good, for God "calls Himself our father, helper, solacer, and protector, so that we will erect no other father, helper, solacer, and protector" (86, 28-30). That, in fact, is why "Jesus Christ has, when He taught us to pray, first told us to say Father, that is: that we should recognize Him as our Father without a doubt, not only with our mouths, but profoundly in our hearts" (88, 12-15). The Christian is confronted first with the uniqueness of God as the ultimate object of his belief, and second, with the fact that his belief must consist in a response to this uniqueness which recognizes no qualification:

> Only those are believers who know truly in their hearts that they should go to God alone in all their affairs. For they know that power over all things is in His hands alone, and that such power can be in the hands of no one else except in His. For they know that there can be no God except Him. Thus help, protection, grace, death, and life may rest in no one's hands except His.
>
> (88,29-33)

This is the first of the two superintending frames of reference within which Zwingli's discussion of images will fit: on the one hand, the uniqueness of God as the object of man's true belief; on the other, man's unconditional response to that object of true belief. "The believer is one who trusts in God alone" (97, 7-8).

### THE DEFINITION OF FALSE BELIEF

But men have never put their whole belief and trust in God. They have merely professed to do so, while turning actually to other people and other things in His stead. Zwingli is acutely conscious of this defect in human nature, just as he is aware of man's inclination to hypocrisy in public worship. The failure to rely ultimately on God alone is a persisting fact of man's spiritual life. People "may well be believers, but not in the true God" (89, 21). Thus what should be the sole object of man's belief has everywhere been fragmented into multiple responses to a congeries of substitutes for Him. All substitutes, however, are immediately recognizable and easily reduced to a single common denominator—namely, anyone or anything to whom man "goes for help, who is his sole comfort and treasure" (89, 18-19); in other words, anyone or anything placed between God and man by man himself: "They are not believers who go to anyone else for help other than to the one, true God. For thus are the believers differentiated from the unbelievers in that the believers, or those who are trusting, go to God alone; but the unbelievers go to the created [*den gschöpfften*]" (88, 29-33).

THE DYNAMICS OF FALSE BELIEF

What, then, is the source of *den gschöpfften?* How are they to be identified specifically as substitutes for God? And in what way do they intervene between God and man? To these three interlocked questions Zwingli returns one answer: all substitutes for God, regardless of their virtually infinite variety, are the inevitable result of a single dynamic process peculiar to man, a process which Zwingli understands and interprets in psychological fashion.

In turning away from God as the sole object of his ultimate belief, man has either consciously or unconsciously put his real trust in creatures and created things. He may, for example, regard his doctor as the one who is alone responsible for the state of his health; he may rely ultimately on political power, or social prestige; he may trust completely in the power of wealth, so that, as Zwingli says, "his gold or possessions are god" (97, 13-14; cf. 14-24). To these manifestations of false belief, all of which are internal and initially unconscious thought-processes, Zwingli assigns the single word *Abgott,* "strange god." His use of *Abgott* is precise and virtually consistent throughout the essay. Whenever he uses the word, he intends to convey the notion of a psychic process in which someone or something important in a man's interior life, regardless of its external form, is displacing God as the object of that man's real faith. What Zwingli had understood loosely as "temptation" (2, 710, 9) in 1523 has deepened by 1525 into a specific pattern of estrangement. Indeed, the word *Abgott* itself designates the process of becoming-estranged-from-God, and must be interpreted as Zwingli's final development of the implications of the phrase "inward idols" (*inneren götzen*) to which he had referred but once in the Second Disputation (2, 710, 7) and only partially explored in ***A Brief Christian Introduction*** (2, 655, 21-25).

Increasingly as these strange gods make themselves felt, and as man becomes more conscious of his reliance on them, he must try eventually to give to them some specific form; the mental process must be pictured. Zwingli is aware that an instinctive need as well as an instinctive capacity for imagining things is so deeply rooted in the human psyche that "what the mind of man takes in hand for himself runs always to phantasy and makes an image [*verbildt*] of the same" (96, 30-31). In fact, "there is no one," he asserts, "who, as soon as he hears God spoken of, or any other thing which he has not already seen, does not picture a form [*gestalt*] for himself" (96, 24-26). Furthermore, the experience of the senses is as ineradicable a need of human existence as the imaginative faculty: "by nature man falls upon those things which are placed in the realm of the senses" (92, 15-16). Thus the movement from an invisible, subjective process, existing initially within man's mind, to a visible, objectified image, is inevitable. The internal strange gods must sooner or later be externalized, and to all forms of such externalization, regardless of their variety, Zwingli assigns the single word *Götze,* "idol." Anyone or anything within man's mind estranging him from true belief in God, thereby initiating false belief, constitutes, as an internal, spiritual phenomenon, an *Abgott,* a strange god; as an external, material phenomenon perpetuating false belief, it is a *Götze,* an "idol" (cf. 96, 10-11). "Where one has strange gods, there one begins to honor them with idols and outward reverence" (106, 13-15). It may be a creature, a human being already existing, or it may be an object brought into existence by man's hands. The *Götzen* are thus defined as "portraits of the *abgötten*" (99, 2); they are the final results of an endless process of human invention (cf. 137, 3), for "the strange god [*der abgot*] always comes before the idols [*dem götzen*]" (133, 27-28). Consequently, "service to idols follows only afterward, when the strange god is already set up in your hearts" (105, 18-19; cf. 132, 6-7). For Zwingli idolatry is therefore not to be understood conventionally. He replies to the iconophiles that if men "have their hope in creatures, then they are idolaters, *although these same creatures are not idols*" (89, 22-23; italics mine). Idolatry thus interpreted, as opposed to true belief, constitutes the second superintending frame of reference for Zwingli's discussion of images.

In 1523, when he had dealt with the problem of music in the ***Interpretation and Substantiation of the Conclusions,*** Zwingli found himself confronted by a fundamentally irreconcilable tension between the ideal of a truly private prayer such as Christ commanded, and the reality of the spiritual and psychological dangers inherent in any form of public worship. In dealing with the problem of the visual arts, he faces a comparable tension. True belief consists in a continuing, single relationship between man and his *creator* God. False belief consists in discontinuous, multiple relationships between man and his several self-*created* substitutes for God (cf. 88, 32-33; 89, 28-29). True belief must be of such an abiding intensity "that it cannot be diminished *by any visible thing*" (92, 14; italics mine). Pressing continually against this assertion, however, as Zwingli recognized, was the fact that men naturally turn to visible things, so that all men are in fact idolators by nature (96, 26-27). He thereby discloses his acute awareness of the tension never absent from the ***Answer***—namely, the conflict, as irreconcilable as that between private prayer and common prayer, between the ideal condition of true belief, permanently beyond human realization, and the reality of man's ever-present idolatry.

Against the tension between the two, Zwingli turns then to the problem of the images themselves: "We are arguing only against those images which have lessened belief in the one God, such as those to this or that saint as a helper, and against the images to which one does reverence" (94, 21-24). Thus Zwingli's discussion is to be conducted on two distinctively different grounds: on the one hand, the relationship which the image holds to those who are in some way or another affected by seeing it; on the other hand, the relationship which the image bears to the person or persons represented or suggested by it. He deals with the first as the central manifestation of popular piety—that is, with the ceremonial and spiritual abuses which the images have induced in the faithful.

### POPULAR PIETY

God commanded men neither to worship images nor to serve them. The iconophiles interpret the commandment to mean merely "that one should not kneel before images because that is an outward thing; and because it is only a ceremony it therefore has nothing to do with the New Testament" (101, 7-10). Zwingli rejoins simply by pointing to the incontrovertible fact that churches everywhere were choked with statues and pictures which the faithful worshiped (cf. 107, 8-109, 30). They bowed to them, knelt before them, burned incense before them, prayed to them; they had even come to believe that certain statues or images in some places or shrines were holier than others. What is this, he argues, if not worship: "why do you bow before idols in church and not bow before images [*bilden*] in your room, but drink, swear, gamble or do even worse before them" (101, 18-21)? Where paintings or statues induce no false hopes and are not thereby revered, where they are simply images (*bilder*), "the likeness [*glychnussen*]" (96, 11-12) of anything that is visible but gives no cause for a religious response, then these cannot be regarded as idols. But paintings and statues in churches do, in fact, induce an immediate religious response. The "danger here is that everything which is in the church becomes from that moment on so great and holy in our eyes that we think it cannot be touched, so dear has it become" (101, 29-32; cf. 104, 12-14; 122, 27-29). Consequently, such images are idols, either because "you hold those in the church to be holier than those elsewhere, or, on the other hand, that you honor them for a purpose other than that which they signify" (101, 22-24). Reverence for the image may thus be induced on two interrelated but distinguishable grounds: first, the physical setting itself, and second, that significance popular piety reads into the images. But for Zwingli architecture cannot confer sanctification; the shrines and churches housing statues and paintings of the saints are simply buildings. Furthermore, the faithful worship statues and images even when they are erected outside churches, because they have come to believe that any statues and paintings can accomplish miracles. A local example was the statue of St. Anne at Ober-Stammheim to which miracles were attributed. It stood in the open and was much frequented for at least one year, if not two, before a chapel was built to house it. Thus the response of uneducated people to the sight of saints' images was sufficient ground for denying their propriety and for abolishing them. Zwingli bluntly reiterated Sebastian Hofmeister's argument during the Second Disputation: "Take the image of St. Anne at Stammenheim. Did men go there before it was made? No. And now that it has been burned do men go there so much? No" (102, 21-24). The behavior of the people was proof sufficient of their idolatry, of their captivity to the senses.

### LEARNED PIETY

Zwingli objected to images also with regard to the relationship which they bore to the person represented or suggested. The learned iconophiles were more sophisticated in their false belief, for they denied that they worshiped the images. Following Bonaventura, Aquinas, and the precepts of the *Summa Rudium,* they maintained that "we honor the images for another reason; the image of Saint Peter for his sake, who is in heaven" (104, 16-17). "I honor no image," they argued; "I also burn no candles before it, except to him whom the image signifies" (104, 17-19). To this traditional argument Zwingli insists first of all that saints, far from being desirous of such veneration, in fact abhor it. "If they were living still today, they would cry out against us: Why do you attribute to us that which is God's alone?" (90, 9-11). Zwingli first proposed this idea in the ***Interpretation and Substantiation of the Conclusions*** (3, 95, 29-34); Hätzer had taken it up in the second of his Answers; Commander Schmid had made it prominent during the Second Disputation. Now Zwingli returns to the theme with even greater vehemence, adducing the example of Paul and Barnabas (Acts 14:8-20), who, because they had healed a cripple, were worshiped by the citizens of Lystra:

> They tore their clothes and fell among the people, crying: "You men! What are you doing? We are mortal men, just as you also, and we teach you so that you may turn from such foolishness (namely, that they had attributed to a creature that which was from God alone) to the living God who has created

> heaven and earth, the sea and all that is therein," and so forth.
>
> [91, 4-9]

Zwingli stresses the fact that Paul and Barnabas were possessed by no "inward idols of temptation"; they had no "strange gods"; they permitted nothing whatsoever to impinge on the exclusiveness of their belief and trust in God. So he reiterates the argument he had advanced earlier in ***A Brief Christian Introduction:*** How could such true believers approve of being worshiped or venerated because they were presumed to possess powers which belonged to God alone, powers which had been attributed falsely to them by their fellow men? For that, Zwingli argues, is what men have done to the saints:

> We have heard that we shall have no other god before our God and Father . . . although we look immediately for a blessed end with St. Barbara and seek a healthy stomach with St. Erasmus, yet we know well that the only god is the true God. But God has given much of this power to the former and the latter pious believers. Yet we have said this without foundation in the Word of God, and we have attributed to these pious, departed Christians that which is God's alone.
>
> [89, 36; 90, 1, 4-9]

The inevitable psychological process of seeking to imagine and picture God, which Zwingli had earlier described, has led men to distribute, as it were, portions of God's power among men and women such as Saint Paul or Saint Barbara, believing them to be saints for false reasons, and thence, because of those false reasons, making them, in effect, gods themselves, because they are worshiped for the special attributes which men have accorded them (cf. 132, 19-21; 136, 34).

It is at this point that the dynamic process by which a strange god eventually becomes externalized is given concrete illustration:

> We all know that one has set up service to idols only because one therefore hopes to get something thereby . . . this one in St. Peter's name that he guard him from despair, that one in St. Niklaus' name that he not drown, and so forth, just as each has his own fear and trouble. But notice: was it right, therefore, that you sought for this or that help from Saints Peter, Niklaus, Gertrude, or Barbara? No. You should not have made them into such idols.
>
> [105, 2-3, 6-11]

If Zwingli's distinctions between strange god, idol, and image are borne in mind, this passage is central for an understanding of the role that religious images play within his dynamic of false belief. A man, for example, is mortally afraid of drowning. When this fear grips him, rather than relying wholly on God's omnipotence he turns to Saint Nicholas to intercede for him with God. The choice of saints was doubtless, by and large, arbitrary at first, depending on the tales told of them.[5] Gradually, however, a relationship between the man's fear of drowning and Saint Nicholas became fixed in his mind to the degree that he removed from God the power to save him from drowning and attached that power permanently and specifically to the Saint. As Zwingli said elsewhere of Saint Christopher, "I do not mean that he is an idol, but that you are allotting to him that which is God's alone" (99, 26-28; cf. 100, 8-10; 132, 19-21). In such fashion true belief was replaced by false belief, the unique union of faith between man and God was broken and Saint Nicholas, as the estranging element, had become—*against his own will* as well as against God's—an *Abgott,* a strange god within the man's mind. Then as the man's instinct to picture things, to make a *gestalt,* became operative and was joined to his need to give to this *gestalt* a sensible form, the process of becoming-estranged-from-God was externalized and objectified in a painting or statue of Saint Nicholas. The decision to make a visible artistic representation of Saint Nicholas was initially idolatrous, however, because it was inspired not by a saint but by an *Abgott.* Thus the whole process of externalization and objectification into an image was idolatrous. Even before the image had been made, it was an idol.[6]

These, then, are the two arguments with which Zwingli rebuts the doctrine that "the honor rendered to the image passes to the prototype": first of all, the saints themselves do not wish to be so honored, and, second, owing to the dynamics of false belief, to represent a saint by any kind of image is in fact to create an idol, even when the image is neither worshiped nor venerated. Both were suggested in the brief commentary on Exodus 20:3-4 which he wrote for ***A Brief Christian Introduction***. Now, after two years of deepening reflection on the problem—not so much against the background of local iconoclasm as in 1523 but rather in the context of systematically defining true Christian belief, what "has to do with the greatest part of our salvation" (95, 1-2)—he had come to the conclusion that God prohibited the making of all images "of all gods, that is: all those that anyone could himself choose for his own solace" (92, 26-27).

### IMAGES OF CHRIST: THE DIVINITY OF CHRIST

Zwingli turns next to the refutation of what he considers "the greatest counter-objection which the idol protectors make" (113, 20)—namely, images of Christ. That objection was, in fact, the crux of the iconophile argument which Compar stated as follows: "Christ is God and man; one may therefore portray Him according to His human nature" (114, 23-24). Zwingli's rejoinder consists in an extended discussion of the two natures and their unity, but although he affirms the unity of Christ, he greatly emphasizes His divinity, to the point, in fact, of depreciating His humanity. Such an emphasis is characteristic of Zwingli's Christology, for he always tended to stress the distinction of the two natures as against their unity, especially as the controversy with Luther over the Real Presence deepened. God is the author of Redemption, and Christ's humanity, even on the Cross, plays, as it were, an auxiliary role. It is the divinity rather than the humanity of Christ that saves mankind: "Redemption is through the deity, although the death is of man" (118, 25-26). Consequently, since even the iconophiles are agreed that God may not be portrayed, then "it follows that one should not and may not portray Christ. For the divinity of Christ may not be portrayed because the deity may and should not be portrayed" (119, 2-5). The propriety or even the possibility of any visible representation of Christ in His divinity is completely denied.

IMAGES OF CHRIST: THE HUMANITY OF CHRIST

Equally emphatic, however, is Zwingli's toleration of images of Christ in His humanity: "Where anyone has a portrait [*bildnus*] of His humanity, that is just as fitting to have as to have other portraits. . . . No one is forbidden from having a portrait of the humanity of Christ" (119, 15-17, 24-25). Thus men may, after all, make images of Christ as man, but with two major qualifications.

First of all, under no circumstances are they to be offered reverence of any sort (118, 14-15; 119, 25-26). If an image of Christ's humanity is made and reverenced, it becomes, like images of the saints, an idol. Moreover, the idolatry thus induced is of the worst possible sort, because man would be putting his faith in a creature rather than the creator. In Zwingli's specialized vocabulary man would be turning Christ Himself into an estranging and separating element from God. Everyone, therefore, "who now has the image of Christ in his house should take care that he not make it into an idol; for as we have already said, with us no pictures become idols faster than those of Christ" (119, 27-28; 120, 1-2).

The second qualification is that such images or portraits of Christ are under no circumstances to be designed for churches, or placed within them. Above all, the crucifix must everywhere be removed, for as Zwingli bluntly observed: "I have never seen in churches a cross displayed without one making it into an idol . . . we call the golden, silver, stone, and wooden crosses our Lord God; we embrace them as if we received solace and comfort from them. As soon as that happens, away with them (120, 2-3; 119, 19-22). On this point Zwingli is adamant. He has abandoned completely the theoretical latitude of the May decree of 1524, just as the Council had abandoned it in practice in June; neither in churches nor in private homes could a symbolic representation of Christ be tolerated longer. But outside the churches, in private homes or public places, images of Christ in His humanity could be displayed. In ***A Brief Christian Introduction*** Zwingli had said with regard to images that "if someone places representations of historic events [*geschichteswyss*] outside the churches, this may be allowed so long as they do not give rise to reverence" (2, 658, 19-20). It had appeared, then, that the word *geschichteswyss* might exclude all possibility of religious art. Both the word and its context were ambiguous, however, and it is quite possible that in 1523 Zwingli was undecided on the question whether such an art was possible. Two years later his position is clear. An art with Christian content is permissible, but only within the severe qualifications on which he insisted. The persons and events of Christian history, its central figure not excluded, are portrayable in visual form only, *geschichteswyss,* purely historical phenomena. Christian representational art is thus voided entirely by Zwingli not only of any liturgical and ecclesiastical content or purpose but also of any spiritual dimension.

REPRESENTATION AND THE WORD

"The portrait of Christ teaches the simple, unlettered man, and incites him to devotion which he would not have if he had not seen the portrait of Christ" (120, 10-12). Compar in that single sentence brought forward the two principal arguments which had sustained the use of images in the medieval West, the didactic one stemming from Pope Gregory and the hortatory one stemming from Saint Bonaventura. To both Zwingli replies with a devastating series of parallel comparisons of the value of the Word and the worthlessness of images, the whole revolving now around the pedagogics of faith.

To begin with, men can learn nothing of the content of God's Word from an image. "Why," Zwingli rhetorically asks, "do we not send images to unbelievers so that they can learn belief from them?" (120, 18-19). Precisely because we would be required to explain what they mean, which in turn requires knowledge of the Word. "If now you show an unbelieving or unlettered child images, then you must teach him with the Word in addition, or he will have looked at the picture in vain" (120, 22-25). For if "you were newly come from the unbelievers and knew nothing of Christ and saw Him painted with the apostles at the Last Supper, or on the Cross, then you would learn nothing from this same picture other than to say: 'He who is pictured there was a good-looking man in spite of it all'" (121, 18-22). Zwingli's witticism is a particularly telling index to his contempt for the Gregorian defense of images. One may have images of Christ, but they are powerless; the "story must be learned only from the Word, and from the painting one learns nothing except the form of the body, the movements or the constitution of the body or face" (121, 26-29).

In 1523 Zwingli had excluded all music from the service of worship on the basis of a threefold argument drawn from Scripture: (1) God had not explicitly commanded it; (2) Christ had instructed men to pray individually and in private; and (3) Saint Paul had urged men to pray to God in their hearts. Two years later Zwingli adduces now virtually the same threefold argument for the denial of any pedagogical value to images: (1) "God has not told us to teach from pictures, but from His Word" (122, 3-4); (2) "If teaching with images assists toward a knowledge of faith, then there is no doubt that Christ would have taught us to make images" (122, 9-11); and (3) "the holy apostles have forbidden us to have idols" (122, 12-13).

Paintings and statues, therefore, as visible, palpable forms appealing to the eye, cannot be the bearers either of spiritual or of educational effects. By the same token, the sensuous experience stimulated in the beholder cannot have a spiritual or educational character. The arts of the eye can neither teach the Holy nor express the Holy. They can portray only the accidents, not the substance, of Christianity, as they are given in the relatives of time and history. Men have thought that they could acquire the substance of true belief from pictures and statues only because for centuries the Papacy taught with them rather than with the Word. In saying that, Zwingli discloses what is for him one of the most important and urgent reasons for the removal of images—namely, that they constitute a barrier to the proper religious education of Zurich. Once they were entirely removed, then Zwingli's goal would be attained: "the hunger for the divine Word would become greater in men, and men would call more earnestly on God for preachers and workers than otherwise occurs" (127, 32-34).

### REPRESENTATION AND TIME

Another traditional argument on which Compar earlier drew for the retention of images had been that enlightened Christians in the sixteenth century could not possibly worship images as had the pagans or even the Israelites when they prostrated themselves before the Golden Calf. Zwingli retorts by maintaining that there is essentially no difference between the pagan idol and the Christian "image," so called, because the latter, as he has demonstrated, is, in fact, an idol too: "The objection that those idols were of gods, and ours not, has long been superseded. Ours are just as much strange gods as theirs" (141, 31-32). Indeed, the only distinction which he can find at all between pagan and Christian practice with regard to images is the fact that "the heathen idols insulted only the true God, but our idols insult the true God and His chosen saints" (111, 16-17). On the other hand, in countering Compar's objection Zwingli stresses that true belief, as he has defined it, existed in the time of Moses as it does now in sixteenth-century Zurich, and so likewise with false belief. The nature of either, in other words, cannot be transformed or bound by time. He presses the argument now against the following statement by Compar:

> A Christian goes across the field. He finds there the Passion of Christ, once, twice, or three or more times in image-niches along the way; whenever he sees them he does honor to Christ's Passion. . . . But when he finds no such images on his path, then he never thinks either of God or His saints. Therefore images are good for us and never evil.
>
> [124, 25-28; 125, 12-14]

Whereas the extraordinary extent to which late medieval piety was captive to the senses is perhaps nowhere better epitomized than in Compar's admission, Zwingli's rejoinder is no less devastating. Service to God is "to be busy in the will of the heavenly father" (125, 22), and that is not a matter of occasion. It is, to the contrary, a life service. "Right, true, brave, and steadfast reverence for God is when a man carries his God with him in his heart, God willing, wherever he goes, even if he nowhere sees a piece of wood with a saint's picture on it" (126, 13-15). The false believer is one whose belief is, in fact, bound by time. He is one who by "looking at images or idols induces devotion for no longer than one sees them and mumbles a meaningless word" (125, 31; 126, 1-2). For such isolated and haphazard moments of false belief and false devotion Zwingli has nothing but scorn, dismissing them contemptuously with the proverb "out of sight, out of mind" (126, 4-5). True belief knows no such passing moments.

Zwingli interrupts his argument with a significant brief excursion on the Sabbath in order to demonstrate that it, too, is not simply an appointed time, but an inner and continuing process. It would be only "an outward thing if we thought the day of the Lord—that is, Sunday—is bound therefore to that day" (129, 3-5). When the Sabbath is not properly understood as an interior spiritual phenomenon with neither beginning nor end, then Zwingli condemns it as a ceremonial, "bound to time [*zyt gebunden*] which is an element of this world, that is, an outward thing" (129, 2-3). And so it is with images because they, too, are ceremonials (130, 1-3). There is no other single passage in the ***Answer*** which concentrates so intensely in one sentence all the aspects of false belief against which he is so vehemently protesting. The two diametrically opposed structures of true belief and false belief which have served as referents for the image problem are incomparably illumined. The prime symbol of true belief is the Word, invisible and heard; the prime symbol of false belief is the image, visible and seen.

THE SACRAMENTAL PROBLEM

The difference between these two forms of belief points finally to the most fundamental reason for Zwingli's opposition to images. The liturgy of the Mass had not always been conducted with the visual splendor of the late Middle Ages. The primitive Church seems not to have regarded such material aids as necessary or important. Yet the attractive power of the image eventually proved irresistible, and its admission by the Church was indeed momentous, not alone for the history of art but also for the history of Christian worship. Piety and worship grew so sensuous that as early as the twelfth and thirteenth centuries a "dominant motif" of the religious life of the people had become "the desire to behold sacred reality with bodily eyes."[7] To that desire the Church had responded by proclaiming, above all else, the dogma of Transubstantiation, and it can scarcely be fortuitous that the authoritative formulation of the Real Presence of Christ and the elaboration of so much of the Mass liturgy should occur in the same centuries.

Both are expressions of that drive toward the palpably real, that insistent demand for the concrete in faith and worship, that attempt to bind the spiritual to the material, which is so profoundly characteristic of the high and late Middle Ages. Within the structure of the liturgy itself there began in this period an intensification of everything that would appeal to the sensibility. Before the twelfth century, for instance, the priest had kissed the altar twice only, upon approaching it and upon leaving it; by 1300 the kiss "was performed every time the celebrant turned around at the altar."[8] Until the eleventh century, altars had been rarely more than three or four feet square; from that time onward, they grew steadily in size, until by the fifteenth century some could be found which were twelve feet long. In the thirteenth century altars became more and more elaborately decorated: the austere *mensa* was gradually giving way to the great reredos-altar of the fourteenth and fifteenth centuries.[9] Altar crosses and candles made their appearance in the twelfth century,[10] and there were significant alterations in the vestments of the priest. Under Innocent III the symbolism of their colors was codified and elaborated. Those which the priest wore to the altar had customarily been interpreted as signifying Christ's Passion. During the thirteenth century an actual cross appeared on the back of the chasuble, a development which meant that "the allegorical presentation of the Crucified could be imaged even in the external figuration."[11] Nor was it enough to satisfy the sense of sight: in the same period the extension of the priest's hands after the consecration came to be understood as an imitation of the arms of Christ stretched out upon the cross, so that the sense of movement, too, was symbolically gratified.[12] Finally, this period saw everywhere conscious efforts to amplify and enrich the musical aspects of liturgical drama.[13] The climax of such multiplication and intensification of all that was sensuous in the liturgy of the Mass was the Elevation of the Host.[14] The faithful of the Middle Ages knew that Christ was really present in the consecrated elements. But they knew, too, that they could actually see only the sacramental appearance of bread and wine, of which the substance was Christ's body and blood. Their insistence upon actually seeing the elements is, perhaps, the supreme expression of the medieval drive for visualizing the sacred. Thus the custom arose toward the close of the twelfth century of elevating the Host so that, although only for a moment, the people might see it. The Lateran proclamation on Transubstantiation served not only to answer this longing to see God, but to intensify it as well. Greatly increased importance was attached to the Feast of Corpus Christi, first officially instituted by Urban IV in 1264,[15] when the people could see the Host not just for a brief moment in a dimly lit church but for a much longer period. In the brightness of day they could follow it with their eyes, and adore it as it was carried through the streets in solemn and splendid procession.

Thus the liturgy of the Mass in the high and late Middle Ages gave rise to an intensely emotional and sensuous experience, the substance of which was mediated by the arts. First of all, the Church was in itself a representation of supernatural reality. Although a structure of stone and wood and glass, its reality lay in the fact that, by virtue of the language employed in the ritual of dedication, the church was, "mystically and liturgically, an image of heaven."[16] Inside the building the worshiper entered another world. The more splendid the interior, the richer the vestments, the more glorious the music, the more elaborate the liturgy, with all its attendant magnificence of sight and sound, of processional movements and odors of incense and burning candles, the nearer the worshiper came to an intimation of heaven itself. And when the priest, the *creator creatoris,* at length raised the Host on high, the worshiper saw Christ: "See the Son of God who, for your sakes, shows His wounds to the Heavenly Father; See the Son of God who, for your sakes, was thus lifted on the Cross; See the Son of God who will come to judge the living and the dead."[17] A more dramatic climax to a sufficiently dramatic spectacle could scarcely be imagined, and this threefold repetition of the exhortation to "see" in Berthold of Regensburg's sermon on the Mass emphasizes the overwhelmingly visual aspect of the religious experience.

Such a spectacle, in the exact sense of the word, was for Zwingli the apogee of idolatry. Christ's human body was something specifically defined and delimited; it was in Heaven, invisible and incommunicable. There was no possibility of a corporeal, material eating of Christ in the bread. He rejected both the Transubstantiation of the medieval church and the Consubstantiation of Luther.[18] The presence of Christ at the Lord's Supper in Zurich could be only a spiritual one, for Christ could be an object of faith only and solely through His divinity, just as His divinity rather than His humanity redeemed mankind. As a result, the spiritual realm was sundered from the material. The faith and worship of the medieval Church had sought to bring the two always closer and closer together. Zwingli strove to divorce them completely. For the faithful in the Middle Ages, viewing the celebration of the liturgy of the Mass was to undergo a multiple sense experience in which sight and sound, smell and movement all were profoundly aroused and implicated. The Zwinglian Sermon Liturgy and the celebration of the Lord's Supper stand in irreconcilable opposition to such a religious experience. Insofar as it was possible, Zwingli eliminated everything sensuous from worship. Music, vestments, incense, ritual gestures, and images—all were of no avail to man precisely because his faith, the only reality, the invisible action of the Holy Spirit in men's hearts, had nothing whatsoever to do with the senses. To the triple exhortation to "see" of Berthold of Regensburg, he would thus have replied: "Faith is from the invisible God and it tends toward the invisible God, and is something completely apart from all that is sensible. Anything that is body, anything that is of the senses, cannot be an object of faith" (3, 798, 14-17). On those two great affirmations—with respect at least to images—rested Zwingli's ***Answer to Valentin Compar***.

*Notes*

[1] *Z,s 3,* 155, 28-184, 31.

[2] K. D. Kluser, *Der Landschreiber Valentin Compar von Uri und sein Streit mit Zwingli,* Historisches Neujahrsblatt herausgegeben von der Gesellschaft für Geschichte und Alterthümer des Kantons Uri, 1 (1895), 38.

[3] Unless indicated to the contrary, all references in the text are to Vol. 4 of Zwingli's works.

[4] *Z,* 3, 900, 1 to 906, 5. This section on images and that in the reply to the Bishop of Constance will not be analyzed, since all the arguments contained in them are incorporated and refined in The *Answer to Valentin Compar.*

[5] Cf. Erasmus' Colloquy, The Franciscans; or, Rich Beggars, *The Whole Familiar Colloquies of Desiderius Erasmus of Rotterdam,* trans. Nathan Bailey (London, 1877), pp. 187-88: "This town abounds with swineherds, by reason of a large wood hard by that produces plenty of acorns, and the people have an opinion that St. Antony takes charge of the hogs, and therefore they worship him, for fear he should grow angry if they neglect him."

[6] Zwingli points out that the individual process described above is exactly paralleled in the religious history of the pagans: "they came to the point where they realized that a God must exist. But that they serve God alone was not enough for them; they gave a portion of the divine power to many and thought these same to be the sun, the moon, Jove, Mercury, and others. That was not enough. After that they also portrayed these same imagined gods of theirs and thus split the one God into many gods (see how the strange god always comes before the idol!), and thereafter also portrayed these gods in all sorts of forms and finally have served and honored the created more than the creator" (Z, 4, 133, 21-30).

[7] Otto von Simson, *The Gothic Cathedral: Origins of Gothic Architecture and the Mediaeval Concept of Order,* Bollingen Series, 48 (New York, 1956), xx.

[8] Joseph A. Jungmann, S.J., *The Mass of the Roman Rite: Its Origins and Development,* trans. Francis A. Brunner, C.SS.R. (New York, 1951), *1,* 107.

[9] Ibid., pp. 109, n. 37; 109-10.

[10] Ibid., p. 109, n. 37.

[11] Ibid., p. 112.

[12] Ibid., p. 107.

[13] Ibid., pp. 123-27.

[14] Ibid., pp. 119-21.

[15] Ibid., p. 122.

[16] Von Simson, *The Gothic Cathedral,* p. 8.

[17] Jungmann, *The Mass of the Roman Rite,* p. 121.

[18] The literature on Zwingli's eucharistical doctrine is large, controversial, and complex; cf. the magisterial survey by J.-V.-M. Pollet, "Zwinglianisme," *Dictionnaire de Théologie Catholique, 15*[2] (Paris, 1950), cols. 3825-42.

**Robert C. Walton (essay date 1967)**

SOURCE: "The Influence of Mediaeval and Humanist Traditions upon Zwingli's View of Society," in *Zwingli's Theocracy,* University of Toronto Press, 1967, pp. 17-29.

[*In this excerpt from his book on Zwingli's ideas on theocracy, Walton explains the influence of humanist traditions on Zwingli's thought.*]

Even if the local traditions which zwingli accepted had not allowed the magistrate an important place in ecclesiastical affairs, the intellectual tradition which molded his thought would have led him to demand it. As it was, the ideas he brought to Zurich fitted the state of affairs in the city remarkably well. For example, his belief that the acquisition of secular authority and wealth had corrupted the clergy was a theme common both to the leading late scholastics and to the humanists of the northern Renaissance, especially Erasmus. Zwingli had come to this conclusion from his study of these sources and, above all, from his knowledge of scripture and from his personal experience. He was one with Erasmus in the desire to put the wealth and power of the church in the hands of the secular magistrate to free the clergy to preach the Gospel.[1] At Zurich the transfer was already well under way, and the earlier achievements of the magistracy doubtless inclined Zwingli to an even more willing acceptance of the government's role in the affairs of the church. Zwingli's ideas, pertinent and sympathetic to the actual situation in Zurich, won the support of a majority, at least in the Great Council, and aided the magistracy in bringing policies begun long before to their full fruition.

Except for the Baptists, no one in the sixteenth century seriously advocated the establishment of a "free church." Indeed, the idea of a magistracy which tolerated numerous sects and reserved for itself a sphere of activity divorced from religious life would have been an unspeakable heresy. The men of the sixteenth century still believed in the *corpus christianum*—the idea that society was a single Christian body.[2] The *corpus christianum* was divided into two realms, the spiritual and the secular, which were ruled by the priesthood and the magistrate. Together they governed the citizens of the Christian world. At the head of both was God, the creator and the sustainer of the Christian body, which existed to realize his purpose. As long as men believed in the *corpus christianum,* they lived in a society which was dominated by a theocratic aim, but not necessarily a society ruled by the clergy.[3]

In the course of the middle ages the relationship between the priesthood and temporal power within the Christian body had been radically altered. The early middle ages were dominated by the theory of Pope Gelasius, which asserted that emperor and priest were supreme in their respective kingdoms.

> There are two things, most august Emperor, by which this world is chiefly ruled: the sacred authority of the priesthood and the royal power. Of these two, the priests carry the greater weight, because they will have to render account in the divine judgment even for the kings of men.[4]

Gelasianism tended to ignore the divine sanction of the emperor and to stress the superiority of the clergy. But neither Pope Gelasius nor his successors tried to claim a decisive role for the clergy in mundane affairs. They sought only to protect their supremacy in ecclesiastical affairs.

Until Gregory VII was raised to the papal throne in 1073 the church was dominated by the German emperors who developed the theory of "royal theocracy." They believed the divine sanction of their office empowered them to intervene in spiritual matters and to claim a position in the earthly hierarchy over the clergy. Gregory VII rejected all that. He denied the sacramental character of the imperial office and announced that clerical authority, due to its nature and function, was superior to secular even in the affairs of the world. Earthly rulers did not receive their authority directly from God; the power they exercised was delegated to them by the pope. The Holy See had in theory, if never completely in practice, placed itself as a mediator between the earthly ruler and God.[5] Thus, the Gelasian theory was replaced by a doctrine which subjected the secular power to the spiritual.

In both the early period of "royal theocracy" and the era of papal supremacy, the tendency to fuse secular and religious authority was apparent. This was the result of the assumption that society had an ultimate and single divine purpose, and, however much the scales may have been tipped towards monarch or pope, the basic idea of the Christian society, oriented to God's will, remained throughout the middle ages.

Although by the sixteenth century the high water-mark of papal authority, as practised by Innocent III or proclaimed by Boniface VIII, was long past, the church remained a secular power. It controlled vast wealth and was deeply involved in political affairs. During the two centuries prior to the sixteenth, the extent to which wealth and power had corrupted the church was revealed in the fiscalism that accompanied the centralization of the church administration. The fourteenth and the fifteenth centuries were eras of rapid growth and centralization for secular government. European rulers sought to curb the financial drain imposed by the See of Peter's fiscalism and to limit the exercise of secular authority by the higher clergy. Developments in Zurich illustrate these efforts. The obvious solution to the problem was found in the establishment of national churches, which, though still loyal in dogma, cult, and adherence to the papacy, were effectively controlled by the local government.

Such far-reaching changes were not carried out without recrimination on both sides. Kings, princes, and magistrates found it necessary to seek authors to defend their policies. These were not hard to find among laymen and theologians. Two of the most important were the clerics, William of Occam, a founding father of the late scholastic *via moderna,* and Marsilio of

Padua. They were active in the early decades of the fourteenth century and elaborated a view of the church which denied it wealth and secular power.

Though both men devoted their intellects to the cause of Lewis the Bavarian and attacked the basis of Pope John XXII's claim to secular power, the main lines of their thought were not similar. Marsilio's hostility to the independent authority of the church and his use of corporate theory to justify the control of the clergy by the secular government reveal his experience as a citizen of Padua and reflect, in part, his native city's solution to the problem of the church's disruptive influence in the affairs of the commune. By identifying the *universitas civium* with the *universitas fidelium,* i.e., the state with the church, Marsilio was able to rationalize the complete subordination of the clergy and all aspects of spiritual life to the authority of a government which represented the will of the people, or better, the "weightier part" (*pars valentior*) of the people. Marsilio rejected *in toto* the pope's claims to the *plentitudo potestatis* which he believed could rest only in the people, and asserted the authority of councils, representing clergy and laity, over the entire ecclesiastical hierarchy.[6] In order to preserve the peace of the state, he denied the clergy any secular function and limited them to their spiritual tasks: the proclamation of the Gospel and the administration of the sacraments.[7] His conclusions were a radical departure from past tradition.

Though Marsilio contributed to a climate of opinion which undoubtedly influenced the development of Zwingli's thought, it is doubtful that he had a direct effect upon Zwingli's intellectual development. Zwingli worked within a similar urban environment and used corporate theory to rationalize the control of the external affairs of the church by the magistracy and to identify the members of the church with the citizenry of Zurich. However, unlike Marsilio, he never gave the government authority over spiritual matters and did not seek to subordinate the clergy merely to preserve the state. Zwingli believed that good citizenship depended upon adherence to the Christian faith, while Marsilio made no such assumption.[8] The similarities between the two views are probably best explained by the fact that both men thought in terms of a communal environment which was dominated by a corporate theory of society and government.

Like Marsilio, Occam rejected the papal claim to unlimited power over all things temporal and spiritual. While recognizing the divine sanction of the pope's authority over the spiritual realm, he denied the pope and the clergy any rights in the secular sphere, except that of demanding the support necessary for them to perform their spiritual functions.[9] By asserting that kings and emperors received their authority from God through the people, not through the pope, and by limiting their power to temporal affairs, Occam sought to delineate the proper function of both the priesthood and the civil authority. He believed that the two were able to coordinate their jurisdiction because both served the same end, "the common good."[10] Occam's theory was far more moderate than Marsilio's and bears comparison with Gelasian dualism.[11]

Occam's view of religious authority and his definition of the church are of particular interest. Although he stressed the fallibility of the pope and asserted the authority of the scripture when he said, "Holy Scripture is not able to err . . . the Pope is able to err," he acknowledged the importance of an extra-scriptural tradition, passed along through the apostles and those who followed them, for the formulation of the truths of faith. He clearly was not the forerunner of Protestant biblicism but he helped to give the question of biblical authority a central place in late mediaeval theology. Occam defined the church as the *congregatio christianorum fidelium* (assembly of faithful christians) and agreed that, when basic issues divided the church, a general council which represented it and derived its authority by delegation from the *congregatio* was superior to the pope.[12] Here again, however, Occam was far more moderate than Marsilio in his defence of councilliar supremacy; he viewed a council only as a portion of the whole church and put it on the same level with "provincial councils." In order for the council's decisions to have full validity, Occam maintained that it required the tacit agreement of all the faithful to its gathering and its actions; nor did he deny that in the normal course of events a pope should summon a council, or that a council which became heretical was subject to the supervision and correction of the pope.[13]

Many of Occam's ideas and much of his terminology were to appear frequently before and during the Reformation. Although it is possible to see certain parallels between Zwingli's definition of the church, his conception of the authority of councils and regional ecclesiastical gatherings, and his explication of the clergy's proper competence, it is difficult to establish a direct connection between Zwingli's thought and that of either Occam or Marsilio. If there was any one person who made a deep impression upon Zwingli, it was Erasmus. A number of Erasmus' ideas, especially those concerning the role of priest and prince in society, indicate that there was a certain amount of common ground between him and the major theorists who had opposed the secular activities of the clergy in the past.[14] In places his statements suggest a possible familiarity with Marsilio or Occam, and it is tempting to speculate that, via Erasmus, Zwingli was indirectly influenced by them.

However, Zwingli may well have had first-hand contact with the writings of Marsilio and Occam or with the work of their followers. When he studied at Vienna it was a centre of Occamist thought and, later at Basel there was opportunity for him to hear representatives of both Thomist and Occamist schools. Most scholars say that Zwingli was more closely associated with Thomism, but he himself refers to having studied both schools.[15] Zwingli no doubt had an interest in, and knowledge of, the Occamist tradition. The climate of opinion generated by the desire to limit the church to its rightful spiritual functions had existed long enough to become part of an accepted critical attitude. Zwingli could not have avoided absorbing some of it.

Various aspects of disaffection with the church were represented in German humanism, dominated by such figures as Erasmus and Hutten; consequently, it is necessary to examine with particular care Zwingli's connection with German humanism. After four centuries, this is not an easy task, but the work is made lighter by our knowledge of Zwingli's library. The three hundred and twenty books and twenty-eight manuscripts which are known to have been in it cover a wide range of topics and reveal Zwingli's contacts with the German humanists. The books included John Hus' *De ecclesia,* and William Bude's *Commentary on the Pandects of Justinian,* which was later influential in forming Calvin's view of the state.[16] There was, of course, Augustine's *City of God,* along with the works of Seneca, Eusebius, Lactantius, Jerome, Aristotle, and Cicero's *De Officiis.*[17] Although copies of Eberlein von Günzburg's pamphlets do not seem to have been in Zwingli's library, he did receive letters from Günzburg, and Günzburg's ideas may have interested him.[18] Günzburg hoped that the end of papal power in Germany would allow the Germanization and democratization of the church. He also sought social reforms for the benefit of the peasants.[19] Thanks to his friends in Basel, Zwingli had a copy of Hutten's edition of Lorenzo Valla's *De Donatione Constantini,* as well as some of Hutten's other pamphlets.[20] Shortly before his death Hutten sought and found refuge with Zwingli, but it is hard to say just what his influence upon Zwingli was; his "nationalist" interests may have strengthened Zwingli's Swiss patriotism. Conrad Celtis could have been another source for the development of Zwingli's patriotism. Usteri believes that Zwingli's first two poems, the ***Ox*** and the ***Labyrinth,*** reflect the influence of the classical, political-patriotic themes stressed by Celtis;[21] but although he was at Vienna while Celtis was lecturing there, he never mentioned him as a teacher and could have derived these ideas from his own studies.

A more important contribution to Zwingli's thoughts on the relationship between the pastor and the magistrate may have come from Melanchthon. In the fall of 1522 the Ravensburg humanist Michael Hummelberg sent Zwingli a copy of Melanchthon's M.A. theses which dealt with the subject of the *"Double Magistracy."*[22] Melanchthon's theses reveal that he still thought within the framework of the *corpus christianum.* The government of the world was twofold, spiritual and corporal (*spirituale et corporale*); corporal government (*regimen*) was civil government and administrated the external law, "the law of the flesh." The magistrates, princes, and judges who controlled civil government were, in Melanchthon's eyes, ordained by God to rule the external realm. He explained that the justice which they administered existed for coercion of those who lacked the spirit of God and that as long as the magistrates did not use the sword contrary to God's law, they did not sin.[23] Their justice, he concluded, was not of life but of death and the punishment of sin.

Melanchthon denied that the spiritual kingdom, which is ruled by God's Word and by those who serve it, had anything to do with secular power. He clarified his conception of the spiritual realm when he said: "They are miserably deceived who consider the [righteousness] of the spirit to be nothing else than the carnal righteousness of the world." This passage makes clear the foundation upon which the dual magistracy is based. It is based upon a twofold righteousness ordained by God, which is necessary because many lack the spirit of God. If they had it, Melanchthon believed, the external law would become unnecessary.[24]

Melanchthon's conception of a dual regimen certainly appeared again in Zwingli. The sharp distinction which the former made between the worldly and the spiritual kingdom resembles Zwingli's division of authority between the magistrate and the pastor. Melanchthon, like Zwingli, justified the two powers in terms of a twofold righteousness established by God. The ideas found in Melanchthon's theses seem to have influenced Zwingli's sermon ***On Divine and Human Righteousness*** which appeared in 1523.[25]

It is to Erasmus, however, that one must look for a solid structure of ideas which enriched Zwingli's political thought. In addition to the Greek New Testament, Zwingli had twenty-three of Erasmus' works in his library and was familiar with ten others. Among these works were the *Complaint of Peace, Enchiridion, The Education of a Christian Prince,* and an edition of Erasmus' collected works published by Froben in 1519.[26]

Alfred Rich's admirable study of the beginnings of Zwingli's theology has shown the vital role which Erasmus played in Zwingli's early theological development. His careful analysis of the reasons for Zwingli's rejection of the Erasmian position in 1520-21 shows that there were certain points of continuity between the two even after the break. Both still saw scripture as the key to the revival of Christianity, though what each assumed the revival meant was radically different.[27] Rich does not consider the possibility that their attitude towards the place of the church in society remained the same. It is beyond the scope of this work to investigate the question thoroughly, but a few citations which indicate that they continued to agree should be mentioned.

Some have said Zwingli derived his principle of congregational participation in church affairs and his general attitude towards hierarchy from Erasmus.[28] The first assertion must be qualified in terms of the corporate tradition which dominated the political ideas of the city government and provided the frame of reference for Zwingli's consideration of the problem of church government which itself was a civil-religious issue. The most that can be said is that if Erasmus did aid Zwingli in formulating a conception of congregational participation in church affairs, his influence was of secondary importance. The corporate tradition of government and the special place occupied by the Zurich Council in the affairs of all local assemblies were clearly far more important in determining Zwingli's solution to this question. The same applies to any general consideration of Erasmus' influence upon his political thought, for the two men worked in radically different contexts.

There is, on the other hand, considerable support for the claim that Erasmus helped to form Zwingli's attitude toward the hierarchy of the church. Erasmus' contempt for the clergy's lack of learning and for the greed and worldliness of the higher clergy was manifest. His bitter criticism of the clerical estate often concentrated upon these failings.

> For one thing, they reckon it the highest degree of piety to have no contact with literature, and hence they see to it that they do not know how to read . . . some of them make a good profit from their dirtiness and mendicancy. . . . Our popes, cardinals and bishops for some time now have earnestly copied the state and practice of princes, and come near to beating them at their own game. . . . Nor do they keep in mind the name they bear, or what the word "bishop" means, labour, vigilance, solicitude. Yet in raking in moneys they truly play the bishop, overseeing everything and overlooking nothing.[29]

Erasmus objected to the confusion of the spiritual office with worldly authority which, he said, caused secularization and neglect of religion. Similar complaints appear more than once in Zwingli's writings. During the First Disputation he discussed the bishop's office:

> And actually it concerns the little word bishop which, when one translates it into German properly, means nothing else than a guardian or supervisor, who should direct attention and care towards his people, being entrusted to instruct them in the divine faith and will, that is, in good German: a pastor.[30]

A comparison of the two definitions reveals that Zwingli and Erasmus share a similar conception of the bishop's task.

Speaking of the pope, Erasmus remarked:

> As to the Supreme Pontiffs who take the place of Christ, if they tried to emulate His life, I mean His poverty, labors, teaching, cross and contempt for safety, if even they thought upon the title of Pope—that is, Father, or the addition "Most Holy," who on earth would be more afflicted . . . It would lose them all that wealth and honor, all those possessions, triumphal progresses, offices . . . In place of these it would bring . . . a thousand troublesome tasks. . . . [31]

Zwingli, writing about the false prophet in ***Der Hirt*** (***The Shepherd***), passed a harsh judgment upon the hierarchy for living like the princes of this world.

> Then it follows that they who have the staff, that is, worldly authority, along with the office of the shepherd are not shepherds but wolves; for Christ has forbidden the shepherd all ruling after the custom and manner of the princes of this world. . . . If they now have the staff which Christ has forbidden them, then they are false shepherds.[32]

The ultimate cause of Erasmus' disgust with the hierarchy was its propensity to cause war rather than to encourage peace, as the clergy should. Erasmus hoped for peace and religious revival in Christian Europe.[33] As he saw the situation, peace was possible if the clergy fulfilled its office and influenced the princes to follow wise policies. Needless to say, his hopes were never realized, but his ideals helped to crystallize Zwingli's opposition to mercenary service and his demand for Swiss neutrality.

Erasmus' pessimism about the clergy mirrored a general feeling which had long been present in European society. Despairing of the clergy's ability to reform itself he turned to the prince for help and assigned him the predominant role in the moral direction of the community. The introduction to the 1518 edition of the *Enchiridion,* written two years after the *Education of a Christian Prince,* gave a definition of the *corpus christianum* which summarized his opinion. He described the Christian body in terms of a series of concentric circles revolving around Christ as the centre. The ecclesiastical hierarchy constituted the inner circle. Much like Occam, Erasmus demanded the withdrawal of the hierarchy from worldly affairs and he based their superiority upon their spiritual function. Though he complained that the princes, the members of the second circle, often behaved like the common people, the members of the third, Erasmus gave them full control of society.[34] When he considered the prince's responsibilities in *The Education of a Christian Prince,* Erasmus said the moral example given by the prince to the people had greater effect than that of churchmen: "The studies and character of priests and bishops are a potent factor in this matter, I admit, but not nearly so much as those of the prince."[35] Erasmus had expressed the same idea in the *Complaint of Peace*. Using terminology reminiscent of Eusebius' description of Constantine as the upholder of God's image on earth, he exalted the authority of the prince: "I call unto you, O ye princes, at whose beck and commandment the matters and business of men most chiefly do depend, and that among men do bear the image of Christ."[36] However, he was careful to show the prince ruled for the common good, not for his own advancement: "[the prince] born for the common good . . . to whom no concern is of longer standing or more dear than the state. . . . The one idea which should concern a prince in ruling . . . the public need, free from all private interests."[37]

Erasmus' view of the service to the common good must have had a familiar ring to Zwingli in Switzerland, where the rising magistracies of the cities had long ago proclaimed in defence of their expanding power their devotion to the common good. The advice Erasmus gave to the princes concerning the conduct of justice indicates how great a moral task he gave to the ruler. Some of these ideas appeared later in Zwingli. Though the ruler to whom they referred was quite different, for Erasmus as for Zwingli, the governor's administration of justice had a didactic function: "Let the prince propose such laws as not only provide punishment in particular for the sources of crime but also have influence against sin itself. . . . The main purpose of law should be to restrain crime by reason rather than by punishment."[38] Speaking of the functions of judges and rulers, Zwingli wrote: "Therefore the judge and rulers are servants of God, they are the schoolmasters."[39]

One piece of advice given to the prince may have played a part in Zwingli's strategy of reform. Erasmus told the prince that the introduction of reforms required time and care.

> However, if the people prove intractable and rebel against what is good for them, then you must bide your time and gradually lead them over to your end. . . . Yet he must not cease his efforts as long as he is able to renew his fight and what he has not accomplished by one method he should try to effect by another.[40]

Although as a diplomat Zwingli was no fool, this maxim might have been in the back of his mind.

There is no doubt that Erasmus was willing to expand the competence of the civil authority to achieve the purification of the church. The argument of a number of scholars, that Erasmus allowed the church to be absorbed into the state which then defined the church's task in terms of its own conception of the common good, has already been noted.[41] Such a claim goes too far. Erasmus assumed that the prince, whose power he wished to enhance, was Christian. By definition, the power any Christian exercised was limited, and those who exercised absolute authority were pagans, not Christians. Erasmus made this point clear enough:

> Never forget that "dominion," "imperial authority," "kingdom," "power," are all pagan terms, not Christian. The ruling power of a Christian state consists only of administration, kindness, and protection. . . . To subject his people through fear, to make them perform servile tasks, to drive them from their possessions, depose them of their goods, and finally even to martyr them—those are the rights of a pagan prince.[42]

Zwingli said much the same thing in the sermon ***The Shepherd*** which was delivered during the Second Disputation: "Seneca also considers royal power as a service; that is, the kingdom or the government is an office of doing good."[43] Erasmus and Zwingli both believed that a Christian prince or magistrate could not be a tyrant. They thought of society as a *corpus christianum* and were willing to trust secular authorities because they assumed that such men were Christian. The ideal bond for the prince and his people was Christian love, which Erasmus hoped the proper education would instill: "But where Christian love unites the people and their prince, then everything is yours that your position demands."[44] This is where Zwingli disagreed with Erasmus. For him, the ability to fulfil the love commandment was the gift of God's grace, not something which could be gained through education.

Erasmus envisaged "a government bound to the model of Christ."[45] By portraying the ruler as the bearer of Christ's image in the world, Erasmus made the exercise of absolute power in the pagan sense impossible. Any ruler who accepted the Erasmian standard had to conform to the principles of divine behaviour. Its essence was defined by Erasmus as the service of the good, an expression of love, and the service of the good excluded the possibility of tyranny. In a world ruled by a "limited" monarch, Erasmus could consider the restoration of a purified church, stripped of all earthly authority and devoted to its spiritual calling. Indeed he could even grant the prince the right to set in order the affairs of the church, when the clergy was unable to do so.[46]

The very fact that Zwingli did not remain an Erasmian, and that his thought developed under very different conditions than that of Erasmus, makes it difficult to assess the importance of Erasmus' view of the state and its ruler upon Zwingli. In seeking a solution to this problem, Moeller's comments upon the subject are helpful. He notes the importance of Erasmus' conception of the state in the thinking of the northern humanists as a whole and states that Zwingli shared the general tendency to view the state as an organism, and that he also used this concept to justify linking directly the tasks of the church and state; but he claims that Zwingli's republicanism was a deviation from Erasmus' ideal state governed by a monarch. Without denying the significance of the humanists' political thought, in particular of Erasmus', Moeller asserts that for Zwingli as for Bucer the city environment in which they worked was a more decisive influence.[47]

Although Zwingli certainly did not derive either his faith in the Christian magistrate, or his belief in the *corpus christianum* from Erasmus, it is possible to conclude that Zwingli's belief in both was reinforced by his study of Erasmus and that Zwingli drew upon Erasmus' ideas and altered them to fit the local situation. Zwingli sought to remove the last vestiges of secular power and wealth from the hands of the clergy to free them for the preaching of the Gospel. He was in practice as willing as Erasmus was in theory to increase the authority of the magistrate. Though he spoke of the Christian magistrate in a different context, he employed terms similar to those used by Erasmus to describe the Christian prince. Zwingli believed that the magistrate could be trusted because he was a Christian magistrate, bound by Christian morality. He and Erasmus both viewed society as Christian and understood the offices of priest, prince, or magistrate as the organs of direction for it. This conception, though not so complete in Zwingli's case that it prevented him from propounding a right of rebellion against the government, explains much of his readiness to depend upon the magistracy for the success of his programme.

Thus, it probably would have shocked Zwingli to hear the product of his work described as a theocracy in the modern sense, i.e., as a society under ecclesiastical direction. All he sought was to restore the balance of authority within Christian society. To achieve this he called for an end to the wealth and power of the clergy. Only when the government was in full control of its rightful domain and the clergy devoted itself to the things of the spirit, could the rule of God be realized. This was Zwingli's "theocratic" ideal.

*Notes*

[1] Geldner argues that Erasmus sought to reduce the church to the position it had held during the first three centuries of its existence. Erasmus believed that it should have no rights in the temporal sphere and that its sole influence should be pedagogical. According to Geldner, Erasmus opposed forceful secularization of the church and hoped that it would divest itself of wealth and power which he said were a burden and the cause of ecclesiastical tyranny. Erasmus felt that the church's Denunciation of secular concerns would free the state from the illegal power exercised by the church. Geldner also asserted that Erasmus defended the prince's right to restore order in the church when the hierarchy failed to do it (Geldner, *Die Staatsauffassung und Fürstenlehre des Erasmus von Rotterdam,* 98-100, 140). Maurer claims that Erasmus' view of the clergy's place in the *corpus christianum* represented a revival of the Franciscan ideal and that the logic of Erasmus' conception led to the absorption of the church by the state (Maurer, *Das Verhältnis des Staates zur Kirche nach humanistische Anschauung vornehmlich bei Erasmus,* 23-5). Moeller asserts that Erasmus placed a religious gloss on the state and incorporated the church in the state as an educational institution (Moeller, 49).

[2] G. Locher, "Die Evangelische Stellung der Reformatoren zum öffentlichen Leben," *Kirchliche Zeitfrage,* Heft 26 (1950), 11-12; "Staat und Politik in der Lehre der Reformaoren," *Reformatio,* I (1952), 204.

[3] cf. *supra* ix.

[4] Quoted in Tellenbach, 33, 34.

[5] *Ibid.,* 35-6, 60, 156, 158.

[6] Gewirth, I, 25-8, 182-3, 291-2, 258, 285-6.

[7] Gewirth I, 207, 295; Seeberg III, 585.

[8] Gewirth I, 293-4.

[9] Boehner, 450-1; Seeberg, III, 587.

[10] Boehner, 445, 460, 463, 464.

[11] Boehner, 468; Oberman, 422.

[12] Oberman, 366, 399, 418; Seeburg III, 587, 588-9.

[13] Gewirth, I, 289, 290.

[14] cf. chap. II, n. 1.

[15] O. Farner I, 215, 218-19, 221-2.

[16] Köhler "Huldrych Zwinglis Bibliothek," *NB,* LXXXIV, 6, 13, 21.

[17] Usteri, "Initia Zwingliana," *TSK,* LVIII (1885), 617, 627; LIX (1886), 98, 103-4; Köhler, *NB,* LXXXIV, 17, 22.

[18] Köhler, *NB,* LXXXIV, 14.

[19] Fife, "Humanistic Currents in the Reformation Era," *GR,* XII, 83.

[20] Köhler, *NB,* LXXXIV, 14, 21.

[21] Usteri, *TSK,* LVIII, 617, 629.

[22] In a letter to Zwingli, written on November 2, 1522, Michael Hummelberg informed him that Luther's answer to Henry VIII's attack had been published. If Zwingli did not have it, Hummelberg offered to get it for him. He advised Zwingli to read, in the meantime, Melanchthon's *Themata*: "In the meantime read these 'Theses Concerning the Double Magistracy' of the Melanchthon and you will see how they have confused the spiritual ministry of the Pope with temporal things" (*Z,* VII, 607, 8-10). Hummelberg's statement implies either that the *Themata* were already in Zwingli's hands or, as the use of *haec* makes more likely, they were being sent along with his letter. Since the work was known to have been in Zwingli's library, it is justifiable to assumed that it arrived sometime later in 1522 and was available to reinforce Zwingli's own views on the matter during the earlier stages of his career as a reformer. Köhler believes that the *Themata* may have influenced what he terms Zwingli's *staatstheoretische Anschauung* (Zwingli's theoretical view of the state); Köhler, *NB,* LXXXIV, 15, 21).

[23] M, I, 595.

[24] M, I, 596.

[25] Köhler, *NB,* LXXXIV, 15, 21.

[26] *Ibid*., 14-15. Egli, "Aus Zwinglis Bibliothek," *ZWI,* II (1907), 181.

[27] Rich, 21-2, 26, 28, 82-3, 151.

[28] Usteri was responsible for both suggestions (*TSK,* LVIII, 669-70). Köhler agrees with Usteri (*NB,* LXXXIV, 29).

[29] Erasmus, *The Praise of Folly,* ed. Hudson, 85-6, 97 (hereafter cited as *PF*).

[30] *Z,* I, 495, 22-496, 1.

[31] *PF,* 98-9.

[32] *Z,* III, 57, 25-8, 31-58, 1.

[33] Rudolf Liechtenhan, "Die Politische Hoffnung des Erasmus und Ihr Zusammenbruch," *Gedenkschrift zum 400 Todestage des Erasmus von Rotterdam,* 152-3, 158.

[34] Geldner, 80-1, 140.

[35] Erasmus, *The Education of a Christian Prince,* ed. Born, 157 (hereafter cited as *ECP*).

[36] Erasmus, *Complaint of Peace,* ed. Hirten, 56.

[37] *ECP,* 162-3, 140.

[38] *Ibid.,* 222.

[39] *Z,* II, 488, 4-5.

[40] *ECP,* 213-14.

[41] Maurer, 23-4.

[42] *ECP,* 175-9.

[43] *Z,* III, 27.

[44] *ECP,* 180.

[45] Enthoven, *NJKA,* XXIV, 316.

[46] Geldner, 84-5, 98-9.

[47] Moeller, 48-9, 51-3.

## Heiko A. Oberman (lecture date 1984)

SOURCE: "Zwingli's Reformation Between Sucess and Failure," in *The Reformation: Roots and Ramifications*, translated by Andrew Colin Gow, T & T Clark, 1994, pp. 183-99.

[*In this essay, originally delivered as a lecture in 1984, Oberman discusses Zwingli's contributions to the Reformation in the political and social context of sixteenth-century Switzerland.*]

### CANTONIZATION AND PAROCHIALISM

Is Zwingli's Reformation anything more than an episode between Luther and Calvin? To claim that it had a world-wide or even a European influence seems presumptuous in the light of recent Reformation history, which assigns Zwingli's Zurich to the 'city Reformation' and characterizes this phenomenon in sociological terms as a process of 'communalization'.

If communalization means the emancipation of the city, which dates back to the late Middle Ages, and in conjunction with this, the 'localization' of the Reformation—as compared to the territorial Reformation of the princes—then the events at Zurich in the years 1519-31 are reduced *de facto* to an internal Swiss affair touching hardly more than the area of the canton. The image of the parochial *Leutpriester* (secular 'people's priest', that is, pastor) of the local church at Zurich fits this interpretation well. Zwingli was able to unite the religious and the political emancipation of the city with such consummate skill that he even ended his life on the battlefield as an *Antistes* (here: chief pastor) without clerical robes, as a cleric in arms, as a member of the citizen militia. Despite the defeat at Kappel in 1531, the Reformation had taken root and been 'naturalized' politically at Zurich to such an extent—according to this view—that Zwingli's legacy was in no danger within the city walls, at least.

This 'bourgeois' interpretation of Zwingli has to be tested critically. There is no doubt that Zwingli was not accorded a comprehensive and balanced interpretation for centuries because he was constantly represented as somehow inadequate when compared to Luther, or as dependent on the Wittenberg reformer. The lasting contribution of the celebrated Zwingli specialist, Gottfried W. Locher, consists in having understood Zwingli on Zwingli's own terms, thus freeing him from the anathema pronounced on him by the Gnesio-Lutherans. The extent and boundaries of Zwingli's influence, however, cannot be ascertained without comparing the reformer of Zurich with Martin Luther,[1] nor without fitting Zwingli into the framework formed by the Strasbourg reformer Martin Bucer, Zwingli's independent successor Heinrich Bullinger and the Genevan pastor of pastors, John Calvin. In the absence of a larger evangelical context, the historian is forced to resort to the equivocal concept of 'Zwinglianism'—which, as the literature demonstrates, can make no claim to precision.[2] To describe Bucer and Bullinger as 'Zwinglians' is a kind of forced baptism. Their association and shared characteristics become clear only when they are compared to Luther, which I will undertake in the third part of this chapter.

### ZURICH: THE PROTOTYPICAL CITY REFORMATION

The term 'communalization of the Reformation'[3] contains an important element of truth, just as the image of Zwingli as a cleric in arms on the battlefield furnishes evidence for the radical and logically consistent redefinition of clerics as citizens, a redefinition which stripped them of their special privileges. This term delineates the field in which Zwingli became a reformer and Zurich an evangelical city. But we ought to recognize the limits set by this urban interpretive framework. The perfect interlocking fit, the smooth co-operation between Zwingli and Zurich postulated in recent trends, but only aspired to by Zwingli, is not borne out by the evidence in the sources. Above all, limiting the sphere of our investigation to the urban theater means losing all ability to perceive and understand Zwingli's regional, indeed his European, importance.

I will concentrate on 'taking inventory' for three decisive years: 1522-3, the year of the evangelical breakthrough; 1527-8, the year of alliances; and the year of crisis, 1530-1, which saw the Kappel War and Zwingli's death.

### 1522-3: THE INTRODUCTION OF THE REFORMATION

It is quite simply an error to imagine that Zwingli was harmoniously integrated into the political power structures of Zurich in the early twenties, and therefore grew 'organically' into the position of political 'helmsman'. This integrationist model is linked in a very unfortunate way to what only seem to be unequivocal key-words: 'biblical theocracy', or Zwingli as the mighty 'prophet', who represents correct belief and the right politics. To the extent that the historian's task is to describe reality, not ideals, these are distortions. They are based on a highly inflated estimate of how firm a consensus and how lasting an understanding were possible between Zwingli and the leading citizens in the council at Zurich. We are obliged to consider Zurich's internal situation briefly if we are to understand Zwingli's political positions and status in the city. The proper place to start is not the Zurich Disputation of 29 January 1523, but the defeat of Marignano (1515) and its critical *domestic* effects on the political structure and power relations in Zurich.

After Marignano, the representatives of the guislds demanded and received greater political responsibility. The city council was forced to commit itself to a policy that allowed no more experiments in foreign policy. Service in foreign armies and the granting of pensions were strictly limited by breaking off all alliances with foreign powers—except the alliance with the Pope, which had been sealed on 9 December 1514.

In 1518, Zwingli's call to Zurich was supported by the papal party, which had grown much stronger since the battle of Marignano. They doubtless knew that their candidate had accompanied the Glarus military contingent in 1513 and 1515 to protect the Pontifical State and that he had left Glarus after the shocking defeat which brought the French party to power.

In the summer of 1521, Zurich once again marched into Italy to secure Parma and Piacenza for the Holy Father. It was to be Zurich's last mercenary expedition. On 11 January 1522, Zurich prohibited mercenary service for foreign powers forever and without exception.[4] The passage of this long-overdue prohibition is often explained with reference to the influence of Zwingli's protests: he had, after all, publicly attacked the rich cardinals who employed Swiss youth and, if necessary, their blood in order to rage unchecked as 'wolves'. However, the decision made on 11 January was based not on Zwingli's attack on *curial* militarism, but on the council's policy of frustrating *French* attempts to hire Zurich mercenaries.

When the expedition to Piacenza was debated in the previous year, the council decided to send mercenary troops to Italy *despite* Zwingli's active opposition: 'agreements must be fulfilled' (*pacta sunt servanda*).

The influence of the *Leutpriester* did not extend very far into the chambers of the city council.

Lent of 1522 saw the 'Lenten scandal' at the Froschauer house. This immediately set off an episcopal visitation, which was in turn supported by the Zurich council—*in spite of* Zwingli's public declarations and the appearance of his first evangelical treatise. Further violation of the Lenten fast was prohibited. 'No-one may eat meat on such days and at such times as have in the past been prohibited, except from necessity.'[5] The council once again took a position opposed to the *Leutpriester*.

The disputations have been cited repeatedly as proof of the close political co-operation between Zwingli and the council. However, they actually hide another series of conflicts.

Zwingli engaged in a 'private' disputation with the wandering Franciscan preacher Franz Lambert. This exchange was set off by Zwingli, who heckled Lambert's sermon at the *Fraumünster* (Cathedral of Our Lady) on 15 July 1520: 'Brother, you are wrong there.'[6] This method of interrupting sermons had already been used successfully by Zwingli's right-hand man, Leo Jud, on numerous occasions, and was quite simply a violation of the policy of 'calm and order' (*Ruhe und Ordnung*) pursued carefully and consistently by the city council. One week later, the opposing parties—Zwingli and the lectors of the three mendicant orders—were summoned before a committee of the Small Council. The Chapter of the *Grossmünster* was included, as well as the two other *Leutpriester* and Konrad Schmid, Bachelor of Theology, probably as an expert witness. (*peritus*). Six months before the clergy of the city and surrounding countryside under Zurich's control were summoned as a group, the council tried to defuse the explosive situation by putting Zwingli into contact with the élite of the old Church. No matter how much this improved Zwingli's status as the representative of his party, the council's decision to allow only preaching in accord with Scripture was still that of a non-partisan authority. Even the disputation that took place six months later, generally known in Zwingli studies as the 'first Zurich disputation', still was not *Zwingli's* disputation, but remained—against his expectations—an affair of the city council.

The city council not only approved these disputations, it organized them. In both cases the council judged the outcome of the disputation—the 'hearing against each other' (*Verhör gegeneinander*). As in 1523, the council ordered, for the sake of 'liberating the city', that preaching *not* be argumentative: 'You are to treat each other in a friendly way.'[7] The authorities still hoped to drain this swamp of poisonous quarrels.

The three events, from the 'Lenten scandal' (April 1522) through the disputation with the monastic dignitaries (21 July 1522) to the great disputation before the council (29 January 1523), mark three steps on the path that led from eliminating the spiritual authority of the Bishop of Constance to establishing the religious jurisdiction of the Zurich council as the final court of appeal.

There is no doubt that Zwingli's influence was growing during this period. When the episcopal delegation from Constance arrived in April 1522 to conduct a visitation on account of the Lenten 'sausage-eating' episode, Zwingli had a hard time getting a hearing from the council.[8] He was summoned before a council committee in July. *Bürgermeister* Marx Röist now took the initiative and tried at first to settle the dispute in as private a way as possible. He felt he could prevent further escalation of tensions by ordering Zwingli and the mendicants to preach along the same lines. Although he was responsible for public order, he wanted to refer the substantive judgement of the theologian's controversy to the Cathedral Chapter of Zurich. When Zwingli protested[9] and his partisans in the council started to bother the *Bürgermeister,* however, the council ordered that all preaching be based on Scripture alone: 'Indeed, you masters of the monastic orders, it is my lords' intention that you should only preach the Holy Gospel from now on, St. Paul and the prophets, which is Holy Writ, and leave Scotus and Thomas and such things alone.'[10]

What is unique and lasting about the subsequent disputation before the council of 29 January 1523, the so-called 'first Zurich disputation'? It is no longer possible to insist that this disputation made Holy Scripture the standard for preaching. Even the formulation of the *Abschied* (the declaration which enjoins scriptural preaching) is no innovation. Nor was it a novelty to hold a disputation before the council: it was merely a stage on the road to urban emancipation from episcopal jurisdiction. Since scholars have read the *Abschied* from Zwingli's perspective and have, therefore, interpreted it as a victory for him, only one phrase has become well-known: that allowing the *Leutpriester* to continue 'as in the past' (*wie bisher*). Although his preaching and theology are thereby acknowledged as 'scriptural' this phrase does not grant Zwingli the exclusive rights nor the spiritual monopoly that he thought it did.

In accordance with the political aims of the Small Council, particularly of *Bürgermeister* Marx Röist, *both* parties were dismissed with the order not to call each other heretics nor to insult each other,[11] under pain of severe punishment. Only when a majority of the Small Council insisted on maintaining their policy of pacification *after* the end of the disputation held in October of 1523 did the Great Council decide to exercise control over not only basic legislation governing preaching, but also over the practical regulations and ordinances concerning correct, licit preaching. Until this time at least, there was no such thing as 'Zwingli's Zurich'. In 1523—while the magistrature was still decisively under the influence of the Small Council in religious matters—there is reason to speak of Zwingli's influence as a preacher, but not of his power as a politician.

One seemingly tiny detail is a clear sign of Zwingli's distance from the council. It has been overlooked in the past, probably because it does not fit into the common image of 'Zwingli's Zurich'. On 20 January 1523, the eminent Swiss humanist Glarean (+1563) complained in a letter from Basel that Zwingli told him the wrong date for the disputation—nine days early: 'Your letter, in which you wrote that the disputation would take place on January 20th, led us completely astray, because I eagerly showed it to my friends everywhere; everyone who read it and has gone to Zurich for no reason will now be angry with me . . . '[12]

Zwingli's letter to Glarean contained yet another error. The *Leutpriester* assumed that he would preside himself after the fashion of a medieval university professor who, according to the university statutes, presides over the disputation concerning the theses he has composed and published. But everything happened differently in this case. The council took such a large part in planning the disputation that Zwingli was not even consulted by the council concerning the date. And not only the *date,* but also the *form* of the disputation was a complete surprise to Zwingli: whereas he had been preparing for *his* disputation, right down to the traditional series of academic theses, *Bürgermeister* Marx Röist and the Small Council pushed their plan through for a 'hearing' of the two sides. Zwingli and the council simply did not co-operate on this matter.

Nevertheless, the disputation held before the council does have two faces. For one, the summons and the *Abschied* fit seamlessly into the policy of peaceable order pursued by the Small Council and directed against Zwingli as well as his adversaries. It was due to Zwingli's theological interpretation and significance that this local event, embedded in city politics, became a spiritual event that reached far beyond the walls and canton of Zurich. The renewal of theology and of the Church was initiated in Zurich on the basis of Holy Scripture; this decision for renewal settled the question once and for all and by proxy, as it were, for all of Christendom: the Holy Spirit does not say one thing today and another tomorrow.[13] That particular roomful of people, therefore, was a Christian assembly.[14] The 'council disputation' became Zwingli's *Council,* representing the entire Church. The council of Zurich merely called a hearing; Zwingli discovered in it the first evangelical General Synod. This redefinition of a hearing as a 'Christian assembly' has epochal significance for the history of the universal Protestant Church. *The event itself is as 'local' as its meaning is 'universal'.* Zwingli speaks of Zurich's 'authority by proxy', but the power of the Reformation in Zurich was not yet that complete.

### 2. 1527: THE CONFEDERACY OF THE EVANGELICALS

Just as it seemed as though the political leadership and the city's pastor might be 'of one heart and soul', the perspectives and strategies of the council and the reformer threatened to split irreconcilably once again.

By necessity Zurich's internal policy sought to resolve tensions within the walls and to avoid all strife with the mercantile class engaged in foreign trade, and with those guilds that had anything to do with the outside—particularly the 'Butchers', who depended on a steady supply of men from the inner cantons of Switzerland to maintain their numbers. All alliances that might involve Zurich in broader conflicts had been abrogated and were to be avoided. Zwingli, however, was keen on new alliances; he saw Zurich merely as the beginning, as a starting point and prototype for the much-needed pacification of Christendom that accompanies obedience to God's Word.

One document merits particular attention because it has preserved Zwingli's all-encompassing view of the Reformation: his plea for an alliance, in the summer of 1527, that would be able to face up to the pan-European expansionism of the Habsburgs. Since Zwingli had failed completely in this attempt by 1529/30, German historians have not been able to refrain from concluding that this idea was nothing but the enthusiastic and naïve plan of an amateur politician hampered by the particular disadvantage of Swiss blinders, without the ability to see beyond the Swiss border. His correspondence with Philip of Hesse, written in a secret code, has even been dismissed as 'a game of cowboys and Indians'. This judgement has been made all the easier by the condemnation of Philip's bigamy common among moralizing historians, a judgement which has tended to eclipse the sharp political vision of Zwingli's correspondent in Hesse, the man who would later be the leader and *spiritus rector* (guiding influence) of the Schmalkaldic Alliance.

Swiss historians have not been so confused in their judgement, and have recognized Zwingli's all-encompassing political ambitions. This judgement is correct. The introduction of the Reformation at Berne (1528) meant much more to him than just another canton won over; it was a decisive step on the way toward a 'true confederacy' (*eine wahre Eidgenossenschaft*). But even this interpretation falls short of the mark. The reformer of Zurich doubtless wanted not just a loose co-operation between Swiss towns and cities at *Tagsatzungen* (federal Diets), but a firmly established Swiss nation (*natio helvetica*). This was achieved both despite and thanks to the Second War of Kappel.

His broader vision, which transcended national boundaries, has not yet been mentioned. On two folio pages, dated by Walther Köhler (+1946) to the summer of 1527, Zwingli set out his political program. It is an impressive sketch for a trans-national confederacy.[15]

In order to place this plan in proper perspective, we must resort to comparisons with modern alliance patterns, such as the ambitious though as-yet unrealized plan, born of the Second World War, to establish an independent European defensive alliance with the goal of guaranteeing European unity, security and independence. The title subsequently added to Zwingli's plan ***Why we ought to unite with Constance, Lindau, Strasbourg etc.***—that is, with the upper Rhine, Lake Constance and Alsace—*under one law* does not immediately reveal everything Zwingli expected of the city's leaders: Zurich ought to think and act not merely with reference to all of Switzerland, but with reference to all of Europe.

Constance and Lindau had been Emperor Maximilian's strategic bases of operations in the Swabian War of 1499, the memory of which was still fresh and terrifying. Nonetheless, these cities should not be thought of as 'hostile foreign parts', Zwingli felt, but rather included in a broadly-based defensive alliance after all unhappy memories and resentment had been put to rest. Like the Landgrave of Hesse, the 'shepherd of Zurich' was capable of thinking on a European scale and opposing to the Habsburg dream of universal empire the alternative vision of a confederate evangelical alliance.

What then, was Zwingli's goal? It was 'one people and one alliance'[16] from Switzerland to Strasbourg. We can add that this confederacy would have constituted precisely the barricade—a kind of *cordon evangèlique*—between Burgundy and Austria, between Habsburg and Habsburg, that Emperor Maximilian had tried to prevent by founding the Swabian Alliance (*Schwäbischer Bund*). The new confederacy would push its way into the power vacuum left by the crumbling Swabian Alliance—but *against* the Emperor. In retrospect, the success of such an alliance would have brought forward the Schmalkaldic War of 1547 by about twenty years—to a time much more favorable in military terms for the evangelical side.

This document is of interest for two reasons. First, it demonstrates yet again how much more Zwingli was than a mere 'City Pastor' (*Stadtpfarrer*). Of equal importance are the theological grounds and arguments with which Zwingli prefaced his plan: although the cause of the Reformation can survive only 'by the power of God' (*uss der kraft gottes*), God generally does not intervene directly in the course of events on earth but makes use of people to provide (his) people with 'help and protection' (*hilff und schirm*). Since God allows this treaty of alliance to be concluded, 'it is clear that he wants to use it for good purposes.'[17]

In the third part of this chapter, we will return to this basic position for the purpose of comparing Zwingli to Luther. Zwingli sums up his entire theology in this single sentence. God directs the history of humanity with consummate power and skill toward the time when human and divine righteousness will grow into unity. God clearly approves of Zwingli's proposed treaty, because it would lead to 'peace, order, equity and justice' ('friden, ruwen, billichkeit und gerechtigkeit'). The all-powerful, just director of history guarantees the efficacy of the Reformation in establishing justice. It is therefore the task of all believers to advance the Reformation with all their might, in the certain knowledge of God's support and of victory. Zwingli's political theology starts from this principle, which in turn makes *Realpolitik* the execution of God's righteous justice, trusting to God's omnipotence.

This fundamental principle does not, however, have anything to do with Zwingli's own experience—quite the contrary! Helmut Meyer has been able to demonstrate, by means of painstaking research, just how closely Zwingli was involved in the deliberations of the city council[18]—even in those of the *Geheimer Rat,* the 'privy council'. However, Zwingli's constant participation in political affairs in the last years of his life and his advancement to the most important committees of Zurich's governmental élite do not refute the thesis that his influence was limited; rather, his overt political 'success' at Zurich minimizes, indeed hides, the extent to which he was isolated in the last years. The Marburg Colloquy (October 1529) was the precondition to a far-reaching evangelical accord with Electoral Saxony and Hesse. Its failure was topped in the following year by the decision of the imperial cities Constance and Strasbourg—without, perhaps even against, Zurich—along with Lindau and Memmingen, to present the Emperor with their own Confession at Augsburg, the *Tetrapolitana*. Zwingli's far-sighted European plan had failed.

His efforts to unite the Swiss 'nation' did seem more successful, to the extent that the five cantons of inner Switzerland (Lucerne, Uri, Schwytz, Unterwalden and Zug) had allowed free preaching of the Gospel. But the victory of the First War of Kappel did not bear fruit, because Zurich decided to join the double-edged Bernese strategic boycott. From Zwingli's perspective, the city of Zurich had refused to seize the opportunity which God had provided.

3. 1531: THE CATASTROPHE OF KAPPEL

Johann Stumpf remarked in his *Chronica* how strongly Zwingli felt he had been left in the lurch by the political élite of Zurich. On 26 July 1531, the reformer announced his resignation and intent to leave Zurich with the explanation that 'the *pensioner* [people drawing pensions] of the Five Cantons are taking the upper hand in Zurich as well'.[19] Threatening to resign strengthened Zwingli's support at first. Stumpf's chronicle (which is not sufficiently appreciated today; it has been labelled 'too partisan') continues: 'This threat frightened many, such that many eyes overflowed with tears.' Three days later the council itself begged him 'to stay with them until death'.[20]

Which is exactly what happened. But it makes absolutely no sense to conclude on this account that Zwingli fell at Kappel as an obedient burgher in the service of the city council. On 9 October, when the Five Cantons were already mobilizing, Zwingli painted in his last sermon a grimly realistic portrait of his hopeless political isolation. Zurich was chained to the Five Cantons by financial interests; all warnings were too late:

> But no loyal warning made to you helps; everything is in vain. The pensioners of the five cantons have too much *ruggen* [backing] in this city. There is a chain, from which I have in the past torn many rings, and broken it, but it is whole now. [Stumpf explains: meaning the secret oligarchy of the well-wishers of the five cantons in Zurich.] This chain will strangle me and many a pious Zuricher. I am finished. You will deliver me into their hands, but you will still knock horns with me.[21]

Zwingli answers in advance—and correctly—the question as to why mighty Zurich put only 3,500 men in the field on 11 October against an opposing force twice as strong. His answer is more convincing than those of modern observers, with their doubtless correct references to the short time available for mobilization and inadequate military tactics and strategy. The defeat was, in fact, a foregone conclusion; as Zwingli predicted, the chain had been made whole again. Five hundred men of Zurich fell in less than an hour.

Zwingli's view of history—that the almighty God would lead the Reformation to its final victory—explains the catastrophic defeat at Kappel. The catastrophe consisted not in military weakness and tactical errors, but in God's refusal, to smash the 'chain' of Zurich's opponents.

The consequences of the Second Kappel War prepared the future course of the Swiss Confederacy, a course that Germany first discovered with the Religious Peace of Augsburg in 1555, reaching its end only after much bloodshed in 1648. The practical political principle that is to this day considered to be a German invention is in fact a product of rational Swiss politics, set out in the Second Peace of Kappel at Deinikon on 16 November 1531: 'Cuius regio, eius religio' (the religion of a territory is determined by its lord).

3. LUTHER AND ZWINGLI

The defeat at Kappel made waves far beyond the narrow confines of the canton and the Swiss Confederacy. A flood of reproaches descended on the fallen chaplain. The harshest reactions came, not surprisingly, from Wittenberg. As late as 1544, Luther thundered that [Zwingli's downfall at] Kappel is the fate of all sects and zealots, 'the terrifying judgement of God, where Zwingli met such a wretched death'.[22] Is this merely Saxon self-righteousness, Luther's stiff-necked certainty that he was right, expressed in terms just as strong and as dogged as ever, thirteen years after Zwingli's death?

These two great reformers were born hardly seven weeks apart—yet they are separated by the space of an entire epoch. In short, Luther was experiencing the End Time; Zwingli lived in modern times. The gap that separated them in theology and piety, in the doctrine of the sacraments and 'Christian' politics had far-reaching consequences. To measure the distance between these epochs, we must go beyond details to the basic question posed by our analysis of Zwingli's influence and activities as *Leutpriester* in Zurich and as a political theologian with European ambitions: the question of God's righteousness and omnipotence.

God's omnipotence is a pressing concern in all Christian thought, and occupies a central position in evangelical theology as well. Luther and Zwingli both interpret God's omnipotence according to a specific and particular paradigm. When Luther speaks of God's omnipotence, he throws his view of the Devil into sharp relief, with considerable consequences for his interpretation of history: human history is not the era, the time of God's omnipotence, but of his powerlessness; the history of the Church, vulnerable to Satan's fury, a fury that will end only with the end of the world.[23]

For the sake of comparison, we will now turn our attention to the reformer of Zurich. I will concentrate on a scholarly-exegetical text: Zwingli's reading of Isaiah, which he presented in the pedagogically innovative form of learned 'prophecy' in 1527 and made public the following year in his preaching. Isaiah 42.8 clearly 'reveals' God alone in his almighty majesty: 'My glory I will not give to another'. This single text, Zwingli argues, smashes all Wittenberg's theology concerning the Lord's Supper. The real presence of the historical Christ on the altar is not biblical, because it requires that Christ be present physically all over the world—*ubique*—at the same time. 'Ubiquity', however, is a characteristic of eternal God, therefore it touches only

Christ's divine—not his bodily, human—nature. Christ's human nature is neither eternal, infinite, nor everywhere (*ubique*) present: God does not give his majesty to any human being.[24]

Scholarly depictions of the controversy over the Lord's Supper have not taken Zwingli's exegesis of Isaiah into account, because of its relative lateness and because it offers nothing new in this area toward distinguishing Zwingli from Luther. This text does, however, express a program that lends it paradigmatic importance for our understanding of the *philosophical* presuppositions of Zwingli's theology. Zwingli breaks God's nature down into its component parts with the logical persuasiveness characteristic of the medieval *via antiqua* (scholastic theology). Rather than present the entire sequence of his argument, I will emphasize only this principle: Ubiquity is an inalienable and non-transferable characteristic of God alone. On this rests his omnipotence: 'However, to be everywhere is a hidden property belonging only to spiritual beings. Indeed, this is where his omnipotence originates.'[25]

Not only can it be proven that God exists, but it can be shown what he logically must be like. God must be ubiquitous, because it is a necessary corollary of his omnipotence. The entire argument is sustained by reasoned, necessary connections, which are revealed in his introductory formulae: 'it is necessary' (*necesse est*), 'therefore' (*ergo*), 'from this, then' (*hinc enim*) and 'it cannot' (*non potest*), along with all the features of a 'proof' in the rationalistic theology that was called the *via antiqua* in the Middle Ages, and which has held Protestant theology captive since the time of Hegel and German Idealism. The *via antiqua* is 'logical' in the sense of a chain of cause and effect that can be followed logically by a thinking person. The *via moderna* broke this chain.

Two key passages from William of Ockham (the *Venerabilis Inceptor*) confirm this: 'It cannot be proved that God is omnipotent, but grasped and held by faith alone.'[26] The 'rational and logical' analysis of God's nature and characteristics comes up against an impenetrable barrier in the form of God's peculiar and particular way of being and perceiving, divine activities which are not structured according to the standards of human logic: 'God's mind is of a different sort than our minds'[27]—impossible for us to grasp.

Here Luther is entirely within the tradition of the *via moderna,* in that he accepts a radical separation between God's wisdom and human thought, and proposes the omnipotence of God as an article of faith. Luther's conclusions lead far beyond Ockham: omnipotent God will lead history to final victory; this can be and is to be believed despite the evidence of reason and of one's conscience, despite the visible and tangible power of the Devil, by faith alone. God's omnipotence is hidden. It functions in history 'by means of its opposite' (*sub contrario*). His power rests, disguised, in the Cross.

In Zwingli's theology, the Devil has already been deposed and overcome; he has been, as it were, de-mythologized. Luther believes that the Devil rules over his world-wide empire with all his might and violence until the last day of the End Time: the Devil is the *rex saeculi,* the king of this world. From Luther's perspective, Zwingli was ensnared in the causal chain of philosophical theology long before he was fettered by the conspiracy of the Zurich pensioners. I would like to close this comparison of Luther and Zwingli with two reflections: a glance backwards and a glance into what might be a less narrow future.

First: Luther's doctrine of the Lord's Supper was not a sudden and inconsistent relapse into the Middle Ages[28] set off by Zwingli; rather, it is based on fundamental decisions which represent a deep gulf between Luther and Zwingli. Therefore we are justified in claiming that the dispute over the doctrine of ubiquity, which was at the center of the Reformation from 1525 on, could have been conducted in a much more fruitful and promising fashion on the basis of the doctrine of divine omnipotence or providence. Ockham's use of the term *sola fide* disentangles theology from the causal web of logical metaphysics. Luther adopted this insight in so far as he believed that God can be perceived only via Scripture—reason can only stand by and gape in amazement. Scripture therefore puts 'believing reason' in its proper place: radical exegesis resists logical necessity. The 'scriptural principle'—believed with great certainty by all involved to be the common basis of the Reformation—was mortgaged from the very beginning to the all-encompassing dispute over the Lord's Supper.

Second: Zwingli's 'evangelical discovery' was characterized by obedient listening to God's biblical call to penance: 'Repent!', reform yourselves. His evangelical ethics grew out of obedient submission to God's omnipotent will to enforce true righteousness in history over against injustice and opposition. In this respect, Zwingli's Reformation had world-wide consequences. Zwingli's death and the catastrophe of Kappel allowed the urban Reformation to expand the evangelical legacy beyond the walls of cities and thereby to move across Europe. In consequence, the Reformation eventually surpassed Zwingli's visionary plan of 1527 by much more than he could ever have hoped.

Zwingli listened to Scripture in a new way, with a sharpened sense of social justice that made the Reformation modern. Luther also listened to Scripture in a new way, but experienced the Reformation eschatologically. His belief in the Devil made him look medieval from the perspective of the Enlightenment, which then set very narrow boundaries to his sphere of influence. The differences between Luther and Zwingli could be papered over by their agreement on the Lord's Supper (the *Abendmahlskonkordie*), but not overcome. The healing of Protestantism throughout the world and the evangelical contribution to the unity of the entire, genuinely catholic ecumenical Church depend on whether or not it is possible to break through the double chain forged by individual reason and individual dogmatism which Luther and Zwingli attacked, each in his own way, with the weapons of the Gospel.

To conclude: Zwingli won Zurich for the Reformation, but gambled with the local Reformation to attempt the Reformation of all Christendom. For this reason alone, Zwingli defies definition as a mere city reformer. The 'counter-reformer' Fabri called him a 'second Luther', 'only more dangerous'. Fabri came from Constance, so he knew all about the political ferment engendered by 'that Swiss reformer' and the threat it posed to Habsburg designs on Europe. Fabri was wrong, however: Zwingli's policy of alliances had no lasting effect. Zwingli became really 'dangerous' to Roman plans to regain control over Europe only after Kappel. Odd as it may seem, this defeat allowed Zurich to exert a powerful influence on the subsequent history of the Christian world.

*Notes*

[1] See Ulrich Gäbler, 'Luthers Beziehungen zu den Oberdeutschen und Schweizern von 1526 bis 1530/31', in: *Leben und Werk Martin Luthers von 1526 bis 1546,* ed. H. Junghans, Göttingen 1983, 481-96, 885-91; and M. Brecht, 'Luthers Beziehungen zu den Oberdeutschen und Schweizern von 1530/31 bis 1546', ibid., 497-517, 891-4.

[2] The monumental study of G. W. Locher, *Die Zwinglische Reformation im Rahmen der europäischen Kirchengeschichte,* Göttingen 1979, even distinguishes between 'late Zwinglianism'—the 'Nachfolger-Tradition' founded by Heinrich Bullinger (584ff.)—and the 'form and legacy' of Zwingli's work, which produce only theological echoes (671 ff.). Locher had to define the concept 'Zwinglianism' in a very broad way in order to describe Martin Bucer as a 'Zwinglian'. See Locher's excellent sketch of John Calvin in *Protestantische Profile. Lebensbilder aus fünf Jahrhunderten,* ed. K. Scholder and D. Kleinmann, Königstein/Ts 1983, 78-93.

[3] See P. Blickle, *Die Reformation im Reich,* Stuttgart 1982, 92; 158.

[4] See E. Egli, *Schweizerische Reformationsgeschichte,* vol. 1, ed. G. Finsler, Zurich 1910, 57.

[5] '. . . dass niemas zuo solichen vorhar verbottnen ziten und tagen on notdurfft sölle fleisch essen' (*Ratsmandat* (city council decree) of 26 February 1523; E. Egli, *Aktensammlung zur Geschichte der Zürcher Reformation in den Jahren 1519-33,* Zurich 1879 [Nieuwkoop 1973], 118, n. 339); cf. the first Lenten decree of 9 April 1522, which is the same in substance.

[6] 'Bruder, da irrest du' (G. Finsler, *Die Chronik des Bernhard Wyss 1519-530,* Basel 1901, 16).

[7] Finsler, *Chronik,* 19.

[8] Cf. *Acta Tiguri,* Zwingli's description of the events from 7-9 April 1522, addressed to Erasmus Fabricius, in: *Huldreich Zwinglis sämtliche Werke* (= *ZW*) 1, 144.5-11; cf. the introduction, 137f.

[9] 'Ich bin in diser statt Zürich bischof und pfarrer und mir ist die seelsorg bevolen; ich han darum geschworen und die münch nit; si sond uf mich acht han und ich nit uf si; dann so dick si predigend, das erlogen ist, so will ich's widerfechten . . .' (Finsler, *Chronik,* 19.)

[10] 'Ja, ir herren von örden, das ist miner herren meinung, daß ir sollend nun fürohin predigen das heilig evangelium, den heiligen Paulum und die propheten, daß die heilige gechrift ist, und lassend den Scotum und Thomam und sollig ding ligen' (ibid.). Zwingli himself reports to Beatus Rhenanus: 'Mandatum erat, ut relictis Thomabus, Scotis reliquisque id farinae doctoribus unis sacris literis nitantur, quae scilicet intra biblia contineantur' (Zurich, 30 July 1522, *ZW* VII, 549.3-5).

[11] 'einanderen hinfür dheins wegs schmützen, ketzeren, noch andere schmachwortt zureden' (*ZW* I, 471.7f.).

[12] 'Mirum in modum fefellit nos charta tua, in qua scripseras XIII. Kalendas Februarias venturam disputationem. Eam cum ubique sedulus apud amicos circumferrem, quidam viderunt ac Tigurum iverunt, fortassis mihi infensi, cum celeritas tua et te et me fefellerit' (*ZW* VIII, 9.1-4).

[13] *ZW* I, 514.9f.

[14] *ZW* I, 495.10f.

[15] *ZW* VI 1, 197-201.

[16] That 'ein volck und pündtnus wurde . . .' (*ZW* VI 1, 201.17).

[17] '[es] ist . . . offembar, das er inn zuo guotem bruchen wil' (*ZW* VI 1, 200.9).

[18] H. Meyer, *Der zweite Kappeler Krieg. Die Krise der Schweizerischen Reformation,* Zurich 1976, 316-23.

[19] Johann Stumpf, *Chronic vom Leben und Werk des Ulrich Zwingli,* ed. L. Weiss, Zurich 1932[2], 166. On

Stumpf's chronicle, see P. Wernle, 'Das Verhältnis der schweizerischen zur deutschen Reformation', in: *Basler Zeitschrift für Geschichte und Altertumskunde* 17 (1918), 227-315, 248-50.

[20] 'Ab dieser red erschrack mencklich, also daß vielen die ougen übergiengend"; they asked him 'by inen zu blyben, bis in den todt' (Stumpf, *Chronica,* 166).

[21] 'Aber es hilft kein getrüwe warnung an üch, sonder ist alles vergebens. Die pensionär der fünf Orten habend zuviel ruggens in diser statt. Es ist ein ketten gemacht, uß der ich bishar mangen ring gerissen und sy oft gebrochen hab, aber jetzund ist sy ganz. (Verstand die heymlich oligarchy der fünf orten gönner Zürich.) Dise kette wirt mir und mengen frommen Zürcher den hals abziehen. Es ist um mich zuthon. Ihr werdend mich ihnen in die händ bringen, aber ihr werdend ein hörnli mit mir abstoßen' (Stumpf, *Chronica,* 169).

[22] 'das schreckliche urteil Gottes, da der Zwingel so jemerlich ward erschlagen' (*WA* 54, 154.17f.).

[23] See ch. 3 above, 'Martin Luther: Between the Middle Ages and Modern Times'.

[24] *ZW* XIV, 336.32-337.15.

[25] 'Ubique autem esse, intima ac sola numinis est proprietas. Hinc enim dimanat omnipotentia' (*ZW* XIV, 337.9-11).

[26] 'Non potest demonstrari quod Deus sit omnipotens, sed sola fide tenetur' (Quodlibet I, q.1 ad 7; *Guillelmi de Ockham. Quodlibeta septem,* ed. J. C. Wey CSB, *Opera Theologica* IX, St. Bonaventure, NY 1980, 11.230f.).

[27] '[I]ntellectio Dei est alterius rationis a nostris intellectionibus' (Quodlibet III, q. 1 ad 3; ibid., 207.202f.).

[28] See also: Oberman, *Werden und Wertung der Reformation,* Tübingen 1979$^2$, 368; English trans.: *Masters of the Reformation,* Cambridge, 1981, 288.

## W. P. Stephens (essay date 1992)

SOURCE: "Zwingli: Theologian and Reformer," in *Zwingli: An Introduction to His Thought*, Oxford at the Clarendon Press, 1992, pp. 138-48.

[*In the following excerpt, Stephens offers an introduction to Zwingli's thinking as a theologian and reformer.*]

Zwingli's theology has many characteristic marks, of which the two most notable are that it is biblical and centred in God. They are not separate, but are intimately related, for the Bible is God's word and not man's and it points to faith in God and not in man.

### *A Biblical Theologian*

The statue of Zwingli by the Wasserkirche in Zurich portrays him with the sword held by the left hand but with the Bible held above it in the right hand. The statue rightly emphasizes the central role of the Bible in Zwingli's reforming ministry. He began his ministry in Zurich on Saturday 1 January 1519, his 35th birthday. He announced that he would begin the next day a continuous exposition of St Matthew, not according to the fathers but according to the scriptures themselves. This action of Zwingli focuses attention on the dominant element in his ministry: the exposition and proclamation of the word.

The preaching of the word meant that the Bible was not God's word in a merely static sense, as something given by God in the past. It was rather for Zwingli the living word of God. Zwingli was to write in ***A Commentary,*** 'Those who are faithful therefore grasp at the word of God, as a shipwrecked man grasps at a plank.' (Z III 670.33-4; *Works* iii. 93.) It was through the preaching of the word that God changed lives and changed society, for in preaching it is God who is the chief actor and not the preacher. Zwingli could therefore say of his preaching in Zurich: 'This is the seed I have sown, Matthew, Luke, Paul, and Peter have watered it, and God has given it splendid increase'. (Z I 285.25-8; *Works* i. 239.)

To the preaching was added the prophecy in June 1525. It combined scholarly exegesis with biblical exposition. It led to a flow of commentaries on the books of the Bible, and it helped to make both ministers and theological students men of the Bible. In this way Zwingli's biblical emphasis was to shape the life of the church in Zurich and beyond. It is this which was fundamental, though the prophecy is interesting for its surprisingly modern combination of ministerial and lay education and its use of a participatory style of learning. Through exegesis and exposition the Bible spoke to the life of people and their community. The prayer used at the beginning asked not only for an illumination of one's mind but also for a consequent transformation of one's life. Scholarship was not to be divorced from piety, both personal and social.

Two years earlier in the first disputation the fundamental role of the Bible in the Reformation was vividly demonstrated in another way. The Bible was placed before the assembly in Hebrew, Latin, and Greek, as a witness to the fact that the criterion of all preaching and teaching is scripture. 'I say that we have here infallible and unprejudiced judges, that is the holy writ, which can neither lie nor deceive. These we have present in Hebrew, Greek, and Latin tongues; these let us take on both sides as fair and just judges.' (Z II 498.2-6; *Selected Works* 56-7.) Moreover the sixty-seven articles which were the subject of debate at the disputation were described as being 'on the basis of scripture, which is called *theopneustos,* that is inspired by God'(Z I 458.3-6).

It was the central role and sole authority of scripture which divided Zwingli from his Catholic opponents in Zurich and beyond. With it he repudiated the authority of the church, expressed in the teaching office of the pope or bishops and in the appeal to the councils and fathers of the church. 'They are impious who embrace the word of man as God's. It is, therefore, madness and utter impiety to put the enactments and decrees of certain men or certain councils upon an equality with the word of God.' (Z III 674.23-5; *Works* iii. 98.) Nevertheless Zwingli could claim in ***An Exposition of the Faith*** that his teaching had the support of the fathers: 'Nor do we make a single assertion for which we have not the authority of the first doctors of the church.' (S IV 69.4-5; LCC xxiv. 278.)

Zwingli's view of scripture, above all his giving attention to the whole of it and not just to certain parts, supplied strength and comprehensiveness to his grasp of the Christian faith. It saved him from the one-sidedness of the anabaptists in neglecting the Old Testament in favour of the New and of Luther in stressing justification to the detriment of sanctification.

Yet alongside the centrality of the Bible there was an astonishing, some would say an excessive, openness to the truth whether or not it came in an explicitly Christian form. Standing in a tradition that runs through Justin Martyr and Augustine, Zwingli did not hesitate to welcome the truth he saw in non-Christian writers—in his case essentially pre-Christian ones. Here one sees in him the profound and continuing influence of humanist scholarship, with its delight in the rediscovered literature of Greece and Rome. (At points, especially in his writing on providence, the priority given to the non-biblical material has raised suspicion about the genuinely biblical nature of Zwingli's theology.) Zwingli, following Augustine, held that all truth comes from God, and therefore its immediate source (whether in Paul or in Plato) is unimportant, compared with its ultimate source (in God). The truth moreover was to be tested by the truth disclosed in Christ and scripture. (A parallel to this may be seen in his controversy with Luther, in which Luther accused him of giving to reason a role superior to that of the word. Zwingli answered the charge precisely by stating that his appeal was not to reason itself, independent of faith, but to the reason of the believing man, in other words to reason rooted in faith.)

For Zwingli all goodness, like all truth, comes from God. Therefore he took with deep seriousness the instances of good men who were not Christian. In his vision of heaven in ***An Exposition of the Faith*** Socrates was to be found as well as Samuel, Aristides as well as Abraham. But good pagans like Socrates were not good or in heaven because of something in them apart from God or independently of his work of redemption in Christ. It was not their goodness that put them there; rather was their goodness evidence that they had been elected by God in Christ before the foundation of the world. Zwingli's placing of particular people in heaven is open to obvious objection, not least in terms of his own theology which allows that we can never know with certainty whether another person is elect. Zwingli's attitude to people (in his case in the past) who were not Christian and to writings which were not dependent on the biblical revelation foreshadows at points some of the modern discussion of the relation of Christianity to other religious faiths and offers some insights for it.

*A Theocentric Theology*

The stress on the Bible was in itself a part of and a witness to the theocentric character of Zwingli's theology. This found distinctive expression in a vital element in Zwingli's theology and preaching: the attack on idolatry. This corresponds in a measure to Luther's attack on justification by works. Idolatry means a placing of one's trust in the creature and not the creator. Jeremiah asserted this in the words: 'They have forsaken me, the fountain of living water, and have hewn out for themselves cisterns, broken cisterns, that can hold no water' (2: 13).

Zwingli's position was expressed in the fifty-first article in 1523: 'He who gives this authority [to remit sins] to the creature takes away the honour that belongs to God and gives it to one who is not God.' (Z 1 464.I-2.) This conviction lay behind his attack on a range of medieval practices and beliefs, such as the intercession of the saints, the use of images, the doing of so-called good works, and a reliance on the sacraments. Zwingli's contrast between faith in God and faith in outward things probably also reflects a negative attitude to outward things which he sees both as leading from God rather than leading to him, and as symbols of what man does rather than of what God does. It is at this point that Zwingli and Luther are in sharpest contrast. Their difference here reflects their different ways of understanding God and creation, and the fact that Zwingli has a Greek as well as a biblical view of the opposition between flesh and spirit.

The theocentric emphasis can be seen also in the sovereignty of God, which shapes the whole of Zwingli's theology. It affects the understanding of God (with a stress on the Spirit and on the divinity rather than the humanity of Christ), of salvation (with a stress on God's providence and election), of church and ministry, and of word and sacrament (with a stress on the inward working of the Spirit rather than the outward means). It is also expressed in his theocratic view of society.

The theocentric emphasis is combined with a strong sense of the opposition of outward and inward, flesh and Spirit, which is part of Zwingli's humanist heritage. (This Greek view exists in Zwingli alongside the biblical opposition of flesh and Spirit, where flesh is the whole person and Spirit is the Holy Spirit.) This combination lies behind Zwingli's view of the sacraments. It separates him from Luther and in a measure from other Reformed theologians, such as Bucer, who combined the two more positively. Of course other influences are also at work here, such as the stress on inwardness in the modern devotion and a reaction against a superstitious regard for externals in much medieval religion.

The opposition of inward and outward was an element in Zwingli's opposition to outward forms in religion. It helps to explain why someone as musical as Zwingli (he played an array of instruments) could banish music and singing from church. Singing could distract from true spiritual worship, just as images inside church could, though not necessarily those outside. In worship as in the whole of life the glory or honour of God was fundamental.

### *Zwingli's Approach to Reformation*

In Zwingli's approach to reformation, teaching and timing were fundamental. He had a strong sense that there was a right moment and a wrong moment for saying or doing something, and in this context he frequently alluded to the danger of casting pearls before swine. His was not the way of the revolutionary—a quick sermon and then out with the hammer and sickle! In his case, let us say, a sermon against idolatry and then out with the hammer to smash the statues and a sickle to slash the pictures. Nor even for him the traditional way of the established church leader, the way of instant legislation, as though changing the church's laws and structures would magically produce reform.

He said of the revolutionaries who wanted to destroy images without more ado, 'Let them first teach their hearers to be upright in the things that pertain to God, and they will immediately see all these objectionable things fall away.' 'Teaching should come first, and the abolition of images follow without disturbance.' (Z III 899.33-5, 906.8-9: *Works* iii. 330, 337.) To misquote Chaucer, he taught and afterwards he wrought. Preaching and persuasion came first, whether by book, or sermon, or public disputation. The persuasion led to pressure from the people for change, and then—at least in many instances—there followed legislation and action. In Zwingli's wise words:

> You can easily persuade an old man to leave his chair if you first put into his hand a staff upon which he can lean, when otherwise he will never listen to you but rather believe that you are trying to entrap him into falling upon the pavement and breaking his head. So the human mind must above all be led to an infallible knowledge of God, and when it has duly attained that, it will easily let go false hopes in created things. (Z III 891.3-8; *Works* iii. 321.)

He advocated that one should first 'restore to their creator the hearts that are given over to this world' before trying to abolish the mass and cast out images (Z V 393.19-22; *Works* ii. 31). He was concerned also about the weak and argued that 'to press on regardless of the weak is the mark not of a strong but of a restless spirit which cannot wait until the poor sheep can catch up behind' (Z IV 255.9-13; LCC xxiv. 158).

With such an approach to reform (at least in outward things), it is not surprising that when changes came they lasted so long. The most notable example is that of organs. They were abolished in 1524 and destroyed in 1527. Apparently Zurich did not have an organ again until over three centuries later in 1848, and even then because of opposition it was not consecrated for five years. Zwingli's church, the Great Minster, did not have one till 1874—350 years after the last one had been played there.

His sense of the right time may express a naturally cautious approach. At several points he held back when others took an initiative. He was present when others broke the Lenten fast in 1522, but he did not break it himself, although he defended those who did. He attacked images before the second disputation in October 1523, but he did not break them as others did, although he afterwards visited in prison those who had done so. He supported marriage for ministers, but although he married early in 1523 he did not make his marriage public until 2 April 1524. He advocated the use of German rather than Latin in worship, but it was Jud who first introduced it, not Zwingli.

### *A Social Reformer*

The Reformation was clearly and fundamentally concerned with people's personal faith in God, but it was also social. In some places it has been fashionable to speak of the Reformation of the sixteenth century as concerned with God and the reformation of the twentieth century as concerned with man. Luther, it is said, wrestled with the question, 'How can I find a gracious God?', whereas we wrestle with the question, 'How can I find a gracious neighbour?' There is a truth in this half-truth, or perhaps a half-truth in this truth. The Reformation of Luther and Zwingli, Bucer and Calvin, was rooted in the discovery of a gracious God. But as there is no fire without heat, so there is no faith without love, no finding a gracious God without becoming a gracious neighbour. For Zwingli as for Luther faith is active in love, but for Zwingli in addition one of the purposes of the law is to show us God's will so that we may live in accordance with it.

Thus the seemingly modern idea that churches or church property should be sold or adapted for the poor is not a new idea. Zwingli, like Bucer, recalled that Ambrose sold chalices to ransom prisoners of war. Furthermore it was natural for Zwingli to tell people to spend their money not on images but on the poor, and to see that monasteries were turned into schools or hospitals or places for the poor. His profoundly biblical (though not literalist) theology enabled him to come afresh to social questions (such as marriage and tyrannicide) and offer new approaches.

*A Political Reformer*

The Reformation, however, was political as well as social. Zwingli's social concern was not simply ambulance work, helping the poor when they were down to stand up, although he was certainly not concerned with a fundamental change in the structure of society as we understand that today. His aim was to build a Christian society, a society ordering its life according to God's word, in which preacher and prince (or in his case the council) were both servants of God.

The political emphasis can be seen in his patriotism. He was an intense patriot years before he was a reformer, and engaged with political questions from the beginning of his ministry. In particular he opposed the mercenary system—attacking those who made a profit from hiring out their fellow countrymen to foreign powers as well as deploring the lowering of moral standards and the self-indulgence that followed from foreign contact and cheap money. These attacks led to his departure from his first parish in Glarus, but helped his later move to Zurich.

In Zurich he dealt directly with social and political issues in his preaching, and did not hesitate to name names in his sermons. He portrayed the minister in terms of the prophet, and encouraged others to engage in a ministry that was social and political. He did this notably in his sermon on the shepherd or pastor, preached to some 350 ministers at the second disputation in October 1523. He used the example of Elijah and Naboth's vineyard to show that the prophet is obliged to challenge those in authority not just when the whole people suffers but also when only one person suffers injustice. In the light of John the Baptist's challenge to Herod he declared:

> From this we learn, that the shepherd must handle and oppose everything which no one else dares to, with no exception, and he must stand before princes, people, and priests, and not allow himself to be frightened by greatness, strength, numbers, nor any means of terror, and at God's command not cease till they are converted . . . (Z III 34.3-5, 35.30-36.2.)

*A Practical Reformer*

There was also a practical element in Zwingli's approach to reformation. Zwingli had no doubt that God's will would prevail, but he stood clearly in the tradition that was to find expression in the famous words ascribed to Cromwell: 'Put your trust in God and keep your powder dry!' One of his most astonishing writings is an actual plan for war, which is well regarded by some military experts. It included detailed instructions about such matters as the disposition of the troops, the time of day or night for attack, and the sort of blasts to be blown on the trumpet. Its concern was not essentially a military one. Its point for Zwingli is clear in its opening words. 'In the name of God! Amen. The author has produced this plan to the honour of God and in the service of the gospel of Christ, so that violence and oppression do not gain control and suppress the fear of God and innocence of life.' (Z III 551.1—5.)

His concern in this was with the preaching of the gospel. That lay behind his ***Plan for a Campaign,*** as it did with the later battle against the five cantons. In June 1529, when Berne was hesitant about war with them, Zwingli wrote about the necessity to secure the preaching of the gospel. 'This is the end I have in view—the enervation of the oligarchy. Unless this takes place neither the truth of the gospel nor its ministers will be safe among us.' (Z X 147.5-7.)

This practical concern lay behind Zwingli's attempts to forge alliances with other states and cities. Yet in 1531 he would not compromise his view of the eucharist (even so far as to subscribe the Tetrapolitan Confession of Bucer) in order to join the Schmalkald League. Yet the league was formed to defend the preaching of the gospel and its members included allies such as Strasbourg and Constance and Philip of Hesse. 'The business of the truth is not to be deserted, even to the sacrifice of our lives. For we do not live to this age, nor to the princes, but to the Lord.' (Z XI 340.2-4.)

Besides the practical and often political approach which distinguished him from Luther, there was a practical approach which in some cases was common to them, in particular the recognition that new forms of worship were needed to give expression to the rediscovery and reformulation of the Christian faith. Recent study has shown something of Zwingli's originality here. A reformation lives only as it finds outward forms which embody what it expresses. It is part of the success of

Zwingli that he and others gave such forms to the Reformation in Zurich, both in worship and in public life.

*A Pastoral Reformer*

There was also a pastoral and corporate dimension to the Reformation. Unlike Erasmus whom he much admired, Zwingli had a congregation with all the demands that that made on him. His theology was not formed in a quiet study, but under constant pressure and in response to religious and political problems at home and abroad. In a letter to Haller in 1523 he referred to having been called away ten times in writing it. He mentioned the demands made on him on all sides; yet he told Haller not to spare him if he could be of use, as soon it would be quieter. (Z VIII 140.30-5.) To Valian in the following year he wrote of the haste in which everything was done as he tried to help people and keep deadlines with the printer, whose eye was on the date of the book fair, adding that he did not have in the house a single copy of a letter. (He was in fact without a secretary.) (Z VIII 166.11-167.6.) A year later he wrote to Vadian of being so busy and suffering so much from headaches that if he did not see his pen go forward, he would hardly know what was happening (Z VIII 314.13-15).

It was under such pressure that Zwingli, the theologian and reformer, worked. But he did not work alone. He had his library; he had the years of careful study both of the Greek New Testament and of the fathers which had preceded his coming to Zurich; he had colleagues such as Jud; and he had a circle of learned friends such as Bucer and Oecolampadius. Ministry was much less isolated from colleagues, and theology less isolated from the life of church and society than it often is today—and what was true for Zwingli in Zurich was equally true for Bucer in Strasbourg and Luther in Wittenberg.

These elements in Zwingli's work as theologian and reformer are not all that could be said about him, though they are characteristic and important. His was a theology that was biblical, yet open to truth wherever it is found. It was centred in God, but in the God who has revealed himself in Christ and who is active through the Spirit. His was a reformation that was educational and practical in method, and personal, social, and political in scope. Both the reformation and the theology sprang from one who was not a solitary, but a partner with others in ministry. His aim in it all can be seen in the last words of ***A Commentary:*** 'All I have said, I have said to the glory of God, and for the benefit of the commonwealth of Christ and the good of the conscience.' His was a theology and ministry which embraced society as well as the individual, but its source and goal were the glory of God.

## FURTHER READING


### Bibliography

Pipkin, H. Wayne. *A Zwingli Bibliography.* Pittsburgh: Pittsburgh Theological Seminary, 1972, 157 p.

Useful English bibliography of work on Zwingli.

### Biography

Farner, Oskar. *Zwingli the Reformer: His Life and Work.* Translated by D. G. Sear. New York: Philosophical Library, 1952, 135 p.

English translation of an early biography of Zwingli.

Gäbler, Ulrich. *Huldrych Zwingli: His Life and Work.* Translated by Ruth Gritsch. Philadelphia: Fortress Press, 1986, 196 p.

Thorough overview of Zwingli's life and work, with extensive bibliographical references for each chapter and topic addressed.

Potter, G. R. *Zwingli.* Cambridge: Cambridge University Press, 1976, 432 p.

Authoritative English-language biography of Zwingli.

### Criticism

Courvoisier, Jaques. *Zwingli: A Reformed Theologian.* Richmond, Va.: John Knox Press, 1963, 101 p.

Study of the main features of Zwingli's theology, concluding that he was "an authentic Reformed theologian in the broadest, as well as the most precise, sense of the term."

Davies, Rupert E. *The Problem of Authority in the Continental Reformers: A Study in Luther, Zwingli, and Calvin.* Westport, Conn.: Greenwood Press Publishers, 1978, 158 p.

Reprint of 1946 comparative study of how each major Reformation figure recognized and treated the problem of the grounding for religious truth.

Eire, Carlos M. N. *War Against the Idols: The Reformation of Worship from Erasmus to Calvin.* Cambridge: Cambridge University Press, 1986, 325 p.

Survey of the Swiss Reformation, including chapters on the humanist tradition and Zwingli.

Furcha, E. J. and Wayne H. Pipkin, eds. *Prophet, Pastor, Protestant: The Work of Huldrych Zwingli after Five Hundred Years.* Alison Park, Penn.: Pickwick Publications, 1984, 191 p.

Collection of essays by important Zwingli scholars.

Grimm, Harold J. "The Growth of Lutheranism." In *The Reformation Era: 1500-1650*, pp. 97-210. 1954. Reprint by Macmillan, 1965.

A highly-regarded work in which Grimm describes the rise of Zwinglianism in Switzerland and Zwingli's conflict with Luther over the meaning of the Eucharist.

Lindberg, Carter. *The European Reformations.* Cambridge, Mass.: Blackwell Publishers, 1996, 444 p.

A comprehensive study of reformation movements throughout Europe; includes a chapter on Zwingli.

Locher, Gottfried W. *Zwingli's Thought: New Perspectives.* Leiden: E. J. Brill, 1981, 394 p.

Collection of essays about Zwingli and aspects of his work by an important German Zwingli scholar.

Rilliet, Jean. *Zwingli: Third Man of the Reformation.* London: Lutterworth Press, 1964, 320 p.

Critical exposition of Zwingli's work and thought.

Stephens, W. P. *The Theology of Huldrych Zwingli.* Oxford: Clarendon, 1986, 348 p.

Analysis and exposition of Zwingli's theological writings.

Walton, Robert. "Zwingli: Founding Father of the Reformed Churches." In *Leaders of the Reformation,* edited by Richard L. DeMolen, pp. 69-98. Selinsgrove, PA: Susquehana University Press, 1984,    p.

Assessment of Zwingli's central role in the Swiss Reformation and the political context of reformation Zurich.

# How to Use This Index

## The main references

Calvino, Italo
1923-1985.....CLC 5, 8, 11, 22, 33, 39, 73; SSC 3

**list all author entries in the following Gale Literary Criticism series:**

***BLC*** = *Black Literature Criticism*
***CLC*** = *Contemporary Literary Criticism*
***CLR*** = *Children's Literature Review*
***CMLC*** = *Classical and Medieval Literature Criticism*
***DA*** = *DISCovering Authors*
***DC*** = *Drama Criticism*
***HLC*** = *Hispanic Literature Criticism*
***LC*** = *Literature Criticism from 1400 to 1800*
***NCLC*** = *Nineteenth-Century Literature Criticism*
***PC*** = *Poetry Criticism*
***SSC*** = *Short Story Criticism*
***TCLC*** = *Twentieth-Century Literary Criticism*
***WLC*** = *World Literature Criticism, 1500 to the Present*

## The cross-references

See also CANR 23; CA 85-88; obituary CA 116

**list all author entries in the following Gale biographical and literary sources:**

***AAYA*** = *Authors & Artists for Young Adults*
***AITN*** = *Authors in the News*
***BEST*** = *Bestsellers*
***BW*** = *Black Writers*
***CA*** = *Contemporary Authors*
***CAAS*** = *Contemporary Authors Autobiography Series*
***CABS*** = *Contemporary Authors Bibliographical Series*
***CANR*** = *Contemporary Authors New Revision Series*
***CAP*** = *Contemporary Authors Permanent Series*
***CDALB*** = *Concise Dictionary of American Literary Biography*
***CDBLB*** = *Concise Dictionary of British Literary Biography*
***DLB*** = *Dictionary of Literary Biography*
***DLBD*** = *Dictionary of Literary Biography Documentary Series*
***DLBY*** = *Dictionary of Literary Biography Yearbook*
***HW*** = *Hispanic Writers*
***JRDA*** = *Junior DISCovering Authors*
***MAICYA*** = *Major Authors and Illustrators for Children and Young Adults*
***MTCW*** = *Major 20th-Century Writers*
***NNAL*** = *Native North American Literature*
***SAAS*** = *Something about the Author Autobiography Series*
***SATA*** = *Something about the Author*
***YABC*** = *Yesterday's Authors of Books for Children*

# Literature Criticism from 1400 to 1800

## Cumulative Indexes

# Literary Criticism Series Cumulative Author Index


**Abasiyanik, Sait Faik** 1906-1954
See Sait Faik
See also CA 123

**Abbey, Edward** 1927-1989 . . . . . . **CLC 36, 59**
See also CA 45-48; 128; CANR 2, 41

**Abbott, Lee K(ittredge)** 1947- . . . . . . **CLC 48**
See also CA 124; CANR 51; DLB 130

**Abe, Kobo**
1924-1993 . . . . . . . . . . **CLC 8, 22, 53, 81; DAM NOV**
See also CA 65-68; 140; CANR 24; MTCW

**Abelard, Peter** c. 1079-c. 1142 . . . **CMLC 11**
See also DLB 115

**Abell, Kjeld** 1901-1961 . . . . . . . . . . . . **CLC 15**
See also CA 111

**Abish, Walter** 1931- . . . . . . . . . . . . . . **CLC 22**
See also CA 101; CANR 37; DLB 130

**Abrahams, Peter (Henry)** 1919- . . . . . **CLC 4**
See also BW 1; CA 57-60; CANR 26; DLB 117; MTCW

**Abrams, M(eyer) H(oward)** 1912- . . . **CLC 24**
See also CA 57-60; CANR 13, 33; DLB 67

**Abse, Dannie**
1923- . . . **CLC 7, 29; DAB; DAM POET**
See also CA 53-56; CAAS 1; CANR 4, 46; DLB 27

**Achebe, (Albert) Chinua(lumogu)**
1930- . . . . . **CLC 1, 3, 5, 7, 11, 26, 51, 75; BLC; DA; DAB; DAC; DAM MST, MULT, NOV; WLC**
See also AAYA 15; BW 2; CA 1-4R; CANR 6, 26, 47; CLR 20; DLB 117; MAICYA; MTCW; SATA 40; SATA-Brief 38

**Acker, Kathy** 1948- . . . . . . . . . . . . . . **CLC 45**
See also CA 117; 122; CANR 55

**Ackroyd, Peter** 1949- . . . . . . . . . . **CLC 34, 52**
See also CA 123; 127; CANR 51; DLB 155; INT 127

**Acorn, Milton** 1923- . . . . . . . . . **CLC 15; DAC**
See also CA 103; DLB 53; INT 103

**Adamov, Arthur**
1908-1970 . . . . **CLC 4, 25; DAM DRAM**
See also CA 17-18; 25-28R; CAP 2; MTCW

**Adams, Alice (Boyd)**
1926- . . . . . . . . . . **CLC 6, 13, 46; SSC 24**
See also CA 81-84; CANR 26, 53; DLBY 86; INT CANR-26; MTCW

**Adams, Andy** 1859-1935 . . . . . . . . . . **TCLC 56**
See also YABC 1

**Adams, Douglas (Noel)**
1952- . . . . . . . . . **CLC 27, 60; DAM POP**
See also AAYA 4; BEST 89:3; CA 106; CANR 34; DLBY 83; JRDA

**Adams, Francis** 1862-1893 . . . . . . . **NCLC 33**

**Adams, Henry (Brooks)**
1838-1918 . . . . . . **TCLC 4, 52; DA; DAB; DAC; DAM MST**
See also CA 104; 133; DLB 12, 47

**Adams, Richard (George)**
1920- . . . . . . . **CLC 4, 5, 18; DAM NOV**
See also AAYA 16; AITN 1, 2; CA 49-52; CANR 3, 35; CLR 20; JRDA; MAICYA; MTCW; SATA 7, 69

**Adamson, Joy(-Friederike Victoria)**
1910-1980 . . . . . . . . . . . . . . . . . . . **CLC 17**
See also CA 69-72; 93-96; CANR 22; MTCW; SATA 11; SATA-Obit 22

**Adcock, Fleur** 1934- . . . . . . . . . . . . . . **CLC 41**
See also CA 25-28R; CAAS 23; CANR 11, 34; DLB 40

**Addams, Charles (Samuel)**
1912-1988 . . . . . . . . . . . . . . . . . . . **CLC 30**
See also CA 61-64; 126; CANR 12

**Addison, Joseph** 1672-1719 . . . . . . . . . **LC 18**
See also CDBLB 1660-1789; DLB 101

**Adler, Alfred (F.)** 1870-1937 . . . . . . **TCLC 61**
See also CA 119

**Adler, C(arole) S(chwerdtfeger)**
1932- . . . . . . . . . . . . . . . . . . . . . . . **CLC 35**
See also AAYA 4; CA 89-92; CANR 19, 40; JRDA; MAICYA; SAAS 15; SATA 26, 63

**Adler, Renata** 1938- . . . . . . . . . . . . **CLC 8, 31**
See also CA 49-52; CANR 5, 22, 52; MTCW

**Ady, Endre** 1877-1919 . . . . . . . . . . . **TCLC 11**
See also CA 107

**Aeschylus**
525B.C.-456B.C. . . . . . . . **CMLC 11; DA; DAB; DAC; DAM DRAM, MST**

**Afton, Effie**
See Harper, Frances Ellen Watkins

**Agapida, Fray Antonio**
See Irving, Washington

**Agee, James (Rufus)**
1909-1955 . . . . **TCLC 1, 19; DAM NOV**
See also AITN 1; CA 108; 148; CDALB 1941-1968; DLB 2, 26, 152

**Aghill, Gordon**
See Silverberg, Robert

**Agnon, S(hmuel) Y(osef Halevi)**
1888-1970 . . . . . . . . . . . . . . . **CLC 4, 8, 14**
See also CA 17-18; 25-28R; CAP 2; MTCW

**Agrippa von Nettesheim, Henry Cornelius**
1486-1535 . . . . . . . . . . . . . . . . . . . . **LC 27**

**Aherne, Owen**
See Cassill, R(onald) V(erlin)

**Ai** 1947- . . . . . . . . . . . . . . . . . . . **CLC 4, 14, 69**
See also CA 85-88; CAAS 13; DLB 120

**Aickman, Robert (Fordyce)**
1914-1981 . . . . . . . . . . . . . . . . . . . **CLC 57**
See also CA 5-8R; CANR 3

**Aiken, Conrad (Potter)**
1889-1973 . . . . . . . . . **CLC 1, 3, 5, 10, 52; DAM NOV, POET; SSC 9**
See also CA 5-8R; 45-48; CANR 4; CDALB 1929-1941; DLB 9, 45, 102; MTCW; SATA 3, 30

**Aiken, Joan (Delano)** 1924- . . . . . . . . **CLC 35**
See also AAYA 1; CA 9-12R; CANR 4, 23, 34; CLR 1, 19; DLB 161; JRDA; MAICYA; MTCW; SAAS 1; SATA 2, 30, 73

**Ainsworth, William Harrison**
1805-1882 . . . . . . . . . . . . . . . . . **NCLC 13**
See also DLB 21; SATA 24

**Aitmatov, Chingiz (Torekulovich)**
1928- . . . . . . . . . . . . . . . . . . . . . . . **CLC 71**
See also CA 103; CANR 38; MTCW; SATA 56

**Akers, Floyd**
See Baum, L(yman) Frank

**Akhmadulina, Bella Akhatovna**
1937- . . . . . . . . . . . **CLC 53; DAM POET**
See also CA 65-68

**Akhmatova, Anna**
1888-1966 . . . . . . . . . . . . **CLC 11, 25, 64; DAM POET; PC 2**
See also CA 19-20; 25-28R; CANR 35; CAP 1; MTCW

**Aksakov, Sergei Timofeyvich**
1791-1859 . . . . . . . . . . . . . . . . . . **NCLC 2**

**Aksenov, Vassily**
See Aksyonov, Vassily (Pavlovich)

**Aksyonov, Vassily (Pavlovich)**
1932- . . . . . . . . . . . . . . . . . . . . **CLC 22, 37**
See also CA 53-56; CANR 12, 48

**Akutagawa, Ryunosuke**
1892-1927 . . . . . . . . . . . . . . . . . . **TCLC 16**
See also CA 117; 154

**Alain** 1868-1951 . . . . . . . . . . . . . . . . **TCLC 41**

**Alain-Fournier** . . . . . . . . . . . . . . . . . . . . **TCLC 6**
See also Fournier, Henri Alban
See also DLB 65

**Alarcon, Pedro Antonio de**
1833-1891 . . . . . . . . . . . . . . . . . . **NCLC 1**

**Alas (y Urena), Leopoldo (Enrique Garcia)**
1852-1901 . . . . . . . . . . . . . . . . . . **TCLC 29**
See also CA 113; 131; HW

**Albee, Edward (Franklin III)**
1928- . . . . . . **CLC 1, 2, 3, 5, 9, 11, 13, 25, 53, 86; DA; DAB; DAC; DAM DRAM, MST; WLC**
See also AITN 1; CA 5-8R; CABS 3; CANR 8, 54; CDALB 1941-1968; DLB 7; INT CANR-8; MTCW

**Alberti, Rafael** 1902- . . . . . . . . . . . . . . **CLC 7**
See also CA 85-88; DLB 108

**Albert the Great** 1200(?)-1280 . . . . **CMLC 16**
See also DLB 115

**Alcala-Galiano, Juan Valera y**
See Valera y Alcala-Galiano, Juan

**Alcott, Amos Bronson** 1799-1888 .. **NCLC 1**
See also DLB 1

**Alcott, Louisa May**
1832-1888 ..... **NCLC 6, 58; DA; DAB; DAC; DAM MST, NOV; WLC**
See also CDALB 1865-1917; CLR 1, 38; DLB 1, 42, 79; DLBD 14; JRDA; MAICYA; YABC 1

**Aldanov, M. A.**
See Aldanov, Mark (Alexandrovich)

**Aldanov, Mark (Alexandrovich)**
1886(?)-1957 ................ **TCLC 23**
See also CA 118

**Aldington, Richard** 1892-1962...... **CLC 49**
See also CA 85-88; CANR 45; DLB 20, 36, 100, 149

**Aldiss, Brian W(ilson)**
1925- ....... **CLC 5, 14, 40; DAM NOV**
See also CA 5-8R; CAAS 2; CANR 5, 28; DLB 14; MTCW; SATA 34

**Alegria, Claribel**
1924- .......... **CLC 75; DAM MULT**
See also CA 131; CAAS 15; DLB 145; HW

**Alegria, Fernando** 1918-........... **CLC 57**
See also CA 9-12R; CANR 5, 32; HW

**Aleichem, Sholom** ............. **TCLC 1, 35**
See also Rabinovitch, Sholem

**Aleixandre, Vicente**
1898-1984 .... **CLC 9, 36; DAM POET; PC 15**
See also CA 85-88; 114; CANR 26; DLB 108; HW; MTCW

**Alepoudelis, Odysseus**
See Elytis, Odysseus

**Aleshkovsky, Joseph** 1929-
See Aleshkovsky, Yuz
See also CA 121; 128

**Aleshkovsky, Yuz** ................. **CLC 44**
See also Aleshkovsky, Joseph

**Alexander, Lloyd (Chudley)** 1924- .. **CLC 35**
See also AAYA 1; CA 1-4R; CANR 1, 24, 38, 55; CLR 1, 5; DLB 52; JRDA; MAICYA; MTCW; SAAS 19; SATA 3, 49, 81

**Alexie, Sherman (Joseph, Jr.)**
1966- .......... **CLC 96; DAM MULT**
See also CA 138; NNAL

**Alfau, Felipe** 1902-............... **CLC 66**
See also CA 137

**Alger, Horatio, Jr.** 1832-1899..... **NCLC 8**
See also DLB 42; SATA 16

**Algren, Nelson** 1909-1981 .... **CLC 4, 10, 33**
See also CA 13-16R; 103; CANR 20; CDALB 1941-1968; DLB 9; DLBY 81, 82; MTCW

**Ali, Ahmed** 1910- ................ **CLC 69**
See also CA 25-28R; CANR 15, 34

**Alighieri, Dante** 1265-1321 .... **CMLC 3, 18**

**Allan, John B.**
See Westlake, Donald E(dwin)

**Allen, Edward** 1948-.............. **CLC 59**

**Allen, Paula Gunn**
1939- .......... **CLC 84; DAM MULT**
See also CA 112; 143; NNAL

**Allen, Roland**
See Ayckbourn, Alan

**Allen, Sarah A.**
See Hopkins, Pauline Elizabeth

**Allen, Woody**
1935- ......... **CLC 16, 52; DAM POP**
See also AAYA 10; CA 33-36R; CANR 27, 38; DLB 44; MTCW

**Allende, Isabel**
1942- .... **CLC 39, 57, 97; DAM MULT, NOV; HLC**
See also AAYA 18; CA 125; 130; CANR 51; DLB 145; HW; INT 130; MTCW

**Alleyn, Ellen**
See Rossetti, Christina (Georgina)

**Allingham, Margery (Louise)**
1904-1966 .................. **CLC 19**
See also CA 5-8R; 25-28R; CANR 4; DLB 77; MTCW

**Allingham, William** 1824-1889 ... **NCLC 25**
See also DLB 35

**Allison, Dorothy E.** 1949- ......... **CLC 78**
See also CA 140

**Allston, Washington** 1779-1843.... **NCLC 2**
See also DLB 1

**Almedingen, E. M.** ................ **CLC 12**
See also Almedingen, Martha Edith von
See also SATA 3

**Almedingen, Martha Edith von** 1898-1971
See Almedingen, E. M.
See also CA 1-4R; CANR 1

**Almqvist, Carl Jonas Love**
1793-1866 ................. **NCLC 42**

**Alonso, Damaso** 1898-1990 ........ **CLC 14**
See also CA 110; 131; 130; DLB 108; HW

**Alov**
See Gogol, Nikolai (Vasilyevich)

**Alta** 1942- ...................... **CLC 19**
See also CA 57-60

**Alter, Robert B(ernard)** 1935-...... **CLC 34**
See also CA 49-52; CANR 1, 47

**Alther, Lisa** 1944-.............. **CLC 7, 41**
See also CA 65-68; CANR 12, 30, 51; MTCW

**Altman, Robert** 1925-............. **CLC 16**
See also CA 73-76; CANR 43

**Alvarez, A(lfred)** 1929-.......... **CLC 5, 13**
See also CA 1-4R; CANR 3, 33; DLB 14, 40

**Alvarez, Alejandro Rodriguez** 1903-1965
See Casona, Alejandro
See also CA 131; 93-96; HW

**Alvarez, Julia** 1950-.............. **CLC 93**
See also CA 147

**Alvaro, Corrado** 1896-1956 ....... **TCLC 60**

**Amado, Jorge**
1912- ....... **CLC 13, 40; DAM MULT, NOV; HLC**
See also CA 77-80; CANR 35; DLB 113; MTCW

**Ambler, Eric** 1909-............ **CLC 4, 6, 9**
See also CA 9-12R; CANR 7, 38; DLB 77; MTCW

**Amichai, Yehuda** 1924- ...... **CLC 9, 22, 57**
See also CA 85-88; CANR 46; MTCW

**Amiel, Henri Frederic** 1821-1881 .. **NCLC 4**

**Amis, Kingsley (William)**
1922-1995 ..... **CLC 1, 2, 3, 5, 8, 13, 40, 44; DA; DAB; DAC; DAM MST, NOV**
See also AITN 2; CA 9-12R; 150; CANR 8, 28, 54; CDBLB 1945-1960; DLB 15, 27, 100, 139; INT CANR-8; MTCW

**Amis, Martin (Louis)**
1949- ................ **CLC 4, 9, 38, 62**
See also BEST 90:3; CA 65-68; CANR 8, 27, 54; DLB 14; INT CANR-27

**Ammons, A(rchie) R(andolph)**
1926- ......... **CLC 2, 3, 5, 8, 9, 25, 57; DAM POET; PC 16**
See also AITN 1; CA 9-12R; CANR 6, 36, 51; DLB 5, 165; MTCW

**Amo, Tauraatua i**
See Adams, Henry (Brooks)

**Anand, Mulk Raj**
1905- ......... **CLC 23, 93; DAM NOV**
See also CA 65-68; CANR 32; MTCW

**Anatol**
See Schnitzler, Arthur

**Anaya, Rudolfo A(lfonso)**
1937- .... **CLC 23; DAM MULT, NOV; HLC**
See also CA 45-48; CAAS 4; CANR 1, 32, 51; DLB 82; HW 1; MTCW

**Andersen, Hans Christian**
1805-1875 ........ **NCLC 7; DA; DAB; DAC; DAM MST, POP; SSC 6; WLC**
See also CLR 6; MAICYA; YABC 1

**Anderson, C. Farley**
See Mencken, H(enry) L(ouis); Nathan, George Jean

**Anderson, Jessica (Margaret) Queale**
............................ **CLC 37**
See also CA 9-12R; CANR 4

**Anderson, Jon (Victor)**
1940- ............ **CLC 9; DAM POET**
See also CA 25-28R; CANR 20

**Anderson, Lindsay (Gordon)**
1923-1994 ................... **CLC 20**
See also CA 125; 128; 146

**Anderson, Maxwell**
1888-1959 ...... **TCLC 2; DAM DRAM**
See also CA 105; 152; DLB 7

**Anderson, Poul (William)** 1926- .... **CLC 15**
See also AAYA 5; CA 1-4R; CAAS 2; CANR 2, 15, 34; DLB 8; INT CANR-15; MTCW; SATA 90; SATA-Brief 39

**Anderson, Robert (Woodruff)**
1917- .......... **CLC 23; DAM DRAM**
See also AITN 1; CA 21-24R; CANR 32; DLB 7

**Anderson, Sherwood**
1876-1941 ....... **TCLC 1, 10, 24; DA; DAB; DAC; DAM MST, NOV; SSC 1; WLC**
See also CA 104; 121; CDALB 1917-1929; DLB 4, 9, 86; DLBD 1; MTCW

**Ashbery, John (Lawrence)** 1927- ...... **CLC 2, 3, 4, 6, 9, 13, 15, 25, 41, 77; DAM POET**
See also CA 5-8R; CANR 9, 37; DLB 5, 165; DLBY 81; INT CANR-9; MTCW

**Ashdown, Clifford**
See Freeman, R(ichard) Austin

**Ashe, Gordon**
See Creasey, John

**Ashton-Warner, Sylvia (Constance)** 1908-1984 ............ **CLC 19**
See also CA 69-72; 112; CANR 29; MTCW

**Asimov, Isaac** 1920-1992 ...... **CLC 1, 3, 9, 19, 26, 76, 92; DAM POP**
See also AAYA 13; BEST 90:2; CA 1-4R; 137; CANR 2, 19, 36; CLR 12; DLB 8; DLBY 92; INT CANR-19; JRDA; MAICYA; MTCW; SATA 1, 26, 74

**Assis, Joaquim Maria Machado de**
See Machado de Assis, Joaquim Maria

**Astley, Thea (Beatrice May)** 1925- ............ **CLC 41**
See also CA 65-68; CANR 11, 43

**Aston, James**
See White, T(erence) H(anbury)

**Asturias, Miguel Angel** 1899-1974 .............. **CLC 3, 8, 13; DAM MULT, NOV; HLC**
See also CA 25-28; 49-52; CANR 32; CAP 2; DLB 113; HW; MTCW

**Atares, Carlos Saura**
See Saura (Atares), Carlos

**Atheling, William**
See Pound, Ezra (Weston Loomis)

**Atheling, William, Jr.**
See Blish, James (Benjamin)

**Atherton, Gertrude (Franklin Horn)** 1857-1948 ............ **TCLC 2**
See also CA 104; 155; DLB 9, 78

**Atherton, Lucius**
See Masters, Edgar Lee

**Atkins, Jack**
See Harris, Mark

**Attaway, William (Alexander)** 1911-1986 ............. **CLC 92; BLC; DAM MULT**
See also BW 2; CA 143; DLB 76

**Atticus**
See Fleming, Ian (Lancaster)

**Atwood, Margaret (Eleanor)** 1939- ..... **CLC 2, 3, 4, 8, 13, 15, 25, 44, 84; DA; DAB; DAC; DAM MST, NOV, POET; PC 8; SSC 2; WLC**
See also AAYA 12; BEST 89:2; CA 49-52; CANR 3, 24, 33; DLB 53; INT CANR-24; MTCW; SATA 50

**Aubigny, Pierre d'**
See Mencken, H(enry) L(ouis)

**Aubin, Penelope** 1685-1731(?) ........ **LC 9**
See also DLB 39

**Auchincloss, Louis (Stanton)** 1917- ............. **CLC 4, 6, 9, 18, 45; DAM NOV; SSC 22**
See also CA 1-4R; CANR 6, 29, 55; DLB 2; DLBY 80; INT CANR-29; MTCW

**Auden, W(ystan) H(ugh)** 1907-1973 ...... **CLC 1, 2, 3, 4, 6, 9, 11, 14, 43; DA; DAB; DAC; DAM DRAM, MST, POET; PC 1; WLC**
See also AAYA 18; CA 9-12R; 45-48; CANR 5; CDBLB 1914-1945; DLB 10, 20; MTCW

**Audiberti, Jacques** 1900-1965 ...... **CLC 38; DAM DRAM**
See also CA 25-28R

**Audubon, John James** 1785-1851 ............ **NCLC 47**

**Auel, Jean M(arie)** 1936- ............ **CLC 31; DAM POP**
See also AAYA 7; BEST 90:4; CA 103; CANR 21; INT CANR-21; SATA 91

**Auerbach, Erich** 1892-1957 ....... **TCLC 43**
See also CA 118; 155

**Augier, Emile** 1820-1889 ........ **NCLC 31**

**August, John**
See De Voto, Bernard (Augustine)

**Augustine, St.** 354-430 ...... **CMLC 6; DAB**

**Aurelius**
See Bourne, Randolph S(illiman)

**Aurobindo, Sri** 1872-1950 ........ **TCLC 63**

**Austen, Jane** 1775-1817 ..... **NCLC 1, 13, 19, 33, 51; DA; DAB; DAC; DAM MST, NOV; WLC**
See also AAYA 19; CDBLB 1789-1832; DLB 116

**Auster, Paul** 1947- ............... **CLC 47**
See also CA 69-72; CANR 23, 52

**Austin, Frank**
See Faust, Frederick (Schiller)

**Austin, Mary (Hunter)** 1868-1934 ................. **TCLC 25**
See also CA 109; DLB 9, 78

**Autran Dourado, Waldomiro**
See Dourado, (Waldomiro Freitas) Autran

**Averroes** 1126-1198 ............. **CMLC 7**
See also DLB 115

**Avicenna** 980-1037 ............. **CMLC 16**
See also DLB 115

**Avison, Margaret** 1918- ............. **CLC 2, 4, 97; DAC; DAM POET**
See also CA 17-20R; DLB 53; MTCW

**Axton, David**
See Koontz, Dean R(ay)

**Ayckbourn, Alan** 1939- ...... **CLC 5, 8, 18, 33, 74; DAB; DAM DRAM**
See also CA 21-24R; CANR 31; DLB 13; MTCW

**Aydy, Catherine**
See Tennant, Emma (Christina)

**Ayme, Marcel (Andre)** 1902-1967 ... **CLC 11**
See also CA 89-92; CLR 25; DLB 72; SATA 91

**Ayrton, Michael** 1921-1975 ......... **CLC 7**
See also CA 5-8R; 61-64; CANR 9, 21

**Azorin** .......................... **CLC 11**
See also Martinez Ruiz, Jose

**Azuela, Mariano** 1873-1952 ..... **TCLC 3; DAM MULT; HLC**
See also CA 104; 131; HW; MTCW

**Baastad, Babbis Friis**
See Friis-Baastad, Babbis Ellinor

**Bab**
See Gilbert, W(illiam) S(chwenck)

**Babbis, Eleanor**
See Friis-Baastad, Babbis Ellinor

**Babel, Isaac**
See Babel, Isaak (Emmanuilovich)

**Babel, Isaak (Emmanuilovich)** 1894-1941(?) ...... **TCLC 2, 13; SSC 16**
See also CA 104; 155

**Babits, Mihaly** 1883-1941 ........ **TCLC 14**
See also CA 114

**Babur** 1483-1530 ................. **LC 18**

**Bacchelli, Riccardo** 1891-1985 ..... **CLC 19**
See also CA 29-32R; 117

**Bach, Richard (David)** 1936- ...... **CLC 14; DAM NOV, POP**
See also AITN 1; BEST 89:2; CA 9-12R; CANR 18; MTCW; SATA 13

**Bachman, Richard**
See King, Stephen (Edwin)

**Bachmann, Ingeborg** 1926-1973 ..... **CLC 69**
See also CA 93-96; 45-48; DLB 85

**Bacon, Francis** 1561-1626 ....... **LC 18, 32**
See also CDBLB Before 1660; DLB 151

**Bacon, Roger** 1214(?)-1292 ...... **CMLC 14**
See also DLB 115

**Bacovia, George** .................. **TCLC 24**
See also Vasiliu, Gheorghe

**Badanes, Jerome** 1937- ........... **CLC 59**

**Bagehot, Walter** 1826-1877 ...... **NCLC 10**
See also DLB 55

**Bagnold, Enid** 1889-1981 ...... **CLC 25; DAM DRAM**
See also CA 5-8R; 103; CANR 5, 40; DLB 13, 160; MAICYA; SATA 1, 25

**Bagritsky, Eduard** 1895-1934 ..... **TCLC 60**

**Bagrjana, Elisaveta**
See Belcheva, Elisaveta

**Bagryana, Elisaveta** ................ **CLC 10**
See also Belcheva, Elisaveta
See also DLB 147

**Bailey, Paul** 1937- ............... **CLC 45**
See also CA 21-24R; CANR 16; DLB 14

**Baillie, Joanna** 1762-1851 ........ **NCLC 2**
See also DLB 93

**Bainbridge, Beryl (Margaret)** 1933- .... **CLC 4, 5, 8, 10, 14, 18, 22, 62; DAM NOV**
See also CA 21-24R; CANR 24, 55; DLB 14; MTCW

**Baker, Elliott** 1922- ............... **CLC 8**
See also CA 45-48; CANR 2

**Baker, Jean H.** ................ **TCLC 3, 10**
See also Russell, George William

**Baker, Nicholson** 1957- ............ **CLC 61; DAM POP**
See also CA 135

**Baker, Ray Stannard** 1870-1946 ... **TCLC 47**
See also CA 118

**Baker, Russell (Wayne)** 1925- ...... **CLC 31**
See also BEST 89:4; CA 57-60; CANR 11, 41; MTCW

**Bakhtin, M.**
See Bakhtin, Mikhail Mikhailovich

**Bakhtin, M. M.**
See Bakhtin, Mikhail Mikhailovich

**Bakhtin, Mikhail**
See Bakhtin, Mikhail Mikhailovich

**Bakhtin, Mikhail Mikhailovich**
1895-1975 .................. **CLC 83**
See also CA 128; 113

**Bakshi, Ralph** 1938(?)- ........... **CLC 26**
See also CA 112; 138

**Bakunin, Mikhail (Alexandrovich)**
1814-1876 ............. **NCLC 25, 58**

**Baldwin, James (Arthur)**
1924-1987 ...... **CLC 1, 2, 3, 4, 5, 8, 13, 15, 17, 42, 50, 67, 90; BLC; DA; DAB; DAC; DAM MST, MULT, NOV, POP; DC 1; SSC 10; WLC**
See also AAYA 4; BW 1; CA 1-4R; 124; CABS 1; CANR 3, 24; CDALB 1941-1968; DLB 2, 7, 33; DLBY 87; MTCW; SATA 9; SATA-Obit 54

**Ballard, J(ames) G(raham)**
1930- .... **CLC 3, 6, 14, 36; DAM NOV, POP; SSC 1**
See also AAYA 3; CA 5-8R; CANR 15, 39; DLB 14; MTCW

**Balmont, Konstantin (Dmitriyevich)**
1867-1943 ................. **TCLC 11**
See also CA 109; 155

**Balzac, Honore de**
1799-1850 ........ **NCLC 5, 35, 53; DA; DAB; DAC; DAM MST, NOV; SSC 5; WLC**
See also DLB 119

**Bambara, Toni Cade**
1939-1995 ...... **CLC 19, 88; BLC; DA; DAC; DAM MST, MULT**
See also AAYA 5; BW 2; CA 29-32R; 150; CANR 24, 49; DLB 38; MTCW

**Bamdad, A.**
See Shamlu, Ahmad

**Banat, D. R.**
See Bradbury, Ray (Douglas)

**Bancroft, Laura**
See Baum, L(yman) Frank

**Banim, John** 1798-1842 ......... **NCLC 13**
See also DLB 116, 158, 159

**Banim, Michael** 1796-1874 ...... **NCLC 13**
See also DLB 158, 159

**Banjo, The**
See Paterson, A(ndrew) B(arton)

**Banks, Iain**
See Banks, Iain M(enzies)

**Banks, Iain M(enzies)** 1954- ....... **CLC 34**
See also CA 123; 128; INT 128

**Banks, Lynne Reid** ................ **CLC 23**
See also Reid Banks, Lynne
See also AAYA 6

**Banks, Russell** 1940- .......... **CLC 37, 72**
See also CA 65-68; CAAS 15; CANR 19, 52; DLB 130

**Banville, John** 1945- ............. **CLC 46**
See also CA 117; 128; DLB 14; INT 128

**Banville, Theodore (Faullain) de**
1832-1891 ................. **NCLC 9**

**Baraka, Amiri**
1934- ........ **CLC 1, 2, 3, 5, 10, 14, 33; BLC; DA; DAC; DAM MST, MULT, POET, POP; DC 6; PC 4**
See also Jones, LeRoi
See also BW 2; CA 21-24R; CABS 3; CANR 27, 38; CDALB 1941-1968; DLB 5, 7, 16, 38; DLBD 8; MTCW

**Barbauld, Anna Laetitia**
1743-1825 ................. **NCLC 50**
See also DLB 107, 109, 142, 158

**Barbellion, W. N. P.** .............. **TCLC 24**
See also Cummings, Bruce F(rederick)

**Barbera, Jack (Vincent)** 1945- ...... **CLC 44**
See also CA 110; CANR 45

**Barbey d'Aurevilly, Jules Amedee**
1808-1889 ........... **NCLC 1; SSC 17**
See also DLB 119

**Barbusse, Henri** 1873-1935 ........ **TCLC 5**
See also CA 105; 154; DLB 65

**Barclay, Bill**
See Moorcock, Michael (John)

**Barclay, William Ewert**
See Moorcock, Michael (John)

**Barea, Arturo** 1897-1957 ......... **TCLC 14**
See also CA 111

**Barfoot, Joan** 1946- .............. **CLC 18**
See also CA 105

**Baring, Maurice** 1874-1945 ........ **TCLC 8**
See also CA 105; DLB 34

**Barker, Clive** 1952- ... **CLC 52; DAM POP**
See also AAYA 10; BEST 90:3; CA 121; 129; INT 129; MTCW

**Barker, George Granville**
1913-1991 ..... **CLC 8, 48; DAM POET**
See also CA 9-12R; 135; CANR 7, 38; DLB 20; MTCW

**Barker, Harley Granville**
See Granville-Barker, Harley
See also DLB 10

**Barker, Howard** 1946- ............ **CLC 37**
See also CA 102; DLB 13

**Barker, Pat(ricia)** 1943- ........ **CLC 32, 94**
See also CA 117; 122; CANR 50; INT 122

**Barlow, Joel** 1754-1812 ......... **NCLC 23**
See also DLB 37

**Barnard, Mary (Ethel)** 1909- ....... **CLC 48**
See also CA 21-22; CAP 2

**Barnes, Djuna**
1892-1982 ... **CLC 3, 4, 8, 11, 29; SSC 3**
See also CA 9-12R; 107; CANR 16, 55; DLB 4, 9, 45; MTCW

**Barnes, Julian (Patrick)**
1946- .................. **CLC 42; DAB**
See also CA 102; CANR 19, 54: DLBY 93

**Barnes, Peter** 1931- ............ **CLC 5, 56**
See also CA 65-68; CAAS 12; CANR 33, 34; DLB 13; MTCW

**Baroja (y Nessi), Pio**
1872-1956 ............. **TCLC 8; HLC**
See also CA 104

**Baron, David**
See Pinter, Harold

**Baron Corvo**
See Rolfe, Frederick (William Serafino Austin Lewis Mary)

**Barondess, Sue K(aufman)**
1926-1977 .................... **CLC 8**
See also Kaufman, Sue
See also CA 1-4R; 69-72; CANR 1

**Baron de Teive**
See Pessoa, Fernando (Antonio Nogueira)

**Barres, Maurice** 1862-1923 ....... **TCLC 47**
See also DLB 123

**Barreto, Afonso Henrique de Lima**
See Lima Barreto, Afonso Henrique de

**Barrett, (Roger) Syd** 1946- ........ **CLC 35**

**Barrett, William (Christopher)**
1913-1992 ................... **CLC 27**
See also CA 13-16R; 139; CANR 11; INT CANR-11

**Barrie, J(ames) M(atthew)**
1860-1937 ............. **TCLC 2; DAB; DAM DRAM**
See also CA 104; 136; CDBLB 1890-1914; CLR 16; DLB 10, 141, 156; MAICYA; YABC 1

**Barrington, Michael**
See Moorcock, Michael (John)

**Barrol, Grady**
See Bograd, Larry

**Barry, Mike**
See Malzberg, Barry N(athaniel)

**Barry, Philip** 1896-1949 .......... **TCLC 11**
See also CA 109; DLB 7

**Bart, Andre Schwarz**
See Schwarz-Bart, Andre

**Barth, John (Simmons)**
1930- ...... **CLC 1, 2, 3, 5, 7, 9, 10, 14, 27, 51, 89; DAM NOV; SSC 10**
See also AITN 1, 2; CA 1-4R; CABS 1; CANR 5, 23, 49; DLB 2; MTCW

**Barthelme, Donald**
1931-1989 ...... **CLC 1, 2, 3, 5, 6, 8, 13, 23, 46, 59; DAM NOV; SSC 2**
See also CA 21-24R; 129; CANR 20; DLB 2; DLBY 80, 89; MTCW; SATA 7; SATA-Obit 62

**Barthelme, Frederick** 1943- ........ **CLC 36**
See also CA 114; 122; DLBY 85; INT 122

**Barthes, Roland (Gerard)**
1915-1980 ................ **CLC 24, 83**
See also CA 130; 97-100; MTCW

**Barzun, Jacques (Martin)** 1907- .... **CLC 51**
See also CA 61-64; CANR 22

**Bashevis, Isaac**
See Singer, Isaac Bashevis

**Bashkirtseff, Marie** 1859-1884 ... **NCLC 27**

**Basho**
See Matsuo Basho

**Bass, Kingsley B., Jr.**
See Bullins, Ed

**Belser, Reimond Karel Maria de** 1929-
See Ruyslinck, Ward
See also CA 152

**Bely, Andrey** .............. **TCLC 7; PC 11**
See also Bugayev, Boris Nikolayevich

**Benary, Margot**
See Benary-Isbert, Margot

**Benary-Isbert, Margot** 1889-1979 ... **CLC 12**
See also CA 5-8R; 89-92; CANR 4; CLR 12; MAICYA; SATA 2; SATA-Obit 21

**Benavente (y Martinez), Jacinto** 1866-1954 ..... **TCLC 3; DAM DRAM, MULT**
See also CA 106; 131; HW; MTCW

**Benchley, Peter (Bradford)** 1940- ..... **CLC 4, 8; DAM NOV, POP**
See also AAYA 14; AITN 2; CA 17-20R; CANR 12, 35; MTCW; SATA 3, 89

**Benchley, Robert (Charles)** 1889-1945 ................ **TCLC 1, 55**
See also CA 105; 153; DLB 11

**Benda, Julien** 1867-1956 ......... **TCLC 60**
See also CA 120; 154

**Benedict, Ruth** 1887-1948 ........ **TCLC 60**

**Benedikt, Michael** 1935- ......... **CLC 4, 14**
See also CA 13-16R; CANR 7; DLB 5

**Benet, Juan** 1927- ................ **CLC 28**
See also CA 143

**Benet, Stephen Vincent** 1898-1943 ...... **TCLC 7; DAM POET; SSC 10**
See also CA 104; 152; DLB 4, 48, 102; YABC 1

**Benet, William Rose** 1886-1950 ...... **TCLC 28; DAM POET**
See also CA 118; 152; DLB 45

**Benford, Gregory (Albert)** 1941- .... **CLC 52**
See also CA 69-72; CANR 12, 24, 49; DLBY 82

**Bengtsson, Frans (Gunnar)** 1894-1954 .................. **TCLC 48**

**Benjamin, David**
See Slavitt, David R(ytman)

**Benjamin, Lois**
See Gould, Lois

**Benjamin, Walter** 1892-1940 ...... **TCLC 39**

**Benn, Gottfried** 1886-1956 ......... **TCLC 3**
See also CA 106; 153; DLB 56

**Bennett, Alan** 1934- ... **CLC 45, 77; DAB; DAM MST**
See also CA 103; CANR 35, 55; MTCW

**Bennett, (Enoch) Arnold** 1867-1931 ................ **TCLC 5, 20**
See also CA 106; 155; CDBLB 1890-1914; DLB 10, 34, 98, 135

**Bennett, Elizabeth**
See Mitchell, Margaret (Munnerlyn)

**Bennett, George Harold** 1930-
See Bennett, Hal
See also BW 1; CA 97-100

**Bennett, Hal** ...................... **CLC 5**
See also Bennett, George Harold
See also DLB 33

**Bennett, Jay** 1912- ............... **CLC 35**
See also AAYA 10; CA 69-72; CANR 11, 42; JRDA; SAAS 4; SATA 41, 87; SATA-Brief 27

**Bennett, Louise (Simone)** 1919- ..... **CLC 28; BLC; DAM MULT**
See also BW 2; CA 151; DLB 117

**Benson, E(dward) F(rederic)** 1867-1940 .................. **TCLC 27**
See also CA 114; DLB 135, 153

**Benson, Jackson J.** 1930- .......... **CLC 34**
See also CA 25-28R; DLB 111

**Benson, Sally** 1900-1972 .......... **CLC 17**
See also CA 19-20; 37-40R; CAP 1; SATA 1, 35; SATA-Obit 27

**Benson, Stella** 1892-1933 ......... **TCLC 17**
See also CA 117; 155; DLB 36, 162

**Bentham, Jeremy** 1748-1832 ..... **NCLC 38**
See also DLB 107, 158

**Bentley, E(dmund) C(lerihew)** 1875-1956 .................. **TCLC 12**
See also CA 108; DLB 70

**Bentley, Eric (Russell)** 1916- ....... **CLC 24**
See also CA 5-8R; CANR 6; INT CANR-6

**Beranger, Pierre Jean de** 1780-1857 ................. **NCLC 34**

**Berdyaev, Nicolas**
See Berdyaev, Nikolai (Aleksandrovich)

**Berdyaev, Nikolai (Aleksandrovich)** 1874-1948 .................. **TCLC 67**
See also CA 120

**Berendt, John (Lawrence)** 1939- .... **CLC 86**
See also CA 146

**Berger, Colonel**
See Malraux, (Georges-)Andre

**Berger, John (Peter)** 1926- ...... **CLC 2, 19**
See also CA 81-84; CANR 51; DLB 14

**Berger, Melvin H.** 1927- .......... **CLC 12**
See also CA 5-8R; CANR 4; CLR 32; SAAS 2; SATA 5, 88

**Berger, Thomas (Louis)** 1924- .......... **CLC 3, 5, 8, 11, 18, 38; DAM NOV**
See also CA 1-4R; CANR 5, 28, 51; DLB 2; DLBY 80; INT CANR-28; MTCW

**Bergman, (Ernst) Ingmar** 1918- .................... **CLC 16, 72**
See also CA 81-84; CANR 33

**Bergson, Henri** 1859-1941 ........ **TCLC 32**

**Bergstein, Eleanor** 1938- ........... **CLC 4**
See also CA 53-56; CANR 5

**Berkoff, Steven** 1937- ............. **CLC 56**
See also CA 104

**Bermant, Chaim (Icyk)** 1929- ...... **CLC 40**
See also CA 57-60; CANR 6, 31

**Bern, Victoria**
See Fisher, M(ary) F(rances) K(ennedy)

**Bernanos, (Paul Louis) Georges** 1888-1948 .................... **TCLC 3**
See also CA 104; 130; DLB 72

**Bernard, April** 1956- ............. **CLC 59**
See also CA 131

**Berne, Victoria**
See Fisher, M(ary) F(rances) K(ennedy)

**Bernhard, Thomas** 1931-1989 .............. **CLC 3, 32, 61**
See also CA 85-88; 127; CANR 32; DLB 85, 124; MTCW

**Berriault, Gina** 1926- ............. **CLC 54**
See also CA 116; 129; DLB 130

**Berrigan, Daniel** 1921- ............. **CLC 4**
See also CA 33-36R; CAAS 1; CANR 11, 43; DLB 5

**Berrigan, Edmund Joseph Michael, Jr.** 1934-1983
See Berrigan, Ted
See also CA 61-64; 110; CANR 14

**Berrigan, Ted** ..................... **CLC 37**
See also Berrigan, Edmund Joseph Michael, Jr.
See also DLB 5, 169

**Berry, Charles Edward Anderson** 1931-
See Berry, Chuck
See also CA 115

**Berry, Chuck** ..................... **CLC 17**
See also Berry, Charles Edward Anderson

**Berry, Jonas**
See Ashbery, John (Lawrence)

**Berry, Wendell (Erdman)** 1934- ............. **CLC 4, 6, 8, 27, 46; DAM POET**
See also AITN 1; CA 73-76; CANR 50; DLB 5, 6

**Berryman, John** 1914-1972 ...... **CLC 1, 2, 3, 4, 6, 8, 10, 13, 25, 62; DAM POET**
See also CA 13-16; 33-36R; CABS 2; CANR 35; CAP 1; CDALB 1941-1968; DLB 48; MTCW

**Bertolucci, Bernardo** 1940- ........ **CLC 16**
See also CA 106

**Bertrand, Aloysius** 1807-1841 .... **NCLC 31**

**Bertran de Born** c. 1140-1215 ..... **CMLC 5**

**Besant, Annie (Wood)** 1847-1933 ... **TCLC 9**
See also CA 105

**Bessie, Alvah** 1904-1985 ........... **CLC 23**
See also CA 5-8R; 116; CANR 2; DLB 26

**Bethlen, T. D.**
See Silverberg, Robert

**Beti, Mongo** .... **CLC 27; BLC; DAM MULT**
See also Biyidi, Alexandre

**Betjeman, John** 1906-1984 ........ **CLC 2, 6, 10, 34, 43; DAB; DAM MST, POET**
See also CA 9-12R; 112; CANR 33; CDBLB 1945-1960; DLB 20; DLBY 84; MTCW

**Bettelheim, Bruno** 1903-1990 ...... **CLC 79**
See also CA 81-84; 131; CANR 23; MTCW

**Betti, Ugo** 1892-1953 ............. **TCLC 5**
See also CA 104; 155

**Betts, Doris (Waugh)** 1932- .... **CLC 3, 6, 28**
See also CA 13-16R; CANR 9; DLBY 82; INT CANR-9

**Bevan, Alistair**
See Roberts, Keith (John Kingston)

**Bialik, Chaim Nachman** 1873-1934 .................. **TCLC 25**

**Bickerstaff, Isaac**
See Swift, Jonathan

**Bidart, Frank** 1939- .............. **CLC 33**
See also CA 140

**Bienek, Horst** 1930- ............ **CLC 7, 11**
See also CA 73-76; DLB 75

**Bierce, Ambrose (Gwinett)**
1842-1914(?) ....... **TCLC 1, 7, 44; DA; DAC; DAM MST; SSC 9; WLC**
See also CA 104; 139; CDALB 1865-1917; DLB 11, 12, 23, 71, 74

**Biggers, Earl Derr** 1884-1933 ..... **TCLC 65**
See also CA 108; 153

**Billings, Josh**
See Shaw, Henry Wheeler

**Billington, (Lady) Rachel (Mary)**
1942- ....................... **CLC 43**
See also AITN 2; CA 33-36R; CANR 44

**Binyon, T(imothy) J(ohn)** 1936- .... **CLC 34**
See also CA 111; CANR 28

**Bioy Casares, Adolfo**
1914- ............... **CLC 4, 8, 13, 88; DAM MULT; HLC; SSC 17**
See also CA 29-32R; CANR 19, 43; DLB 113; HW; MTCW

**Bird, Cordwainer**
See Ellison, Harlan (Jay)

**Bird, Robert Montgomery**
1806-1854 .................. **NCLC 1**

**Birney, (Alfred) Earle**
1904- ........... **CLC 1, 4, 6, 11; DAC; DAM MST, POET**
See also CA 1-4R; CANR 5, 20; DLB 88; MTCW

**Bishop, Elizabeth**
1911-1979 ...... **CLC 1, 4, 9, 13, 15, 32; DA; DAC; DAM MST, POET; PC 3**
See also CA 5-8R; 89-92; CABS 2; CANR 26; CDALB 1968-1988; DLB 5, 169; MTCW; SATA-Obit 24

**Bishop, John** 1935- .............. **CLC 10**
See also CA 105

**Bissett, Bill** 1939- .......... **CLC 18; PC 14**
See also CA 69-72; CAAS 19; CANR 15; DLB 53; MTCW

**Bitov, Andrei (Georgievich)** 1937- ... **CLC 57**
See also CA 142

**Biyidi, Alexandre** 1932-
See Beti, Mongo
See also BW 1; CA 114; 124; MTCW

**Bjarme, Brynjolf**
See Ibsen, Henrik (Johan)

**Bjornson, Bjornstjerne (Martinius)**
1832-1910 ................ **TCLC 7, 37**
See also CA 104

**Black, Robert**
See Holdstock, Robert P.

**Blackburn, Paul** 1926-1971 ...... **CLC 9, 43**
See also CA 81-84; 33-36R; CANR 34; DLB 16; DLBY 81

**Black Elk**
1863-1950 ..... **TCLC 33; DAM MULT**
See also CA 144; NNAL

**Black Hobart**
See Sanders, (James) Ed(ward)

**Blacklin, Malcolm**
See Chambers, Aidan

**Blackmore, R(ichard) D(oddridge)**
1825-1900 .................. **TCLC 27**
See also CA 120; DLB 18

**Blackmur, R(ichard) P(almer)**
1904-1965 ................. **CLC 2, 24**
See also CA 11-12; 25-28R; CAP 1; DLB 63

**Black Tarantula**
See Acker, Kathy

**Blackwood, Algernon (Henry)**
1869-1951 .................. **TCLC 5**
See also CA 105; 150; DLB 153, 156

**Blackwood, Caroline** 1931-1996 ... **CLC 6, 9**
See also CA 85-88; 151; CANR 32; DLB 14; MTCW

**Blade, Alexander**
See Hamilton, Edmond; Silverberg, Robert

**Blaga, Lucian** 1895-1961 .......... **CLC 75**

**Blair, Eric (Arthur)** 1903-1950
See Orwell, George
See also CA 104; 132; DA; DAB; DAC; DAM MST, NOV; MTCW; SATA 29

**Blais, Marie-Claire**
1939- ....... **CLC 2, 4, 6, 13, 22; DAC; DAM MST**
See also CA 21-24R; CAAS 4; CANR 38; DLB 53; MTCW

**Blaise, Clark** 1940- ............... **CLC 29**
See also AITN 2; CA 53-56; CAAS 3; CANR 5; DLB 53

**Blake, Nicholas**
See Day Lewis, C(ecil)
See also DLB 77

**Blake, William**
1757-1827 ....... **NCLC 13, 37, 57; DA; DAB; DAC; DAM MST, POET; PC 12; WLC**
See also CDBLB 1789-1832; DLB 93, 163; MAICYA; SATA 30

**Blake, William J(ames)** 1894-1969 ... **PC 12**
See also CA 5-8R; 25-28R

**Blasco Ibanez, Vicente**
1867-1928 ....... **TCLC 12; DAM NOV**
See also CA 110; 131; HW; MTCW

**Blatty, William Peter**
1928- ............. **CLC 2; DAM POP**
See also CA 5-8R; CANR 9

**Bleeck, Oliver**
See Thomas, Ross (Elmore)

**Blessing, Lee** 1949- ............... **CLC 54**

**Blish, James (Benjamin)**
1921-1975 .................. **CLC 14**
See also CA 1-4R; 57-60; CANR 3; DLB 8; MTCW; SATA 66

**Bliss, Reginald**
See Wells, H(erbert) G(eorge)

**Blixen, Karen (Christentze Dinesen)**
1885-1962
See Dinesen, Isak
See also CA 25-28; CANR 22, 50; CAP 2; MTCW; SATA 44

**Bloch, Robert (Albert)** 1917-1994 ... **CLC 33**
See also CA 5-8R; 146; CAAS 20; CANR 5; DLB 44; INT CANR-5; SATA 12; SATA-Obit 82

**Blok, Alexander (Alexandrovich)**
1880-1921 .................. **TCLC 5**
See also CA 104

**Blom, Jan**
See Breytenbach, Breyten

**Bloom, Harold** 1930- ............. **CLC 24**
See also CA 13-16R; CANR 39; DLB 67

**Bloomfield, Aurelius**
See Bourne, Randolph S(illiman)

**Blount, Roy (Alton), Jr.** 1941- ..... **CLC 38**
See also CA 53-56; CANR 10, 28; INT CANR-28; MTCW

**Bloy, Leon** 1846-1917 ............ **TCLC 22**
See also CA 121; DLB 123

**Blume, Judy (Sussman)**
1938- ... **CLC 12, 30; DAM NOV, POP**
See also AAYA 3; CA 29-32R; CANR 13, 37; CLR 2, 15; DLB 52; JRDA; MAICYA; MTCW; SATA 2, 31, 79

**Blunden, Edmund (Charles)**
1896-1974 ................ **CLC 2, 56**
See also CA 17-18; 45-48; CANR 54; CAP 2; DLB 20, 100, 155; MTCW

**Bly, Robert (Elwood)**
1926- .......... **CLC 1, 2, 5, 10, 15, 38; DAM POET**
See also CA 5-8R; CANR 41; DLB 5; MTCW

**Boas, Franz** 1858-1942 ........... **TCLC 56**
See also CA 115

**Bobette**
See Simenon, Georges (Jacques Christian)

**Boccaccio, Giovanni**
1313-1375 .......... **CMLC 13; SSC 10**

**Bochco, Steven** 1943- ............. **CLC 35**
See also AAYA 11; CA 124; 138

**Bodenheim, Maxwell** 1892-1954 ... **TCLC 44**
See also CA 110; DLB 9, 45

**Bodker, Cecil** 1927- .............. **CLC 21**
See also CA 73-76; CANR 13, 44; CLR 23; MAICYA; SATA 14

**Boell, Heinrich (Theodor)**
1917-1985 .... **CLC 2, 3, 6, 9, 11, 15, 27, 32, 72; DA; DAB; DAC; DAM MST, NOV; SSC 23; WLC**
See also CA 21-24R; 116; CANR 24; DLB 69; DLBY 85; MTCW

**Boerne, Alfred**
See Doeblin, Alfred

**Boethius** 480(?)-524(?) .......... **CMLC 15**
See also DLB 115

**Bogan, Louise**
1897-1970 .......... **CLC 4, 39, 46, 93; DAM POET; PC 12**
See also CA 73-76; 25-28R; CANR 33; DLB 45, 169; MTCW

**Bogarde, Dirk** .................... **CLC 19**
See also Van Den Bogarde, Derek Jules Gaspard Ulric Niven
See also DLB 14

**Brandes, Georg (Morris Cohen)** 1842-1927 .................. **TCLC 10**
See also CA 105

**Brandys, Kazimierz** 1916- ......... **CLC 62**

**Branley, Franklyn M(ansfield)** 1915- ...................... **CLC 21**
See also CA 33-36R; CANR 14, 39; CLR 13; MAICYA; SAAS 16; SATA 4, 68

**Brathwaite, Edward Kamau** 1930- ........... **CLC 11; DAM POET**
See also BW 2; CA 25-28R; CANR 11, 26, 47; DLB 125

**Brautigan, Richard (Gary)** 1935-1984 .... **CLC 1, 3, 5, 9, 12, 34, 42; DAM NOV**
See also CA 53-56; 113; CANR 34; DLB 2, 5; DLBY 80, 84; MTCW; SATA 56

**Brave Bird, Mary** 1953-
See Crow Dog, Mary (Ellen)
See also NNAL

**Braverman, Kate** 1950- ........... **CLC 67**
See also CA 89-92

**Brecht, Bertolt** 1898-1956 ...... **TCLC 1, 6, 13, 35; DA; DAB; DAC; DAM DRAM, MST; DC 3; WLC**
See also CA 104; 133; DLB 56, 124; MTCW

**Brecht, Eugen Berthold Friedrich**
See Brecht, Bertolt

**Bremer, Fredrika** 1801-1865 ..... **NCLC 11**

**Brennan, Christopher John** 1870-1932 .................. **TCLC 17**
See also CA 117

**Brennan, Maeve** 1917- ............. **CLC 5**
See also CA 81-84

**Brentano, Clemens (Maria)** 1778-1842 .................. **NCLC 1**
See also DLB 90

**Brent of Bin Bin**
See Franklin, (Stella Maraia Sarah) Miles

**Brenton, Howard** 1942- ........... **CLC 31**
See also CA 69-72; CANR 33; DLB 13; MTCW

**Breslin, James** 1930-
See Breslin, Jimmy
See also CA 73-76; CANR 31; DAM NOV; MTCW

**Breslin, Jimmy** ................. **CLC 4, 43**
See also Breslin, James
See also AITN 1

**Bresson, Robert** 1901- ............ **CLC 16**
See also CA 110; CANR 49

**Breton, Andre** 1896-1966 ..... **CLC 2, 9, 15, 54; PC 15**
See also CA 19-20; 25-28R; CANR 40; CAP 2; DLB 65; MTCW

**Breytenbach, Breyten** 1939(?)- ...... **CLC 23, 37; DAM POET**
See also CA 113; 129

**Bridgers, Sue Ellen** 1942- ......... **CLC 26**
See also AAYA 8; CA 65-68; CANR 11, 36; CLR 18; DLB 52; JRDA; MAICYA; SAAS 1; SATA 22, 90

**Bridges, Robert (Seymour)** 1844-1930 ....... **TCLC 1; DAM POET**
See also CA 104; 152; CDBLB 1890-1914; DLB 19, 98

**Bridie, James** ..................... **TCLC 3**
See also Mavor, Osborne Henry
See also DLB 10

**Brin, David** 1950- ................ **CLC 34**
See also CA 102; CANR 24; INT CANR-24; SATA 65

**Brink, Andre (Philippus)** 1935- .................... **CLC 18, 36**
See also CA 104; CANR 39; INT 103; MTCW

**Brinsmead, H(esba) F(ay)** 1922- .... **CLC 21**
See also CA 21-24R; CANR 10; MAICYA; SAAS 5; SATA 18, 78

**Brittain, Vera (Mary)** 1893(?)-1970 ................. **CLC 23**
See also CA 13-16; 25-28R; CAP 1; MTCW

**Broch, Hermann** 1886-1951 ....... **TCLC 20**
See also CA 117; DLB 85, 124

**Brock, Rose**
See Hansen, Joseph

**Brodkey, Harold (Roy)** 1930-1996 .. **CLC 56**
See also CA 111; 151; DLB 130

**Brodsky, Iosif Alexandrovich** 1940-1996
See Brodsky, Joseph
See also AITN 1; CA 41-44R; 151; CANR 37; DAM POET; MTCW

**Brodsky, Joseph** .. **CLC 4, 6, 13, 36, 50; PC 9**
See also Brodsky, Iosif Alexandrovich

**Brodsky, Michael Mark** 1948- ..... **CLC 19**
See also CA 102; CANR 18, 41

**Bromell, Henry** 1947- ............. **CLC 5**
See also CA 53-56; CANR 9

**Bromfield, Louis (Brucker)** 1896-1956 ................. **TCLC 11**
See also CA 107; 155; DLB 4, 9, 86

**Broner, E(sther) M(asserman)** 1930- ...................... **CLC 19**
See also CA 17-20R; CANR 8, 25; DLB 28

**Bronk, William** 1918- ............ **CLC 10**
See also CA 89-92; CANR 23; DLB 165

**Bronstein, Lev Davidovich**
See Trotsky, Leon

**Bronte, Anne** 1820-1849 .......... **NCLC 4**
See also DLB 21

**Bronte, Charlotte** 1816-1855 ..... **NCLC 3, 8, 33, 58; DA; DAB; DAC; DAM MST, NOV; WLC**
See also AAYA 17; CDBLB 1832-1890; DLB 21, 159

**Bronte, Emily (Jane)** 1818-1848 .... **NCLC 16, 35; DA; DAB; DAC; DAM MST, NOV, POET; PC 8; WLC**
See also AAYA 17; CDBLB 1832-1890; DLB 21, 32

**Brooke, Frances** 1724-1789 .......... **LC 6**
See also DLB 39, 99

**Brooke, Henry** 1703(?)-1783 ......... **LC 1**
See also DLB 39

**Brooke, Rupert (Chawner)** 1887-1915 ....... **TCLC 2, 7; DA; DAB; DAC; DAM MST, POET; WLC**
See also CA 104; 132; CDBLB 1914-1945; DLB 19; MTCW

**Brooke-Haven, P.**
See Wodehouse, P(elham) G(renville)

**Brooke-Rose, Christine** 1926- ...... **CLC 40**
See also CA 13-16R; DLB 14

**Brookner, Anita** 1928- ........... **CLC 32, 34, 51; DAB; DAM POP**
See also CA 114; 120; CANR 37; DLBY 87; MTCW

**Brooks, Cleanth** 1906-1994 ..... **CLC 24, 86**
See also CA 17-20R; 145; CANR 33, 35; DLB 63; DLBY 94; INT CANR-35; MTCW

**Brooks, George**
See Baum, L(yman) Frank

**Brooks, Gwendolyn** 1917- ...... **CLC 1, 2, 4, 5, 15, 49; BLC; DA; DAC; DAM MST, MULT, POET; PC 7; WLC**
See also AITN 1; BW 2; CA 1-4R; CANR 1, 27, 52; CDALB 1941-1968; CLR 27; DLB 5, 76, 165; MTCW; SATA 6

**Brooks, Mel** ...................... **CLC 12**
See also Kaminsky, Melvin
See also AAYA 13; DLB 26

**Brooks, Peter** 1938- .............. **CLC 34**
See also CA 45-48; CANR 1

**Brooks, Van Wyck** 1886-1963 ...... **CLC 29**
See also CA 1-4R; CANR 6; DLB 45, 63, 103

**Brophy, Brigid (Antonia)** 1929-1995 ............. **CLC 6, 11, 29**
See also CA 5-8R; 149; CAAS 4; CANR 25, 53; DLB 14; MTCW

**Brosman, Catharine Savage** 1934- .... **CLC 9**
See also CA 61-64; CANR 21, 46

**Brother Antoninus**
See Everson, William (Oliver)

**Broughton, T(homas) Alan** 1936- ... **CLC 19**
See also CA 45-48; CANR 2, 23, 48

**Broumas, Olga** 1949- .......... **CLC 10, 73**
See also CA 85-88; CANR 20

**Brown, Charles Brockden** 1771-1810 ................ **NCLC 22**
See also CDALB 1640-1865; DLB 37, 59, 73

**Brown, Christy** 1932-1981 ......... **CLC 63**
See also CA 105; 104; DLB 14

**Brown, Claude** 1937- ..... **CLC 30; BLC; DAM MULT**
See also AAYA 7; BW 1; CA 73-76

**Brown, Dee (Alexander)** 1908- ......... **CLC 18, 47; DAM POP**
See also CA 13-16R; CAAS 6; CANR 11, 45; DLBY 80; MTCW; SATA 5

**Brown, George**
See Wertmueller, Lina

**Brown, George Douglas** 1869-1902 .................. **TCLC 28**

**Burroughs, Edgar Rice** 1875-1950 .... **TCLC 2, 32; DAM NOV**
See also AAYA 11; CA 104; 132; DLB 8; MTCW; SATA 41

**Burroughs, William S(eward)** 1914- ....... **CLC 1, 2, 5, 15, 22, 42, 75; DA; DAB; DAC; DAM MST, NOV, POP; WLC**
See also AITN 2; CA 9-12R; CANR 20, 52; DLB 2, 8, 16, 152; DLBY 81; MTCW

**Burton, Richard F.** 1821-1890.... **NCLC 42**
See also DLB 55

**Busch, Frederick** 1941- ... **CLC 7, 10, 18, 47**
See also CA 33-36R; CAAS 1; CANR 45; DLB 6

**Bush, Ronald** 1946- .............. **CLC 34**
See also CA 136

**Bustos, F(rancisco)**
See Borges, Jorge Luis

**Bustos Domecq, H(onorio)**
See Bioy Casares, Adolfo; Borges, Jorge Luis

**Butler, Octavia E(stelle)** 1947- ..... **CLC 38; DAM MULT, POP**
See also AAYA 18; BW 2; CA 73-76; CANR 12, 24, 38; DLB 33; MTCW; SATA 84

**Butler, Robert Olen (Jr.)** 1945- ............ **CLC 81; DAM POP**
See also CA 112; DLB 173; INT 112

**Butler, Samuel** 1612-1680 .......... **LC 16**
See also DLB 101, 126

**Butler, Samuel** 1835-1902 ...... **TCLC 1, 33; DA; DAB; DAC; DAM MST, NOV; WLC**
See also CA 143; CDBLB 1890-1914; DLB 18, 57, 174

**Butler, Walter C.**
See Faust, Frederick (Schiller)

**Butor, Michel (Marie Francois)** 1926- ............. **CLC 1, 3, 8, 11, 15**
See also CA 9-12R; CANR 33; DLB 83; MTCW

**Buzo, Alexander (John)** 1944-...... **CLC 61**
See also CA 97-100; CANR 17, 39

**Buzzati, Dino** 1906-1972 .......... **CLC 36**
See also CA 33-36R

**Byars, Betsy (Cromer)** 1928-....... **CLC 35**
See also AAYA 19; CA 33-36R; CANR 18, 36; CLR 1, 16; DLB 52; INT CANR-18; JRDA; MAICYA; MTCW; SAAS 1; SATA 4, 46, 80

**Byatt, A(ntonia) S(usan Drabble)** 1936- ... **CLC 19, 65; DAM NOV, POP**
See also CA 13-16R; CANR 13, 33, 50; DLB 14; MTCW

**Byrne, David** 1952-............... **CLC 26**
See also CA 127

**Byrne, John Keyes** 1926-
See Leonard, Hugh
See also CA 102; INT 102

**Byron, George Gordon (Noel)** 1788-1824 ..... **NCLC 2, 12; DA; DAB; DAC; DAM MST, POET; PC 16; WLC**
See also CDBLB 1789-1832; DLB 96, 110

**Byron, Robert** 1905-1941......... **TCLC 67**

**C. 3. 3.**
See Wilde, Oscar (Fingal O'Flahertie Wills)

**Caballero, Fernan** 1796-1877..... **NCLC 10**

**Cabell, Branch**
See Cabell, James Branch

**Cabell, James Branch** 1879-1958 ... **TCLC 6**
See also CA 105; 152; DLB 9, 78

**Cable, George Washington** 1844-1925 ............ **TCLC 4; SSC 4**
See also CA 104; 155; DLB 12, 74; DLBD 13

**Cabral de Melo Neto, Joao** 1920- .......... **CLC 76; DAM MULT**
See also CA 151

**Cabrera Infante, G(uillermo)** 1929- ..... **CLC 5, 25, 45; DAM MULT; HLC**
See also CA 85-88; CANR 29; DLB 113; HW; MTCW

**Cade, Toni**
See Bambara, Toni Cade

**Cadmus and Harmonia**
See Buchan, John

**Caedmon** fl. 658-680............. **CMLC 7**
See also DLB 146

**Caeiro, Alberto**
See Pessoa, Fernando (Antonio Nogueira)

**Cage, John (Milton, Jr.)** 1912- ..... **CLC 41**
See also CA 13-16R; CANR 9; INT CANR-9

**Cain, G.**
See Cabrera Infante, G(uillermo)

**Cain, Guillermo**
See Cabrera Infante, G(uillermo)

**Cain, James M(allahan)** 1892-1977 ............. **CLC 3, 11, 28**
See also AITN 1; CA 17-20R; 73-76; CANR 8, 34; MTCW

**Caine, Mark**
See Raphael, Frederic (Michael)

**Calasso, Roberto** 1941- ........... **CLC 81**
See also CA 143

**Calderon de la Barca, Pedro** 1600-1681 ............... **LC 23; DC 3**

**Caldwell, Erskine (Preston)** 1903-1987 ........ **CLC 1, 8, 14, 50, 60; DAM NOV; SSC 19**
See also AITN 1; CA 1-4R; 121; CAAS 1; CANR 2, 33; DLB 9, 86; MTCW

**Caldwell, (Janet Miriam) Taylor (Holland)** 1900-1985 ............. **CLC 2, 28, 39; DAM NOV, POP**
See also CA 5-8R; 116; CANR 5

**Calhoun, John Caldwell** 1782-1850 ................. **NCLC 15**
See also DLB 3

**Calisher, Hortense** 1911- ..... **CLC 2, 4, 8, 38; DAM NOV; SSC 15**
See also CA 1-4R; CANR 1, 22; DLB 2; INT CANR-22; MTCW

**Callaghan, Morley Edward** 1903-1990 ..... **CLC 3, 14, 41, 65; DAC; DAM MST**
See also CA 9-12R; 132; CANR 33; DLB 68; MTCW

**Callimachus** c. 305B.C.-c. 240B.C......... **CMLC 18**

**Calvin, John** 1509-1564 ............ **LC 37**

**Calvino, Italo** 1923-1985 ..... **CLC 5, 8, 11, 22, 33, 39, 73; DAM NOV; SSC 3**
See also CA 85-88; 116; CANR 23; MTCW

**Cameron, Carey** 1952- ............ **CLC 59**
See also CA 135

**Cameron, Peter** 1959-............. **CLC 44**
See also CA 125; CANR 50

**Campana, Dino** 1885-1932........ **TCLC 20**
See also CA 117; DLB 114

**Campanella, Tommaso** 1568-1639 .... **LC 32**

**Campbell, John W(ood, Jr.)** 1910-1971 ................... **CLC 32**
See also CA 21-22; 29-32R; CANR 34; CAP 2; DLB 8; MTCW

**Campbell, Joseph** 1904-1987 ....... **CLC 69**
See also AAYA 3; BEST 89:2; CA 1-4R; 124; CANR 3, 28; MTCW

**Campbell, Maria** 1940-...... **CLC 85; DAC**
See also CA 102; CANR 54; NNAL

**Campbell, (John) Ramsey** 1946- ............... **CLC 42; SSC 19**
See also CA 57-60; CANR 7; INT CANR-7

**Campbell, (Ignatius) Roy (Dunnachie)** 1901-1957 .................. **TCLC 5**
See also CA 104; 155; DLB 20

**Campbell, Thomas** 1777-1844 .... **NCLC 19**
See also DLB 93; 144

**Campbell, Wilfred**................ **TCLC 9**
See also Campbell, William

**Campbell, William** 1858(?)-1918
See Campbell, Wilfred
See also CA 106; DLB 92

**Campion, Jane**.................... **CLC 95**
See also CA 138

**Campos, Alvaro de**
See Pessoa, Fernando (Antonio Nogueira)

**Camus, Albert** 1913-1960 .... **CLC 1, 2, 4, 9, 11, 14, 32, 63, 69; DA; DAB; DAC; DAM DRAM, MST, NOV; DC 2; SSC 9; WLC**
See also CA 89-92; DLB 72; MTCW

**Canby, Vincent** 1924-............. **CLC 13**
See also CA 81-84

**Cancale**
See Desnos, Robert

**Canetti, Elias** 1905-1994 ....... **CLC 3, 14, 25, 75, 86**
See also CA 21-24R; 146; CANR 23; DLB 85, 124; MTCW

**Canin, Ethan** 1960-............... **CLC 55**
See also CA 131; 135

**Cannon, Curt**
See Hunter, Evan

**Cape, Judith**
See Page, P(atricia) K(athleen)

**Capek, Karel**
1890-1938 ...... **TCLC 6, 37; DA; DAB; DAC; DAM DRAM, MST, NOV; DC 1; WLC**
See also CA 104; 140

**Capote, Truman**
1924-1984 ...... **CLC 1, 3, 8, 13, 19, 34, 38, 58; DA; DAB; DAC; DAM MST, NOV, POP; SSC 2; WLC**
See also CA 5-8R; 113; CANR 18; CDALB 1941-1968; DLB 2; DLBY 80, 84; MTCW; SATA 91

**Capra, Frank** 1897-1991........... **CLC 16**
See also CA 61-64; 135

**Caputo, Philip** 1941-.............. **CLC 32**
See also CA 73-76; CANR 40

**Card, Orson Scott**
1951- ...... **CLC 44, 47, 50; DAM POP**
See also AAYA 11; CA 102; CANR 27, 47; INT CANR-27; MTCW; SATA 83

**Cardenal, Ernesto**
1925- .......... **CLC 31; DAM MULT, POET; HLC**
See also CA 49-52; CANR 2, 32; HW; MTCW

**Cardozo, Benjamin N(athan)**
1870-1938 .................. **TCLC 65**
See also CA 117

**Carducci, Giosue** 1835-1907....... **TCLC 32**

**Carew, Thomas** 1595(?)-1640........ **LC 13**
See also DLB 126

**Carey, Ernestine Gilbreth** 1908-.... **CLC 17**
See also CA 5-8R; SATA 2

**Carey, Peter** 1943-......... **CLC 40, 55, 96**
See also CA 123; 127; CANR 53; INT 127; MTCW

**Carleton, William** 1794-1869...... **NCLC 3**
See also DLB 159

**Carlisle, Henry (Coffin)** 1926-...... **CLC 33**
See also CA 13-16R; CANR 15

**Carlsen, Chris**
See Holdstock, Robert P.

**Carlson, Ron(ald F.)** 1947-......... **CLC 54**
See also CA 105; CANR 27

**Carlyle, Thomas**
1795-1881 ....... **NCLC 22; DA; DAB; DAC; DAM MST**
See also CDBLB 1789-1832; DLB 55; 144

**Carman, (William) Bliss**
1861-1929 ............. **TCLC 7; DAC**
See also CA 104; 152; DLB 92

**Carnegie, Dale** 1888-1955 ........ **TCLC 53**

**Carossa, Hans** 1878-1956......... **TCLC 48**
See also DLB 66

**Carpenter, Don(ald Richard)**
1931-1995 ................... **CLC 41**
See also CA 45-48; 149; CANR 1

**Carpentier (y Valmont), Alejo**
1904-1980 ............. **CLC 8, 11, 38; DAM MULT; HLC**
See also CA 65-68; 97-100; CANR 11; DLB 113; HW

**Carr, Caleb** 1955(?)-.............. **CLC 86**
See also CA 147

**Carr, Emily** 1871-1945........... **TCLC 32**
See also DLB 68

**Carr, John Dickson** 1906-1977 ...... **CLC 3**
See also CA 49-52; 69-72; CANR 3, 33; MTCW

**Carr, Philippa**
See Hibbert, Eleanor Alice Burford

**Carr, Virginia Spencer** 1929-....... **CLC 34**
See also CA 61-64; DLB 111

**Carrere, Emmanuel** 1957- ......... **CLC 89**

**Carrier, Roch**
1937- ... **CLC 13, 78; DAC; DAM MST**
See also CA 130; DLB 53

**Carroll, James P.** 1943(?)-......... **CLC 38**
See also CA 81-84

**Carroll, Jim** 1951- ............... **CLC 35**
See also AAYA 17; CA 45-48; CANR 42

**Carroll, Lewis** ........... **NCLC 2, 53; WLC**
See also Dodgson, Charles Lutwidge
See also CDBLB 1832-1890; CLR 2, 18; DLB 18, 163; JRDA

**Carroll, Paul Vincent** 1900-1968.... **CLC 10**
See also CA 9-12R; 25-28R; DLB 10

**Carruth, Hayden**
1921- ...... **CLC 4, 7, 10, 18, 84; PC 10**
See also CA 9-12R; CANR 4, 38; DLB 5, 165; INT CANR-4; MTCW; SATA 47

**Carson, Rachel Louise**
1907-1964 ........ **CLC 71; DAM POP**
See also CA 77-80; CANR 35; MTCW; SATA 23

**Carter, Angela (Olive)**
1940-1992 ...... **CLC 5, 41, 76; SSC 13**
See also CA 53-56; 136; CANR 12, 36; DLB 14; MTCW; SATA 66; SATA-Obit 70

**Carter, Nick**
See Smith, Martin Cruz

**Carver, Raymond**
1938-1988 ......... **CLC 22, 36, 53, 55; DAM NOV; SSC 8**
See also CA 33-36R; 126; CANR 17, 34; DLB 130; DLBY 84, 88; MTCW

**Cary, Elizabeth, Lady Falkland**
1585-1639 ................... **LC 30**

**Cary, (Arthur) Joyce (Lunel)**
1888-1957 ................ **TCLC 1, 29**
See also CA 104; CDBLB 1914-1945; DLB 15, 100

**Casanova de Seingalt, Giovanni Jacopo**
1725-1798 ................... **LC 13**

**Casares, Adolfo Bioy**
See Bioy Casares, Adolfo

**Casely-Hayford, J(oseph) E(phraim)**
1866-1930 ............ **TCLC 24; BLC; DAM MULT**
See also BW 2; CA 123; 152

**Casey, John (Dudley)** 1939-........ **CLC 59**
See also BEST 90:2; CA 69-72; CANR 23

**Casey, Michael** 1947-.............. **CLC 2**
See also CA 65-68; DLB 5

**Casey, Patrick**
See Thurman, Wallace (Henry)

**Casey, Warren (Peter)** 1935-1988... **CLC 12**
See also CA 101; 127; INT 101

**Casona, Alejandro**................. **CLC 49**
See also Alvarez, Alejandro Rodriguez

**Cassavetes, John** 1929-1989........ **CLC 20**
See also CA 85-88; 127

**Cassill, R(onald) V(erlin)** 1919-... **CLC 4, 23**
See also CA 9-12R; CAAS 1; CANR 7, 45; DLB 6

**Cassirer, Ernst** 1874-1945 ........ **TCLC 61**

**Cassity, (Allen) Turner** 1929- .... **CLC 6, 42**
See also CA 17-20R; CAAS 8; CANR 11; DLB 105

**Castaneda, Carlos** 1931(?)-......... **CLC 12**
See also CA 25-28R; CANR 32; HW; MTCW

**Castedo, Elena** 1937- ............. **CLC 65**
See also CA 132

**Castedo-Ellerman, Elena**
See Castedo, Elena

**Castellanos, Rosario**
1925-1974 ...... **CLC 66; DAM MULT; HLC**
See also CA 131; 53-56; DLB 113; HW

**Castelvetro, Lodovico** 1505-1571..... **LC 12**

**Castiglione, Baldassare** 1478-1529 ... **LC 12**

**Castle, Robert**
See Hamilton, Edmond

**Castro, Guillen de** 1569-1631........ **LC 19**

**Castro, Rosalia de**
1837-1885 ...... **NCLC 3; DAM MULT**

**Cather, Willa**
See Cather, Willa Sibert

**Cather, Willa Sibert**
1873-1947 ........ **TCLC 1, 11, 31; DA; DAB; DAC; DAM MST, NOV; SSC 2; WLC**
See also CA 104; 128; CDALB 1865-1917; DLB 9, 54, 78; DLBD 1; MTCW; SATA 30

**Catton, (Charles) Bruce**
1899-1978 ................... **CLC 35**
See also AITN 1; CA 5-8R; 81-84; CANR 7; DLB 17; SATA 2; SATA-Obit 24

**Catullus** c. 84B.C.-c. 54B.C. ..... **CMLC 18**

**Cauldwell, Frank**
See King, Francis (Henry)

**Caunitz, William J.** 1933-1996 ..... **CLC 34**
See also BEST 89:3; CA 125; 130; 152; INT 130

**Causley, Charles (Stanley)** 1917-..... **CLC 7**
See also CA 9-12R; CANR 5, 35; CLR 30; DLB 27; MTCW; SATA 3, 66

**Caute, David** 1936-.... **CLC 29; DAM NOV**
See also CA 1-4R; CAAS 4; CANR 1, 33; DLB 14

**Cavafy, C(onstantine) P(eter)**
1863-1933 .... **TCLC 2, 7; DAM POET**
See also Kavafis, Konstantinos Petrou
See also CA 148

**Cavallo, Evelyn**
See Spark, Muriel (Sarah)

**Child, Philip** 1898-1978 ........ **CLC 19, 68**
See also CA 13-14; CAP 1; SATA 47

**Childers, (Robert) Erskine** 1870-1922 .................. **TCLC 65**
See also CA 113; 153; DLB 70

**Childress, Alice** 1920-1994 .... **CLC 12, 15, 86, 96; BLC; DAM DRAM, MULT, NOV; DC 4**
See also AAYA 8; BW 2; CA 45-48; 146; CANR 3, 27, 50; CLR 14; DLB 7, 38; JRDA; MAICYA; MTCW; SATA 7, 48, 81

**Chislett, (Margaret) Anne** 1943-.... **CLC 34**
See also CA 151

**Chitty, Thomas Willes** 1926-....... **CLC 11**
See also Hinde, Thomas
See also CA 5-8R

**Chivers, Thomas Holley** 1809-1858 ................. **NCLC 49**
See also DLB 3

**Chomette, Rene Lucien** 1898-1981
See Clair, Rene
See also CA 103

**Chopin, Kate** ......... **TCLC 5, 14; DA; DAB; SSC 8**
See also Chopin, Katherine
See also CDALB 1865-1917; DLB 12, 78

**Chopin, Katherine** 1851-1904
See Chopin, Kate
See also CA 104; 122; DAC; DAM MST, NOV

**Chretien de Troyes** c. 12th cent. - ............... **CMLC 10**

**Christie**
See Ichikawa, Kon

**Christie, Agatha (Mary Clarissa)** 1890-1976 ...... **CLC 1, 6, 8, 12, 39, 48; DAB; DAC; DAM NOV**
See also AAYA 9; AITN 1, 2; CA 17-20R; 61-64; CANR 10, 37; CDBLB 1914-1945; DLB 13, 77; MTCW; SATA 36

**Christie, (Ann) Philippa**
See Pearce, Philippa
See also CA 5-8R; CANR 4

**Christine de Pizan** 1365(?)-1431(?).... **LC 9**

**Chubb, Elmer**
See Masters, Edgar Lee

**Chulkov, Mikhail Dmitrievich** 1743-1792 ..................... **LC 2**
See also DLB 150

**Churchill, Caryl** 1938-... **CLC 31, 55; DC 5**
See also CA 102; CANR 22, 46; DLB 13; MTCW

**Churchill, Charles** 1731-1764......... **LC 3**
See also DLB 109

**Chute, Carolyn** 1947-............. **CLC 39**
See also CA 123

**Ciardi, John (Anthony)** 1916-1986 ........... **CLC 10, 40, 44; DAM POET**
See also CA 5-8R; 118; CAAS 2; CANR 5, 33; CLR 19; DLB 5; DLBY 86; INT CANR-5; MAICYA; MTCW; SATA 1, 65; SATA-Obit 46

**Cicero, Marcus Tullius** 106B.C.-43B.C.............. **CMLC 3**

**Cimino, Michael** 1943-........... **CLC 16**
See also CA 105

**Cioran, E(mil) M.** 1911-1995....... **CLC 64**
See also CA 25-28R; 149

**Cisneros, Sandra** 1954- ..... **CLC 69; DAM MULT; HLC**
See also AAYA 9; CA 131; DLB 122, 152; HW

**Cixous, Helene** 1937-............. **CLC 92**
See also CA 126; CANR 55; DLB 83; MTCW

**Clair, Rene**...................... **CLC 20**
See also Chomette, Rene Lucien

**Clampitt, Amy** 1920-1994 ... **CLC 32; PC 17**
See also CA 110; 146; CANR 29; DLB 105

**Clancy, Thomas L., Jr.** 1947-
See Clancy, Tom
See also CA 125; 131; INT 131; MTCW

**Clancy, Tom**..... **CLC 45; DAM NOV, POP**
See also Clancy, Thomas L., Jr.
See also AAYA 9; BEST 89:1, 90:1

**Clare, John** 1793-1864 ............ **NCLC 9; DAB; DAM POET**
See also DLB 55, 96

**Clarin**
See Alas (y Urena), Leopoldo (Enrique Garcia)

**Clark, Al C.**
See Goines, Donald

**Clark, (Robert) Brian** 1932-........ **CLC 29**
See also CA 41-44R

**Clark, Curt**
See Westlake, Donald E(dwin)

**Clark, Eleanor** 1913-1996 ....... **CLC 5, 19**
See also CA 9-12R; 151; CANR 41; DLB 6

**Clark, J. P.**
See Clark, John Pepper
See also DLB 117

**Clark, John Pepper** 1935- .... **CLC 38; BLC; DAM DRAM, MULT; DC 5**
See also Clark, J. P.
See also BW 1; CA 65-68; CANR 16

**Clark, M. R.**
See Clark, Mavis Thorpe

**Clark, Mavis Thorpe** 1909-........ **CLC 12**
See also CA 57-60; CANR 8, 37; CLR 30; MAICYA; SAAS 5; SATA 8, 74

**Clark, Walter Van Tilburg** 1909-1971 ................... **CLC 28**
See also CA 9-12R; 33-36R; DLB 9; SATA 8

**Clarke, Arthur C(harles)** 1917- ............ **CLC 1, 4, 13, 18, 35; DAM POP; SSC 3**
See also AAYA 4; CA 1-4R; CANR 2, 28, 55; JRDA; MAICYA; MTCW; SATA 13, 70

**Clarke, Austin** 1896-1974 ...... **CLC 6, 9; DAM POET**
See also CA 29-32; 49-52; CAP 2; DLB 10, 20

**Clarke, Austin C(hesterfield)** 1934- .......... **CLC 8, 53; BLC; DAC; DAM MULT**
See also BW 1; CA 25-28R; CAAS 16; CANR 14, 32; DLB 53, 125

**Clarke, Gillian** 1937- ............. **CLC 61**
See also CA 106; DLB 40

**Clarke, Marcus (Andrew Hislop)** 1846-1881 ................. **NCLC 19**

**Clarke, Shirley** 1925-............. **CLC 16**

**Clash, The**
See Headon, (Nicky) Topper; Jones, Mick; Simonon, Paul; Strummer, Joe

**Claudel, Paul (Louis Charles Marie)** 1868-1955 ................ **TCLC 2, 10**
See also CA 104

**Clavell, James (duMaresq)** 1925-1994 ............. **CLC 6, 25, 87; DAM NOV, POP**
See also CA 25-28R; 146; CANR 26, 48; MTCW

**Cleaver, (Leroy) Eldridge** 1935- ..... **CLC 30; BLC; DAM MULT**
See also BW 1; CA 21-24R; CANR 16

**Cleese, John (Marwood)** 1939- ..... **CLC 21**
See also Monty Python
See also CA 112; 116; CANR 35; MTCW

**Cleishbotham, Jebediah**
See Scott, Walter

**Cleland, John** 1710-1789 ............ **LC 2**
See also DLB 39

**Clemens, Samuel Langhorne** 1835-1910
See Twain, Mark
See also CA 104; 135; CDALB 1865-1917; DA; DAB; DAC; DAM MST, NOV; DLB 11, 12, 23, 64, 74; JRDA; MAICYA; YABC 2

**Cleophil**
See Congreve, William

**Clerihew, E.**
See Bentley, E(dmund) C(lerihew)

**Clerk, N. W.**
See Lewis, C(live) S(taples)

**Cliff, Jimmy**...................... **CLC 21**
See also Chambers, James

**Clifton, (Thelma) Lucille** 1936- .............. **CLC 19, 66; BLC; DAM MULT, POET; PC 17**
See also BW 2; CA 49-52; CANR 2, 24, 42; CLR 5; DLB 5, 41; MAICYA; MTCW; SATA 20, 69

**Clinton, Dirk**
See Silverberg, Robert

**Clough, Arthur Hugh** 1819-1861.. **NCLC 27**
See also DLB 32

**Clutha, Janet Paterson Frame** 1924-
See Frame, Janet
See also CA 1-4R; CANR 2, 36; MTCW

**Clyne, Terence**
See Blatty, William Peter

**Cobalt, Martin**
See Mayne, William (James Carter)

**Cobbett, William** 1763-1835 ..... **NCLC 49**
See also DLB 43, 107, 158

**Coburn, D(onald) L(ee)** 1938- . . . . . . **CLC 10**
See also CA 89-92

**Cocteau, Jean (Maurice Eugene Clement)** 1889-1963 . . . . **CLC 1, 8, 15, 16, 43; DA; DAB; DAC; DAM DRAM, MST, NOV; WLC**
See also CA 25-28; CANR 40; CAP 2; DLB 65; MTCW

**Codrescu, Andrei** 1946- . . . . . . . . . . . **CLC 46; DAM POET**
See also CA 33-36R; CAAS 19; CANR 13, 34, 53

**Coe, Max**
See Bourne, Randolph S(illiman)

**Coe, Tucker**
See Westlake, Donald E(dwin)

**Coetzee, J(ohn) M(ichael)** 1940- . . . . . . **CLC 23, 33, 66; DAM NOV**
See also CA 77-80; CANR 41, 54; MTCW

**Coffey, Brian**
See Koontz, Dean R(ay)

**Cohan, George M.** 1878-1942 . . . . . **TCLC 60**

**Cohen, Arthur A(llen)** 1928-1986 . . . . . . . . . . . . . . . . . **CLC 7, 31**
See also CA 1-4R; 120; CANR 1, 17, 42; DLB 28

**Cohen, Leonard (Norman)** 1934- . . . . **CLC 3, 38; DAC; DAM MST**
See also CA 21-24R; CANR 14; DLB 53; MTCW

**Cohen, Matt** 1942- . . . . . . . . . . **CLC 19; DAC**
See also CA 61-64; CAAS 18; CANR 40; DLB 53

**Cohen-Solal, Annie** 19(?)- . . . . . . . . . **CLC 50**

**Colegate, Isabel** 1931- . . . . . . . . . . . . **CLC 36**
See also CA 17-20R; CANR 8, 22; DLB 14; INT CANR-22; MTCW

**Coleman, Emmett**
See Reed, Ishmael

**Coleridge, Samuel Taylor** 1772-1834 . . . . . **NCLC 9, 54; DA; DAB; DAC; DAM MST, POET; PC 11; WLC**
See also CDBLB 1789-1832; DLB 93, 107

**Coleridge, Sara** 1802-1852 . . . . . . . **NCLC 31**

**Coles, Don** 1928- . . . . . . . . . . . . . . . . **CLC 46**
See also CA 115; CANR 38

**Colette, (Sidonie-Gabrielle)** 1873-1954 . . . . . . . . . . . . . **TCLC 1, 5, 16; DAM NOV; SSC 10**
See also CA 104; 131; DLB 65; MTCW

**Collett, (Jacobine) Camilla (Wergeland)** 1813-1895 . . . . . . . . . . . . . . . . **NCLC 22**

**Collier, Christopher** 1930- . . . . . . . . . **CLC 30**
See also AAYA 13; CA 33-36R; CANR 13, 33; JRDA; MAICYA; SATA 16, 70

**Collier, James L(incoln)** 1928- . . . . . . . . . . . . **CLC 30; DAM POP**
See also AAYA 13; CA 9-12R; CANR 4, 33; CLR 3; JRDA; MAICYA; SAAS 21; SATA 8, 70

**Collier, Jeremy** 1650-1726 . . . . . . . . . . . **LC 6**

**Collier, John** 1901-1980 . . . . . . . . . . . **SSC 19**
See also CA 65-68; 97-100; CANR 10; DLB 77

**Collingwood, R(obin) G(eorge)** 1889(?)-1943 . . . . . . . . . . . . . . . . **TCLC 67**
See also CA 117; 155

**Collins, Hunt**
See Hunter, Evan

**Collins, Linda** 1931- . . . . . . . . . . . . . . **CLC 44**
See also CA 125

**Collins, (William) Wilkie** 1824-1889 . . . . . . . . . . . . . . . **NCLC 1, 18**
See also CDBLB 1832-1890; DLB 18, 70, 159

**Collins, William** 1721-1759 . . . . . . . . . **LC 4; DAM POET**
See also DLB 109

**Collodi, Carlo** 1826-1890 . . . . . . . . **NCLC 54**
See also Lorenzini, Carlo
See also CLR 5

**Colman, George**
See Glassco, John

**Colt, Winchester Remington**
See Hubbard, L(afayette) Ron(ald)

**Colter, Cyrus** 1910- . . . . . . . . . . . . . . **CLC 58**
See also BW 1; CA 65-68; CANR 10; DLB 33

**Colton, James**
See Hansen, Joseph

**Colum, Padraic** 1881-1972 . . . . . . . . . **CLC 28**
See also CA 73-76; 33-36R; CANR 35; CLR 36; MAICYA; MTCW; SATA 15

**Colvin, James**
See Moorcock, Michael (John)

**Colwin, Laurie (E.)** 1944-1992 . . . . . . . . . . . **CLC 5, 13, 23, 84**
See also CA 89-92; 139; CANR 20, 46; DLBY 80; MTCW

**Comfort, Alex(ander)** 1920- . . . . . . . . . . . . . **CLC 7; DAM POP**
See also CA 1-4R; CANR 1, 45

**Comfort, Montgomery**
See Campbell, (John) Ramsey

**Compton-Burnett, I(vy)** 1884(?)-1969 . . . . . . **CLC 1, 3, 10, 15, 34; DAM NOV**
See also CA 1-4R; 25-28R; CANR 4; DLB 36; MTCW

**Comstock, Anthony** 1844-1915 . . . . **TCLC 13**
See also CA 110

**Comte, Auguste** 1798-1857. . . . . . . **NCLC 54**

**Conan Doyle, Arthur**
See Doyle, Arthur Conan

**Conde, Maryse** 1937- . . . . . . . **CLC 52, 92; DAM MULT**
See also Boucolon, Maryse
See also BW 2

**Condillac, Etienne Bonnot de** 1714-1780 . . . . . . . . . . . . . . . . . . . **LC 26**

**Condon, Richard (Thomas)** 1915-1996 . . . . . . . . . **CLC 4, 6, 8, 10, 45; DAM NOV**
See also BEST 90:3; CA 1-4R; 151; CAAS 1; CANR 2, 23; INT CANR-23; MTCW

**Confucius** 551B.C.-479B.C. . . . . . . . **CMLC 19; DA; DAB; DAC; DAM MST**

**Congreve, William** 1670-1729 . . . . . . . . **LC 5, 21; DA; DAB; DAC; DAM DRAM, MST, POET; DC 2; WLC**
See also CDBLB 1660-1789; DLB 39, 84

**Connell, Evan S(helby), Jr.** 1924- . . . . . . . **CLC 4, 6, 45; DAM NOV**
See also AAYA 7; CA 1-4R; CAAS 2; CANR 2, 39; DLB 2; DLBY 81; MTCW

**Connelly, Marc(us Cook)** 1890-1980 . . . . . . . . . . . . . . . . . . . . **CLC 7**
See also CA 85-88; 102; CANR 30; DLB 7; DLBY 80; SATA-Obit 25

**Connor, Ralph** . . . . . . . . . . . . . . . . . . **TCLC 31**
See also Gordon, Charles William
See also DLB 92

**Conrad, Joseph** 1857-1924 . . . . **TCLC 1, 6, 13, 25, 43, 57; DA; DAB; DAC; DAM MST, NOV; SSC 9; WLC**
See also CA 104; 131; CDBLB 1890-1914; DLB 10, 34, 98, 156; MTCW; SATA 27

**Conrad, Robert Arnold**
See Hart, Moss

**Conroy, Donald Pat(rick)** 1945- . . . **CLC 30, 74; DAM NOV, POP**
See also AAYA 8; AITN 1; CA 85-88; CANR 24, 53; DLB 6; MTCW

**Constant (de Rebecque), (Henri) Benjamin** 1767-1830 . . . . . . . . . . . . . . . . . **NCLC 6**
See also DLB 119

**Conybeare, Charles Augustus**
See Eliot, T(homas) S(tearns)

**Cook, Michael** 1933- . . . . . . . . . . . . . **CLC 58**
See also CA 93-96; DLB 53

**Cook, Robin** 1940- . . . . **CLC 14; DAM POP**
See also BEST 90:2; CA 108; 111; CANR 41; INT 111

**Cook, Roy**
See Silverberg, Robert

**Cooke, Elizabeth** 1948- . . . . . . . . . . . **CLC 55**
See also CA 129

**Cooke, John Esten** 1830-1886 . . . . . **NCLC 5**
See also DLB 3

**Cooke, John Estes**
See Baum, L(yman) Frank

**Cooke, M. E.**
See Creasey, John

**Cooke, Margaret**
See Creasey, John

**Cook-Lynn, Elizabeth** 1930- . . . . . . . . . . **CLC 93; DAM MULT**
See also CA 133; NNAL

**Cooney, Ray** . . . . . . . . . . . . . . . . . . . . . **CLC 62**

**Cooper, Douglas** 1960- . . . . . . . . . . . . **CLC 86**

**Cooper, Henry St. John**
See Creasey, John

**Cooper, J(oan) California** . . . . . . . . . . . . . . . **CLC 56; DAM MULT**
See also AAYA 12; BW 1; CA 125; CANR 55

**Cooper, James Fenimore** 1789-1851 . . . . . . . . . . . . **NCLC 1, 27, 54**
See also CDALB 1640-1865; DLB 3; SATA 19

**Coover, Robert (Lowell)** 1932- .......... **CLC 3, 7, 15, 32, 46, 87; DAM NOV; SSC 15**
See also CA 45-48; CANR 3, 37; DLB 2; DLBY 81; MTCW

**Copeland, Stewart (Armstrong)** 1952- .......... **CLC 26**

**Coppard, A(lfred) E(dgar)** 1878-1957 .......... **TCLC 5; SSC 21**
See also CA 114; DLB 162; YABC 1

**Coppee, Francois** 1842-1908 ...... **TCLC 25**

**Coppola, Francis Ford** 1939- ....... **CLC 16**
See also CA 77-80; CANR 40; DLB 44

**Corbiere, Tristan** 1845-1875 ..... **NCLC 43**

**Corcoran, Barbara** 1911- .......... **CLC 17**
See also AAYA 14; CA 21-24R; CAAS 2; CANR 11, 28, 48; DLB 52; JRDA; SAAS 20; SATA 3, 77

**Cordelier, Maurice**
See Giraudoux, (Hippolyte) Jean

**Corelli, Marie** 1855-1924 ......... **TCLC 51**
See also Mackay, Mary
See also DLB 34, 156

**Corman, Cid** .......... **CLC 9**
See also Corman, Sidney
See also CAAS 2; DLB 5

**Corman, Sidney** 1924-
See Corman, Cid
See also CA 85-88; CANR 44; DAM POET

**Cormier, Robert (Edmund)** 1925- .... **CLC 12, 30; DA; DAB; DAC; DAM MST, NOV**
See also AAYA 3, 19; CA 1-4R; CANR 5, 23; CDALB 1968-1988; CLR 12; DLB 52; INT CANR-23; JRDA; MAICYA; MTCW; SATA 10, 45, 83

**Corn, Alfred (DeWitt III)** 1943- .... **CLC 33**
See also CA 104; CAAS 25; CANR 44; DLB 120; DLBY 80

**Corneille, Pierre** 1606-1684 .... **LC 28; DAB; DAM MST**

**Cornwell, David (John Moore)** 1931- .......... **CLC 9, 15; DAM POP**
See also le Carre, John
See also CA 5-8R; CANR 13, 33; MTCW

**Corso, (Nunzio) Gregory** 1930- ... **CLC 1, 11**
See also CA 5-8R; CANR 41; DLB 5, 16; MTCW

**Cortazar, Julio** 1914-1984 ...... **CLC 2, 3, 5, 10, 13, 15, 33, 34, 92; DAM MULT, NOV; HLC; SSC 7**
See also CA 21-24R; CANR 12, 32; DLB 113; HW; MTCW

**CORTES, HERNAN** 1484-1547 ..... **LC 31**

**Corwin, Cecil**
See Kornbluth, C(yril) M.

**Cosic, Dobrica** 1921- .......... **CLC 14**
See also CA 122; 138

**Costain, Thomas B(ertram)** 1885-1965 .......... **CLC 30**
See also CA 5-8R; 25-28R; DLB 9

**Costantini, Humberto** 1924(?)-1987 .......... **CLC 49**
See also CA 131; 122; HW

**Costello, Elvis** 1955- .......... **CLC 21**

**Cotter, Joseph Seamon Sr.** 1861-1949 .......... **TCLC 28; BLC; DAM MULT**
See also BW 1; CA 124; DLB 50

**Couch, Arthur Thomas Quiller**
See Quiller-Couch, Arthur Thomas

**Coulton, James**
See Hansen, Joseph

**Couperus, Louis (Marie Anne)** 1863-1923 .......... **TCLC 15**
See also CA 115

**Coupland, Douglas** 1961- ....... **CLC 85; DAC; DAM POP**
See also CA 142

**Court, Wesli**
See Turco, Lewis (Putnam)

**Courtenay, Bryce** 1933- .......... **CLC 59**
See also CA 138

**Courtney, Robert**
See Ellison, Harlan (Jay)

**Cousteau, Jacques-Yves** 1910- ...... **CLC 30**
See also CA 65-68; CANR 15; MTCW; SATA 38

**Coward, Noel (Peirce)** 1899-1973 .......... **CLC 1, 9, 29, 51; DAM DRAM**
See also AITN 1; CA 17-18; 41-44R; CANR 35; CAP 2; CDBLB 1914-1945; DLB 10; MTCW

**Cowley, Malcolm** 1898-1989 ....... **CLC 39**
See also CA 5-8R; 128; CANR 3, 55; DLB 4, 48; DLBY 81, 89; MTCW

**Cowper, William** 1731-1800 ...... **NCLC 8; DAM POET**
See also DLB 104, 109

**Cox, William Trevor** 1928- ....... **CLC 9, 14, 71; DAM NOV**
See also Trevor, William
See also CA 9-12R; CANR 4, 37, 55; DLB 14; INT CANR-37; MTCW

**Coyne, P. J.**
See Masters, Hilary

**Cozzens, James Gould** 1903-1978 .......... **CLC 1, 4, 11, 92**
See also CA 9-12R; 81-84; CANR 19; CDALB 1941-1968; DLB 9; DLBD 2; DLBY 84; MTCW

**Crabbe, George** 1754-1832 ....... **NCLC 26**
See also DLB 93

**Craddock, Charles Egbert**
See Murfree, Mary Noailles

**Craig, A. A.**
See Anderson, Poul (William)

**Craik, Dinah Maria (Mulock)** 1826-1887 .......... **NCLC 38**
See also DLB 35, 163; MAICYA; SATA 34

**Cram, Ralph Adams** 1863-1942 .... **TCLC 45**

**Crane, (Harold) Hart** 1899-1932 ....... **TCLC 2, 5; DA; DAB; DAC; DAM MST, POET; PC 3; WLC**
See also CA 104; 127; CDALB 1917-1929; DLB 4, 48; MTCW

**Crane, R(onald) S(almon)** 1886-1967 .......... **CLC 27**
See also CA 85-88; DLB 63

**Crane, Stephen (Townley)** 1871-1900 ....... **TCLC 11, 17, 32; DA; DAB; DAC; DAM MST, NOV, POET; SSC 7; WLC**
See also CA 109; 140; CDALB 1865-1917; DLB 12, 54, 78; YABC 2

**Crase, Douglas** 1944- .......... **CLC 58**
See also CA 106

**Crashaw, Richard** 1612(?)-1649 ...... **LC 24**
See also DLB 126

**Craven, Margaret** 1901-1980 .......... **CLC 17; DAC**
See also CA 103

**Crawford, F(rancis) Marion** 1854-1909 .......... **TCLC 10**
See also CA 107; DLB 71

**Crawford, Isabella Valancy** 1850-1887 .......... **NCLC 12**
See also DLB 92

**Crayon, Geoffrey**
See Irving, Washington

**Creasey, John** 1908-1973 .......... **CLC 11**
See also CA 5-8R; 41-44R; CANR 8; DLB 77; MTCW

**Crebillon, Claude Prosper Jolyot de (fils)** 1707-1777 .......... **LC 28**

**Credo**
See Creasey, John

**Creeley, Robert (White)** 1926- ..... **CLC 1, 2, 4, 8, 11, 15, 36, 78; DAM POET**
See also CA 1-4R; CAAS 10; CANR 23, 43; DLB 5, 16, 169; MTCW

**Crews, Harry (Eugene)** 1935- .......... **CLC 6, 23, 49**
See also AITN 1; CA 25-28R; CANR 20; DLB 6, 143; MTCW

**Crichton, (John) Michael** 1942- .... **CLC 2, 6, 54, 90; DAM NOV, POP**
See also AAYA 10; AITN 2; CA 25-28R; CANR 13, 40, 54; DLBY 81; INT CANR-13; JRDA; MTCW; SATA 9, 88

**Crispin, Edmund** .......... **CLC 22**
See also Montgomery, (Robert) Bruce
See also DLB 87

**Cristofer, Michael** 1945(?)- ........ **CLC 28; DAM DRAM**
See also CA 110; 152; DLB 7

**Croce, Benedetto** 1866-1952 ...... **TCLC 37**
See also CA 120; 155

**Crockett, David** 1786-1836 ....... **NCLC 8**
See also DLB 3, 11

**Crockett, Davy**
See Crockett, David

**Crofts, Freeman Wills** 1879-1957 .......... **TCLC 55**
See also CA 115; DLB 77

**Croker, John Wilson** 1780-1857 .. **NCLC 10**
See also DLB 110

**Davies, Rhys** 1903-1978 . . . . . . . . . . . **CLC 23**
See also CA 9-12R; 81-84; CANR 4; DLB 139

**Davies, (William) Robertson** 1913-1995 . . . . . **CLC 2, 7, 13, 25, 42, 75, 91; DA; DAB; DAC; DAM MST, NOV, POP; WLC**
See also BEST 89:2; CA 33-36R; 150; CANR 17, 42; DLB 68; INT CANR-17; MTCW

**Davies, W(illiam) H(enry)** 1871-1940 . . . . . . . . . . . . . . . . . . . **TCLC 5**
See also CA 104; DLB 19, 174

**Davies, Walter C.**
See Kornbluth, C(yril) M.

**Davis, Angela (Yvonne)** 1944- . . . . . . . . . . **CLC 77; DAM MULT**
See also BW 2; CA 57-60; CANR 10

**Davis, B. Lynch**
See Bioy Casares, Adolfo; Borges, Jorge Luis

**Davis, Gordon**
See Hunt, E(verette) Howard, (Jr.)

**Davis, Harold Lenoir** 1896-1960 . . . . **CLC 49**
See also CA 89-92; DLB 9

**Davis, Rebecca (Blaine) Harding** 1831-1910 . . . . . . . . . . . . . . . . . . . **TCLC 6**
See also CA 104; DLB 74

**Davis, Richard Harding** 1864-1916 . . . . . . . . . . . . . . . . . . **TCLC 24**
See also CA 114; DLB 12, 23, 78, 79; DLBD 13

**Davison, Frank Dalby** 1893-1970 . . . **CLC 15**
See also CA 116

**Davison, Lawrence H.**
See Lawrence, D(avid) H(erbert Richards)

**Davison, Peter (Hubert)** 1928- . . . . . **CLC 28**
See also CA 9-12R; CAAS 4; CANR 3, 43; DLB 5

**Davys, Mary** 1674-1732 . . . . . . . . . . . . . **LC 1**
See also DLB 39

**Dawson, Fielding** 1930- . . . . . . . . . . . . **CLC 6**
See also CA 85-88; DLB 130

**Dawson, Peter**
See Faust, Frederick (Schiller)

**Day, Clarence (Shepard, Jr.)** 1874-1935 . . . . . . . . . . . . . . . . . . **TCLC 25**
See also CA 108; DLB 11

**Day, Thomas** 1748-1789 . . . . . . . . . . . . . **LC 1**
See also DLB 39; YABC 1

**Day Lewis, C(ecil)** 1904-1972 . . . . . . . . . . . . . . **CLC 1, 6, 10; DAM POET; PC 11**
See also Blake, Nicholas
See also CA 13-16; 33-36R; CANR 34; CAP 1; DLB 15, 20; MTCW

**Dazai, Osamu** . . . . . . . . . . . . . . . . . . . **TCLC 11**
See also Tsushima, Shuji

**de Andrade, Carlos Drummond**
See Drummond de Andrade, Carlos

**Deane, Norman**
See Creasey, John

**de Beauvoir, Simone (Lucie Ernestine Marie Bertrand)**
See Beauvoir, Simone (Lucie Ernestine Marie Bertrand) de

**de Brissac, Malcolm**
See Dickinson, Peter (Malcolm)

**de Chardin, Pierre Teilhard**
See Teilhard de Chardin, (Marie Joseph) Pierre

**Dee, John** 1527-1608 . . . . . . . . . . . . . . **LC 20**

**Deer, Sandra** 1940- . . . . . . . . . . . . . . . **CLC 45**

**De Ferrari, Gabriella** 1941- . . . . . . . . **CLC 65**
See also CA 146

**Defoe, Daniel** 1660(?)-1731 . . . . **LC 1; DA; DAB; DAC; DAM MST, NOV; WLC**
See also CDBLB 1660-1789; DLB 39, 95, 101; JRDA; MAICYA; SATA 22

**de Gourmont, Remy(-Marie-Charles)**
See Gourmont, Remy (-Marie-Charles) de

**de Hartog, Jan** 1914- . . . . . . . . . . . . . **CLC 19**
See also CA 1-4R; CANR 1

**de Hostos, E. M.**
See Hostos (y Bonilla), Eugenio Maria de

**de Hostos, Eugenio M.**
See Hostos (y Bonilla), Eugenio Maria de

**Deighton, Len** . . . . . . . . . . . . . **CLC 4, 7, 22, 46**
See also Deighton, Leonard Cyril
See also AAYA 6; BEST 89:2; CDBLB 1960 to Present; DLB 87

**Deighton, Leonard Cyril** 1929-
See Deighton, Len
See also CA 9-12R; CANR 19, 33; DAM NOV, POP; MTCW

**Dekker, Thomas** 1572(?)-1632 . . . . . **LC 22; DAM DRAM**
See also CDBLB Before 1660; DLB 62, 172

**Delafield, E. M.** 1890-1943 . . . . . . . **TCLC 61**
See also Dashwood, Edmee Elizabeth Monica de la Pasture
See also DLB 34

**de la Mare, Walter (John)** 1873-1956 . . . . **TCLC 4, 53; DAB; DAC; DAM MST, POET; SSC 14; WLC**
See also CDBLB 1914-1945; CLR 23; DLB 162; SATA 16

**Delaney, Franey**
See O'Hara, John (Henry)

**Delaney, Shelagh** 1939- . . . . . . . . . . **CLC 29; DAM DRAM**
See also CA 17-20R; CANR 30; CDBLB 1960 to Present; DLB 13; MTCW

**Delany, Mary (Granville Pendarves)** 1700-1788 . . . . . . . . . . . . . . . . . . . . **LC 12**

**Delany, Samuel R(ay, Jr.)** 1942- . . . . . . . . . . . . **CLC 8, 14, 38; BLC; DAM MULT**
See also BW 2; CA 81-84; CANR 27, 43; DLB 8, 33; MTCW

**De La Ramee, (Marie) Louise** 1839-1908
See Ouida
See also SATA 20

**de la Roche, Mazo** 1879-1961 . . . . . . **CLC 14**
See also CA 85-88; CANR 30; DLB 68; SATA 64

**Delbanco, Nicholas (Franklin)** 1942- . . . . . . . . . . . . . . . . . . . . . **CLC 6, 13**
See also CA 17-20R; CAAS 2; CANR 29, 55; DLB 6

**del Castillo, Michel** 1933- . . . . . . . . . **CLC 38**
See also CA 109

**Deledda, Grazia (Cosima)** 1875(?)-1936 . . . . . . . . . . . . . . . . **TCLC 23**
See also CA 123

**Delibes, Miguel** . . . . . . . . . . . . . . . . . **CLC 8, 18**
See also Delibes Setien, Miguel

**Delibes Setien, Miguel** 1920-
See Delibes, Miguel
See also CA 45-48; CANR 1, 32; HW; MTCW

**DeLillo, Don** 1936- . . . . . **CLC 8, 10, 13, 27, 39, 54, 76; DAM NOV, POP**
See also BEST 89:1; CA 81-84; CANR 21; DLB 6, 173; MTCW

**de Lisser, H. G.**
See De Lisser, H(erbert) G(eorge)
See also DLB 117

**De Lisser, H(erbert) G(eorge)** 1878-1944 . . . . . . . . . . . . . . . . . . **TCLC 12**
See also de Lisser, H. G.
See also BW 2; CA 109; 152

**Deloria, Vine (Victor), Jr.** 1933- . . . . . . . . . . **CLC 21; DAM MULT**
See also CA 53-56; CANR 5, 20, 48; MTCW; NNAL; SATA 21

**Del Vecchio, John M(ichael)** 1947- . . . . . . . . . . . . . . . . . . . . . . . **CLC 29**
See also CA 110; DLBD 9

**de Man, Paul (Adolph Michel)** 1919-1983 . . . . . . . . . . . . . . . . . . **CLC 55**
See also CA 128; 111; DLB 67; MTCW

**De Marinis, Rick** 1934- . . . . . . . . . . . **CLC 54**
See also CA 57-60; CAAS 24; CANR 9, 25, 50

**Dembry, R. Emmet**
See Murfree, Mary Noailles

**Demby, William** 1922- . . . . . **CLC 53; BLC; DAM MULT**
See also BW 1; CA 81-84; DLB 33

**Demijohn, Thom**
See Disch, Thomas M(ichael)

**de Montherlant, Henry (Milon)**
See Montherlant, Henry (Milon) de

**Demosthenes** 384B.C.-322B.C. . . . **CMLC 13**

**de Natale, Francine**
See Malzberg, Barry N(athaniel)

**Denby, Edwin (Orr)** 1903-1983 . . . . . **CLC 48**
See also CA 138; 110

**Denis, Julio**
See Cortazar, Julio

**Denmark, Harrison**
See Zelazny, Roger (Joseph)

**Dennis, John** 1658-1734 . . . . . . . . . . . . **LC 11**
See also DLB 101

**Dennis, Nigel (Forbes)** 1912-1989.... **CLC 8**
See also CA 25-28R; 129; DLB 13, 15; MTCW

**De Palma, Brian (Russell)** 1940-.... **CLC 20**
See also CA 109

**De Quincey, Thomas** 1785-1859 ... **NCLC 4**
See also CDBLB 1789-1832; DLB 110; 144

**Deren, Eleanora** 1908(?)-1961
See Deren, Maya
See also CA 111

**Deren, Maya** .................... **CLC 16**
See also Deren, Eleanora

**Derleth, August (William)**
1909-1971 .................. **CLC 31**
See also CA 1-4R; 29-32R; CANR 4; DLB 9; SATA 5

**Der Nister** 1884-1950............ **TCLC 56**

**de Routisie, Albert**
See Aragon, Louis

**Derrida, Jacques** 1930-......... **CLC 24, 87**
See also CA 124; 127

**Derry Down Derry**
See Lear, Edward

**Dersonnes, Jacques**
See Simenon, Georges (Jacques Christian)

**Desai, Anita**
1937- ........... **CLC 19, 37, 97; DAB; DAM NOV**
See also CA 81-84; CANR 33, 53; MTCW; SATA 63

**de Saint-Luc, Jean**
See Glassco, John

**de Saint Roman, Arnaud**
See Aragon, Louis

**Descartes, Rene** 1596-1650 ...... **LC 20, 35**

**De Sica, Vittorio** 1901(?)-1974 ..... **CLC 20**
See also CA 117

**Desnos, Robert** 1900-1945........ **TCLC 22**
See also CA 121; 151

**Destouches, Louis-Ferdinand**
1894-1961 ................ **CLC 9, 15**
See also Celine, Louis-Ferdinand
See also CA 85-88; CANR 28; MTCW

**de Tolignac, Gaston**
See Griffith, D(avid Lewelyn) W(ark)

**Deutsch, Babette** 1895-1982 ....... **CLC 18**
See also CA 1-4R; 108; CANR 4; DLB 45; SATA 1; SATA-Obit 33

**Devenant, William** 1606-1649 ....... **LC 13**

**Devkota, Laxmiprasad**
1909-1959 .................. **TCLC 23**
See also CA 123

**De Voto, Bernard (Augustine)**
1897-1955 .................. **TCLC 29**
See also CA 113; DLB 9

**De Vries, Peter**
1910-1993 .... **CLC 1, 2, 3, 7, 10, 28, 46; DAM NOV**
See also CA 17-20R; 142; CANR 41; DLB 6; DLBY 82; MTCW

**Dexter, John**
See Bradley, Marion Zimmer

**Dexter, Martin**
See Faust, Frederick (Schiller)

**Dexter, Pete**
1943- ......... **CLC 34, 55; DAM POP**
See also BEST 89:2; CA 127; 131; INT 131; MTCW

**Diamano, Silmang**
See Senghor, Leopold Sedar

**Diamond, Neil** 1941- ............. **CLC 30**
See also CA 108

**Diaz del Castillo, Bernal** 1496-1584 .. **LC 31**

**di Bassetto, Corno**
See Shaw, George Bernard

**Dick, Philip K(indred)**
1928-1982 ............ **CLC 10, 30, 72; DAM NOV, POP**
See also CA 49-52; 106; CANR 2, 16; DLB 8; MTCW

**Dickens, Charles (John Huffam)**
1812-1870 ...... **NCLC 3, 8, 18, 26, 37, 50; DA; DAB; DAC; DAM MST, NOV; SSC 17; WLC**
See also CDBLB 1832-1890; DLB 21, 55, 70, 159, 166; JRDA; MAICYA; SATA 15

**Dickey, James (Lafayette)**
1923- ........ **CLC 1, 2, 4, 7, 10, 15, 47; DAM NOV, POET, POP**
See also AITN 1, 2; CA 9-12R; CABS 2; CANR 10, 48; CDALB 1968-1988; DLB 5; DLBD 7; DLBY 82, 93; INT CANR-10; MTCW

**Dickey, William** 1928-1994 ...... **CLC 3, 28**
See also CA 9-12R; 145; CANR 24; DLB 5

**Dickinson, Charles** 1951-.......... **CLC 49**
See also CA 128

**Dickinson, Emily (Elizabeth)**
1830-1886 ....... **NCLC 21; DA; DAB; DAC; DAM MST, POET; PC 1; WLC**
See also CDALB 1865-1917; DLB 1; SATA 29

**Dickinson, Peter (Malcolm)**
1927- .................... **CLC 12, 35**
See also AAYA 9; CA 41-44R; CANR 31; CLR 29; DLB 87, 161; JRDA; MAICYA; SATA 5, 62

**Dickson, Carr**
See Carr, John Dickson

**Dickson, Carter**
See Carr, John Dickson

**Diderot, Denis** 1713-1784 .......... **LC 26**

**Didion, Joan**
1934- .. **CLC 1, 3, 8, 14, 32; DAM NOV**
See also AITN 1; CA 5-8R; CANR 14, 52; CDALB 1968-1988; DLB 2, 173; DLBY 81, 86; MTCW

**Dietrich, Robert**
See Hunt, E(verette) Howard, (Jr.)

**Dillard, Annie**
1945- .......... **CLC 9, 60; DAM NOV**
See also AAYA 6; CA 49-52; CANR 3, 43; DLBY 80; MTCW; SATA 10

**Dillard, R(ichard) H(enry) W(ilde)**
1937- ......................... **CLC 5**
See also CA 21-24R; CAAS 7; CANR 10; DLB 5

**Dillon, Eilis** 1920-1994............ **CLC 17**
See also CA 9-12R; 147; CAAS 3; CANR 4, 38; CLR 26; MAICYA; SATA 2, 74; SATA-Obit 83

**Dimont, Penelope**
See Mortimer, Penelope (Ruth)

**Dinesen, Isak**........ **CLC 10, 29, 95; SSC 7**
See also Blixen, Karen (Christentze Dinesen)

**Ding Ling**........................ **CLC 68**
See also Chiang Pin-chin

**Disch, Thomas M(ichael)** 1940-... **CLC 7, 36**
See also AAYA 17; CA 21-24R; CAAS 4; CANR 17, 36, 54; CLR 18; DLB 8; MAICYA; MTCW; SAAS 15; SATA 54

**Disch, Tom**
See Disch, Thomas M(ichael)

**d'Isly, Georges**
See Simenon, Georges (Jacques Christian)

**Disraeli, Benjamin** 1804-1881 .. **NCLC 2, 39**
See also DLB 21, 55

**Ditcum, Steve**
See Crumb, R(obert)

**Dixon, Paige**
See Corcoran, Barbara

**Dixon, Stephen** 1936-..... **CLC 52; SSC 16**
See also CA 89-92; CANR 17, 40, 54; DLB 130

**Dobell, Sydney Thompson**
1824-1874 ................. **NCLC 43**
See also DLB 32

**Doblin, Alfred** ................... **TCLC 13**
See also Doeblin, Alfred

**Dobrolyubov, Nikolai Alexandrovich**
1836-1861 .................. **NCLC 5**

**Dobyns, Stephen** 1941-............ **CLC 37**
See also CA 45-48; CANR 2, 18

**Doctorow, E(dgar) L(aurence)**
1931- ..... **CLC 6, 11, 15, 18, 37, 44, 65; DAM NOV, POP**
See also AITN 2; BEST 89:3; CA 45-48; CANR 2, 33, 51; CDALB 1968-1988; DLB 2, 28, 173; DLBY 80; MTCW

**Dodgson, Charles Lutwidge** 1832-1898
See Carroll, Lewis
See also CLR 2; DA; DAB; DAC; DAM MST, NOV, POET; MAICYA; YABC 2

**Dodson, Owen (Vincent)**
1914-1983 ............. **CLC 79; BLC; DAM MULT**
See also BW 1; CA 65-68; 110; CANR 24; DLB 76

**Doeblin, Alfred** 1878-1957........ **TCLC 13**
See also Doblin, Alfred
See also CA 110; 141; DLB 66

**Doerr, Harriet** 1910- ............. **CLC 34**
See also CA 117; 122; CANR 47; INT 122

**Domecq, H(onorio) Bustos**
See Bioy Casares, Adolfo; Borges, Jorge Luis

**Domini, Rey**
See Lorde, Audre (Geraldine)

**Dominique**
See Proust, (Valentin-Louis-George-Eugene-) Marcel

**Don, A**
See Stephen, Leslie

**Donaldson, Stephen R.**
1947- ............ **CLC 46; DAM POP**
See also CA 89-92; CANR 13, 55; INT CANR-13

**Donleavy, J(ames) P(atrick)**
1926- ............. **CLC 1, 4, 6, 10, 45**
See also AITN 2; CA 9-12R; CANR 24, 49; DLB 6, 173; INT CANR-24; MTCW

**Donne, John**
1572-1631 ....... **LC 10, 24; DA; DAB; DAC; DAM MST, POET; PC 1**
See also CDBLB Before 1660; DLB 121, 151

**Donnell, David** 1939(?)- ........... **CLC 34**

**Donoghue, P. S.**
See Hunt, E(verette) Howard, (Jr.)

**Donoso (Yanez), Jose**
1924-1996 ........... **CLC 4, 8, 11, 32; DAM MULT; HLC**
See also CA 81-84; 155; CANR 32; DLB 113; HW; MTCW

**Donovan, John** 1928-1992 ......... **CLC 35**
See also CA 97-100; 137; CLR 3; MAICYA; SATA 72; SATA-Brief 29

**Don Roberto**
See Cunninghame Graham, R(obert) B(ontine)

**Doolittle, Hilda**
1886-1961 ..... **CLC 3, 8, 14, 31, 34, 73; DA; DAC; DAM MST, POET; PC 5; WLC**
See also H. D.
See also CA 97-100; CANR 35; DLB 4, 45; MTCW

**Dorfman, Ariel**
1942- ....... **CLC 48, 77; DAM MULT; HLC**
See also CA 124; 130; HW; INT 130

**Dorn, Edward (Merton)** 1929-... **CLC 10, 18**
See also CA 93-96; CANR 42; DLB 5; INT 93-96

**Dorsan, Luc**
See Simenon, Georges (Jacques Christian)

**Dorsange, Jean**
See Simenon, Georges (Jacques Christian)

**Dos Passos, John (Roderigo)**
1896-1970 ...... **CLC 1, 4, 8, 11, 15, 25, 34, 82; DA; DAB; DAC; DAM MST, NOV; WLC**
See also CA 1-4R; 29-32R; CANR 3; CDALB 1929-1941; DLB 4, 9; DLBD 1; MTCW

**Dossage, Jean**
See Simenon, Georges (Jacques Christian)

**Dostoevsky, Fedor Mikhailovich**
1821-1881 ...... **NCLC 2, 7, 21, 33, 43; DA; DAB; DAC; DAM MST, NOV; SSC 2; WLC**

**Doughty, Charles M(ontagu)**
1843-1926 .................. **TCLC 27**
See also CA 115; DLB 19, 57, 174

**Douglas, Ellen** .................... **CLC 73**
See also Haxton, Josephine Ayres; Williamson, Ellen Douglas

**Douglas, Gavin** 1475(?)-1522 ........ **LC 20**

**Douglas, Keith** 1920-1944 ........ **TCLC 40**
See also DLB 27

**Douglas, Leonard**
See Bradbury, Ray (Douglas)

**Douglas, Michael**
See Crichton, (John) Michael

**Douglas, Norman** 1868-1952 ...... **TCLC 68**

**Douglass, Frederick**
1817(?)-1895 .... **NCLC 7, 55; BLC; DA; DAC; DAM MST, MULT; WLC**
See also CDALB 1640-1865; DLB 1, 43, 50, 79; SATA 29

**Dourado, (Waldomiro Freitas) Autran**
1926- .................... **CLC 23, 60**
See also CA 25-28R; CANR 34

**Dourado, Waldomiro Autran**
See Dourado, (Waldomiro Freitas) Autran

**Dove, Rita (Frances)**
1952- ....... **CLC 50, 81; DAM MULT, POET; PC 6**
See also BW 2; CA 109; CAAS 19; CANR 27, 42; DLB 120

**Dowell, Coleman** 1925-1985 ........ **CLC 60**
See also CA 25-28R; 117; CANR 10; DLB 130

**Dowson, Ernest (Christopher)**
1867-1900 .................. **TCLC 4**
See also CA 105; 150; DLB 19, 135

**Doyle, A. Conan**
See Doyle, Arthur Conan

**Doyle, Arthur Conan**
1859-1930 ......... **TCLC 7; DA; DAB; DAC; DAM MST, NOV; SSC 12; WLC**
See also AAYA 14; CA 104; 122; CDBLB 1890-1914; DLB 18, 70, 156; MTCW; SATA 24

**Doyle, Conan**
See Doyle, Arthur Conan

**Doyle, John**
See Graves, Robert (von Ranke)

**Doyle, Roddy** 1958(?)- ............ **CLC 81**
See also AAYA 14; CA 143

**Doyle, Sir A. Conan**
See Doyle, Arthur Conan

**Doyle, Sir Arthur Conan**
See Doyle, Arthur Conan

**Dr. A**
See Asimov, Isaac; Silverstein, Alvin

**Drabble, Margaret**
1939- ........ **CLC 2, 3, 5, 8, 10, 22, 53; DAB; DAC; DAM MST, NOV, POP**
See also CA 13-16R; CANR 18, 35; CDBLB 1960 to Present; DLB 14, 155; MTCW; SATA 48

**Drapier, M. B.**
See Swift, Jonathan

**Drayham, James**
See Mencken, H(enry) L(ouis)

**Drayton, Michael** 1563-1631 ......... **LC 8**

**Dreadstone, Carl**
See Campbell, (John) Ramsey

**Dreiser, Theodore (Herman Albert)**
1871-1945 ....... **TCLC 10, 18, 35; DA; DAC; DAM MST, NOV; WLC**
See also CA 106; 132; CDALB 1865-1917; DLB 9, 12, 102, 137; DLBD 1; MTCW

**Drexler, Rosalyn** 1926- .......... **CLC 2, 6**
See also CA 81-84

**Dreyer, Carl Theodor** 1889-1968.... **CLC 16**
See also CA 116

**Drieu la Rochelle, Pierre(-Eugene)**
1893-1945 .................. **TCLC 21**
See also CA 117; DLB 72

**Drinkwater, John** 1882-1937...... **TCLC 57**
See also CA 109; 149; DLB 10, 19, 149

**Drop Shot**
See Cable, George Washington

**Droste-Hulshoff, Annette Freiin von**
1797-1848 .................. **NCLC 3**
See also DLB 133

**Drummond, Walter**
See Silverberg, Robert

**Drummond, William Henry**
1854-1907 .................. **TCLC 25**
See also DLB 92

**Drummond de Andrade, Carlos**
1902-1987 ................... **CLC 18**
See also Andrade, Carlos Drummond de
See also CA 132; 123

**Drury, Allen (Stuart)** 1918- ........ **CLC 37**
See also CA 57-60; CANR 18, 52; INT CANR-18

**Dryden, John**
1631-1700 ........ **LC 3, 21; DA; DAB; DAC; DAM DRAM, MST, POET; DC 3; WLC**
See also CDBLB 1660-1789; DLB 80, 101, 131

**Duberman, Martin** 1930- ........... **CLC 8**
See also CA 1-4R; CANR 2

**Dubie, Norman (Evans)** 1945- ...... **CLC 36**
See also CA 69-72; CANR 12; DLB 120

**Du Bois, W(illiam) E(dward) B(urghardt)**
1868-1963 ........ **CLC 1, 2, 13, 64, 96; BLC; DA; DAC; DAM MST, MULT, NOV; WLC**
See also BW 1; CA 85-88; CANR 34; CDALB 1865-1917; DLB 47, 50, 91; MTCW; SATA 42

**Dubus, Andre**
1936- ......... **CLC 13, 36, 97; SSC 15**
See also CA 21-24R; CANR 17; DLB 130; INT CANR-17

**Duca Minimo**
See D'Annunzio, Gabriele

**Ducharme, Rejean** 1941- .......... **CLC 74**
See also DLB 60

**Duclos, Charles Pinot** 1704-1772 ..... **LC 1**

**Dudek, Louis** 1918- ........... **CLC 11, 19**
See also CA 45-48; CAAS 14; CANR 1; DLB 88

**Edwards, Jonathan**
1703-1758 .......... **LC 7; DA; DAC; DAM MST**
See also DLB 24

**Efron, Marina Ivanovna Tsvetaeva**
See Tsvetaeva (Efron), Marina (Ivanovna)

**Ehle, John (Marsden, Jr.)** 1925-.... **CLC 27**
See also CA 9-12R

**Ehrenbourg, Ilya (Grigoryevich)**
See Ehrenburg, Ilya (Grigoryevich)

**Ehrenburg, Ilya (Grigoryevich)**
1891-1967 ............ **CLC 18, 34, 62**
See also CA 102; 25-28R

**Ehrenburg, Ilyo (Grigoryevich)**
See Ehrenburg, Ilya (Grigoryevich)

**Eich, Guenter** 1907-1972 .......... **CLC 15**
See also CA 111; 93-96; DLB 69, 124

**Eichendorff, Joseph Freiherr von**
1788-1857 .................. **NCLC 8**
See also DLB 90

**Eigner, Larry**...................... **CLC 9**
See also Eigner, Laurence (Joel)
See also CAAS 23; DLB 5

**Eigner, Laurence (Joel)** 1927-1996
See Eigner, Larry
See also CA 9-12R; 151; CANR 6

**Einstein, Albert** 1879-1955 ....... **TCLC 65**
See also CA 121; 133; MTCW

**Eiseley, Loren Corey** 1907-1977..... **CLC 7**
See also AAYA 5; CA 1-4R; 73-76; CANR 6

**Eisenstadt, Jill** 1963- ............. **CLC 50**
See also CA 140

**Eisenstein, Sergei (Mikhailovich)**
1898-1948 .................. **TCLC 57**
See also CA 114; 149

**Eisner, Simon**
See Kornbluth, C(yril) M.

**Ekeloef, (Bengt) Gunnar**
1907-1968 ....... **CLC 27; DAM POET**
See also CA 123; 25-28R

**Ekelof, (Bengt) Gunnar**
See Ekeloef, (Bengt) Gunnar

**Ekwensi, C. O. D.**
See Ekwensi, Cyprian (Odiatu Duaka)

**Ekwensi, Cyprian (Odiatu Duaka)**
1921- ...... **CLC 4; BLC; DAM MULT**
See also BW 2; CA 29-32R; CANR 18, 42; DLB 117; MTCW; SATA 66

**Elaine**.......................... **TCLC 18**
See also Leverson, Ada

**El Crummo**
See Crumb, R(obert)

**Elia**
See Lamb, Charles

**Eliade, Mircea** 1907-1986 ......... **CLC 19**
See also CA 65-68; 119; CANR 30; MTCW

**Eliot, A. D.**
See Jewett, (Theodora) Sarah Orne

**Eliot, Alice**
See Jewett, (Theodora) Sarah Orne

**Eliot, Dan**
See Silverberg, Robert

**Eliot, George**
1819-1880 ..... **NCLC 4, 13, 23, 41, 49; DA; DAB; DAC; DAM MST, NOV; WLC**
See also CDBLB 1832-1890; DLB 21, 35, 55

**Eliot, John** 1604-1690 ............. **LC 5**
See also DLB 24

**Eliot, T(homas) S(tearns)**
1888-1965 ..... **CLC 1, 2, 3, 6, 9, 10, 13, 15, 24, 34, 41, 55, 57; DA; DAB; DAC; DAM DRAM, MST, POET; PC 5; WLC 2**
See also CA 5-8R; 25-28R; CANR 41; CDALB 1929-1941; DLB 7, 10, 45, 63; DLBY 88; MTCW

**Elizabeth** 1866-1941 ............. **TCLC 41**

**Elkin, Stanley L(awrence)**
1930-1995 ...... **CLC 4, 6, 9, 14, 27, 51, 91; DAM NOV, POP; SSC 12**
See also CA 9-12R; 148; CANR 8, 46; DLB 2, 28; DLBY 80; INT CANR-8; MTCW

**Elledge, Scott**..................... **CLC 34**

**Elliot, Don**
See Silverberg, Robert

**Elliott, Don**
See Silverberg, Robert

**Elliott, George P(aul)** 1918-1980..... **CLC 2**
See also CA 1-4R; 97-100; CANR 2

**Elliott, Janice** 1931-.............. **CLC 47**
See also CA 13-16R; CANR 8, 29; DLB 14

**Elliott, Sumner Locke** 1917-1991 ... **CLC 38**
See also CA 5-8R; 134; CANR 2, 21

**Elliott, William**
See Bradbury, Ray (Douglas)

**Ellis, A. E.**........................ **CLC 7**

**Ellis, Alice Thomas**................ **CLC 40**
See also Haycraft, Anna

**Ellis, Bret Easton**
1964- ......... **CLC 39, 71; DAM POP**
See also AAYA 2; CA 118; 123; CANR 51; INT 123

**Ellis, (Henry) Havelock**
1859-1939 .................. **TCLC 14**
See also CA 109

**Ellis, Landon**
See Ellison, Harlan (Jay)

**Ellis, Trey** 1962-................. **CLC 55**
See also CA 146

**Ellison, Harlan (Jay)**
1934- ...... **CLC 1, 13, 42; DAM POP; SSC 14**
See also CA 5-8R; CANR 5, 46; DLB 8; INT CANR-5; MTCW

**Ellison, Ralph (Waldo)**
1914-1994 ........ **CLC 1, 3, 11, 54, 86; BLC; DA; DAB; DAC; DAM MST, MULT, NOV; WLC**
See also AAYA 19; BW 1; CA 9-12R; 145; CANR 24, 53; CDALB 1941-1968; DLB 2, 76; DLBY 94; MTCW

**Ellmann, Lucy (Elizabeth)** 1956-.... **CLC 61**
See also CA 128

**Ellmann, Richard (David)**
1918-1987 ................... **CLC 50**
See also BEST 89:2; CA 1-4R; 122; CANR 2, 28; DLB 103; DLBY 87; MTCW

**Elman, Richard** 1934-............. **CLC 19**
See also CA 17-20R; CAAS 3; CANR 47

**Elron**
See Hubbard, L(afayette) Ron(ald)

**Eluard, Paul**.................. **TCLC 7, 41**
See also Grindel, Eugene

**Elyot, Sir Thomas** 1490(?)-1546 ..... **LC 11**

**Elytis, Odysseus**
1911-1996 .... **CLC 15, 49; DAM POET**
See also CA 102; 151; MTCW

**Emecheta, (Florence Onye) Buchi**
1944- .. **CLC 14, 48; BLC; DAM MULT**
See also BW 2; CA 81-84; CANR 27; DLB 117; MTCW; SATA 66

**Emerson, Ralph Waldo**
1803-1882 ..... **NCLC 1, 38; DA; DAB; DAC; DAM MST, POET; WLC**
See also CDALB 1640-1865; DLB 1, 59, 73

**Eminescu, Mihail** 1850-1889 ..... **NCLC 33**

**Empson, William**
1906-1984 ........ **CLC 3, 8, 19, 33, 34**
See also CA 17-20R; 112; CANR 31; DLB 20; MTCW

**Enchi Fumiko (Ueda)** 1905-1986.... **CLC 31**
See also CA 129; 121

**Ende, Michael (Andreas Helmuth)**
1929-1995 ................... **CLC 31**
See also CA 118; 124; 149; CANR 36; CLR 14; DLB 75; MAICYA; SATA 61; SATA-Brief 42; SATA-Obit 86

**Endo, Shusaku**
1923-1996 .......... **CLC 7, 14, 19, 54; DAM NOV**
See also CA 29-32R; 153; CANR 21, 54; MTCW

**Engel, Marian** 1933-1985.......... **CLC 36**
See also CA 25-28R; CANR 12; DLB 53; INT CANR-12

**Engelhardt, Frederick**
See Hubbard, L(afayette) Ron(ald)

**Enright, D(ennis) J(oseph)**
1920- ................... **CLC 4, 8, 31**
See also CA 1-4R; CANR 1, 42; DLB 27; SATA 25

**Enzensberger, Hans Magnus**
1929- ....................... **CLC 43**
See also CA 116; 119

**Ephron, Nora** 1941- ........... **CLC 17, 31**
See also AITN 2; CA 65-68; CANR 12, 39

**Epsilon**
See Betjeman, John

**Epstein, Daniel Mark** 1948- ........ **CLC 7**
See also CA 49-52; CANR 2, 53

**Epstein, Jacob** 1956- ............. **CLC 19**
See also CA 114

**Epstein, Joseph** 1937-............ **CLC 39**
See also CA 112; 119; CANR 50

**Epstein, Leslie** 1938- ............ **CLC 27**
See also CA 73-76; CAAS 12; CANR 23



Author Index

**Equiano, Olaudah** 1745(?)-1797 .......... **LC 16; BLC; DAM MULT**
See also DLB 37, 50

**Erasmus, Desiderius** 1469(?)-1536.... **LC 16**

**Erdman, Paul E(mil)** 1932- ........ **CLC 25**
See also AITN 1; CA 61-64; CANR 13, 43

**Erdrich, Louise** 1954- ....... **CLC 39, 54; DAM MULT, NOV, POP**
See also AAYA 10; BEST 89:1; CA 114; CANR 41; DLB 152; MTCW; NNAL

**Erenburg, Ilya (Grigoryevich)**
See Ehrenburg, Ilya (Grigoryevich)

**Erickson, Stephen Michael** 1950-
See Erickson, Steve
See also CA 129

**Erickson, Steve** .................. **CLC 64**
See also Erickson, Stephen Michael

**Ericson, Walter**
See Fast, Howard (Melvin)

**Eriksson, Buntel**
See Bergman, (Ernst) Ingmar

**Ernaux, Annie** 1940- ............. **CLC 88**
See also CA 147

**Eschenbach, Wolfram von**
See Wolfram von Eschenbach

**Eseki, Bruno**
See Mphahlele, Ezekiel

**Esenin, Sergei (Alexandrovich)** 1895-1925 .................. **TCLC 4**
See also CA 104

**Eshleman, Clayton** 1935-........... **CLC 7**
See also CA 33-36R; CAAS 6; DLB 5

**Espriella, Don Manuel Alvarez**
See Southey, Robert

**Espriu, Salvador** 1913-1985......... **CLC 9**
See also CA 154; 115; DLB 134

**Espronceda, Jose de** 1808-1842... **NCLC 39**

**Esse, James**
See Stephens, James

**Esterbrook, Tom**
See Hubbard, L(afayette) Ron(ald)

**Estleman, Loren D.** 1952- ...... **CLC 48; DAM NOV, POP**
See also CA 85-88; CANR 27; INT CANR-27; MTCW

**Eugenides, Jeffrey** 1960(?)- ........ **CLC 81**
See also CA 144

**Euripides** c. 485B.C.-406B.C. ......... **DC 4**
See also DA; DAB; DAC; DAM DRAM, MST

**Evan, Evin**
See Faust, Frederick (Schiller)

**Evans, Evan**
See Faust, Frederick (Schiller)

**Evans, Marian**
See Eliot, George

**Evans, Mary Ann**
See Eliot, George

**Evarts, Esther**
See Benson, Sally

**Everett, Percival L.** 1956- ......... **CLC 57**
See also BW 2; CA 129

**Everson, R(onald) G(ilmour)** 1903- ....................... **CLC 27**
See also CA 17-20R; DLB 88

**Everson, William (Oliver)** 1912-1994 ............... **CLC 1, 5, 14**
See also CA 9-12R; 145; CANR 20; DLB 5, 16; MTCW

**Evtushenko, Evgenii Aleksandrovich**
See Yevtushenko, Yevgeny (Alexandrovich)

**Ewart, Gavin (Buchanan)** 1916-1995 ................ **CLC 13, 46**
See also CA 89-92; 150; CANR 17, 46; DLB 40; MTCW

**Ewers, Hanns Heinz** 1871-1943 ... **TCLC 12**
See also CA 109; 149

**Ewing, Frederick R.**
See Sturgeon, Theodore (Hamilton)

**Exley, Frederick (Earl)** 1929-1992 ................. **CLC 6, 11**
See also AITN 2; CA 81-84; 138; DLB 143; DLBY 81

**Eynhardt, Guillermo**
See Quiroga, Horacio (Sylvestre)

**Ezekiel, Nissim** 1924-............ **CLC 61**
See also CA 61-64

**Ezekiel, Tish O'Dowd** 1943- ....... **CLC 34**
See also CA 129

**Fadeyev, A.**
See Bulgya, Alexander Alexandrovich

**Fadeyev, Alexander**.............. **TCLC 53**
See also Bulgya, Alexander Alexandrovich

**Fagen, Donald** 1948-............. **CLC 26**

**Fainzilberg, Ilya Arnoldovich** 1897-1937
See Ilf, Ilya
See also CA 120

**Fair, Ronald L.** 1932-............. **CLC 18**
See also BW 1; CA 69-72; CANR 25; DLB 33

**Fairbairns, Zoe (Ann)** 1948- ....... **CLC 32**
See also CA 103; CANR 21

**Falco, Gian**
See Papini, Giovanni

**Falconer, James**
See Kirkup, James

**Falconer, Kenneth**
See Kornbluth, C(yril) M.

**Falkland, Samuel**
See Heijermans, Herman

**Fallaci, Oriana** 1930-............. **CLC 11**
See also CA 77-80; CANR 15; MTCW

**Faludy, George** 1913-............. **CLC 42**
See also CA 21-24R

**Faludy, Gyoergy**
See Faludy, George

**Fanon, Frantz** 1925-1961 ............. **CLC 74; BLC; DAM MULT**
See also BW 1; CA 116; 89-92

**Fanshawe, Ann** 1625-1680.......... **LC 11**

**Fante, John (Thomas)** 1911-1983 ... **CLC 60**
See also CA 69-72; 109; CANR 23; DLB 130; DLBY 83

**Farah, Nuruddin** 1945- ..... **CLC 53; BLC; DAM MULT**
See also BW 2; CA 106; DLB 125

**Fargue, Leon-Paul** 1876(?)-1947 ... **TCLC 11**
See also CA 109

**Farigoule, Louis**
See Romains, Jules

**Farina, Richard** 1936(?)-1966 ....... **CLC 9**
See also CA 81-84; 25-28R

**Farley, Walter (Lorimer)** 1915-1989 ................... **CLC 17**
See also CA 17-20R; CANR 8, 29; DLB 22; JRDA; MAICYA; SATA 2, 43

**Farmer, Philip Jose** 1918-....... **CLC 1, 19**
See also CA 1-4R; CANR 4, 35; DLB 8; MTCW

**Farquhar, George** 1677-1707 ....... **LC 21; DAM DRAM**
See also DLB 84

**Farrell, J(ames) G(ordon)** 1935-1979 .................... **CLC 6**
See also CA 73-76; 89-92; CANR 36; DLB 14; MTCW

**Farrell, James T(homas)** 1904-1979 ......... **CLC 1, 4, 8, 11, 66**
See also CA 5-8R; 89-92; CANR 9; DLB 4, 9, 86; DLBD 2; MTCW

**Farren, Richard J.**
See Betjeman, John

**Farren, Richard M.**
See Betjeman, John

**Fassbinder, Rainer Werner** 1946-1982 ................... **CLC 20**
See also CA 93-96; 106; CANR 31

**Fast, Howard (Melvin)** 1914- ............ **CLC 23; DAM NOV**
See also AAYA 16; CA 1-4R; CAAS 18; CANR 1, 33, 54; DLB 9; INT CANR-33; SATA 7

**Faulcon, Robert**
See Holdstock, Robert P.

**Faulkner, William (Cuthbert)** 1897-1962 ..... **CLC 1, 3, 6, 8, 9, 11, 14, 18, 28, 52, 68; DA; DAB; DAC; DAM MST, NOV; SSC 1; WLC**
See also AAYA 7; CA 81-84; CANR 33; CDALB 1929-1941; DLB 9, 11, 44, 102; DLBD 2; DLBY 86; MTCW

**Fauset, Jessie Redmon** 1884(?)-1961 ........ **CLC 19, 54; BLC; DAM MULT**
See also BW 1; CA 109; DLB 51

**Faust, Frederick (Schiller)** 1892-1944(?) ..... **TCLC 49; DAM POP**
See also CA 108; 152

**Faust, Irvin** 1924-................. **CLC 8**
See also CA 33-36R; CANR 28; DLB 2, 28; DLBY 80

**Fawkes, Guy**
See Benchley, Robert (Charles)

**Fearing, Kenneth (Flexner)** 1902-1961 ................... **CLC 51**
See also CA 93-96; DLB 9

**Fecamps, Elise**
See Creasey, John

**Federman, Raymond** 1928- ...... **CLC 6, 47**
See also CA 17-20R; CAAS 8; CANR 10, 43; DLBY 80

**Federspiel, J(uerg) F.** 1931- ........ **CLC 42**
See also CA 146

**Feiffer, Jules (Ralph)**
1929- ...... **CLC 2, 8, 64; DAM DRAM**
See also AAYA 3; CA 17-20R; CANR 30; DLB 7, 44; INT CANR-30; MTCW; SATA 8, 61

**Feige, Hermann Albert Otto Maximilian**
See Traven, B.

**Feinberg, David B.** 1956-1994 ...... **CLC 59**
See also CA 135; 147

**Feinstein, Elaine** 1930- ............ **CLC 36**
See also CA 69-72; CAAS 1; CANR 31; DLB 14, 40; MTCW

**Feldman, Irving (Mordecai)** 1928- .... **CLC 7**
See also CA 1-4R; CANR 1; DLB 169

**Fellini, Federico** 1920-1993 ..... **CLC 16, 85**
See also CA 65-68; 143; CANR 33

**Felsen, Henry Gregor** 1916- ....... **CLC 17**
See also CA 1-4R; CANR 1; SAAS 2; SATA 1

**Fenton, James Martin** 1949- ....... **CLC 32**
See also CA 102; DLB 40

**Ferber, Edna** 1887-1968 ........ **CLC 18, 93**
See also AITN 1; CA 5-8R; 25-28R; DLB 9, 28, 86; MTCW; SATA 7

**Ferguson, Helen**
See Kavan, Anna

**Ferguson, Samuel** 1810-1886 ..... **NCLC 33**
See also DLB 32

**Fergusson, Robert** 1750-1774 ....... **LC 29**
See also DLB 109

**Ferling, Lawrence**
See Ferlinghetti, Lawrence (Monsanto)

**Ferlinghetti, Lawrence (Monsanto)**
1919(?)- ............. **CLC 2, 6, 10, 27; DAM POET; PC 1**
See also CA 5-8R; CANR 3, 41; CDALB 1941-1968; DLB 5, 16; MTCW

**Fernandez, Vicente Garcia Huidobro**
See Huidobro Fernandez, Vicente Garcia

**Ferrer, Gabriel (Francisco Victor) Miro**
See Miro (Ferrer), Gabriel (Francisco Victor)

**Ferrier, Susan (Edmonstone)**
1782-1854 .................. **NCLC 8**
See also DLB 116

**Ferrigno, Robert** 1948(?)- .......... **CLC 65**
See also CA 140

**Ferron, Jacques** 1921-1985 ... **CLC 94; DAC**
See also CA 117; 129; DLB 60

**Feuchtwanger, Lion** 1884-1958 ..... **TCLC 3**
See also CA 104; DLB 66

**Feuillet, Octave** 1821-1890 ...... **NCLC 45**

**Feydeau, Georges (Leon Jules Marie)**
1862-1921 ..... **TCLC 22; DAM DRAM**
See also CA 113; 152

**Ficino, Marsilio** 1433-1499 ......... **LC 12**

**Fiedeler, Hans**
See Doeblin, Alfred

**Fiedler, Leslie A(aron)**
1917- .................. **CLC 4, 13, 24**
See also CA 9-12R; CANR 7; DLB 28, 67; MTCW

**Field, Andrew** 1938- .............. **CLC 44**
See also CA 97-100; CANR 25

**Field, Eugene** 1850-1895 ......... **NCLC 3**
See also DLB 23, 42, 140; DLBD 13; MAICYA; SATA 16

**Field, Gans T.**
See Wellman, Manly Wade

**Field, Michael** .................. **TCLC 43**

**Field, Peter**
See Hobson, Laura Z(ametkin)

**Fielding, Henry**
1707-1754 ...... **LC 1; DA; DAB; DAC; DAM DRAM, MST, NOV; WLC**
See also CDBLB 1660-1789; DLB 39, 84, 101

**Fielding, Sarah** 1710-1768 ........... **LC 1**
See also DLB 39

**Fierstein, Harvey (Forbes)**
1954- ..... **CLC 33; DAM DRAM, POP**
See also CA 123; 129

**Figes, Eva** 1932- ................. **CLC 31**
See also CA 53-56; CANR 4, 44; DLB 14

**Finch, Robert (Duer Claydon)**
1900- ....................... **CLC 18**
See also CA 57-60; CANR 9, 24, 49; DLB 88

**Findley, Timothy**
1930- ...... **CLC 27; DAC; DAM MST**
See also CA 25-28R; CANR 12, 42; DLB 53

**Fink, William**
See Mencken, H(enry) L(ouis)

**Firbank, Louis** 1942-
See Reed, Lou
See also CA 117

**Firbank, (Arthur Annesley) Ronald**
1886-1926 .................. **TCLC 1**
See also CA 104; DLB 36

**Fisher, M(ary) F(rances) K(ennedy)**
1908-1992 ................ **CLC 76, 87**
See also CA 77-80; 138; CANR 44

**Fisher, Roy** 1930- ................ **CLC 25**
See also CA 81-84; CAAS 10; CANR 16; DLB 40

**Fisher, Rudolph**
1897-1934 ........... **TCLC 11; BLC; DAM MULT**
See also BW 1; CA 107; 124; DLB 51, 102

**Fisher, Vardis (Alvero)** 1895-1968.... **CLC 7**
See also CA 5-8R; 25-28R; DLB 9

**Fiske, Tarleton**
See Bloch, Robert (Albert)

**Fitch, Clarke**
See Sinclair, Upton (Beall)

**Fitch, John IV**
See Cormier, Robert (Edmund)

**Fitzgerald, Captain Hugh**
See Baum, L(yman) Frank

**FitzGerald, Edward** 1809-1883 .... **NCLC 9**
See also DLB 32

**Fitzgerald, F(rancis) Scott (Key)**
1896-1940 ....... **TCLC 1, 6, 14, 28, 55; DA; DAB; DAC; DAM MST, NOV; SSC 6; WLC**
See also AITN 1; CA 110; 123; CDALB 1917-1929; DLB 4, 9, 86; DLBD 1; DLBY 81; MTCW

**Fitzgerald, Penelope** 1916- ... **CLC 19, 51, 61**
See also CA 85-88; CAAS 10; DLB 14

**Fitzgerald, Robert (Stuart)**
1910-1985 ................... **CLC 39**
See also CA 1-4R; 114; CANR 1; DLBY 80

**FitzGerald, Robert D(avid)**
1902-1987 ................... **CLC 19**
See also CA 17-20R

**Fitzgerald, Zelda (Sayre)**
1900-1948 .................. **TCLC 52**
See also CA 117; 126; DLBY 84

**Flanagan, Thomas (James Bonner)**
1923- .................... **CLC 25, 52**
See also CA 108; CANR 55; DLBY 80; INT 108; MTCW

**Flaubert, Gustave**
1821-1880 ........ **NCLC 2, 10, 19; DA; DAB; DAC; DAM MST, NOV; SSC 11; WLC**
See also DLB 119

**Flecker, Herman Elroy**
See Flecker, (Herman) James Elroy

**Flecker, (Herman) James Elroy**
1884-1915 .................. **TCLC 43**
See also CA 109; 150; DLB 10, 19

**Fleming, Ian (Lancaster)**
1908-1964 ...... **CLC 3, 30; DAM POP**
See also CA 5-8R; CDBLB 1945-1960; DLB 87; MTCW; SATA 9

**Fleming, Thomas (James)** 1927- .... **CLC 37**
See also CA 5-8R; CANR 10; INT CANR-10; SATA 8

**Fletcher, John** 1579-1625...... **LC 33; DC 6**
See also CDBLB Before 1660; DLB 58

**Fletcher, John Gould** 1886-1950... **TCLC 35**
See also CA 107; DLB 4, 45

**Fleur, Paul**
See Pohl, Frederik

**Flooglebuckle, Al**
See Spiegelman, Art

**Flying Officer X**
See Bates, H(erbert) E(rnest)

**Fo, Dario** 1926- ..... **CLC 32; DAM DRAM**
See also CA 116; 128; MTCW

**Fogarty, Jonathan Titulescu Esq.**
See Farrell, James T(homas)

**Folke, Will**
See Bloch, Robert (Albert)

**Follett, Ken(neth Martin)**
1949- ...... **CLC 18; DAM NOV, POP**
See also AAYA 6; BEST 89:4; CA 81-84; CANR 13, 33, 54; DLB 87; DLBY 81; INT CANR-33; MTCW

**Fontane, Theodor** 1819-1898 ..... **NCLC 26**
See also DLB 129

**Friedman, B(ernard) H(arper)** 1926- . . . . . . . . . . . . . . . . . . . . . . . . **CLC 7**
See also CA 1-4R; CANR 3, 48

**Friedman, Bruce Jay** 1930- . . . . **CLC 3, 5, 56**
See also CA 9-12R; CANR 25, 52; DLB 2, 28; INT CANR-25

**Friel, Brian** 1929- . . . . . . . . . . . **CLC 5, 42, 59**
See also CA 21-24R; CANR 33; DLB 13; MTCW

**Friis-Baastad, Babbis Ellinor** 1921-1970 . . . . . . . . . . . . . . . . . . . . **CLC 12**
See also CA 17-20R; 134; SATA 7

**Frisch, Max (Rudolf)** 1911-1991 . . . . . **CLC 3, 9, 14, 18, 32, 44; DAM DRAM, NOV**
See also CA 85-88; 134; CANR 32; DLB 69, 124; MTCW

**Fromentin, Eugene (Samuel Auguste)** 1820-1876 . . . . . . . . . . . . . . . . . **NCLC 10**
See also DLB 123

**Frost, Frederick**
See Faust, Frederick (Schiller)

**Frost, Robert (Lee)** 1874-1963 . . . . **CLC 1, 3, 4, 9, 10, 13, 15, 26, 34, 44; DA; DAB; DAC; DAM MST, POET; PC 1; WLC**
See also CA 89-92; CANR 33; CDALB 1917-1929; DLB 54; DLBD 7; MTCW; SATA 14

**Froude, James Anthony** 1818-1894 . . . . . . . . . . . . . . . . . **NCLC 43**
See also DLB 18, 57, 144

**Froy, Herald**
See Waterhouse, Keith (Spencer)

**Fry, Christopher** 1907- . . . . . **CLC 2, 10, 14; DAM DRAM**
See also CA 17-20R; CAAS 23; CANR 9, 30; DLB 13; MTCW; SATA 66

**Frye, (Herman) Northrop** 1912-1991 . . . . . . . . . . . . . . **CLC 24, 70**
See also CA 5-8R; 133; CANR 8, 37; DLB 67, 68; MTCW

**Fuchs, Daniel** 1909-1993 . . . . . . . . **CLC 8, 22**
See also CA 81-84; 142; CAAS 5; CANR 40; DLB 9, 26, 28; DLBY 93

**Fuchs, Daniel** 1934- . . . . . . . . . . . . . . **CLC 34**
See also CA 37-40R; CANR 14, 48

**Fuentes, Carlos** 1928- . . . . . . **CLC 3, 8, 10, 13, 22, 41, 60; DA; DAB; DAC; DAM MST, MULT, NOV; HLC; SSC 24; WLC**
See also AAYA 4; AITN 2; CA 69-72; CANR 10, 32; DLB 113; HW; MTCW

**Fuentes, Gregorio Lopez y**
See Lopez y Fuentes, Gregorio

**Fugard, (Harold) Athol** 1932- . . . . . . . . . **CLC 5, 9, 14, 25, 40, 80; DAM DRAM; DC 3**
See also AAYA 17; CA 85-88; CANR 32, 54; MTCW

**Fugard, Sheila** 1932- . . . . . . . . . . . . . **CLC 48**
See also CA 125

**Fuller, Charles (H., Jr.)** 1939- . . . . **CLC 25; BLC; DAM DRAM, MULT; DC 1**
See also BW 2; CA 108; 112; DLB 38; INT 112; MTCW

**Fuller, John (Leopold)** 1937- . . . . . . . **CLC 62**
See also CA 21-24R; CANR 9, 44; DLB 40

**Fuller, Margaret** . . . . . . . . . . . . . . **NCLC 5, 50**
See also Ossoli, Sarah Margaret (Fuller marchesa d')

**Fuller, Roy (Broadbent)** 1912-1991 . . . . . . . . . . . . . . . . . **CLC 4, 28**
See also CA 5-8R; 135; CAAS 10; CANR 53; DLB 15, 20; SATA 87

**Fulton, Alice** 1952- . . . . . . . . . . . . . . . **CLC 52**
See also CA 116

**Furphy, Joseph** 1843-1912 . . . . . . . . **TCLC 25**

**Fussell, Paul** 1924- . . . . . . . . . . . . . . . **CLC 74**
See also BEST 90:1; CA 17-20R; CANR 8, 21, 35; INT CANR-21; MTCW

**Futabatei, Shimei** 1864-1909 . . . . . . **TCLC 44**

**Futrelle, Jacques** 1875-1912 . . . . . . **TCLC 19**
See also CA 113; 155

**Gaboriau, Emile** 1835-1873 . . . . . . **NCLC 14**

**Gadda, Carlo Emilio** 1893-1973 . . . . **CLC 11**
See also CA 89-92

**Gaddis, William** 1922- . . . . . **CLC 1, 3, 6, 8, 10, 19, 43, 86**
See also CA 17-20R; CANR 21, 48; DLB 2; MTCW

**Gage, Walter**
See Inge, William (Motter)

**Gaines, Ernest J(ames)** 1933- . . . . . . . . . **CLC 3, 11, 18, 86; BLC; DAM MULT**
See also AAYA 18; AITN 1; BW 2; CA 9-12R; CANR 6, 24, 42; CDALB 1968-1988; DLB 2, 33, 152; DLBY 80; MTCW; SATA 86

**Gaitskill, Mary** 1954- . . . . . . . . . . . . . **CLC 69**
See also CA 128

**Galdos, Benito Perez**
See Perez Galdos, Benito

**Gale, Zona** 1874-1938 . . . . . . **TCLC 7; DAM DRAM**
See also CA 105; 153; DLB 9, 78

**Galeano, Eduardo (Hughes)** 1940- . . . **CLC 72**
See also CA 29-32R; CANR 13, 32; HW

**Galiano, Juan Valera y Alcala**
See Valera y Alcala-Galiano, Juan

**Gallagher, Tess** 1943- . . **CLC 18, 63; DAM POET; PC 9**
See also CA 106; DLB 120

**Gallant, Mavis** 1922- . . . . . . . . . . . . **CLC 7, 18, 38; DAC; DAM MST; SSC 5**
See also CA 69-72; CANR 29; DLB 53; MTCW

**Gallant, Roy A(rthur)** 1924- . . . . . . . **CLC 17**
See also CA 5-8R; CANR 4, 29, 54; CLR 30; MAICYA; SATA 4, 68

**Gallico, Paul (William)** 1897-1976 . . . **CLC 2**
See also AITN 1; CA 5-8R; 69-72; CANR 23; DLB 9, 171; MAICYA; SATA 13

**Gallo, Max Louis** 1932- . . . . . . . . . . . **CLC 95**
See also CA 85-88

**Gallois, Lucien**
See Desnos, Robert

**Gallup, Ralph**
See Whitemore, Hugh (John)

**Galsworthy, John** 1867-1933 . . . . . . **TCLC 1, 45; DA; DAB; DAC; DAM DRAM, MST, NOV; SSC 22; WLC 2**
See also CA 104; 141; CDBLB 1890-1914; DLB 10, 34, 98, 162

**Galt, John** 1779-1839 . . . . . . . . . . . . **NCLC 1**
See also DLB 99, 116, 159

**Galvin, James** 1951- . . . . . . . . . . . . . . . **CLC 38**
See also CA 108; CANR 26

**Gamboa, Federico** 1864-1939 . . . . . . **TCLC 36**

**Gandhi, M. K.**
See Gandhi, Mohandas Karamchand

**Gandhi, Mahatma**
See Gandhi, Mohandas Karamchand

**Gandhi, Mohandas Karamchand** 1869-1948 . . . . . **TCLC 59; DAM MULT**
See also CA 121; 132; MTCW

**Gann, Ernest Kellogg** 1910-1991 . . . . **CLC 23**
See also AITN 1; CA 1-4R; 136; CANR 1

**Garcia, Cristina** 1958- . . . . . . . . . . . . . **CLC 76**
See also CA 141

**Garcia Lorca, Federico** 1898-1936 . . . **TCLC 1, 7, 49; DA; DAB; DAC; DAM DRAM, MST, MULT, POET; DC 2; HLC; PC 3; WLC**
See also CA 104; 131; DLB 108; HW; MTCW

**Garcia Marquez, Gabriel (Jose)** 1928- . . . . **CLC 2, 3, 8, 10, 15, 27, 47, 55, 68; DA; DAB; DAC; DAM MST, MULT, NOV, POP; HLC; SSC 8; WLC**
See also AAYA 3; BEST 89:1, 90:4; CA 33-36R; CANR 10, 28, 50; DLB 113; HW; MTCW

**Gard, Janice**
See Latham, Jean Lee

**Gard, Roger Martin du**
See Martin du Gard, Roger

**Gardam, Jane** 1928- . . . . . . . . . . . . . . **CLC 43**
See also CA 49-52; CANR 2, 18, 33, 54; CLR 12; DLB 14, 161; MAICYA; MTCW; SAAS 9; SATA 39, 76; SATA-Brief 28

**Gardner, Herb(ert)** 1934- . . . . . . . . . . **CLC 44**
See also CA 149

**Gardner, John (Champlin), Jr.** 1933-1982 . . . . . **CLC 2, 3, 5, 7, 8, 10, 18, 28, 34; DAM NOV, POP; SSC 7**
See also AITN 1; CA 65-68; 107; CANR 33; DLB 2; DLBY 82; MTCW; SATA 40; SATA-Obit 31

**Gardner, John (Edmund)** 1926- . . . . . . . . . . . . **CLC 30; DAM POP**
See also CA 103; CANR 15; MTCW

**Gardner, Miriam**
See Bradley, Marion Zimmer

**Gardner, Noel**
See Kuttner, Henry

Author Index

**Gardons, S. S.**
See Snodgrass, W(illiam) D(e Witt)

**Garfield, Leon** 1921-1996.......... **CLC 12**
See also AAYA 8; CA 17-20R; 152; CANR 38, 41; CLR 21; DLB 161; JRDA; MAICYA; SATA 1, 32, 76; SATA-Obit 90

**Garland, (Hannibal) Hamlin** 1860-1940 ........... **TCLC 3; SSC 18**
See also CA 104; DLB 12, 71, 78

**Garneau, (Hector de) Saint-Denys** 1912-1943 .................. **TCLC 13**
See also CA 111; DLB 88

**Garner, Alan** 1934- ....... **CLC 17; DAB; DAM POP**
See also AAYA 18; CA 73-76; CANR 15; CLR 20; DLB 161; MAICYA; MTCW; SATA 18, 69

**Garner, Hugh** 1913-1979 .......... **CLC 13**
See also CA 69-72; CANR 31; DLB 68

**Garnett, David** 1892-1981 .......... **CLC 3**
See also CA 5-8R; 103; CANR 17; DLB 34

**Garos, Stephanie**
See Katz, Steve

**Garrett, George (Palmer)** 1929- .................. **CLC 3, 11, 51**
See also CA 1-4R; CAAS 5; CANR 1, 42; DLB 2, 5, 130, 152; DLBY 83

**Garrick, David** 1717-1779 ....... **LC 15; DAM DRAM**
See also DLB 84

**Garrigue, Jean** 1914-1972 ........ **CLC 2, 8**
See also CA 5-8R; 37-40R; CANR 20

**Garrison, Frederick**
See Sinclair, Upton (Beall)

**Garth, Will**
See Hamilton, Edmond; Kuttner, Henry

**Garvey, Marcus (Moziah, Jr.)** 1887-1940 ............ **TCLC 41; BLC; DAM MULT**
See also BW 1; CA 120; 124

**Gary, Romain** .................... **CLC 25**
See also Kacew, Romain
See also DLB 83

**Gascar, Pierre**.................... **CLC 11**
See also Fournier, Pierre

**Gascoyne, David (Emery)** 1916- .... **CLC 45**
See also CA 65-68; CANR 10, 28, 54; DLB 20; MTCW

**Gaskell, Elizabeth Cleghorn** 1810-1865 .. **NCLC 5; DAB; DAM MST**
See also CDBLB 1832-1890; DLB 21, 144, 159

**Gass, William H(oward)** 1924- ... **CLC 1, 2, 8, 11, 15, 39; SSC 12**
See also CA 17-20R; CANR 30; DLB 2; MTCW

**Gasset, Jose Ortega y**
See Ortega y Gasset, Jose

**Gates, Henry Louis, Jr.** 1950- .......... **CLC 65; DAM MULT**
See also BW 2; CA 109; CANR 25, 53; DLB 67

**Gautier, Theophile** 1811-1872 ............... **NCLC 1, 59; DAM POET; SSC 20**
See also DLB 119

**Gawsworth, John**
See Bates, H(erbert) E(rnest)

**Gay, Oliver**
See Gogarty, Oliver St. John

**Gaye, Marvin (Penze)** 1939-1984 ... **CLC 26**
See also CA 112

**Gebler, Carlo (Ernest)** 1954- ....... **CLC 39**
See also CA 119; 133

**Gee, Maggie (Mary)** 1948-......... **CLC 57**
See also CA 130

**Gee, Maurice (Gough)** 1931-....... **CLC 29**
See also CA 97-100; SATA 46

**Gelbart, Larry (Simon)** 1923- ... **CLC 21, 61**
See also CA 73-76; CANR 45

**Gelber, Jack** 1932-........ **CLC 1, 6, 14, 79**
See also CA 1-4R; CANR 2; DLB 7

**Gellhorn, Martha (Ellis)** 1908- .. **CLC 14, 60**
See also CA 77-80; CANR 44; DLBY 82

**Genet, Jean** 1910-1986 ...... **CLC 1, 2, 5, 10, 14, 44, 46; DAM DRAM**
See also CA 13-16R; CANR 18; DLB 72; DLBY 86; MTCW

**Gent, Peter** 1942-................ **CLC 29**
See also AITN 1; CA 89-92; DLBY 82

**Gentlewoman in New England, A**
See Bradstreet, Anne

**Gentlewoman in Those Parts, A**
See Bradstreet, Anne

**George, Jean Craighead** 1919-...... **CLC 35**
See also AAYA 8; CA 5-8R; CANR 25; CLR 1; DLB 52; JRDA; MAICYA; SATA 2, 68

**George, Stefan (Anton)** 1868-1933 ................ **TCLC 2, 14**
See also CA 104

**Georges, Georges Martin**
See Simenon, Georges (Jacques Christian)

**Gerhardi, William Alexander**
See Gerhardie, William Alexander

**Gerhardie, William Alexander** 1895-1977 .................... **CLC 5**
See also CA 25-28R; 73-76; CANR 18; DLB 36

**Gerstler, Amy** 1956-.............. **CLC 70**
See also CA 146

**Gertler, T.** ....................... **CLC 34**
See also CA 116; 121; INT 121

**gfgg**......................... **CLC XvXzc**

**Ghalib**......................... **NCLC 39**
See also Ghalib, Hsadullah Khan

**Ghalib, Hsadullah Khan** 1797-1869
See Ghalib
See also DAM POET

**Ghelderode, Michel de** 1898-1962 .... **CLC 6, 11; DAM DRAM**
See also CA 85-88; CANR 40

**Ghiselin, Brewster** 1903- .......... **CLC 23**
See also CA 13-16R; CAAS 10; CANR 13

**Ghose, Zulfikar** 1935-............. **CLC 42**
See also CA 65-68

**Ghosh, Amitav** 1956- ............. **CLC 44**
See also CA 147

**Giacosa, Giuseppe** 1847-1906 ...... **TCLC 7**
See also CA 104

**Gibb, Lee**
See Waterhouse, Keith (Spencer)

**Gibbon, Lewis Grassic** ............. **TCLC 4**
See also Mitchell, James Leslie

**Gibbons, Kaye** 1960- ......... **CLC 50, 88; DAM POP**
See also CA 151

**Gibran, Kahlil** 1883-1931 .... **TCLC 1, 9; DAM POET, POP; PC 9**
See also CA 104; 150

**Gibran, Khalil**
See Gibran, Kahlil

**Gibson, William** 1914- ........ **CLC 23; DA; DAB; DAC; DAM DRAM, MST**
See also CA 9-12R; CANR 9, 42; DLB 7; SATA 66

**Gibson, William (Ford)** 1948- ......... **CLC 39, 63; DAM POP**
See also AAYA 12; CA 126; 133; CANR 52

**Gide, Andre (Paul Guillaume)** 1869-1951 ........ **TCLC 5, 12, 36; DA; DAB; DAC; DAM MST, NOV; SSC 13; WLC**
See also CA 104; 124; DLB 65; MTCW

**Gifford, Barry (Colby)** 1946-....... **CLC 34**
See also CA 65-68; CANR 9, 30, 40

**Gilbert, W(illiam) S(chwenck)** 1836-1911 ..... **TCLC 3; DAM DRAM, POET**
See also CA 104; SATA 36

**Gilbreth, Frank B., Jr.** 1911-....... **CLC 17**
See also CA 9-12R; SATA 2

**Gilchrist, Ellen** 1935- ........ **CLC 34, 48; DAM POP; SSC 14**
See also CA 113; 116; CANR 41; DLB 130; MTCW

**Giles, Molly** 1942- ............... **CLC 39**
See also CA 126

**Gill, Patrick**
See Creasey, John

**Gilliam, Terry (Vance)** 1940-....... **CLC 21**
See also Monty Python
See also AAYA 19; CA 108; 113; CANR 35; INT 113

**Gillian, Jerry**
See Gilliam, Terry (Vance)

**Gilliatt, Penelope (Ann Douglass)** 1932-1993 ........... **CLC 2, 10, 13, 53**
See also AITN 2; CA 13-16R; 141; CANR 49; DLB 14

**Gilman, Charlotte (Anna) Perkins (Stetson)** 1860-1935 ........ **TCLC 9, 37; SSC 13**
See also CA 106; 150

**Gilmour, David** 1949-............. **CLC 35**
See also CA 138, 147

**Gilpin, William** 1724-1804....... **NCLC 30**

**Gilray, J. D.**
See Mencken, H(enry) L(ouis)

**Gilroy, Frank D(aniel)** 1925- . . . . . . . . **CLC 2**
See also CA 81-84; CANR 32; DLB 7

**Ginsberg, Allen**
1926- . . . . . . **CLC 1, 2, 3, 4, 6, 13, 36, 69; DA; DAB; DAC; DAM MST, POET; PC 4; WLC 3**
See also AITN 1; CA 1-4R; CANR 2, 41; CDALB 1941-1968; DLB 5, 16, 169; MTCW

**Ginzburg, Natalia**
1916-1991 . . . . . . . . . . . **CLC 5, 11, 54, 70**
See also CA 85-88; 135; CANR 33; MTCW

**Giono, Jean** 1895-1970. . . . . . . . . . **CLC 4, 11**
See also CA 45-48; 29-32R; CANR 2, 35; DLB 72; MTCW

**Giovanni, Nikki**
1943- . . . . . . **CLC 2, 4, 19, 64; BLC; DA; DAB; DAC; DAM MST, MULT, POET**
See also AITN 1; BW 2; CA 29-32R; CAAS 6; CANR 18, 41; CLR 6; DLB 5, 41; INT CANR-18; MAICYA; MTCW; SATA 24

**Giovene, Andrea** 1904-. . . . . . . . . . . . . **CLC 7**
See also CA 85-88

**Gippius, Zinaida (Nikolayevna)** 1869-1945
See Hippius, Zinaida
See also CA 106

**Giraudoux, (Hippolyte) Jean**
1882-1944 . . . . **TCLC 2, 7; DAM DRAM**
See also CA 104; DLB 65

**Gironella, Jose Maria** 1917- . . . . . . . **CLC 11**
See also CA 101

**Gissing, George (Robert)**
1857-1903 . . . . . . . . . . . . **TCLC 3, 24, 47**
See also CA 105; DLB 18, 135

**Giurlani, Aldo**
See Palazzeschi, Aldo

**Gladkov, Fyodor (Vasilyevich)**
1883-1958 . . . . . . . . . . . . . . . . . . **TCLC 27**

**Glanville, Brian (Lester)** 1931- . . . . . . **CLC 6**
See also CA 5-8R; CAAS 9; CANR 3; DLB 15, 139; SATA 42

**Glasgow, Ellen (Anderson Gholson)**
1873(?)-1945 . . . . . . . . . . . . . . . **TCLC 2, 7**
See also CA 104; DLB 9, 12

**Glaspell, Susan** 1882(?)-1948 . . . . . . **TCLC 55**
See also CA 110; 154; DLB 7, 9, 78; YABC 2

**Glassco, John** 1909-1981 . . . . . . . . . . . **CLC 9**
See also CA 13-16R; 102; CANR 15; DLB 68

**Glasscock, Amnesia**
See Steinbeck, John (Ernst)

**Glasser, Ronald J.** 1940(?)- . . . . . . . . **CLC 37**

**Glassman, Joyce**
See Johnson, Joyce

**Glendinning, Victoria** 1937- . . . . . . . . **CLC 50**
See also CA 120; 127; DLB 155

**Glissant, Edouard**
1928- . . . . . . . **CLC 10, 68; DAM MULT**
See also CA 153

**Gloag, Julian** 1930- . . . . . . . . . . . . . . **CLC 40**
See also AITN 1; CA 65-68; CANR 10

**Glowacki, Aleksander**
See Prus, Boleslaw

**Gluck, Louise (Elisabeth)**
1943- . . . . . . . . . . . . . . **CLC 7, 22, 44, 81; DAM POET; PC 16**
See also CA 33-36R; CANR 40; DLB 5

**Gobineau, Joseph Arthur (Comte) de**
1816-1882 . . . . . . . . . . . . . . . . . **NCLC 17**
See also DLB 123

**Godard, Jean-Luc** 1930- . . . . . . . . . . . **CLC 20**
See also CA 93-96

**Godden, (Margaret) Rumer** 1907- . . . **CLC 53**
See also AAYA 6; CA 5-8R; CANR 4, 27, 36, 55; CLR 20; DLB 161; MAICYA; SAAS 12; SATA 3, 36

**Godoy Alcayaga, Lucila** 1889-1957
See Mistral, Gabriela
See also BW 2; CA 104; 131; DAM MULT; HW; MTCW

**Godwin, Gail (Kathleen)**
1937- . . . . . . . . . . . . **CLC 5, 8, 22, 31, 69; DAM POP**
See also CA 29-32R; CANR 15, 43; DLB 6; INT CANR-15; MTCW

**Godwin, William** 1756-1836. . . . . . **NCLC 14**
See also CDBLB 1789-1832; DLB 39, 104, 142, 158, 163

**Goebbels, Josef**
See Goebbels, (Paul) Joseph

**Goebbels, (Paul) Joseph**
1897-1945 . . . . . . . . . . . . . . . . . . **TCLC 68**
See also CA 115; 148

**Goebbels, Joseph Paul**
See Goebbels, (Paul) Joseph

**Goethe, Johann Wolfgang von**
1749-1832 . . . . . . . . **NCLC 4, 22, 34; DA; DAB; DAC; DAM DRAM, MST, POET; PC 5; WLC 3**
See also DLB 94

**Gogarty, Oliver St. John**
1878-1957 . . . . . . . . . . . . . . . . . . **TCLC 15**
See also CA 109; 150; DLB 15, 19

**Gogol, Nikolai (Vasilyevich)**
1809-1852 . . . . . . . . **NCLC 5, 15, 31; DA; DAB; DAC; DAM DRAM, MST; DC 1; SSC 4; WLC**

**Goines, Donald**
1937(?)-1974 . . . . . . . . . . . **CLC 80; BLC; DAM MULT, POP**
See also AITN 1; BW 1; CA 124; 114; DLB 33

**Gold, Herbert** 1924- . . . . . . . **CLC 4, 7, 14, 42**
See also CA 9-12R; CANR 17, 45; DLB 2; DLBY 81

**Goldbarth, Albert** 1948- . . . . . . . . . **CLC 5, 38**
See also CA 53-56; CANR 6, 40; DLB 120

**Goldberg, Anatol** 1910-1982 . . . . . . . **CLC 34**
See also CA 131; 117

**Goldemberg, Isaac** 1945- . . . . . . . . . . **CLC 52**
See also CA 69-72; CAAS 12; CANR 11, 32; HW

**Golding, William (Gerald)**
1911-1993 . . . . **CLC 1, 2, 3, 8, 10, 17, 27, 58, 81; DA; DAB; DAC; DAM MST, NOV; WLC**
See also AAYA 5; CA 5-8R; 141; CANR 13, 33, 54; CDBLB 1945-1960; DLB 15, 100; MTCW

**Goldman, Emma** 1869-1940 . . . . . . . **TCLC 13**
See also CA 110; 150

**Goldman, Francisco** 1955- . . . . . . . . . . **CLC 76**

**Goldman, William (W.)** 1931- . . . . **CLC 1, 48**
See also CA 9-12R; CANR 29; DLB 44

**Goldmann, Lucien** 1913-1970 . . . . . . **CLC 24**
See also CA 25-28; CAP 2

**Goldoni, Carlo**
1707-1793 . . . . . . . . **LC 4; DAM DRAM**

**Goldsberry, Steven** 1949- . . . . . . . . . . **CLC 34**
See also CA 131

**Goldsmith, Oliver**
1728-1774 . . . . . . **LC 2; DA; DAB; DAC; DAM DRAM, MST, NOV, POET; WLC**
See also CDBLB 1660-1789; DLB 39, 89, 104, 109, 142; SATA 26

**Goldsmith, Peter**
See Priestley, J(ohn) B(oynton)

**Gombrowicz, Witold**
1904-1969 . . . . . . . . . . . **CLC 4, 7, 11, 49; DAM DRAM**
See also CA 19-20; 25-28R; CAP 2

**Gomez de la Serna, Ramon**
1888-1963 . . . . . . . . . . . . . . . . . . . . **CLC 9**
See also CA 153; 116; HW

**Goncharov, Ivan Alexandrovich**
1812-1891 . . . . . . . . . . . . . . . . . . **NCLC 1**

**Goncourt, Edmond (Louis Antoine Huot) de**
1822-1896 . . . . . . . . . . . . . . . . . . **NCLC 7**
See also DLB 123

**Goncourt, Jules (Alfred Huot) de**
1830-1870 . . . . . . . . . . . . . . . . . . **NCLC 7**
See also DLB 123

**Gontier, Fernande** 19(?)- . . . . . . . . . . **CLC 50**

**Goodman, Paul** 1911-1972 . . . . **CLC 1, 2, 4, 7**
See also CA 19-20; 37-40R; CANR 34; CAP 2; DLB 130; MTCW

**Gordimer, Nadine**
1923- . . . . **CLC 3, 5, 7, 10, 18, 33, 51, 70; DA; DAB; DAC; DAM MST, NOV; SSC 17**
See also CA 5-8R; CANR 3, 28; INT CANR-28; MTCW

**Gordon, Adam Lindsay**
1833-1870 . . . . . . . . . . . . . . . . . **NCLC 21**

**Gordon, Caroline**
1895-1981 . . . **CLC 6, 13, 29, 83; SSC 15**
See also CA 11-12; 103; CANR 36; CAP 1; DLB 4, 9, 102; DLBY 81; MTCW

**Gordon, Charles William** 1860-1937
See Connor, Ralph
See also CA 109

**Gordon, Mary (Catherine)**
1949- . . . . . . . . . . . . . . . . . . . . **CLC 13, 22**
See also CA 102; CANR 44; DLB 6; DLBY 81; INT 102; MTCW

Author Index

**Gordon, Sol** 1923- ................ **CLC 26**
See also CA 53-56; CANR 4; SATA 11

**Gordone, Charles**
1925-1995 ..... **CLC 1, 4; DAM DRAM**
See also BW 1; CA 93-96; 150; CANR 55; DLB 7; INT 93-96; MTCW

**Gorenko, Anna Andreevna**
See Akhmatova, Anna

**Gorky, Maxim** ......... **TCLC 8; DAB; WLC**
See also Peshkov, Alexei Maximovich

**Goryan, Sirak**
See Saroyan, William

**Gosse, Edmund (William)**
1849-1928 .................. **TCLC 28**
See also CA 117; DLB 57, 144

**Gotlieb, Phyllis Fay (Bloom)**
1926- ....................... **CLC 18**
See also CA 13-16R; CANR 7; DLB 88

**Gottesman, S. D.**
See Kornbluth, C(yril) M.; Pohl, Frederik

**Gottfried von Strassburg**
fl. c. 1210- ................. **CMLC 10**
See also DLB 138

**Gould, Lois** .................... **CLC 4, 10**
See also CA 77-80; CANR 29; MTCW

**Gourmont, Remy (-Marie-Charles) de**
1858-1915 .................. **TCLC 17**
See also CA 109; 150

**Govier, Katherine** 1948- ........... **CLC 51**
See also CA 101; CANR 18, 40

**Goyen, (Charles) William**
1915-1983 ............ **CLC 5, 8, 14, 40**
See also AITN 2; CA 5-8R; 110; CANR 6; DLB 2; DLBY 83; INT CANR-6

**Goytisolo, Juan**
1931- ..... **CLC 5, 10, 23; DAM MULT; HLC**
See also CA 85-88; CANR 32; HW; MTCW

**Gozzano, Guido** 1883-1916 ......... **PC 10**
See also CA 154; DLB 114

**Gozzi, (Conte) Carlo** 1720-1806 .. **NCLC 23**

**Grabbe, Christian Dietrich**
1801-1836 ................. **NCLC 2**
See also DLB 133

**Grace, Patricia** 1937- ............. **CLC 56**

**Gracian y Morales, Baltasar**
1601-1658 .................... **LC 15**

**Gracq, Julien** .................. **CLC 11, 48**
See also Poirier, Louis
See also DLB 83

**Grade, Chaim** 1910-1982 .......... **CLC 10**
See also CA 93-96; 107

**Graduate of Oxford, A**
See Ruskin, John

**Graham, John**
See Phillips, David Graham

**Graham, Jorie** 1951- .............. **CLC 48**
See also CA 111; DLB 120

**Graham, R(obert) B(ontine) Cunninghame**
See Cunninghame Graham, R(obert) B(ontine)
See also DLB 98, 135, 174

**Graham, Robert**
See Haldeman, Joe (William)

**Graham, Tom**
See Lewis, (Harry) Sinclair

**Graham, W(illiam) S(ydney)**
1918-1986 ................... **CLC 29**
See also CA 73-76; 118; DLB 20

**Graham, Winston (Mawdsley)**
1910- ....................... **CLC 23**
See also CA 49-52; CANR 2, 22, 45; DLB 77

**Grahame, Kenneth**
1859-1932 ............ **TCLC 64; DAB**
See also CA 108; 136; CLR 5; DLB 34, 141; MAICYA; YABC 1

**Grant, Skeeter**
See Spiegelman, Art

**Granville-Barker, Harley**
1877-1946 ...... **TCLC 2; DAM DRAM**
See also Barker, Harley Granville
See also CA 104

**Grass, Guenter (Wilhelm)**
1927- ..... **CLC 1, 2, 4, 6, 11, 15, 22, 32, 49, 88; DA; DAB; DAC; DAM MST, NOV; WLC**
See also CA 13-16R; CANR 20; DLB 75, 124; MTCW

**Gratton, Thomas**
See Hulme, T(homas) E(rnest)

**Grau, Shirley Ann**
1929- .............. **CLC 4, 9; SSC 15**
See also CA 89-92; CANR 22; DLB 2; INT CANR-22; MTCW

**Gravel, Fern**
See Hall, James Norman

**Graver, Elizabeth** 1964- ........... **CLC 70**
See also CA 135

**Graves, Richard Perceval** 1945- .... **CLC 44**
See also CA 65-68; CANR 9, 26, 51

**Graves, Robert (von Ranke)**
1895-1985 ...... **CLC 1, 2, 6, 11, 39, 44, 45; DAB; DAC; DAM MST, POET; PC 6**
See also CA 5-8R; 117; CANR 5, 36; CDBLB 1914-1945; DLB 20, 100; DLBY 85; MTCW; SATA 45

**Graves, Valerie**
See Bradley, Marion Zimmer

**Gray, Alasdair (James)** 1934- ...... **CLC 41**
See also CA 126; CANR 47; INT 126; MTCW

**Gray, Amlin** 1946- ............... **CLC 29**
See also CA 138

**Gray, Francine du Plessix**
1930- ............ **CLC 22; DAM NOV**
See also BEST 90:3; CA 61-64; CAAS 2; CANR 11, 33; INT CANR-11; MTCW

**Gray, John (Henry)** 1866-1934 .... **TCLC 19**
See also CA 119

**Gray, Simon (James Holliday)**
1936- .................. **CLC 9, 14, 36**
See also AITN 1; CA 21-24R; CAAS 3; CANR 32; DLB 13; MTCW

**Gray, Spalding** 1941- .. **CLC 49; DAM POP**
See also CA 128

**Gray, Thomas**
1716-1771 ...... **LC 4; DA; DAB; DAC; DAM MST; PC 2; WLC**
See also CDBLB 1660-1789; DLB 109

**Grayson, David**
See Baker, Ray Stannard

**Grayson, Richard (A.)** 1951- ....... **CLC 38**
See also CA 85-88; CANR 14, 31

**Greeley, Andrew M(oran)**
1928- ............... **CLC 28; DAM POP**
See also CA 5-8R; CAAS 7; CANR 7, 43; MTCW

**Green, Anna Katharine**
1846-1935 .................. **TCLC 63**
See also CA 112

**Green, Brian**
See Card, Orson Scott

**Green, Hannah**
See Greenberg, Joanne (Goldenberg)

**Green, Hannah** .................... **CLC 3**
See also CA 73-76

**Green, Henry** 1905-1973 ..... **CLC 2, 13, 97**
See also Yorke, Henry Vincent
See also DLB 15

**Green, Julian (Hartridge)** 1900-
See Green, Julien
See also CA 21-24R; CANR 33; DLB 4, 72; MTCW

**Green, Julien** ................ **CLC 3, 11, 77**
See also Green, Julian (Hartridge)

**Green, Paul (Eliot)**
1894-1981 ...... **CLC 25; DAM DRAM**
See also AITN 1; CA 5-8R; 103; CANR 3; DLB 7, 9; DLBY 81

**Greenberg, Ivan** 1908-1973
See Rahv, Philip
See also CA 85-88

**Greenberg, Joanne (Goldenberg)**
1932- .................... **CLC 7, 30**
See also AAYA 12; CA 5-8R; CANR 14, 32; SATA 25

**Greenberg, Richard** 1959(?)- ....... **CLC 57**
See also CA 138

**Greene, Bette** 1934- .............. **CLC 30**
See also AAYA 7; CA 53-56; CANR 4; CLR 2; JRDA; MAICYA; SAAS 16; SATA 8

**Greene, Gael** ...................... **CLC 8**
See also CA 13-16R; CANR 10

**Greene, Graham**
1904-1991 .... **CLC 1, 3, 6, 9, 14, 18, 27, 37, 70, 72; DA; DAB; DAC; DAM MST, NOV; WLC**
See also AITN 2; CA 13-16R; 133; CANR 35; CDBLB 1945-1960; DLB 13, 15, 77, 100, 162; DLBY 91; MTCW; SATA 20

**Greer, Richard**
See Silverberg, Robert

**Gregor, Arthur** 1923- .............. **CLC 9**
See also CA 25-28R; CAAS 10; CANR 11; SATA 36

**Gregor, Lee**
See Pohl, Frederik

**Gregory, Isabella Augusta (Persse)** 1852-1932 .................. **TCLC 1**
See also CA 104; DLB 10

**Gregory, J. Dennis**
See Williams, John A(lfred)

**Grendon, Stephen**
See Derleth, August (William)

**Grenville, Kate** 1950- ............. **CLC 61**
See also CA 118; CANR 53

**Grenville, Pelham**
See Wodehouse, P(elham) G(renville)

**Greve, Felix Paul (Berthold Friedrich)** 1879-1948
See Grove, Frederick Philip
See also CA 104; 141; DAC; DAM MST

**Grey, Zane** 1872-1939 ........ **TCLC 6; DAM POP**
See also CA 104; 132; DLB 9; MTCW

**Grieg, (Johan) Nordahl (Brun)** 1902-1943 .................. **TCLC 10**
See also CA 107

**Grieve, C(hristopher) M(urray)** 1892-1978 .... **CLC 11, 19; DAM POET**
See also MacDiarmid, Hugh; Pteleon
See also CA 5-8R; 85-88; CANR 33; MTCW

**Griffin, Gerald** 1803-1840 ........ **NCLC 7**
See also DLB 159

**Griffin, John Howard** 1920-1980.... **CLC 68**
See also AITN 1; CA 1-4R; 101; CANR 2

**Griffin, Peter** 1942- .............. **CLC 39**
See also CA 136

**Griffith, D(avid Lewelyn) W(ark)** 1875(?)-1948 ................ **TCLC 68**
See also CA 119; 150

**Griffith, Lawrence**
See Griffith, D(avid Lewelyn) W(ark)

**Griffiths, Trevor** 1935- ......... **CLC 13, 52**
See also CA 97-100; CANR 45; DLB 13

**Grigson, Geoffrey (Edward Harvey)** 1905-1985 ................ **CLC 7, 39**
See also CA 25-28R; 118; CANR 20, 33; DLB 27; MTCW

**Grillparzer, Franz** 1791-1872...... **NCLC 1**
See also DLB 133

**Grimble, Reverend Charles James**
See Eliot, T(homas) S(tearns)

**Grimke, Charlotte L(ottie) Forten** 1837(?)-1914
See Forten, Charlotte L.
See also BW 1; CA 117; 124; DAM MULT, POET

**Grimm, Jacob Ludwig Karl** 1785-1863 .................. **NCLC 3**
See also DLB 90; MAICYA; SATA 22

**Grimm, Wilhelm Karl** 1786-1859 .. **NCLC 3**
See also DLB 90; MAICYA; SATA 22

**Grimmelshausen, Johann Jakob Christoffel von** 1621-1676 ................ **LC 6**
See also DLB 168

**Grindel, Eugene** 1895-1952
See Eluard, Paul
See also CA 104

**Grisham, John** 1955- .. **CLC 84; DAM POP**
See also AAYA 14; CA 138; CANR 47

**Grossman, David** 1954- ........... **CLC 67**
See also CA 138

**Grossman, Vasily (Semenovich)** 1905-1964 ................... **CLC 41**
See also CA 124; 130; MTCW

**Grove, Frederick Philip** ............ **TCLC 4**
See also Greve, Felix Paul (Berthold Friedrich)
See also DLB 92

**Grubb**
See Crumb, R(obert)

**Grumbach, Doris (Isaac)** 1918- ................. **CLC 13, 22, 64**
See also CA 5-8R; CAAS 2; CANR 9, 42; INT CANR-9

**Grundtvig, Nicolai Frederik Severin** 1783-1872 ................. **NCLC 1**

**Grunge**
See Crumb, R(obert)

**Grunwald, Lisa** 1959- ............. **CLC 44**
See also CA 120

**Guare, John** 1938- .............. **CLC 8, 14, 29, 67; DAM DRAM**
See also CA 73-76; CANR 21; DLB 7; MTCW

**Gudjonsson, Halldor Kiljan** 1902-
See Laxness, Halldor
See also CA 103

**Guenter, Erich**
See Eich, Guenter

**Guest, Barbara** 1920- ............. **CLC 34**
See also CA 25-28R; CANR 11, 44; DLB 5

**Guest, Judith (Ann)** 1936- .... **CLC 8, 30; DAM NOV, POP**
See also AAYA 7; CA 77-80; CANR 15; INT CANR-15; MTCW

**Guevara, Che** ............. **CLC 87; HLC**
See also Guevara (Serna), Ernesto

**Guevara (Serna), Ernesto** 1928-1967
See Guevara, Che
See also CA 127; 111; DAM MULT; HW

**Guild, Nicholas M.** 1944- .......... **CLC 33**
See also CA 93-96

**Guillemin, Jacques**
See Sartre, Jean-Paul

**Guillen, Jorge** 1893-1984 ...... **CLC 11; DAM MULT, POET**
See also CA 89-92; 112; DLB 108; HW

**Guillen, Nicolas (Cristobal)** 1902-1989 .......... **CLC 48, 79; BLC; DAM MST, MULT, POET; HLC**
See also BW 2; CA 116; 125; 129; HW

**Guillevic, (Eugene)** 1907- .......... **CLC 33**
See also CA 93-96

**Guillois**
See Desnos, Robert

**Guillois, Valentin**
See Desnos, Robert

**Guiney, Louise Imogen** 1861-1920 ................. **TCLC 41**
See also DLB 54

**Guiraldes, Ricardo (Guillermo)** 1886-1927 .................. **TCLC 39**
See also CA 131; HW; MTCW

**Gumilev, Nikolai Stephanovich** 1886-1921 .................. **TCLC 60**

**Gunesekera, Romesh** ............... **CLC 91**

**Gunn, Bill** ....................... **CLC 5**
See also Gunn, William Harrison
See also DLB 38

**Gunn, Thom(son William)** 1929- ............ **CLC 3, 6, 18, 32, 81; DAM POET**
See also CA 17-20R; CANR 9, 33; CDBLB 1960 to Present; DLB 27; INT CANR-33; MTCW

**Gunn, William Harrison** 1934(?)-1989
See Gunn, Bill
See also AITN 1; BW 1; CA 13-16R; 128; CANR 12, 25

**Gunnars, Kristjana** 1948- .......... **CLC 69**
See also CA 113; DLB 60

**Gurganus, Allan** 1947- ............ **CLC 70; DAM POP**
See also BEST 90:1; CA 135

**Gurney, A(lbert) R(amsdell), Jr.** 1930- .... **CLC 32, 50, 54; DAM DRAM**
See also CA 77-80; CANR 32

**Gurney, Ivor (Bertie)** 1890-1937 ... **TCLC 33**

**Gurney, Peter**
See Gurney, A(lbert) R(amsdell), Jr.

**Guro, Elena** 1877-1913........... **TCLC 56**

**Gustafson, Ralph (Barker)** 1909-.... **CLC 36**
See also CA 21-24R; CANR 8, 45; DLB 88

**Gut, Gom**
See Simenon, Georges (Jacques Christian)

**Guterson, David** 1956- ............ **CLC 91**
See also CA 132

**Guthrie, A(lfred) B(ertram), Jr.** 1901-1991 ................... **CLC 23**
See also CA 57-60; 134; CANR 24; DLB 6; SATA 62; SATA-Obit 67

**Guthrie, Isobel**
See Grieve, C(hristopher) M(urray)

**Guthrie, Woodrow Wilson** 1912-1967
See Guthrie, Woody
See also CA 113; 93-96

**Guthrie, Woody** ................... **CLC 35**
See also Guthrie, Woodrow Wilson

**Guy, Rosa (Cuthbert)** 1928- ........ **CLC 26**
See also AAYA 4; BW 2; CA 17-20R; CANR 14, 34; CLR 13; DLB 33; JRDA; MAICYA; SATA 14, 62

**Gwendolyn**
See Bennett, (Enoch) Arnold

**H. D.** ........ **CLC 3, 8, 14, 31, 34, 73; PC 5**
See also Doolittle, Hilda

**H. de V.**
See Buchan, John

**Haavikko, Paavo Juhani** 1931- .................... **CLC 18, 34**
See also CA 106

**Habbema, Koos**
See Heijermans, Herman

**Harris, Mark** 1922- . . . . . . . . . . . . . . **CLC 19**
See also CA 5-8R; CAAS 3; CANR 2, 55; DLB 2; DLBY 80

**Harris, (Theodore) Wilson** 1921-. . . . **CLC 25**
See also BW 2; CA 65-68; CAAS 16; CANR 11, 27; DLB 117; MTCW

**Harrison, Elizabeth Cavanna** 1909-
See Cavanna, Betty
See also CA 9-12R; CANR 6, 27

**Harrison, Harry (Max)** 1925- . . . . . . **CLC 42**
See also CA 1-4R; CANR 5, 21; DLB 8; SATA 4

**Harrison, James (Thomas)**
1937- . . . . . . . **CLC 6, 14, 33, 66; SSC 19**
See also CA 13-16R; CANR 8, 51; DLBY 82; INT CANR-8

**Harrison, Jim**
See Harrison, James (Thomas)

**Harrison, Kathryn** 1961- . . . . . . . . . . **CLC 70**
See also CA 144

**Harrison, Tony** 1937-. . . . . . . . . . . . . **CLC 43**
See also CA 65-68; CANR 44; DLB 40; MTCW

**Harriss, Will(ard Irvin)** 1922- . . . . . . **CLC 34**
See also CA 111

**Harson, Sley**
See Ellison, Harlan (Jay)

**Hart, Ellis**
See Ellison, Harlan (Jay)

**Hart, Josephine**
1942(?)- . . . . . . . . . . **CLC 70; DAM POP**
See also CA 138

**Hart, Moss**
1904-1961 . . . . . . **CLC 66; DAM DRAM**
See also CA 109; 89-92; DLB 7

**Harte, (Francis) Bret(t)**
1836(?)-1902 . . . . **TCLC 1, 25; DA; DAC; DAM MST; SSC 8; WLC**
See also CA 104; 140; CDALB 1865-1917; DLB 12, 64, 74, 79; SATA 26

**Hartley, L(eslie) P(oles)**
1895-1972 . . . . . . . . . . . . . . . . . **CLC 2, 22**
See also CA 45-48; 37-40R; CANR 33; DLB 15, 139; MTCW

**Hartman, Geoffrey H.** 1929- . . . . . . . **CLC 27**
See also CA 117; 125; DLB 67

**Hartmann von Aue**
c. 1160-c. 1205 . . . . . . . . . . . . . **CMLC 15**
See also DLB 138

**Hartmann von Aue** 1170-1210. . . . **CMLC 15**

**Haruf, Kent** 1943- . . . . . . . . . . . . . . . **CLC 34**
See also CA 149

**Harwood, Ronald**
1934- . . . . **CLC 32; DAM DRAM, MST**
See also CA 1-4R; CANR 4, 55; DLB 13

**Hasek, Jaroslav (Matej Frantisek)**
1883-1923 . . . . . . . . . . . . . . . . . . **TCLC 4**
See also CA 104; 129; MTCW

**Hass, Robert** 1941-. . . . . **CLC 18, 39; PC 16**
See also CA 111; CANR 30, 50; DLB 105

**Hastings, Hudson**
See Kuttner, Henry

**Hastings, Selina**. . . . . . . . . . . . . . . . . . **CLC 44**

**Hatteras, Amelia**
See Mencken, H(enry) L(ouis)

**Hatteras, Owen** . . . . . . . . . . . . . . . . . . **TCLC 18**
See also Mencken, H(enry) L(ouis); Nathan, George Jean

**Hauptmann, Gerhart (Johann Robert)**
1862-1946 . . . . . . **TCLC 4; DAM DRAM**
See also CA 104; 153; DLB 66, 118

**Havel, Vaclav**
1936- . . . . . . . . . . . . . . . . **CLC 25, 58, 65; DAM DRAM; DC 6**
See also CA 104; CANR 36; MTCW

**Haviaras, Stratis** . . . . . . . . . . . . . . . . . . **CLC 33**
See also Chaviaras, Strates

**Hawes, Stephen** 1475(?)-1523(?) . . . . . **LC 17**

**Hawkes, John (Clendennin Burne, Jr.)**
1925- . . . . . . **CLC 1, 2, 3, 4, 7, 9, 14, 15, 27, 49**
See also CA 1-4R; CANR 2, 47; DLB 2, 7; DLBY 80; MTCW

**Hawking, S. W.**
See Hawking, Stephen W(illiam)

**Hawking, Stephen W(illiam)**
1942- . . . . . . . . . . . . . . . . . . . . . . . **CLC 63**
See also AAYA 13; BEST 89:1; CA 126; 129; CANR 48

**Hawthorne, Julian** 1846-1934 . . . . . **TCLC 25**

**Hawthorne, Nathaniel**
1804-1864 . . . . . . . **NCLC 39; DA; DAB; DAC; DAM MST, NOV; SSC 3; WLC**
See also AAYA 18; CDALB 1640-1865; DLB 1, 74; YABC 2

**Haxton, Josephine Ayres** 1921-
See Douglas, Ellen
See also CA 115; CANR 41

**Hayaseca y Eizaguirre, Jorge**
See Echegaray (y Eizaguirre), Jose (Maria Waldo)

**Hayashi Fumiko** 1904-1951 . . . . . . . **TCLC 27**

**Haycraft, Anna**
See Ellis, Alice Thomas
See also CA 122

**Hayden, Robert E(arl)**
1913-1980 . . . . . . **CLC 5, 9, 14, 37; BLC; DA; DAC; DAM MST, MULT, POET; PC 6**
See also BW 1; CA 69-72; 97-100; CABS 2; CANR 24; CDALB 1941-1968; DLB 5, 76; MTCW; SATA 19; SATA-Obit 26

**Hayford, J(oseph) E(phraim) Casely**
See Casely-Hayford, J(oseph) E(phraim)

**Hayman, Ronald** 1932-. . . . . . . . . . . . **CLC 44**
See also CA 25-28R; CANR 18, 50; DLB 155

**Haywood, Eliza (Fowler)**
1693(?)-1756 . . . . . . . . . . . . . . . . . . . **LC 1**

**Hazlitt, William** 1778-1830 . . . . . . **NCLC 29**
See also DLB 110, 158

**Hazzard, Shirley** 1931- . . . . . . . . . . . **CLC 18**
See also CA 9-12R; CANR 4; DLBY 82; MTCW

**Head, Bessie**
1937-1986 . . . . . . . . . . **CLC 25, 67; BLC; DAM MULT**
See also BW 2; CA 29-32R; 119; CANR 25; DLB 117; MTCW

**Headon, (Nicky) Topper** 1956(?)- . . . **CLC 30**

**Heaney, Seamus (Justin)**
1939- . . . . . . **CLC 5, 7, 14, 25, 37, 74, 91; DAB; DAM POET**
See also CA 85-88; CANR 25, 48; CDBLB 1960 to Present; DLB 40; DLBY 95; MTCW

**Hearn, (Patricio) Lafcadio (Tessima Carlos)**
1850-1904 . . . . . . . . . . . . . . . . . . . **TCLC 9**
See also CA 105; DLB 12, 78

**Hearne, Vicki** 1946- . . . . . . . . . . . . . . **CLC 56**
See also CA 139

**Hearon, Shelby** 1931-. . . . . . . . . . . . . **CLC 63**
See also AITN 2; CA 25-28R; CANR 18, 48

**Heat-Moon, William Least**. . . . . . . . . . **CLC 29**
See also Trogdon, William (Lewis)
See also AAYA 9

**Hebbel, Friedrich**
1813-1863 . . . . **NCLC 43; DAM DRAM**
See also DLB 129

**Hebert, Anne**
1916- . . . . . . . . . . . . **CLC 4, 13, 29; DAC; DAM MST, POET**
See also CA 85-88; DLB 68; MTCW

**Hecht, Anthony (Evan)**
1923- . . . . . . **CLC 8, 13, 19; DAM POET**
See also CA 9-12R; CANR 6; DLB 5, 169

**Hecht, Ben** 1894-1964 . . . . . . . . . . . . . **CLC 8**
See also CA 85-88; DLB 7, 9, 25, 26, 28, 86

**Hedayat, Sadeq** 1903-1951. . . . . . . . **TCLC 21**
See also CA 120

**Hegel, Georg Wilhelm Friedrich**
1770-1831 . . . . . . . . . . . . . . . . . **NCLC 46**
See also DLB 90

**Heidegger, Martin** 1889-1976 . . . . . . **CLC 24**
See also CA 81-84; 65-68; CANR 34; MTCW

**Heidenstam, (Carl Gustaf) Verner von**
1859-1940 . . . . . . . . . . . . . . . . . . . **TCLC 5**
See also CA 104

**Heifner, Jack** 1946- . . . . . . . . . . . . . . **CLC 11**
See also CA 105; CANR 47

**Heijermans, Herman** 1864-1924 . . . **TCLC 24**
See also CA 123

**Heilbrun, Carolyn G(old)** 1926-. . . . . **CLC 25**
See also CA 45-48; CANR 1, 28

**Heine, Heinrich** 1797-1856 . . . . **NCLC 4, 54**
See also DLB 90

**Heinemann, Larry (Curtiss)** 1944- . . **CLC 50**
See also CA 110; CAAS 21; CANR 31; DLBD 9; INT CANR-31

**Heiney, Donald (William)** 1921-1993
See Harris, MacDonald
See also CA 1-4R; 142; CANR 3

**Heinlein, Robert A(nson)**
1907-1988 ...... **CLC 1, 3, 8, 14, 26, 55; DAM POP**
See also AAYA 17; CA 1-4R; 125; CANR 1, 20, 53; DLB 8; JRDA; MAICYA; MTCW; SATA 9, 69; SATA-Obit 56

**Helforth, John**
See Doolittle, Hilda

**Hellenhofferu, Vojtech Kapristian z**
See Hasek, Jaroslav (Matej Frantisek)

**Heller, Joseph**
1923- .... **CLC 1, 3, 5, 8, 11, 36, 63; DA; DAB; DAC; DAM MST, NOV, POP; WLC**
See also AITN 1; CA 5-8R; CABS 1; CANR 8, 42; DLB 2, 28; DLBY 80; INT CANR-8; MTCW

**Hellman, Lillian (Florence)**
1906-1984 ...... **CLC 2, 4, 8, 14, 18, 34, 44, 52; DAM DRAM; DC 1**
See also AITN 1, 2; CA 13-16R; 112; CANR 33; DLB 7; DLBY 84; MTCW

**Helprin, Mark**
1947- .............. **CLC 7, 10, 22, 32; DAM NOV, POP**
See also CA 81-84; CANR 47; DLBY 85; MTCW

**Helvetius, Claude-Adrien**
1715-1771 .................... **LC 26**

**Helyar, Jane Penelope Josephine** 1933-
See Poole, Josephine
See also CA 21-24R; CANR 10, 26; SATA 82

**Hemans, Felicia** 1793-1835 ...... **NCLC 29**
See also DLB 96

**Hemingway, Ernest (Miller)**
1899-1961 .... **CLC 1, 3, 6, 8, 10, 13, 19, 30, 34, 39, 41, 44, 50, 61, 80; DA; DAB; DAC; DAM MST, NOV; SSC 1; WLC**
See also AAYA 19; CA 77-80; CANR 34; CDALB 1917-1929; DLB 4, 9, 102; DLBD 1; DLBY 81, 87; MTCW

**Hempel, Amy** 1951- .............. **CLC 39**
See also CA 118; 137

**Henderson, F. C.**
See Mencken, H(enry) L(ouis)

**Henderson, Sylvia**
See Ashton-Warner, Sylvia (Constance)

**Henley, Beth** ............... **CLC 23; DC 6**
See also Henley, Elizabeth Becker
See also CABS 3; DLBY 86

**Henley, Elizabeth Becker** 1952-
See Henley, Beth
See also CA 107; CANR 32; DAM DRAM, MST; MTCW

**Henley, William Ernest**
1849-1903 ................... **TCLC 8**
See also CA 105; DLB 19

**Hennissart, Martha**
See Lathen, Emma
See also CA 85-88

**Henry, O.** ........ **TCLC 1, 19; SSC 5; WLC**
See also Porter, William Sydney

**Henry, Patrick** 1736-1799 .......... **LC 25**

**Henryson, Robert** 1430(?)-1506(?).... **LC 20**
See also DLB 146

**Henry VIII** 1491-1547 ............. **LC 10**

**Henschke, Alfred**
See Klabund

**Hentoff, Nat(han Irving)** 1925- ..... **CLC 26**
See also AAYA 4; CA 1-4R; CAAS 6; CANR 5, 25; CLR 1; INT CANR-25; JRDA; MAICYA; SATA 42, 69; SATA-Brief 27

**Heppenstall, (John) Rayner**
1911-1981 ................... **CLC 10**
See also CA 1-4R; 103; CANR 29

**Herbert, Frank (Patrick)**
1920-1986 ...... **CLC 12, 23, 35, 44, 85; DAM POP**
See also CA 53-56; 118; CANR 5, 43; DLB 8; INT CANR-5; MTCW; SATA 9, 37; SATA-Obit 47

**Herbert, George**
1593-1633 .............. **LC 24; DAB; DAM POET; PC 4**
See also CDBLB Before 1660; DLB 126

**Herbert, Zbigniew**
1924- ......... **CLC 9, 43; DAM POET**
See also CA 89-92; CANR 36; MTCW

**Herbst, Josephine (Frey)**
1897-1969 ................... **CLC 34**
See also CA 5-8R; 25-28R; DLB 9

**Hergesheimer, Joseph**
1880-1954 ................... **TCLC 11**
See also CA 109; DLB 102, 9

**Herlihy, James Leo** 1927-1993 ...... **CLC 6**
See also CA 1-4R; 143; CANR 2

**Hermogenes** fl. c. 175- ........... **CMLC 6**

**Hernandez, Jose** 1834-1886...... **NCLC 17**

**Herodotus** c. 484B.C.-429B.C..... **CMLC 17**

**Herrick, Robert**
1591-1674 ..... **LC 13; DA; DAB; DAC; DAM MST, POP; PC 9**
See also DLB 126

**Herring, Guilles**
See Somerville, Edith

**Herriot, James**
1916-1995 ........ **CLC 12; DAM POP**
See also Wight, James Alfred
See also AAYA 1; CA 148; CANR 40; SATA 86

**Herrmann, Dorothy** 1941- ......... **CLC 44**
See also CA 107

**Herrmann, Taffy**
See Herrmann, Dorothy

**Hersey, John (Richard)**
1914-1993 .... **CLC 1, 2, 7, 9, 40, 81, 97; DAM POP**
See also CA 17-20R; 140; CANR 33; DLB 6; MTCW; SATA 25; SATA-Obit 76

**Herzen, Aleksandr Ivanovich**
1812-1870 ................. **NCLC 10**

**Herzl, Theodor** 1860-1904 ........ **TCLC 36**

**Herzog, Werner** 1942- ............ **CLC 16**
See also CA 89-92

**Hesiod** c. 8th cent. B.C.- ......... **CMLC 5**

**Hesse, Hermann**
1877-1962 .... **CLC 1, 2, 3, 6, 11, 17, 25, 69; DA; DAB; DAC; DAM MST, NOV; SSC 9; WLC**
See also CA 17-18; CAP 2; DLB 66; MTCW; SATA 50

**Hewes, Cady**
See De Voto, Bernard (Augustine)

**Heyen, William** 1940- ......... **CLC 13, 18**
See also CA 33-36R; CAAS 9; DLB 5

**Heyerdahl, Thor** 1914- ............ **CLC 26**
See also CA 5-8R; CANR 5, 22; MTCW; SATA 2, 52

**Heym, Georg (Theodor Franz Arthur)**
1887-1912 ................... **TCLC 9**
See also CA 106

**Heym, Stefan** 1913- .............. **CLC 41**
See also CA 9-12R; CANR 4; DLB 69

**Heyse, Paul (Johann Ludwig von)**
1830-1914 ................... **TCLC 8**
See also CA 104; DLB 129

**Heyward, (Edwin) DuBose**
1885-1940 ................. **TCLC 59**
See also CA 108; DLB 7, 9, 45; SATA 21

**Hibbert, Eleanor Alice Burford**
1906-1993 ......... **CLC 7; DAM POP**
See also BEST 90:4; CA 17-20R; 140; CANR 9, 28; SATA 2; SATA-Obit 74

**Hichens, Robert S.** 1864-1950..... **TCLC 64**
See also DLB 153

**Higgins, George V(incent)**
1939- ............... **CLC 4, 7, 10, 18**
See also CA 77-80; CAAS 5; CANR 17, 51; DLB 2; DLBY 81; INT CANR-17; MTCW

**Higginson, Thomas Wentworth**
1823-1911 ................. **TCLC 36**
See also DLB 1, 64

**Highet, Helen**
See MacInnes, Helen (Clark)

**Highsmith, (Mary) Patricia**
1921-1995 ........... **CLC 2, 4, 14, 42; DAM NOV, POP**
See also CA 1-4R; 147; CANR 1, 20, 48; MTCW

**Highwater, Jamake (Mamake)**
1942(?)- ..................... **CLC 12**
See also AAYA 7; CA 65-68; CAAS 7; CANR 10, 34; CLR 17; DLB 52; DLBY 85; JRDA; MAICYA; SATA 32, 69; SATA-Brief 30

**Highway, Tomson**
1951- ..... **CLC 92; DAC; DAM MULT**
See also CA 151; NNAL

**Higuchi, Ichiyo** 1872-1896....... **NCLC 49**

**Hijuelos, Oscar**
1951- .... **CLC 65; DAM MULT, POP; HLC**
See also BEST 90:1; CA 123; CANR 50; DLB 145; HW

**Hikmet, Nazim** 1902(?)-1963....... **CLC 40**
See also CA 141; 93-96

**Hildegard von Bingen**
1098-1179 ................. **CMLC 20**
See also DLB 148

**Hildesheimer, Wolfgang** 1916-1991 .................... **CLC 49**
See also CA 101; 135; DLB 69, 124

**Hill, Geoffrey (William)** 1932- ... **CLC 5, 8, 18, 45; DAM POET**
See also CA 81-84; CANR 21; CDBLB 1960 to Present; DLB 40; MTCW

**Hill, George Roy** 1921- ............ **CLC 26**
See also CA 110; 122

**Hill, John**
See Koontz, Dean R(ay)

**Hill, Susan (Elizabeth)** 1942- .. **CLC 4; DAB; DAM MST, NOV**
See also CA 33-36R; CANR 29; DLB 14, 139; MTCW

**Hillerman, Tony** 1925- ............. **CLC 62; DAM POP**
See also AAYA 6; BEST 89:1; CA 29-32R; CANR 21, 42; SATA 6

**Hillesum, Etty** 1914-1943 ........ **TCLC 49**
See also CA 137

**Hilliard, Noel (Harvey)** 1929- ...... **CLC 15**
See also CA 9-12R; CANR 7

**Hillis, Rick** 1956- ................ **CLC 66**
See also CA 134

**Hilton, James** 1900-1954 ......... **TCLC 21**
See also CA 108; DLB 34, 77; SATA 34

**Himes, Chester (Bomar)** 1909-1984 .... **CLC 2, 4, 7, 18, 58; BLC; DAM MULT**
See also BW 2; CA 25-28R; 114; CANR 22; DLB 2, 76, 143; MTCW

**Hinde, Thomas** ................. **CLC 6, 11**
See also Chitty, Thomas Willes

**Hindin, Nathan**
See Bloch, Robert (Albert)

**Hine, (William) Daryl** 1936- ....... **CLC 15**
See also CA 1-4R; CAAS 15; CANR 1, 20; DLB 60

**Hinkson, Katharine Tynan**
See Tynan, Katharine

**Hinton, S(usan) E(loise)** 1950- ........ **CLC 30; DA; DAB; DAC; DAM MST, NOV**
See also AAYA 2; CA 81-84; CANR 32; CLR 3, 23; JRDA; MAICYA; MTCW; SATA 19, 58

**Hippius, Zinaida** .................. **TCLC 9**
See also Gippius, Zinaida (Nikolayevna)

**Hiraoka, Kimitake** 1925-1970
See Mishima, Yukio
See also CA 97-100; 29-32R; DAM DRAM; MTCW

**Hirsch, E(ric) D(onald), Jr.** 1928-... **CLC 79**
See also CA 25-28R; CANR 27, 51; DLB 67; INT CANR-27; MTCW

**Hirsch, Edward** 1950- ......... **CLC 31, 50**
See also CA 104; CANR 20, 42; DLB 120

**Hitchcock, Alfred (Joseph)** 1899-1980 ................... **CLC 16**
See also CA 97-100; SATA 27; SATA-Obit 24

**Hitler, Adolf** 1889-1945 .......... **TCLC 53**
See also CA 117; 147

**Hoagland, Edward** 1932- .......... **CLC 28**
See also CA 1-4R; CANR 2, 31; DLB 6; SATA 51

**Hoban, Russell (Conwell)** 1925- .......... **CLC 7, 25; DAM NOV**
See also CA 5-8R; CANR 23, 37; CLR 3; DLB 52; MAICYA; MTCW; SATA 1, 40, 78

**Hobbes, Thomas** 1588-1679 ......... **LC 36**
See also DLB 151

**Hobbs, Perry**
See Blackmur, R(ichard) P(almer)

**Hobson, Laura Z(ametkin)** 1900-1986 ................. **CLC 7, 25**
See also CA 17-20R; 118; CANR 55; DLB 28; SATA 52

**Hochhuth, Rolf** 1931- ..... **CLC 4, 11, 18; DAM DRAM**
See also CA 5-8R; CANR 33; DLB 124; MTCW

**Hochman, Sandra** 1936- .......... **CLC 3, 8**
See also CA 5-8R; DLB 5

**Hochwaelder, Fritz** 1911-1986 ...... **CLC 36; DAM DRAM**
See also CA 29-32R; 120; CANR 42; MTCW

**Hochwalder, Fritz**
See Hochwaelder, Fritz

**Hocking, Mary (Eunice)** 1921- ..... **CLC 13**
See also CA 101; CANR 18, 40

**Hodgins, Jack** 1938- .............. **CLC 23**
See also CA 93-96; DLB 60

**Hodgson, William Hope** 1877(?)-1918 ................ **TCLC 13**
See also CA 111; DLB 70, 153, 156

**Hoeg, Peter** 1957- ................ **CLC 95**
See also CA 151

**Hoffman, Alice** 1952- ............ **CLC 51; DAM NOV**
See also CA 77-80; CANR 34; MTCW

**Hoffman, Daniel (Gerard)** 1923- .................. **CLC 6, 13, 23**
See also CA 1-4R; CANR 4; DLB 5

**Hoffman, Stanley** 1944- ............. **CLC 5**
See also CA 77-80

**Hoffman, William M(oses)** 1939- ... **CLC 40**
See also CA 57-60; CANR 11

**Hoffmann, E(rnst) T(heodor) A(madeus)** 1776-1822 ........... **NCLC 2; SSC 13**
See also DLB 90; SATA 27

**Hofmann, Gert** 1931- ............. **CLC 54**
See also CA 128

**Hofmannsthal, Hugo von** 1874-1929 .... **TCLC 11; DAM DRAM; DC 4**
See also CA 106; 153; DLB 81, 118

**Hogan, Linda** 1947- .......... **CLC 73; DAM MULT**
See also CA 120; CANR 45; NNAL

**Hogarth, Charles**
See Creasey, John

**Hogarth, Emmett**
See Polonsky, Abraham (Lincoln)

**Hogg, James** 1770-1835 .......... **NCLC 4**
See also DLB 93, 116, 159

**Holbach, Paul Henri Thiry Baron** 1723-1789 ..................... **LC 14**

**Holberg, Ludvig** 1684-1754 .......... **LC 6**

**Holden, Ursula** 1921- ............. **CLC 18**
See also CA 101; CAAS 8; CANR 22

**Holderlin, (Johann Christian) Friedrich** 1770-1843 ............ **NCLC 16; PC 4**

**Holdstock, Robert**
See Holdstock, Robert P.

**Holdstock, Robert P.** 1948- ........ **CLC 39**
See also CA 131

**Holland, Isabelle** 1920- ........... **CLC 21**
See also AAYA 11; CA 21-24R; CANR 10, 25, 47; JRDA; MAICYA; SATA 8, 70

**Holland, Marcus**
See Caldwell, (Janet Miriam) Taylor (Holland)

**Hollander, John** 1929- ...... **CLC 2, 5, 8, 14**
See also CA 1-4R; CANR 1, 52; DLB 5; SATA 13

**Hollander, Paul**
See Silverberg, Robert

**Holleran, Andrew** 1943(?)- ......... **CLC 38**
See also CA 144

**Hollinghurst, Alan** 1954- ....... **CLC 55, 91**
See also CA 114

**Hollis, Jim**
See Summers, Hollis (Spurgeon, Jr.)

**Holly, Buddy** 1936-1959 ......... **TCLC 65**

**Holmes, John**
See Souster, (Holmes) Raymond

**Holmes, John Clellon** 1926-1988.... **CLC 56**
See also CA 9-12R; 125; CANR 4; DLB 16

**Holmes, Oliver Wendell** 1809-1894 ................ **NCLC 14**
See also CDALB 1640-1865; DLB 1; SATA 34

**Holmes, Raymond**
See Souster, (Holmes) Raymond

**Holt, Victoria**
See Hibbert, Eleanor Alice Burford

**Holub, Miroslav** 1923- ............. **CLC 4**
See also CA 21-24R; CANR 10

**Homer** c. 8th cent. B.C.- ..... **CMLC 1, 16; DA; DAB; DAC; DAM MST, POET**

**Honig, Edwin** 1919- .............. **CLC 33**
See also CA 5-8R; CAAS 8; CANR 4, 45; DLB 5

**Hood, Hugh (John Blagdon)** 1928- ..................... **CLC 15, 28**
See also CA 49-52; CAAS 17; CANR 1, 33; DLB 53

**Hood, Thomas** 1799-1845......... **NCLC 16**
See also DLB 96

**Hooker, (Peter) Jeremy** 1941- ...... **CLC 43**
See also CA 77-80; CANR 22; DLB 40

**hooks, bell** ....................... **CLC 94**
See also Watkins, Gloria

**Hope, A(lec) D(erwent)** 1907- .... **CLC 3, 51**
See also CA 21-24R; CANR 33; MTCW

**Hope, Brian**
See Creasey, John

**Hunt, (James Henry) Leigh** 1784-1859 . . . . . . **NCLC 1; DAM POET**

**Hunt, Marsha** 1946- . . . . . . . . . . . . . . **CLC 70**
See also BW 2; CA 143

**Hunt, Violet** 1866-1942 . . . . . . . . . . **TCLC 53**
See also DLB 162

**Hunter, E. Waldo**
See Sturgeon, Theodore (Hamilton)

**Hunter, Evan**
1926- . . . . . . . . . **CLC 11, 31; DAM POP**
See also CA 5-8R; CANR 5, 38; DLBY 82; INT CANR-5; MTCW; SATA 25

**Hunter, Kristin (Eggleston)** 1931- . . . **CLC 35**
See also AITN 1; BW 1; CA 13-16R; CANR 13; CLR 3; DLB 33; INT CANR-13; MAICYA; SAAS 10; SATA 12

**Hunter, Mollie** 1922- . . . . . . . . . . . . . **CLC 21**
See also McIlwraith, Maureen Mollie Hunter
See also AAYA 13; CANR 37; CLR 25; DLB 161; JRDA; MAICYA; SAAS 7; SATA 54

**Hunter, Robert** (?)-1734 . . . . . . . . . . . . . **LC 7**

**Hurston, Zora Neale**
1903-1960 . . . . **CLC 7, 30, 61; BLC; DA; DAC; DAM MST, MULT, NOV; SSC 4**
See also AAYA 15; BW 1; CA 85-88; DLB 51, 86; MTCW

**Huston, John (Marcellus)**
1906-1987 . . . . . . . . . . . . . . . . . . **CLC 20**
See also CA 73-76; 123; CANR 34; DLB 26

**Hustvedt, Siri** 1955- . . . . . . . . . . . . . . **CLC 76**
See also CA 137

**Hutten, Ulrich von** 1488-1523 . . . . . . . **LC 16**

**Huxley, Aldous (Leonard)**
1894-1963 . . . . . **CLC 1, 3, 4, 5, 8, 11, 18, 35, 79; DA; DAB; DAC; DAM MST, NOV; WLC**
See also AAYA 11; CA 85-88; CANR 44; CDBLB 1914-1945; DLB 36, 100, 162; MTCW; SATA 63

**Huysmans, Charles Marie Georges**
1848-1907
See Huysmans, Joris-Karl
See also CA 104

**Huysmans, Joris-Karl** . . . . . . . . . . . . . . **TCLC 7**
See also Huysmans, Charles Marie Georges
See also DLB 123

**Hwang, David Henry**
1957- . . . . **CLC 55; DAM DRAM; DC 4**
See also CA 127; 132; INT 132

**Hyde, Anthony** 1946- . . . . . . . . . . . . . **CLC 42**
See also CA 136

**Hyde, Margaret O(ldroyd)** 1917- . . . **CLC 21**
See also CA 1-4R; CANR 1, 36; CLR 23; JRDA; MAICYA; SAAS 8; SATA 1, 42, 76

**Hynes, James** 1956(?)- . . . . . . . . . . . . **CLC 65**

**Ian, Janis** 1951- . . . . . . . . . . . . . . . . . **CLC 21**
See also CA 105

**Ibanez, Vicente Blasco**
See Blasco Ibanez, Vicente

**Ibarguengoitia, Jorge** 1928-1983 . . . . **CLC 37**
See also CA 124; 113; HW

**Ibsen, Henrik (Johan)**
1828-1906 . . . . . . . **TCLC 2, 8, 16, 37, 52; DA; DAB; DAC; DAM DRAM, MST; DC 2; WLC**
See also CA 104; 141

**Ibuse Masuji** 1898-1993 . . . . . . . . . . **CLC 22**
See also CA 127; 141

**Ichikawa, Kon** 1915- . . . . . . . . . . . . . . **CLC 20**
See also CA 121

**Idle, Eric** 1943- . . . . . . . . . . . . . . . . . . **CLC 21**
See also Monty Python
See also CA 116; CANR 35

**Ignatow, David** 1914- . . . . . . **CLC 4, 7, 14, 40**
See also CA 9-12R; CAAS 3; CANR 31; DLB 5

**Ihimaera, Witi** 1944- . . . . . . . . . . . . . **CLC 46**
See also CA 77-80

**Ilf, Ilya** . . . . . . . . . . . . . . . . . . . . . . . . . **TCLC 21**
See also Fainzilberg, Ilya Arnoldovich

**Illyes, Gyula** 1902-1983 . . . . . . . . . . . . **PC 16**
See also CA 114; 109

**Immermann, Karl (Lebrecht)**
1796-1840 . . . . . . . . . . . . . . . **NCLC 4, 49**
See also DLB 133

**Inclan, Ramon (Maria) del Valle**
See Valle-Inclan, Ramon (Maria) del

**Infante, G(uillermo) Cabrera**
See Cabrera Infante, G(uillermo)

**Ingalls, Rachel (Holmes)** 1940- . . . . . **CLC 42**
See also CA 123; 127

**Ingamells, Rex** 1913-1955 . . . . . . . . **TCLC 35**

**Inge, William (Motter)**
1913-1973 . . **CLC 1, 8, 19; DAM DRAM**
See also CA 9-12R; CDALB 1941-1968; DLB 7; MTCW

**Ingelow, Jean** 1820-1897 . . . . . . . . **NCLC 39**
See also DLB 35, 163; SATA 33

**Ingram, Willis J.**
See Harris, Mark

**Innaurato, Albert (F.)** 1948(?)- . . **CLC 21, 60**
See also CA 115; 122; INT 122

**Innes, Michael**
See Stewart, J(ohn) I(nnes) M(ackintosh)

**Ionesco, Eugene**
1909-1994 . . . . **CLC 1, 4, 6, 9, 11, 15, 41, 86; DA; DAB; DAC; DAM DRAM, MST; WLC**
See also CA 9-12R; 144; CANR 55; MTCW; SATA 7; SATA-Obit 79

**Iqbal, Muhammad** 1873-1938 . . . . . **TCLC 28**

**Ireland, Patrick**
See O'Doherty, Brian

**Iron, Ralph**
See Schreiner, Olive (Emilie Albertina)

**Irving, John (Winslow)**
1942- . . . . . **CLC 13, 23, 38; DAM NOV, POP**
See also AAYA 8; BEST 89:3; CA 25-28R; CANR 28; DLB 6; DLBY 82; MTCW

**Irving, Washington**
1783-1859 . . . . . **NCLC 2, 19; DA; DAB; DAM MST; SSC 2; WLC**
See also CDALB 1640-1865; DLB 3, 11, 30, 59, 73, 74; YABC 2

**Irwin, P. K.**
See Page, P(atricia) K(athleen)

**Isaacs, Susan** 1943- . . . **CLC 32; DAM POP**
See also BEST 89:1; CA 89-92; CANR 20, 41; INT CANR-20; MTCW

**Isherwood, Christopher (William Bradshaw)**
1904-1986 . . . . . . . . **CLC 1, 9, 11, 14, 44; DAM DRAM, NOV**
See also CA 13-16R; 117; CANR 35; DLB 15; DLBY 86; MTCW

**Ishiguro, Kazuo**
1954- . . . . . . **CLC 27, 56, 59; DAM NOV**
See also BEST 90:2; CA 120; CANR 49; MTCW

**Ishikawa, Hakuhin**
See Ishikawa, Takuboku

**Ishikawa, Takuboku**
1886(?)-1912 . . . . . . . . . . . . . . . **TCLC 15; DAM POET; PC 10**
See also CA 113; 153

**Iskander, Fazil** 1929- . . . . . . . . . . . . . **CLC 47**
See also CA 102

**Isler, Alan** . . . . . . . . . . . . . . . . . . . . . . . **CLC 91**

**Ivan IV** 1530-1584 . . . . . . . . . . . . . . . . **LC 17**

**Ivanov, Vyacheslav Ivanovich**
1866-1949 . . . . . . . . . . . . . . . . . . **TCLC 33**
See also CA 122

**Ivask, Ivar Vidrik** 1927-1992 . . . . . . . **CLC 14**
See also CA 37-40R; 139; CANR 24

**Ives, Morgan**
See Bradley, Marion Zimmer

**J. R. S.**
See Gogarty, Oliver St. John

**Jabran, Kahlil**
See Gibran, Kahlil

**Jabran, Khalil**
See Gibran, Kahlil

**Jackson, Daniel**
See Wingrove, David (John)

**Jackson, Jesse** 1908-1983 . . . . . . . . . **CLC 12**
See also BW 1; CA 25-28R; 109; CANR 27; CLR 28; MAICYA; SATA 2, 29; SATA-Obit 48

**Jackson, Laura (Riding)** 1901-1991
See Riding, Laura
See also CA 65-68; 135; CANR 28; DLB 48

**Jackson, Sam**
See Trumbo, Dalton

**Jackson, Sara**
See Wingrove, David (John)

**Jackson, Shirley**
1919-1965 . . . . . . . . **CLC 11, 60, 87; DA; DAC; DAM MST; SSC 9; WLC**
See also AAYA 9; CA 1-4R; 25-28R; CANR 4, 52; CDALB 1941-1968; DLB 6; SATA 2

**Jacob, (Cyprien-)Max** 1876-1944 . . . **TCLC 6**
See also CA 104

**Jacobs, Jim** 1942- . . . . . . . . . . . . . . . . **CLC 12**
See also CA 97-100; INT 97-100

**Jacobs, W(illiam) W(ymark)**
1863-1943 . . . . . . . . . . . . . . . . . . **TCLC 22**
See also CA 121; DLB 135

**Jacobsen, Jens Peter** 1847-1885 . . **NCLC 34**

**Kauffman, Janet** 1945- ............ **CLC 42**
See also CA 117; CANR 43; DLBY 86

**Kaufman, Bob (Garnell)** 1925-1986 ................... **CLC 49**
See also BW 1; CA 41-44R; 118; CANR 22; DLB 16, 41

**Kaufman, George S.** 1889-1961 ...... **CLC 38; DAM DRAM**
See also CA 108; 93-96; DLB 7; INT 108

**Kaufman, Sue** ................... **CLC 3, 8**
See also Barondess, Sue K(aufman)

**Kavafis, Konstantinos Petrou** 1863-1933
See Cavafy, C(onstantine) P(eter)
See also CA 104

**Kavan, Anna** 1901-1968 ...... **CLC 5, 13, 82**
See also CA 5-8R; CANR 6; MTCW

**Kavanagh, Dan**
See Barnes, Julian (Patrick)

**Kavanagh, Patrick (Joseph)** 1904-1967 ................... **CLC 22**
See also CA 123; 25-28R; DLB 15, 20; MTCW

**Kawabata, Yasunari** 1899-1972 ............ **CLC 2, 5, 9, 18; DAM MULT; SSC 17**
See also CA 93-96; 33-36R

**Kaye, M(ary) M(argaret)** 1909- ..... **CLC 28**
See also CA 89-92; CANR 24; MTCW; SATA 62

**Kaye, Mollie**
See Kaye, M(ary) M(argaret)

**Kaye-Smith, Sheila** 1887-1956 ..... **TCLC 20**
See also CA 118; DLB 36

**Kaymor, Patrice Maguilene**
See Senghor, Leopold Sedar

**Kazan, Elia** 1909- ........... **CLC 6, 16, 63**
See also CA 21-24R; CANR 32

**Kazantzakis, Nikos** 1883(?)-1957 ........... **TCLC 2, 5, 33**
See also CA 105; 132; MTCW

**Kazin, Alfred** 1915- ........... **CLC 34, 38**
See also CA 1-4R; CAAS 7; CANR 1, 45; DLB 67

**Keane, Mary Nesta (Skrine)** 1904-1996
See Keane, Molly
See also CA 108; 114; 151

**Keane, Molly** ..................... **CLC 31**
See also Keane, Mary Nesta (Skrine)
See also INT 114

**Keates, Jonathan** 19(?)- ........... **CLC 34**

**Keaton, Buster** 1895-1966 ......... **CLC 20**

**Keats, John** 1795-1821 ........ **NCLC 8; DA; DAB; DAC; DAM MST, POET; PC 1; WLC**
See also CDBLB 1789-1832; DLB 96, 110

**Keene, Donald** 1922- ............. **CLC 34**
See also CA 1-4R; CANR 5

**Keillor, Garrison** .................. **CLC 40**
See also Keillor, Gary (Edward)
See also AAYA 2; BEST 89:3; DLBY 87; SATA 58

**Keillor, Gary (Edward)** 1942-
See Keillor, Garrison
See also CA 111; 117; CANR 36; DAM POP; MTCW

**Keith, Michael**
See Hubbard, L(afayette) Ron(ald)

**Keller, Gottfried** 1819-1890 ....... **NCLC 2**
See also DLB 129

**Kellerman, Jonathan** 1949- ............ **CLC 44; DAM POP**
See also BEST 90:1; CA 106; CANR 29, 51; INT CANR-29

**Kelley, William Melvin** 1937- ...... **CLC 22**
See also BW 1; CA 77-80; CANR 27; DLB 33

**Kellogg, Marjorie** 1922- ............ **CLC 2**
See also CA 81-84

**Kellow, Kathleen**
See Hibbert, Eleanor Alice Burford

**Kelly, M(ilton) T(erry)** 1947- ...... **CLC 55**
See also CA 97-100; CAAS 22; CANR 19, 43

**Kelman, James** 1946- .......... **CLC 58, 86**
See also CA 148

**Kemal, Yashar** 1923- .......... **CLC 14, 29**
See also CA 89-92; CANR 44

**Kemble, Fanny** 1809-1893 ....... **NCLC 18**
See also DLB 32

**Kemelman, Harry** 1908-1996 ........ **CLC 2**
See also AITN 1; CA 9-12R; 155; CANR 6; DLB 28

**Kempe, Margery** 1373(?)-1440(?) ..... **LC 6**
See also DLB 146

**Kempis, Thomas a** 1380-1471 ....... **LC 11**

**Kendall, Henry** 1839-1882 ....... **NCLC 12**

**Keneally, Thomas (Michael)** 1935- ...... **CLC 5, 8, 10, 14, 19, 27, 43; DAM NOV**
See also CA 85-88; CANR 10, 50; MTCW

**Kennedy, Adrienne (Lita)** 1931- ..... **CLC 66; BLC; DAM MULT; DC 5**
See also BW 2; CA 103; CAAS 20; CABS 3; CANR 26, 53; DLB 38

**Kennedy, John Pendleton** 1795-1870 .................. **NCLC 2**
See also DLB 3

**Kennedy, Joseph Charles** 1929-
See Kennedy, X. J.
See also CA 1-4R; CANR 4, 30, 40; SATA 14, 86

**Kennedy, William** 1928- ... **CLC 6, 28, 34, 53; DAM NOV**
See also AAYA 1; CA 85-88; CANR 14, 31; DLB 143; DLBY 85; INT CANR-31; MTCW; SATA 57

**Kennedy, X. J.** .................. **CLC 8, 42**
See also Kennedy, Joseph Charles
See also CAAS 9; CLR 27; DLB 5; SAAS 22

**Kenny, Maurice (Francis)** 1929- .......... **CLC 87; DAM MULT**
See also CA 144; CAAS 22; NNAL

**Kent, Kelvin**
See Kuttner, Henry

**Kenton, Maxwell**
See Southern, Terry

**Kenyon, Robert O.**
See Kuttner, Henry

**Kerouac, Jack** ..... **CLC 1, 2, 3, 5, 14, 29, 61**
See also Kerouac, Jean-Louis Lebris de
See also CDALB 1941-1968; DLB 2, 16; DLBD 3; DLBY 95

**Kerouac, Jean-Louis Lebris de** 1922-1969
See Kerouac, Jack
See also AITN 1; CA 5-8R; 25-28R; CANR 26, 54; DA; DAB; DAC; DAM MST, NOV, POET, POP; MTCW; WLC

**Kerr, Jean** 1923- ................. **CLC 22**
See also CA 5-8R; CANR 7; INT CANR-7

**Kerr, M. E.** .................... **CLC 12, 35**
See also Meaker, Marijane (Agnes)
See also AAYA 2; CLR 29; SAAS 1

**Kerr, Robert** ..................... **CLC 55**

**Kerrigan, (Thomas) Anthony** 1918- ...................... **CLC 4, 6**
See also CA 49-52; CAAS 11; CANR 4

**Kerry, Lois**
See Duncan, Lois

**Kesey, Ken (Elton)** 1935- ...... **CLC 1, 3, 6, 11, 46, 64; DA; DAB; DAC; DAM MST, NOV, POP; WLC**
See also CA 1-4R; CANR 22, 38; CDALB 1968-1988; DLB 2, 16; MTCW; SATA 66

**Kesselring, Joseph (Otto)** 1902-1967 ..... **CLC 45; DAM DRAM, MST**
See also CA 150

**Kessler, Jascha (Frederick)** 1929- .... **CLC 4**
See also CA 17-20R; CANR 8, 48

**Kettelkamp, Larry (Dale)** 1933- .... **CLC 12**
See also CA 29-32R; CANR 16; SAAS 3; SATA 2

**Key, Ellen** 1849-1926 ........... **TCLC 65**

**Keyber, Conny**
See Fielding, Henry

**Keyes, Daniel** 1927- ............. **CLC 80; DA; DAC; DAM MST, NOV**
See also CA 17-20R; CANR 10, 26, 54; SATA 37

**Keynes, John Maynard** 1883-1946 .................. **TCLC 64**
See also CA 114; DLBD 10

**Khanshendel, Chiron**
See Rose, Wendy

**Khayyam, Omar** 1048-1131 .... **CMLC 11; DAM POET; PC 8**

**Kherdian, David** 1931- ........... **CLC 6, 9**
See also CA 21-24R; CAAS 2; CANR 39; CLR 24; JRDA; MAICYA; SATA 16, 74

**Khlebnikov, Velimir** ............. **TCLC 20**
See also Khlebnikov, Viktor Vladimirovich

**Khlebnikov, Viktor Vladimirovich** 1885-1922
See Khlebnikov, Velimir
See also CA 117

**Khodasevich, Vladislav (Felitsianovich)** 1886-1939 .................. **TCLC 15**
See also CA 115

**Kielland, Alexander Lange** 1849-1906 .................... **TCLC 5**
See also CA 104

**Kiely, Benedict** 1919- .......... **CLC 23, 43**
See also CA 1-4R; CANR 2; DLB 15

**Kienzle, William X(avier)** 1928- ............ **CLC 25; DAM POP**
See also CA 93-96; CAAS 1; CANR 9, 31; INT CANR-31; MTCW

**Kierkegaard, Soren** 1813-1855.... **NCLC 34**

**Killens, John Oliver** 1916-1987..... **CLC 10**
See also BW 2; CA 77-80; 123; CAAS 2; CANR 26; DLB 33

**Killigrew, Anne** 1660-1685........... **LC 4**
See also DLB 131

**Kim**
See Simenon, Georges (Jacques Christian)

**Kincaid, Jamaica** 1949- .............. **CLC 43, 68; BLC; DAM MULT, NOV**
See also AAYA 13; BW 2; CA 125; CANR 47; DLB 157

**King, Francis (Henry)** 1923- .......... **CLC 8, 53; DAM NOV**
See also CA 1-4R; CANR 1, 33; DLB 15, 139; MTCW

**King, Martin Luther, Jr.** 1929-1968 .... **CLC 83; BLC; DA; DAB; DAC; DAM MST, MULT**
See also BW 2; CA 25-28; CANR 27, 44; CAP 2; MTCW; SATA 14

**King, Stephen (Edwin)** 1947- ............. **CLC 12, 26, 37, 61; DAM NOV, POP; SSC 17**
See also AAYA 1, 17; BEST 90:1; CA 61-64; CANR 1, 30, 52; DLB 143; DLBY 80; JRDA; MTCW; SATA 9, 55

**King, Steve**
See King, Stephen (Edwin)

**King, Thomas** 1943- ..... **CLC 89; DAC; DAM MULT**
See also CA 144; NNAL

**Kingman, Lee**..................... **CLC 17**
See also Natti, (Mary) Lee
See also SAAS 3; SATA 1, 67

**Kingsley, Charles** 1819-1875 ..... **NCLC 35**
See also DLB 21, 32, 163; YABC 2

**Kingsley, Sidney** 1906-1995........ **CLC 44**
See also CA 85-88; 147; DLB 7

**Kingsolver, Barbara** 1955- ......... **CLC 55, 81; DAM POP**
See also AAYA 15; CA 129; 134; INT 134

**Kingston, Maxine (Ting Ting) Hong** 1940- .... **CLC 12, 19, 58; DAM MULT, NOV**
See also AAYA 8; CA 69-72; CANR 13, 38; DLB 173; DLBY 80; INT CANR-13; MTCW; SATA 53

**Kinnell, Galway** 1927- ........... **CLC 1, 2, 3, 5, 13, 29**
See also CA 9-12R; CANR 10, 34; DLB 5; DLBY 87; INT CANR-34; MTCW

**Kinsella, Thomas** 1928- ......... **CLC 4, 19**
See also CA 17-20R; CANR 15; DLB 27; MTCW

**Kinsella, W(illiam) P(atrick)** 1935- .............. **CLC 27, 43; DAC; DAM NOV, POP**
See also AAYA 7; CA 97-100; CAAS 7; CANR 21, 35; INT CANR-21; MTCW

**Kipling, (Joseph) Rudyard** 1865-1936 ...... **TCLC 8, 17; DA; DAB; DAC; DAM MST, POET; PC 3; SSC 5; WLC**
See also CA 105; 120; CANR 33; CDBLB 1890-1914; CLR 39; DLB 19, 34, 141, 156; MAICYA; MTCW; YABC 2

**Kirkup, James** 1918- .............. **CLC 1**
See also CA 1-4R; CAAS 4; CANR 2; DLB 27; SATA 12

**Kirkwood, James** 1930(?)-1989 ...... **CLC 9**
See also AITN 2; CA 1-4R; 128; CANR 6, 40

**Kirshner, Sidney**
See Kingsley, Sidney

**Kis, Danilo** 1935-1989 ............ **CLC 57**
See also CA 109; 118; 129; MTCW

**Kivi, Aleksis** 1834-1872......... **NCLC 30**

**Kizer, Carolyn (Ashley)** 1925- ..... **CLC 15, 39, 80; DAM POET**
See also CA 65-68; CAAS 5; CANR 24; DLB 5, 169

**Klabund** 1890-1928.............. **TCLC 44**
See also DLB 66

**Klappert, Peter** 1942-............. **CLC 57**
See also CA 33-36R; DLB 5

**Klein, A(braham) M(oses)** 1909-1972 ........ **CLC 19; DAB; DAC; DAM MST**
See also CA 101; 37-40R; DLB 68

**Klein, Norma** 1938-1989 .......... **CLC 30**
See also AAYA 2; CA 41-44R; 128; CANR 15, 37; CLR 2, 19; INT CANR-15; JRDA; MAICYA; SAAS 1; SATA 7, 57

**Klein, T(heodore) E(ibon) D(onald)** 1947- ...................... **CLC 34**
See also CA 119; CANR 44

**Kleist, Heinrich von** 1777-1811 .............. **NCLC 2, 37; DAM DRAM; SSC 22**
See also DLB 90

**Klima, Ivan** 1931-..... **CLC 56; DAM NOV**
See also CA 25-28R; CANR 17, 50

**Klimentov, Andrei Platonovich** 1899-1951
See Platonov, Andrei
See also CA 108

**Klinger, Friedrich Maximilian von** 1752-1831 .................. **NCLC 1**
See also DLB 94

**Klopstock, Friedrich Gottlieb** 1724-1803 ................. **NCLC 11**
See also DLB 97

**Knebel, Fletcher** 1911-1993........ **CLC 14**
See also AITN 1; CA 1-4R; 140; CAAS 3; CANR 1, 36; SATA 36; SATA-Obit 75

**Knickerbocker, Diedrich**
See Irving, Washington

**Knight, Etheridge** 1931-1991 ............. **CLC 40; BLC; DAM POET; PC 14**
See also BW 1; CA 21-24R; 133; CANR 23; DLB 41

**Knight, Sarah Kemble** 1666-1727 ..... **LC 7**
See also DLB 24

**Knister, Raymond** 1899-1932...... **TCLC 56**
See also DLB 68

**Knowles, John** 1926- ...... **CLC 1, 4, 10, 26; DA; DAC; DAM MST, NOV**
See also AAYA 10; CA 17-20R; CANR 40; CDALB 1968-1988; DLB 6; MTCW; SATA 8, 89

**Knox, Calvin M.**
See Silverberg, Robert

**Knox, John** c. 1505-1572........... **LC 37**
See also DLB 132

**Knye, Cassandra**
See Disch, Thomas M(ichael)

**Koch, C(hristopher) J(ohn)** 1932- ... **CLC 42**
See also CA 127

**Koch, Christopher**
See Koch, C(hristopher) J(ohn)

**Koch, Kenneth** 1925- ....... **CLC 5, 8, 44; DAM POET**
See also CA 1-4R; CANR 6, 36; DLB 5; INT CANR-36; SATA 65

**Kochanowski, Jan** 1530-1584........ **LC 10**

**Kock, Charles Paul de** 1794-1871 ................. **NCLC 16**

**Koda Shigeyuki** 1867-1947
See Rohan, Koda
See also CA 121

**Koestler, Arthur** 1905-1983 ....... **CLC 1, 3, 6, 8, 15, 33**
See also CA 1-4R; 109; CANR 1, 33; CDBLB 1945-1960; DLBY 83; MTCW

**Kogawa, Joy Nozomi** 1935- ...... **CLC 78; DAC; DAM MST, MULT**
See also CA 101; CANR 19

**Kohout, Pavel** 1928-.............. **CLC 13**
See also CA 45-48; CANR 3

**Koizumi, Yakumo**
See Hearn, (Patricio) Lafcadio (Tessima Carlos)

**Kolmar, Gertrud** 1894-1943....... **TCLC 40**

**Komunyakaa, Yusef** 1947-...... **CLC 86, 94**
See also CA 147; DLB 120

**Konrad, George**
See Konrad, Gyoergy

**Konrad, Gyoergy** 1933- ...... **CLC 4, 10, 73**
See also CA 85-88

**Konwicki, Tadeusz** 1926-..... **CLC 8, 28, 54**
See also CA 101; CAAS 9; CANR 39; MTCW

**Koontz, Dean R(ay)** 1945- ...... **CLC 78; DAM NOV, POP**
See also AAYA 9; BEST 89:3, 90:2; CA 108; CANR 19, 36, 52; MTCW

**Kopit, Arthur (Lee)**
1937- ..... **CLC 1, 18, 33; DAM DRAM**
See also AITN 1; CA 81-84; CABS 3; DLB 7; MTCW

**Kops, Bernard** 1926- ............... **CLC 4**
See also CA 5-8R; DLB 13

**Kornbluth, C(yril) M.** 1923-1958.... **TCLC 8**
See also CA 105; DLB 8

**Korolenko, V. G.**
See Korolenko, Vladimir Galaktionovich

**Korolenko, Vladimir**
See Korolenko, Vladimir Galaktionovich

**Korolenko, Vladimir G.**
See Korolenko, Vladimir Galaktionovich

**Korolenko, Vladimir Galaktionovich**
1853-1921 .................. **TCLC 22**
See also CA 121

**Korzybski, Alfred (Habdank Skarbek)**
1879-1950 .................. **TCLC 61**
See also CA 123

**Kosinski, Jerzy (Nikodem)**
1933-1991 .... **CLC 1, 2, 3, 6, 10, 15, 53, 70; DAM NOV**
See also CA 17-20R; 134; CANR 9, 46; DLB 2; DLBY 82; MTCW

**Kostelanetz, Richard (Cory)** 1940- .. **CLC 28**
See also CA 13-16R; CAAS 8; CANR 38

**Kostrowitzki, Wilhelm Apollinaris de**
1880-1918
See Apollinaire, Guillaume
See also CA 104

**Kotlowitz, Robert** 1924- ............ **CLC 4**
See also CA 33-36R; CANR 36

**Kotzebue, August (Friedrich Ferdinand) von**
1761-1819 ................ **NCLC 25**
See also DLB 94

**Kotzwinkle, William** 1938- ... **CLC 5, 14, 35**
See also CA 45-48; CANR 3, 44; CLR 6; DLB 173; MAICYA; SATA 24, 70

**Kozol, Jonathan** 1936- ............ **CLC 17**
See also CA 61-64; CANR 16, 45

**Kozoll, Michael** 1940(?)- .......... **CLC 35**

**Kramer, Kathryn** 19(?)- ........... **CLC 34**

**Kramer, Larry** 1935- .. **CLC 42; DAM POP**
See also CA 124; 126

**Krasicki, Ignacy** 1735-1801 ....... **NCLC 8**

**Krasinski, Zygmunt** 1812-1859 .... **NCLC 4**

**Kraus, Karl** 1874-1936 ............ **TCLC 5**
See also CA 104; DLB 118

**Kreve (Mickevicius), Vincas**
1882-1954 .................. **TCLC 27**

**Kristeva, Julia** 1941- ............. **CLC 77**
See also CA 154

**Kristofferson, Kris** 1936- .......... **CLC 26**
See also CA 104

**Krizanc, John** 1956- .............. **CLC 57**

**Krleza, Miroslav** 1893-1981 ......... **CLC 8**
See also CA 97-100; 105; CANR 50; DLB 147

**Kroetsch, Robert**
1927- ............ **CLC 5, 23, 57; DAC; DAM POET**
See also CA 17-20R; CANR 8, 38; DLB 53; MTCW

**Kroetz, Franz**
See Kroetz, Franz Xaver

**Kroetz, Franz Xaver** 1946- ........ **CLC 41**
See also CA 130

**Kroker, Arthur** 1945- ............. **CLC 77**

**Kropotkin, Peter (Aleksieevich)**
1842-1921 .................. **TCLC 36**
See also CA 119

**Krotkov, Yuri** 1917- .............. **CLC 19**
See also CA 102

**Krumb**
See Crumb, R(obert)

**Krumgold, Joseph (Quincy)**
1908-1980 ................... **CLC 12**
See also CA 9-12R; 101; CANR 7; MAICYA; SATA 1, 48; SATA-Obit 23

**Krumwitz**
See Crumb, R(obert)

**Krutch, Joseph Wood** 1893-1970.... **CLC 24**
See also CA 1-4R; 25-28R; CANR 4; DLB 63

**Krutzch, Gus**
See Eliot, T(homas) S(tearns)

**Krylov, Ivan Andreevich**
1768(?)-1844 ................ **NCLC 1**
See also DLB 150

**Kubin, Alfred (Leopold Isidor)**
1877-1959 .................. **TCLC 23**
See also CA 112; 149; DLB 81

**Kubrick, Stanley** 1928- ............ **CLC 16**
See also CA 81-84; CANR 33; DLB 26

**Kumin, Maxine (Winokur)**
1925- ..... **CLC 5, 13, 28; DAM POET; PC 15**
See also AITN 2; CA 1-4R; CAAS 8; CANR 1, 21; DLB 5; MTCW; SATA 12

**Kundera, Milan**
1929- ............ **CLC 4, 9, 19, 32, 68; DAM NOV; SSC 24**
See also AAYA 2; CA 85-88; CANR 19, 52; MTCW

**Kunene, Mazisi (Raymond)** 1930- ... **CLC 85**
See also BW 1; CA 125; DLB 117

**Kunitz, Stanley (Jasspon)**
1905- .................. **CLC 6, 11, 14**
See also CA 41-44R; CANR 26; DLB 48; INT CANR-26; MTCW

**Kunze, Reiner** 1933- .............. **CLC 10**
See also CA 93-96; DLB 75

**Kuprin, Aleksandr Ivanovich**
1870-1938 .................. **TCLC 5**
See also CA 104

**Kureishi, Hanif** 1954(?)- ........... **CLC 64**
See also CA 139

**Kurosawa, Akira**
1910- .......... **CLC 16; DAM MULT**
See also AAYA 11; CA 101; CANR 46

**Kushner, Tony**
1957(?)- ........ **CLC 81; DAM DRAM**
See also CA 144

**Kuttner, Henry** 1915-1958 ........ **TCLC 10**
See also CA 107; DLB 8

**Kuzma, Greg** 1944- ................ **CLC 7**
See also CA 33-36R

**Kuzmin, Mikhail** 1872(?)-1936 .... **TCLC 40**

**Kyd, Thomas**
1558-1594 ....... **LC 22; DAM DRAM; DC 3**
See also DLB 62

**Kyprianos, Iossif**
See Samarakis, Antonis

**La Bruyere, Jean de** 1645-1696 ...... **LC 17**

**Lacan, Jacques (Marie Emile)**
1901-1981 ................... **CLC 75**
See also CA 121; 104

**Laclos, Pierre Ambroise Francois Choderlos de** 1741-1803 .............. **NCLC 4**

**La Colere, Francois**
See Aragon, Louis

**Lacolere, Francois**
See Aragon, Louis

**La Deshabilleuse**
See Simenon, Georges (Jacques Christian)

**Lady Gregory**
See Gregory, Isabella Augusta (Persse)

**Lady of Quality, A**
See Bagnold, Enid

**La Fayette, Marie (Madelaine Pioche de la Vergne Comtes** 1634-1693 ....... **LC 2**

**Lafayette, Rene**
See Hubbard, L(afayette) Ron(ald)

**Laforgue, Jules**
1860-1887 ........ **NCLC 5, 53; PC 14; SSC 20**

**Lagerkvist, Paer (Fabian)**
1891-1974 .......... **CLC 7, 10, 13, 54; DAM DRAM, NOV**
See also Lagerkvist, Par
See also CA 85-88; 49-52; MTCW

**Lagerkvist, Par** .................. **SSC 12**
See also Lagerkvist, Paer (Fabian)

**Lagerloef, Selma (Ottiliana Lovisa)**
1858-1940 ................ **TCLC 4, 36**
See also Lagerlof, Selma (Ottiliana Lovisa)
See also CA 108; SATA 15

**Lagerlof, Selma (Ottiliana Lovisa)**
See Lagerloef, Selma (Ottiliana Lovisa)
See also CLR 7; SATA 15

**La Guma, (Justin) Alex(ander)**
1925-1985 ........ **CLC 19; DAM NOV**
See also BW 1; CA 49-52; 118; CANR 25; DLB 117; MTCW

**Laidlaw, A. K.**
See Grieve, C(hristopher) M(urray)

**Lainez, Manuel Mujica**
See Mujica Lainez, Manuel
See also HW

**Laing, R(onald) D(avid)**
1927-1989 ................... **CLC 95**
See also CA 107; 129; CANR 34; MTCW

**Lamartine, Alphonse (Marie Louis Prat) de**
1790-1869 ..... **NCLC 11; DAM POET; PC 16**

**Lamb, Charles**
1775-1834 ....... **NCLC 10; DA; DAB; DAC; DAM MST; WLC**
See also CDBLB 1789-1832; DLB 93, 107, 163; SATA 17

**Lamb, Lady Caroline** 1785-1828 .. **NCLC 38**
See also DLB 116

**Lamming, George (William)**
1927- ............. **CLC 2, 4, 66; BLC; DAM MULT**
See also BW 2; CA 85-88; CANR 26; DLB 125; MTCW

**L'Amour, Louis (Dearborn)**
1908-1988 .... **CLC 25, 55; DAM NOV, POP**
See also AAYA 16; AITN 2; BEST 89:2; CA 1-4R; 125; CANR 3, 25, 40; DLBY 80; MTCW

**Lampedusa, Giuseppe (Tomasi) di** ... **TCLC 13**
See also Tomasi di Lampedusa, Giuseppe

**Lampman, Archibald** 1861-1899 .. **NCLC 25**
See also DLB 92

**Lancaster, Bruce** 1896-1963 ........ **CLC 36**
See also CA 9-10; CAP 1; SATA 9

**Landau, Mark Alexandrovich**
See Aldanov, Mark (Alexandrovich)

**Landau-Aldanov, Mark Alexandrovich**
See Aldanov, Mark (Alexandrovich)

**Landis, Jerry**
See Simon, Paul (Frederick)

**Landis, John** 1950- ............... **CLC 26**
See also CA 112; 122

**Landolfi, Tommaso** 1908-1979 ... **CLC 11, 49**
See also CA 127; 117

**Landon, Letitia Elizabeth**
1802-1838 ................. **NCLC 15**
See also DLB 96

**Landor, Walter Savage**
1775-1864 ................. **NCLC 14**
See also DLB 93, 107

**Landwirth, Heinz** 1927-
See Lind, Jakov
See also CA 9-12R; CANR 7

**Lane, Patrick**
1939- ........... **CLC 25; DAM POET**
See also CA 97-100; CANR 54; DLB 53; INT 97-100

**Lang, Andrew** 1844-1912 ......... **TCLC 16**
See also CA 114; 137; DLB 98, 141; MAICYA; SATA 16

**Lang, Fritz** 1890-1976 ............ **CLC 20**
See also CA 77-80; 69-72; CANR 30

**Lange, John**
See Crichton, (John) Michael

**Langer, Elinor** 1939- ............. **CLC 34**
See also CA 121

**Langland, William**
1330(?)-1400(?) ...... **LC 19; DA; DAB; DAC; DAM MST, POET**
See also DLB 146

**Langstaff, Launcelot**
See Irving, Washington

**Lanier, Sidney**
1842-1881 ...... **NCLC 6; DAM POET**
See also DLB 64; DLBD 13; MAICYA; SATA 18

**Lanyer, Aemilia** 1569-1645 ...... **LC 10, 30**
See also DLB 121

**Lao Tzu** ....................... **CMLC 7**

**Lapine, James (Elliot)** 1949- ....... **CLC 39**
See also CA 123; 130; CANR 54; INT 130

**Larbaud, Valery (Nicolas)**
1881-1957 ................... **TCLC 9**
See also CA 106; 152

**Lardner, Ring**
See Lardner, Ring(gold) W(ilmer)

**Lardner, Ring W., Jr.**
See Lardner, Ring(gold) W(ilmer)

**Lardner, Ring(gold) W(ilmer)**
1885-1933 ................ **TCLC 2, 14**
See also CA 104; 131; CDALB 1917-1929; DLB 11, 25, 86; MTCW

**Laredo, Betty**
See Codrescu, Andrei

**Larkin, Maia**
See Wojciechowska, Maia (Teresa)

**Larkin, Philip (Arthur)**
1922-1985 .... **CLC 3, 5, 8, 9, 13, 18, 33, 39, 64; DAB; DAM MST, POET**
See also CA 5-8R; 117; CANR 24; CDBLB 1960 to Present; DLB 27; MTCW

**Larra (y Sanchez de Castro), Mariano Jose de**
1809-1837 ................. **NCLC 17**

**Larsen, Eric** 1941- ............... **CLC 55**
See also CA 132

**Larsen, Nella**
1891-1964 ............. **CLC 37; BLC; DAM MULT**
See also BW 1; CA 125; DLB 51

**Larson, Charles R(aymond)** 1938- ... **CLC 31**
See also CA 53-56; CANR 4

**Las Casas, Bartolome de** 1474-1566 .. **LC 31**

**Lasker-Schueler, Else** 1869-1945 .. **TCLC 57**
See also DLB 66, 124

**Latham, Jean Lee** 1902- .......... **CLC 12**
See also AITN 1; CA 5-8R; CANR 7; MAICYA; SATA 2, 68

**Latham, Mavis**
See Clark, Mavis Thorpe

**Lathen, Emma** ..................... **CLC 2**
See also Hennissart, Martha; Latsis, Mary J(ane)

**Lathrop, Francis**
See Leiber, Fritz (Reuter, Jr.)

**Latsis, Mary J(ane)**
See Lathen, Emma
See also CA 85-88

**Lattimore, Richmond (Alexander)**
1906-1984 .................... **CLC 3**
See also CA 1-4R; 112; CANR 1

**Laughlin, James** 1914- ............ **CLC 49**
See also CA 21-24R; CAAS 22; CANR 9, 47; DLB 48

**Laurence, (Jean) Margaret (Wemyss)**
1926-1987 ........ **CLC 3, 6, 13, 50, 62; DAC; DAM MST; SSC 7**
See also CA 5-8R; 121; CANR 33; DLB 53; MTCW; SATA-Obit 50

**Laurent, Antoine** 1952- ........... **CLC 50**

**Lauscher, Hermann**
See Hesse, Hermann

**Lautreamont, Comte de**
1846-1870 .......... **NCLC 12; SSC 14**

**Laverty, Donald**
See Blish, James (Benjamin)

**Lavin, Mary** 1912-1996 .. **CLC 4, 18; SSC 4**
See also CA 9-12R; 151; CANR 33; DLB 15; MTCW

**Lavond, Paul Dennis**
See Kornbluth, C(yril) M.; Pohl, Frederik

**Lawler, Raymond Evenor** 1922- .... **CLC 58**
See also CA 103

**Lawrence, D(avid) H(erbert Richards)**
1885-1930 .... **TCLC 2, 9, 16, 33, 48, 61; DA; DAB; DAC; DAM MST, NOV, POET; SSC 4, 19; WLC**
See also CA 104; 121; CDBLB 1914-1945; DLB 10, 19, 36, 98, 162; MTCW

**Lawrence, T(homas) E(dward)**
1888-1935 .................. **TCLC 18**
See also Dale, Colin
See also CA 115

**Lawrence of Arabia**
See Lawrence, T(homas) E(dward)

**Lawson, Henry (Archibald Hertzberg)**
1867-1922 .......... **TCLC 27; SSC 18**
See also CA 120

**Lawton, Dennis**
See Faust, Frederick (Schiller)

**Laxness, Halldor** .................. **CLC 25**
See also Gudjonsson, Halldor Kiljan

**Layamon** fl. c. 1200- ............ **CMLC 10**
See also DLB 146

**Laye, Camara**
1928-1980 ........... **CLC 4, 38; BLC; DAM MULT**
See also BW 1; CA 85-88; 97-100; CANR 25; MTCW

**Layton, Irving (Peter)**
1912- .... **CLC 2, 15; DAC; DAM MST, POET**
See also CA 1-4R; CANR 2, 33, 43; DLB 88; MTCW

**Lazarus, Emma** 1849-1887 ........ **NCLC 8**

**Lazarus, Felix**
See Cable, George Washington

**Lazarus, Henry**
See Slavitt, David R(ytman)

**Lea, Joan**
See Neufeld, John (Arthur)

**Leacock, Stephen (Butler)**
1869-1944 .. **TCLC 2; DAC; DAM MST**
See also CA 104; 141; DLB 92

**Lear, Edward** 1812-1888 ......... **NCLC 3**
See also CLR 1; DLB 32, 163, 166; MAICYA; SATA 18

**Lear, Norman (Milton)** 1922- ...... **CLC 12**
See also CA 73-76

**Leavis, F(rank) R(aymond)**
1895-1978 .................. **CLC 24**
See also CA 21-24R; 77-80; CANR 44; MTCW

**Leavitt, David** 1961- ... **CLC 34; DAM POP**
See also CA 116; 122; CANR 50; DLB 130; INT 122

**Lester, Richard** 1932- . . . . . . . . . . . . . **CLC 20**

**Lever, Charles (James)**
1806-1872 . . . . . . . . . . . . . . . . . **NCLC 23**
See also DLB 21

**Leverson, Ada** 1865(?)-1936(?) . . . . **TCLC 18**
See also Elaine
See also CA 117; DLB 153

**Levertov, Denise**
1923- . . . . . . **CLC 1, 2, 3, 5, 8, 15, 28, 66; DAM POET; PC 11**
See also CA 1-4R; CAAS 19; CANR 3, 29, 50; DLB 5, 165; INT CANR-29; MTCW

**Levi, Jonathan** . . . . . . . . . . . . . . . . . . . **CLC 76**

**Levi, Peter (Chad Tigar)** 1931- . . . . . **CLC 41**
See also CA 5-8R; CANR 34; DLB 40

**Levi, Primo**
1919-1987 . . . . . . . . **CLC 37, 50; SSC 12**
See also CA 13-16R; 122; CANR 12, 33; MTCW

**Levin, Ira** 1929- . . . . . **CLC 3, 6; DAM POP**
See also CA 21-24R; CANR 17, 44; MTCW; SATA 66

**Levin, Meyer**
1905-1981 . . . . . . . . . **CLC 7; DAM POP**
See also AITN 1; CA 9-12R; 104; CANR 15; DLB 9, 28; DLBY 81; SATA 21; SATA-Obit 27

**Levine, Norman** 1924- . . . . . . . . . . . . **CLC 54**
See also CA 73-76; CAAS 23; CANR 14; DLB 88

**Levine, Philip**
1928- . . . . . . . . . . . **CLC 2, 4, 5, 9, 14, 33; DAM POET**
See also CA 9-12R; CANR 9, 37, 52; DLB 5

**Levinson, Deirdre** 1931- . . . . . . . . . . . **CLC 49**
See also CA 73-76

**Levi-Strauss, Claude** 1908- . . . . . . . . **CLC 38**
See also CA 1-4R; CANR 6, 32; MTCW

**Levitin, Sonia (Wolff)** 1934- . . . . . . . **CLC 17**
See also AAYA 13; CA 29-32R; CANR 14, 32; JRDA; MAICYA; SAAS 2; SATA 4, 68

**Levon, O. U.**
See Kesey, Ken (Elton)

**Levy, Amy** 1861-1889. . . . . . . . . . . **NCLC 59**
See also DLB 156

**Lewes, George Henry**
1817-1878 . . . . . . . . . . . . . . . . . **NCLC 25**
See also DLB 55, 144

**Lewis, Alun** 1915-1944. . . . . . . . . . . . **TCLC 3**
See also CA 104; DLB 20, 162

**Lewis, C. Day**
See Day Lewis, C(ecil)

**Lewis, C(live) S(taples)**
1898-1963 . . . . . **CLC 1, 3, 6, 14, 27; DA; DAB; DAC; DAM MST, NOV, POP; WLC**
See also AAYA 3; CA 81-84; CANR 33; CDBLB 1945-1960; CLR 3, 27; DLB 15, 100, 160; JRDA; MAICYA; MTCW; SATA 13

**Lewis, Janet** 1899- . . . . . . . . . . . . . . . **CLC 41**
See also Winters, Janet Lewis
See also CA 9-12R; CANR 29; CAP 1; DLBY 87

**Lewis, Matthew Gregory**
1775-1818 . . . . . . . . . . . . . . . . . **NCLC 11**
See also DLB 39, 158

**Lewis, (Harry) Sinclair**
1885-1951 . . . . . **TCLC 4, 13, 23, 39; DA; DAB; DAC; DAM MST, NOV; WLC**
See also CA 104; 133; CDALB 1917-1929; DLB 9, 102; DLBD 1; MTCW

**Lewis, (Percy) Wyndham**
1884(?)-1957 . . . . . . . . . . . . . . . **TCLC 2, 9**
See also CA 104; DLB 15

**Lewisohn, Ludwig** 1883-1955. . . . . . **TCLC 19**
See also CA 107; DLB 4, 9, 28, 102

**Leyner, Mark** 1956- . . . . . . . . . . . . . . **CLC 92**
See also CA 110; CANR 28, 53

**Lezama Lima, Jose**
1910-1976 . . . . **CLC 4, 10; DAM MULT**
See also CA 77-80; DLB 113; HW

**L'Heureux, John (Clarke)** 1934- . . . . **CLC 52**
See also CA 13-16R; CANR 23, 45

**Liddell, C. H.**
See Kuttner, Henry

**Lie, Jonas (Lauritz Idemil)**
1833-1908(?) . . . . . . . . . . . . . . . . . **TCLC 5**
See also CA 115

**Lieber, Joel** 1937-1971. . . . . . . . . . . . . **CLC 6**
See also CA 73-76; 29-32R

**Lieber, Stanley Martin**
See Lee, Stan

**Lieberman, Laurence (James)**
1935- . . . . . . . . . . . . . . . . . . . . . **CLC 4, 36**
See also CA 17-20R; CANR 8, 36

**Lieksman, Anders**
See Haavikko, Paavo Juhani

**Li Fei-kan** 1904-
See Pa Chin
See also CA 105

**Lifton, Robert Jay** 1926- . . . . . . . . . . **CLC 67**
See also CA 17-20R; CANR 27; INT CANR-27; SATA 66

**Lightfoot, Gordon** 1938- . . . . . . . . . . . **CLC 26**
See also CA 109

**Lightman, Alan P.** 1948- . . . . . . . . . . **CLC 81**
See also CA 141

**Ligotti, Thomas (Robert)**
1953- . . . . . . . . . . . . . . . . **CLC 44; SSC 16**
See also CA 123; CANR 49

**Li Ho** 791-817. . . . . . . . . . . . . . . . . . . . **PC 13**

**Liliencron, (Friedrich Adolf Axel) Detlev von**
1844-1909 . . . . . . . . . . . . . . . . . . **TCLC 18**
See also CA 117

**Lilly, William** 1602-1681 . . . . . . . . . . . **LC 27**

**Lima, Jose Lezama**
See Lezama Lima, Jose

**Lima Barreto, Afonso Henrique de**
1881-1922 . . . . . . . . . . . . . . . . . . **TCLC 23**
See also CA 117

**Limonov, Edward** 1944- . . . . . . . . . . . **CLC 67**
See also CA 137

**Lin, Frank**
See Atherton, Gertrude (Franklin Horn)

**Lincoln, Abraham** 1809-1865. . . . . **NCLC 18**

**Lind, Jakov** . . . . . . . . . . . . **CLC 1, 2, 4, 27, 82**
See also Landwirth, Heinz
See also CAAS 4

**Lindbergh, Anne (Spencer) Morrow**
1906- . . . . . . . . . . . . **CLC 82; DAM NOV**
See also CA 17-20R; CANR 16; MTCW; SATA 33

**Lindsay, David** 1878-1945 . . . . . . . . **TCLC 15**
See also CA 113

**Lindsay, (Nicholas) Vachel**
1879-1931 . . . . . . . . **TCLC 17; DA; DAC; DAM MST, POET; WLC**
See also CA 114; 135; CDALB 1865-1917; DLB 54; SATA 40

**Linke-Poot**
See Doeblin, Alfred

**Linney, Romulus** 1930- . . . . . . . . . . . **CLC 51**
See also CA 1-4R; CANR 40, 44

**Linton, Eliza Lynn** 1822-1898. . . . **NCLC 41**
See also DLB 18

**Li Po** 701-763 . . . . . . . . . . . . . . . . . . **CMLC 2**

**Lipsius, Justus** 1547-1606 . . . . . . . . . . **LC 16**

**Lipsyte, Robert (Michael)**
1938- . . . . . . . . . . . . . **CLC 21; DA; DAC; DAM MST, NOV**
See also AAYA 7; CA 17-20R; CANR 8; CLR 23; JRDA; MAICYA; SATA 5, 68

**Lish, Gordon (Jay)** 1934- . . **CLC 45; SSC 18**
See also CA 113; 117; DLB 130; INT 117

**Lispector, Clarice** 1925-1977 . . . . . . . **CLC 43**
See also CA 139; 116; DLB 113

**Littell, Robert** 1935(?)- . . . . . . . . . . . **CLC 42**
See also CA 109; 112

**Little, Malcolm** 1925-1965
See Malcolm X
See also BW 1; CA 125; 111; DA; DAB; DAC; DAM MST, MULT; MTCW

**Littlewit, Humphrey Gent.**
See Lovecraft, H(oward) P(hillips)

**Litwos**
See Sienkiewicz, Henryk (Adam Alexander Pius)

**Liu E** 1857-1909 . . . . . . . . . . . . . . . . **TCLC 15**
See also CA 115

**Lively, Penelope (Margaret)**
1933- . . . . . . . . . **CLC 32, 50; DAM NOV**
See also CA 41-44R; CANR 29; CLR 7; DLB 14, 161; JRDA; MAICYA; MTCW; SATA 7, 60

**Livesay, Dorothy (Kathleen)**
1909- . . . . . . . . . . . . **CLC 4, 15, 79; DAC; DAM MST, POET**
See also AITN 2; CA 25-28R; CAAS 8; CANR 36; DLB 68; MTCW

**Livy** c. 59B.C.-c. 17 . . . . . . . . . . . . **CMLC 11**

**Lizardi, Jose Joaquin Fernandez de**
1776-1827 . . . . . . . . . . . . . . . . . **NCLC 30**

**Llewellyn, Richard**
See Llewellyn Lloyd, Richard Dafydd Vivian
See also DLB 15

**Llewellyn Lloyd, Richard Dafydd Vivian** 1906-1983 .................. **CLC 7, 80**
See also Llewellyn, Richard
See also CA 53-56; 111; CANR 7; SATA 11; SATA-Obit 37

**Llosa, (Jorge) Mario (Pedro) Vargas**
See Vargas Llosa, (Jorge) Mario (Pedro)

**Lloyd Webber, Andrew** 1948-
See Webber, Andrew Lloyd
See also AAYA 1; CA 116; 149; DAM DRAM; SATA 56

**Llull, Ramon** c. 1235-c. 1316..... **CMLC 12**

**Locke, Alain (Le Roy)** 1886-1954 .................. **TCLC 43**
See also BW 1; CA 106; 124; DLB 51

**Locke, John** 1632-1704 .......... **LC 7, 35**
See also DLB 101

**Locke-Elliott, Sumner**
See Elliott, Sumner Locke

**Lockhart, John Gibson** 1794-1854 .................. **NCLC 6**
See also DLB 110, 116, 144

**Lodge, David (John)** 1935- ............ **CLC 36; DAM POP**
See also BEST 90:1; CA 17-20R; CANR 19, 53; DLB 14; INT CANR-19; MTCW

**Loennbohm, Armas Eino Leopold** 1878-1926
See Leino, Eino
See also CA 123

**Loewinsohn, Ron(ald William)** 1937- ........................ **CLC 52**
See also CA 25-28R

**Logan, Jake**
See Smith, Martin Cruz

**Logan, John (Burton)** 1923-1987..... **CLC 5**
See also CA 77-80; 124; CANR 45; DLB 5

**Lo Kuan-chung** 1330(?)-1400(?)...... **LC 12**

**Lombard, Nap**
See Johnson, Pamela Hansford

**London, Jack**.. **TCLC 9, 15, 39; SSC 4; WLC**
See also London, John Griffith
See also AAYA 13; AITN 2; CDALB 1865-1917; DLB 8, 12, 78; SATA 18

**London, John Griffith** 1876-1916
See London, Jack
See also CA 110; 119; DA; DAB; DAC; DAM MST, NOV; JRDA; MAICYA; MTCW

**Long, Emmett**
See Leonard, Elmore (John, Jr.)

**Longbaugh, Harry**
See Goldman, William (W.)

**Longfellow, Henry Wadsworth** 1807-1882 ..... **NCLC 2, 45; DA; DAB; DAC; DAM MST, POET**
See also CDALB 1640-1865; DLB 1, 59; SATA 19

**Longley, Michael** 1939-........... **CLC 29**
See also CA 102; DLB 40

**Longus** fl. c. 2nd cent. -........... **CMLC 7**

**Longway, A. Hugh**
See Lang, Andrew

**Lonnrot, Elias** 1802-1884........ **NCLC 53**

**Lopate, Phillip** 1943- ............. **CLC 29**
See also CA 97-100; DLBY 80; INT 97-100

**Lopez Portillo (y Pacheco), Jose** 1920- ........................ **CLC 46**
See also CA 129; HW

**Lopez y Fuentes, Gregorio** 1897(?)-1966 ................. **CLC 32**
See also CA 131; HW

**Lorca, Federico Garcia**
See Garcia Lorca, Federico

**Lord, Bette Bao** 1938- ............ **CLC 23**
See also BEST 90:3; CA 107; CANR 41; INT 107; SATA 58

**Lord Auch**
See Bataille, Georges

**Lord Byron**
See Byron, George Gordon (Noel)

**Lorde, Audre (Geraldine)** 1934-1992 .......... **CLC 18, 71; BLC; DAM MULT, POET; PC 12**
See also BW 1; CA 25-28R; 142; CANR 16, 26, 46; DLB 41; MTCW

**Lord Jeffrey**
See Jeffrey, Francis

**Lorenzini, Carlo** 1826-1890
See Collodi, Carlo
See also MAICYA; SATA 29

**Lorenzo, Heberto Padilla**
See Padilla (Lorenzo), Heberto

**Loris**
See Hofmannsthal, Hugo von

**Loti, Pierre** ..................... **TCLC 11**
See also Viaud, (Louis Marie) Julien
See also DLB 123

**Louie, David Wong** 1954- ......... **CLC 70**
See also CA 139

**Louis, Father M.**
See Merton, Thomas

**Lovecraft, H(oward) P(hillips)** 1890-1937 .... **TCLC 4, 22; DAM POP; SSC 3**
See also AAYA 14; CA 104; 133; MTCW

**Lovelace, Earl** 1935-............. **CLC 51**
See also BW 2; CA 77-80; CANR 41; DLB 125; MTCW

**Lovelace, Richard** 1618-1657........ **LC 24**
See also DLB 131

**Lowell, Amy** 1874-1925 .... **TCLC 1, 8; DAM POET; PC 13**
See also CA 104; 151; DLB 54, 140

**Lowell, James Russell** 1819-1891 .. **NCLC 2**
See also CDALB 1640-1865; DLB 1, 11, 64, 79

**Lowell, Robert (Traill Spence, Jr.)** 1917-1977 ... **CLC 1, 2, 3, 4, 5, 8, 9, 11, 15, 37; DA; DAB; DAC; DAM MST, NOV; PC 3; WLC**
See also CA 9-12R; 73-76; CABS 2; CANR 26; DLB 5, 169; MTCW

**Lowndes, Marie Adelaide (Belloc)** 1868-1947 .................. **TCLC 12**
See also CA 107; DLB 70

**Lowry, (Clarence) Malcolm** 1909-1957 ................ **TCLC 6, 40**
See also CA 105; 131; CDBLB 1945-1960; DLB 15; MTCW

**Lowry, Mina Gertrude** 1882-1966
See Loy, Mina
See also CA 113

**Loxsmith, John**
See Brunner, John (Kilian Houston)

**Loy, Mina** .... **CLC 28; DAM POET; PC 16**
See also Lowry, Mina Gertrude
See also DLB 4, 54

**Loyson-Bridet**
See Schwob, (Mayer Andre) Marcel

**Lucas, Craig** 1951- ................ **CLC 64**
See also CA 137

**Lucas, George** 1944-.............. **CLC 16**
See also AAYA 1; CA 77-80; CANR 30; SATA 56

**Lucas, Hans**
See Godard, Jean-Luc

**Lucas, Victoria**
See Plath, Sylvia

**Ludlam, Charles** 1943-1987..... **CLC 46, 50**
See also CA 85-88; 122

**Ludlum, Robert** 1927- ... **CLC 22, 43; DAM NOV, POP**
See also AAYA 10; BEST 89:1, 90:3; CA 33-36R; CANR 25, 41; DLBY 82; MTCW

**Ludwig, Ken**...................... **CLC 60**

**Ludwig, Otto** 1813-1865.......... **NCLC 4**
See also DLB 129

**Lugones, Leopoldo** 1874-1938 ..... **TCLC 15**
See also CA 116; 131; HW

**Lu Hsun** 1881-1936 ...... **TCLC 3; SSC 20**
See also Shu-Jen, Chou

**Lukacs, George** ................... **CLC 24**
See also Lukacs, Gyorgy (Szegeny von)

**Lukacs, Gyorgy (Szegeny von)** 1885-1971
See Lukacs, George
See also CA 101; 29-32R

**Luke, Peter (Ambrose Cyprian)** 1919-1995 ................... **CLC 38**
See also CA 81-84; 147; DLB 13

**Lunar, Dennis**
See Mungo, Raymond

**Lurie, Alison** 1926-........ **CLC 4, 5, 18, 39**
See also CA 1-4R; CANR 2, 17, 50; DLB 2; MTCW; SATA 46

**Lustig, Arnost** 1926-............. **CLC 56**
See also AAYA 3; CA 69-72; CANR 47; SATA 56

**Luther, Martin** 1483-1546 ........ **LC 9, 37**

**Luxemburg, Rosa** 1870(?)-1919.... **TCLC 63**
See also CA 118

**Luzi, Mario** 1914-................ **CLC 13**
See also CA 61-64; CANR 9; DLB 128

**L'Ymagier**
See Gourmont, Remy (-Marie-Charles) de

**Lynch, B. Suarez**
See Bioy Casares, Adolfo; Borges, Jorge Luis

**Lynch, David (K.)** 1946- . . . . . . . . . . . **CLC 66**
See also CA 124; 129

**Lynch, James**
See Andreyev, Leonid (Nikolaevich)

**Lynch Davis, B.**
See Bioy Casares, Adolfo; Borges, Jorge Luis

**Lyndsay, Sir David** 1490-1555 . . . . . . **LC 20**

**Lynn, Kenneth S(chuyler)** 1923- . . . . **CLC 50**
See also CA 1-4R; CANR 3, 27

**Lynx**
See West, Rebecca

**Lyons, Marcus**
See Blish, James (Benjamin)

**Lyre, Pinchbeck**
See Sassoon, Siegfried (Lorraine)

**Lytle, Andrew (Nelson)** 1902-1995 . . **CLC 22**
See also CA 9-12R; 150; DLB 6; DLBY 95

**Lyttelton, George** 1709-1773 . . . . . . . . **LC 10**

**Maas, Peter** 1929- . . . . . . . . . . . . . . . **CLC 29**
See also CA 93-96; INT 93-96

**Macaulay, Rose** 1881-1958 . . . . . **TCLC 7, 44**
See also CA 104; DLB 36

**Macaulay, Thomas Babington**
1800-1859 . . . . . . . . . . . . . . . . . **NCLC 42**
See also CDBLB 1832-1890; DLB 32, 55

**MacBeth, George (Mann)**
1932-1992 . . . . . . . . . . . . . . . . **CLC 2, 5, 9**
See also CA 25-28R; 136; DLB 40; MTCW; SATA 4; SATA-Obit 70

**MacCaig, Norman (Alexander)**
1910- . . . . . **CLC 36; DAB; DAM POET**
See also CA 9-12R; CANR 3, 34; DLB 27

**MacCarthy, (Sir Charles Otto) Desmond**
1877-1952 . . . . . . . . . . . . . . . . . . **TCLC 36**

**MacDiarmid, Hugh**
. . . . . . . . . . . **CLC 2, 4, 11, 19, 63; PC 9**
See also Grieve, C(hristopher) M(urray)
See also CDBLB 1945-1960; DLB 20

**MacDonald, Anson**
See Heinlein, Robert A(nson)

**Macdonald, Cynthia** 1928- . . . . . . **CLC 13, 19**
See also CA 49-52; CANR 4, 44; DLB 105

**MacDonald, George** 1824-1905 . . . . . **TCLC 9**
See also CA 106; 137; DLB 18, 163; MAICYA; SATA 33

**Macdonald, John**
See Millar, Kenneth

**MacDonald, John D(ann)**
1916-1986 . . . . . . . . . . . . . **CLC 3, 27, 44; DAM NOV, POP**
See also CA 1-4R; 121; CANR 1, 19; DLB 8; DLBY 86; MTCW

**Macdonald, John Ross**
See Millar, Kenneth

**Macdonald, Ross** . . . . . **CLC 1, 2, 3, 14, 34, 41**
See also Millar, Kenneth
See also DLBD 6

**MacDougal, John**
See Blish, James (Benjamin)

**MacEwen, Gwendolyn (Margaret)**
1941-1987 . . . . . . . . . . . . . . . . **CLC 13, 55**
See also CA 9-12R; 124; CANR 7, 22; DLB 53; SATA 50; SATA-Obit 55

**Macha, Karel Hynek** 1810-1846 . . **NCLC 46**

**Machado (y Ruiz), Antonio**
1875-1939 . . . . . . . . . . . . . . . . . . . **TCLC 3**
See also CA 104; DLB 108

**Machado de Assis, Joaquim Maria**
1839-1908 . . . . . **TCLC 10; BLC; SSC 24**
See also CA 107; 153

**Machen, Arthur** . . . . . . . . . . . **TCLC 4; SSC 20**
See also Jones, Arthur Llewellyn
See also DLB 36, 156

**Machiavelli, Niccolo**
1469-1527 . . . . . . . . **LC 8, 36; DA; DAB; DAC; DAM MST**

**MacInnes, Colin** 1914-1976 . . . . . . **CLC 4, 23**
See also CA 69-72; 65-68; CANR 21; DLB 14; MTCW

**MacInnes, Helen (Clark)**
1907-1985 . . . . . **CLC 27, 39; DAM POP**
See also CA 1-4R; 117; CANR 1, 28; DLB 87; MTCW; SATA 22; SATA-Obit 44

**Mackay, Mary** 1855-1924
See Corelli, Marie
See also CA 118

**Mackenzie, Compton (Edward Montague)**
1883-1972 . . . . . . . . . . . . . . . . . . . **CLC 18**
See also CA 21-22; 37-40R; CAP 2; DLB 34, 100

**Mackenzie, Henry** 1745-1831 . . . . **NCLC 41**
See also DLB 39

**Mackintosh, Elizabeth** 1896(?)-1952
See Tey, Josephine
See also CA 110

**MacLaren, James**
See Grieve, C(hristopher) M(urray)

**Mac Laverty, Bernard** 1942- . . . . . . . **CLC 31**
See also CA 116; 118; CANR 43; INT 118

**MacLean, Alistair (Stuart)**
1922-1987 . . . . . . . . . . **CLC 3, 13, 50, 63; DAM POP**
See also CA 57-60; 121; CANR 28; MTCW; SATA 23; SATA-Obit 50

**Maclean, Norman (Fitzroy)**
1902-1990 . . . . . . . . **CLC 78; DAM POP; SSC 13**
See also CA 102; 132; CANR 49

**MacLeish, Archibald**
1892-1982 . . . . . . . . . . . **CLC 3, 8, 14, 68; DAM POET**
See also CA 9-12R; 106; CANR 33; DLB 4, 7, 45; DLBY 82; MTCW

**MacLennan, (John) Hugh**
1907-1990 . . . . . . . . **CLC 2, 14, 92; DAC; DAM MST**
See also CA 5-8R; 142; CANR 33; DLB 68; MTCW

**MacLeod, Alistair**
1936- . . . . . . **CLC 56; DAC; DAM MST**
See also CA 123; DLB 60

**MacNeice, (Frederick) Louis**
1907-1963 . . . . . . **CLC 1, 4, 10, 53; DAB; DAM POET**
See also CA 85-88; DLB 10, 20; MTCW

**MacNeill, Dand**
See Fraser, George MacDonald

**Macpherson, James** 1736-1796 . . . . . . **LC 29**
See also DLB 109

**Macpherson, (Jean) Jay** 1931- . . . . . . **CLC 14**
See also CA 5-8R; DLB 53

**MacShane, Frank** 1927- . . . . . . . . . . . **CLC 39**
See also CA 9-12R; CANR 3, 33; DLB 111

**Macumber, Mari**
See Sandoz, Mari(e Susette)

**Madach, Imre** 1823-1864 . . . . . . . . **NCLC 19**

**Madden, (Jerry) David** 1933- . . . . **CLC 5, 15**
See also CA 1-4R; CAAS 3; CANR 4, 45; DLB 6; MTCW

**Maddern, Al(an)**
See Ellison, Harlan (Jay)

**Madhubuti, Haki R.**
1942- . . . . . . . . . . . . . . . **CLC 6, 73; BLC; DAM MULT, POET; PC 5**
See also Lee, Don L.
See also BW 2; CA 73-76; CANR 24, 51; DLB 5, 41; DLBD 8

**Maepenn, Hugh**
See Kuttner, Henry

**Maepenn, K. H.**
See Kuttner, Henry

**Maeterlinck, Maurice**
1862-1949 . . . . . . **TCLC 3; DAM DRAM**
See also CA 104; 136; SATA 66

**Maginn, William** 1794-1842 . . . . . . . **NCLC 8**
See also DLB 110, 159

**Mahapatra, Jayanta**
1928- . . . . . . . . . . **CLC 33; DAM MULT**
See also CA 73-76; CAAS 9; CANR 15, 33

**Mahfouz, Naguib (Abdel Aziz Al-Sabilgi)**
1911(?)-
See Mahfuz, Najib
See also BEST 89:2; CA 128; CANR 55; DAM NOV; MTCW

**Mahfuz, Najib** . . . . . . . . . . . . . . . . . **CLC 52, 55**
See also Mahfouz, Naguib (Abdel Aziz Al-Sabilgi)
See also DLBY 88

**Mahon, Derek** 1941- . . . . . . . . . . . . . . **CLC 27**
See also CA 113; 128; DLB 40

**Mailer, Norman**
1923- . . . . . . **CLC 1, 2, 3, 4, 5, 8, 11, 14, 28, 39, 74; DA; DAB; DAC; DAM MST, NOV, POP**
See also AITN 2; CA 9-12R; CABS 1; CANR 28; CDALB 1968-1988; DLB 2, 16, 28; DLBD 3; DLBY 80, 83; MTCW

**Maillet, Antonine** 1929- . . . . . . **CLC 54; DAC**
See also CA 115; 120; CANR 46; DLB 60; INT 120

**Mais, Roger** 1905-1955 . . . . . . . . . . . **TCLC 8**
See also BW 1; CA 105; 124; DLB 125; MTCW

**Maistre, Joseph de** 1753-1821 . . . . **NCLC 37**

**Maitland, Frederic** 1850-1906 . . . . . **TCLC 65**

**Maitland, Sara (Louise)** 1950- . . . . . . **CLC 49**
See also CA 69-72; CANR 13

**Major, Clarence**
1936- . . . . . . . . . . . . **CLC 3, 19, 48; BLC; DAM MULT**
See also BW 2; CA 21-24R; CAAS 6; CANR 13, 25, 53; DLB 33

**Marshall, Paule**
1929- .............. **CLC 27, 72; BLC; DAM MULT; SSC 3**
See also BW 2; CA 77-80; CANR 25; DLB 157; MTCW

**Marsten, Richard**
See Hunter, Evan

**Marston, John**
1576-1634 ....... **LC 33; DAM DRAM**
See also DLB 58, 172

**Martha, Henry**
See Harris, Mark

**Martial** c. 40-c. 104 ............... **PC 10**

**Martin, Ken**
See Hubbard, L(afayette) Ron(ald)

**Martin, Richard**
See Creasey, John

**Martin, Steve** 1945- .............. **CLC 30**
See also CA 97-100; CANR 30; MTCW

**Martin, Valerie** 1948- ............. **CLC 89**
See also BEST 90:2; CA 85-88; CANR 49

**Martin, Violet Florence**
1862-1915 .................. **TCLC 51**

**Martin, Webber**
See Silverberg, Robert

**Martindale, Patrick Victor**
See White, Patrick (Victor Martindale)

**Martin du Gard, Roger**
1881-1958 .................. **TCLC 24**
See also CA 118; DLB 65

**Martineau, Harriet** 1802-1876.... **NCLC 26**
See also DLB 21, 55, 159, 163, 166; YABC 2

**Martines, Julia**
See O'Faolain, Julia

**Martinez, Jacinto Benavente y**
See Benavente (y Martinez), Jacinto

**Martinez Ruiz, Jose** 1873-1967
See Azorin; Ruiz, Jose Martinez
See also CA 93-96; HW

**Martinez Sierra, Gregorio**
1881-1947 .................. **TCLC 6**
See also CA 115

**Martinez Sierra, Maria (de la O'LeJarraga)**
1874-1974 .................. **TCLC 6**
See also CA 115

**Martinsen, Martin**
See Follett, Ken(neth Martin)

**Martinson, Harry (Edmund)**
1904-1978 .................. **CLC 14**
See also CA 77-80; CANR 34

**Marut, Ret**
See Traven, B.

**Marut, Robert**
See Traven, B.

**Marvell, Andrew**
1621-1678 ...... **LC 4; DA; DAB; DAC; DAM MST, POET; PC 10; WLC**
See also CDBLB 1660-1789; DLB 131

**Marx, Karl (Heinrich)**
1818-1883 ................. **NCLC 17**
See also DLB 129

**Masaoka Shiki** .................. **TCLC 18**
See also Masaoka Tsunenori

**Masaoka Tsunenori** 1867-1902
See Masaoka Shiki
See also CA 117

**Masefield, John (Edward)**
1878-1967 .... **CLC 11, 47; DAM POET**
See also CA 19-20; 25-28R; CANR 33; CAP 2; CDBLB 1890-1914; DLB 10, 19, 153, 160; MTCW; SATA 19

**Maso, Carole** 19(?)- .............. **CLC 44**

**Mason, Bobbie Ann**
1940- .......... **CLC 28, 43, 82; SSC 4**
See also AAYA 5; CA 53-56; CANR 11, 31; DLB 173; DLBY 87; INT CANR-31; MTCW

**Mason, Ernst**
See Pohl, Frederik

**Mason, Lee W.**
See Malzberg, Barry N(athaniel)

**Mason, Nick** 1945- ............... **CLC 35**

**Mason, Tally**
See Derleth, August (William)

**Mass, William**
See Gibson, William

**Masters, Edgar Lee**
1868-1950 ...... **TCLC 2, 25; DA; DAC; DAM MST, POET; PC 1**
See also CA 104; 133; CDALB 1865-1917; DLB 54; MTCW

**Masters, Hilary** 1928- ............ **CLC 48**
See also CA 25-28R; CANR 13, 47

**Mastrosimone, William** 19(?)- ...... **CLC 36**

**Mathe, Albert**
See Camus, Albert

**Matheson, Richard Burton** 1926- ... **CLC 37**
See also CA 97-100; DLB 8, 44; INT 97-100

**Mathews, Harry** 1930- .......... **CLC 6, 52**
See also CA 21-24R; CAAS 6; CANR 18, 40

**Mathews, John Joseph**
1894-1979 ...... **CLC 84; DAM MULT**
See also CA 19-20; 142; CANR 45; CAP 2; NNAL

**Mathias, Roland (Glyn)** 1915- ...... **CLC 45**
See also CA 97-100; CANR 19, 41; DLB 27

**Matsuo Basho** 1644-1694 ............ **PC 3**
See also DAM POET

**Mattheson, Rodney**
See Creasey, John

**Matthews, Greg** 1949- ............ **CLC 45**
See also CA 135

**Matthews, William** 1942- .......... **CLC 40**
See also CA 29-32R; CAAS 18; CANR 12; DLB 5

**Matthias, John (Edward)** 1941- ...... **CLC 9**
See also CA 33-36R

**Matthiessen, Peter**
1927- ............ **CLC 5, 7, 11, 32, 64; DAM NOV**
See also AAYA 6; BEST 90:4; CA 9-12R; CANR 21, 50; DLB 6, 173; MTCW; SATA 27

**Maturin, Charles Robert**
1780(?)-1824 ................ **NCLC 6**

**Matute (Ausejo), Ana Maria**
1925- ........................ **CLC 11**
See also CA 89-92; MTCW

**Maugham, W. S.**
See Maugham, W(illiam) Somerset

**Maugham, W(illiam) Somerset**
1874-1965 ....... **CLC 1, 11, 15, 67, 93; DA; DAB; DAC; DAM DRAM, MST, NOV; SSC 8; WLC**
See also CA 5-8R; 25-28R; CANR 40; CDBLB 1914-1945; DLB 10, 36, 77, 100, 162; MTCW; SATA 54

**Maugham, William Somerset**
See Maugham, W(illiam) Somerset

**Maupassant, (Henri Rene Albert) Guy de**
1850-1893 ..... **NCLC 1, 42; DA; DAB; DAC; DAM MST; SSC 1; WLC**
See also DLB 123

**Maupin, Armistead**
1944- ............ **CLC 95; DAM POP**
See also CA 125; 130; INT 130

**Maurhut, Richard**
See Traven, B.

**Mauriac, Claude** 1914-1996 ......... **CLC 9**
See also CA 89-92; 152; DLB 83

**Mauriac, Francois (Charles)**
1885-1970 ....... **CLC 4, 9, 56; SSC 24**
See also CA 25-28; CAP 2; DLB 65; MTCW

**Mavor, Osborne Henry** 1888-1951
See Bridie, James
See also CA 104

**Maxwell, William (Keepers, Jr.)**
1908- ....................... **CLC 19**
See also CA 93-96; CANR 54; DLBY 80; INT 93-96

**May, Elaine** 1932- ............... **CLC 16**
See also CA 124; 142; DLB 44

**Mayakovski, Vladimir (Vladimirovich)**
1893-1930 ................ **TCLC 4, 18**
See also CA 104

**Mayhew, Henry** 1812-1887 ...... **NCLC 31**
See also DLB 18, 55

**Mayle, Peter** 1939(?)- ............. **CLC 89**
See also CA 139

**Maynard, Joyce** 1953- ............ **CLC 23**
See also CA 111; 129

**Mayne, William (James Carter)**
1928- ....................... **CLC 12**
See also CA 9-12R; CANR 37; CLR 25; JRDA; MAICYA; SAAS 11; SATA 6, 68

**Mayo, Jim**
See L'Amour, Louis (Dearborn)

**Maysles, Albert** 1926- ............ **CLC 16**
See also CA 29-32R

**Maysles, David** 1932- ............. **CLC 16**

**Mazer, Norma Fox** 1931- ......... **CLC 26**
See also AAYA 5; CA 69-72; CANR 12, 32; CLR 23; JRDA; MAICYA; SAAS 1; SATA 24, 67

**Mazzini, Guiseppe** 1805-1872 .... **NCLC 34**

**McAuley, James Phillip**
1917-1976 .................. **CLC 45**
See also CA 97-100

**McBain, Ed**
See Hunter, Evan

**McBrien, William Augustine**
1930- . . . . . . . . . . . . . . . . . . . . . . . **CLC 44**
See also CA 107

**McCaffrey, Anne (Inez)**
1926- . . . . . . **CLC 17; DAM NOV, POP**
See also AAYA 6; AITN 2; BEST 89:2; CA 25-28R; CANR 15, 35, 55; DLB 8; JRDA; MAICYA; MTCW; SAAS 11; SATA 8, 70

**McCall, Nathan** 1955(?)- . . . . . . . . . . **CLC 86**
See also CA 146

**McCann, Arthur**
See Campbell, John W(ood, Jr.)

**McCann, Edson**
See Pohl, Frederik

**McCarthy, Charles, Jr.** 1933-
See McCarthy, Cormac
See also CANR 42; DAM POP

**McCarthy, Cormac** 1933- . . . . . **CLC 4, 57, 59**
See also McCarthy, Charles, Jr.
See also DLB 6, 143

**McCarthy, Mary (Therese)**
1912-1989 . . . . . . **CLC 1, 3, 5, 14, 24, 39, 59; SSC 24**
See also CA 5-8R; 129; CANR 16, 50; DLB 2; DLBY 81; INT CANR-16; MTCW

**McCartney, (James) Paul**
1942- . . . . . . . . . . . . . . . . . . . . **CLC 12, 35**
See also CA 146

**McCauley, Stephen (D.)** 1955- . . . . . **CLC 50**
See also CA 141

**McClure, Michael (Thomas)**
1932- . . . . . . . . . . . . . . . . . . . . . **CLC 6, 10**
See also CA 21-24R; CANR 17, 46; DLB 16

**McCorkle, Jill (Collins)** 1958- . . . . . . **CLC 51**
See also CA 121; DLBY 87

**McCourt, James** 1941- . . . . . . . . . . . . . **CLC 5**
See also CA 57-60

**McCoy, Horace (Stanley)**
1897-1955 . . . . . . . . . . . . . . . . . . **TCLC 28**
See also CA 108; 155; DLB 9

**McCrae, John** 1872-1918 . . . . . . . . . **TCLC 12**
See also CA 109; DLB 92

**McCreigh, James**
See Pohl, Frederik

**McCullers, (Lula) Carson (Smith)**
1917-1967 . . . . **CLC 1, 4, 10, 12, 48; DA; DAB; DAC; DAM MST, NOV; SSC 24; WLC**
See also CA 5-8R; 25-28R; CABS 1, 3; CANR 18; CDALB 1941-1968; DLB 2, 7, 173; MTCW; SATA 27

**McCulloch, John Tyler**
See Burroughs, Edgar Rice

**McCullough, Colleen**
1938(?)- . . . . **CLC 27; DAM NOV, POP**
See also CA 81-84; CANR 17, 46; MTCW

**McDermott, Alice** 1953- . . . . . . . . . . **CLC 90**
See also CA 109; CANR 40

**McElroy, Joseph** 1930- . . . . . . . . . **CLC 5, 47**
See also CA 17-20R

**McEwan, Ian (Russell)**
1948- . . . . . . . . . **CLC 13, 66; DAM NOV**
See also BEST 90:4; CA 61-64; CANR 14, 41; DLB 14; MTCW

**McFadden, David** 1940- . . . . . . . . . . . **CLC 48**
See also CA 104; DLB 60; INT 104

**McFarland, Dennis** 1950- . . . . . . . . . **CLC 65**

**McGahern, John**
1934- . . . . . . . . . . . **CLC 5, 9, 48; SSC 17**
See also CA 17-20R; CANR 29; DLB 14; MTCW

**McGinley, Patrick (Anthony)**
1937- . . . . . . . . . . . . . . . . . . . . . . . **CLC 41**
See also CA 120; 127; INT 127

**McGinley, Phyllis** 1905-1978 . . . . . . **CLC 14**
See also CA 9-12R; 77-80; CANR 19; DLB 11, 48; SATA 2, 44; SATA-Obit 24

**McGinniss, Joe** 1942- . . . . . . . . . . . . . **CLC 32**
See also AITN 2; BEST 89:2; CA 25-28R; CANR 26; INT CANR-26

**McGivern, Maureen Daly**
See Daly, Maureen

**McGrath, Patrick** 1950- . . . . . . . . . . . **CLC 55**
See also CA 136

**McGrath, Thomas (Matthew)**
1916-1990 . . . . **CLC 28, 59; DAM POET**
See also CA 9-12R; 132; CANR 6, 33; MTCW; SATA 41; SATA-Obit 66

**McGuane, Thomas (Francis III)**
1939- . . . . . . . . . . . . . . . . **CLC 3, 7, 18, 45**
See also AITN 2; CA 49-52; CANR 5, 24, 49; DLB 2; DLBY 80; INT CANR-24; MTCW

**McGuckian, Medbh**
1950- . . . . . . . . . . . **CLC 48; DAM POET**
See also CA 143; DLB 40

**McHale, Tom** 1942(?)-1982 . . . . . . . **CLC 3, 5**
See also AITN 1; CA 77-80; 106

**McIlvanney, William** 1936- . . . . . . . . . **CLC 42**
See also CA 25-28R; DLB 14

**McIlwraith, Maureen Mollie Hunter**
See Hunter, Mollie
See also SATA 2

**McInerney, Jay**
1955- . . . . . . . . . . . . **CLC 34; DAM POP**
See also AAYA 18; CA 116; 123; CANR 45; INT 123

**McIntyre, Vonda N(eel)** 1948- . . . . . **CLC 18**
See also CA 81-84; CANR 17, 34; MTCW

**McKay, Claude**
. . . . . . . . . **TCLC 7, 41; BLC; DAB; PC 2**
See also McKay, Festus Claudius
See also DLB 4, 45, 51, 117

**McKay, Festus Claudius** 1889-1948
See McKay, Claude
See also BW 1; CA 104; 124; DA; DAC; DAM MST, MULT, NOV, POET; MTCW; WLC

**McKuen, Rod** 1933- . . . . . . . . . . . . . **CLC 1, 3**
See also AITN 1; CA 41-44R; CANR 40

**McLoughlin, R. B.**
See Mencken, H(enry) L(ouis)

**McLuhan, (Herbert) Marshall**
1911-1980 . . . . . . . . . . . . . . . **CLC 37, 83**
See also CA 9-12R; 102; CANR 12, 34; DLB 88; INT CANR-12; MTCW

**McMillan, Terry (L.)**
1951- . . . . . . . **CLC 50, 61; DAM MULT, NOV, POP**
See also BW 2; CA 140

**McMurtry, Larry (Jeff)**
1936- . . . . . . . . . . **CLC 2, 3, 7, 11, 27, 44; DAM NOV, POP**
See also AAYA 15; AITN 2; BEST 89:2; CA 5-8R; CANR 19, 43; CDALB 1968-1988; DLB 2, 143; DLBY 80, 87; MTCW

**McNally, T. M.** 1961- . . . . . . . . . . . . **CLC 82**

**McNally, Terrence**
1939- . . . **CLC 4, 7, 41, 91; DAM DRAM**
See also CA 45-48; CANR 2; DLB 7

**McNamer, Deirdre** 1950- . . . . . . . . . . **CLC 70**

**McNeile, Herman Cyril** 1888-1937
See Sapper
See also DLB 77

**McNickle, (William) D'Arcy**
1904-1977 . . . . . . **CLC 89; DAM MULT**
See also CA 9-12R; 85-88; CANR 5, 45; NNAL; SATA-Obit 22

**McPhee, John (Angus)** 1931- . . . . . . **CLC 36**
See also BEST 90:1; CA 65-68; CANR 20, 46; MTCW

**McPherson, James Alan**
1943- . . . . . . . . . . . . . . . . . . . . **CLC 19, 77**
See also BW 1; CA 25-28R; CAAS 17; CANR 24; DLB 38; MTCW

**McPherson, William (Alexander)**
1933- . . . . . . . . . . . . . . . . . . . . . . . **CLC 34**
See also CA 69-72; CANR 28; INT CANR-28

**Mead, Margaret** 1901-1978 . . . . . . . . **CLC 37**
See also AITN 1; CA 1-4R; 81-84; CANR 4; MTCW; SATA-Obit 20

**Meaker, Marijane (Agnes)** 1927-
See Kerr, M. E.
See also CA 107; CANR 37; INT 107; JRDA; MAICYA; MTCW; SATA 20, 61

**Medoff, Mark (Howard)**
1940- . . . . . . . . **CLC 6, 23; DAM DRAM**
See also AITN 1; CA 53-56; CANR 5; DLB 7; INT CANR-5

**Medvedev, P. N.**
See Bakhtin, Mikhail Mikhailovich

**Meged, Aharon**
See Megged, Aharon

**Meged, Aron**
See Megged, Aharon

**Megged, Aharon** 1920- . . . . . . . . . . . . . **CLC 9**
See also CA 49-52; CAAS 13; CANR 1

**Mehta, Ved (Parkash)** 1934- . . . . . . . **CLC 37**
See also CA 1-4R; CANR 2, 23; MTCW

**Melanter**
See Blackmore, R(ichard) D(oddridge)

**Melikow, Loris**
See Hofmannsthal, Hugo von

**Melmoth, Sebastian**
See Wilde, Oscar (Fingal O'Flahertie Wills)

**Meltzer, Milton** 1915- . . . . . . . . . . . . **CLC 26**
See also AAYA 8; CA 13-16R; CANR 38; CLR 13; DLB 61; JRDA; MAICYA; SAAS 1; SATA 1, 50, 80

**Melville, Herman**
1819-1891 . . . . . **NCLC 3, 12, 29, 45, 49; DA; DAB; DAC; DAM MST, NOV; SSC 1, 17; WLC**
See also CDALB 1640-1865; DLB 3, 74; SATA 59

**Menander**
c. 342B.C.-c. 292B.C. . . . . . . . . **CMLC 9; DAM DRAM; DC 3**

**Mencken, H(enry) L(ouis)**
1880-1956 . . . . . . . . . . . . . . . . . . **TCLC 13**
See also CA 105; 125; CDALB 1917-1929; DLB 11, 29, 63, 137; MTCW

**Mercer, David**
1928-1980 . . . . . . . **CLC 5; DAM DRAM**
See also CA 9-12R; 102; CANR 23; DLB 13; MTCW

**Merchant, Paul**
See Ellison, Harlan (Jay)

**Meredith, George**
1828-1909 . . **TCLC 17, 43; DAM POET**
See also CA 117; 153; CDBLB 1832-1890; DLB 18, 35, 57, 159

**Meredith, William (Morris)**
1919- . . **CLC 4, 13, 22, 55; DAM POET**
See also CA 9-12R; CAAS 14; CANR 6, 40; DLB 5

**Merezhkovsky, Dmitry Sergeyevich**
1865-1941 . . . . . . . . . . . . . . . . . . **TCLC 29**

**Merimee, Prosper**
1803-1870 . . . . . . . . . . . . **NCLC 6; SSC 7**
See also DLB 119

**Merkin, Daphne** 1954- . . . . . . . . . . . . **CLC 44**
See also CA 123

**Merlin, Arthur**
See Blish, James (Benjamin)

**Merrill, James (Ingram)**
1926-1995 . . . . **CLC 2, 3, 6, 8, 13, 18, 34, 91; DAM POET**
See also CA 13-16R; 147; CANR 10, 49; DLB 5, 165; DLBY 85; INT CANR-10; MTCW

**Merriman, Alex**
See Silverberg, Robert

**Merritt, E. B.**
See Waddington, Miriam

**Merton, Thomas**
1915-1968 . . **CLC 1, 3, 11, 34, 83; PC 10**
See also CA 5-8R; 25-28R; CANR 22, 53; DLB 48; DLBY 81; MTCW

**Merwin, W(illiam) S(tanley)**
1927- . . . . . . **CLC 1, 2, 3, 5, 8, 13, 18, 45, 88; DAM POET**
See also CA 13-16R; CANR 15, 51; DLB 5, 169; INT CANR-15; MTCW

**Metcalf, John** 1938- . . . . . . . . . . . . . . **CLC 37**
See also CA 113; DLB 60

**Metcalf, Suzanne**
See Baum, L(yman) Frank

**Mew, Charlotte (Mary)**
1870-1928 . . . . . . . . . . . . . . . . . . . **TCLC 8**
See also CA 105; DLB 19, 135

**Mewshaw, Michael** 1943- . . . . . . . . . . . **CLC 9**
See also CA 53-56; CANR 7, 47; DLBY 80

**Meyer, June**
See Jordan, June

**Meyer, Lynn**
See Slavitt, David R(ytman)

**Meyer-Meyrink, Gustav** 1868-1932
See Meyrink, Gustav
See also CA 117

**Meyers, Jeffrey** 1939- . . . . . . . . . . . . **CLC 39**
See also CA 73-76; CANR 54; DLB 111

**Meynell, Alice (Christina Gertrude Thompson)**
1847-1922 . . . . . . . . . . . . . . . . . . . **TCLC 6**
See also CA 104; DLB 19, 98

**Meyrink, Gustav** . . . . . . . . . . . . . . . . . **TCLC 21**
See also Meyer-Meyrink, Gustav
See also DLB 81

**Michaels, Leonard**
1933- . . . . . . . . . . . . . . **CLC 6, 25; SSC 16**
See also CA 61-64; CANR 21; DLB 130; MTCW

**Michaux, Henri** 1899-1984 . . . . . . **CLC 8, 19**
See also CA 85-88; 114

**Michelangelo** 1475-1564. . . . . . . . . . . . **LC 12**

**Michelet, Jules** 1798-1874 . . . . . . . **NCLC 31**

**Michener, James A(lbert)**
1907(?)- . . . . . . . . . . **CLC 1, 5, 11, 29, 60; DAM NOV, POP**
See also AITN 1; BEST 90:1; CA 5-8R; CANR 21, 45; DLB 6; MTCW

**Mickiewicz, Adam** 1798-1855 . . . . . **NCLC 3**

**Middleton, Christopher** 1926- . . . . . . **CLC 13**
See also CA 13-16R; CANR 29, 54; DLB 40

**Middleton, Richard (Barham)**
1882-1911 . . . . . . . . . . . . . . . . . . **TCLC 56**
See also DLB 156

**Middleton, Stanley** 1919- . . . . . . . . **CLC 7, 38**
See also CA 25-28R; CAAS 23; CANR 21, 46; DLB 14

**Middleton, Thomas**
1580-1627 . . . . . . . **LC 33; DAM DRAM, MST; DC 5**
See also DLB 58

**Migueis, Jose Rodrigues** 1901- . . . . . **CLC 10**

**Mikszath, Kalman** 1847-1910 . . . . . **TCLC 31**

**Miles, Josephine (Louise)**
1911-1985 . . . . . . . . **CLC 1, 2, 14, 34, 39; DAM POET**
See also CA 1-4R; 116; CANR 2, 55; DLB 48

**Militant**
See Sandburg, Carl (August)

**Mill, John Stuart** 1806-1873 . . **NCLC 11, 58**
See also CDBLB 1832-1890; DLB 55

**Millar, Kenneth**
1915-1983 . . . . . . . . **CLC 14; DAM POP**
See also Macdonald, Ross
See also CA 9-12R; 110; CANR 16; DLB 2; DLBD 6; DLBY 83; MTCW

**Millay, E. Vincent**
See Millay, Edna St. Vincent

**Millay, Edna St. Vincent**
1892-1950 . . . . . . **TCLC 4, 49; DA; DAB; DAC; DAM MST, POET; PC 6**
See also CA 104; 130; CDALB 1917-1929; DLB 45; MTCW

**Miller, Arthur**
1915- . . . . **CLC 1, 2, 6, 10, 15, 26, 47, 78; DA; DAB; DAC; DAM DRAM, MST; DC 1; WLC**
See also AAYA 15; AITN 1; CA 1-4R; CABS 3; CANR 2, 30, 54; CDALB 1941-1968; DLB 7; MTCW

**Miller, Henry (Valentine)**
1891-1980 . . . . **CLC 1, 2, 4, 9, 14, 43, 84; DA; DAB; DAC; DAM MST, NOV; WLC**
See also CA 9-12R; 97-100; CANR 33; CDALB 1929-1941; DLB 4, 9; DLBY 80; MTCW

**Miller, Jason** 1939(?)- . . . . . . . . . . . . . **CLC 2**
See also AITN 1; CA 73-76; DLB 7

**Miller, Sue** 1943- . . . . . **CLC 44; DAM POP**
See also BEST 90:3; CA 139; DLB 143

**Miller, Walter M(ichael, Jr.)**
1923- . . . . . . . . . . . . . . . . . . . . . **CLC 4, 30**
See also CA 85-88; DLB 8

**Millett, Kate** 1934- . . . . . . . . . . . . . . . **CLC 67**
See also AITN 1; CA 73-76; CANR 32, 53; MTCW

**Millhauser, Steven** 1943- . . . . . . . **CLC 21, 54**
See also CA 110; 111; DLB 2; INT 111

**Millin, Sarah Gertrude** 1889-1968 . . **CLC 49**
See also CA 102; 93-96

**Milne, A(lan) A(lexander)**
1882-1956 . . . . . . . **TCLC 6; DAB; DAC; DAM MST**
See also CA 104; 133; CLR 1, 26; DLB 10, 77, 100, 160; MAICYA; MTCW; YABC 1

**Milner, Ron(ald)**
1938- . . . . . **CLC 56; BLC; DAM MULT**
See also AITN 1; BW 1; CA 73-76; CANR 24; DLB 38; MTCW

**Milosz, Czeslaw**
1911- . . . . . . . . **CLC 5, 11, 22, 31, 56, 82; DAM MST, POET; PC 8**
See also CA 81-84; CANR 23, 51; MTCW

**Milton, John**
1608-1674 . . . . . . **LC 9; DA; DAB; DAC; DAM MST, POET; WLC**
See also CDBLB 1660-1789; DLB 131, 151

**Min, Anchee** 1957- . . . . . . . . . . . . . . . **CLC 86**
See also CA 146

**Minehaha, Cornelius**
See Wedekind, (Benjamin) Frank(lin)

**Miner, Valerie** 1947- . . . . . . . . . . . . . **CLC 40**
See also CA 97-100

**Minimo, Duca**
See D'Annunzio, Gabriele

**Minot, Susan** 1956- . . . . . . . . . . . . . . **CLC 44**
See also CA 134

**Minus, Ed** 1938- . . . . . . . . . . . . . . . . . **CLC 39**

**Miranda, Javier**
See Bioy Casares, Adolfo

**Mirbeau, Octave** 1848-1917. . . . . . . **TCLC 55**
See also DLB 123

**Miro (Ferrer), Gabriel (Francisco Victor)** 1879-1930 .................. **TCLC 5**
See also CA 104

**Mishima, Yukio** ....... **CLC 2, 4, 6, 9, 27; DC 1; SSC 4**
See also Hiraoka, Kimitake

**Mistral, Frederic** 1830-1914 ...... **TCLC 51**
See also CA 122

**Mistral, Gabriela**............ **TCLC 2; HLC**
See also Godoy Alcayaga, Lucila

**Mistry, Rohinton** 1952-...... **CLC 71; DAC**
See also CA 141

**Mitchell, Clyde**
See Ellison, Harlan (Jay); Silverberg, Robert

**Mitchell, James Leslie** 1901-1935
See Gibbon, Lewis Grassic
See also CA 104; DLB 15

**Mitchell, Joni** 1943-.............. **CLC 12**
See also CA 112

**Mitchell, Joseph (Quincy)** 1908-1996 ................... **CLC 98**
See also CA 77-80; 152

**Mitchell, Margaret (Munnerlyn)** 1900-1949 ...... **TCLC 11; DAM NOV, POP**
See also CA 109; 125; CANR 55; DLB 9; MTCW

**Mitchell, Peggy**
See Mitchell, Margaret (Munnerlyn)

**Mitchell, S(ilas) Weir** 1829-1914 .. **TCLC 36**

**Mitchell, W(illiam) O(rmond)** 1914- ...... **CLC 25; DAC; DAM MST**
See also CA 77-80; CANR 15, 43; DLB 88

**Mitford, Mary Russell** 1787-1855.. **NCLC 4**
See also DLB 110, 116

**Mitford, Nancy** 1904-1973......... **CLC 44**
See also CA 9-12R

**Miyamoto, Yuriko** 1899-1951 ..... **TCLC 37**

**Mo, Timothy (Peter)** 1950(?)-...... **CLC 46**
See also CA 117; MTCW

**Modarressi, Taghi (M.)** 1931-...... **CLC 44**
See also CA 121; 134; INT 134

**Modiano, Patrick (Jean)** 1945-..... **CLC 18**
See also CA 85-88; CANR 17, 40; DLB 83

**Moerck, Paal**
See Roelvaag, O(le) E(dvart)

**Mofolo, Thomas (Mokopu)** 1875(?)-1948 .......... **TCLC 22; BLC; DAM MULT**
See also CA 121; 153

**Mohr, Nicholasa** 1935-..... **CLC 12; DAM MULT; HLC**
See also AAYA 8; CA 49-52; CANR 1, 32; CLR 22; DLB 145; HW; JRDA; SAAS 8; SATA 8

**Mojtabai, A(nn) G(race)** 1938- ................ **CLC 5, 9, 15, 29**
See also CA 85-88

**Moliere** 1622-1673 ..... **LC 28; DA; DAB; DAC; DAM DRAM, MST; WLC**

**Molin, Charles**
See Mayne, William (James Carter)

**Molnar, Ferenc** 1878-1952 ..... **TCLC 20; DAM DRAM**
See also CA 109; 153

**Momaday, N(avarre) Scott** 1934- ..... **CLC 2, 19, 85, 95; DA; DAB; DAC; DAM MST, MULT, NOV, POP**
See also AAYA 11; CA 25-28R; CANR 14, 34; DLB 143; INT CANR-14; MTCW; NNAL; SATA 48; SATA-Brief 30

**Monette, Paul** 1945-1995.......... **CLC 82**
See also CA 139; 147

**Monroe, Harriet** 1860-1936....... **TCLC 12**
See also CA 109; DLB 54, 91

**Monroe, Lyle**
See Heinlein, Robert A(nson)

**Montagu, Elizabeth** 1917-........ **NCLC 7**
See also CA 9-12R

**Montagu, Mary (Pierrepont) Wortley** 1689-1762 ............... **LC 9; PC 16**
See also DLB 95, 101

**Montagu, W. H.**
See Coleridge, Samuel Taylor

**Montague, John (Patrick)** 1929- .................... **CLC 13, 46**
See also CA 9-12R; CANR 9; DLB 40; MTCW

**Montaigne, Michel (Eyquem) de** 1533-1592 ...... **LC 8; DA; DAB; DAC; DAM MST; WLC**

**Montale, Eugenio** 1896-1981 ........ **CLC 7, 9, 18; PC 13**
See also CA 17-20R; 104; CANR 30; DLB 114; MTCW

**Montesquieu, Charles-Louis de Secondat** 1689-1755 ..................... **LC 7**

**Montgomery, (Robert) Bruce** 1921-1978
See Crispin, Edmund
See also CA 104

**Montgomery, L(ucy) M(aud)** 1874-1942 ............ **TCLC 51; DAC; DAM MST**
See also AAYA 12; CA 108; 137; CLR 8; DLB 92; DLBD 14; JRDA; MAICYA; YABC 1

**Montgomery, Marion H., Jr.** 1925- .. **CLC 7**
See also AITN 1; CA 1-4R; CANR 3, 48; DLB 6

**Montgomery, Max**
See Davenport, Guy (Mattison, Jr.)

**Montherlant, Henry (Milon) de** 1896-1972 .... **CLC 8, 19; DAM DRAM**
See also CA 85-88; 37-40R; DLB 72; MTCW

**Monty Python**
See Chapman, Graham; Cleese, John (Marwood); Gilliam, Terry (Vance); Idle, Eric; Jones, Terence Graham Parry; Palin, Michael (Edward)
See also AAYA 7

**Moodie, Susanna (Strickland)** 1803-1885 ................. **NCLC 14**
See also DLB 99

**Mooney, Edward** 1951-
See Mooney, Ted
See also CA 130

**Mooney, Ted** ..................... **CLC 25**
See also Mooney, Edward

**Moorcock, Michael (John)** 1939- .................. **CLC 5, 27, 58**
See also CA 45-48; CAAS 5; CANR 2, 17, 38; DLB 14; MTCW

**Moore, Brian** 1921- ...... **CLC 1, 3, 5, 7, 8, 19, 32, 90; DAB; DAC; DAM MST**
See also CA 1-4R; CANR 1, 25, 42; MTCW

**Moore, Edward**
See Muir, Edwin

**Moore, George Augustus** 1852-1933 ........... **TCLC 7; SSC 19**
See also CA 104; DLB 10, 18, 57, 135

**Moore, Lorrie** .............. **CLC 39, 45, 68**
See also Moore, Marie Lorena

**Moore, Marianne (Craig)** 1887-1972 .... **CLC 1, 2, 4, 8, 10, 13, 19, 47; DA; DAB; DAC; DAM MST, POET; PC 4**
See also CA 1-4R; 33-36R; CANR 3; CDALB 1929-1941; DLB 45; DLBD 7; MTCW; SATA 20

**Moore, Marie Lorena** 1957-
See Moore, Lorrie
See also CA 116; CANR 39

**Moore, Thomas** 1779-1852........ **NCLC 6**
See also DLB 96, 144

**Morand, Paul** 1888-1976 .. **CLC 41; SSC 22**
See also CA 69-72; DLB 65

**Morante, Elsa** 1918-1985........ **CLC 8, 47**
See also CA 85-88; 117; CANR 35; MTCW

**Moravia, Alberto**....... **CLC 2, 7, 11, 27, 46**
See also Pincherle, Alberto

**More, Hannah** 1745-1833 ....... **NCLC 27**
See also DLB 107, 109, 116, 158

**More, Henry** 1614-1687............. **LC 9**
See also DLB 126

**More, Sir Thomas** 1478-1535 .... **LC 10, 32**

**Moreas, Jean**.................... **TCLC 18**
See also Papadiamantopoulos, Johannes

**Morgan, Berry** 1919-.............. **CLC 6**
See also CA 49-52; DLB 6

**Morgan, Claire**
See Highsmith, (Mary) Patricia

**Morgan, Edwin (George)** 1920-..... **CLC 31**
See also CA 5-8R; CANR 3, 43; DLB 27

**Morgan, (George) Frederick** 1922- ...................... **CLC 23**
See also CA 17-20R; CANR 21

**Morgan, Harriet**
See Mencken, H(enry) L(ouis)

**Morgan, Jane**
See Cooper, James Fenimore

**Morgan, Janet** 1945- ............. **CLC 39**
See also CA 65-68

**Morgan, Lady** 1776(?)-1859...... **NCLC 29**
See also DLB 116, 158

**Morgan, Robin** 1941-.............. **CLC 2**
See also CA 69-72; CANR 29; MTCW; SATA 80

**Morgan, Scott**
See Kuttner, Henry

**Morgan, Seth** 1949(?)-1990 ........ **CLC 65**
See also CA 132

**Morgenstern, Christian** 1871-1914 .................. **TCLC 8**
See also CA 105

**Morgenstern, S.**
See Goldman, William (W.)

**Moricz, Zsigmond** 1879-1942 ..... **TCLC 33**

**Morike, Eduard (Friedrich)** 1804-1875 ................ **NCLC 10**
See also DLB 133

**Mori Ogai** ...................... **TCLC 14**
See also Mori Rintaro

**Mori Rintaro** 1862-1922
See Mori Ogai
See also CA 110

**Moritz, Karl Philipp** 1756-1793 ...... **LC 2**
See also DLB 94

**Morland, Peter Henry**
See Faust, Frederick (Schiller)

**Morren, Theophil**
See Hofmannsthal, Hugo von

**Morris, Bill** 1952-................ **CLC 76**

**Morris, Julian**
See West, Morris L(anglo)

**Morris, Steveland Judkins** 1950(?)-
See Wonder, Stevie
See also CA 111

**Morris, William** 1834-1896 ....... **NCLC 4**
See also CDBLB 1832-1890; DLB 18, 35, 57, 156

**Morris, Wright** 1910-... **CLC 1, 3, 7, 18, 37**
See also CA 9-12R; CANR 21; DLB 2; DLBY 81; MTCW

**Morrison, Chloe Anthony Wofford**
See Morrison, Toni

**Morrison, James Douglas** 1943-1971
See Morrison, Jim
See also CA 73-76; CANR 40

**Morrison, Jim** .................... **CLC 17**
See also Morrison, James Douglas

**Morrison, Toni** 1931- ........ **CLC 4, 10, 22, 55, 81, 87; BLC; DA; DAB; DAC; DAM MST, MULT, NOV, POP**
See also AAYA 1; BW 2; CA 29-32R; CANR 27, 42; CDALB 1968-1988; DLB 6, 33, 143; DLBY 81; MTCW; SATA 57

**Morrison, Van** 1945- ............. **CLC 21**
See also CA 116

**Mortimer, John (Clifford)** 1923- ...... **CLC 28, 43; DAM DRAM, POP**
See also CA 13-16R; CANR 21; CDBLB 1960 to Present; DLB 13; INT CANR-21; MTCW

**Mortimer, Penelope (Ruth)** 1918-.... **CLC 5**
See also CA 57-60; CANR 45

**Morton, Anthony**
See Creasey, John

**Mosher, Howard Frank** 1943-...... **CLC 62**
See also CA 139

**Mosley, Nicholas** 1923-........ **CLC 43, 70**
See also CA 69-72; CANR 41; DLB 14

**Mosley, Walter** 1952- ..... **CLC 97; DAM MULT, POP**
See also AAYA 17; BW 2; CA 142

**Moss, Howard** 1922-1987 .......... **CLC 7, 14, 45, 50; DAM POET**
See also CA 1-4R; 123; CANR 1, 44; DLB 5

**Mossgiel, Rab**
See Burns, Robert

**Motion, Andrew (Peter)** 1952-...... **CLC 47**
See also CA 146; DLB 40

**Motley, Willard (Francis)** 1909-1965 .................. **CLC 18**
See also BW 1; CA 117; 106; DLB 76, 143

**Motoori, Norinaga** 1730-1801 .... **NCLC 45**

**Mott, Michael (Charles Alston)** 1930-.................... **CLC 15, 34**
See also CA 5-8R; CAAS 7; CANR 7, 29

**Mountain Wolf Woman** 1884-1960 .................. **CLC 92**
See also CA 144; NNAL

**Moure, Erin** 1955- ............... **CLC 88**
See also CA 113; DLB 60

**Mowat, Farley (McGill)** 1921- ...... **CLC 26; DAC; DAM MST**
See also AAYA 1; CA 1-4R; CANR 4, 24, 42; CLR 20; DLB 68; INT CANAR-24; JRDA; MAICYA; MTCW; SATA 3, 55

**Moyers, Bill** 1934- ............... **CLC 74**
See also AITN 2; CA 61-64; CANR 31, 52

**Mphahlele, Es'kia**
See Mphahlele, Ezekiel
See also DLB 125

**Mphahlele, Ezekiel** 1919- ..... **CLC 25; BLC; DAM MULT**
See also Mphahlele, Es'kia
See also BW 2; CA 81-84; CANR 26

**Mqhayi, S(amuel) E(dward) K(rune Loliwe)** 1875-1945 ............ **TCLC 25; BLC; DAM MULT**
See also CA 153

**Mrozek, Slawomir** 1930-........ **CLC 3, 13**
See also CA 13-16R; CAAS 10; CANR 29; MTCW

**Mrs. Belloc-Lowndes**
See Lowndes, Marie Adelaide (Belloc)

**Mtwa, Percy** (?)-................ **CLC 47**

**Mueller, Lisel** 1924-........... **CLC 13, 51**
See also CA 93-96; DLB 105

**Muir, Edwin** 1887-1959 .......... **TCLC 2**
See also CA 104; DLB 20, 100

**Muir, John** 1838-1914 ........... **TCLC 28**

**Mujica Lainez, Manuel** 1910-1984 .................. **CLC 31**
See also Lainez, Manuel Mujica
See also CA 81-84; 112; CANR 32; HW

**Mukherjee, Bharati** 1940- ............ **CLC 53; DAM NOV**
See also BEST 89:2; CA 107; CANR 45; DLB 60; MTCW

**Muldoon, Paul** 1951- ........ **CLC 32, 72; DAM POET**
See also CA 113; 129; CANR 52; DLB 40; INT 129

**Mulisch, Harry** 1927-............. **CLC 42**
See also CA 9-12R; CANR 6, 26

**Mull, Martin** 1943-............... **CLC 17**
See also CA 105

**Mulock, Dinah Maria**
See Craik, Dinah Maria (Mulock)

**Munford, Robert** 1737(?)-1783 ....... **LC 5**
See also DLB 31

**Mungo, Raymond** 1946-........... **CLC 72**
See also CA 49-52; CANR 2

**Munro, Alice** 1931- ...... **CLC 6, 10, 19, 50, 95; DAC; DAM MST, NOV; SSC 3**
See also AITN 2; CA 33-36R; CANR 33, 53; DLB 53; MTCW; SATA 29

**Munro, H(ector) H(ugh)** 1870-1916
See Saki
See also CA 104; 130; CDBLB 1890-1914; DA; DAB; DAC; DAM MST, NOV; DLB 34, 162; MTCW; WLC

**Murasaki, Lady** .................. **CMLC 1**

**Murdoch, (Jean) Iris** 1919- ...... **CLC 1, 2, 3, 4, 6, 8, 11, 15, 22, 31, 51; DAB; DAC; DAM MST, NOV**
See also CA 13-16R; CANR 8, 43; CDBLB 1960 to Present; DLB 14; INT CANR-8; MTCW

**Murfree, Mary Noallles** 1850-1922 ................... **SSC 22**
See also CA 122; DLB 12, 74

**Murnau, Friedrich Wilhelm**
See Plumpe, Friedrich Wilhelm

**Murphy, Richard** 1927-........... **CLC 41**
See also CA 29-32R; DLB 40

**Murphy, Sylvia** 1937-............. **CLC 34**
See also CA 121

**Murphy, Thomas (Bernard)** 1935-... **CLC 51**
See also CA 101

**Murray, Albert L.** 1916- .......... **CLC 73**
See also BW 2; CA 49-52; CANR 26, 52; DLB 38

**Murray, Les(lie) A(llan)** 1938- ........... **CLC 40; DAM POET**
See also CA 21-24R; CANR 11, 27

**Murry, J. Middleton**
See Murry, John Middleton

**Murry, John Middleton** 1889-1957 .................. **TCLC 16**
See also CA 118; DLB 149

**Musgrave, Susan** 1951- ........ **CLC 13, 54**
See also CA 69-72; CANR 45

**Musil, Robert (Edler von)** 1880-1942 ....... **TCLC 12, 68; SSC 18**
See also CA 109; CANR 55; DLB 81, 124

**Muske, Carol** 1945- .............. **CLC 90**
See also Muske-Dukes, Carol (Anne)

**Muske-Dukes, Carol (Anne)** 1945-
See Muske, Carol
See also CA 65-68; CANR 32

**Musset, (Louis Charles) Alfred de** 1810-1857 .................. **NCLC 7**

**My Brother's Brother**
See Chekhov, Anton (Pavlovich)

**Myers, L. H.** 1881-1944.......... **TCLC 59**
See also DLB 15

**Myers, Walter Dean** 1937- ..... **CLC 35; BLC; DAM MULT, NOV**
See also AAYA 4; BW 2; CA 33-36R; CANR 20, 42; CLR 4, 16, 35; DLB 33; INT CANR-20; JRDA; MAICYA; SAAS 2; SATA 41, 71; SATA-Brief 27

**Myers, Walter M.**
See Myers, Walter Dean

**Myles, Symon**
See Follett, Ken(neth Martin)

**Nabokov, Vladimir (Vladimirovich)** 1899-1977 ..... **CLC 1, 2, 3, 6, 8, 11, 15, 23, 44, 46, 64; DA; DAB; DAC; DAM MST, NOV; SSC 11; WLC**
See also CA 5-8R; 69-72; CANR 20; CDALB 1941-1968; DLB 2; DLBD 3; DLBY 80, 91; MTCW

**Nagai Kafu**...................... **TCLC 51**
See also Nagai Sokichi

**Nagai Sokichi** 1879-1959
See Nagai Kafu
See also CA 117

**Nagy, Laszlo** 1925-1978............ **CLC 7**
See also CA 129; 112

**Naipaul, Shiva(dhar Srinivasa)** 1945-1985 ..... **CLC 32, 39; DAM NOV**
See also CA 110; 112; 116; CANR 33; DLB 157; DLBY 85; MTCW

**Naipaul, V(idiadhar) S(urajprasad)** 1932- .... **CLC 4, 7, 9, 13, 18, 37; DAB; DAC; DAM MST, NOV**
See also CA 1-4R; CANR 1, 33, 51; CDBLB 1960 to Present; DLB 125; DLBY 85; MTCW

**Nakos, Lilika** 1899(?)- ............ **CLC 29**

**Narayan, R(asipuram) K(rishnaswami)** 1906- ....... **CLC 7, 28, 47; DAM NOV**
See also CA 81-84; CANR 33; MTCW; SATA 62

**Nash, (Frediric) Ogden** 1902-1971 ....... **CLC 23; DAM POET**
See also CA 13-14; 29-32R; CANR 34; CAP 1; DLB 11; MAICYA; MTCW; SATA 2, 46

**Nathan, Daniel**
See Dannay, Frederic

**Nathan, George Jean** 1882-1958 ... **TCLC 18**
See also Hatteras, Owen
See also CA 114; DLB 137

**Natsume, Kinnosuke** 1867-1916
See Natsume, Soseki
See also CA 104

**Natsume, Soseki** ............... **TCLC 2, 10**
See also Natsume, Kinnosuke

**Natti, (Mary) Lee** 1919-
See Kingman, Lee
See also CA 5-8R; CANR 2

**Naylor, Gloria** 1950- ..... **CLC 28, 52; BLC; DA; DAC; DAM MST, MULT, NOV, POP**
See also AAYA 6; BW 2; CA 107; CANR 27, 51; DLB 173; MTCW

**Neihardt, John Gneisenau** 1881-1973 .................. **CLC 32**
See also CA 13-14; CAP 1; DLB 9, 54

**Nekrasov, Nikolai Alekseevich** 1821-1878 ................. **NCLC 11**

**Nelligan, Emile** 1879-1941........ **TCLC 14**
See also CA 114; DLB 92

**Nelson, Willie** 1933-.............. **CLC 17**
See also CA 107

**Nemerov, Howard (Stanley)** 1920-1991 ............ **CLC 2, 6, 9, 36; DAM POET**
See also CA 1-4R; 134; CABS 2; CANR 1, 27, 53; DLB 5, 6; DLBY 83; INT CANR-27; MTCW

**Neruda, Pablo** 1904-1973 ..... **CLC 1, 2, 5, 7, 9, 28, 62; DA; DAB; DAC; DAM MST, MULT, POET; HLC; PC 4; WLC**
See also CA 19-20; 45-48; CAP 2; HW; MTCW

**Nerval, Gerard de** 1808-1855 ..... **NCLC 1; PC 13; SSC 18**

**Nervo, (Jose) Amado (Ruiz de)** 1870-1919 ................. **TCLC 11**
See also CA 109; 131; HW

**Nessi, Pio Baroja y**
See Baroja (y Nessi), Pio

**Nestroy, Johann** 1801-1862...... **NCLC 42**
See also DLB 133

**Neufeld, John (Arthur)** 1938- ...... **CLC 17**
See also AAYA 11; CA 25-28R; CANR 11, 37; MAICYA; SAAS 3; SATA 6, 81

**Neville, Emily Cheney** 1919-....... **CLC 12**
See also CA 5-8R; CANR 3, 37; JRDA; MAICYA; SAAS 2; SATA 1

**Newbound, Bernard Slade** 1930-
See Slade, Bernard
See also CA 81-84; CANR 49; DAM DRAM

**Newby, P(ercy) H(oward)** 1918- .......... **CLC 2, 13; DAM NOV**
See also CA 5-8R; CANR 32; DLB 15; MTCW

**Newlove, Donald** 1928- ............ **CLC 6**
See also CA 29-32R; CANR 25

**Newlove, John (Herbert)** 1938-..... **CLC 14**
See also CA 21-24R; CANR 9, 25

**Newman, Charles** 1938-.......... **CLC 2, 8**
See also CA 21-24R

**Newman, Edwin (Harold)** 1919- .... **CLC 14**
See also AITN 1; CA 69-72; CANR 5

**Newman, John Henry** 1801-1890 ................ **NCLC 38**
See also DLB 18, 32, 55

**Newton, Suzanne** 1936- ........... **CLC 35**
See also CA 41-44R; CANR 14; JRDA; SATA 5, 77

**Nexo, Martin Andersen** 1869-1954 .................. **TCLC 43**

**Nezval, Vitezslav** 1900-1958 ...... **TCLC 44**
See also CA 123

**Ng, Fae Myenne** 1957(?)-.......... **CLC 81**
See also CA 146

**Ngema, Mbongeni** 1955- .......... **CLC 57**
See also BW 2; CA 143

**Ngugi, James T(hiong'o)**........ **CLC 3, 7, 13**
See also Ngugi wa Thiong'o

**Ngugi wa Thiong'o** 1938- ..... **CLC 36; BLC; DAM MULT, NOV**
See also Ngugi, James T(hiong'o)
See also BW 2; CA 81-84; CANR 27; DLB 125; MTCW

**Nichol, B(arrie) P(hillip)** 1944-1988 ................... **CLC 18**
See also CA 53-56; DLB 53; SATA 66

**Nichols, John (Treadwell)** 1940-.... **CLC 38**
See also CA 9-12R; CAAS 2; CANR 6; DLBY 82

**Nichols, Leigh**
See Koontz, Dean R(ay)

**Nichols, Peter (Richard)** 1927- .................. **CLC 5, 36, 65**
See also CA 104; CANR 33; DLB 13; MTCW

**Nicolas, F. R. E.**
See Freeling, Nicolas

**Niedecker, Lorine** 1903-1970 .... **CLC 10, 42; DAM POET**
See also CA 25-28; CAP 2; DLB 48

**Nietzsche, Friedrich (Wilhelm)** 1844-1900 ........... **TCLC 10, 18, 55**
See also CA 107; 121; DLB 129

**Nievo, Ippolito** 1831-1861 ....... **NCLC 22**

**Nightingale, Anne Redmon** 1943-
See Redmon, Anne
See also CA 103

**Nik. T. O.**
See Annensky, Innokenty Fyodorovich

**Nin, Anais** 1903-1977 ...... **CLC 1, 4, 8, 11, 14, 60; DAM NOV, POP; SSC 10**
See also AITN 2; CA 13-16R; 69-72; CANR 22, 53; DLB 2, 4, 152; MTCW

**Nishiwaki, Junzaburo** 1894-1982 .... **PC 15**
See also CA 107

**Nissenson, Hugh** 1933-........... **CLC 4, 9**
See also CA 17-20R; CANR 27; DLB 28

**Niven, Larry** ...................... **CLC 8**
See also Niven, Laurence Van Cott
See also DLB 8

**Niven, Laurence Van Cott** 1938-
See Niven, Larry
See also CA 21-24R; CAAS 12; CANR 14, 44; DAM POP; MTCW

**Nixon, Agnes Eckhardt** 1927-...... **CLC 21**
See also CA 110

**Nizan, Paul** 1905-1940........... **TCLC 40**
See also DLB 72

**Nkosi, Lewis** 1936- ..... **CLC 45; BLC; DAM MULT**
See also BW 1; CA 65-68; CANR 27; DLB 157

**Okigbo, Christopher (Ifenayichukwu)** 1932-1967 .......... **CLC 25, 84; BLC; DAM MULT, POET; PC 7**
See also BW 1; CA 77-80; DLB 125; MTCW

**Okri, Ben** 1959- ................. **CLC 87**
See also BW 2; CA 130; 138; DLB 157; INT 138

**Olds, Sharon** 1942- ..... **CLC 32, 39, 85; DAM POET**
See also CA 101; CANR 18, 41; DLB 120

**Oldstyle, Jonathan**
See Irving, Washington

**Olesha, Yuri (Karlovich)** 1899-1960 .................... **CLC 8**
See also CA 85-88

**Oliphant, Laurence** 1829(?)-1888 ............... **NCLC 47**
See also DLB 18, 166

**Oliphant, Margaret (Oliphant Wilson)** 1828-1897 ................. **NCLC 11**
See also DLB 18, 159

**Oliver, Mary** 1935-......... **CLC 19, 34, 98**
See also CA 21-24R; CANR 9, 43; DLB 5

**Olivier, Laurence (Kerr)** 1907-1989 .................. **CLC 20**
See also CA 111; 150; 129

**Olsen, Tillie** 1913- ..... **CLC 4, 13; DA; DAB; DAC; DAM MST; SSC 11**
See also CA 1-4R; CANR 1, 43; DLB 28; DLBY 80; MTCW

**Olson, Charles (John)** 1910-1970 ..... **CLC 1, 2, 5, 6, 9, 11, 29; DAM POET**
See also CA 13-16; 25-28R; CABS 2; CANR 35; CAP 1; DLB 5, 16; MTCW

**Olson, Toby** 1937- ............... **CLC 28**
See also CA 65-68; CANR 9, 31

**Olyesha, Yuri**
See Olesha, Yuri (Karlovich)

**Ondaatje, (Philip) Michael** 1943- ........ **CLC 14, 29, 51, 76; DAB; DAC; DAM MST**
See also CA 77-80; CANR 42; DLB 60

**Oneal, Elizabeth** 1934-
See Oneal, Zibby
See also CA 106; CANR 28; MAICYA; SATA 30, 82

**Oneal, Zibby** .................... **CLC 30**
See also Oneal, Elizabeth
See also AAYA 5; CLR 13; JRDA

**O'Neill, Eugene (Gladstone)** 1888-1953 ...... **TCLC 1, 6, 27, 49; DA; DAB; DAC; DAM DRAM, MST; WLC**
See also AITN 1; CA 110; 132; CDALB 1929-1941; DLB 7; MTCW

**Onetti, Juan Carlos** 1909-1994 .... **CLC 7, 10; DAM MULT, NOV; SSC 23**
See also CA 85-88; 145; CANR 32; DLB 113; HW; MTCW

**O Nuallain, Brian** 1911-1966
See O'Brien, Flann
See also CA 21-22; 25-28R; CAP 2

**Oppen, George** 1908-1984 .... **CLC 7, 13, 34**
See also CA 13-16R; 113; CANR 8; DLB 5, 165

**Oppenheim, E(dward) Phillips** 1866-1946 ................. **TCLC 45**
See also CA 111; DLB 70

**Origen** c. 185-c. 254 ........... **CMLC 19**

**Orlovitz, Gil** 1918-1973 ........... **CLC 22**
See also CA 77-80; 45-48; DLB 2, 5

**Orris**
See Ingelow, Jean

**Ortega y Gasset, Jose** 1883-1955 ..... **TCLC 9; DAM MULT; HLC**
See also CA 106; 130; HW; MTCW

**Ortese, Anna Maria** 1914- ......... **CLC 89**

**Ortiz, Simon J(oseph)** 1941- .......... **CLC 45; DAM MULT, POET; PC 17**
See also CA 134; DLB 120; NNAL

**Orton, Joe** ............ **CLC 4, 13, 43; DC 3**
See also Orton, John Kingsley
See also CDBLB 1960 to Present; DLB 13

**Orton, John Kingsley** 1933-1967
See Orton, Joe
See also CA 85-88; CANR 35; DAM DRAM; MTCW

**Orwell, George** ..... **TCLC 2, 6, 15, 31, 51; DAB; WLC**
See also Blair, Eric (Arthur)
See also CDBLB 1945-1960; DLB 15, 98

**Osborne, David**
See Silverberg, Robert

**Osborne, George**
See Silverberg, Robert

**Osborne, John (James)** 1929-1994 ..... **CLC 1, 2, 5, 11, 45; DA; DAB; DAC; DAM DRAM, MST; WLC**
See also CA 13-16R; 147; CANR 21; CDBLB 1945-1960; DLB 13; MTCW

**Osborne, Lawrence** 1958- ......... **CLC 50**

**Oshima, Nagisa** 1932- ............ **CLC 20**
See also CA 116; 121

**Oskison, John Milton** 1874-1947 ..... **TCLC 35; DAM MULT**
See also CA 144; NNAL

**Ossoli, Sarah Margaret (Fuller marchesa d')** 1810-1850
See Fuller, Margaret
See also SATA 25

**Ostrovsky, Alexander** 1823-1886 .............. **NCLC 30, 57**

**Otero, Blas de** 1916-1979.......... **CLC 11**
See also CA 89-92; DLB 134

**Otto, Whitney** 1955-.............. **CLC 70**
See also CA 140

**Ouida** ......................... **TCLC 43**
See also De La Ramee, (Marie) Louise
See also DLB 18, 156

**Ousmane, Sembene** 1923- .... **CLC 66; BLC**
See also BW 1; CA 117; 125; MTCW

**Ovid** 43B.C.-18(?) ... **CMLC 7; DAM POET; PC 2**

**Owen, Hugh**
See Faust, Frederick (Schiller)

**Owen, Wilfred (Edward Salter)** 1893-1918 ...... **TCLC 5, 27; DA; DAB; DAC; DAM MST, POET; WLC**
See also CA 104; 141; CDBLB 1914-1945; DLB 20

**Owens, Rochelle** 1936-............. **CLC 8**
See also CA 17-20R; CAAS 2; CANR 39

**Oz, Amos** 1939- ......... **CLC 5, 8, 11, 27, 33, 54; DAM NOV**
See also CA 53-56; CANR 27, 47; MTCW

**Ozick, Cynthia** 1928- .... **CLC 3, 7, 28, 62; DAM NOV, POP; SSC 15**
See also BEST 90:1; CA 17-20R; CANR 23; DLB 28, 152; DLBY 82; INT CANR-23; MTCW

**Ozu, Yasujiro** 1903-1963 .......... **CLC 16**
See also CA 112

**Pacheco, C.**
See Pessoa, Fernando (Antonio Nogueira)

**Pa Chin** ......................... **CLC 18**
See also Li Fei-kan

**Pack, Robert** 1929-............... **CLC 13**
See also CA 1-4R; CANR 3, 44; DLB 5

**Padgett, Lewis**
See Kuttner, Henry

**Padilla (Lorenzo), Heberto** 1932- ... **CLC 38**
See also AITN 1; CA 123; 131; HW

**Page, Jimmy** 1944-............... **CLC 12**

**Page, Louise** 1955-............... **CLC 40**
See also CA 140

**Page, P(atricia) K(athleen)** 1916- .... **CLC 7, 18; DAC; DAM MST; PC 12**
See also CA 53-56; CANR 4, 22; DLB 68; MTCW

**Page, Thomas Nelson** 1853-1922.... **SSC 23**
See also CA 118; DLB 12, 78; DLBD 13

**Paget, Violet** 1856-1935
See Lee, Vernon
See also CA 104

**Paget-Lowe, Henry**
See Lovecraft, H(oward) P(hillips)

**Paglia, Camille (Anna)** 1947-....... **CLC 68**
See also CA 140

**Paige, Richard**
See Koontz, Dean R(ay)

**Pakenham, Antonia**
See Fraser, (Lady) Antonia (Pakenham)

**Palamas, Kostes** 1859-1943 ........ **TCLC 5**
See also CA 105

**Palazzeschi, Aldo** 1885-1974....... **CLC 11**
See also CA 89-92; 53-56; DLB 114

**Paley, Grace** 1922- ....... **CLC 4, 6, 37; DAM POP; SSC 8**
See also CA 25-28R; CANR 13, 46; DLB 28; INT CANR-13; MTCW

**Palin, Michael (Edward)** 1943- ..... **CLC 21**
See also Monty Python
See also CA 107; CANR 35; SATA 67

**Palliser, Charles** 1947- . . . . . . . . . . . . . **CLC 65**
See also CA 136

**Palma, Ricardo** 1833-1919 . . . . . . . . **TCLC 29**

**Pancake, Breece Dexter** 1952-1979
See Pancake, Breece D'J
See also CA 123; 109

**Pancake, Breece D'J** . . . . . . . . . . . . . . . **CLC 29**
See also Pancake, Breece Dexter
See also DLB 130

**Panko, Rudy**
See Gogol, Nikolai (Vasilyevich)

**Papadiamantis, Alexandros**
1851-1911 . . . . . . . . . . . . . . . . . . **TCLC 29**

**Papadiamantopoulos, Johannes** 1856-1910
See Moreas, Jean
See also CA 117

**Papini, Giovanni** 1881-1956 . . . . . . . **TCLC 22**
See also CA 121

**Paracelsus** 1493-1541 . . . . . . . . . . . . . . **LC 14**

**Parasol, Peter**
See Stevens, Wallace

**Parfenie, Maria**
See Codrescu, Andrei

**Parini, Jay (Lee)** 1948- . . . . . . . . . . . **CLC 54**
See also CA 97-100; CAAS 16; CANR 32

**Park, Jordan**
See Kornbluth, C(yril) M.; Pohl, Frederik

**Parker, Bert**
See Ellison, Harlan (Jay)

**Parker, Dorothy (Rothschild)**
1893-1967 . . . . . . . . . . . . . . . **CLC 15, 68; DAM POET; SSC 2**
See also CA 19-20; 25-28R; CAP 2; DLB 11, 45, 86; MTCW

**Parker, Robert B(rown)**
1932- . . . . . . **CLC 27; DAM NOV, POP**
See also BEST 89:4; CA 49-52; CANR 1, 26, 52; INT CANR-26; MTCW

**Parkin, Frank** 1940- . . . . . . . . . . . . . **CLC 43**
See also CA 147

**Parkman, Francis, Jr.**
1823-1893 . . . . . . . . . . . . . . . . . **NCLC 12**
See also DLB 1, 30

**Parks, Gordon (Alexander Buchanan)**
1912- . . . **CLC 1, 16; BLC; DAM MULT**
See also AITN 2; BW 2; CA 41-44R; CANR 26; DLB 33; SATA 8

**Parnell, Thomas** 1679-1718 . . . . . . . . . . **LC 3**
See also DLB 94

**Parra, Nicanor**
1914- . . . . . . **CLC 2; DAM MULT; HLC**
See also CA 85-88; CANR 32; HW; MTCW

**Parrish, Mary Frances**
See Fisher, M(ary) F(rances) K(ennedy)

**Parson**
See Coleridge, Samuel Taylor

**Parson Lot**
See Kingsley, Charles

**Partridge, Anthony**
See Oppenheim, E(dward) Phillips

**Pascal, Blaise** 1623-1662 . . . . . . . . . . . **LC 35**

**Pascoli, Giovanni** 1855-1912 . . . . . . **TCLC 45**

**Pasolini, Pier Paolo**
1922-1975 . . . . . . . . . **CLC 20, 37; PC 17**
See also CA 93-96; 61-64; DLB 128; MTCW

**Pasquini**
See Silone, Ignazio

**Pastan, Linda (Olenik)**
1932- . . . . . . . . . . . **CLC 27; DAM POET**
See also CA 61-64; CANR 18, 40; DLB 5

**Pasternak, Boris (Leonidovich)**
1890-1960 . . . . . . **CLC 7, 10, 18, 63; DA; DAB; DAC; DAM MST, NOV, POET; PC 6; WLC**
See also CA 127; 116; MTCW

**Patchen, Kenneth**
1911-1972 . . . **CLC 1, 2, 18; DAM POET**
See also CA 1-4R; 33-36R; CANR 3, 35; DLB 16, 48; MTCW

**Pater, Walter (Horatio)**
1839-1894 . . . . . . . . . . . . . . . . . . **NCLC 7**
See also CDBLB 1832-1890; DLB 57, 156

**Paterson, A(ndrew) B(arton)**
1864-1941 . . . . . . . . . . . . . . . . . . **TCLC 32**
See also CA 155

**Paterson, Katherine (Womeldorf)**
1932- . . . . . . . . . . . . . . . . . . . . **CLC 12, 30**
See also AAYA 1; CA 21-24R; CANR 28; CLR 7; DLB 52; JRDA; MAICYA; MTCW; SATA 13, 53

**Patmore, Coventry Kersey Dighton**
1823-1896 . . . . . . . . . . . . . . . . . . **NCLC 9**
See also DLB 35, 98

**Paton, Alan (Stewart)**
1903-1988 . . . . . . **CLC 4, 10, 25, 55; DA; DAB; DAC; DAM MST, NOV; WLC**
See also CA 13-16; 125; CANR 22; CAP 1; MTCW; SATA 11; SATA-Obit 56

**Paton Walsh, Gillian** 1937-
See Walsh, Jill Paton
See also CANR 38; JRDA; MAICYA; SAAS 3; SATA 4, 72

**Paulding, James Kirke** 1778-1860 . . **NCLC 2**
See also DLB 3, 59, 74

**Paulin, Thomas Neilson** 1949-
See Paulin, Tom
See also CA 123; 128

**Paulin, Tom** . . . . . . . . . . . . . . . . . . . . . **CLC 37**
See also Paulin, Thomas Neilson
See also DLB 40

**Paustovsky, Konstantin (Georgievich)**
1892-1968 . . . . . . . . . . . . . . . . . . . **CLC 40**
See also CA 93-96; 25-28R

**Pavese, Cesare**
1908-1950 . . . . . **TCLC 3; PC 13; SSC 19**
See also CA 104; DLB 128

**Pavic, Milorad** 1929- . . . . . . . . . . . . . **CLC 60**
See also CA 136

**Payne, Alan**
See Jakes, John (William)

**Paz, Gil**
See Lugones, Leopoldo

**Paz, Octavio**
1914- . . . . . . . **CLC 3, 4, 6, 10, 19, 51, 65; DA; DAB; DAC; DAM MST, MULT, POET; HLC; PC 1; WLC**
See also CA 73-76; CANR 32; DLBY 90; HW; MTCW

**p'Bitek, Okot**
1931-1982 . . . . . . . . . . . . . **CLC 96; BLC; DAM MULT**
See also BW 2; CA 124; 107; DLB 125; MTCW

**Peacock, Molly** 1947- . . . . . . . . . . . . . **CLC 60**
See also CA 103; CAAS 21; CANR 52; DLB 120

**Peacock, Thomas Love**
1785-1866 . . . . . . . . . . . . . . . . . **NCLC 22**
See also DLB 96, 116

**Peake, Mervyn** 1911-1968 . . . . . . . **CLC 7, 54**
See also CA 5-8R; 25-28R; CANR 3; DLB 15, 160; MTCW; SATA 23

**Pearce, Philippa** . . . . . . . . . . . . . . . . . . **CLC 21**
See also Christie, (Ann) Philippa
See also CLR 9; DLB 161; MAICYA; SATA 1, 67

**Pearl, Eric**
See Elman, Richard

**Pearson, T(homas) R(eid)** 1956- . . . . **CLC 39**
See also CA 120; 130; INT 130

**Peck, Dale** 1967- . . . . . . . . . . . . . . . . **CLC 81**
See also CA 146

**Peck, John** 1941- . . . . . . . . . . . . . . . . . **CLC 3**
See also CA 49-52; CANR 3

**Peck, Richard (Wayne)** 1934- . . . . . . **CLC 21**
See also AAYA 1; CA 85-88; CANR 19, 38; CLR 15; INT CANR-19; JRDA; MAICYA; SAAS 2; SATA 18, 55

**Peck, Robert Newton**
1928- . . **CLC 17; DA; DAC; DAM MST**
See also AAYA 3; CA 81-84; CANR 31; JRDA; MAICYA; SAAS 1; SATA 21, 62

**Peckinpah, (David) Sam(uel)**
1925-1984 . . . . . . . . . . . . . . . . . . . **CLC 20**
See also CA 109; 114

**Pedersen, Knut** 1859-1952
See Hamsun, Knut
See also CA 104; 119; MTCW

**Peeslake, Gaffer**
See Durrell, Lawrence (George)

**Peguy, Charles Pierre**
1873-1914 . . . . . . . . . . . . . . . . . . **TCLC 10**
See also CA 107

**Pena, Ramon del Valle y**
See Valle-Inclan, Ramon (Maria) del

**Pendennis, Arthur Esquir**
See Thackeray, William Makepeace

**Penn, William** 1644-1718 . . . . . . . . . . . **LC 25**
See also DLB 24

**Pepys, Samuel**
1633-1703 . . . . . **LC 11; DA; DAB; DAC; DAM MST; WLC**
See also CDBLB 1660-1789; DLB 101

**Percy, Walker**
1916-1990 . . . . **CLC 2, 3, 6, 8, 14, 18, 47, 65; DAM NOV, POP**
See also CA 1-4R; 131; CANR 1, 23; DLB 2; DLBY 80, 90; MTCW

**Perec, Georges** 1936-1982 ......... **CLC 56**
See also CA 141; DLB 83

**Pereda (y Sanchez de Porrua), Jose Maria de** 1833-1906 .................. **TCLC 16**
See also CA 117

**Pereda y Porrua, Jose Maria de**
See Pereda (y Sanchez de Porrua), Jose Maria de

**Peregoy, George Weems**
See Mencken, H(enry) L(ouis)

**Perelman, S(idney) J(oseph)** 1904-1979 ...... **CLC 3, 5, 9, 15, 23, 44, 49; DAM DRAM**
See also AITN 1, 2; CA 73-76; 89-92; CANR 18; DLB 11, 44; MTCW

**Peret, Benjamin** 1899-1959 ....... **TCLC 20**
See also CA 117

**Peretz, Isaac Loeb** 1851(?)-1915... **TCLC 16**
See also CA 109

**Peretz, Yitzkhok Leibush**
See Peretz, Isaac Loeb

**Perez Galdos, Benito** 1843-1920... **TCLC 27**
See also CA 125; 153; HW

**Perrault, Charles** 1628-1703 ......... **LC 2**
See also MAICYA; SATA 25

**Perry, Brighton**
See Sherwood, Robert E(mmet)

**Perse, St.-John** .............. **CLC 4, 11, 46**
See also Leger, (Marie-Rene Auguste) Alexis Saint-Leger

**Perutz, Leo** 1882-1957........... **TCLC 60**
See also DLB 81

**Peseenz, Tulio F.**
See Lopez y Fuentes, Gregorio

**Pesetsky, Bette** 1932-............. **CLC 28**
See also CA 133; DLB 130

**Peshkov, Alexei Maximovich** 1868-1936
See Gorky, Maxim
See also CA 105; 141; DA; DAC; DAM DRAM, MST, NOV

**Pessoa, Fernando (Antonio Nogueira)** 1888-1935 ........... **TCLC 27; HLC**
See also CA 125

**Peterkin, Julia Mood** 1880-1961.... **CLC 31**
See also CA 102; DLB 9

**Peters, Joan K.** 1945-............. **CLC 39**

**Peters, Robert L(ouis)** 1924-........ **CLC 7**
See also CA 13-16R; CAAS 8; DLB 105

**Petofi, Sandor** 1823-1849........ **NCLC 21**

**Petrakis, Harry Mark** 1923-........ **CLC 3**
See also CA 9-12R; CANR 4, 30

**Petrarch** 1304-1374 .... **CMLC 20; DAM POET; PC 8**

**Petrov, Evgeny** .................. **TCLC 21**
See also Kataev, Evgeny Petrovich

**Petry, Ann (Lane)** 1908- ...... **CLC 1, 7, 18**
See also BW 1; CA 5-8R; CAAS 6; CANR 4, 46; CLR 12; DLB 76; JRDA; MAICYA; MTCW; SATA 5

**Petursson, Halligrimur** 1614-1674 .... **LC 8**

**Philips, Katherine** 1632-1664........ **LC 30**
See also DLB 131

**Philipson, Morris H.** 1926-........ **CLC 53**
See also CA 1-4R; CANR 4

**Phillips, Caryl** 1958- .......... **CLC 96; DAM MULT**
See also BW 2; CA 141; DLB 157

**Phillips, David Graham** 1867-1911 .................. **TCLC 44**
See also CA 108; DLB 9, 12

**Phillips, Jack**
See Sandburg, Carl (August)

**Phillips, Jayne Anne** 1952- ............ **CLC 15, 33; SSC 16**
See also CA 101; CANR 24, 50; DLBY 80; INT CANR-24; MTCW

**Phillips, Richard**
See Dick, Philip K(indred)

**Phillips, Robert (Schaeffer)** 1938-... **CLC 28**
See also CA 17-20R; CAAS 13; CANR 8; DLB 105

**Phillips, Ward**
See Lovecraft, H(oward) P(hillips)

**Piccolo, Lucio** 1901-1969.......... **CLC 13**
See also CA 97-100; DLB 114

**Pickthall, Marjorie L(owry) C(hristie)** 1883-1922 ................. **TCLC 21**
See also CA 107; DLB 92

**Pico della Mirandola, Giovanni** 1463-1494 .................... **LC 15**

**Piercy, Marge** 1936- ......... **CLC 3, 6, 14, 18, 27, 62**
See also CA 21-24R; CAAS 1; CANR 13, 43; DLB 120; MTCW

**Piers, Robert**
See Anthony, Piers

**Pieyre de Mandiargues, Andre** 1909-1991
See Mandiargues, Andre Pieyre de
See also CA 103; 136; CANR 22

**Pilnyak, Boris** .................. **TCLC 23**
See also Vogau, Boris Andreyevich

**Pincherle, Alberto** 1907-1990 ..... **CLC 11, 18; DAM NOV**
See also Moravia, Alberto
See also CA 25-28R; 132; CANR 33; MTCW

**Pinckney, Darryl** 1953- ........... **CLC 76**
See also BW 2; CA 143

**Pindar** 518B.C.-446B.C......... **CMLC 12**

**Pineda, Cecile** 1942-............. **CLC 39**
See also CA 118

**Pinero, Arthur Wing** 1855-1934 ..... **TCLC 32; DAM DRAM**
See also CA 110; 153; DLB 10

**Pinero, Miguel (Antonio Gomez)** 1946-1988 ................. **CLC 4, 55**
See also CA 61-64; 125; CANR 29; HW

**Pinget, Robert** 1919- ........ **CLC 7, 13, 37**
See also CA 85-88; DLB 83

**Pink Floyd**
See Barrett, (Roger) Syd; Gilmour, David; Mason, Nick; Waters, Roger; Wright, Rick

**Pinkney, Edward** 1802-1828 ..... **NCLC 31**

**Pinkwater, Daniel Manus** 1941-.... **CLC 35**
See also Pinkwater, Manus
See also AAYA 1; CA 29-32R; CANR 12, 38; CLR 4; JRDA; MAICYA; SAAS 3; SATA 46, 76

**Pinkwater, Manus**
See Pinkwater, Daniel Manus
See also SATA 8

**Pinsky, Robert** 1940- .. **CLC 9, 19, 38, 94; DAM POET**
See also CA 29-32R; CAAS 4; DLBY 82

**Pinta, Harold**
See Pinter, Harold

**Pinter, Harold** 1930- ..... **CLC 1, 3, 6, 9, 11, 15, 27, 58, 73; DA; DAB; DAC; DAM DRAM, MST; WLC**
See also CA 5-8R; CANR 33; CDBLB 1960 to Present; DLB 13; MTCW

**Piozzi, Hester Lynch (Thrale)** 1741-1821 ................ **NCLC 57**
See also DLB 104, 142

**Pirandello, Luigi** 1867-1936 ...... **TCLC 4, 29; DA; DAB; DAC; DAM DRAM, MST; DC 5; SSC 22; WLC**
See also CA 104; 153

**Pirsig, Robert M(aynard)** 1928- ........ **CLC 4, 6, 73; DAM POP**
See also CA 53-56; CANR 42; MTCW; SATA 39

**Pisarev, Dmitry Ivanovich** 1840-1868 ................ **NCLC 25**

**Pix, Mary (Griffith)** 1666-1709....... **LC 8**
See also DLB 80

**Pixerecourt, Guilbert de** 1773-1844 ................ **NCLC 39**

**Plaidy, Jean**
See Hibbert, Eleanor Alice Burford

**Planche, James Robinson** 1796-1880 ................ **NCLC 42**

**Plant, Robert** 1948- .............. **CLC 12**

**Plante, David (Robert)** 1940- ....... **CLC 7, 23, 38; DAM NOV**
See also CA 37-40R; CANR 12, 36; DLBY 83; INT CANR-12; MTCW

**Plath, Sylvia** 1932-1963 ..... **CLC 1, 2, 3, 5, 9, 11, 14, 17, 50, 51, 62; DA; DAB; DAC; DAM MST, POET; PC 1; WLC**
See also AAYA 13; CA 19-20; CANR 34; CAP 2; CDALB 1941-1968; DLB 5, 6, 152; MTCW

**Plato** 428(?)B.C.-348(?)B.C..... **CMLC 8; DA; DAB; DAC; DAM MST**

**Platonov, Andrei** ................ **TCLC 14**
See also Klimentov, Andrei Platonovich

**Platt, Kin** 1911- ................ **CLC 26**
See also AAYA 11; CA 17-20R; CANR 11; JRDA; SAAS 17; SATA 21, 86

**Plautus** c. 251B.C.-184B.C. .......... **DC 6**

**Plick et Plock**
See Simenon, Georges (Jacques Christian)

**Pritchett, V(ictor) S(awdon)**
1900- .............. **CLC 5, 13, 15, 41; DAM NOV; SSC 14**
See also CA 61-64; CANR 31; DLB 15, 139; MTCW

**Private 19022**
See Manning, Frederic

**Probst, Mark** 1925- .............. **CLC 59**
See also CA 130

**Prokosch, Frederic** 1908-1989.... **CLC 4, 48**
See also CA 73-76; 128; DLB 48

**Prophet, The**
See Dreiser, Theodore (Herman Albert)

**Prose, Francine** 1947-............. **CLC 45**
See also CA 109; 112; CANR 46

**Proudhon**
See Cunha, Euclides (Rodrigues Pimenta) da

**Proulx, E. Annie** 1935- ........... **CLC 81**

**Proust, (Valentin-Louis-George-Eugene-) Marcel**
1871-1922 ........ **TCLC 7, 13, 33; DA; DAB; DAC; DAM MST, NOV; WLC**
See also CA 104; 120; DLB 65; MTCW

**Prowler, Harley**
See Masters, Edgar Lee

**Prus, Boleslaw** 1845-1912 ........ **TCLC 48**

**Pryor, Richard (Franklin Lenox Thomas)**
1940- ....................... **CLC 26**
See also CA 122

**Przybyszewski, Stanislaw**
1868-1927 .................. **TCLC 36**
See also DLB 66

**Pteleon**
See Grieve, C(hristopher) M(urray)
See also DAM POET

**Puckett, Lute**
See Masters, Edgar Lee

**Puig, Manuel**
1932-1990 ........ **CLC 3, 5, 10, 28, 65; DAM MULT; HLC**
See also CA 45-48; CANR 2, 32; DLB 113; HW; MTCW

**Purdy, Al(fred Wellington)**
1918- .......... **CLC 3, 6, 14, 50; DAC; DAM MST, POET**
See also CA 81-84; CAAS 17; CANR 42; DLB 88

**Purdy, James (Amos)**
1923- ............ **CLC 2, 4, 10, 28, 52**
See also CA 33-36R; CAAS 1; CANR 19, 51; DLB 2; INT CANR-19; MTCW

**Pure, Simon**
See Swinnerton, Frank Arthur

**Pushkin, Alexander (Sergeyevich)**
1799-1837 ..... **NCLC 3, 27; DA; DAB; DAC; DAM DRAM, MST, POET; PC 10; WLC**
See also SATA 61

**P'u Sung-ling** 1640-1715 ............ **LC 3**

**Putnam, Arthur Lee**
See Alger, Horatio, Jr.

**Puzo, Mario**
1920- ..... **CLC 1, 2, 6, 36; DAM NOV, POP**
See also CA 65-68; CANR 4, 42; DLB 6; MTCW

**Pygge, Edward**
See Barnes, Julian (Patrick)

**Pym, Barbara (Mary Crampton)**
1913-1980 ............. **CLC 13, 19, 37**
See also CA 13-14; 97-100; CANR 13, 34; CAP 1; DLB 14; DLBY 87; MTCW

**Pynchon, Thomas (Ruggles, Jr.)**
1937- ..... **CLC 2, 3, 6, 9, 11, 18, 33, 62, 72; DA; DAB; DAC; DAM MST, NOV, POP; SSC 14; WLC**
See also BEST 90:2; CA 17-20R; CANR 22, 46; DLB 2, 173; MTCW

**Qian Zhongshu**
See Ch'ien Chung-shu

**Qroll**
See Dagerman, Stig (Halvard)

**Quarrington, Paul (Lewis)** 1953-.... **CLC 65**
See also CA 129

**Quasimodo, Salvatore** 1901-1968 ... **CLC 10**
See also CA 13-16; 25-28R; CAP 1; DLB 114; MTCW

**Quay, Stephen** 1947- ............. **CLC 95**

**Quay, The Brothers**
See Quay, Stephen; Quay, Timothy

**Quay, Timothy** 1947-............. **CLC 95**

**Queen, Ellery**.................. **CLC 3, 11**
See also Dannay, Frederic; Davidson, Avram; Lee, Manfred B(ennington); Marlowe, Stephen; Sturgeon, Theodore (Hamilton); Vance, John Holbrook

**Queen, Ellery, Jr.**
See Dannay, Frederic; Lee, Manfred B(ennington)

**Queneau, Raymond**
1903-1976 ........... **CLC 2, 5, 10, 42**
See also CA 77-80; 69-72; CANR 32; DLB 72; MTCW

**Quevedo, Francisco de** 1580-1645.... **LC 23**

**Quiller-Couch, Arthur Thomas**
1863-1944 .................. **TCLC 53**
See also CA 118; DLB 135, 153

**Quin, Ann (Marie)** 1936-1973....... **CLC 6**
See also CA 9-12R; 45-48; DLB 14

**Quinn, Martin**
See Smith, Martin Cruz

**Quinn, Peter** 1947-............... **CLC 91**

**Quinn, Simon**
See Smith, Martin Cruz

**Quiroga, Horacio (Sylvestre)**
1878-1937 ..... **TCLC 20; DAM MULT; HLC**
See also CA 117; 131; HW; MTCW

**Quoirez, Francoise** 1935-........... **CLC 9**
See also Sagan, Francoise
See also CA 49-52; CANR 6, 39; MTCW

**Raabe, Wilhelm** 1831-1910 ....... **TCLC 45**
See also DLB 129

**Rabe, David (William)**
1940- ...... **CLC 4, 8, 33; DAM DRAM**
See also CA 85-88; CABS 3; DLB 7

**Rabelais, Francois**
1483-1553 ...... **LC 5; DA; DAB; DAC; DAM MST; WLC**

**Rabinovitch, Sholem** 1859-1916
See Aleichem, Sholom
See also CA 104

**Rachilde** 1860-1953 ............. **TCLC 67**
See also DLB 123

**Racine, Jean**
1639-1699 .... **LC 28; DAB; DAM MST**

**Radcliffe, Ann (Ward)**
1764-1823 ............... **NCLC 6, 55**
See also DLB 39

**Radiguet, Raymond** 1903-1923 .... **TCLC 29**
See also DLB 65

**Radnoti, Miklos** 1909-1944 ....... **TCLC 16**
See also CA 118

**Rado, James** 1939-............... **CLC 17**
See also CA 105

**Radvanyi, Netty** 1900-1983
See Seghers, Anna
See also CA 85-88; 110

**Rae, Ben**
See Griffiths, Trevor

**Raeburn, John (Hay)** 1941-........ **CLC 34**
See also CA 57-60

**Ragni, Gerome** 1942-1991 ......... **CLC 17**
See also CA 105; 134

**Rahv, Philip** 1908-1973 ........... **CLC 24**
See also Greenberg, Ivan
See also DLB 137

**Raine, Craig** 1944- ............... **CLC 32**
See also CA 108; CANR 29, 51; DLB 40

**Raine, Kathleen (Jessie)** 1908- ... **CLC 7, 45**
See also CA 85-88; CANR 46; DLB 20; MTCW

**Rainis, Janis** 1865-1929.......... **TCLC 29**

**Rakosi, Carl**...................... **CLC 47**
See also Rawley, Callman
See also CAAS 5

**Raleigh, Richard**
See Lovecraft, H(oward) P(hillips)

**Raleigh, Sir Walter** 1554(?)-1618 .... **LC 31**
See also CDBLB Before 1660; DLB 172

**Rallentando, H. P.**
See Sayers, Dorothy L(eigh)

**Ramal, Walter**
See de la Mare, Walter (John)

**Ramon, Juan**
See Jimenez (Mantecon), Juan Ramon

**Ramos, Graciliano** 1892-1953 ..... **TCLC 32**

**Rampersad, Arnold** 1941-.......... **CLC 44**
See also BW 2; CA 127; 133; DLB 111; INT 133

**Rampling, Anne**
See Rice, Anne

**Ramsay, Allan** 1684(?)-1758 ........ **LC 29**
See also DLB 95

**Ramuz, Charles-Ferdinand**
1878-1947 .................. **TCLC 33**

**Rand, Ayn**
1905-1982 ...... **CLC 3, 30, 44, 79; DA; DAC; DAM MST, NOV, POP; WLC**
See also AAYA 10; CA 13-16R; 105; CANR 27; MTCW

**Randall, Dudley (Felker)**
1914- ...... **CLC 1; BLC; DAM MULT**
See also BW 1; CA 25-28R; CANR 23; DLB 41

**Randall, Robert**
See Silverberg, Robert

**Ranger, Ken**
See Creasey, John

**Ransom, John Crowe**
1888-1974 ......... **CLC 2, 4, 5, 11, 24; DAM POET**
See also CA 5-8R; 49-52; CANR 6, 34; DLB 45, 63; MTCW

**Rao, Raja** 1909- ... **CLC 25, 56; DAM NOV**
See also CA 73-76; CANR 51; MTCW

**Raphael, Frederic (Michael)**
1931- ..................... **CLC 2, 14**
See also CA 1-4R; CANR 1; DLB 14

**Ratcliffe, James P.**
See Mencken, H(enry) L(ouis)

**Rathbone, Julian** 1935- ........... **CLC 41**
See also CA 101; CANR 34

**Rattigan, Terence (Mervyn)**
1911-1977 ....... **CLC 7; DAM DRAM**
See also CA 85-88; 73-76; CDBLB 1945-1960; DLB 13; MTCW

**Ratushinskaya, Irina** 1954- ........ **CLC 54**
See also CA 129

**Raven, Simon (Arthur Noel)**
1927- ....................... **CLC 14**
See also CA 81-84

**Rawley, Callman** 1903-
See Rakosi, Carl
See also CA 21-24R; CANR 12, 32

**Rawlings, Marjorie Kinnan**
1896-1953 .................. **TCLC 4**
See also CA 104; 137; DLB 9, 22, 102; JRDA; MAICYA; YABC 1

**Ray, Satyajit**
1921-1992 ... **CLC 16, 76; DAM MULT**
See also CA 114; 137

**Read, Herbert Edward** 1893-1968.... **CLC 4**
See also CA 85-88; 25-28R; DLB 20, 149

**Read, Piers Paul** 1941- ...... **CLC 4, 10, 25**
See also CA 21-24R; CANR 38; DLB 14; SATA 21

**Reade, Charles** 1814-1884 ........ **NCLC 2**
See also DLB 21

**Reade, Hamish**
See Gray, Simon (James Holliday)

**Reading, Peter** 1946- ............. **CLC 47**
See also CA 103; CANR 46; DLB 40

**Reaney, James**
1926- ...... **CLC 13; DAC; DAM MST**
See also CA 41-44R; CAAS 15; CANR 42; DLB 68; SATA 43

**Rebreanu, Liviu** 1885-1944 ....... **TCLC 28**

**Rechy, John (Francisco)**
1934- ............... **CLC 1, 7, 14, 18; DAM MULT; HLC**
See also CA 5-8R; CAAS 4; CANR 6, 32; DLB 122; DLBY 82; HW; INT CANR-6

**Redcam, Tom** 1870-1933 ......... **TCLC 25**

**Reddin, Keith**.................... **CLC 67**

**Redgrove, Peter (William)**
1932- ..................... **CLC 6, 41**
See also CA 1-4R; CANR 3, 39; DLB 40

**Redmon, Anne**................... **CLC 22**
See also Nightingale, Anne Redmon
See also DLBY 86

**Reed, Eliot**
See Ambler, Eric

**Reed, Ishmael**
1938- ........ **CLC 2, 3, 5, 6, 13, 32, 60; BLC; DAM MULT**
See also BW 2; CA 21-24R; CANR 25, 48; DLB 2, 5, 33, 169; DLBD 8; MTCW

**Reed, John (Silas)** 1887-1920 ...... **TCLC 9**
See also CA 106

**Reed, Lou**....................... **CLC 21**
See also Firbank, Louis

**Reeve, Clara** 1729-1807 ......... **NCLC 19**
See also DLB 39

**Reich, Wilhelm** 1897-1957........ **TCLC 57**

**Reid, Christopher (John)** 1949-..... **CLC 33**
See also CA 140; DLB 40

**Reid, Desmond**
See Moorcock, Michael (John)

**Reid Banks, Lynne** 1929-
See Banks, Lynne Reid
See also CA 1-4R; CANR 6, 22, 38; CLR 24; JRDA; MAICYA; SATA 22, 75

**Reilly, William K.**
See Creasey, John

**Reiner, Max**
See Caldwell, (Janet Miriam) Taylor (Holland)

**Reis, Ricardo**
See Pessoa, Fernando (Antonio Nogueira)

**Remarque, Erich Maria**
1898-1970 .... **CLC 21; DA; DAB; DAC; DAM MST, NOV**
See also CA 77-80; 29-32R; DLB 56; MTCW

**Remizov, A.**
See Remizov, Aleksei (Mikhailovich)

**Remizov, A. M.**
See Remizov, Aleksei (Mikhailovich)

**Remizov, Aleksei (Mikhailovich)**
1877-1957 .................. **TCLC 27**
See also CA 125; 133

**Renan, Joseph Ernest**
1823-1892 ................. **NCLC 26**

**Renard, Jules** 1864-1910 ......... **TCLC 17**
See also CA 117

**Renault, Mary**.............. **CLC 3, 11, 17**
See also Challans, Mary
See also DLBY 83

**Rendell, Ruth (Barbara)**
1930- ......... **CLC 28, 48; DAM POP**
See also Vine, Barbara
See also CA 109; CANR 32, 52; DLB 87; INT CANR-32; MTCW

**Renoir, Jean** 1894-1979 ........... **CLC 20**
See also CA 129; 85-88

**Resnais, Alain** 1922-.............. **CLC 16**

**Reverdy, Pierre** 1889-1960 ........ **CLC 53**
See also CA 97-100; 89-92

**Rexroth, Kenneth**
1905-1982 ...... **CLC 1, 2, 6, 11, 22, 49; DAM POET**
See also CA 5-8R; 107; CANR 14, 34; CDALB 1941-1968; DLB 16, 48, 165; DLBY 82; INT CANR-14; MTCW

**Reyes, Alfonso** 1889-1959 ........ **TCLC 33**
See also CA 131; HW

**Reyes y Basoalto, Ricardo Eliecer Neftali**
See Neruda, Pablo

**Reymont, Wladyslaw (Stanislaw)**
1868(?)-1925 ................. **TCLC 5**
See also CA 104

**Reynolds, Jonathan** 1942- ....... **CLC 6, 38**
See also CA 65-68; CANR 28

**Reynolds, Joshua** 1723-1792 ........ **LC 15**
See also DLB 104

**Reynolds, Michael Shane** 1937- .... **CLC 44**
See also CA 65-68; CANR 9

**Reznikoff, Charles** 1894-1976 ....... **CLC 9**
See also CA 33-36; 61-64; CAP 2; DLB 28, 45

**Rezzori (d'Arezzo), Gregor von**
1914- ....................... **CLC 25**
See also CA 122; 136

**Rhine, Richard**
See Silverstein, Alvin

**Rhodes, Eugene Manlove**
1869-1934 .................. **TCLC 53**

**R'hoone**
See Balzac, Honore de

**Rhys, Jean**
1890(?)-1979 .... **CLC 2, 4, 6, 14, 19, 51; DAM NOV; SSC 21**
See also CA 25-28R; 85-88; CANR 35; CDBLB 1945-1960; DLB 36, 117, 162; MTCW

**Ribeiro, Darcy** 1922- ............. **CLC 34**
See also CA 33-36R

**Ribeiro, Joao Ubaldo (Osorio Pimentel)**
1941- ..................... **CLC 10, 67**
See also CA 81-84

**Ribman, Ronald (Burt)** 1932- ....... **CLC 7**
See also CA 21-24R; CANR 46

**Ricci, Nino** 1959-................ **CLC 70**
See also CA 137

**Rice, Anne** 1941- ..... **CLC 41; DAM POP**
See also AAYA 9; BEST 89:2; CA 65-68; CANR 12, 36, 53

**Rice, Elmer (Leopold)**
1892-1967 .... **CLC 7, 49; DAM DRAM**
See also CA 21-22; 25-28R; CAP 2; DLB 4, 7; MTCW

**Rice, Tim(othy Miles Bindon)** 1944- ........ **CLC 21**
See also CA 103; CANR 46

**Rich, Adrienne (Cecile)** 1929- .... **CLC 3, 6, 7, 11, 18, 36, 73, 76; DAM POET; PC 5**
See also CA 9-12R; CANR 20, 53; DLB 5, 67; MTCW

**Rich, Barbara**
See Graves, Robert (von Ranke)

**Rich, Robert**
See Trumbo, Dalton

**Richard, Keith** ........ **CLC 17**
See also Richards, Keith

**Richards, David Adams** 1950- ........ **CLC 59; DAC**
See also CA 93-96; DLB 53

**Richards, I(vor) A(rmstrong)** 1893-1979 ........ **CLC 14, 24**
See also CA 41-44R; 89-92; CANR 34; DLB 27

**Richards, Keith** 1943-
See Richard, Keith
See also CA 107

**Richardson, Anne**
See Roiphe, Anne (Richardson)

**Richardson, Dorothy Miller** 1873-1957 ........ **TCLC 3**
See also CA 104; DLB 36

**Richardson, Ethel Florence (Lindesay)** 1870-1946
See Richardson, Henry Handel
See also CA 105

**Richardson, Henry Handel** ........ **TCLC 4**
See also Richardson, Ethel Florence (Lindesay)

**Richardson, John** 1796-1852 ........ **NCLC 55; DAC**
See also DLB 99

**Richardson, Samuel** 1689-1761 ...... **LC 1; DA; DAB; DAC; DAM MST, NOV; WLC**
See also CDBLB 1660-1789; DLB 39

**Richler, Mordecai** 1931- ....... **CLC 3, 5, 9, 13, 18, 46, 70; DAC; DAM MST, NOV**
See also AITN 1; CA 65-68; CANR 31; CLR 17; DLB 53; MAICYA; MTCW; SATA 44; SATA-Brief 27

**Richter, Conrad (Michael)** 1890-1968 ........ **CLC 30**
See also CA 5-8R; 25-28R; CANR 23; DLB 9; MTCW; SATA 3

**Ricostranza, Tom**
See Ellis, Trey

**Riddell, J. H.** 1832-1906 ........ **TCLC 40**

**Riding, Laura** ........ **CLC 3, 7**
See also Jackson, Laura (Riding)

**Riefenstahl, Berta Helene Amalia** 1902-
See Riefenstahl, Leni
See also CA 108

**Riefenstahl, Leni** ........ **CLC 16**
See also Riefenstahl, Berta Helene Amalia

**Riffe, Ernest**
See Bergman, (Ernst) Ingmar

**Riggs, (Rolla) Lynn** 1899-1954 ..... **TCLC 56; DAM MULT**
See also CA 144; NNAL

**Riley, James Whitcomb** 1849-1916 ...... **TCLC 51; DAM POET**
See also CA 118; 137; MAICYA; SATA 17

**Riley, Tex**
See Creasey, John

**Rilke, Rainer Maria** 1875-1926 ........ **TCLC 1, 6, 19; DAM POET; PC 2**
See also CA 104; 132; DLB 81; MTCW

**Rimbaud, (Jean Nicolas) Arthur** 1854-1891 ..... **NCLC 4, 35; DA; DAB; DAC; DAM MST, POET; PC 3; WLC**

**Rinehart, Mary Roberts** 1876-1958 ........ **TCLC 52**
See also CA 108

**Ringmaster, The**
See Mencken, H(enry) L(ouis)

**Ringwood, Gwen(dolyn Margaret) Pharis** 1910-1984 ........ **CLC 48**
See also CA 148; 112; DLB 88

**Rio, Michel** 19(?)- ........ **CLC 43**

**Ritsos, Giannes**
See Ritsos, Yannis

**Ritsos, Yannis** 1909-1990..... **CLC 6, 13, 31**
See also CA 77-80; 133; CANR 39; MTCW

**Ritter, Erika** 1948(?)- ........ **CLC 52**

**Rivera, Jose Eustasio** 1889-1928... **TCLC 35**
See also HW

**Rivers, Conrad Kent** 1933-1968...... **CLC 1**
See also BW 1; CA 85-88; DLB 41

**Rivers, Elfrida**
See Bradley, Marion Zimmer

**Riverside, John**
See Heinlein, Robert A(nson)

**Rizal, Jose** 1861-1896........ **NCLC 27**

**Roa Bastos, Augusto (Antonio)** 1917- ..... **CLC 45; DAM MULT; HLC**
See also CA 131; DLB 113; HW

**Robbe-Grillet, Alain** 1922- ...... **CLC 1, 2, 4, 6, 8, 10, 14, 43**
See also CA 9-12R; CANR 33; DLB 83; MTCW

**Robbins, Harold** 1916- ........ **CLC 5; DAM NOV**
See also CA 73-76; CANR 26, 54; MTCW

**Robbins, Thomas Eugene** 1936-
See Robbins, Tom
See also CA 81-84; CANR 29; DAM NOV, POP; MTCW

**Robbins, Tom** ........ **CLC 9, 32, 64**
See also Robbins, Thomas Eugene
See also BEST 90:3; DLBY 80

**Robbins, Trina** 1938- ........ **CLC 21**
See also CA 128

**Roberts, Charles G(eorge) D(ouglas)** 1860-1943 ........ **TCLC 8**
See also CA 105; CLR 33; DLB 92; SATA 88; SATA-Brief 29

**Roberts, Elizabeth Madox** 1886-1941 ........ **TCLC 68**
See also CA 111; DLB 9, 54, 102; SATA 33; SATA-Brief 27

**Roberts, Kate** 1891-1985 ........ **CLC 15**
See also CA 107; 116

**Roberts, Keith (John Kingston)** 1935- ........ **CLC 14**
See also CA 25-28R; CANR 46

**Roberts, Kenneth (Lewis)** 1885-1957 ........ **TCLC 23**
See also CA 109; DLB 9

**Roberts, Michele (B.)** 1949- ........ **CLC 48**
See also CA 115

**Robertson, Ellis**
See Ellison, Harlan (Jay); Silverberg, Robert

**Robertson, Thomas William** 1829-1871 .... **NCLC 35; DAM DRAM**

**Robinson, Edwin Arlington** 1869-1935 ........ **TCLC 5; DA; DAC; DAM MST, POET; PC 1**
See also CA 104; 133; CDALB 1865-1917; DLB 54; MTCW

**Robinson, Henry Crabb** 1775-1867 ........ **NCLC 15**
See also DLB 107

**Robinson, Jill** 1936- ........ **CLC 10**
See also CA 102; INT 102

**Robinson, Kim Stanley** 1952- ...... **CLC 34**
See also CA 126

**Robinson, Lloyd**
See Silverberg, Robert

**Robinson, Marilynne** 1944- ........ **CLC 25**
See also CA 116

**Robinson, Smokey** ........ **CLC 21**
See also Robinson, William, Jr.

**Robinson, William, Jr.** 1940-
See Robinson, Smokey
See also CA 116

**Robison, Mary** 1949- ........ **CLC 42, 98**
See also CA 113; 116; DLB 130; INT 116

**Rod, Edouard** 1857-1910 ........ **TCLC 52**

**Roddenberry, Eugene Wesley** 1921-1991
See Roddenberry, Gene
See also CA 110; 135; CANR 37; SATA 45; SATA-Obit 69

**Roddenberry, Gene** ........ **CLC 17**
See also Roddenberry, Eugene Wesley
See also AAYA 5; SATA-Obit 69

**Rodgers, Mary** 1931- ........ **CLC 12**
See also CA 49-52; CANR 8, 55; CLR 20; INT CANR-8; JRDA; MAICYA; SATA 8

**Rodgers, W(illiam) R(obert)** 1909-1969 ........ **CLC 7**
See also CA 85-88; DLB 20

**Rodman, Eric**
See Silverberg, Robert

**Rodman, Howard** 1920(?)-1985..... **CLC 65**
See also CA 118

**Rodman, Maia**
See Wojciechowska, Maia (Teresa)

**Rodriguez, Claudio** 1934- ........ **CLC 10**
See also DLB 134

**Roelvaag, O(le) E(dvart)**
1876-1931 .................. **TCLC 17**
See also CA 117; DLB 9

**Roethke, Theodore (Huebner)**
1908-1963 ...... **CLC 1, 3, 8, 11, 19, 46; DAM POET; PC 15**
See also CA 81-84; CABS 2; CDALB 1941-1968; DLB 5; MTCW

**Rogers, Thomas Hunton** 1927- ..... **CLC 57**
See also CA 89-92; INT 89-92

**Rogers, Will(iam Penn Adair)**
1879-1935 ...... **TCLC 8; DAM MULT**
See also CA 105; 144; DLB 11; NNAL

**Rogin, Gilbert** 1929-.............. **CLC 18**
See also CA 65-68; CANR 15

**Rohan, Koda** .................... **TCLC 22**
See also Koda Shigeyuki

**Rohmer, Eric**..................... **CLC 16**
See also Scherer, Jean-Marie Maurice

**Rohmer, Sax** ..................... **TCLC 28**
See also Ward, Arthur Henry Sarsfield
See also DLB 70

**Roiphe, Anne (Richardson)**
1935- ...................... **CLC 3, 9**
See also CA 89-92; CANR 45; DLBY 80; INT 89-92

**Rojas, Fernando de** 1465-1541 ...... **LC 23**

**Rolfe, Frederick (William Serafino Austin Lewis Mary)** 1860-1913...... **TCLC 12**
See also CA 107; DLB 34, 156

**Rolland, Romain** 1866-1944....... **TCLC 23**
See also CA 118; DLB 65

**Rolle, Richard** c. 1300-c. 1349 ... **CMLC 21**
See also DLB 146

**Rolvaag, O(le) E(dvart)**
See Roelvaag, O(le) E(dvart)

**Romain Arnaud, Saint**
See Aragon, Louis

**Romains, Jules** 1885-1972.......... **CLC 7**
See also CA 85-88; CANR 34; DLB 65; MTCW

**Romero, Jose Ruben** 1890-1952 ... **TCLC 14**
See also CA 114; 131; HW

**Ronsard, Pierre de**
1524-1585 ............... **LC 6; PC 11**

**Rooke, Leon**
1934- ......... **CLC 25, 34; DAM POP**
See also CA 25-28R; CANR 23, 53

**Roper, William** 1498-1578.......... **LC 10**

**Roquelaure, A. N.**
See Rice, Anne

**Rosa, Joao Guimaraes** 1908-1967... **CLC 23**
See also CA 89-92; DLB 113

**Rose, Wendy**
1948- .... **CLC 85; DAM MULT; PC 13**
See also CA 53-56; CANR 5, 51; NNAL; SATA 12

**Rosen, Richard (Dean)** 1949-....... **CLC 39**
See also CA 77-80; INT CANR-30

**Rosenberg, Isaac** 1890-1918....... **TCLC 12**
See also CA 107; DLB 20

**Rosenblatt, Joe** ................... **CLC 15**
See also Rosenblatt, Joseph

**Rosenblatt, Joseph** 1933-
See Rosenblatt, Joe
See also CA 89-92; INT 89-92

**Rosenfeld, Samuel** 1896-1963
See Tzara, Tristan
See also CA 89-92

**Rosenstock, Sami**
See Tzara, Tristan

**Rosenstock, Samuel**
See Tzara, Tristan

**Rosenthal, M(acha) L(ouis)**
1917-1996 ................... **CLC 28**
See also CA 1-4R; 152; CAAS 6; CANR 4, 51; DLB 5; SATA 59

**Ross, Barnaby**
See Dannay, Frederic

**Ross, Bernard L.**
See Follett, Ken(neth Martin)

**Ross, J. H.**
See Lawrence, T(homas) E(dward)

**Ross, Martin**
See Martin, Violet Florence
See also DLB 135

**Ross, (James) Sinclair**
1908- ...... **CLC 13; DAC; DAM MST; SSC 24**
See also CA 73-76; DLB 88

**Rossetti, Christina (Georgina)**
1830-1894 ..... **NCLC 2, 50; DA; DAB; DAC; DAM MST, POET; PC 7; WLC**
See also DLB 35, 163; MAICYA; SATA 20

**Rossetti, Dante Gabriel**
1828-1882 ........ **NCLC 4; DA; DAB; DAC; DAM MST, POET; WLC**
See also CDBLB 1832-1890; DLB 35

**Rossner, Judith (Perelman)**
1935- .................. **CLC 6, 9, 29**
See also AITN 2; BEST 90:3; CA 17-20R; CANR 18, 51; DLB 6; INT CANR-18; MTCW

**Rostand, Edmond (Eugene Alexis)**
1868-1918 ...... **TCLC 6, 37; DA; DAB; DAC; DAM DRAM, MST**
See also CA 104; 126; MTCW

**Roth, Henry** 1906-1995 ....... **CLC 2, 6, 11**
See also CA 11-12; 149; CANR 38; CAP 1; DLB 28; MTCW

**Roth, Joseph** 1894-1939.......... **TCLC 33**
See also DLB 85

**Roth, Philip (Milton)**
1933- ...... **CLC 1, 2, 3, 4, 6, 9, 15, 22, 31, 47, 66, 86; DA; DAB; DAC; DAM MST, NOV, POP; WLC**
See also BEST 90:3; CA 1-4R; CANR 1, 22, 36, 55; CDALB 1968-1988; DLB 2, 28, 173; DLBY 82; MTCW

**Rothenberg, Jerome** 1931-....... **CLC 6, 57**
See also CA 45-48; CANR 1; DLB 5

**Roumain, Jacques (Jean Baptiste)**
1907-1944 ............ **TCLC 19; BLC; DAM MULT**
See also BW 1; CA 117; 125

**Rourke, Constance (Mayfield)**
1885-1941 .................. **TCLC 12**
See also CA 107; YABC 1

**Rousseau, Jean-Baptiste** 1671-1741 ... **LC 9**

**Rousseau, Jean-Jacques**
1712-1778 ....... **LC 14, 36; DA; DAB; DAC; DAM MST; WLC**

**Roussel, Raymond** 1877-1933 ..... **TCLC 20**
See also CA 117

**Rovit, Earl (Herbert)** 1927-......... **CLC 7**
See also CA 5-8R; CANR 12

**Rowe, Nicholas** 1674-1718........... **LC 8**
See also DLB 84

**Rowley, Ames Dorrance**
See Lovecraft, H(oward) P(hillips)

**Rowson, Susanna Haswell**
1762(?)-1824 ................ **NCLC 5**
See also DLB 37

**Roy, Gabrielle**
1909-1983 .... **CLC 10, 14; DAB; DAC; DAM MST**
See also CA 53-56; 110; CANR 5; DLB 68; MTCW

**Rozewicz, Tadeusz**
1921- ......... **CLC 9, 23; DAM POET**
See also CA 108; CANR 36; MTCW

**Ruark, Gibbons** 1941- ............. **CLC 3**
See also CA 33-36R; CAAS 23; CANR 14, 31; DLB 120

**Rubens, Bernice (Ruth)** 1923-... **CLC 19, 31**
See also CA 25-28R; CANR 33; DLB 14; MTCW

**Rubin, Harold**
See Robbins, Harold

**Rudkin, (James) David** 1936- ...... **CLC 14**
See also CA 89-92; DLB 13

**Rudnik, Raphael** 1933-............. **CLC 7**
See also CA 29-32R

**Ruffian, M.**
See Hasek, Jaroslav (Matej Frantisek)

**Ruiz, Jose Martinez** ............... **CLC 11**
See also Martinez Ruiz, Jose

**Rukeyser, Muriel**
1913-1980 .......... **CLC 6, 10, 15, 27; DAM POET; PC 12**
See also CA 5-8R; 93-96; CANR 26; DLB 48; MTCW; SATA-Obit 22

**Rule, Jane (Vance)** 1931-.......... **CLC 27**
See also CA 25-28R; CAAS 18; CANR 12; DLB 60

**Rulfo, Juan**
1918-1986 .... **CLC 8, 80; DAM MULT; HLC**
See also CA 85-88; 118; CANR 26; DLB 113; HW; MTCW

**Rumi, Jalal al-Din** 1297-1373 .... **CMLC 20**

**Runeberg, Johan** 1804-1877...... **NCLC 41**

**Runyon, (Alfred) Damon**
1884(?)-1946 ................ **TCLC 10**
See also CA 107; DLB 11, 86, 171

**Rush, Norman** 1933-.............. **CLC 44**
See also CA 121; 126; INT 126

**Rushdie, (Ahmed) Salman**
1947- ..... **CLC 23, 31, 55; DAB; DAC; DAM MST, NOV, POP**
See also BEST 89:3; CA 108; 111; CANR 33; INT 111; MTCW

**Rushforth, Peter (Scott)** 1945- ..... **CLC 19**
See also CA 101

**Ruskin, John** 1819-1900 .......... **TCLC 63**
See also CA 114; 129; CDBLB 1832-1890; DLB 55, 163; SATA 24

**Russ, Joanna** 1937- .............. **CLC 15**
See also CA 25-28R; CANR 11, 31; DLB 8; MTCW

**Russell, George William** 1867-1935
See Baker, Jean H.
See also CA 104; 153; CDBLB 1890-1914; DAM POET

**Russell, (Henry) Ken(neth Alfred)** 1927- ...................... **CLC 16**
See also CA 105

**Russell, Willy** 1947- .............. **CLC 60**

**Rutherford, Mark** ................ **TCLC 25**
See also White, William Hale
See also DLB 18

**Ruyslinck, Ward** 1929- ........... **CLC 14**
See also Belser, Reimond Karel Maria de

**Ryan, Cornelius (John)** 1920-1974 ... **CLC 7**
See also CA 69-72; 53-56; CANR 38

**Ryan, Michael** 1946- ............. **CLC 65**
See also CA 49-52; DLBY 82

**Rybakov, Anatoli (Naumovich)** 1911- .................... **CLC 23, 53**
See also CA 126; 135; SATA 79

**Ryder, Jonathan**
See Ludlum, Robert

**Ryga, George** 1932-1987 .. **CLC 14; DAC; DAM MST**
See also CA 101; 124; CANR 43; DLB 60

**S. S.**
See Sassoon, Siegfried (Lorraine)

**Saba, Umberto** 1883-1957 ........ **TCLC 33**
See also CA 144; DLB 114

**Sabatini, Rafael** 1875-1950 ....... **TCLC 47**

**Sabato, Ernesto (R.)** 1911- ....... **CLC 10, 23; DAM MULT; HLC**
See also CA 97-100; CANR 32; DLB 145; HW; MTCW

**Sacastru, Martin**
See Bioy Casares, Adolfo

**Sacher-Masoch, Leopold von** 1836(?)-1895 ............... **NCLC 31**

**Sachs, Marilyn (Stickle)** 1927- ..... **CLC 35**
See also AAYA 2; CA 17-20R; CANR 13, 47; CLR 2; JRDA; MAICYA; SAAS 2; SATA 3, 68

**Sachs, Nelly** 1891-1970 ........ **CLC 14, 98**
See also CA 17-18; 25-28R; CAP 2

**Sackler, Howard (Oliver)** 1929-1982 .................. **CLC 14**
See also CA 61-64; 108; CANR 30; DLB 7

**Sacks, Oliver (Wolf)** 1933- ........ **CLC 67**
See also CA 53-56; CANR 28, 50; INT CANR-28; MTCW

**Sade, Donatien Alphonse Francois Comte** 1740-1814 ................ **NCLC 47**

**Sadoff, Ira** 1945- .................. **CLC 9**
See also CA 53-56; CANR 5, 21; DLB 120

**Saetone**
See Camus, Albert

**Safire, William** 1929- ............. **CLC 10**
See also CA 17-20R; CANR 31, 54

**Sagan, Carl (Edward)** 1934-1996.... **CLC 30**
See also AAYA 2; CA 25-28R; 155; CANR 11, 36; MTCW; SATA 58

**Sagan, Francoise** ........ **CLC 3, 6, 9, 17, 36**
See also Quoirez, Francoise
See also DLB 83

**Sahgal, Nayantara (Pandit)** 1927- ... **CLC 41**
See also CA 9-12R; CANR 11

**Saint, H(arry) F.** 1941- ........... **CLC 50**
See also CA 127

**St. Aubin de Teran, Lisa** 1953-
See Teran, Lisa St. Aubin de
See also CA 118; 126; INT 126

**Sainte-Beuve, Charles Augustin** 1804-1869 ................. **NCLC 5**

**Saint-Exupery, Antoine (Jean Baptiste Marie Roger) de** 1900-1944 .... **TCLC 2, 56; DAM NOV; WLC**
See also CA 108; 132; CLR 10; DLB 72; MAICYA; MTCW; SATA 20

**St. John, David**
See Hunt, E(verette) Howard, (Jr.)

**Saint-John Perse**
See Leger, (Marie-Rene Auguste) Alexis Saint-Leger

**Saintsbury, George (Edward Bateman)** 1845-1933 .................. **TCLC 31**
See also DLB 57, 149

**Sait Faik** ....................... **TCLC 23**
See also Abasiyanik, Sait Faik

**Saki** ................... **TCLC 3; SSC 12**
See also Munro, H(ector) H(ugh)

**Sala, George Augustus** ........... **NCLC 46**

**Salama, Hannu** 1936- ............. **CLC 18**

**Salamanca, J(ack) R(ichard)** 1922- ..................... **CLC 4, 15**
See also CA 25-28R

**Sale, J. Kirkpatrick**
See Sale, Kirkpatrick

**Sale, Kirkpatrick** 1937- ........... **CLC 68**
See also CA 13-16R; CANR 10

**Salinas, Luis Omar** 1937- ..... **CLC 90; DAM MULT; HLC**
See also CA 131; DLB 82; HW

**Salinas (y Serrano), Pedro** 1891(?)-1951 ................ **TCLC 17**
See also CA 117; DLB 134

**Salinger, J(erome) D(avid)** 1919- ...... **CLC 1, 3, 8, 12, 55, 56; DA; DAB; DAC; DAM MST, NOV, POP; SSC 2; WLC**
See also AAYA 2; CA 5-8R; CANR 39; CDALB 1941-1968; CLR 18; DLB 2, 102, 173; MAICYA; MTCW; SATA 67

**Salisbury, John**
See Caute, David

**Salter, James** 1925- ......... **CLC 7, 52, 59**
See also CA 73-76; DLB 130

**Saltus, Edgar (Everton)** 1855-1921 ................... **TCLC 8**
See also CA 105

**Saltykov, Mikhail Evgrafovich** 1826-1889 ................. **NCLC 16**

**Samarakis, Antonis** 1919- .......... **CLC 5**
See also CA 25-28R; CAAS 16; CANR 36

**Sanchez, Florencio** 1875-1910 ..... **TCLC 37**
See also CA 153; HW

**Sanchez, Luis Rafael** 1936- ........ **CLC 23**
See also CA 128; DLB 145; HW

**Sanchez, Sonia** 1934- ...... **CLC 5; BLC; DAM MULT; PC 9**
See also BW 2; CA 33-36R; CANR 24, 49; CLR 18; DLB 41; DLBD 8; MAICYA; MTCW; SATA 22

**Sand, George** 1804-1876 ........ **NCLC 2, 42, 57; DA; DAB; DAC; DAM MST, NOV; WLC**
See also DLB 119

**Sandburg, Carl (August)** 1878-1967 .... **CLC 1, 4, 10, 15, 35; DA; DAB; DAC; DAM MST, POET; PC 2; WLC**
See also CA 5-8R; 25-28R; CANR 35; CDALB 1865-1917; DLB 17, 54; MAICYA; MTCW; SATA 8

**Sandburg, Charles**
See Sandburg, Carl (August)

**Sandburg, Charles A.**
See Sandburg, Carl (August)

**Sanders, (James) Ed(ward)** 1939- ... **CLC 53**
See also CA 13-16R; CAAS 21; CANR 13, 44; DLB 16

**Sanders, Lawrence** 1920- ............ **CLC 41; DAM POP**
See also BEST 89:4; CA 81-84; CANR 33; MTCW

**Sanders, Noah**
See Blount, Roy (Alton), Jr.

**Sanders, Winston P.**
See Anderson, Poul (William)

**Sandoz, Mari(e Susette)** 1896-1966 .................. **CLC 28**
See also CA 1-4R; 25-28R; CANR 17; DLB 9; MTCW; SATA 5

**Saner, Reg(inald Anthony)** 1931- .... **CLC 9**
See also CA 65-68

**Sannazaro, Jacopo** 1456(?)-1530 ...... **LC 8**

**Sansom, William** 1912-1976 ...... **CLC 2, 6; DAM NOV; SSC 21**
See also CA 5-8R; 65-68; CANR 42; DLB 139; MTCW

**Santayana, George** 1863-1952 ..... **TCLC 40**
See also CA 115; DLB 54, 71; DLBD 13

**Santiago, Danny** .................. **CLC 33**
See also James, Daniel (Lewis)
See also DLB 122

**Santmyer, Helen Hoover** 1895-1986 ................... **CLC 33**
See also CA 1-4R; 118; CANR 15, 33; DLBY 84; MTCW

**Santos, Bienvenido N(uqui)** 1911-1996 ...... **CLC 22; DAM MULT**
See also CA 101; 151; CANR 19, 46

**Shaw, Irwin**
1913-1984 . . . . . . . . . . . . . **CLC 7, 23, 34; DAM DRAM, POP**
See also AITN 1; CA 13-16R; 112; CANR 21; CDALB 1941-1968; DLB 6, 102; DLBY 84; MTCW

**Shaw, Robert** 1927-1978 . . . . . . . . . . . **CLC 5**
See also AITN 1; CA 1-4R; 81-84; CANR 4; DLB 13, 14

**Shaw, T. E.**
See Lawrence, T(homas) E(dward)

**Shawn, Wallace** 1943- . . . . . . . . . . . . **CLC 41**
See also CA 112

**Shea, Lisa** 1953- . . . . . . . . . . . . . . . . . **CLC 86**
See also CA 147

**Sheed, Wilfrid (John Joseph)**
1930- . . . . . . . . . . . . . . . . **CLC 2, 4, 10, 53**
See also CA 65-68; CANR 30; DLB 6; MTCW

**Sheldon, Alice Hastings Bradley**
1915(?)-1987
See Tiptree, James, Jr.
See also CA 108; 122; CANR 34; INT 108; MTCW

**Sheldon, John**
See Bloch, Robert (Albert)

**Shelley, Mary Wollstonecraft (Godwin)**
1797-1851 . . . . **NCLC 14, 59; DA; DAB; DAC; DAM MST, NOV; WLC**
See also CDBLB 1789-1832; DLB 110, 116, 159; SATA 29

**Shelley, Percy Bysshe**
1792-1822 . . . . . . . **NCLC 18; DA; DAB; DAC; DAM MST, POET; PC 14; WLC**
See also CDBLB 1789-1832; DLB 96, 110, 158

**Shepard, Jim** 1956- . . . . . . . . . . . . . . **CLC 36**
See also CA 137; SATA 90

**Shepard, Lucius** 1947- . . . . . . . . . . . . **CLC 34**
See also CA 128; 141

**Shepard, Sam**
1943- . . . . . . . . . **CLC 4, 6, 17, 34, 41, 44; DAM DRAM; DC 5**
See also AAYA 1; CA 69-72; CABS 3; CANR 22; DLB 7; MTCW

**Shepherd, Michael**
See Ludlum, Robert

**Sherburne, Zoa (Morin)** 1912- . . . . . . **CLC 30**
See also AAYA 13; CA 1-4R; CANR 3, 37; MAICYA; SAAS 18; SATA 3

**Sheridan, Frances** 1724-1766 . . . . . . . . . **LC 7**
See also DLB 39, 84

**Sheridan, Richard Brinsley**
1751-1816 . . . . . . . . **NCLC 5; DA; DAB; DAC; DAM DRAM, MST; DC 1; WLC**
See also CDBLB 1660-1789; DLB 89

**Sherman, Jonathan Marc** . . . . . . . . . . . **CLC 55**

**Sherman, Martin** 1941(?)- . . . . . . . . . **CLC 19**
See also CA 116; 123

**Sherwin, Judith Johnson** 1936- . . . **CLC 7, 15**
See also CA 25-28R; CANR 34

**Sherwood, Frances** 1940- . . . . . . . . . . **CLC 81**
See also CA 146

**Sherwood, Robert E(mmet)**
1896-1955 . . . . . . **TCLC 3; DAM DRAM**
See also CA 104; 153; DLB 7, 26

**Shestov, Lev** 1866-1938 . . . . . . . . . . **TCLC 56**

**Shevchenko, Taras** 1814-1861 . . . . **NCLC 54**

**Shiel, M(atthew) P(hipps)**
1865-1947 . . . . . . . . . . . . . . . . . . **TCLC 8**
See also CA 106; DLB 153

**Shields, Carol** 1935- . . . . . . . . . **CLC 91; DAC**
See also CA 81-84; CANR 51

**Shields, David** 1956- . . . . . . . . . . . . . . **CLC 97**
See also CA 124; CANR 48

**Shiga, Naoya** 1883-1971 . . . **CLC 33; SSC 23**
See also CA 101; 33-36R

**Shilts, Randy** 1951-1994 . . . . . . . . . . **CLC 85**
See also AAYA 19; CA 115; 127; 144; CANR 45; INT 127

**Shimazaki, Haruki** 1872-1943
See Shimazaki Toson
See also CA 105; 134

**Shimazaki Toson** . . . . . . . . . . . . . . . . . . **TCLC 5**
See also Shimazaki, Haruki

**Sholokhov, Mikhail (Aleksandrovich)**
1905-1984 . . . . . . . . . . . . . . . . . **CLC 7, 15**
See also CA 101; 112; MTCW; SATA-Obit 36

**Shone, Patric**
See Hanley, James

**Shreve, Susan Richards** 1939- . . . . . . **CLC 23**
See also CA 49-52; CAAS 5; CANR 5, 38; MAICYA; SATA 46; SATA-Brief 41

**Shue, Larry**
1946-1985 . . . . . . **CLC 52; DAM DRAM**
See also CA 145; 117

**Shu-Jen, Chou** 1881-1936
See Lu Hsun
See also CA 104

**Shulman, Alix Kates** 1932- . . . . . . **CLC 2, 10**
See also CA 29-32R; CANR 43; SATA 7

**Shuster, Joe** 1914- . . . . . . . . . . . . . . . **CLC 21**

**Shute, Nevil** . . . . . . . . . . . . . . . . . . . . . . **CLC 30**
See also Norway, Nevil Shute

**Shuttle, Penelope (Diane)** 1947- . . . . . **CLC 7**
See also CA 93-96; CANR 39; DLB 14, 40

**Sidney, Mary** 1561-1621 . . . . . . . . . . . **LC 19**

**Sidney, Sir Philip**
1554-1586 . . . . . **LC 19; DA; DAB; DAC; DAM MST, POET**
See also CDBLB Before 1660; DLB 167

**Siegel, Jerome** 1914-1996 . . . . . . . . . **CLC 21**
See also CA 116; 151

**Siegel, Jerry**
See Siegel, Jerome

**Sienkiewicz, Henryk (Adam Alexander Pius)**
1846-1916 . . . . . . . . . . . . . . . . . . . **TCLC 3**
See also CA 104; 134

**Sierra, Gregorio Martinez**
See Martinez Sierra, Gregorio

**Sierra, Maria (de la O'LeJarraga) Martinez**
See Martinez Sierra, Maria (de la O'LeJarraga)

**Sigal, Clancy** 1926- . . . . . . . . . . . . . . . . **CLC 7**
See also CA 1-4R

**Sigourney, Lydia Howard (Huntley)**
1791-1865 . . . . . . . . . . . . . . . . . **NCLC 21**
See also DLB 1, 42, 73

**Siguenza y Gongora, Carlos de**
1645-1700 . . . . . . . . . . . . . . . . . . . . . **LC 8**

**Sigurjonsson, Johann** 1880-1919 . . . **TCLC 27**

**Sikelianos, Angelos** 1884-1951 . . . . **TCLC 39**

**Silkin, Jon** 1930- . . . . . . . . . . . . **CLC 2, 6, 43**
See also CA 5-8R; CAAS 5; DLB 27

**Silko, Leslie (Marmon)**
1948- . . . . . . . . . . **CLC 23, 74; DA; DAC; DAM MST, MULT, POP**
See also AAYA 14; CA 115; 122; CANR 45; DLB 143; NNAL

**Sillanpaa, Frans Eemil** 1888-1964 . . . **CLC 19**
See also CA 129; 93-96; MTCW

**Sillitoe, Alan**
1928- . . . . . . . . . . **CLC 1, 3, 6, 10, 19, 57**
See also AITN 1; CA 9-12R; CAAS 2; CANR 8, 26, 55; CDBLB 1960 to Present; DLB 14, 139; MTCW; SATA 61

**Silone, Ignazio** 1900-1978 . . . . . . . . . . **CLC 4**
See also CA 25-28; 81-84; CANR 34; CAP 2; MTCW

**Silver, Joan Micklin** 1935- . . . . . . . . **CLC 20**
See also CA 114; 121; INT 121

**Silver, Nicholas**
See Faust, Frederick (Schiller)

**Silverberg, Robert**
1935- . . . . . . . . . . . . . **CLC 7; DAM POP**
See also CA 1-4R; CAAS 3; CANR 1, 20, 36; DLB 8; INT CANR-20; MAICYA; MTCW; SATA 13, 91

**Silverstein, Alvin** 1933- . . . . . . . . . . . **CLC 17**
See also CA 49-52; CANR 2; CLR 25; JRDA; MAICYA; SATA 8, 69

**Silverstein, Virginia B(arbara Opshelor)**
1937- . . . . . . . . . . . . . . . . . . . . . . . **CLC 17**
See also CA 49-52; CANR 2; CLR 25; JRDA; MAICYA; SATA 8, 69

**Sim, Georges**
See Simenon, Georges (Jacques Christian)

**Simak, Clifford D(onald)**
1904-1988 . . . . . . . . . . . . . . . . . **CLC 1, 55**
See also CA 1-4R; 125; CANR 1, 35; DLB 8; MTCW; SATA-Obit 56

**Simenon, Georges (Jacques Christian)**
1903-1989 . . . . . . . **CLC 1, 2, 3, 8, 18, 47; DAM POP**
See also CA 85-88; 129; CANR 35; DLB 72; DLBY 89; MTCW

**Simic, Charles**
1938- . . . . . . . . . . . . **CLC 6, 9, 22, 49, 68; DAM POET**
See also CA 29-32R; CAAS 4; CANR 12, 33, 52; DLB 105

**Simmel, Georg** 1858-1918 . . . . . . . . **TCLC 64**

**Simmons, Charles (Paul)** 1924- . . . . . **CLC 57**
See also CA 89-92; INT 89-92

**Simmons, Dan** 1948- . . . **CLC 44; DAM POP**
See also AAYA 16; CA 138; CANR 53

**Simmons, James (Stewart Alexander)**
1933- . . . . . . . . . . . . . . . . . . . . . . . . **CLC 43**
See also CA 105; CAAS 21; DLB 40

**Simms, William Gilmore** 1806-1870 .................. **NCLC 3**
See also DLB 3, 30, 59, 73

**Simon, Carly** 1945-............... **CLC 26**
See also CA 105

**Simon, Claude** 1913- .... **CLC 4, 9, 15, 39; DAM NOV**
See also CA 89-92; CANR 33; DLB 83; MTCW

**Simon, (Marvin) Neil** 1927- ........... **CLC 6, 11, 31, 39, 70; DAM DRAM**
See also AITN 1; CA 21-24R; CANR 26, 54; DLB 7; MTCW

**Simon, Paul (Frederick)** 1941(?)- ... **CLC 17**
See also CA 116; 153

**Simonon, Paul** 1956(?)- ........... **CLC 30**

**Simpson, Harriette**
See Arnow, Harriette (Louisa) Simpson

**Simpson, Louis (Aston Marantz)** 1923- .... **CLC 4, 7, 9, 32; DAM POET**
See also CA 1-4R; CAAS 4; CANR 1; DLB 5; MTCW

**Simpson, Mona (Elizabeth)** 1957-... **CLC 44**
See also CA 122; 135

**Simpson, N(orman) F(rederick)** 1919- ....................... **CLC 29**
See also CA 13-16R; DLB 13

**Sinclair, Andrew (Annandale)** 1935- ..................... **CLC 2, 14**
See also CA 9-12R; CAAS 5; CANR 14, 38; DLB 14; MTCW

**Sinclair, Emil**
See Hesse, Hermann

**Sinclair, Iain** 1943-............... **CLC 76**
See also CA 132

**Sinclair, Iain MacGregor**
See Sinclair, Iain

**Sinclair, Irene**
See Griffith, D(avid Lewelyn) W(ark)

**Sinclair, Mary Amelia St. Clair** 1865(?)-1946
See Sinclair, May
See also CA 104

**Sinclair, May**.................. **TCLC 3, 11**
See also Sinclair, Mary Amelia St. Clair
See also DLB 36, 135

**Sinclair, Roy**
See Griffith, D(avid Lewelyn) W(ark)

**Sinclair, Upton (Beall)** 1878-1968 ...... **CLC 1, 11, 15, 63; DA; DAB; DAC; DAM MST, NOV; WLC**
See also CA 5-8R; 25-28R; CANR 7; CDALB 1929-1941; DLB 9; INT CANR-7; MTCW; SATA 9

**Singer, Isaac**
See Singer, Isaac Bashevis

**Singer, Isaac Bashevis** 1904-1991 .... **CLC 1, 3, 6, 9, 11, 15, 23, 38, 69; DA; DAB; DAC; DAM MST, NOV; SSC 3; WLC**
See also AITN 1, 2; CA 1-4R; 134; CANR 1, 39; CDALB 1941-1968; CLR 1; DLB 6, 28, 52; DLBY 91; JRDA; MAICYA; MTCW; SATA 3, 27; SATA-Obit 68

**Singer, Israel Joshua** 1893-1944 ... **TCLC 33**

**Singh, Khushwant** 1915-........... **CLC 11**
See also CA 9-12R; CAAS 9; CANR 6

**Sinjohn, John**
See Galsworthy, John

**Sinyavsky, Andrei (Donatevich)** 1925- ........................ **CLC 8**
See also CA 85-88

**Sirin, V.**
See Nabokov, Vladimir (Vladimirovich)

**Sissman, L(ouis) E(dward)** 1928-1976 ................. **CLC 9, 18**
See also CA 21-24R; 65-68; CANR 13; DLB 5

**Sisson, C(harles) H(ubert)** 1914-..... **CLC 8**
See also CA 1-4R; CAAS 3; CANR 3, 48; DLB 27

**Sitwell, Dame Edith** 1887-1964 .............. **CLC 2, 9, 67; DAM POET; PC 3**
See also CA 9-12R; CANR 35; CDBLB 1945-1960; DLB 20; MTCW

**Sjoewall, Maj** 1935-................ **CLC 7**
See also CA 65-68

**Sjowall, Maj**
See Sjoewall, Maj

**Skelton, Robin** 1925-............. **CLC 13**
See also AITN 2; CA 5-8R; CAAS 5; CANR 28; DLB 27, 53

**Skolimowski, Jerzy** 1938-......... **CLC 20**
See also CA 128

**Skram, Amalie (Bertha)** 1847-1905 .................. **TCLC 25**

**Skvorecky, Josef (Vaclav)** 1924- ........... **CLC 15, 39, 69; DAC; DAM NOV**
See also CA 61-64; CAAS 1; CANR 10, 34; MTCW

**Slade, Bernard**................. **CLC 11, 46**
See also Newbound, Bernard Slade
See also CAAS 9; DLB 53

**Slaughter, Carolyn** 1946-.......... **CLC 56**
See also CA 85-88

**Slaughter, Frank G(ill)** 1908- ...... **CLC 29**
See also AITN 2; CA 5-8R; CANR 5; INT CANR-5

**Slavitt, David R(ytman)** 1935-.... **CLC 5, 14**
See also CA 21-24R; CAAS 3; CANR 41; DLB 5, 6

**Slesinger, Tess** 1905-1945 ........ **TCLC 10**
See also CA 107; DLB 102

**Slessor, Kenneth** 1901-1971........ **CLC 14**
See also CA 102; 89-92

**Slowacki, Juliusz** 1809-1849 ..... **NCLC 15**

**Smart, Christopher** 1722-1771 ... **LC 3; DAM POET; PC 13**
See also DLB 109

**Smart, Elizabeth** 1913-1986........ **CLC 54**
See also CA 81-84; 118; DLB 88

**Smiley, Jane (Graves)** 1949- ......... **CLC 53, 76; DAM POP**
See also CA 104; CANR 30, 50; INT CANR-30

**Smith, A(rthur) J(ames) M(arshall)** 1902-1980 .............. **CLC 15; DAC**
See also CA 1-4R; 102; CANR 4; DLB 88

**Smith, Adam** 1723-1790............ **LC 36**
See also DLB 104

**Smith, Alexander** 1829-1867 ..... **NCLC 59**
See also DLB 32, 55

**Smith, Anna Deavere** 1950-........ **CLC 86**
See also CA 133

**Smith, Betty (Wehner)** 1896-1972... **CLC 19**
See also CA 5-8R; 33-36R; DLBY 82; SATA 6

**Smith, Charlotte (Turner)** 1749-1806 ................. **NCLC 23**
See also DLB 39, 109

**Smith, Clark Ashton** 1893-1961 .... **CLC 43**
See also CA 143

**Smith, Dave**................... **CLC 22, 42**
See also Smith, David (Jeddie)
See also CAAS 7; DLB 5

**Smith, David (Jeddie)** 1942-
See Smith, Dave
See also CA 49-52; CANR 1; DAM POET

**Smith, Florence Margaret** 1902-1971
See Smith, Stevie
See also CA 17-18; 29-32R; CANR 35; CAP 2; DAM POET; MTCW

**Smith, Iain Crichton** 1928- ........ **CLC 64**
See also CA 21-24R; DLB 40, 139

**Smith, John** 1580(?)-1631 ........... **LC 9**

**Smith, Johnston**
See Crane, Stephen (Townley)

**Smith, Joseph, Jr.** 1805-1844 .... **NCLC 53**

**Smith, Lee** 1944-............. **CLC 25, 73**
See also CA 114; 119; CANR 46; DLB 143; DLBY 83; INT 119

**Smith, Martin**
See Smith, Martin Cruz

**Smith, Martin Cruz** 1942- ..... **CLC 25; DAM MULT, POP**
See also BEST 89:4; CA 85-88; CANR 6, 23, 43; INT CANR-23; NNAL

**Smith, Mary-Ann Tirone** 1944-..... **CLC 39**
See also CA 118; 136

**Smith, Patti** 1946- ............... **CLC 12**
See also CA 93-96

**Smith, Pauline (Urmson)** 1882-1959 .................. **TCLC 25**

**Smith, Rosamond**
See Oates, Joyce Carol

**Smith, Sheila Kaye**
See Kaye-Smith, Sheila

**Smith, Stevie** ....... **CLC 3, 8, 25, 44; PC 12**
See also Smith, Florence Margaret
See also DLB 20

**Smith, Wilbur (Addison)** 1933-..... **CLC 33**
See also CA 13-16R; CANR 7, 46; MTCW

**Smith, William Jay** 1918- .......... **CLC 6**
See also CA 5-8R; CANR 44; DLB 5; MAICYA; SAAS 22; SATA 2, 68

**Smith, Woodrow Wilson**
See Kuttner, Henry

**Smolenskin, Peretz** 1842-1885.... **NCLC 30**

**Smollett, Tobias (George)** 1721-1771 .. **LC 2**
See also CDBLB 1660-1789; DLB 39, 104

**Snodgrass, W(illiam) D(e Witt)**
1926- ............ **CLC 2, 6, 10, 18, 68; DAM POET**
See also CA 1-4R; CANR 6, 36; DLB 5; MTCW

**Snow, C(harles) P(ercy)**
1905-1980 ....... **CLC 1, 4, 6, 9, 13, 19; DAM NOV**
See also CA 5-8R; 101; CANR 28; CDBLB 1945-1960; DLB 15, 77; MTCW

**Snow, Frances Compton**
See Adams, Henry (Brooks)

**Snyder, Gary (Sherman)**
1930- .. **CLC 1, 2, 5, 9, 32; DAM POET**
See also CA 17-20R; CANR 30; DLB 5, 16, 165

**Snyder, Zilpha Keatley** 1927- ...... **CLC 17**
See also AAYA 15; CA 9-12R; CANR 38; CLR 31; JRDA; MAICYA; SAAS 2; SATA 1, 28, 75

**Soares, Bernardo**
See Pessoa, Fernando (Antonio Nogueira)

**Sobh, A.**
See Shamlu, Ahmad

**Sobol, Joshua** ..................... **CLC 60**

**Soderberg, Hjalmar** 1869-1941 .... **TCLC 39**

**Sodergran, Edith (Irene)**
See Soedergran, Edith (Irene)

**Soedergran, Edith (Irene)**
1892-1923 .................. **TCLC 31**

**Softly, Edgar**
See Lovecraft, H(oward) P(hillips)

**Softly, Edward**
See Lovecraft, H(oward) P(hillips)

**Sokolov, Raymond** 1941- ........... **CLC 7**
See also CA 85-88

**Solo, Jay**
See Ellison, Harlan (Jay)

**Sologub, Fyodor** .................. **TCLC 9**
See also Teternikov, Fyodor Kuzmich

**Solomons, Ikey Esquir**
See Thackeray, William Makepeace

**Solomos, Dionysios** 1798-1857 ... **NCLC 15**

**Solwoska, Mara**
See French, Marilyn

**Solzhenitsyn, Aleksandr I(sayevich)**
1918- ...... **CLC 1, 2, 4, 7, 9, 10, 18, 26, 34, 78; DA; DAB; DAC; DAM MST, NOV; WLC**
See also AITN 1; CA 69-72; CANR 40; MTCW

**Somers, Jane**
See Lessing, Doris (May)

**Somerville, Edith** 1858-1949 ...... **TCLC 51**
See also DLB 135

**Somerville & Ross**
See Martin, Violet Florence; Somerville, Edith

**Sommer, Scott** 1951- ............. **CLC 25**
See also CA 106

**Sondheim, Stephen (Joshua)**
1930- ....... **CLC 30, 39; DAM DRAM**
See also AAYA 11; CA 103; CANR 47

**Sontag, Susan**
1933- ............ **CLC 1, 2, 10, 13, 31; DAM POP**
See also CA 17-20R; CANR 25, 51; DLB 2, 67; MTCW

**Sophocles**
496(?)B.C.-406(?)B.C. .... **CMLC 2; DA; DAB; DAC; DAM DRAM, MST; DC 1**

**Sordello** 1189-1269 ............. **CMLC 15**

**Sorel, Julia**
See Drexler, Rosalyn

**Sorrentino, Gilbert**
1929- ............ **CLC 3, 7, 14, 22, 40**
See also CA 77-80; CANR 14, 33; DLB 5, 173; DLBY 80; INT CANR-14

**Soto, Gary**
1952- ....... **CLC 32, 80; DAM MULT; HLC**
See also AAYA 10; CA 119; 125; CANR 50; CLR 38; DLB 82; HW; INT 125; JRDA; SATA 80

**Soupault, Philippe** 1897-1990 ...... **CLC 68**
See also CA 116; 147; 131

**Souster, (Holmes) Raymond**
1921- ... **CLC 5, 14; DAC; DAM POET**
See also CA 13-16R; CAAS 14; CANR 13, 29, 53; DLB 88; SATA 63

**Southern, Terry** 1924(?)-1995 ....... **CLC 7**
See also CA 1-4R; 150; CANR 1, 55; DLB 2

**Southey, Robert** 1774-1843 ....... **NCLC 8**
See also DLB 93, 107, 142; SATA 54

**Southworth, Emma Dorothy Eliza Nevitte**
1819-1899 ................ **NCLC 26**

**Souza, Ernest**
See Scott, Evelyn

**Soyinka, Wole**
1934- ....... **CLC 3, 5, 14, 36, 44; BLC; DA; DAB; DAC; DAM DRAM, MST, MULT; DC 2; WLC**
See also BW 2; CA 13-16R; CANR 27, 39; DLB 125; MTCW

**Spackman, W(illiam) M(ode)**
1905-1990 ................... **CLC 46**
See also CA 81-84; 132

**Spacks, Barry (Bernard)** 1931- ..... **CLC 14**
See also CA 154; CANR 33; DLB 105

**Spanidou, Irini** 1946- ............. **CLC 44**

**Spark, Muriel (Sarah)**
1918- ..... **CLC 2, 3, 5, 8, 13, 18, 40, 94; DAB; DAC; DAM MST, NOV; SSC 10**
See also CA 5-8R; CANR 12, 36; CDBLB 1945-1960; DLB 15, 139; INT CANR-12; MTCW

**Spaulding, Douglas**
See Bradbury, Ray (Douglas)

**Spaulding, Leonard**
See Bradbury, Ray (Douglas)

**Spence, J. A. D.**
See Eliot, T(homas) S(tearns)

**Spencer, Elizabeth** 1921- .......... **CLC 22**
See also CA 13-16R; CANR 32; DLB 6; MTCW; SATA 14

**Spencer, Leonard G.**
See Silverberg, Robert

**Spencer, Scott** 1945- ............. **CLC 30**
See also CA 113; CANR 51; DLBY 86

**Spender, Stephen (Harold)**
1909-1995 ...... **CLC 1, 2, 5, 10, 41, 91; DAM POET**
See also CA 9-12R; 149; CANR 31, 54; CDBLB 1945-1960; DLB 20; MTCW

**Spengler, Oswald (Arnold Gottfried)**
1880-1936 .................. **TCLC 25**
See also CA 118

**Spenser, Edmund**
1552(?)-1599 .... **LC 5; DA; DAB; DAC; DAM MST, POET; PC 8; WLC**
See also CDBLB Before 1660; DLB 167

**Spicer, Jack**
1925-1965 ............. **CLC 8, 18, 72; DAM POET**
See also CA 85-88; DLB 5, 16

**Spiegelman, Art** 1948- ............ **CLC 76**
See also AAYA 10; CA 125; CANR 41, 55

**Spielberg, Peter** 1929- ............. **CLC 6**
See also CA 5-8R; CANR 4, 48; DLBY 81

**Spielberg, Steven** 1947- ........... **CLC 20**
See also AAYA 8; CA 77-80; CANR 32; SATA 32

**Spillane, Frank Morrison** 1918-
See Spillane, Mickey
See also CA 25-28R; CANR 28; MTCW; SATA 66

**Spillane, Mickey** ................ **CLC 3, 13**
See also Spillane, Frank Morrison

**Spinoza, Benedictus de** 1632-1677 .... **LC 9**

**Spinrad, Norman (Richard)** 1940- ... **CLC 46**
See also CA 37-40R; CAAS 19; CANR 20; DLB 8; INT CANR-20

**Spitteler, Carl (Friedrich Georg)**
1845-1924 .................. **TCLC 12**
See also CA 109; DLB 129

**Spivack, Kathleen (Romola Drucker)**
1938- ........................ **CLC 6**
See also CA 49-52

**Spoto, Donald** 1941- .............. **CLC 39**
See also CA 65-68; CANR 11

**Springsteen, Bruce (F.)** 1949- ...... **CLC 17**
See also CA 111

**Spurling, Hilary** 1940- ............ **CLC 34**
See also CA 104; CANR 25, 52

**Spyker, John Howland**
See Elman, Richard

**Squires, (James) Radcliffe**
1917-1993 ..................... **CLC 51**
See also CA 1-4R; 140; CANR 6, 21

**Srivastava, Dhanpat Rai** 1880(?)-1936
See Premchand
See also CA 118

**Stacy, Donald**
See Pohl, Frederik

**Stael, Germaine de**
See Stael-Holstein, Anne Louise Germaine Necker Baronn
See also DLB 119

**Stael-Holstein, Anne Louise Germaine Necker Baronn** 1766-1817 .......... **NCLC 3**
See also Stael, Germaine de

**Stafford, Jean** 1915-1979 ... **CLC 4, 7, 19, 68**
See also CA 1-4R; 85-88; CANR 3; DLB 2, 173; MTCW; SATA-Obit 22

**Stafford, William (Edgar)** 1914-1993 ... **CLC 4, 7, 29; DAM POET**
See also CA 5-8R; 142; CAAS 3; CANR 5, 22; DLB 5; INT CANR-22

**Staines, Trevor**
See Brunner, John (Kilian Houston)

**Stairs, Gordon**
See Austin, Mary (Hunter)

**Stannard, Martin** 1947- .......... **CLC 44**
See also CA 142; DLB 155

**Stanton, Maura** 1946- ............ **CLC 9**
See also CA 89-92; CANR 15; DLB 120

**Stanton, Schuyler**
See Baum, L(yman) Frank

**Stapledon, (William) Olaf** 1886-1950 .................. **TCLC 22**
See also CA 111; DLB 15

**Starbuck, George (Edwin)** 1931-1996 ....... **CLC 53; DAM POET**
See also CA 21-24R; 153; CANR 23

**Stark, Richard**
See Westlake, Donald E(dwin)

**Staunton, Schuyler**
See Baum, L(yman) Frank

**Stead, Christina (Ellen)** 1902-1983 ......... **CLC 2, 5, 8, 32, 80**
See also CA 13-16R; 109; CANR 33, 40; MTCW

**Stead, William Thomas** 1849-1912 .................. **TCLC 48**

**Steele, Richard** 1672-1729 .......... **LC 18**
See also CDBLB 1660-1789; DLB 84, 101

**Steele, Timothy (Reid)** 1948- ....... **CLC 45**
See also CA 93-96; CANR 16, 50; DLB 120

**Steffens, (Joseph) Lincoln** 1866-1936 .................. **TCLC 20**
See also CA 117

**Stegner, Wallace (Earle)** 1909-1993 ... **CLC 9, 49, 81; DAM NOV**
See also AITN 1; BEST 90:3; CA 1-4R; 141; CAAS 9; CANR 1, 21, 46; DLB 9; DLBY 93; MTCW

**Stein, Gertrude** 1874-1946 ...... **TCLC 1, 6, 28, 48; DA; DAB; DAC; DAM MST, NOV, POET; WLC**
See also CA 104; 132; CDALB 1917-1929; DLB 4, 54, 86; MTCW

**Steinbeck, John (Ernst)** 1902-1968 ...... **CLC 1, 5, 9, 13, 21, 34, 45, 75; DA; DAB; DAC; DAM DRAM, MST, NOV; SSC 11; WLC**
See also AAYA 12; CA 1-4R; 25-28R; CANR 1, 35; CDALB 1929-1941; DLB 7, 9; DLBD 2; MTCW; SATA 9

**Steinem, Gloria** 1934- ............. **CLC 63**
See also CA 53-56; CANR 28, 51; MTCW

**Steiner, George** 1929- ............ **CLC 24; DAM NOV**
See also CA 73-76; CANR 31; DLB 67; MTCW; SATA 62

**Steiner, K. Leslie**
See Delany, Samuel R(ay, Jr.)

**Steiner, Rudolf** 1861-1925 ........ **TCLC 13**
See also CA 107

**Stendhal** 1783-1842 .... **NCLC 23, 46; DA; DAB; DAC; DAM MST, NOV; WLC**
See also DLB 119

**Stephen, Leslie** 1832-1904 ........ **TCLC 23**
See also CA 123; DLB 57, 144

**Stephen, Sir Leslie**
See Stephen, Leslie

**Stephen, Virginia**
See Woolf, (Adeline) Virginia

**Stephens, James** 1882(?)-1950 ...... **TCLC 4**
See also CA 104; DLB 19, 153, 162

**Stephens, Reed**
See Donaldson, Stephen R.

**Steptoe, Lydia**
See Barnes, Djuna

**Sterchi, Beat** 1949- ............... **CLC 65**

**Sterling, Brett**
See Bradbury, Ray (Douglas); Hamilton, Edmond

**Sterling, Bruce** 1954- ............. **CLC 72**
See also CA 119; CANR 44

**Sterling, George** 1869-1926 ....... **TCLC 20**
See also CA 117; DLB 54

**Stern, Gerald** 1925- .............. **CLC 40**
See also CA 81-84; CANR 28; DLB 105

**Stern, Richard (Gustave)** 1928- ... **CLC 4, 39**
See also CA 1-4R; CANR 1, 25, 52; DLBY 87; INT CANR-25

**Sternberg, Josef von** 1894-1969..... **CLC 20**
See also CA 81-84

**Sterne, Laurence** 1713-1768 ...... **LC 2; DA; DAB; DAC; DAM MST, NOV; WLC**
See also CDBLB 1660-1789; DLB 39

**Sternheim, (William Adolf) Carl** 1878-1942 .................. **TCLC 8**
See also CA 105; DLB 56, 118

**Stevens, Mark** 1951- ............. **CLC 34**
See also CA 122

**Stevens, Wallace** 1879-1955 ........ **TCLC 3, 12, 45; DA; DAB; DAC; DAM MST, POET; PC 6; WLC**
See also CA 104; 124; CDALB 1929-1941; DLB 54; MTCW

**Stevenson, Anne (Katharine)** 1933- ..................... **CLC 7, 33**
See also CA 17-20R; CAAS 9; CANR 9, 33; DLB 40; MTCW

**Stevenson, Robert Louis (Balfour)** 1850-1894 ..... **NCLC 5, 14; DA; DAB; DAC; DAM MST, NOV; SSC 11; WLC**
See also CDBLB 1890-1914; CLR 10, 11; DLB 18, 57, 141, 156, 174; DLBD 13; JRDA; MAICYA; YABC 2

**Stewart, J(ohn) I(nnes) M(ackintosh)** 1906-1994 .............. **CLC 7, 14, 32**
See also CA 85-88; 147; CAAS 3; CANR 47; MTCW

**Stewart, Mary (Florence Elinor)** 1916- ............... **CLC 7, 35; DAB**
See also CA 1-4R; CANR 1; SATA 12

**Stewart, Mary Rainbow**
See Stewart, Mary (Florence Elinor)

**Stifle, June**
See Campbell, Maria

**Stifter, Adalbert** 1805-1868 ...... **NCLC 41**
See also DLB 133

**Still, James** 1906- ................ **CLC 49**
See also CA 65-68; CAAS 17; CANR 10, 26; DLB 9; SATA 29

**Sting**
See Sumner, Gordon Matthew

**Stirling, Arthur**
See Sinclair, Upton (Beall)

**Stitt, Milan** 1941- ................ **CLC 29**
See also CA 69-72

**Stockton, Francis Richard** 1834-1902
See Stockton, Frank R.
See also CA 108; 137; MAICYA; SATA 44

**Stockton, Frank R.** ................ **TCLC 47**
See also Stockton, Francis Richard
See also DLB 42, 74; DLBD 13; SATA-Brief 32

**Stoddard, Charles**
See Kuttner, Henry

**Stoker, Abraham** 1847-1912
See Stoker, Bram
See also CA 105; DA; DAC; DAM MST, NOV; SATA 29

**Stoker, Bram** 1847-1912 ........ **TCLC 8; DAB; WLC**
See also Stoker, Abraham
See also CA 150; CDBLB 1890-1914; DLB 36, 70

**Stolz, Mary (Slattery)** 1920- ....... **CLC 12**
See also AAYA 8; AITN 1; CA 5-8R; CANR 13, 41; JRDA; MAICYA; SAAS 3; SATA 10, 71

**Stone, Irving** 1903-1989 ......... **CLC 7; DAM POP**
See also AITN 1; CA 1-4R; 129; CAAS 3; CANR 1, 23; INT CANR-23; MTCW; SATA 3; SATA-Obit 64

**Stone, Oliver (William)** 1946- ...... **CLC 73**
See also AAYA 15; CA 110; CANR 55

**Stone, Robert (Anthony)** 1937- .................. **CLC 5, 23, 42**
See also CA 85-88; CANR 23; DLB 152; INT CANR-23; MTCW

**Stone, Zachary**
See Follett, Ken(neth Martin)

**Thomas, D(onald) M(ichael)**
1935- . . . . . . . . . . . . . . . . . **CLC 13, 22, 31**
See also CA 61-64; CAAS 11; CANR 17, 45; CDBLB 1960 to Present; DLB 40; INT CANR-17; MTCW

**Thomas, Dylan (Marlais)**
1914-1953 . . . **TCLC 1, 8, 45; DA; DAB; DAC; DAM DRAM, MST, POET; PC 2; SSC 3; WLC**
See also CA 104; 120; CDBLB 1945-1960; DLB 13, 20, 139; MTCW; SATA 60

**Thomas, (Philip) Edward**
1878-1917 . . . . . . **TCLC 10; DAM POET**
See also CA 106; 153; DLB 19

**Thomas, Joyce Carol** 1938- . . . . . . . . **CLC 35**
See also AAYA 12; BW 2; CA 113; 116; CANR 48; CLR 19; DLB 33; INT 116; JRDA; MAICYA; MTCW; SAAS 7; SATA 40, 78

**Thomas, Lewis** 1913-1993 . . . . . . . . . **CLC 35**
See also CA 85-88; 143; CANR 38; MTCW

**Thomas, Paul**
See Mann, (Paul) Thomas

**Thomas, Piri** 1928- . . . . . . . . . . . . . . . **CLC 17**
See also CA 73-76; HW

**Thomas, R(onald) S(tuart)**
1913- . . . . . . . . . . . . **CLC 6, 13, 48; DAB; DAM POET**
See also CA 89-92; CAAS 4; CANR 30; CDBLB 1960 to Present; DLB 27; MTCW

**Thomas, Ross (Elmore)** 1926-1995 . . **CLC 39**
See also CA 33-36R; 150; CANR 22

**Thompson, Francis Clegg**
See Mencken, H(enry) L(ouis)

**Thompson, Francis Joseph**
1859-1907 . . . . . . . . . . . . . . . . . . **TCLC 4**
See also CA 104; CDBLB 1890-1914; DLB 19

**Thompson, Hunter S(tockton)**
1939- . . . . . . . **CLC 9, 17, 40; DAM POP**
See also BEST 89:1; CA 17-20R; CANR 23, 46; MTCW

**Thompson, James Myers**
See Thompson, Jim (Myers)

**Thompson, Jim (Myers)**
1906-1977(?) . . . . . . . . . . . . . . . . . **CLC 69**
See also CA 140

**Thompson, Judith** . . . . . . . . . . . . . . . . . **CLC 39**

**Thomson, James**
1700-1748 . . . . . **LC 16, 29; DAM POET**
See also DLB 95

**Thomson, James**
1834-1882 . . . . . **NCLC 18; DAM POET**
See also DLB 35

**Thoreau, Henry David**
1817-1862 . . . . . **NCLC 7, 21; DA; DAB; DAC; DAM MST; WLC**
See also CDALB 1640-1865; DLB 1

**Thornton, Hall**
See Silverberg, Robert

**Thucydides** c. 455B.C.-399B.C. . . . **CMLC 17**

**Thurber, James (Grover)**
1894-1961 . . . . **CLC 5, 11, 25; DA; DAB; DAC; DAM DRAM, MST, NOV; SSC 1**
See also CA 73-76; CANR 17, 39; CDALB 1929-1941; DLB 4, 11, 22, 102; MAICYA; MTCW; SATA 13

**Thurman, Wallace (Henry)**
1902-1934 . . . . . . . . . . . . . **TCLC 6; BLC; DAM MULT**
See also BW 1; CA 104; 124; DLB 51

**Ticheburn, Cheviot**
See Ainsworth, William Harrison

**Tieck, (Johann) Ludwig**
1773-1853 . . . . . . . . . . . . . . . **NCLC 5, 46**
See also DLB 90

**Tiger, Derry**
See Ellison, Harlan (Jay)

**Tilghman, Christopher** 1948(?)- . . . . . **CLC 65**

**Tillinghast, Richard (Williford)**
1940- . . . . . . . . . . . . . . . . . . . . . . . **CLC 29**
See also CA 29-32R; CAAS 23; CANR 26, 51

**Timrod, Henry** 1828-1867 . . . . . . . **NCLC 25**
See also DLB 3

**Tindall, Gillian** 1938- . . . . . . . . . . . . . . **CLC 7**
See also CA 21-24R; CANR 11

**Tiptree, James, Jr.** . . . . . . . . . . . . . **CLC 48, 50**
See also Sheldon, Alice Hastings Bradley
See also DLB 8

**Titmarsh, Michael Angelo**
See Thackeray, William Makepeace

**Tocqueville, Alexis (Charles Henri Maurice Clerel Comte)** 1805-1859 . . . . . **NCLC 7**

**Tolkien, J(ohn) R(onald) R(euel)**
1892-1973 . . . . . . . **CLC 1, 2, 3, 8, 12, 38; DA; DAB; DAC; DAM MST, NOV, POP; WLC**
See also AAYA 10; AITN 1; CA 17-18; 45-48; CANR 36; CAP 2; CDBLB 1914-1945; DLB 15, 160; JRDA; MAICYA; MTCW; SATA 2, 32; SATA-Obit 24

**Toller, Ernst** 1893-1939 . . . . . . . . . . **TCLC 10**
See also CA 107; DLB 124

**Tolson, M. B.**
See Tolson, Melvin B(eaunorus)

**Tolson, Melvin B(eaunorus)**
1898(?)-1966 . . . . . . . . . . . **CLC 36; BLC; DAM MULT, POET**
See also BW 1; CA 124; 89-92; DLB 48, 76

**Tolstoi, Aleksei Nikolaevich**
See Tolstoy, Alexey Nikolaevich

**Tolstoy, Alexey Nikolaevich**
1882-1945 . . . . . . . . . . . . . . . . . . **TCLC 18**
See also CA 107

**Tolstoy, Count Leo**
See Tolstoy, Leo (Nikolaevich)

**Tolstoy, Leo (Nikolaevich)**
1828-1910 . . . . . . **TCLC 4, 11, 17, 28, 44; DA; DAB; DAC; DAM MST, NOV; SSC 9; WLC**
See also CA 104; 123; SATA 26

**Tomasi di Lampedusa, Giuseppe** 1896-1957
See Lampedusa, Giuseppe (Tomasi) di
See also CA 111

**Tomlin, Lily** . . . . . . . . . . . . . . . . . . . . . . **CLC 17**
See also Tomlin, Mary Jean

**Tomlin, Mary Jean** 1939(?)-
See Tomlin, Lily
See also CA 117

**Tomlinson, (Alfred) Charles**
1927- . . . . . . . . . . . . . **CLC 2, 4, 6, 13, 45; DAM POET; PC 17**
See also CA 5-8R; CANR 33; DLB 40

**Tonson, Jacob**
See Bennett, (Enoch) Arnold

**Toole, John Kennedy**
1937-1969 . . . . . . . . . . . . . . . . **CLC 19, 64**
See also CA 104; DLBY 81

**Toomer, Jean**
1894-1967 . . . . . . **CLC 1, 4, 13, 22; BLC; DAM MULT; PC 7; SSC 1**
See also BW 1; CA 85-88; CDALB 1917-1929; DLB 45, 51; MTCW

**Torley, Luke**
See Blish, James (Benjamin)

**Tornimparte, Alessandra**
See Ginzburg, Natalia

**Torre, Raoul della**
See Mencken, H(enry) L(ouis)

**Torrey, E(dwin) Fuller** 1937- . . . . . . . **CLC 34**
See also CA 119

**Torsvan, Ben Traven**
See Traven, B.

**Torsvan, Benno Traven**
See Traven, B.

**Torsvan, Berick Traven**
See Traven, B.

**Torsvan, Berwick Traven**
See Traven, B.

**Torsvan, Bruno Traven**
See Traven, B.

**Torsvan, Traven**
See Traven, B.

**Tournier, Michel (Edouard)**
1924- . . . . . . . . . . . . . . . **CLC 6, 23, 36, 95**
See also CA 49-52; CANR 3, 36; DLB 83; MTCW; SATA 23

**Tournimparte, Alessandra**
See Ginzburg, Natalia

**Towers, Ivar**
See Kornbluth, C(yril) M.

**Towne, Robert (Burton)** 1936(?)- . . . . **CLC 87**
See also CA 108; DLB 44

**Townsend, Sue** 1946- . . **CLC 61; DAB; DAC**
See also CA 119; 127; INT 127; MTCW; SATA 55; SATA-Brief 48

**Townshend, Peter (Dennis Blandford)**
1945- . . . . . . . . . . . . . . . . . . . . . **CLC 17, 42**
See also CA 107

**Tozzi, Federigo** 1883-1920 . . . . . . . . **TCLC 31**

**Traill, Catharine Parr**
1802-1899 . . . . . . . . . . . . . . . . . **NCLC 31**
See also DLB 99

**Trakl, Georg** 1887-1914 . . . . . . . . . . . **TCLC 5**
See also CA 104

**Transtroemer, Tomas (Goesta)**
1931- . . . . . . . . **CLC 52, 65; DAM POET**
See also CA 117; 129; CAAS 17

**Transtromer, Tomas Gosta**
See Transtroemer, Tomas (Goesta)

**Traven, B.** (?)-1969 . . . . . . . . . . . . . **CLC 8, 11**
See also CA 19-20; 25-28R; CAP 2; DLB 9, 56; MTCW

**Treitel, Jonathan** 1959- . . . . . . . . . . . **CLC 70**

**Tremain, Rose** 1943-. . . . . . . . . . . . . . **CLC 42**
See also CA 97-100; CANR 44; DLB 14

**Tremblay, Michel**
1942- . . . . . . **CLC 29; DAC; DAM MST**
See also CA 116; 128; DLB 60; MTCW

**Trevanian** . . . . . . . . . . . . . . . . . . . . . . . . **CLC 29**
See also Whitaker, Rod(ney)

**Trevor, Glen**
See Hilton, James

**Trevor, William**
1928- . . . . . **CLC 7, 9, 14, 25, 71; SSC 21**
See also Cox, William Trevor
See also DLB 14, 139

**Trifonov, Yuri (Valentinovich)**
1925-1981 . . . . . . . . . . . . . . . . . . . **CLC 45**
See also CA 126; 103; MTCW

**Trilling, Lionel** 1905-1975 . . . . **CLC 9, 11, 24**
See also CA 9-12R; 61-64; CANR 10; DLB 28, 63; INT CANR-10; MTCW

**Trimball, W. H.**
See Mencken, H(enry) L(ouis)

**Tristan**
See Gomez de la Serna, Ramon

**Tristram**
See Housman, A(lfred) E(dward)

**Trogdon, William (Lewis)** 1939-
See Heat-Moon, William Least
See also CA 115; 119; CANR 47; INT 119

**Trollope, Anthony**
1815-1882 . . . . . **NCLC 6, 33; DA; DAB; DAC; DAM MST, NOV; WLC**
See also CDBLB 1832-1890; DLB 21, 57, 159; SATA 22

**Trollope, Frances** 1779-1863 . . . . . **NCLC 30**
See also DLB 21, 166

**Trotsky, Leon** 1879-1940 . . . . . . . . . **TCLC 22**
See also CA 118

**Trotter (Cockburn), Catharine**
1679-1749 . . . . . . . . . . . . . . . . . . . . . **LC 8**
See also DLB 84

**Trout, Kilgore**
See Farmer, Philip Jose

**Trow, George W. S.** 1943- . . . . . . . . . **CLC 52**
See also CA 126

**Troyat, Henri** 1911- . . . . . . . . . . . . . . **CLC 23**
See also CA 45-48; CANR 2, 33; MTCW

**Trudeau, G(arretson) B(eekman)** 1948-
See Trudeau, Garry B.
See also CA 81-84; CANR 31; SATA 35

**Trudeau, Garry B.** . . . . . . . . . . . . . . . . . **CLC 12**
See also Trudeau, G(arretson) B(eekman)
See also AAYA 10; AITN 2

**Truffaut, Francois** 1932-1984 . . . . . . . **CLC 20**
See also CA 81-84; 113; CANR 34

**Trumbo, Dalton** 1905-1976 . . . . . . . . **CLC 19**
See also CA 21-24R; 69-72; CANR 10; DLB 26

**Trumbull, John** 1750-1831 . . . . . . . **NCLC 30**
See also DLB 31

**Trundlett, Helen B.**
See Eliot, T(homas) S(tearns)

**Tryon, Thomas**
1926-1991 . . . . . . **CLC 3, 11; DAM POP**
See also AITN 1; CA 29-32R; 135; CANR 32; MTCW

**Tryon, Tom**
See Tryon, Thomas

**Ts'ao Hsueh-ch'in** 1715(?)-1763 . . . . . . . **LC 1**

**Tsushima, Shuji** 1909-1948
See Dazai, Osamu
See also CA 107

**Tsvetaeva (Efron), Marina (Ivanovna)**
1892-1941 . . . . . . . . . **TCLC 7, 35; PC 14**
See also CA 104; 128; MTCW

**Tuck, Lily** 1938- . . . . . . . . . . . . . . . . . **CLC 70**
See also CA 139

**Tu Fu** 712-770 . . . . . . . . . . . . . . . . . . . . . **PC 9**
See also DAM MULT

**Tunis, John R(oberts)** 1889-1975 . . . **CLC 12**
See also CA 61-64; DLB 22, 171; JRDA; MAICYA; SATA 37; SATA-Brief 30

**Tuohy, Frank** . . . . . . . . . . . . . . . . . . . . . **CLC 37**
See also Tuohy, John Francis
See also DLB 14, 139

**Tuohy, John Francis** 1925-
See Tuohy, Frank
See also CA 5-8R; CANR 3, 47

**Turco, Lewis (Putnam)** 1934- . . . **CLC 11, 63**
See also CA 13-16R; CAAS 22; CANR 24, 51; DLBY 84

**Turgenev, Ivan**
1818-1883 . . . . . . . **NCLC 21; DA; DAB; DAC; DAM MST, NOV; SSC 7; WLC**

**Turgot, Anne-Robert-Jacques**
1727-1781 . . . . . . . . . . . . . . . . . . . . **LC 26**

**Turner, Frederick** 1943- . . . . . . . . . . . **CLC 48**
See also CA 73-76; CAAS 10; CANR 12, 30; DLB 40

**Tutu, Desmond M(pilo)**
1931- . . . . . **CLC 80; BLC; DAM MULT**
See also BW 1; CA 125

**Tutuola, Amos**
1920- . . . . . . . . . . . . **CLC 5, 14, 29; BLC; DAM MULT**
See also BW 2; CA 9-12R; CANR 27; DLB 125; MTCW

**Twain, Mark**
. . . . . **TCLC 6, 12, 19, 36, 48, 59; SSC 6; WLC**
See also Clemens, Samuel Langhorne
See also DLB 11, 12, 23, 64, 74

**Tyler, Anne**
1941- . . . . . . . . **CLC 7, 11, 18, 28, 44, 59; DAM NOV, POP**
See also AAYA 18; BEST 89:1; CA 9-12R; CANR 11, 33, 53; DLB 6, 143; DLBY 82; MTCW; SATA 7, 90

**Tyler, Royall** 1757-1826 . . . . . . . . . . **NCLC 3**
See also DLB 37

**Tynan, Katharine** 1861-1931 . . . . . . . **TCLC 3**
See also CA 104; DLB 153

**Tyutchev, Fyodor** 1803-1873 . . . . . **NCLC 34**

**Tzara, Tristan**
1896-1963 . . . . . . . **CLC 47; DAM POET**
See also Rosenfeld, Samuel; Rosenstock, Sami; Rosenstock, Samuel
See also CA 153

**Uhry, Alfred**
1936- . . . . . **CLC 55; DAM DRAM, POP**
See also CA 127; 133; INT 133

**Ulf, Haerved**
See Strindberg, (Johan) August

**Ulf, Harved**
See Strindberg, (Johan) August

**Ulibarri, Sabine R(eyes)**
1919- . . . . . . . . . . **CLC 83; DAM MULT**
See also CA 131; DLB 82; HW

**Unamuno (y Jugo), Miguel de**
1864-1936 . . . **TCLC 2, 9; DAM MULT, NOV; HLC; SSC 11**
See also CA 104; 131; DLB 108; HW; MTCW

**Undercliffe, Errol**
See Campbell, (John) Ramsey

**Underwood, Miles**
See Glassco, John

**Undset, Sigrid**
1882-1949 . . . . . . . . . **TCLC 3; DA; DAB; DAC; DAM MST, NOV; WLC**
See also CA 104; 129; MTCW

**Ungaretti, Giuseppe**
1888-1970 . . . . . . . . . . . . . . **CLC 7, 11, 15**
See also CA 19-20; 25-28R; CAP 2; DLB 114

**Unger, Douglas** 1952- . . . . . . . . . . . . . **CLC 34**
See also CA 130

**Unsworth, Barry (Forster)** 1930- . . . . **CLC 76**
See also CA 25-28R; CANR 30, 54

**Updike, John (Hoyer)**
1932- . . . . . . **CLC 1, 2, 3, 5, 7, 9, 13, 15, 23, 34, 43, 70; DA; DAB; DAC; DAM MST, NOV, POET, POP; SSC 13; WLC**
See also CA 1-4R; CABS 1; CANR 4, 33, 51; CDALB 1968-1988; DLB 2, 5, 143; DLBD 3; DLBY 80, 82; MTCW

**Upshaw, Margaret Mitchell**
See Mitchell, Margaret (Munnerlyn)

**Upton, Mark**
See Sanders, Lawrence

**Urdang, Constance (Henriette)**
1922- . . . . . . . . . . . . . . . . . . . . . . . **CLC 47**
See also CA 21-24R; CANR 9, 24

**Uriel, Henry**
See Faust, Frederick (Schiller)

**Uris, Leon (Marcus)**
1924- . . . . **CLC 7, 32; DAM NOV, POP**
See also AITN 1, 2; BEST 89:2; CA 1-4R; CANR 1, 40; MTCW; SATA 49

**Urmuz**
See Codrescu, Andrei

**Urquhart, Jane** 1949- . . . . . . . . **CLC 90; DAC**
See also CA 113; CANR 32

**Ustinov, Peter (Alexander)** 1921- . . . . **CLC 1**
See also AITN 1; CA 13-16R; CANR 25, 51; DLB 13

**Vaculik, Ludvik** 1926- . . . . . . . . . . . . . **CLC 7**
See also CA 53-56

**Valdez, Luis (Miguel)**
1940- . . . . . **CLC 84; DAM MULT; HLC**
See also CA 101; CANR 32; DLB 122; HW

**Valenzuela, Luisa**
1938- . . . **CLC 31; DAM MULT; SSC 14**
See also CA 101; CANR 32; DLB 113; HW

**Valera y Alcala-Galiano, Juan**
1824-1905 . . . . . . . . . . . . . . . . . . **TCLC 10**
See also CA 106

**Valery, (Ambroise) Paul (Toussaint Jules)**
1871-1945 . . . . . . . . . . . . . . . **TCLC 4, 15; DAM POET; PC 9**
See also CA 104; 122; MTCW

**Valle-Inclan, Ramon (Maria) del**
1866-1936 . . . . . **TCLC 5; DAM MULT; HLC**
See also CA 106; 153; DLB 134

**Vallejo, Antonio Buero**
See Buero Vallejo, Antonio

**Vallejo, Cesar (Abraham)**
1892-1938 . . . . . . . . . . . . . . . **TCLC 3, 56; DAM MULT; HLC**
See also CA 105; 153; HW

**Vallette, Marguerite Eymery**
See Rachilde

**Valle Y Pena, Ramon del**
See Valle-Inclan, Ramon (Maria) del

**Van Ash, Cay** 1918- . . . . . . . . . . . . . . **CLC 34**

**Vanbrugh, Sir John**
1664-1726 . . . . . . . **LC 21; DAM DRAM**
See also DLB 80

**Van Campen, Karl**
See Campbell, John W(ood, Jr.)

**Vance, Gerald**
See Silverberg, Robert

**Vance, Jack** . . . . . . . . . . . . . . . . . . . . . **CLC 35**
See also Vance, John Holbrook
See also DLB 8

**Vance, John Holbrook** 1916-
See Queen, Ellery; Vance, Jack
See also CA 29-32R; CANR 17; MTCW

**Van Den Bogarde, Derek Jules Gaspard Ulric Niven** 1921-
See Bogarde, Dirk
See also CA 77-80

**Vandenburgh, Jane** . . . . . . . . . . . . . . . . **CLC 59**

**Vanderhaeghe, Guy** 1951- . . . . . . . . . **CLC 41**
See also CA 113

**van der Post, Laurens (Jan)**
1906-1996 . . . . . . . . . . . . . . . . . . . . **CLC 5**
See also CA 5-8R; 155; CANR 35

**van de Wetering, Janwillem** 1931- . . **CLC 47**
See also CA 49-52; CANR 4

**Van Dine, S. S.** . . . . . . . . . . . . . . . . . . **TCLC 23**
See also Wright, Willard Huntington

**Van Doren, Carl (Clinton)**
1885-1950 . . . . . . . . . . . . . . . . . **TCLC 18**
See also CA 111

**Van Doren, Mark** 1894-1972 . . . . . **CLC 6, 10**
See also CA 1-4R; 37-40R; CANR 3; DLB 45; MTCW

**Van Druten, John (William)**
1901-1957 . . . . . . . . . . . . . . . . . . . **TCLC 2**
See also CA 104; DLB 10

**Van Duyn, Mona (Jane)**
1921- . . . . . . . **CLC 3, 7, 63; DAM POET**
See also CA 9-12R; CANR 7, 38; DLB 5

**Van Dyne, Edith**
See Baum, L(yman) Frank

**van Itallie, Jean-Claude** 1936- . . . . . . . **CLC 3**
See also CA 45-48; CAAS 2; CANR 1, 48; DLB 7

**van Ostaijen, Paul** 1896-1928 . . . . . **TCLC 33**

**Van Peebles, Melvin**
1932- . . . . . . . . **CLC 2, 20; DAM MULT**
See also BW 2; CA 85-88; CANR 27

**Vansittart, Peter** 1920- . . . . . . . . . . . **CLC 42**
See also CA 1-4R; CANR 3, 49

**Van Vechten, Carl** 1880-1964 . . . . . . **CLC 33**
See also CA 89-92; DLB 4, 9, 51

**Van Vogt, A(lfred) E(lton)** 1912- . . . . . **CLC 1**
See also CA 21-24R; CANR 28; DLB 8; SATA 14

**Varda, Agnes** 1928- . . . . . . . . . . . . . . **CLC 16**
See also CA 116; 122

**Vargas Llosa, (Jorge) Mario (Pedro)**
1936- . . . . **CLC 3, 6, 9, 10, 15, 31, 42, 85; DA; DAB; DAC; DAM MST, MULT, NOV; HLC**
See also CA 73-76; CANR 18, 32, 42; DLB 145; HW; MTCW

**Vasiliu, Gheorghe** 1881-1957
See Bacovia, George
See also CA 123

**Vassa, Gustavus**
See Equiano, Olaudah

**Vassilikos, Vassilis** 1933- . . . . . . . . . **CLC 4, 8**
See also CA 81-84

**Vaughan, Henry** 1621-1695 . . . . . . . . . **LC 27**
See also DLB 131

**Vaughn, Stephanie** . . . . . . . . . . . . . . . . **CLC 62**

**Vazov, Ivan (Minchov)**
1850-1921 . . . . . . . . . . . . . . . . . **TCLC 25**
See also CA 121; DLB 147

**Veblen, Thorstein (Bunde)**
1857-1929 . . . . . . . . . . . . . . . . . **TCLC 31**
See also CA 115

**Vega, Lope de** 1562-1635 . . . . . . . . . . . **LC 23**

**Venison, Alfred**
See Pound, Ezra (Weston Loomis)

**Verdi, Marie de**
See Mencken, H(enry) L(ouis)

**Verdu, Matilde**
See Cela, Camilo Jose

**Verga, Giovanni (Carmelo)**
1840-1922 . . . . . . . . . . . **TCLC 3; SSC 21**
See also CA 104; 123

**Vergil**
70B.C.-19B.C. . . . . . **CMLC 9; DA; DAB; DAC; DAM MST, POET; PC 12**

**Verhaeren, Emile (Adolphe Gustave)**
1855-1916 . . . . . . . . . . . . . . . . . **TCLC 12**
See also CA 109

**Verlaine, Paul (Marie)**
1844-1896 . . . . . . . . . . . . . . . **NCLC 2, 51; DAM POET; PC 2**

**Verne, Jules (Gabriel)**
1828-1905 . . . . . . . . . . . . . . . . **TCLC 6, 52**
See also AAYA 16; CA 110; 131; DLB 123; JRDA; MAICYA; SATA 21

**Very, Jones** 1813-1880 . . . . . . . . . . . **NCLC 9**
See also DLB 1

**Vesaas, Tarjei** 1897-1970 . . . . . . . . . . **CLC 48**
See also CA 29-32R

**Vialis, Gaston**
See Simenon, Georges (Jacques Christian)

**Vian, Boris** 1920-1959 . . . . . . . . . . . . **TCLC 9**
See also CA 106; DLB 72

**Viaud, (Louis Marie) Julien** 1850-1923
See Loti, Pierre
See also CA 107

**Vicar, Henry**
See Felsen, Henry Gregor

**Vicker, Angus**
See Felsen, Henry Gregor

**Vidal, Gore**
1925- . . . . . **CLC 2, 4, 6, 8, 10, 22, 33, 72; DAM NOV, POP**
See also AITN 1; BEST 90:2; CA 5-8R; CANR 13, 45; DLB 6, 152; INT CANR-13; MTCW

**Viereck, Peter (Robert Edwin)**
1916- . . . . . . . . . . . . . . . . . . . . . . . **CLC 4**
See also CA 1-4R; CANR 1, 47; DLB 5

**Vigny, Alfred (Victor) de**
1797-1863 . . . . . . **NCLC 7; DAM POET**
See also DLB 119

**Vilakazi, Benedict Wallet**
1906-1947 . . . . . . . . . . . . . . . . . **TCLC 37**

**Villiers de l'Isle Adam, Jean Marie Mathias Philippe Auguste Comte**
1838-1889 . . . . . . . . . . **NCLC 3; SSC 14**
See also DLB 123

**Villon, Francois** 1431-1463(?) . . . . . . . **PC 13**

**Vinci, Leonardo da** 1452-1519 . . . . . . . **LC 12**

**Vine, Barbara** . . . . . . . . . . . . . . . . . . . . **CLC 50**
See also Rendell, Ruth (Barbara)
See also BEST 90:4

**Vinge, Joan D(ennison)**
1948- . . . . . . . . . . . . . . . . **CLC 30; SSC 24**
See also CA 93-96; SATA 36

**Violis, G.**
See Simenon, Georges (Jacques Christian)

**Visconti, Luchino** 1906-1976 . . . . . . . **CLC 16**
See also CA 81-84; 65-68; CANR 39

**Vittorini, Elio** 1908-1966 . . . . . . **CLC 6, 9, 14**
See also CA 133; 25-28R

**Vizinczey, Stephen** 1933- . . . . . . . . . . **CLC 40**
See also CA 128; INT 128

**Vliet, R(ussell) G(ordon)**
1929-1984 . . . . . . . . . . . . . . . . . . **CLC 22**
See also CA 37-40R; 112; CANR 18

**Vogau, Boris Andreyevich** 1894-1937(?)
See Pilnyak, Boris
See also CA 123

**Vogel, Paula A(nne)** 1951- . . . . . . . . . **CLC 76**
See also CA 108

**Voight, Ellen Bryant** 1943- . . . . . . . . **CLC 54**
See also CA 69-72; CANR 11, 29, 55; DLB 120

**Voigt, Cynthia** 1942- . . . . . . . . . . . . . **CLC 30**
See also AAYA 3; CA 106; CANR 18, 37, 40; CLR 13; INT CANR-18; JRDA; MAICYA; SATA 48, 79; SATA-Brief 33

**Voinovich, Vladimir (Nikolaevich)** 1932- . . . . . . . . . . . . . . . . . . . . **CLC 10, 49**
See also CA 81-84; CAAS 12; CANR 33; MTCW

**Vollmann, William T.** 1959- . . . . . . **CLC 89; DAM NOV, POP**
See also CA 134

**Voloshinov, V. N.**
See Bakhtin, Mikhail Mikhailovich

**Voltaire** 1694-1778 . . . . . **LC 14; DA; DAB; DAC; DAM DRAM, MST; SSC 12; WLC**

**von Daeniken, Erich** 1935- . . . . . . . . **CLC 30**
See also AITN 1; CA 37-40R; CANR 17, 44

**von Daniken, Erich**
See von Daeniken, Erich

**von Heidenstam, (Carl Gustaf) Verner**
See Heidenstam, (Carl Gustaf) Verner von

**von Heyse, Paul (Johann Ludwig)**
See Heyse, Paul (Johann Ludwig von)

**von Hofmannsthal, Hugo**
See Hofmannsthal, Hugo von

**von Horvath, Odon**
See Horvath, Oedoen von

**von Horvath, Oedoen**
See Horvath, Oedoen von

**von Liliencron, (Friedrich Adolf Axel) Detlev**
See Liliencron, (Friedrich Adolf Axel) Detlev von

**Vonnegut, Kurt, Jr.** 1922- . . . . . . **CLC 1, 2, 3, 4, 5, 8, 12, 22, 40, 60; DA; DAB; DAC; DAM MST, NOV, POP; SSC 8; WLC**
See also AAYA 6; AITN 1; BEST 90:4; CA 1-4R; CANR 1, 25, 49; CDALB 1968-1988; DLB 2, 8, 152; DLBD 3; DLBY 80; MTCW

**Von Rachen, Kurt**
See Hubbard, L(afayette) Ron(ald)

**von Rezzori (d'Arezzo), Gregor**
See Rezzori (d'Arezzo), Gregor von

**von Sternberg, Josef**
See Sternberg, Josef von

**Vorster, Gordon** 1924- . . . . . . . . . . . . **CLC 34**
See also CA 133

**Vosce, Trudie**
See Ozick, Cynthia

**Voznesensky, Andrei (Andreievich)** 1933- . . . . . . **CLC 1, 15, 57; DAM POET**
See also CA 89-92; CANR 37; MTCW

**Waddington, Miriam** 1917- . . . . . . . . **CLC 28**
See also CA 21-24R; CANR 12, 30; DLB 68

**Wagman, Fredrica** 1937- . . . . . . . . . . . **CLC 7**
See also CA 97-100; INT 97-100

**Wagner, Richard** 1813-1883. . . . . . . **NCLC 9**
See also DLB 129

**Wagner-Martin, Linda** 1936- . . . . . . . **CLC 50**

**Wagoner, David (Russell)** 1926- . . . . . . . . . . . . . . . . . . . **CLC 3, 5, 15**
See also CA 1-4R; CAAS 3; CANR 2; DLB 5; SATA 14

**Wah, Fred(erick James)** 1939- . . . . . . **CLC 44**
See also CA 107; 141; DLB 60

**Wahloo, Per** 1926-1975 . . . . . . . . . . . . **CLC 7**
See also CA 61-64

**Wahloo, Peter**
See Wahloo, Per

**Wain, John (Barrington)** 1925-1994 . . . . . . . . . . . **CLC 2, 11, 15, 46**
See also CA 5-8R; 145; CAAS 4; CANR 23, 54; CDBLB 1960 to Present; DLB 15, 27, 139, 155; MTCW

**Wajda, Andrzej** 1926- . . . . . . . . . . . . . **CLC 16**
See also CA 102

**Wakefield, Dan** 1932- . . . . . . . . . . . . . . **CLC 7**
See also CA 21-24R; CAAS 7

**Wakoski, Diane** 1937- . . . . . . . . . . . **CLC 2, 4, 7, 9, 11, 40; DAM POET; PC 15**
See also CA 13-16R; CAAS 1; CANR 9; DLB 5; INT CANR-9

**Wakoski-Sherbell, Diane**
See Wakoski, Diane

**Walcott, Derek (Alton)** 1930- . . . . **CLC 2, 4, 9, 14, 25, 42, 67, 76; BLC; DAB; DAC; DAM MST, MULT, POET**
See also BW 2; CA 89-92; CANR 26, 47; DLB 117; DLBY 81; MTCW

**Waldman, Anne** 1945- . . . . . . . . . . . . . **CLC 7**
See also CA 37-40R; CAAS 17; CANR 34; DLB 16

**Waldo, E. Hunter**
See Sturgeon, Theodore (Hamilton)

**Waldo, Edward Hamilton**
See Sturgeon, Theodore (Hamilton)

**Walker, Alice (Malsenior)** 1944- . . . . . . . **CLC 5, 6, 9, 19, 27, 46, 58; BLC; DA; DAB; DAC; DAM MST, MULT, NOV, POET, POP; SSC 5**
See also AAYA 3; BEST 89:4; BW 2; CA 37-40R; CANR 9, 27, 49; CDALB 1968-1988; DLB 6, 33, 143; INT CANR-27; MTCW; SATA 31

**Walker, David Harry** 1911-1992. . . . **CLC 14**
See also CA 1-4R; 137; CANR 1; SATA 8; SATA-Obit 71

**Walker, Edward Joseph** 1934-
See Walker, Ted
See also CA 21-24R; CANR 12, 28, 53

**Walker, George F.** 1947- . . . . . . . . **CLC 44, 61; DAB; DAC; DAM MST**
See also CA 103; CANR 21, 43; DLB 60

**Walker, Joseph A.** 1935- . . . . **CLC 19; DAM DRAM, MST**
See also BW 1; CA 89-92; CANR 26; DLB 38

**Walker, Margaret (Abigail)** 1915- . . . . **CLC 1, 6; BLC; DAM MULT**
See also BW 2; CA 73-76; CANR 26, 54; DLB 76, 152; MTCW

**Walker, Ted** . . . . . . . . . . . . . . . . . . . . . **CLC 13**
See also Walker, Edward Joseph
See also DLB 40

**Wallace, David Foster** 1962- . . . . . . . **CLC 50**
See also CA 132

**Wallace, Dexter**
See Masters, Edgar Lee

**Wallace, (Richard Horatio) Edgar** 1875-1932 . . . . . . . . . . . . . . . . . . **TCLC 57**
See also CA 115; DLB 70

**Wallace, Irving** 1916-1990 . . . . . **CLC 7, 13; DAM NOV, POP**
See also AITN 1; CA 1-4R; 132; CAAS 1; CANR 1, 27; INT CANR-27; MTCW

**Wallant, Edward Lewis** 1926-1962 . . . . . . . . . . . . . . . . . **CLC 5, 10**
See also CA 1-4R; CANR 22; DLB 2, 28, 143; MTCW

**Walley, Byron**
See Card, Orson Scott

**Walpole, Horace** 1717-1797. . . . . . . . . . **LC 2**
See also DLB 39, 104

**Walpole, Hugh (Seymour)** 1884-1941 . . . . . . . . . . . . . . . . . . . **TCLC 5**
See also CA 104; DLB 34

**Walser, Martin** 1927- . . . . . . . . . . . . . **CLC 27**
See also CA 57-60; CANR 8, 46; DLB 75, 124

**Walser, Robert** 1878-1956 . . . . . . . . . . **TCLC 18; SSC 20**
See also CA 118; DLB 66

**Walsh, Jill Paton**. . . . . . . . . . . . . . . . . . **CLC 35**
See also Paton Walsh, Gillian
See also AAYA 11; CLR 2; DLB 161; SAAS 3

**Walter, Villiam Christian**
See Andersen, Hans Christian

**Wambaugh, Joseph (Aloysius, Jr.)** 1937- . . . . **CLC 3, 18; DAM NOV, POP**
See also AITN 1; BEST 89:3; CA 33-36R; CANR 42; DLB 6; DLBY 83; MTCW

**Ward, Arthur Henry Sarsfield** 1883-1959
See Rohmer, Sax
See also CA 108

**Ward, Douglas Turner** 1930- . . . . . . . **CLC 19**
See also BW 1; CA 81-84; CANR 27; DLB 7, 38

**Ward, Mary Augusta**
See Ward, Mrs. Humphry

**Ward, Mrs. Humphry** 1851-1920 . . . . . . . . . . . . . . . . . . **TCLC 55**
See also DLB 18

**Ward, Peter**
See Faust, Frederick (Schiller)

**Warhol, Andy** 1928(?)-1987 . . . . . . . . **CLC 20**
See also AAYA 12; BEST 89:4; CA 89-92; 121; CANR 34

**Warner, Francis (Robert le Plastrier)** 1937- . . . . . . . . . . . . . . . . . . . . . . . **CLC 14**
See also CA 53-56; CANR 11

**Warner, Marina** 1946- . . . . . . . . . . . . **CLC 59**
See also CA 65-68; CANR 21, 55

**Warner, Rex (Ernest)** 1905-1986. . . . **CLC 45**
See also CA 89-92; 119; DLB 15

**Wergeland, Henrik Arnold** 1808-1845 .................. **NCLC 5**

**Wersba, Barbara** 1932-........... **CLC 30**
See also AAYA 2; CA 29-32R; CANR 16, 38; CLR 3; DLB 52; JRDA; MAICYA; SAAS 2; SATA 1, 58

**Wertmueller, Lina** 1928- .......... **CLC 16**
See also CA 97-100; CANR 39

**Wescott, Glenway** 1901-1987....... **CLC 13**
See also CA 13-16R; 121; CANR 23; DLB 4, 9, 102

**Wesker, Arnold** 1932- ............. **CLC 3, 5, 42; DAB; DAM DRAM**
See also CA 1-4R; CAAS 7; CANR 1, 33; CDBLB 1960 to Present; DLB 13; MTCW

**Wesley, Richard (Errol)** 1945-....... **CLC 7**
See also BW 1; CA 57-60; CANR 27; DLB 38

**Wessel, Johan Herman** 1742-1785 .... **LC 7**

**West, Anthony (Panther)** 1914-1987 .................. **CLC 50**
See also CA 45-48; 124; CANR 3, 19; DLB 15

**West, C. P.**
See Wodehouse, P(elham) G(renville)

**West, (Mary) Jessamyn** 1902-1984 ................. **CLC 7, 17**
See also CA 9-12R; 112; CANR 27; DLB 6; DLBY 84; MTCW; SATA-Obit 37

**West, Morris L(anglo)** 1916-..... **CLC 6, 33**
See also CA 5-8R; CANR 24, 49; MTCW

**West, Nathanael** 1903-1940 ..... **TCLC 1, 14, 44; SSC 16**
See also CA 104; 125; CDALB 1929-1941; DLB 4, 9, 28; MTCW

**West, Owen**
See Koontz, Dean R(ay)

**West, Paul** 1930- .......... **CLC 7, 14, 96**
See also CA 13-16R; CAAS 7; CANR 22, 53; DLB 14; INT CANR-22

**West, Rebecca** 1892-1983 .. **CLC 7, 9, 31, 50**
See also CA 5-8R; 109; CANR 19; DLB 36; DLBY 83; MTCW

**Westall, Robert (Atkinson)** 1929-1993 ................... **CLC 17**
See also AAYA 12; CA 69-72; 141; CANR 18; CLR 13; JRDA; MAICYA; SAAS 2; SATA 23, 69; SATA-Obit 75

**Westlake, Donald E(dwin)** 1933- .......... **CLC 7, 33; DAM POP**
See also CA 17-20R; CAAS 13; CANR 16, 44; INT CANR-16

**Westmacott, Mary**
See Christie, Agatha (Mary Clarissa)

**Weston, Allen**
See Norton, Andre

**Wetcheek, J. L.**
See Feuchtwanger, Lion

**Wetering, Janwillem van de**
See van de Wetering, Janwillem

**Wetherell, Elizabeth**
See Warner, Susan (Bogert)

**Whale, James** 1889-1957 ......... **TCLC 63**

**Whalen, Philip** 1923- .......... **CLC 6, 29**
See also CA 9-12R; CANR 5, 39; DLB 16

**Wharton, Edith (Newbold Jones)** 1862-1937 ...... **TCLC 3, 9, 27, 53; DA; DAB; DAC; DAM MST, NOV; SSC 6; WLC**
See also CA 104; 132; CDALB 1865-1917; DLB 4, 9, 12, 78; DLBD 13; MTCW

**Wharton, James**
See Mencken, H(enry) L(ouis)

**Wharton, William (a pseudonym)** ......................... **CLC 18, 37**
See also CA 93-96; DLBY 80; INT 93-96

**Wheatley (Peters), Phillis** 1754(?)-1784 .... **LC 3; BLC; DA; DAC; DAM MST, MULT, POET; PC 3; WLC**
See also CDALB 1640-1865; DLB 31, 50

**Wheelock, John Hall** 1886-1978 .... **CLC 14**
See also CA 13-16R; 77-80; CANR 14; DLB 45

**White, E(lwyn) B(rooks)** 1899-1985 .. **CLC 10, 34, 39; DAM POP**
See also AITN 2; CA 13-16R; 116; CANR 16, 37; CLR 1, 21; DLB 11, 22; MAICYA; MTCW; SATA 2, 29; SATA-Obit 44

**White, Edmund (Valentine III)** 1940- ........... **CLC 27; DAM POP**
See also AAYA 7; CA 45-48; CANR 3, 19, 36; MTCW

**White, Patrick (Victor Martindale)** 1912-1990 .. **CLC 3, 4, 5, 7, 9, 18, 65, 69**
See also CA 81-84; 132; CANR 43; MTCW

**White, Phyllis Dorothy James** 1920-
See James, P. D.
See also CA 21-24R; CANR 17, 43; DAM POP; MTCW

**White, T(erence) H(anbury)** 1906-1964 .................. **CLC 30**
See also CA 73-76; CANR 37; DLB 160; JRDA; MAICYA; SATA 12

**White, Terence de Vere** 1912-1994 ................... **CLC 49**
See also CA 49-52; 145; CANR 3

**White, Walter F(rancis)** 1893-1955 .................. **TCLC 15**
See also White, Walter
See also BW 1; CA 115; 124; DLB 51

**White, William Hale** 1831-1913
See Rutherford, Mark
See also CA 121

**Whitehead, E(dward) A(nthony)** 1933- ........................ **CLC 5**
See also CA 65-68

**Whitemore, Hugh (John)** 1936-..... **CLC 37**
See also CA 132; INT 132

**Whitman, Sarah Helen (Power)** 1803-1878 ................ **NCLC 19**
See also DLB 1

**Whitman, Walt(er)** 1819-1892 ..... **NCLC 4, 31; DA; DAB; DAC; DAM MST, POET; PC 3; WLC**
See also CDALB 1640-1865; DLB 3, 64; SATA 20

**Whitney, Phyllis A(yame)** 1903- ........... **CLC 42; DAM POP**
See also AITN 2; BEST 90:3; CA 1-4R; CANR 3, 25, 38; JRDA; MAICYA; SATA 1, 30

**Whittemore, (Edward) Reed (Jr.)** 1919- ......................... **CLC 4**
See also CA 9-12R; CAAS 8; CANR 4; DLB 5

**Whittier, John Greenleaf** 1807-1892 .............. **NCLC 8, 59**
See also DLB 1

**Whittlebot, Hernia**
See Coward, Noel (Peirce)

**Wicker, Thomas Grey** 1926-
See Wicker, Tom
See also CA 65-68; CANR 21, 46

**Wicker, Tom** ..................... **CLC 7**
See also Wicker, Thomas Grey

**Wideman, John Edgar** 1941- ......... **CLC 5, 34, 36, 67; BLC; DAM MULT**
See also BW 2; CA 85-88; CANR 14, 42; DLB 33, 143

**Wiebe, Rudy (Henry)** 1934- ............ **CLC 6, 11, 14; DAC; DAM MST**
See also CA 37-40R; CANR 42; DLB 60

**Wieland, Christoph Martin** 1733-1813 ................ **NCLC 17**
See also DLB 97

**Wiene, Robert** 1881-1938......... **TCLC 56**

**Wieners, John** 1934-.............. **CLC 7**
See also CA 13-16R; DLB 16

**Wiesel, Elie(zer)** 1928- ...... **CLC 3, 5, 11, 37; DA; DAB; DAC; DAM MST, NOV**
See also AAYA 7; AITN 1; CA 5-8R; CAAS 4; CANR 8, 40; DLB 83; DLBY 87; INT CANR-8; MTCW; SATA 56

**Wiggins, Marianne** 1947-.......... **CLC 57**
See also BEST 89:3; CA 130

**Wight, James Alfred** 1916-
See Herriot, James
See also CA 77-80; SATA 55; SATA-Brief 44

**Wilbur, Richard (Purdy)** 1921- ... **CLC 3, 6, 9, 14, 53; DA; DAB; DAC; DAM MST, POET**
See also CA 1-4R; CABS 2; CANR 2, 29; DLB 5, 169; INT CANR-29; MTCW; SATA 9

**Wild, Peter** 1940-................ **CLC 14**
See also CA 37-40R; DLB 5

**Wilde, Oscar (Fingal O'Flahertie Wills)** 1854(?)-1900 .... **TCLC 1, 8, 23, 41; DA; DAB; DAC; DAM DRAM, MST, NOV; SSC 11; WLC**
See also CA 104; 119; CDBLB 1890-1914; DLB 10, 19, 34, 57, 141, 156; SATA 24

**Wilder, Billy** .................... **CLC 20**
See also Wilder, Samuel
See also DLB 26

**Wilder, Samuel** 1906-
See Wilder, Billy
See also CA 89-92

**Wilder, Thornton (Niven)**
1897-1975 ...... **CLC 1, 5, 6, 10, 15, 35, 82; DA; DAB; DAC; DAM DRAM, MST, NOV; DC 1; WLC**
See also AITN 2; CA 13-16R; 61-64; CANR 40; DLB 4, 7, 9; MTCW

**Wilding, Michael** 1942- ........... **CLC 73**
See also CA 104; CANR 24, 49

**Wiley, Richard** 1944- ............. **CLC 44**
See also CA 121; 129

**Wilhelm, Kate** ..................... **CLC 7**
See also Wilhelm, Katie Gertrude
See also CAAS 5; DLB 8; INT CANR-17

**Wilhelm, Katie Gertrude** 1928-
See Wilhelm, Kate
See also CA 37-40R; CANR 17, 36; MTCW

**Wilkins, Mary**
See Freeman, Mary Eleanor Wilkins

**Willard, Nancy** 1936- ........... **CLC 7, 37**
See also CA 89-92; CANR 10, 39; CLR 5; DLB 5, 52; MAICYA; MTCW; SATA 37, 71; SATA-Brief 30

**Williams, C(harles) K(enneth)**
1936- ........ **CLC 33, 56; DAM POET**
See also CA 37-40R; DLB 5

**Williams, Charles**
See Collier, James L(incoln)

**Williams, Charles (Walter Stansby)**
1886-1945 ............... **TCLC 1, 11**
See also CA 104; DLB 100, 153

**Williams, (George) Emlyn**
1905-1987 ...... **CLC 15; DAM DRAM**
See also CA 104; 123; CANR 36; DLB 10, 77; MTCW

**Williams, Hugo** 1942- ............. **CLC 42**
See also CA 17-20R; CANR 45; DLB 40

**Williams, J. Walker**
See Wodehouse, P(elham) G(renville)

**Williams, John A(lfred)**
1925- ... **CLC 5, 13; BLC; DAM MULT**
See also BW 2; CA 53-56; CAAS 3; CANR 6, 26, 51; DLB 2, 33; INT CANR-6

**Williams, Jonathan (Chamberlain)**
1929- ....................... **CLC 13**
See also CA 9-12R; CAAS 12; CANR 8; DLB 5

**Williams, Joy** 1944- .............. **CLC 31**
See also CA 41-44R; CANR 22, 48

**Williams, Norman** 1952- .......... **CLC 39**
See also CA 118

**Williams, Sherley Anne**
1944- ..... **CLC 89; BLC; DAM MULT, POET**
See also BW 2; CA 73-76; CANR 25; DLB 41; INT CANR-25; SATA 78

**Williams, Shirley**
See Williams, Sherley Anne

**Williams, Tennessee**
1911-1983 ..... **CLC 1, 2, 5, 7, 8, 11, 15, 19, 30, 39, 45, 71; DA; DAB; DAC; DAM DRAM, MST; DC 4; WLC**
See also AITN 1, 2; CA 5-8R; 108; CABS 3; CANR 31; CDALB 1941-1968; DLB 7; DLBD 4; DLBY 83; MTCW

**Williams, Thomas (Alonzo)**
1926-1990 ................... **CLC 14**
See also CA 1-4R; 132; CANR 2

**Williams, William C.**
See Williams, William Carlos

**Williams, William Carlos**
1883-1963 .... **CLC 1, 2, 5, 9, 13, 22, 42, 67; DA; DAB; DAC; DAM MST, POET; PC 7**
See also CA 89-92; CANR 34; CDALB 1917-1929; DLB 4, 16, 54, 86; MTCW

**Williamson, David (Keith)** 1942- .... **CLC 56**
See also CA 103; CANR 41

**Williamson, Ellen Douglas** 1905-1984
See Douglas, Ellen
See also CA 17-20R; 114; CANR 39

**Williamson, Jack** .................. **CLC 29**
See also Williamson, John Stewart
See also CAAS 8; DLB 8

**Williamson, John Stewart** 1908-
See Williamson, Jack
See also CA 17-20R; CANR 23

**Willie, Frederick**
See Lovecraft, H(oward) P(hillips)

**Willingham, Calder (Baynard, Jr.)**
1922-1995 ................. **CLC 5, 51**
See also CA 5-8R; 147; CANR 3; DLB 2, 44; MTCW

**Willis, Charles**
See Clarke, Arthur C(harles)

**Willy**
See Colette, (Sidonie-Gabrielle)

**Willy, Colette**
See Colette, (Sidonie-Gabrielle)

**Wilson, A(ndrew) N(orman)** 1950- .. **CLC 33**
See also CA 112; 122; DLB 14, 155

**Wilson, Angus (Frank Johnstone)**
1913-1991 .. **CLC 2, 3, 5, 25, 34; SSC 21**
See also CA 5-8R; 134; CANR 21; DLB 15, 139, 155; MTCW

**Wilson, August**
1945- ....... **CLC 39, 50, 63; BLC; DA; DAB; DAC; DAM DRAM, MST, MULT; DC 2**
See also AAYA 16; BW 2; CA 115; 122; CANR 42, 54; MTCW

**Wilson, Brian** 1942- .............. **CLC 12**

**Wilson, Colin** 1931- ............ **CLC 3, 14**
See also CA 1-4R; CAAS 5; CANR 1, 22, 33; DLB 14; MTCW

**Wilson, Dirk**
See Pohl, Frederik

**Wilson, Edmund**
1895-1972 .......... **CLC 1, 2, 3, 8, 24**
See also CA 1-4R; 37-40R; CANR 1, 46; DLB 63; MTCW

**Wilson, Ethel Davis (Bryant)**
1888(?)-1980 ........... **CLC 13; DAC; DAM POET**
See also CA 102; DLB 68; MTCW

**Wilson, John** 1785-1854.......... **NCLC 5**

**Wilson, John (Anthony) Burgess** 1917-1993
See Burgess, Anthony
See also CA 1-4R; 143; CANR 2, 46; DAC; DAM NOV; MTCW

**Wilson, Lanford**
1937- ..... **CLC 7, 14, 36; DAM DRAM**
See also CA 17-20R; CABS 3; CANR 45; DLB 7

**Wilson, Robert M.** 1944- ......... **CLC 7, 9**
See also CA 49-52; CANR 2, 41; MTCW

**Wilson, Robert McLiam** 1964- ..... **CLC 59**
See also CA 132

**Wilson, Sloan** 1920- .............. **CLC 32**
See also CA 1-4R; CANR 1, 44

**Wilson, Snoo** 1948- ............... **CLC 33**
See also CA 69-72

**Wilson, William S(mith)** 1932- ..... **CLC 49**
See also CA 81-84

**Winchilsea, Anne (Kingsmill) Finch Counte**
1661-1720 ..................... **LC 3**

**Windham, Basil**
See Wodehouse, P(elham) G(renville)

**Wingrove, David (John)** 1954- ...... **CLC 68**
See also CA 133

**Winters, Janet Lewis** .............. **CLC 41**
See also Lewis, Janet
See also DLBY 87

**Winters, (Arthur) Yvor**
1900-1968 ............... **CLC 4, 8, 32**
See also CA 11-12; 25-28R; CAP 1; DLB 48; MTCW

**Winterson, Jeanette**
1959- ............ **CLC 64; DAM POP**
See also CA 136

**Winthrop, John** 1588-1649.......... **LC 31**
See also DLB 24, 30

**Wiseman, Frederick** 1930- ......... **CLC 20**

**Wister, Owen** 1860-1938 ......... **TCLC 21**
See also CA 108; DLB 9, 78; SATA 62

**Witkacy**
See Witkiewicz, Stanislaw Ignacy

**Witkiewicz, Stanislaw Ignacy**
1885-1939 ................... **TCLC 8**
See also CA 105

**Wittgenstein, Ludwig (Josef Johann)**
1889-1951 .................. **TCLC 59**
See also CA 113

**Wittig, Monique** 1935(?)- .......... **CLC 22**
See also CA 116; 135; DLB 83

**Wittlin, Jozef** 1896-1976 .......... **CLC 25**
See also CA 49-52; 65-68; CANR 3

**Wodehouse, P(elham) G(renville)**
1881-1975 ... **CLC 1, 2, 5, 10, 22; DAB; DAC; DAM NOV; SSC 2**
See also AITN 2; CA 45-48; 57-60; CANR 3, 33; CDBLB 1914-1945; DLB 34, 162; MTCW; SATA 22

**Woiwode, L.**
See Woiwode, Larry (Alfred)

**York, Simon**
See Heinlein, Robert A(nson)

**Yorke, Henry Vincent** 1905-1974 . . . **CLC 13**
See also Green, Henry
See also CA 85-88; 49-52

**Yosano Akiko** 1878-1942 . . **TCLC 59; PC 11**

**Yoshimoto, Banana** . . . . . . . . . . . . . . . . **CLC 84**
See also Yoshimoto, Mahoko

**Yoshimoto, Mahoko** 1964-
See Yoshimoto, Banana
See also CA 144

**Young, Al(bert James)**
1939- . . . . . **CLC 19; BLC; DAM MULT**
See also BW 2; CA 29-32R; CANR 26; DLB 33

**Young, Andrew (John)** 1885-1971 . . . . **CLC 5**
See also CA 5-8R; CANR 7, 29

**Young, Collier**
See Bloch, Robert (Albert)

**Young, Edward** 1683-1765 . . . . . . . . . . . **LC 3**
See also DLB 95

**Young, Marguerite (Vivian)**
1909-1995 . . . . . . . . . . . . . . . . . . . **CLC 82**
See also CA 13-16; 150; CAP 1

**Young, Neil** 1945- . . . . . . . . . . . . . . . . **CLC 17**
See also CA 110

**Young Bear, Ray A.**
1950- . . . . . . . . . . **CLC 94; DAM MULT**
See also CA 146; NNAL

**Yourcenar, Marguerite**
1903-1987 . . . . . . . . . **CLC 19, 38, 50, 87; DAM NOV**
See also CA 69-72; CANR 23; DLB 72; DLBY 88; MTCW

**Yurick, Sol** 1925- . . . . . . . . . . . . . . . . . **CLC 6**
See also CA 13-16R; CANR 25

**Zabolotskii, Nikolai Alekseevich**
1903-1958 . . . . . . . . . . . . . . . . . . **TCLC 52**
See also CA 116

**Zamiatin, Yevgenii**
See Zamyatin, Evgeny Ivanovich

**Zamora, Bernice (B. Ortiz)**
1938- . . . . . **CLC 89; DAM MULT; HLC**
See also CA 151; DLB 82; HW

**Zamyatin, Evgeny Ivanovich**
1884-1937 . . . . . . . . . . . . . . . . **TCLC 8, 37**
See also CA 105

**Zangwill, Israel** 1864-1926 . . . . . . . . **TCLC 16**
See also CA 109; DLB 10, 135

**Zappa, Francis Vincent, Jr.** 1940-1993
See Zappa, Frank
See also CA 108; 143

**Zappa, Frank** . . . . . . . . . . . . . . . . . . . . . **CLC 17**
See also Zappa, Francis Vincent, Jr.

**Zaturenska, Marya** 1902-1982 . . . . **CLC 6, 11**
See also CA 13-16R; 105; CANR 22

**Zelazny, Roger (Joseph)**
1937-1995 . . . . . . . . . . . . . . . . . . . **CLC 21**
See also AAYA 7; CA 21-24R; 148; CANR 26; DLB 8; MTCW; SATA 57; SATA-Brief 39

**Zhdanov, Andrei A(lexandrovich)**
1896-1948 . . . . . . . . . . . . . . . . . . **TCLC 18**
See also CA 117

**Zhukovsky, Vasily** 1783-1852 . . . . **NCLC 35**

**Ziegenhagen, Eric** . . . . . . . . . . . . . . . . . **CLC 55**

**Zimmer, Jill Schary**
See Robinson, Jill

**Zimmerman, Robert**
See Dylan, Bob

**Zindel, Paul**
1936- . . . . . **CLC 6, 26; DA; DAB; DAC; DAM DRAM, MST, NOV; DC 5**
See also AAYA 2; CA 73-76; CANR 31; CLR 3; DLB 7, 52; JRDA; MAICYA; MTCW; SATA 16, 58

**Zinov'Ev, A. A.**
See Zinoviev, Alexander (Aleksandrovich)

**Zinoviev, Alexander (Aleksandrovich)**
1922- . . . . . . . . . . . . . . . . . . . . . . . **CLC 19**
See also CA 116; 133; CAAS 10

**Zoilus**
See Lovecraft, H(oward) P(hillips)

**Zola, Emile (Edouard Charles Antoine)**
1840-1902 . . . . . . **TCLC 1, 6, 21, 41; DA; DAB; DAC; DAM MST, NOV; WLC**
See also CA 104; 138; DLB 123

**Zoline, Pamela** 1941- . . . . . . . . . . . . . **CLC 62**

**Zorrilla y Moral, Jose** 1817-1893 . . **NCLC 6**

**Zoshchenko, Mikhail (Mikhailovich)**
1895-1958 . . . . . . . . . . **TCLC 15; SSC 15**
See also CA 115

**Zuckmayer, Carl** 1896-1977 . . . . . . . . **CLC 18**
See also CA 69-72; DLB 56, 124

**Zuk, Georges**
See Skelton, Robin

**Zukofsky, Louis**
1904-1978 . . . . . . . **CLC 1, 2, 4, 7, 11, 18; DAM POET; PC 11**
See also CA 9-12R; 77-80; CANR 39; DLB 5, 165; MTCW

**Zweig, Paul** 1935-1984 . . . . . . . . . **CLC 34, 42**
See also CA 85-88; 113

**Zweig, Stefan** 1881-1942 . . . . . . . . . **TCLC 17**
See also CA 112; DLB 81, 118

**Zwingli, Huldreich** 1484-1531 . . . . . . . **LC 37**

# *LC* Cumulative Nationality Index


**AFGHAN**
Babur **18**

**AMERICAN**
Bradstreet, Anne **4, 30**
Edwards, Jonathan **7**
Eliot, John **5**
Franklin, Benjamin **25**
Hopkinson, Francis **25**
Knight, Sarah Kemble **7**
Munford, Robert **5**
Penn, William **25**
Taylor, Edward **11**
Washington, George **25**
Wheatley (Peters), Phillis **3**
Winthrop, John **31**

**BENINESE**
Equiano, Olaudah **16**

**CANADIAN**
Marie de l'Incarnation **10**

**CHINESE**
Lo Kuan-chung **12**
P'u Sung-ling **3**
Ts'ao Hsueh-ch'in **1**
Wu Ch'eng-en **7**
Wu Ching-tzu **2**

**DANISH**
Holberg, Ludvig **6**
Wessel, Johan Herman **7**

**DUTCH**
Erasmus, Desiderius **16**
Lipsius, Justus **16**
Spinoza, Benedictus de **9**

**ENGLISH**
Addison, Joseph **18**
Andrewes, Lancelot **5**
Arbuthnot, John **1**
Aubin, Penelope **9**
Bacon, Francis **18, 32**
Beaumont, Francis **33**
Behn, Aphra **1, 30**
Boswell, James **4**
Bradstreet, Anne **4, 30**
Brooke, Frances **6**
Bunyan, John **4**
Burke, Edmund **7, 36**
Butler, Samuel **16**
Carew, Thomas **13**
Cary, Elizabeth, Lady Falkland **30**
Cavendish, Margaret Lucas **30**
Caxton, William , **17**
Chapman, George **22**
Charles I **13**
Chatterton, Thomas **3**
Chaucer, Geoffrey **17**
Churchill, Charles **3**
Cleland, John **2**
Collier, Jeremy **6**
Collins, William **4**
Congreve, William **5, 21**
Crashaw, Richard **24**
Daniel, Samuel **24**
Davys, Mary **1**
Day, Thomas **1**
Dee, John **20**
Defoe, Daniel **1**
Dekker, Thomas **22**
Delany, Mary (Granville Pendarves) **12**
Dennis, John **11**
Devenant, William **13**
Donne, John **10, 24**
Drayton, Michael **8**
Dryden, John **3, 21**
Elyot, Sir Thomas **11**
Equiano, Olaudah **16**
Fanshawe, Ann **11**
Farquhar, George **21**
Fielding, Henry **1**
Fielding, Sarah **1**
Fletcher, John **33**
Foxe, John **14**
Garrick, David **15**
Gray, Thomas **4**
Hakluyt, Richard **31**
Hawes, Stephen **17**
Haywood, Eliza (Fowler) **1**
Henry VIII **10**
Herbert, George **24**
Herrick, Robert **13**
Hobbes, Thomas **36**
Howell, James **13**
Hunter, Robert **7**
Johnson, Samuel **15**
Jonson, Ben(jamin) **6, 33**
Julian of Norwich **6**
Kempe, Margery **6**
Killigrew, Anne **4**
Kyd, Thomas **22**
Langland, William **19**
Lanyer, Aemilia **10, 30**
Lilly, William **27**
Locke, John **7**
Lovelace, Richard **24**
Lyttelton, George **10**
Malory, (Sir) Thomas **11**
Manley, (Mary) Delariviere **1**
Marlowe, Christopher **22**
Marston, John **33**
Marvell, Andrew **4**

# Literary Criticism Series Cumulative Topic Index



This index lists all topic entries in Gale's *Classical and Medieval Literature Criticism, Contemporary Literary Criticism, Literature Criticism from 1400 to 1800, Nineteenth-Century Literature Criticism,* and *Twentieth-Century Literary Criticism.*

Topic Index

# *LC* Cumulative Title Index

Title Index

Title Index

**Title Index**

Title Index

Title Index

Title Index

**3**:38
"An Epode" (Jonson) **33**:174
*L'epreuve* (Marivaux) **4**:358, 364, 369, 371-72
"Equité des Vieux Gaulois" (Ronsard) **6**:410
*Erasmus Montanus* (Holberg) **6**:269, 272, 274-77, 283-85
"Êrh-lang Sou-shan-t'u Ko" (Wu Ch'eng-en) **7**:397
*Eriphyle* (Voltaire) **14**:397
*Der erste Beernhäuter* (Grimmelshausen) **6**:247
*Eruditissimi viri Guilielmi Rossei opus elegans* (More) **10**:365, 369, 409; **32**:331, 332
"La Española inglesa" (Cervantes) **6**:171; **23**:95, 99
"Espiración" (Quevedo) **23**:178
*L'Esprit* (Helvetius)
See *De l'esprit*
*L'esprit des moeurs* (Voltaire) **14**:328
*Esprit du clergé* (Holbach) **14**:153
*Esprit du judaïsme* (Holbach) **14**:154
"L'esprit fort" (Perrault) **2**:253
*Essai sur la poésie épique* (Voltaire)
See *Essay upon the Epic Poetry of the European Nations from Homer down to Milton*
*Essai sur la Vie de Sénèque* (Diderot) **26**:74, 119
*Essai sur le goût* (Marmontel) **2**:214, 222
*Essai sur le mérite et la vertu* (Diderot) **26**:117, 119
*Essai sur les causes qui peuvent affecter les esprits et les caractères* (Montesquieu) **7**:348, 358
*Essai sur les moeurs* (Voltaire) **14**:334, 353, 358, 364, 380, 383-88, 395, 402
*Essai sur les préjugés* (Holbach) **14**:152, 154, 168
*Essai sur les révolutions de la musique en France* (Marmontel) **2**:222
*Essai sur les romans* (Marmontel) **2**:213, 215, 220
*Essai sur l'histoire générale et sur les moeurs et l'esprit des nations* (Voltaire) **14**:411
*Essai sur l'origine des connaissances humaines* (Condillac) **26**:5-6, 8-11, 13-14, 23, 25, 27, 29-31, 40-1, 44, 47-8, 50-6, 59
*Essai sur l'origine des connoissances humaines* (Condillac)
See *Essai sur l'origine des connaissances humaines*
*Essai sur l'origine des langues* (Rousseau) **14**:292, 294-95
*Les essais de Messire Michel Seigneur de Montaigne* (Montaigne) **8**:189, 191-94, 196-97, 199, 201-06, 210, 212-14, 216-20, 223, 225, 229-31, 233-42, 244, 247
*Essais de Theodicee* (Leibniz) **35**:130, 142, 148, 164, 166-67, 171-72, 175
*Essais sur la peinture* (Diderot) **26**:69, 120, 124-25, 127, 163
*Essais sur le règnes de Claude et de Néron* (Diderot) **26**:119
"Essay" (Prior)
See "Essay upon Opinion"
*An Essay concerning Human Understanding* (Locke) **7**:236, 238-39, 244, 246-48, 251, 253, 255-56, 258, 266, 269, 271-72, 281, 284-91, 296; **35**:197-267
*An Essay concerning the True Original, Extent, and End of Civil Government* (Locke) **7**:273
*An Essay for the Understanding of St. Paul's Epistles by Consulting St. Paul Himself* (Locke) **7**:282-83
*Essay of Dramatic Poesy* (Dryden)
See *Of Dramatick Poesie: An Essay*
"Essay of Heroic Plays" (Dryden)
See "Of Heroic Plays"
"An Essay of Heroic Plays" (Dryden) **3**:236
*Essay on Comedy* (Farquhar)
See *Discourse Upon Comedy*
*Essay on Conversation* (Fielding) **1**:234
"An Essay on Criticism" (Pope) **3**:263-64, 267-70, 273, 275-76, 291, 295, 307, 313, 322, 324-28, 337
*Essay on Dramatic Discourse Concerning Satire* (Dryden) **21**:111-12, 115
"Essay on Homer" (Parnell) **3**:253
"Essay on Learning" (Prior)
See "Essay upon Learning"
*An Essay on Man* (Pope) **3**:269, 272-73, 276, 279, 287-89, 291, 297, 300, 304, 306-07, 313, 315-16, 318-19, 326, 334, 337
*An Essay on publick Spirit* (Dennis)
See *An Essay upon Public Spirit; being a Satire in Prose upon the Manners and Luxury of the Times, the chief Sources of our present Parties and Divisions*
"Essay on the Different Styles of Poetry" (Parnell) **3**:255
*An Essay on the Genius of Shakespear* (Dennis) **11**:16, 19, 21, 30, 32, 38-9
"Essay on the Georgics" (Addison) **18**:20
*An Essay on the Human Soul* (Marat) **10**:231
"Essay on the Imagination" (Addison) **18**:58, 62
*Essay on the Knowledge of the Characters of Men* (Moritz) **1**:234
*An Essay on the Navy* (Dennis) **11**:19
*An Essay on the Operas, after the Italian manner, which are about to be established on the English Stage: with some Reflections on the Damage which they may bring to the Public* (Dennis) **11**:15, 19, 26
*Essay on the Origin of Human Knowledge* (Condillac)
See *Essai sur l'origine des connaissances humaines*
*Essay on the Origin of Knowledge* (Condillac)
See *Essai sur l'origine des connaissances humaines*
*Essay on the Prejudices and the Influence of Opinions on Customs and the Happiness of Mankind* (Holbach)
See *Essai sur les préjugés*
"Essay on the Real Secret of the Freemasons" (Cleland) **2**:53
*Essay on the Sublime and Beautiful* (Burke)
See *A Philosophical Enquiry into the Origin of Our Ideas of the Sublime and Beautiful*
*An Essay on the Theatre* (Goldsmith) **2**:126
*An Essay towards an Abridgement of the English History* (Burke) **7**:49
*An Essay Towards the Present and Future Peace of Europe By the Establishment of an European Dyet, Parliament, or Estates* (Penn) **25**:302-03, 342, 346
"An Essay upon Acting" (Garrick) **15**:122
*Essay upon Human Understanding* (Condillac)
See *Essai sur l'origine des connaissances humaines*
"Essay upon Learning" (Prior) **4**:465, 467, 474
"Essay upon Opinion" (Prior) **4**:467-71
*An Essay upon Projects* (Defoe) **1**:160
*An Essay upon Public Spirit; being a Satire in Prose upon the Manners and Luxury of the Times, the chief Sources of our present Parties and Divisions* (Dennis) **11**:8-9, 15, 17, 19, 26
*Essay upon the Civil Wars of France* (Voltaire) **14**:382
*Essay upon the Epic Poetry of the European Nations from Homer down to Milton* (Voltaire) **14**:349-50, 352
*Essayes in Divinity* (Donne) **10**:40, 76-7, 83
*Essays* (Bacon) **18**:104, 108, 110, 114-15, 116, 118, 123-24, 128, 132-34, 136-37, 141-42, 146, 149, 178-79, 183, 187, 192; **32**:118, 136, 183
*Essays* (Hume) **7**:145, 167
*Essays* (Montagu)
See *The Nonsense of Common-Sense*
*Essays* (Montaigne)
See *Les essais de Messire Michel Seigneur de Montaigne*
*Essays and Poems and Simplicity, a Comedy* (Montagu) **9**:271, 276, 279
*Essays and Treatises on Several Subjects* (Hume) **7**:153
*Essays, Moral and Political* (Hume) **7**:152, 189
*Essays Moral, Political, and Literary* (Hume) **7**:163
*Essays on Painting* (Diderot)
See *Essais sur la peinture*
*Essays on the Law of Nature* (Locke) **35**:209, 229
*Essays upon Several Moral Subjects* (Collier) **6**:200, 227
*Essays upon Wit* (Addison) **18**:7, 18, 60
*Esther* (Andreae) **32**:101
*Esther* (Racine) **28**:295-97, 313, 315, 344, 346, 349, 351-53, 355-56, 358, 371-72, 381-82, 384
*Est-il bon? Est-il méchant?* (Diderot) **26**:103, 110, 117, 119, 137, 143
*La Estrelle* (Vega) **23**:343, 350, 402-03
*Westward Ho* (Dekker) **22**:88, 104, 106, 110-111, 125-6, 132
"Etenim res Creatae exerto Capite observantes expectant revelationem filiorum Dei" (Vaughan) **27**:306
"Eternity" (Herrick) **13**:334, 358
*Eternity* (Smart)
See *On the Eternity of the Supreme Being*
"Etesia absent" (Vaughan) **27**:362
*Ethic* (Spinoza)
See *Ethic ordine geometrico demonstrata*
*Ethic ordine geometrico demonstrata* (Spinoza) **9**:397-99, 402-04, 408, 415-17, 419-26, 428, 431-36, 438-39, 441-42, 444-47
"Ethick Epistles" (Pope)
See "Epistles to Several Persons"
*Ethics* (Leibniz) **35**:132
*Ethocratie* (Holbach) **14**:152, 155-56, 160, 174
"Eton" (Gray)
See "Ode on a Distant Prospect of Eton College"
"Eton College Ode" (Gray)
See "Ode on a Distant Prospect of Eton College"
*L'étourdi* (Moliere) **10**:260, 275-77, 280, 283, 286-87, 293, 309-10; **28**:255-58, 260-61, 265-67
*Les Etrennes* (Lesage)
See *Turcaret*
*Eugenia and Adelaide* (Sheridan) **7**:371, 378
*Eurydice Hiss'd* (Fielding) **1**:220

Title Index

Title Index

Title Index

Title Index

Title Index

Title Index

Title Index

Title Index

Title Index

Title Index

Title Index

Title Index

Title Index

Title Index

Title Index

ISBN 0-7876-1131-X

9 780787 611316